THE GERMAN REVOLUTION, 1917-1923

HISTORICAL MATERIALISM BOOK SERIES

Editorial board

PAUL BLACKLEDGE, Leeds - SEBASTIAN BUDGEN, Paris
JIM KINCAID, Leeds - STATHIS KOUVELAKIS, Paris
MARCEL VAN DER LINDEN, Amsterdam
CHINA MIÉVILLE, London - PAUL REYNOLDS, Lancashire

THE GERMAN REVOLUTION
1917-1923

By

Pierre Broué

Translated by John Archer and
Edited by Ian Birchall and Brian Pearce
With an Introduction by Eric D. Weitz

BRILL
LEIDEN · BOSTON
2005

This book is printed on acid-free paper.

Original title: La révolution en Allemagne, 1917-1923
© Pierre Broué, Les Editions de Minuit, 1971

Library of Congress Cataloging-in-Publication Data

Broué, Pierre.
  [Révolution en Allemagne, 1917-1923. English]
  The German Revolution / by Pierre Broué ; [translated by John Archer and edited by Ian Birchall and Brian Pearce].
    p. cm. — (Historical materialism book series, ISSN 1570-1522 ; 5)
  Includes bibliographical references and index.
  ISBN 90-04-13940-0 (alk. paper)
  1. Germany—Politics and government—1918-1933. 2. World War, 1914-1918—Germany. 3. Kommunistische Partei Deutschlands—History. 4. Germany—History—Revolution, 1918. I. Title. II. Series.

DD240.B81613 2004
943.085—dc22

2004040884

ISSN   1570–1522
ISBN   90 04 13940 0

© Copyright 2005 by Koninklijke Brill NV, Leiden, The Netherlands

All rights reserved. No part of this publication may be reproduced, translated, stored in a retrieval system, or transmitted in any form or by any means, electronic, mechanical, photocopying, recording or otherwise, without prior written permission from the publisher.

Authorization to photocopy items for internal or personal use is granted by Koninklijke Brill provided that the appropriate fees are paid directly to The Copyright Clearance Center, 222 Rosewood Drive, Suite 910 Danvers, MA 01923, USA. Fees are subject to change.

PRINTED IN THE NETHERLANDS

CONTENTS

PART ONE

FROM WAR TO REVOLUTION: THE VICTORY AND DEFEAT OF ULTRA-LEFTISM

PART TWO

THE ATTEMPT TO DEFINE THE ROLE OF A COMMUNIST PARTY

PART THREE

From the Conquest of the Masses to a Defeat Without a Fight

PART FOUR

AN UNDERTAKING CONDEMNED BY HISTORY?

Abbreviations and Acronyms

AAU – Allgemeine Arbeiter-Union, 'unionist' organisation of an ultra-leftist tendency.

ADGB – Allgemeiner Deutscher Gewerkschaftsbund, workers' trade-union confederation.

AfA – Allgemeiner freier Angestelltenbund, white-collar trade-union confederation.

Agit-prop – Department of the Central Committee for propaganda and agitation.

Bezirk – Party district; grouped together to form Oberbezirk, subdivided into Unterbezirk.

BL – Bezirksleitung, Party leadership in a district.

Comintern – Communist International.

DMV – Deutscher Metallarbeitverband, metalworkers' union.

IKD – Internationale Kommunisten Deutschlands, organisation of the 'left radicals' in 1918, successor to the ISD.

Inprekorr – Internationale Presse-Korrespondenz, Comintern information bulletin.

ISD – Internationale Sozialisten Deutschlands, organisation of the 'left radicals' before 1918.

ISR – Red International of Labour Unions.

KAG – Kommunistische Arbeitsgemeinschaft, group organised by Levi and his supporters in the summer of 1921.

KAP (or KAPD) – Kommunistische Arbeiterpartei Deutschlands, left-Communist party founded in 1920.

KJVD – Kommunistischer Jugendverband Deutschlands, organisation of the Communist Party youth.

KO – Kampforganisation, combat group of the KPD(S).

KPD – Kommunistische Partei Deutschlands, name of the Communist Party from November to December 1920 and after August 1921.

KPD(S) – Kommunistische Partei Deutschlands (Spartakusbund), name of the Communist Party from January 1919 to November 1920.

KPO (or KPD-O) Kommunistische Partei Deutschlands (Opposition), organisation of the 'right' Communists, with Brandler, after 1929.

Leninbund – Lenin League, organisation of the 'left' Communists, with Urbahns, after 1928.

Oberbezirk – See Bezirk.

Orgburo – Organisation Bureau of the Zentrale.

Orgesch – Organisation Escherisch, extreme right-wing terrorist group.

Orgleiter – Party member with organisational responsibility.

Polburo – Political bureau of the Zentrale.

Polleiter – Communist Party member with political responsibility.

Profintern – Red International of Labour Unions.

SAP (or SAPD) – Sozialistische Arbeiterpartei Deutschlands, left Social-Democratic Party from 1931.

SED – Sozialistische Einheitspartei Deutschlands, party formed from the fusion of the Communist and Social-Democratic Parties in East Germany.

SPD – Sozialistische Partei Deutschlands, name of the Social-Democratic Party until 1922.

Teno – Technische Nothilfe, technical emergency service, organisation of strike-beakers.

Unterbezirk – See Bezirk.

USPD – Unabhängige Sozialdemokratische Partei Deutschlands, Independent Social-Democratic Party.

USPD (Linke) – Independent Social-Democratic Party (Left), name of the Independent Party from the Halle Congress to the Fusion Congress with the KPD.

VKPD – Vereinigte Kommunistische Partei Deutschlands, name of the United Communist Party from December 1920 (fusion with the USPD) to August 1921 (Jena Congress).

VSPD – Vereinigte Sozialdemokratische Partei Deutschlands, name of the United Social-Democratic Party after the reintegration of the Independents in 1922.

Zentrale – Centre, leadership of the Communist Party, composed of leading members resident at the centre.

Zentralausschuss – Central Committee, broader leadership body of the Party including representatives from the various regions.

Eric D. Weitz
Foreword to the English Edition

Pierre Broué's history of the German Revolution
is a remarkable achievement. Written long before
key archives became available in the 1990s, Broué
managed to write a detailed and moving history of
the radical Left in Germany amid the conflagration
of war and revolution. Written in France, *The German
Revolution* was also a product of the global left-
wing upsurge of the 1960s and early 1970s, a period
when many activists and academics began to
rediscover and rewrite the history of the Left from
the founding of the Second International in the 1880s
to the antifascist resistance movements of the 1940s.
The years that Broué covers in depth were those of
the most widespread popular insurgency in Europe
since the revolutions of 1848. They were marked
by the carnage of World War I, the great antiwar
strikes in so many European countries, the Russian
Revolutions of 1917, and the swell of revolutions and
class-based civil wars that ran all across the continent
from 1918 to 1923. These were the years also when,
in the wake of the Bolshevik Revolution, Communist
Parties were founded and the Social-Democratic-
Communist split became virtually unbridgeable.

For Broué, the Bolshevik Revolution remained
the correct model of revolutionary practice and V.I.
Lenin the key strategist and thinker. The tragedy in
Germany was that it lacked comparable leaders and
a sufficiently developed consciousness among the

workers. While the German Left had its powerful figures and devoted, experienced activists, they could never constitute a strong enough nucleus within the labour movement and, in any case, failed to work out a consistent and effective revolutionary strategy. Broué writes of the many heroic struggles of German workers: the antiwar strikes of 1917 and 1918, the revolutionary overthrow of the Imperial government in 1918, the waves of strikes and armed uprisings that continually punctuated the period from 1918 to 1923. But the ultimate defeat in 1923 was a world-shattering event. It marked not only the end of any hopes for a socialist Germany in this period. It also meant that the Bolshevik Revolution would remain isolated. Left to its own devices, the Soviet Union turned in on itself. In Broué's account, the degeneration of the revolutionary movement into Stalinism was a result not of the ideological and political presuppositions of Leninism, but of the historical defeat of the working class abroad, especially in Germany. Had the German proletariat triumphed, Germany's higher technical and cultural levels would have contributed mightily to the development of socialism in the Soviet Union and beyond. The defeat of 1923 was world-shattering in another sense: its reverberations came in 1933 with the counterrevolution triumphant, the rise to power of Hitler and the Nazi Party.

Broué provides a wealth of fascinating detail. He uses to great effect virtually all the materials that were accessible to him at the time, including long-forgotten memoirs and newspaper accounts. His narrative is often gripping: the great working-class upsurge that overthrew the Imperial government in November 1918, the debates within the Spartacist group leading up to the founding of the Communist Party of Germany (KPD) in the very first days of 1919, the struggles for the possession of the streets and factories, the continual back and forth between the emissaries of the Russian Communist Party and their German counterparts. There are also trenchant biographical portraits. For Broué, Rosa Luxemburg and Karl Liebknecht were, of course, the main figures, and despite certain criticisms, his admiration of them is untrammelled. Their assassinations in 1919 marked an irreparable blow to the young Communist Party still struggling to find its bearings. He also evaluates highly their successor as head of the KPD, Paul Levi, despite his split with the Party in 1921. These are well-known figures; what is even more striking in Broué's text is the many portraits of lower-level leaders and activists, the cadres who kept the Party going despite its many defeats.

The German Revolution was written in the 1970s, when academic scholarship on the German labour movement and the German Revolution was in its boom phase. In French, Broué's work stood almost alone.[1] But scores, and even hundreds, of studies appeared in German and English in this period. Most depart sharply from Broué's key analytical points.

The scholarship of from the late 1960s into the 1980s was fuelled largely by the development of social history, which turned the analytical gaze from high politics and élite members of society to the common people. In West Germany, 'historical social science', emanating preeminently from Bielefeld University, provided the dominant paradigm.[2] In the English-speaking world, the great inspiration came from E.P. Thompson's *The Making of the English Working Class*.[3] The English-language scholarship especially brought workers into play as agents of their own history, while the German-language scholarship focused more on the structural constitution of class society and the constraints and possibilities of popular activism. Despite the huge variety of individual works in both languages, the result by the 1990s was an infinitely richer depiction of the conditions of working-class life and the characteristics of labour activism.[4] East-German historical research helped this trend by producing some works that were empirically rich, but overall, the discipline of history was too wedded to official régime interpretations of the past to really contribute to the excitement and innovations in scholarship.[5]

But another result, totally unanticipated in the social history scholarship of the time, was to call into question the very concept of class and the notion of the proletariat as a more or less homogeneous actor in history.[6] In Broué's

---

[1] The exceptions in French are the works of Gilbert Badia, such as, *Le Spartakisme, les dernières années de Rosa Luxemburg et de Karl Liebknecht, 1914–1919* (Paris: l'Arche, 1967).

[2] A good example dealing specifically with labour is Jürgen Kocka, *Klassengesellschaft im Krieg: Deutsche Sozialgeschichte 1914–1918* (Göttingen: Vandenhoeck & Ruprecht, 1973).

[3] E.P. Thompson, *The Making of the English Working Class* (New York: Pantheon, 1964).

[4] The grand syntheses in German are contained in the series, *Geschichte der Arbeiter und der Arbeiterbewegung in Deutschland seit dem Ende des 18. Jahrhunderts*, edited by Gerhard A Ritter. For the period covered by Broué's study, the relevant volume is Heinrich August Winkler, *Von der Revolution zur Stabilisierung: Arbeiter und Arbeiterbewegung in der Weimarer Republik 1918 bis 1924* (Berlin: J. H. W. Dietz Nachf., 1984).

[5] Notable examples of East German scholarship on German labour include Erwin Könneman and Hans-Joachim Krusch, *Aktionseinheit contra Kapp-Putsch* (Berlin: Dietz, 1972), and Hartmut Zwahr (eds.), *Die Konstituierung der deutschen Arbeiterklasse von den dreissiger bis zu den siebziger Jahren des 19. Jahrhunderts* (Berlin: Akademie-Verlag, 1981).

[6] For the best critique, see Katheeln Canning, 'Gender and the Politics of Class Formation: Rethinking German Labor History', *American Historical Review*, 97, 3, 1992:

account, there is a working class in the singular, just as there is a capitalist class in the singular. Each has its own interests, which are unmediated reflections of their respective positions in the class hierarchy. But most of the academic scholarship demonstrated that the working class was a highly complex entity, divided by gender, skill, religion, region, and politics. The Social-Democratic and Communist Parties presumed to speak for the working class, but their relationship to their class base was always tenuous. The parties sought to channel, educate, and discipline their members; they were not just the unmediated expression of the working class, which, in any case, hardly existed in the singular.[7]

By all accounts, the workers councils were the key institutions that emerged in the German Revolution, as they had been in the Bolshevik Revolution. Much of the historical debate has centred on the question of just how radical were the councils.[8] Broué is deeply attentive to the political conflicts within the labour movement in the early months of the Revolution, but he most definitely upholds the radical potential of the councils. By the end of the scholarly wave in the late 1980s, a far more restrained view had become predominant. In this reading, the councils were never revolutionary; most of them simply turned over day-to-day power to state bureaucrats and backed the Social-Democratic Party. In the wake of the disasters of World War I, the vast majority of the councils simply sought to administer an orderly transition to a new democratic government and a peacetime economy.[9] Yet Broué is correct, it seems to me, to emphasise the *potential* of the councils, and not just their immediate conservatism.[10] Certainly, there is evidence enough of efforts to turn them into effective agencies of power, if not in the immediate weeks and months of the Revolution, then during the socialisation strikes in spring 1919 and the general strike that defeated the Kapp Putsch in spring 1920.

736–68, and idem, *Languages of Labor and Gender: Female Factory Work in Germany, 1850–1914* (Ithaca: Cornell University Press, 1994).

   [7] For an account of the prewar labour movement that reflects this position, see Eric D. Weitz, *Creating German Communism, 1890–1990: From Popular Protests to Socialist State* (Princeton: Princeton University Press, 1997), pp. 18–61, and, generally, David E. Barclay and Eric D. Weitz (eds.) *Between Reform and Revolution: German Socialism and Communism from 1840 to 1990* (New York: Berghahn Books, 1998).

   [8] The two important, early works that stimulated the debate were Eberhard Kolb, *Die Arbeiterräte in der deutschen Innenpolitik* (Düsseldorf: Droste, 1962), and Peter von Oertzen, *Betriebsräte in der Novemberrevolution* (Düsseldorf: Droste, 1963)

   [9] For this position, see Winkler, *Von der Revolution zur Stabilisierung*.

   [10] See also Weitz, *Creating German Communism*.

For all his attentiveness to the manifestations of popular protest, Broué misses one central element that has been highlighted in the scholarship since around 1990: women's activism, notably around issues of consumption, but also in the workplace.[11] Clearly, this is a result of the surge in women's and gender history over the last few decades. Broué is fixated on the workplace and the working class. Yet there was a whole realm of popular activism in marketplaces, unemployment offices, and coal depots. No less than the police forces and civilian officials, the overwhelmingly male leadership of the trade unions and workers' parties had no idea how to address these protests. They could envision the new society based on labour's participation and control over the production process, but they could not imagine how a new society could be built upon women's protests. Later, the KPD would also develop an uneasy and unclear relationship to such efforts. It sometimes supported any manifestation of protest against the existing society, but its proletarian heart remained committed to the mines and factories as the sites of 'real' activism.[12]

And what about the Party itself? The KPD was the first mass-based Communist Party to emerge outside of the Soviet Union. The Soviet leaders placed enormous hopes on a German revolution. The German comrades basked in the glow of these expectations. Until the disastrous defeat of 1933, they ranked just behind the Russians in the Comintern. But the KPD also came increasingly under the sway of the Soviets, as was the case with all Communist Parties around the globe. This, too, was a result of the great defeat of 1923. Ironically, here Broué is in line with commentators such as Hermann Weber, who view the Stalinisation of the KPD as developing very early and as substantially complete by 1928.[13] More recent histories, situated more firmly in the social history of the German working class, have challenged this

---

[11] See, for example, Ute Daniel, *Arbeiterfrauen in der Kriegsgesellschaft: Beruf, Familie und Politik im Ersten Weltkrieg* (Göttingen: Vandenhoeck and Ruprecht, 1989); Karen Hagemann, *Frauenalltag und Männerpolitik: Alltagsleben und gesellschaftliches Handeln von Arbeiterfrauen in der Weimar Republik* (Bonn: J.H.W. Dietz Nachf., 1990); Karin Hartewig, *Das unberechenbare Jahrzehnt: Bergarbeiter und ihre Familien im Ruhrgebiet* (Munich: Beck, 1993); Atina Grossmann, *Reforming Sex: The German Movement for Birth Control and Abortion Reform, 1920–1950* (New York: Oxford University Press, 1995); and Belinda Davis, *Home Fires Burning: Food, Politics, and Everyday Life in World War I Berlin* (Chapel Hill: University of North Carolina Press, 2000).

[12] See Weitz, *Creating German Communism*, pp. 188–232.

[13] Among many other works, see Weber's magnum opus, *Die Wandlung des deutschen Kommunismus: Die Stalinisierung der KPD in der Weimarer Republik*, 2 vols. (Frankfurt am Main: Europäische Verlagsanstalt, 1969).

approach.[14] Instead, they have argued that the character of the KPD had very much to do with domestic social and political factors. Notably, the urban working-class milieu in Germany decisively shaped the KPD, partly by giving it its activist hue, partly by solidifying a split between Social Democrats and Communists that ran through local communities and the workplace as well as the political parties. Other factors, like the tendency to view the male proletarian as the essential actor and male combativeness as the key revolutionary virtue, also decisively shaped the nature of the KPD, and these characteristics had roots in Germany and Europe as well as in the Soviet Union. In other words, it is too narrow a perspective to view the history of German Communism through the lens of Moscow. It is one of the great virtues of Broué's study that he explores in intricate detail German developments at the level of both high politics and popular activism. But, after 1923, he argues, the history of German Communism was determined in Moscow. In fact, there was always a complex interaction between Comintern and Soviet régime directives, on the one hand, and the proclivities and practices of German Communists, on the other.

A great deal has changed in the world since the original French publication of *The German Revolution*. Communist régimes no longer exist in Europe, and few are their advocates. The confidence in the triumph of socialism and communism that animated Broué's work is shared by fewer and fewer people. The political field has become vastly more complicated with the decline of traditional parties in Europe, including those of the classical labour movement, and the rise of new social movements, such as feminism and environmentalism. Scholarly controversies are different from those that fuelled the many studies on German labour from the late 1960s into the 1980s. German Communist archives are open for investigation, and have enabled scholars to write much more finely-honed depictions of the KPD and its successor, the Socialist Unity Party (SED). Yet Pierre Broué's study remains a highly valuable contribution to the literature and a testament to what a creative scholar can produce even without the free run of the archives.

---

[14] See Klaus-Michael Mallmann, *Kommunisten in der Weimarer Republik* (Darmstadt: Wissenschaftliche Buchgesellschaft, 1999), and Weitz, *Creating German Communism*.

Suggestions for Further Reading[15]

Source publications and reference works

Bauer, Franz J. (ed.), *Die Regierung Eisner 1918/19. Ministerratsprotokolle und Dokumente*, Düsseldorf: Droste Verlag, 1987.

Bernstein, Eduard, *Die deutsche Revolution von 1918/19. Geschichte der Entstehung und ersten Arbeitsperiode der deutschen Republik*, edited by Heinrich August Winkler, annotated by Teresa Löwe, Bonn: Verlag J.H.W. Dietz Nachf., 1998.

Bock, Hans Manfred, 'Bericht über den Gründungsparteitag der KAPD am 4. und 5. April 1920 in Berlin', *Jahrbuch Arbeiterbewegung*, 5, 1977: 185–242.

Crusius, R., G. Schiefelbein and M. Wilke (eds.), *Die Betriebsräte in der Weimarer Republik*, 2 Volumes, Berlin: Verlag Olle & Wolter, 1978.

Groß-Berliner Arbeiter- und Soldatenräte in der Revolution 1918/19. Dokumente der Vollversammlungen und des Vollzugsrates.

Vol. 1: Gerhard Engel et.al. (eds.), *Vom Ausbruch der Revolution bis zum 1. Reichsrätekongreß*, Berlin: Akademie-Verlag, 1993.

Vol. 2: Gerhard Engel et al. (eds.), *Vom Reichsrätekongreß bis zum Generalstreikbeschluß am 3. März 1919*, Berlin: Akademie-Verlag, 1997.

Heinrich Potthoff and Hermann Weber (eds.), *Die SPD-Fraktion in der Nationalversammlung, 1919–1920*, Düsseldorf: Droste Verlag, 1986.

Quellen zur Geschichte der deutschen Gewerkschaftsbewegung im 20. Jahrhundert.

Vol. 1: Klaus Schönhoven (ed.), *Die Gewerkschaften in Weltkrieg und Revolution 1914–1919*, Cologne: Bund-Verlag, 1985.

Vol. 2: Michael Ruck (ed.), *Die Gewerkschaften in den Anfangsjahren der Republik 1919–1923*, Cologne: Bund-Verlag, 1985.

Quellen zur Geschichte der Rätebewegung in Deutschland.

Vol. 1: Eberhard Kolb with Reinhard Rürup (eds.), *Der Zentralrat der Deutschen Sozialistischen Republik, 19.12.1918–8.4.1919*. Leiden: Brill, 1968.

Vol. 2: Eberhard Kolb and Klaus Schönhoven (eds.), *Regionale und lokale Räteorganisationen in Württemberg*, Düsseldorf: Droste Verlag, 1976.

Vol. 3: Peter Brandt and Reinhard Rürup (eds.), *Arbeiter-, Soldaten- und Volksräte in Baden, 1918/19*, Düsseldorf: Droste Verlag, 1980.

Sabine Roß, *Biographisches Handbuch der Reichsrätekongresse 1918/19*, Düsseldorf: Droste Verlag, 2000.

Weber, Hermann (ed.), *Die Gründung der KPD. Protokoll und Materialien des Gründungsparteitages der Kommunistischen Partei Deutschlands 1918/19*, Berlin: Dietz Verlag, 1993.

Studies of developments in Germany

Arnold, Volker, *Rätebewegung und Rätetheorien in der Novemberrevolution. Räte als Organisationsformen des Kampfes und der Selbstbestimmung*, Second revised edition, Hamburg: Junius Verlag, 1985.

Bahne, Siegfried, 'Die Erwerbslosenpolitik der KPD in der Weimarer Republik', in *Vom Elend der Handarbeit: Probleme historischer Unterschichtenforschung*, edited by Hans Mommsen and Wilfried Schulze, Stuttgart: Klett-Cotta, 1981.

---

[15] Compiled by Marcel van der Linden and Eric D. Weitz.

Barclay, David E. and Eric D. Weitz (eds.), *Between Reform and Revolution: Studies in German Socialism and Communism from 1840 to 1990*, Providence: Berghahn, 1996.

Bauer, Karin, *Clara Zetkin und die proletarische Frauenbewegung*, Berlin: Oberbaum, 1978.

Bayerlein, Bruno, Leonid G. Babičenko, Fridrich Firsov, and Aleksandr Ju. Vatlin (eds.), *Deutscher Oktober, 1923. Ein Revolutionsplan und sein Scheitern*, Berlin: Aufbau Verlag, 2003.

Bock, Hans Manfred. *Syndikalismus und Linkskommunismus von 1918 bis 1923. Ein Beitrag zur Sozial- und Ideengeschichte der frühen Weimarer Republik*, Second edition, Darmstadt: Wissenschaftliche Buchgesellschaft, 1993.

Bodek, Richard, 'Communist Music in the Streets: Politics and Perceptions in Berlin at the End of the Weimar Republic', in *Elections, Mass Politics, and Social Change in Modern Germany: New Perspectives*, edited by Larry Eugene Jones and James Retallack, Cambridge: Cambridge University Press, 1992.

Canning, Kathleen. 'Gender and the Politics of Class Formation: Rethinking German Labor History', *American Historical Review*, 97, 3, 1992: 736–68.

Crew, David, 'A Social Republic? Social Democrats, Communists, and the Weimar Welfare State, 1919–1933', in *Between Reform and Revolution: Studies in German Socialism and Communism from 1840 to 1990*, edited by David E. Barclay and Eric D. Weitz, Providence: Berghahn, 1996.

Daniel, Ute, *Arbeiterfrauen in der Kriegsgesellschaft: Beruf, Familie und Politik im Ersten Weltkrieg*, Göttingen: Vandenhoeck & Ruprecht, 1989.

Davis, Belinda, *Home Fires Burning: Food, Politics, and Everyday Life in World War I Berlin*, Chapel Hill: Univerity of North Carolina Press, 2000.

Dobson, Sean, *Authority and Upheaval in Leipzig, 1910–1920. The Story of a Relationship*, New York: Columbia University Press, 2001.

Dreetz, Dieter, Klaus Gessner and Heinz Sperling, *Bewaffnete Kämpfe in Deutschland 1918–1923*, Berlin: Militärverlag der Deutschen Demokratischen Republik, 1988.

Feldman, Gerald D., Eberhard Kolb and Reinhard Rürup, 'Die Massenbewegung der Arbeiterschaft in Deutschland nach dem Ersten Weltkrieg', *Politische Vierteljahrschrift*, 13, 3, 1972: 84–105.

—— et al., *Die Anpassung an die Inflation / The Adaption to Inflation*, Berlin and New York: Walter de Gruyter, 1986.

Fischer, Conan J., *The German Communists and the Rise of Nazism*, New York: St. Martin's Press, 1991.

Fülberth, Georg, *Die Beziehungen zwischen SPD und KPD in der Kommunalpolitik der Weimarer Periode 1918/19 bis 1933*, Cologne: Pahl-Rugenstein, 1985.

Gietinger, Klaus, *Eine Leiche im Landwehrkanal. Die Ermordung der Rosa L.* Mainz: Decaton Verlag, 1993.

Grau, Bernhard, *Kurt Eisner 1867–1919. Eine Biographie*, Munich: Verlag C.H. Beck, 2001.

Grossmann, Atina, *Reforming Sex: The German Movement for Birth Control and Abortion Reform, 1920–1950*, New York: Oxford University Press, 1995.

Guttsmann, W. L., *Workers' Culture in Weimar Germany: Between Tradition and Commitment*, New York: Berg, 1990.

Hagemann, Karen, *Frauenalltag und Männerpolitik: Alltagsleben und gesellschaftliches Handeln von Arbeiterfrauen in der Weimarer Republik*, Bonn: J.H.W. Dietz Nachf., 1990.

Harman, Chris, *The Lost Revolution: Germany 1918–1923*, London: Bookmarks, 1982.

Hartewig, Karin, *Das unberechenbare Jahrzehnt. Bergarbeiter und ihre Familien im Ruhrgebiet 1914–1924*, Munich: Verlag C.H. Beck, 1993.

Heer-Kleinert, Lore, *Die Gewerkschaftspolitik der KPD in der Weimarer Republik*, Frankfurt a. M.: Campus, 1983.

Herlemann, Beatrix, *Die Kommunalpolitik der KPD im Ruhrgebeit 1924–1933*, Wuppertal: Peter Hammer, 1977.

Kluge, Ulrich, *Soldatenräte und Revolution. Studien zur Militärpolitik in Deutschland 1918/19*, Göttingen: Vandenhoeck & Ruprecht, 1975.

——, *Die deutsche Revolution 1918/1919*, Frankfurt am Main: Suhrkamp Verlag, 1985.

Koch-Baumgarten, Sigrid, *Aufstand der Avantgarde. Die Märzaktion der KPD 1921*, Frankfurt am Main and New York: Campus Verlag, 1986.

Kolb, Eberhard, *Die Arbeiterräte in der deutschen Innenpolitik 1918–1919*, Expanded edition, Frankfurt am Main [etc.]: Ullstein, 1978.

—— (ed.), *Friedrich Ebert als Reichspräsident. Amtsführung und Amtsverständnis*, Munich: Oldenbourg Verlag, 1997.

Kontos, Silvia, *'Die Partei kämpft wie ein Mann': Frauenpolitik der KPD in der Weimarer Republik*, Frankfurt am Main: Roter Stern, 1979.

Krause, Hartfrid, *USPD: Geschichte der Unabhängigen Sozialdemokratischen Partei Deutschlands*, Frankfurt am Main: Europäische Verlags-Anstalt, 1975.

Krumpholz, Ralf, *Wahrnehmung und Politik. Die Bedeutungs des Ordnungsdenkens für das politische Handeln am Beispiel der deutschen Revolution von 1918–1920*, Münster: Lit Verlag, 1998.

Lehnert, Detlef, *Sozialdemokratie und Novemberrevolution. Die Neuordnungsdebatte 1918/19 in der politischen Publizistik von SPD und USPD*, Frankfurt am Main and New York: Campus Verlag, 1983.

Linse, Ulrich, *Die entschiedene Jugend 1919–1921. Deutschlands erste revolutionäre Schüler- und Studentenbewegung*, Frankfurt am Main: Dipa-Verlag, 1981.

Lucas, Erhard, *Märzrevolution im Ruhrgebiet. März/April 1920*, 3 Volumes, Frankfurt am Main: Verlag Roter Stern, 1970–8.

——, *Zwei Formen von Radikalismus in der deutschen Arbeiterbewegung*, Frankfurt am Main: Verlag Roter Stern, 1976.

Luz, Rudolf, *KPD, Weimarer Staat und politische Einheit der Arbeiterbewegung in der Nachkriegskrise 1919–1922/23*, Konstanz: Hartung-Gorre Verlag, 1987.

Mason, Tim, *Nazism, Fascism and the Working Class: Essays by Tim Mason*, edited by Jane Caplan, Cambridge: Cambridge University Press, 1995.

Mallmann, Klaus-Michael, *Kommunisten in der Weimarer Republik*, Darmstadt: Wissenschaftliche Buchgesellschaft, 1999.

Mommsen, Hans, *Die verspielte Freiheit: Der Weg der Republik von Weimar in den Untergang 1918 bis 1933*, Frankfurt a. M.: Propyläen, 1990.

Pelz, William A., *The Spartakusbund and the German Working Class Movement 1914–1919*, Lewiston: The Edwin Mellen Press, 1987.

Peterson, Larry, *German Communism, Workers' Protest, and Labor Unions. The Politics of the United Front in Rhineland-Westphalia 1920–1924*, Dordrecht: Kluwer Academic Publishers, 1993.

Peukert, Detlev J.K., *Die Weimarer Republik: Krisenjahre der klassischen Moderne*, Frankfurt a. M.: Suhrkamp, 1987.

——, *Jugend zwischen Krieg und Krise. Lebenswelten von Arbeiterjungen in der Weimarer Republik*, Cologne: Bund-Verlag, 1987.

Rosenhaft, Eve, *Beating the Fascists? The German Communists and Political Violence, 1929–1933*, Cambridge: Cambridge University Press, 1983.

Rouette, Susanne, *Sozialpolitik als Geschlechterpolitik. Die Regulierung der*

Frauenarbeit nach dem Ersten Weltkrieg, Frankfurt am Main and New York: Campus Verlag, 1993.

Ruck, Michael, *Die Freien Gewerkschaften im Ruhrkampf 1923*, Cologne: Bund-Verlag, 1986.

Rürup, Reinhard, 'Demokratischer Revolution und "dritter Weg": Die deutsche Revolution von 1918/19 in den neueren wissenschaftlichen Diskussion', *Geschichte und Gesellschaft*, 9, 2, 1983: 278–301.

Rurup, Reinhard (ed.), *Arbeiter- und Soldatenräte im rheinisch-westfälischen Industriegebiet. Studien zur Geschichte der Revolution 1918/19*, Wuppertal: Verlag Peter Hammer, 1975.

Schöck, Eva Cornelia, *Arbeitslosigkeit und Rationalisierung: Die Lage der Arbeiter und die kommunistische Gewerkschaftspolitik 1920–1928*, Frankfurt a. M.: Campus, 1977.

Schönhoven, Klaus, *Reformismus und Radikalismus: Gespaltene Arbeiterbewegun im Weimarer Sozialstaat*, Munich: DTV, 1989.

Schumann, Dirk, *Politische Gewalt in der Weimarer Republik 1918–1933. Kampf um die Straße und Furcht vor dem Bürgerkrieg*, Essen: Klartext, 2001.

Seligmann, Michael, *Aufstand der Räte. Die erste bayerische Räterepublik vom 7. April 1919*, Grafenau: Trotzdem Verlag, 1989.

Stolle, Uta, *Arbeiterpolitik im Betrieb: Frauen und Männer, Reformisten und Radikale, Fach- und Massenarbeiter bei Bayer, BASF, Bosch und in Solingen (1900–1933)*, Frankfurt a. M.: Campus, 1980.

Tenfelde, Klaus (ed.), *Arbeiter im 20. Jahrhundert*, Stuttgart: Klett-Cotta, 1991.

——, *Proletarische Provinz: Radikalisierung und Widerstand in Penzberg/Oberbayern 1900–1945*, Munich: Oldenbourg, 1982.

Weber, Hermann, *Kommunismus in Deutschland 1918–1945*, Darmstadt: Wissenschaftliche Buchgesellschaft, 1983.

Weber, Stefan, *Ein kommunistischer Putsch? Märzaktion 1921 in Mitteldeutschland*, Berlin: Dietz, 1991.

Weinhauer, Klaus, *Alltag und Arbeitskampf im Hamburger Hafen. Sozialgeschichte der Hamburger Hafenarbeiter 1914–1933*, Paderborn: Ferdinand Schöningh, 1994.

Weitz, Eric D., *Creating German Communism, 1890–1990: From Popular Protests to Socialist State*, Princeton: Princeton University Press, 1997.

——, *Popular Communism: Political Strategies and Social Histories in the Formation of the German, French, and Italian Communist Parties, 1919–1948*, Western Societies Program Occasional Paper no. 31, Ithaca: Cornell University Institute for European Studies, 1992.

——. '"Rosa Luxemburg Belongs To Us!": German Communism and the Luxemburg Legacy', *Central European History*, 27, 1, 1994: 27–64.

Robert F. Wheeler, *USPD und Internationale. Sozialistischer Internationalismus in der Zeit der Revolution*, Frankfurt am Main: Ullstein Verlag, 1975.

Winkler, Heinrich August, *Der Schein der Normalität: Arbeiter und Arbeiterbewegung in der Weimarer Republik 1924 bis 1930*, Berlin: J.H.W. Dietz Nachf., 1988.

——, *Von der Revolution zur Stabilisierung: Arbeiter und Arbeiterbewegung in der Weimarer Republik 1918 bis 1924*, Berlin: J.H.W. Dietz Nachf., 1984.

——, *Der Weg in die Katastrophe: Arbeiter und Arbeiterbewegung in der Weimarer Republik 1930 bis 1933*, Berlin: J.H.W. Dietz Nachf., 1990.

Wunderer, Hartmann, 'Materialien zur Soziologie der Mitgliedschaft und Wählerschaft der KPD zur Zeit der Weimarer Republik', *Gesellschaft*, 5, 1975: 257–81.

Studies of international connections

Berger, Stefan, and David Broughton (eds.), *The Force of Labour. The Western European Labour Movement and the Working Class in the Twentieth Century*, Oxford and Washington, DC: Berg, 1995.

Bertrand, Charles (ed.), *Revolutionary Situations in Europe, 1917–1922. Germany, Italy, Austria-Hungary*, Montreal: Interuniversity Centre for European Studies, 1977.

Broué, Pierre, *Histoire de l'Internationale Communiste 1919–1943*, Paris: Fayard.

Carsten, Francis L., *Revolution in Central Europe, 1918–1919*, Berkeley: University of California Press, 1972.

Cronin, James E., and Carmen Sirianni (eds), *Work, Community, and Power. The Experience of Labor in Europe and America, 1900–1925*, Philadelphia: Temple University Press, 1983.

Gluckstein, Donny, *The Western Soviets. Workers' Councils versus Parliament 1915–1920*, London: Bookmarks, 1985.

Haimson, Leopold H., and Giulio Sapelli (eds.), *Strikes, Social Conflict and the First World War. An International Perspective*, Milan: Feltrinelli, 1992.

Haimson, Leopold H., and Charles Tilly (eds.), *Strikes, Wars, and Revolutions in an International Perspective. Strike Waves in the Late Nineteenth and Early Twentieth Centuries*, Cambridge: Cambridge University Press, 1989.

Linden, Marcel van der, 'Communist Parties: The First Generation (1918–1923)', in *Transnational Labour History: Explorations*. Aldershot: Ashgate, 2003.

Löwenthal, Richard, 'The "Missing Revolution" in Industrial Societies: Comparative Reflections on a German Problem', in: Volker R. Berghahn and Martin Kitchen (eds.), *Germany in the Age of Total War*, London: Croom Helm, 1981.

Post, Ken, *Revolution's Other World. Communism and the Periphery, 1917–39*, Basingstoke and New York: Macmillan Press, 1997.

Schmitt, Hans A. (ed.), *Neutral Europe between War and Revolution 1917–23*. Charlottesville: University of Virginia Press, 1988.

Vatlin, Alexander. 'The Testing-Ground of World Revolution: Germany in the 1920s', in Tim Rees and Andrew Thorpe (eds.), *International Communism and the Communist International 1919–43*, Manchester and New York: Manchester University Press, 1998.

Wrigley, Chris (ed.), *Challenges of Labour: Central and Western Europe 1917–1920*, London: Routledge, 1993.

Preface

In 1970, in the great lecture theatre of the Polytechnic Museum in Moscow, one of the main cities of the United Socialist States of Europe, a history lecture is being given dealing with the Russian Revolution which opened the way for the victory of socialism in Europe. The professor-fitter has just recalled the difficult conditions of the struggle during the first years of the Soviet state, the obstacles created by the rural and backward nature of the country and its initial isolation. He explains:

> If the revolution in the West had been delayed too long, this situation could have led to an aggressive socialist war by Russia, supported by the European proletariat, against the capitalist West. This did not happen because the proletarian revolution was by this time already knocking at the door owing to its own inner development.[1]

After a long period of instances of dual power, especially in Germany, the capture of power by workers' councils in several industrial centres gave the signal for a bitter civil war from which the German workers emerged victorious. But this victory unleashed an attack by the capitalist governments of France and Poland. The Red Army of the Soviet Union responded, whilst the imperialist regiments,

---

[1] E. Preobrazhensky, *From NEP to Socialism*, London, 1973, p. 99.

undermined from within by revolutionary propaganda, melted in the fire of the German Revolution. Now it was the turn of the French and Polish workers to rise. The European revolution triumphed, and the United Socialist States of Europe were established. The lecturer concludes:

> New Soviet Europe opened a fresh page in economic development. The industrial technique of Germany was united with Russian agriculture, and on the territory of Europe there began rapidly to develop and become consolidated a new economic organism, revealing enormous possibilities and a mighty breakthrough to the expansion of the productive forces. And along with this, Soviet Russia, which previously had outstripped Europe politically, now modestly took its place as an economically backward country behind the advanced industrial countries of the proletarian dictatorship.[2]

In 1922, the young Communist leader Preobrazhensky imagined that this would be how, half a century later, a new generation would be taught about the unfolding of the final struggle, the first episodes of which his contemporaries were living through. It was still no more than a picture of the future presented in the form of a literary fiction. However, a year later, one of the main leaders of Soviet Russia, the President of the Communist International, Grigory Zinoviev, wrote in *Pravda*, the central organ of the Russian Communist Party, a series of articles on the coming German Revolution:

> The German events are developing with the inexorability of fate. The path which it took the Russian Revolution twelve years to cover, from 1906 to 1917, will have taken the German Revolution five years, from 1918 to 1923. In the course of the last few days, events have speeded up even more. First of all, the 'coalition', then the 'grand coalition', thereafter the Kornilov episode, the cabinet of specialists, of personalities, and now, once again something like a 'grand coalition' – in short an endless whirlwind of governments. This is what was happening 'above'. But 'below', the masses are seething with excitement, and the fight which, in a short period, will decide Germany's future, is about to begin. The proletarian revolution is knocking at Germany's door; you would have to be blind not to see it. The coming events will have a *world-historical meaning*. Very soon, everyone will see that this autumn of 1923 is a turning-point, not just for the history of Germany, but for the history of the whole world. With trembling hands, the

---

[2] Ibid., p. 123.

proletariat is turning the vital page of the world-wide struggle of the proletariat. A new chapter is opening in the history of the proletarian world revolution.[3]

The President of the International added:

> The key fact is that the German Revolution will have a powerful industrial base.... In this sense, Lenin's words remain correct: 'In Western Europe', he said, 'and above all in countries like Germany, it will be much more difficult to begin the proletarian revolution than in Russia. But it will be much easier to continue and complete it.' ... The German proletariat no longer runs the risk of taking power prematurely. The conditions for the victory of the proletarian revolution in Germany have long been ripe.... The German Revolution will have the advantage of the full assistance of the Russian experience, and it will not repeat the mistakes of the Russian Revolution ... As for the wonderful energy which twenty million German proletarians, steeled, educated and organised, will be able to display in the final struggle for socialism, we cannot yet have the remotest conception of it.[4]

Lenin and his comrades in the Bolshevik Party led in Russia a revolution which in their eyes was only a struggle of the vanguard. But the main battle did not take place, and the Russian vanguard remained isolated. The German Revolution – the decisive phase for all revolutionaries of the time – finally failed, after five years of ups and downs.

Since that time, many commentators have drawn conclusions which suited their ideology or their politics; some have seen the superior revolutionary qualities of the Russian people, the new Messiah; others have discovered the deep democratic sentiments – or alternatively, the congenital militarisation – of the German people; and all have noted the illusions of the utopians who believed they could transplant into a Western country, in the heart of an advanced society, the experience of the Russian October Revolution.

Writing on the eve of the Second World War, an eminent Germanist judged that the aborted German Revolution had consisted of 'no more than a disturbed interval of which the cause could be discovered in the temporary crisis of nervous disequilibrium produced by the physical privations of the

---

[3] G. Sinowjew (G. Zinoviev), *Probleme der Deutschen Revolution*, Hamburg, 1923, pp. 1–2.

[4] Ibid., pp. 7–11.

war, and the physical collapse consequent on the defeat and collapse of the Reich'.[5] Others had tried to explain the Paris Commune by what they called 'the mass psychosis of the besieged'. But this author, apparently attached to the democratic ideal, gave a more specifically political explanation of the failure of the revolution:

> Very rapidly, the organised German worker understood the fundamental difference which separated Germany from Russia, and sensed the irreparable catastrophe that would have been produced in Germany, a land of developed and scientifically organised industry, by the sudden establishment of full-blooded communism such as had been achieved in Russia.[6]

It seems worthwhile to recall these comments, inasmuch as, in fact, the revolution in Germany was supplanted by a counter-revolution which, a few years later, under the name of Hitlerism, was to launch on the world an assault of barbarism such that we may wonder to what other 'catastrophe' it could be compared, even by an 'organised worker'! We shall encounter the men of this counter-revolution in the course of our pages: Faupel, the staff officer who tricked the delegates from the soldiers' councils, and who, twenty years later, was to command the Condor Legion in Spain; Canaris, the naval officer who assisted the escape of one of the murderers of Rosa Luxemburg, and twenty years later was to command the Abwehr; the political officer, power behind the throne to better-known generals, Major Kurt von Schleicher, briefly Chancellor in 1932; and also Adolf Hitler and Hermann Goering, Krupp, Thyssen and I.G. Farben. The battle fought in Germany between 1918 and 1923 shaped our past, and undoubtedly weighs on our present.

It also concerns our future. From 1918 to 1923, in revolutionary Germany, the struggle was not street-fighting and the storming of barricades everyday; it was not waged exclusively with machine-guns, mortars and flame-throwers. It was also, and above all, the hidden struggle in the factories, the mines, the community centres, the unions and the parties, in public meetings and committees, in political and economic strikes, in street demonstrations, polemics and theoretical debates. It was a class struggle and above all a struggle within the working class; what was at stake was the building, in Germany and in the world, of a revolutionary party which was fully determined to change

---

[5] H. Lichtenberger, *L'Allemagne nouvelle*, 1936, p. 12.
[6] Ibid., pp. 11–12.

the world. The road leading to this goal is neither straight nor simple, nor even easy to perceive. Between 'ultra-leftism' and 'opportunism', between 'sectarianism' and 'revisionism', between 'activism' and 'passivity', the German revolutionaries toiled greatly, and in vain, to trace their path to the future, to discover, sometimes through their own negative experiences, sometimes in the successful example of their Russian comrades, the means to ensure the seizure of power by the working class in their country.

Many of the key documents we needed to illuminate this attempt were lacking: political necessities have, for the time being, condemned them to lie dormant in archives to which we have been refused access. Far from the least of the problems posed in this narrative of the aborted birth of a 'mass' communist party is the role played by the Communist International, and, within that International, by the Bolshevik Party in power in Russia.

Chapter One
The Battlefield

Today we have one soldier in five, in a few years time we shall have one in three, by 1900 the army, hitherto the most outstandingly Prussian element in Germany, will have a socialist majority. That is coming about as if by fate. The Berlin government can see it happening just as clearly as we can, but it is powerless.

Thus Friedrich Engels, the companion-in-arms of Marx, and with him the founder of scientific socialism, wrote in the early 1890s in his analysis of the prospects before the German workers' movement. He envisaged only one remaining serious obstacle – war:

A war would change all that. . . . But if war is to break out . . . one thing is certain. This war, in which 15 to 20 million armed men would slaughter one another and devastate Europe as it has never been devastated before – this war would either lead to the immediate triumph of socialism, or it would lead to such an upheaval in the old order of things, it would leave behind it everywhere such a heap of ruins, that the old capitalist society would become more impossible than ever, and the social revolution, set back by 10 or 15 years, would only be all the more radical and more rapidly implemented.[1]

---

[1] F. Engels, 'Socialism in Germany', in K. Marx and F. Engels, *Collected Works*, Volume 27, Moscow, 1990, pp. 240–5.

Engels thus expected Germany to be at the centre of the battlefield on which proletariat and bourgeoisie would face each other in the final conflict.

An advanced capitalist country

Marx and Engels considered that the preconditions for socialism were predicated upon the development of the forces of production within the capitalist system, the numerical increase and concentration of the proletariat, and the ability of the proletariat to develop its class consciousness and forms of organisation. According to this analysis, Germany at the start of the twentieth century was one of those advanced countries in which the prospects for victory of the revolution were both closest and most realistic.

Germany experienced a profound economic transformation in the closing years of the nineteenth century and the opening years of the twentieth. Its natural resources in coal, the basis of an industrial economy at that time, its extremely rapid demographic expansion, which had resulted by 1913 in a population of 67.8 million, and its long-established commercial development which had accumulated the necessary capital for an industrial revolution that had raised Germany within a few decades into the ranks of the most advanced capitalist countries. With a production of 190 million tonnes in 1913, Germany was the second-largest coal producer in the world. With a production of 27 million tonnes of iron – which was not sufficient to meet its needs – Germany held the first place in Europe. Its coal and potash mines – 10 million tonnes being extracted in 1913 – enabled it to reach the first rank with the output of its chemical industry. From 1890 onwards, Germany was the first European state to undertake on an industrial scale the exploitation of the new sources of energy, electricity and the internal combustion engine. On the eve of 1914, it led Europe in the production of electrical appliances. Not only was German industrial preponderance so clearly marked that in this field it could be compared only with the USA, but it showed a remarkable capacity for using new technologies and procedures. No other country had initiated a system of scientific research so closely linked to industrial applications. In research laboratories and in establishments of technical education, Germany was in the vanguard of progress and of the scientific organisation of production.[2]

---

[2] P. Renouvin, *L'Empire allemand de 1890 à 1918*, Volume 1, pp. 11–25.

The German economy, like the British or the American, can serve for the study of the imperialist phase of capitalism, even though the belated character of its development meant that it lacked a colonial empire like that of France or Britain. In 1913, the value of its external trade was 22.5 million marks, double that of France, and 85 per cent of that of Britain.[3] It had commercial connections with the entire world, and as it could no longer absorb all of its products in its internal market, it sought outlets for them across the globe.

An incomplete bourgeois revolution

The German state is a very recent creation. For a long time it was a question only of 'the Germanies'. The movement of nationalities which shook Europe in the nineteenth century seemed in 1848 to be drawing Germany along the road of realising its unity by revolutionary means. But the German bourgeoisie had neither the boldness nor the confidence in its own strength of the French bourgeoisie in 1789. Threatened by the proletarian movement which was taking shape on the extreme Left of the democratic movement, it preferred security behind the ramparts of the monarchical state to a popular-democratic adventure. It made its choice between political liberalism and the profits which the unification of the country under the Prussian fist ensured. It has been said that German unity was erected in the years 1852–57 'on coal and iron',[4] and that 'Saint Manchester was the godfather at the baptism of the new Reich'. But it was the Prussian army, led by Bismarck, which inscribed German unity in the reality of frontiers and law. In this way, Prussia stamped on unified Germany the imprint of its double aspect, that of the triumphant bourgeoisie more absorbed in the pursuit of profits than in 'sterile political games', and that of the landed gentry of the East, the junkers in their helmets and boots, whose arrogance and military strength were to make Europe tremble after the 1860s.

This double aspect could be seen in the complexity of the Imperial Constitution. The Reich was not a unitary state; it was a federation, made up of twenty-five states – from Prussia, which had more than half the population

---

[3] Ibid., p. 17.
[4] A parody of Bismarck's remark that Germany would be unified by 'blood and iron'. [Translator's note.]

and nine-tenths of the mining and metallurgical resources, to tiny principalities of 50,000 inhabitants, by way of Bavaria, Saxony and Württemberg with a few million inhabitants, and the three 'free cities' of Hamburg, Bremen and Lübeck.[5] Each of these states retained its own constitution. Prussia had its king, who was also the German emperor. Bavaria, Saxony and Württemberg had their own kings, Baden and Hesse their grand dukes, and the free cities their senates. Each had legislative assemblies, with a nominated upper chamber and an elected lower chamber. The electoral system varied from one state to another: Württemberg adopted universal suffrage, while Baden gave the right to vote to all who paid taxes. In Bavaria and Hesse, one could vote if one paid a charge. The Landtag in Prussia was elected by a complicated system of 'classes' into which electors were grouped according to their property.[6] In Cologne in 1908, this system gave the same electoral weight to 370 rich electors in the first class as to 22,324 electors in the third – as well as, in the 58th section of Berlin in 1903, to a certain Herr Heffte, a manufacturer of sausages and the single elector in the first class, the right to form a class for himself alone.[7]

The Imperial government was in charge of matters concerning the whole country: foreign relations, the army and the navy, post and telegraphs, commerce, customs and communications. The Emperor, who wielded very extensive executive powers, delegated them to an Imperial Chancellor responsible to him. Legislative power was shared between the Bundesrat, made up of delegates from the states, and the Reichstag, a national assembly elected by universal suffrage. In practice, the way in which the constituency boundaries were drawn (which favoured rural electors), the custom of holding elections on workdays (which prevented many wage-earning electors from going to the poll), 'official' candidatures, and the absence of payment for deputies, restricted the effectiveness of the electoral principle. The powers of the Reichstag were constrained. It could not initiate legislation, it could not pass any without the agreement of the Bundesrat and it could not depose the Chancellor even when a majority of its members opposed him.[8]

---

[5] Renouvin, Volume 2, op. cit., p. 104.
[6] Ibid., pp. 105–6.
[7] A classic example, taken from H. Moysset, *L'esprit public en Allemagne vingt ans après Bismarck*, Paris, 1911.
[8] Renouvin, Volume 2, op. cit., p. 107.

This régime – neither parliamentary nor democratic – was characterised, moreover, by the dominant position of Prussia in the Imperial government. The King of Prussia was the Emperor and the Prussian Prime Minister was the Imperial Chancellor. The seventeen Prussian delegates to the Bundesrat could stop any measure which displeased their government, from which they received an imperative mandate.[9] Nothing was possible in the Reich without the agreement of this government, which itself was the product of the 'class' electoral system in the Prussian Landtag. Prussia continued to be the bastion of a warrior-aristocracy of junkers. The officer corps was a proud caste of warriors combining the arrogance of a feudal baron with the superiority of a technician. They personally pledged allegiance to the Emperor, and were convinced that they had been entrusted with a sacred mission to defend the state. The junkers formed the overwhelming majority of the higher cadres in the state, and their mentality prevailed in the military hierarchy. It was the same in the Imperial bureaucracy. The federal civil servants were mostly Prussian, cast in the same mould as the military chiefs, whose conception of authority and whose arrogance they shared. It was to this caste that the Emperor could hand over absolute power by decreeing martial law – 'a state of siege' – which suspended all constitutional liberties and guarantees, and installed nothing less than a military dictatorship.

A pre-socialist society

In reality, this political structure was an enormous anachronism in relation to the country's social evolution: one of the contradictions which makes revolutions necessary. The social structure of Germany presented all the characteristics of a society ready for socialism. Whereas, in 1871, one-third of the Germans lived in cities, two-thirds did so in 1910. The population, of which the overwhelming majority consisted of working-class people, was concentrated in very large cities, of which, in 1910, 23 had more than 200,000 inhabitants. Greater Berlin had 4.2 million, Hamburg 930,000, Munich and Leipzig 600,000, Cologne 500,000, Essen and Düsseldorf between 300,000 and 350,000, and Bremen and Chemnitz between 250,000 and 300,000.[10] In central and southern Germany, there were many small and medium-sized peasant

---

[9] Ibid., p. 109.
[10] Renouvin, Volume 1, op. cit., pp. 69–70.

holdings, but over the territory as a whole there were 3.3 million agricultural workers, and the large estates, of which 369 included more than 1,000 hectares each, covered a quarter of the whole cultivated area.[11] This medieval survival created the possibility of the alliance, dear to Marxists, between the urban proletariat and the poor peasants, the rural proletariat.

By dispossessing the middle bourgeoisie, and monopolising the instruments of production in a few hands, the concentration of the economy in the hands of a few industrial magnates seemed to have created the conditions for the socialisation of industry. Mining was dominated by Emil Kirdorf, the chairman of the Gelsenkirchen mines and director of coal syndicate of Rhineland-Westphalia, which in 1913 controlled 87 per cent of coal production.[12] The Fritz Thyssen *Konzern* was a model of vertical concentration, it possessed coal and iron-ore mines, blast furnaces, rolling mills and metalworking plants. Krupp employed over 70,000 workers, of whom more than 41,000 worked in its establishments in Essen alone. This was effectively a closed city, with its own streets, police force, fire brigade, and 150 kilometres of internal railways.[13] In the chemical industry, Badische Anilin employed over 10,000 workers in Ludwigshafen.[14] The rest of chemical production was controlled by two firms, the fusion of which in 1916 was to lead to the birth of I.G. Farben.[15] Electrical equipment was dominated by Siemens and by Rathenau's AEG, which in the Berlin region employed 71,000 workers in ten plants. Two shipping companies, the Hamburg-Amerika Line and the Norddeutscher Lloyd, provided 40 per cent of maritime transport.[16]

The fusion of banking capital with industrial capital was more thorough than anywhere else, except in the USA. The banks dominated economic activity, and 74 per cent of banking business was concentrated in five large establishments in Berlin.[17]

The magnates – Kirdorf, Thyssen, Krupp, Hugenberg, Stinnes, von Siemens, Rathenau, Ballin and Helfferich – formed the top of a very thin stratum, some 75,000 heads of families representing between 200,000 and 250,000 persons,

---

[11] Ibid., p. 71.
[12] Ibid., p. 31.
[13] G. Raphael, *Krupp et Thyssen*, Paris, 1925, p. 211.
[14] Renouvin, Volume 1, op. cit., p. 27.
[15] C. Bettelheim, *L'Économie allemande sous le nazisme*, Paris, 1946, p. 67, n. 2.
[16] Renouvin, Volume 1, op. cit., pp. 28, 65.
[17] Ibid., pp. 32–3.

whom we may regard, with Sombart, as the rich bourgeoisie, whose annual incomes exceeded 12,500 marks. With the middle bourgeoisie, consisting of 650,000 heads of families and between 2 and 2.5 million people with annual incomes of 3,000 to 12,000 marks, these upper, governing classes formed no more than around four or five per cent of the population. At the other end of the social scale, Sombart calculated that in 1907 there were 8.64 million industrial workers, 1.7 million wage-earners in trade and transport, and 2.3 million minor white-collar workers in industry and trade, about 12.5 millions in all. He drew the conclusion that the proletariat, in the broad sense of the term, including women and children, made up between 67 and 68 per cent of the total population. At the end of his study of German society, Edmond Vermeil stated that 'on the eve of 1914, the Germany of Wilhelm II was a country three-quarters proletarianised'.[18]

The general increase in the standard of living had been to the advantage, and then only up to 1908, of a relatively thin layer of highly-skilled workers, a real 'labour aristocracy',[19] the role of which is by no means always a conservative one, because many socialist educators and organisers have emerged from its ranks. However, the German proletariat had nothing in common with the still immature, wretched and prostrate proletariat which filled the factories at the beginning of the industrial revolution. Relatively well-educated, familiar with technology and machines, with a sense of collective work and responsibility, with a taste for organisation, the German proletarians were modern workers, able to defend their immediate interests, to devote themselves to militant activity, and to become conscious of a society which treated them merely as tools, and also aware that their solidarity made them into a force which could change their lives and that of the petty bourgeoisie, who capitalist concentration crushed, and who they judged, with some reason, could become their allies in struggle.

---

[18] E. Vermeil, *L'Allemagne contemporaine, sociale, politique, culturelle (1890–1950)*, Volume 1, Paris, 1952, pp. 92–4.

[19] Henri Burgelin writes that 'it is possible that certain categories of workers, especially the unskilled, did not see any increase in their real standard of living' (*La Société allemande, 1871–1968*, Paris, 1969, p. 91). Since 1934 no new study has covered the material dealt with in J. Kuczynski's *Die Entwicklung der Lage der Arbeitschaft*, Basel, 1934.

War or revolution

The general features of Germany as an advanced capitalist country and its political structure ensured that it was a battlefield favourable to the workers' struggles. Not only was the working class the only social force able to complete the democratic revolution in Germany, by destroying the anachronistic power of the landed aristocracy and the privileges of the army and the state bureaucracy, but in the course of this struggle the working class was inevitably led to present its own candidature for the succession to the old ruling class, and to demand power for itself in the name of all the exploited. The struggle to democratise political life, for the extension of universal suffrage, required that the constitutional framework be broken; it called for a class struggle which could end only in an armed struggle and in the violent destruction of the officer corps, the bulwark of the state. Article 68 of the Constitution clearly expressed its very essence, because it excluded the hypothesis of a peaceful transformation by the parliamentary road, it was the opposite of that suggested by the evolution of the political structures in Britain at that time.

From this point of view, the conditions – military, social and political – in which German unity had been achieved, the efforts of Bismarck simultaneously to preserve the power of the junkers and to expand the bourgeoisie's field of operations, resulted in Germany being deprived of those safety-valves that operated in other advanced countries: a political structure based upon universal suffrage, parliamentarism and a democratic ideology. In other words, the rulers of Germany deprived themselves of the most effective means of protecting capitalist property.

The international position of German imperialism suffered from the same insecurity. Germany's industrial development took place in a period when the riches of the world were nearly all shared out, and German imperialism was denied the advantage of having those extra safety valves, namely markets in the colonial empires which other powers dominated. Historians usually emphasise the role of Anglo-German competition as one the main factors which caused the Great War. Indeed, from 1890 onwards, Great Britain experienced the first signs of the decline of its world leadership. The USA and Germany surpassed it in terms of production in several departments. Its exports were more and more exclusively directed towards industrially backward countries, and on this ground Britain ran up against German industry. Germany, the second industrial state in the world, was almost sure of winning in conditions of free competition, but a large part of the world was closed to its direct expansion. And at the same time, the colonial empire which it needed could not be formed without a fight. The Anglo-German rivalry in the field of naval armaments has to be considered from this angle, as has the systematic opposition of British diplomacy to the establishment of German supremacy in Europe. The stake in the struggle was a world too small for the needs of the contenders. This struggle arose out of the need of capitalism itself to expand. War was inevitable now that the division of the world was completed, and the pressure of the latest-comer, German imperialism, called this into question. From the beginning of the century, the choice was between civil war and world revolution, or imperialist war, which, as Engels had foreseen, could in turn be transformed into revolution and civil war.

Nationalism or socialism

In 1912, the Congress of the Socialist International in Basel agreed afresh on a declaration which outlined the tasks of the International, its constituent parties and the working class in each country in the case of the outbreak of war:

> If war is declared, the working classes in the countries affected, as well as their parliamentary representatives, have the duty to mobilise their forces to prevent hostilities from breaking out, with the support of the coordinating activity of the International Bureau, by applying those means which will seem the most effective to them, means which evidently will vary according to the more or less aggravated turn which the class struggle may take and in relation to the general political situation. If, in spite of their efforts, war should break out, their duty is to struggle actively for a speedy end to the fighting, and to make every effort to use the economic and political crisis which the war causes to rouse the people, and in this way to speed up the abolition of the rule of the capitalist class.[20]

---

[20] Text of the amendment moved by Lenin and Luxemburg at the Stuttgart Congress, in J. Braunthal, *Geschichte der Internationale*, Volume 1, Hanover, 1961–3, pp. 370, 372.

The ruling classes in Germany, confronted with such a socialist, internationalist, proletarian position as this, in a country increasingly mechanised homogenised and proletarianised, and where the industrial proletariat held such an important place, was obliged on pain of death to 'reconcile the proletariat with the Reich' – to use Vermeil's phrase[21] – by convincing the proletariat that it was an integral part of the national community. This is the meaning of the efforts expended by the apostles of 'social Christianity', such as Monsignor Ketteler or the Reverend Stöcker, of the 'national socialism' of Friedrich Naumann, or the 'social policy' of Wilhelm II.[22] Here we have the role of the nationalist ideology, based on the feverish and anxious national feeling of a people which had had to fight for national unity before seeing this unity bestowed upon it, on pride in its gigantic economic achievements, on the superior culture of 'a chosen people', and on a feeling of frustration as a power that had come too late to the division of the world. Education, the press and propaganda conveyed this message.

Vermeil has shown how national socialism and Hitlerite anti-Semitism had their roots in the efforts of the ruling classes to tear the proletarian masses away from any internationalist, revolutionary ideology. At the opening of the twentieth century, anti-Semitism (which August Bebel called 'the socialism of fools') had been the means for diverting the anger of the petty bourgeoisie who were crushed by the development of big capital, and were threatened with being driven down into the proletariat. The ruling classes in Germany had no other means of surviving than by going forward to conquer the world, and no other way to win over the proletariat but to lead it – as Vermeil writes – 'into the ambience of fanatical nationalism'.[23]

Marxists considered that the first stages on the road to the socialist revolution in Germany were the struggle for the class consciousness of the proletariat, and the organisation of the proletariat as a class in the socialist party, a section of the International. Nobody can dispute that Engels's optimism could be justified by the successes which had been won on this road, and, in the first place, in the building of that great workers' organisation, the German Social-Democratic Party, as it was before 1914.

---

[21] Vermeil, op. cit., p. 114.
[22] Ibid., pp. 101, 104.
[23] Ibid., p. 114.

Chapter Two
Social Democracy Before 1914

The split between Social Democrats and Communists, the basis for which had existed since August 1914, when almost every socialist party supported its government on the outbreak of the First World War, and which was realised in 1919 with the establishment of the Communist International, has projected a distorting light on the history of the International. Many writers, politicians and historians who have attempted to discover the roots of this significant split treat it as a phenomenon which could have been foreseen. Although the tensions and debates within the International prior to 1914 were implicit pointers to a split, few if any socialists desired a schism. The Russian Bolshevik faction, the nucleus of the future world Communist movement, regarded itself as no more than a Russian faction constructing a workers' social-democratic party – which in the language of those times meant 'revolutionary Marxist' – in the given historical conditions of the empire of the Tsars. When Lenin was polemicising in 1905 against Peter Struve, he angrily denied that he wanted to split the Party:

> When and where did I call the 'revolutionism of Bebel and Kautsky' opportunism? When and where did I ever claim to have created any sort of special trend in international social democracy *not identical* with the trend of Bebel and Kautsky? When and where have there been brought to

light differences between me, on the one hand, and Bebel and Kautsky, on
the other – differences even slightly approximating in gravity the differences
between Bebel and Kautsky, for instance, on the agrarian question in Breslau?[1]

The indignation of the Bolshevik leader in 1905 was legitimate. Despite many
discussions and differences, he maintained this attitude until 1914, and let
slip no occasion to pay homage to German Social Democracy, the model of
that 'revolutionary social democracy' which he wished to construct in Russia,
in opposition to those he regarded as the opportunists, whom he wished to
exclude from the Party only because they denied the necessity for its existence
and wished to 'liquidate' it.

A model of revolutionary social democracy

Lenin believed up to the Stuttgart Congress in 1907 that German Social
Democracy 'had always upheld the revolutionary standpoint in Marxism'.[2]
When he condemned the German delegates at that congress for their
opportunism, he concurred fully with Kautsky's criticism of them. He
maintained this position right up to the eve of the First World War. On
6 August 1913, he ended an article in *Pravda* devoted to the life and work of
August Bebel with these lines:

> The period of preparation and the mustering of working-class forces is in
> all countries a necessary stage in the development of the world emancipation
> struggle of the proletariat, and nobody can compare with August Bebel as
> a brilliant personification of the peculiarities and tasks of that period. Himself
> a worker, he proved able to break his own road to sound socialist convictions,
> and became a model workers' leader, a representative and participant in
> the mass struggle of the wage-slaves of capital for a better social system.[3]

On 4 April 1914, Lenin sharply criticised the opportunist positions which the
trade-union leader Karl Legien had defended during his visit to the USA,
but he again hailed 'the great services' performed by German Social Democracy,

---

[1] V.I. Lenin, 'The Two Tactics of Social Democracy in the Democratic Revolution',
Collected Works, Volume 9, Moscow, 1972, p. 66.
[2] V.I. Lenin, 'The International Socialist Congress in Stuttgart', *Collected Works*,
Volume 13, Moscow, 1978, p. 85.
[3] V.I. Lenin, 'August Bebel', *Collected Works*, Volume 19, Moscow, 1977, p. 300.

its 'strictly formulated theory', its 'mass organisation, newspapers, trade unions, political associations'.[4]

Amongst those who were central to the founding of the Communist International, perhaps Trotsky alone had glimpsed the destiny of German Social Democracy. He wrote, after the 1905 Revolution, in his book *Results and Prospects*:

> The function of the socialist parties was and is to revolutionise the consciousness of the working class, just as the development of capitalism revolutionised social relations. But the work of agitation and organisation amongst the ranks of the proletariat has an internal inertia. The European socialist parties, particularly the largest of them, the German Social-Democratic Party, have developed their conservatism in proportion as the great masses have embraced socialism and the more these masses have become organised and disciplined. As a consequence of this, social democracy as an organisation embodying the political experience of the proletariat may at a certain moment become a direct obstacle to open conflict between the workers and bourgeois reaction.[5]

In fact, the criticisms of German Social Democracy from within the Second International arose not from revolutionaries but from opportunists such as the French Socialists. The German leaders had been the pupils of Marx and Engels, their direct successors at the head of the world socialist movement. No one could dispute the 'right of succession' of men such as Kautsky[6] and Bebel.[7] The latter personified the organisation of the German working class in the period when capitalism was rapidly expanding. This worker, a turner in the metallurgical industry, a deputy in the Reichstag in 1871, launched the slogan 'War on the Palaces' at the very moment when Bismarck's troops were

---

[4] V.I. Lenin, 'What Should Not be Copied From the German Labour Movement', *Collected Works*, Volume 20, Moscow, 1977, p. 257.

[5] L.D. Trotsky, 'Results and Prospects', *The Permanent Revolution and Results and Prospects*, New York, 1974, p. 114. He was later to write: 'I did not expect the official leaders of the International, in case of war, to prove themselves capable of serious revolutionary initiative. At the same time I could not even admit the idea that the social democracy would simply cower on its belly before a nationalist militarism.' (L.D. Trotsky, *My Life*, Harmondsworth, 1979, p. 241.)

[6] See Karl Renner's *Karl Kautsky. Skizze zur Geschichte der geistigen und politischen Entwicklung der deutschen Arbeiterklasse*, Berlin, 1929.

[7] There is as yet no biography of Bebel worthy of his historical significance. See his memoirs, *Aus meinem Leben*, Berlin, 1910–14.

helping those of Thiers to crush the fighters of the Paris Commune. Twice imprisoned and twice sentenced, he was the soul of the resistance to the anti-socialist laws in the last third of the nineteenth century, the patient builder, the broad-shouldered fighter who tirelessly recruited, trained and convinced crowds of workers, by his solid arguments and his calm confidence in the struggle, that they must take their destiny into their own hands.

Fourteen years younger than Bebel was the Austrian, Karl Kautsky, born in 1854. He embodied the intellectual ambition of scientific socialism. By the side of Bebel the practitioner, he was the theoretician, the scholar, who gave clear guidance to the party and the masses alike. In Switzerland, he had edited the *Sozialdemokrat*, which activists distributed clandestinely in Germany at the time of Bismarck's anti-socialist Exceptional Laws. He was a friend and disciple of Engels, and continued in the columns of *Die Neue Zeit*, the Party's theoretical journal, the work of the founders of scientific socialism. His adversaries called him the 'Pope' of social democracy, and said that he claimed to be infallible. The fact is that his authority was immense and his prestige considerable. He seemed to be the agile brain of a firm arm.

A new universe

In forty years, despite persecution and prosecutions, the German Social Democrats succeeded in organising the workers in every field, not merely in respect of political action in every form, but also in respect of short-term demands, and the organisation of the workers' leisure pursuits, education and culture. The activists of the SPD provided the working class with a real organising framework. They were the *Vertrauensmänner*, the trusted representatives of the party in the localities or the workplaces, trade-union delegates, and elected officials of trade unions, cooperatives and mass organisations at all levels. Within the state and in opposition to it, the followers of Marx and Engels constructed a party so powerful that it formed a real state within the state.

The SPD had 1,085,905 members in 1914. In the legislative elections in 1912, its candidates collected more than 4,250,000 votes. The trade unions which it had brought into existence, and for which it provided the leadership, had over two million members and an annual income of 88 million marks. Around it, its activists knew how to build a broad network of parallel organisations; these organised at different levels nearly all wage-earners, and extended into every sphere of social life: associations of socialist women, the youth movement, people's universities, libraries and reading societies, leisure organisations and open-air movements, publishing houses, newspapers, journals and magazines. This edifice rested upon the solid framework of a competent, efficient administrative and technical apparatus, experienced in modern methods of management and propaganda. On its 90 daily papers, the Party employed 267 full-time journalists and 3,000 manual and clerical workers, managers, commercial directors and representatives. The majority of the leading members, especially the Executive (the *Parteivorstand*), and the central offices, all the responsible people in the different states, and the majority of the secretaries of the local organisations, were full-time functionaries of the Party, professionals appointed by it, devoting all their time to it, as were the majority of its elected representatives, its 110 deputies in the Reichstag, the 220 deputies which it had in the various Landtags, and its 2,886 elected municipal councillors. The leaders of the trade-union federations, the craft unions or the local groups, who had themselves become professionals over the years, were overwhelmingly members of the Party.

Such a large movement, organised on a class basis in Imperial Germany, could not be regarded as a common-or-garden political machine, nor even as the model of a 'workers' party' in a parliamentary democracy. Ruth Fischer wrote:

> The German social democrats were able to realize a type of organization that was more than a loosely knit association of individuals coming together temporarily for temporary aims, more than a party for the defence of labor interests. The German Social Democratic Party became a way of life. It was much more than a political machine; it gave the German worker dignity and status in a world of his own. The individual worker lived in his party, the party penetrated into the workers' everyday habits. His ideas, his reactions, his attitudes, were formed out of this integration of his person with his collective.[8]

Whether considered as a world or a counter-society, German Social Democracy, with its traditions, practices and ceremonies, sometimes similar to those of religious bodies, provided not just a political attitude or a way of thinking, but a framework, a way of living and of feeling. That is how we can explain that tendencies as widely divergent as those personified by Eduard Bernstein

---

[8] R. Fischer, *Stalin and German Communism*, Cambridge, MA., 1948, p. 4.

and Rosa Luxemburg could coexist within the same organisation. That is how we can understand why Luxemburg, the leader of the revolutionary wing of German Social Democracy, could write in her polemic against the conception of the party which Lenin developed in *What Is to Be Done?*: 'The fact is that the social democracy is not *joined* to the organisation of the proletariat. It is itself the proletariat.'[9]

Reform or revolution

Although the SPD was fully engaged in all the great battles of ideas in respect of strategy and tactics which raged in the international workers' movement, its organisational unity was never affected.

Whilst the other socialist movements in Europe fragmented in quarrels which often seemed Byzantine, German Social Democracy presented the spectacle of a cohesive party in which all manner of tendencies cohabited, the equivalents of which elsewhere would have taken the form of rival parties. Since the fusion at the Gotha Congress of 1875 of Bebel and Wilhelm Liebknecht's Social-Democratic Workers' Party with Ferdinand Lassalle's General Association of German Workers, tendencies had arisen within the SPD, tendencies in which a specialist of the French workers' movement would easily have detected the German equivalents of 'possibilists', 'Guesdists', 'Blanquists' and 'Allemanists'. But they remained in the same party, and lived in the same world, and this gave their disagreements a special complexion, because debates which are settled by compromises, and which are to lead to action, are more fruitful than dialogues of the deaf.

Marx had been worried by the important concessions which his followers had made to Lassalle in the Gotha Programme.[10] When, in 1878, Bismarck tried to crush the young party under the blows of his Exceptional Laws, one current in it declared itself in favour of accepting the restrictions which the law imposed. But this current, inspired by Karl Höchberg, which presented its ideas as being 'realistic', was quickly overcome by the Marxists. Without rejecting either the possibilities for legal expression, however limited they

---

[9] R. Luxemburg, 'Leninism or Marxism', *The Russian Revolution and Leninism or Marxism?*, Ann Arbor, 1961, p. 89.

[10] Marx's 'Critique of the Gotha Programme', which he wrote in 1875, was first published by Engels in 1891. See F. Mehring, *Geschichte der deutschen Sozialdemokratie*, Volume 2, Berlin, 1960, pp. 48–51.

might be (as the impatient elements, the forerunners of the future ultra-leftists, proposed), the Social Democrats were also to wage an illegal campaign of propaganda, agitation and organisation, which enabled the Party to continue to grow despite the repression.[11]

The socialists had to adjust their activities when the Exceptional Laws were annulled in 1891. In opposition, on the one hand, to the 'youth' who advocated boycotting elections and a permanent policy of the offensive, as well as, on the other hand, to the right wing of Georg von Vollmar who wanted to reorient the Party towards 'possibilism' and exclusively electoral struggle, the leadership secured victory, in the programme adopted at the Erfurt Congress, for the conception developed by Kautsky. Kautsky did not renounce the maximum programme, the socialist revolution, which the expansion of capitalism had made a distant prospect, but laid down that the Party could and must fight for the demands of a minimum programme, partial aims, and political, economic and social reforms, and must work to consolidate the political and economic power of the workers' movement, whilst raising the consciousness of the working class.[12]

In this way, the dichotomy was created which distinguished the maximum programme – revolution and socialism – from the minimum programme of reforms which could be realised within the framework of the existing capitalist régimes. This separation was to dominate the theory and practice of social democracy for decades.

The first serious attack on the theoretical level against the Marxist foundations of the Erfurt Programme started in 1898, and originated from within the leading nucleus of the Party, from a friend of Engels, an organiser of the illegal press in the time of the Exceptional Laws. This was the 'revisionism' of Eduard Bernstein. He based himself upon his observations of the preceding twenty years, during which capitalism had developed peacefully, and he questioned Marx's perspective that the contradictions of capitalism would sharpen. At the same time, he questioned the philosophical foundations of Marxism, dialectical materialism. Bernstein believed that socialism was no longer the dialectical solution of these contradictions, imposed by the conscious struggle of the working class. He now saw socialism as being the result of the free choice of people, independently of their economic and social

---

[11] Ibid., pp. 556, 577, 579–81.
[12] Ibid., pp. 563–4, 676–8, 681–3.

conditioning, as a moral option instead of a social necessity. He counterposed to what he regarded as outdated revolutionary phraseology the realistic search for reforms, for which the working class should sink itself into a broad democratic movement with important sections of the bourgeoisie.[13]

The 'Bernstein affair', the debate which opened in this way, was both very sharp and very rich. Kautsky devoted himself to refuting the economic arguments of Bernstein,[14] and by his side the group of radical defenders of Marxism found a spokesperson of high quality in Rosa Luxemburg. She breathed new life into the revolutionary forces when she proposed her own interpretation of the Erfurt combination of minimum and maximum demands: the dilemma of 'reform or revolution' was meaningless, because the struggle for reforms could only have revolutionary resolution, and could only be carried out by Social Democrats with this perspective.[15] The Dresden Congress in 1903 closed the debate, at least formally, by condemning the attempt of the revisionists to 'replace the policy of conquering power through victory by a policy which accommodates itself to the existing order'.[16]

Nonetheless, the debate was to continue throughout the following years. The Russian Revolution of 1905 struck the German Social Democrats like a thunderbolt. Kautsky wrote that it was 'the event which many of us had come to believe to be impossible after we had waited in vain so long for it'.[17] It coincided with a spontaneous agitation within the working class which culminated in the same year in the widespread unofficial strike of the Ruhr miners.[18] A new conflict developed between the trade-union full-timers and the radical elements. The former, for fear of adventurism, tried to hold back the workers' struggles, and refused to politicise them. The latter concurred with Luxemburg that the 'political general strike' was an effective means of raising the political consciousness of large numbers of previously backward workers, and was thus one of the essential weapons of the socialist movement. Bebel's motion on the political general strike was carried at the Jena Congress

---

[13] C.E. Schorske, *German Social Democracy, 1905–1917*, Cambridge, MA., 1955, pp. 16–20. See E. Bernstein, *Die Voraussetzungen des Sozialismus und die Aufgaben der Sozialdemokratie*, Stuttgart, 1909.

[14] Schorske, op. cit., pp. 19–20, and Kautsky, *Bernstein und das sozialdemokratische Programm, Eine Antikritik*, Stuttgart, 1899.

[15] Schorske, op. cit., pp. 21–2, and R Luxemburg, *Sozialreform und Revolution*, Leipzig, 1899.

[16] Quoted by Schorske, op. cit., pp. 23–4.

[17] K. Kautsky, *Der politische Massenstreik*, Berlin, 1914, p. 109.

[18] Schorske, op. cit., pp. 35–7.

in September 1905.[19] The radicals seemed to have carried the day against the new revisionists, who thereafter regrouped in the trade unions round Legien, who, for his part, had announced that the general strike was 'general nonsense'.

In reality, the battlefield had changed during these few years. The congress debates no longer reflected it faithfully, as the real battle was developing in a muffled way within the Party and trade-union apparatus. At the Mannheim Congress in 1906, the trade-union leaders won the support of Bebel for a resolution which placed the trade-unions and the Party on a basis of equality, by providing for obligatory consultation between the two organisations on matters of common interest.[20] This annulled the vote at Jena. One of the radical newspapers, the *Leipziger Volkszeitung*, could write: 'The revisionism which we killed in the party is reviving with greater vigour than ever in the trade unions.'[21] Luxemburg summed up the new relations between unions and Party in the phrase attributed to a peasant (the unions) who tells his wife (the Party): 'When we agree, you decide. When we don't agree, I decide.'[22] The revisionist Eduard David rejoiced: 'The short flowering of revolutionism has, most fortunately, passed. . . . The party can now devote itself to positively exploiting and extending its parliamentary power.'[23]

When the leadership of the SPD concluded the Jena compromise with the leaders of the trade unions, it categorically turned its back on the Party's identification with revolution, and its references to revolution in the ensuing debates were few and far between. From that time onwards, it was the 'Centre', at an equal distance from the new revisionism – which was fed by the success of imperialism and intended to adapt the party to what it called the 'modern' economy – and from radicalism, which was sustained from 1910 by growing economic difficulties and by the workers' strikes in response to them.

Moreover, the Party suffered a serious defeat in the general elections of 1907, and the leaders persuaded themselves that, before they could think of important or lasting success, they must win the petty-bourgeois voters whom they considered to be frightened by excessively revolutionary phraseology. Kautsky was the theoretician of the centrist leadership. However, the debates

[19] Ibid., pp. 42–4.
[20] *Protokoll über die Verhandlungen des Parteitages der Sozialdemokratischen Partei Deutschlands, 1905*, pp. 131–2.
[21] Quoted in Schorske, op. cit., p. 52.
[22] *Protokoll über die Verhandlungen des Parteitages der Sozialdemokratischen Partei Deutschlands, 1906*, p. 315.
[23] Quoted in Schorske, op. cit., p. 53.

on the national question and anti-militarism, not to mention those on imperialism in connection with the Morocco affair, and on how to win electoral reform and universal suffrage in Prussia, led to the emergence of an ever-closer alliance between the Right and the Centre. This led to the coalescence of a left-wing current which placed increasing emphasis on the problems of the Party's internal functioning, to the degree that, in 1912, it was accused of factional activities.

The years of economic expansion in Europe had come to an end, and Germany and its fellow European countries had entered a period of crisis with the rise of inter-imperialist rivalries and the intensification of class conflict. The SPD Centre remained sceptical of the chances of a revolution, and was anxious about becoming involved in anything which could threaten the unity of the Party at the moment when reformist practice was no longer obtaining the reforms which justified it. It tried to contain all the centrifugal tendencies by continuing legal day-to-day activities together with a formal attachment to revolutionary perspectives, as it had done in the period of the Erfurt Congress, but now in a very different context.

The Party bureaucracy

The analyses of sociologists such as Max Weber and Robert Michels,[24] and the furious attacks by French Socialists such as Charles Andler, have contributed to painting a somewhat schematic picture of German Social Democracy. They tried to explain the victory of revisionism in its ranks by depicting the SPD as a sclerotic, bureaucratised organisation, fundamentally conservative, tightly subjected to an apparatus of politically-limited functionaries, and consequently integrated into the society which it originally claimed to be struggling against and transforming.

There is a real basis for these accusations. The Executive, which had been strengthened at the demand of the radicals in the period of the struggle against revisionism, was dominated by full-timers who in practice were not subject to control. The Executive appointed and paid the local and regional secretaries who made up the hierarchy which contained all the activity of the

---

[24] R. Michels, *Zur Soziologie des Parteiwesens in der modernen Demokratie*, Leipzig, 1911; 'Die deutsche Sozialdemokratie. Parteimitgliedschaft une soziale Zusammen-setzung', *Archiv für Sozialwissenschaft und Sozialpolitik*, Volume 23, 1906, pp. 471–556.

organisations in a fine-meshed net. Discipline was strict, and the elected members or the representatives in the mass organisations were subject to tight control in the Party fractions which the full-time members of the leadership controlled. The Executive also nominated the candidates in elections, made the careers of the full-timers, transferred functionaries, technicians, instructors and journalists, and conducted the electoral campaigns, which were their main business, like military operations.

Michels explained this complete centralisation of the apparatus and the reign of strict discipline as the result of the victory of conservatism in the ideology of the Party from 1906 onwards. However, these same characteristics led Lenin to regard the German Party as the model of revolutionary social democracy. In his opinion, Bebel and the activists of his generation had realised the aim, which the Bolsheviks proclaimed but had not yet attained, of a disciplined, centralised mass party which would constitute the framework for a workers' army firmly led by a professional general staff. From this point of view, German Social Democracy was the object of the somewhat envious admiration of the few Russian émigrés who had the good fortune to familiarise themselves with its functioning.

The contradiction existed only in appearance. Carl Schorske remarks in his discussion of the sociologists and of Michels in particular: 'The purposes for which – and the circumstances under which – the bureaucracy was constructed were far stronger forces for conservatism than the mere fact that the functionaries were salaried.'[25] The professional revolutionaries who had built the Bolshevik faction in order to bring revolutionary consciousness and social-democratic organisation to the Russian working class did so in conditions of illegality and repression which hardly gave them the possibility or even the temptation to adapt themselves to, or to integrate themselves into, Tsarist society. They had maintained their revolutionary objective, which might have seemed even more remote than in Germany, in the forefront of their general propaganda, whilst they strongly centralised their organisation – yet no conservatism found its way into their daily practice. On the contrary, the apparatus of German Social Democracy, which did not reject in principle its long-term revolutionary objective any more than the Russian Bolsheviks, was constructed entirely between 1906 and 1909.

---

[25] Schorske, op. cit., p. 127.

In this period, it was seeking electoral effectiveness, to increase the number of votes won and candidates elected, during a period of relative social calm and reflux of the working class, and it was preoccupied with ensuring that internal conflicts did not weaken its electoral impact, and that the revolutionary phraseology of its radical wing or the demands of the least-favoured workers did not scare off potential voters amongst the democratic petty bourgeoisie and the most conservative strata of the workers. The revisionism of Bernstein and the reformism of the leaders of the trade unions had taken root in an economic conjuncture which encouraged optimistic beliefs in continued, peaceful progress.

This was what Zinoviev was to do his best to demonstrate by means of a study of the statistics which were published by the organisation in Greater Berlin in 1907. He was trying, after the event, to explain the change in the nature of the Party and the 'treachery' of its leaders in 1914, and emphasised that, at that date, the percentage of members who were definitely not wage-earners – 'self-employed workers' including proprietors of inns and taverns, barbers, artisans, traders and even small-scale manufacturers – could be estimated at 9.8 per cent. The specific political weight of these elements was all the greater because the Party was orienting its electoral effort and adapting its language in order to win this clientèle. The counterweight was insubstantial; only 14.9 per cent of the members of the Party figure in the statistics under the simple label of 'workers', or to be more precise, unskilled workers, who, in fact, made up the mass of the working class.[26]

The core of the Party's supporters was composed of skilled workers who had a trade, whom Zinoviev called 'the labour aristocracy'.[27] It was from their ranks that the Party's full-time staff was recruited, an apparatus of some thousands of privileged functionaries,[28] who often held more than one job and salary, and controlled promotions in the Party's apparatus – its press, treasury and mass organisations – in brief, what Zinoviev called 'the labour bureaucracy'. He defined this as a caste which tried to hide the fact that it existed, but which had its own clearly defined interests. Its aim was 'order and peace', the social status quo, which gave an increasingly conservative character to the Party's policies. He drew the conclusion that the members

---

[26] G. Sinowjew (Zinoviev), *Der Krieg und die Krise des Sozialismus*, German edition, 1924, pp. 548–9. The first edition appeared in Petrograd in 1917.

[27] Ibid.

[28] Estimated by Zinoviev at about 4,000 (ibid., p. 510).

of this caste were, in reality, emissaries of the bourgeoisie within the ranks of the proletariat.[29]

Carl Schorske arrived at a very similar analysis and conclusions, though he formulated them differently, in his study of the manner in which conservatism seeped into the party:

> What the party functionary wanted above all else was peace and unity in the organisation. In the riven condition of the party, this made him a natural opponent of both criticism and change. And as the pressure for change came increasingly from the left, the functionary identified himself increasingly with the right.[30]

He stressed that this phenomenon could be sensed particularly in the functioning of the Party, and especially in the preparation of the congresses. The workers in the big cities, who generally were radicals, were swamped by the representatives of less sharply proletarian and revolutionary organisations. At the congress of the Land of Württemberg in 1911, the 8,659 members of the Stuttgart organisation, nearly all workers, were represented by 43 delegates, whilst the 723 Party members in small towns and villages had 49 delegates. In the same Land in 1912, the 17,000 members in Stuttgart and Cannstadt had 90 delegates, whilst 5,000 others from non-proletarian centres had 224 delegates.[31] The state executives accordingly relied for support on the majority of delegates from semi-rural units, which felt more heavily the pressure of the state and the ruling classes, and thereby held in check the local units in the workers' centres, in a framework very precisely based no longer on the workplace but on the electoral constituencies.

Konrad Haenisch, who at the time was the radical editor of the *Dortmunder Arbeiterzeitung* in a stronghold of very radical miners, wrote to one of his friends in 1910 that, 'despite the unanimous and repeated votes of confidence of the miners' organisation', his conditions of work had become so intolerable under the control of those whom he called the 'high bureaucrats [*Oberbonzen*]' that he was going to give up his job. After being elected to a responsible post by a conference of the Party, he was removed from it by the regional executive at the direct demand of the trade-union full-timers.[32]

---

[29] Ibid., pp. 507, 532.
[30] Schorske, op. cit., p. 127.
[31] Ibid., pp. 130–1.
[32] Ibid., p. 134.

A study of the composition of the supreme organ of the Party, its national congress, reveals the same phenomenon. In 1911, 52 per cent of the members, those in districts with more than 8,000 members each – in principle, the working-class centres – were represented by only 27 per cent of the delegates. The general ratio of representation varied from one delegate per 57 members in the small units of the Party, to one delegate per 5,700 in those of the great industrial cities.[33] The industrial proletariat was under-represented in the decision-making organisations, and this is not the least important cause of the repeated defeats of the radicals in the congresses after 1905. This situation was desired and systematically exploited by the men who held the levers of command in the apparatus. Such men were often former proletarians whose rise to professional functions amounted to a real social promotion.

Historically, the Social-Democratic bureaucracy was personified by Fritz Ebert,[34] who became Secretary in 1906 at the age of 36, and Chairman of the Party in 1913 after Bebel died. This former saddler, who joined the Party when very young, had a noteworthy talent for organisation. At first, he was a manual worker in the shipyards in Bremen, and then manager of a Party canteen which was a centre of Social-Democratic propaganda. In 1900, he was a full-timer, a member of the Party secretariat in Bremen responsible for labour problems, where he won the reputation of being an efficient official. When elected General Secretary, he made himself the champion of modern methods of organisation, introduced telephones, stenographers and typists into the dusty offices, multiplying reports and questionnaires, card-indexes and circulars. Schorske writes of him: 'Colourless, cool, determined, industrious and intensely practical, Ebert had all those characteristics which were to make of him, *mutatis mutandis*, the Stalin of social democracy.'[35]

It was Ebert who constructed the apparatus, and in whom the revisionists finally placed their confidence. In 1911, he had the support of Legien and the trade-union leaders against Haase – whom Bebel supported – for the succession to the chairmanship vacated by the veteran radical Singer.[36] He was defeated on this occasion,[37] but was to succeed Bebel himself two years later, this time

---

[33] Ibid., pp. 138–9.
[34] G. Kotowski, *Friedrich Ebert. Eine politische Biographie*, Volume 1, Wiesbaden, 1963.
[35] Schorske, op. cit., p. 124.
[36] Ibid., pp. 211–12.
[37] K.R. Collins, 'The Election of Hugo Haase to the Co-Chairmanship of the Prewar German Social Democracy', *International Review of Social History*, no. 2, 1968, pp. 174–88.

without difficulty. His lieutenants, the other bosses of the apparatus, seem at first sight to be less dull. Otto Braun, of working-class origin, had belonged in his youth to the left-wing opposition group which opposed the Erfurt Programme. Later a journalist in Königsberg, he subsequently kept his distance from the great theoretical disputes in the Party. The former compositor Philip Scheidemann had become a journalist in Hesse; he was a talented agitator, and passed for a radical until he was elected to the Executive, but he too had stood back from the great debates, and did not speak at any of the three congresses to which he was delegated between 1906 and 1911. In the Reichstag, he became the Party fraction's expert on stock-rearing.[38]

At first, one may feel surprised at the importance of the role which such insipid personalities played in a movement as broad and as important as Social Democracy. The fact is that Ebert, Braun, Scheidemann and the others found themselves placed in what was in a certain sense a privileged position, between opposed class forces. The economic transformation of Germany and the relative social peace in Europe, interrupted only by the revolution in the Russian Empire in 1905, the advances in social legislation, which were won by Social Democracy and the trade unions, together with the prospects of social advancement and individual success which the workers' organisations and their closed world offered to capable members of the working class, all nourished the revisionist tendencies.

These tendencies were fundamentally opposed to Marxism, in particular the tendency which favoured a 'national-socialist' movement, in which the standard of living of the German workers was considered to be linked to the prosperity of 'its' capitalists and the expansion of German imperialism.

Such perspectives were developed in the wake of Bernstein's revisionism, but much more crudely and cynically, and without the idealism and the moral preoccupations which inspired him.[39] These people were 'socialists' for whom the working classes were in league with capitalism, with its colonial and military policies, defensive in principle, but offensive where necessary. If the German Empire were drawn into a war, whether it be offensive or defensive, the German workers could under no circumstances desire its defeat.

---

[38] Schorske, op. cit., pp. 206–8, 280.
[39] Perspectives similar to those of Bernstein's were developed and applied from that time onward by the representatives of the current which Charles Andler called 'neo-Lassallean'.

Noske, a former woodcutter who had become a Party functionary and then a deputy, expressed more clearly than anyone else this repudiation of the very foundations of proletarian internationalism, when he declared in the Reichstag that the socialists were not 'vagabonds without a fatherland', and called on the deputies of the bourgeois parties to give the German workers sound reasons for being soldiers of Germany.[40] The forces at work behind Noske were not disguising themselves.

The junker and Prussian Minister for War, von Einem, grasped the opportunity which this speech offered, and called upon Bebel to repudiate the anti-militarist writings of his comrade, Karl Liebknecht.[41] Indeed, it was through Noske and the Prussian minister as intermediaries that the SPD was to be brought to engage in the debate on the national question and, in particular, the problem of national defence. The Imperial High Court was to pronounce when it sentenced Karl Liebknecht to eighteen months in prison.[42]

[40] Schorske, op. cit., p. 77.
[41] Ibid., p. 78.
[42] W. Bartel, *Die Linken in der deutschen Sozialdemokratie im Kampf gegen Militarismus und Krieg*, East Berlin, 1958, pp. 75–7.

Chapter Three
The Lefts in German Social Democracy

Before 1914, no Social Democrat, whatever his or her occasional criticisms of the Party leadership, would have dared to argue that it had abandoned its class positions and the perspectives of its maximum programme. However, it cannot be denied that a radical bloc took shape on the Left. It was politically confused, but it nonetheless showed the existence of general unease.

Criticisms on this level were particularly numerous and lively during the Party Congress in 1913. One delegate came to the rostrum to declare that, in the factories, many workers thought that the leaders 'had become too close to bourgeois ideals'.[1] Another declared: 'Thanks to the process of consolidating the organisation, of centralisation . . ., the comrades taken individually now don't see the overall picture, and, more and more, it is the full-timer, the secretary, who alone has the power to control the whole mechanism.'[2]

During the last years preceding the First World War, moreover, there were growing signs of a deep division between the leaders and the 'led', and a constant deterioration in their relations. In 1910, amid the discussion on electoral reform in Prussia, *Vorwärts* and *Die Neue Zeit* refused to publish the articles by

---

[1] *Protokoll über die Verhandlungen des Parteitages der Sozialdemokratischen Partei Deutschlands, 1913*, p. 287.
[2] Ibid., pp. 246–7.

Luxemburg in favour of the mass strike, and thus created a significant precedent for censorship by the Party leadership.[3] In 1912, on the occasion of a reorganisation of the editorship of *Die Neue Zeit*, Kautsky succeeded in removing the function of writing the editorial of the theoretical journal from the old radical Franz Mehring.[4] Then, in 1913, the executive procured the expulsion of one of its sharpest critics, Karl Radek, by means of very poor arguments and especially by a retrospective procedure unprecedented in the practice of German Social Democracy.[5]

Moreover, at the same time, the opposition of those who at the time were called 'left radicals [*Linksradikalen*]' tended to depart from the loyal forms to which it had hitherto been confined. In the debate on reforming the Party institutions in 1912, Georg Ledebour and his radical deputy friends organised what was effectively a faction on the Left. It was not without reason that the Executive accused them of breaking discipline.[6] On the eve of the First World War, the left-radical elements assembled themselves within the Party organisations in which they enjoyed a strong presence. Fritz Westmeyer, the radical leader in Stuttgart, brought in the radical Artur Crispien to edit the *Schwäbische Tageblatt*.[7] Finally, the first issue of a bulletin published by Julian Marchlewski, Franz Mehring and Rosa Luxemburg appeared in December 1913, which was clearly intended to regroup the resolute left-wing oppositionists.[8]

Brilliant but marginal personalities

History has essentially retained two names, those of Rosa Luxemburg and Karl Liebknecht, whom their shared struggle during the First World War and their tragic deaths during the same night of January 1919 were to link forever. But, in reality, they are only two of the most important figures in a current which separated itself step by step from the journalists and theoreticians who gathered around Kautsky in the course of the 'Bernstein affair' and the struggle against revisionism.

---

[3] Schorske, op. cit., p. 182.
[4] Ibid., p. 253.
[5] Ibid., pp. 253ff.
[6] Ibid., pp. 217–9.
[7] W. Keil, *Erlebnisse eines Sozialdemokraten*, Volume 1, Stuttgart, 1947–8, p. 262.
[8] This bulletin, the first issue of which appeared on 27 December 1913, was a weekly 'press correspondence' of modest dimensions (P. Nettl, *Rosa Luxemburg*, abridged edition, London, 1969, pp. 313–15).

Karl Liebknecht,[9] who some were later to make the personification of German Bolshevism, was born into the Party. His father was Wilhelm Liebknecht, one of the Party's founders. A lawyer and a militant youth organiser, he championed, particularly at the time of the Jena Congress in 1905, the anti-militarist struggle, whose necessity and principles were set forth in his celebrated pamphlet *Militarism and Anti-Militarism*, which was submitted to the first youth congress in Mannheim in 1906.[10] The prosecutions which its publication earned for him, and his sentence to eighteen months' imprisonment made him both the symbol of the socialists' struggle against the army and the bogey of the nationalists.

In the Party, he defended the independence of the youth organisations against the Executive, and promoted the idea of appealing to the youth to join the revolutionary struggle. He was also the protector and defender of all the socialists who had left Eastern Europe to seek refuge in Germany. Trotsky, who knew him during these years, wrote of him: 'His was an impulsive, passionate and heroic nature; he had, moreover, real political intuition, a sense of the masses and of the situation, and an incomparable courage of initiative.'[11] His qualities did not have much prestige in prewar Social Democracy. He was a standard-bearer rather than a leader, an agitator rather than a theoretician. He had not yet met a situation big enough to match his powers, and he was not an apparatus man. The functionaries and the parliamentarians – those who from this time on manipulated what we can call the 'public opinion' of the Party – treated him with the condescension which in their eyes was deserved by his behaviour as an unmanageable child with a venerated name.[12]

In the years around 1910, Franz Mehring[13] was at the centre of the weekly meetings of the Left in Berlin.[14] Born in 1846, this historian of literature and highly-reputed critic had at first been a democrat, and became a Social Democrat only in the period of the Exceptional Laws. He was for a long time the editor of the *Leipziger Volkszeitung* and wrote the editorials in *Die Neue*

---

[9] K.W. Meyer, *Karl Liebknecht: Man Without a Country*, Washington, 1957.

[10] K. Liebknecht, *Militarism and Anti-Militarism*, Cambridge, MA., 1972.

[11] Trotsky, *My Life*, op. cit., p. 222.

[12] Ibid., p. 223.

[13] T. Höhle, *Franz Mehring. Sein Weg zum Marxismus 1869–1891*, 1958; Joseph Schleifstein, *Franz Mehring. Sein marxistisches Schaffen 1891–1919*, East Berlin, 1959.

[14] These meetings took place on Fridays at the Rheingold restaurant (Trotsky, *My Life*, op. cit., p. 219).

Zeit, but broke from Kautsky in 1910 to draw nearer to Luxemburg. He was without doubt the clearest-headed of all the left critics,[15] but his age and his intellectual training nonetheless prevented him from being a real leader of a tendency or a faction.

Another leading figure of the radical wing of Social Democracy, Clara Zetkin, had followed a similar course.[16] She too had become a Social Democrat at the time of the Exceptional Laws. Born in 1857, she lived for several years in emigration in France, where she met most of the European socialist leaders. She was head of the socialist women's organisation and editor of its organ, *Die Gleichheit*. Bound by close friendship to Luxemburg, she was, like Mehring, one of the prestigious figures to remain faithful to the revolutionary tradition.

Nonetheless, these personalities, who were generally respected and whose names were widely known in the Party and its periphery, could not form the axis for the regroupment of an opposition. This axis was in fact to be formed of activists of foreign origin.

Anton Pannekoek, a Dutch astronomer with a worldwide reputation, played an important role in German Social Democracy. He was invited in 1906 to teach in the central Party school in Berlin, but had to refuse under threat of expulsion from Germany. He nevertheless established himself in Germany, especially in Bremen, for several years, and contributed to forming a generation of revolutionary activists there.[17] In 1909, he wrote *Die taktischen Differenzen in der Arbeiterbewegung* [*Tactical Differences in the Workers' Movement*] in which he emphasised the existence of different strata in the working class, and the influence of the bourgeoisie and the petty bourgeoisie in the labour movement.

He was one of the first to apply to German Social Democracy the analysis, earlier confined by Marxists to the Anglo-Saxon labour movement, of the existence of a privileged stratum in the working class as the principal source of opportunism.[18] In 1912, he engaged in a polemic with Kautsky, especially in his article 'Mass Action and Revolution'. Here, he criticised the practice of the Party leadership and the theoretical justification for it which Kautsky

---

[15] He refused to accept that there existed any current of revolutionaries other than the Russians in the Socialist International (ibid.).

[16] L. Dornemann, *Klara Zetkin. Ein Lebensbild*, East Berlin, 1959.

[17] S. Bricianer (ed.), *Pannekoek et les conseils ouvriers*, Paris, 1969, pp. 45–6.

[18] A. Pannekoek, *Die taktischen Differenzen in der Arbeiterbewegung*, Hamburg, 1909; extracts in Bricianer (ed.), op. cit., pp. 52–98.

provided in his writings. Against Kautsky, he stressed the need to destroy the bourgeois state by proletarian mass action.[19] He insisted on the need for anti-militarist activity by Social Democracy, and emphasised that the working class must struggle for power now that the imperialist epoch had been reached. Whilst he was a theoretician and educator in the German Party, he maintained close contacts with his Dutch comrades, members of the Tribunist group, who had broken in 1909 from official Social Democracy to form a small dissident group with a revolutionary programme, the Sociaal Democratische Partij.[20]

The Bolsheviks alone in the international movement supported the Tribunist group, which included, along with Anton Pannekoek, the poet Herman Gorter and the writer Henrietta Roland-Holst. Since that time, many commentators have emphasised the close links between the analyses and perspectives outlined by Lenin and Pannekoek. These qualify them to be considered as two of the most representative theoreticians of the international left wing, the elements of which were forming within the Social-Democratic movement.[21]

Julian Karski – whose real name was Marchlewski – was the comrade of another celebrated exile named Helphand and known as Parvus, a brilliant theoretician who became a businessman just before the First World War.[22] Karski played an important role as a journalist, first in Dresden and then on the *Leipziger Volkszeitung*, as a populariser of Marxist thought and method, and in the service of the Party leaders as a specialist on the socialist movement in Eastern Europe. After 1910, he also became critical of the opportunist turn of Kautsky's politics, his theoretical justifications, his analysis of imperialism, and his pacifist and gradualist slogans for a parliamentary conquest of the state.[23] In 1913, he wrote in his own name and those of Luxemburg and Mehring lines which read like a verdict:

> Here is what it is all about. We three – and myself in particular, I insist –
> we take the view that the Party is passing through an internal crisis which
> is infinitely more serious than that which it experienced when revisionism

---

[19] A. Pannekoek, 'Massenaktion une Revolution', *Die Neue Zeit*, Volume 30, no. 2, pp. 541–50, 585–593, 609–19; extracts in Bricianer (ed.), op. cit., pp. 106–12.
[20] Ibid., pp. 42–3.
[21] See in particular H. Schurer, 'Anton Pannekoek and the Origins of Leninism', *The Slavonic and East European Review*, Volume 41 (no. 97), June 1963, pp. 327–44.
[22] Z.A.B. Zeman and W.B. Scharlau, *The Merchant of Revolution: The Life of Alexander I. Helphand (Parvus) 1867–1924*, London, 1965.
[23] H. Schumacher, *Sie nannten ihn Karski*, East Berlin, 1964.

first appeared. These words may seem to be excessive, but I am convinced that the Party is in danger of sinking into complete atrophy if it continues down this road. Faced with such a situation, there is only one slogan for a revolutionary party: the most vigorous and merciless self-criticism.[24]

Rosa Luxemburg

However, none of these men inspired so much respect and on occasion fear and hatred in the leadership of the Party and the trade unions, as the frail, sickly woman of foreign origin who appeared along with Kautsky as one of the two theoreticians of German Social Democracy at the beginning of this century.

Rosa Luxemburg[25] was born in 1870 in Poland, of an impoverished Jewish family. She was won to socialism when very young, and emigrated to Switzerland in 1888, where she became linked with another émigré Polish activist, Leo Jogiches, known as Tyszka. Together, they founded and led the Social Democracy of the Kingdom of Poland and Lithuania (SDKPiL), and played an important role in Warsaw during the Russian Revolution in 1905–6, which earned them many months in prison.

However, from 1898, and except for the 'Polish' period of the revolution of 1905–6, it was above all by her activity in German Social Democracy and her participation in the great theoretical debates that Luxemburg – who was naturalised German by means of a marriage of convenience – won her stripes, her reputation and solid friendships and enmities. Her name is inseparable from the history of the 'Bernstein affair', and the theoretical struggle against revisionism and for 'the defence of Marxism'. On that occasion, she published her famous pamphlet, *Reform or Revolution*.[26] It was she also, in particular through her work, *The Mass Strike, the Political Party and the Trade Unions*,[27] who opened the debate on 'the mass strike' in the German Party and on the results and lessons of the first Russian Revolution.

---

[24] Letter to Hans Block, 16 December 1913, in E. Meyer, 'Zur Loslösung vom Zentrum in der Vorkriegszeit', *Die Internationale*, no. 5, 1927, pp. 153–8.

[25] Main biographies are Paul Frölich, *Rosa Luxemburg*, London, 1940; and Peter Nettl, *Rosa Luxemburg*, two volumes, London, 1966 (abridged edition, 1969); also one by a leader of the SED, Fred Oelssner, *Rosa Luxemburg. Eine Kritische biographische Skizze*, Berlin, 1952.

[26] Luxemburg, *Sozialreform oder Revolution*, op. cit.

[27] R. Luxemburg, *Massenstreik, Partei und Gewerkschaften*, Hamburg, 1906.

From 1910, like Pannekoek, Mehring and Karski, she broke off her collaboration with Kautsky, which had also been a close personal friendship. She counterposed to his increasingly revisionist analyses and perspectives her own analyses of imperialism and mass action. She was prosecuted in 1913 for an anti-militarist statement in the course of a speech in a Party meeting in Bockenheim,[28] and found herself in the limelight in the early months of 1914 both as a victim of repression and as a speaker at large mass meetings in the campaign of protest and defence of the Party.[29] In the interval, she taught for several years at the central Party school in Berlin, and made a great impression on her students, even when they did not share her opinions.[30]

She was an important figure at all the congresses of the International, and generally carried the votes of Polish Social Democracy in exile. She was also a member of the International Socialist Bureau. However, she was never able to establish within the SPD either a permanent platform based on the support of a newspaper or a journal, or a stable audience wider than the handful of friends and supporters around her. But she was able to make herself felt in a milieu which was basically hostile to her, and difficult for a woman of foreign origin to penetrate. She had excellent relations with Bebel and Wilhelm Liebknecht as well as with the Kautskys, and won the respect of them all as much by the power of her intelligence as by her talents as a polemicist and orator. This sensitive woman with her artistic temperament had the daring of the greatest thinkers. Lenin was later to hail her as 'an eagle'.[31] They had been the co-authors of an important amendment to Bebel's resolution on war which he moved at the Stuttgart Congress in 1907, and we may conclude, retrospectively, that before the First World War they were the figureheads of the international social-democratic Left.

Nonetheless, these two independent personalities conflicted on a certain number of important theoretical and practical questions. Following the publication of Lenin's *What Is to Be Done?*, the arguments of which she judged to represent a disastrous tendency towards centralisation, which she called 'Blanquism' and 'Jacobinism', she wrote in opposition to Lenin:

[28] Nettl, op. cit., p. 481.
[29] Ibid., pp. 482–4.
[30] Ibid., pp. 390–6.
[31] V.I. Lenin, 'Notes of a Publicist', Collected *Works*, Volume 33, Moscow, 1976, p. 210.

However, social-democratic activity is carried on under radically different conditions. It arises historically out of the elementary class struggle. It spreads and develops in accordance with the following dialectical contradiction. The proletarian army is recruited and becomes aware of its objectives in the course of the struggle itself. The activity of the party organization, the growth of the proletarians' awareness of the objectives of the struggle and the struggle itself, are not different things separated chronologically and mechanically. They are only different aspects of the same process. Except for the general principles of the struggle, there do not exist for the social democracy detailed sets of tactics which a central committee can teach the party membership in the same way as troops are instructed in their training camps. Furthermore, the range of influence of the socialist party is constantly fluctuating with the ups and downs of the struggle in the course of which the organization is created and grows. For this reason, social-democratic centralism cannot be based on the mechanical subordination and blind obedience of the party membership to the leading party centre. . . . Social-democratic centralism . . . can only be the concentrated will of the individuals and groups representative of the most class-conscious, militant, advanced sections of the working class. . . . It is the rule of the majority within its own party.[32]

She came out very firmly against the conception of centralism which Lenin defended:

Evidently, the important thing for the social democracy is not the preparation of a set of directives all ready for future policy. It is important, firstly, to encourage a correct historic appreciation of the forms of struggle corresponding to the given situations, and, secondly, to maintain an understanding of the relativity of the current phase and the inevitable increase of revolutionary tension as the final goal of the class struggle is approached. . . . Granting, as Lenin wants, such absolute powers of a negative character to the top organ of the party, we strengthen, to a dangerous extent, the conservatism inherent in such an organ. . . . The ultra-centralism asked by Lenin is full of the sterile spirit of the overseer. It is not a positive and creative spirit. Lenin's concern is not so much to make the activity of the

[32] Luxemburg, *Leninism or Marxism*, op. cit., pp. 87–9.

party more fruitful as to control the party – to narrow the movement rather than to develop it, to bind rather than to unify it.[33]

Her well-known conclusion has sometimes, if very incorrectly, been considered as the essence of her differences with Bolshevism: 'Historically, the errors committed by a truly revolutionary movement are infinitely more fruitful than the infallibility of the cleverest central committee.'[34]

This polemic, which was soon rendered obsolete, does not possess the major importance which many historians and commentators suggest.[35] Nonetheless, it enables us to assess the difference which separated the thinking of Luxemburg from the Bolsheviks and their conception of the party. It is important at the same time to remember Luxemburg's attachment to the SPD as such and to its unity, on both the national and the international planes. She never ceased, in fact, to think what she wrote to her old friend Henrietta Roland-Holst in 1908:

> A split amongst Marxists – which is not to be confused with differences of opinion – is fatal. Now that you want to leave the Party, I wish with all my strength to prevent you from doing so. . . . Your resignation from the SDAP would mean simply that you are leaving the social-democratic movement. This, you must not do; none of us must do that! We cannot be outside the organisation, out of contact with the masses. The worst of workers' parties is better than nothing![36]

The conflict between Luxemburg and Lenin over centralisation and the role of the party did not prevent them from carrying on a united struggle against opportunism at the Stuttgart Congress in 1907, nor from maintaining cordial personal relations thereafter. However, when Luxemburg broke with Kautsky after 1910, accusing him of opening the road to a new kind of revisionism, she was not supported by any of the Russian Social Democrats and least of

---

[33] Ibid., pp. 93–4.

[34] Ibid., p. 108.

[35] See in particular what Lenin himself wrote in 1908 about *What Is to Be Done?* in his preface to a collection of his articles (V.I. Lenin, 'Preface to the Collection *Twelve Years*', *Collected Works*, Volume 13, op. cit., pp. 94–113).

[36] Reproduced in H. Roland-Holst Van der Schalk, *Rosa Luxemburg. Ihr Leben und Wirken*, p. 221. [The SDAP, the Social-Democratic Workers' Party, was the socialist party in the Netherlands, which Roland-Holst, Pannekoek and Gorter left in 1909. Editor's note]

all Lenin, who thought that her accusations were exaggerated.[37] When, in 1913, she published *The Accumulation of Capital*, the fruits of her thinking as a teacher of political economy, she was sharply attacked, not only by Pannekoek, but by Lenin, who regarded her thesis – that expanded capitalist production is impossible in a closed economy and necessitates the plunder of precapitalist economies[38] – as 'fundamentally incorrect'.

When Luxemburg thought that she had demonstrated both the necessity of imperialism and its fragility in the face of the mass resistance which it provokes, Lenin attacked her on the grounds that she made revolutionary activity an objective phenomenon, and passed silently over the role of Social Democracy as a revolutionary leadership. Finally, in 1914, the International Socialist Bureau concerned itself with the question of the Russian Party, which Lenin had wanted and for which he had worked since 1912 against the Mensheviks whom he called the 'liquidators', Luxemburg agreed with Kautsky in condemning what they called Lenin's 'splitting' policy, and spoke in favour of reuniting Russian Social Democracy.[39] The congress which was projected for 1914 but never held because of the outbreak of war would undoubtedly have witnessed a discussion on the Russian question in which Luxemburg and Lenin would once again have been at odds.

The division of the Lefts: the Radek affair

The division of the Lefts in Germany, which was linked with the divisions of the international social-democratic Left, are clearly illustrated by what has come to be called the 'Radek affair'. Karl Radek, whose real name was Karl Sobelsohn[40] and came to be called 'Radek' from the time of the 'affair', was born in Austrian Galicia. In the German Party, he was a freelance or, to put it better, an 'outsider'. Originally an activist in the Polish Socialist Party, he joined the SDKPiL in 1904. He took part in the 1905 Revolution in Warsaw, where he was in charge of the Party's newspaper, *Czerwony Sztandar*. Then, after being arrested and escaping, he took refuge in Germany, in Leipzig, where he worked on the *Leipziger Volkszeitung* from 1908, and then in Bremen in 1911, where he worked on the *Bremer Bürgerzeitung*, and attracted attention

---

[37] Nettl, op. cit., Volume 1, p. 433.
[38] Summarised in Nettl, op. cit., Volume 2, pp. 532–4.
[39] Ibid., pp. 592–5.
[40] H. Schurer, 'Radek and the German Revolution', *Survey*, no. 53, October 1964.

by the sharpness of his pen. He polemicised not only against the nationalist tendencies in Social Democracy, but against the pacifist illusions of the Centre. This young man was one of those who attacked Kautsky's analysis of imperialism in the columns of *Die Neue Zeit* itself in May 1912.[41]

The 'Radek affair' broke out in 1912. Radek went to Göppingen at the invitation of Thalheimer, with whom he was friendly, to replace him temporarily in control of the local radical newspaper *Freie Volkszeitung*, which had long been in financial difficulty, mainly because of its hostility to the revisionist leaders in Württemberg. Radek raised a national scandal by accusing the executive of acting in concert with the revisionists in their attempt to strangle the newspaper. At the same time, he was excluded from the SDKPiL because of his support for the opposition on the Party committee in Warsaw. In 1912, he was expelled on the charge of having formerly stolen money, books and clothes from Party comrades.[42] The German Party's Congress in 1912 had raised the question of Radek's membership, which was contested by the Executive, without settling it. The Congress in 1913 took note of the fact that he had been excluded from its fraternal Polish party. After deciding that in principle no one who had been excluded from one party could join another party of the International, the Congress decided to apply this rule retrospectively to Radek.

Luxemburg was the intermediary of the Polish Party in its dealings with the German Executive, and she assisted Radek's enemies, such was her hostility to him. Marchlewski supported her. But Pannekoek and his friends in Bremen unconditionally backed Radek, whilst Karl Liebknecht also supported him on principle, because he saw the executive 'making an example of him' in the process of taking reprisals against those who criticised its opportunism. At the level of the International, Lenin and Trotsky for their part rallied to the defence of Radek, who appealed to the Congress.[43] The War was to leave the affair unresolved, but it was not without later repercussions.

---

[41] K. Radek, 'Unser Kampf gegen den Imperialismus', in *In den Reihen der deutschen Revolution*, pp. 156–76.

[42] There is a detailed account of the Radek affair in the Polish Party in Nettl, op. cit., Volume 2, pp. 574–7.

[43] Schorske, op. cit. pp. 255–6; R. Fischer, op. cit., pp. 201–3; H. Schurer, op. cit., passim. Radek's point of view, set out in *Meine Abrechnung*, Bremen, 1913, is well presented by Rudolf Franz, 'Der Fall Radek von 1913', *Das Forum*, Volume 4, no. 5, February 1920, pp. 389–93.

It is significant that the leaders of the German Left were so divided on the occasion of the first trial of strength inside the Party, over an attempt to discipline a left-wing opponent, and, moreover, that some on the Left had been willing to see a fellow left-winger disciplined. The solidarity amongst members of a tendency against the bureaucratic apparatus did not exist here. Indeed, for the SPD's members, there was no sign of any coherent and enduring left-wing group.

But elements did exist

It would be tempting to draw the conclusion that the Left consisted essentially of intellectuals, Party journalists, writers and teachers, people such as Paul Lensch, Konrad Haenisch, August Thalheimer, Paul Frölich, Heinrich Ströbel and Ernst Meyer, who had been collaborators of Luxemburg, Mehring or Marchlewski in the press, or Luxemburg's students in the central Party school. But that would be an excessively restricted view. Wilhelm Pieck, who had moved from Bremen to Berlin, where he became the secretary of the school, Friedrich Westmeyer in Stuttgart, and Wilhelm Koenen in Halle were Party workers, full-timers, trained as professionals and members of the apparatus. For it was these militant workers, trade-union activists and Party members, who gave the union leaders a hard time in the wildcat strikes,[44] which had become more frequent and tended to become more general in the run-up to the First World War. They included Heinrich Teuber, a miner from Bochum, Fritz Heckert, the leader of the building workers in Chemnitz, engineers such as Robert Dissmann in Stuttgart, Josef Ernst in Hagen in the Ruhr, or Otto Brass in Remscheid or Richard Müller the turner in Berlin.

These radical left-wing activists held strong positions on the eve of the War. In certain industrial centres, they enjoyed majority support amongst the Party members and in the local Party apparatus. They also enjoyed great prestige and a wide following in the Party and in the working class through their publications. This could be seen in the success of Luxemburg's speaking tour in 1914 after the legal action brought against her.[45] They also enjoyed great influence within the groups of young socialists both inside and outside the Party, which came under attack from both the Party bureaucracy and the forces of the state.

---

[44] Nettl, op. cit., Volume 2, p. 478.
[45] See *Rosa Luxemburg gegen den deutschen Militarismus*, East Berlin, 1960.

It was within this milieu, which was greatly influenced by Karl Liebknecht, and was inspired by the anti-militarist feelings he strove to encourage, that many young activists were educated, and they often studied under Luxemburg in the school in Berlin: Willi Münzenberg who was for the moment in exile in Switzerland, Walter Stoecker, Edwin Hoernle, Jakob Walcher, Wilhelm Koenen, Paul Frölich and Georg Schumann, to name but a few.

These activists drew closer in 1914, although they did not form a group, in producing propaganda calling for the mass strike, denouncing imperialism and the arms race, and criticising the pacifist slogan of disarmament which Kautsky advanced. They played a major role in the rising tide of economic strikes, meetings and workers' demonstrations against war, and in the defence of Luxemburg. But what really formed the common foundation of their struggle as socialist activists was their deeply-held belief that the socialist revolution was the only solution to imperialism and war, and that the spontaneous action of the masses was the only decisive force in politics. However, as Luxemburg wrote, this was to be carried on in a 'truly democratic party', as she believed the SPD to be.[46]

The German left radicals had been in conflict for years with the authoritarian organisation of their own party. They concluded that centralisation was the main obstacle to the radicalisation of the masses and to the development of revolutionary activity. In this they disagreed with Lenin. They were aware that revisionism was advancing in the ranks of the Party, and particularly in its leadership. They knew that the trade-union bureaucrats and their conservative views were gaining influence in its leading bodies. However, they were convinced of the revolutionary character of the imperialist period, and were tireless critics of the opportunism of the leaders and of their authoritarian methods. Like Luxemburg, they believed that there were no recipes for organisation:

> We cannot secure ourselves in advance against all possibilities of opportunist deviation. Such dangers can be overcome only by the movement itself – certainly with the aid of Marxist theory, but only after the dangers in question have taken tangible form in practice.[47]

This fundamental conception of activity, this identification of the Party with the mass movement, and their deep devotion to the organisation in which,

---

[46] Nettl, op. cit., Volume 2, p. 479.
[47] Luxemburg, *Leninism or Marxism?*, op. cit., p. 106.

despite its bureaucratic excrescences, they continued to see the expression of the revolutionary social-democratic workers' movement, led them to reject the prospect of organising in a faction. They rejected the possibility of setting up, even in an informal and loosely-defined manner, a revolutionary tendency in German or international social democracy which would bring them into association with the Bolsheviks. Consequently, they had even more reason to oppose any split in the Party or the International.

No one as yet had faced up to this question, even as a working hypothesis. It had been raised, and then only tentatively, either by anarchist activists such as Landauer or by a journalist such as Franz Pfemfert, both of whom were outside the workers' movement.[48] But it was precisely this question which was put on the agenda, firstly by the outbreak of the First World War, and then by the support for national defence in their respective countries by the leaders of German Social Democracy and of the other great parties of the International. Kautsky was not mistaken when he wrote to his old associate, Victor Adler, on 8 October 1913: 'There is here a certain uneasiness, a hesitant search for new paths, something must come out of it . . . even Rosa's supporters cannot answer the question of knowing what is to be done.'[49]

---

[48] The writer Franz Pfemfert published from 1911 onwards the weekly *Die Aktion*. He supported the left elements round Rosa Luxemburg, but called for 'a new workers' party' (H.M. Bock, *Syndikalismus und Linkskommunismus von 1918–1923*, Meisenheim/ Glain, 1969, p. 47).

[49] Quoted in V. Adler, *Briefswechsel mit August Bebel und Karl Kautsky*, Vienna, 1954, p. 582.

PART ONE

FROM WAR TO REVOLUTION: THE VICTORY AND DEFEAT OF ULTRA-LEFTISM

Chapter Four

The War and the Crisis of Social Democracy

On 31 July 1914, the International Socialist Bureau issued its call for a struggle against war, and Jean Jaurès fell under the bullets of Raoul Villain. On 1 August, the German government declared war on Russia, and proclaimed a state of emergency. On 2 August, the executive of the German Social-Democratic Party met to define the attitude of the members of the Reichstag on the question of voting for the war credits which the Chancellor, Bethmann-Hollweg, demanded.

The leaders were deeply divided. The old revisionist David and the Party Secretary, Scheidemann, spoke in favour of voting for the war credits.[1] Haase and Ledebour called for a hostile vote consistent with the principled positions of the Party. After discussion, the decision was deferred to the following day. At the meeting of the Social-Democratic fraction in the Reichstag, the Right attacked first. David made much of the danger which the Russian autocracy posed to German liberties. He emphasised the danger that, in the reigning atmosphere of war fever, the Party might be declared illegal if it voted against. He declared that he had decided not to accept group discipline when voting on a question of such importance.[2]

---

[1] K. Liebknecht, *Klassenkampf gegen den Krieg*, Berlin, 1919, p. 14.
[2] Ibid., pp. 55, 87.

Those opposed to voting for the credits were far from showing the same determination. When the fraction decided by 78 votes against 14 to vote for the war credits, the 14 opponents – amongst whom were Haase, Ledebour, Liebknecht and Otto Rühle – agreed to respect discipline on the following day. Moreover, at the session of the Reichstag on 4 August, it was Hugo Haase, as Chairman of the Party and spokesperson of the fraction, who informed the Chancellor of the Social Democrats' unanimous support for the government's war policy.

He justified this gesture by the concern for national defence of a people devoted to liberty and culture, and threatened by Tsarist despotism. He expressed the wish that, when the security of Germany had been assured by arms, the belligerents could as quickly as possible conclude a durable peace which would guarantee the friendship between peoples. When the SPD voted for the credits and approved the War, it also declared its attachment to the International, to socialism and to peace. A page in world history had been turned.[3]

The meaning and the consequences of 4 August

With the advantage of hindsight, it is easy to demonstrate that the vote on 4 August was the logical consequence of the Social Democrats' political development during the preceding years. However, the news came as a shock to many well-informed contemporaries. Lenin doubted for a moment the veracity of the issue of *Vorwärts* which announced the vote, and considered that the German General Staff might have forged it.[4] As recently as 25 July, less than ten days earlier, the Party had solemnly declared in a manifesto:

> The class-conscious workers of Germany, in the name of humanity and civilisation, send up a strong protest against the war-mongers. . . . Not a drop of the blood of a German soldier can be sacrificed to the thirst for power of the governing group in Austria and imperialist appetites for profit.[5]

---

[3] Frölich, Lindau and Thomas (eds), *Illustrierte Geschichte der deutschen Revolution*, Berlin, 1929, p. 99; Philip Scheidemann, *Memoiren eines Sozialdemokraten*, Volume 1, Dresden, 1928, pp. 257–8.

[4] Trotsky, *My Life*, op. cit., p. 276.

[5] Quoted in C. Grünberg, *Die Internationale und der Weltkrieg*, Volume 1, Leipzig, 1916, p. 51.

On 30 July, in the face of the seemingly irresistible succession of events, the Executive had thrown up its hands and talked about 'useless efforts' and 'having done its duty'. But, even then, it had not yet placed to its lips the bugle that called for war to defend 'endangered civilisation'.[6]

We still lack documents today about the real motives of the Social-Democratic leaders, whether they expressed them or not, and about their intimate thoughts during this crucial week. Scheidemann has confessed that he was greatly impressed by the size of the chauvinist demonstrations in Berlin.[7] A letter and notes by Ebert express his fear that the War and the eventual reawakening of the Russian workers' movement would give new force to the plans of 'the Rosa group'.[8] It certainly seems that fear was the dominating sentiment. By the evening of 30 July, Ebert and Otto Braun had left for Switzerland with the Party's treasury.[9] In applying the state of siege, the military authorities had dictatorial powers. It seemed clear that, from one day to the next, they could destroy the gigantic edifice which had been so patiently built up, abolish the social conquests, destroy the organisations, and close the press, that they could arrest members and leaders, and with one stroke of the pen erase all the results of decades of Social-Democratic activity.

The terrible pressure of the news media, the established authorities and the state apparatus, and the brutal resurgence of elemental chauvinism seemed to create an irresistible current. Not having been accustomed to isolation, to struggling against the stream, and still less to brutal repression and illegality, many members were tempted to succumb to this mood. Some could not withstand it. In a few hours, Konrad Haenisch disavowed his years of struggle in the front rank of the radicals, and joined the camp of the patriots, declaring that in this way he had settled 'a conflict between two souls'.[10] This phenomenon was neither unique nor new; Carl Schorske recalls in that connection the other 'Fourth of August', that night in 1789, when the French nobility surrendered its privileges, and 'publicly renounced its own principles of social organization'.[11]

---

[6] Ibid., pp. 63–4.
[7] Scheidemann, op. cit., p. 235.
[8] F. Ebert, *Schriften*, Volume 1, Dresden, 1926, p. 309; see also D.K. Buse, 'Ebert and the Coming of World War One: A Month From his Diary', *International Review of Social History*, no. 3, 1968, pp. 430–48.
[9] Scheidemann, op. cit., p. 245.
[10] Quoted by E. Prager, *Geschichte der USPD*, Berlin, 1921, p. 34.
[11] Schorske, op. cit., p. 290.

Indeed, a new period opened in August 1914. Henceforth, it was not possible for either the German Social Democrats or the French Socialists to look forward, at any rate in the immediate future, to a peaceful road to socialism at the moment when the inter-imperialist contradictions had led to armed conflict. To leaders who were caught by surprise in their routine, who were confronted with choices the implications of which they were perhaps unable to grasp, on the threshold of events which they could not even imagine, the new situation brought doubt, hesitation and confusion. The government did the rest. In the closing days of July, the Ministry of the Interior occupied itself in soothing the leaders of the trade unions, assuring them that they had nothing to fear, that the fatherland needed all its sons, and them in particular.[12]

Through the mouths of the right-wing Social Democrats, the German bourgeoisie offered an attractive solution, in the form of the survival of the Party organisations and, even better, of their becoming 'official', with their role recognised as necessary, so that 'civil peace' could be maintained in the face of the external danger. Once again, but with more convincing arguments, the ruling classes offered to the workers' leaders a role in society which they justified by promoting the existence of a national interest shared by workers and employers, and by the integration of the working class and its party into the national community, the German fatherland.

On 2 August, the trade unions made an agreement with the employers that there were to be no strikes or lock-outs, and that all collective agreements would be extended for the duration of hostilities.[13] On 3 August, about thirty deputies, supporters of David and Scheidemann, decided that, whatever happened, they would vote for the war credits, confident that the trade-union leaders would support them.[14] The promises of the government that there would be 'a new orientation' after the War, and the assurances that no measures would be taken against the workers' organisations as long as they played the game, together with glimpses of possible new political careers, served to tip the scales.

Those who were hesitant rallied to the Right. As to the fourteen deputies who wished to vote against the war credits and the War, the grip of the ideology of 'unity' and their attachment to the Party and 'party patriotism' were so powerful that none of them resolved to infringe the discipline of the

---

[12] P. Umbreit, *Die deutschen Gewerkschaften im Weltkrieg*, Berlin, 1917, p. 21.
[13] Ibid., pp. 21–30.
[14] Grünberg, op. cit., p. 73.

fraction. Haase and even Liebknecht respected the decision which had been reached by a majority, even though some members of the fraction had announced in advance that they would not accept discipline if the decision went against them.

The turn was much more decisive than those people who submitted to 'the Party' believed it to be. The Social Democrats joined in the War, giving it their blessing. The falseness of their declarations about attachment to principles, the international solidarity of the workers, peace and socialism, assurances about the purely defensive character of the War, and the indignant denials that there would be any annexations, was now clear. Their words were exposed as a paltry rhetorical cover for a reality that consisted of shrapnel, bombs, machine guns, poison gas and imperialist aims. The Social-Democratic leaders soon became as 'annexationist' as the military and political chiefs. They assured the German workers that Wilhelm II's army was defending the prospects of socialism and its future victory in Europe when it fought against Tsarism and British imperialism. In France, the Socialists in turn declared that German militarism and pan-German imperialism had to be destroyed if the possibility of socialism were to be ensured. The International died on 4 August 1914.

The first acts of resistance

No one has ever doubted the importance of these events or the magnitude of the Party's turn. But disagreements arise when it comes to framing an analysis. Franz Borkenau has contested what he calls the 'communist' thesis that the leaders 'betrayed'. He has devoted himself to demonstrating the power of the 'patriotic wave' which swept Germany and elsewhere, across the frontiers of party convictions. He sees in it the proof that, in the modern world, political passions are aroused less by class antagonisms than by those between nations. He wrote on the situation in Germany: 'The leaders did exactly what the masses wanted, and, had they acted otherwise, would have found no mass support. . . . The revolutionary proletariat proved to be a myth.'[15] His thesis on this point repeats exactly what Kautsky was to say from 1914.[16] But a thorough examination demonstrates its fragility. True, there

---

[15] F. Borkenau, *World Communism*, Michigan, 1962, pp. 58–9.
[16] Notably in his *Sozialismus und Krieg*, Prague, 1937.

can be no dispute about what Kautsky and Borkenau call 'the apathy of the masses'. The decision to vote for war credits did not meet open resistance on the part of the workers, whether Party members or not. It was not opposed by any movement, strike, demonstration or large-scale refusal to carry out orders for mobilisation, nor by any mutiny by reservists. Nonetheless, these remarks are no more than observations, and cannot claim to be explanations.

It is clear that what Borkenau calls 'the masses' are no more than a large number of individuals whose feelings and reactions, and whose willingness to struggle or to capitulate, can only be expressed collectively through an organisation. Before 4 August 1914, the SPD was this organisation, the organisation of the German workers. On 4 August 1914, the leaders of this party and the trade unions decided, over the heads of 'the masses' and without consulting them, that they accepted and would support the government's war policy. This was the result of a long process which had dispossessed the masses of any control over their own organisations. After that, where and when could the masses have opposed such decisions? This is the question which the revolutionaries and Lenin in particular raised immediately after 4 August 1914.

The attitude of the German working class to the War was, in fact, not at all determined by open discussion in general meetings held in full freedom. They were under pressure from two sides; at the top, in meetings between leaders under threat of the state of siege, and at the base, individually faced by a mobilisation notice and under threat of court-martial, with any strike or demonstration forbidden by the government, the Party and the unions alike. In the face of the threat of arrest and summary conviction, the socialist worker who wanted to express his opposition to the War not only was deprived of the support of his organisation, but also found it lined up on the same side as his class adversary. In reality, the question of the attitude of 'the masses' cannot be raised independently of that of the 'chiefs'.

Replying in 1915 to the arguments of Kautsky, Lenin stressed that it is absurd to put the question as if 'the "masses", "in retaliation" to war, should make a revolution "within 24 hours", and institute "socialism" . . ., or otherwise the "masses" would be revealing "spinelessness and treachery"':

> . . . a revolution cannot be 'made', that revolutions *develop* from objectively
> (that is, independently of the will of parties and classes) mature crises and
> turns in history, that without organisation the masses lack unity of will, and
> that the struggle against a centralised state's powerful terrorist military

organisation is a difficult and lengthy business. Owing to the treachery of their leaders, the masses *could not* do anything at the crucial moment, whereas this 'handful' of leaders *were in an excellent position* and in duty bound to vote against the war credits, take a stand against a 'class truce' and justification of the war, express themselves in favour of the defeat of *their own* governments, set up an international apparatus for the purpose of carrying on propaganda in favour of fraternisation in the trenches, organise the publication of illegal literature on the necessity of starting revolutionary activities, etc.[17]

From this point of view, it is significant that the resistance to class collaboration and to 'civil peace', otherwise known as maintaining the proletarian class struggle, found expression in the Germany of 1914 only where radicals had effective responsibilities, controlled sectors of the apparatus or positions in the press, and where an organisation, or part of one, could express the opposition of the activists and part of the 'masses' to the chauvinist policies of the national leaderships. This happened in Brunswick, where Thalheimer was responsible for *Volksfreund*, and in Württemberg where Westmeyer controlled the Party organisation in Stuttgart and Crispien ran the *Schwäbische Tageblatt*. It happened also around and through the big radical daily newspapers, *Leipziger Volkszeitung, Bremer Bürgerzeitung* and even intermittently *Vorwärts*.[18] Nor was it accidental that the first illegal publication to express proletarian opposition to the War came from a Party unit, that of the Berlin constituency of Niederbarnim, nor that it was produced by three activists who had the means to assemble, print and distribute information, that is to say, the embryo of an organisation. In fact, beginning in December 1914, Paul Schwenk (a member of the editorial staff of *Vorwärts*), the bookbinder Otto Gabel (the secretary of the organisation in Niederbarnim), and the leader of the socialist women in Berlin, Martha Arendsee, published duplicated documents and material which enabled an albeit restricted circle of activists to acquaint themselves with the theses of the opponents of the policy of the 'sacred union'.[19]

---

[17] V.I. Lenin, 'The Collapse of the Second International', *Collected Works*, Volume 21, Moscow, 1977, pp. 240–1.

[18] See the chronology in *Illustrierte Geschichte der deutschen Revolution*, op. cit., pp. 515–18, for an account of persecution of the press.

[19] M. Arendsee, *Unter der roten Fahne*, East Berlin, 1958, pp. 75–81; P. Schwenk, 'Lenin, Mehring und das Niederbarnimer Referentenmaterial', *Beiträge zur Geschichte der deutschen Arbeiterbewegung*, no. 1, 1960, pp. 158–63.

Julian Marchlewski, Rosa Luxemburg's old comrade, recalled how she thought for one moment how it might be possible to stimulate a sudden outburst in the ranks of the militants and to give organised form to spontaneous resistance which she believed already existed in clandestinity, by publishing and circulating a manifesto signed by well-known personalities in the Party. But the 'message in a bottle' technique could not serve as a substitute for organised activity, as Leo Jogiches argued against her. Of the dozens of militants whom she invited to meet at her apartment to work out the proposed manifesto, only seven came, and only two of those were nationally known personalities – Franz Mehring and Paul Lensch. Lensch, in any case, would not sign anything, and was soon to go over to the Party leadership.[20] Liebknecht, for his part, had not agreed in the Reichstag to accept discipline in order to break it immediately. Nonetheless, Luxemburg persisted. They decided to call another meeting, for which they sent out more than three hundred telegrams. Clara Zetkin alone replied without evasion or reservation. The idea had to be dropped.[21]

The German revolutionaries found themselves completely atomised. They were, moreover, to learn to their cost that, in a party which they still regarded as being theirs, they could be subjected to repression which reinforced that of the state and the police. The prohibition of all demonstrations and public meetings decreed on 1 August was a foretaste of the measures that would be used to silence the opponents of the War. The Party Executive was to extend this state of siege into the Party itself. The experience of Karl Liebknecht in this connection was as decisive for him personally as for the future of the German Left.

At the beginning of August, he still believed that the opportunities for self-expression by the opposition inside the Party would remain intact, and that it was reasonable to hope to arrive at a regeneration by way of an internal political discussion. It was within this perspective that he suggested to the Executive that a meeting be organised against the propaganda for annexations, which he hoped to make the starting point for the correction of what he still regarded as the mistake of 4 August.[22] The Executive refused.

---

[20] See Marchlewski's memoirs, *Bulletin communiste*, no. 3, 20 January 1921, pp. 40–5.
[21] *Die Revolution*, no. 2, 1924, cited in G. Badia, 'L'Attitude de la gauche sociale-démocrate allemande dans les premiers mois de la guerre', *Le Mouvement social*, no. 49, 1964, p. 84.
[22] Ibid.

At the end of August, he entered occupied Belgium, and learned about the atrocities which the German army had committed. On 3 September, he protested against a Bremen newspaper which had written about the SPD's parliamentary fraction being unanimous on 3 August.[23] On 21 September, he went to Stuttgart to meet political friends who had invited him there. The military authorities prohibited the public meeting which had been planned, but he had a long discussion with activists who reproached him for his vote in the Reichstag on 4 August. He revealed to them what had been discussed in the fraction, and the existence of an opposition on the question of the credits, and recognised his mistake: 'Your criticisms are absolutely justified . . . I ought to have shouted "No!" in the plenary session of the Reichstag. I made a serious mistake.'[24]

Liebknecht was censured by the Executive for having disclosed this information. He replied on 10 October by appealing to the democratic tradition of the Party, which, as he wrote, permitted 'any comrade . . . to take up a position even against the highest authorities'.[25] The military court opened proceedings against him on 17 October in respect of events going back to before the War. On 10 November, the organ of the building workers' union, edited by the revisionist Winnig, called for him to be expelled. As Schorske wrote: 'The changed relationship of the party to the state demanded that that it keep its opposition under control, that it maintain the *Burgfrieden* within the labor movement.'[26]

The military authorities and the Party apparatus both worked in the same direction. Already on 5 August, the Executive had postponed the Party congress for the duration of the War, consequently exercising powers with which it had been granted for use in the eventuality of totally different circumstances.[27] The military authorities banned the meetings of activists in Stuttgart on 21 September, in München-Gladbach on 4 November, in Leipzig on the 24th, and in Altona on the 29th, but elsewhere it was the Party secretaries who prevented general meetings from being held, by simply refusing to call them.

In Hamburg, a single general meeting covering four districts was held, because the radicals called it themselves over the heads of the regular

[23] Ibid., pp. 85–6.
[24] *Dokumente und Materialen zur Geschichte der deutschen Arbeiterbewegung*, Volume 1, East Berlin, 1958, p. 35, n. 5.
[25] Liebknecht, *Klassenkampf gegen den Krieg*, op. cit., pp. 17, 23–4.
[26] Schorske, op. cit., p. 297.
[27] Grünberg, op. cit., p. 41.

bodies.[28] The radical newspapers were gagged one after another by this double repression: *Rheinische Zeitung* was suspended for two days on 11 September, *Volksblatt* in Bochum was closed down on the 20th, *Echo vom Rheinfall* and *Dantziger Zeitung* on the 25th.[29] Several of the editorial workers on *Vorwärts* – Cünow, Däumig and Hilferding – had declared that they disagreed with the Executive,[30] and the paper was suspended on 21 September for three days, and indefinitely on the 28th.[31] The military authorities only authorised its reappearance on 1 October when Haase and Richard Fischer approached them and undertook on behalf of the Party that the paper would no longer speak of the 'class struggle'.[32] In November, it was the Party Executive in Württemberg which cleared out the radical leadership from Crispien and Walcher's *Schwäbische Tageblatt*, and installed the revisionist Wilhelm Keil in control.[33]

It was obvious to the clearer-headed among the opposition that every means was to be used to gag them, and that they would be denied any chance of addressing the rank and file of the Party. They therefore had to consider preparing to act publicly as far as they could. This meant breaking discipline. The decision to do so was a painful one for these men and women for whom the Party had been the world and the reason for their existence. They felt that they were trampling underfoot part of themselves, and their health often suffered severely.[34]

Faced with the collapse of his last illusions, with his nerves shaken by the importance of the gesture, but aware that he owed it to those who had not given up the socialist ideal, Liebknecht decided to take the decisive step. Only one means of expression remained open to him, that of voting against the war credits, of voting against the decision of his party. There was a dramatic discussion in Lebedour's apartment on the night of 1–2 December, but he could not convince any of the other oppositional deputies that it was necessary at all costs to resolve to make this spectacular gesture.[35] In the

---

[28] *Illustrierte Geschichte der deutschen Revolution*, op. cit., p. 515.
[29] Schorske, op. cit., p. 298.
[30] *Illustrierte Geschichte der deutschen Revolution*, op. cit., p. 515.
[31] Prager, op. cit., pp. 30–32.
[32] *Illustrierte Geschichte der deutschen Revolution*, op. cit., p. 515.
[33] Keil, op. cit., Volume 1, pp. 306–17.
[34] All the opposition leaders from Haase to Luxemburg, by way of Zetkin and Mehring, had serious difficulties with their health during this period.
[35] Liebknecht, *Klassenkampf gegen den Krieg*, op. cit., pp. 41, 89.

Reichstag on 3 December, he alone voted against the credits, and in this way made himself the symbol of the opposition and the rallying-centre for its scattered forces.

This act started the split, although its completion took years, and the conditions under which it was consummated were confused, reflecting the hesitations of those who opposed the pro-war turn of the Party leaders on 4 August, and took up the fight against it.

The Bolsheviks declare their position

Lenin and the exiled Bolshevik leaders were the first to take up a clear position towards the consequences of 4 August. It was around 24 August that Lenin drafted the document 'The Tasks of Revolutionary Social Democracy in the European War', which spelt out the essentials of the Bolsheviks' orientation in the years to come.[36]

In Lenin's opinion, there was no doubt about the 'bourgeois, imperialist and dynastic' character of the War. The position of the Social-Democratic leaders was a 'sheer betrayal of socialism'.[37] Not that they could have prevented the war by adopting other attitudes, but because they abandoned the class position of the working class in the face of an imperialist war:

> . . . the workers' parties . . . did not oppose the governments' criminal conduct, but called upon the working class to *identify* its position with that of the imperialist governments. The leaders of the International committed an act of treachery against socialism by voting for war credits, by reiterating the chauvinist ('patriotic') slogans of the bourgeoisie of their 'own' countries, by justifying and defending the war, by joining the bourgeois governments of the belligerent countries, and so on and so forth. . . . The responsibility for thus disgracing socialism falls primarily on the German social democrats, who were the strongest and most influential party in the Second International.[38]

The defection of the leaders of the principal parties in the International to the positions of the imperialist bourgeoisie had far-reaching historic

---

[36] V.I. Lenin, 'The Tasks of Revolutionary Social Democracy in the European War', *Collected Works*, Volume 21, op. cit., pp. 15–23.
[37] Ibid., p. 16.
[38] V.I. Lenin, 'The War and Russian Social Democracy', *Collected Works*, Volume 21, op. cit., pp. 23–4.

significance: it pointed to the 'ideological and political bankruptcy' of the International.[39] Lenin indicated the true cause without hesitation: 'This collapse has been mainly caused by the actual prevalence in it [the International] of petit-bourgeois opportunism, the bourgeois nature and the danger of which have long been indicated by the finest representatives of the revolutionary proletariat of all countries.'[40] In his opinion, the opportunist current, which revealed itself before the War in the various forms of reformism, class collaboration, pacifism and concern for legality and parliamentary perspectives, was crowned in the adoption, in the face of the War, of a chauvinist ideology which was really the result of the social pressure of privileged strata of the proletariat, the labour aristocracy and the bureaucracy of the Party and trade-union full-time officials:

> Opportunism was engendered in the course of decades by the special features in the period of the development of capitalism, when the comparatively peaceful and cultured life of a stratum of privileged workmen 'bourgeoisified' them, gave them crumbs from the table of their national capitalists, and isolated them from the suffering, misery and revolutionary temper of the impoverished and ruined masses. The imperialist war is the direct continuation and culmination of this state of affairs, because this is a war for the *privileges* of the great power nations, for the repartition of colonies, and domination over other nations.[41]

The defection of the opportunist leaders into the imperialist camp when the war broke out entailed, therefore, a major reorientation on the part of the revolutionary social democrats. The imperialist war had profound historical significance in respect of both the working class and revolutionary perspectives. Lenin wrote:

> In Europe socialism has emerged from a comparatively peaceful stage that is confined within narrow and national limits. With the outbreak of the war of 1914–15, it entered the stage of revolutionary action; there can be no doubt that the time has come for a complete break with opportunism, for its expulsion from the workers' parties.[42]

---

[39] V.I. Lenin, 'The Tasks of Revolutionary Social Democracy in the European War', op. cit., p. 16.
[40] Ibid.
[41] V.I. Lenin, 'The Collapse of the Second International', op. cit., pp. 242–3.
[42] Ibid., p. 249.

In itself, the European war marked 'the beginning of a new epoch',[43] in which the task of the working class was to fight for power and for socialism:

> The conversion of the present imperialist war into a civil war is the only correct proletarian slogan, one that follows from the experience of the [Paris] Commune, and outlined in the Basle resolution (1912); it has been dictated by all the conditions of an imperialist war between highly-developed bourgeois countries.[44]

This new perspective demanded that under no circumstances could the call for 'unity' be used to tolerate the existence of opportunist wings in workers' parties.

Moreover, Lenin understood that the leaders of the Social-Democratic Parties – those 'tens of thousands of leaders, officials and privileged workers', who had been 'demoralised by legalism', and who had 'disorganised the million-strong army of the social-democratic proletariat'[45] – had much to lose, on the basis of narrow self-interest, if the workers' organisations were dissolved.

The problem, therefore, was not that of the unity of the working class, which remained 'its greatest weapon in the struggle for the socialist revolution',[46] but rather that of its revolutionary unity, which required that opportunism, that alien class element, be eliminated: 'One must be blind not to see bourgeois and petit-bourgeois influence on the proletariat as the main and fundamental cause of the International's disgrace and collapse in 1914.'[47]

In September 1914, the Bolsheviks' Central Committee made a call for a new, Third International, in view of the bankruptcy of the Second International: 'Today, following 1914, unity of the proletarian struggle for the socialist revolution demands that the workers' parties separate themselves completely from the parties of the opportunists.'[48] They also declared:

---

[43] V.I. Lenin, 'Dead Chauvinism and Living Socialism', *Collected Works*, Volume 21, op. cit., p. 98.

[44] V.I. Lenin, 'The War and Russian Social Democracy', op. cit., p. 34.

[45] V.I. Lenin, 'How the Police and the Reactionaries Protect the Unity of the German Social Democracy', *Collected Works*, Volume 21, op. cit., p. 130.

[46] V.I. Lenin, 'What Next?', *Collected Works*, Volume 21, op. cit., p. 109.

[47] V.I. Lenin, 'How the Police and the Reactionaries Protect the Unity of the German Social Democracy', op. cit., p. 131.

[48] V.I. Lenin, 'What Next?', op. cit., p. 111.

The Second International is dead, overcome by opportunism. Down with opportunism, and long live the Third International, purged not only of 'turncoats' . . ., but of opportunism as well. The Second International did its share of useful preparatory work in preliminarily organising the proletarian masses during the long 'peaceful' period of the most brutal capitalist slavery and the most rapid capitalist progress in the last third of the nineteenth and the beginning of the twentieth centuries. To the Third International falls the task of organising the proletarian forces for a revolutionary onslaught against the capitalist governments, for civil war against the bourgeoisie of all countries, for the capture of political power, for the triumph of socialism.[49]

But the Bolsheviks were almost completely isolated. Sufficient forces did not exist in 1914 to carry through on the international scale the split which was necessary for both the construction of revolutionary parties and a revolutionary International. Lenin wrote in *Socialism and War*:

It is perfectly obvious that to create an *international* Marxist organisation, there must be a readiness to form independent Marxist parties in the *various* countries. As a country with the oldest and strongest working-class movement, Germany is of decisive importance. The immediate future will show whether the conditions are mature for the formation of a new and Marxist International. If they are, our party will gladly join such a Third International, purged of opportunism and chauvinism. If they are not, then that will show that a more-or-less protracted period of evolution is needed for that purging to be effective. Our party will form the extreme opposition within the old International, pending the time when the conditions in the various countries make possible the formation of an international workingmen's association standing on the basis of revolutionary Marxism.[50]

In the light of the necessity to act on the international plane, Lenin and the Bolsheviks made every effort to widen their small group of allies in the international movement. There were the Dutch, grouped round *De Tribune*, including Pannekoek, who had returned to his own country when war was declared. There were the Bremen activists who collaborated with the *Bremer-*

---

[49] V.I. Lenin, 'The Position and Tasks of the Socialist International', *Collected Works*, Volume 21, op. cit., p. 41.

[50] V.I. Lenin, 'Socialism and War', *Collected Works*, Volume 21, op. cit., p. 330.

Bürgerzeitung, and were in touch with Radek and Pannekoek.[51] There was the little group in Berlin round Julian Borchardt, who published *Lichtstrahlen*,[52] and was also in touch with Radek and the Bremen people.

Lenin was to place much hope, as his correspondence with Radek shows,[53] in the possibility that a revolutionary group called *Stern* would be formed, but in the end this did not happen. He made great efforts with these different activists to establish an international journal, *Vorbote*, which Pannekoek would be responsible for producing, and in which he was to publish an interesting analysis of the social roots of the opportunism in the workers' movement.[54] Nonetheless, Lenin was to admit, in a letter to the Dutchman David Wijnkoop in July 1915, that the most favourable moment had perhaps not yet come for a split in German Social Democracy, and it was all the more necessary to fight to obtain in all countries a complete break with opportunism.[55] At the same time, he urged Radek to get from the Germans a statement of their ideological position, a clear, full and precise declaration of principles, and said: '. . . the Dutch + ourselves + the Left Germans + 0, and that won't be too bad, for *later* it will not be zero, but everyone'.[56]

It was with the same purpose that Lenin and his allies in European social democracy took part in the Zimmerwald Conference in September 1915, where they formed the nucleus of what became known as the Zimmerwald Left. Radek reported on this conference in *Lichtstrahlen*, and wrote that it was a 'first step towards the reconstruction of the International', and that the revolutionary militants who supported it, despite the pacifist ambiguities expressed by many of the participants, 'did so starting from the idea that it was impossible immediately to form a combat organisation out of the debris of the old International'.[57]

---

[51] Bock, op. cit., pp. 66–72.

[52] Ibid., pp. 72–7.

[53] V.I. Lenin, 'To Karl Radek', *Collected Works*, Volume 36, Moscow, 1971, pp. 329–36.

[54] See in particular 'Zur Einführung', and 'Der Imperialismus und die Aufgaben des Proletariats', *Vorbote*, no. 1, January 1916, of which Bricianer gives a summary and excerpts, op. cit., pp. 121–8.

[55] V.I. Lenin, 'To David Wijnkoop', *Collected Works*, Volume 35, Moscow, 1976, pp. 191–2.

[56] V.I. Lenin, 'To Karl Radek', op. cit., p. 330.

[57] K. Radek, 'Der erste Schritt', *Lichtstrahlen*, 3 October 1915, pp. 3–5.

Repression and radicalisation

Despite his age, Liebknecht was called up into a territorial unit on 7 February 1915.[58] The military authorities were worried because they feared his influence, and kept transferring him from one unit to another. The restrictions upon his freedom of movement, however, rendered him less dangerous for the Party leaders.

This did not prevent him from drafting in May 1915 a leaflet which advanced the celebrated formula, 'the main enemy is at home',[59] which Lenin was to hail as the ideal revolutionary formula.[60] A few days later, Luxemburg was arrested to serve her sentence.[61] Newspapers and journalists suffered blow after blow. In February, *Volkszeitung* in Königsberg was suspended for three weeks. In March, the Magdeburg *Volksstimme* was suspended, the *Bergische Arbeitsstimme*, and the *Sozialdemocratische Zeitung* in Remscheid were banned. In May, a former editor in the *Freie Presse* was arrested.[62] The repression continued. In April 1916, *Lichtstrahlen* was banned,[63] and, on 17 October of the same year, *Vorwärts* was seized by the military authorities, and handed over to the Party Executive.[64]

In a general way, the Social-Democratic leadership played a role as auxiliary police in the policy of 'civil peace'. Heavy industry and the General Staff worked hand-in-hand to organise a war economy, the burden of which was carried by the working people. Public expenditure was financed by inflation. The prices of foodstuffs rose by fifty per cent in the first two years, whilst wages remained static.[65] The trade-union leader, Winnig, went so far as to declare: 'Above the momentary interests of the wage-earners, there stands national independence and the desire for economy on the part of the whole people.'[66]

Soon everyone's earnings, even those of skilled workers, tended towards a 'minimum diet', which itself was gravely endangered by rationing and shortages. Bread was put on ration on 1 February 1915. Next, it was the turn

---

[58] *Illustrierte Geschichte der deutschen Revolution*, op. cit., p. 515.
[59] Text in *Dokumente und Materialen*, Volume 2/1, op. cit., pp. 162–6.
[60] V.I. Lenin, 'Socialism and War', op. cit., p. 326.
[61] *Vorwärts*, 20 February 1915.
[62] *Illustrierte Geschichte der deutschen Revolution*, op. cit., p. 515.
[63] Bock, op. cit., p. 73.
[64] *Dokumente und Materialen*, Volume 2/1, op. cit., p. 490.
[65] *Illustrierte Geschichte der deutschen Revolution*, op. cit., pp. 123–6.
[66] Cited in ibid., p. 113.

of fat, meat and potatoes. There was the terrible 'turnip winter' of 1915–16. Ration cards entitled holders – if the supplies were in the shops – to 1.5 kg of bread, 2.5 kg of potatoes, 80 grams of butter, 250 grams of meat, 180 grams of sugar and half an egg per week. This total provided one-third of the necessary calories.[67] Working people, soldiers and sailors, and the civil population suffered from hunger, but the former radical, Paul Lensch, wrote that rationing was a measure of 'war socialism'.[68] As for dividends, they rose on a regular basis.[69]

It was a long time since anyone could regard the War as the fresh, joyous expedition that led straight to Paris. The war of the trenches, buried in mud and cold, silenced heroic declamations. Overcrowded hospitals, the spectacle of mutilated young men, the ever-lengthening lists of dead and missing 'fallen on the field of honour', sounded the death-knell of the illusions which the Social Democrats had encouraged in 1914. There would be no 'new orientation', nor even any future for the millions of young Germans who were perishing on every front. The desire for peace would perhaps have expressed itself amongst the masses if the straitjacket of repression had not tightened daily.

On 28 May 1915, over a thousand women demonstrated for peace in front of the Reichstag.[70] On 2 December 1916, the Reichstag adopted the law on mobilisation, the *Hilfsdienstgesetz*, which tied the worker to the workplace. Every man between the ages of 17 and 60 not already in the armed forces was obliged to report to the authorities with a certificate of employment or a certificate provided by a preceding employer. In the latter case, he was directed within a fortnight to a place of work. If he refused or left his work, he risked a sentence of up to a year in prison.[71]

Nothing remained of the conquests made by German working class or of the liberties which their leaders had called upon them to defend by means of the War. Despite the repression, their anger increasingly found expression. In November 1915 incidents occurred in Stuttgart, and women demonstrated against the high cost of living. At the same time, in Leipzig, the police put down attempts to demonstrate against the price of meat. In

---

[67] Ibid., p. 125. There is a full study of the problems of food supplies in A. Sayous, 'L'Épuisement économique de l'Allemagne entre 1914 et 1918', *Revue historique*, January-March 1940, pp. 66–75.

[68] Cited in *Illustrierte Geschichte der deutschen Revolution*, op. cit., p. 113.

[69] Ibid., pp. 123–4.

[70] *Dokumente und Materialen*, Volume 2/1, op. cit., pp. 167–8.

[71] *Illustrierte Geschichte der deutschen Revolution*, op. cit., p. 128.

Berlin on 2 February 1916, there were incidents in front of empty shops.[72] On 1 May 1916, the *Internationale* group called a demonstration against the imperialist war.[73] Several thousands of workers and young people gathered round Liebknecht when he spoke in the Potsdamer Platz.[74] He was arrested, but 55,000 workers in the munitions factories in Berlin struck on 28 June,[75] the day he appeared in court. They were followed by working people in Brunswick, whilst in Bremen there were street demonstrations.[76]

In July 1916, the miners of Borbeck in the Ruhr struck work for higher pay, and they were followed elsewhere in the Ruhr during that summer. On 16 August in Essen, a group of workers demonstrated with shouts of 'Long Live Liebknecht!'. There were real hunger-riots in Hamburg. Repression struck again. Karski was arrested on 28 June, Ernst Meyer on 3 August, and Mehring on 15 August. Liebknecht had been sentenced in the lower court to two-and-a-half years in a fortress, and this was increased on appeal to four-and-a-half years.[77]

It was no longer possible to hide the deepening of social tensions. The military and political leaders could not claim a victory for the 'sacred union', but made up for it by attacking the 'agitators'. The mass opposition encouraged and occasionally engendered organisations at a very basic level, which enabled the masses to express themselves and to act. The socialist movement came back to life through violent convulsions after the stupor of August 1914. In a letter to Victor Adler, Kautsky admitted: 'Extremism corresponds to the present needs of the uneducated masses. Today in the trenches, Liebknecht is the most popular man.'[78]

The left-wing oppositions

Very slowly, the efforts of the German revolutionaries, the left radicals, to organise began to have practical results. The small nucleus of friends who had met immediately after 4 August around Luxemburg held together and

---

[72] Ibid., p. 516.
[73] Text in *Dokumente und Materialen*, Volume 2/1, op. cit., pp. 373–5.
[74] Report in ibid., pp. 376–8.
[75] E. Winkler, 'Die Berliner Obleutebewegung im Jahre 1916', *Zeitschrift für Gewissenschaft*, East Berlin, no. 11, 1968, p. 1427; Bartel, op. cit., p. 323.
[76] Bartel, op. cit., pp. 323–4.
[77] *Illustrierte Geschichte der deutschen Revolution*, op. cit., pp. 312, 331, 516.
[78] Adler, op. cit., p. 630.

grew. At the outset, it included Luxemburg herself, Liebknecht, Jogiches and Marchlewski, her old comrades from Polish Social Democracy, Mehring and Zetkin, who were her personal friends, Paul Levi, who had been her lawyer since 1913, Meyer and Ströbel, the journalists from *Vorwärts*, and the Berlin activists whom Liebknecht brought in – Wilhelm Pieck, the second secretary of the Party in Berlin, whose contacts as a member of the apparatus were valuable, Paul Lange and Hermann and Käthe Duncker.[79]

Despite the presence of activists of Eastern European origin, this group had only limited experience of clandestine activity. All its members were known to the authorities and they were closely shadowed. They managed to undertake clandestine propaganda work only when, after several months, the Dunckers made contact with the leaders of the Party group in Niederbarnim, who offered to provide technical help. The first leaflet was drafted by Marchlewski; it was a polemical article against Haenisch[80] which the Niederbarnim comrades ran off on a duplicator at night in one of their apartments, before sending them to addresses from Clara Zetkin's card-index.

For the moment, the group had two aims. Firstly, it wanted to break the silence which could lead activists abroad to conclude that the German Social Democrats were unanimous in their support for the chauvinist policy of their leaders. Secondly, its members wished to build a genuine organisation. Liebknecht, Luxemburg, Mehring and Zetkin addressed Swiss socialist papers to make known their condemnation of the chauvinist declarations which the revisionists Südekum and Richard Fischer had made. Liebknecht, Luxemburg and Mehring sent Christmas greetings to the *Labour Leader* in London; Mehring declared that the struggle for peace and against annexations could not be separated from the class struggle, and that it would be waged in Germany, 'with the leaders if they wished, without them if they did nothing, and against them if they resisted'.[81]

Soon afterwards, the Niederbarnim comrades distributed within the Party the text of the speech by Liebknecht opposing the vote for war credits.[82] At the end of December, Hugo Eberlein undertook to set up the basis of an

[79] Bartel, op. cit., pp. 190–1; H. Wohlgemuth, *Die Entstehung der KPD*, East Berlin, 1968, pp. 64–5.

[80] H. Schumacher (op. cit., p. 134, n. 107) has shown that Paul Schwenk was mistaken in attributing this article to Mehring.

[81] *Dokumente und Materialen*, Volume 2/1, op. cit., pp. 31, 77.

[82] Liebknecht, *Klassenkampf gegen den Krieg*, op. cit., p. 17; *Dokumente und Materialen*, Volume 2/1, op. cit., p. 64.

organisation: an internal network in the Party, including an agent in each workplace and one person responsible in each locality for contact with the centre for distributing the writings of the opposition.

By around mid-1915, the group was in contact with over three hundred localities.[83] On 5 January 1915, another member of the central nucleus, Artur Crispien, sent an organising circular to members who were believed to be reliable, and got replies within a few days from Dresden, Duisburg, Munich and Danzig, as well as from such influential activists as Westmeyer and Dissman.[84] The first conference was held on 5 May in Berlin in Pieck's apartment. The organising work was sufficiently advanced for the activists to sketch out a regional organisation, so that the structure of the secret network within the Party could be improved.[85]

Successes and severe blows alternated in the secret struggle of these too prominent activists. Luxemburg's appeal was rejected, and she was imprisoned for two months in February 1915. Nonetheless, she produced from prison a contribution to the first issue of the journal, *Die Internationale*, which the group had decided to produce, and which she and Mehring edited. It was printed on the presses of a Party paper in the Ruhr, and appeared with contributions from Zetkin, Thalheimer, Ströbel, Käthe Duncker, Paul Lange and Liebknecht. But the journal was immediately banned.[86] At the same moment, the Württemberg activist Jakob Walcher was arrested and charged with distributing a subversive leaflet. The decision of the court which sentenced him emphasised that his political line was opposed to that of his Party.[87]

The year 1915 was very hard. Clara Zetkin was arrested on her return from the International Women's Conference in Berne.[88] She was released in October, but her health was very bad, and she took hardly any part in the

---

[83] Institute of Marxism-Leninism of the Central Committee of the SED (IML ZPA), East Berlin, *Wilhelm Pieck. Mappe, Dokumente du KPD 1914*, 1929, NL 36/2. Substantial excerpts in G. Badia, *Le Spartakisme*, Paris, 1967, pp. 326–37.

[84] Wohlgemuth, op. cit., p. 98.

[85] Bartel, op. cit., p. 222; and IML-ZPA, NL 36/2. Those present were Pieck, Liebknecht, Mehring, Käthe and Hermann Duncker, Geithner, Rühle, Paul Levi, Crispien, Berten, Merkel and Gäbel.

[86] See Wohlgemuth's introduction to the facsimile reprint of this issue of *Die Internationale*, East Berlin, 1965.

[87] *Illustrierte Geschichte der deutschen Revolution*, op. cit., p. 142.

[88] Bartel, op. cit., p. 250; *Illustrierte Geschichte der deutschen Revolution*, op. cit., p. 516.

opposition's activity.[89] In Stuttgart, seven activists, including Friedrich Westmeyer and a youth, Hans Tittel, were arrested and charged.[90] In Berlin, Pieck made contact with some young workers influenced by the Saxon building worker Fritz Globig,[91] but he was arrested after the women's demonstration outside the Reichstag.[92] In the autumn, it was the turn of Meyer, and of Eberlein. In the end, despite his age, Friedrich Westmeyer was called up into the army, and was to die in a hospital near the front.[93]

Political activity amongst the émigrés and in the Swiss workers' movement closely affected the German movement, because the first international regroupments took place in Switzerland. Willi Münzenberg had been the Secretary of the Swiss socialist youth for several years, and had maintained contacts with Germany, both with Bremen and with Saxony. At the beginning of the War, he was working with the Rhinelander, Walter Stoecker. Ten countries were represented at the youth conference which was held in Berne at Easter 1915; German groups in Stuttgart, Göppingen and Karlsruhe sent delegates. The resolution moved by a Bolshevik won only three votes with thirteen against. But the conference decided to break from the Vienna Bureau, and proclaimed itself the Independent Youth International, with Münzenberg as its international secretary. On 1 September 1915, the first issue of its journal, *Jugend-Internationale*, appeared with articles by Hoernle, Liebknecht, Kollontai and Radek. Liebknecht, Mehring, Paul Frölich and Georg Schumann helped to distribute it in Germany.[94]

At the time of the international socialist conference in Zimmerwald, the opponents of the war were divided equally between a centrist majority tending towards pacifism, and a Left which was identified by its acceptance of the Bolshevik theses. Five Germans were present: Adolf Hoffmann and Ledebour on one side, and Meyer and Thalheimer, representing the *Internationale* group, on the other, all voted with the majority. Borchardt, the editor of *Lichtstrahlen*, alone lined up with Lenin in the Zimmerwald Left.[95]

[89] *Illustrierte Geschichte der deutschen Revolution*, op. cit., p. 142.
[90] *Dokumente und Materialen*, Volume 2/1, op. cit., pp. 201–6.
[91] Arendsee, op. cit., p. 92.
[92] *Illustrierte Geschichte der deutschen Revolution*, op. cit., p. 515.
[93] Ibid., pp. 142, 515.
[94] W. Münzenberg, *Die Dritte Front*, Berlin, 1930, pp. 43, 156–65, 204–7.
[95] Bartel, op. cit., p. 237.

In June 1915, more than 750 well-known activists, editors of newspapers, full-time officials and trade-union leaders, addressed a protest to the Party Executive against its policy.[96] The text was drafted in Liebknecht's apartment by himself, Meyer, Ströbel, Marchlewski, Hermann Duncker and Mehring, as well as Laukant, Heinrich Laufenberg and Ledebour.[97] On 1 January 1916, the *Internationale* group held a conference in Liebknecht's apartment. The twelve delegates[98] adopted as the basis for their activity the document *The Crisis of Social Democracy*, which Luxemburg had drafted in prison. This fiercely criticised 'civil peace' as well as pacifist illusions, and declared that peace could result only from revolutionary activity by the working class.[99] On 19 March, a larger conference was held, again in Berlin, with seventeen delegates from Berlin itself.[100] This conference took up an extremely clear attitude towards the newly-emerging centrist opposition, and was in fact the beginning of the future Spartacus group.

Lenin subjected the documents of the *Internationale* group to a detailed criticism, especially the *Junius Pamphlet* which Luxemburg had written in prison. The essential divergence lay in the fact that the Germans set peace as their aim, rather than civil war. Lenin attacked 'Junius' for an analysis that was based on the past, centred around the perspective of a return to the prewar situation, and to the unfolding of the class struggle within the framework of bourgeois democracy, whilst he believed that the War had opened up the epoch of revolutions.[101] Nonetheless, the call for class struggle during a war was a revolutionary act of great importance. When the Spartacus group, following Liebknecht, declared that the main enemy was at home, it took its place in the revolutionary wing which was gradually taking shape within the international socialist movement.

---

[96] Text in *Dokumente und Materialen*, Volume 2/1, op. cit., pp. 169–73.

[97] Amongst those who signed were many future Communist leaders, such as Brandler, Brass, Däumig, Eberlein, Heckert, Lange, Merges, Paul Neumann, Rühle, Thalheimer and Walcher, as well as future leaders of the Independents, Crispien, Robert Dissmann and Ledebour.

[98] K. Duncker, Eberlein, Knief, Liebknecht, Lindau, Mehring, Meyer, Minster, Rühle, Schumann, August and Bertha Thalheimer (*Illustrierte Geschichte der deutschen Revolution*, op. cit., p. 135). See also Bartel, op. cit., pp. 270–5; and Wohlgemuth, op. cit., pp. 167–71.

[99] *Dokumente und Materialen*, Volume 2/1, op. cit., pp. 279–82.

[100] This conference became known after the discovery in 1948 of the notes of one of the participants, Ohloff. U. Plener, 'Die Märzkonferenz der Spartakusgruppe, ein Markstein auf dem Wege zur Gründung der KPD', *Beiträge zur Geschichte der deutschen Arbeiterbewegung*, East Berlin, 1961, no. 4, pp. 812–41.

[101] See in particular V.I. Lenin, 'The *Junius Pamphlet*', *Collected Works*, Volume 22, Moscow, 1977, pp. 305–19.

Moreover, a few days after the conference, Otto Rühle published in *Vorwärts* a sensational article in support of a split in the Social-Democratic movement,[102] which so far had been defended only by Borchardt's paper,[103] and he had been arrested. The activists had been working towards a split in the youth organisations, as shown by the efforts of, for example, Fritz Globig and his comrades in Berlin[104] to organise the young workers on an independent basis. At Easter, under cover of a conference of nature-lovers, they held a national conference of the oppositional youth in an inn near Jena. Liebknecht, Rühle, Hoernle and Schumann took part, and the conference adopted theses drafted by Liebknecht.[105] The revolutionaries succeeded in establishing such legal papers as *Arbeiterpolitik* in Bremen and *Sozialdemokrat* in Stuttgart.[106] They also published illegal papers more or less regularly, such as the *Spartacus Letters*, but also *Der Kampf* in Duisberg and Hamburg.[107]

As it grew, the opposition encountered problems, both in respect of contacts with centrist oppositionists, who were increasingly numerous and active within the parliamentary group, and over differences in respect of its own perspectives. Some wanted to work towards proclaiming a new party, and to cut all their links with Social Democracy. Luxemburg opposed them. In her opinion, they should stay in the Party as long as they could, take care not to become a sect, and work to draw the workers into struggle.[108] Already in January, Johann Knief in Bremen, Rühle and Lindau had declared for a split.[109] The demonstration of 1 May 1916 had corresponded to Luxemburg's conception of mass action, whilst the leaflet drafted by Liebknecht had been printed and distributed by young activists,[110] which pointed to a certain degree of organisation.

The strike on 28 June seemed to confirm this line; workers with whom the revolutionaries had no direct influence carried out during the War the type

---

[102] 'Zur Parteispaltung', *Vorwärts*, 12 January 1916; *Dokumente und Materialen*, Volume 2/1, op. cit., pp. 301–7.

[103] Bock, op. cit., p. 74.

[104] Arendsee, op. cit., p. 103.

[105] *Illustrierte Geschichte der deutschen Revolution*, op. cit., p. 131; Bartel, op. cit., p. 307.

[106] Controlled by Walcher, Hoernle, Crispien and Rück (*Illustrierte Geschichte der deutschen Revolution*, op. cit., p. 143).

[107] Ibid.

[108] Frölich, op. cit., p. 277; Wohlgemuth, op. cit., p. 186.

[109] F. Globig, . . . *aber verbunden sind wir machtig*, East Berlin, 1958, p. 138; Wohlgemuth, op. cit., p. 169.

[110] Arendsee, op. cit., pp. 101–2.

of political strike which the revisionists believed to be impossible even in peacetime. Nonetheless, despite the efforts of the organiser, Jogiches, and of Levi, who went to Switzerland and made contacts there,[111] the Spartacus group (as it was now called) remained numerically weak, and did not succeed in capitalising in numerical terms upon the sympathy which Liebknecht's prestige won for it.[112] Some of its members, such as Heckert and Brandler in Chemnitz, exerted real influence because they had trade-union positions,[113] but the group itself remained a fairly loose network with insecure connections which arrests or mobilisation could break at any moment.

In reality, there were several organisations. In Berlin, the *Lichtstrahlen* group was organised as the International Socialists of Germany (ISD), but repression and then the evolution of its principal figure, Borchardt, soon disappointed those – notably Lenin – who were counting on its development.[114] In the north-west, several groups began to organise in association with *Die Internationale*, whilst at the same time they maintained their links with Radek in Switzerland. In Hamburg, the historian Heinrich Laufenberg, who had been a centrist before the war, had taken a stand against the War. He maintained an active small clandestine group along with such other activists as Fritz Wolffheim, a former member of the Industrial Workers of the World in the USA, Rudolf Lindau, Wilhelm Düwell, and Paul Frölich. By its side, an organisation of 'free youth' formed on a socialist, anti-militarist and internationalist basis carried on agitation and propaganda work under cover of leisure and open-air activities. Thanks to the support of underground leaders, it recruited widely amongst working-class youth, but had no contact with the underground groups.[115]

In Bremen, where the radicals had always enjoyed considerable influence – Pieck had been secretary there, and Pannekoek had lived there for six years – Johann Knief, a former schoolteacher who had become a Party instructor and editorial worker on *Bremer-Bürgerzeitung*, had much influence amongst young workers. The cadres of the Party knew Radek personally, and he continued

---

[111] Beradt, op. cit., p. 17, finds it important to defend Levi against his right-wing critics by explaining the political purpose of his visits to Switzerland.

[112] Prestige which rose still higher after he was sentenced.

[113] S. Beckert, 'Die Linken in Chemnitz im Kampf gegen den Opportunismus für die Herausbildung einer neuen revolutionären Partei', *Beiträge zur Geschichte der deutschen Arbeiterbewegung*, no. 1, 1967, pp. 109ff.

[114] On Lenin's hopes, see V.I. Lenin, 'To Karl Radek', op. cit., pp. 334–6.

[115] *Vorwärts und nicht vergessen*, East Berlin, 1958, pp. 235, 253.

to influence them strongly by correspondence. Knief was able to maintain a weekly discussion circle in the Party, at which he would defend revolutionary theses, distributing the articles by Radek, Lenin and Trotsky which were appearing in the Swiss press.[116] He was able to build up a clandestine nucleus of young activists, which had a certain influence amongst the dockers.

One of his supporters, a young journalist named Eildermann, maintained regular relations with the youth organisations in Dresden and in Stuttgart, and even with a group of soldiers in the 75th Infantry Regiment, organised by a Bremen shoemaker, Carl Jannack. Whilst on leave in the autumn of 1915, Jannack told Knief that his comrades were in favour of a split and of founding a revolutionary party. Eildermann was delegated from Bremen to the Jena conference in 1916. In the same year, the Bremen revolutionaries, having definitively broken from the centrist team which ran *Bremer-Bürgerzeitung*, had collected money from the workers in the naval dockyards to buy the press for the new weekly which they were soon to bring out, *Arbeiterpolitik*. Their leaders took part in the conference of *Die Internationale*, maintained contact with Borchardt and the ISD, and with the Zimmerwald Left through Radek. During Easter 1916, they had a long discussion with Ernst Meyer about their work, when he visited them from Berlin.[117]

In Berlin, the work of the activists in Niederbarnim, which had started within the Party, was quickly taken over by a new opposition which started in the trade unions, that of the 'revolutionary delegates', the successors in the Berlin factories of the well-known 'men of confidence' of the SPD.[118] It was the war which marked them, and gave them a special character. When 'civil peace' was proclaimed, in fact, several leading figures in the metalworkers' union (the DMV) in Berlin attended a meeting called by the leader of the turners' branch, the Social Democrat Richard Müller, in order to organise a struggle in the union against the employers, over the heads of the reformist leaders who supported the war policy, namely Oskar Cohen and Siering. They received so wide a hearing that in March 1916, only Müller's firm refusal to stand stopped him being elected to head the union in Berlin.[119]

---

[116] Ibid., p. 142.
[117] Ibid., pp. 143–8, 169.
[118] On this, see W. Tormin, *Zwischen Rätediktatur und sozialer Demokratie*, Düsseldorf, 1954, pp. 40–44; P. von Oertzen, *Betriebsräte in der Novemberrevolution*, Düsseldorf, 1964, pp. 71–8; Winkler, op. cit., pp. 1422–35. See also the memoirs of Richard Müller, *Vom Kaiserreich zur Republik*, Berlin, 1924–5.
[119] R. Müller, op. cit., pp. 59–60.

Müller was later to regret letting this opportunity slip, but the group for the moment preferred semi-clandestine activity in the union apparatus to direct assumption of responsibilities. The original nucleus, the existence of which was to surprise many people in 1918, acted in a climate of conspiracy. It methodically recruited reliable members from amongst the trade-union representatives in the workplaces and different crafts. The members of the network buried themselves with securing key positions. They took advantage of the legal cover provided by the turners' union and acted in the union as a well-organised fraction, but always kept close links with the workers in the factories and the workshops, becoming capable of checking on the way a delegates' congress went, and, insisting on full freedom of discussion.

They constituted a unique kind of organisation, neither a trade union nor a party, but a clandestine group in the trade unions and the Party alike. As the leading circle of the revolutionary delegates, they succeeded several times in expressing the workers' will to resist the state and the Party apparatus, and in concretely expressing in activity their demands and their readiness to struggle. The principal nucleus, the 'centre', never numbered more than fifty members,[120] but thanks to the turners, who were well situated in every workplace, as a small but well-knit and disciplined phalanx in the delegates' meetings, they could set in motion, with the help of some hundreds of men whom they directly influenced, tens and later hundreds of thousands of Berlin workers, by enabling them to make their own decisions about active initiatives which corresponded with their aspirations.

These metalworkers, who were specialists on relatively high pay because the firms which employed them were on full-time war work, were certainly the finest people in Social Democracy and in the prewar trade-union movement. Unknown in 1914, by the end of the War they were to be the accepted leaders of the workers of Berlin and, despite their relative youth, the cadres of the revolutionary socialist movement. Their principal leader, Richard Müller, was linked to Ledebour and leaned towards the centrist opposition, which led him to try to prevent polemics breaking out in their ranks between the different tendencies in the opposition.[121] Three of them at least, Bruno Peters, Otto Franke and Hermann Grothe were either members of the Spartacus group,

---

[120] According to von Oertzen (op. cit., p. 74), who provides convincing arguments against the figure of 80 to 100 put forward by Tormin, op. cit., p. 42.

[121] R. Müller, op. cit., p. 66.

or were soon to join it.[122] The rest, the majority of whom became Communists in 1919–20, were close to the Spartacists, such as Paul Eckert, Paul Wegmann, Richard Nowakowski, Hans Pfeiffer, Paul Neumann, Heinrich Malzahn, Neuendorf, Otto Tost, Paul Scholze, Fritz Winguth, Richard Schöttler, Paul Weyer and Anton Grylewicz.[123] Their circle was broadened by activists who were not factory workers, such as Ottomar Geschke, who ran a hostel for young workers.[124] This circle, which was constantly renewed by individual mobilisations and demobilisations, organised in June 1916 the strike in solidarity with Liebknecht by 55,000 Berlin metalworkers.[125]

It was a flexible network which relied on the mutual trust of activists working in legal organisations. The circle of the revolutionary delegates was in reality a candidate for the leadership of the Berlin workers. It was successfully to challenge the SPD and the unions several times for this, without, however, having the ambition of becoming an independent political leadership or of splitting the unions.

Revolutionaries who opposed a split

The positions of the revolutionary opposition in Germany, then, were very far from expressing what the Bolsheviks were expecting. To be sure, the little group in Bremen did from time to time publish articles by Bukharin, Radek or Lenin, and was ready to accept as a whole Lenin's analyses of the bankruptcy of the Second International and the necessity for a new International. The *Internationale* group, which agreed that the Second International was bankrupt, recognised that the Third International was historically necessary, but refused to prepare for it by a split:

---

[122] Von Oertzen, op. cit., p. 73, and recollections of the earliest activists in *Vorwärts und nicht vergessen*, op. cit., pp. 269ff., 349ff. On Grothe, see his biography in H. Weber, *Der Gründungsparteitag der KPD*, Frankfurt-am-Main, 1969, p. 317.

[123] See biographies in Appendix.

[124] Von Oertzen (op. cit.), also implies that Paul Scholze was a member of the Spartacist group, which is possible, but for which there is no documentary evidence. In any case, he did not join the KPD(S) in January 1919. J.S. Drabkin considers as 'revolutionary activists at work amongst the revolutionary delegates' Franke, Schöttler, Nowakowski and Hans Pfeiffer (*Die Novemberrevolution 1918 in Deutschland*, Berlin, 1968, p. 448).

[125] Winkler, op. cit., pp. 1429–30. It seems to have remained the case throughout the war that the police could never penetrate this circle; at all events, there is no report on them in the documents published by Leo Stern.

The new International which must be born after the bankruptcy of its predecessor can only be born on the basis of the class struggles of the working-class masses of the most important countries. . . . It must be born from below. . . . German social democracy, the bankruptcy of which has only proved its weakness – which has long existed – must undergo a complete internal change if it wishes one day to lead the proletarian masses in conformity with its historic mission.

Its transformation into an active revolutionary force cannot be achieved merely by programmes and manifestos, by a mechanical discipline or by outdated organisational forms, but only by the propagation of class consciousness and the resolute initiative of the masses . . . which presupposes the transformation of the bureaucratic system of the party into a democratic system, in which the full-timers will be the instruments of the masses.[126]

In fact, Luxemburg drew lessons from the bankruptcy of the Second International which did little to bring her nearer to Lenin's standpoint on organisation. She wrote:

It is precisely the powerful organisation, precisely the much-lauded discipline of the German social democracy, which enabled a handful of parliamentarians to command this organisation of four million people to turn around in 24 hours, and defend the very fortress which the organisation was designed to attack. . . . The more effective the education, the organisation and the famous discipline . . . so much more effective today is the war-effort of German social democracy.[127]

Convinced that the revolutionaries must be organised in a party and in an International, she did not believe that this historic task could be achieved in any and every situation, and especially not in the absence of any mass movement:

Men do not make their history as they would like, but they do make it themselves. The activity of the working class depends on the degree of maturity which social evolution has achieved. But social evolution does not advance beyond the working class. It is the driving force of it and the cause,

---

[126] *Spartakusbriefe*, Berlin, 1958, pp. 137–9.
[127] R. Luxemburg, 'The Reconstruction of the International', *Ausgewählte Reden und Schriften*, Volume 2, p. 521.

as much as the product and the result. Its activity itself is a determining factor in History. And if we cannot jump over historical evolution, we certainly can accelerate or slow down this evolution. . . . The victory of the socialist proletariat is bound to the iron laws of History, to the thousand stages of an earlier evolution filled with suffering and with too many delays. But this victory cannot be won if there does not leap, from the mass of the material conditions which History has accumulated, the spark, the conscious will of the great masses.[128]

The revolutionaries in the *Internationale* group therefore accepted a very different perspective from that of the Bolsheviks. Their task was to restore the old house, to drive the Eberts and Scheidemanns out, and to win back the Party for its members. For that purpose, whilst awaiting the inevitable uprising of the masses, their propaganda would help both to enlighten it, and to provide an analysis of it. But the immediate, 'mechanical' split which the Bolsheviks advocated and which certain elements in Germany influenced by them were beginning to advocate, seemed to them to be a remedy worse than the disease. Jogiches wrote that it would result in cutting off the revolutionaries from 'the best comrades in the Party', and in plunging them into impotence.[129] Luxemburg wrote:

> It is always possible to walk out of small sects or small coteries, and, if one does not want to stay there, to apply oneself to building new sects and new coteries. But it is only an irresponsible daydream to want to liberate the whole mass of the working class from the very weighty and dangerous yoke of the bourgeoisie by a simple 'walk-out'.[130]

In fact, she claimed that such an initiative would fail to address the root of the problem: the liberation of the proletariat passes through their liberation from 'parliamentary cretinism' and from the superstition of the 'party card'. She wrote:

---

[128] R. Luxemburg, 'The Crisis of Social Democracy', *Ausgewählte Reden und Schriften*, Volume 2, p. 269.

[129] See in particular the letter from Jogiches to Heckert and Brandler in September 1916, quoted by Wohlgemuth, op. cit., p. 193.

[130] 'Gracchus', 'Open Letter to Our Political Friends', *Der Kampf*, Duisburg, no. 31, 6 January 1917, in *Dokumente und Materialen*, Volume 2/1, op. cit., p. 525.

> The liquidation of the heap of organised decay which today calls itself Social Democracy is not a private affair which depends on the personal decision of one or several groups. It will occur inevitably as the result of the World War.[131]

In reality, just as the decisions of August 1914 had demonstrated that the SPD was not only 'the movement of the class itself' but also an apparatus which could defect to the camp of the class enemy, so the events of 1917 were to reveal the futility of the perspectives of restoring or reforming the Party. The split in Social Democracy was in fact to take place, partly, to be sure, as a consequence of the 'pressure of the masses', but above all on the initiative of the apparatus. It was to take place, not between revolutionaries and reformists, but amongst the reformists. In this way, it once again created confusion in the ranks of the revolutionaries, who had not been able either to foresee or to prepare for it.

---

[131] Ibid.

Chapter Five

The Foundation of the Independent Social-Democratic Party

There were two other German Social Democrats besides Borchardt from *Lichtstrahlen* and Ernst Meyer and Bertha Thalheimer from *Internationale* at the Zimmerwald conference. They were Georg Ledebour and Adolf Hoffmann, both Reichstag deputies and well-known figures on the radical Left, for which they had often spoken in the prewar polemics against the revisionists and the reformists. At Zimmerwald, they supported the theses of the majority, which Lenin characterised as 'centrist'. Contrary to the opinion expressed by Franz Borkenau, that the War provoked regroupments on entirely new bases,[1] the old oppositions, apart from a few individual defections, reappeared immediately after August 1914. The fourteen deputies who on 3 August had supported the position of voting against war credits took much the same approach as the radical bloc. They reflected the radicals' attachment to the Erfurt Programme and their principled stand that called upon all socialists to reject any collaboration with the bourgeois state.

But the sharpness of the contradictions which the war opened up, plus Liebknecht's initiatives, raised new problems, and opened new perspectives which the old left bloc had never envisaged. When

---

[1] Borkenau, op. cit., p. 61.

Liebknecht refused to bow before the discipline of the Party and appealed to the masses to act independently over its head, he effectively fragmented the radical bloc, a process of which he was aware: 'What is needed now is open agitation and clarification, not seeking agreement on a middle position.'[2]

The reaction of the other opposition deputies could not fail to be sharp. Starting from the night of 1–2 December 1914, when Liebknecht separated from those who thereafter were called the centrists, polemics raged amongst the former radicals. Haase and his friends, like Ledebour and Adolf Hoffmann, regarded Liebknecht as having acted like an irresponsible sectarian, and having provided the executive with a pretext for disciplinary actions which could only confuse the issues in the necessary internal discussions. Liebknecht retorted that when the opposition, anxious to appear loyal, bowed before the decisions of the Executive, they became its accomplices. The centrists accepted this risk. In their eyes, the Party was still their party, whatever its errors, and the vote on 4 August was one such error, aggravated by subsequent errors about annexations. In their opinion, the political struggle to regenerate the Party had to be waged within it, with respect for its constitution and its traditions.

A loyal opposition

The Executive understood this situation perfectly. For the moment, it needed to retain those oppositionists who had decided not to cause a scandal. It could use them in its efforts to isolate Liebknecht and his supporters, portraying the latter as sabotaging unity, and as 'enemies of the Party'. The existence of a loyal opposition had the effect of disproving Liebknecht's charge that his act of indiscipline was the only way to express his opposition. The Executive accordingly decided on 3 February 1915 to authorise a certain form of public opposition, and to permit deputies who could not conscientiously accept discipline and vote for war credits to absent themselves when the vote was taken. In the Reichstag session on 20 March, the deputy Otto Rühle joined Liebknecht in voting against the war credits, whilst Haase and his friends walked out of the chamber before the vote.[3]

---

[2] Liebknecht, *Klassenkampf gegen den Krieg*, op. cit., pp. 51–2.
[3] Prager, op. cit., pp. 53–4, 60.

Whilst the supporters of the majority stressed the patriotic character of the War and the need for 'civil peace' to ensure national defence, the centrist minority stressed that the Social Democrats were seeking an honourable compromise and a peace without annexations or indemnities, and were showing their attachment to democratic liberties. Liebknecht and his comrades refused to play this game. They criticised the thesis of 'peace without annexations', which they analysed as an off-shoot of Kautsky's prewar idea of 'universal disarmament', a mere left-wing cover for the majority's war policy.

Events seemed to be proving Liebknecht to be right. In 1915, it was clear that the War had come to stay, that the rulers of Germany had a programme of annexations, and that the Social-Democratic Executive was far from repudiating it. The attacks on democratic rights, the police repression, and the deterioration in the conditions of the workers eased the task of all the oppositionists, and the centrists were to harden their criticism and to express it for the first time outside of the Party. In March, Haase and Stadthagen denounced in the Reichstag the state of siege, censorship and the anti-working-class character of the régime's domestic policy. Ledebour denounced the oppression of the national minorities in the occupied regions.[4] Haase accused the government's policy of exacerbating class differences. These criticisms echoed a rising discontent, but were still located within the framework of the war policy. Haase was arguing that abuses which threatened the morale of the defenders of the fatherland had to be corrected.[5]

Three months later, the centrists faced the SPD Executive's endorsement of the government's open declaration of annexationist policies. In order to prevent Liebknecht from formally protesting against them, the centrists decided to take a further step, following the protest of 9 June 1915 drafted by Liebknecht, Ströbel, Marchlewski, Meyer and others.[6] Bernstein, Haase and Kautsky published in *Leipziger Volkszeitung* what was really a manifesto of the loyal opposition, entitled 'The Tasks of the Hour'.[7] They refrained from criticising the position which the Party adopted in August 1914, but now declared that

---

[4] Schorske, op. cit., p. 303.
[5] *Stenographische Berichte der Verhandlungen des deutschen Reichstages*, Volume 306, p. 46. Prager (op. cit., pp. 56–7) does not note the nationalist phrases.
[6] *Dokumente und Materialen*, Volume 2/1, op. cit., p. 169, n. 1.
[7] 'Das Gebot der Stunde', *Leipziger Volkszeitung*, 19 June 1915; Prager, op. cit., pp. 72–4.

the moment had come, with the security of Germany ensured and its frontiers protected, for placing the accent on that part of the Social-Democratic programme which had hitherto been sidelined, but which was now more relevant than ever, namely the return to the status quo of before 1914, by a peace without annexations.

The text did not mention the class struggle, but it affirmed that the Party should refuse to declare its confidence in the Bethmann-Hollweg government, and suggested that the Party should take the initiative in a campaign for peace. Despite the anodyne character of these proposals, the government became anxious. After all, these three men taken together symbolised the whole of prewar Social Democracy. *Leipziger Volkszeitung* was suppressed.[8] The Executive, for its part, went through the motions of jettisoning ballast; on 15 December, Scheidemann put a question to the Chancellor about his programme of annexations.[9] The tone of his intervention and the content of the reply by Bethmann-Hollweg gave the centrists the impression that they were witnessing a piece of play-acting, and that the Executive had already approved the programme. This provoked some them into breaking discipline, and when war credits were voted on 29 December 1915, 22 Social-Democratic deputies left the sitting to avoid voting, but 20 remained and voted against.[10]

The first serious breach between the Executive and the loyal opposition had just taken place. On 29 December, the loyal opposition published a declaration in which it justified its attitude by saying that, in conformity with the Party tradition, there could be no question of expressing confidence in the government to carry out a policy of peace, now that Germany's frontiers were secure. The Executive made its contribution on 12 January, by expelling Liebknecht from the parliamentary group, an undisguised threat to the other rebels.[11]

But signs of discontent in the Party were growing. The leading committee [Zentralvorstand] in Greater Berlin approved the declaration of the minority by 41 votes to 17. Ledebour won for it the approval of a large minority of 320 Party officials in the sixth constituency in Berlin. Similar votes took place

---

[8] Bartel, op. cit., p. 240, n. 1.
[9] P. Scheidemann, *Der Zusammenbruch*, Berlin, 1921, pp. 30–2; *Stenographische Berichte*, Volume 306, p. 443.
[10] Prager, op. cit., pp. 87–8.
[11] Ibid., pp. 87, 90.

in Leipzig, Halle and Bremen.[12] Part of the apparatus seemed to be joining the loyal opposition. This was what their followers in the working class demanded from them. Haase was a lawyer, and his profession put him in day-to-day contact with the repression. He decided that he could no longer make any concession over civil liberties.[13] On 24 May 1916, he made a violent speech in the Reichstag against the state of siege, and the minority voted with him against its renewal. The answer came at once: the fraction expelled them, by 53 votes to 33.[14]

Towards the split in the Party

The 33 deputies who were expelled formed the Collective for Social-Democratic Work [Sozialdemokratische Arbeitsgemeinschaft] in the Reichstag.[15] The split in the parliamentary group had been effected. In principle, there was still a single party, but in reality there were two parliamentary groups and three tendencies.

The revolutionaries and the pacifists did not seem to be close to agreement. Since December 1915, Liebknecht had been avoided by the deputies who now supported the Collective.[16] In the course of a meeting which took place in Neukölln, they refused to take part in the demonstration which he and his comrades were preparing for 1 May.[17] In Bremen the deputy Henke, a member of the Haase group, broke off relations with Knief and Frölich, who were preparing to found *Arbeiterpolitik*.[18] The first of the Spartacus letters contained violent attacks on the centrists. From that time onwards, the two tendencies were in competition, each trying to extend its influence in the Party.[19]

The actions of the Executive brought them closer together. Starting in March, the Executive started a violent campaign to recover control of the organisation. This culminated in September with the holding of a national conference on

---

[12] Ibid., p. 91.

[13] Schorske, op. cit., p. 309.

[14] Prager, op. cit., pp. 94–6.

[15] Text of the statement in ibid., p. 96.

[16] Liebknecht, *Klassenkampf gegen den Krieg*, op. cit., pp. 90–92; 'Die Dezembermänner von 1915', *Spartakusbriefe*, op. cit., pp. 86–91.

[17] *Spartakusbriefe*, op. cit., pp. 165–6.

[18] *Unter der roten Fahne*, East Berlin, 1958, pp. 90–1.

[19] Kautsky wrote to Adler on 7 August 1916: 'The danger to us from the Spartacus group is great. . . . If the Left of the fraction had demonstrated by declaring its independence a year ago, as I wanted it to do, the Spartacus group today would have no importance.' (Adler, op. cit., p. 361.)

the theme of Party unity. In October, the military authorities seized *Vorwärts*, the fortress of the centrists round Hilferding, and handed it to the Executive, who made it its own principal organ under the control of Hermann Müller.[20]

The Berlin workers in the Party who sympathised with the opposition were not to forget what they regarded as an act of piracy, and as the symbol of the break from socialist principles on the part of the Social-Democratic leaders. When the Reichstag discussed the law about mobilising manpower, Haase called it 'a second anti-socialist law'.[21] His group accused the supporters of the majority who voted for it, and the trade-union leaders who accepted it, of 'forging the chains of the proletariat'.[22] The adoption of this law during the 'turnip winter' lifted the Party crisis to its height. The Party was tearing itself apart under the pressure of conflicting class forces: the ruling classes acting through the Executive as their intermediary, and the working people compelling the centrists to express their will to resist. The Executive found itself facing the consequences of its own policy. Its only course was to impose inside the Party the same state of siege as already weighed upon the country. As for the loyal opposition, it had to defend itself, and cease to be loyal on pain of death.

A national conference of the oppositions was organised in Berlin on 7 January 1917 on the initiative of the Collective for Social-Democratic Work. The problem was to agree on measures to be taken to defend the minorities, to defend activists threatened with expulsion, and to protect their newspapers from the threat of seizure.[23] All the currents were represented there, and of the 157 delegates, 35 were Spartacists.[24] No one suggested taking the initiative in a split. On behalf of the Spartacists, Meyer suggested refusing to pay membership fees over to the Executive, as the Stuttgart and Bremen organisations had already done.[25] The majority of the delegates declined to follow him on this course, which they regarded as very likely to lead to a split. The only result of the conference was that a resolution was carried calling for the maintenance of 'permanent contacts' between the oppositions in order to develop their influence 'within the framework of the constitution

---

[20] Prager, op. cit., pp. 116–19.
[21] *Stenographische Berichte*, Volume 308, pp. 2290–4.
[22] *Protokoll über die Verhandlungen des Gründungsparteitages der USP*, 1917, p. 88.
[23] Ibid., pp. 97–8; Prager, op. cit., p. 124.
[24] Prager, op. cit., p. 125.
[25] *Protokoll USP*, 1917, op. cit., p. 99; Prager, op. cit., pp. 125–6.

of the Party'.[26] This received 111 votes, against 34 for a Spartacist motion, and six for a document from Borchardt.[27]

The response of the Executive, ten days later, showed how inane these precautions were. On 16 January, it announced that the opposition 'had placed itself outside the Party' by holding this conference, which it regarded as 'factional'. It instructed the local organisations to take all necessary measures – contrary to the constitution – against the 'saboteurs', who were to be expelled with the least possible delay.[28] The purge was carried out in a high-handed fashion. Where the supporters of the Executive had a majority in the leading committees, the minority was expelled. Where the oppositionists held the levers of power, the Executive expelled the local organisation *en bloc* and formed a new one with people whom it could trust in control. Ninety-one local organisations were expelled in this way, with the overwhelming majority of the activists in Berlin, Leipzig, Bremen and Brunswick.[29] Nothing now remained for the oppositionists but to act upon the Executive's *fait accompli*. The opposition had a split forced upon it, and, in the course of a congress held in Gotha at Easter 1917 it decided to form the Independent Social-Democratic Party of Germany (USPD).

The formation of the Independent Social-Democratic Party

In this way, the SPD split during the crucial year of the War, against the declared will of practically all the leaders of the opposition. It was neither a matter of a few leaders splitting off, nor of the secession of some local organisations. The Party was divided from top to bottom. Some 170,000 members stayed with the old firm, whilst the new party claimed 120,000.[30] Amongst the latter were the best-known leaders of every prewar tendency, Liebknecht and Luxemburg, Haase and Ledebour, Kautsky and Hilferding, and even Bernstein. The split was neither prepared nor desired by the

---

[26] The text is given in Prager, op. cit., pp. 126–7.

[27] Ibid., p. 126.

[28] Ibid., pp. 129–30, *Protokoll über die Verhandlungen des Parteitages der Sozialdemokratischen Partei Deutschlands, 1917*, p. 36.

[29] Prager, op. cit., pp. 130–1.

[30] *Illustrierte Geschichte der deutschen Revolution*, op. cit., p. 148. Ossip Flechtheim mentions another estimate, that of Drahn, who attributes 248,000 members to the SPD and 100,000 to the USPD. He notes that, according to Ebert, the USPD had 14,000 members in Berlin as against 12,000 for the SPD (O.K. Flechtheim, *Die KPD in der Weimarer Republik*, Offenbach, 1948, p. 109).

oppositionists; it resulted from the combined pressure of the rise in working-class indignation and the determination of the Executive, in the service of the war policy, to throttle all resistance. The leaders of the new party, who had fought for years with the avowed object of avoiding a split, paradoxically found themselves at the head of a party which resulted from a split.

The presence of the Spartacist militants in the ranks of the USPD is no less surprising, since it followed the sharp struggle against the centrists and the loyal opposition. Since December 1915, all their documents had stressed the need for a well-defined political demarcation from the centrists. In a resounding article in *Vorwärts*, which won the warm approval of Lenin,[31] Otto Rühle had spoken out in favour of a split, because he felt that the centrists and revolutionaries could not work together in the same organisation.[32]

In March 1916, when the Spartacists welcomed the foundation of the Collective for Social-Democratic Work in the Reichstag, they were careful to distance themselves from its pacifist politics. They wrote: 'The slogan is neither split nor unity, a new party or the old one, but the reconquest of the Party from below, by the revolt of the masses, who must take their organisations and their instruments in hand.'[33] Meyer developed this position at the conference of the opposition in January 1917:

> The opposition will remain in the Party not only in order to resist the politics of the majority with pen and activity, but in order to interpose itself, to protect the masses from the Imperial policy which is being practised clandestinely by Social Democracy, and in order to use the Party as a recruiting ground for the working-class anti-militarist policy. . . . We remain in the Party only to the extent that we can wage the class struggle there against the Executive. From the moment when we are seriously prevented from doing so, we shall not wish to remain. But we are not for the split.[34]

However, the determination of the Executive to force the split opened up the development which the Spartacists feared. There were many who thought that the moment had come also to break with the centrists. Already at the

---

[31] V.I. Lenin, 'The Tasks of the Opposition in France', *Collected Works*, Volume 22, op. cit., pp. 127–30.

[32] *Vorwärts*, 12 January 1916; reproduced in *Dokumente und Materialen*, Volume 2/1, op. cit., pp. 301–5.

[33] 'Nüchterne Prüfung und scharfe Entscheidung', *Dokumente und Materialen*, Volume 2/1, op. cit., pp. 328–33.

[34] E. Meyer, *Spartakus im Kriege*, Berlin, 1927, p. 14.

conference of 1 December 1916, Johann Knief, a delegate from Bremen, supported by Rudolf Lindau from Hamburg, had demanded that the opposition should set itself the aim of building an independent revolutionary party.[35] A few weeks later, the Bremen activists decided to stop paying their contributions to the Executive, and to act autonomously.[36] In the columns of their paper, *Arbeiterpolitik,* Karl Radek defended the idea of constructing a revolutionary party by a decisive break from the centrists: 'The idea of constructing a party jointly with the centrists is a dangerous utopia. Whether the circumstances are favourable or not, the left radicals must construct their own party if they wish to fulfil their historic mission.'[37] Many Spartacists were of the same mind. This was the original position of Heckert and his comrades from Chemnitz,[38] and of the Württemberg militants whom Jogiches set himself to win with such success. It was also the standpoint of Paul Levi, who in February 1917 wrote an article for *Arbeiterpolitik,* stating that he was a member of the *Internationale* group. He called for a sharp, clear break from the centrists.[39]

Everything depended on what the *Internationale* people would decide to do in this situation which they had neither desired nor foreseen. The left radicals in Bremen recognised this:

> The left radicals face a big decision. The biggest responsibility rests in the hands of the *Internationale* group, the most active and the largest group, which we see as the nucleus of the future radical party of the Left, despite the criticisms which we have had to make of it. We frankly admit that without it, we and the ISD will not be able for the foreseeable future to construct a party capable of acting. The radical Left depends on the *Internationale* group in order for the struggle to be carried on in an orderly manner, under its own banner if not, as yet, as a small army. Otherwise, the struggle for clarification amongst the various left oppositions within the workers' movement will be delayed even longer.[40]

But the Spartacist leaders did not reach a decision. They were convinced that the authorities had decided to stifle their voice by any means; they feared

---

[35] Globig, op. cit., p. 138.
[36] *Unter der roten Fahne,* op. cit., p. 90.
[37] 'Unterm eigenen Banner', *Arbeiterpolitik,* nos 8 and 9, 1917, in *In den Reihen der Deutschen Revolution,* op. cit., p. 411.
[38] Beckert, op. cit., pp. 109ff.
[39] PL, 'Wir und die andern', *Arbeiterpolitik,* no. 9, 1917.
[40] *Arbeiterpolitik,* no. 10, 10 March 1917.

being isolated from the masses if they did not have the cover of a legal party. And they decided to join the USPD, despite the reservations of many of them, the members from Württemberg in particular, to whom Jogiches wrote to remind them that the group had clearly rejected forming an independent party which might well degenerate quickly into a sect.[41]

These reservations were expressed even at the congress at which the Party was founded. A member from Duisberg, Rosi Wolfstein, announced that she was deeply suspicious of the centrists.[42] In the name of the group, Fritz Rück declared that he intended to preserve inside the new party the utmost freedom of movement, and said that they must fight for the widest possible autonomy of the organisations at the base of the party against the 'apparatus', and spoke in favour of a 'revolutionary policy', not only in words but in deeds.[43]

The clearest result of the Spartacists' decision was to divide the revolutionary minority (the ISD and Borchardt did not join the USPD),[44] and especially to enable the USPD to benefit from the enormous prestige which Karl Liebknecht had won by his courageous struggle against the War.

At first glance, the adherence of people like Kautsky, Bernstein and Wurm, who were regarded as the right wing of the centrists, was no less surprising. It was known that they thought that the essential factor was the struggle for a compromise peace, which would, moreover, be the only means of avoiding serious revolutionary disturbances. It was known that they were convinced that this struggle had no chance of winning if it was not led by the old SPD. They had firmly opposed the creation of a new party even after the first mass expulsions.

Many of the centrists like them would have preferred to have avoided the proclamation of a party at Gotha, and would have been satisfied with the label of the 'organisation of the opposition', which had the double advantage in their eyes of keeping alive the perspective of regenerating the old party, and of closing the road to the revolutionaries who wanted the construction of a new party and a new International. It seems likely that Kautsky and

---

[41] Extracts from his letter in *Illustrierte Geschichte der deutschen Revolution*, op. cit., pp. 147–8.

[42] *Leipziger Volkszeitung*, 15 April 1917.

[43] *Protokoll USP, 1917*, op. cit., pp. 19–23. The Spartacist speaker provoked various interruptions by quoting with approval what Radek had written before the War (pp. 62–7).

[44] Statement from Bremen and Hamburg in *Dokumente und Materialen*, Volume 2/1, op. cit., p. 605.

Bernstein only decided to join the new organisation after consulting friends, in order to act as a counter-weight to the Spartacists and help to limit their influence there.[45]

At the Gotha Congress, Kautsky and the former revisionists Bernstein and Eisner were finally to line up with Haase defending the retention of the old title for the new organisation. Kautsky declared that the new party 'would be a continuation'. He claimed that it was really the 'government socialists' who had abandoned the Party, betrayed its programme, and deserted its mission. What for him was a 'fall-back' position was no doubt the real feeling of most of the delegates. Haase, who had the ear of the Congress, sincerely wanted a new party, which would correct what it would now consider to be the mistake of August 1914, and return to the line which it should never have abandoned, 'unity to lead the class struggle vigorously and effectively'.[46]

In this sense, it was the old party that he wanted to revive, the pre-1914 party in its political composition and its factional conflicts; the revolutionaries Liebknecht and Luxemburg had their place there at the side of the revisionist Bernstein. Ledebour distinguished himself by the sharpness – even bitterness – of his attacks on the Spartacists and what he called their 'nihilism'. He supported the principle of national defence, and he called for popular pressure to be directed on the government for peace negotiations to be opened. He developed at the Congress his conception of a negotiated peace – very much along the lines of the US President Woodrow Wilson – for self-determination of nations, for arbitration, general disarmament and prohibition of secret diplomacy.[47]

The overwhelming majority of the members of the new party shared the sentiments of the delegates to the foundation conference; that they must fight at the same time for democracy and socialism, in other words, raise again the banner of Social Democracy which the 'majority' had trodden underfoot, once again reconciling the minimum programme and the revolutionary objective. The Gotha Congress solemnly re-adopted the old Erfurt Programme,[48] and this gave full meaning to the act of the Party's foundation. The delegates regarded their task as reviving the old SPD and its old methods of struggle, its tradition of opposition and refusal of collaboration with the state, but also

---

[45] Schorske, op. cit., pp. 314–5.
[46] *Protokoll USP, 1917*, op. cit., pp. 39–40, 49.
[47] Ibid., p. 56.
[48] Ibid., p. 47.

its scepticism about the proletarian revolution, which it always regarded as desirable but out of reach.

The new party was to be different to the prewar organisation in one important respect. This was its structure, its degree of centralisation, and the role of its apparatus. The majority of the delegates were convinced that all the deleterious aspects had been due to the way in which the old party had been organised. They decided to restrict the powers of the full-time officials on the leading committees by granting them only consultative status. These leading committees were renamed committees of action [Aktionausschuss]. The secretaries of local or regional organisations were henceforth to be recruited and paid directly by the organisation which employed them, and not by the national leadership. The latter was also no longer to possess the title deeds to the property of the Party's enterprises, in particular in its press. Moreover, the national leadership was to have at its side a council [Beirat] consisting of people elected from the different regions, which had to be consulted before any important decision could be taken.[49]

As Schorske noted, the centrists remained firmly fixed in the past even in their efforts at innovation. They conceived of problems of organisation only in the terms in which they had experienced them in the course of the years immediately prior to the outbreak of the War, and they set themselves to preventing the rebirth of a bureaucratic apparatus with an opportunistic perspective. However, they did this during a serious wave of repression and the emergence of a revolutionary situation which probably called for real centralisation. But the Spartacists went even further in their opposition to centralisation. They called not only for the number of full-timers and the financial resources of the centre to be reduced to a minimum, but also for complete freedom of expression and action for regional and especially local organisations. One of their spokesmen, the young Fritz Rück, spelt it out: 'We want to be free to pursue our own policy.'[50]

We can explain why the Spartacists joined the USPD under these conditions. Liebknecht said in the following year that they joined 'in order to push it

---

[49] Ibid., p. 48. The draft of the proposed structure was presented by Wilhelm Dittmann. The leadership consisted of Dittmann, Haase, Hofer, Laukant, Ledebour, Wengels and Luise Zietz. Ernst Meyer was defeated in the election. The Beirat included Dissmann, Paul Dittmann, Fleissner, Grütz, Henke, Sepp Oerter and Schnellbacher (Prager, op. cit., p. 154).

[50] *Protokoll USP, 1917*, pp. 22–6, 29.

forward, to get it within the reach of our whip, and to win the best elements of it',[51] and because it offered the best field of work for people who had difficulty expressing themselves publicly as a tendency.

But these explanations settle only some of the problems. The attitude of the Spartacists towards the new party can only be explained by their conception of the proletarian revolution, which they had elaborated in the struggle against bureaucratic centralisation, and which showed little concern for the question of organisation. This is where one can locate the roots of their differences, not merely with the Bolsheviks on the international plane, but also on the national plane with the left radicals in Bremen. Had they not been convinced that the masses would spontaneously find the forms of organisation adequate to the course of their actions, and that the role of the party was no more than to enlighten them and stimulate them to action, then the Spartacists would have formed their own organisation, or at least solidly organised their own faction within the USPD – something which they did not do.

Schorske comments on the organisational structure which the Party adopted at Gotha:

> The Independents thus deprived themselves of any organizational instrument by which the spontaneous mass actions of the revolution, once begun, could be unified and consolidated into a single political striking force. The frustrating experience of yesterday had blinded the revolutionary leaders of tomorrow.[52]

The left wing breaks up

The left radicals had energetically opposed the decision of the Spartacists to join the new party. In February 1917 at a meeting in Bremen, Knief called for a complete ideological and organisational break with the social patriots and the centrists alike:

> The split in the Party which the social patriot leaders carried through imperatively demands the sharpest struggle against the social patriots and the centre of the Party within the unions and the cooperatives as well. It then further requires the immediate regrouping of all the left-radical elements

---

[51] *Bericht über den Gründungsparteitag der Kommunistischen Partei Deutschlands (Sparta-kusbund) 30 December 1918 to 1 January 1919*, Berlin, nd (1919), p. 4.
[52] Schorske, op. cit., p. 321.

in a workers' party, and finally the preparing of an international meeting of the socialist working class to continue the work of Zimmerwald and Kienthal.[53]

In early March 1917, the left-radical groups in Bremen, Hamburg, Hanover and Rüstringen declared in favour of breaking from the Centre and constructing an independent party of the left radicals.[54] Borchardt took the same position, and justified it by the need to eliminate all 'leaders' from the workers' movement.[55]

Immediately after the Gotha Congress, the Bremen and Hamburg groups issued an appeal for the construction of an independent revolutionary organisation.[56] *Arbeiterpolitik* announced in July: 'The *Internationale* group is dead. . . . The solid basis for the new international socialist party in Germany exists. A group of comrades have formed themselves into an action committee to take the first practical steps to form the new party.'[57]

Finally, in August 1917, a conference of the left-radical groups, with delegates from Bremen, Berlin, Frankfurt-am-Main, Rüstringen, Moers and Neustadt, met in Berlin with the perspective of creating an 'international socialist party'.[58] The resolution which the conference accepted emphasised for the first time the need to resist the division of the workers' movement between parties and trade unions. It pronounced itself in favour of organising workers' associations [Einheitsorganisationen], a position profoundly different from that of the Bolsheviks, whose adherents the left radicals had hitherto appeared to be. Moreover, at the same time, Julian Borchardt declared in a pamphlet that a revolution in Germany was quite impossible.[59] Otto Rühle, who was still a deputy in the Reichstag, joined the International Socialists, along with the activists in Dresden and Pirna who supported him.

The first result, then, of the split in Social Democracy and of the foundation of the USPD, was a split in the revolutionary Left, and a good deal of confusion. However, some positive elements emerged. In Switzerland, the influence of

---

[53] *Arbeiterpolitik*, no. 8, 24 February 1917, in *Dokumente und Materialen*, Volume 2/1, op. cit., p. 571.

[54] *Arbeiterpolitik*, no. 10, 10 March 1917, in ibid., p. 573.

[55] Ibid., p. 578.

[56] *Arbeiterpolitik*, no. 18, 5 May 1917, in ibid., p. 605.

[57] *Arbeiterpolitik*, no. 30, 28 July 1917.

[58] Wohlgemuth (op. cit., p. 219) gives the first account of this conference, never previously mentioned in any account.

[59] J. Borchardt, *Revolutionshoffnung!* (not consulted).

the Bolsheviks on the émigré German revolutionaries had grown considerably in this period. The *Jugend-Internationale*, run by Willi Münzenberg, smuggled Bolshevik texts into Germany, and many young militants, whether Spartacists or left radicals, thereby came under the influence of Lenin.[60] And Paul Levi accepted the invitation of Zinoviev to join the bureau of the Zimmerwald Left as a German representative.[61]

Levi had been introduced by Radek to Lenin, who regarded him at this time as 'already a Bolshevik'.[62] When Lenin started the long journey back to Russia in April 1917, Levi was the first to sign the manifesto of the internationalists, under his pseudonym of Paul Hartstein. This supported the journey which was organised with the consent of the German government; it declared that the 'Russian revolutionaries wanted to return to Russia for the sole purpose of working for the revolution there', and that, 'by this action, they will help the workers of all countries and especially in Germany and Austria to begin the revolutionary struggle against their governments'.[63] Soon afterwards, Levi returned to Germany, where he played an important role at the head of the Spartacus group, and collaborated with the independent *Sozialdemokrat* of Frankfurt, under the pseudonym of Hartlaub.[64]

As for Radek, he left Switzerland at the same time as Lenin, and was to stay in Stockholm with Vorovsky and Hanecki. Together they organised the production of two journals, *Bote der Russischen Revolution* and *Russische Korrespondenz-Pravda*, which were to publish in Germany Bolshevik documents and information from Russia.[65]

---

[60] Münzenberg, op. cit., pp. 197–204.

[61] At the Olten conference, according to Henri Guilbeaux, *Du Kremlin au Cherche-Midi*, Paris, 1933, p. 106.

[62] V.I. Lenin, 'A Letter to the German Communists', *Collected Works*, Volume 32, Moscow, 1975, p. 516.

[63] 'Déclaration des internationalistes faite à Berne le 7 avril 1917', *Demain*, no. 13, May 1917.

[64] C. Beradt, *Paul Levi*, Frankfurt-am-Main, 1969, p. 18.

[65] Schurer, op. cit., p. 65.

Chapter Six

The Rise of the Revolutionary Movement

The year of 1917 marked the fundamental turning point in the First World War. The Russian Revolution was the most spectacular manifestation of the crisis which shook all the warring countries. In Germany, this crisis revealed itself in the first instance by the formation of the Independent Social-Democratic Party, which reflected a division in the working class. After February 1917, the problem which had already been posed at the level of theory by both Lenin and Luxemburg – the construction of a revolutionary party in Germany and a new international – was now posed as a practical issue.

The turning point at the start of 1917

The battles in 1916 were very costly. Between February and December, 240,000 German soldiers fell before Verdun, without the General Staff gaining their desired objective. At the end of December, the forces of the Entente counter-attacked. The German generals called for the resources which they considered to be necessary for victory. Hindenburg became commander-in-chief and Ludendorff quarter master-general. They were to impose submarine warfare on the civilian statesmen, a dangerous weapon because it aroused public opinion in neutral countries against Germany. It could be effective if it led to a rapid collapse of the resistance of the Entente, but after beginning in January it had clearly failed by April.[1]

The winter was terrible; food froze in cellars.[2] The potato harvest in 1916 fell to 23 million tonnes from the prewar figure of 46 million, and six million tonnes never reached the official market.[3] The black market flourished, and the opulence of speculators was a standing insult to the workers' districts and to the emaciated soldiers who emerged from time to time on leave from the hell of the battlefield. Peasant discontent began to express itself in a 'hesitation waltz' by the Catholic Centre, which flirted in the Reichstag with the outlook of the opposition.

Under these conditions, the Russian Revolution in February was to reverberate loudly. At first sight, it seemed to raise the chances of a German victory, because it put one of Germany's adversaries almost completely out of action. This is what the revisionist David said; he stressed that the revolution had been possible only because it followed the collapse of the power of the autocracy, for which the German war effort could clearly take the credit.[4] But the event only appeared to serve the interests of those who wanted to fight 'to the end' for victory. The censorship, of course, concealed the essential aspects of the news from Russia, but every German was soon to learn, at least in outline, that the Tsarist autocracy, which war propaganda had long been presenting as 'Enemy Number One' had been brought down by a popular revolution. The problem of war aims raised itself afresh. The appeal of the Petrograd Soviet for peace – which was highlighted by the warmongers for the purpose of claiming that a German victory was near – showed that the reality of Germany's war aims differed greatly from what Ebert and Scheidemann had said they were.

Above all, the activities of the Russian workers and peasants, despite the lack of information, served as an example to their German counterparts. Not only was a victorious revolution possible, but it could lead to the end of the slaughter elsewhere than in Russia as well. In the Council of Ministers, the Minister for the Interior spoke of 'the intoxicating effect of the Russian Revolution'; the Under-Secretary of State Helfferich reported on his discussions

---

[1] G. Badia, *Histoire de l'Allemagne contemporaine*, Volume 1, Paris, 1962, pp. 67–8.
[2] Ibid., p. 69.
[3] Sayous, op. cit.
[4] *Stenographische Berichte*, Volume 311, p. 3980.

with the trade unions, and declared that, according to them, 'the public agitation raised by the difficulties of the food supply and the revolutionary movement in Russia may become a tempest that the government cannot control'.[5]

The Revolution stimulated political clarification in the workers' movement, forcing people to adopt a standpoint. In the Reichstag, Haase asked the government: 'Does the Chancellor want the German masses to end up speaking Russian?'[6] Ledebour commented at Gotha on the attitude of the centrists:

> We Social Democrats of the opposition have not ignored what is going on in the East. We have used the opportunity to point out to the government and the bourgeois parties that it is high time to draw the lessons. . . . We have declared that if this state of things continues, there will inevitably come about in our country, in Germany, events such as have happened in Russia.[7]

The Spartacist, Fritz Heckert, declared, for his part, that the 'German proletariat must draw the lessons of the Russian Revolution and take their own destiny in hand',[8] whilst Clara Zetkin stated in a letter to the Congress:

> The action of the people of Russia is written before our congress in letters of fire. The ardent spirit and driving force of this action is the young working class under the leadership of a social democracy which itself has known how to hold high and pure the banner of international socialism in time of war. I hope and I desire that your deliberations and your decisions will be worthy of this historic event of the century! Let us put ourselves under the tutelage of the historic mistress of every people and every age: the revolution.[9]

The workers' reaction seems to have confirmed what the revolutionaries thought. The Imperial authorities and the trade-union leaders busied themselves as hard as they could with defusing the explosive elements which they could see in the situation. A report from the prefect of police to the military commander of Berlin, dated 23 February, stated: 'Today nearly all the trade-union activists in the metalworkers' union who can be regarded as setting

---

[5] Quoted by Badia, op. cit., no. 4, pp. 70–1.
[6] *Stenographische Berichte*, Volume 309, p. 2888.
[7] *Protokoll USP, 1917*, p. 60.
[8] Ibid., p. 67.
[9] Ibid., p. 50.

the opinion in the factories are politically members of the opposition and largely members of the Spartacist group, whose slogan is: "End the War by Strikes!"' In the same context, he detailed the attitude of the heads of the trade-union apparatus:

> The trade-union leaders Cohen and Siering are powerless in the face of the power of the extremist trade-union activists, and are compelled to submit to them, because their own positions and re-election are at stake. This is why Siering is acting completely on the line of these extremists, agitating in various meetings . . . which wins him the sympathy of the extremists.[10]

In the approaching trial of strength the Imperial authorities were counting on the leaders of the unions. The Under-Secretary of State Wahnschaffe wrote to Ludendorff on 24 February: 'We can hardly win the war without the industrial workers. Now no one has as much influence on them, by a long way, as the trade-union leaders. Without these leaders, and even more so against them, nothing can be done.'[11]

The strikes in April 1917

The clandestine organisations prepared for mass action, the conditions for which seemed to have now arisen. In Berlin in the first days of April, the Spartacists distributed a leaflet which called for a mass protest, and quoted the example of the Russian workers, who had managed to bring down Tsarism and found 'a democratic republic'.[12] In Leipzig, a leaflet apparently from the same source also welcomed the Russian Revolution, and ended: 'Take your own destiny in hand! Power will be yours if you are united!'[13] There were work stoppages in Hamburg, Magdeburg, Bremen and Nuremberg. In Berlin, the revolutionary delegates judged that the moment had come for action which would make possible at first a mobilisation of the masses, and, at a later stage, the conditions for broadening the spread of their appeal and increasing the number of workers involved in action. They decided to take advantage of a meeting of the metalworkers' union in Berlin on 15 April to

---

[10] *Dokumente und Materialen*, Volume 2/1, op. cit., pp. 554–6.
[11] Ibid., p. 559.
[12] Ibid., pp. 630–33.
[13] K. Mammach, *Der Einfluss der russischen Februarrevolution und der Grossen Sozialistischen Oktoberrevolution auf die deutsche Arbeiterklasse*, East Berlin, 1955, p. 25.

propose a motion in favour of a strike for better food.[14] The trade-union officials discovered what was being planned, and discreetly arranged for the arrest on the 13th of Richard Müller, the secret organiser of the revolutionary metalworkers and the official representative of the turners.[15] The news did not reach the workers until the day of the meeting.

That day, a movement had already begun in Leipzig. On 12 April, women demanded bread in a demonstration in front of the town hall; the police arrested 16 demonstrators. On the 13th, the Saxon government appealed to people to be calm and to accept unavoidable restrictive measures. On the following day, more than 500 workers converged on the town hall demanding an improvement of the food supply. They were allowed in, and there were promises that measures would be taken.[16]

On the morning of 15 April, it was announced that the weekly bread ration would be cut from 1,350g to 450g. The news was accompanied by communiqués hailing the success of submarine warfare.[17] When the metalworkers met, they decided to take action. Cohen and Siering quickly took the lead, and proposed a strike for the following day, the 16th, for the food supply to be improved.[18] The revolutionary delegates had been outflanked. They approved the leaders' initiative, but called further for the action to be kept up until Müller was released. Cohen replied that he could not accept alone the responsibility of leading such a difficult operation; he called for and obtained the election of a strike committee to conduct negotiations together with him.[19]

On the 16th, *Vorwärts* did not condemn the strike, but warned against the danger which agitation might mean for the 'peace policy' which, so it claimed, was being elaborated. 'The mad hope of seeing events like those in Russia', declared the Social-Democratic daily, 'could cost the lives of hundreds of thousands of men on the battlefield.'[20] Meanwhile, mass meetings were held in all the factories. By nine o'clock, 300 firms were on strike. The trade unions said that there was a confirmed total of 200,000 strikers, and the real figure

---

[14] R. Müller, op. cit., pp. 80–81.
[15] Ibid., p. 82.
[16] Mammach, op. cit., p. 24.
[17] Müller, op. cit., p. 79.
[18] Mammach, op. cit., p. 35; Müller, op. cit., p. 82.
[19] Müller, op. cit., p. 83; A. Schreiner et al., *Revolutionäre Ereignisse und Probleme in Deutschland während der Periode der Grossen Sozialistischen Oktoberrevolution 1917–1918*, East Berlin, 1957, pp. 33ff.
[20] *Vorwärts*, 16 April 1917.

seems to have been about 300,000.[21] The streets began to fill with demonstrations formed spontaneously behind a variety of slogans, many of them political.

The elected committee met at the office of the union and produced a smaller commission. By the side of Alwin Körsten, who represented the general leadership of the unions, and Cohen and Siering, the metalworkers' leaders, there were eight factory delegates, at least two of whom, Otto Tost from Schwartzkopf and Franz Fischer from DWM, were members of the clandestine revolutionary nucleus. The delegation which they formed was received at once by the commissioner for food supply, Michaelis, who promised that a municipal food committee, on which the unions would be represented, would be formed. The workers' delegates demanded guarantees that no one would be punished, and insisted that Müller be set free, and the commissioner referred them to the military authorities. The interview lasted five hours.[22]

Things went the same way in Leipzig. On the morning of the 16th, handwritten leaflets were distributed in nearly all the workplaces, calling on the workers to hold a meeting in the lunch-break to decide whether to strike.[23] The agitation continued in the factories throughout the morning, and forced the trade-union leaders to take an initiative; the metalworkers' union called a public meeting in the Brauereigarten in Leipzig-Stotteritz. Work generally stopped by midday, and at three o'clock more than 10,000 workers gathered to hear a speech from the leader of the metalworkers, Arthur Lieberasch.

He declared that the demonstration on the 14th had shown the leaders that they must give the workers the possibility to express their demands. But when he called for a return to work next day, he provoked a storm of protest. Amid the uproar, a resolution was finally agreed: it called for increased rations of food and coal, but also spelt out six political demands – a fact of the highest importance. These called on the government to declare for a peace without annexations, for censorship to be abolished, for the state of siege to be lifted, for the conscription of labour to end, for political prisoners to be freed, and for universal suffrage to be introduced at all levels.[24] The meeting decided that the resolution must be delivered personally to the Chancellor in Berlin, and elected a delegation on the spot, consisting of two officials from the metalworkers' union and three representatives of the USPD.

---

[21] Schreiner, op. cit., p. 24.
[22] Ibid., pp. 37–9.
[23] Mammach, op. cit., p. 25.
[24] Ibid., pp. 26–7.

Meanwhile, another meeting was proceeding in the Vorgarten. A worker hailed the Russian Revolution, saying that the meeting itself proved that it was possible in Germany to copy its example. That evening, the trade-union leaders urged the military authorities at all costs not to intervene, because that would give the movement an 'anarchist' character, which they would no longer be able to control.[25] In Berlin, the strike committee confirmed its decision to continue the action until Müller was set free.[26]

On 17 April, the atmosphere grew even more tense. The Social-Democratic leaders Bauer and Scheidemann worked hard to convince Helfferich and General Groener that it was their duty to receive the delegation of the Leipzig strikers, despite the fact that it was advancing political demands. To refuse would lead to 'useless bloodshed', whilst it would cost nothing to receive the delegation and appease it.[27]

The Spartacists distributed leaflets calling on the workers to take up the demands of the Leipzig strikers, and to broaden the struggle on that basis. Körsten, Cohen and Siering were received by the High Command. They came back with the assurance that Müller was to be released with the least possible delay. There was then a very lively discussion in the committee. Many delegates, most of whom belonged to the USPD, wanted to raise again the Leipzig political demands. Cohen retorted that the strike must be ended, that to continue it would be to put at risk the gains which he had won, that the committee had no mandate to go further, that another general meeting would be needed to decide on a new strike platform, and, finally, that he was personally opposed on principle to the unions taking up political positions. In the end, he narrowly won the day. The meeting refused to adopt the Leipzig political demands, and decided to call for a return to work on the next day, the morning of the 18th.[28] The delegation of Leipzig strikers, having returned from Berlin where it had been received, took the same position. In principle, the strike was over.

However, work did not recommence immediately. On the 17th, the USPD deputies in Berlin took part in factory meetings, and called for the struggle to continue on the basis of the Leipzig programme. The popular old comrade Adolf Hoffmann welcomed the revolutionary example of Russia at a workers'

---

[25] Ibid., pp. 28–9.
[26] Schreiner, op. cit., pp. 40–1.
[27] P. Scheidemann, *Der Zussammenbruch*, op. cit., p. 65.
[28] Schreiner, op. cit., pp. 44–5, 49; Müller, op. cit., p. 83.

meeting in the Knorr-Bremse plant. On the following day, he and Haase were present at a meeting of the workers at DWM, where Siering in vain pleaded for a return to work: 'We must not end in division what we began in unity.' Other Independent deputies, Vogtherr, Dittmann and Büchner, argued for the strike to continue. In the end, over 50,000 workers were for continuing the strike, and they denounced the 'betrayal' of the movement by the leaders.[29]

In most of the factory meetings, the slogan of electing workers' councils was raised 'like at Leipzig' – this is how legends are born! – with representatives of the USPD. The DWM strikers elected a strike committee led by revolutionary delegates, Franz Fischer and Bruno Peters. The Knorr-Bremse strikers decided after five hours' discussion to put the demand for Liebknecht to be released at the head of their demands. They elected a workers' council over which the revolutionary Paul Scholze presided, and which at once issued a call for workers' councils to be elected in every firm.[30] However, it was a minority of workers who kept the movement going, and, despite the warnings of Scheidemann who feared a 'backlash', the military authorities intervened, placing the workers in the enterprises on strike under military discipline, and arresting the leaders, including Peters, Fischer and Scholze.[31] Order was soon restored, and work was resumed.

A few days later, General Groener, as the head of the armaments section of the General Staff, issued an appeal to the workers:

> Read and re-read again the letter of Marshal Hindenburg, and you will recognise your worst enemies. They are not away near Arras, on the Aisne, or in Champagne, nor are they in London. . . . Our worst enemies are in our midst . . . the agitators for strikes. . . . Whoever goes on strike when our armies are facing the enemy is a cur.[32]

The trade unions backed him, in *Vorwärts* of 27 April: 'Strikes must be avoided. . . . An early peace is dependent upon the improvement of Germany's capacity to resist.'[33] However, the workers' reaction was to be very different. Three years later, Müller recalled this episode, no doubt with a trace of

---

[29] Schreiner, op. cit., pp. 49, 52; Müller, op. cit., p. 83.
[30] Schreiner, op. cit., pp. 53, 59–60.
[31] Mammach, op. cit., pp. 39–40.
[32] Poster reproduced in *Dokumente und Materialen*, Volume 2/1, op. cit., p. 629.
[33] *Vorwärts*, April 27, 1917, in *Dokumente und Materialen*, Volume 2/1, op. cit., pp. 626–8.

nostalgia: 'The revolutionary delegates and everyone who was working against the War could not have accomplished by their propaganda what Groener's appeal did for them.'[34]

A stage had passed. The masses had delivered their first attack. The Independent Social Democrats, who were at the same time conducting discussions with a view to a parliamentary coalition that could end the war, had won a great deal of prestige. In the eyes of ever-widening sections of the people, they were appearing as the champions of a mass struggle for peace, and this struggle would have revolutionary consequences, thanks to the very conditions in which it was developing.

The revolutionary organisation of the sailors

A spontaneous revolutionary outburst in the navy was to turn to the USPD for leadership. A wide range of factors coincided to produce active centres of agitation aboard the warships. The crews included a majority of skilled workers, most often metalworkers, who were class-conscious and had experience of class struggle. The circumstances of the War, which kept the ships in port, enabled the sailors to maintain close contacts with the workers in the docks and shipyards, to circulate books, leaflets and newspapers, to exchange ideas, and to organise discussions. The conditions of life, the concentration of proletarians in confined spaces, and the qualities of daring and the collective spirit which they promoted rendered the harsh conditions endured by the sailors and stokers increasingly intolerable. All this occurred within the combination of inactivity and the absurd disciplinary drills imposed by a particularly reactionary officer corps.[35]

Right from the start of the War, there were some groups of people in the navy who read the radical press, in particular the *Leipziger Volkszeitung*. In 1915, the paper had made a vague suggestion that a central organisation was needed in the fleet to bring together the scattered socialist groups.[36] The movement died down, and then reawakened after the winter of 1916–17, especially under the influence of the Russian Revolution, in which young petty-officers, sailors and stokers, workers by origin and Social Democrats by education, saw before them the road that led to peace.

---

[34] Müller, op. cit., p. 85.
[35] Schreiner, op. cit., pp. 187–9.
[36] Bartel, op. cit., pp. 96–8.

On the cruiser *Friedrich der Grosse*, a small group of men met regularly in the boiler room or the munitions store. The stoker Willy Sachse and the sailor Max Reichpietsch read and discussed pamphlets by Marx and Bebel, and circulated copies of the Erfurt Programme. Ashore at Wilhelmshaven, they made contact with crews from other ships. They learned in 1917 that canteen committees were being introduced on all warships for the purpose of supervising the feeding of the crews, and that they were to include sailors' representatives. They grasped the opportunity on offer, and proceeded to build a secret organisation, the League of Soldiers and Sailors.[37]

They utilised the activity of the canteen committees in the same way as the workers in the factories used their delegates, and in a few weeks they had succeeded in forming a very flexible network of trusted people covering the whole fleet. This was led by clandestine committees first formed on the *Friedrich der Grosse* and then on the *Prinz Regent Luitpold*, with links formed on land. The political force behind the enterprise was Reichpietsch, and he did not hide from his comrades what he intended: 'We must make it perfectly clear to everyone that the canteen commissions are the first step towards constructing sailors' councils on the Russian model.'[38]

They could soon claim the credit for the victorious hunger strike on a cruiser, and Reichpietsch estimated that his organisation was ready to start a mass movement for peace in the fleet. But he judged it to be necessary, before going further, to establish a connection with the USPD, to which he was looking for perspectives and coordination in a common struggle. In mid-June, whilst on leave, he contacted the Party in Berlin, and met its leaders, Dittmann and Luise Zietz at the Party office, and then Haase, Vogtherr and Dittmann again, who received him at the Reichstag.[39]

The work which Reichpietsch and his comrades undertook was extremely dangerous, and required perfect organisation, clandestinity and secrecy, substantial finance, and many other precautions. The old Social-Democratic parliamentarians to whom he turned for help and direction had not the slightest idea of these requirements. To be sure, Zietz did exclaim: 'We ought to stand in shame before these sailors; they are much more advanced than we are.' But no more than the others could she raise herself above the

---

[37] Ibid., pp. 104–7.
[38] Quoted by A Schreiner, *Zur Geschichte der deutschen Aussenpolitik*, Berlin, 1952, Volume 1, p. 400.
[39] Schreiner, *Revolutionäre Ereignisse*, op. cit., pp. 106–7, 113–14.

routine perspective of reformist, electoralist practice. Dittmann regretted that he could not supply pamphlets of his speech against the state of siege to the sailors free of charge, because the Party treasurer had not provided for the possibility. He discouraged Reichpietsch from trying to form Party branches on the ships; since, according to the Party's rules, people in the armed forces did not pay subscriptions, the Party centre was uninterested in their formal membership.[40]

Nonetheless, he gave the sailors membership forms to fill in and return, despite the fact that the slightest political activity on their part would, if discovered, lead to their being court-martialled! Whilst he did not advise forming sailors' branches, he did propose that they should join the existing branches in the ports which carried on legal public activities, and he asked Reichpietsch to take the initiative in founding a Party branch in Wilhelmshaven. In general, he said, the sailors should not keep in contact with the national leadership, but, wherever possible, should remain in touch with local organisations. To be sure, Dittmann made clear to Reichpietsch the dangers in what he was doing, but told him that he would do better in any case to appear under his own name in the official activities of the Party on land.[41]

As for political perspectives, Haase and Dittmann told him about the forthcoming conference of the Socialist International to be held in Stockholm, and conceded that a movement for peace in the fleet would reinforce the positions of the socialist supporters of peace there.[42] In a word, they told him that, whilst they were sceptical about the possibilities for action which he foresaw, there could be no question of dissuading him from being involved in them. In any case, they did not warn him at all of the real risks which this movement of sailors was running, and they actually compounded these risks by recklessly widening the scope of their contacts with irresponsible civilians.

Reichpietsch took what he was offered. Consumed with the desire for action, he returned to his ship and assured his comrades that the deputies whom he had met were in favour of a revolutionary struggle for peace, and were convinced of the decisive role which a general strike of the fleet would play. The organisation widened further when a committee led by Beckers and Köbis was founded on the *Prinz Regent* and undertook to build an organisation

---

[40] Ibid., pp. 115–17.
[41] Ibid., p. 117.
[42] Ibid.

on the ships anchored at Kiel. On 25 July 1917, a central leadership, the clandestine *Flottenzentrale*, was set up, with more than 5,000 sailors grouped under its leadership. To his comrades, Reichpietsch summed up the perspective: a movement had to be organised in the fleet to provide arguments for the Independent delegates at Stockholm, and, if nothing came out of the conference, the revolutionary sailors 'will put to the soldiers the slogan: "Arise! Let us break our chains as the Russians have done!"' He added: 'Each of us knows what he will have to do.'[43]

There were more and more incidents, because the sailors were aware of their strength, proud of their organisation, and confident of winning support. On the 19th, there was a hunger-strike on the *Prinz Regent Luitpold*, a large-scale walk-out without permission from the *Pillau* on the 20th, a walk-out without permission of 49 men from the *Prinz Regent Luitpold* on 1 August, and the 'great disembarkation' by 400 crew members of the *Prinz Regent* on 2 August.[44] This time, the apparatus of repression was ready to go into action. It knew everything. The 'ringleaders' were arrested. On 26 August, a court-martial pronounced five death sentences, and on 5 September Alwin Köbis and Reichpietsch were shot.[45]

A few weeks later, Lenin wrote that this revolutionary movement marked 'the growth of the world revolution'[46] and that it constituted one of the 'indisputable symptoms' of 'a great turning point', of 'the eve of a worldwide revolution'.[47] The approaching tragedy in Germany was summed up in this drama, in the contrast between the readiness of the young workers in uniform to act, and the impotence of leaders crushed by responsibilities, and convinced that the future of humanity could be settled in terms of subscriptions, local branches and speeches in parliamentary assemblies.

The aftermath of the October Revolution

The revolutionary sailors in Russia were more successful than their German brothers. The victorious October Revolution was soon to answer the problems of the day in another way, and to lead to new political regroupments. The

---

[43] Ibid., pp. 124–6, 135, 140.
[44] C. Vidil, *Les Mutineries de la marine allemande*, Paris, 1931, p. 104.
[45] Ibid., p. 111.
[46] V.I. Lenin, 'Letter to the Bolshevik Comrades Attending the Congress of Soviets of the Northern Region', *Collected Works*, Volume 26, Moscow, 1977, p. 182.
[47] V.I. Lenin, 'The Crisis has Matured', *Collected Works*, Volume 26, op. cit., p. 74.

leadership of the USPD hailed it in the *Leipziger Volkszeitung* on 12 November: 'The working class has taken political power in Russia. This is an event of world significance. Never has the working class faced such an important task as this.'[48]

On 14 November, the same newspaper wrote: 'We German workers are with all our hearts with our Russian comrades in struggle in these days. They are also fighting for our cause. They are the vanguard of humanity, the vanguard of peace.'[49]

In reality, the USPD was deeply divided about the stance it should take towards the Revolution and the new Soviet régime. On the 12th, its leaders called on the workers to follow the Russian example and 'prepare to demonstrate for a peace without annexations'.[50] But on the 15th, Kautsky put the question in the *Leipziger Volkszeitung*, 'How is it going to finish?', and concluded, 'in social and political decomposition, in chaos'.[51] On 30 November, Zetkin explained the significance of the Revolution which gave state power to the soviets, workers' organisations,[52] but on 24 December, Bernstein violently attacked the Bolshevik dictatorship,[53] and from the 17th onwards the *Leipziger Volkszeitung* gave space to the Menshevik Stein to present severe criticisms of the new revolutionary régime.[54]

The Bolsheviks regarded the victory of the revolution in Russia merely as the first stage of a worldwide revolution. The celebrated decree of 26 December 1917 recalled this. Under the names of Lenin and Trotsky, the Soviet régime offered its help by all possible means, including money, to the international left wing of the workers' movement in all countries.[55] When on 26 November, the German-Russian peace negotiations at Brest-Litovsk began, the Bolsheviks produced systematic propaganda addressed to the German soldiers and workers which was intended to speed up the inevitable revolutionary explosion. Radek directed a press bureau in the People's Commissariat of Foreign Affairs. With the help of social-democratic activists recruited in the prisoner-of-war camps, he organised the distribution, particularly by air, of hundreds of

---

[48] *Leipziger Volkszeitung*, 12 November 1917.
[49] *Leipziger Volkszeitung*, 14 November 1917.
[50] *Leipziger Volkszeitung*, 12 November 1917.
[51] *Leipziger Volkszeitung*, 15 November 1917.
[52] *Leipziger Volkszeitung*, women's supplement, 30 November 1917.
[53] *Leipziger Volkszeitung*, 24 December 1917.
[54] *Leipziger Volkszeitung*, 17 and 27 December 1917.
[55] Bunyan and Fisher, *The Bolshevik Revolution 1917–1918*, p. 285.

thousands of leaflets, reproducing the Soviet government's peace appeal, and then edited a journal, *Die Fackel* [*The Torch*], run off in half a million copies and distributed all along the front.[56]

The German military leaders were alarmed by this propaganda, drafted in simple, direct language, and by the effect which it had amongst troops who hitherto had been well controlled. Their attitude hardened, they withdrew the facilities for fraternisation which had been conceded in the course of the armistice negotiations, and they did their best to reach a rapid conclusion, and to exploit to the full the need of the Bolsheviks for peace. On 10 January 1918, General Hoffmann announced to the Russian delegates the conditions of the ultimatum, which were to provoke a fraught discussion about the peace amongst the Bolshevik leaders and the first serious crisis in the Party. However, Trotsky was able to use the discussions at Brest as a platform from which the Russian working people called for help to their brothers in the warring countries, particularly in the empires of Central Europe.[57] Their call was heard; on 14 January, a strike broke out in the Manfred Weiss arms factory in Csepel in Budapest. In a few days, it spread to all the industrial enterprises in Austria and Hungary.[58]

This was the beginning of what Franz Borkenau, who cannot be suspected of exaggeration on the point, calls 'the greatest revolutionary movement of properly proletarian origin which the modern world has seen', a movement which, according to the same writer, was 'to shake the Central Powers to their foundations'.[59]

The strikes of January 1918

The combativity of the workers had risen continuously since October 1917. News of the negotiations at Brest warmed the workers' hearts. Many militants agreed with what Liebknecht wrote from prison:

> Thanks to the Russian delegates, Brest has become a revolutionary platform
> with reverberations felt far and wide. It has denounced the Central European
> powers. It has exposed the German spirit of brigandage, lying, cunning and

---

[56] Fischer, op. cit., pp. 30–1.
[57] E.H. Carr, *The Bolshevik Revolution*, Volume 3, London, 1952, pp. 29–32.
[58] Borkenau, op. cit., pp. 91–2.
[59] Ibid., p. 92.

hypocrisy. It has delivered a crushing judgement on the peace policy of the German Majority, a policy which is not so much hypocritical as cynical.[60]

In the first fortnight of January, Spartacist militants distributed a leaflet calling for a general strike, and denouncing the illusion that the separate peace with Russia could be a step towards general peace.[61] Towards the middle of the month, there was a joint meeting of the revolutionary delegates, the leaders of the USPD, and its deputies in the Reichstag and the Prussian Landtag. Müller reported on the situation of the Berlin working class. He concluded that a general strike for political demands could be called, and declared that the workers were ready for it, but that they were waiting to be summoned by the USPD.[62] The participants in the meeting were divided, and sometimes disagreed violently. A minority, for which Ströbel spoke, came out against any action, and declared that Müller was mistaken about the state of mind of the workers, who, in reality, were completely passive. The majority agreed with Haase in thinking that a general strike was necessary to impose peace, but refused to run the risk of getting the Party banned, which he said would certainly follow if they issued a call for one.

These hesitations were not to the taste of Ledebour and Adolf Hoffmann, who said that they were prepared to sign a strike call personally if the Party refused to do so.[63] In the end, they reached a compromise: a text drafted by Haase calling for a three-day strike[64] would be signed, not by the Party as such, but by the deputies, and would go into the factories as a leaflet.[65] Yet the deputies still hesitated; two days later, the fraction altered the text and deleted any mention of a strike,[66] although the Party activists continued to publicise the slogan by word of mouth. After fruitless negotiations to get the leaflet printed illegally by the Spartacists, the text was finally published on 10 January. In particular, it declared:

> If the working people do not express their will, it can appear that the masses of the German people approve the acts of the ruling class. . . . The

---

[60] *Politische Aufzeichnungen aus seinem Nachlass*, pp. 51–2. [By 'majority', Liebknecht means the SPD. Editor's note]
[61] *Dokumente und Materialen*, Volume 2/2, East Berlin, 1967, pp. 67–70.
[62] Müller, op. cit., p. 101.
[63] Ibid.
[64] This detail comes from a Spartacist report on the strikes, usually attributed to Jogiches (*Dokumente und Materialen*, Volume 2/2, op. cit., p. 132).
[65] Müller, op. cit., p. 102.
[66] *Dokumente und Materialen*, Volume 2/2, op. cit., p. 132.

time has come for you to raise your voice for a peace without annexations
and indemnities, on the basis of the right of peoples to self-determination.
It is up to you.[67]

Meanwhile, the circle of revolutionary delegates had gone on to prepare for
the strike, the idea of which was favourably received in the factories in which
information about the strikes in Central Europe was circulating. They fixed
the start for Monday, 28 January, but did not make the decision public in
order to avoid any preventative repression.[68] However, a Spartacist leaflet
issued in the week preceding that date, which carried news of the strike wave
in Austria-Hungary and 'the workers' council of Vienna elected on the Russian
model', announced: 'Monday, 28 January, the general strike begins!'[69] It warned
workers against the majority 'fight-to-the-bitter-end' socialists, whom it
recommended should on no account be elected to the councils: 'These wolves
in sheep's clothing are a danger to the movement much more serious than
the Prussian police.'[70]

In this climate, the general meeting of the Berlin turners was held on
Sunday, 27 January. At the proposal of Müller, with no shouting or applause,
it decided unanimously to start the strike on the following day in the morning,
when the workers were arriving for work and to hold general meetings on
the spot to elect delegates. These delegates were then to meet at the trade-
union centre and nominate the leadership of the strike. The lessons of April
1917 had not been forgotten.[71] On the morning of the 28th, there were 400,000
people on strike in Berlin, and general meetings were held in all the factories,
with the turners and the revolutionary delegates being elected with
overwhelming majorities. At midday, as arranged, the 414 delegates elected
in the factories met.

Müller put before them a seven-point programme, close to the demands
of the Leipzig strikers in 1917: peace without annexations or indemnities, on
the basis of the right of the peoples to self-determination, as defined at Brest
by the Russian delegates; representation of workers in the peace negotiations;
improvements in the food supply; lifting of the state of siege; restoration of

---

[67] Müller, op. cit., p. 102.
[68] Ibid.
[69] *Dokumente und Materialen*, Volume 2/2, op. cit., p. 71.
[70] Ibid., p. 73.
[71] R. Müller, op. cit., p. 102.

freedom of expression and assembly; laws restricting female and child labour; an end to military control in the factories; liberation of political prisoners; and democratisation of the state at all levels, beginning with equal and universal suffrage at the age of 20 in the Prussian Landtag.[72] The meeting then elected an Action Committee of eleven members, all belonging to the nucleus of the revolutionary delegates: Scholze and Tost, already known for their role in the strike of April 1917, Eckert, Neuendorf, Blumenthal, Malzahn, Kraatz, Zimmermann, Tirpitz, Cläre Casper and, of course, Müller.[73]

The meeting decided to invite the USPD to send three of its representatives to speak to the Action Committee.[74] At that point, a Spartacist proposed extending the same invitation to the SPD, in order (as he said) to 'expose' them.[75] The proposal was at first defeated by a majority of two, but was finally adopted after an intervention by Müller,[76] who feared that the movement would be presented and denounced as 'divisive' were the SPD not invited.

The Action Committee met at once. It included, besides the elected eleven, Haase, Ledebour and Dittmann from the USPD, and Ebert, Scheidemann and Braun from the SPD. Müller was in the chair. Ebert immediately demanded the right to speak, demanded that the number of representatives of parties be equal to that of the striking workers, and declared that some of the demands which had just been carried by vote were unacceptable. The elected eleven refused to put into question what the workers' meeting had just decided. However, the meeting was suddenly interrupted by the information – which was false – that the police were on their way to the trade-union centre. When

---

[72] Ibid. See the account of the beginning of the strike at AEG Hennigsdorf in P. Blumenthal, 'Die AEG Arbeiter demonstrieren für Karl Liebknecht', *1918. Erinnerungen von Veteranen der deutschen Gewerkschaftsbewegung an die Novemberrevolution (1914–1920),* Berlin, 1949, pp. 73–4.

[73] Jogiches wrote about them: 'Ten men workers and one woman, all trade unionists of the opposition (not full-timers), influential in their milieu. . . . Their political position mostly USPD but not in a clear way. They are in fact trade unionists rather than political people. Amongst them were two who had been in the strike for Liebknecht, and one from our group [presumably Paul Scholze].' (*Dokumente und Materialen,* Volume 2/2, op. cit., p. 133.)

[74] The invitation to the Independents, to 'Ledebourski' (as Jogiches called him) was given in order to wrong-foot a metalworkers' full-timer who supported the majority. His name was Wuschek, and he had just arrived with a declaration from the 'majority' leadership calling for a united action (*Dokumente und Materialen,* Volume 2/2, op. cit., p. 133.)

[75] Müller, op. cit., p. 103.

[76] Jogiches specifies: 'a member of our tendency aiming to confuse'.

the moment of panic had passed it was noticed that the three SPD delegates had departed. That evening, the military command banned factory meetings and the election of strike committees. The number of strikers reached 500,000.[77]

On 29 January, the Committee of Action met again. Scheidemann announced that in the interval he had made some contacts, and that the Under-Secretary of State for the Interior was disposed to receive a delegation, on the condition that it consisted only of parliamentarians, as the strikers' delegates had no legal status as representatives. Scheidemann insisted that it was necessary to open these negotiations, as they could benefit the movement on the issue of food supplies. The majority of the Committee agreed to negotiate, but rejected the conditions made by the Under-Secretary. It nominated Scholze, Müller, Haase and Scheidemann to meet him.

This delegation was kept waiting at the Ministry, and twice lost Scheidemann in the corridors. In the end, the two deputies were received alone, not by the Under-Secretary, but by a civil servant. To make things easier, Scholze and Müller stayed in the waiting room. The only information that the delegation brought back was that the work of the Action Committee was declared to be illegal, and could lead to criminal proceedings.[78]

Vorwärts was banned on 30 January. The authorities said that it had 'propagated false news' when it announced that there were 300,000 people on strike. This, however, was a great advantage, as it helped to rebuild its prestige.

Here and there the strikers clashed with the police. The Action Committee issued a leaflet calling for the strike to be extended: 'The movement must be strengthened so that the government will yield to our just demands.'[79] It called for street demonstrations and an open-air meeting in Treptow Park on the 31st. On the night of 30–1 January, the military command had big red posters put up announcing that the state of siege had been tightened and that special courts-martial had been set up. Five thousand non-commissioned officers were drafted into the capital to support the police. In the morning, the first incidents took place between striking workers and tramdrivers who refused to strike. Civil war could be sensed in the air.[80] Jogiches described it

---

[77] Müller, op. cit., pp. 103–4.
[78] Ibid., p. 106.
[79] Ibid., pp. 106–7.
[80] Ibid.

thus: 'Like a revolutionary breeze, a certain readiness, but no one knew what to do. After each clash with the police we heard people say: "Comrades, we shall come back with arms tomorrow."'[81]

The tramway system was sabotaged,[82] and the first arrests followed. Ebert spoke at the meeting in Treptow Park in defiance of the military authorities' ban:

> It is the duty of the workers to support their brothers and their fathers who are at the front and to make the best possible weapons for them . . . as the English and French workers are doing for their brothers at the front in their working hours. . . . Victory is the dearest wish of all Germans.[83]

He was called a 'scab' and 'traitor' by the crowd, but he declared that he supported the strikers' demands, by which he meant their economic demands.

The police did not attempt to arrest him, but Dittmann was 'caught in the act' of calling for subversion, and he was later sentenced to five years in a fortress. In the afternoon, Scheidemann and Ebert proposed to the Action Committee that negotiations with the government be opened through the trade union leaders whom the Chancellor was willing to receive.[84] The members of the Committee were disoriented. As Jogiches pointed out, 'they didn't know what to do with all this revolutionary energy'.[85] They were aware of the trap which was being set for them with the negotiations, but they contented themselves with declaring that only the strikers' delegates could effectively negotiate on behalf of the strikers.[86]

The government pressed home its advantage. On 1 February, the military High Command announced that it would impose martial law in the factories if work was not resumed by 4 February. At the Committee of Action, the SPD deputies insisted that work must be quickly resumed. They said that great dangers threatened the workers, because the military authorities were preparing a clampdown, and that continuing with the strike would make things worse. Once again, they set about trying – this time with the support of Haase – to arrange for the Chancellor to authorise another mass meeting of the strikers.

---

[81] *Dokumente und Materialen*, Volume 2/2, op. cit., p. 134.
[82] Ibid.
[83] Quoted by K. Brammer, *Der Prozess des Reichspräsidenten*, pp. 68–9.
[84] Müller, op. cit., p. 107.
[85] *Dokumente und Materialen*, Volume 2/2, op. cit., p. 134.
[86] Müller, op. cit., p. 107.

The Chancellor replied that he would only do so on condition that the delegates undertook to ensure that the meeting would decide on an immediate return to work![87]

Isolated on the Action Committee, the revolutionary delegates refused to go down the road which Haase and Scheidemann suggested, and unanimously rejected the proposal that the trade-union leaders should mediate. But, ultimately, the movement had been badly organised, and the Action Committee was cut off from the mass of the strikers, which meant that the only information they received was about the repression.[88] The Spartacists pressed for the strike to be hardened, which could lead to armed struggle. However, the Berlin strikers were isolated in the Reich, the soldiers remained disciplined. Nothing pointed to a possible fraternisation of troops and workers. There was only one way out left open to Müller and his comrades: to put an end to the strike without negotiations, and to recognise defeat and retreat. That is what they did. The Action Committee issued a call for work to be resumed on 3 February.[89]

Aftermath of the strike of January 1918

Ebert recalled his role in the January 1918 strike in a court case some years later against a nationalist who accused him of having 'betrayed the fatherland' in the midst of war:

> The radical leadership had got the upper hand in the munitions factories in Berlin. Supporters of our party whom the radicals had terrorised into stopping work came to the Executive to ask it to send members into the strike leadership. . . . I entered the strike leadership with the firmly-determined intention of bringing the strike to an end as soon as possible, and in this way saving the country from disaster.[90]

The Social-Democratic leaders repeated on a much larger scale the manoeuvre which Cohen and Siering had pulled off in April 1917. They achieved their aim, without appearing in the eyes of the majority of the strikers as actually having broken the strike. When work was resumed, the Social-Democratic press gave its policy a reasonable-socialist, 'national' hallmark, which could

---

[87] Ibid., pp. 108–9.
[88] *Dokumente und Materialen*, Volume 2/2, op. cit., p. 135.
[89] Müller, op. cit., p. 110.
[90] Brammer, op. cit., p. 21.

justify the prudent course it advocated in Germany, by savagely attacking the Bolsheviks, and condemning the 'extremism' which the Russian example inspired. Otto Braun, writing in *Vorwärts*, declared unequivocally to the Bolsheviks that their hopes for a German revolution had no basis in reality, and that the German working class categorically renounced violence.[91]

This defeat was rich in lessons for the revolutionary minority. Richard Müller described the dominant feeling amongst the workers: 'We need arms. We need propaganda in the army. Revolution is the only way out.'[92] The Spartacists drew the lessons of the experience of the Action Committee in their leaflets. Jogiches wrote on their behalf:

> Thanks to parliamentary cretinism, to their desire to apply ready-made procedures to every industrial dispute, and especially through fear of the masses, but more especially – and this is not the least important reason – because, right from the start, the Independents could not conceive of the strike except as a simple movement of protest, the Committee was restricted by the influence of the deputies to trying to get into discussion with the government, instead of rejecting negotiation in any form, and unleashing the energies of the masses in the most varied forms.[93]

The Spartacists emphasised that the leadership in the struggles should be placed in the hands of elected workers' councils, and that the revolutionaries should win over the soldiers. They distributed a special leaflet to the soldiers in the Berlin garrison.[94] Many worker activists shared these conclusions: 'In dealing with the reactionaries, we must learn to speak Russian.'[95] They soon devoted themselves to popularising the slogan of the Russian Revolution: 'Workers' and Soldiers' Councils.'[96]

During this period, the Spartacists printed eight leaflets with a print-run of between 20,000 and 100,000 copies each. This was an impressive performance for an illegal organisation.[97] Nonetheless, they recognised that they were neither sufficiently organised nor clearly oriented. Jogiches wrote: 'It appears

---

[91] *Vorwärts*, 15 February 1918.
[92] Müller, op. cit., p. 110.
[93] *Dokumente und Materialen*, Volume 2/2, op. cit., p. 134.
[94] Excerpts in Bartel, *Revolutionäre Ereignisse*, op. cit., p. 168; it was attached to Jogiches's report, but is not included in *Dokumente und Materialen*.
[95] *Dokumente und Materialen*, Volume 2/2, op. cit., p. 99.
[96] Ibid., pp. 137–8.
[97] Ibid., p. 136.

that there were a great many of our supporters amongst the delegates. . . . However, they were scattered, they had no plan of action, and they were lost in the crowd. Moreover, most of them did not see things very clearly.'[98]

Whilst waiting for the workers to draw the lessons of defeat and to rebuild their forces, the price of the defeat had to be paid straightaway. Some 50,000 Berlin workers, about 10 per cent of the strikers, found their special exemptions cancelled, and were called up into the armed forces. Amongst them were 'ringleaders' like Müller, who was the first to go.[99] The police set out to hunt down the revolutionaries, and, during March, managed to arrest Jogiches, who was in hiding in Neukölln.[100] The Spartacist organisation was beheaded by these arrests. The government's hands were free. On 18 February, the German army launched an attack on the Eastern front, and its striking success forced the Soviet government to submit to the German demands, which caused grave difficulties for it, and helped to pave the way for the convulsions of the Civil War.[101]

In the Reichstag, the Majority Social Democrats abstained from voting on the Treaty of Brest-Litovsk.[102] The generals confidently declared that victory was within their reach, with the food supply guaranteed by the grain from Ukraine.[103] The offensive on the Western front was to begin on 21 March.

Between March and November 1918, 192,447 people were to be killed in the war, 421,340 were missing or imprisoned, 860,287 were wounded, and there would be 300,000 more civilian deaths than in 1917, whilst the infant mortality rate was to double.[104]

---

[98] Ibid., p. 135.

[99] L. Stern, *Die Auswirkungen der grossen sozialistischen Oktoberrevolution auf Deutschland*, Volume 2, East Berlin, 1959, pp. 488.

[100] L. Stern, *Die Auswirkungen der grossen sozialistischen Oktoberrevolution auf Deutschland*, Volume 4, East Berlin, 1959, pp. 1363, 1365. At the same time, two of his comrades were arrested, two of his closest collaborators, the soldier Willi Budich and Willi Leow, who together had been in charge in Berlin of the revolutionary propaganda directed to the soldiers in the garrison.

[101] Carr, op. cit., pp. 47ff.

[102] *Stenographische Berichte*, 22 March 1918, p. 573.

[103] Bartel, *Revolutionäre Ereignisse*, op. cit., p. 180.

[104] Ibid., p. 183.

Chapter Seven
Problems of the World Revolution

The momentous events of 4 August 1914 had raised
fundamental strategic and tactical problems for the
world socialist movement. The Russian Revolution
of 1917 posed them in their full sharpness. In Germany,
during the first three years of the War, the problems
of the revolutionary party and the seizure of state
power seemed to exist solely within the domain of
theory. The victory of the Bolsheviks in October 1917
was a verification in practice of their perspectives,
and put these questions on the agenda as concrete,
immediate tasks. Under the conditions of the War,
however, the initial tasks facing revolutionaries were
theoretical discussions, hindered by difficulties in
obtaining information.

The problem of the split before 1917

The overriding point in the theses which Rosa
Luxemburg drafted and which the conference
of the *Internationale* group adopted on 1 January
1916 had been expressed in the twelfth thesis, the
consequence of the analysis of the bankruptcy of the
Second International:

> In view of the betrayal, by the official
> representatives of the socialist parties in the
> principal countries, of the aims and interests of
> the working class; in view of their passage from
> the camp of the working-class International to

the political camp of the imperialist bourgeoisie; it is vitally necessary for socialism to build a new workers' International, which will take into its own hands the leadership and coordination of the revolutionary class struggle against world imperialism.[1]

Lenin emphasised in his critique of the *Junius Pamphlet* that this dominant thesis lost all its practical application if it was not accompanied by the decision to break, in each country, from the centrist and social-pacifist leaderships in order to group together in struggle those who would form the future International.

Radek was the first to develop in *Arbeiterpolitik* the theoretical arguments in favour of revolutionaries forcing the split in the socialist movement. He started by showing how the leaderships of the various social-democratic parties had all identified themselves since the declaration of war with 'social imperialism'. He showed that the very simple argument in favour of the split – that the unity of the socialist movement behind the social-imperialist leaders meant unity with imperialism – was rejected by certain revolutionaries – Luxemburg was his prime target – some of whom believed that the consequences of the war would lead to the regeneration of the Party as a whole, whilst others believed that a split organised before the masses became conscious of the treachery of the leaders would be ineffective, resulting in the isolation of the revolutionaries.[2]

He directly confronted one of the most solid myths in the German socialist movement, when he emphasised that workers' unity was not a 'good thing in itself', any more, necessarily, than splits were 'a bad thing'. In fact, the history of the workers' movement was that of a long succession of splits which resulted not from chance or some whim of History, but from the pressure of adverse social forces. He reviewed the main features of the successive splits in the Chartist movement and of the German movement at the time of Lassalle and the First International. He drew the conclusion: 'Firstly, the divergent orientations within the workers' movement are always rooted in social differences, differences which have led to splits. Secondly, never has it been possible to recover quickly from these splits. The process of unification has always been a long process of struggle.'[3]

---

[1] *Dokumente und Materielen*, Volume 2/1, op. cit., p. 281.
[2] K. Radek, 'Einheit oder Spaltung', *Arbeiterpolitik*, nos. 4, 8 and 10, 1916, in *In den Reihen der deutschen Revolution*, op. cit., pp. 336–8.
[3] Ibid., p. 315.

The same was true of the contemporary crisis of social democracy. The 'policy of 4 August' was in fact an international phenomenon, which necessarily had common roots in London, St Petersburg, Paris and Vienna. These roots – which, for example, explained the alignment of German 'socialism' with the traditional positions of the British trade unions towards the imperialist policies of their bourgeoisie – were to be sought in the existence and the pressure of a 'labour aristocracy' in the labour movement:

> The upper stratum of the German working class acquired relatively high wages, thanks to the impetuous development of German industry. The system of social insurance which the state or the unions provided offered it relatively secure living conditions. We can say that this stratum had a share in bourgeois culture. It had already been declaring for over fifteen years, through the mouths of the revisionists and the trade-union leaders, that it had more than its chains to lose.[4]

In fact, the essential forces in the camp of revisionism were not so much the petty-bourgeois elements, particularly in the south, as the trade-union leaders who supported this petty-bourgeois line. They relied on the privileges which had been won to oppose every attempt to organise large-scale movements of the workers to defend their political rights and to fight for their economic demands. As Radek wrote in 'Unity or Split': 'They based their resistance to the romantic revolutionaries on a claim that such actions were impossible, but in reality what they expressed was the labour aristocracy's fear of seeing their conquests endangered.'[5] In the same perspective, the revisionists and trade-union leaders had supported the colonial policy of the German bourgeoisie.

Consequently, it was not by chance that the policy of 4 August carried the day in the labour movement in countries like Germany, Britain and France which had experienced a fairly profound development of a labour aristocracy. Even in countries like Italy and Russia, where the labour aristocracy formed only a very thin stratum, we saw groups of 'social patriots' based on a nucleus of skilled workers who thought in purely reformist terms, and who lined up with their own bourgeoisie for that reason. The revolutionaries knew all this before the War, but they had underestimated its effects:

---

[4] Ibid., p. 317.
[5] Ibid., p. 318.

> We believed that this policy expressed only the illusions of the leaders, which would be dissipated under the sharpened pressure of class antagonisms. Experience has shown that we were mistaken. In the first place, this was not the policy of the leaders alone; it had behind it a whole category of workers who wanted nothing other than what the leaders wanted. It would be a fatal illusion to try to say that there are not masses behind the leaders, or that, if they are behind them, it is simply because they are not enlightened enough. *The split goes through the masses of workers themselves.*[6]

Some wrongly believed that the War would soon dispel the daydreams of the social-imperialists, and that the unity of the workers must be preserved at all costs in order that, when events had shown the revolutionaries to be correct, the entire working class would rapidly recover its unity in the course of struggle. For, whilst it was true that imperialism would be forced increasingly to restrict the privileges of the labour aristocracy, and in this way undermine the basis of reformism, the fact remained that an ideology anchored in a stratum of society would not be dissipated in a few years.

To begin with, at the given time, the bourgeoisie had decided to utilise the social-patriotic leaders, the spokesmen for the labour aristocracy, to maintain and to conceal its own rule. The 'socialists' were to become ministers, to occupy positions in the apparatus of the bourgeois state, and to seek, by obtaining minor concessions, to divide the working class so that it could not carry on a united revolutionary fight. If the revolutionary activists remained within the Party for the purpose of carrying on the struggle against the social-imperialists, they would, by that act, abandon their role as the vanguard in the proletarian struggle:

> If the formal unity of the Party remains unbroken, if the social-imperialists dominate the Party and determine its policy, we shall be obliged either to give up the struggle against the class enemy for some years, or to carry it on without regard to the slogans of the imperialist leaderships. In the former case, if we abandon the struggle against the external enemy and if we restrict ourselves to criticising the social-imperialists, this criticism loses all meaning; it will be wiped out and annulled by what we would have to do in the Reichstag, in the trade-union movement, by our abstaining from action to

---

[6] Ibid., p. 320.

convince the working masses that our criticism is correct. In the other case, the social-imperialists will very quickly expel us from the Party. No majority in the Party can tolerate for a long time a minority which condemns its policy as a betrayal of its basic principles. It will still less tolerate this group placing itself in opposition to all that it does, and it will call on the masses to act against such a group.[7]

Radek goes on to say that, even if the revolutionaries became the majority following a congress, they could not take the risk of keeping in the Party the opportunists who were really class enemies. Consequently, the revolutionaries would have to expel the opportunists along with those amongst the workers – and there would be some – who continued to support them: 'Whichever way we turn, there will be a split.'[8] Therefore, he continues, they must consciously prepare for it. It will be the only way to organise the struggle against imperialist war, the bourgeoisie and its agents in the labour movement. The sooner it is expressed practically in terms of organisation, as it has been expressed in people's thoughts since 1914, the sooner the damage will be repaired, the sooner the revolutionary unity of the working class will be re-established.

A similar effort in the field of theoretical research led Marchlewski, in his criticism of the theses on peace adopted by the SPD, to analyse the position of the opportunists on the question of the state. He counterposed to them the position of Marx and Engels, who saw the state as the instrument through which the power of a class is exercised. Marchlewski took the same approach as Lenin, who was working at the same time on *The State and Revolution*. He declared: 'The workers must struggle against the state. They cannot realise their ideal, which is based on the liberty and equality of human beings, without breaking the class-rule of the state.'[9]

This was the way that some of the German revolutionaries came to approach the outlook of the Bolsheviks, with whom they had only tenuous links and no common organisation. The Russian Revolution was to contribute consistency and weight to their ideas.

---

[7] Ibid., pp. 323–4.
[8] Ibid., p. 325.
[9] 'Theses on the Question of Peace', *Spartakus im Kriege*, p. 58.

The influence of the Russian Revolution

The Russian Revolution's influence can be traced in the German labour movement from 1917, not merely in the theoretical and practical positions of the German revolutionaries, but in the direction in which large masses of workers moved, and in the way that the term 'workers' councils [*Arbeiterräte*]', the German rendering of the Russian 'soviets', entered the vernacular. These were the signs of subterranean movements which were preparing revolutionary explosions.

From this point of view, Russia in 1917 was not remote. Our problem, however, is how, in this period of European war and state censorship, the German workers and in particular the revolutionary groups could become aware of the Russian experience. Likewise, we have to show the efforts of the Bolsheviks, once they were in power, to try to win to their views revolutionaries who were far from being in agreement with them on every level, and in particular to convince them that their first duty was to form a new party – which the Spartacists had up to now refused to consider.

Faced with the difficulty of establishing links with the various European countries, the Bolsheviks did not neglect the opportunity offered by the presence on Russian soil of some two million prisoners of war, amongst whom were 165,000 German soldiers, and 2,000 German officers.[10] The situation was favourable after the February Revolution. Many prisoners were social-democratic activists whose sympathies could not fail to be with the workers and peasants, and with those parties which aimed at ending the imperialist war. Neither the Mensheviks nor the Socialist Revolutionaries, who were more or less paralysed by their policy of the 'sacred union', could in practice manage to mount propaganda like that of the Bolsheviks amongst the prisoners of war.

Small underground groups of social-democratic activists had been formed here and there in Russia before the February Revolution. They developed immediately after the Revolution when many German prisoners of war went over to the Bolsheviks.[11] But after October everything went forward on a much wider scale, and the Bolsheviks made every attempt to capitalise upon their earlier efforts. They also organised widespread agitation for

---

[10] R. Dix, 'Deutsche Internationalisten bei der Errichtung und Verteidigung der Sowjetmacht', *Beiträge zur Geschichte der deutschen Arbeiterbewegung*, no. 3, 1966, p. 495.
[11] Ibid., pp. 485, 496.

fraternisation with the German forces along the whole front.[12] Radek, who had returned to Russia immediately after the insurrection, encouraged systematic propaganda, agitation and organisation amongst the prisoners of every nationality, and began with those who spoke German. In December 1917, his principal instrument, the German-language *Die Fackel* [*The Torch*], began to appear.[13] The Federation of Internationalist Prisoners of War, followed by the formation at a conference in Moscow of the German group of the Russian Communist Party (Bolsheviks) were the first practical results of this effort to construct nuclei of foreign Communists.[14] Whilst the signing of the Brest-Litovsk Treaty put an end to this work of recruitment, at the same time it would enable its full benefit to be felt, because many prisoners influenced by the Russian Communists returned to their homelands. The troops themselves frequently carried the revolutionary virus to the rear or to the other fronts.[15]

Around Radek there appeared men who were to form in Russia the general staff of the first nucleus of the German-speaking Communists, Rothkegel from Hamburg, Josef Böhm from Bremen, the Austrian Karl Tomann, a former trade-union official,[16] the social-democratic activist Hermann Osterloh,[17] and a young journalist who was the inspiration of a pacifist movement, Ernst Reuter, whom the Soviet government appointed as a commissar in the republic of the Volga Germans.[18] There was also a railway worker, the son of German émigrés, Nicholas Krebs, who had been a Bolshevik since 1916.[19] Their politico-military struggle in the areas under German army occupation brought other recruits, such as the schoolteacher Wilhelm Zaisser, a reserve lieutenant, who went over to the Ukrainian partisans with his unit.[20]

---

[12] K.L. Seleznev, 'Bolshevistskaiia agitatsia i revolutsionnoe dvizhenie v Germanskoi Armii na vostochnoe fronte v 1918g', in *Noyabre'skaia Revolutiutsiia v Germanii*, Moscow, 1960, pp. 271–328.

[13] Ibid., pp. 276–7.

[14] Dix, op. cit., p. 495. It is noteworthy that there is no reference to Radek in this essay.

[15] D.S. Davidovich, *Revolutsionnii Krisis 1923 g V Germanii I Gamburgskoe vosstanie*, Moscow, 1963, pp. 133–4, mentions the influence exercised by Bolshevik propaganda on the reserve officer Ernst Schneller, who was to become a communist on his return.

[16] Dix, op. cit., p. 495.

[17] W. Brandt and R. Lowenthal, *Ernst Reuter. Ein Leben für die Freiheit*, Munich, 1957, pp. 109, 129.

[18] He was later known in the KPD(S) of which he even became General Secretary in 1921 for a few months. See Brandt and Lowenthal, op. cit., p. 112.

[19] At this time, Krebs russified his name as Rakov; he was later active in Germany as 'Felix Wolf'.

[20] He was later a military leader in the fighting in the Ruhr, and served in Spain

The links with the German revolutionary movement were considerably eased when diplomatic relations were established between the Soviet government and Germany immediately after the Brest-Litovsk Treaty was signed. Bukharin himself stayed for some time in the embassy.[21] The Soviet ambassador, Adolf Joffe, was an old, experienced revolutionary activist, and perfectly understood the reason for his mission. Already at Brest-Litovsk, he amicably remarked to Count Czernin: 'I hope that we shall soon manage to unleash a revolution in your country.'[22] When he arrived in Berlin in April 1918, he showed his gift for the spectacular gesture when he refused to present his letters of accreditation to the Kaiser, and sent out invitations to his first reception to the principal leaders of the USPD and the revolutionaries, including those who were in prison.[23] He was active in every field; he bought information which he passed on to the German revolutionaries, and he provided them with money and advice.[24]

By his side was another activist who had experience of underground work, Mieczislaw Bronski,[25] a Pole, a former companion of Lenin in Switzerland, and one of the pillars of the Zimmerwald Left.[26]

The Soviet embassy was an important means of communication. It had strong financial resources and exceptional material means for the period, and it could ensure rapid contact with Petrograd under the cover of diplomatic immunity. All this facilitated conspiratorial work, and at the same time direct political contact between the secret or semi-secret Germans and the victorious Russian revolutionaries.[27] The Soviet embassy employed German activists in its various services, and especially in its telegraphic service, Rosta. In this

---

as 'General Gomez'. On the 1918 episode, rarely referred to, see A. Marty, *La Révolte de la Mer Noire*, Paris, 1939, p. 72.

[21] In particular he was to be there at the end of October 1918 (Stern, op. cit., Volume 4, p. 1661).

[22] Quoted by Carr, op. cit., p. 71.

[23] Ibid., p. 76.

[24] L. Fischer, *Men and Politics*, London, 1941, p. 31.

[25] Carr, op. cit., p. 135.

[26] Amongst other members of the active diplomatic staff in the German movement, the German police reports mention Zagorsky, who was said to be in charge of contact with the USPD leaders; Marcel Rosenberg, who dealt with all press questions (and was in 1936 to be the ambassador of the USSR in Spain, until he disappeared in the great purges); and Mme Markowski, who dealt with relations with the youth organisations. The same sources report that Joffe tried in vain to get as his 'economic adviser' Karski-Marchlewski, and could only get him repatriated (Stern, op. cit., p. 1365).

[27] Joffe states that he handed over to Barth several hundred thousand marks to assist with the preparation of the insurrection (*Izvestia*, 6 December 1918).

way, these activists had a legal cover and full freedom of action. In such a position were Emil Eichhorn, a former director of the SPD's press bureau and a leader of the USPD, Ernst Meyer, formerly a journalist on *Vorwärts* and a leading Spartacist,[28] as well as Eugen Leviné, another Spartacist activist. One of the leading Independents, Oscar Cohn, was the embassy's lawyer and its agent in all its financial operations.[29]

Even though the embassy was not the channel for propaganda literature, as the German government was to describe it some months later, it was a place of refuge, a centre of influence and an information agency.[30] The change in the nature of the relations between Germany and Russia is expressed in the fact that a report on conditions in Germany, much more complete than that in the clandestine *Spartacus Letters*, could appear in Petrograd in *Welt-revolution*, the organ of the German section of the Bolshevik Party.[31]

The efforts of the Bolsheviks

The Bolsheviks were convinced that Germany was the decisive centre of the European revolution. They saw the Russian Revolution as the first stage in the world revolution, which would find a decisive and early field of battle in Germany. During 1918, it was the 'delay' of the German Revolution which would form the background for the discussion amongst the Bolsheviks around the problem of the separate peace with Germany and the Treaty of Brest-Litovsk. It was the perspective of the German Revolution which dictated the outlines of the foreign policy of the Soviet government.

Right from the February Revolution, the Bolsheviks considered the building of links with Germany and establishing a German organisation as a primary question. In the course of his journey to Russia, Lenin entrusted to Vorovsky, Hanecki and Radek, who remained in Stockholm, the duty of running the foreign bureau of the Central Committee. One of its tasks was to circulate in Germany *Russische Korrespondenz-Prawda*, which carried information about Russia and the arguments of the Bolsheviks.[32] In his *April Theses*, which

---

[28] See biographies in the Appendix.

[29] Carr, op. cit., p. 77.

[30] For example, the very day after Liebknecht was released, it was known in Moscow that he was in political agreement with the Bolsheviks.

[31] I.M. Krivoguz, *'Spartak' i obrazovanie Kommunisticheskoi partii Germanii*, Moscow, 1962, p. 136.

[32] W. Imig, 'Zur Hilfe Lenins für die deutschen Linken', *Beiträge zur Geschichte der deutschen Arbeiterbewegung*, no. 5/6, 1963, pp. 810ff.

he submitted to the Party on his arrival, Lenin paid homage to Liebknecht and the activity of the German revolutionaries, and described the left internationalists Münzenberg, Radek and Hartstein as 'true internationalists', 'representatives of the revolutionary internationalist mass, and not their corrupters'. Moreover: 'It is we who must found, and right now, without delay, a *new*, revolutionary, proletarian International, or rather, we must not fear to acknowledge publicly that this new International is *already established and operating*.'[33]

The Soviet historian Krivoguz states that over 60,000 leaflets were brought secretly into Germany in the summer of 1917 alone.[34] The activists of the Youth International grouped around Münzenberg in Switzerland ensured that Lenin's article 'The Military Policy of the Revolutionary Proletariat', which he had handed to them before he left for Russia, was circulated in Germany. By way of both Stockholm and Switzerland, several thousands of copies of *The State and Revolution* arrived in Germany.[35]

At the end of August 1917, Lenin urged the foreign bureau of the Central Committee to do their utmost to organise an international conference of the Left:

> The Bolsheviks, the PSD, the Dutch, *Arbeiterpolitik*, *Demain*, there is already a sufficient *nucleus*. . . . The resolutions of the conference of the Bolsheviks (24–29 April 1917) and of their congress (July 1917) . . . the draft new programme of the same party – there is a sufficient *ideological basis* (adding *Vorbote*, *Tribune*, *Arbeiterpolitik* and others) to be able to present the whole world with clear answers to the questions raised by imperialism, and to accuse the social-chauvinists and the Kautskyans.[36]

He believed that the principal political attack had to be directed against the centrists and especially Kautsky, whom he judged to be his most dangerous adversary, because, whilst formally he had broken from the social-chauvinists, in reality he defended their policies, and all his efforts were directed to preventing the bacillus of Bolshevism from infecting the German working class. This was the perspective in which Lenin drafted in 1918 – essentially

---

[33] V.I. Lenin, 'The Tasks of the Proletariat in Our Revolution', *Collected Works*, Volume 24, Moscow, 1977, p. 82.

[34] Krivoguz, op. cit., p. 63.

[35] Imig, op. cit., pp. 809–10, 814–55.

[36] V.I. Lenin, 'To the Bureau of the Central Committee Abroad', *Collected Works*, Volume 35, op. cit., pp. 321–2.

to convince the German revolutionary activists – his pamphlet *The Proletarian Revolution and the Renegade Kautsky*, in which he put forward the Bolshevik Revolution as a model:

> These [Bolshevik] tactics were the only internationalist tactics, because they did the utmost possible in one country *for* the development, support and awakening of the revolution *in all countries*. These tactics have been justified by their enormous success, for Bolshevism ... has become *world* Bolshevism, has produced an idea, a theory, a programme and tactics which differ concretely and in practice from those of social-chauvinism and social-pacifism ... the mass of workers in all countries are realising more and more clearly every day that Bolshevism has indicated the right road of escape from the horrors of the war and imperialism, that Bolshevism *can serve as a model of tactics for all.*[37]

Lenin realised at the beginning of October 1918 that the German situation was maturing more quickly than his pamphlet was being printed, and drafted a ten-page summary which he sent to Chicherin, asking him to get it distributed in Germany as quickly as possible (which would best be done through Switzerland).[38] This document, which bears the same title as the pamphlet, closes with the following remark:

> Europe's greatest misfortune and danger is that it has *no* revolutionary party. It has parties of traitors like the Scheidemanns ..., and of servile souls like Kautsky. But it has no revolutionary party. Of course, a mighty, popular revolutionary movement might rectify this deficiency, but it is nevertheless a serious misfortune and a grave danger. That is why we must do out utmost to expose renegades like Kautsky, thereby supporting the revolutionary *groups* of genuinely internationalist workers, who are to be found in *all* countries. The proletariat will very soon turn away from the traitors and renegades and follow these groups, drawing and training leaders from their midst.[39]

---

[37] V.I. Lenin, 'The Proletarian Revolution and the Renegade Kautsky', *Collected Works*, Volume 28, Moscow, 1977, pp. 293–4.

[38] Imig, op. cit., p. 818.

[39] V.I. Lenin, 'The Proletarian Revolution and the Renegade Kautsky', *Collected Works*, Volume 28, op. cit., p. 112. The article appeared in *Pravda* on 11 October 1918.

The response of the German revolutionaries

The German revolutionaries enthusiastically hailed the revolution in Russia from February 1917 onward. It greatly encouraged them, because it clearly showed that the working masses could enter into struggle against the bourgeoisie, and that victory was possible. In her message to the foundation conference of the USPD, Zetkin spoke of this 'greatly encouraging event'.[40] Luxemburg wrote from her prison that 'these magnificent events' acted upon her 'like an elixir of life'.[41] In her manuscript on the Russian Revolution, she wrote: 'In this Lenin and Trotsky and their friends were the *first*, those who went ahead as an example to the proletariat of the world; they are still the *only ones* who can cry with [Ulrich] von Hutten: 'I have dared!' This is the essential and *enduring* in Bolshevik policy.'[42]

On this ground, the Spartacists and the left radicals in Bremen were in full agreement. On 17 November, the editors of *Arbeiterpolitik* enthusiastically hailed the seizure of power by the workers' and soldiers' councils.[43] On 15 December, Johann Knief explained in the same publication why the Russian Revolution had been able to advance so quickly and be victorious: 'Uniquely and exclusively because there existed in Russia an independent party of the extreme Left which from the beginning unfurled the banner of socialism, and fought under the sign of the social revolution.'[44] He added that the victory of the Bolsheviks clearly showed why the Spartacists were wrong, and why they should make a clear break from the centrists in the USPD, and start constructing a revolutionary party.

The example of the Russian Revolution and Lenin's arguments found an echo amongst the Spartacists, and, on 3 June 1918, Mehring, as a veteran, addressed an open letter to the Bolsheviks in which he declared that he fully supported their policies. He strongly criticised the USPD's perspective of reconstructing the prewar SPD and of using 'the old, well-tried tactics'. This he called 'reactionary utopianism'. He called for the construction of a new International, and made a self-criticism: 'We have been mistaken on just one point: we joined the Independent Party when it was formed, in the hope of

---

[40] *Protokoll USP, 1917*, op. cit., p. 50.
[41] R. Luxemburg, *Briefe an Freunde*, Zürich, 1950, p. 157.
[42] Luxemburg, *The Russian Revolution and Leninism or Marxism?*, op. cit., p. 80.
[43] *Arbeiterpolitik*, no. 46, 17 November 1917, *Dokumente und Materielen*, Volume 2/2, op. cit., pp. 15–18.
[44] 'Eine dringende Notwendigkeit', *Arbeiterpolitik*, no. 50, 15 December 1917, *Dokumente und Materielen*, Volume 2/2, op. cit., pp 43–7.

pushing it forward. We had to give that up as hopeless.'[45] He developed the same themes at greater length in a series of articles entitled 'The Bolsheviks and Us', which were published in *Leipziger Volkszeitung* from 10 June 1918 onwards. He showed that the Bolsheviks were working within the perspectives which Marx drew up from his analysis of the Paris Commune, and that the dictatorship of the proletariat was being realised in Russia in the form of soviets. He added that in Germany this perspective required that the workers should take power through the workers' councils. He also said that the perspective of world revolution required the construction of a new International, with the Bolsheviks forming the core.[46] In the women's supplement of the same daily paper, Zetkin developed the idea of the exercising of power by the workers' councils, which would be the 'soviet' form of the proletarian revolution in Germany.[47]

But this important evolution on the part of some of the most responsible Spartacists did not lead to any major rethink in respect of the organisation of their group. We would need a great deal of optimism to follow the Soviet historian Krivoguz in concluding that 'in fact the split between the Spartacist League and the Independents was complete by the summer of 1918'.[48]

The principal reason lies no doubt in Luxemburg's reservations about the policies of the Bolsheviks. She criticised the policy of terror and persecution of the other tendencies which claimed to be socialist, and she also criticised the agrarian policy of the Bolsheviks, which she claimed to be creating the danger of a capitalist revival. But she especially criticised the foreign policy of Soviet Russia and the acceptance of the peace of Brest-Litovsk, which risked delaying the end of the war and the outbreak of the German Revolution.[49]

---

[45] Open letter published in *Mitteilungs-Blatt des Verbandes der sozialdemokratischen Wahlvereine Berlins und Umgegend*, no. 16, 21 July 1918, reproduced in *Dokumente und Materielen*, Volume 2/2, op. cit., pp. 158–62.

[46] *Leipziger Volkszeitung*, 31 May, 1 and 10 June 1918.

[47] *Leipziger Volkszeitung*, women's supplement, no. 30, 9 August 1918.

[48] Krivoguz, op. cit., p. 105.

[49] In August-September 1918, she drafted a violent attack on the policies of the Bolsheviks in respect of the Treaty of Brest-Litovsk, and intended this to become a 'Spartacus Letter'. By common agreement, Levi, Leviné and Ernst Meyer refused to publish it (see *Die Rote Fahne*, 15 January 1922). According to what he wrote in 1922, Levi visited her in prison at Breslau, and managed to convince her to withdraw it from publication. As he was leaving, she handed him the manuscript of *Die Russische Revolution* and said: 'It was for you that I wrote this pamphlet, and if I manage to convince you alone, my labor will not have been useless.' (Paul Levi, 'Introduction' to *The Russian Revolution*, pp. 1–2.)

The penultimate 'Spartacus Letter' was entitled 'The Russian Tragedy'. It expressed a belief which apparently was widely held amongst German leftists that the Russian Revolution was doomed to be crushed in the near future, because it was isolated and, in a certain sense, premature. An editorial note makes this clear:

> These fears result from the objective situation of the Bolsheviks, and not from their subjective behaviour. We reproduce this article only because of its conclusion: without the German Revolution, the Russian Revolution remains in danger, and the fight for socialism in this world-wide war is futile. There is only *one* solution: the large-scale uprising of the German working class.[50]

The revolution advances more quickly than the revolutionaries

The revolution was to arrive before the revolutionaries could break their routine, get free from the vice of repression, and draw in practice the conclusions which three years of struggle in Russia and elsewhere had imposed on them. It was to come essentially from military defeat. By 18 July, the General Staff knew that the German army, which had been forced onto the defensive by Foch's attack and the use of tanks on the Western front, no longer had any reasonable chance of victory. Ludendorff himself accepted that the War had to end.[51]

This awareness in leading circles went alongside a complementary decision, that the apparatus of the régime must be democratised. 'Parliamentarisation' would ensure that the representatives of the political parties would be forced to share the responsibility for decisions which the military defeat made unavoidable.[52] Majority Social Democrats and Catholics of the Centre Party opened the perspective of participating in a government of national union which could negotiate with the Entente on the basis of President Wilson's 'Fourteen Points'. This became an accomplished fact on 4 October, with the entry into the new government, just formed by Prince Max of Baden, the new Chancellor, of the Catholic deputy Mathias Erzberger, and of Philip Scheidemann as ministers without portfolio.[53] The SPD relied on the promise by

---

[50] *Spartakusbriefe*, op. cit., p. 453.
[51] Badia, op. cit., p. 93.
[52] Ibid., p. 95.
[53] Drabkin, op. cit., pp. 82–3.

the Prince that they would proceed to 'democratisation', to 'parliamentarisation', as the final defence against subversion.

The leading circles in Germany saw 'subversion' as the principal danger. The army on the Eastern front had shown itself to be useless for carrying on the War, corroded as it was by the virus of revolution. This evolution confirmed the forecast which Liebknecht had made in jail at Luckau, just after military law was introduced: 'We shall see what harvest will ripen from the seeds that those in power are sowing today.'[54]

The Kaiser was terrified by the reports which reached him about 'the large number of desertions, cases of insubordination and red flags appearing on trains carrying soldiers on leave'.[55] These troops had to be isolated by a 'cordon sanitaire', and the restoration of their reliability would take time.[56] Police reports described both the growing discontent amongst workers and wide sections of the civil population, and the prestige enjoyed by the Russian Revolution.

Yet the building of the revolutionary organisation lagged behind the audacious political analyses and perspectives of the revolutionaries, and they were unable to take advantage either of the revolutionary ferment that was rising throughout 1918, or of the technical and financial help which the Russians gave them from April onwards. The revolutionaries in Bremen no longer had a single activist in the shipyards or the port industries where they had once enjoyed a solid base.[57] In Berlin, the Spartacist group in Constituency Six, which covered Charlottenburg and Berlin-Moabit and went as far as Spandau, had only seven members.[58] The Spartacist leadership had been broken up by the arrests following the January strikes, with Jogiches, Heckert and many others being apprehended.[59] Pieck, hunted by the police, had fled to Holland. The central work of the group – the publication of the *Letters* and leaflets – rested on a few individuals around Levi, who had returned from Switzerland,[60] and Meyer.

---

[54] *Die Aktion*, no. 29, 19 July 1919.

[55] Kaiser Wilhelm II, *Ereignisse und Gestalten aus den jahren 1917–1918*, cited in Badia, op. cit., p. 81.

[56] Badia, op. cit., p. 81.

[57] E. Kolb, *Die Arbeiterräte in der deutschen Innenpolitik*, Düsseldorf, 1962, p. 79.

[58] Interview with the leader of the group, Karl Retzlaw, in H. Weber, op. cit., pp. 20–1, n. 41.

[59] *Vorwärts und nicht vergessen*, op. cit., pp. 468–9.

[60] Paul Frölich writes that Levi 'had taken over the running of *Spartakus* after Leo Jogiches' arrest in March 1918' (Frölich, *Rosa Luxemburg*, op. cit., p. 241). We can rely

Zetkin and Mehring, though still standard-bearers, were no longer physically able to lead the hard life of the underground. This situation weighed heavily on the morale of the leaders, who failed to appreciate how quickly the situation was developing and did not foresee important events in 1918. This is clear from the letter which Meyer addressed to Lenin on 7 September 1918:

> We have had to await the signs of revolutionary movements in Germany, and we await them as impatiently as you. Fortunately, all my friends have become much more optimistic. In any case, we cannot look forward to more important activities, neither immediately nor in the near future. But for the winter we have bigger plans, and the situation here is going to support our activity.[61]

The truth is that the revolutionaries did not feel that they had a grip on events.

However, the organisation of the revolutionary youth gave them grounds for hope. During the spring of 1918, the League of Free Youth emerged from the fusion of two organisations in Berlin which had arisen from the reaction against the SPD's chauvinist policies. These were the Berliner Jugendbildungverein, at the head of which Max Köhler replaced Fritz Globig, both Spartacists, and the Vereinigung Arbeiterjugend, organised by the USPD, but led by Walter Stoecker in close association with Willi Münzenberg.[62] On 5 May 1918, the League of Free Youth assembled over 2,000 people to an illegal meeting near Stolpe to commemorate the centenary of the birth of Karl Marx.[63] The fusion in Berlin encouraged unification on a national scale. During the summer, there were secret conferences in many parts of the country to prepare the unification of the youth organisations of different radical groups, all affiliated to the Youth International which Münzenberg was leading from Switzerland. The USPD youth, in whose ranks the influence of Ernst Däumig prevailed, took a pro-Bolshevik position: they too popularised the slogan of the seizure of power through revolutionary councils.[64]

---

on this evidence, which comes from one who was deeply opposed to Levi, but who was concerned for objectivity in his historical work.

[61] IML, Moscow, Collection 19; *Dokumente und Materielen*, Volume 2/2, op. cit., p. 195.

[62] Globig, op. cit., pp. 232–3.

[63] Ibid.; *Unter der roten Fahne*, op. cit., p. 106.

[64] *Unter der roten Fahne*, op. cit., p. 107.

The revolutionary delegates in Berlin had suffered heavily from the repression which followed the January strikes. To prepare for any eventuality, every leader selected a replacement, but Müller was not lucky when he chose Emil Barth. Barth was a metalworker who had been discharged from the army; a capable speaker, but soon revealed as a conceited braggart. The political leadership of their group was thereafter formed by two of the principal USPD leaders in Berlin, neither of whom was a factory worker. One was Georg Ledebour, the great opponent of the Spartacists, and the other was the journalist Ernst Däumig, formerly a non-commissioned officer in the French Foreign Legion. He found himself entrusted with the tasks of organising revolutionary propaganda in the garrison, and forming armed detachments with a view to insurrection.[65]

This work had hardly begun by September 1918. Däumig's contacts were no more than some individuals in the barracks, and arms amounted to a few dozen revolvers.[66] It was only at the last moment that, thanks to the efforts of two activists in the group of revolutionary delegates in Berlin, Cläre Derfert-Casper and Arthur Schöttler, the Berlin revolutionaries provided themselves with weapons through workers in the arsenals around Suhl.[67]

So, irrespective of whether they had fought during the War for peace through a revolution, or for a revolution through a struggle for peace, the German revolutionaries had not succeeded – and in the majority had not even tried – to build what was needed as early as 1914, an organisation of their own which could meet the needs and the aspirations of the masses, find agreement on slogans, and centralise their activity. Peace and revolution overtook them.

---

[65] Müller, op. cit., pp. 126–7.
[66] Ibid.
[67] *Vorwärts und nicht vergessen*, op. cit., pp. 296ff.; recollections of Hermann Grothe, *1918. Erinnerungen von Veteranen*, Berlin, 1949, pp. 333, 409–10.

Chapter Eight

The November Revolution

The revolution which exploded in Germany during the first days of November 1918 seems at first sight to confirm the expectations and the opinions of Rosa Luxemburg. The working masses were finding their way to revolutionary action despite their leaders, and often against them, almost completely independently of the revolutionary organisations, which were overtaken by the event, in the absence of any unifying slogan and, finally, of any leadership. At the same time, as if in accordance with the Spartacists' clandestine appeals, the revolution appeared to be moving towards a new form of state power based upon workers' and soldiers' councils, on the model of the Russian soviets. Taken up by millions of people, the slogan of the councils became a potent material force.

The leaders and the military defeat

The political and military leaders in Germany felt the approaching storm. The defeat at Montdidier on the Western front on 8 August showed that any hope of military victory was in vain, and that the leaders no longer had any grip on the conduct of the War, which had become a 'game of chance'. In mid-August, the Kaiser held a conference with his Chancellor, Hertling, the army chiefs Hindenburg and Ludendorff, and the Emperor of Austria: they all agreed to seek the most favourable moment to sue for peace. The Secretary of State, Hintze, informed President Wilson that the German government wished to negotiate on the basis of a return to the status quo ante.[1]

In September, the situation worsened on the fronts held by Germany's Austro-Hungarian and Bulgarian allies. The military chiefs became more insistent. On 29 September, Hindenburg and Ludendorff informed the Chancellor that the situation on the Eastern front had become desperate, and expressed the wish that the government be broadened to provide the most solid base for negotiations.[2] They in fact shared with Hintze the idea that 'we must forestall an upheaval from below by a revolution from above'.[3] Their aim was to form a government representative of the existing majority in the Reichstag with, in particular, the inclusion of Social-Democratic ministers.

Chancellor Hertling resigned, and Wilhelm II summoned to take his place Prince Max of Baden, a progressive grandee tinged with the reputation of being a liberal. The Prince chose his ministers from amongst the deputies of the parties which supported a policy of immediate negotiations. The SPD nominated Bauer and Scheidemann.[4] On 4 October, the government of Max of Baden proposed to President Wilson that an armistice be concluded on the basis of the 'Fourteen Points'. On 8 November, he sent to the Allies the delegation charged with concluding the armistice. Already the military chiefs – especially Ludendorff – were talking about 'unacceptable' conditions, and were trying to throw the responsibility for the peace onto the shoulders of 'the politicians'. Nonetheless, they made no effort to obstruct it. In their eyes, the revolutionary threat was very real. Everything depended to a large extent on the SPD, which for the time being was working all out in favour of a peaceful domestic solution. *Vorwärts* even campaigned to show that 'Russian solutions' were not practicable in Germany: 'The Russian Revolution swept away democracy and replaced it with the dictatorship of the workers' and soldiers' councils. The Social-Democratic Party unequivocally rejects Bolshevik theory and methods for Germany, and declares its commitment to democracy.'[5] On 4 November, Ebert telephoned the Secretary of State

---

[1] Badia, op. cit., Volume 1, pp. 93–4.

[2] Ibid., pp. 94–5.

[3] Quoted in F. Payer, *Von Bethmann-Hollweg bis Ebert. Erinnerungen und Bilder*, Frankfurt-am-Main, 1923, p. 82.

[4] See the internal discussions of the SPD leadership in H. Müller, *Die November-revolution*, Berlin, 1931, pp. 10–11.

[5] 'Dictatorship or Democracy', *Vorwärts*, 21 October 1918.

Wahnschaffe, assuring him that the trade unions would use all their power to calm the workers.[6]

The first cracks

Already in September, there was increasing evidence of growing radicalisation. At the conference of the USPD, Haase, Dittmann and Hilferding had some difficulty getting the slogan of the dictatorship of the proletariat rejected, and spent much effort denouncing the 'romantic taste for the Bolshevik Revolution'.[7] Kautsky expounded the same themes as *Vorwärts*.[8] Haase confessed to Däumig that he had no idea of what was going to happen.[9] An enthusiastic Lenin wrote to the Spartacists on 18 October: 'Now the decisive hour is at hand . . .'.[10]

On 7 October, the Spartacists held a conference in Berlin, and delegates from the Bremen communists took part. The conference analysed the situation in Germany as 'a revolutionary situation in which the problems which the German bourgeoisie could not solve in the revolution of 1848 are being posed in a new way'. It declared the solidarity of the coming revolution with the Russian Revolution, and drew up an immediate programme which included an amnesty for all, civilians and members of the armed forces, who had opposed the War, the abolition of conscription of labour, and the lifting of the state of siege. Its programme of action included the cancellation of all war loans, expropriation of the banks, mines and factories, shorter working hours, increased wages for the low-paid, the seizure of large and medium rural estates, the abolition of military law, the transfer of enforcement of discipline to delegates elected by soldiers, the right of soldiers to organise and hold meetings, the abolition of courts martial, the immediate release of those sentenced, the abolition of the death penalty or forced labour for political or military offences, the allocation of food to be administered by workers' delegates, the abolition of the *Länder*, and the abolition of the royal and princely dynasties. To realise this programme, the conference called for 'the formation of councils of workers and soldiers where they do not already

---

[6] Prinz Max von Baden, *Erinnerungen und Dokumente*, Stuttgart-Berlin, 1928, p. 571.
[7] Tormin, op. cit., p. 32.
[8] K. Kautsky, *The Dictatorship of the Proletariat*, Ann Arbor, 1964.
[9] E. Barth, *Aus der Werkstatt der deutschen Revolution*, Berlin, 1919, p. 35.
[10] V.I. Lenin, 'To the Members of the Spartacus Group', *Collected Works*, Volume 35, op. cit., p. 369.

exist'.[11] The revolutionaries were announcing their candidature for the leadership of the forthcoming revolution.

The Social-Democratic ministers were aware of the danger, and their contributions to the discussions in the Cabinet took up this theme.[12] They insisted that the amnesty for political prisoners be decreed quickly.[13] They believed that Liebknecht in particular must be released, because imprisonment was winning him the halo of a martyr. To be sure, this course would be risky, but it was necessary if they were to convince the working class of the commitment of the new government to 'democratisation'. Scheidemann convinced his colleagues, despite the opposition of the army chiefs. They decided to free the Spartacist leader on 21 October.[14] In the days which followed, some hundreds of activists were freed, including those who had been in prison for years.

At a meeting of trade-union leaders in Berlin on the evening of 22 October, with Alwin Körsten in the chair, the metalworker Paul Eckert was allowed to speak, and announced the astounding news: 'Karl Liebknecht has been freed, he will arrive in Berlin tomorrow at five o'clock in the afternoon.'[15] The majority of the delegates showed their satisfaction by singing the *Internationale*, and the police intervened.[16]

The next day, several thousand people, closely shepherded by a large force of police, waited for the freed prisoner, and gave him a triumphal welcome. Like an activist hungry for action, he plunged into the battle as soon as he left the Potsdam station. In the same square where he had been arrested two years before, he harangued the crowd, hailed the example of the Russian Revolution, and called for proletarian revolution in Germany.[17] That same evening, the Soviet ambassador Joffe put on a spectacular reception for him, and read a congratulatory telegram from Lenin, to which Liebknecht replied. Other German activists, Walcher, Haase, Barth, Globig and Rühle, spoke.[18] Many of those present, representatives of the various revolutionary

---

[11] *Dokumente und Materialen*, Volume 2/2, op. cit., pp. 228–43.
[12] See the discussions in K. Westarp, *Die Regierung des Prinzen Max von Baden*, Berlin, 1923, passim.
[13] Ibid., sessions of 6 October, p. 88, 10 October, p. 129, 12 October, pp. 129, 167.
[14] Ibid., p. 305; Max von Baden, op. cit., p. 476.
[15] According to O Franke, *Vorwärts und nicht vergessen*, op. cit., pp. 273–4.
[16] Ibid.
[17] Arendsee, op. cit., p. 108.
[18] Ibid., p. 110.

organisations, believed that Liebknecht, the heroic symbol of the revolutionary movement, would be able to unify the diverse groups.

Yet, paradoxically, Liebknecht stood alone. He believed that there was no more time to be lost and that the Revolution had been delayed too long, but he also knew that he could provide it only with a banner, not a general staff. His Spartacist comrades could not play that role. To be sure, Otto Franke was well-rooted in the nucleus of revolutionary delegates.[19] Levi had been at work for several months, and served as a link with the radicals in Bremen.[20] Pieck had returned from Holland on 26 October to resume his activities.[21] But these still were leaders without troops, at least in the key city of Berlin, where there were no more than fifty of them.[22]

The real vanguard of the forces in the factories was organised in the ranks of the USPD under the leadership of the centrists with whom Liebknecht had crossed swords so often, and particularly in the nucleus of the revolutionary delegates from the factories. The problem arose of establishing a direct link with them.

The USPD leaders took the initiative. They knew that they risked being overwhelmed by the activists, and they wanted simultaneously to control Liebknecht and to exploit his prestige. So they offered to coopt him onto the leadership of their party.[23] The proposal was tempting from several points of view. The USPD had numerous activists in its ranks, and had major publishing outlets. But Liebknecht was not prepared to make an unprincipled compromise. He asked for guarantees, for a congress to be called which he believed would denounce the past procrastination of the centrist leadership, and that the USPD recognise that the Spartacists had been correct during the preceding years. He had no wish to run the risk of being a hostage in the leadership. But the USPD leaders were not ready to make such a concession, which amounted to political suicide. They agreed only to draft a declaration of

---

[19] Ibid., pp. 270–73.

[20] Beradt, op. cit., p. 18.

[21] Arendsee, op. cit., p. 30.

[22] K. Radek, 'November, Eine kleine Seite aus meinen Erinnerungen', *Archiv für Sozialgeschichte*, no. 2, 1962, p. 132 (originally in *Krasnaia Nov*, no. 10, 1926).

[23] Liebknecht's notebook: extracts in *Illustrierte Geschichte der deutschen Revolution*, op. cit., p. 203; and Pieck, *Correspondance Internationale*, no. 136, 14 November 1928, p. 1507. According to Drabkin (op. cit., pp. 102–3), the Karl Liebknecht Collection at the IML in Moscow contains a typed copy with the manuscript note 'Tagebuch von Karl Liebknecht?' at the end. He specifies that it was extracts from this text that appeared in the *Illustrierte Geschichte*.

intent, recognising that their point of view had come close to that of the Spartacists. Liebknecht did not think that this was enough, and declined the cooptation, but he agreed to be invited to attend the meetings of the USPD's Executive whenever an important decision had to be taken.[24]

Nothing remained for him but to turn towards the revolutionary delegates, who could supply him with a cadre and a wide network across all the factories in the capital, in short, an instrument for revolutionary action. He encountered no difficulty from this side. On 26 October the nucleus decided to transform itself into a provisional workers' council, and coopted three Spartacists, Liebknecht, Pieck and Meyer.[25] This improvised revolutionary leadership proceeded at once to discuss the situation and to consider perspectives, drawing the conclusion that they must be prepared for immediate action in the case that Max of Baden's government rejected peace discussions and issued a call for national defence.[26]

But Liebknecht was not satisfied with this analysis. He regarded it as purely passive, and even dependent upon the enemy's initiative. He refused to go along with the delegates, who declared that the masses were not ready to fight, at least unless the government provoked them. He saw proof of the opposite in the initiatives which were occurring across the country, and in the combativity of the youth, who had just held their congress in Berlin on 26–7 October. On the evening of the 26th, 2,000 people demonstrated in Hamburg, and twice that number in Friedrichshafen on the 27th. On the evening of the 27th, after speaking at a USPD meeting at the *Andreas Festsäle*, he led several hundred workers and youth towards the city centre, where they clashed with the police.[27] He believed that it was by activities of this kind, relying on the most combative elements, that the mobilisation of the masses would be achieved.

Liebknecht tried hard to convince the revolutionary delegates of this. During the day on 28 October, he had a long discussion with Däumig and Barth. He said that whatever happened, even if the government did not try to prolong the war in the name of 'national defence', the revolutionaries were obliged

---

[24] *Illustrierte Geschichte der deutschen Revolution*, op. cit., p. 203. *Vorwärts* of 29 November devotes an article to the relations between Liebknecht and the USPD, which, it argues, could only be established on a confused basis.

[25] *Illustrierte Geschichte der deutschen Revolution*, op. cit., p. 203; Pieck, op. cit., p. 1507.

[26] *Illustrierte Geschichte der deutschen Revolution*, op. cit., p. 203.

[27] Ibid., p. 87.

to mobilise the masses by means of meetings and demonstrations which would make them become aware of their strength, and would raise the level of their consciousness and their will to victory. Däumig and Barth hesitated, and came near to accusing Liebknecht of wishful thinking. In the end, they agreed only to hold meetings, and categorically rejected the suggestion of street demonstrations.[28]

At the full session that evening, the delegates accepted Pieck's proposal to distribute a leaflet calling on workers to ignore the notices being circulated calling on them to join the colours.[29] Liebknecht repeated his proposal systematically to organise meetings and street demonstrations, and proposed to concentrate them, as a start, on 3 November. Däumig, Barth and Müller opposed the proposal. In their opinion, it ran the risk of engaging prematurely in the decisive battle. They declared that the revolutionaries must strike only when they could be sure of success, and one of them referred ironically to Liebknecht's plan as 'revolutionary gymnastics'.[30]

In reality, Liebknecht's opponents in the provisional council were only repeating the arguments which the leaders of the USPD, who were no less opposed to open activity, were developing at the same time. Liebknecht tried in vain to convince them. He said that the mass movement could only develop in the streets, and that the leaders' duty was to lead them there as soon as possible. He added that those who retreated behind the argument that the relation of forces was still unfavourable were actually shrinking from a necessary confrontation because the situation would only become favourable to the revolutionaries from the moment when they joined battle. In particular, the soldiers would respect discipline and would carry out the orders of the officers as long as they did not have a serious prospect of revolution before them. It was only in the streets, by fraternising with the workers in uniform, that the workers could overcome the armed forces, materially superior but politically inferior when facing the united action of the working class.[31]

On 2 November, a joint meeting was held of the leaders of the USPD and the revolutionary delegates. Ledebour introduced an officer of the Second Guards' battalion, Lieutenant Waltz, who had come to him to say that he

---

[28] Ibid., p. 203.
[29] Ibid.
[30] Ibid. Drabkin (op. cit., p. 104), following the original version of Liebknecht's notebook, specifies that it was Barth.
[31] *Illustrierte Geschichte der deutschen Revolution*, op. cit., p. 203.

would place himself and his unit at the disposal of the revolutionary general staff for an insurrection.[32] Those present enthusiastically welcomed this newcomer who brought them armed forces and weapons, and at last made a successful insurrection conceivable. Waltz, under the alias of Lindner, was attached to Däumig in the technical preparations – military and strategic – for the coming insurrection.[33] However, the reports of the factory delegates remained pessimistic. Of the 120,000 workers which the network controlled, only 75,000 at the most were ready to respond by strikes and demonstrations at the first call of the leaders.[34] Could anyone imagine an insurrection occurring without a general strike taking place first? The leaders were also divided on this question.

Haase was enthusiastically backed by Müller in proposing to fix the date of the armed insurrection for 11 November, and to prepare for it immediately. Ledebour retorted that this proposal was no more than a cover for evasion and a refusal to act. In his opinion, the insurrection should be fixed for the next day but one, 4 November. Liebknecht, who, according to Pieck's testimony, had discussed the problem with the Russians in the embassy, opposed both proposals. In effect, he categorically rejected any suggestion which could lead to unleashing the armed insurrection without the necessary preparation and mobilisation of the masses.

In his view, they should issue the slogan of a general strike, and let the strikers themselves decide on organising armed demonstrations for an immediate peace, lifting of the state of siege, proclamation of the socialist republic, and a government of workers' and soldiers' councils. He declared that it was only in the course of the general strike that 'the level of activity would have to be raised by increasingly daring measures up to insurrection'.[35] In the vote, Ledebour's motion was rejected by 22 votes to 19, and Liebknecht's motion by 46 to 5. Nothing remained but Haase's motion, which amounted to a decision to wait.[36]

The outcome of this last discussion was a serious defeat for Liebknecht. The intervention of the Spartacist leader in the general staff of the revolutionary delegates could not overcome the hesitations of the majority of the factory

---

[32] Ibid.
[33] H. Müller, op. cit., p. 94.
[34] Pieck, op. cit., p. 1507.
[35] Ibid.; *Illustrierte Geschichte der deutschen Revolution*, op. cit., p. 203.
[36] Ibid.

delegates, nor, above all, the reservations or hostility of the USPD leaders. Not only was no progress made in respect of organisation and activities, but Liebknecht himself seemed to be morally a prisoner of the contradictions which, through the delegates, were gripping the USPD.

However, the situation differed elsewhere. The Spartacists occupied strong positions in the USPD in Stuttgart. One of their members, Fritz Rück, held the chair of the party executive in Württemberg, and they controlled the regional newspaper, *Der Sozialdemokrat*. Already in September, they were in a position to control a network of factory delegates, through a secret action committee of five members, which included Thalheimer and Rück himself.[37] Rück wrote:

> The problem is to set the masses into motion. This can only be done by starting in the factories. Our officially having joined the Independent Party, however politically distasteful it may be to us, leaves our hands free, and enables us to construct in the factories a well-knit system of people whom we can trust, under the cover of organising the legal party.[38]

Rück took part in the Spartacist conference on 7 October. After his return, on the 16th, he secretly brought together forty factory delegates to help organise an insurrection.[39] On the following day, the censors suspended *Sozialdemokrat* for a fortnight after Rück had taken the responsibility of ignoring their instructions. But the group had an underground press, and on 30 October, the local USPD voted to issue a manifesto in favour of calling a central meeting of a pre-parliament of workers' and soldiers' councils, and of organising a street demonstration.

During the night of 30–1 October, the workers on the night shift in the Daimler plant held a meeting to hear Rück, who appealed to them secretly to elect a workers' council. On 2 November, two delegates from the Stuttgart action committee who had taken part in the debates of the revolutionary delegates in Berlin, returned with the information that the insurrection would be fixed for 4 November.[40] The leaflets were printed on the night of 2–3 November. The council elected at Daimler was opened to delegates from

---

[37] Kolb, op. cit., p. 63.
[38] 'Journal of a Spartacist', *Illustrierte Geschichte der deutschen Revolution*, op. cit., p. 182.
[39] *Illustrierte Geschichte der deutschen Revolution*, op. cit., p. 82.
[40] Kolb, op. cit., p. 63; *Illustrierte Geschichte der deutschen Revolution*, op. cit., p. 182.

other plants, and decided on a general strike on the 4th, which was a success. The city-wide workers' council, formed from the enlarged Daimler council, elected a committee, chose Rück as its chairman, and decided on the election of workers' councils in all the factories. The committee decided to publish a journal, *Die Rote Fahne* [*The Red Flag*], which immediately called for a council republic to be established in Germany.[41]

But the movement that was born in Stuttgart remained isolated. The Berlin revolutionaries had decided to wait. The workers' council in Stuttgart controlled the city, where there were gigantic demonstrations, but was dangerously exposed, because the governmental and legal authorities in the *Land* remained in place. The workers in the Zeppelin plant in Friedrichshafen were influenced by the propaganda coming from Daimler, and had just formed their workers' council. Thalheimer and Rück went there to coordinate the activity, but were arrested *en route*.[42] The members of the Stuttgart council, deprived of their leaders and momentarily disoriented, were arrested in turn. The first battle of the vanguard was short, and the police everywhere were ready to respond.

In every large city they arrested activists, charging them with – of all things – offences committed during the January strikes. On 5 November, the Prussian police arranged a discovery of considerable amounts of propaganda material in the Soviet diplomatic bag, and the Reich government gave Joffe and the Soviet representatives in the embassy in Berlin six hours to leave German territory.[43] Was this a symbolic measure, to sever the links between the Russian Revolution of yesterday and the German Revolution of tomorrow? In any case, it was too late, because already the calendar of the revolution had been determined by the actions of the sailors in Kiel.

---

[41] Kolb, op. cit., p. 64. The report of the decisions of the Stuttgart workers' council on 4 November is in *Die Rote Fahne* of 5 November 1918, *Dokumente und Materialen*, Volume 2/2, op. cit., pp. 285–6.

[42] Kolb, op. cit., p. 65.

[43] *Die Regierung des Prinzen Max von Baden*, op. cit., pp. 541–5. According to *Berliner Tageblatt* of 7 November, the seized propaganda material included a pamphlet by Radek entitled *The Collapse of Imperialism and the Task of the International Working Class*, based on a speech in Moscow on 7 October, as well as the text of a leaflet distributed in the Daimler plant at Stuttgart a few days earlier.

The wave from Kiel

On 28 October, the crews of the naval vessels anchored at Wilhelmshaven moved into action. An order to prepare to go to sea gave rise to disturbing rumours that the General Staff was preparing to make a last stand to defend its honour in the North Sea. There were several demonstrations on board, with about a thousand men arrested and disembarked, and five warships were sent to Kiel.[44]

The movement was triggered by anxiety about the fate of the arrested men. The sailors remembered the fate of the mutineers in 1917, and sought support from the workers. On 1 November, they met in the trade-union centre in Kiel, and decided to hold a public meeting the next day.[45] On 2 November, police occupied the trade-union centre, and the sailors gathered on the parade ground. One of them, Karl Artelt, a USPD member who had been sentenced to five months imprisonment in 1917, proposed organising a street demonstration on the next day, and the sailors called for support in hand-written leaflets.[46]

On 3 November, there were several thousand sailors and soldiers intending to demonstrate, though their numbers were small compared with the size of the garrison. The demonstration was forbidden, and military units patrolled the town. Despite an appeal for calm from a trade-union official, the sailors decided to demonstrate in the streets. They ran into a patrol which opened fire; there were nine killed and twenty-nine wounded. The resulting shock set the men of the garrison in Kiel into motion, since now the sailors could not turn back.[47]

Meetings aboard ships took place that night. Artelt took the initiative of getting the first sailors' council of the German Revolution elected on board a torpedo-boat. In the early morning, he found himself at the head of a committee appointed by 20,000 men. The officers were overwhelmed. Admiral Souchon, the commander of the base, agreed to all the demands which Artelt presented to him in the name of his comrades: the abolition of saluting, shorter periods of service, more leave, the release of those arrested. That night the whole of the garrison was organised in a network of soldiers' councils. The red flag floated over the naval vessels, and many officers had been arrested

---

[44] Kolb, op. cit., p. 71.
[45] *Vorwärts und nicht vergessen*, op. cit., p. 91.
[46] Ibid., p. 92.
[47] Ibid., pp. 72–3.

by their men. On shore, the USPD and the SPD jointly called for a general strike and then for a workers' council to be formed which would fuse with the sailors' council.

The SPD leader Gustav Noske, whom the government appointed Governor of Kiel, hastened to recognise the authority of the new workers' and soldiers' council in order to calm the sailors, and to restrict the spread of the militancy.[48] By 6 November, calm seemed to have returned.

However, the Kiel mutiny set off a major blaze. The widespread fear of reprisals forced the sailors to widen the movement. In Cuxhaven, a USPD activist, Karl Baier, a worker conscripted into the navy, alerted the small network of trusted comrades which he had formed when he learned what was happening in Kiel. The sailors met in the trade-union centre on the night of 6 November. They elected a soldiers' council at the same time as the workers in the factories were preparing to establish a workers' council, of which Kraatz, who had been one of the organisers of the January strike in Berlin, was the chairman. The new council of workers and soldiers called for help from Hamburg, and Wilhelm Düwell was sent to assist them.[49] In Wilhelmshaven on the next day, 7 November, a demonstration of sailors led by a stoker, Bernhard Kuhnt, before the War a full-time Party worker in Chemnitz, set off a general strike. The same evening, workers and soldiers elected a council in which the SPD had a majority, with Kuhnt in the chair.[50]

In Bremen, nearly all of the revolutionary activists were either in prison or in the army, and the impulse had to come from outside. On 4 November, a mass meeting addressed by the USPD deputy Henke took place, which demanded an armistice, the abdication of the Kaiser, and lifting of the state of siege.[51] But the following days were calm. However, on 6 November, a train carrying arrested sailors broke down in the station. They escaped into the city and the shipyards, and appealed to the working people for help.[52] There was a spontaneous demonstration, and leading Independents placed themselves at its head. The prison doors were opened, and an Independent, Frasunkiewicz, called for workers' and soldiers' councils to be elected. The slogan of a socialist republic was well-received, but the meeting broke up

---

[48] H. Müller, op. cit., p. 26; Gustav Noske, *Von Kiel bis Kapp*, Berlin, 1920, pp. 8–24.
[49] Arendsee, op. cit., pp. 108–22.
[50] Kolb, op. cit., p. 78.
[51] *Illustrierte Geschichte der deutschen Revolution*, op. cit., p. 116.
[52] Ibid., pp. 116–7.

without having decided anything.[53] Only on 7 November did the strike, which began in the shipyards on the Weser, become general, and workers' councils were elected in all the factories. The central workers' and soldiers' council for the city was set up on 9 November.[54]

In Hamburg, on the evening of 5 November, the USPD held a meeting which had been arranged well in advance. Dittmann resisted the sailors who called for a demonstration to be organised for the release of those arrested, and secured the defeat of a motion by Wilhelm Düwell in favour of the election of workers' councils.[55] During the night, a leading seaman named Friedrich Zeller refused to accept defeat, and organised a group of sailors to seek support on the quayside. During the night, about a hundred people installed themselves in the trade-union centre, and issued an appeal for a central demonstration at midday.[56] During the morning, in response to the initiative of some activists – in particular the youth leader, Friedrich Peter, a deserter who had returned secretly to Hamburg – this was organised, and a provisional workers' council was formed at the trade-union centre, with two presidents at its head, Zeller and the local USPD leader, Kallweit.[57]

The improvised general staff of the Revolution sent detachments to occupy all the barracks. Peter met his death in an exchange of shots in front of one of them.[58] Forty thousand demonstrators gathered at the appointed hour. A USPD leader won applause when he called for the seizure of political power by the council of workers and soldiers. The left radical Fritz Wolffheim won approval for the slogan of a republic of councils, and Wilhelm Düwell for that of the dismissal of the local commanding general and the conversion of industry from wartime to peacetime production.[59] In the evening, the council of workers and soldiers was formed under the chairmanship of Heinrich Laufenberg, the left radical.[60] Meanwhile, Frölich, at the head of a group of armed sailors, occupied the offices and the printworks of the daily *Hamburger Echo*, and published there the first number of the newspaper of the workers' and soldiers' council of Hamburg, also entitled *Die Rote Fahne*.[61] He wrote:

---

[53] Kolb, op. cit., p. 79.
[54] *Illustrierte Geschichte der deutschen Revolution*, op. cit., p. 117.
[55] Kolb, op. cit., p. 77.
[56] Ibid.
[57] *Illustrierte Geschichte der deutschen Revolution*, op. cit., p. 113.
[58] Ibid., p. 191.
[59] Ibid., p. 193.
[60] Kolb, op. cit., p. 77.
[61] Arendsee, op. cit., p. 251.

'This is the beginning of the German Revolution, of the world revolution. Hail the most powerful action of the world revolution! Long live socialism! Long live the German workers' republic! Long live world Bolshevism!'[62]

The Revolution spreads like wildfire

The movement which began in the coastal cities spread irresistibly. On 6 November in Düsseldorf, there was fighting around a trainload of prisoners that stopped in the station, and the council of workers and soldiers was formed on the spot.[63]

In Bavaria, the movement was not initiated by the sailors, but by a revolutionary group working in the ranks of the USPD. Eisner, a former revisionist who had become a radical by way of pacifism, organised in Munich a discussion circle in which about a hundred workers and intellectuals took part. From amongst them were recruited the first members of the USPD in Bavaria. By the summer of 1918, there were barely 400 of them, but they were the educated cadres who exerted a decisive influence on the workers in the Krupp plant, and who could assemble a solid network of reliable supporters in the other enterprises. Moreover, they had close links with the wing of the Peasant League which was led by the blind man Gandorfer and sympathised with socialism. Eisner prepared for the Revolution by systematically using the desire of the masses for peace. On 7 November, he led a peace demonstration in the streets of Munich, in the course of which a decision was taken for a general strike and an attack on the barracks. The King of Bavaria fled, and Eisner became the President of the workers' and soldiers' council of the Bavarian Republic.[64]

In Halle, worker activists of the city marched off the train at the head of mutinous sailors on 6 November.[65] They won over the soldiers of the 14th Regiment of light infantry, and mounted attacks on the other barracks. A sailor, Karl Meseberg, a former local activist and member of the USPD, took the chair of the soldiers' council; it soon fused with the workers' council which had arisen from the activity of a network of delegates led by the

---

[62] *Illustrierte Geschichte der deutschen Revolution*, op. cit., p. 192.
[63] Arendsee, op. cit., pp. 472–7.
[64] Kolb, pp. 67–70.
[65] Arendsee, op. cit., p. 367.

Independents: the Independent Otto Kilian was chairman of the workers' and soldiers' council.[66]

In Erfurt, a strike on 7 November in solidarity with the Kiel mutineers made factory meetings possible, and a central council for the city was elected after a mass meeting on the same day.[67] In Hanau that same day, a demonstration of workers clashed with the police when a workers' and soldiers' council was formed with Schnellbacher, a Spartacist, in the chair.[68] Again, on 7 November, in Brunswick, sailors from outside the city organised a demonstration and forced the opening of the prison gates, whilst the striking workers appointed a workers' council. On 8 November, the ruling prince abdicated and the Spartacist August Merges, chairman of the workers' and soldiers' council, assumed the title of President of the Socialist Republic of Brunswick.[69]

In Leipzig, there was a small Spartacist group with about twenty-five members. They tried in vain to persuade a USPD meeting on 7 November to call a general strike. But, on the same day, some sailors from the ports organised the first street demonstrations, and appealed to the soldiers to act. The barracks were taken on 8 November, and a workers' and soldiers' council was proclaimed. In Chemnitz the day passed almost peacefully. Fritz Heckert returned on 8 November, and, through his leading positions in the building trade union and the USPD, he succeeded in organising simultaneously the strike and the election of a workers' and soldiers' council, which included Majority Social Democrats. He was elected its chairman on 9 November.[70]

The revolutionaries in Berlin continued to hesitate throughout these decisive days. The nucleus of the delegates met on 4 November, when the news from Kiel was announced. Liebknecht and Pieck proposed to begin the action on 8 or 9 November. But the majority of the delegates refused to call for a strike because these were workers' pay-days. They confined themselves to sending emissaries to the provinces, and to entrusting Pieck to draft a leaflet on the events in Kiel. There was another meeting on 6 November, when Liebknecht, who in the interval had been busy with unavailing attempts in private to

---

[66] *Illustrierte Geschichte der deutschen Revolution*, op. cit., p. 135.
[67] Arendsee, op. cit., pp. 426–7.
[68] F. Schnellbacher, *Hanau in der Revolution*, p. 13, cited in *Illustrierte Geschichte der Novemberrevolution in Deutschland*, op. cit., pp. 128–9.
[69] *Illustrierte Geschichte der deutschen Revolution*, op. cit., p. 130.
[70] Arendsee, op. cit., pp. 406–8, 469–70.

convince Däumig, repeated his insistence that the insurrection had to be preceded and prepared for by street demonstrations. He was again outvoted. The insurrection was called for 11 November at the earliest.

On 7 November, the Executive of the USPD met at the Party headquarters with the leaders of the revolutionary delegates and several representatives from provincial cities. Otto Brass, from Remscheid, and Dittmann sharply criticised the decisions which had been reached on the preceding day, for they did not think that the situation was ripe. Haase was still more reserved; he did not believe in the Revolution, and said that the Kiel revolt was an 'impulsive explosion', and that he had promised Noske not to do anything which could compromise the 'unity' between the two Social-Democratic Parties. Liebknecht once more repeated his proposal, and this time he had the support of the delegate from Düsseldorf. But the feelings in the meeting were rising high, and he vehemently denounced what he called 'the crude mechanical method of people who want to manufacture a revolution'. Once again, Däumig, Barth and Müller opposed him, and the decision for an insurrection on 11 November was confirmed. It was decided that the USPD Executive would take responsibility for it is a public appeal, but there was to be no action before 'the day'.[71]

The Majority Social Democrats felt the approach of the storm more acutely than anyone else. Since 23 October, their ministers in the government had been calling for Wilhelm II to abdicate.[72] On 31 October, Scheidemann and Ebert, and on 3 November a joint delegation from the Party and the trade unions,[73] told the Chancellor that the Kaiser had to go. Konrad Haenisch explained this attitude in a private letter:

> The problem is to resist the Bolshevik Revolution, which is rising, ever more threatening, and which means chaos. The Imperial question is closely linked to that of Bolshevism. We must sacrifice the Kaiser to save the country. This has absolutely nothing to do with dogmatic republicanism.[74]

Finally, the SPD presented an ultimatum to the government: if the Emperor did not abdicate by 8 November, they could no longer accept responsibility for what might happen.[75]

---

[71] Pieck, op. cit., p. 1507.
[72] P. Scheidemann, *Memoiren eines Sozialdemokraten*, Volume 2, Dresden, 1928 p. 262.
[73] Max von Baden, op. cit., pp. 539, 591.
[74] Quoted by Kolb, op. cit., p. 32.
[75] H. Müller, op. cit., p. 45.

On the morning of 8 November, Otto Franke and Liebknecht reached an agreement. They were uneasy, because time was passing. It was becoming increasingly difficult to hold back the workers, who were losing patience, and were in danger of launching isolated actions. Moreover, the police were closing in on the conspirators, and could thus behead the movement. In the end, also, the Majority Party, which was watching which way the wind was blowing, was getting ready to take control of the uprising and thereby neutralise it. From that point, every minute lost involved considerable risk to the revolutionaries – and Liebknecht did his utmost to convince Dittmann of this.[76]

When the delegates met again at the appointed time in their usual centre, they learned that their military specialist Lindner – Lieutenant Waltz – had been arrested, and decided to move their meeting to a room in the Reichstag.[77] Whilst they were on their way, Däumig was arrested; he had the plans for the insurrection in his briefcase. Luise Zietz, who was with him, managed to get away and gave the alarm. From that time, there could be no retreat because the police now had enough evidence to arrest everyone. Yet the USPD leaders – without Haase, who had gone to Kiel as a conciliator – still hesitated. In Liebknecht's absence, it was Barth who prevailed; they decided to draft, and to distribute as a leaflet, a call for an insurrection to overthrow the Imperial régime and establish a republic of councils. This would carry ten signatures, those of Liebknecht and Pieck, of Haase, Ledebour and Brühl, and of the revolutionary delegates, Barth, Franke, Eckert, Wegmann and Neuendorf.[78]

Liebknecht was not present, as he and his Spartacist comrades had decided to face the USPD and the delegates with an *fait accompli*, and to reject their procrastination. In company with Ernst Meyer and in the name of the Spartacist League, he was drafting another leaflet – which also would bear his signature – calling on the workers to fight for the conciliar republic and to join with the Russian working class in the fight for world revolution.[79] He was still not aware that the repression had finally driven his allies to cross the Rubicon.

That evening, the representatives of the SPD in the factories reported to the Party leaders. They declared unanimously that in every factory the workers

---

[76] *Illustrierte Geschichte der deutschen Revolution*, op. cit., p. 204.
[77] Pieck, op. cit., p. 1507.
[78] Ibid., p. 1508. Text in Barth, op. cit., p. 53.
[79] Pieck, op. cit., p. 1508. Text in *Dokumente und Materialen*, Volume 2/2, op. cit., pp. 324–5.

were ready to act on 9 November, and that there could no longer be any question of holding them back.[80] The calls to battle would go out to men who wished to fight.

That point marks the beginning of the Revolution. Those who wanted it and were trying hard to prepare it; those who wanted it but doubted whether they could start it, and thus wanted it to be provoked; and those who did not want it and had resisted it to the last moment – all were to leap aboard the juggernaut. The news from every part of Germany on the night of 8–9 November confirmed it: here the sailors and there the soldiers organised demonstrations, whilst workers came out on strike. Workers' and soldiers' councils were elected. The prisons were attacked and opened. The red flag, emblem of the world revolution, floated over the public buildings.

Berlin, 9 November

Leaflets calling for insurrection had been distributed in every workplace since dawn. Workers held meetings across the city, and assembled in all the industrial districts to march to the city centre. E.O. Volkmann writes in an often-quoted passage:

> The day which Marx and his friend desired all their lives had come at last. The Revolution was on the march in the capital of the empire. The firm tread, in step, of the workers' battalions echoed in the streets. They came from Spandau, from the workers' districts, from the north and east, and marched towards the city centre, the symbol of imperial power. To the fore were Barth's assault troops, revolvers and grenades in their hands, with the women and children preceding them. Then came the masses in tens of thousands, radicals, Independents, Majority socialists, all mingled together.[81]

The morning issue of *Vorwärts*, to be sure, warned against 'ill-considered action'[82] but the Majority Social Democrats took care not to place themselves in opposition to an irresistible current. Their factory representatives had met Ebert again early in the morning, and had quite unequivocally told him that

---

[80] H. Müller, op. cit., p. 45.

[81] E.O. Volkmann, *La Révolution allemande*, Paris, 1933, pp. 35–6. Cläre Derfert-Casper mentions in her memoirs a different and more probable order: 'In front, the armed men, then men without weapons, and in the rear the women.' (*Illustrierte Geschichte der deutschen Revolution*, op. cit., p. 149.)

[82] *Vorwärts*, 9 November 1918. A few hours later, a supplement called for a general strike.

the masses were following the Independents and were escaping completely from the influence of the Majority. What had to be avoided at all costs was the eventuality of the garrison resisting, thus leading to fighting in the streets. Then the worst could happen, there would be a bloody revolution, and the extremists would have power in their hands. Indeed, there were incidents where soldiers had been confined to barracks. An officer of the Naumburg Light Infantry regiment told *Vorwärts* that his men were ready to fire on the crowd. This is what the Majority Social Democrats wanted to avoid at all costs. Otto Wels went to the Alexander barracks, though warned not to do so; he spoke to the men from the roof of a motor car, and managed to convince them not to fire on the people, but on the contrary to march with them in this peaceful revolution.[83]

The other regiments in the garrison followed the example of the light infantry. A staff officer, Lieutenant Colin Ross, told Ebert that the High Command had given the order not to shoot.[84] *Vorwärts* put out a special leaflet: 'They Will Not Shoot'.[85] In the event, only one barracks opened fire. Amongst the demonstrators there were four deaths, including one of the Spartacists' youth leaders in Berlin, Erich Habersaath, a worker at Schwartzkopf.[86] Despite this episode, everything passed off in perfect order. The Majority Social Democrats, defeated in the factories, made up their losses in the barracks. When a body of workers led by former editorial staff of the daily paper tried to seize *Vorwärts* – the memory of its confiscation still rankled – they ran into an armed barricade mounted by machine-gunners from the Naumburg light infantry who had joined the Revolution two hours earlier.[87]

The meeting of the representatives of the SPD accepted Ebert's suggestion that they should propose to the Independents that they share the responsibilities of government.[88] However, Ebert, Scheidemann and Otto Braun waited several hours for a meeting of the USPD leaders, which in the end never took place.[89] Amongst the USPD leaders present, Dittmann was ready to accept the Majority's proposal, but Ledebour violently opposed it.[90] He immediately informed the group of revolutionary delegates, who discussed the question

[83] H. Müller, op. cit., pp. 46–8.
[84] Ibid., p. 49.
[85] Ibid., p. 48.
[86] *Illustrierte Geschichte der deutschen Revolution*, op. cit., p. 206.
[87] H. Müller, op. cit., p. 49.
[88] Ibid., p. 50.
[89] *Illustrierte Geschichte der deutschen Revolution*, op. cit., p. 208.
[90] H. Müller, op. cit., p. 50; Pieck, op. cit., p. 1058.

without being able to reach agreement. An improvised council of war around Barth shared out tasks; Liebknecht joined the columns that were marching on the Imperial Palace, Eichhorn headed for the police headquarters, whilst Adolf Hoffmann, a popular figure, reached the city hall at the head of the workers.[91]

At *Vorwärts* they hastened to assemble an action committee – it was soon renamed a workers' and soldiers' council – consisting of twelve factory workers, all party members, plus Ebert, Braun, Wels and Eugen Ernst.[92] It was this council which launched the call in the midday edition of *Vorwärts* for a general strike, and for the insurrection to establish a social republic.[93] The Social-Democrats signed their leaflets with the magic words 'workers' council', 'soldiers' council', 'people's committee'.

The Independents discussed the Majority's proposals at great length, but they had still reached no conclusion by midday, when Ebert, Scheidemann, Braun and the trade-union leader Heller were received by Max of Baden, who announced the abdication of Wilhelm II.[94] Ebert expressed some reservations about the future of the Imperial régime, but agreed to accept the post of Chancellor of the Reich within the framework of the Constitution. He at once issued an appeal for calm and discipline, and demanded that order be maintained.[95] At one o'clock, he told the USPD about the new situation, and repeated his offer of a share of governmental responsibilities. Oskar Cohn asked him whether he was ready to take Liebknecht into his government, to which he replied that his party excluded no-one. The Independents continued their discussion, and promised to reply at six o'clock.[96]

During this time, the victorious crowd, full of enthusiasm and feeling its power, flooded the streets of Berlin, waved banners, chanted slogans, and rushed to support leaders who offered it an objective. The infantry guarding the police headquarters surrendered without a struggle to Eichhorn's followers, and handed over their weapons to the attackers. Six hundred political prisoners were set free, and Eichhorn took over the office of the police chief and his functions.[97] Since one o'clock the Moabit prison had, under the assault of

---

[91] Pieck, op. cit., p. 1058.
[92] H. Müller, op. cit., p. 59.
[93] *Dokumente und Materialen*, Volume 2/2, op. cit., p. 230.
[94] H. Müller, op. cit., p. 51.
[95] *Dokumente und Materialen*, Volume 2/2, op. cit., p. 333.
[96] H. Müller, op. cit., p. 52.
[97] Emil Eichhorn, *Meine Tätigkeit im Berliner Polizeipräsidium und mein Anteil an den Januar-Ereignissen*, Berlin, 1919, p. 8.

soldiers and armed workers, been forced to open its gates and to let free many political prisoners, civilians and military, including Leo Jogiches, the organiser of the Spartacists.

A handful of officers tried to organise resistance in front of the university and later in front of the Prussian State Library. The crowd swept them away, and the Reichstag buildings surrendered without a shot being fired.[98] Tens of thousands of Berlin workers massed in front of the building; Scheidemann spoke from a balcony and tried to preach calm, but he then yielded to the shouting, and made the decision to proclaim the Republic – an almost revolutionary initiative for which Ebert was to criticise him sharply.[99] A little later, at the Imperial Palace, Liebknecht, who had already been speaking from the roof of a motor car, had the 'German Socialist Republic' proclaimed by acclamation. Then he went on to the balcony of the dwelling-place of the Hohenzollerns and announced:

> The rule of capitalism, which turned Europe into a cemetery, is henceforward broken. We remember our Russian brothers. They told us when they left: 'If within a month you haven't done as we did, we shall break with you.' It only took four days. We must not imagine that our task is ended because the past is dead. We now have to strain our strength to construct the workers' and soldiers' government and a new proletarian state, a state of peace, joy and freedom for our German brothers and our brothers throughout the whole world. We stretch out our hands to them, and call on them to carry to completion the world revolution. Those of you who want to see the free German Socialist Republic and the German Revolution, raise your hands![100]

A forest of arms was raised.

The revolutionary leaders continued their discussions. Ledebour firmly opposed any collaboration with the SPD, and seemed at first to win a majority to support him. But there soon appeared the first delegations of soldiers. Some were spontaneous, but others, very numerous, were organised by the SPD, like the one led by Max Cohen-Reuss, an old Party supporter who had only recently become a soldier. They all insisted upon unity of the socialists, and their alliance in the government to defend the Revolution, peace and

---

[98] *Illustrierte Geschichte der deutschen Revolution*, op. cit., p. 152.
[99] H. Müller, op. cit., p. 53; Scheidemann, op. cit., Volume 2, p. 313.
[100] *Vossische Zeitung*, 10 November 1918; *Illustrierte Geschichte der deutschen Revolution*, op. cit., pp. 209–10.

brotherhood. Other delegations, particularly of workers, had their own grounds for calling on Liebknecht to join the government, as a guarantee of the will of the German Revolution for peace. When Liebknecht arrived late in the afternoon, he estimated that the USPD could not categorically refuse all collaboration with the SPD, as Ledebour proposed, without running the risk of being misunderstood, and of appearing to the masses to be enemies of the unity which they desired.[101]

He won the support of Müller and Däumig for imposing six conditions: proclamation of the German Socialist Republic, legislative, executive and judicial power to be in the hands of elected representatives of workers and soldiers, no bourgeois ministers, participation by the USPD to be limited to the time needed to conclude the armistice, technical ministries under the control of a purely political departmental staff, and equal representation of the socialist parties in the cabinet.[102] Ledebour alone declared that he opposed participation even on these conditions.[103]

The reply of the USPD leaders was finally communicated to the SPD at eight o'clock in the evening. In the meantime, the latter had tried a new initiative, and declared that the delegation to sign the armistice would not set out until the government had been formed. The SPD's answer reached the USPD at nine o'clock. The leaders of Ebert's party accepted the last two conditions, and rejected the first four. In their opinion, nothing but a constituent assembly, elected by universal suffrage, could decide the nature of the German régime, and the provisional government should remain in place until that assembly was convened and elected. They declared above all that they opposed any 'class dictatorship', and wanted bourgeois parties to join the government.[104]

The USPD leaders were deeply divided, and, deprived throughout of the advice of Haase, they put off their decision until the next day.[105] That evening there appeared in Berlin two daily newspapers of the extreme Left, published on the presses of the great dailies which had been occupied during the day, the USPD's *Die Internationale*, and the Spartacists' *Die Rote Fahne*.[106]

---

[101] Pieck, op. cit., p. 1058.
[102] *Illustrierte Geschichte der deutschen Revolution*, op. cit., p. 210; *Vorwärts*, 10 November 1918.
[103] Pieck, op. cit., p. 1058.
[104] H. Müller, op. cit., p. 57; *Vorwärts*, 10 November 1919.
[105] H. Müller, op. cit., p. 58.
[106] Pieck, op. cit., p. 1058.

At 10 o'clock in the evening, the revolutionary delegates, joined by several hundred representatives of the insurgent workers, met, with Barth in the chair, in the great meeting hall of the Reichstag. The assembly regarded itself provisionally as the workers' and soldiers' council of the capital, and called for meetings in the factories and the barracks on the next day, 10 November, at 10 o'clock in the morning. They would elect delegates, one per 1,000 workers and one per battalion, to the general assembly projected for five o'clock in the evening at the Busch Circus, to appoint the new revolutionary government.[107] The Majority Social Democrats made no protest, although this decision threatened all that they had won during the day, but they were to devote the night to preparing for this decisive battle.

The Ebert government

Wels had played a central role during 9 November. His largely improvised action had in fact enabled the SPD to find the support which they needed in the Berlin garrison. A group of officers including Colin Ross signed an appeal to the officers to collaborate in maintaining order, and to support the new government.[108] The problem now for the SPD was to organise this support systematically, and to make use of it for the mass meeting in the Busch Circus.

During the night of 9–10 November, Wels drafted and had printed in 40,000 copies a leaflet addressed 'to the men of the troops who support the policy of *Vorwärts*'.[109] Ebert appointed him military commandant of the capital,[110] and Colonel Reinhard issued orders to all the commanders of units to allow men accredited by him to enter the barracks.[111] The theme of the activity of Wels's people lies in the banner headline in *Vorwärts*: 'No Fratricidal Struggle'.[112]

Haase arrived during the night. At first, he inclined towards refusing participation, but he changed his mind when the executive met at 10 o'clock the next morning, and insisted that the USPD must not create an obstacle to agreement amongst socialists by adhering in full to the conditions laid down the preceding day. Neither Liebknecht nor the leaders of the revolutionary

---

[107] Ibid.; H. Müller, op. cit., p. 58.
[108] Text in H. Müller, op. cit., p. 61.
[109] Ibid., p. 62.
[110] Ibid., p. 82.
[111] Kolb, op. cit., p. 117.
[112] *Vorwärts*, 10 November 1918.

delegates were present, because they were busy with preparations for meetings and assemblies in the factories, but Liebknecht, who had been kept informed of what was going on, announced that he would not join the government if the USPD reneged on its conditions.[113] The negotiations went on without him. In the end, at half past one that afternoon, the representatives of the two Social-Democratic Parties agreed on a text:

> The cabinet is formed exclusively of Social Democrats, who are people's commissars with equal rights. This does not apply to holders of ministerial portfolios, technical assistants to the cabinet, which alone determines policy. Each ministry is controlled by two members of the Social-Democratic Parties, with equal powers. Political power is in the hands of the workers' and soldiers' councils, which will very soon be convened to a meeting representing the whole Reich. The question of the constituent assembly will not be posed before the new order, which is today being established by the revolution, has been consolidated, and it will be the subject of later discussions.[114]

The leaders of the two parties also agreed on names; Ebert, Scheidemann and Landsberg, nominated by the SPD on the preceding day, were to be joined by Dittmann, Haase and Barth for the USPD.[115]

At two o'clock, Wels brought together in the *Vorwärts* premises the representatives of his party in the factories and the soldiers' delegates, in order to prepare for the Busch Circus meeting, which at all costs had to endorse the agreement between the Party leaderships. He explained to the soldiers that they should defend the right of 'the whole people' against the supporters of the rule of the councils alone, and they should demand that a national assembly be elected. One of the leaders at his side recognised in the crowd of soldiers the son of a Party veteran. That is how Brutus Molkenbuhr became the leader of the soldiers who supported the Majority.[116]

The meeting began late. Over 1,500 delegates occupied the hall, the workers in the gallery and the soldiers down below surrounded the platform. The atmosphere was stormy; speakers were frequently interrupted, people brandished weapons, and there were fist fights. There were hardly any

---

[113] *Illustrierte Geschichte der deutschen Revolution*, op. cit., p. 211.
[114] Ibid., pp. 210–11.
[115] H. Müller, op. cit., p. 65.
[116] Ibid., pp. 69–70.

stewards, and a certain number of people without mandates were let in. Several times scuffles broke out, and it was feared that shots might be exchanged. Barth was in the chair in his capacity as representative of the 'workers' council', and he easily won confirmation of a secretariat which had perhaps already been negotiated, with Lieutenant Waltz as Vice-Chairman and Brutus Molkenbuhr as Secretary.[117] He then called on Ebert to explain the situation: 'The conditions of the armistice which the capitalists and imperialists of the Entente are imposing are very hard, but we must accept them to put an end to the slaughter.'[118] He announced to the delegates that the two Social-Democratic Parties agreed to form a government on a basis of equality, with no bourgeois ministers. Haase followed him, speaking in the same sense, and confirmed the agreement.

Liebknecht was very calm but incisive. His task was not easy, because he had the vast majority of the soldiers against him, breaking into his speech with interruptions and insults, even threatening him with their weapons, and shouting 'Unity! Unity!' at every one of his attacks on the Majority Social Democrats. He warned the delegates against illusions about unity, recalling how the SPD – 'these people who today are with the Revolution, and were its enemies only the day before yesterday' – had collaborated with the General Staff, and denounced the manoeuvres which aimed at using the soldiers against the workers. He repeated: 'The counter-revolution is already on the move, it is already in action, and is here in our midst.'[119]

The election of the Executive Committee of the councils in Berlin gave rise to a confused battle. Barth first proposed to elect the bureau of the assembly, nine soldiers and nine workers. Müller presented a list prepared by the revolutionary delegates which included the members of the nucleus who had prepared the insurrection, and, alongside the principal delegates, Barth, Ledebour, Liebknecht and Luxemburg. But the soldiers protested loudly at this. The Social-Democratic delegate Büchel then demanded that there should be parity of representation between the two workers' parties. Ebert supported him, whilst Barth and Müller opposed the proposal.

---

[117] We have followed here the account given in *Vossische Zeitung*, 11 November 1918, which we have compared with those given by H. Müller (op. cit., pp. 70–2); and R. Müller (op. cit., pp. 36–7). A stenographic record of this meeting exists in the Berlin IML. Extracts from this are cited by Drabkin, op. cit., pp. 165–7.

[118] *Vossische Zeitung*, 11 November 1918.

[119] Cited by Drabkin, op. cit., p. 166.

The soldiers brandished their weapons and chanted 'Parity! Parity!', and Ebert put on a show of withdrawing the Büchel proposal. But then a printworker declared that no newspapers would appear if a parity government was not set up. A soldiers' delegate said that the soldiers would form their own Executive if parity were not agreed. The demand of parity of the workers' representation was unreasonable, because in the factories the SPD was far from being as well represented as the USPD. Therefore the bureau, with the unanimous support of the SPD, advanced a compromise proposal: nine from the USPD and three from the SPD, to represent the workers.

But the soldiers, whom Wels's people had organised, continued their obstruction. In the end, Barth gave way and advanced a proposal which met their demands: an Executive made up of twelve soldiers' delegates, Majority Social Democrats or men under their influence, and twelve workers' delegates, six SPD and six USPD. Liebknecht, whose name was proposed along with that of Pieck and Luxemburg for the USPD list, indignantly refused, and protested against this gross violation of the most elementary democracy, in which a rowdy minority was absolutely preventing the majority from declaring its position through a vote. In the end, six members of the nucleus of revolutionary delegates agreed to stand as candidates to represent the 'independent' faction of the revolutionary delegates. These were Barth, Müller, Ledebour, Eckert, Wegmann and Neuendorf. After a brief recess, Müller came forward to propose to the assembly in the name of those elected, that the list of six People's Commissars who had already been nominated by their respective parties be endorsed, and the sitting ended.[120]

Thus the second day of the German Revolution found the Majority Social Democrats, who had done their utmost to prevent it, winning an indisputable victory. Their leader Ebert, Chancellor of the Reich by the grace of Max of Baden, People's Commissar by that of the general staffs of the two Social-Democratic Parties, found his position endorsed by the first assembly of the councils in the capital, so that he became, at one and the same time, head of the legal government and of the revolutionary government!

We should, however, not exaggerate the importance of the defeat of the revolutionaries on the second day of the revolution; it had only just begun. This, at any rate, was what Moscow thought. Spontaneous demonstrations of

---

[120] Ibid., pp. 165–7.

satisfaction took place there, and Radek was to write later: 'Tens of thousands of workers broke out into wild cheers. I have never seen anything like it. Late in the evening, workers and red soldiers were still parading. The world revolution had come. Our isolation was at an end.'[121]

---

[121] Radek, *November*, op. cit., p. 121.

Chapter Nine

The Period of Dual Power

Western historians generally claim that the German Revolution of November 1918 was not a real revolution. They stress the insignificance of the activity of the German councils, their improvised nature, their hesitant behaviour, and, finally, their powerlessness. Comparing them with the events in Russia, they draw the conclusion that the German councils were not real soviets, but ephemeral organisations, transitory forms born out of a passing infatuation and a rather romantic fashion.[1]

The official interpretations in the German Democratic Republic have led certain historians to analogous positions. Whilst both the Bolsheviks and the Spartacists in 1918 had seen in the development in Germany of the workers' and soldiers' councils proof of the proletarian character of the German Revolution, a specialist in East Germany actually stated during a public discussion that the German councils were 'organs of the power of the bourgeoisie', in certain cases from the very start.[2]

For the Western historians, the problem is to show that a soviet revolution, a state apparatus formed on the basis of a pyramid of councils, in an advanced country, was effectively utopian. For the others, the

---

[1] Those who support this thesis usually refer to the councils in Munich, as they did resemble the model which these historians suppose was the norm.

[2] W. Kleen, 'Über die Rolle der Räte in der Novemberrevolution', *Zeitschrifte für Gewissenschaft*, no. 2, 1956, pp. 326–30.

task is to prove that no revolution could have a proletarian character without the 'firm leadership' of a party 'of a Marxist-Leninist type'. Both of these theses are partisan, but both express some truth; what was lacking in the German soviets in 1918 was the concerted activity of patient explanation which the Bolsheviks carried on in Russia, which enabled them to strengthen the soviets and their authority between February and October, and to win the majority in the soviets so that they could become a weapon in the struggle for power.

But it would be a mistake to go on to compare the German councils in November 1918 to the Russian soviets in November 1917. We need to compare them first to the soviets in February 1917; both had emerged from largely spontaneous activity before the great political debate about power had developed. Despite the weakness of their organisation, the German revolutionaries played a more important role in the formation of the councils than the Bolsheviks did in the formation of the soviets. Moreover, the bourgeoisie recognised this factor, both in Germany and in the countries of the Entente.

In reality, the chances of a German soviet revolution appeared on 9 November 1918 to be more serious than those of a Russian soviet revolution in February 1917. To be sure, the councils in all the workers' centres were divided between the two influences of the SPD and the USPD. In Russia, the Mensheviks and the Socialist Revolutionaries were in the majority across the country, including on the Petrograd Soviet. In Germany, on the contrary, the revolutionaries, left Independents, International Communists and Spartacists, partisans of the dictatorship of the proletariat, led some of the most important councils. Müller in Berlin, Kurt Eisner in Munich, Rück in Stuttgart, Heckert in Chemnitz, Lipinski in Leipzig, Merges in Brunswick, Laufenberg in Hamburg, all were chairmen of councils of workers and soldiers, the authority of which spread over whole regions. For the rest, there was apparently neither more nor less disorder in the tumultuous birth of the German councils than there had been in that of the soviets, or than there was to be in 1936 in the committees or *consejos* in Spain.

The councils of workers and soldiers

The essential difference between the German councils in November 1918 and the soviets in February 1917 lies in the place which the old workers' parties and trade unions occupied in them. This is explained in the first place by the different traditions in the two countries, which in Russia saw soviets become the form of organisation *par excellence*, whilst in Germany the political and trade-union organisations had been for a long time a permanent and determining factor in working-class life.

In Cologne, after trying to create a committee [Wohlfahrtsausschuss] to include representatives of the bourgeois parties, amongst them Dr Konrad Adenauer,[3] the local leaders of the Social-Democratic Parties ended by forming a workers' council, in the course of a meeting on 8 November, which was ratified by acclamation in a meeting that afternoon. In Kassel, the council and its action committee were formed on the 9th following discussions between the trade unions and the two workers' parties, and were confirmed on the 13th by an assembly of 600 delegates elected by workers and soldiers. In Breslau, on the 9th, the SPD and the Catholic Centre Party invited the USPD to join them in forming a 'people's committee' in which Paul Löbe, a Social Democrat, was to preside. This committee was 'elected' on the 13th by a meeting of 30,000. A similar procedure resulted in workers' councils including representatives of the Centre and of the Christian trade unions in Duisberg, Recklinghausen and Bielefeld, where the operation was carried through by the Social Democrat Carl Severing.[4]

In general, these procedures remained exceptional, and could only be used where the revolutionary movement had been manipulated or pre-empted by the initiatives of the politicians or the reformist apparatus. Whatever confusion existed amongst the revolutionaries over the precise definition of councils, all agreed that they had to be democratic, and this bluntly contradicted any idea of rigged elections or votes by acclamation. Most of the time, the working people wanted an elected council. The Social Democrats, ever loyal to their 'democratic principle', wanted elections on a territorial basis, by districts; suffrage was 'universal', and public figures, such as members of the apparatus, could, as in ordinary elections, defeat candidates known for their class positions. Thus, in Dresden, where elections by districts were organised by the provisional council, they gave 47 seats out of 50 in the workers' 'college' and 40 seats out of 50 in the soldiers' 'college' to the SPD.[5] The workers' and soldiers'

---

[3] Tormin, op. cit., p. 59.
[4] Kolb, op. cit., pp. 83, 91–2.
[5] Ibid., p. 96.

council in Dresden, under the chairmanship of Neuring, a Social-Democratic trade unionist, was thereafter one of the most conservative.[6]

Elsewhere, the elections were held in the factories according to the principle of the dictatorship of the proletariat, where the right to vote was organised on the basis of units of production. In Berlin, the workers elected one delegate per thousand votes in the big factories, and one delegate per part of a thousand elsewhere.[7] In Frankfurt-am-Main, the figure was one per 400, in Hamburg and Leipzig it was one per 600, in Stuttgart one per 300, and in Bremen one per 180.[8]

In many places, SPD members demanded that the elections in the factories be boycotted. In Brunswick, they demanded as a precondition, whatever the outcome of the vote, a pledge of equal representation on the Executive. They met with refusal and therefore did not stand, and 5,454 electors chose 25 names from a list of 50 drawn up by the provisional committee. In Stuttgart, on the contrary, after the members of the first provisional council were arrested, the SPD obtained a clear majority in the elections, with 155 delegates out of 300 seats, as against 90 for the USPD. In Leipzig, no Majority organisation had existed since the split, and nearly all those who were elected belonged to the USPD. In the Weser shipyards in Bremen, the left radicals won 24 seats against the SPD's 13 and the USPD's nine, and the SPD members took their seats. But, in Hamburg, they only agreed to take part at the last moment, when the other groups promised them representation on the Executive.[9]

Whenever there appeared a majority against them in the workplace elections, the local SPD and trade-union leaders called for unity and appealed to the Berlin agreement of 9 November to get parity of representation on the executive. These demands, however, did not contradict the concerns of those elected, as the participation of representatives of parties and trade unions in the councils served to strengthen their authority. In Leipzig, the Executive included, besides 10 workers and 10 soldiers, three representatives of the USPD. That in Hamburg included 18 elected members, nine from each college, and 12 representatives of organisations, three from each political party, the SPD, the USPD and the left radicals, and three from the local trade unions.

---

[6] *Illustrierte Geschichte der Weber Revolution*, op. cit., p. 381.
[7] Drabkin, op. cit., p. 159.
[8] Kolb, op. cit., pp. 94–6.
[9] Ibid., pp. 95–6.

Events in most places followed the course of those in Berlin; the Independents surrendered proportional representation, to their own disadvantage, and agreed to parity on the Executive, even when they had a majority in the council, as in Frankfurt-am-Main, Dortmund, Erfurt and the majority of industrial cities. Only when the SPD either did not exist or refused to join in did they form the Executive, for example in Bremen, Leipzig, Halle and Düsseldorf. The SPD, however, was not interested in parity where it was strong. In Stuttgart, the USPD had only four seats out of a total of 15.[10]

In the pyramid of councils from the workplace to the locality, the influence of the SPD and the trade-union apparatus became stronger the closer to the summit. They therefore worked hard in the weeks which followed the establishment of the councils to form regional councils in which they kept a majority, simply by adding the councils which they controlled, or in which they enjoyed parity.

It is not surprising, therefore, in these conditions, that many of the initiatives of the councils in November were limited to the framework of the constitution or to the level of proclamations, and were satisfied to oscillate between the anti-soviet line of the SPD, and the 'hesitation waltz' of the USPD. For all that, some of the councils clearly expressed the will to construct a state of a new, strictly soviet, kind. A few councils abolished the existing institutions. In Chemnitz, Leipzig and Gotha, they declared the municipal councils dissolved, and in Hamburg, Bremen and Koenigsberg they dissolved the traditional institutions of Senate and Burghers.[11] Other councils did this without even saying so, contenting themselves with driving out of their committees senior bureaucrats or traditionally-elected people.

The council in Bremen went further, and prohibited any meeting or demonstration in favour of the re-establishment of the Senate or of elections to the National Assembly.[12] The council in Neukölln, which was dominated by the Spartacists, prohibited all activity by the old organisations, and declared the police force dissolved. This Berlin district was denounced in the press as being the test-bed for the dictatorship of the proletariat.[13] The situation was

---

[10] Ibid.

[11] M. Einhorn, 'Zur Rolle der Räte im November und Dezember 1918', *Zeitschrifte für Gewissenschaft*, no. 3, 1956, p. 548; on Hamburg, see R.A. Comfort, *Revolutionary Hamburg*, Stanford, 1966, p. 46. The measure was to be rescinded shortly afterwards (ibid., p. 48).

[12] *Illustrierte Geschichte der deutschen Revolution*, op. cit., p. 195.

[13] *Vossische Zeitung*, 4 December 1918.

not dissimilar in Britz, Mariendorf and Tempelhof. A conference of councils of workers and soldiers for the Niederbarnim constituency on 18 November called for such measures to be introduced throughout Germany.[14]

In the Ruhr, a conference of the councils in Lower Rhineland and Western Westphalia was held on 20 November, and adopted a motion by the Independent Otto Brass for all existing state structures to be dissolved, and for power to pass to the councils. A programme of action for the councils laid down what this meant – the disarming of the police, the construction of a red guard, the organisation of a security force, and the control of justice, food supplies, etc. This was carried out or at least embarked upon in every city where revolutionary Independents and Spartacists held the majority in the council, in Düsseldorf, Gelsenkirchen, Hamborn, Müllheim, Solingen, Essen, etc. The workers' and soldiers' council in Gotha dissolved the Landtag and formed a Land government.[15]

An important development which signified the will of the revolutionaries to create an alternative centre of power was the formation by the councils of their own armed force or police.[16] There were workers' guards in Frankfurt-am-Main and Hildenburghausen,[17] workers' volunteers in Düsseldorf,[18] a security force in Hamburg[19] and, most often, red guards, the nuclei of which were formed by mutinous sailors, for example, under the leadership of the non-commissioned officer Lunsmann[20] in Bremen, in Halle the 'security regiment', led by the former officer Fritz Ferchlandt and the 'red sailor' Karl Meseberg,[21] and in Brunswick, a guard numbering a thousand.[22]

Lastly, in the councils led by revolutionaries, the Executives provided themselves with structures suited to the tasks of government, with individuals or commissions responsible for finance, public security, food supplies, labour problems, and so on. They took upon themselves powers at every level, those of the judiciary as well as of the legislature or the executive, in accordance with the very character of soviet power. The workers' and soldiers' council in Essen seized and closed down the *Rheinischer Westfälischer Zeitung* on

---

[14] *Illustrierte Geschichte der deutschen Revolution*, op. cit., p. 193.
[15] Ibid., pp. 195–8.
[16] H. Oeckel, *Die revolutionäre Volkswehr 1918–1919*, East Berlin, 1968.
[17] Einhorn, op. cit., p. 549.
[18] *Vorwärts und nicht vergessen*, op. cit., p. 48.
[19] Kolb, op. cit., p. 295; Comfort, op. cit., p. 53.
[20] *Illustrierte Geschichte der deutschen Revolution*, op. cit., p. 239.
[21] *Vorwärts und nicht vergessen*, op. cit., p. 368.
[22] Kolb, op. cit., p. 294.

3 December, and a few days later the *Essener Allgemeine Zeitung*. The council in Hanau prohibited any dismissals, and imposed the eight-hour working day. That in Mülheim decreed pay increases of 80 per cent,[23] and that in Leipzig took possession of the press and propaganda department of the military command.[24] The most alert politicians were not mistaken; Hermann Müller was to write that the republic of Neukölln was on the way towards bringing about 'a class dictatorship like that in Soviet Russia'.[25]

Throughout Germany, the revolutionaries who took part in the activities of the councils were at the forefront of the battle for an alternative structure of power. The early days of November unexpectedly provided one single contrary example, that of Württemberg, where for several days all the workers' parties, including the Spartacists, collaborated in a provisional structure which enjoyed a legal authority, the 'provisional government' of Württemberg, which was empowered by the Landtag immediately after the Revolution. Two Spartacist activists held responsible posts in it. August Thalheimer, who had just been freed from prison, was in charge of finance and Albert Schreiner in charge of war.[26] But the Spartacist Zentrale reacted sharply, and a letter signed by Jogiches explained to the Württembergers that it would be a serious mistake to share responsibilities of government with the SPD in the given circumstances.[27] Thalheimer immediately resigned, and was soon followed by Schreiner.[28]

The parties and the councils

It is indicative of the dash and vigour of the conciliar movement that no one tried at first to oppose the formation of councils or to contest their authority. Here and there, the representatives of the bourgeois parties were glad when the protection of the Social Democrats kept a little place open for them.[29] The High Command itself recognised the existence of the soldiers'

---

[23] *Illustrierte Geschichte der deutschen Revolution*, op. cit., pp. 194–6.
[24] Ibid., p. 198.
[25] H. Müller, op. cit., pp. 141–2.
[26] *Kreuz-Zeitung*, 11 November 1918, and for a commentary on this matter, see Drabkin, in *Noyabrskaya Revoliutsiia v Germanii*, op. cit., pp. 374–6.
[27] The full text of this letter, dated 11 November and addressed to Thalheimer, was published for the first time by Drabkin, *Noyabrskaya Revoliutsiia v Germanii*, op. cit., pp. 377–8.
[28] W. Keil, *Erlebnisse eines Sozialdemokraten*, Volume 2, Stuttgart, 1948, p. 107.
[29] We have already seen the case of Cologne, where the burgomaster Konrad

councils. At the headquarters in Spa, Lieutenant-Colonel Faupel received their delegates; he described to them the immense task of getting the troops back home from the Western front, and asked them to collaborate with the officers.[30] The authority of the councils was recognised to varying degrees by the imperial authorities, the administration, the police, the courts and the military commands.

However, one of the first initiatives taken against the power of the workers' and soldiers' councils was the forming of citizens' councils, which were sometimes divided into professional councils for doctors, lawyers, judges and even landowners and priests.[31] In Cologne, for example, whilst the *Kölnische Zeitung* said that the bourgeoisie was ready to support the new power structures,[32] a number of the city's businessmen founded the Hansabund, the purpose of which was to form citizens' councils.[33] The *Deutsche Zeitung* approved this appeal, and wrote that councils alone would not suffice, but that 'confronted by "one-sided" workers' guards, it is necessary to organise "civic guards"'.[34]

The bourgeois parties and the authorities accepted the councils as a real power, though a very transitory one, which conferred a provisional legitimacy on existing authorities which had no longer any constitutional standing: the aim was to use them to change the situation to their advantage. That, briefly, was the viewpoint of the Social Democrats. They considered that the councils were transitory institutions, relevant only to the period of the fall of the Imperial régime, and that they must relinquish the power which they had seized, because they represented only part of the population. Friedrich Stampfer explained this in *Vorwärts* on 13 November: 'We have been victorious, but we have not been victorious for ourselves alone. We have been victorious for the entire people. That is why our slogan is not "All power to the soviets", but "All power to the whole people".'[35]

Adenauer played an important role as president of the *Wohlfahrtsausschuss*; in Breslau, out of 100 people elected to the council, 34 belonged to bourgeois parties (Drabkin, op. cit., p. 226).

[30] J.W. Wheeler-Bennett, *The Nemesis of Power*, London, 1954, p. 26.

[31] Drabkin, op. cit., p. 225. In Bonn, the workers' and soldiers' council was to fuse with that of the citizens (*Kölnische Zeitung*, 12 November 1918, evening edition).

[32] *Kölnische Zeitung*, 12 November 1918 (morning edition).

[33] Drabkin, *Die Novemberrevolution 1918 in Deutschland*, op. cit., p. 224.

[34] *Deutsche Zeitung*, 13 November 1918.

[35] *Vorwärts*, 13 November 1918.

Within this perspective, the role of the councils henceforth was to help establish a new 'democratic' régime, based on the election by universal suffrage of a national assembly, which would have constituent power, and which alone could express the will of 'the people'.

On this basis, that of the struggle for the rapid convocation of a constituent assembly which would strip the councils of their power, and establish a democratic constitution, the SPD was the spearhead of a coalition bringing together the entire array of old political forces and, behind them, the possessing classes. We cannot fail to be struck by the speed with which the authorities and politicians merged into this 'democratic' movement, in order to fight against the Revolution and to defend order and property. Conservatives and reactionaries proclaimed themselves from one day to the next to be republicans and democrats, partisans of 'the sovereignty of the people', which hitherto had seemed to be the least of their concerns.

Kreuz-Zeitung's old motto 'Forward for God, King and Country!' disappeared, and the paper called for universal suffrage.[36] The Catholic Centre renamed itself the People's Christian Democratic Party. The conservatives regrouped in the People's National German Party, which included in its programme universal suffrage, parliamentary government, and freedom of publication and opinion. The fusion of the old Progressives with part of the old National Liberals produced the German Democratic Party. The remainder of the National Liberals, under the presidency of Gustav Stresemann and with the support of Stinnes, Vögler, Röchling and other business magnates, floated the German People's Party. Junkers and bourgeois dressed themselves in democratic clothes, because the main objective was first to get rid of the councils.[37]

On this question there were no major differences within the government. Max of Baden and Ebert were agreed, and the declaration of 10 November provided for the election of a constituent assembly. The USPD's 'People's Commissars' were to raise technical objections, discuss the suitability of different dates and ask for time to 'prepare' the electoral campaign, but they chose the parliamentary republic in preference to the system of councils and the dictatorship of the proletariat.[38] Nonetheless, unanimity did not reign in the USPD on this point. The party's left wing – the leaders in Berlin and the

---

[36] Drabkin, op. cit., p. 296, n. 307.
[37] Ibid., pp. 293–6.
[38] Kolb, op. cit., pp. 157ff.

revolutionary delegates – fought for several months for the concept of power to the councils, and on this point at least agreed with the Spartacists.

In fact, the only ideologically coherent opposition to the programme of calling a constituent assembly came from the Spartacists. Luxemburg explained this clearly in *Die Rote Fahne*, which had reappeared:

> The choice today is not between democracy and dictatorship. The question which history has placed on the agenda is: *bourgeois* democracy or *socialist* democracy. For the dictatorship of the proletariat is democracy in the socialist sense of the term. The dictatorship of the proletariat does not mean bombs, putsches, riots or 'anarchy', as the agents of capitalism claim. It means using every means of political power to construct socialism, to expropriate the capitalist class, in agreement with and by the will of the revolutionary majority of the proletariat, in the spirit of socialist democracy. Without the conscious will and the conscious activity of the majority of the proletariat, there can be no socialism. A class organisation is needed to sharpen this consciousness, to organise this activity: the parliament of the proletarians of town and country.[39]

But the revolutionaries themselves were divided over the meaning and practical implications of this principled position. To be sure, they all believed, as Luxemburg was to declare at the Foundation Congress of the German Communist Party, that the workers' and soldiers' councils, like the Russian soviets, formed 'the watchword of the world revolution', 'the ABC of the revolution today', and the characteristic which distinguished the revolution in 1918 from the bourgeois revolutions which preceded it.[40] But disagreements began when it was a question of deciding what revolutionaries should do within councils in which they were in a minority.

In Dresden, the left radicals followed Otto Rühle on 16 November in resigning *en bloc* from the workers' and soldiers' council in the city; they thought that they should not be there because they found themselves in a minority, facing a coalition of SPD and USPD elected representatives, whom they summarily qualified as 'counter-revolutionaries'.[41] By this spectacular gesture, they rejected the perspective which Luxemburg was to trace when

---

[39] *Die Rote Fahne*, 20 November 1918.
[40] *Der Gründungsparteitag der KPD, Protokoll und Materialen*, Frankfurt am Main, 1969, p. 183.
[41] Text in *Dokumente und Materialen*, Volume 2/2, op. cit., pp. 403–4.

she said: 'It is from below that we shall undermine the bourgeois state, by acting so that the public powers, legislative and administrative, shall no longer be separate, but combined, and by placing them in the hands of the workers' and soldiers' councils.'[42]

The drama and the historic weakness of the German workers' and soldiers' councils is ultimately bound up with the fact that there did not exist a real 'conciliar party', to encourage and invigorate them, and to take part in the struggle for conciliar power, which the Bolsheviks were able to do between February and October 1917. On the decisive problem of 'constituent assembly or councils', the leaders of the right wing of the USPD, Haase, Dittmann, and so on, adopted, with a few fine differences, the positions of the SPD. The left-wing Independents, organised separately, generally shared the conception of the leading Spartacists. The Spartacists themselves were divided between the leading nucleus, which worked within the perspective that it was necessary to win the masses, and the impatient elements who gave up the task of convincing the masses. This confusion and the absence of a revolutionary organisation to lead a consistent struggle for winning the majority in the councils and for the seizure of state power by the councils, left the field clear for the enemies of the councils who were at work within them.

In Hamburg, only a few days after having announced their dissolution, the workers' and soldiers' council re-established the Burghers and the Senate as administrative organs. In the same city, the former officer Frederick Baumann was appointed by a member of the Senate named Petersen to struggle against the 'extremists' within the workers' and soldiers' council itself. He soon became a member of it by way of the soldiers' council, and he joined forces with the SPD to 'eliminate gradually the radicals from all their positions of control over the military or the police'. He even succeeded in getting himself put in charge of the red guard intended to protect the council.[43]

By collaborating with the old institutions, whose revival was assisted by the existence of the central government, the councils were being driven into a corner. Financial needs had them by the throat. They were undermined and eaten up from within. Soon, as Luxemburg wrote, 'they let slip the greatest part of the positions they had won on 9 November'.[44] They could not hold

---

[42] *Der Gründungsparteitag der KPD*, op. cit., p. 99.
[43] Comfort, op. cit., pp. 47, 52–3.
[44] 'Speech on the Programme', *Der Gründungsparteitag der KPD*, op. cit., p. 184.

out for long even where they resisted. The 'conciliar power' which was proclaimed in Neukölln on 6 December was annulled on the 11th by the executive of the councils in Berlin.[45] On 16 December, the Prussian government reintroduced the old institutions in Neukölln on the same day as the first congress of German 'soviets' opened in Berlin.[46]

The fact is that, despite its defeat, the German bourgeoisie was unquestionably more vigorous than the feeble Russian bourgeoisie in 1917. It had at its disposal an instrument of rare quality, the officer corps, and above all the total support of the flexible, experienced apparatus of Social Democracy, which would know how to defend effectively what it called 'order' against 'chaos', and 'freedom' against 'dictatorship'. It confirmed Liebknecht's warning on 10 November by finally enabling the positions of the counter-revolution to triumph within the very heart of the councils. Finally, the German bourgeoisie enjoyed the solid support of the armies of the Entente, the threatening shadow of which hung over this whole period of the German Revolution.

The bourgeois government

The assembly of the delegates of workers and soldiers at the Busch Circus on 10 November handed power to the six 'People's Commissars', who had for some hours been the Reich cabinet. Ebert, who was in this way installed by the Berlin 'soviet' as the President of the Council of People's Commissars, had already since the previous day been the Chancellor of the Reich appointed by Prince Max of Baden. In this way, the state of dual power resulted in a single summit, a two-faced government, soviet for the workers, bourgeois and legal from the standpoint of the state apparatus, the ruling classes, the army and the Entente, from which its representative Erzberger had, since 8 November, been appealing for the material means to fight Bolshevism.[47]

There can be no dispute today about the deal which was concluded between Chancellor Ebert and the army chiefs in these November days; even if the version about the telephone conversation between General Wilhelm Groener and Ebert on the night of 9–10 November can no longer be formally accepted.[48]

---

[45] H. Müller, op. cit., p. 142.
[46] Ibid., p. 219.
[47] Badia, Volume 1, op. cit., p. 119.
[48] On this question see L. Berthold and H. Neef, *Militarismus und Opportunismus gegen die Novemberrevolution*, East Berlin, 1958, and the comments on the telephone conversation reported by E.O. Volkmann (pp. 23–4).

On 10 November, Marshal Hindenburg telegraphed to the army chiefs that the General Staff had decided to collaborate with the Chancellor to 'avert the spread of terrorist Bolshevism in Germany'.[49] Groener appears to have been the prime mover of the agreement, and several years later he was to justify himself against right-wing critics when he declared:

> The officer corps could only cooperate with a government which undertook the struggle against Bolshevism. . . . Ebert had made up his mind on this. . . . We made an alliance against Bolshevism. . . . There existed no other party which had enough influence upon the masses to enable the re-establishment of a governmental power with the help of the army.[50]

The state apparatus and the bureaucracy continued to function under the authority of Ebert. Already on 9 November, he had called upon all state officials to remain at their posts.[51] On 13 November, a proclamation by the Council of People's Commissioners laid down that the Bundesrat, the legislative second chamber of the Imperial Constitution, that of the princes, would continue to 'be authorised to exercise without change in the future the functions laid upon it according to the laws and decrees of the Reich'.[52] All the administrative personnel, the whole body of high functionaries selected under the Imperial régime, remained in place.

Under the authority of the People's Commissars and, theoretically, the control of the elected members of the Executive of the Councils, with the representatives of the two Social-Democratic Parties, the bourgeois ministers retained their portfolios; General von Scheüch remained at the War Ministry, Dr Solf at Foreign Affairs, Schiffer, of the Centre, at the Ministry of Finance, and the Democrat Hugo Preuss as Secretary of State for the Interior.[53] Between the 9th and the 10th, Ebert had placed his own men in key posts at the top of the administration. His friend Baake was head of the Chancellery. The councillor Simons was put in charge of inspecting the mail so that the Chancellor would receive whatever post seemed important to him, even if it related to the sphere of reponsibility of another People's Commissar.[54]

---

[49] *Dokumente und Materialen*, Volume 2/2, op. cit., p. 357.
[50] W. Groener, *Lebenserinnerungen*, Göttingen, 1957, p. 467.
[51] *Vorwärts*, 10 November 1918.
[52] *Vorwärts*, 14 November 1918.
[53] *Vorwärts*, 15 November 1918.
[54] Kolb, op. cit., pp. 122–3.

The economic power of the bourgeoisie remained intact. To be sure, on 12 November, the first proclamation of the people's Commissars, established the foundation of the new régime including an amnesty for political offences, lifting of the state of siege and censorship, permitting freedom of opinion and the right of women to vote, and allowing for right to vote at the age of twenty. It also took a number of important measures dealing with the regulation and protection of work, a pledge to limit the working day to eight hours, the extension of the system of social insurance, the introduction of unemployment pay, and schemes to build workers' housing.[55] But these were no more than measures to preserve the existing society and to protect property, adopted in the fear which the workers' movement inspired amongst the bourgeoisie. This was so much the case that on 15 November, the most responsible representatives of the employers, Hugo Stinnes, Vögler, Hugenberg, Rathenau and Siemens, signed an agreement with the trade unions to form 'a community of labour', accepting all the demands which they had obstinately rejected until then, namely, an eight-hour day without loss of pay, the fixing of working conditions by collective agreement, the recognition of trade-union representatives in workplaces and an end to company unions, the election of committees in all enterprises employing more than fifty people to supervise the application of collective agreements, and the introduction, at all levels, of parity commissions for arbitration.[56]

A bourgeois commentator was to say that the agreement had one great merit: 'It forms a strong bulwark against any attempt to overthrow our social system by violence.'[57] A Socialisation Commission was created, with representatives of all the parties, trade unions and employers' organisations.[58] Nothing came of it, except, for the bourgeoisie, the gain of a useful period of time.

Defence of the property of the big capitalists was not a popular slogan, and the socialists had to defend the capitalist régime by talking about 'socialisation'. They also defended it by appealing to 'press freedom' to protect the big newspaper firms against the revolutionary workers, as in the case of

[55] *Dokumente und Materialen*, Volume 2/2, op. cit., pp. 365–6.
[56] Text in ibid., pp. 393–6.
[57] Leibrock, *Die Volkwirtschaftliche Bedeutung der deutschen Arbeitergeberverbände*, p. 65, cited by Badia, op. cit., p. 114.
[58] Drabkin, op. cit., p. 313, who had access to the archives of the Commission, lists its members as Kautsky, Hilferding, Cunow, the trade-union leaders Hué and Umbreit, some academics and the electricity boss Walter Rathenau.

the *Berliner Lokalanzeiger* when the Spartacists seized it. The capitalists were able to utilise freely their buildings, their plant and their capital not merely to present their political programme, but to prepare psychologically and materially for the civil war which they felt to be inevitable.

In this way the initiative of Eduard Stadtler, a former prisoner of war in Russia, to create an 'anti-Bolshevik centre', was to be supported with large sums of money, part of which was supplied by Helfferich, the head of the Deutsche Bank, for printing in hundreds of thousands of copies leaflets and pamphlets which often were real incitements to murder against the Spartacists, 'the Bolshevik terror', chaos, the Jews, and 'Bloody Rosa'.[59] The 'General Secretariat' which Stadtler founded served as cover for an even more effective body, the Anti-Bolshevik League, which organised its own intelligence service, and set up, in its founder's words, an 'active anti-communist counter-espionage organisation'.[60]

After November the propagation of news remained in the hands of anti-working-class forces, thanks to the slogan of 'freedom of the press' which was orchestrated by the Social Democrats and the forces which supported them. Whilst such newspapers as *Vossische Zeitung, Berliner Tageblatt, Kreuz-Zeitung* and others continued to appear, supported by considerable funds, the workers' revolutionary organisations, which could count only on the contributions of working people, and thus were forced into silence or to presenting their viewpoint, with very inadequate resources, against the crushing weight of the coalition. The 'free press' even censored, with the government's agreement, the proclamations and resolutions of the Berlin Executive of the Councils. The press agencies likewise remained in private hands, and Ebert appointed his own son to head the semi-official government agency.[61] We can understand how, under these conditions, nearly the entire press, and certainly all of those publications which claimed to present 'news', could from mid-November not merely support the government in calling for the Constitutional Assembly, but could also orchestrate a systematic campaign to discredit the workers' and soldiers' councils.

---

[59] Drabkin (ibid., p. 482) mentions in particular the series of pamphlets *Antispartakus;* between 10,000 and 100,000 of each of these were published.

[60] Ibid., p. 482. Drabkin points out the use by Stadtler of the term 'national socialism' amongst his objectives.

[61] Kolb, op. cit., p. 183.

The Berlin Executive Committee

During the first month of the Revolution, the Council of People's Commissars, which had been put into power by the councils in November, engaged in a bitter struggle for influence against the Berlin council of workers and soldiers, familiarly known as the Executive [Vollzugsrat]. A recent historian has stressed the paradox which meant that this organ, which was the product of the defeat of the revolutionaries under the pressure of the soldiers in the Busch Circus and had a majority of socialists from Ebert's party, became during the weeks that followed the expression of the revolutionaries' efforts to consolidate the rule of the councils, and to counterpose the beginning of a radical orientation to the pro-bourgeois approach of the People's Commissars.[62]

The Executive Council met in surroundings totally different from those of the Council of Commissars. Whilst the members of the latter were installed in the ministries, where, despite gestures of resistance from some, they were quickly assimilated by the officials and procedures of the administration, the Executive Council was installed in the building of the Prussian Landtag, in the heart of the Revolution. It was continually subject to the pressures of the street, 'to what the Revolution wrote on the walls', to recall the expression of its chairman Richard Müller.[63] It expressed at the same time the ambition of its most active members, the nucleus of the revolutionary delegates, to make it the 'Petrograd Soviet' of the German Revolution.[64] It also reflected the confidence of the working people of Berlin, who appealed to it at every turn, because they regarded it as belonging to them. The atmosphere there was so revolutionary that the most moderate of Social Democrats were often persuaded by their colleagues or by workers' delegations to go much further than they wished.[65]

The Executive Council was initially formed of a majority of SPD members and sympathisers. 'Parity' only applied to the people whom the soldiers

---

[62] H.E. Friedlander, 'Conflict of Revolutionary Authority: Provisional Government Berlin Soviet, November–December 1918', *International Review of Social History*, Volume 7, no. 2, 1962, pp. 163–76. There is another comprehensive study, by the Soviet historian S.I. Lenzner, 'Ispolnitelnii Komitet Berlinskikh Rabochikh I Soldatchikh Sovetov (10 noyabrya-16 dekabriya 1918g)' in *Noyabrzskaya Revoliutsiia v Germanii*, op. cit., pp. 98–139.

[63] *Allgemeine Kongress der Arbeiter- und Soldaten-Räte Deutschlands, vom 16 bis 21 Dezember im Abgeordnetenhause zu Berlin, Stenographischer Bericht*, Berlin, n.d. (1919), column 149.

[64] H. Müller, op. cit., p. 104.

[65] Friedlander, op. cit., p. 173.

elected. But unreliable elected members were replaced fairly soon by reliable activists. The nucleus remained stable after 13 November.[66] The Chairmen were Richard Müller – a concession to the Berlin workers – and, for the soldiers, Brutus Molkenbuhr, who after two days replaced the first Chairman, Captain Von Beerfelde.[67] The leaders of the Social-Democratic fraction were one of the soldiers' delegates, Max Cohen-Reuss, a later arrival, and Hermann Müller, who sat as a 'workers' delegate'.[68] The leaders of the revolutionary fraction were Ledebour and Däumig, and behind them were the nucleus of the revolutionary delegates who led the strikes in 1917–18, people such as Eckert, Neuendorff and Wegmann. Around them were the revolutionary engineering workers whom the Berlin working class knew, and who were now undertaking a whole range of responsibilities, including Paul Scholze, who chaired the meetings of the group of delegates, Nowakowski, Paul Neumann, Heinrich Malzahn and Max Urich, who managed the secretariat of the council.[69] The Social Democrats were Party full-timers or trade-union officials, such as Gustav Heller and Oskar Rusch, the latter of whom was to move quickly to the left and join the USPD.

The soldiers' delegates were different. Apart from Hans Paasche, an interesting young bourgeois figure, son of a National Liberal businessman elected President of the Reichstag, who became a revolutionary by way of pacifism,[70] they politically followed Social Democracy. They were barely politicised, and some were frank careerists who took advantage of the situation, found jobs in the ministries for their girlfriends or pals on the pretext of exercising 'control', and obstructed all serious work through their irresponsibility.[71] There were real adventurers like Colin Ross, Ebert and Wels's agent in the soldiers' councils, who was to be thrown out in December for his contacts with monarchists, and was later to become an adviser to Hitler on geopolitics.[72] Otto Strobel was the author of an anti-Semitic article, signed

---

[66] The USPD's workers' delegates were Barth, Ledebour, Däumig, Eckert, Neuendorf, Wegmann and Richard Müller; the SPD's workers' delegates were Hermann Müller, Buchel, Hirt, Heller, Julich, Maynz and Oskar Rusch. The soldiers' delegates were von Beerfelde, Molkenbuhr, Gerhardt, Paasche. Waltz, Bergmann, Portner, Strobel, Lidtke, Hertel, Lemper, Köller, Eckmann and Guntzel (Lenzner, op. cit., p. 101).

[67] H. Müller, op. cit., p. 92. It was said that Von Beerfelde wanted to arrest the Minister for War.

[68] Ibid., p. 91.

[69] Brandt and Lowenthal, op. cit., p. 120.

[70] H. Müller, op. cit., p. 99.

[71] Ibid., pp. 92–3, 97–8; R. Müller, Volume 2, op. cit., pp. 53, 154–6.

[72] H. Müller, op. cit., pp. 96–7. Rudolf Coper says that Colin Ross was 'a high-class

not merely with his name but with his title as a council member, which appeared in a reactionary daily newspaper.[73] Lieutenant Waltz had perhaps dreamed (as Hermann Müller suggests) of becoming 'Marshal of the German Revolution', but was discovered at the end of November to have become an informer when he was arrested on 8 November, and to have supplied the police with the plan of the insurrection and thus the means to arrest Däumig.[74]

The incidents which these individual cases provoked took up hours of precious time in the Executive Council. Waltz, whom Richard Müller expelled without any formal procedure, had the impudence to protest and to plead extenuating circumstances. He admitted before the soldiers' council to being guilty of nothing more than 'stupidities', and managed in this way to group in his support a minority which imposed two nights' sessions of discussion on the delegates from the councils of the garrison.[75]

Despite its good intentions and despite enjoying the confidence of the Berlin workers, the Executive Council was unable to organise its own work or even to create its own apparatus. It claimed simultaneously to supervise and control the cabinet of the Reich and the Prussian government, to give political leadership to the Berlin councils, to act as a centre for the 10,000 councils in the country, to settle labour problems, and to provide a revolutionary orientation on affairs in general. It quickly sank into disorder, a state of affairs which was maintained by the hostility of the government and the state bureaucracy, as well as sabotage by the administration, which made all kinds of demands upon it whilst starving it of resources. Its discussions were constantly interrupted by delegations. It was buried in correspondence which the Chairmen spent their time signing without having read.[76] It was unable to establish priorities in respect of the vast number of tasks facing it, and it did not listen to the stern warning of Hermann Müller: 'An organism which has the ambition to go down in history on the same level as the Committee of Public Safety in the great French Revolution must take care not to become a section of the labour department.'[77]

---

spy', 'welcome in all sections of society' (*Failure of a Revolution*, Cambridge, 1954, p. 114).

[73] H. Müller, op. cit., p. 97; the article, entitled 'An das deutsche Volk vom Gelehrten bis zum Arbeiter', appeared in *Deutsche Tageszeitung* on 13 December 1918.

[74] H. Müller, op. cit., p. 93.

[75] Ibid., pp. 93–7; *Freiheit*, 29 November 1918; *Vorwärts*, 29 November 1918; *Die Rote Fahne*, 30 November 1918.

[76] Friedlander, op. cit., p. 174.

[77] H. Müller, op. cit., p. 111.

The conflict of powers

As soon as it began its work in the evening of 10 November, the Executive Council adopted, on the motion of Eckert, a proclamation addressed to 'the working people': 'The old Germany is no more. . . . Germany has become a socialist republic. The holders of political power are the workers' and soldiers' councils.'[78]

The government which was elected on the same day had the task of concluding the armistice. The other tasks were the socialist transformation of the economy and the restoration of peace by way of unity of the working people. The proclamation hailed the example which the working people of Russia had given, and pointed out that the revolutionary régime could not reconstruct in a day what years of war had destroyed, but that it was the only power which could carry out the necessary reconstruction. It did not say a word about the possibility of calling a national assembly.

Vorwärts did not publish the Executive's proclamation. But the governmental programme mentioned the method of voting for the National Assembly. Two successive articles by Stampfer pointed in the same direction: the government must come from 'the whole people', and not from the workers and soldiers alone.[79] The differences sharpened because, on 11 November, the Executive published a decree in which it defined its own powers: 'All the communal and regional authorities of the Reich and the military authorities continue to function. All orders which come from these authorities will be regarded as being in the name of the Executive Council.'[80] This was an attack on the powers of the Council of the People's Commissars and at the same time an involuntary support to the attempts to salvage the state apparatus, which was to cover itself with the authority of the Executive of the Councils, in order first to survive and then to retaliate.

The question, amongst others, was to find out whether the Executive would be able to organise any coercive forces. On 12 November, Däumig proposed that a red guard be created;[81] the motion was carried by twenty-one votes to one, with the Majority Social Democrats voting in favour. The next day's papers carried an appeal from the Executive which was a first move to put the proposal into practice: 'We need your help. Two thousand working-class

---

[78] *Vossische Zeitung*, 11 November 1918.
[79] *Vorwärts*, 13 and 14 November 1918.
[80] *Vossische Zeitung*, 12 November 1918.
[81] H. Müller, op. cit., p. 128; R. Müller, Volume 2, op. cit., pp. 82ff.

comrades, mature socialists, politically organised and with military training, must take on the protection of the Revolution.'[82]

Applicants were invited to present themselves at the trade-union headquarters that very day. But they were not to be enlisted. The opposition on the Right immediately objected, through the voice of Colin Ross. A meeting of delegates of soldiers' councils, in the barracks of the Alexandra Guards regiment, rejected the Social Democrat Rusch, who supported the suggestion of forming a red guard in the name of defending the Revolution. The soldiers saw the proposal to arm civilians as a gesture of hostility towards them. The representative of the Fusilier Guards regiment declared that soldiers did not support any party, because they belonged to the fatherland. The meeting turned down the proposal to create a red guard.[83] In a communiqué published at two o'clock in the morning, the Executive declared that it took note that the troops in Berlin, while declaring their allegiance to the Socialist Republic, at the same time opposed the creation of a red guard; accordingly, it 'provisionally' gave up the proposal.[84]

The defeat of the Executive on this central question, and its prompt retreat, encouraged its enemies, who pressed their advantage home. Late in the afternoon of 14 November a meeting of soldiers was arranged at the Reichstag to discuss this question. Ebert spoke, declaring that there could be no question of forming a red guard; the decision of the Executive would be final: 'Workers and soldiers, civil servants and bourgeois, are all behind the government. We have nothing to fear.'[85] Wels followed him and, as the new military commander of the city, appealed for discipline. To the soldiers who raised the problem of pay, the representatives of the government replied they must take this problem to the Executive Committee. The meeting confirmed the opposition of the soldiers' councils to the idea of a red guard, and condemned the Executive for having 'exceeded its powers' by proposing one in the first place.

On 16 November, the problem of security and public order was raised this time by the governmental bodies. Barth brought it into the Cabinet council, and it was discussed that afternoon by Ebert, Barth, representatives of the Executive, and the ministers concerned. Barth declared that it was necessary within a week to recruit 10,000 men, 3,000 for Eichhorn's security force, 3,000

---

[82] *Deutsche Tageszeitung*, 13 November 1918.
[83] *8 Uhr-Abendblatt*, 13 November 1918; Coper, op. cit. p. 114.
[84] *Vossische Zeitung*, 14 November 1918.
[85] *Berliner Lokalanzeiger*, 15 November 1918.

to be at the disposal of the city commandant, and 4,000 to guard the railway stations and sort out the demobilised soldiers.[86] Next day, Wels announced the formation of a 'republican defence force', to consist of between 13,000 and 15,000 men, and to be recruited by calling for volunteers.[87] Volunteers flowed in, and so did donations from bourgeois circles, to finance this force for the purpose of maintaining order.[88] The Executive suffered a double defeat: the government had organised to its own advantage the armed force which it had refused to let the Executive organise, and it had struck a powerful blow at the prestige of the latter. In the following days, Eichhorn was to appeal in vain for his forces to be increased. In the end, after several weeks the recruits came, as Wegmaun had suggested, from lists prepared on 13 November for the red guard;[89] by this time Wels's forces were by far the larger.

On 16 November, Däumig renewed the battle in the Executive on the problem of political perspectives. He said that the Revolution had destroyed the old system of government, but that it had not built up any other, and he called for clear measures and a decisive choice between a 'bourgeois-democratic' and a 'socialist' republic. He protested against the activity of the government, which tended to escape from the control of the Executive, appointing Secretaries and Under-Secretaries of State, and issuing proclamations; and he demanded legislative and executive power for the Executive elected by the councils. He moved a resolution which condemned 'the efforts of the German bourgeoisie to convene as quickly as possible a constituent assembly' as a means 'to rob the working people of the fruits of the Revolution', and proposed that a Central Council representing the entire Reich be convened at once 'to study a new constitution from the standpoint of proletarian democracy'. He warned the Executive that if it supported the governmental project of calling a constituent assembly, it would be signing its own death-warrant and that of the councils.[90]

Däumig's motion was immediately and energetically opposed by Ross and Hermann Müller. The latter said that Däumig's point of view was 'anti-democratic', because it aimed at building up a 'class dictatorship of the

---

[86] Drabkin, op. cit., p. 233.
[87] Ibid.; *Vorwärts*, 18 November 1918; *Dokumente und Materialen*, Volume 2/2, op. cit., p. 415.
[88] Drabkin, op. cit., p. 233.
[89] Ibid., p. 234.
[90] Drabkin, p. 237; R. Müller, Volume 2, op. cit., pp. 82ff., 127–8.

proletariat against the majority of the people'. He put it clearly: 'We cannot here go towards such a dictatorship as exists in Russia',[91] and moved an amendment which stressed the provisional character of the existence of the councils: it stressed that the quicker the Constituent Assembly was convened, the sooner there would be a socialist majority at the head of the nation. These arguments failed to convince every member of his own party. Däumig's motion was just defeated by twelve votes to ten, with the soldiers' delegate Hans Paasch and the two Social-Democratic workers' delegates, Büchel and Julich, voting for it.[92] Hermann Müller then accepted Däumig's motion in his own name, with an addition about the future constitution which the Central Council would adopt: 'This constitution will be submitted to a constituent assembly convened by the Central Council.'[93]

After a confused discussion in which Barth changed his position, the text of the new resolution was adopted by nine votes to seven.[94] The Executive had opened the road to its own dissolution and that of the councils as organs of power, whilst the likes of Richard Müller, a supporter of power to the councils, voted for their liquidation in the belief that a compromise was being reached.[95] The Majority exploited the confusion immediately. On the same day as this discussion took place, Landsberg declared in an interview that the government had already reached a decision about convening the Constituent Assembly.[96] On the following day, *Vorwärts* announced that the Cabinet had already fixed the date of the elections as 2 February.[97] On 18 November, *Freiheit* protested and denied the statement,[98] evidently on behalf of the USPD ministers, but on the 19th the organ of the USPD had to admit that the question of the Constituent Assembly had been discussed on the 17th and had been thoroughly settled in principle, whilst it maintained that no date had yet been decided.[99] Meanwhile, for two days already, the Social-Democratic press headed by *Vorwärts* had plunged deeply into the campaign for the early convocation of the Constituent Assembly.

---

[91] Cited in Drabkin, op. cit., p. 239.
[92] Cited in ibid., p. 240.
[93] H. Müller, op. cit., p. 128.
[94] Cited in Drabkin, op. cit., p. 240.
[95] Ibid., p. 241.
[96] *Vossische Zeitung*, 16 November 1918.
[97] *Vorwärts*, 17 November 1918.
[98] *Freiheit*, 18 November 1918.
[99] *Freiheit*, 19 November 1918.

The Executive recognised the mistake which it had made on the 18th. Richard Müller was to speak later about a 'confused' position which 'made it look ridiculous'.[100] The Executive tried to win back the lost ground by turning towards those who had mandated it, the delegates of the workers' and soldiers' councils who had appointed it on 10 November. It recalled them to the Busch Circus for the 18th.

Addressing this assembly, Richard Müller presented a report on the activity of the Executive. He did his best to present the resolution of 16 November by placing the emphasis on the role of the councils and the dangers which too early a calling of the Constituent Assembly could involve:

> If we now convene the Constituent Assembly, that would be the death sentence for the workers' and soldiers' councils. They would eliminate themselves. That they must not do. We must ensure our own rule, if necessary by force. Whoever supports the National Assembly forces the struggle upon us. I say this clearly: I have risked my life for the Revolution, and I am ready to do it again. The National Assembly is the road to the rule of the bourgeoisie, the road to conflict. That road goes over my dead body. When I say that, I know that some of the members of the Executive agree with me, as well as all the working people who took part in preparing the Revolution, and I do not doubt that I have a majority of working people at my side.[101]

Herman Müller intervened in a reassuring spirit: the Majority Social Democrats also wanted a social republic, but the question could not be settled in a meeting like this one, because neither of the two workers' parties had rejected the principle of convening the Constituent Assembly. This did not frighten him, he had confidence in the German people and in the will which it would express when it voted.[102] Haase said that the conquests of the Revolution had nothing to fear from universal suffrage in a country in which the workers formed the majority; alluding to Russia, he warned his hearers to be on guard against 'false' conceptions resulting from 'foreign examples'.[103] Kaliski, a Social

---

[100] R. Müller, op. cit., Volume 2, p. 83.
[101] *Protokolle der Versammlungen der Arbeiter- und Soldatenräte Gross-Berlin*, Volume 1, cited in Drabkin, op. cit., pp. 241–4, extracts complementing the report which appeared in *Vorwärts* of 20 November 1918.
[102] *Vorwärts*, 20 November 1918.
[103] Ibid.; Drabkin, p. 243.

Democrat, said that a revolution without democracy would open the way to another war.[104]

Ledebour replied that the working class today held the power, and should not run the slightest risk of losing it. He opposed the idea that real democracy could exist under a capitalist system, it was necessary to begin by breaking down the foundations of capitalism.[105]

Liebknecht energetically defended himself against his adversaries' charge that he was an enemy of 'unity'. He was for unity and clarity. In reply to the question, 'What are we to do?', he called upon all who wanted to carry the Revolution forward, to construct socialism, to unite, because the powerful armed counter-revolution was on the march. He appealed to working people to defend their power, to be aware that 'traitors' were at work amongst them, and never to forget that the emancipation of their class could result only from their own activity. He was especially applauded when he insisted on the need for clear positions, a thinly-veiled criticism of the confusion in the Executive.[106]

A certain number of delegates intervened to attack Richard Müller's report on activity from another angle. On 15 November, Müller and Molkenbuhr, as joint presidents, had signed a declaration in which they entrusted to the trade-union organisations the representation of the economic interests of the workers.[107] That same day, the local trade-union commission in Berlin, led by the Majority Social Democrat Körsten, decided that the action committees in the workplaces should all be wound up and re-elected.[108] This initiative favoured the employers, who were struggling against the efforts of the workers' committees to exert over their activities a control which neither they nor the trade-union leaders liked.[109] Several factory delegates criticised the Executive for having in this way handed over the monopoly of representing the working people to the very people who 'for four years had betrayed them'.[110] Richard Müller had to promise to review the question.[111]

His reply in concluding the debate was entirely centred on the criticisms from the Left:

---

[104] Drabkin, op. cit., p. 243.
[105] *Vorwärts*, 20 November 1918.
[106] Drabkin, op. cit., pp. 243–4.
[107] Ibid., pp. 235–6.
[108] *Dokumente und Materialen*, Volume 2/2, op. cit., p. 401.
[109] Drabkin, op. cit., p. 236.
[110] Ibid., pp. 236–7.
[111] Ibid., p. 237.

Whilst I sit on the Executive, I shall fight for the Constituent National Assembly to come only when there is no more danger to the conquests of the Revolution. . . . You know what we want in the Executive, and we shall be watchful that the conquests of the Revolution are not lost. When comrade Haase declared that the government must go forward . . . you may be confident that we, the Executive, will push it forward, and we know very well how to push it, as very recent past events have shown.[112]

The resolution of 16 November was not put to the vote of the assembly, but was referred back to the Executive with other documents. It was not even published, because the government forbade the Wolff telegraphic agency to make it known.[113] The *Berliner Tageblatt* reported on the assembly in the Busch circus, and summed the problem up in this way: 'Along with the question of the Constituent Assembly, the question is posed – who governs in Germany? Is the supreme authority in the hands of the government, or really in the hands of the workers' and soldiers' councils?'[114]

The bourgeois and Social-Democratic press posed the problem in this way, because the bourgeoisie was beginning to feel that it had the strength to settle it in a way favourable to itself, that is, to the government. The Executive was doomed to fight a disorderly defensive battle. It retreated step by step, and it was driven day by day from its positions. On 18 November, there was a joint meeting of the two Councils at the chancellery.[115] Ebert made an immediate attack on the demands of the Executive and its encroachments on the authority of the government, when it was only a Berlin organisation. This provoked protests even from the Social-Democratic members of the Executive. Dittmann proposed quickly electing a central all-Germany council.[116] Landsberg, a supporter of the Majority, admitted that the Council of the People's Commissars and the Cabinet drew their authority from the Executive of the councils which had appointed them, and could recall them, but he argued that it could not permit any interference in the domain of executive power without in this way forming a 'counter-government', which meant anarchy.[117]

---

[112] Cited in ibid., p. 244.
[113] Ibid., p. 244.
[114] *Berliner Tageblatt*, 19 November 1918.
[115] Kolb, op. cit., p. 134; Drabkin, op. cit., pp. 245–9, the latter summarises the official record which is kept in the central archives of the Reich in Potsdam (Reichskanzlei, no. 2482, 28ff.).
[116] Drabkin, op. cit., p. 246.
[117] Ibid., pp. 246–7.

Däumig protested against the 'absolutist' conception held by the defenders of the authority of the Cabinet, and he demanded that the Executive be granted powers of effective control.[118] On the subject of the National Assembly, Ebert denied that a date for it to meet had been fixed.[119] The USPD ministers did their best to reach a compromise. In the end, a commission was appointed to be responsible for laying down the limits of the authority of each body on the basis of a stable agreement that the decisions of the Council of People's Commissars were immediately applicable, and that the Executive could intervene only in the case of a disagreement.[120] On 23 November, as a result of the work of the commission, a declaration by the Executive laid down the new constitutional order for the 'initial transition period'. Power lay with the workers' and soldiers' councils, the functions of which were being carried out for the Reich by the Berlin Executive, until a Central Council for the whole country was elected, and executive power was delegated to the Council of the People's Commissars.[121]

On 23 November, the Executive accordingly enlarged itself by taking in representatives of different regions and of the army. It now had twenty-five additional members, mostly Majority Social Democrats, such as the young Kurt Schumacher, who represented soldiers disabled in the war. But it also drew in some revolutionaries, such as Karl Baier, a sailor from Cuxhaven, and von Lojewski, a soldier from Spandau, whom Fritz Heckert from Saxony was soon to join as a participant from time to time.[122]

But the initiative came too late. The Social-Democratic and bourgeois press already knew how to exploit against the Berlin Executive the ever-latent hostility to the capital. It hinted that the Executive aspired to be a dictator, and wanted to set itself against universal suffrage.[123] The same themes that had been used against the Paris Commune reappeared. The Executive came under fire from every side.[124] Its enemies said that the Entente did not recognise it, and that to recognise its authority implied the risk of breaking the armistice.[125]

---

[118] Ibid., p. 247.
[119] Ibid.
[120] Ibid.
[121] *Dokumente und Materialen*, Volume 2/2, op. cit. p. 459.
[122] H. Müller, op. cit., pp. 105–6.
[123] Friedlander, op. cit., p. 168.
[124] See Chapter 7 of Kolb, op. cit., 'Die Diskreditierung der Arbeiterräte durch die Presse'.
[125] Friedlander, op. cit., p. 168.

The government press agency spoke of 800 million marks being spent on the workers' councils, and this became 1,800 million marks spent by the Executive.[126] On the other hand, the press did not say a word about the report of the treasurer, Max Maynz.[127]

The all-German conference of regional prime ministers declared on 25 November for convening the National Assembly.[128] The Council of People's Commissars, after much dealing between supporters of the Majority and Independent socialists, fixed the date for elections to the Assembly as 16 February 1919,[129] whilst the Executive decided, on 23 November, to convene in Berlin for 16 December a meeting of delegates of councils from all parts of the Reich.[130] Preparation for this meeting coincided with a redoubled press campaign against the Berlin Executive and its radical leaders. *Vorwärts* raged against 'Corpse-Müller', the 'walking corpse', in allusion to his speech on 18 November. They attacked 'Richard the First' and 'the junkers on the other side'.[131] Not surprisingly, the attempted putsch on 6 December by monarchist elements, which was openly aimed at the executive, used the classical argument of the anti-Semites when it called the Executive's headquarters in the Prussian Landtag a 'synagogue'.[132]

The Berlin Executive Council was already defeated before the congress of the Councils met to elect a new Central Council and to settle finally the question of the power of the councils. The Council of People's Commissars could permit itself to turn back at the frontiers the Russians whom it had invited, Bukharin, Joffe, Rakovsky, Ignatov and Radek, representing the All-Russia Congress of Soviets.[133] Luxemburg was to write, with her ferocious pen, the epitaph of the Berlin Executive Council, this revolutionary organism which she called 'the sarcophagus of the revolution', and 'the fifth wheel of the cart of the crypto-capitalist governmental clique':

> It is clear that it was in the Executive Council and in the workers' and soldiers' councils that the masses should have discovered their role. But

---

[126] Ibid.; Kolb, op. cit., p. 191.
[127] Friedlander, op. cit., p. 169.
[128] Kolb, op. cit., p. 132.
[129] Ibid., p. 133.
[130] *Dokumente und Materialen*, Volume 2/2, op. cit., pp. 462–4.
[131] See in particular 'Der lebende Leichnam', *Vorwärts*, 5 December; 'Richard I Wilhelms Ersatz', *Vorwärts*, 18 December 1918.
[132] R. Müller, Volume 2, op. cit., pp. 157–8; H. Müller, op. cit., p. 109.
[133] Brandt and Lowenthal, op. cit., p. 112; Scheidemann, *Der Zusammenbruch*, op. cit., p. 227.

their organ, the organ of the proletarian revolution is reduced to a state of total impotence. Power has slipped out of its hands, to pass into those of the bourgeoisie. No organ of political power lets power escape of its own free will, without having made some mistake. It is the passivity and the indolence of the Executive Committee which has made possible the game of Ebert and Scheidemann.[134]

This was a severe verdict, but no one was to contest it. The 'Petrograd Soviet' of the German Revolution was finally defeated. Its president, Richard Müller, was to bury it himself in his own way by calling it the 'maid of all work' of the Revolution.[135]

The Congress of the Councils

The Congress of the Workers' and Soldiers' Councils revealed the size of the political defeat which the revolutionaries had suffered in six weeks. A total of 489 delegates took part, 405 sent by workers' councils, and 84 by those of soldiers.[136] Out of the whole, there were only 179 factory and office workers. There were 71 intellectuals and 164 'professionals', journalists, deputies or full-timers in parties or trade unions.[137] Representatives of the apparatus heavily outnumbered those representing factory workers. The Majority Social Democrats had a clear majority, with 288 delegates against 90 Independents, of whom only 10 were Spartacists. The best known of them were Heckert and Leviné. There were also 11 'united revolutionaries', around Laufenberg from Hamburg, 25 democrats and 75 non-party.[138] Ebert's proposals had a majority in advance. On the day that it opened, *Vorwärts*, setting out the perspective of calling the Constituent Assembly, took the liberty of waxing ironic at the expense of the Spartacists, and asked whether they would, in conformity with their policy of power to the councils, accept the decision of the councils to surrender power.[139]

---

[134] *Die Rote Fahne*, 11 December 1918.
[135] Cited in H. Müller, op. cit., p. 111.
[136] *Allgemeiner Kongress*, op. cit., pp. 198ff.; *Illustrierte Geschichte der deutschen Revolution*, op. cit., p. 249.
[137] *Illustrierte Geschichte der deutschen Revolution*, op. cit., p. 250.
[138] Ibid., pp. 249–50.
[139] *Vorwärts*, 16 December 1918; *Dokumente und Materialen*, Volume 2/2, op. cit., p. 621.

Neither Karl Liebknecht nor Rosa Luxemburg were delegates. In Berlin, eligibility was reserved to those whose names were on the lists of people who worked in factories or in military units. The Presidium proposed that they be invited in a consultative capacity, but this was immediately rejected without discussion.[140] When the matter was raised some hours later by a delegate from Württemberg, it was rejected after sharp exchanges.[141] Nothing was left for the Spartacists but to try to influence the Congress from outside. They had foreseen this, and had organised demonstrations and delegations of demonstrators at the opening and in recesses.

In alliance with the revolutionary delegates, they organised a huge meeting at the opening of the Congress, followed by a procession and the sending of a delegation in the name of 250,000 Berlin workers who had gathered at their summons. The revolutionary delegate Paul Weyer was admitted to the Congress, and he read out the demands of the demonstrators: proclamation of a united socialist republic, workers' and soldiers' power, the exercise of governmental power by an Executive elected by the Central Council, the recall of Ebert's Council of People's Commissars, measures to purge and disarm counter-revolutionaries, arming of the workers, and an appeal to the workers of the whole world to construct their councils to carry out the tasks of the world revolution.[142]

But the Congress remained unmoved. The President of the session, Leinert, declared that he had taken note of the demands, and would take account of them in his decisions. Whilst the crowd of demonstrators made its way through the streets of Berlin, Richard Müller resumed his report which had been interrupted by the arrival of the delegation. On 18 December, it was also on the initiative of the Spartacists that a delegation of soldiers from seventeen units was to come, under the leadership of Dorrenbach, to list their demands about the army and discipline. This time the reception was openly hostile, and the Majority threatened to leave the hall. There was to be another demonstration on 18 December, this time of Berlin workers on strike.[143] But, despite the crowds which they could bring together, the Spartacists and the revolutionary delegates did not succeed when they organised these 'journées' – on the model of the French Revolution of which they perhaps

---

[140] *Allgemeiner Kongress*, op. cit., Column 12.
[141] Ibid., Columns 53–8.
[142] Ibid., Columns 19ff.
[143] Ibid., Columns 123ff., 144ff.

were thinking – which could have influenced a hesitant or undecided assembly. The stakes were down, and the First Congress of the Councils was to develop more or less as Ebert and his friends had foreseen.

The only surprise in fact came over the difficult problem of the demands of the soldiers, which their delegates, including the Social Democrats among them, wanted to impose. Ebert had secretly undertaken to the General Staff that he would not let these questions be mentioned in the Congress. The adoption of the 'seven Hamburg points' – themselves a compromise suggested by the Social Democrat, Lamp'l – was to mark the starting-point for threats directed at the government by the General Staff, and, in the long run, of the great crisis of December, which the decomposition of the army during the preceding weeks had opened.[144]

For the rest, and in particular for the question of the nature of power, the councils and the Constituent Assembly, the debates in the Congress took on an academic, not to say parliamentary, character. Max Cohen-Reuss defended the thesis of early convocation of the Constituent Assembly elected by universal suffrage. According to him, this method of election would be a great victory for socialism, because it had been unsuccessfully demanded in Germany since well before the Erfurt Programme. The socialists needed it because they needed an impregnable central power to oppose the strong bourgeoisie, and a government resulting from free elections to oppose the Entente. Cohen had no doubt about the outcome of the elections: it was because the Constituent Assembly would have a socialist majority that its election would be the shortest route to establishing the socialist régime in Germany.

The Social Democrats had decided to prevent their 'pure, clear, good socialist universe' from being 'disfigured and sabotaged by Bolshevik distortions'. According to Cohen, socialism would be brought about by a socialist government elected by the whole people. When the councils had convened the Constituent Assembly, they would bring their special mission to an end, and could then take their natural place in social life by playing an important role in production.[145]

Däumig presented the counter-report. He emphasised that to adopt Cohen's text would mean the death sentence for the councils. He recalled their appearance and development in Russia and then in Germany, and

---

[144] See Chapter 12.
[145] *Allgemeiner Kongress*, op. cit., Columns 209ff.

declared that they were 'the organisational form of the modern revolution', the proletarian form of democracy. The supporters of the Majority tried by every means to destroy them, and presented them as a real bogey by equating them with dictatorship. The Russian experience would not necessarily be repeated in Germany, because in Germany, unlike rural Russia, the dictatorship of the councils would obviously be that of the working-class majority. To socialism from above, as recommended by Cohen, he counterposed socialism from below, born out of workers' activity in the workplace. He ended by declaring his faith in the system of councils which, according to him, would sooner or later impose itself.[146]

There were no new arguments in the debate. The only controversial problem was the date of the Constituent Assembly, which the Independents wanted to postpone as long as they could, in order that the socialists would, as they said, have more time 'to enlighten the masses' still in the grip of bourgeois ideology. In the end, there were three different motions. One, from Geyer and Laufenberg, proposed the date 16 March, and won 50 votes. Another, from Ebert and Haase, resulting from a compromise in the Council of People's Commissars, won hardly more. The proposal of Max Cohen to fix the date for 19 January was adopted by 400 votes to 50.[147] About half of the USPD delegates followed Haase and voted for it, whilst some of the rest lined up in opposition with Ledebour, Däumig and others such as Richard Müller. On the following day, a motion by Däumig which stated that the councils remained the basis of supreme authority in legislative and executive matters, and that a second congress would be needed before the adoption of a new constitution, was defeated by 344 votes to 98.[148]

The Congress of the Councils clearly declared that it opposed 'conciliar power'. Däumig could well call it 'a suicide club'.[149] Ebert's Majority, after having won a striking victory on the very territory of its opponents, crowned it by passing Lündemann's amendment, which turned to the advantage of the People's Commissars alone the authority which was devolved in principle to the Central Council.[150] Learning from experience, Richard Müller and the other leaders of the revolutionary delegates succeeded in persuading

---

[146] Ibid., Columns 226ff.
[147] According to Tormin, op. cit., p. 99.
[148] *Allgemeiner Kongress*, op. cit., Column 300.
[149] Ibid., Column 227.
[150] Ibid., Column 292.

the majority of the USPD delegates that they must henceforth boycott this powerless Central Council.[151] Soviet power could be no more than a bad joke from the moment when it was embodied in people who described themselves as its determined opponents.

Throughout Germany, the revolutionaries organised meetings and demonstrations, and at their instigation resolutions were carried and protests organised against the decision of the Congress of Councils. On 21 December in Berlin, Pieck, Liebknecht, Duncker and Paul Scholze, representing the revolutionary delegates, called for struggle against its decisions, and for an implacable fight against the Ebert-Scheidemann government.[152] The question, however, was not posed, and still less solved, of whether the fight should proceed in the long term through re-election of the councils and winning a majority in them, or whether henceforward the revolutionaries must pursue the struggle which had begun over a month earlier, against the convocation of the Constituent Assembly, by going over the heads of the existing councils – in other words, fighting in the immediate future for a conciliar form of power which the councils themselves did not want.

This question was to dominate the political life of Germany up to the elections. The differences which it provoked were to leave their mark on the whole German Communist movement for a long time.

---

[151] R. Müller, Volume 2, op. cit., p. 223; Prager, op. cit., p. 185; *Freiheit*, 2 December 1918.

[152] Reports in *Die Rote Fahne*, 22 December 1918.

Chapter Ten

The Crisis in the Socialist Movement

The severe judgement which Rosa Luxemburg pronounced on the activity of the Berlin Executive Council leaves historians dissatisfied. It is impossible, from the standpoint of the revolutionaries, to lay full responsibility for the defeat on Richard Müller and his friends. The powerlessness of the radicals in the Executive and the inability of this 'organ of political power', as she called it, to go beyond purely propagandist activity were not and could not have been the fault of the elected members of the Berlin councils alone. The same characteristics were to be found in the work of the other revolutionary groups. The weak representation of the supporters of conciliar power even at the Congress of the Councils proved that their indisputable early influence had declined, and that, in this decisive period, they were unable to reach the heart of the mass movement.

The Spartacus League in the USPD

The problem was not a new one for the Spartacists. We remember the political struggle which Luxemburg waged in 1916 against the members of her group who wanted to bring an independent organisation into existence, and her efforts to prevent the formation of what she called, in advance, a 'sect', cut off from the broad masses organised in the SPD. We recall that in 1917, the revolutionaries adopted different attitudes towards the USPD. Most of the Spartacists joined the new party, despite the resistance of the Württembergers, but the left radicals in Bremen, Hamburg and Berlin refused.

On the eve of the Revolution, in the summer of 1918, these differences seemed to have been toned down. Many activists regarded entering the USPD as less positive since Kautsky, the theoretician of the party, took his stand for 'democracy' and against 'Bolshevism'. We have seen how Franz Mehring wrote that this entry had been a mistake, and, with the return of Paul Levi, who had been won to Bolshevism in Switzerland and was close to the Bremen activists, the perspectives for founding an independent revolutionary party became clearer. The joint conference in October seemed to foreshadow a fusion which would take place after the break which now seemed inevitable between the Spartacus League and the USPD.

However, events did not fulfil this expectation. When Liebknecht was freed, he agreed to appear as a standard-bearer for the Independents, and to take part in the meetings of its Executive. The reason for his attitude is simple: he believed that the Spartacists did not have the means to intervene in industry – the territory on which the decisive battle was being fought. This was why he and Pieck chose to integrate themselves into the nucleus which formed the real leadership of the Berlin working class, the revolutionary delegates, the majority of whom were members of the USPD. Liebknecht saw activists such as Wegmann, Eckert, Neuendorff and Nowakowski, rather than Däumig and Richard Müller, as the people through whom he could reach the masses. The sympathy of these men for the Russian Revolution and the revolutionary programme was well known.

On 10 November, a group of armed Spartacists, bearing an order from the Berlin Executive of the Councils signed by Richard Müller and von Beerfelde, and led by Hermann Duncker, took possession of the printing works of the big daily newspaper, *Berliner Lokalanzeiger*.[1] Luxemburg, who arrived in Berlin shortly afterwards, sharply criticised this initiative of theirs, publishing a daily for which they did not have the resources, and with an orientation with which she disagreed.[2] On the evening of 11 November, at the Hotel Excelsior,

---

[1] See on this episode 'Protestschreiben der Vereinigung Grossstädtischer Zeitungsverleger vom 15 November 1918 gegen die Drucklegung der *Roten Fahne* in der druckerei des Berliner Lokal-Anzeigers', *Dokumente und Materialen*, Volume 2/2, op. cit., pp. 389–92.

[2] Frölich, op. cit., p. 264.

the leading Spartacists in Berlin improvised a conference and sketched out a programme.[3] Jogiches' letter to Thalheimer[4] provides an idea of their analysis. They believed that the revolution was still just a soldiers' mutiny. Undertaken by soldiers who were tired of military service, it was based on their demands, it had essentially been led by soldiers, and the social aspects had been relegated to second place. To be sure, it was useful that it had helped to break the spearhead of the counter-revolution within the army, but the counter-revolution still enjoyed in the 'governmental socialists' an asset all the more important in that they retained the confidence of a not inconsiderable section of the working class.

The role of the revolutionaries, as they saw it, was to enlighten the masses through agitation and propaganda. It was to help the masses to go systematically through the experience of the real role of the Social Democrats by pushing them forward in struggles – especially strikes – of an economic character on such burning questions as food rationing, unemployment and 'the real economic chaos which necessarily follows the war'. Any collaboration with the Majority Social Democrats would only make the experience of the masses more difficult: 'In a word, historically speaking, the moment when we take the lead is not at the beginning, but at the end of the revolution.'[5]

This analysis was the basis on which Luxemburg defended her viewpoint, according to which the Spartacists should stay as long as possible in the USPD, in order in the first instance to gain support and recruit members, but with the longer-term aim of winning the majority. Her opinion prevailed, and the group, which had become the Spartacus League, remained a propaganda group within the USPD.

Nonetheless, the group started to build an organisation and devised a plan of work.[6] A central leadership, the Zentrale, was appointed, including Liebknecht, Luxemburg, Mehring, Jogiches, Ernst Meyer, Hermann and Käthe Duncker, Wilhelm Pieck, Paul Levi, Paul Lange, plus Thalheimer who was to return from Stuttgart, and Eberlein[7] who was called back from Danzig.

---

[3] *1918, Erinnerungen von Veteranen*, op. cit., p. 21; *Vorwärts und nicht vergessen*, op. cit., p. 49. According to Drabkin (op. cit., p. 197) those present were Eberlein, Lange, Levi, Mehring, Meyer and Thalheimer.

[4] Reproduced by J.S. Drabkin in *Noiabrskaia Revoliutsiia v Germanii*, Moscow, 1960, pp. 377–8.

[5] Ibid., p. 378.

[6] *Vorwärts und nicht vergessen*, op. cit., pp. 51–2.

[7] Ibid., p. 52.

Liebknecht, Luxemburg, Thalheimer, Levi and Lange, reinforced by Fritz Rück, who had also to be brought from Stuttgart, found themselves charged with producing *Die Rote Fahne*. Jogiches saw to questions of organisation, Eberlein to finance, and Pieck to building the League in Berlin. The Dunckers received the responsibility of work amongst the youth, Karl Schulz was to organise propaganda amongst the soldiers, and, finally, Ernst Meyer took control of a press bureau.[8] In the project which Luxemburg outlined, plans were made to produce a whole series of publications, a theoretical journal, specialised periodicals for youth and women, an agitational sheet for soldiers, and a press correspondence bulletin.[9]

None of this was to be achieved by the intended dates. In the days which followed, the forces of the group were fully engaged in the battle to defend the daily *Die Rote Fahne*. The owners of the *Lokalanzeiger* took legal action, the Berlin Executive retreated, von Beerfelde resigned, and the Spartacists had to surrender the print works.[10] *Die Rote Fahne* only reappeared on 18 November, and was produced by an expensive firm of printers. Printing and selling 'agitation cards' at 50 pfennigs each[11] – there were no subscriptions – could not bring in the necessary resources. During the first week of the workers' and soldiers' councils in the country, there was no large-scale Spartacist propaganda work. However, Liebknecht was to express the opinion of the Zentrale on the scale of the task which awaited the revolutionaries, when he wrote on 20 November on the subject of the councils:

> The working people who are elected are often only imperfectly enlightened, have only weak class consciousness, and are even hesitant, irresolute, lacking in energy, so that they [the councils] have hardly any revolutionary character, or that their political struggle against the agents of the old régime is hardly visible.[12]

Masses and party

The process by which large masses of people change direction in a revolutionary period is a complex one, and, in particular, does not develop in a straight

---

[8] Weber, op. cit., p. 29.
[9] *Vorwärts und nicht vergessen*, op. cit., pp. 52–3.
[10] Ibid., p. 50. See also *Berliner Lokalanzeiger*, 15 November 1918; *Kölnische Zeitung*, 17 November 1918; and *Die Rote Fahne*, 18 November 1918.
[11] Weber, op. cit., p. 30.
[12] *Die Rote Fahne*, 20 November 1918.

line, when these masses are constantly being increased by hundreds of thousands of individuals who are awakening to political life. Their experience, which sometimes is concentrated in only a few weeks, demands that the political organisations which hope to take advantage of them have quick reflexes and especially great clarity of analysis. In Germany in 1918, the positions of the workers' parties and of the competing currents within them contributed rather to increasing the confusion.

In principle, two workers' political organisations claiming to be socialist offered themselves to the German working people in November and December – the old SPD, which people still called the Majority, even in places where it no longer had the majority, and the USPD. Both were in government, both were on the Executive Council, both claimed to be both for socialism and for the November Revolution which had carried them to power. The differences between them were not striking at first glance; nearly all the decisions of the Cabinet were taken unanimously, and *Freiheit* used language very close to that of *Vorwärts*, a few nuances excepted.

But the situation became complicated as soon as one was no longer satisfied with official declarations, and examined the real differences within these parties, and above all the differences of behaviour in practice between some of their representatives and others. Within the USPD there was, in the first place, the Spartacus League, which had its own daily paper and its own policy. On 10 November, the refusal of Liebknecht to join the Ebert-Scheidemann-Haase government made the Spartacus League a third leadership, or at least a formal opposition to the line which the other two were following. In reality, there were more tendencies than that. In the SPD, by the side of the authentic right wing of Ebert and Scheidemann, who were actually allied to the General Staff, and were consciously fighting to liquidate the councils, for a bourgeois republic to be set up and an alliance against Bolshevism with the Entente, we must distinguish a left wing, unorganised but made up of many members for whom such an alliance, had they heard about it, would be inconceivable, and who honestly believed in the pacifist socialist perspectives which people like Cohen-Reuss developed. This 'Left' was to reveal itself more vigorously during the following weeks in the hostility which many members and even leaders displayed to an even more markedly right-wing policy, namely the cooperation between Noske and the Free Corps.[13]

---

[13] See Chapter 12.

Within the USPD, the 'Right' consisted essentially of the leading nucleus of which Haase and Dittmann were the spokesmen, and which was actually very close to the Social-Democratic 'Left'. It really desired a parliamentary democracy, but dreamt of reconciling it with the institutionalised existence of workers' councils, which would have 'a share' of the power. Like the Social-Democratic Left, it provided a cover for the policy of Ebert and of the Right, whilst from time to time it distanced itself from them and sharply attacked them, at least verbally, on points of detail such as the date of the elections or their relations with the General Staff. The Left of the Independents, which included Däumig, Ledebour and the circle of revolutionary delegates round Richard Müller, did not, of course, have the same intransigent attitude to the Council of People's Commissars or the Berlin Executive as Liebknecht did, but it upheld the prewar radical revolutionary positions, and added to them the demand for conciliar power as a concrete perspective, which clearly put them in the camp of unconditional supporters of the Russian Revolution and its adherents.

The leaders of the Spartacus League agreed with the Left of the Independents on a bitter struggle against the Right in the Party, for strengthening the power of the councils, and against the perspective of convening the National Assembly. But they were not so committed to political work in the traditional trade unions, on which, moreover, many activitists, were now turning their backs. Finally, whilst they intended to take part in elections when there were called, they did not have the support of the majority of the members of the League on this point. In fact, the tendency which Arthur Rosenberg calls 'the utopian current' revealed itself in the ranks of the Spartacus League as it did in the ranks of the revolutionary organisations attached to the IKD. We prefer to call 'an ultra-left tendency' those who totally rejected any common work with the 'social traitors' and their accomplices – a very wide conception – and who thought that political power would come via the barrels of the rifles in the hands of the armed working people within the following few weeks at the most.

We may agree with Arthur Rosenberg in regretting that the German workers' movement could not break quickly enough from the organisational forms and tendencies inherited from the War, nor restructure itself along the lines of the real differences. Perhaps the 'democratic' wing of Haase and Dittmann could have acted as an effective counterweight to the right wing around Ebert in a reformist Social-Democratic Party. Perhaps 'revolutionary social democracy', ranging from Ledebour through Liebknecht to the leftists, could have coordinated at least to some extent the efforts of organisation and the struggles of the supporters of conciliar power. But the fact is that the revolutionary elements were not able to being about this clarification whilst there was still time.

In any case, immediately after the November Revolution, an important section of those who had formed the workers' vanguard had turned their backs on the old party. The organising cadres of the class had often turned to the USPD. In many large industrial centres, it was true that this party exerted the principal influence on the workers in large factories. The bitterness which resulted from the political disputes during the War, the memory of the SPD's policy of supporting the General Staff against its own opposition – for example, the seizure of *Vorwärts* – ruled out for these workers the reunification which their leaders were increasingly desiring (even if they dared not formulate it openly), confronted as they were with the prospect of a soviet-style revolution which they did not want. The great majority of the working-class cadres found themselves, so to speak, trapped in Haase's party, the policy of which did not differ substantially from Ebert's, but which at the same time at least formally was the party of Liebknecht and Luxemburg.

At the same time, there were millions of people who had turned to the SPD. They were workers who hitherto had remained outside political activity, demobilised soldiers, petty-bourgeois people on whom the War and the defeat had inflicted grave suffering, and young people of all social origins who hoped for a rapid improvement in their living conditions as well as a democratic reorganisation of the country. The SPD was seen by the broadest masses as the incarnation of the Revolution, because it was that party which the Revolution had brought to power and which promised them not only peace, democracy and socialism for tomorrow, but, more importantly, to get there without fresh suffering, without revolution or civil war.

The rallying of bourgeois parties and forces to the programme which the SPD formulated, and the general atmosphere of fraternity to which all those declarations gave birth, created a climate of confidence and unity, and almost of unanimity. The revolutionaries seemed to be trouble-makers to the wide strata of people who desired a form of democratic socialism. In their eyes, it was only the revolutionaries whose outcries, violence, 'excesses' and invective, and the accusations of 'betrayal' which they hurled at the leaders, who endangered the 'unity' needed to consolidate the Revolution, and thereby they put the Revolution in jeopardy. The Majority Social Democrats exploited to the full, against the Spartacists, this desire for unity amongst the barely politicised, inexperienced masses whom they drew around themselves and organised, just as they had done with the soldiers' delegates in November, presenting the Spartacists in their propaganda as 'disrupters'.

Vanguard or militant minority?

The revolutionary minority itself was becoming radicalised, and all the more when it had the feeling of being drawn into a political unanimity which would be fatal to it. Part of it regrouped around the Spartacus League, although the process which led it to do so was perfectly spontaneous. Working-class elements whom the dominating power of the Social-Democratic and trade-union bureaucracy had turned against any organisational form, pacifist activists who saw their main enemy in the 'general-staff socialists', young people who believed only in the force of arms, a whole stratum of the disaffected, rebels, fighters and purists, who saw the principal obstacle to the victory of the Revolution in the bureaucratic apparatuses – they were all fascinated by the Russian Revolution. They knew little of the long experience of the Bolsheviks, and for them Bolshevism was summed up in armed insurrection and the use of revolutionary violence as the cure-all for the problem of imperialist, militarist violence. In 1920, Paul Levi outlined the composition of the Spartacus League to the Second Congress of the Communist International: 'Groups which had formed themselves in the course of the revolutionary development all over Germany, most of the time with no clear political ideas, most often attracted by the name of Karl Liebknecht . . . groups of people who had never been organised on a political level before.'[14]

The danger which threatened the Spartacus League lay in this isolation which was imposed upon it as much by the results of the initiatives of its own forces as by the efforts of the large parties which feared it. The spearhead of these forces tended to be elements who were isolated not only from the mass organisations, but from the working class itself and its traditions. They were young people, impatient and inexperienced, convinced that their mission was not that of a vanguard, with the role of patient explanation, but that of a militant minority.

---

[14] Report to the Second Congress, Levi Archives, P124/8, p. 3.

Jogiches informed Thalheimer after 9 November that Luxemburg was aware that the revolt must be transformed into a social revolution, but this meant the entry of the working class on a mass scale into the strife on the basis of its own class demands. This was why she welcomed with hope and even with enthusiasm the beginning of action by workers for economic demands, which revealed itself through the strikes which broke out across the country at the end of November. *Die Rote Fahne* wrote on 15 November:

> The civil war which everyone is doing their best, in agony and anxiety, to keep out of the Revolution, is not letting itself be kept out. The civil war is nothing but a different name for the class war, and the idea that we could arrive at socialism by way of the decrees of a parliamentary majority is nothing but an absurd petty-bourgeois illusion.[15]

The class action of workers for their economic demands as employees of capital is indeed one of the routes by which working people can be led most quickly to lose the illusions which they hold regarding parties that wield power in their name. The government of People's Commissars genuinely feared workers' demands, and busied itself with preventing strikes. Barth himself was responsible for labour questions in the Cabinet, and he begged the workers not to 'debase the Revolution to a movement for wages'.[16]

In this perspective, the struggle of revolutionaries for influence in the unions took on extreme importance. The grip on the trade-union apparatus maintained by the most conservative elements and counter-revolutionary elements of the SPD, was very strong. It was further strengthened by the fact that millions of workers had recently joined, knowing little about politics, but interested first and foremost in defending their material conditions. The majority of Spartacist activists and of the revolutionaries of the IKD confused the organisations with their leaders. They denounced trade unions with hatred and contempt, as agencies of the bourgeoisie, or as outdated forms of organisation. They appealed to class-conscious working people to organise outside of them.

Confronted with calls for workers to leave the unions which were issued by some local branches, the old Spartacist nucleus in the union organisations hesitated to express an opinion, whilst at the same time conceding that it

---

[15] *Die Rote Fahne*, 27 November 1918.
[16] *Die Rote Fahne*, 28 November 1918.

was necessary 'to liquidate the trade unions'. These hesitations cost them dearly, because it was through the channel of the trade unions, which many revolutionary activists no longer tried to influence from within, that the SPD undertook to win the new strata of workers, and to regain their influence.

The Spartacus League breaks with the Independents

The struggle between the two powers traced a line of fundamental cleavage between those who supported conciliar power and the supporters of a constituent assembly. This line was soon to cut through the heart of the USPD, despite the efforts of its leaders to temporise. On 18 November, at the Busch Circus, Haase came out in favour of the principle of the Constituent Assembly, but insisted on the need to avoid convening it prematurely.[17] Hilferding, in the columns of *Freiheit*, explained that the administration had to be democratised and the economy socialised before the Assembly was convened.[18] On 27 November, the USPD Executive published a declaration in which it asserted that the Constituent Assembly should only be convened 'if the technical and political conditions, were fulfilled, if in itself it authentically expressed the will of the enlightened people'.[19]

In *Die Rote Fahne*, Luxemburg subjected the position of the Party to a rigorous criticism, stating that full clarification was necessary, and called for a special conference to be held to discuss this central question.[20]

From then on, the internal conflict took up nearly all the attention and energy of the USPD activists. The final surrender to Ebert by Haase and his colleagues on the question of setting the date for the elections on 16 February shed new light on the preceding discussions. It reinforced the position of the supporters of a special congress, and embarrassed those who did not want such a congress at any price because the mere act of calling it would represent a retreat on their part. Calling the congress would of itself mean turning to the Left and eliminating the Haase leadership. *Die Rote Fahne* concentrated its fire on the USPD leadership, and tried to mobilise the members to force

---

[17] *Vorwärts*, 20 November 1918.
[18] *Freiheit,* 18 November 1918.
[19] *Freiheit*, 27 November 1918; *Dokumente und Materialen*, Volume 2/2, op. cit., pp. 494–6.
[20] *Die Rote Fahne*, 29 November 1918; *Dokumente und Materialen*, Volume 2/2, op. cit., pp. 497–500.

the holding of the congress. In fact, the Spartacists would be able to take the leadership in the course of a battle in which they were in a position to bring together all the forces of the Left of the Party. The leadership continued to oppose the demand, using technical arguments which really expressed a political choice. Calling a congress, it insisted, would hold up the serious preparation of their electoral campaign. The Spartacists were accused of sabotaging the work of the Party.

Very quickly the feeling grew that the USPD was heading for a split, almost by mutual consent. Ströbel in *Freiheit* on 8 December, and Breitscheid in *Der Sozialist* on the 12th declared that the differences between the two wings of the party were insurmountable. On 12 December, the general meeting of the USPD in Stuttgart declared for the re-election of the workers' and soldiers' councils, and for conciliar power.[21] Berlin gave still more hope for the Spartacists; their people worked closely with the revolutionary delegates, and on a number of occasions the workers in the big factories in their thousands attended Spartacist meetings and demonstrations and applauded their speakers, Liebknecht, Levi and Pieck. On 14 December, civil war nearly broke out in the USPD. *Die Rote Fahne* published a draft programme, 'What Does the Spartacus League Want?', written jointly by Levi and Luxemburg.[22] At the same time, *Freiheit* attacked the Bolsheviks and Spartacists under the headline 'German Tactics for a German Revolution', and identified convening the Constituent Assembly as the immediate revolutionary task.[23]

On 15 December, immediately before the meeting of the Congress of the Councils, the Berlin conference of the USPD was held, to take a decision on the matter of the special party congress. The debate covered the whole range of political problems. Haase spoke for the Executive, defending the policy of collaborating with Ebert and Scheidemann, and justifying the decision of the government to convene the Assembly. He called on the conference to recognise the fact that the majority of the country was at that time behind Ebert, and that the game of democracy must be played in order to construct a new social order in which the councils would have their place in the constitution, by the side of an assembly elected by universal suffrage. According to Haase,

---

[21] *Die Rote Fahne*, 15 December 1918; *Dokumente und Materialen*, Volume 2/2, op. cit., pp. 595–6.
[22] *Die Rote Fahne*, 14 December 1918. On Levi's role in drawing it up, see Beradt, op. cit., p. 24.
[23] *Freiheit*, 14 December 1918.

the proposals of the Spartacists were no more than a caricature of the slogans of the Bolsheviks shipped into Germany, whereas the situation was profoundly different, in the first place because Germany was an advanced country, and secondly, because the international situation required the election of a representative assembly in Germany. He accused the Spartacists of helping the counter-revolutionaries, who used them to frighten the petty bourgeoisie by brandishing the spectre of dictatorship and terror. He appealed to the Spartacists to draw the necessary conclusions about their differences from the rest of the Party, and to leave an organisation in which there was no longer a place for them.[24]

Luxemburg presented the case against Haase, in the form of a violent attack on the work of Ebert's government. She said that Haase was not wrong when he said that the masses were behind Ebert. But he did not say that they were there because, amongst other reasons, the Independents supported Ebert, and Haase was a member of his government. Let Haase and his friends break with Ebert and leave his government, then the masses will no doubt begin to see more clearly and to understand what forces are concealing themselves – more and more unsuccessfully – behind Ebert. Luxemburg spoke sarcastically about Haase's profession of democratic faith: 'If it is a question of democratic principle, then let us have some democracy first in our own party! First call the congress, so that the masses can say whether they still want this government!'[25]

Liebknecht and Eberlein spoke in support of her, and Hilferding and Ströbel defended the position of Haase. In the closing vote, a resolution from Hilferding spelling out that the Party's principal task was to prepare for elections was counterposed to Luxemburg's motion for a special congress. The former was carried by 485 votes to 185.[26] The Left was defeated in what it regarded as its bastion. *Freiheit* was to carry a headline 'Clarity at Last', and the principal newspapers of the Independents hailed the event.

But the USPD had practically exploded. Whilst Dittmann, Haase and Hilferding stood by Ebert, the Independent delegates from the provinces, people such as Brass, Curt Geyer and Wilhelm Koenen, worked with the Berlin revolutionaries, and about forty of them agreed on the first day to meet as a faction with Liebknecht.[27] In most of the votes, the USPD divided into

---

[24] *Freiheit*, 16 December 1918.
[25] Ibid.; *Dokumente und Materialen*, Volume 2/2, op. cit., pp. 603–6.
[26] Ibid.
[27] *Illustrierte Geschichte der Novemberrevolution in Deutschland*, Berlin, 1968, p. 246.

two nearly equal parts. At the end of the congress, the decision to boycott the Executive Council, which Richard Müller carried, created an intolerable situation for the Independent ministers.

On 21 November, the revolutionary delegates met with the Party's representatives in the big factories in the capital. This gathering demanded almost unanimously that a special congress be held before the end of December, that Haase and his colleagues resign from the government, and that an anti-parliamentarian electoral campaign be organised. It expressly denounced the policy of Barth in the Cabinet, declaring that it no longer had confidence in him, and denied him the right to represent them in the future.[28] It is very likely that it was during the same meeting that the revolutionary delegates elected an action committee of five, in which Ledebour and Däumig, the left Independents, joined Liebknecht and Pieck, the Spartacists, with Paul Scholze in the chair.[29] The main question on the agenda was the formation of a new party based on the Spartacists and the revolutionary delegates, and drawing in numerous elements from the Independents.

Already at the demonstration on 16 December in front of the Reichstag, the metalworker Richard Nowakowski, one of the most influential of the revolutionary delegates, had welcomed the demonstrators, 'in the name of the USPD and of the Spartacist League'.[30] At the moment when the question of finally leaving the USPD and forming a new party faced the Spartacists, they could reasonably hope to attract the leading nucleus of the revolutionary delegates, and, through them, the vanguard of the Berlin working class, the leaders and organisers of the class in the factories. They tried to go faster, and on 22 December, Wilhelm Pieck wrote in the name of the League to the USPD to demand that within three days it call a congress which would meet before the end of the month.[31] The reply was, of course, known in advance, and the question of constructing a revolutionary party was finally posed less than two months after the Revolution began.

---

[28] *Die Rote Fahne*, 23 December 1918; *Dokumente und Materialen*, Volume 2/2, op. cit., p. 645.
[29] *Vorwärts und nicht vergessen*, op. cit., p. 61; Pieck, and after him numerous authors, put this meeting on 18 December, for which there is no documentary evidence.
[30] *Die Rote Fahne*, 17 December 1918.
[31] *Die Rote Fahne*, 24 December 1918; *Dokumente und Materialen*, Volume 2/2, op. cit., pp. 646–7.

Convergent and contradictory tendencies

In the eyes of the bourgeoisie, this party already existed. The press indiscriminately applied the label 'Spartacist' to all the extremist groups, and hardly drew any distinctions amongst the people whom it did its best to present as 'the men with knives between their teeth'. The reality was that neither the Russian Revolution nor the November Revolution had succeeded in completely reconciling the groups which had disagreed before and especially during the War about how to prepare and carry through the proletarian revolution in Germany.

The 'left radicals' – the Bremen people and the group to which this name was applied in Berlin – had shown a tendency towards unification. A conference in Bremen on 23 November decided to found a new organisation, the International Communists of Germany (IKD).[32] They had some local influence, particularly in the shipyards and amongst the port workers. They had always opposed revolutionaries joining the USPD, and regarded what had happened as a striking confirmation – was not their principal adversary in Bremen, Alfred Henke, the strongest supporter of Haase in the big port, and consequently the government's attorney? At the same time, they were aware that in Germany as a whole, they did not have sufficient forces to form by themselves even the embryo of a new revolutionary party.

As in 1917, they gave critical support to the Spartacists, and stated that they would back any initiative on its part in the direction of an independent organisation of revolutionaries by way of a definite break from the centrists.[33] They adopted the name of 'Communists' unanimously after a speech by Johann Knief. In this they showed both their attachment to the Russian Revolution, and their determination to throw away 'the dirty shirt', to break from the past and from discredited labels. They fought to widen and deepen the power of the councils, and to federate the communist groups in Germany. The left radicals of Hamburg, their neighbours, so near to them politically that historians have often confused them, joined the IKD at this point, as well as the remains in Berlin of Borchardt's group, which the young writer Werner Möller was leading.

The Spartacists were gradually organising themselves. The League had had the beginnings of an apparatus since 11 November, publications, offices which

---

[32] *Der Kommunist*, Bremen, 28 November 1918; *Dokumente und Materialen*, Volume 2/2, op. cit., pp. 456–8.
[33] Ibid., p. 456.

it had several times to vacate, and contribution cards which it sold. Outside Berlin, it had contacts with nearly all the important centres, in Bavaria, Brunswick, Chemnitz, Dresden, Leipzig, Upper Silesia, East Prussia, Stuttgart, Thuringia and Hanau, as well as the Ruhr where 'the Communist Workers' Party of Essen-Ruhr (members of the Spartacus League)' had just been formed. In these regions, the League's contacts reflected the revolutionaries' influence prior to the November Revolution.[34] Since then, they had established new contacts and formed new groups in Beuthen, Brandenburg, Erfurt, Frankfurt-am-Main, Kiel, Munich, Nuremberg and Solingen.[35] However, it was still organisationally what the 'group' had been, a fairly loose network around a small nucleus of political leaders.

Nowhere did the Spartacists form an organised faction, nowhere did they undertake systematic work to build their faction or even an organised tendency either in the workers' councils[36] or in the USPD, where their work rested on the propaganda of *Die Rote Fahne* and on the prestige and activity of their most prominent members. At the same time, however, the League held to its conception of revolutionary agitation and moving the masses into action, and worked to mobilise the broad masses of workers whose spontaneous action it hoped to enlighten and inspire. To this effect it organised many meetings and demonstrations.

In order to counterbalance the almost exclusive influence of the Majority socialists on the soldiers and their councils, it founded on 15 November the League of Red Soldiers, on the initiative of a group of their members who until then had specialised in work amongst the youth, Karl Schulz, Peter Maslowski and Willi Budich.[37] This group published three times a week a special sheet, *Der Rote Soldat*.[38] Liebknecht, an indefatigable agitator, spoke everywhere that revolutionary ideas could find an echo. Entire columns of the slim *Die Rote Fahne* were devoted to calls for gatherings, meetings, demonstrations, and processions of soldiers, unemployed, deserters and men on leave. The fact is that the Spartacists had neither the power nor, doubtless,

---

[34] *Illustrierte Geschichte der Novemberrevolution in Deutschland*, op. cit., p. 284.

[35] Ibid., p. 283.

[36] See the replies given to Radek by Liebknecht on the organisation at the beginning of December (Radek, *November*, op. cit., p. 132).

[37] *Die Rote Fahne*, 18 November 1918; B. Gross, *Willi Münzenberg*, Stuttgart, 1967, p. 89.

[38] *Der Rote Soldat*, no. 1, 23 November 1918.

the desire to control these demonstrations, and they often provided the opportunity for dubious elements to engage in violent, futile and even harmful incidents. The leaders knew the dangers for the image which they wanted to give of their movement, coming from the untimely enthusiasm of elements often foreign to the industrial working class who claimed to be supporters of their organisation. Luxemburg admitted in *Die Rote Fahne* the danger from the initiatives of the déclassé elements of whom there were large numbers in the capital: 'They disfigure our socialist aims, fully aware and knowing very well what they are doing, and are trying to divert our socialist aims into lumpen-proletarian adventures, leading the masses astray.'[39]

Similarly, the communists of the IKD expressed their anxiety about the initiatives which they regarded as 'revolutionary impatience'; they declared that there could be no question of even thinking of replacing Ebert by a government of revolutionaries which was not solidly based on a majority in the councils.[40]

The anxious revolutionaries were unable to turn the tide. To begin with, the impression which the Spartacists' demonstrations created, the large numbers of people whom they attracted, gave to the leaders and the participants alike a false impression of their power. Liebknecht might get the impression from the crowds which applauded him that he ruled the streets, when, for lack of a real organisation, he was not master even of his own troops, especially when they were intoxicated with their numbers and their shouting. There was no question of giving lectures or courses in 'theory' to these impatient, hard men who had come out of the War; they wanted clear slogans that would enthuse them, they wanted action. Accordingly, every Spartacist meeting, the speakers attacked the Ebert government, denounced its collaboration with the General Staff, and called for it to be brought down. The crowds who listened to them were being radicalised, in a sense, in isolation, and their will to act grew in inverse proportion to the influence of the revolutionaries in the councils, so that they were in the end ready to sweep them away if the councils rejected their leadership.

The Social Democrats and army chiefs exploited this situation by systematically trying to provoke incidents which enabled them to denounce the Spartacists for their 'violence' before the mass of moderate working people.

---

[39] *Die Rote Fahne*, 18 November 1918.
[40] *Der Kommunist*, Dresden, no. 5, 1918, *Dokumente und Materialen*, Volume 2/2, op. cit., pp. 614–5.

On 21 November, after three simultaneous meetings addressed by Liebknecht, Luxemburg and Levi,[41] the participants joined together for a demonstration outside the police headquarters; some soldiers on a vehicle opened fire.[42] On 6 December, supporters of Wels fired on a demonstration of the League of Red Soldiers, killing fourteen people, and wounding many, including Budich.[43]

Following a protest demonstration on the following day, a group of soldiers occupied the editorial premises of *Die Rote Fahne*, arrested Liebknecht, and tried to take him away.[44] The Spartacist leaflets and *Die Rote Fahne* denounced 'Bloody Wels'. The demonstrators were more and more numerous, and appeared to be more determined: 150,000 on 8 December,[45] and over 250,000 on the 16th, the day when the Congress of Councils opened.[46] That day, Levi's speech called for determination, coolness and calm; if the Congress failed to fulfil its historic mission and called the Constituent Assembly, the working people who supported conciliar power would know how to bring that régime down, as they had brought down the old régime.[47] But Liebknecht, who spoke after him, got thunderous applause when he called for purging the 'nests of counter-revolution', in the front ranks of which he placed the 'Ebert-Scheidemann government'.[48]

When the incidents of 'Bloody Christmas' took place between the army and the Berlin workers,[49] it was Spartacist elements who, on their own initiative, attacked the *Vorwärts* building[50] and then printed, under the title *Red Vorwärts*, leaflets calling for the Ebert government to be overthrown and for it to be replaced by 'real socialists, that is, communists',[51] and then addressed an ultimatum to the government in the name of 'the revolutionary workers and

---

[41] *Die Rote Fahne*, 22 November 1918; resolution in *Dokumente und Materialen*, Volume 2/2, op. cit., p. 444.

[42] *Die Rote Fahne*, 22 November 1918.

[43] *Die Rote Fahne*, 7 and 8 December 1918; *Illustrierte Geschichte der deutschen Revolution*, op. cit., pp. 242–5; *Illustrierte Geschichte der Novemberrevolution in Deutschland*, op. cit., p. 235; K. Wrobel, *Der Sieg der Arbeiter und Matrosen*, Berlin, 1958, p. 50.

[44] *Die Rote Fahne*, 8 December 1918; *Illustrierte Geschichte der deutschen Revolution*, op. cit., p. 246.

[45] *Die Rote Fahne*, 9 December 1918.

[46] *Die Rote Fahne*, 17 December 1918; *Dokumente und Materialen*, Volume 2/2, op. cit., pp. 622–5.

[47] *Dokumente und Materialen*, Volume 2/2, op. cit., p. 623.

[48] Ibid., p. 624.

[49] See Chapter 12.

[50] Leaflet in *Dokumente und Materialen*, Volume 2/2, op. cit., pp. 660–2. At the trial of Ledebour, Ernest Meyer was to describe the anger of Luxemburg and Liebknecht when they learnt of this initiative (*Ledebour Prozess*, Berlin, 1919, p. 516).

[51] *Dokumente und Materialen*, Volume 2/2, op. cit., pp. 663–4.

soldiers of Greater Berlin'.[52] In fact, two distinct political lines appeared in the activity of the Spartacists during these days in December, when the capital went through an almost uninterrupted succession of demonstrations, fights and riots.

On the one hand, Luxemburg explained in *Die Rote Fahne* the position of the Party Zentrale, to the effect that the ruling classes had, after regrouping behind Ebert, provisionally won a victory, which meant that the workers were obliged to join the electoral campaign, utilising it as a platform to mobilise the masses.[53] On the other, the League of Red Soldiers, on the day following the decision of the Councils' Congress, called for a struggle which could only mean preventive action against the elections, and hence a struggle to overthrow the government.[54]

Luxemburg, with Jogiches and Levi, who shared her viewpoint on the question of the Constituent Assembly, were in a definite minority in the Spartacist League, where the ultra-left current in favour of boycotting the elections was in a large majority, even though no vote had yet enabled the respective strengths of the currents to be measured. The situation was the same within the IKD; Johann Knief, who spoke in favour of taking part in a campaign which had now become inevitable in the framework of the elections, was on the point of being swamped by the supporters of the boycott, at the head of whom stood Paul Frölich and Felix Schmidt.[55] The same differences were to be found in the group of the revolutionary delegates: it was to decide a few days later by 26 votes to 16 to accept the accomplished fact, and consequently to take part in the elections in the form of an anti-electoralist electoral struggle.[56]

Concern to avoid adventures and ultra-left initiatives was greatest amongst the representatives of the factories. On 26 December, a general meeting of revolutionary delegates and convenors of the big factories drew a balance sheet of the Christmas events. They declared that they understood the bitterness of the revolutionary workers who had tried to take back *Vorwärts*, which the army chiefs had stolen from the proletariat in 1916, but the resolution voted

---

[52] Ibid., p. 665.
[53] 'Die Wahlen zur Nationalversammlung', *Die Rote Fahne*, 23 December 1918; *Dokumente und Materialen*, Volume 2/2, op. cit., pp. 648–50.
[54] Leaflet in ibid., pp. 642–4.
[55] *Vorwärts und nicht vergessen*, op. cit., pp. 175–6.
[56] *Bericht über dem Gründungsparteitag der KPD*, op. cit., p. 47.

for declared that the occupation of the building was untimely, and called for it to be evacuated. This declaration, signed by Scholze, Nowakowski and Paul Weyer was published in *Die Rote Fahne*.[57] The differences were now obvious and public, and the question of the attitude towards the elections for the Constituent Assembly which the Congress of Councils had adopted provoked new divisions in the revolutionary movement.

---

[57] *Die Rote Fahne*, 17 December 1918; *Dokumente und Materialen*, Volume 2/2, op. cit., pp. 666–7. Wilhelm Pieck (op. cit., p. 61) writes that this resolution, inspired by Ernst Däumig, was a manoeuvre directed against the Spartacists. In fact, it was directed against the ultra-left initiatives, of which the Spartacists had no monopoly, but on the contrary it was perfectly within the line defined by the Zentrale, particularly in the draft programme published in *Die Rote Fahne* on 14 December.

Chapter Eleven

The Foundation of the Communist Party of Germany

The foundation of the Communist Party of Germany was carried out in this atmosphere of political confusion amongst the revolutionary vanguard. The preparations for it coincided with the arrival in Berlin of three of the delegates sent by Moscow to represent Soviet Russia at the Congress of the Councils of Berlin. They had been turned back at the frontier, and had succeeded in crossing it secretly.[1] All three were destined to play a role in the new party. The most important was Karl Radek; the other two, Krebs (also known as 'Rakov' and 'Felix Wolf') and Ernst Reuter-Friesland, had been won to Bolshevism in Russia itself.

The choice of these emissaries was doubtless unfortunate. Felix Wolf did not know Germany. Friesland was also unknown to the old Spartacus nucleus and even to the radical movement, with whom he had had no contact before the War. Radek, on the other hand, was intimately involved in the whole history of the German Left, but it was precisely this fact that made his presence hardly opportune from certain points of view. To be sure, he had connections with the Bremen communists. But a

---

[1] Brandt and Lowenthal, op. cit., p. 113; Radek, op. cit., pp. 128–32. Hermann Osterloh, one of the leaders of the prisoners of war and of the German section, was a member of the delegation, but was not able to get into Germany (ibid., p. 122).

strong personal animosity existed between him and Luxemburg and Jogiches. This arose out of differences within Polish Social Democracy, and had been fed by the 'Radek affair' just before the war. However, he enjoyed the advantage of his connections with Paul Levi in Switzerland during the War. Levi is said to have pacified the anger of Luxemburg, who fulminated against the sending of a 'commissar'.[2] He welcomed, introduced and escorted Radek. Then, above all, it has to be recognised that the envoys from Moscow, irrespective of their personalities, had on their side the fact that they were trusted by the Bolshevik Party, the leaders of the Russian Revolution, and this simple fact conferred on them an immense authority in the eyes of the German revolutionaries. Radek wrote a lively, emotional account of his meeting with the German leaders. Apart from embarrassment in the first moments, the memories of past quarrels did not seem to weigh heavily against the tasks of the hour. After an exchange of views about the situation in Russia – the presence of her friend Dzerzhinsky at the head of the Cheka surprised Luxemburg – and on the German political questions of the moment, the discussion turned to the attitude to be taken towards the calling of the Constituent Assembly, and towards the need to form a Communist Party.[3]

Preliminary discussions

At that moment the principal obstacles came, not from the Spartacists but from the 'Communists' of the IKD. The latter had not forgotten the disagreements in 1917 about the USPD, nor their disappointment when the Spartacists decided in November to stay within that party. Johann Knief opposed fusion with the Spartacists, despite the decisions which had just been reached by the conference of the IKD. He put his position bluntly to Radek, who had come to Bremen. He believed that the Ebert-Haase government would soon be swamped by the mass movement, and that the most probable replacement would be a government further to the left, of Ledebour, Liebknecht and Luxemburg, born out of what he called 'revolutionary impatience', and this would raise the danger that the supporters of the councils and the real communists would be discredited. He believed that the hour of the genuine revolutionaries – himself and his supporters – would sound only after that

---

[2] Beradt, op. cit., p. 43, with no reference to any document.
[3] Radek, *November*, op. cit., pp. 132–4.

government had failed. Moreover, whilst he was in favour of a Bolshevik Party being formed in Germany, he thought that such a party could not possibly include Luxemburg and her supporters, whom he believed to be alien to the spirit of Bolshevism. At the same time, he told Radek that the proletarian revolution could win in Germany only on the basis of a broad mass movement, and that the firm centralism which Jogiches would not fail to initiate in a party formed with the Spartacists would be a real problem. The discussion between the two men was a hard one, but it ended in a compromise: rather than come into opposition to the spokesman of the Bolsheviks in the person of his old friend Radek, Knief was to refrain from intervening and putting his personal position.[4]

The second conference of the IKD was finally held in Berlin during 15–17 December, with delegates from Bremen and Hamburg, the Rhineland, Saxony, Bavaria, Württemberg and Berlin, with the remains of the Borchardt group, but without its leader, Knief's friends and supporters, Frölich, Laufenberg and Otto Rühle. The majority of the delegates accepted that the forthcoming break of the Spartacists from the Independents had removed the principal difference and the essential obstacle to forming a unified party.[5] Knief spoke to propose that the revolutionaries should participate in the election campaign for the Constituent Assembly, but he was in a minority. He then took this opportunity of refusing to be delegated to the fusion conference. Frölich, who wanted to boycott the election, was mandated to represent the Bremen communists in the new unified leadership.[6] Radek eloquently expounded his arguments for fusion, which he said was overdue.[7] Certain fundamental questions which divided the Spartacists from the Bremen communists, such as that of the trade unions, do not seem to have been tackled at all.

Moreover, the Spartacist leadership was also divided. Luxemburg and Jogiches appear to have been hostile at the beginning to fusion with the 'communists', and Jogiches appears even to have opposed it vigorously to the end. In fact, he believed that they should stay in the USPD until its next congress, in order on that occasion to attract all the elements of the Left

---

[4] Ibid., p. 135.

[5] *Der Kommunist*, Bremen, no. 5, 1918; *Dokumente und Materialen*, Volume 2/2, op. cit., pp. 609–13 for the resolution adopted.

[6] *Vorwärts und nicht vergessen*, op. cit., p. 176.

[7] *Illustrierte Geschichte der deutschen Revolution*, op. cit., p. 264; Jogiches was also present.

who would remain in the Party were the Spartacists to break prematurely. Clara Zetkin was to say on this subject in 1921: 'Shortly beforehand, I had a conversation with comrade Luxemburg. She herself and comrade Jogiches, still more vigorously, believed that it was only after the Independent Social-Democratic Party congress that we should break with it, and form ourselves into a communist party.'[8]

Zetkin was not present at the Foundation Congress; moreover she declared that she was not informed that it was to take place. According to Fritz Heckert, she is said to have cried out, 'What imbeciles!', when she heard that the decision had been taken.[9] But, here too, the intervention of Radek, with the prestige of the October Revolution behind him, was decisive, and Luxemburg let herself be convinced not to wait for the USPD's congress in order to split. Nonetheless, she revealed important disagreements concerning the name which the new party was to adopt. Eberlein, whose evidence on the point is confirmed by that of Levi, summed up her position in these words:

> The Russian Communist Party is still the only one in the International. The parties of the Second International are going to oppose it without mercy. The duty of the communists is to tear the socialist parties of Western Europe away from the Second International in order to found a new, revolutionary International. The Russian Communist Party will not succeed in doing that by itself. There is a deep gulf between it and the socialist parties of the West, especially the French, English and American. It is for us, the German revolutionaries, to be the means of unity between the revolutionaries of Eastern Europe and the still-reformist socialists of the West. It is for us to hasten the breakaway of these socialists from reformism. We shall do our duty better as a 'socialist party'. If we present ourselves as a 'communist party', the closeness of our links with the Russians will complicate our task in the West.[10]

In the end, the Zentrale rejected by four votes to three, with Paul Levi abstaining, the proposal of Luxemburg to call the new party 'Socialist'.[11] On 29 December 1918 – the same day as the Independents left the Ebert government

---

[8] *Protokoll des III Kongresses der Kommunistischen Internationale (Moskau, 22 Juni bis 12 Juli 1921)*, Hamburg, 1921, p. 668.

[9] Ibid., pp. 541, 669.

[10] 'Spartakus und die Dritte Internationale', *Inprekorr*, no. 28, 29 February 1924, pp. 306–7.

[11] Ibid., p. 307.

– the conference of the Spartacus League approved by 80 votes to three the proposal to leave the Social-Democratic Party to found a communist party.[12] The unification of the Spartacus League and the IKD and the foundation of a German Communist Party had been achieved. It remained to be seen what left-wing elements of the USPD would join it, and especially what positions it would take on the problems that confronted it at the end of 1918.

Commenting on the positions of Willi Münzenberg in the Youth International, Johann Knief wrote on 24 December that they were not yet 'in the spirit of the communists'.[13] In his opinion, the principal difference was between Spartacists and communists. However, the Founding Congress was to show that in reality the ultra-leftists won the day in the new party over the Spartacists personified by Luxemburg as well as over the communists represented by Knief, for the leaders of the ultra-left current came both from the Spartacists, for instance the Berliners Schröder and Wendel, and from the IKD, such as Otto Rühle, Frölich and Werner Möller.

The victory of the ultra-leftists at the Founding Congress of the KPD(S)

The Congress met in Berlin on 30 December 1918. There were 83 delegates from the Spartacus League, and 29 from the IKD. The capital was still rumbling from the violent incidents at Christmas. The resignation of the Independent ministers seemed to be opening a new stage in the radicalisation of the masses. Paul Levi was later to describe the atmosphere in these terms:

> The air of Berlin . . . was filled with revolutionary tension. . . . There was no one who did not feel that the immediate future would see further great demonstrations and actions. . . . The delegates who represented these hitherto-unorganised masses who had come to us exclusively in action, through it and for it, just could not understand that any new action, which could easily be foreseen, might end not in victory but in retreat. They did not consider, even in their worst dreams, following a tactic which would have left them a margin of manoeuvre if they needed to retreat.[14]

---

[12] *1918. Erinnerungen von Veteranen*, op. cit., pp. 23–4. The three votes against were those of Jogiches, Werner Hirsch and a delegate from Mühleim, Meister, probably in fact Minster (*Die Rote Fahne*, 30 December 1928).

[13] *Der Kommunist*, Bremen, 24 December 1918, cited in Gross, op. cit., p. 88.

[14] Report to the Second Congress of the Comintern, Levi Archives, P124/8, p. 4.

Liebknecht delivered the opening speech. This dealt with 'the crisis in the Independent Social-Democratic Party', and with the decision to be reached in respect of building a new party. His tone was very hard. He retraced the political past of the centrist opposition, in which he said numerous revisionists were to be found, both amongst the leaders and amongst the mass of the membership, and he characterised its past activity as 'parliamentary cretinism'. He attacked the growth of the 'puerile and mechanistic' conception which had prevailed in the preparing of the November insurrection, with the 'failure to understand the supreme importance of mass action itself, and overestimation of bureaucratic, parliamentary and other activities'. He recalled that, in the past, the Spartacists had enjoyed total freedom of action in the USPD, and stated: 'We joined the USPD in order to drive forward through our efforts all those who could be driven, in order to make the best elements advance, and to unite them in order to win over the largest possible revolutionary forces, and to organise them in a single, revolutionary, proletarian party. . . . It was a labour of Sisyphus.'[15]

Having indicted the Independents, the 'fig leaf' for Ebert and Scheidemann since 9 December, and having recalled the refusal of the Executive to call the party congress, he drew the conclusion that the USPD was moribund, and that the mass of its members who were not preparing to break from it were in the process of returning to the camp of the Majority socialists. He therefore advocated a clear and immediate break and the foundation of a new party, and moved a motion in this sense. The name 'Communist Party of Germany (Spartacus)' was preferred, after a brief discussion, to those of 'Workers' Communist Party of Germany' and 'Revolutionary Communist Party of Germany' proposed by the preparatory commission.[16]

Radek then spoke in the name of the Russian Soviet government. He outlined bluntly the situation of Russia, and took pains to point out the difficulties which awaited a weak party, born nonetheless at an auspicious time, that of the most serious world crisis. He ended by opening the perspective of the International:

---

[15] *Der Gründungsparteitag der KPD*, op. cit., pp. 52–6. We refer to this text, established by Hermann Weber according to the stenographic record discovered in Levi's archives, rather than to the very incomplete *Bericht über den Gründungsparteitag* (op. cit.) written up during the repression following the January Days by secretaries who attended the sessions.

[16] Ibid., pp. 63–6.

German Social Democracy is dead. It was once the authority throughout the world. It now has no more authority, and from now on, no section of the International will have the authority which the German section once had. The International will be a league of working classes, in which each will know why it is fighting and will follow its own road, which nevertheless will be the same as that of the others.[17]

On the afternoon of 30 December, the task fell to Paul Levi of presenting the position of the Zentrale on the question of the elections to the Constituent Assembly. He began by explaining a point on which, it seemed, all the delegates agreed: the role which the German bourgeoisie and its agents expected the Constituent Assembly to play. He declared: 'The road to the victory of the proletariat can pass only over the corpse of the National Assembly.' But he then added almost immediately: 'Despite all that, we propose to you that we do not stand aside from the elections to the National Assembly.'[18]

From that moment, his speech was subjected to violent interruptions and vehement objections. He tried to show how the presence of Communist deputies in parliament, unlike the old Social-Democratic practices, could help revolutionary struggles, and he quoted the example of the Russians who participated in the elections to the Constituent Assembly before they dissolved it. Someone shouted: 'Let's do that!' He replied: 'What leads you to believe that the whole of Germany is today at as advanced a level of the revolution as the comrade believes?' He thought that the workers could effectively overthrow the Assembly in Berlin, in Rhineland-Westphalia and in Upper Silesia. But these districts were not the whole of Germany. The revolutionaries did not have the strength to organise a boycott, which would only damage them. He was still being interrupted when he went on:

> The question is very serious. We see the situation in this way: the decision on this question may influence the fate of our movement for months. . . . So think about the situation as it is: the National Assembly is going to meet. It will meet and you cannot stop it. For months it will dominate all political life in Germany. You will not be able to prevent all eyes from being fixed on it, you will not be able to prevent even the best of your supporters from

---

[17] Ibid., p. 86. This curious description of the International bears no resemblance to the 'world party of revolution' desired by Lenin. Radek was later to formulate very different definitions.

[18] Ibid., p. 90.

being interested in it, seeking information, forecasting and wanting to know what will happen in the National Assembly. It will be in the consciousness of the German workers, and confronted with this fact, do you want to stay outside and work from the outside? Comrades, you want to dissolve the National Assembly. What will you say if the National Assembly meets in a place like Schilda?[19]

Another heckler then shouted that if the Assembly did install itself in a small town, it would thereby condemn itself. This enabled Levi to answer that no social force ever condemns itself, especially when it is a force as powerful as the German bourgeoisie, and that it was the duty of the Communists – who did not believe that the bourgeoisie would commit suicide – to fight wherever they must for the Revolution, and to regroup the workers for the Revolution. There can be no doubt that the young Spartacist speaker achieved a great feat of oratory. But the majority of the delegates were convinced that 'power is in the street', and they would not let the slightest doubt be expressed on this subject.

Levi's speech opened up a stormy debate which divided the Congress into two unequal parts. Luxemburg confessed her bitterness in the face of the 'extremism' of the majority and its tendency to 'neglect the necessary calm, seriousness and reflection'. In her turn, she pointed to the example of Russia. She recalled that the German Revolution had only just begun, whilst that of October 1917 had begun in 1905, and declared that the masses in Germany, who had not had enough time to develop the power of their councils, were not mature enough to overthrow the Constituent Assembly. She exposed the contradictions in the argument of the supporters of a boycott, who feared the effects of the elections on the consciousness of the masses, and who nonetheless thought that the masses were sufficiently conscious to prevent them from being held.[20] Käthe Duncker told the majority of the delegates that they wanted 'to lance a boil which had not yet ripened'.[21] Heckert waxed ironic about the caution of the radicals and the leftists during the War, and stressed that, even where they had their greatest strength, the Communists were still a minority, and that the majority followed Ebert and Scheidemann.

---

[19] Ibid., pp. 93, 95. We know that, in order to avoid the political pressure of Berlin's workers, the Assembly was to meet in Weimar.
[20] Ibid., pp. 99–104.
[21] Ibid., p. 113.

He proposed participation in the elections with a single list for the whole of Germany consisting solely of the names of Liebknecht and Luxemburg.[22] Liebknecht did not conceal his hesitations, which were well-known, but, because he was disciplined in relation to the Zentrale, he recalled at some length his own role in the Reichstag in mobilising the masses against the War. All these contributions were received coolly by the delegates, even when they were not interrupted.

But they wildly applauded the most leftist speakers such as Otto Rühle, who declared that the proletariat did not have to encumber itself with the Constituent Assembly, 'a new corpse', and that they must finish with 'compromises and opportunism'. In an effort to refute the arguments of Levi about the use of parliament as a platform, he declared: 'Today we have other platforms. The street is the huge platform that we have won and which we shall not abandon, even if they shoot at us.'[23] Participation in the elections, in the eyes of this supporter of 'street power', meant renouncing the revolution. He counterposed a short-term, insurrectionary perspective to Levi's position: 'If it [the Assembly] went to Schilda, we would have to establish ourselves as the new government in Berlin. We still have a fortnight.'[24]

Many of the speeches were in the same style. Leviné said that the Spartacists, who were too weak either to participate or to boycott, should concentrate their forces on agitation in favour of workers' and soldiers' councils,[25] but others spoke of the need to keep their hands unsullied, of the possibility that the masses would not understand them, and denounced the proposal to participate as a sharp turn or even a descent into opportunism. At the end of the debate, the Congress rejected Levi's proposal, and by 62 votes to 23 adopted the counter-proposal moved by Otto Rühle; the Communist Party would not take part in the elections. At this point in the discussion and following this vote, which pleased the left radicals, Karl Becker on behalf of the IKD announced that his group had decided to join the new party.[26] The first day of the Congress ended with an important victory for the leftist wing.

---

[22] Ibid., pp. 113–7.

[23] Ibid., p. 98. On 10 January 1919, Rühle was to call a street demonstration in Dresden. It was met outside the premises of the Social-Democratic newspaper by gunfire which left 12 dead and 52 wounded. Rühle was to be arrested, then released when order was restored (Drabkin, op. cit., pp. 521–2).

[24] *Der Gründungsparteitag der KPD*, op. cit., p. 98.

[25] Ibid., pp. 109–13.

[26] Ibid., pp. 135–6.

On the second day, Lange opened the discussion on 'the economic struggle'. The spokesman of the Zentrale, more cautious than Levi, denounced the conservative role of the trade-union bureaucracies and their efforts to convert the factory committees into simple appendages of the employers' structures, but avoided formulating an opinion about whether revolutionaries should join and conduct militant activity within the traditional trade unions.[27] Several delegates were to criticise him for this. Rieger, from Berlin, thought that belonging to the Communist Party was incompatible with being in a trade-union organisation.[28] Frölich declared that it was impossible to win the unions from within, and that the slogan 'Leave the unions!' must be advanced. He proposed building 'workers' unions' in the workplaces, abolishing once and for all the frontier between the Party and the trade unions.[29] Heckert opposed Frölich's arguments, and emphasised that large masses joined the unions and that it was necessary not to confuse the role of the unions with that of the factory committees, and warned against the dangers of the slogan of leaving the unions.[30] Luxemburg criticised the position of Frölich on the 'workers' unions' for trying to combine two old forms – party and union – instead of concentrating the proletarian forces on the new forms, workers' councils and factory councils. She was not completely satisfied with the slogan 'Leave the unions!', but agreed that the liquidation of the unions was on the agenda.[31] She proposed to refer the question to a commission, and the Congress, less passionate than the preceding day, supported her.[32]

The Congress applauded Luxemburg at length on the following day during and after her speech on the Party programme, although it was a clear condemnation of the ultra-left orientation of the majority. The formation of the Communist Party marked the time 'when the entire socialist programme' had to be 'established upon a new foundation', and the 'urgent duty' was to replace it 'upon the foundations laid by Marx and Engels in 1848' with the *Communist Manifesto*. She declared:

> Genuine Marxism turns its weapons against those who seek to falsify it.
> Burrowing like a mole beneath the foundations of capitalist society, it has

---

[27] Ibid., pp. 138, 149.
[28] Ibid., p. 159.
[29] Ibid., pp. 152–4.
[30] Ibid., pp. 160–2.
[31] Ibid., pp. 162–4.
[32] Ibid., p. 165.

worked so well that the larger part of the German proletariat is marching today under our banner, the storm-riding standard of revolution. Even in the opposite camp, even where the counter-revolution still seems to rule, we have adherents and future comrades-in-arms.[33]

Humanity faced the choice between a descent into barbarism or salvation through socialism, the historic necessity for its survival. This is the framework within which the situation in Germany had to be analysed: 'The revolution of 9 November was characterised by inadequacy and weakness. . . . What happened on 9 November was to a very small extent the victory of a new principle; it was little more than a collapse of the extant system of imperialism.' Despite the appearance of the workers' and soldiers' councils, 'the slogan of the Revolution', which enabled it 'to be numbered amongst proletarian socialist revolutions', the first phase of the Revolution was characterised by illusions, the illusion of the proletariat and the soldiers about 'their belief in the possibility of unity under the banner of what passes by the name of socialism', the illusion spread by Ebert that 'socialism' flaunted in that way could effectively put a brake on the class struggle. The shootings on 6 and 24 December had dissipated illusions on both sides: 'But it is in truth a great gain for the proletariat that naught beyond these rags and tatters remains from the first phase of the revolution, for there is nothing so destructive as illusion, whereas nothing can be of greater use to the revolution than naked truth.'[34]

Luxemburg said that the second phase of the Revolution had begun with the development and the generalising of the strikes:

> Now I regard it as the very essence of this revolution that strikes will become more and more extensive, until they constitute at last the focus of the revolution. Thus we shall have an economic revolution, and therewith a socialist revolution. The struggle for socialism has to be fought out by the masses, by the masses alone, breast to breast against capitalism; it has to be fought out by those in every occupation, by every proletarian against his employer. Thus only can it be a socialist revolution.[35]

It was during this second phase that the Scheidemann government would disappear. Luxemburg insisted on what she saw as the necessary antidote to the illusions apparently held by the delegates:

---

[33] R. Luxemburg, *Spartacus*, Colombo, 1966, pp. 1, 3, 7.
[34] Ibid., pp. 11–12.
[35] Ibid., p. 14.

We must not again fall into the illusion of the first phase of the revolution, that of 9 November; we must not think that when we wish to bring about a socialist revolution it will suffice to overthrow the capitalist government and to set up another in its place. . . . We must build from below upwards, until the workers' and soldiers' councils gather so much strength that the overthrow of the Ebert-Scheidemann or any similar government will be merely the final act in the drama.[36]

Her speech ended with a warning against those who dreamed of overthrowing the Ebert government at one blow:

Our scripture reads: In the beginning was the deed. Action for us means that the workers' and soldiers' councils must realise their mission and must learn how to become the sole public authorities throughout the realm. Thus only can we mine the ground so effectively as to make everything ready for the revolution which will crown our work. . . . My meaning was that history is not going to make our revolution an easy matter like the bourgeois revolutions. In those revolutions, it sufficed to overthrow that official power at the centre and to replace a dozen or so of persons in authority. . . . It is thus characteristic of the modern proletarian revolution, that we must effect the conquest of political power, not from above, but from beneath. . . . I shall make no attempt to foretell how much time will be required. Who amongst us cares about the time, so long only as our lives suffice to bring it to pass? Enough for us to know clearly the work we have to do; and to the best of my ability I have endeavoured to sketch, in broad outline, the work that lies before us.[37]

A few minutes later, the Congress accepted the draft programme published in *Die Rote Fahne*, which unambiguously declared:

The Spartacus League will refuse to take power merely in the footsteps of the present government when Scheidemann and Ebert have burnt themselves out. . . . If the Spartacus League takes power, it will be in the form of the clear, indubitable will of the great majority of the proletarian masses, in the whole of Germany, and in no other way than in the form of their conscious support of the perspectives, the aims and the methods of struggle advocated

---

[36] Ibid., pp. 19–20.
[37] Ibid., pp. 21–2.

by the League. . . . The victory of Spartacus is to be found, not at the beginning but at the end of the revolution.'[38]

The importance of the Foundation Congress

Several witnesses have recorded the bitterness and pessimism which Leo Jogiches expressed on the morrow of the Congress. In his opinion, the decision to reject taking part in the elections to the Constituent Assembly was clear proof that the foundation of the Party, with the people whom it brought together, was premature.[39] With the agreement of Luxemburg, he asked Zetkin to refrain from joining the Communist Party until she had been able to speak at the next congress of the USPD.[40] Radek was perhaps less pessimistic, although he could not help feeling that he was not dealing with a real party; he was to write later that 'the Congress sharply revealed the youthfulness and inexperience of the Party'.[41] The dominating sentiment at the Congress was its affirmation of total solidarity with the Russian Revolution, which was not a negligible factor. But its links with the masses were very weak. Only Liebknecht was completely optimistic; in his eyes, the youth were with the Spartacists, and he was convinced that the relationship of forces would quickly change from the moment when the Independents had been forced to leave the government.[42]

The fact that the Congress could simultaneously reject the proposal of the Zentrale, expressed by Levi, to take part in the elections, and adopt the programme which Luxemburg presented was indisputably a display of political inconsistency. Moreover, it appears that the dominant leftist current in the Congress did not try to take over the leadership; it was the old Spartacist team, less Mehring, who was ill, and with the addition of Frölich, a representative of the old IKD, who kept the reins in their hands.[43] Doubtless,

---

[38] *Der Gründungsparteitag der KPD*, op. cit., p. 301.
[39] Frölich, op. cit., p. 345.
[40] *Protokoll des III Kongresses der Kommunistischen Internationale*, op. cit., p. 668.
[41] Radek, *November*, op. cit., p. 136.
[42] Ibid.
[43] Those elected to the Zentrale were Hermann Duncker, Käte Duncker, Eberlein, Frölich, Lange, Jogiches, Levi, Liebknecht, Luxemburg, Meyer, Pieck, Thalheimer (*Bericht über den Gründungsparteitag der KPD*, op. cit., p. 45). The corresponding passage, missing in Levi's papers, is reproduced in *Der Gründungsparteitag der KPD*, op. cit., pp. 261–2. Bricianer is therefore wrong when he says (op. cit., p. 158, n. 1) that Paul Levi was a member of the Zentrale in spring 1919 because he had been 'coopted'.

the old Spartacist leaders thought that they had enough influence to restrain the Party from implementing some of the adventurist policies demanded in some of the Congress decisions. There seems to be nothing to suppose that, as Rosenberg suggests, they were tempted to split in order to escape the leftist majority of which they had effectively become hostages.[44]

The structure of the new party was extremely loose, indeed non-existent, and was in any case much closer to that of the USPD than that of the Bolsheviks. The proof of this is provided by Eberlein's organisational report; he found the task of talking about membership cards and subscriptions very hard after the political discussions of the opening days. His report broke away from the electoralist traditions of Social Democracy, because the organisation was to be based on local and workplace groups, while at the same time it was marked with the old hostility of the radicals to centralisation:

> We think that we must put an end to the old system which subordinates the localities to the centre, and feel that the different local and workplace organisations should be fully independent. They should be independent in their activities, and should not always wait for orders from above. . . . The Zentrale assumes principally the task of ensuring an intellectual and political leadership, and of summarising what happens outside the Party.[45]

This report was barely discussed. The exchanges of views and a brief altercation between Ernst Meyer and Karl Becker revealed moreover that the two groups were totally unprepared in this area, and that their conceptions of organisation were unclear. The organisational foundations of the new party were referred for study and to be decided at the next congress. The election of the Zentrale did not automatically make it the leadership of a real party at the national level.

However, the most serious consequence of the decisions taken on 31 December is to be found in the setback to the discussions with the Berlin revolutionary delegates, which were actually proceeding during the Congress. The stakes were high. Liebknecht said that these men were 'the best and most active of the Berlin proletariat', that they were head and shoulders above the high-priests who formed the USPD's cadres, and that the work he had done with them was 'the happiest chapter in his party history'.[46]

---

[44] Rosenberg, op. cit., p. 322.
[45] *Der Gründungsparteitag der KPD*, op. cit., p. 248.
[46] Ibid., pp. 276–7.

The discussions proceeded between a Spartacist delegation led by Liebknecht and a delegation of the nucleus of the revolutionary delegates which included Däumig and Ledebour, Richard Müller, Nowakowski, Eckert and Scholze.[47] They were interrupted several times so that the representatives of the delegates could report to those who mandated them, and could consult them. The Spartacists' delegates were full of hope for the outcome of the negotiations, knowing that these activists, who were formally members of the USPD, were close to the Spartacists, and that they formed an independent group with its own political line and discipline. But Däumig and Ledebour, who were the activists' political advisers and real leaders, never concealed their mistrust, which in Ledebour's case became outright hostility. They both launched an immediate attack, saying that the principal question was participation in the elections to the Constituent Assembly. But a first obstacle arose when the revolutionary delegates preposed that five of them should take part in the commission of the Party Congress on programme and organisation. In this way the representation of the Berlin activists would have been increased, but the Congress was not ready to accept that prospect.[48] Richard Müller reopened the debate with a blunt declaration that joint work depended on the Spartacists giving up their 'old putschist tactic' and their reliance on street demonstrations. Liebknecht replied that on this matter Richard Müller was making himself the spokesman of *Vorwärts*.[49] It is evident that the events at Christmas and the *Red Vorwärts* affair deeply affected the delegates; despite their sympathy for the ideas which the Spartacists defended, and despite their attachment to Liebknecht after weeks of joint work, the representatives of the factories were hostile to the adventurist elements who inspired such activities and claimed to represent Spartacism. Arthur Rosenberg writes: 'Däumig, Ledebour and Richard Müller really wanted to follow a communist policy, but wanted to have nothing to do with the sort of people whom the public regarded as Spartacists.'[50] This formula was doubtless a more accurate description of the average delegate than of the three named leaders, who Liebknecht moreover stressed were not in complete agreement with each other, as Ledebour came over as a determined enemy, whilst Däumig was always very fraternal and close.[51]

---

[47] Ibid., p. 270.
[48] Ibid., p. 271.
[49] Ibid.
[50] Rosenberg, op. cit., p. 323.
[51] *Der Gründungsparteitag der KPD, Protokoll und Materialen*, op. cit., p. 275.

Whatever the facts may have been, the conditions which the revolutionary delegates laid down were an expression of this deep distrust. They demanded that the decision to boycott the elections be dropped, that the programme commission be formed on a parity basis, that the 'street tactics' be precisely and jointly defined, that their representatives should have access to press and leaflet committees, and finally that any reference to 'Spartacus' should be removed from the name of the new party.[52] Undoubtedly, no old Bolshevik would have objected to these conditions, and no old Spartacist would have been strongly opposed. But, to the majority of the Congress, they were not acceptable, and their ironic attitude towards these negotiations was, moreover, one of the symptoms which Radek found to be the most alarming.[53]

Liebknecht and his Communist delegation did not need even to report to and consult with the Congress to be aware that the negotiations had broken down; the Congress had in fact been hostile right from the beginning to fusion with the delegates, and there was no debate on this fundamental question.[54]

This was without doubt the major failure of the German Communists. The foundation of a real Communist Party in Germany in 1919 would have been difficult to conceive without the participation of these worker-delegates who possessed the confidence of the Berlin proletariat, whose struggles they had led during the War and the revolutionary days. Only a few individuals, Paul Eckert, Fritz Winguth and Paul Weyer, were to join the KPD(S). The nucleus of the delegates and the thousands of activists whom they influenced turned their backs on what they believed to be an unwarranted split.[55]

The Spartacist leaders were isolated from these militant organisers of the working class, the genuinely indispensable cadres of a workers' revolutionary party, and, as they were doubtless aware, they had no foothold in the industrial workers' movement. On the other hand, the admirable fighters in the Berlin

---

[52] Ibid., p. 273.

[53] Radek, *November*, op. cit., p. 136.

[54] Bricianer (op. cit., p. 142) believes that this fact justifies him in writing that Liebknecht persisted 'against the will of the majority in carrying out *in secret* futile negotiations with certain Independent leaders and left trade union officials' (our emphasis).

[55] The archives of the IML-ZPA in Berlin contain the protocol of the meeting of delegates on 1 January after negotiations were broken off. Drabkin (op. cit., pp. 461–2, n. 6) summarises the debates. Ledebour, Wegmann, Eckert and Däumig declared in favour of founding a new revolutionary party, which would present itself in the elections; a minority was for entering the KPD; the majority finally opted to stay in the USPD.

factories were deprived of political leadership, or, rather, were lured behind the unsure leaders of the USPD Left, and were to become entangled in the contradictory demands of a situation that was infinitely more complicated than that during the War, in the course of which they had won their stripes and their authority. Between these two groups, whose very closeness deepened their rivalry, there appeared in the explosive situation the risk of competition between them, which was considerably increased by the ultra-left spirit which permeated all the political groups, each trying to show itself as more 'left' than the other. The new-born Communist Party was from the start isolated from the masses, and it was doomed to impotence before it had swung into action. The events of January and the assassination of Liebknecht and Luxemburg were to finish it off. The task of building links with the working masses had to be started all over again.

Nonetheless, when Lenin heard that the Congress had taken place, even though he did not know either what had happened or what it meant, he expressed his delight on 12 January, in the 'Open Letter to the Workers of Europe and America' which he was then in the process of drafting:

> The *foundation* of a genuinely proletarian, genuinely internationalist, genuinely revolutionary Third International, the *Communist International*, became *a fact* when the German Spartacus League, with such world-known and world-famous leaders, with such staunch working-class champions as Liebknecht, Rosa Luxemburg, Clara Zetkin and Franz Mehring, made a clean break with socialists like Scheidemann. . . . It became a fact when the Spartacus League changed its name to the Communist Party of Germany. Though it has not yet been officially inaugurated, the Third International actually exists.[56]

---

[56] V.I. Lenin, 'Letter to the Workers of Europe and America', *Collected Works*, Volume 28, pp. 429–30. The text, which was completed on 21 January, the date on which Lenin was told of the murder of the two German leaders, was published in *Pravda* on 24 January 1919.

Chapter Twelve
The Uprising of January 1919

In his biography of Rosa Luxemburg, Paul Frölich says that she did not permit herself to share the apprehensions and the pessimism of Leo Jogiches following the Founding Congress: 'Rosa simply declared that a new-born child always squalled at first. . . . [S]he expressed her firm conviction that the new party would eventually find the right path despite all its errors, because it embraced the best core of the German proletariat.'[1]

In reality, the pessimism of Jogiches was no less justified than the optimism of his comrade. The situation presented contradictory aspects. Despite the weaknesses of the new party, and despite the defeat of the revolutionaries in the councils, a very deep current, the same as what the leftists in the Spartacus League were expressing in their own way, was radicalising the militant Berlin workers and dispelling the illusions of November. Above all, the situation of the Ebert government seemed to have become more precarious day by day since the Congress of the Councils. The army was decomposing and falling out of the grasp of the officers, whose openly counter-revolutionary undertakings were increasingly raising the masses against them, and forcing even the Independents to break up the

---

[1] Frölich, op. cit., pp. 281–2.

coalition which, as good conciliators, they had hitherto done their best to preserve. Time was working for the Revolution.

December: a month of unrest

At the beginning of December, Luxemburg had commented on the strike movement in her celebrated article 'Acheron has Begun to Flow'.[2] The economic movement of the workers tore away the democratic and, up to that point, purely political mask of the November Revolution, and raised the problems of the day in class terms before the least enlightened masses. Many saw a clear sign when on 8 December, the workers' and soldiers' council in Mülheim arrested Fritz Thyssen, the younger Stinnes and several other leading capitalists.[3]

Another indication of radicalisation was the break-up of the army, the divorce between the government and the General Staff on the one hand and the soldiers' councils on the other, which called into question the authority of the Council of People's Commissars, and deprived the traditional state apparatus and the ruling classes of their best-tempered weapon.

The High Command met its first political defeat in the army at Ems on 1 December. The GHQ had convened a congress of the councils of the front-line soldiers, which it hoped to induce to agree to the programme of the high command: rapid calling of the Constituent Assembly; the power of the councils to be abolished; the authority of officers to be re-established; and civilians to be disarmed under the control of officers. However, Barth was unexpectedly present at the congress, and to some extent he turned the situation around. The delegates decided to send representatives to the Executive in Berlin, and adopted subversive resolutions calling for external marks of respect – saluting – to be abolished when off-duty, and for the soldiers' councils to be re-elected.[4]

The High Command became anxious because the decision of the congress at Ems showed that the soldiers' councils were slipping out of its control. The growing anxiety in the camp of the counter-revolution led to the initiatives of 6 December, which themselves were a powerful factor in radicalising the

---

[2] *Die Rote Fahne*, 27 November 1918.
[3] *Dokumente und Materialen*, Volume 2/2, op. cit., p. 563.
[4] *Vorwärts*, 2 December 1918; Barth, op. cit., pp. 80–1; *Illustrierte Geschichte der deutschen Revolution*, op. cit., p. 228.

masses in Berlin and turning them against the Ebert government. A garrison troop in Berlin, theoretically under the orders of Wels, marched on 5 December to the Chancellery, and there hailed Ebert. Suppe, a NCO, announced that the soldiers believed in Ebert, and would support him in the struggle against 'reaction' and 'terrorism'. Ebert thanked them in the name of the government.[5] The next day, around four o'clock in the afternoon, an armed body of soldiers led by a NCO named Fischer occupied the premises of the Executive of the councils and arrested its members. Another troop, commanded by a NCO named Spiero, went to the Chancellery and announced that it intended to nominate Ebert as President of the Republic.[6] Finally, in the evening, soldiers of the garrison fired with machine-guns on a demonstration of the League of Red Soldiers.[7]

The operation was not well led, and no doubt had no great significance in itself; the soldiers involved were not sure about what was going on, and a speech was enough to confuse them. But it was a symptom of a certain state of mind; it was followed the next day by the arrest of Liebknecht in the office of *Die Rote Fahne*,[8] and is evidence of an anxiety which revealed itself in the scale of the response to it over the following days. On 8 December, there were 100,000 demonstrators, and the workers organised punitive expeditions.[9] Eichhorn instituted an enquiry whose findings increased anxiety, and pointed suspicion at people around Ebert; it seems that not only Count Wolff-Metternich, whom the protection of Wels had placed at the head of the People's Naval Division a few days before, was compromised, but also Colin Ross himself, who resigned at this point, and Ebert's private secretary, Moser.[10] The Majority Social Democrats in the government, who had been accused of feebleness up to that time, now began to be suspected of complicity.

At that particular time, Ebert was being put under great pressure by the army chiefs. They were losing patience, and he yielded to some of their demands, whilst doing his utmost to hide the fact. This is why he agreed,

[5] *Vorwärts*, 6 December 1918.
[6] *Vorwärts*, 7 December 1918.
[7] *Die Rote Fahne*, 7 December 1918; K. Wrobel, *Der Sieg der Arbeiter und Matrosen*, Berlin, 1958, p. 30.
[8] *Die Rote Fahne*, 8 December 1918.
[9] Wrobel, op. cit., p. 30, gives an account, based on eye-witness reports, of an attack on the Hotel Bristol in the Unter den Linden, carried out by workers from Neukölln.
[10] A summary of the enquiry (the main points of which are to be found in the daily press and in Eichhorn, op. cit.) is in Coper, op. cit., pp. 154–6.

after an urgent intervention by Hindenburg in a letter of 8 December, that ten divisions from the front and under the firm control of their officers should enter the capital.[11] Their commander, General Lequis, outlined a battle-plan: disarm civilians, search the unreliable districts, and summarily execute anyone 'who illegally exercises functions of authority'.[12] But Ebert protested against any plans that could trigger conflicts in Berlin, when their outcome remained unpredictable. Major von Schleicher worked out a compromise on the basis of which the soldiery would restrict themselves for the moment to a march through the city in good order, from which 'a psychological shock' was to be expected, and the disarmament would be postponed to a later date.[13] The solemn entry of the troops gave Ebert the chance to make a speech in which he declared that the German army had not been defeated by the enemy[14] – a strong support for the legend that Germany had been 'stabbed in the back' by the revolutionaries. But the generals very quickly dropped their plan, for the troops were escaping from their control. General Groener was to explain later: 'The soldiers so much desired to go home that one could do nothing with these ten divisions. The programme of purging Berlin of the Bolshevik elements and of ordering arms to be handed in could not be carried out.'[15]

The army had returned from the front in good order, but could not hold together when idle, nor in the atmosphere in the rear, especially in Berlin. General Lequis even admitted that 'the influence of the extraordinary propaganda of the Spartacists is making itself felt'.[16] Benoist-Méchin writes: 'As soon as these divisions arrived in Berlin, they fell apart and collapsed. One by one, the regiments were won by the contagion and went over to the revolution.'[17] It was clear that the army could not be used for fighting in the streets; another instrument had to be found.

---

[11] Evidence of General Groener to the Munich trial, cited in G. Ritter and S. Miller, *Die deutsche Revolution*, Frankfurt-am-Main, 1968, p. 125.
[12] Cited in Berthold and Neef, op. cit., p. 165.
[13] Wheeler Bennett, op. cit., p. 31.
[14] *Vorwärts*, 11 December 1918.
[15] Cited in G. Badia, *Les Spartakistes*, Paris, 1966, p. 171.
[16] *Vossische Zeitung*, 25 December 1918.
[17] Benoist-Méchin, *Histoire de l'armée allemande*, Volume 1, Paris, 1936, p. 101.

Battles around the army

The decisions which the Congress of the Councils, which was in other respects under the influence of Ebert, adopted regarding the army indicate the feeling amongst wide masses of working people which the delegates only partially expressed. Even when they supported Ebert's policy, they were not prepared to follow him in his collaboration with the officer corps, which appeared to them to be an anti-democratic force, whereas they wanted a form of socialism which would be democratic.

Under the pressure of a demonstration of soldiers of the Berlin garrison, of which Dorrenbach made himself the spokesman,[18] the Congress of Councils voted for a resolution moved by the Social Democrat Lamp'l from Hamburg. The 'Seven Hamburg Points' were agreed despite Ebert. They were a real sentence of death on the old army: abolition of marks of rank, abolition of discipline and of wearing uniform when off-duty, abolition of external marks of respect, election of officers by the soldiers, and transfer of the army command to the soldiers' councils.[19] Hindenburg was warned by his observer, Major von Harbou, and informed Ebert that he would not agree to the 'assassination' of the German army, and would refuse to permit the decision of the Congress to be implemented. He sent out a circular to that effect.[20]

On 20 December, two emissaries from Hindenburg, General Groener and Major von Schleicher, in full uniform, met Ebert and Landsberg, and then, with the People's Commissars, tried to convince the Central Council.[21] They insisted that demobilisation must not be delayed, and that the final decisions must be left to the Constituent Assembly. Again on 28 December, Haase was to protest against the capitulation of Ebert and the non-application of the decisions of the Congress, in a joint session of the Council of Commissars and the Central Council.[22] During this time, tensions were rising in Berlin, where there were rumours that a military *coup d'état* was being prepared.

The clash was to take place over the troop of sailors who had become the People's Naval Division.[23] A contingent from Cuxhaven had joined a first

---

[18] *Allgemeiner Kongress*, op. cit., column 123ff.
[19] Ibid., column 181.
[20] Groener, op. cit., p. 475.
[21] Ibid.; H. Müller, op. cit., p. 184; *Der Zentralrat der deutschen sozialistischen Republik, 19 Dezember 1918–8 April 1919, vom ersten zum zweiten Rätekongress*, Leiden, 1968, pp. 44–54.
[22] *Der Zentralrat*, op. cit., p. 78, n. 38.
[23] Wrobel (op. cit.), presents the account which is most favourable to the sailors. But the other versions do not differ significantly.

group which came from Kiel at the beginning of November. This troop was under the command successively of Otto Tost, Count Wolff-Metternich and then Fritz Radtke, and was used by Wels as a police force. He stationed it in the Marstall, the stables of the palace, and entrusted it with bringing the castle back under control, which was held by 'uncontrollables'.[24]

Relations deteriorated in December. The sailors, probably under the influence of the former Lieutenant Dorrenbach, who was close to Liebknecht, became radicalised, and the division joined the demonstration of the Spartacists and the League of Red Soldiers on 21 December.[25] The Prussian Minister of Finance protested against the numbers of this division being increased, and called for it to evacuate the castle and the Marstall.[26] The People's Commissars demanded that its numbers be reduced from 3,000 to 600 men, but the sailors demanded that the redundant men be integrated into the defence forces of the Republic.[27] To cut matters short, Wels warned that they would not be paid until the numbers had been brought down to the figure intended.[28] The councils of the soldiers of the garrison of the capital demanded that the strength of the division be increased.[29]

Negotiations developed in a very tense atmosphere. According to the sailors, Wels had threatened their leader, Radtke, that he might use Lequis's troops against them.[30] An agreement was finally reached on 21 December: the sailors agreed to vacate the premises and return the keys to Wels, and he, in exchange, undertook to pay them what was owed.[31] On 23 December, the sailors evacuated the palace, and returned the keys to Barth.[32] Barth approached Wels about paying the sailors, and Wels referred him to Ebert. The sailors went to the Chancellery, but could not find Ebert there, and gave free rein to their anger; they closed the doors, blocked the telephone exchange, and marched on the Kommandantur to demand their money.[33]

---

[24] *Illustrierte Geschichte der deutschen Revolution*, op. cit., p. 254.
[25] Ibid., p. 264; H. Müller, op. cit., p. 227.
[26] *Illustrierte Geschichte der deutschen Revolution*, op. cit., p. 255; H. Müller, op. cit., p. 227.
[27] H. Müller, op. cit., p. 227.
[28] *Illustrierte Geschichte der deutschen Revolution*, op. cit., p. 255.
[29] Resolution in H. Müller, op. cit., p. 226.
[30] *Illustrierte Geschichte der deutschen Revolution*, op. cit., p. 255.
[31] H. Müller, op. cit., p. 266.
[32] *Illustrierte Geschichte der deutschen Revolution*, op. cit., p. 255; H. Müller, op. cit., p. 228.
[33] H. Müller, op. cit., pp. 256, 228.

On the way, they came under fire, which they returned, and were then machine-gunned from an armoured car under Wels's command. There were three dead and many wounded. Convinced that they had been led into a trap, they arrested Wels and two of his colleagues as hostages, and shut them up in the Marstall. Dorrenbach succeeded in convincing them that they should evacuate the Chancellery. However, Ebert had meanwhile appealed for help to the High Command, Lequis's troops were sent out with very strict orders to restore calm and break up the naval division, and they occupied the Chancellery that evening.[34] An armed confrontation seemed probable, but Barth and then Ebert placed themselves between the sailors and the soldiers. In the end, the sailors agreed to fall back to the Marstall.[35] At three o'clock in the morning, they set free their hostages, except Wels. But orders had been given to Captain Pabst of the Guards Cavalry Division, to attack the Marstall in order to free the hostages. At seven o'clock in the morning, they began to shell the Marstall, which they had encircled. The shelling went on for two hours.[36]

The sound of gunfire had alerted the Berlin workers, who gathered in their districts and marched towards the centre. At the moment when Captain Pabst, who believed he was on the point of victory, gave the sailors twenty minutes to lay down their arms, the crowd took him in the rear. Benoist-Méchin relates:

> The multitude advanced like a tide to fling itself upon the barrier of soldiers which General Lequis had posted to defend the shock troops. They asked the soldiers whether they were not ashamed of making common cause with the officers against the people. The soldiers hesitated and were quickly overrun. Some threw down their rifles, and others were disarmed by the demonstrators. The barrier was broken down in the twinkling of an eye, and the crowd rushed shouting at the rear of the Guards Cavalry posted in front of the Marstall.[37]

It was a disaster for the officers, whom Eichhorn's men only saved with great difficulty from being lynched. The government not only had to pay the sailors,

---

[34] *Illustrierte Geschichte der deutschen Revolution*, op. cit., p. 256; H. Müller, op. cit., p. 229.
[35] *Illustrierte Geschichte der deutschen Revolution*, op. cit., p. 256, stresses Barth's role, whilst Müller stresses that of Ebert.
[36] *Illustrierte Geschichte der deutschen Revolution*, op. cit., p. 258; H. Müller, op. cit., p. 230.
[37] Benoist-Méchin, volume 1, op. cit., p. 118.

but also to withdraw the Lequis division from Berlin. Wels left the garrison command, and Anton Fischer took his place.[38]

The great loser in this affair was Ebert. The Berlin workers saw him as the accomplice of the military. In the Cabinet, the Independent ministers became refractory. They themselves were under pressure from their followers, who called on them to break with the 'traitors' and 'promoters of counter-revolution', and demanded explanations at least. Who gave the order to attack the Marstall, when the problem was in the course of being settled? Did the Social Democrats approve the initiatives of Winnig, who in the East was participating in an anti-Bolshevik crusade in the Baltic states? Did Ebert and his colleagues intend to apply the 'Seven Hamburg Points'? These questions were raised in the Central Council,[39] and the Independents regarded the explanations that they received as inadequate. They refused to share the responsibility which their Majority colleagues accepted for the events of 24 December, and on 29 December decided that Haase, Barth and Dittmann should resign.[40] Their comrades in the Prussian government did likewise.[41]

This gesture had all the effect which Luxemburg had expected when she had demanded of Haase a fortnight earlier that he withdraw from the government. The resignation of the Independent Commissars, which resulted from the radicalisation of the Berlin masses, was also a factor in speeding up that process. But it also pushed the Majority towards greater dependence on the army chiefs.

Towards civil war

The departure of Haase and his colleagues deprived Ebert, at least in Berlin, of valuable support. The crowd which accompanied to the cemetery on 29 December the bodies of the sailors who had been killed at Christmas carried a huge banner: 'We accuse Ebert, Landsberg and Scheidemann of murdering the sailors.'[42] However, on the same day, the SPD organised a counter-demonstration, apparently still more numerous,[43] bearing the slogan, 'Down

---

[38] H. Müller, op. cit., p. 232.
[39] *Der Zentralrat*, op. cit., pp. 85–6, 89–94.
[40] *Freiheit*, 29 December 1918.
[41] *Der Zentralrat*, op. cit., pp. 185–6.
[42] R. Müller, *Der Bürgerkrieg in Deutschland*, Berlin, 1925, p. 20.
[43] This is what Heckert claimed at the Congress (*Der Gründungsparteitag der KPD*, op. cit., p. 116); he estimated the number of these demonstrators at 160,000.

with the Bloody Dictatorship of the Spartacist League!'[44] Both sides were preparing for civil war.

The process of radicalisation of the Berlin workers was profound but, above all, contradictory. The November Revolution had been victorious without a real battle; it had reinforced the myth of unity, and had sown the illusion that everything would be easy. In two months, the workers of the capital had become aware of their strengths, and at the same time of their weaknesses. The conquests which they had thought secure had escaped them at the precise moment when they understood how powerful they were. On 6 December, they began to learn the inspiring effectiveness of tens and hundreds of thousands of people shoulder to shoulder in the streets. If they were so numerous on 16 December when they answered the call of the Spartacists to demonstrate outside the Congress of Councils – to the surprise of the organisers themselves – it was because, having tested their strength, they were now trying vaguely to make use of it, in order to check what they perceived as a retreat, without being able to explain it except as a 'betrayal'. It was like this in July 1917 in Petrograd. As Trotsky put it: 'Before they could find the path to a change of the personal composition of the soviets, the workers and soldiers tried to subject the soviets to their will by the method of direct action.'[45]

In this situation, the appeals of the USPD and those even of *Die Rote Fahne* to take part in the electoral campaign seemed a ridiculous way to fight against an adversary who had mortars, machine-guns and grenades, but whom they now knew was not invincible in street battles. After the Christmas days, the workers of Berlin made their leap forward without concerning themselves with the rest of Germany. They were driven by a vague awareness that immediate revolutionary violence was their only effective weapon against counter-revolutionary violence. On this point, they agreed with the Spartacist leaders: the Revolution was in danger, and they would have to fight.

However, the ways and means of this combat remained obscure to most of them. A workers' insurrection could hardly count on an organised military force. The Spartacists and the League of Red Soldiers called for a red guard to be formed, though they could neither lead nor staff it. The League of Red Soldiers had some units, and Eichhorn had his security forces. The garrison

---

[44] R. Müller, *Der Bürgerkrieg*, op. cit., p. 21.
[45] L.D. Trotsky, *History of the Russian Revolution*, London, 1977, p. 576.

at Spandau, which was influenced by the Spartacist von Lojevski regarded itself – and was regarded – as a revolutionary formation. Dorrenbach, who was linked to Liebknecht, enjoyed unchallenged authority with the sailors of the People's Naval Division, though they were far from seeing themselves as 'Spartacists' or even sympathisers.[46] In any case, these units were scattered and far from in political agreement. They lacked both a general staff and close contact with the workers in the big factories. The armed proletariat in Berlin was definitely not a proletarian army. It was a crowd with the impulses and passion of a crowd, whilst its autonomous detachments believed in the effectiveness of action by active minorities. From this point of view, the successive occupations of *Vorwärts* have led to many arguments. We cannot deny that 'uncontrollable elements' or even provocateurs played a role, but that does not explain everything. Interventions of that kind are effective and attract attention only in a favourable situation and in particular in the midst of an impatient crowd where only the language of a revolutionary novice can touch the heart of the demonstrators, because it echoes their own feelings.

The break-up of the coalition government and the dispersion of the myth of unity, together with the suicide of the councils at their own congress, left the Berlin workers with nothing but their weapons and a sharp feeling of imminent danger for which they could see no political remedy. In December 1918 in Berlin, as in Petrograd in July 1917, the radicalised masses saw in armed struggle the simplifying short cut which would cut the Gordian knot of the political arguments in which they no longer wanted to be involved. But, in Berlin, there was no Bolshevik Party to open up a perspective of political struggle, nor to lead them into a necessary retreat after the setbacks of the first armed demonstrations and the consequences thereof, which could easily have been foreseen.

There were swings of opinion amongst the revolutionary leaders. The revolutionary delegates condemned the occupation of *Vorwärts*, but the KPD(S) Congress also rejected the analysis of Levi and Luxemburg. Those who should have been leaders were giving contradictory signals to those who were looking for a way forward, and their differences could be seen. This was a factor that severely affected the desire of the masses to advance, as Trotsky noted: 'More

---

[46] After *Die Rote Fahne* described them as solid supporters of the proletarian revolution, representatives of the division replied in *Vorwärts* that they had 'nothing to do with the Spartacists' (Bock, op. cit., p. 112).

than anything else, indecisiveness in their leaders exhausts the nerves of the masses. Fruitless waiting impels them to more and more insistent knockings at that door which will not open to them, or to actual outbreaks of despair.'[47]

However, at this moment the counter-revolution found precisely what the revolutionaries lacked, a leadership able to analyse the relation of forces, and an instrument, a trained, disciplined force. The leader was no longer Ebert, who had been buffeted in the storms of December. It was a member of his party, a Social-Democratic deputy who for many years had enjoyed the confidence of the officer corps, Gustav Noske. He now joined the government with Rudolf Wissell and Paul Löbe, to replace the Independents who had resigned.[48] This man was determined. 'One of us has to do the job of executioner', he declared.[49]

There could be no more question of relying on the traditional army to restore order. Since the Lequis misadventure, it did not exist. However, some officers who foresaw that the army would crumble had been occupying themselves for several weeks in saving certain élite units from the disaster. Following a conference on 6 December at the headquarters of General Sixte von Arnim, General Maercker had formed within his unit 'a Free Corps of volunteer light infantry', like those which had been formed in the East to combat Bolshevism.[50] The Maercker formations were intended for civil war; they were organised, armed and trained for this purpose. The men who composed them were volunteers receiving special pay, and prepared for specific tasks: 'Occupation of stations and control points, protection of depots of *matériel* and munitions, policing ports, defending public premises, clearing streets and open spaces, and taking buildings by assault.'[51] When they joined they took a special oath of loyalty 'to the provisional government of Chancellor Ebert' until the Constituent Assembly had formed a 'definitive government'.[52] When the conflict over the Marstall broke out on 24 December in Berlin,

---

[47] Trotsky, *History of the Russian Revolution*, op. cit., pp. 518–19.
[48] The semi-official representative of President Wilson, Dresel, wrote that Noske was an energetic man, capable of repressing the putsch or the disorders which, moreover, he foresaw (cited by Drabkin, op. cit., p. 442). The same author stresses (pp. 423–42) the link between the formation of the Free Corps and a foreign policy of rapprochement with the Entente and of military struggle against the Bolsheviks, especially in the Baltic states.
[49] Noske, op. cit., p. 68.
[50] Benoist-Méchin, Volume 1, op. cit., p. 142.
[51] Ibid., p. 143.
[52] L. Maercker, *Vom Kaiserheer zur Reichswehr*, Leipzig, 1922, p. 53.

General Maercker already had available 4,000 volunteers. They were installed near Berlin, but a long way from its crowds, in the camp at Zossen. On 4 January, Ebert and Noske were invited by General von Lüttwitz, who had replaced Lequis, to review these men whom they regarded with amazement because they were 'real soldiers'. Noske leaned over to Ebert and said: 'Don't worry! Now you will see that the wheel is going to turn!'[53]

At this point, General von Lüttwitz had over 80,000 men under his command around Berlin.[54] There can be doubt that their officers counted on using them in the capital.[55] Time was perhaps working for the Revolution; the problem for its conscious enemies was to strike decisively whilst they had the means to do so, and not let it advance.

The Eichhorn affair

The Eichhorn affair was what provided the pretext for the trial of strength, and it was seized by both sides. The police chief in the November Revolution was an old Social-Democratic activist, an old radical, one of the founders of the USPD. He was often called 'the German Caussidière' in memory of 1848 – and for the Majority Social Democrats, he was one of the men to be brought down. They had tolerated until then his presence in the police headquarters because they did not have the power to depose him without destroying the coalition government. But the resignation of the Independents left their hands free in this respect. As a homogeneous government, they were determined to appoint their own people to executive positions. Having made up their minds on repression, they could not tolerate at the police headquarters a man whose sympathies with the revolutionaries were known.

Nonetheless, they acted with prudence. On 29 December, their trusted agent, Anton Fischer, made contact with some of Eichhorn's collaborators, and put to them coded proposals based on their agreeing to join the units of which he was in charge.[56] Then on 1 January, *Vorwärts* launched the

---

[53] Ibid., p. 64.
[54] Drabkin, op. cit., p. 480.
[55] General Groener was later to declare that Noske had appealed to Ebert on 29 December to 'lead troops against the Spartacists' (*Der Dolchstossprozess in München*, Munich, 1925, p. 225).
[56] *Illustrierte Geschichte der deutschen Revolution*, op. cit., p. 260.

attack on Eichhorn in nothing less than a campaign of defamation. It accused him of having received 'Russian gold' as an employee of the Rosta, having illegally bought arms, and possessing stolen foodstuffs. The Social-Democratic newspaper declared that the presence of Eichhorn in his post was 'a danger to public security'.[57] On 3 January, Eichhorn was summoned to the Prussian Ministry of the Interior, where he was accused by a privy councillor, Doyé, a collaborator of the Social-Democratic Minister of the Interior Hirsch, of the worst misdeeds, from swindling to armed robbery. On 4 January, the Prussian Cabinet, on the proposal of Hirsch, decided to dismiss him and to replace him with the Social Democrat Ernst.[58] However, Eichhorn refused to give way,[59] and he had the support of the organisations of the Left in Berlin, from the Independents to the IKD by way of the Spartacists and the revolutionary delegates.

Arthur Rosenberg has tried to account for Eichhorn's attitude and his refusal to abandon his post, and concludes that it cannot be explained rationally, speaking of Eichhorn's 'caprices'. The resignation of the Independent Eichhorn ought, in his view, to have naturally followed that of the Independent ministers; it was not conceivable that a position of such importance could remain in the hands of a man whose hostility to the Majority Social Democrats and whose sympathies with the revolutionaries were so well-known. Nor did the Independents have any right to stress the importance of this key position; with this kind of reasoning they should never have called for their own ministers to resign.[60]

In reality, the question was not situated on the juridical plane where Rosenberg locates it. When Eichhorn refused to yield his place to Ernst, he was responding to the sentiment of the Berlin workers, for in their eyes he and his force, which had been strengthened in recent weeks by reliable activists, constituted one of their last guarantees against the counter-revolutionary undertakings which enjoyed the goodwill of the government, if not more than that. The news of his dismissal provoked an explosion of anger which expressed itself in resolutions, strikes and demonstrations.[61]

---

[57] *Vorwärts*, 1 January 1919.
[58] Kolb, op. cit., pp. 226–7.
[59] See his own explanation in Eichhorn, op. cit., pp. 60ff.
[60] Rosenberg, op. cit., p. 325.
[61] *Illustrierte Geschichte der Novemberrevolution in Deutschland*, op. cit., p. 308.

The revolutionary delegates met on the evening of 4 January, and, for once, were all in agreement: the retreat had lasted long enough, and an action to reverse it was needed. This was exactly what the Communist Zentrale thought, and they proposed to issue a call for a general strike. Luxemburg insisted that there was no question of going beyond a simple protest strike, and that at the same time they had to know both how far Ebert was ready to go and how the workers in the other regions of Germany would react.[62] A year-and-a-half later, a Communist who was present was to say:

> In the evening of 4 January, the KPD Zentrale discussed the situation which the measure against Eichhorn had brought about. There was complete agreement on how to appreciate the situation. Everyone present thought that it would be senseless to try to take over the government: a government supported by the proletariat would not have lasted for more than a fortnight. Consequently, the members of the Zentrale all agreed that they had to avoid any slogans which necessarily would have meant overthrowing the government of that time. Our slogans had to be formulated as follows: cancel the dismissal of Eichhorn; disarm the counter-revolutionary troops (Suppe's guards, etc.); and arm the workers. None of these slogans implied bringing down the government, not even that of arming the proletariat, in a situation in which this government also still possessed a measure of support amongst the proletariat, which could not be ignored. We all agreed about that; these minimum slogans had to be defended with the greatest possible energy. It had to be the necessary result of a powerful act of revolutionary will. . . . This was the sense in which we launched our call for the demonstration.[63]

In fact, some disagreements remained, although they were not expressed, and were probably not yet even perceived. Liebknecht confided to one of his comrades, outside the meeting: 'Our government is still impossible, it is true, but a Ledebour government based on the revolutionary delegates is already now possible.'[64] Luxemburg was of the opinion, which seemed reasonable, that even if they could aim at bringing down the Ebert government in Berlin,

---

[62] Müller, *Der Bürgerkrieg*, op. cit., p. 30.
[63] *Die Rote Fahne*, 5 September 1920. Levi was probably the author of this article; in any case it expresses his point of view.
[64] Radek, *October*, op. cit., p. 137.

such an initiative would be senseless, because the provinces were not ready to follow. Circumstances were to ensure that this divergence widened.

For the moment, agreement was not hard to reach in the revolutionary leaderships. On the morning of 5 January, the USPD in Berlin, the revolutionary delegates and the Communist Party distributed a joint leaflet calling for a demonstration at two o'clock in the Siegesallee: 'Your freedom is at stake! Your future is at stake! The fate of the Revolution is at stake! Long live international revolutionary socialism!'[65] The Berlin organisation was calling for a demonstration and nothing more. The sole aim was, as their leaflet pointed out, 'to show that the revolutionary spirit of the November days is not extinguished',[66] and not to take up positions for a battle. This battle was approaching, but not immediately. It was the response of the masses to the call for the demonstration which would indicate what to do next.[67]

But the protest developed on a scale which surprised the organisers themselves. The heart of the capital was occupied by hundreds of thousands of demonstrators, all the way from the Siegesallee to the Alexanderplatz, where, from the balcony of the police headquarters, Ledebour, Liebknecht, Däumig and Eichhorn himself acknowledged the power of the assembled workers, and hailed this vast display of their determination. Eichhorn said: 'I got my job from the Revolution, and I shall give it up only to the Revolution.'[68]

A year later, the Communist leader already quoted recalled this demonstration:

> What we saw [that day] in Berlin was perhaps the largest proletarian mass action in history. We do not believe that there were demonstrations on this scale in Russia. From the Roland statue to the Siegesallee, the proletarians were marching, rank upon rank. There were marchers far away in the Tiergarten. They had brought their weapons, and they carried their red banners. They were ready to do anything and to give anything, even their lives. It was an army of 200,000 such as no Ludendorff had never seen.[69]

---

[65] The full text of the leaflet is in *Dokumente und Materialen*, Volume 2/2, op. cit., pp. 9–10.
[66] Ibid., p. 10.
[67] Statement by Ledebour, *Ledebour-Prozess*, op. cit., pp. 4ff.
[68] *Die Rote Fahne*, 6 January 1919.
[69] *Die Rote Fahne*, 5 September 1920.

For the organisers of the demonstration, the number of demonstrators, their determination and willingness to struggle were a new factor. Not only was the revolutionary spirit of November not dead, but it had never been so alive. The broadest Berlin masses wanted to fight; they would not allow their demonstration to be a gesture with no future.

A step on the road to insurrection

Our Communist witness continues his account:

> It was then that the incredible happened. The masses were there very early, from nine o'clock, in the cold and the fog. The leaders were in session somewhere, deliberating. The fog grew heavier, and the masses were still waiting. But the leaders deliberated. Midday came, bringing hunger as well as cold. And the leaders deliberated. The masses were delirious with excitement. They wanted action, something to relieve their delirium. No one knew what. The leaders deliberated. The fog grew thicker, and with it came twilight. The masses returned sadly homeward. They had wanted some great event, and they had done nothing. And the leaders deliberated. They had deliberated in the Marstall. They continued in the police headquarters, and they were still deliberating. The workers stood outside on the empty Alexanderplatz, their rifles in their hands, and with their light and heavy machine guns. Inside the leaders deliberated. At the police headquarters, the guns were aimed, there were sailors at every corner, and in all the rooms overlooking the street there was a seething mass of soldiers, sailors and workers. Inside the leaders were sitting, deliberating. They sat all evening, and they sat all night, and they deliberated. And they were sitting at dawn the next morning – and still deliberating. The groups came back to the Siegesallee again, and the leaders were still sitting and deliberating. They deliberated and deliberated and deliberated.[70]

Those deliberating were the Berlin leadership of the USPD, Ledebour, Däumig, Eichhorn's deputy Grylewicz, the revolutionary delegates, Scholze and others, and two members of the Communist Zentrale, Karl Liebknecht and Wilhelm Pieck.[71] The problem which they were debating was indeed a complicated

---

[70] Ibid.
[71] The fullest account of the ensuing discussions is to be found in R. Müller, *Der Bürgerkrieg*, op. cit., pp. 30ff.

one. They all felt that a retreat on their part in the Eichhorn affair would be a great disappointment to the Berlin workers, that it would not be understood, and that it would no doubt lead to discouragement and loss of forces. They also thought that they could not fight by half-measures, and that, if there was a battle, it would be a decisive one. Many amongst them thought that the best form of defence was attack. People were saying that the forces of order were showing hesitation, and that Fischer's men refused to obey when he ordered them to seize the police headquarters.

The Communist Zentrale had not met since the preceding evening, when it had unanimously thought that they could and should get Eichhorn's dismissal reversed, the counter-revolutionary troops disarmed, and even the proletariat armed. They all thought it would have been wrong to issue slogans which could provoke a fight to bring the Ebert government down. But since then there had been the great demonstration, and Liebknecht and Pieck could reasonably think that the situation had progressed.

Amongst the other leading figures present,[72] many thought that they could easily seize power, a question which they approached only in terms of the military relation of forces. Were the revolutionaries sufficiently organised to join a fight which could not fail to be the decisive battle? This was the opinion of Dorrenbach. He was a talented agitator with great influence over the sailors of the division stationed in the Marstall, and declared that the sailors were only waiting for a sign to struggle alongside the workers to bring the Ebert government down. He added that, according to his information, the largest part of the Berlin garrison was in a similar frame of mind. He ended by saying that he knew from a reliable source that several thousand men, encamped at Spandau with 2,000 machine-guns and 20 field-guns, were ready to march on the capital: they must go forward. Ledebour was convinced, and Liebknecht threw the weight of his prestige into the balance; they both thought that it was no longer enough to protest against the dismissal of Eichhorn, but that they must launch a struggle for power since this was possible.[73]

The unusual alliance of Ledebour and Liebknecht was decisive. The meeting did not take into account the warning by a soldiers' delegate, Albrecht, who

---

[72] Namely, revolutionary delegates and left Independents. Some were there with several different mandates, such as Anton Grylewicz, revolutionary delegate, vice-chairman of the USPD at Berlin and Eichhorn's deputy. H. Weber, *Die Wandlung des deutschen Kommunismus*, Volume 2, Frankfurt-am-Main, 1969, p. 145.

[73] *Illustrierte Geschichte der deutschen Revolution*, op. cit., p. 274; Müller, *Der Bürgerkrieg*, op. cit., pp. 30–8, 46.

disputed not merely Dorrenbach's evaluation of the state of mind of the garrison, but also his confidence in the attitude of the sailors.[74] Richard Müller, who chaired the meeting, thought like Liebknecht that the masses were in the process of taking the revolutionary road, but he disputed that the moment had come to launch in Berlin an attack which at best could end only in a victory in the capital alone, for a vanguard isolated from the rest of the country.[75]

Däumig supported him, saying that it was not a matter of seizing power just for a few days in an ephemeral Berlin Commune, but of winning conclusively on the national scale. But, this time, Richard Müller and Däumig were in a minority. They only got six votes.[76] So, almost unanimously, the meeting decided to test the possibility of overthrowing the government. For this purpose it appointed a 'revolutionary committee' of fifty-two members to lead the movement, and, as soon as necessary, to elevate itself into a provisional revolutionary government pending the re-election of the councils and a new congress being called. At its head were three chairmen with equal rights, Ledebour, Liebknecht and Paul Scholze.[77] It was too heavy a structure, doomed to impotence. Däumig again denounced adventurism, refused to share any responsibility for it, and left the hall.

At the same moment, there occurred an incident, the consequences of which were decisive, but on which there remains much more light to be shed. A group of armed workers acting independently once again occupied the *Vorwärts* building.[78] Other groups during the night occupied in turn the principal publishing and newspaper firms,[79] probably in the hope of hardening the

---

[74] Ibid., and H. Müller, op. cit., p. 252.

[75] H. Müller, op. cit., p. 253.

[76] Both Robert and Hermann Müller name Däumig, Robert Müller, Eckert, Neuendorf, Rusch and Malzahn.

[77] *Illustrierte Geschichte der deutschen Revolution*, op. cit., p. 275; *Ledebour Prozess*, op. cit., p. 53.

[78] *Illustrierte Geschichte der deutschen Revolution*, op. cit., pp. 280–1, specifies that the initiative was taken in the course of the actual demonstration outside the police headquarters by a café waiter called Alfred Roland, later exposed as an *agent provocateur*. The fact was confirmed by an inquiry by the Prussian Landtag, by several statements at Ledebour's trial, and was endorsed by Richard Müller (Drabkin, op. cit., p. 486, n. 23). But it is undeniable that ultra-left elements who were in no way *provocateurs* took part in this occupation from the very beginning; the best-known was the writer Werner Möller, one of the leaders of the IKD in Berlin before the founding of the KPD(S). Bock (op. cit., p. 435) says that he was one of the leaders of leftist activism in the capital.

[79] Namely, the press firms Büxenstein, Scherle, Mosse and Ullstein, and the telegraphic

conflict. It is hardly likely that these people thought they could settle the problem of expropriating the capitalist press by such commando operations. Ledebour later said about these initiatives: 'This mass action faced us with *a fait accompli.*'[80] But at the same moment, he was himself to face the Berlin workers with *a fait accompli* of a still more far-reaching effect.

The struggle to bring down the government

Whilst these events were developing in the streets of the capital, the clumsy Revolutionary Committee harnessed itself to the preparatory work. There is little evidence of what it accomplished, and that comes down to calling a fresh demonstration for Monday, 6 January at 11am.[81] A large presence of workers would demand a call for a general strike. It then drafted a proclamation – at that stage typewritten – to be issued at the moment of taking power:

> The Ebert-Scheidemann government has made itself intolerable. The undersigned Revolutionary Committee representing revolutionary workers and soldiers (Independent Social-Democratic Party and Communist Party) announces that it has been deposed. The undersigned Revolutionary Committee provisionally assumes the functions of government. Comrades! Workers! Close ranks round the decisions of the Revolutionary Committee! Signed: Liebknecht, Ledebour, Scholze.[82]

But this appeal never saw the light of day. The ground was slipping away beneath the feet of the Revolutionary Committee. The Marstall sailors protested against an enterprise in which they had been involved against their will,[83] and they attacked Dorrenbach for having committed them without their having been consulted.[84] They made the Revolutionary Committee leave

---

agency Wolff. At the head of those occupying Mosse was a certain Drach, whom a message from Eisner stated to be a 'spy' for Ludendorff (Drabkin, op. cit., p. 486, n. 23).

[80] *Ledebour-Prozess*, op. cit., p. 62.

[81] The appeal was signed by the revolutionary delegates, the Central Executive of the USPD for Greater Berlin and the Zentrale of the KPD(S), and the name of the Revolutionary Committee (*Freiheit*, 6 January 1919; *Dokumente und Materialen*, Volume 2/2, op. cit., p. 136).

[82] Photocopy of the original in *Illustrierte Geschichte der deutschen Revolution*, op. cit., p. 272. Liebknecht had signed on behalf of Ledebour, who was absent.

[83] *Freiheit*, 10 January 1919; *Dokumente und Materialen*, Volume 2/2, op. cit., p. 136.

[84] *Ledebour-Prozess*, op. cit., pp. 189–94; E. Waldman, *The Spartacist Uprising of 1919 and the Crisis of the German Socialist Movement*, Milwaukee, 1958, p. 176.

the Marstall where it was meeting,[85] and set free its prisoners including Anton Fischer, who had been arrested early in the morning as a measure of precaution.[86] A detachment of 300 men, led by the sailor Lemmgen, went to occupy the Ministry of War on the orders of the Revolutionary Committee. The Under-Secretary of State demanded a written order, and the leader of the detachment went to ask for one. Before bringing it back, he had a nap; tired of waiting, his men dispersed.[87] The unfolding of events on 6 January dissipated the illusions of the preceding day. Our Communist witness wrote: 'These masses were not ready to take power. Apart from their own initiatives, men should have placed themselves at their head, and their first revolutionary act should have been to put an end to the deliberations of the leaders in the police headquarters.'[88]

Despite the hundreds of thousands of strikers, there were altogether less than 10,000 men determined to fight. These were Eichhorn's forces, the detachments which occupied the newspaper offices and print works, and those who occupied *Vorwärts*, whom the Communists and Independents Eugen Leviné, Werner Möller, Otto Brass and Haberland, the chairman of the Neukölln committee, came to reinforce and control.[89] The mass of the Berlin workers were ready to strike and demonstrate, but not to engage in armed struggle.

By the evening of 6 January, many people could see that the movement was in retreat, and that the idea that they could take power was a serious mistake. The Central Committee of the councils and its Berlin Executive both approved the dismissal of Eichhorn.[90] Noske was installed in the headquarters of the Free Corps, and was preparing his counter-attack. There was crisis at the Communist Zentrale. Radek, who at the urging of Luxemburg had gone into hiding when the action began, sent a message through Duncker to the Zentrale strongly advising that they call for the strikers to go back to work and immediately start a campaign for the re-election of the workers' councils.[91]

---

[85] Müller, *Der Bürgerkrieg*, op. cit., p. 87.
[86] *Illustrierte Geschichte der deutschen Revolution*, op. cit., p. 280.
[87] Ibid., p. 276; *Ledebour-Prozess*, op. cit., pp. 278ff.; Drabkin, op. cit., p. 488, n. 28.
[88] *Die Rote Fahne*, 5 September 1920.
[89] *Illustrierte Geschichte der deutschen Revolution*, op. cit., p. 281; Drabkin, op. cit., p. 495.
[90] Only Däumig and Richard Müller, in the absence of Malzahn, having voted against. *Dokumente und Materialen*, Volume 2/3, op. cit., p. 15.
[91] Radek, *November*, op. cit., pp. 137–8.

Luxemburg replied to him that the Independents were preparing to capitulate, and that the Communists should not make their task easier by sounding the alarm for a retreat, a move which, however, she also believed to be necessary.[92] Jogiches wanted the Zentrale to disavow Liebknecht and Pieck who had acted without a mandate and outside all Party discipline from the evening of 5 January onwards, but the Zentrale hesitated to make a disavowal which would have come out in the midst of battle and risked being misunderstood.[93] The Independents were no less divided. Their National Executive sent Oskar Cohn and Luise Zietz to convince the Berliners, and especially Ledebour, that they had to negotiate, which the Revolutionary Committee finally agreed to do by 51 votes to 10.[94]

Negotiations began during the night of 6–7 January. The Independents wanted an armistice, one clause of which would provide for the buildings occupied by the revolutionaries to be evacuated. The government made unconditional evacuation a precondition for any agreement.[95] Its position was improving by the hour with the reflux and disorientation in the ranks of the workers' vanguard, whilst confidence was rising on the other side. On the night of 5–6 January, the SPD executive issued a leaflet entitled *Extra-Blatt-Vorwärts* – which made clear its intentions. It described 'the armed bands of the Spartacus League' as 'madmen and criminals' who threatened the German workers with 'murder, bloody civil war, anarchy and famine'.[96] On 6 January, Noske, who had given police powers to General von Lüttwitz, prepared the intervention of the Free Corps.[97] A meeting was held in front of the chancellery, addressed by Ebert and Scheidemann, denouncing the attempts to erect 'the dictatorship of Liebknecht and Rosa Luxemburg', and calling on all citizens for help.[98]

A few hours later, there began in the Reichstag building the establishment of a 'Social-Democratic' army unit; on 8 January, two regiments of six companies each were organised at the Reichstag, with the *Vorwärts* journalist Kuttner

---

[92] Ibid., p. 138.

[93] *Illustrierte Geschichte der deutschen Revolution*, op. cit., p. 283; P. Levi, *Was ist das Verbrechen?*, Berlin, 1921, pp. 33–4.

[94] *Illustrierte Geschichte der deutschen Revolution*, op. cit., p. 284; H. Müller, op. cit., p. 262.

[95] H. Müller, op. cit., p. 262.

[96] Text in ibid., pp. 254–5.

[97] Noske, op. cit., pp. 69ff.

[98] Cited in Drabkin, op. cit., p. 490.

and Colonel Gramthow of the War Ministry.[99] On the same day, the ministers met – outside their ministries – and took measures for battle. Noske, who was appointed Commander-in-Chief, decided to concentrate the Free Corps in the Lichterfeld zone.[100] On the evening of 8 January, the negotiations were broken off, with each side holding firm to its positions.

The government then issued an appeal to the people of Berlin announcing its intention to fight violence by violence, and to 'put a stop to oppression and anarchy'.[101] From the revolutionary side, Liebknecht visited the men who were occupying *Vorwärts* – amongst whom was his son Wilhelm – and denounced before them the desertion of the Independent leaders.[102] On 9 January, the revolutionary delegates, the representatives of the KPD(S), and three of the Berlin executive of the USPD replied to the proclamation of the government with a call 'Arise in a General Strike! To Arms!':

> The situation is clear. . . . The salvation of the whole future of the working class, of the whole social revolution, is at stake. Scheidemann and Ebert are publicly calling on their supporters and on the bourgeoisie to struggle against you, the workers. . . . There is no choice! We must fight to the end! Arise for the General Strike! Come out into the streets for the final fight, for victory![103]

The League of Red Soldiers, for its part, called on the armed workers to assemble in the streets to fight.[104]

The majority of the Berlin workers were not ready to take part in nor even to endorse the civil war which was on the point of breaking out between the two camps – both of which equally claimed to be socialist. Meetings and assemblies were held in the factories, and nearly all came out in favour of immediately stopping all the fighting and an end to the 'fratricidal struggles'; demanding the unity of all the currents claiming to be socialist. A meeting called in the Humboldthain on the morning of the 9th with the workers from Schwartzkopf and AEG was held under the slogan: 'Workers, unite, if not with your leaders, at least over their heads.'[105]

---

[99] Ibid., p. 490, n. 35.
[100] Ibid., p. 91.
[101] Leaflet cited in ibid., p. 496; *Reichsanzeiger*, no. 7, 9 January 1919.
[102] F. Zikelsky, *Mein Gewehr in meiner Hand*, East Berlin, 1958, pp. 144–5.
[103] *Dokumente und Materialen*, Volume 2/3, op. cit., pp. 33–4.
[104] Cited in Drabkin, op. cit., p. 498.
[105] Cited in ibid., p. 499.

A delegation from these demonstrators went to the Central Council, where Max Cohen himself echoed their anxiety, and as a result was immediately called to order by the Chairman, Leinert.[106] Right-wing Independents and Majority Social Democrats, for different reasons, took advantage of this desire for peace all the better to denounce the extremist adventurists. But the movement was largely spontaneous. It was under its pressure that the negotiations which the Independents had clamoured for were resumed on the evening of 9 January. They were to continue until the 11th with a government delegation led by Hermann Müller.[107]

In the interval, however, time had worked in favour of the government, which had decided at all costs to take firm action. On 8 January, its forces reoccupied the Anhalt station and the administration building of the railways, which had been occupied since the preceding day. On 9 January, they reoccupied the official Reich printing establishment, and besieged the *Vorwärts* print-works. There, Brutus Molkenbuhr confirmed to the officer-in-charge of the operation that his orders were indeed to recover it by force.[108] On 10 January, the Guards regiments went into attack in Spandau, which was a bastion of the insurrection and posed a threat to the rear of the forces of repression. The chairman of the workers' council was killed in the fighting, and the chairman of the soldiers' council, a former editor of *Leipziger Volkszeitung*, the Spartacist Max von Lojevski, was arrested and murdered with his fellow-prisoners.[109]

During the night of 10–11 January, whilst the negotiations were proceeding, one of the negotiators, Georg Ledebour, was arrested along with the Spartacist leader, Ernst Meyer.[110] On the morning of 11 January, the troops commanded by Major von Stephani began to shell the *Vorwärts* building.[111] After two hours, the besieged hoisted a white flag and sent a delegation, the members of which were arrested. The officer gave the occupiers ten minutes to come out unconditionally. Several prisoners were murdered on the spot, amongst them Werner Möller and the journalist Fernbach. Later in the evening, the soldiers recaptured the Wolff news agency building and the last of the occupied

---

[106] *Der Zentralrat*, op. cit., pp. 287–8.
[107] *Illustrierte Geschichte der deutschen Revolution*, op. cit., p. 284; H. Müller, op. cit., p. 262, etc.
[108] *Illustrierte Geschichte der deutschen Revolution*, op. cit., p. 285.
[109] Ibid., pp. 285–6.
[110] Ibid., p. 286.
[111] Ibid., p. 288.

publishing establishments. Finally, on 12 January, they launched an attack on the police headquarters, in which 300 insurgents were still holding out. Their leader, the Communist Justus Braun, was struck down along with several of his companions.[112]

The brutality of the offensive by Noske's men and the pressure from the factories to end fratricidal fighting were enough to disorganise the mediocre leadership of the Revolutionary Committee, the last meeting of which seems to have been on 9 January. The Zentrale of the KPD(S) also was totally disorganised. It had had no contact with Liebknecht for several days; he was spending his time with the Independent leaders. Levi and Radek were meeting in the latter's home; they were aware that the leadership was paralysed and that it was powerless in the face of the decisions which clearly had to be taken. On 9 January, they elaborated a plan to intervene together in the workers' meetings, to propose a retreat and the evacuation of the occupied premises, which seemed to them to be the only way to halt the threatening repression. But they gave up this idea – an initiative as individual as that of Liebknecht and Pieck – when they learned that it was too late, because the troops were already on the move.[113] On 9 January, Radek wrote to the Zentrale a letter which Levi was to take to them:

> In your pamphlet about your programme, *What Does the Spartacus League Want?*, you declare that you only want to seize power if you have the majority of the working class behind you. This fundamentally correct point of view is founded on the simple fact that the workers' government cannot be formed without the backing of the mass organisation of the proletariat. Today, the only mass organisations to be considered, the workers' and soldiers' councils, have no strength except on paper. Consequently, it is not the party of struggle, the Communist Party, which heads them, but the social-patriots or the Independents. In such a situation, there is absolutely no question of dreaming of the proletariat possibly taking power. If as a result of a putsch, the government fell into your hands, you would be cut off from the provinces, and would be swept away in a few hours.[114]

---

[112] Ibid., pp. 288–90.

[113] Radek, *November*, op. cit., p. 138.

[114] Cited in *Illustrierte Geschichte der deutschen Revolution*, op. cit., p. 282. Radek was subsequently interrogated at length by the German police about this letter. The original was to be found in the Thomas archives, which were used for the production of the *Illustrierte Geschichte*, but which disappeared in the Nazi period.

He therefore thought the initiative which had been taken, with the approval of the Party's representatives, was a serious mistake:

> In this situation, the action on which the revolutionary delegates decided on Saturday as a reply to the attack by the social-patriotic government upon the police headquarters should have had the character only of an act of protest. The proletarian vanguard, exasperated by the policy of the government and badly led by the revolutionary delegates, whose political in experience made them unable to grasp the relation of forces in the Reich as a whole, has in its zeal transformed the movement of protest into a struggle for power. This permits Ebert and Scheidemann to strike a blow at the movement in Berlin which can weaken the movement as a whole.[115]

Radek used the example of the Bolsheviks in July 1917. He categorically insisted that the Communist leaders must accept their responsibilities, which meant taking the initiative before the masses of a call to retreat:

> The only force able to call a halt and to prevent this disaster is you, the Communist Party. You have enough perspicacity to know that this struggle is hopeless. Your members Levi and Duncker have told me that you know this. . . . Nothing can stop him who is weaker from retreating before a stronger force. In July 1917, we were infinitely stronger than you are today, and we held back the masses with all our might, and, when we did not succeed, with a tremendous effort we then led a retreat from a hopeless struggle.[116]

No one can dispute that Radek's analysis coincided with a sentiment which was extremely widely held amongst the Berlin workers, who were determined to defend themselves against counter-revolutionary undertakings, but were disoriented by the incoherent policy of the revolutionary leaders and by the civil war between the different workers' parties. The same day as Radek sent his letter to the Zentrale, 40,000 workers from the AEG, Schwartzkopf and several other factories met in Humboldthain and elected a commission of eight members, two from each party and two from the revolutionary delegates,[117] to organise a campaign on the slogans which they had adopted: withdraw the present leaders and replace them with 'uncompromised' ones, dissolve the army General Staff, suppress all ranks, and demobilise the army.[118]

---

[115] Ibid.
[116] Ibid.
[117] *Der Zentralrat*, op. cit., p. 277.
[118] Ibid., p. 295.

The following day, 15,000 workers in Spandau demanded that the People's Commissars stand down, that committees be formed at all levels on the basis of parity from the representatives of the three parties – Majority, Independent and Communist – and that the workers' and soldiers' councils be re-elected.[119] In the following days, there was a flood of resolutions to the same effect, all demanding the removal of Ebert and Scheidemann, that another Independent be appointed police chief, and a government of the three workers' parties be formed.[120] The fact that numerous Social-Democratic militants supported these proposals showed the depth of the desire for unity, and how the Berlin working class was hostile to what it saw as fratricidal strife. Had the Zentrale adopted Radek's proposals, it would have enabled the Communist Party to avoid being directly or indirectly blamed for the continued fighting, to draw into a necessary retreat the confused Independents and revolutionary delegates, and to isolate within the SPD those who demanded repression against the extreme Left, the conscious allies of the army General Staff.

But the Spartacist leaders – including Luxemburg – judged the situation differently. They were to make a point of honour of resistance and maintaining the occupation of *Vorwärts*, and thus vying with the revolutionary delegates and the left Independents in out-bidding each other on the Left. They were to let the Independents profit from exploiting the aspiration for unity, from which, in the end, the Majority Social Democrats alone benefited, because they succeeded in making people believe that the Communists alone were hostile to forming an alliance of workers in these circumstances. By committing themselves to a half-begun insurrection, they were to leave the opponents of Ebert in the SPD disarmed in the face of a policy of repression when no other solution seemed available.[121]

Levi defended Radek's view in the debate which followed at the Zentrale. Jogiches went further and demanded that the action of Liebknecht and Pieck be publicly repudiated in *Die Rote Fahne*. Though Luxemburg shared his sentiment – according to Paul Levi, she said that it would no longer be possible

---

[119] Ibid., p. 296.

[120] See Leinert's reports on the resolutions received, ibid., pp. 308, 326.

[121] Max Cohen, who on several occasions expressed his anxiety at the soldiers' initiatives, reflected to some extent within the Central Council the apprehensions of workers from Ebert's party at the alliance of their leaders with the Free Corps. Molkenbuhr himself was to draw up a violent indictment of Noske and his allies by quoting the minutes of the Executive of 15 January (Drabkin, op. cit., p. 509).

to go on working in future with Liebknecht[122] – this public repudiation was never carried out. On 10 January, Wilhelm Pieck addressed to the revolutionary delegates and the committee of action, in the name of the Zentrale of the KPD(S), a letter announcing that the party was withdrawing its representatives from the committee. The letter criticised the revolutionary delegates for their 'uncertainty and irresolution', as well as for having 'engaged in demoralising, disorganising, paralysing discussions', thus giving the impression that the struggle should go on.[123] It was probably after this discussion that Luxemburg wrote for *Die Rote Fahne* a full-scale attack on the Independents:

> Once more the USPD has played the role of guardian angel of the counter-revolution. Haase and Dittmann may well have resigned from the Ebert government, but on the street they pursue the same policy as they did in government. They act as a screen for the Scheidemanns. . . . Above all, the coming weeks must be devoted to liquidating the USPD, this rotting corpse, the decomposition of which poisons the Revolution.[124]

She wrote on 8 January:

> Germany has until now been the classical land of organisation. Here we are fanatical about organisation and make a parade of it. Everything must be sacrificed to 'the organisation': good sense, our aims and the capacity of the movement to act. What do we see today? At decisive moments of the Revolution, this vaunted talent for organisation fails in the most pitiable way.[125]

On 11 January, she wrote:

> The absence of leadership, the non-existence of a centre to organise the Berlin working class, cannot continue. If the cause of the Revolution is to advance, if the victory of the proletariat, of socialism, is to be anything but a dream, the revolutionary workers must set up leading organisations able to guide and to utilise the combative energy of the masses.[126]

---

[122] Levi, op. cit., pp. 33–4.

[123] *Die Rote Fahne*, 13 January 1919, *Dokumente und Materialen*, Volume 2/3, op. cit., pp. 41–2.

[124] *Die Rote Fahne*, 11 January 1919; *Dokumente und Materialen*, Volume 2/3, op. cit., pp. 47–9.

[125] *Die Rote Fahne*, 6 January 1919, *Dokumente und Materialen*, Volume 2/3, op. cit., pp. 23–6.

[126] *Die Rote Fahne*, 11 January 1919, *Dokumente und Materialen*, Volume 2/3, op. cit., pp. 47–51.

Thus, Luxemburg seems, under the influence of these days of revolutionary struggle, to have approached the conception of the revolutionary party which she had until then opposed.[127] In a last article, she tried to draw a balance-sheet of the 'Spartacus Week'.[128] She had no doubt, she repeated, that it was impossible to expect 'a decisive victory of the proletarian revolution', the fall of the Ebert-Scheidemann government, and 'the installation of the socialist dictatorship'. The cause was to be found in the lack of maturity of the Revolution, the absence of coordination between the revolutionary centres – 'common action would give a wholly new dimension to the attacks and to the response of the Berlin proletariat' – and the fact that the economic struggles were only just beginning. In these conditions, they should ask themselves whether the preceding week had been 'a mistake'. She did not think so, because she believed that the workers had been provoked:

> The revolutionary workers were obliged to take up arms, because they faced the violent provocation of Ebert and Scheidemann. It was a question of honour for the revolution to repel that attack immediately, with all its strength, if they did not want the counter-revolution to be encouraged to take a fresh step forward, if they did not want the ranks of the revolutionary proletariat and the credit of the German Revolution within the International to be shaken.[129]

In Luxemburg's opinion, the formal end of the struggle in defeat was to be explained by 'the contradiction between the task to be undertaken and the absence, at that stage of the Revolution, of the preconditions enabling it to be fulfilled'. But history teaches that the road to socialism is 'paved with defeats', and that defeats lead to victory for those who are capable of drawing their lessons:

> Leadership was lacking. But one can and one must install a new leadership, a leadership that has come out of the masses and which the masses choose. . . . The masses rose to the level of their task. They made this defeat into a link in the series of historic defeats which form the pride and the

---

[127] Badia (*Les Spartakistes*, op. cit., p. 261), writes: 'It is nonetheless the case that Rosa Luxemburg felt the need, at the head of the revolution, for a body to guide and orient the action, imposing its will on the masses. Is that not a step towards the Leninist conception of the party of the working class?' It is difficult to go along with this, both as far as Luxemburg's thought is concerned, and in the allegedly 'Leninist' conception of a party 'imposing' its will on the masses.

[128] *Die Rote Fahne*, 14 January 1919; *Dokumente und Materialen*, Volume 2/3, op. cit., pp. 71–5.

[129] Ibid.

strength of international socialism. This is why victory will flower from the soil of this defeat.[130]

Despite this declaration of faith, the title which Luxemburg gave her article, 'Order Reigns in Berlin', summed up the situation in all its brutality. The leadership of the Communist Party had not been able to prevent the crushing of the movement which it had helped to unleash, and which it had done nothing to prevent or to check. It had no doubt let slip for a long time the chance of a struggle for a united class-front against the leaders who were in alliance with the generals. It was to pay dearly for the ultra-left action which had been undertaken without adequate reflection by Liebknecht and the majority of the revolutionary delegates – the same people who a few days earlier were criticising the Spartacists for their 'putschist tactic'.

The double assassination

The Free Corps had indeed decided to strike at the head, and were actively seeking the revolutionary leaders. Dorrenbach, Emil Eichhorn and Paul Scholze succeeded in getting out of the capital,[131] but Luxemburg and Liebknecht stayed there. Luxemburg was still working in the editorial office of *Die Rote Fahne* when Noske's troops attacked the *Vorwärts* building, and Levi had great difficulty in persuading her that her life was in danger and that she had a duty to hide. Liebknecht revealed the same lack of awareness, and was insisting at that very moment that arrangements be made for a public meeting at which Luxemburg and he would speak in the name of the Party. In the end, they both consented to hide, but refused to leave Berlin when repression was beating down the workers.[132] They took refuge first in Neukölln on 12–13 January, and then at the flat of a sympathiser in Wilmersdorf. This was where Luxemburg discovered from reading *Vorwärts* that Liebknecht had signed the notorious document of the Revolutionary Committee.[133] She said to him: 'Karl, is that our programme?'[134] Silence fell between them.

---

[130] Ibid.

[131] Rosenberg, op. cit., p. 331; Badia, *Les Spartakistes*, op. cit., p. 249.

[132] Radek, op. cit., p. 138. On 15 January, the Central Committee was to learn from Max Cohen of the arrest of an elderly sister-in-law of Liebknecht, and of that of a girl who had lived in Rosa Luxemburg's house (*Der Zentralrat*, op. cit., pp. 415–16).

[133] A facsimile of the text was published by *Vorwärts* on 14 January.

[134] Paul Levi was to write: 'None of those present will ever forget the scene during which Rosa Luxemburg presented to Liebknecht the document signed "The Provisional Government, Ledebour, Liebknecht, Scholze".' ('Rosa Luxemburg und Karl Liebknecht

It was in this apartment that they were arrested, along with Wilhelm Pieck, who had brought them false papers, on the evening of 15 January. All three were taken to the Hotel Eden, the centre where the staff of the Guards division were installed, and were interrogated by Captain Pabst. During the night, Liebknecht first and then Luxemburg left the hotel under escort, to be imprisoned in the Moabit. On 16 January, *Vorwärts* was the only daily paper to announce in its morning edition the arrest of the two Communist leaders. In a note, it congratulated itself on the 'generosity' of the victors, who had known how to defend 'order, human life, and law against force'.[135]

Nonetheless, the midday editions announced in large headlines the news that Liebknecht and Luxemburg were dead, the former struck down whilst trying to escape, and the latter lynched by unknown persons who stopped the vehicle during her transfer to Moabit. A communiqué from the Guards division supplied details, which for the moment were the only source of information. Liebknecht, struck in the head by an unknown person, was wounded whilst leaving the Hotel Eden; he had taken advantage of a breakdown of the car, had tried to flee into the Tiergarten, and had been shot after the usual summons. As for Luxemburg, who had been knocked down by the crowd outside the Hotel Eden and carried away unconscious, she had been taken away from her guards and finished off. Liebknecht's body was in the morgue, but that of Luxemburg had not been recovered.[136]

The truth emerged bit by bit. It was the soldiers who had killed their prisoners, after apparently having seriously maltreated them during their questioning. Liebknecht, who came out first, was struck in the back of the neck with a rifle-butt by the soldier Runge, and thrown bleeding into a car, which took him into the Tiergarten where his escort finished him off. Naval Lieutenant Z. von Pflugk-Hartung directed the whole operation. The body was later deposited at the Zoo police station as 'an unidentified corpse'. Luxemburg, who was already in a very bad state, was struck by Runge in the same way, taken away unconscious, and killed. Her body was weighted with stones, and then thrown into the canal, which yielded it up only months later. This operation was directed by Lieutenant Vogel.[137]

---

zum Gedächtnis', *Der Klassenkampf*, no. 2, 15 January 1929, p. 34) Rosi Wolfstein reported to JP Nettl the comment mentioned here (Nettl, Volume 2, op. cit., p. 767).

[135] *Vorwärts*, 16 January 1919 (morning edition).

[136] Press extracts in E. Hannover-Drück and H. Hannover, *Der Mord an Rosa Luxemburg und Karl Liebknecht*, Frankfurt-am-Main, 1965, pp. 35–45.

[137] Ibid., pp. 45–8.

Some months later, in May 1919, a court martial sentenced Runge to two years and Vogel to two-and-a-half years, and acquitted von Pflugk-Hartung.[138] Vogel escaped thanks to the complicity of one of his judges, Lieutenant Commander Canaris,[139] and succeeded in getting abroad.

The consequences of this double murder are incalculable. To be sure, despite the efforts of Jogiches and Levi, who devoted immense effort to the enquiry, no direct responsibility of any Social-Democratic leader can be established. But their moral responsibility is overwhelming. Two days before, *Vorwärts* had published what was nothing less than a call for the murder of 'Karl, Rosa and partners, not one dead, not one, amongst the dead'.[140] It was men gathered, armed, and in the end protected by Noske and the Social-Democratic ministers who carried out the assassinations. Scheidemann was to say: 'You see how their own terrorist tactic has done for them themselves!'[141] After that, there was always the blood of Liebknecht and Luxemburg between German Social Democrats and Communists.

The young Communist Party was deprived simultaneously of its best political leader and its most prestigious spokesman. Luxemburg and Liebknecht were known to every German worker, and enjoyed high standing throughout the international movement. Alone of all the Communists outside Russia, they had the stature to discuss as equals with the Bolshevik leaders, and to have been a counterweight to their authority in the International that was soon to be founded. Moreover, the statements by Runge and particularly the declarations by Captain Pabst tended to cast terrible suspicions on Pieck, who was spared by the killers. These suspicions were to make necessary a Party enquiry, the conclusions of which are still being discussed.[142]

---

[138] Ibid., p. 116; record of the trial, pp. 59–120.

[139] *Illustrierte Geschichte der deutschen Revolution*, op. cit., p. 305. This officer, who had played a role in the repression of the revolutionary sailors in 1917, was covered for by his supervisors. As an admiral, he was to become head of the Abwehr under the Third Reich.

[140] *Vorwärts*, 13 January 1919; facsimile of the poem 'Das Leichenhaus' ('The Morgue'), *Illustrierte Geschichte der deutschen Revolution*, op. cit., p. 331.

[141] Scheidemann, *Memoiren eines Sozialdemokraten*, Volume 2, op. cit., p. 348.

[142] G. Nollau, *Die Internationale: Wurzeln und Erscheinungsformen des proletarischen Internationalismus*, Cologne, 1969, p. 332, with a statement by Pabst to the author, dated 30 November 1959; Erich Wollenberg is one of the sources of the version according to which Hans Kippenberger, in charge of the enquiry, is said to have paid with his life for the information gathered against Pieck on this occasion, at the time of the Moscow Trials (E. Wollenberg, *Der Apparat*, Bonn, 1952, pp. 76–8).

The double murder not only rendered unbridgeable the gulf between the Majority Social Democrats and the revolutionaries. It also convinced the revolutionaries that their only mistake had been to procrastinate. Several months of cruel experience were needed for the isolated detachments of German Communists to convince themselves that their mistakes were of a different order.

PART TWO

THE ATTEMPT TO DEFINE THE ROLE OF A COMMUNIST PARTY

Chapter Thirteen

The Noske Period

The fighting in January 1919 in Berlin brought to an end the first phase of the revolution, the phase of the democratic illusions, as Rosa Luxemburg put it, or, if you prefer, that of the belief in the peaceful transition to socialism. Two months of Social-Democratic government had solved none of the problems which workers encountered, and satisfied none of their hopes. To be sure, peace had returned. But, for all that, people were still dying in all the cities of Germany. Cold and hunger were as bad as during the worst times of the War. Universal suffrage had not of itself settled any of the economic difficulties. The economy seemed to be worn out by the strain of the years of war, dislocated by the shocks of the defeat and the Revolution, indeed collapsing. Factories were closing, unemployment was rising. In Berlin, there were 180,000 out of work in January, and 500,000 in March. Transport of goods came to a standstill, as people could not afford to buy them. The black market continued to flourish, enriching the dealers and corrupting every social class. A world was disintegrating which no words could revive. What was to follow it?

The working class thought it had won a victory, but saw it slip away. Some saw the very face of their worst enemies behind those who were their recognised leaders. The era of promises and belief in an easy future vanished. Again they were at war –

another kind of war – in which one fought or went under. Some of the workers no longer believed in trees of liberty or universal embraces, and succumbed to nihilism or took up the rifle. Other workers were desperately trying to fight for their interests, only to be confronted by the employers, the officer corps and those professional soldiers who had chosen the profession of civil war, men without hope who knew only how to obey and to fight, the 'damned souls', the product of four years of war.

That was the first half of the picture. The other half was that the workers' struggles changed their character after January. There were fewer parades and demonstrations, but there were hard-fought strikes. Fewer political slogans, but demands around basic economic issues. Here and there, the workers went on fighting arms in hand, either because they still wanted to attack the press, or because someone wanted to disarm them. However, day after day, and week after week, the revolutionary assault troops grew weaker under the pressure of defeat and disappointment. The attacks fragmented at the same time as awareness grew that only a general struggle, led and coordinated by a single centre, could overcome the determination of the possessing classes. But, in a situation in which its intervention would have been decisive and it could have found everything it needed to grow rapidly, the Communist Party was practically absent from the scene.

The assassination of Liebknecht and Luxemburg was not the only blow suffered by the KPD(S). Franz Mehring survived the double murder by only a few weeks. His impaired health could not resist the shock.[1] At the same time, Johann Knief, who had been consumptive as a result of the war years, took to his bed; he was to die after a long secret period of suffering.[2] Radek was hunted by the entire police force, was arrested on 12 February, feared for his life for some days, and finally obtained a refuge in a prison cell where he enjoyed the prestige of a man through whom one could open a discussion with the Russians.[3] Leo Jogiches once again tried to bring together the fragments of the organisation, and escaped the police who sought him for more than two months. However, in March, he was arrested and, on the usual pretext of 'trying to escape', was shot down.[4] Eugen Leviné, who had escaped from

---

[1] He finally died on 29 January 1919 (*Illustrierte Geschichte der deutschen Revolution,* op. cit., p. 519).

[2] Bock (op. cit., p. 432) specifies that he died on 6 April 1919, following an operation for appendicitis.

[3] Radek, *November,* op. cit., passim.

[4] *Illustrierte Geschichte der deutschen Revolution,* op. cit., p. 367.

the massacre of the defenders of the *Vorwärts* building in January, an organiser and speaker, always where the fighting was hottest, was sent by the Zentrale to Bavaria, where he was captured after the republic of councils in Munich was crushed, tried, sentenced to death, and shot.[5]

There was no organisation that was centralised or even homogeneous, but only groups, individuals and tendencies, to lead the struggle, political as well as military, against the Free Corps, and to denounce the Majority Party and the trade-union leaders. A new leadership of struggle emerged, which did not include any Communists. The efforts of the Berlin revolutionary delegates were supported and widened by those of other activists in other industrial districts, like them generally trade-union cadres and members of the USPD. At the time of the Congress of the Councils in Berlin in December 1918, contacts were established around the Berliners with men who were recognised leaders of broad sections of advanced workers, Otto Brass of the metalworkers' union in the Ruhr, and Wilhelm Koenen of Halle.[6] In the Ruhr and Central Germany, the workers' councils had from the beginning had a less strictly political character than in the rest of the country, but perhaps a broader basis. In any case, they had preserved their role as centres of working-class activity: the economic demands came from them. During the second phase of the Revolution it was the struggle for socialisation that was to draw hundreds of thousands of workers, including Social Democrats, into strike action and then into armed struggle.

The January wave

The West German historian Eberhard Kolb characterises January 1919 as the month of 'communist putsches'.[7] This is a frequent but disputable claim. The putsches in January throughout the whole of Germany were real putsches only if we accept that the Berlin uprising was one. In fact, most of the time, the actions of the revolutionary activists presented the same characteristics as that in Berlin, that is a limited attack, a battle only halfway engaged in, often inspired by a defensive reflex, and more like an angry gesture than a conspiracy. Most often these actions came down to armed demonstrations

---

[5] Sentenced on 4 June 1919, he was executed on 6 June (*Illustrierte Geschichte der deutschen Revolution*, op. cit., p. 396).

[6] *Vorwärts und nicht vergessen*, op. cit., p. 397.

[7] Kolb, op. cit., p. 315.

and attempts to occupy the premises of Social-Democratic or right-wing newspapers. Sometimes they began in order to support the revolutionaries in Berlin, and sometimes to protest at the repression against them. They quickly collapsed, generally broken by the action of Social-Democratic local authorities and the intervention of the ordinary police forces or bourgeois militias.

On 9 January, in Dresden, a revolutionary demonstration approaching the premises of a Social-Democratic newspaper was broken up by the police. On 10 January, there was another demonstration, this time in force, and the police fired on it, killing fifteen of the demonstrators. Two days later, all activities of the KPD(S) were banned.[8] In Stuttgart on 10 January, there was an armed demonstration, the premises of *Neue Tageblatt* were occupied, and a revolutionary sheet was produced; then Lieutenant Hahn, elected by the soldiers' councils and placed by the Social Democrats at the head of the police, had all the leading Communists in Württemberg – Edwin Hoernle, Fritz Rück, Willi Münzenberg and Albert Schreiner – arrested for 'conspiracy'.[9]

In Leipzig, the Communists took the lead in demonstrations of the unemployed, and printed leaflets on the premises of a newspaper which they occupied. The workers' and soldiers' council, with a strong Independent majority, denounced their action, and made them leave the place.[10] In Duisberg, a Communist named Rogg, who was chairman of the workers' and soldiers' council, authorised and approved the seizure of a Social-Democratic newspaper, and for that he was repudiated by the council and deprived of his position.[11]

Elsewhere, the game ended in a draw, at least for the time being. In Hamburg, a demonstration of revolutionaries ended in the sack of the *Hamburger Echo* on 9 January. The following day there was a large Social-Democratic counter-demonstration; the police arrested Laufenberg, the chairman of the local council, and the workers' militia had to intervene to free him. On 11 January, there was a clash between two demonstrations, and a pitched battle in front of the city hall between Social-Democratic demonstrators and 'red' militias. Laufenberg had to promise an early re-election of the council by universal

[8] Ibid., pp. 315–6.
[9] *Illustrierte Geschichte der deutschen Revolution*, op. cit., p. 376; Kolb, op. cit., p. 315.
[10] Kolb, op. cit., p. 299; *Vorwärts und nicht vergessen*, op. cit., p. 411.
[11] Kolb, op. cit., p. 315.

suffrage.[12] In Halle, each camp in turn seemed to be near to winning. The army reoccupied the barracks, and the workers' and soldiers' council arranged to be protected by a militia organised round Meseberg's red sailors. There were exchanges of fire every day. On 12 January, the soldiers attempted to destroy the 'Red Kommandantur', and were driven back. On 16 January, they arrested Meseberg, but had to release him the next day under the threat of the machine-guns of Ferchlandt, who commanded the red guard.[13]

The revolutionary elements were unable to seize power except in Düsseldorf and Bremen. In Düsseldorf, the workers' militia, which was called 'the security regiment', took the initiative on the night of 9–10 January, occupied the strategic points, and arrested the leading counter-revolutionaries. The council elected an executive of five members, with Karl Schmidt, an Independent, as chairman, whilst Seidel, a Communist, took charge of the police. In Bremen, the workers' council was re-elected on 6 January. The USPD received 8,520 votes and 58 seats, the Social Democrats 14,680 votes and 113 seats, and the Communists 7190 votes and 57 seats. Independents and Communists, therefore, had a narrow majority, and the Social Democrats refused to take their seats. After feverish negotiations between leaders, at the end of a street demonstration, Frasunkiewicz, an Independent, proclaimed the Republic of the Councils on the territory of Bremen. An executive was chosen, of nine People's Commissars, of whom four were Communists. On the 14th, the workers' militia intervened to repress an attempted putsch supported by the chairman of the soldiers' council. The new revolutionary government permitted the elections to the Constituent Assembly to proceed on the 19th, but hardened its attitude in the face of a threat of armed intervention. Breitmeyer, a Communist, took control of the police, whilst the council sent Jannack and Karl Becker, both Communists, to make contact respectively with the revolutionary authorities in Leipzig and Hamburg to seek their for help.[14] Noske had heard that the Ruhr miners threatened to strike if the Free Corps attacked Bremen, but decided to take the risk. The Gerstenberg division reconquered the city in 48 hours and killed a hundred people. By the evening of the 4th, Noske's order reigned in Bremen.[15]

---

[12] *Vorwärts und nicht vergessen*, op. cit., p. 259; Comfort, op. cit., p. 54.
[13] *Vorwärts und nicht vergessen*, op. cit., pp. 370–1.
[14] Ibid., pp. 184, 198–9, 202, 484.
[15] *Vorwärts*, 5 January 1919.

The Ruhr miners' strike

For a few days, there was a real possibility that Bremen and the Ruhr might join forces in the struggle. In the Ruhr, agitation had risen consistently since November; strikes and incidents multiplied. At the end of December, revolutionary elements, left Independents or Communists, won the majority in several cities, including Hamborn, Mülheim and Oberhausen.[16] Workers' militias were organised in most places, and the first clash with them came before Hagen, on 9 January, where the Free Corps of Captain Lichtschlag was forced to withdraw.[17]

The workers' agitation was centred around the question of the socialisation of industry. The Congress of the Councils had decided that it should be carried through quickly, beginning with the coal mines. On 11 January, the workers' and soldiers' council in Essen unanimously decided to occupy the premises of the employers' organisation and install its own control commissions. Their concern was to take concrete measures to apply the socialisation on which they had decided during the preceding day.[18] Throughout the region, the Social Democrats followed the movement, some because they supported the old demand for socialisation, and others because they realised that if they clashed with the workers when the agitation was in full flood, there was a chance that the elections to the National Assembly might not be held. A regional conference of workers' and soldiers' councils was held in Essen on 13 January which approved the initiative taken by the council in Essen, and appointed a commission to prepare to socialise the mines.[19] This was the 'Commission of Nine', three Social Democrats, three Independents and three Communists.[20] The representatives of the three parties issued a joint appeal to the miners to return to work because the mines were to be seized from the employers.[21] Accepting the Communist Hammer's proposal, it was agreed to proceed to the election of workers' representatives in every mine in order to set up the pyramidal structure of councils throughout the coal-field.[22]

---

[16] *Illustrierte Geschichte der deutschen Revolution*, op. cit., pp. 314–5.

[17] Ibid., p. 115.

[18] Von Oertzen, op. cit., p. 213.

[19] Spethmann, op. cit., pp. 149ff.; *Illustrierte Geschichte der deutschen Revolution*, op. cit., pp. 313ff.

[20] *Illustrierte Geschichte der deutschen Revolution*, op. cit., pp. 313ff.; Von Oertzen, op. cit., p. 113; the appeal of the 'Commission of Nine' for socialisation is in *Dokumente und Materialien*, Volume 2/3, op. cit., pp. 56–8.

[21] *Dokumente und Materialien*, Volume 2/3, op. cit., p. 59.

[22] *Illustrierte Geschichte der deutschen Revolution*, op. cit., p. 317.

The Ebert government announced that it agreed to the demands of the miners, and it appointed as Reich commissioners in Rhineland-Westphalia the senior civil servant Röhrig, the magnate Vögler and the trade unionist Hué.[23] Neither Hué nor Limbertz, a leader of the Social Democrats, concealed that their first concern was to calm down the workers' agitation in this key sector,[24] and on 19 January, the elections to the Constituent Assembly proceeded normally throughout the Ruhr.

On 19 January, Noske obtained approval by the assembly of a decree provisionally organising the army, and the Reichswehr command was entrusted to him as Minister of War. The seven Hamburg points were abolished, the power of the councils was annulled, and the authority of the officers restored.[25] At the same time, he prepared the counter-offensive and liquidation of the councils.[26] On the evening of 27 January, the councils in Wilhelmshaven, which were being led by a young Communist teacher from Bremen named Jörn, were crushed by an élite force, Captain Ehrhardt's naval brigade.[27] The Gerstenberg division – a Free Corps of 3,000 men – set off in the direction of Bremen.[28] Feelings ran very high along the coast, and the Majority Social-Democratic representatives joined in the protests in every council. The Social-Democratic daily paper in Hamburg, the *Hamburger Echo*, opposed its own executive when it denounced the danger of the moment: 'Prussian militarism is on the point of receiving the powers with which it can strangle the whole revolution.'[29]

The executive of the council in Hamburg voted by a large majority to mobilise military formations, including armed workers, to 'support Bremen by every military means'.[30] The Gerstenberg force reached Bremen on 3 February, and completed the disarming of the militias on the 5th. Bremers-haven fell in turn on the 9th.[31] In Hamburg, the Social-Democratic Party gave up resistance. But hardly was the Republic of Councils liquidated in Bremen before the whole of the Ruhr began to move again.

---

[23] Ibid., p. 318.
[24] See quotations from their speeches, ibid., p. 318.
[25] Text in Ritter and Miller, op. cit., pp. 188–90.
[26] Noske, op. cit., pp. 78–9.
[27] *Illustrierte Geschichte der deutschen Revolution*, op. cit., p. 341.
[28] Ibid., p. 342.
[29] *Hamburger Echo*, 31 January 1919, cited by Comfort, op. cit., p. 70.
[30] Ibid., p. 70.
[31] Ibid., pp. 345–6.

On 6 February, the regional conference of councils appointed Karski, whom the KPD(S) Zentrale had just sent to the Ruhr, to advise the 'Commission of Nine'. On the 7th, the soldiers' council of the Seventh Army Corps, which was based near Münster, was disturbed by rumours that the coal barons had reached agreement with Noske, and had contributed large sums of money for the 'reconquest' of the mining area by the troops of General von Watter. It decided to ignore the decree of 19 January, and to declare itself the supreme authority in the region. On the orders of Noske, von Watter sent the Lichtschlag Free Corps to Münster. The members of the soldiers' council were arrested, and a new council was 'elected'. The Free Corps then marched on Hervest-Dorten, where a leading citizen had just been assassinated, and took possession of it on the 15th, after a short struggle which left dead thirty-six of the defenders. The chairman of the workers' council, a Communist named Fest, was charged with murder without the flimsiest of grounds, and was murdered by the soldiers who arrested him. In the meantime, on 14 January, a new regional conference in Essen threatened to call a general strike if the troops of General von Watter were not withdrawn from the mining area. The murder of Fest and the Lichtschlag action brought things to a head. A conference of the delegates of the most radical councils, convened in haste in Mülheim, called for a general strike on 16 January.[32]

The Social Democrats were led by Limbertz, and they counter-attacked at the Essen conference on 19 January. Before any discussion, they demanded that the Mülheim conference be repudiated, and having been defeated, they left the meeting hall. The 170 remaining delegates, of whom 28 were Social Democrats, voted for a general strike until the troops were withdrawn. The same day, 19 people were killed in Elberfeld and two in Essen. On 20 January, there was fighting across the region, in Gelsenkirchen, Bochum and Bottrop, where there were 72 dead. The situation was very confused. The last-minute retreat of the Social Democrats and the intervention of the troops gave the advantage of surprise to the repression. There were 183,000 strikers on the 20th, but only 142,000 on the 22nd.[33]

The regional leaders of the councils, particularly the Independent Baade, thought it wiser to accept the overtures of General von Watter, who said that he would be satisfied with the disarming of the militias and the resumption

---

[32] *Illustrierte Geschichte der deutschen Revolution*, op. cit., pp. 320–2.
[33] Ibid., pp. 322–4.

of work. The negotiations were conducted in Münster, and agreement was reached. The strike was called off, and an armistice was concluded. Forty-eight hours later, General von Watter declared that the workers had broken it, and the Lichtschlag Free Corps resumed the attack.[34] The combativity of the workers of the Ruhr was, for the moment, broken.

Elsewhere the wave was rising afresh. On 21 February, Kurt Eisner, the Independent who led the councils in Bavaria, was assassinated by a young officer.[35] When the Mannheim council of workers and soldiers, led by Hermann Remmele, an Independent, and Stolzenburg, a Communist, learned this news, they proclaimed a conciliar republic.[36] In Leipzig, the left Independents won a majority in the council, and Curt Geyer replaced Seger as its chairman.[37] And above all, on 24 February a general strike broke out in Central Germany.

The general strike

Since December, the left Independents in Central Germany, Koenen, Bernhard Düwell, the Berliners with Richard Müller, and the Ruhr people with Otto Brass, had been trying to coordinate their activities.[38] In fact, in the absence of a solid revolutionary organisation, they were to fail, and their plans to build a general movement remained unfulfilled.

Nonetheless, the movement in Central Germany was remarkable for the organisational efforts and the clear-headed determination of its leaders, the left Independents Wilhelm Koenen and Bernhard Düwell. They succeeded in gathering around the nucleus of the miners most of the decisive workers' organisations in the region, railwaymen, workers in the chemical industry, including those in Leuna where Wilhelm Koenen's brother Bernhard was chairman of the workers' council. In January, they succeeded in organising a provisional regional workers' council, which decided on the 17th to place under its control the mining operations in the Halle region.[39] Elections to councils were held in all the mines on the 27th. On the 29th, a conference of the councils in the region was held, and Wilhelm Koenen presented a report

---

[34] Ibid., p. 326.
[35] Ibid.
[36] *Vorwärts und nicht vergessen*, op. cit., pp. 515–18, 536.
[37] Kolb, op. cit., p. 299.
[38] Ibid., p. 125.
[39] Von Oertzen, op. cit., p. 136.

on socialisation.[40] In this way, unity between the workers of the Ruhr and those of the Central Region was prepared.

The signal for the action – the general strike – had to be given by the Congress of Councils, which was originally to be held in February, and which alone would have the necessary authority for such a movement of national dimensions.[41] But this conference was put off under the pressure of the Social Democrats, and the initiatives of the Free Corps and of General von Watter in the Ruhr were to force a change in plans. As the Ruhr strike was coming to an end, and as the representatives of the Essen conference were preparing to negotiate, the delegates from Central Germany met in Halle to issue the call for the general strike to start on 24 February, and called on the Berlin workers to join them. The conference was elected by the working people in all the big enterprises, and by a number of those working in small ones. Half of the delegates were Independents, and Communists and Majority Social Democrats shared the rest equally. The essential aim was 'socialisation from below', the 'democratisation of the workplace'.[42]

The strike was nearly total in the Halle district on the 24th, and it spread to Saxony on the 25th.[43] In Leipzig, the workers who were consulted gave 34,012 votes for and 5,320 against.[44] Curt Geyer, at the head of the 'Limited Committee of Five', had strategic points occupied by the workers' militias who were ready to defend 'the Council Republic' and the strike.[45] On 26 February, the Social Democrats and bourgeois elements replied with a 'counter-strike'; civil servants, doctors, tradesmen, stopped work in turn.[46] At this moment, Noske ordered General Maercker to restore order in Halle in order to smash the centre of the burgeoning strike movement.[47] The results of the elections to the workers' council of Greater Berlin were to show that the strike was threatening to spread to the capital, where Independents and Communists together had the majority.[48]

---

[40] Ibid., pp. 136–7.
[41] Ibid., p. 86, n. 2.
[42] *Illustrierte Geschichte der deutschen Revolution*, op. cit., p. 373; Von Oertzen, op. cit., p. 143.
[43] *Dokumente und Materialen*, Volume 2/3, op. cit., p. 200.
[44] Ibid., p. 201.
[45] Kolb, op. cit., p. 299.
[46] Benoist-Méchin, op. cit., p. 226.
[47] Ibid., pp. 226–7.
[48] *Illustrierte Geschichte der deutschen Revolution*, op. cit., p. 359.

Maercker's 3,500-strong light infantry arrived in Halle on the morning of 1 March. They were immediately overwhelmed, were in danger of being dispersed and disarmed by the crowd, and retreated to the barracks.[49] The next day, an officer in civilian clothes on a spying mission was recognised and lynched by the crowd. Maercker then ordered that anyone who resisted was to be shot on the spot.[50] Wilhelm Koenen just escaped being kidnapped at night,[51] but Karl Meseberg was less fortunate, as he was arrested by soldiers and disappeared. His body was discovered on the 19th; he too had been 'shot whilst trying to escape'. The strike was weakening by 5 March, and it ended on the 7th.[52]

It was at this point that the movement broke out in Berlin. On 21 February, the KPD(S) Zentrale had in *Die Rote Fahne* appealed to the workers to gather in the factories, in meetings and if possible, in demonstrations to voice their hostility to the intervention of the Free Corps in the Ruhr.[53] On 27 February, the workers in the state enterprises at Spandau called for a strike in solidarity with the workers of Central Germany, proposing a minimum programme which included pay increases, the establishment of a revolutionary tribunal to try the military chiefs, and immediate elections to the factory councils.[54]

On 28 February, the general meeting of the workers' councils in Berlin took place. Under the pressure of a delegation which included representatives of the workers in AEG in Henningsdorf, who were members of all three workers' parties,[55] it began to discuss the possibility of a general strike in solidarity with the strikers in Central and Northern Germany, but was quickly stopped by the pressure of the Social Democrats.[56] Before it broke up, it elected a new Executive; the Independents won 305 votes, the Majority 271, the KPD(S) 99, and the Democrats 95. Seven Independents, seven Majority socialists, two Communists and one Democrat won seats.[57] In the new Executive, the

---

[49] Ibid., p. 376; Benoist-Méchin, op. cit., p. 227.
[50] Benoist-Méchin, op. cit., pp. 228–9.
[51] *Vorwärts und nicht vergessen*, op. cit., pp. 402–3.
[52] *Illustrierte Geschichte der deutschen Revolution*, op. cit., p. 377.
[53] *Die Rote Fahne*, 21 February 1918; *Dokumente und Materialen*, Volume 2/3, op. cit., pp. 181–2.
[54] *Die Rote Fahne*, 1 March 1919; *Dokumente und Materialen*, Volume 2/3, op. cit., p. 202.
[55] *Dokumente und Materialen*, Volume 2/3, op. cit., p. 204.
[56] *Illustrierte Geschichte der deutschen Revolution*, op. cit., p. 359 adds the detail that the meeting ended at 3:00 pm, since the premises had to be made available for a dance.
[57] *Illustrierte Geschichte der deutschen Revolution*, op. cit., p. 359. The elections in the

Independents and the Communists together had the majority, and they faced the problem of the general strike. It was clear that they had no chance of success unless the Social Democrats supported it. But the Social Democrats were doing their best to prevent the workers in Berlin from moving into action, as much by their own proposals as by their warnings. On 1 March, the Social-Democratic fraction in the National Assembly presented a resolution calling for socialisation, and the government published a scheme to that end on 3 March. The representatives of the Majority in the Berlin workers' council sent a delegation to Weimar on the 2nd, and in *Vorwärts* on the 3rd they published a warning against the general strike.[58]

Die Rote Fahne published on the same day an appeal signed by the Central Committee of the KPD(S), its fraction in the workers' and soldiers' councils of Greater Berlin, the Communist delegates in the big factories, and the district leadership in Greater Berlin:[59] 'The hour has returned. The dead are rising again!' The appeal reviewed the past months and stressed: 'The Eberts, Scheidemanns and Noskes are mortal enemies of the Revolution. . . . The Revolution cannot go forward except over the tomb of "Majority" Social Democracy.'[60]

With this perspective, it appealed to the workers of Berlin to launch the general strike, on the slogans of re-election of the councils in all the factories, disarming of the counter-revolutionary gangs, restoration of the right to assemble, formation of a red guard, withdrawal of troops from all the occupied industrial zones, release of political prisoners, arrest of the murderers of Liebknecht and Luxemburg, prosecution and condemnation of the military chiefs and the 'Majority' leaders as 'betrayers of the Revolution' and accomplices in the January murders, an immediate peace, and renewal of diplomatic relations with the Soviet Republic.

The Communist leaders urged the working people to meet, to organise their strike, and to contribute to the necessary discussions in the factories: 'Do not let yourselves be drawn into fresh gun-fights! Noske is waiting just for that to provoke fresh bloodshed!'[61]

---

factories had been conducted on the basis of competing lists, and not on the basis of 'agreement' and 'parity' as in November.

[58] *Illustrierte Geschichte der deutschen Revolution*, op. cit., p. 359.

[59] *Die Rote Fahne*, 3 March 1919; *Dokumente und Materialen*, Volume 2/3, op. cit., pp. 282–6.

[60] *Dokumente und Materialen*, Volume 2/3, op. cit., pp. 282–4.

[61] Ibid., p. 285. Noske had returned during the night of 1–2 March (Noske, op. cit., p. 101).

On the same day, 3 March, several mass meetings of workers in big factories in the capital, in particular Knorr-Bremse in Lichtenberg, carried resolutions in this tone. The delegations from Siemens, Spandau, Schwartzkopf and other places met at the same time as the Berlin council, and decided to go together to demand that the call for a general strike be issued. Their pressure on the meeting was decisive, and the decision in favour of a general strike was carried by a very large majority, including nearly all the Social-Democratic delegates.[62] The resolution called for the councils to be recognised, for the seven Hamburg points to be put into effect, for political prisoners to be released, Ledebour at their head, for the state of siege to be lifted, for all those involved in political murders to be arrested, for a workers' guard to be organised, for all the Free Corps to be dissolved, and for political and economic relations to be renewed with the Soviet government.[63] The Executive decided that the strike would apply to all newspapers, excepting an information organ to be published under its own responsibility.[64]

However, the next day, the Communist representatives withdrew from the committee which functioned as the strike leadership. Despite their protests, Richard Müller defended the principle that the Majority delegates – who had voted for the strike – should participate in its leadership, in the name of democracy. Herfurt,[65] speaking for the Communist fraction on 4 March, declared:

> The general strike is directed against the government which the Social-Democratic Party heads, and against its policy. To take representatives of this policy into the leadership of the strike is to betray the strike and the Revolution. The results of this betrayal are revealed today. Almost the entire counter-revolutionary press appears, including *Vorwärts*, whilst the revolutionary press does not. The German Communist Party refuses to bear, in any way whatever, the responsibility for this betrayal. It withdraws its members from the Executive in order to demonstrate its most energetic protest.[66]

---

[62] *Illustrierte Geschichte der deutschen Revolution*, op. cit., p. 360.

[63] *Dokumente und Materialen*, Volume 2/3, op. cit., p. 389.

[64] *Illustrierte Geschichte der deutschen Revolution*, op. cit., p. 360. The first issue appeared on 4 March under the title *Mitteilungsblatt des Vollzugsrats der Arbeiter- und Soldatenräte Grossberlins*.

[65] At the time, one of the left-wing leaders of the KPD in Berlin. He was to go over to the opposition, then to the ultra-left KAPD and to Laufenberg's Communist League, before being exposed as a *provocateur* working for the Reichswehr (*Freiheit*, 25 March 1921).

[66] *Dokumente und Materialen*, Volume 2/3, op. cit., p. 291.

On the day when the strike was announced, 3 March, the Prussian government proclaimed a state of siege, 'in order to protect the working people of Greater Berlin from the terrorist undertakings of a minority, and to spare it from famine'.[67] Noske was invested with full civil and military powers. He banned all public open-air meetings and all demonstrations or processions, as well as the appearance of any new periodicals, and warned that any infringements would be put down by force, and could lead to courts martial.[68] During the night of 3–4 March, there were incidents between the police and the workers in several parts of Berlin.[69] There was looting of several shops, which the revolutionaries were to denounce as the work of provocateurs.[70] On the morning of 4 March, Noske seized on a pretext to order the Free Corps to march on Berlin.[71]

That day a huge crowd gathered early in the afternoon in the Alexanderplatz, close to the police headquarters. Anger grew quickly when the news arrived of incidents at Spandau; the Free Corps had disarmed the soldiers who were guarding the machine-guns depot, and there had been firing.[72] A unit of the Free Corps commanded by von Lüttwitz tried to drive into the crowd; the officer commanding it was roughly handled, and tanks intervened and fired on the crowd to clear the area. 'There was a terrible massacre.'[73] At the Executive Committee, Richard Müller in the name of the strikers dissociated himself from trouble-makers and looters. The Communist Party produced a leaflet warning against attempts to divert the movement down the road of 'military putsches'.[74]

The situation became still worse on 5 March, when the Free Corps attacked a detachment of the naval division at the Lehrt station. A delegation of sailors went to the police headquarters to demand to be recognised as guardians of the building, as a guarantee of good faith. Von Lüttwitz refused, and on the way out one of the delegation, Rudolf Klöppel, was killed by a shot in the

---

[67] Noske, op. cit., p. 103.
[68] Ibid., p. 104.
[69] *Illustrierte Geschichte der deutschen Revolution*, op. cit., p. 361. Noske (op. cit., p. 105) even speaks of '32 police stations attacked'.
[70] Benoist-Méchin (op. cit., p. 234) attributes this looting to 'dubious elements', but says that the intervention of 'provocateurs' is unlikely. *Illustrierte Geschichte der deutschen Revolution*, op. cit., p. 362, advances the opposite opinion.
[71] Noske, op. cit., p. 106.
[72] *Illustrierte Geschichte der deutschen Revolution*, op. cit., p. 363.
[73] Benoist-Méchin, op. cit., p. 236.
[74] *Dokumente und Materialen*, Volume 2/3, op. cit., p. 292.

back. The incident was decisive: the majority of the sailors turned against the Free Corps and began to fight them, arms in hand, whilst some of them dealt out to the crowd the stocks of arms which they held.[75] On 6 March, the forces of von Lüttwitz, tanks, machine-guns, mortars and artillery, launched an attack on the Marstall and the building occupied by the naval division.[76] A leaflet issued by the Communist Party stressed that the armed fighting was the act of the sailors and certain republican defence units, which in January had stabbed the working people in the back: 'We are fighting for socialism and against capitalism. Their leaders are fighting for their positions in the armed forces against their employers with whom they have fallen out. There is all that and more to divide us from them. . . . Between them and us there is no political solidarity.'[77]

On the same day, there were stormy debates at the meeting of the workers' council. The Independents suggested hardening the strike by extending it to the supply of water, gas and electricity. The Social-Democratic delegates were violently opposed. Finding themselves in a minority, they walked out of the meeting, resigned from the strike committee, issued an appeal for the strike to be called off, and distributed it by means of leaflets and posters.[78] The Berlin trade-union commission, which the Social Democrats controlled, adopted the same line. They all denounced the proposed measure as 'adventurist', and said that it would hit only the workers' districts and make the strike unpopular there. The majority was reduced, and Richard Müller in turn resigned from the strike committee.[79] The troops of von Lüttwitz immediately struck back. They occupied the power-houses which supplied the bourgeois quarters, and used the Technische Nothilfe,[80] the strike-breakers' organisation,

---

[75] *Illustrierte Geschichte der deutschen Revolution*, op. cit., p. 362; Benoist-Méchin, op. cit., p. 237.

[76] Benoist-Méchin, op. cit., pp. 237–9.

[77] The leaflet is mentioned in *Illustrierte Geschichte der deutschen Revolution*, op. cit., p. 362; and reproduced in Noske, op. cit., p. 110. The Soviet historian V.F. Chelike says that the attitude of the Zentrale of the KPD(S) and of Paul Levi during the March days in Berlin was like that of the Communists in Munich, whom the latter was to treat as 'putschists'. But the documents which he quotes are not convincing, compared with all those which are known from elsewhere ('Nachalo Martovskikh boev 1919 v Berline', *Noiabrskaia Revoliutsiia v Germanii*, op. cit., pp. 168–9). We should remember (note 65) that the representative of the Communist fraction, the ultra-leftist Herfurt, who refused to sit on the strike committee, was in the service of the Reichswehr, a fact of which the Soviet historian seems to be unaware.

[78] *Illustrierte Geschichte der deutschen Revolution*, op. cit., p. 364.

[79] Ibid.

[80] Coper, op. cit., p. 241.

to restore normal service. The strike was defeated as much by Noske as by the Social Democrats' desertion. The general meeting of the councils declared on 7 March that it favoured a return to work subject to five conditions:

- No punishments for acts committed during the strike.
- Release of persons detained for acts committed during the strike.
- Withdrawal of soldiers from occupied factories.
- Withdrawal of the Free Corps from Berlin.
- End of the state of siege and abolition of special military courts.[81]

By the morning of 8 March, the fighting was drawing to an end. Sailors and workers had been driven from the city centre where they had for some time been sniping from roofs. The strike committee accepted defeat and, after fruitless talks with Noske, issued the order to resume work unconditionally.[82] The last sector in which order was not yet completely restored was Lichtenberg, and alarming rumours were circulating about the fate of its garrison. During the morning of 9 March, the editors in Berlin of the *Berliner Zeitung am Mittag* were informed by a senior military official that the police headquarters in Lichtenberg had been stormed, and its seventy occupants savagely killed. The editor hesitated to publish such information, but received a second telephone call from councillor Doyé, one of the top officials in the Ministry of the Interior, who confirmed that the information was correct and demanded that it be published immediately, if necessary in a special edition. The truth was that five policemen had met their deaths in the course of street brawls.[83] But Noske seized the opportunity which was offered and for which evidently preparations had been made; he had the following posted on the walls of Berlin: 'The brutality and bestiality of the Spartacists who fight against us compel me to give the following order: any person who is caught with arms in his hands in the struggle against the government will be shot on the spot.'[84]

That evening and the following day, 10 March, the press showed no restraint in its attacks on the 'assassins'. *Vorwärts* declared that the decision was 'the only possible reply to the Lichtenberg atrocities'.[85] An order of the day

---

[81] *Dokumente und Materialen*, Volume 2/3, op. cit., pp. 302–3.
[82] *Illustrierte Geschichte der deutschen Revolution*, op. cit., p. 364.
[83] Ibid., p. 365; Benoist-Méchin, op. cit., p. 241.
[84] Noske (op. cit., p. 120) says this was the source of the 'rumour', the number of victims having been increased tenfold.
[85] Benoist-Méchin, op. cit., p. 242. Noske (op. cit., p. 109) only quotes the second half of the sentence.

announced that anyone in whose house arms were found would be shot on the spot.[86] With this orchestration, the real massacre began, the only one that week, and it was perpetrated precisely by those who denounced the imaginary one in Lichtenberg. Noske was to admit in his memoirs to a figure of 1,200 civilian victims.[87] The revolutionaries believed that the real figure was nearer to 3,000, several hundreds of whom were shot without trial.[88] What was claimed to be the 'Lichtenberg massacre' had a counterpart, unfortunately a real one, in shooting of 29 sailors who had been arrested by surprise when they went to collect their pay.[89] The executioner was Lieutenant Marloh, who picked them out from amongst several hundred prisoners 'because they looked intelligent'. He had been ordered by Colonel Reinhard to shoot '150 of them if necessary'.[90] Noske was to write: 'Such a sad thing could happen only in an atmosphere soaked in blood.'[91]

Leo Jogiches was amongst the nameless victims. He was arrested on 10 March, and shot down for 'trying to escape' by Sergeant Tamschik, in charge of a police station.[92]

The last centres of revolt are crushed

The Ruhr had recommenced work at the moment when Central Germany began to strike. The strike in Berlin began when the workers in Central Germany were returning to the factories and the mines. At the very moment when the last fighting died down in the capital, the Ruhr was once more coming to the boil.

At the beginning of March, the Social Democrats who had left the Commission of Nine began at once after the elections to campaign violently against it, and in particular against Karski. They accused him of leading the Commission, in the interests of Bolshevism, to sabotage the coal-mines, and then of calling the strike just when the principle of nationalisation had been

---

[86] Benoist-Méchin, op. cit., p. 242.
[87] Noske, op. cit., p. 110.
[88] *Illustrierte Geschichte der deutschen Revolution*, op. cit., p. 367, and Benoist-Méchin, op. cit., p. 247, estimate the number of civilian wounded at 10,000.
[89] *Illustrierte Geschichte der deutschen Revolution*, op. cit., p. 369.
[90] Ibid., pp. 369–71. Here is a striking parallel with the episode of the execution of supporters of the Paris Commune by General Galliffet in 1871.
[91] Noske, op. cit., p. 110.
[92] *Illustrierte Geschichte der deutschen Revolution*, op. cit., p. 367.

won. At the same time, bourgeois guards and Free Corps were at work attacking the most stubborn workers' centres. Yet throughout March, the temperature was rising in the mines and in the metalworking industries. The miners' union threatened to expel anyone who took part in a conference of councils due to meet in Essen on 30 March. The 475 delegates, representing 195 mines, decided with only eight votes against, and in consideration of the betrayal of the movement in January by the union organisation, to found a new organisation, the German Miners' Union. Unanimously, they decided to strike on 1 April with the same demands as those of the Berlin strikes in March.[93]

They elected a Central Committee of nine members, five Independents, including Teuber, and four Communists.[94] The general strike was to continue through April in the Ruhr, and was to be marked by 'simple bloody repression' as Rudolf Coper put it.[95] On 7 April, Severing, a Social Democrat, was appointed Reich Commissioner in the Ruhr.[96] On the 9th, Lichtschlag had the Nine arrested in Essen.[97] Powerful opposition revealed itself at all the meetings of the miners' union, and the number of strikers rose from 158,592 on 1 April to 307,205 on the 15th, according to the 'Majority' trade union. On 15 April, the Free Corps entered guns in hand the hall where the new clandestine leadership of the strike was meeting, shot down the delegates who tried to get away, and arrested the remainder.

Forty-five people were killed in Düsseldorf, and there were punitive expeditions against Hagen and Remscheid, and against Dortmund and Bochum, where hunger riots were put down. The resistance of the population, who were deeply affected, began to weaken. By 20 April, there were no more than 128,776 strikers, and the movement slowly died.[98] At the beginning of May the order of Hugenberg, Vögler, Krupp and Thyssen once more reigned in the Ruhr.

Bourgeois order was soon to reign throughout Germany. On 6 April, the socialist government had Alwin Brandes, the leader of the Independents, with two of his comrades, arrested in Magdeburg. The workers' militias, the 'guard

---

[93] Ibid., pp. 29–31, 327–9; *Dokumente und Materialen*, Volume 2/3, op. cit., pp. 343–4.
[94] *Illustrierte Geschichte der deutschen Revolution*, op. cit., p. 329.
[95] Coper, op. cit., p. 243.
[96] *Illustrierte Geschichte der deutschen Revolution*, op. cit., p. 331.
[97] Ibid., p. 332.
[98] Ibid., p. 333.

regiment' led by Artelt, who had been head of the mutineers in Kiel in November, struck back by taking two hostages, the minister Landsberg and General von Kleist.[99] German Maercker's forces marched on the city, and occupied it on 10 April. They dispersed a demonstration of workers, killing seven,[100] freed the hostages, disarmed the militiamen, and arrested the leaders of the Independents.[101] However, on 12 April, leaving three battalions behind, they moved on towards Brunswick, where the council, under the inspiration of the Independent Sepp Oerter, could call on reliable militias, and had just started a strike of railwaymen.[102] The infantry were reinforced by the naval brigade of Captain Ehrhardt: they attacked on 17 April, and the city fell without resistance. The principal revolutionary leaders were arrested, but Eichhorn and Dorrenbach, who had taken refuge in Brunswick after the January days, again escaped from the Free Corps.[103]

The turn of the workers of Saxony was soon to come. On 12 April, a demonstration of war-wounded in Dresden degenerated into fighting. Neuring, who earlier had been chairman of the workers' and soldiers' council in the city, and was now War Minister in the government of Saxony, refused to discuss their demands with a delegation which included a Communist. He was lynched and thrown into the Elbe.[104] Noske proclaimed a state of siege.[105] From Magdeburg, General Maercker sent Lieutenant-Colonel Faupel with 1,500 men, but the latter was to confine himself to surrounding Dresden, because he estimated that his forces were insufficient.[106] His arrival hardened the leaders in Leipzig. Under the energetic leadership of a 'Committee of Five', led by Curt Geyer and his Party comrade, the trade unionist Artur Lieberasch, they prepared for a resistance based on calling a general strike in reply to the first attack.[107] Leipzig was said to be guarded by 60,000 armed

---

[99] Ibid., p. 378, Benoist-Méchin, op. cit., p. 283.
[100] Benoist-Méchin, op. cit., pp. 286–7.
[101] *Illustrierte Geschichte der deutschen Revolution*, op. cit., p. 380.
[102] Benoist-Méchin, op. cit., p. 290; Kolb, op. cit., pp. 294–5.
[103] *Illustrierte Geschichte der deutschen Revolution*, op. cit., p. 381; Noske, op. cit., pp. 127–9.
[104] *Illustrierte Geschichte der deutschen Revolution*, op. cit., p. 382; Noske, op. cit., pp. 144–5.
[105] Noske, op. cit., p. 145.
[106] Benoist-Méchin, op. cit., p. 342.
[107] Appeal for resistance by the Leipzig USPD in *Dokumente und Materialen*, Volume 2/3, op. cit., pp. 395–8.

militiamen, and was perfectly calm.[108] *Die Rote Fahne* and the KPD(S) Zentrale had sought refuge there. On the night of 10 May, the 'Committee of Five', thinking the danger was over, announced that they were lifting the night watch. The following night, Maercker's infantry entered the city by surprise and occupied it, and rigorously broke the general strike called in protest. They went on to take Eisenach on 19 May, and succeeded there in capturing Dorrenbach, who was to be killed in the Moabit prison as Jogiches had been – and by the same warder.[109] Then they took Erfurt, which was led by the workers' council under Petzold, an Independent.[110]

However, by this time, the centre of activity had moved on towards Bavaria. The assassination of Kurt Eisner had opened a period of extreme confusion, with a government headed by Hoffmann, a Social Democrat. On 7 April, a council republic was proclaimed in Munich by a curious coalition which included Independents, anarchists, and even the Majority socialist Schneppenhorst, who was a minister. No entirely satisfactory explanation of this strange initiative has yet been made possible, and the thesis that it was a provocation cannot be definitely rejected. The Communists in Munich, who had recently been reorganised under the energetic leadership of Eugene Leviné,[111] denounced the 'masquerade', this 'pseudo-council republic', as having no prospect other than a struggle which could not be won, and would provide a welcome pretext for the Free Corps to intervene.

Given these conditions, it is hard to understand why the Communists accepted responsibility for defending the power of the councils in Munich in response to a counter-revolutionary attempt at a putsch on 13 April,[112] when the prospects were not changed fundamentally by the fact that the Communists had won a secure majority in the factory councils of the Bavarian capital. An executive committee headed by Leviné undertook to organise a hopeless defence.[113] A success by the Bavarian 'red army', led by the poet Ernst Toller,

---

[108] Kolb, op. cit., p. 300.

[109] *Illustrierte Geschichte der deutschen Revolution*, op. cit., pp. 368, 382–3.

[110] A Mitchell, *Revolution in Bavaria 1918–1919*, Princeton, 1965, pp. 305–7.

[111] Ibid., p. 309. On 18 March, the Zentrale led by Levi had written to him, saying that at all costs he should avoid providing any pretext for a military intervention (ibid., p. 308). Leviné had arrived in Munich on 5 March, and had purged the Party there, reorganising it on the basis of factory cells, and putting an end to the close collaboration with the anarchists which had gone on before his arrival, under the leadership of Max Levien (ibid., p. 308).

[112] Ibid., pp. 318–20; H. Beyer, *Von der Novemberrevolution zur Räterepublik in München*, East Berlin, 1957, pp. 93–7.

[113] Beyer, op. cit., pp. 97–102.

caused the Hoffmann government to call in the Free Corps. The Munich revolutionaries, divided to the last minute by quarrels which they tried to settle by means of putsches, were to fight desperately against General von Oven's men, amongst whom the Ehrhardt naval brigade was conspicuous. The soldiers cleared up the last islands of resistance with flame-throwers.[114]

During the final hours, the execution of ten monarchist conspirators, and the arrest as hostages of several hundred leading citizens on the order of the young Communist commander of the red army, Rudolf Egelhofer, served to feed the legend that hostages had been murdered on a large scale by these heirs of the Paris Commune, and played in Munich the same role as the 'Lichtenberg massacre' in Berlin. Several hundred Bavarian revolutionaries were executed without trial, including Egelhofer and Gandorfer. Landauer was beaten to death. Toller and Mühsam, the anarchist poet, were given severe sentences. Leviné was portrayed as a Bolshevik agent, tried by court martial, sentenced to death, and shot.[115] Before his judges he made the celebrated declaration: 'We Communists are all dead men on suspended sentence!'[116]

Down the years, the propaganda of the popular press and the right wing was to make the revolution in Munich a bogey, as a time of upheaval when common criminals ran riot. Munich, the bastion of reaction, was to become the cradle of Nazism.

With the conciliar republic in Munich, the German Revolution, which had begun on 7 November 1918, seemed to be reaching its end. The whole postwar wave of revolution was ebbing, without having flowed beyond the borders of the defeated countries. With it disappeared the illusions which had grown up in this period that the working class would be able easily to take power.

The Soviet Republic of Hungary was proclaimed peacefully by Béla Kun on 21 March 1919, and had seemed for a moment to show that the European revolution was advancing rapidly. Austria was covered with workers' councils. There also the Social Democrats refused to fight for power for the councils, and rallied instead to the National Assembly.[117] The Communist Party seemed

---

[114] *Illustrierte Geschichte der deutschen Revolution*, op. cit., p. 396; Benoist-Méchin, op. cit., pp. 335–7.

[115] Mitchell, op. cit., pp. 330–1; Beyer, op. cit., pp. 136–8.

[116] *Die Aktion*, 1919, p. 485. His speech to the court has been republished in eye-witness accounts and commentaries, edited by T. Dorst and H. Neubauer, *Die Münchner Räterepublik*, Frankfurt-am-Main, 1966, pp. 157–67.

[117] Introduction by Y. Bourdet to M. Adler, *Démocratie et conseils ouvriers*, Paris, 1966, pp. 33–5.

to be advancing by giant strides, rising from 10,000 to 50,000 members between March and May.[118] In Slovakia, a Soviet republic was proclaimed.[119] However, as Yves Bourdet wrote: '. . . by refusing to take power, the Austrian socialists broke the chain of the social revolution. If they had acted differently, the three workers' republics could have come to each others' aid, and without doubt would have aroused an irresistible revolutionary spirit that would have spread through all Europe.'[120]

Neither the Austrian nor the Hungarian Communists were capable of understanding this fact. Béla Kun, who was criticised later by the Russian communists for having united with the Hungarian Social Democrats, tried to force the course of history in Vienna. In mid-May 1919, his emissary, Ernst Bettelheim, arrived in Vienna with considerable sums of money and a claim to be acting on behalf of the Communist International. Bettelheim was an enthusiastic novice, of the type of the German ultra-leftists. On 26 May, he persuaded an enlarged central committee to form a 'directory' of three members to be responsible for the seizure of power. The 'Committee of Revolutionary Soldiers', of which he was the driving force, prepared an insurrection for 15 June, a date fixed by the armistice commission for a large-scale reduction of the workers' militias.[121] However, on 13 June, the Social-Democratic leaders, who had wind of the plot, began to prepare preventive action. Otto Bauer, who was Secretary of State for Foreign Affairs, persuaded the Allies to cancel the clause about partially disarming the militias, which would have led to an uprising by the armed militiamen who feared unemployment.[122] On the initiative of Friedrich Adler, the workers' council in Vienna, in which the Communists were only a minority of about a tenth, denounced the proposed insurrection. That same evening, the Communist directory overruled Bettelheim and countermanded his instructions.[123] Kun telegraphed in vain that 'everything is ready', and that the question was 'one of life and death'.[124] The Communist leaders decided to organise, in place of the proposed insurrection, a large

---

[118] L. Laurat, 'Le Parti communiste autrichien', in J. Freymond (ed.), *Contributions à l'histoire du Comintern*, Geneva, 1965, p. 77.

[119] Ibid.

[120] Bourdet, op. cit., p. 32.

[121] Laurat, op. cit., p. 77.

[122] Ibid., p. 78; Bourdet, op. cit., p. 34.

[123] Laurat, op. cit., pp. 78–81; Bourdet, op. cit., p. 35.

[124] O. Bauer, *Die Österreichische Revolution*, pp. 140–2; E. Bettelheim, *Der Kampf*, 1919, pp. 646–9, cited in J. Braunthal, *Geschichte der Internationale*, Volume 2, Hanover, 1963, p. 162.

demonstration. But on the night of 14–15 June, several hundred Communists were arrested throughout the country. This turned the demonstration into a riot, with twenty people being killed and hundreds wounded on the 15th.[125]

The defeat in Vienna doomed the 'Budapest Commune'. Kun's government was up against insurmountable economic difficulties. It lacked experience, and it was seized by the throat by the peasants' opposition to the measures of war communism, as well as by a counter-revolution which could count on foreign support. It was under heavy pressure from the Allied armies, which had agents even in its headquarters. Kun's government fell on 1 August by handing its resignation to the Budapest soviet. A few days later, Romanian troops entered the Hungarian capital, where the government of Admiral Horthy was installed. The white terror began.[126]

Order reigned again throughout Central Europe. The connection had not been made between the revolutions in Germany, Austria and Hungary and that in Russia. Nonetheless, throughout Europe – and especially in Germany – revolutionaries were continuing to organise themselves, carrying on the task started during the War. Many considered that the delay in doing this had been one of the main causes for the bloody defeat.

---

[125] Laurat, op. cit., pp. 78–81; Bourdet, op. cit., p. 35. What was to be known as 'Bettelheimerei' was subjected as early as October 1920 to a ferocious critique by Arnold Struthahn – Karl Radek – who developed his attacks on this 'putschist' and 'semi-Blanquist' conception, alien to communism, in 'Die Lehren eines Putschversuches', *Die Kommunistische Internationale*, no. 9, October 1920.

[126] Borkenau, op. cit., pp. 130–3.

Chapter Fourteen
Stabilisation in Germany and World Revolution

The formation of the Communist International was taking place as the first phase of the German Revolution was being closed with rifle-fire and flame-throwers. The Bolsheviks started laying its foundations immediately after the Revolution in Germany in November 1918. They considered that the existence of the German Communist Party provided the necessary and sufficient conditions for the establishment of the Communist International,[1] and the first concrete task was to proclaim it. However, the time required for the circulation of documents and the movement of people meant that by the time the Communist International was formally set up, the real founders of the German party had been assassinated.

In December 1918 Eduard Fuchs, a lawyer and member of the Spartacus League, made his way to Moscow carrying a letter addressed by Luxemburg to Lenin.[2] Some days later, Lenin took the first initiatives which were to result in the foundation conference of the Communist International.[3] However, the road ahead was not a straight one. Luxemburg

---

[1] See Chapter 8.
[2] R. Stolyarova, 'Der Aufruf Zum 1 Kongress der KI', *Zeitschrift für Geschichtswissenschaft*, no. 11, 1968, p. 1397. The text of the letter, dated 20 December 1918, had been published in *Pravda*, 2 February 1919.
[3] V.I. Lenin, 'To G.V. Chicherin', *Collected Works*, Volume 42, Moscow, 1971, pp. 119–22.

had been won to the idea that a new International was historically necessary, but judged that the moment for it had not yet come. Eberlein reports that, two days before the Founding Conference of the KPD(S), she had voiced her opposition to any immediate proclamation:

> The existence of a new revolutionary International capable of acting depends
> on the existence of several revolutionary parties in Western Europe. . . .
> The foundation of the International at a time when there is only one
> Communist Party, and that recently founded, could only weaken the idea
> of a revolutionary International.[4]

This point of view, which Jogiches defended after Luxemburg was assassinated, prevailed in the Zentrale when it met at the beginning of January to reach an agreement on the reply to be given to the invitation from the Bolshevik party to the international conference in Moscow.[5] The delegates[6] were mandated to vote against founding the new International, and – if we are to believe Ernst Meyer on the matter[7] – were instructed to leave the conference if the new International were to be proclaimed against the opposition of the German party. In the end, the difficulties due to communication and to the tasks which the leadership of the young party had to shoulder meant that Eberlein alone reached Moscow, where he took part (under the pseudonym of Max Albert) in the work of the conference, and opposed the foundation of the International, which his party believed to be premature.[8] He tells us: 'The Russian comrades, especially Trotsky, Bukharin and Rakovsky, did their utmost to convince me that immediate action was necessary. In the end, Lenin decided that, if the German party maintained its opposition, the foundation of the International would be deferred.'[9]

---

[4] H. Eberlein, 'Spartakus und die III Internationale', *Inprekorr*, no. 28, 29 February 1924, p. 307.

[5] H. Weber, *Der Deutsche Kommunismus*, Cologne, 1963, p. 198, n. 54.

[6] According to the traditional version, there were two delegates, Eberlein and Leviné. According to a statement by Leviné's widow, the latter was due to go to Moscow, not as a delegate, but as a representative of Rosta (H. Weber, *Die Wandlung des deutschen Kommunismus*, Volume 1, Frankfurt-am-Main, 1969, p. 30).

[7] *Bericht über den 5 Parteitag der Kommunistischen Partei Deutschlands (Sektion der Kommunistischen Internationale) vom 1 bis 3 November 1920 in Berlin*, Berlin, 1921, p. 27.

[8] *Der I Kongress der Kommunistischen Internationale. Protokoll der Verhandlungen in Moskau vom 2 bis 19 März 1919*, Hamburg, 1921, p. 76.

[9] H. Eberlein, 'Spartakus und die III Internationale', *Inprekorr*, no. 28, 29 February 1924, p. 307.

Apparently, chance was to decide the question otherwise. A fiery speech by the Austrian Communist Steinhardt, who had arrived after the conference began, and who described the revolutionary uprising in Central Europe, the news, perhaps, that Jogiches had been assassinated, another impassioned appeal from Rakovsky and, in particular, the pressure of this enthusiastic gathering, finally influenced Eberlein, who contented himself with abstaining in the decisive vote.[10] The Communist International was founded. Zinoviev was its President, and Moscow was its headquarters, two important factors the implications of which were not understood at the time. They all thought, with Trotsky, that:

> Whilst today Moscow is the centre of the Third International, tomorrow – we are perfectly convinced – the centre will move to the West, to Berlin, Paris or London. Whilst it is with joy that the workers of Russia have welcomed within the Kremlin walls the representatives of the workers of the world, it is with even greater joy that they will send their representatives to the Second Congress of the Communist International in one of the capitals of Western Europe. A congress in Berlin or Paris would mean the complete victory of the proletarian revolution in Europe and probably in the whole world.[11]

The Bolshevik, like the majority of the revolutionaries in the world, believed that the German Revolution had not perished in the early months of 1919, and that it would rise again with all its power. The only problem was that of the time-scale.

How Radek appreciated the situation

Of all the Bolshevik leaders, Radek alone had direct knowledge of the first phase of the German Revolution, part of which he had witnessed. When his prison régime was relaxed, he wrote from his cell on 11 March to the writer Alfons Paquet, who was travelling in Soviet Russia. After saying that he opposed the January uprising – 'It is not possible to seize power if we do not have the majority of the working class behind us.'[12] – he emphasised what

---

[10] *Der I Kongress der KI*, p. 134.
[11] *Izvestia*, 1 May 1919.
[12] The full text of the letter is reproduced in the introduction to A. Paquet, *Der Geist der russischen Revolution*, Leipzig, 1919, p. vii.

had most impressed him in the course of the German Revolution. The masses had instinctively directed themselves towards organising workers' councils, towards soviet forms in the strict sense. The phenomenon was all the more remarkable in that no intensive propaganda in favour of the councils had been carried out. Radek said that in such conditions, the defeat of the Revolution could not be attributed to the masses themselves, but only to the conditions in which they had to fight, as it happened, without organisation: 'In Germany, a big revolutionary party is lacking. The Communists are first of all a leadership, but not a party with a tradition, such as we were in Russia in 1917.'[13]

Comparison with the Russian Revolution enabled a better understanding of the specific problems of the German Revolution as it developed:

> We never had battles to fight like those in January or of today in which so much blood and wealth are so absurdly sacrificed. We had authority amongst the masses. We kept them in hand. But the German Communists do not yet hold them, and that is what this gunning and rioting means. We had with us mass organisations, trade unions, revolutionary from the start or born of the revolution itself. The German unions, the pride of the German working class, the concentrated expression of their organisational genius, were born in a period of political stagnation and of economic development. Consequently they were reformist. The strength of the organisation had not been formed in the course of the Revolution, and the Revolution, before it has provided itself with new organisations, has dispersed its forces chaotically. Worse, the organisations which the German working class inherited took their stand on the side of the bourgeoisie, and formed the basis for the counter-revolution. That is why the Revolution has this savage, uncontrolled character. Moreover there is this point: we advanced to power along the road of a struggle for peace, and the army was with us. The bourgeoisie could not strike at us by using mercenaries, as it did in Germany. And, finally, the bourgeoisie in Germany is much stronger than it was in Russia.[14]

This did not mean, Radek said, that the Revolution had no chance of success in Germany, but that the struggle there would be much longer: 'The civil war will be much more desperate and destructive in Germany than in

---

[13] Ibid., p. viii.
[14] Ibid., pp. vii–ix.

Russia. You are well enough acquainted with me to know how sadly I write that.'[15]

Hope resided in the perspective of the world revolution which would draw new strength from the inevitable rise of the revolutionary wave in the victorious countries:

> No one can know how quickly things will develop in the countries of the Entente. Meanwhile, the German and the Russian working classes will find themselves side by side – not, however, for a war against the Entente, as I had believed in October, because the Entente can no longer wage a war, and the Revolution does not need one. . . . As soon as an energetic workers' government appears in Germany, the elements of disorganisation will quickly be overcome precisely thanks to these traditions of organisation which today have such different results. . . . This perspective is the only one which enables me to rise above the feeling which oppresses my mind in the face of this endless, aimless blood-letting.[16]

The Weimar Republic

The German Republic was formed in the first six months of 1919, whilst Noske's Free Corps were in action. But in a certain sense, the formation of the Weimar Republic was the prolongation of the November Republic, the fruit of the efforts of millions of German workers, including those who placed their trust in Ebert and Noske in the hope of a united, democratic Germany.

Indeed, we may regard the first result of the November Revolution as the fulfilment of the bourgeois revolution which was aborted midway through the nineteenth century. The Weimar Constitution did not confine itself to preserving the unity of the Reich. Following the formulation of Hugo Preuss, who masterminded its drafting, it 'consecrated, reinforced and strengthened it'.[17] It made Germany a unitary state, decentralised and composed of a reduced number of regions [Länder], the rulers of which controlled local affairs. The Reich government had jurisdiction over internal and external politics, finances, telecommunications and rail and river transport.

---

[15] Ibid., p. ix.
[16] Ibid., pp. x–xi. This letter was written whilst the Berlin proletariat was suffering Noske's attacks on the March strike.
[17] Quoted by P. Benaerts, *L'Unité allemande*, p. 158.

The completion of the bourgeois revolution can be seen likewise in the organisation of political life. The Constitution guaranteed the fundamental rights which it spelled out: equality before the law, inviolability of the person and the home, privacy of letters and telephone conversations, freedom of thought and of opinion, of press and meeting, the representation of minorities, and universal suffrage.

Legislative power was divided between two assemblies. The Reichsrat was made up of delegates from the Länder nominated by their governments, which themselves were the product of Landtags elected by universal suffrage. The powers of the Reichsrat were limited to a suspensive veto. An economic council, the Reichswirtschaftsrat, studied the social and economic aspects of draft legislation, on which it also could take an initiative; the trade unions of industrial and white-collar workers were represented on it on the same basis as the employers' organisations. The Social Democrats saw in the introduction of the Reichswirtschaftsrat proof of the social character of the new democracy. The Reichstag was predominant in the legislative process. It was elected for four-year periods, by universal suffrage by the citizens of both sexes of over twenty years of age, on the basis of a system of redistributive proportional representation. Ministers and the Chancellor were responsible to the Reichstag.

The powers of the President were considerable. He was elected, like the Reichstag, by the whole body of the German electors, for a seven-year term, and could be re-elected. The President appointed the Chancellor and, following the Chancellor's proposals, the various Ministers. He promulgated the laws, and before doing so could demand a referendum if he so desired, or if one-tenth of the electors demanded it. He was the head of the diplomatic corps, the bureaucracy and the armed forces. Article 48 of the Constitution conferred on the President the possibility of exercising a full-blown dictatorship, and made him in a real sense the successor to the Kaiser. He could, by decree, proclaim a state of siege, set up special courts, take all measures necessary to the security of the Reich, and dissolve the Reichstag. The institution of the President constituted for the ruling class, and for their spearhead, the army, their ultimate safeguard. All the democratic provisions, in the last analysis, were only secondary to Article 48, which gave the state sufficient strength to break any attempt at revolution or even any disquieting democratic development within the framework of the Constitution. Thus, the activities of Noske's Free Corps, the repression in Berlin in March, and later the installation of the dictatorship of Hitler, all took place within the framework of the Constitution, which its defenders presented at the time as 'the most democratic constitution in the world'.

The governmental coalition

The role which the Majority Social Democrats had played since 1918 indicated that they would be at the centre of the political life of the Assembly, in which they claimed they would have a majority. In reality, the SPD had won 11.5 million votes out of the 30 million votes cast on 19 January 1919, and only 39 per cent of the seats. But there could be no question of their right-wing partners excluding them from the responsibilities of power in such an unstable situation. They had, for their part, decided to continue to 'accept their responsibilities', which meant parliamentary coalitions with the bourgeois parties. Moreover, the latter showed goodwill, because Ebert was elected President of the Republic by 277 votes out of 328. The first Chancellor to succeed him was to be Scheidemann, and then their Party comrade Gustav Bauer. The Social-Democratic ministers were in a minority in the governments, but Noske retained the decisive War Ministry under both of these Chancellors.

Not all the bourgeois forces took part. On the extreme Right, the German Nationals led by Helfferich of the Deutsche Bank and Hugenberg, the administrator of the Krupp enterprises, could call upon enormous financial resources and a powerful newspaper press. The People's Party displayed the same conservatism, the same nationalism, the same anti-Semitism, but showed themselves desirous of opening up the possibility of good business relations with the Entente countries. At their head stood other industrial magnates, such as Hugo Stinnes, whose combine extended its tentacles widely, the banker Riesser, President of the Hansa League, the banker Cuno, successor to Ballin at the head of the Hamburg-Amerika line, and, especially, Gustav Stresemann, the former general secretary of the Union of Saxon Industrialists. They also could command enormous resources in information and propaganda.

The parliamentary majority which supported the Scheidemann and Bauer governments began with the Democrats, whose clientele extended more widely into the petty bourgeoisie, even though their leaders were businessmen, bankers such as Melchior and Dornberg, and the representatives of the two great powers of the electrical industry, Walter Rathenau of AEG and Karl Friedrich von Siemens. The Centre Party, which had now become the Christian

People's Party, remained the party of the Catholic church, and undertook to be the propagandist for class collaboration and 'the community of interests' between employers and workers, particularly through the role played by the Christian trade unions. Its newspapers *Germania* and *Völkische Zeitung* published in Cologne were read by members of all social classes, including workers. Its leaders, Mathias Erzberger, Josef Wirth and Fehrenbach, came from the middle bourgeoisie.

The new coalition faced serious difficulties. As a result of the wartime blockade, the place of Germany in the world market was occupied by the Allies. The economic system had been stretched to the extreme during the War, and was worn out. The end of hostilities revealed how deeply it had suffered. There were no more military orders to help sustain industry, and at the same time the mass of demobilised soldiers swelled the army of the unemployed. Capital equipment was worn out. Capital began to leave the country, whilst the burdens on the national finances became crushing. Industrial concentration grew to insane proportions; the fortunes of the Thyssens and the Krupps had multiplied five-fold during the war. That of Stinnes had swollen from thirty million marks to one milliard. The 'barons' of big capital were the real masters of Germany. They dictated their conditions to a parliamentary coalition which had no course other than to bow before them. Soon the social measures which had been adopted on the morrow of the November Revolution were breached by rising inflation, and were wiped out by rising unemployment. The mass of the German people were paying for the crushing cost of the War. Revolution remained on the agenda, even though everyone now realised that it would be a very difficult road to travel.

Revolution only postponed

The Bolsheviks too considered that the German Revolution was only postponed. In 1919, they continued to endorse Lenin's declaration in the preceding year at the All-Russian Congress of Soviets:

> . . . we are not merely a weak and backward people, we are the people who have been able – not because of any special services or historical predestination, but because of a definite conjunction of historic circumstances – who have been able to accept the honour of raising the banner of the international socialist revolution. I am well aware, comrades, that the banner is in weak hands, I have said that outright several times already, and the

workers of the most backward country will not be able to hold that banner unless the workers of all advanced countries come to their aid. The socialist reforms that we have accomplished are far from perfect, they are weak and insufficient; they will serve as a guide to the advanced West European workers who will say to themselves: 'The Russians haven't made a very good beginning on the job that has to be done.'[18]

It is interesting to compare the analysis which Paul Levi made in 1919 with the viewpoint of Lenin. He noted the deep radicalisation of the proletarian vanguard in Germany, despite the passivity of the majority of the workers, and emphasised the conditions which were contributing to the development of the world revolution: 'It is objective conditions which have driven the German proletariat with iron determination towards the Revolution, despite its being poorly equipped for it, and little inclined to it.'[19] He drew a balance sheet of the first wave in Germany, and explained:

> It is in Germany that the fate of the world revolution will be decided, not because the German proletariat possess some imaginary superiority, but because, since the Revolution of 9 November, the German bourgeoisie remains as dangerous as before, for its organisational talents, its strength and its brutality . . . and because it has become still more dangerous by clothing itself in the new and seductive garment of Social Democracy. . . . It is because of the threat which German militarism and the German bourgeoisie present to the world revolution that today we regard Germany as the heart of the world revolution and the battleground on which its destiny will be decided.[20]

Trotsky, however, tried to explain what the Bolsheviks thereafter called the 'delay' of the German Revolution, in an article in *Pravda* on 23 April 1919. He rejected the analogy with the Russian Revolution, and emphasised that the decisive factor in the setback to the first wave was the role played by Social Democracy:

---

[18] V.I. Lenin, 'Report on Ratification of the Peace Treaty', *Collected Works*, Volume 27, Moscow, 1977, p. 188.
[19] 'La marche de la Révolution en Allemagne', *Revue communiste*, no. 2, April 1920, p. 142.
[20] Ibid.

History once again exhibited to the world one of its dialectic contradictions: precisely because the German working class had expended most of its energy in the previous epoch upon self-sufficient organisational construction . . . precisely because of this, in a new epoch, at the moment of its transition to open revolutionary struggle for power the German working class proved to be extremely defenceless organisationally.[21]

Trotsky, like Radek, held the opinion that the specific characteristics of the German Revolution were explained by the absence of a Communist Party comparable to the Bolshevik Party:

It [the German working class] is compelled not only to fight for power but to create its organisation and train future leaders in the very course of this struggle. True, in the conditions of the revolutionary epoch this work of education is being done at a feverish pace, but time is nevertheless needed to accomplish it. In the absence of a centralised revolutionary party with a combat leadership whose authority is universally accepted by the working masses; in the absence of leading combat nuclei and leaders, tried in action and tested in experience throughout the various centres and regions of the proletarian movement; this movement upon breaking out into the streets became of necessity intermittent, chaotic, creeping in character. These erupting strikes, insurrections and battles represent at present the only form accessible for the purpose of openly mobilising the forces of the German proletariat, freed from the old party's yoke; and at the same time they represent under the given conditions the sole means of educating new leaders and building the new party.[22]

He emphasised that this process of party building did not start from scratch. The historic gains, the proletarian tradition and the Marxist imprint of the Social-Democratic movement remained. The foundations of the new party would stand upon them: 'The political and cultural level of the German workers, their organisational habits and capabilities are superlative. . . . Tens of thousands of worker-leaders . . . are awakening and rising to their full stature.'[23]

---

[21] L.D. Trotsky, 'A Creeping Revolution', *The First Five Years of the Communist International*, Volume 1, London, 1973, p. 69.
[22] Ibid., p. 70.
[23] Ibid., p. 71.

The troops of the future victorious revolution, the mass of the advanced workers, were to be won by the Communists within the USPD, on which Trotsky wrote:

> If the historical assignment of Kautsky-Haase's Independent party consists in introducing vacillation amongst the ranks of the government party and supplying refuge for its frightened, desperate or indignant elements, then contrariwise, the stormy movement in which our Spartacist brothers-in-arms are playing such an heroic role will, as one of its effects, lead to the uninterrupted demolition from the left of the Independent party whose best and most self-sacrificing elements are being drawn into the communist movement.[24]

The victory of the Revolution lay at the end of this reconquest: 'The stubborn, unabated, erupting and re-erupting, creeping revolution is clearly approaching the critical moment when, having mobilised and trained all its forces in advance for combat, the revolution will deal the class enemy the final mortal blow.'[25]

Deep movements in the working class

One of the factors which enables us to measure the importance of the shifts of opinion in the German working class in this period can be found in the results of the general elections on 19 January.

The first observation which strikes us is the total failure of the ultra-left boycott endorsed by the founding conference of the KPD(S). Nearly 36 million people voted, about two-and-a-half times as many as in 1912. About two-thirds of them were voting for the first time. Some 54 per cent of them were women. Over 83 per cent of those entitled to vote took part, a percentage higher than that reached in earlier consultations, and indeed higher than was to be reached again.[26]

The second striking observation is that the forecast which the supporters of Ebert had advanced before the elections during their campaign for the calling of the Constituent Assembly, was refuted. The two 'socialist' parties received 13.8 million votes, less than the total vote of 16.5 million for the

---

[24] Ibid.
[25] Ibid.
[26] Drabkin, op. cit., p. 543.

bourgeois parties. It is true that these elections were held after some months of 'socialist' government which had been disappointing from many points of view. But the real reasons for the victory of the bourgeois parties were the same as the opponents of the Constituent Assembly had denounced in November and December. The great capitalist firms had contributed lavishly to the electoral fund which they had started in 1908. The four big banks, Deutsche Bank, Dresdner Bank, Darmstädter Bank and Disconto-Gesellschaft, alone paid in over 30 million marks to the electoral treasuries of the various parties.[27] Moreover, the elections were conducted in an atmosphere of repression under the régime of the state of siege. Noske recalled in his memoirs the meaningful picture presented on the Sunday when voting took place in the working-class district of Neukölln, with machine-guns mounted in the public squares and the streets patrolled by soldiers with levelled rifles.[28]

When that is said, the voting on 19 January showed, despite the adverse circumstances, a strong trend to the left, compared with the results of prewar elections. The two Social-Democratic Parties together received 46 per cent of the vote, whereas the united SPD of 1912 won at best only 34.8 per cent. Still more interesting is the comparison constituency by constituency.

J.S. Drabkin, who has attentively studied the electoral statistics, remarks first on the impressive progress of the SPD in the rural, less industrialised areas, compared with the elections of 1912: in East Prussia, 50.1 per cent against 14.8 per cent; in West Prussia, 34.2 per cent against 9.7 per cent; and in Pomerania, 41 per cent against 24 per cent. Secondly, Ebert's party lost heavily in some of the most important industrial districts. In the district of Halle-Merseburg, where the SPD had won 42.6 per cent of the votes in 1912, in January 1919 they received only 16.3 per cent, whilst the Independents gathered 44.1 per cent. In Leipzig, the 55 per cent Social-Democratic vote of 1912 became 20.7 per cent for the Majority Social Democrats, and 38.6 per cent for the Independents. In Düsseldorf, the corresponding figures were 42 per cent in 1912, and 34.6 per cent and 22.5 per cent in 1919. In Thuringia, the corresponding figures were 47.5 per cent in 1912, and 34.6 per cent and 22.5 per cent in 1919. In these industrial regions, the total of the Social-Democratic votes exceeded an absolute majority, but very often it was the Independents who received the larger share of the workers' votes. The

---

[27] Ibid., p. 539.
[28] Noske, op. cit., p. 75.

electoral results in Berlin appeared particularly significant from this point of view. There the SPD had received 75.3 per cent of the votes in 1912, and only 36.4 per cent in 1919, when the Independents won 27.6 per cent. In the workers' districts of Wedding and Friedrichshain, the two parties received practically the same number of votes. Drabkin emphasises this double movement of the votes for the SPD, who gained in rural areas, and declined, with considerable competition from the Independents, in the industrial regions. He concludes that the petty-bourgeois vote for the SPD in 1919 was higher than in 1912.[29]

Even though this conclusion may be well-founded, part of the working class continued to support the party of Ebert, especially in small towns. It was in the great industrial centres that the Independents began to gather working-class majorities behind their candidates, and to cut into some of the most solid positions of their adversary. The important fact is that in this period, which undoubtedly had the character of precarious stabilisation, the Communist Party was underground and in deep crisis, and apparently unable to compete with the other workers' parties.

---

[29] Drabkin, op. cit., pp. 546–7.

Chapter Fifteen
The Communist Party After January 1919

The crushing of the January 1919 uprising dealt a severe blow to the KPD(S). In the following months, its members were engaged on every front, in the front ranks of every struggle, without coordination or centralisation. Despite the fact that the KPD(S) had been proclaimed, the working class did not yet have a revolutionary party, but only scattered fragments, which the leadership elected in January did not succeed in unifying.

Paul Levi

The Zentrale was re-constituted in the early days of March. Paul Levi, who succeeded the great victims of January, was relatively new in the movement, but there was no opposition to him, at any rate for the moment. He was the son of a banker in Hechingen, and, at the age of 36, was of a generation younger than the founders of the Spartacus League. Before the war, he had been a lawyer in Frankfurt, joined the SPD, and been elected as a municipal councillor. But he became an activist only after he had met Rosa Luxemburg in September 1913 and had undertaken her defence in the trial which followed her Bockenheim speech.[1] She introduced him to the small circle of

---

[1] Beradt, op. cit., pp. 12–15.

revolutionaries who repudiated the *union sacrée*. After being called up for military service, he was one of the first correspondents of the group which was formed on the evening of 4 August 1914, and he was very harshly treated in the army.[2] Still in uniform, he was to be one of the twelve delegates at the conference held on 5 March 1915 in Pieck's apartment in Berlin.[3] At the end of 1916, having been discharged from the army, he went to Switzerland, where the welcome he received from the émigré internationalist circles showed that he was regarded as an important figure in the German revolutionary movement. He expressed a lively hostility not merely to the social-chauvinists, but also to the centrists, which drew him to the attention of the Bolsheviks.[4] Lenin in his correspondence deplored certain of his tendencies which were later to be called ultra-leftist,[5] and was to write, years later, after Levi had broken from the Communist movement: 'I made Levi's acquaintance through Radek in Switzerland in 1915 or 1916. At that time, Levi was already a Bolshevik.'[6]

It was indeed Radek who introduced him to Lenin and Zinoviev. In December 1916, with Guilbeaux and Sokolnikov, he was one of the founders of the International Socialist Group which was to publish the significantly-named journal *La Nouvelle Internationale* [*The New International*].[7] He took the pseudonym 'Paul Hartstein', and under that name, on Zinoviev's invitation, on 1 February, he joined the bureau of the Zimmerwald Left at the conference in Olten.[8] He was a valuable contact as much for Radek, that outlaw of the German workers' movement, as for Lenin, who was always seeking a way into Germany. Levi proved himself an ally of the Bolsheviks in the discussions of 1917, because he called in the columns of *Arbeiterpolitik* for a break with the centrists.[9] He signed the manifesto of the internationalists when Lenin left Switzerland to return to Russia, and he then returned to Germany, where he became one of the editors of the *Spartacus Letters*, and a leader of the Spartacus League.

---

[2] He was stationed with a territorial unit in the Vosges, and underwent a long hunger-strike against the 'disciplinary' conditions in his unit.

[3] Bartel, op. cit., p. 222.

[4] Guilbeaux, op. cit., p. 106.

[5] V.I. Lenin, 'To Inessa Armand', *Collected Works*, Volume 35, op. cit., p. 265.

[6] V.I. Lenin, 'A Letter to the German Communists', *Collected Works*, Volume 32, op. cit., p. 516.

[7] Guilbeaux, op. cit., p. 108; Gankin and Fisher, *The Bolsheviks and the World War*, Stanford, 1960, p. 565. The first issue included an editorial by Loriot, 'Towards the Third International' (*La Nouvelle Internationale*, no. 1, 1 May 1917).

[8] Guilbeaux, op. cit., p. 127; on his presence, see the statement by Münzenberg, cited in Gankin and Fisher, op. cit., p. 538.

[9] See Chapter 5.

After the November Revolution, he was a member of the Zentrale, one of the editors of *Die Rote Fahne*, and one of the Spartacists' best orators. He welcomed Radek, with whom he was linked by months of living together and comradeship in Davos,[10] and he assisted in the renewal of contacts between the Bolshevik representative and the Spartacist leaders.[11] At the foundation conference of the KPD(S), he found himself entrusted with the thankless task of presenting the report on the National Assembly – which made him a favourite target for the ultra-leftists, who said that he was after a place as a deputy. In January, he maintained contact with Radek, and did his utmost to convince the Zentrale that it must sharply condemn the adventurist policy of Liebknecht and Pieck.[12] Like Pieck, Eberlein and Jogiches, he was arrested and with them he recovered his freedom a few hours after Luxemburg and Liebknecht were assassinated, an event he learned of at the beginning of his interrogation.[13] In the following days, he and Jogiches were the mainstays of the enquiry into the double assassination, and after Jogiches was murdered he alone could replace him. On the morrow of the so-called 'Lichtenberg massacre', the Free Corps put a price of 20,000 marks on his head.[14]

In the Party, Levi was criticised for his bourgeois lifestyle, the housekeeper who opened the door,[15] his refined tastes, his collection of Chinese jade,[16] his passion for Egyptology, the learned editions of old books which he read in the original languages and quoted from memory in his speeches, his taste for references to Roman history, from the Gracchi to Catilina, and then for his 'Don Juanism',[17] for a certain intellectual arrogance, for haughty

---

[10] According to a private letter quoted by Beradt (op. cit., p. 19), Levi and Radek shared accommodation, and were both in the village when they heard of the outbreak of the Russian Revolution. Levi, who was beginning to learn Russian, heard Radek tell his wife: 'Revoliutsiia v Rossii!'

[11] Radek, *November*, op. cit., pp. 132–3, which show that Levi introduced him to everybody.

[12] See Chapter 9.

[13] P. Levi, 'Rosa Luxemburg und Karl Liebknecht zum Gedächtnis', *Der Klassenkampf*, no. 2, 15 January 1919, p. 33.

[14] *Protokoll des III Kongresses der Kommunistischen Internationale*, op. cit., p. 296.

[15] Ypsilon, *Stalintern*, p. 44.

[16] K. Radek, *Soll die Vereinigte Kommunistische Partei Deutschlands eine Massenpartei der revolutionären Aktion oder zentristische Partei des Wartens sein?*, second edition, Hamburg, 1921, p. 103.

[17] Helmut Gruber speaks of the presence at his funeral of 'young women in fur coats of whom more than one could have decked herself in widow's weeds', and points out that 'Levi is the revolutionary hero of a detective novel who is compromised by his sex life' (H. Gruber, 'Paul Levi and the Comintern', *Survey*, no. 53, October 1964, p. 70).

manners, and for touchiness and a lack of warmth in his relations with people. Nonetheless, in these hours of such drama for the small party, his good qualities came to the fore, his intelligence and culture, his moral courage and his recognition of his responsibilities. He felt the strain of the burden of illegal work, but he accomplished it better than the others. His authority and his activities gave him a commanding position. From March 1919, the leadership of the Party was in his hands.[18]

Levi was amongst those who saw the January action as a monumental mistake. It was probably he who wrote the article laying the responsibility for what happened, out of party patriotism, on Ledebour alone:

> Ledebour wanted to take power in a combination of circumstances in which nearly all the conditions for the dictatorship of the proletariat were absent. The working class was partly behind Scheidemann, partly behind Haase, and partly behind – Ledebour. In such a situation, giving a revolutionary action an aim which could not be achieved – as surely as we can count five fingers on a hand – we must call 'putschism'.[19]

He had just taken over the leadership of the illegal party when he wrote to Lenin from Leipzig, where the Zentrale had sought refuge after the bloody week in Berlin, signing with his Swiss pseudonym, Paul Hartstein.[20] He described the situation, the exasperation and the impotence of the working class, the cold determination of the counter-revolutionaries to exterminate the revolutionary movement, and especially the dangers which that movement posed to itself:

> We shall in all circumstances do everything we can to hold our people in check so that they will not give the government the chance to make another bloodbath. . . . In Germany there exists a syndicalist current. . . . It is often difficult to restrain our people from committing such stupidities. Above all, we have within our organisation some who favour staging a coup d'état.[21]

---

[18] After Levi had broken in 1921 from the KPD, Radek tried to play down his activity. He wrote in *Soll die Vereinigte Kommunistische Partei Deutschlands* (op. cit., pp. 101–2) that Levi had held the leading role in the Zentrale only because Jogiches, as a foreigner, had to disguise himself, and because, after March, Thalheimer, 'a recognised intellectual', was not an orator. Nonetheless he acknowledged that Levi 'had responsibility for the leadership' after the death of Jogiches, and that he had to be persuaded to keep it.

[19] *Die Rote Fahne*, 15 January and 5 September 1920.

[20] P. Levi, *Zwischen Spartakus und Sozialdemokratie*, Frankfurt-am-Main, 1969, pp. 19–22.

[21] Ibid., p. 20.

He told Lenin about the progress that had been made by the USPD in the recent months, and also provided him with details of the complicity of the Independent leaders with Ebert, as if he feared that the Russians might be taken in by the manoeuvres of the Independents, who publicly professed sympathy for the Russian Revolution, and he expressed a desire that the Bolsheviks should condemn sharply the policy of Kautsky and of the USPD. Two days earlier, when the news was announced that the Hungarian Soviet Republic had been formed in Budapest, he explained his anxieties in an implicit comparison with the uprising in Berlin:

> The new Hungarian Revolution, which has replaced bourgeois democracy by the republic of councils, is not the immediate prize of a battle in which the Hungarian proletariat has defeated the Hungarian bourgeoisie and landowners. It is not the result of a pitched battle between the proletariat and the bourgeoisie, in which the latter has been brought down. It is simply the result of the fact that the Hungarian bourgeoisie has collapsed. There is no other word for it. It has foundered in shame and degradation, and all that remains is the proletariat.[22]

The unification reached in Budapest between the Communists and the Social Democrats who declared that they accepted the dictatorship of the councils did not seem to him to bode well:

> At the beginning of our revolution we too had the union of all the socialists. The blackguards who betrayed the Hungarian proletariat as Ebert and Scheidemann betrayed the German proletariat, are today enthusiastic for the republic of the councils and the dictatorship of the Hungarian proletariat. This is a danger which from today onwards threatens the Hungarian Revolution, and we must denounce it in the interests of our Hungarian brothers as well as those of the German movement.[23]

Neither did Levi approve the decision of the Communists in Munich led by Leviné to establish a government of councils in which they alone formed the core, against the instructions given to them. He wrote to the Swiss Communists:

---

[22] *Freiheit* (Hanau), 24 March 1919, cited by Levi in 'Die Lehren der Ungarischen Revolution', *Die Internationale*, no. 24, 24 June 1920, p. 32.

[23] Ibid., p. 33.

> We believe that our comrades in Munich have been doubly mistaken. They let themselves be led into defending this caricature of a council republic which at first they had not taken seriously. . . . Then they permitted this defensive action to be transformed into an offensive action without any need to do so, because they were not content with preventing the right-wing coup, but went on to the dictatorship of the councils without concerning themselves in the least with the rest of the country.[24]

He was soon to draw a general balance sheet:

> It was a mistake to believe that a handful of assault troops of the proletariat could fulfil the historic task which falls to the proletariat. Berlin and Leipzig, Halle and Erfurt, Bremen and Munich have exposed this putschism in experience, and show that only the whole of the proletarian class of town and country can take possession of political power.[25]

His experience of the Party led him finally to conclude that the conditions in which it was founded in December 1918 were a heavy handicap to its development. From that point on, the Spartacists were cut off from the hundreds of thousands of workers who had joined the USPD.[26] The Spartacists had thereafter joined with adventurist, ultra-left, 'putschist' elements which Levi held responsible, through their inexperience, irresponsibility and impatience for the defeats in 1919 and the sad situation of the Party, which illegality prevented from winning the real workers' vanguard. Very quickly he was to wonder how the errors of the Foundation Congress were to be corrected, the anarchist and syndicalist tendencies eliminated, and contact with the workers renewed.

Heinrich Brandler

Levi was not alone in the young party to hold his opinion. The survivors of the Zentrale were with him, with the possible exception of Paul Frölich, who

---

[24] *Le Phare*, no. 1, 1 September 1919, pp. 29–30.

[25] 'Reinigung', *Die Internationale*, no. 15/16, 1 November 1919, p. 283.

[26] For example, within the Berlin workers' council, where all the Independent delegates were left-wingers from the revolutionary delegates, they were the target of attacks and insults from the Communists. This is indicated in a report signed 'Markovski' addressed to Bukharin in September 1919. It fell into the hands of the police, and was reproduced from the *Deutsche Allgemeine Zeitung* in *Freiheit*, 25 October 1919. This was doubtless the Mrs Markovski already mentioned in Chapter 4.

nevertheless supported the Zentrale against the ultra-left adventurists.[27] He had the full support of Clara Zetkin who, in conformity with what had been agreed in December with Luxemburg and Jogiches, was present at the USPD congress in March in order to break from it and to join the KPD(S).[28] He also appears to have had the unreserved support of the most numerous local organisation, the one in Chemnitz. In this working-class city in Saxony, it was by 1,000 votes to three that the members of the USPD decided in January to break from the Independent leadership and to join the Communist Party behind their local leaders, Fritz Heckert and Heinrich Brandler, both old Spartacists.

In March, when the USPD began to reconstruct a local organisation in Chemnitz, the Communist Party already had over 10,000 members in the city.[29] There it was not, as in the other centres, a small activist minority, but, when all the necessary allowances are made, a mass party with important positions in the working class, especially in the building workers' union. The party's organ, Der Kämpfer, spoke out against what it called 'adventures', and advocated for the immediate future a policy of workers' unity in action. In July it emphasised:

> Putsches, riots and revolts serve no good purpose. On the contrary, they assist the counter-revolution. To work in unity, with clear awareness of the objective, at rallying the working class, which is still not capable of much political action, such is the road to follow, a difficult one no doubt, but the only one.[30]

The leader of the Communists in Chemnitz was Heinrich Brandler. He was a building worker aged 38 and a veteran of the SPD and the trade-union movement. He alone had had experience since November 1918 of the activity of a mass communist organisation within workers' councils. He openly opposed the ultra-leftists of the utopian wing of the Party, and he adhered to the Spartacist tradition of seeking the unity of the class by way of struggle, in agreement with the Bolshevik theory of the soviets. He wrote

---

[27] According to Freiheit, 20 November 1919, he published in September a pamphlet entitled The Syndicalist Disorder.

[28] Protokoll des III Kongresses der Kommunistischen Internationale, op. cit., p. 668.

[29] W. Berthold, 'Die Kämpfeti der Chemnitzer Arbeiter gegen die militaristiche Reaktion im August 1919', Beiträge zur Geschichte der deutschen Arbeiterbewegung, no. 1, 1962, p. 127.

[30] Der Kämpfer, 5 July 1919.

in *Kommunistische Zeitfragen* that the workers' councils were the means both of unifying the working class and of reaching its final objective, communism:

> This unity of the working class will in the first place be the result of the victorious struggle for power itself. It will create itself, it is not given. The realisation of this unity of the proletarian class in the widest sense of the term is a task on which the victory of the social revolution depends. A means by which this unity can be achieved is the formation of councils. No organisation, political party, trade union or consumers' cooperative is in a position by itself to bring about this unity of the whole class. These organisations today have enormous significance and an exceptional historical role. But in this struggle for complete political power, for transformation of the entire capitalist social order, they are not sufficient, because they are necessarily never able to bring together more than part of the class. Things are different with the councils. The organisation of the councils is as vast as the capitalist mode of production itself. It is through organising councils that every last one of the exploited workers can easily understand and take his place in the whole movement.[31]

Comprehension of this key question, which was the very basis of the Bolsheviks' theory of the soviets, went along with recognition that the revolution was in retreat. The first confrontation between the ultra-leftists and the supporters of Levi took place at the secret conference of the KPD(S) held in Frankfurt-am-Main on 16–17 August.[32] Willi Münzenberg, who since being released from prison was carrying on the fight against those whom he called 'the Party bureaucrats', developed a thesis which considered that the Party's field of activity should be the revolutionary councils in the factories. He thoroughly denounced 'parliamentarism', by which he meant participation in elections and in parliament. Levi replied, expressing the viewpoint of the Zentrale, justifying it by a different analysis of the situation and of the relation of forces:

> To all appearances, the Revolution has come to a standstill, so that one could say that it has spent itself. We are at the end of an epoch, the epoch which

---

[31] *Kommunistische Zeitfragen* (Chemnitz), no. 1, nd (1919), cited by K.H. Tjaden, *Struktur und Funktion der KPD-Opposition (KPO)*, Maisenheim/Glain, 1964, p. 6.

[32] Minutes in the Levi Archives, P55/9.

began on 9 November and which led to the Revolution being defeated. . . .
We have entered the phase in which the Revolution is unravelling, and we
cannot expect to see great mass movements in the immediate future.[33]

Radek

In the same month of August 1919, Karl Radek's prison régime had been
relaxed, and Levi was able to establish regular contact with him for several
months. The two men had known each other for years. They had the same
evaluation of the January uprising, and they shared the same hostility to
ultra-leftism. This reinforcement was valuable to Levi, because Radek was
the emissary of the Bolshevik Party, and brought him both advice and moral
support. During the months which he had spent in Germany, Radek had been
able to grasp the magnitude of the task which faced the German revolutionaries.
He had just informed Alfons Paquet that the road of the Bolsheviks had been
strewn with roses compared with that of the German Communists.[34] He did
not expect victory to be immediate: 'The world revolution is a very slow
process, and we can expect more than one defeat. I do not doubt that, in each
country, the proletariat will be obliged to construct its dictatorship and then
see it collapse several times before final victory.'[35]

Radek and Levi had long discussions, and exchanged an abundant
correspondence. Radek insisted on the importance of work in the trade unions,
in which millions of working people were assembled, and on which the
Communists had so far systematically turned their backs. He believed that
it was vital that the Party should understand the mistake which the majority
had made on this point at the Foundation Congress. Levi recognised that
Radek's position was well-founded, though whilst he agreed to call upon
activists not to leave the unions, he still refused to urge those who had left
the unions to return to them, or to persuade those who refused to join to
enter them, by launching the slogan: 'All Into the Unions!'[36]

---

[33] Ibid., reproduced in Beradt, op. cit., p. 32; Gross, op. cit., pp. 100–1, also used it.
[34] Paquet, op. cit., p. viii.
[35] K. Radek, *Zur Taktik des Kommunismus: Ein Schreiben an den Oktoberparteitag der
KPD 1919*, Berlin, 1919, p. 5.
[36] Radek, *Soll die Vereinigte Kommunistische Partei Deutschlands*, op. cit., p. 102.

The discussion of the Bavarian experience also divided them. Levi refused to approve of Leviné's action in launching the Party into a battle which he knew to be lost. Radek believed that Leviné had no other course to take, because the Communists must always be with the workers when the latter are fighting their class enemy. Finally, Levi wanted to give up the leadership of the Party. He said that it was too much for him to carry this task through under the burden of the mistrust and hostility of the ultra-left elements of the organisation. Radek tried to convince him to stay at his post. He even told him that to retire would be to desert his post, an act for which, in the course of a revolution, a leader would be shot. Levi was convinced.[37]

A pamphlet based on these discussions, and completed by Radek in his prison cell in the Lehrerstrasse in November 1919, marks an important point in the history of Communism in Germany. *The Development of the World Revolution and the Tactics of the Communist Parties in the Struggle for the Dictatorship of the Proletariat* was the first attempt to apply to Western Europe the analyses which made possible the victory of the revolution in Russia. Radek, a prisoner of the state, began by recalling that the basis for the prospect of world revolution lay not in the desire of the Communists for it, but in the growing objective contradictions of imperialism, and therefore resulted from an analysis of the world economic and political situation as well as the tendencies of its development. Similarly, insurmountable contradictions facing the bourgeoisie, which obliged it to impose its own dictatorship upon the working class, meant that it would itself contribute to dispersing the democratic illusions of the masses and making them recognise that only the 'dictatorship of the majority of the working people', namely, the dictatorship of the proletariat, was able to put an end to the dictatorship of the bourgeoisie over them.[38]

This analysis led to the conclusion that the Communist Parties were to propose to the working class tactics and a strategy which were not based on a short campaign, but, on the contrary, had as their axis a long war, in which the defensive followed the offensive, and in which the Party was not to neglect any of the weapons at its disposal. The illusion of a quick victory arose from the incorrect interpretation of the lessons of the Russian Revolution, the conditions of which, although within an identical historical framework, were

---

[37] Ibid., pp. 101–3.
[38] K. Radek, *Die Entwicklung der Weltrevolution und die Taktik der Kommunistischen Parteien im Kampf um die Diktatur des Proletariats,* Berlin, 1919, pp. 5–10, 12.

by no means the same as those of the European revolution. In the first place, the War, which in Russia had mobilised the peasantry at the side of the proletariat, had now ended. In any case, the peasantry in the West was far less homogeneous than the Russian peasantry. Furthermore, the Russian bourgeoisie was young, weak, deeply subject to foreign capital, and had only attained power for the first time in March 1917, in war conditions which compelled it to share power with the army. But the European bourgeoisie was old, well organised on the basis of economic concentration, rich with the experience of decades of rule, and, lastly, had learned from the Russian experience. The Russian proletariat carried out its revolution arms in hand in the midst of war, but the Western proletariat had surrendered its arms upon demobilisation, at the same time as the bourgeoisie was arming its special formations, and in the West the workers had to launch their first attacks bare-handed. Finally, in the developed countries, illusions about the capacity of capitalism to overcome its crisis were stronger, especially amongst the privileged stratum of the labour aristocracy; although in the long run this stratum could only join with the proletariat as a whole, there could be no disputing that the next great struggles of the proletariat would have a reformist character, and, therefore, the process of transforming the consciousness of the masses would be a long one.[39]

The question of the economic and political struggles had to be raised within this analysis. One could not be separated from the other, for fear of risking a fall into either 'syndicalist' or 'putschist' deviations, each as dangerous as the other. Every partial struggle had to be waged within both of these fields, because the outcome of the struggle would be decided only when the working class 'mobilised in these battles, full of revolutionary will, seizes the organs of power from the bourgeois minority'.[40]

In this long struggle, the one necessary precondition for success (or for victory at the least cost) was the existence of Communist Parties, which would be able to analyse the different stages of the struggles in relation to their outcome and to the final objective. The 'syndicalists' contented themselves with phrases when they said that the masses led their own battles: the masses led the battles, but on the basis of their experience and with the slogans that were offered to them. Only the Communist Party could draw the lessons of

---

[39] Ibid., pp. 15–18.
[40] Ibid., p. 20.

their experiences and advance clear slogans: 'The Communist Party is the party of free discussion in the pauses between the struggles, not a discussion club in the heat of the struggle, but a leadership. It is the general staff of the proletarian revolution, and it cannot give orders, but can only persuade.'[41]

Elsewhere than in Russia, the Communist Parties were too young still to understand all their tasks. The first of these lay in taking stock of their forces and their means of intervention. In Germany, they had first to take account of the existence of mass trade unions which organised more than six million workers and were under the leadership of counter-revolutionaries,[42] and then of the strength of the SPD and the USPD, which together had a crushing superiority over the illegal Communist Party, with its little more than 80,000 members.

On the basis of this analysis of the real relation of forces, Radek polemicised against the ultra-leftists, who did not concern themselves with finding out how to win at least some of that crushing majority of workers whom the Communists did not organise:

> The puerile conception according to which there are on one side the small Communist Parties and on the other side the counter-revolutionaries, and empty space between them, on the basis of which we could begin to form our organisations for world revolution – this conception has nothing to do with the method of communism. It results from infantile communist sectarianism.[43]

The Communist Parties had to avoid behaving like sects of preachers. They had to be able to form their own organisation, draw up their own programme, and work out their own tactics, all in the course of joining in partial struggles. They generally started from a purely propagandist basis, and had to resist another infantile temptation, that of putschism, which sought to carry out the final task of the struggle at its very start. They also had to avoid sectarianism, which led them to boycott elections, and ultimately to base their struggle on the feelings of a very small minority. At the same time – and here it is certain that we have an echo of the conversation with Levi – the Communists, whilst fighting against putschism and sectarianism, had to avoid falling into the

---

[41] Ibid., p. 22.
[42] Ibid., p. 23.
[43] Ibid., p. 25.

opposite extreme of passivity. They had the duty at all times to seek to set the masses in movement.[44]

Radek formulated a precise criticism of the Zentrale on this subject:

> At the moment when Noske mobilised his white guards against Munich, the German proletariat was still too weak to ensure that the council republic in Munich was victorious by a general uprising in support of its aims. But if, during the fighting, the revolutionary parties had put their solidarity with Munich at the centre of the movement through meetings, demonstrations and strikes, it could perhaps have forced the government to refrain from the bloodbath. . . . The Communist Party is not the party that waits for the great upheaval of the future, but the party that strengthens and radicalises the activity of the proletariat.[45]

On the basis of this fundamental principle, he denounced the slogan of the ultra-leftists in favour of leaving the trade unions. Leaving the unions meant divorcing the Communists from the masses, isolating themselves, shutting themselves up as a sect, and depriving themselves of the possibility of winning in action the workers who were not yet Communists but who wanted to fight to defend their living conditions. For the Communist Parties this was a life-and-death question. Every attempt at a split in the working class was contrary, in the strictest sense of the word, to the interests of communism. Radek wrote of the need to 'educate' the proletarian masses, and especially insisted on the central role of factory councils and of the slogan of 'workers' control of production', which alone could educate the masses and prepare them to exercise power.[46]

Finally, Radek addressed himself to the problem which during the next year was to provoke an intense struggle in the KPD(S) over the key question of its strategy towards the vacillating elements in socialism, that is to say, the centrist parties and therefore, in Germany, the USPD:

> We think that it is less a matter of pushing the left-wing elements to split with the centrists than a matter of helping them to drive out the right-wing leaders from the central and local structures, and in this way to construct

---

[44] Ibid., pp. 28–30.
[45] Ibid., pp. 30–1. In 1921, Radek was again to use the formulation of 'the party that waits' in his famous pamphlet against Levi, *Soll die Vereinigte Kommunistische Partei Deutschlands*, op. cit.
[46] Radek, *Die Entwicklung der Weltrevolution*, op. cit., pp. 32–7, 45–9.

a large Communist Party from the fusion of the two communist armies of the proletariat. If the Communist Party succeeds in overcoming the anarcho-syndicalist elements in its ranks and adopting a *firm, politically active course*, if in every specific political activity it manages to confront the Independent Party with the alternative, either to take part in activities in favour of the evident needs of the revolutionary working masses or to lose its influence, the masses of workers in the Independent Party, the USPD, will be obliged in practice to form a bloc with the Communist Party. The leaders of the right wing of the USPD would not be able to participate in such a bloc for long, and would be forced to leave the Party or be doomed to total impotence. But . . . such a development will be possible only if the KPD fights to achieve clarity in its conceptions, and becomes the point of ideological regroupment for the German workers' movement. If it does not succeed, the tactic on which its founding conference resolved will not applicable: it will not provoke the break-up of the other parties, but itself will experience splits and collapse.[47]

And the prisoner in the Lehrerstrasse ended his pamphlet, as if he were already addressing the 'left' activists of the USPD, with an appeal to strengthen the Communist International, 'in which all the revolutionary tendencies of the old International meet', and to defend the Russian Revolution: '"Think in continents!" is what Joseph Chamberlain urged the British imperialists to do. "Think in continents and in centuries!" is the appeal of the Communist International.'[48]

The discussion which developed around this document was to reach its peak on the international level in Lenin's pamphlet about 'left-wing communism'. In Germany, the document was regarded as expressing the point of view of the Bolsheviks. In reality, whilst Bronski, who had returned from Moscow, agreed with Radek that 'the first wave had spent itself' and that now it was necessary 'to organise the masses in preparation for the next wave',[49] Bukharin in Moscow disagreed, and believed that in Germany power could still be won by armed force in an early insurrection.[50] Indeed, he was

---

[47] Ibid., p. 56.
[48] Ibid., pp. 64, 66.
[49] Radek, *November*, op. cit., p. 156
[50] Ibid., p. 162. Bukharin led the Left Communists in 1918 on the question of the 'separate peace' of Brest-Litovsk, and supported leftist positions at least up to 1921. It was only later that he was to become the standard-bearer of the 'Right'.

not alone in this belief. In fact there were many communists in Europe who drew conclusions completely opposed to those of Levi and Radek from the defeats of 1919. In the first place, there were such communists within the KPD(S) in Germany itself, as was to be expected.

The ultra-leftists in the KPD(S)

As isolated actions revealed themselves more and more as doomed to defeat, even the most zealous of the Communists began to question their ideas. The 'combativity of the masses' which had served as a justification for their own revolutionary impatience, was disappearing. Denunciations of betrayals by the Social-Democratic leaders were quickly shown to be insufficient for reawakening the thirst for action amongst the mass of working people. These people, who had believed that power was within their reach, now set about searching for short cuts, for new recipes which could enable them either to overcome the apathy of the masses, or to make the Revolution in spite of it.

The great majority of the activists were to be found in this ultra-left current, the same tendency that had carried the day at the Foundation Congress of the Party. The events of January 1919 only strengthened their determination and their hatred of the opportunists and the leaders of the Majority socialists and the trade unions. This current did not express itself exclusively through the leaders of the IKD, such as the former Saxon deputy Otto Rühle, or Karl Becker in Bremen and Fritz Wolffheim and Laufenberg in Hamburg. It also included such people as Willi Münzenberg, who had largely been trained under the influence of Lenin in Switzerland, old Spartacists such as Mergis in Brunswick, and the leaders of the Berlin Communist organisation, Wendel and Karl Schröder. They all expressed the same impatience, the same exasperation, and a bewildered quest for new means of action. They all alike totally rejected 'compromises' such as participation in 'bourgeois parliaments'. They favoured the boycotting of elections as a class weapon, as well as propaganda in favour of boycotts as a means by which to free the masses from their bourgeois-democratic illusions.[51] They all believed that the trade unions were corporatist and reformist, and had become the 'watchdogs' of capitalism, that they served to mis-direct the spontaneous struggle of

---

[51] *Freiheit*, the journal of the USPD, published on 11 September a resolution passed by the Berlin members of the KPD(S), and stated that it expressed the real outlook of the KPD(S), which ran counter to that of the Zentrale.

the working people, and that revolutionaries must struggle to destroy them as obstacles to class consciousness and the revolutionary struggle. They all counterposed 'the masses' to 'the leaders', 'spontaneous' activity to 'organisation', which they regarded as inevitably 'bureaucratic'. They all took advantage of the federalist form of organisation which had been adopted at the Party's Foundation Congress, and of the conditions of illegality, to assert the autonomy of the local groups, the independence and political initiatives of the 'rank-and-file' activists, and to challenge the leading role of the Zentrale.[52]

In Hamburg, the current developed, under the influence of Wolffheim, the former member of the Industrial Workers of the World, to which Bock gave the description of 'unionist', a term which he preferred to that generally used, of 'syndicalist'. Its central idea was the need to put an end to the traditional separation of organisations and the division of labour between party and trade union: the 'unions' should be the only workers' organisations, and should assume both economic and political functions, the basis of which was the factory, and the highest body the industrial union. The Hamburg Communist newspaper, *Kommunistische Arbeiter-Zeitung*, declared in favour of such a 'revolutionary factory organisation' in February 1919. The campaign in favour of this concept accompanied systematic denunciations of the traditional trade unions and support for attempts to split them which would give birth to such 'unions'. Wolffheim justified this policy on theoretical grounds. The traditional unions had corresponded to the historical period of development of capitalism, and had enabled the gathering of the class on the basis of its economic demands, but from now on, in the period of destruction of capitalism, they were obstacles which had to be overthrown on the road of

---

[52] 'Report of the Zentrale to the Executive of the Communist International on the Question of Organisation', cited in V. Mujbegović, *Komunisticka Partija Nemacke v Periodu Posleratne Krize 1918–1923*, Belgrade, 1968, pp. 166–7, n. 5. It stresses the absence of interest in organisation as such in the Communist ranks: 'In July 1919, the party had 100,000 adherents in Germany, of whom only a few were really Communists. Essentially it was the general hostility to the Noske régime which brought the workers to us. It was impossible to consolidate the Party on such a basis. The units of the Party have not functioned, dues have not been paid. Such a situation cannot be explained only by the conditions of our party's illegality, but also by the very widespread idea amongst German workers that the government could not maintain itself for more than a few weeks or months, and that there was only one step between this situation and the dictatorship of the workers' councils. It was this incorrect interpretation of the situation which enabled us to conclude that comrades considered that intensive work in the organisation was useless. It has been possible to eliminate only gradually this aversion from organisational work.'

the Revolution. The Hamburg Communists proposed to wind up the traditional unions and share out their funds amongst the unemployed. In August, the KPD(S) Hamburg district organisation declared that membership of the Party was incompatible with membership of the traditional trade unions.[53]

The ultra-leftists considered that both of the traditional forms of organisation had collapsed along with the opportunists. From now on, the task was to overcome the actual division of the proletariat, which was scattered amongst reformist parties and corporatist trade unions, and everywhere subject to the authority of 'leaders'. That could be achieved by gathering them together 'at the base', in their workplace, in 'unions' based on the factories in which every distinction between trade-union and political activity would be wiped out, and the sole programmatic foundation would consist of accepting the idea of the dictatorship of the workers' councils as the only force leading to socialism.

The activists in Bremen, whose spokesman in this matter was Karl Becker,[54] as well as Karl Schröder and Wendel in Berlin, did not call into question the necessity of the Communist Party. Indeed, they considered that it should create, support and spread the 'unions'. On 7 October, at the meeting of the workers' councils of Berlin, the KPD(S) faction, whose spokesman was Rasch, appealed to the Independents to counterpose to the 'revolutionising' of the traditional trade unions the perspective of constructing revolutionary factory organisations, and declared that it would withdraw from the meeting if its viewpoint was not accepted. All the efforts of the left Independents, Richard Müller, Malzahn, Neumann and Däumig in the meeting (the Majority Social Democrats had ceased to attend the workers' council meetings months earlier) were in vain in the face of the determination of the Berlin Communists, who spoke of the 'betrayal' of the official unions and the 'success' of the Allgemeine Arbeiter-Union, the 'unionist' organisation of the leftists.[55]

---

[53] Bock, op. cit., pp. 124–30.
[54] Ibid., p. 130.
[55] The account of this discussion is published in *Freiheit*, 8 October 1919. Däumig appealed to the authority of Radek on the question whether revolutionaries should work in the traditional trade unions, and received the answer from the Communists that 'Radek doesn't know anything about Germany!'. A Communist named Peters appealed to his comrades not to show themselves 'irresponsible' by withdrawing from the meeting. A statement by the Zentrale a few days later officially disavowed the behaviour and the political positions of the Berlin Communists (*Freiheit*, 13 October 1919).

In fact, when many Communists criticised their own version of revolutionary Marxism, and tried desperately to force a success after a year of cruel defeats, they simply rediscovered tendencies very close to the anarchist and syndicalist currents which Marxism had defeated within the workers' movement, but which were reborn under the pressure of defeat and of impotence in the face of the labour bureaucracies – though under slogans and through practices which they believed to be 'new'. Levi regarded these theories as 'a regression to the dawn of the workers' movement'.[56]

Levi was convinced that the evil was widespread, and he tried at first to regain hold of the threads of an organisation which existed only on paper. This was the object of the conference of April 1919, at which the organisation was divided into twenty-two geographical districts, each led by a secretary whose mission was 'to group together all the communist elements', the majority of whom were still scattered about in the ranks of the Independents, 'to improve the organisational links between the comrades' and 'to organise local groups'.[57]

But the debates at the conference of August 1919 showed Levi that he had to act in a more radical way.[58] He was sure that he did not command the means to compel the left elements to accept discipline under the authority of the Zentrale, so he resolved on a split. For him, the main task was to return the Party to the road of Marxism, which first meant correcting the decisions of the Foundation Congress. The crucial factor was to have at his disposal an organisation built on Marxist foundations, however small it might be. Having determined to use his position at the head of the Zentrale, he went forward determined if necessary to expel the majority of the members in order to cure the party of its 'disorder'. This was the spirit in which he made the arrangements for the KPD(S)'s Second Congress, which opened on 20 October 1919, and was held in the neighbourhood of Heidelberg, its location and cover being changed each day.

Learning from the experience of the early months of 1919 as well as that of the Foundation Congress, Levi at first tried hard to change the method of representation of the local groups, of which the numerically largest (the ones that supported him, like the Chemnitz group) had been under-represented,

---

[56] Levi Archives, P24/8, f8.
[57] 'Report of the Zentrale to the Executive of the Communist International on the Question of Organisation', cited in Mujbegović, op. cit., p. 165, n. 1.
[58] Levi Archives, P55/9.

because at the Foundation Congress any group of more than 250 members was represented by a maximum of three delegates, irrespective of its size.[59] He took seriously the role of the leadership as a 'centre', and his initiatives were marked by a conception which was in effect much more centralist than that of the First Congress.[60] In this way, he brought about the dissolution of the League of Red Soldiers, which had become the refuge of the ultra-leftists and the most adventurist elements, a real 'red guard' within and on the fringes of the Party.[61] This measure appears to have been taken without provoking any immediate protest, but, adopted as it was in the difficult conditions of illegality, it was soon to be denounced by its opponents as a pledge of good behaviour by Levi to the Noske government, and a first step towards capitulation.

The Heidelberg Congress

As soon as the Congress opened, Levi went over to the offensive. His address consisted of a summary of Communist principles, an analysis of the political situation, and an attack on the theses of the Hamburg people, whom he presented as 'syndicalists'. The Zentrale proposed to begin by discussing and adopting certain principles on which the activity of the Party was to be based, and then to examine the specific questions in the discussion, by way of the theses which the Zentrale presented on parliamentarism and the trade-union question. The theses on principles stressed that the Revolution could not consist of a single 'isolated blow', that it was 'a process of rise and decline, of ebb and flow', the result of a desperate struggle by a class 'which is not yet fully conscious of its tasks or its strength'.[62] The task of the Communists was, precisely, to develop this consciousness, and their duty lay in using

---

[59] See the text on the draft statute drawn up in the spring of 1919 in Weber, *Der Gründungsparteitag der KPD*, op. cit., on the basis of documents in the Paul Levi Archives, pp. 304–9.

[60] *Bericht über den 3 Parteitag der Kommunistischen Partei Deutschlands am 25 und 26 Februar, 1920*, Berlin, 1920, p. 41; *Die Rote Fahne*, 28 December 1921; Bock, op. cit., pp. 139ff., mentions on several occasions the 'measures' or the 'policy' of centralisation on the part of Levi between March and August 1919, without providing any specific examples of them.

[61] The Communist elements of these Kampforganisationen (KO) were to become one of the bases of support for the opposition and then for the KAPD (Bock, op. cit., pp. 419–20).

[62] *Bericht über den 2 Parteitag der Kommunistischen Partei Deutschlands (Spartakusbund) vom 20 bis 24 Oktober, 1919*, Berlin, 1919, p. 61.

every means to succeed in doing so, including participation in elections and especially in militant activity in the traditional trade unions. The theses denounced the supporters of the 'workers' unions' as 'petty-bourgeois utopians' who believed that 'movements of the masses can be provoked on the basis of a particular organisational form, and therefore that the Revolution is a question of an organisational form'.[63]

The first discussion revealed the tactic of the Zentrale; it divided its opponents. They might be united in their opposition to parliamentarism and the traditional trade unions, but they were separated by more profound differences of principle, in particular on the role of the Communist Party. For that reason, Wolffheim tried to turn the situation back in his favour by a change in the agenda, so that parliamentarism and the traditional unions would be debated first, and principles afterwards. Levi had simple arguments to defend the agenda: discussion and agreement on principles were necessary preliminaries, on the basis of which the other questions could be settled in clarity. The Congress accepted the agenda proposed by the Zentrale by 24 votes to 19.[64] The Congress then resolved by 23 votes to 18 that members of the Zentrale were to have the right to vote.[65]

The ultra-leftists were halted in their tracks. The habits of the past and the disorganisation caused by the blows of repression had led them to underestimate the possible threat posed to them by the Zentrale which had been elected at the First Congress, and which consisted of activists who were actually in a minority both at the Congress and in the Party itself. Clearly, it intended to expel the most resolute of its opponents. Laufenberg said that the discussion had not been a political one; he declared that Levi had brandished the bogey of syndicalism merely in order to provoke a split, and that Levi needed this split in order to make possible a rapprochement with the left Independents and a policy of parliamentarism. He said that the theses which Levi had presented would not stand the slightest chance of being adopted by the activists of the Party if they were acquainted with them. Wolffheim in turn complained that the Zentrale had never made any effort to discuss with the Hamburg organisation. He said that the only criticisms which the latter had received were about money, and that he was only now

---

[63] Ibid., p. 30.

[64] Ibid. This decision ensured in advance that Levi's theses would be adopted, but, as it was taken after he had delivered his report, it is clear that the delegates were fully aware of what was at stake when they reached their decision.

[65] *Bericht über den 2 Parteitag der KPD*, op. cit., p. 31.

discovering that there were political differences. In fact, the very ground on which these speakers took their stand revealed that the stroke which Levi had prepared had succeeded. Amongst the other delegates, Schnellbacher declared that the Party found itself confronted anew with the old debate 'between Marx and Bakunin'.[66]

Münzenberg was in the ranks of those who opposed participation in elections, and criticised what he believed to be the 'overly propagandist activity' of the Zentrale, but he did not make anti-parliamentarism an issue of principle. In particular, he opposed the 'federalist' conception of the Party which Hamburg advocated: 'The federalist character of the isolated struggles in Germany has clearly revealed the dangers of federalism.'[67]

The theses on principles and on tactics were put to the vote in succession, and were adopted. The motion which condemned passive resistance and sabotage as forms of activity was carried very narrowly, by 25 votes to 23. Levi moved that it was necessary for clarity and coherence to expel those who opposed the theses on principles, and this was carried by 21 votes to 20. The theses as a whole were finally adopted by 31 votes to 18. The delegates of the opposition, Laufenberg, Wolffheim, Rühle, Schröder, Wendel, Becker and others were not to return to the Congress. The same evening, after a discussion, the opposition rejected a proposal from Wolffheim and Laufenberg immediately to create a new party. Nevertheless, the path to a split was opened.[68]

It remained to Levi to overcome the 'buffer' group, led by Münzenberg and Georg Schumann. Whilst they accepted the theses on tactics and principles and declared that they were faithful to the Marxist and Bolshevik conception of the party, they continued to oppose participation in elections. But the delegates clearly adopted the theses which Levi presented, and the principle of electoral participation. The theses which were later carried on the question of the traditional trade unions laid down that the Communists should work actively within the traditional trade unions in order to win the masses of workers from the trade-union bureaucracy, which formed the principal obstacle to the development of revolutionary consciousness. Communists were obliged to remain in the traditional trade unions as long as they could win fighters for the revolution there.[69]

---

[66] Ibid., pp. 33–8.
[67] Ibid., p. 44.
[68] Ibid., pp. 42, 44, 60–2.
[69] Ibid., pp. 48, 51, 62–7.

Levi had won the first round in his struggle to put the KPD(S) back on course when he obtained from the Second Congress a correction of the most harmful decisions of its Foundation Congress. He explained this in a statement dated 28 November 1919 addressed to all Party members.[70]

Radek and Lenin oppose the split

In a letter sent from his prison cell to the Party Congress, Radek had agreed in every essential point with Levi's theses, which in any case expressed the content of their discussions. He stated what he believed to be the essential lessons of the Russian Revolution, which were as much about participating in elections and militant activity in the traditional trade unions as about the centralisation of the Party.[71] But he was, on the contrary, very much surprised on the eve of the Congress to learn, thanks to a letter from Bronski which was brought to the jail by Elfriede Friedländer, who had emigrated in August 1919 from Austria,[72] that Levi intended to expel those who opposed his theses on principles. Radek in turn used Bronski's messenger to try by a last-minute letter to dissuade Levi from precipitating a split. Levi did not take this message into account.[73]

Radek was to write – though much later – that the Heidelberg theses included some 'opportunistic formulations', and he was no doubt all the more sensitive to the form which the split in preparation would take because many of his old comrades and supporters in Bremen, with Karl Becker at their head, and even, in Hamburg, the Russian Communist Zaks-Gladniev – who worked politically under the name of Fritz Sturm – were in the ranks of the opposition which had been outvoted in Heidelberg, on the grounds that they supported Wolffheim and Laufenberg against the KPD(S). Radek wrote that he was renewing his contact with them in order to organise the struggle against Laufenberg and his group on a better basis, and to save for the Communist

---

[70] Levi Archives, P19/2.
[71] K. Radek, *Zur Taktik des Kommunismus: Ein Schreiben an den Oktober-Parteitag der KPD*, Berlin, 1919.
[72] Elfriede Eisler, who married Paul Friedländer, was a leader of the Socialist Youth in Austria, and had taken part in founding the Austrian Communist Party. She was expelled from its leadership in July 1919, was to settle in August in Berlin, and from that time on was active under the name of Ruth Fischer, borrowed from her mother.
[73] Radek, *November*, op. cit., pp. 157ff.

movement activists whom he valued because he had at least partially been their educator.[74]

The Bolsheviks could not fail to recognise that the Heidelberg theses corresponded to their own politics. Nor could they refuse to support them unreservedly. But they nonetheless sharply condemned the split in the Party. Lenin learned the news by wireless, and on 18 October addressed the German Zentrale to tell them that the ultra-left opposition which they had encountered was no more than a sign of youth and inexperience, and that it was preferable to open discussion with them rather than exclude them in advance from any serious debate. He did not know the precise conditions in which the Congress had taken place, and he expressed himself with great prudence on formal questions, though he did make it clear: 'If the split was inevitable, efforts should be made not to deepen it, but to approach the executive committee of the Third International for mediation and to make the "lefts" formulate their differences in theses and in a pamphlet.'[75]

Whilst he confirmed that he agreed on the fundamental issues, he implored the German leadership to spare no effort to re-establish the unity of the German Communist Party. His position was exactly the same as Radek's, even though there had not been the slightest collaboration between them. But Levi had firmly decided to go all the way with a split.

---

[74] Radek, *Soll die Vereinigte KPD*, op. cit., p. 104.
[75] V.I. Lenin, 'To the Communist Comrades Who Belonged to the United Communist Party of Germany and Have Now Formed a New Party', *Collected Works*, Volume 30, Moscow, 1977, pp. 89–90.

Chapter Sixteen
The Ultra-Left Opposition and the Split

The days which followed the Heidelberg Congress
hardly seemed to favour Levi and the Zentrale.
Radek sharply condemned the idea of a split in the
Party, the Bolsheviks' position suggested that their
attitude towards party splits could change, and
it was clear that the majority of Party members
remained faithful to the champions of ultra-leftism.
In fact, the opposition gained some sympathy when
they denounced the 'bureaucratic' measures taken
against them, and the determination of the Zentrale
to drive all its opponents out of the Party. The
conditions of secrecy in which this internal crisis
developed lent plausibility to the charge that Levi
wanted to forge an electoral alliance with the USPD,
and that excluding the ultra-leftists was the price to
be paid for this.

A party in pieces

With the exception of Chemnitz, the largest districts
had supported the opposition in its battle on the eve
of the Heidelberg Congress. They remained firmly
in its hands, and rejected by large majorities the
theses which the Congress adopted. In Essen, for
example, only 43 members out of a total of 2,000
supported the Zentrale's theses.[1] In Hamburg, Bremen,

---

[1] Bock, op. cit., p. 227.

Berlin and Dresden, which were strongholds of the opposition, the Zentrale took the initiative of calling meetings of the members to submit for their approval the decisions of the Congress, and to persuade them to disavow the local comrades. The results were poor, indeed catastrophic.[2]

To believe Ruth Fischer, for example, in the Berlin-Brandenburg district, which claimed 12,000 members on the eve of Heidelberg, only 36 were present to hear Wilhelm Pieck present his report.[3] In Berlin, the split was finalised by a district conference on 4 January, during which the district leaders called for the conference decisions to be repudiated.[4] After months of conflict, in March 1920, the district controlled by the Zentrale had only 800 members.[5] Nonetheless, the Central Committee meeting on 4–5 January proceeded to apply the decisions of the Heidelberg Congress. It expelled *en bloc* all the districts and organisations where conferences had rejected the theses and refused to agree to the expulsion of the delegates of the opposition. From February 1920, the districts of the North, the North-East, West Saxony and Berlin-Brandenburg were expelled. Other organisations, such as those in Thuringia and in Elberfeld-Barmen, were in the process of being expelled.[6] The members who remained loyal to the Zentrale – the frontier between the 'Party' and the 'opposition' lacked precision – were, for all that, not of the highest quality. At the Karlsruhe congress in February 1920, Heinrich Brandler, just returned from the Ruhr, did not hesitate to state:

> We do not yet have a party. . . . What exists in Rhineland-Westphalia is worse than if we had nothing. . . . It will not be possible quickly to build the Communist Party there. . . . What has happened has discredited our name and our party. . . . The result is that our men have not the least authority amongst the working people.[7]

Eberlein questioned this judgement during the debate, but he revealed that there no longer existed any organisation controlled by the Zentrale in such places as Hamburg, Bremen, Hanover, Dresden and Magdeburg, and that a

---

[2] Ibid., p. 226.
[3] Fischer, op. cit., p. 119.
[4] *Freiheit*, 6 January 1920.
[5] *Bericht über den 2 Parteitag der KPD*, op. cit., p. 38; supporters of the KPD consider this figure to be an exaggeration.
[6] Ibid., pp. 7, 32.
[7] Ibid., pp. 16–17.

number of local groups had broken off all relations with it.[8] In fact, outside of Stuttgart, where the membership had risen since Heidelberg from 4,600 to 5,300,[9] and Chemnitz, where it had risen from 14,000 to 16,000,[10] the KPD(S) now only existed in the form of small local groups.

National Bolshevism

However, the developments within the opposition were to assist the Zentrale, particularly the startling positions adopted by Wolffheim and Laufenberg, who had been Levi's principal targets during and since the Congress.

Ever since October 1918, these two local leaders in Hamburg had advanced the position within their local organisation that the Revolution had to be transformed into a people's revolutionary war against the imperialists of the Entente, in alliance with Soviet Russia. In May 1919, they had with exceptional virulence opposed the projected signature by the German government of the Versailles treaty, which they regarded as a capitulation to world imperialism.[11] However, during the run-up to the Heidelberg Congress, they had not insisted on this perspective, but had resisted participation in elections and work in the trade unions, in favour of building their 'new unions', and had opposed the centralisation of the Party. At Heidelberg, Levi attacked them as 'syndicalists', but he made no reference to their support for a revolutionary war.

However, as soon as the Heidelberg Congress had ended, the members in Hamburg tried to unify the opposition behind themselves and to win it to their new-found nationalist positions. The Communist organ in Hamburg, *Kommunistische Arbeiter-Zeitung*, issued a call for the opposition organisations to regroup:

> All the organs of the German Communist Party who think that the dictatorship of the proletariat should be the dictatorship of the working class and not that of the Party leaders, and who think that the revolutionary acts of the masses are not ordered from above by a group of leaders, but

---

[8] Ibid., pp. 33–6.
[9] *Bericht über den 3 Parteitag der KPD*, op. cit., p. 37.
[10] Ibid., p. 35.
[11] Bock, op. cit., p. 275.

must proceed from the will of the masses themselves and be prepared by gathering the revolutionary workers, on the level of organisation, in the revolutionary mass organisations on the basis of the widest democracy, are invited to contact the Party organisation in Hamburg.[12]

On 3 November, the Hamburg district published as a supplement to *Kommunistische Arbeiter-Zeitung* a document written by Wolffheim and Laufenberg entitled *People's Revolutionary War or Counter-Revolutionary Civil War: First Communist Address to the German Working Class*.[13] Here they defended the thesis that the German nation was 'proletarianised', and that an alliance of the nation-proletariat with the Russian Revolution was necessary for a revolutionary war against the Entente. They stated their thesis with greater precision in a second pamphlet, *Communism Versus Spartacism*,[14] in which they combined an explanation of the need for 'civil peace' – the bourgeoisie having to accept the leading role of the proletariat in order to save the nation – with furious attacks on Paul Levi. They even went so far as anti-Semitism, when they called him 'the Judas of the German Revolution', and accused him of having 'stabbed Germany in the back' by his defeatist propaganda in 1918.[15]

Wolffheim and Laufenberg were criticised even within the opposition, where Friedrich Wendel was to be the only leading member to support them. The leaders of the International and of the KPD(S) sharply attacked them:[16] it was Radek who hit upon the name 'national Bolshevism' for their theory. However, they continued to participate in the organisation of the opposition, of which they were the most spectacular figures in late 1919 and early 1920.

Pannekoek's attempt at theoretical explanation

At the moment when Wolffheim and Laufenberg were beginning to discredit themselves as spokesmen for the German left opposition, the German leftists received the reinforcement of the Dutch communists Hermann Gorter and Anton Pannekoek. At the end of November 1918, Gorter arrived in Berlin,

---

[12] Cited in ibid., p. 225.
[13] Published as a pamphlet in Hamburg in 1919, under the title *Revolutionärer Volkskrieg oder Konterrevolutionärer Bürgerkrieg*.
[14] Published as a pamphlet in Hamburg in 1920 under the title *Kommunismus gegen Spartakismus*.
[15] Ibid., pp. 3–4, cited in Bock, op. cit., p. 277.
[16] See in particular K. Radek and A. Thalheimer, *Gegen den Nationalbolschewismus*, Berlin, 1920.

where he worked with the ultra-left elements. He particularly influenced Karl Schröder, he made himself the theoretician of 'workplace revolutionary organisations', and he probably was one of those who in February 1920 spread the idea of the Allgemeine Arbeiter-Union (General Workers' Union), the first attempt to unify the 'unionist' unions on a national level.[17]

Pannekoek returned to Germany at about the same time. He rejoined his former comrades in Bremen and Berlin, and worked on the press of the IKD, and then in that of the ultra-left local organisations of the KPD(S).[18] Straight after the Heidelberg Congress, he applied himself to the task of explaining theoretically the differences between the Zentrale and the leftists. This led to a series of articles entitled 'The Differences on Tactics and Organisation', and above all to his essay 'World Revolution and Communist Tactics', published under the pseudonym of K. Horner.[19] The majority of the ultra-leftists were soon, forgetting their impatience in 1919, to fall in behind Pannekoek's analysis, denouncing the opportunism of the German Zentrale and the leaders of the Third International and the Russian Party, in a polemic essentially aimed at Radek.

Pannekoek drew from the first months of the German Revolution a conclusion opposed to that of the ultra-leftists in that period. In his opinion, the German experience really brought out 'the nature of the forces which would necessarily make the revolution in Western Europe a slow arduous process'.[20] Believing – as Levi declared at the Frankfurt conference in August 1919 – that Germany had entered a phase of stagnation, he wrote:

> There then emerge two main tendencies. . . . The one current seeks to revolutionise and clarify people's minds by word and deed, and to this end tries to pose the new principles in the sharpest possible contrast to the old received conceptions. The other current attempts to draw the masses still on the sidelines into practical activity, and therefore emphasises points of agreement rather than points of difference in an attempt to avoid as far as is possible anything that might deter them. The first strives for a clear, sharp separation amongst the masses, the second for unity; the first current

---

[17] Bock, op. cit., p. 429.
[18] Ibid., pp. 436–7.
[19] 'Weltrevolution und Kommunistische Taktik', *Kommunismus*, nos. 28–29, 1 August 1920, pp. 976–1018; substantial extracts in French in Bricianer (ed.), op. cit., pp. 163–201; reproduced in full in D.A. Smart, *Pannekoek and Gorter's Marxism*, London, 1978.
[20] Smart, op. cit., p. 98.

may be termed the radical tendency, the second the opportunist one. Given the current situation in Western Europe, with the revolution encountering powerful obstacles on the one hand and the Soviet Union's staunch resistance to the Entente governments' efforts to overthrow it making a powerful impression upon the masses on the other, we can expect a greater influx into the Third International of workers' groups until now undecided; and as a result, opportunism will doubtless become a powerful force in the Communist International.[21]

Pannekoek considered that the new opportunism revolved around the idea that a party, large or small, could by itself bring about a revolution:

A revolution can no more be made by a big mass party or coalition of different parties than by a small radical party. It breaks out spontaneously amongst the masses. . . . In contrast with the strong, sharp emphasis on the new principles – soviet system and dictatorship – which distinguish communism from social democracy, opportunism in the Third International relies as far as possible upon the forms and struggle taken over from the Second International. After the Russian Revolution had replaced parliamentary activity with the soviet system and built up the trade union movement on the basis of the factory, the first impulse in Western Europe was to follow this example. The Communist Party of Germany boycotted the elections for the national assembly and campaigned for immediate or gradual organisational separation from the trade unions. When the revolution slackened and stagnated in 1919, however, the central committee of the KPD introduced a different tactic which amounted to opting for parliamentarism and supporting the old trade union confederations against the industrial unions.[22]

The cause of the victory of the German bourgeoisie over the Revolution in 1918–19 lay in the 'hidden power' of 'the bourgeoisie's ideological hold over the proletariat': 'Because the proletarian masses were still completely governed by a bourgeois mentality, they restored the hegemony of the bourgeoisie with their own hands after it had collapsed.'[23]

---

[21] Ibid., pp. 98–9.
[22] Ibid., pp. 100–2.
[23] Ibid., p. 103.

The example of the German Revolution made it easier to understand the problems of the proletarian revolution in a country where the bourgeois mode of production and a high level of culture had existed for centuries:

> The concrete forces which in our view make up the hegemony of bourgeois conceptions can be seen at work in the case of Germany: in reverence for abstract slogans like 'democracy'; in the power of old habits of thought and programme points, such as the realisation of socialism through parliamentary leaders and a socialist government; in the lack of proletarian self-confidence . . . but above all, in their trust in the party, in the organisation, and in the leaders who for decades had incarnated their struggle, their revolutionary goals, their idealism.[24]

Pannekoek rejected the thesis of the 'active minority' and the illusion that power was within the grasp of the revolutionaries. He believed that the problem was to develop within the proletariat the basis for the permanent exercise of power by their class. This would be a long, difficult task, which would oblige revolutionaries to reconsider the perspectives not only of Marx, but of the Bolsheviks too, as far as the revolution in advanced countries was concerned:

> New countries, where the masses are not poisoned by the fug of a bourgeois ideology, where the beginnings of industrial development have raised the mind from its former slumber and a communist sense of solidarity has awoken, where the raw materials are available to use the most advanced technology inherited from capitalism for a renewal of the traditional forms of production, where oppression elicits the development of the qualities fostered by struggle, but where no over-powerful bourgeoisie can obstruct this process of regeneration – it is such countries that will be the centres of the new communist world.[25]

This was an original analysis, pessimistic about the immediate future, but optimistic for the longer term. The only point which it shared with the ultra-left ideology as it had shown itself in the opposition so far, seemed to be its hostility to forming parties which recognised the role of 'leaders', and which admitted the possibility of revolutionary work in bourgeois parliaments and

---

[24] Ibid., p. 107.
[25] Ibid., p. 137.

reformist trade unions. The views of Pannekoek were at the opposite end of the spectrum to Laufenberg's forecast in November, which assessed the Heidelberg Congress and accused the Zentrale of 'lack of confidence in the masses' because it refused to act as if the problem of power ought to be settled during the coming winter.[26]

However, this was not the principal contradiction in the opposition, which had to adopt a position in relation to the Russian Revolution and to the role of Communist Parties, as well as, more concretely, to the German Party and to joining the Third International.

The opposition in crisis

A current was developing in the opposition which can be called conciliatory, partly under the influence of Pannekoek, probably also under that of Radek, who was leaning with his full weight on his old comrades in Bremen, and partly under the effect of the reaction against the nationalist theses. Immediately after the appeal from the Hamburg leaders, the responsible figures in Bremen reacted against the 'national Bolsheviks'. They were to condemn them without ambiguity, and they set up an information bureau for the whole opposition.[27] On 23 December 1919, this bureau, based firmly on the 8,000 members of oppositional Communist organisations in Bremen, issued an appeal which was a reasoned attempt to avoid a split. It called for a Party conference to be held at the end of January, and for all its organisations to be represented there, irrespective of their attitude towards the theses adopted at Heidelberg. This conference would pursue the discussion which had begun and had been prematurely interrupted at Heidelberg, with an undertaking on the part of the Zentrale to renounce any ideas of a split, expulsions or other similar measures.[28]

Karl Becker presented the view of the 'Marxist' minority of the Communists in Bremen in February 1920, when the General Workers' Union (AAU) was founded. He rejected the idea that a 'union' formed in this way could substitute itself for the Communist Party, and stressed that such 'unions' should be seen simply as a more democratic form of industrial union.[29]

---

[26] Cited in Bock, op. cit., p. 146.
[27] Ibid., p. 225.
[28] Ibid., p. 226.
[29] Ibid., p. 190.

The Third Congress of the KPD(S) was held at the end of the month in Karlsruhe. A group expelled from the Bremen district proposed amendments to the Heidelberg resolutions.[30] At the same time, the Bremen Communists sharply condemned the attitudes of Wolffheim and Laufenberg, and declared that they did not intend to split. The same congress saw one of those responsible for *Kommunistische Arbeiter-Zeitung*, Karl Eulert, declare that the editors of the paper and many other members in Hamburg were devoted to Party unity.[31] Meanwhile, Franz Pfemfert proclaimed from his side that 'the KPD(S) was bankrupt', and moved closer to Otto Rühle, who was himself moving towards anarchism by way of syndicalism. Rühle used the cover of 'anti-authoritarian communism' to advocate federalism, intolerance of discipline, the cult of spontaneity (which he regarded as 'proletarian'), in place of discipline, centralisation and organisation, which he regarded as essentially 'bourgeois'. He declared himself for 'socialism without leaders, state or domination'.[32]

It is understandable that faced with these conditions, the Zentrale made a very firm stand at the Karlsruhe Congress. Despite the anxieties of Walcher, who believed that expulsions would be useless and would only delay the return to the Party of healthy elements in the opposition,[33] the Congress confirmed the Heidelberg decisions. It refused to debate with the Bremen Communists so long as they had not broken every link with the 'petty-bourgeois nationalist' group of Wolffheim and Laufenberg.[34] The ultra-left opposition seemed to be decomposing, and the Zentrale could count on the reinforced pressure which the Executive Committee of the Communist International (ECCI) would exert on the opposition when it invited its representatives to Moscow for a direct discussion.[35] The opposition was held together solely by a shared hostility to the members of the Zentrale, and by a range of principled differences with it that were based on deeply divergent analyses. It seemed unable to embark upon a process of clarification, as this would mean an open break within its own ranks, and appeared to be even less capable of organising a new party.

---

[30] Ibid., p. 226; *Bericht über den 3 Parteitag der KPD*, op. cit., p. 7.
[31] *Bericht über den 3 Parteitag der KPD*, op. cit., pp. 22–3.
[32] Cited in E. Eisner, *Gegen die Bürger im Marxpelz. Die anti-Autoritären 'Linken' in der Arbeiterbewegung*, Cologne, 1968, pp. 23–4.
[33] *Bericht über den 3 Parteitag der KPD*, op. cit., p. 17.
[34] Ibid., p. 7.
[35] By letter of 7 February 1920 (ibid., p. 14).

Chapter Seventeen
The Problem of Centrism

Why were the German workers, who had plenty of
experience since 1918 of the consequences of Social-
Democratic policies, not attracted towards the KPD(S),
even though they looked positively towards the
example of Russia? This is to be explained by the
deep differences which divided the Party, and by
the conditions of illegality in which the discussions
took place. Levi explained in Moscow in 1920:

> The masses which are deserting the once
> all-powerful Social Democracy in hundreds
> of thousands had the choice between the
> Independent Social-Democratic Party, which
> continued to be legal throughout the period,
> and the German Communist Party, which was
> illegal at this time, and was sometimes completely
> removed from the political scene. It is quite clear
> that under such conditions, the Independent
> Social-Democratic Party would necessarily
> become the main organisation of the
> revolutionary masses.[1]

Most of the older revolutionary social democrats and
radicals, and most of the youth who had been won
for the Revolution by the War, the Russian Revolution,
and the November Revolution and its aftermath,
remained in the party of Haase and Dittmann. Tens
and hundreds of thousands of others had joined it

---

[1] Levi Archives, P124/8, p. 2.

since then. The USPD, which had 100,000 members when the Revolution began, had over 300,000 by March 1919. Only in Chemnitz had Brandler and Heckert been able, in January 1919, to draw almost all the Independent workers into the KPD(S).[2]

Communism gets a new opportunity

Despite the confusion and differences which placed its leaders at odds with each other on every question, the USPD had won a real majority of the advanced workers during 1919. In particular, its members held solid positions in the trade unions, and these helped to make it the axis around which the opponents of class collaboration gathered. At the tenth congress of the unions in Nuremberg during 30 June–5 July 1919, two members of the USPD, Robert Dissmann and Richard Müller, spoke in opposition to the policy of joint consultation and class collaboration, called for the agreements with the employers to be broken off, and demanded a return to class-struggle trade unionism.[3] They won the support of 179 delegates, against 445 in the general commission, in the vote of confidence in the outgoing leadership, and 181 votes against 420 at the end of the debate on perspectives.[4] At the metalworkers' congress in Stuttgart, an opposition led by the same Independent activists succeeded in getting the policy of the outgoing leadership condemned by 194 votes to 129. They also won a majority for a class-struggle orientation which would immediately be expressed by the resignation of the trade-union representatives from all the joint committees with the employers.[5]

This was unprecedented. Once the metalworkers' union had moved into the hands of Dissmann and a team which united nearly all the former revolutionary delegates in Berlin,[6] whole sectors of the trade-union movement broke from the reformist politics of the Majority Social Democrats, and came over to the Independents.

---

[2] Bock, op. cit., p. 88.

[3] *Protokoll der Verhandlungen des 10 Kongresses der Gewerkschaften Deutschlands Nürnberg Juni-Juli 1919*, Berlin, 1919; speeches by Dissmann, pp. 327–42, and Richard Müller, pp. 434–52.

[4] Ibid., pp. 404–502.

[5] *Die Vierzehnte ordentliche Generalversammlung des Deutschen Metallarbeiterverbandes in Stuttgart 1919*, Stuttgart, 1919, pp. 19, 182.

[6] Amongst the former revolutionary delegates who turned their backs on the old trade unions, we can mention only one, namely, Paul Weyer, a militant supporter of the 'new unions', who much later joined the KPD(S) and was ultimately expelled in 1924 (Bock, op. cit., pp. 185, 187).

In Berlin, the Majority lost the leadership of the metalworkers' union. Their place was taken by the Independents Oskar Rusch and Otto Tost, who immediately took control of the council of trade unions in the capital.[7] The same happened in the printing industry union; its journal *Graphischer Block* from September spoke for the whole of the left opposition in the unions. From May, in Halle, the executive of the local council of trade unions was under the control of Bovitsky, a left Independent, and his comrade Lemke ran its local secretariat. The trade-union positions of these people, Dissmann, Richard Müller, Rusch, Tost, Niederkirchner, Malzahn and Neumann in the metalworkers, Böttcher in the printers and Teuber in the miners, were all the more secure in that the Communists did not challenge them from the Left.[8]

Since November 1918, the Communists had practically no presence within the unions, some being absent on principle, but others because they had been expelled. They were active in organising numerous 'new unions' like the Ruhr miners' union which was formed in Essen in March 1919.[9] When the activists of the KPD(S) remained in the traditional trade unions, it was also not uncommon for them to avoid taking on responsibilities, for reasons of doctrinal purity. Sepp Miller, for example, was elected to the national leadership of the metalworkers' union at the Frankfurt congress because he was the unchallenged leader of the metalworkers in Bremen, but refused to take his seat, in order to avoid having 'to sit at the same table' as the 'social traitors'.[10]

Levi was impressed by the results which the Independents had achieved in their trade-union work. He believed that the irresponsibility of the putschist elements, whose leaders he had just expelled, had kept the principal leaders of the left-wing Independents away from the foundation of the KPD(S), and that the masses of workers who had gathered subsequently around them[11] had only done so because the KPD(S) was illegal,[12] and because its adventurism

---

[7] *Freiheit*, 19 October 1919; F. Opel, *Der Deutsche Metallarbeiterverband während des ersten Weltkrieges und der Revolution*, Frankfurt-am-Main, 1958, p. 85.

[8] We should note that Fritz Winguth was an exception. He also emerged from the group of the revolutionary delegates, and joined the KPD(S). From July 1919, he had responsibilities in the metalworkers' union apparatus (Weber, *Der Gründungsparteitag der KPD*, op. cit., p. 335).

[9] *Illustrierte Geschichte der deutschen Revolution*, op. cit., p. 329.

[10] *Vorwärts und nicht vergessen*, op. cit., p. 210.

[11] According to Dittmann (*Freiheit*, 2 December 1919), its membership had risen from 300,000 to 750,000 between March and December 1919.

[12] Levi Archives, P124/8, p. 2.

deterred them.[13] Levi was convinced that the possibilities of building a communist movement in Germany, and consequently the possibility of a proletarian revolution, depended on whether the KPD(S) could win the left Independents and their mass base. He thought that the 'aberration' in the historical development of the movement in Germany – the fact that a revolutionary nucleus had not been formed before the War, and that the KPD(S) had been founded in the worst possible conditions in January 1919, with an ultra-left orientation which cut it off from the advanced workers – would be corrected in this way.[14]

The birth of the USPD Left

However, a certain interval of time was needed for a left-wing current, clearly oriented towards communism, to take form within the USPD and accept the position of the Communist International as a guarantee and a counterweight to the practice of the German Communists, which they thoroughly rejected. In May 1919, after the KPD(S)'s Second Congress, Clara Zetkin, as expected, had broken from the USPD, and joined the KPD(S).[15] In opposition to Haase, the representative of the Party leadership, the group in Berlin with the revolutionary delegates at its head, followed Däumig and Richard Müller in denouncing the 'opportunism' and the 'reformism' of the leaders. Their ideas were all the better received because, in the atmosphere of repression which Noske's people had created, the Party leadership's championing of the Constituent Assembly, which had just met, and the perspective of 'socialist reunification', which it had still openly voiced a month earlier,[16] were not an attractive proposition. However, the Left remained confused, like its leadership. Däumig presented a counter-statement expounding at length what he called 'the system of councils',[17] closely influenced by the soviet organisational scheme, which he counterposed to the old parliamentary system. On this point at least, he raised no differences with the Communist slogan of power

---

[13] According in particular to *Freiheit*, 8 October 1919, it was people like Malzahn, Eckert, Neumann and Däumig who defended the position of the Bolsheviks on work in trade unions against members of the KPD(S) in the general meetings of the Berlin council.

[14] Levi Archives, P124/8, pp. 2–3.

[15] C. Zetkin, *Ausgewählte Reden und Schriften*, Volume 2, East Berlin, 1957–60, p. xiii.

[16] See in particular R Hilferding, 'Die Einigung des Proletariats', *Freiheit*, 9 February 1919.

[17] Text of his report and his reply in E. Däumig, *Das Rätesystem*, Berlin, 1919, p. 37.

to the councils, but he stressed that he deeply disagreed with what he called the Communists' 'putschist tactics'. He warned the delegates against the danger which the Communists represented in a period when the masses were being radicalised. If the USPD did not declare its support for councils, the KPD(S) would grow at its expense.[18]

The final resolution resulted from a compromise. As Eugen Prager emphasises,[19] it expressed at the same time the outlooks of both the two opposing tendencies within the Party. It recalled that the Party was founded on the basis of the old Erfurt Programme. It explained that, in the light of the recent revolutionary experiences, it supported 'the system of councils', which united the workers in the factories, gave the proletariat the right 'self-management in industry, in local authorities and in the state', and prepared for 'the transformation of the economy'.[20] It stated that the aim of the Party was 'the dictatorship of the proletariat', which was defined as 'the representation of the great majority of the people'. It did not preclude any method of political or economic struggle to arrive at the Party's objective, 'including parliamentarism', although it condemned 'ill-considered violence'.[21] It ended by calling for 'the reconstruction of the workers' International on the basis of a revolutionary-socialist policy in the spirit of the international conferences in Zimmerwald and Kienthal'.[22]

The right wing of the Party emerged at an advantage from the USPD's Second Congress. It retained the leadership on the basis of a compromise which did not tie its hands, and which permitted it to pursue its own policy. The final resolution was typical of a centrist party in that it left the real differences unresolved. Däumig received 104 votes as Party Chairmen coming immediately after Haase, who won 159; he refused to share the responsibility with Haase and offered his resignation to the Congress, which replaced him with Crispien.[23] During the months which followed, the resistance of the Right to the rising pressure of the Left, the reluctance of most of the Party's newspapers to defend the 'compromise', and, finally, the resumption of relations with socialist parties abroad, were to aggravate the differences.

---

[18] Ibid., p. 15.
[19] Prager, op. cit., p. 194.
[20] Cited in ibid., p. 193.
[21] Ibid.
[22] Ibid., p. 194.
[23] Ibid., p. 195.

The resolution of the March Congress was in fact the basis on which the USPD worked for the 'reconstruction' of the International which Kautsky advocated. This was nothing other than the reconstruction of the Second International on its pre-1914 basis, combined with an all-round mutual amnesty. In February 1919 in Berne, the USPD's delegation, led by Haase and Kautsky, had supported, along with the majority of delegates, a resolution which by implication condemned 'dictatorship', that is, Bolshevism.[24] In Lucerne in August, the Independent delegates lined up in the minority which wanted to keep the door open to the Communists, but despite the support by their own congress for the dictatorship of the proletariat, they continued to condemn violent methods.[25] The failure of these conferences to set in place promptly some genuine international structures, or even to agree on the need for them, undermined the efforts of the 'reconstructors'. Immediately after the Lucerne conference, Kautsky had to admit that the idea of joining the Third International was winning increasing numbers of adherents.[26]

The bulk of the Party's members could not accept with indifference joining an International which would tolerate the presence of German Social Democrats, the 'Noske socialists'. Moreover, the proclamation of the Communist International – which the Independent leaders, including those of the Left, had unanimously condemned as at least 'premature' – exerted an undeniable attraction. That International had the advantage of the prestige of the October Revolution, and there was the strong opposition among the Party's members to any moves that appeared to isolate Russia. Such factors contributed to strengthen the left wing, which was by now beginning to act as an organised tendency.[27]

A new generation of leaders was emerging. These were people for whom the experience of November and the months of reaction which followed had taught the need for a hard revolutionary line, a serious organisation, and the construction of a genuine International of parties ready for combat. Now, younger people were joining the old Berlin nucleus of people such as Däumig, Richard Müller and Adolf Hoffmann, from whom Ledebour separated himself

---

[24] J. Braunthal, *Geschichte der Internationale*, Volume 2, op. cit., pp. 168–73.

[25] Ibid., pp. 174–6; J.W. Hulse, *The Forming of the Communist International*, Stanford, 1964, p. 96.

[26] *Freiheit*, 20 August 1919.

[27] Prager (op. cit., p. 202) dates the start of this organisation in the first months of 1919. Radek (*November*, op. cit., p. 162) says that just before he left for Russia at the end of 1919, he had a long discussion with Däumig, who said that he was in favour of a split in his Party.

because of his anti-Bolshevism. These newcomers, including Wilhelm Koenen, Anton Grylewicz, Bernhard Düwell, Stoecker, Curt Geyer, Böttcher and Remmele, often came from the Socialist Youth, had been active during the War and the Revolution, had all been organisers of councils and leaders in revolutionary committees, and were much less influenced by the ideas and practices of the prewar Party. As they saw things, the question of fusing with the KPD(S), entangled as it was in a crisis which its own sectarianism was making worse, was not in itself an issue,[28] although they attached great importance to the question of their Party's relations with the Communist International.

The question of the International arose at the USPD's conference in Jena on 9–10 September 1919, over the Party's attendance at the conference in Geneva which aimed to resuscitate the Second International. Already the progress made by the Left was clear; influential newspapers such as the *Hamburger Volkszeitung*, edited by the talented Wilhelm Herzog, or the *Gothaer Volksblatt*, declared their support for affiliation to the Third International and fusion with the KPD(S), along with general members' meetings in Halle and Zella-Mehlis, and increasingly determined minorities in most areas.[29] The new relation of forces was clear from the course of the discussion. Hilferding spoke for the leadership, that is, for the right wing. Reversing his previous outlook, on this occasion he opposed reunification with the SPD. He also opposed joining the Second International, which was in the process of being reconstructed. But he was no less opposed to joining the Third International, which he thought had no better chance of surviving than the Soviet Union itself. One does not board a sinking ship. If by some miracle the Communist International was to develop, it would find itself totally controlled by the Russian Communists. His conclusion therefore indicated a centrist path:

> The Party leadership has decided to enter into relations with all the groups of the Left, in order to make a joint approach with them to the Bolsheviks with a view to an understanding. . . . Time will help us, and bring nearer the moment when it will be possible to create an International capable of becoming an instrument of revolution.[30]

---

[28] At the beginning of 1920, Curt Geyer could still write: 'the Left of the Independents has no need of a fusion between parties. The Independents are the mass revolutionary Party in Germany.' ('Nach dem Parteitag', *Das Forum*, no. 4, January 1920, p. 268.)

[29] H. Naumann, 'Dokumente zum 45 Jahrestag der Gründung der KI', *Beiträge zur Geschichte der deutschen Arbeiterbewegung*, no. 9, 1964, pp. 285–97.

[30] *Freiheit*, 11 September 1919.

This procedure was well-conceived; to ignore the Third International, to form an international bloc with a certain number of other parties of the Left and only then to approach the Bolsheviks would have the practical result of turning the situation in favour of the Independents. If the coming congress were to follow Hilferding, the USPD would be the principal instrument of the initiative that the Swiss Socialist Party had launched just after the Lucerne conference, which was to 'reconstruct' the International on the pre-1914 basis after platonically condemning social chauvinism, a centrist solution which would be the same as that of the Vienna Union of Socialist Parties, which its Communist opponents called the 'Two-and-a-Half International'.

Walter Stoecker spoke for the Left, and demanded that the problem of joining the Third International be discussed and studied. The world working-class movement above all needed clarity. Hilferding was offering it an ambiguous solution which was merely an attempt to safeguard the possibility of a future general reconciliation on the basis of a mutual amnesty. The great lesson of the collapse of the Second International in 1914 was that 'a new International, constructed on an entirely new base . . . on a clear revolutionary base', was needed, in order to 'undertake and lead the struggle against world capitalism'. The foundation of a new International in Moscow was a fact, whether one thought it premature or not. He added that the defence of the Russian Revolution was the first present duty of revolutionaries:

> It is our duty to stand by our Russian brothers and comrades by every possible means and with all our strength, whatever we may think about some aspects of their tactics. To be joined by a Party like ours, with a million members, would doubtless be a considerable moral reinforcement for the Russians. Moreover, such reinforcement is in line with our own interest, because the fall of the Russian council republic would set off a dangerous wave of reaction throughout Europe.[31]

The Left made further progress between the Jena conference in September 1919 and the Leipzig Congress in December 1919.[32] Many general meetings and group conferences called for the Party to join the Third International, and favoured the dictatorship of the proletariat against the parliamentary

---

[31] Ibid.; Stoecker, *Die proletarische Internationale*, p. 23.
[32] Anton Grylewicz became vice-chairman of the Berlin organisation of the USPD for some months before taking its leadership (Weber, *Die Wandlung des deutschen Kommunismus*, Volume 2, op. cit., p. 145).

Regime. This tendency won important results at the Congress. To begin with, all reference to the necessity of 'winning the majority' disappeared from the Party's action programme. This had been the pretext on which the right wing based their refusal to take power until after they won an electoral majority. The document went on to lay down that 'the dictatorship of the proletariat' could be based only on the 'system of councils', and that activity of a parliamentary kind must in any case be subordinated to the requirements of the essential means of action, the action of the masses. On this point, reservations about the Soviet régime and a condemnation of the Red Terror – which was excusable in Russia because of the specific conditions of the Civil War – were concessions to the Right which provoked the anger of the Bolsheviks.[33]

The result of the debate on international affiliation was less definite. The Congress decided by 227 votes to 54 to break with the Second International,[34] but rejected Stoecker's motion to join the Third International by 170 votes to 111.[35] In the end, a compromise solution, midway between the positions of Hilferding and Stoecker, was adopted, again by 227 votes to 54.[36] After having put on record that the Party agreed with the Communist International on the fundamental problems of the revolution and of socialism, it called for the construction of a revolutionary International capable of action and bringing together, in addition to the parties already in the Third International, 'the social-revolutionary parties in other countries'. In the event that the latter kept their distance, the USPD would then have to open discussions alone to join the 'Moscow International'.[37]

This was a decisive turning point. Once again, Radek intervened to point out its importance, and to tell the German Communists what was required of them.[38] In his opinion, the Leipzig Congress was 'a victory for the worker masses' in the USPD over their opportunistic leaders,[39] but a victory which had to be consolidated. For the USPD could take its place in the International

---

[33] Prager, op. cit., pp. 209–11.

[34] *Unabhängige Sozialdemokratische Partei: Protokoll über die Verhandlungen des ausserordentlichen Parteitags in Leipzig, 30 November to 6 December 1919*, Berlin, nd, p. 399.

[35] Ibid., pp. 39–40; result of the votes, p. 399. The motion was also signed by Brass, Koenen, Rosenfeld and Toni Sender.

[36] Ibid., p. 399.

[37] Ibid., pp. 534–5. The motion resulted from a compromise between Hilferding and Ledebour.

[38] A. Struthahn, 'Der Parteitag der Unabhängigen', *Die Internationale*, no. 19–20, 2 February 1920, pp. 22–32.

[39] Ibid., p. 25.

genuinely – and not just formally – only if it became a fighting Party, and that transformation depended partly on the KPD(S). Radek explained in February 1920: 'It is only to the extent that the Communist Party surmounts its own crisis that it will be able to help the Independent workers to overcome the crisis of their Party and thus create the basis for reuniting the German's revolutionary proletariat.'[40] It was therefore necessary to correct many of the criticisms in the Communist press, which often went on treating the USPD as if the Leipzig Congress had not taken place, and as if the Independents still adhered to the positions they had held in 1919. Some Communists persisted in raising the question of a split to the level of an eternal principle, whereas the German proletariat could not be victorious unless it mustered its forces on a revolutionary basis. It was this task and this task alone which was on the agenda in Germany, albeit in a concrete form which could not yet be determined. According to Radek, the Communist tactic in relation to this fundamental aim should now be determined by recognising two facts: 'Firstly, that the mass of the Independents are Communists, and secondly, that there is in their leadership a left wing which wants sincerely to take the revolutionary road.'[41]

Despite the reservations within the ranks of the KPD(S), the question of a fusion between the Communists and the left Independents was beginning to be posed by way of the possibility of the USPD affiliating to the Third International. Such a perspective was a deadly threat to the USPD's right wing, which moreover had just lost its most influential leader, Hugo Haase, who had been assassinated on the steps of the Reichstag by an extreme right-winger.[42] The USPD's leaders, Dittmann, Crispien and Hilferding, were trapped between the impossibility of reunification with the 'Noske socialists', whose reformist convictions they fundamentally shared, but whose brutal methods they condemned, and the dangers which they foresaw along the Moscow road. They were forced on to the defensive. They brandished the bogey of a split in the Party, and the phantom of the Spartacist 'adventurists', they accused Geyer and Stoecker of working closely with Levi, and of being agents of the KPD(S) and organisers of a pro-Communist faction in their own Party.[43]

---

[40] Ibid., p. 32.
[41] Ibid.
[42] Prager, op. cit., pp. 205–6. He was struck down on 8 October, and was to die, after a protracted agony, on 7 November (*Freiheit*, 8 October and 8 November 1919).
[43] Prager, op. cit., p. 208, even speaks of 'Communist cells within the Independent Party'.

Above all, they did their best to convince the decisive sector of their supporters, the activists who maintained the opposition to Legien, that 'joining Moscow' would lead them, like the Spartacists, down the road towards splits in the unions and possibly their destruction. From that point of view, the conduct of many Communist activists provided them with a weighty argument – even though it had recently been condemned by the theses on the trade-union question carried at the Heidelberg Congress.[44]

Many Independents, even left-wingers and supporters of joining the Communist International, did not want a split which would weaken their Party. They thought that the normal evolution which had taken people like Bernstein towards the Majority Social Democrats and had removed several right-wing elements from the leadership in Leipzig, would conclude with the driving back of Kautsky and his supporters, whether openly or not, without any formal expulsions such as customarily led to a massive loss of members. They also expressed reservations about the Bolsheviks' principles of organisational centralisation. They remained sensitive – in accord with the German radical tradition – to all the arguments about the danger of a dictatorship over the Party by the bureaucratic apparatus, and even about the need to preserve the independence of the trade unions from the Party. Despite all Levi's efforts, there were powerful antagonisms, both personal and political, dividing Communist leaders from those of the left Independents. The latter believed that the course of events which had made their party a mass party and the KPD(S) a sect retrospectively proved that they had been right at the time of the split in 1918.[45]

A discussion with Lenin begins

These problems as a whole were to be tackled in late 1919 and early 1920 in a political debate – indirect and at a distance, but public – between Lenin and the German Communists. Lenin had written 'Greetings to Italian, French

---

[44] It is significant that the report on the internal situation of the USPD at the Leipzig congress, along with sharp attacks essentially aimed at Geyer and Stoecker for their links with Paul Levi, was delivered by none other than Robert Dissmann, the leader of the metalworkers' union (Prager, op. cit., pp. 207–8).

[45] Däumig was to develop these arguments from the platform at the Second Comintern Congress in the summer of 1920 (*Der Zweite Kongress der Kommunistischen Internationale, Protokoll der Verhandlungen vom 19 Juli in Petrograd und vom 23 Juli bis 7 August 1920 in Moskau*, Hamburg, 1921, p. 271).

and German Communists' on 10 October 1919, and had opened a debate on some of the questions which he thought were essential for the German revolutionary movement. In particular, he took up the question of the split within the KPD(S) and its relations with the Independents.

He declared his 'unreserved admiration' for 'the heroic struggle' of the Berlin newspaper *Die Rote Fahne* – the paper of the Zentrale – and attacked the social-chauvinists and the centrists who took pleasure from the split in the Communist ranks. He regarded the differences between Communists, in a context of rapid growth and violent persecution, simply as growing pains:

> The differences amongst the communists are differences between representatives of a mass movement that has grown with incredible rapidity; and the communists have a single, common, granite-like foundation – recognition of the proletarian revolution, and of the struggle against bourgeois-democratic illusions and bourgeois-democratic parliamentarism, and recognition of the dictatorship of the proletariat and soviet power.[46]

He referred to the past differences in the Bolshevik faction and Party, and did his best at the same time to persuade the German Communists as a whole that the split was not necessary, that the Zentrale was right, and the opposition was mistaken:

> This would be an obvious mistake, and a bigger mistake still would be to retreat from the ideas of Marxism and its practical line (a strong, centralised political Party) to the ideas and practice of syndicalism. It is necessary to work for the Party's participation in bourgeois parliaments, in reactionary trade unions, and in 'works' councils' that have been mutilated and castrated in Scheidemann fashion, for the Party to be wherever workers are to be found, wherever it is possible to talk to workers, to influence the working masses.[47]

Lenin counterposed this principled unity of Communists to the artificial unity of the Independents, whose left wing he particularly attacked:

> The masses are abandoning the Scheidemanns and going over to the Kautskys, being attracted by their left wing ... and this left wing combines – in unprincipled and cowardly fashion – the old prejudices of the petty-

---

[46] VI Lenin, 'Greetings to Italian, French and German Communists', *Collected Works*, Volume 30, op. cit., p. 55.
[47] Ibid., p. 66.

bourgeoisie about parliamentary democracy with communist recognition of the proletarian revolution, the dictatorship of the proletariat, and soviet power.[48]

The German Communist leaders found Lenin's position highly embarrassing. On the one hand, he once again condemned the split which they had carried out against their own left wing. On the other hand, he denounced the left wing of the Independents whom they wanted to attract. The leaders of the Independents immediately seized upon it, and Crispien repeated this analysis. August Thalheimer did his best to reply in a pamphlet which republished Lenin's 'Greetings' letter, the circular of the ECCI of 1 September 1919, and his own comments.[49]

Thalheimer began by denying that Lenin's letter could be taken as a final judgement on the left wing of the USPD, to the extent that Lenin himself admitted that he had only poor information about Germany, and to the extent also that it had been written before the Leipzig Congress, which had created a new situation. He explained the position of the KPD(S) on the USPD's left wing:

> They have gone astray along with the masses. They have developed with the masses, they will go on developing with them, and they will make many mistakes with them. Our attitude towards their mistakes and weaknesses will, as in the past, be one of frank and blunt criticism. But we have no thought of putting them into the same sack, on the moral and intellectual plane, as the betrayers of socialism, as the fossils from the period of purely parliamentarian stagnation of the German workers' movement.[50]

He thus informed Lenin that the German Communists by no means confused the leaders of the Left, such as Däumig, Koenen or Stoecker, with people such as Kautsky, Hilferding and Crispien, who formed the right wing of the USPD. Thalheimer then discussed the split which had taken place with the leftists. He said that the German Communists also believed that purely tactical questions should not provoke splits in a Communist Party. From this point of view, the German Party had set an example at its Foundation Congress, where the ultra-left decisions of its majority did not threaten its unity.

---

[48] Ibid., p. 54.
[49] A. Thalheimer, *Der Weg der Revolution*, 1920, in which his reply summarises and quotes from Crispien's comments. The Berlin leftists had given widespread publicity to Lenin's attacks on the Independent Left: see the speech by Kruger to an assembly of the Berlin councils (*Freiheit*, 20 December 1919).
[50] Thalheimer, op. cit., p. 18.

Nonetheless, he declared that at the Heidelberg Congress, it was not tactical questions that were at stake:

> In truth, these tactical questions, especially in their Hamburg coloration, led to positions which denied the very basis of the Party. To convert the Party into a propaganda society, and later to prepare to dissolve it into the mass of workplace organisations, in which the clear political content which the Party had won during the year would have been once more dissolved into the fog of confusion – all this was leading the Party to its doom. Many comrades had not recognised this danger. The duty of the Party Zentrale was to deal with these issues, most energetically, before it was too late.[51]

Thalheimer, far from agreeing with Lenin that the Heidelberg split was a retreat or a backward move for the German Party, declared that it was a positive act: 'It is not only significant from the standpoint of the German Revolution. It is the first step by which the German Party can show the working class of the Western countries the tactical problems which will confront them in one form or another.'[52] Politely, but firmly, he rejected the argument of authority, the universal value of the Russian example: 'The historical surroundings in Germany are much nearer to the conditions in the Western countries than those in Russia. Our experiences in respect of tactical questions will consequently be of special value for the Westerners.'[53]

The split from the leftists and the desire to win the left wing of the USPD demonstrated a method of constructing a Communist Party that was different from the one followed in Russia, where conditions were not the same.

Radek, who had lived through the defeat of the German Revolution after the victory in Russia, generalised the first lessons of these experiences, and developed Thalheimer's criticism of the leftists:

> A Communist Party cannot be victorious before the majority of the proletariat is ready to take power. But it can launch important proletarian actions, such as demonstrations and mass strikes if, on concrete questions of the workers' daily life, the majority of the class is ready for such partial actions, despite the fact that it does not yet agree upon the necessity of the dictatorship of the proletariat.[54]

---

[51] Ibid., p. 19.
[52] Ibid.
[53] Ibid.
[54] K. Radek, 'Die Entwicklung der deutschen Revolution und die Aufgaben der KP', *Kommunistische Räte-Korrespondenz*, nos. 21–22, 20 November 1919.

Brandler had learnt in Chemnitz the mobilising value of workers' unity in struggle. He had resisted ultra-left impatience, and had sought a revolutionary road which avoided the dilemma of 'all or nothing'. The balance sheet of ultra-left activity was particularly negative in Germany. It led him to seek slogans that were adapted to the workers' current consciousness but were able to help them learn through engaging in decisive political experiences, in other words, to win them gradually to Communism in action. He explained to the first congress of factory councils the necessity for what became known as 'transitional slogans':

> We cannot make the Revolution with people as we would like them to be. We must make it, or at least start to make it, with people as they are. It is in the course of the Revolution itself that people begin to change themselves. . . . The problem is to . . . set concrete tasks before them which correspond to what they can do at that point. I attach much importance to this. We must determine the aim of the stages. To understand what the final socialist objective means does not help at all now. What we need to know is: 'What do we have to do, today and tomorrow, to bring us nearer to this objective?'[55]

In order to apply this line, the KPD(S) did not have to turn towards the ultra-leftists and the things they did 'for honour's sake', nor to those who confused the mass of the workers in the USPD with the bureaucrats such as Crispien who led them. If it aimed to approach the masses whom the reformist, opportunist leaders were deceiving, if it aimed to make progress amongst the mass of trade-union members and to win the left wing of the Independents, it first had to differentiate itself unambiguously from the ultra-left currents. This was why Thalheimer rejected Lenin's suggestion that they should have reversed the split that took place at Heidelberg. He regarded this split as a necessary surgical operation. But, at the same time, he conceded that there was a place for tactical differences in a real Communist Party – which the KPD(S) could then become. However, he pointed out that the road of the KPD(S) towards the victory of the proletariat appeared to be slower, more painful and more difficult to chart than that of the Bolsheviks, whose experience he freely admitted to be both older and richer. He stressed:

---

[55] Cited in Tjaden, op. cit., p. 10.

The experiences of the two roads and the two parties which have united have already shown themselves to be valuable for the positive development of the workers' parties in the West. Communist Russia and communist Germany have still to resolve together enormous tasks in matters of tactics as well as of practical politics.[56]

In this way, this first public long-distance discussion began to unfold between Russian and German Communists, on a basis of equality, on the question of how to win the masses to revolutionary politics. However, the course of the class struggle in Germany was soon to pose the problems in new terms, not only in respect of the relations between the Communists and the workers organised in the other workers' parties and in the trade unions, but in respect of the relations between the German and Russian Communists.

---

[56] Thalheimer, op. cit., p. 20.

Chapter Eighteen
The Kapp Putsch

The installation of a republican régime had not fundamentally changed the structures of Imperial Germany. For the big capitalists, the landed gentry and the generals it was a last resort, a necessary evil, at least until the workers came to their senses. For the workers it was, in general, a sad disappointment. Less than a year after the Revolution from which they expected bread, peace and liberty, bread was dear, liberty was precarious, and peace was imposed by *Diktat*.

The political problem, therefore, was posed in the same terms as the Marxists of Engels's generation had posed it, with a greater sharpness due to the sufferings of the War and the postwar period. Nationalism continued more than ever to be the essential ideological weapon of the possessing classes. The fact that the War had ended in defeat, and that the terms of the peace had been dictated by the victors, enabled all the ills which troubled Germany to be blamed on foreign capitalists and imperialists, as well as on to their accomplices – Spartacists and others – who had 'stabbed in the back' the 'glorious, undefeated army'.

The Treaty of Versailles

The terms of the Versailles Treaty provided substantial support for propaganda on this theme.

The negotiations amongst the Allies had been long. They could agree only on one factor, that of preserving in Germany a rampart against Bolshevism, whether in the form of internal subversion or in that of the threat from the Soviet Republic. Otherwise, their aims were contradictory. French designs on the Ruhr and desire for European hegemony ran into opposition to the Anglo-American coalition which favoured a solvent Germany which could be a counterweight in Europe to French ambitions.

The treaty was a compromise amongst the Allies. It was to contribute to strengthening the nationalist and pan-Germanist tendencies in Germany which it claimed to be uprooting. Germany lost all its colonies, one-eighth of its territory, and one-tenth of its prewar population. Its military land forces were reduced to an army of 100,000 men, a professional army not large enough to tackle a foreign power, but well-suited for a civil war. The Allies would occupy the Rhineland and three bridgeheads which opened Germany to them for fifteen years, whilst Germany's southern and eastern frontiers remained forti-fied. German property abroad and part of its navy were confiscated. Until the Allies decided on the final figure which could be expected by way of reparations, Germany was obliged to make interim payments in gold and deliveries of commodities. Finally, those responsible for the war policy and the principal 'war criminals' were to be handed over to the Allied authorities to be judged by international tribunals.

The German Communists agreed with the Communist International in regarding the Versailles peace as a continuation of the War, an example of imperialist brigandage. It offered a temporary respite for the imperialists, a delay in the revolution in the Entente countries; and their response to the imperialist peace was the same as it had been to the imperialist war – the struggle for world revolution. The nationalists, from their point of view, emphasised the aspects of the Treaty which they saw as odious: the French designs on the Ruhr, the encouragement of 'separatist' tendencies aimed at breaking up Germany, the humiliation of reparations, and the foreign occu-pation, especially the use by the French army of African troops, which they called 'the black shame'. They emphasised the national humiliation, the 'colo-nisation' of Germany, and the treatment of its inhabitants as 'negro people', and they declared that to hand over the war leaders, as the Allies demanded, was not compatible with German honour.

These sentiments were widely echoed in every stratum of the population, and induced many politicians strongly to reject the Treaty. Scheidemann was one of these. He resigned just before the vote on signing the Treaty in the Reichstag, and was replaced by his Party comrade Bauer. Noske argued for signing the Treaty, and rejected the suggestions from Captain Pabst about installing a military dictatorship with a view to national resistance.[1]

The officer corps as a whole recognised that capitulation was the only way out. They may have hoped for some gesture 'for the sake of honour'. General Groener retained his position so that the Treaty could be signed in accordance with the conditions which the army dictated, but he then resigned, like Hindenburg, in the interests of unity.[2] A commission was set up to organise the peacetime army, under the leadership of General von Seeckt.

The Kapp-von Lüttwitz Putsch

The officers were particularly sensitive to the danger posed by Allied demands that 'war criminals' were to be extradited. They informed Noske of this on 26 July 1919,[3] and he supported them unreservedly. But the blast of discontent and ill-feeling which these demands provoked was soon supplemented by the return of the Free Corps who had since 1919 been fighting the Red Army in the Baltic states, and who the Allies had insisted must be withdrawn, having made sure that they would be replaced. In the front rank of the military men, who were thinking more and more in terms of staging a putsch, stood General von Lüttwitz, the officer commanding the armed forces in Berlin, who saw himself as the successor to Hindenburg and the guardian of the traditions and the honour of the army.[4]

The fate of the Free Corps was not the only source of anxiety. The reduction in the size of the forces, which the peace treaty imposed, concerned all ranks of the military. If the élite troops were dissolved, the fate of a substantial part of the military establishment would be settled by the same stroke. The naval brigade led by Captain Ehrhardt, who was based in Doberitz, at the gates of Berlin,[5] was to serve as a test case. General von Lüttwitz assured its leader that he would not permit that 'in such a stormy period such a force should

---

[1] Noske, op. cit., p. 200.
[2] Wheeler-Bennett, op. cit., p. 60; W. von Lüttwitz, *Im Kampf gegen die November revolution*, Berlin, 1934, p. 86.
[3] Wheeler-Bennett, op. cit., pp. 71–2.
[4] See the portrait of him, ibid., pp. 61–2.
[5] Noske, op. cit., p. 203.

be broken up'.[6] He criticised the 'weakness' of the government in the face of the 'Bolshevik menace', and talked openly about a coup d'état. The Berlin police chief, Colonel Arens, tried to dissuade him by arranging an interview with him and the leaders of the right wing in parliament.[7]

The Right was campaigning for the National Assembly to be dissolved and for a new election to the presidency of the Republic, but did not manage to convince him that his projects were imprudent. The General believed only in the strength of his battalions, and thought that the elections would go all the better if he had swept the politicians away beforehand. So he embarked on a conspiracy, the principal figures in which, alongside him, were Ehrhardt, Ludendorff and a civilian named Wolfgang Kapp, the director of agriculture in Prussia, who represented the junkers and highly-placed imperial civil servants.[8] It was a risky enterprise, either premature or too late; the authorities knew nearly everything about it, but it had the advantage of having accomplices in all the key state positions.[9]

The Cabinet met on 12 August. It examined the situation, and postponed the necessary decisions to its meeting on the 15th.[10] That same day, however Noske issued warrants for the arrest of the most conspicuous conspirators, such as Captain Pabst.[11] General von Lüttwitz was forced back onto the defensive, and withdrew to the camp in Doberitz. The senior officer whom Noske had entrusted with security at the camp telephoned to say that von Lüttwitz had arrived, and returned with the assurance that all was calm.[12] That same night, the Ehrhardt brigade set off to march towards the centre of Berlin.

The insurgents issued an ultimatum which called for Ebert to be dismissed, for the Reichstag to be dissolved and new elections to be held, and, in the meantime, a cabinet of technicians to be established with a general at the War Ministry. Noske called a meeting of the military chiefs who were not involved

---

[6] Volkmann, op. cit., p. 273.

[7] J. Erger, *Der Kapp Lüttwitz Putsch*, Düsseldorf, 1967, p. 117.

[8] The first meeting between Kapp and von Lüttwitz had taken place on 21 August 1919 (von Lüttwitz, op. cit., p. 97).

[9] The police prefect, Ernst, knew what was going on. Kapp had had an interview on 11 March 1920 with the well-known government adviser on police affairs, Doyé, whom he was to appoint Under-Secretary for the Interior in his government (ibid., p. 133).

[10] Erger, op. cit., p. 133.

[11] Benoist-Méchin, Volume 2, op. cit., p. 86.

[12] Erger, op. cit., p. 136.

in the plot, in his office at 1.30am, and received the reply that there was no question of armed resistance being organised. The Council of Ministers met at three o'clock, and finally decided to evacuate the capital, leaving only two of its members behind, one of whom was Vice-Chancellor Schiffer.[13] Before dawn, nearly all the government and over 200 deputies were on the road to Dresden, where they hoped to find protection with General Maercker.[14]

In the early hours of the morning, Ehrhardt's men occupied Berlin, and flew the Imperial flag on the public buildings. Kapp was installed in the Chancellery, and he issued his first decrees, proclaiming a state of siege, suspending all newspapers, and appointing General von Lüttwitz as commander-in-chief. By midday he could believe that all the military headquarters and all the police forces in the Berlin military region had joined his enterprise. The members of the government were not happy about the attitude of General Maercker, and took to the road again, this time towards Stuttgart, where they thought that they could count on General Bergmann.[15] By the evening of the 13th, it seemed that the putsch had succeeded without bloodshed, because nowhere had either the army or the police showed signs of opposing it, and the authorities in the north and east had recognised the new government.

How the putsch was crushed

Whilst the government was taking flight, resistance was nonetheless being organised. In the morning, Legien convened a meeting of the General Commission of the trade unions, and at 11 o'clock this body called for a general strike.[16] Wels, who was one of the few Social-Democratic leaders to stay behind, had drafted and printed a poster, to which he attached the signatures of the Social-Democratic ministers, who obviously had never been consulted.[17] This called for a general strike on the theme of unity against counter-revolution and for the defence of the Republic.[18] The Independents also called on the workers to support the general strike, 'for liberty, for

---

[13] Ibid., pp. 140–3, 149.
[14] Benoist-Méchin, Volume 2, op. cit., p. 93.
[15] Ibid., pp. 97–8.
[16] J. Varain, *Freie Gewerkschaften, Sozialdemokratie und Staat*, Düsseldorf, 1956, p. 73.
[17] O. Braun, *Von Weimar zu Hitler*, Hamburg, 1949, p. 94.
[18] Facsimile in *Illustrierte Geschichte der deutschen Revolution*, op. cit., p. 469.

revolutionary socialism, and against military dictatorship and the restoration of the monarchy'.[19] Legien held discussions with the object of forming a general strike committee, which would be made up from all the workers' organisations, and the authority of which could be much wider than that of the General Commission of the trade unions alone. But agreement could not be reached. The Majority socialists, Wels and his comrades, wanted to defend what they regarded as 'the government of the Republic', whilst the Independents made it quite clear that there could be no possibility of their defending the government of Ebert and Noske.[20]

So there would be two 'central strike committees' in Berlin, one around Legien, with the All-German General Trade Unions (ADGB), the Free Trade Unions (AFA) and the civil servants' association, and the SPD, and the other which brought together the leaders of the trade unions in Berlin, Rusch and his comrades, and the leaders of the Independents.[21] The KPD(S) was to join it later.[22]

The initiative in the struggle was taken by Legien. At dawn on 13 March, he refused to flee, criticised the attitude of the Social-Democratic leaders, and threw his whole authority and influence as head of the union apparatus behind the general strike. He had always opposed the idea of a general strike; he was the prudent reformist, the patriarch of the revisionists, the incarnation of decades of class collaboration – and yet he decided to go 'underground' and to make contact with everyone, including the Communists, who could ensure the defeat of the putsch. Moreover, he showed that he was more in touch with the masses at this juncture than the Communists were. In the absence of Paul Levi, who was serving a jail sentence of one year, under the pressure of the Berlin leaders, Friesland and Budich, who tended towards

---

[19] Ibid., pp. 468–9.

[20] Varain, op. cit., p. 173; according to Wels, as quoted by Erger, op. cit., p. 196, the Independents refused to act jointly with the Majority because the latter were really responsible for what was happening.

[21] In fact, only the second called itself the central strike leadership (Erger, op. cit., p. 197).

[22] The KPD(S) explained that it criticised the Independent strike committee because it did not call for workers' councils to be formed immediately (*Illustrierte Geschichte der deutschen Revolution*, op. cit., p. 496). It was only on 17 March that four representatives of the KPD(S) – Pieck, Walcher, Lange and Thalheimer – joined this central committee, and they stayed there for only four days. (Naumann and Voigtländer, 'Zum Problem einer Arbeiterregierung nach dem Kapp-Putsch', *Beiträge zur Geschichte der deutschen Arbeiterbewegung*, no. 3, 1963, p. 469, n. 32.)

ultra-leftism, and against the opposition of Jakob Walcher alone,[23] the KPD(S) leadership published an appeal, probably drafted by Bronski, which *Die Rote Fahne* published on 14 March. This expressed the belief that for the moment there was no point in opposing the military putsch; the real struggle was for power, and that lay in the future:

> Should the working people in these circumstances go in for the general strike? Yesterday, the working class was still shackled with Ebert and Noske's chains, and disarmed. In the worst of conditions, it cannot act. We believe our duty to be to speak out clearly. The working class will undertake to struggle against the military dictatorship in the circumstances and by the means which it will judge to be appropriate. These circumstances do not yet exist.[24]

But the German workers did not hear this appeal for passivity. On 14 March, a Sunday, it was possible to judge the ardour and the scope of the their resistance. One after another the trains ceased to move. By five o'clock in the evening, there were in Berlin no trams, no water, no gas and no electricity. Skirmishes between soldiers and workers were breaking out nearly everywhere. Workers had already responded on the previous day. In Chemnitz, a committee of action was formed, including the trade unions and all the workers' parties, on the initiative of the Communists under Brandler's leadership. It seized the initiative, in the absence of troops, and formed a workers' militia, the Arbeiterwehr, which occupied the station, post office and city hall.

In Leipzig, negotiations between the political parties began, but the Communists refused to sign the document calling for the general strike which the other organisations drafted. The first violent incidents took place on the night of 13–14 March between police and demonstrating workers in Dortmund.[25] The first battles took place in the Ruhr on the 14th. General von Watter ordered his troops to march on Hagen, where the workers were arming themselves; Social Democrats and Independents issued a joint call for a general strike.[26] In Leipzig, the Free Corps opened fire on a workers'

---

[23] Fischer, op. cit., p. 126; *Bericht über den 4 Parteitag der Kommunistischen Partei Deutschlands am 14 und 15 April*, Berlin, 1920, p. 43.

[24] *Die Rote Fahne*, 14 March 1920, *Illustrierte Geschichte der deutschen Revolution*, op. cit., pp. 467–8.

[25] *Illustrierte Geschichte der deutschen Revolution*, op. cit., p. 495.

[26] Ibid., p. 496.

demonstration, 22 people were killed, and the fight went on.[27] In Chemnitz, the workers' organisations decided immediately to recruit 3,000 men to the workers' militia.[28] In Berlin, the KPD(S) Zentrale recognised its mistake, and drafted a new appeal, which was distributed as a leaflet on the 15th, but it still remained behind the development of the struggle in that it did not call for the arming of the proletariat:

> For the general strike! Down with the military dictatorship! All power to the workers' councils!. . . . In the councils, the Communists will fight for the dictatorship of the proletariat, for the republic of councils! Working people! Do not take to the streets! Meet in your workplaces every day! Do not let the White Guards provoke you![29]

The reality was that by the 15th, the Kapp-Lüttwitz government was completely paralysed. The Belgian socialist Louis De Brouckère wrote: 'The general strike now grips them with its terrible, silent power.'[30]

Nothing moved in Berlin, where the Regime could not get a single poster printed. In the Ruhr, on the contrary, when the Lichtschlag Free Corps began to move, it immediately came under attack from bands of armed workers.[31] In the same way, there was fighting in Leipzig, Frankfurt, Halle and Kiel. The sailors in Wilhelmshaven mutinied, and arrested Admiral von Leventzow and 400 officers.[32] In Chemnitz, still under the leadership of the Communists, a committee of action formed of representatives of the workers' parties called on the workers to elect their delegates to workers' factory councils.[33] A few hours later, these delegates, elected by 75,000 workers on a basis of lists and proportional representation, in turn elected the workers' council of the city, ten Communists, nine Social Democrats, one Independent and one Democrat.[34] Brandler was one of the three chairmen of this revolutionary body, the authority and prestige of which extended through a whole industrial region where the

---

[27] Ibid., p. 489.

[28] H. Brandler, *Die Aktion gegen den Kapp-Putsch in Westsachsen*, Berlin, 1920, p. 7.

[29] Distributed as a leaflet on 15 March, *Illustrierte Geschichte der deutschen Revolution*, op. cit., p. 468.

[30] L. De Brouckère, *La Contre-révolution en Allemagne*, p. 46, quoted by Benoist-Méchin, Volume 2, op. cit., p. 100.

[31] *Illustrierte Geschichte der deutschen Revolution*, op. cit., p. 496.

[32] Ibid., p. 481; Benoist-Méchin, Volume 2, op. cit., p. 101.

[33] Brandler, op. cit., pp. 7–8.

[34] Ibid., p. 21. These delegates were made up of 691 Communists, 603 Social Democrats, 100 Independents and 95 Democrats.

forces of repression were disarmed or neutralised, and the workers were armed.[35] He was to write, not without pride:

> In Chemnitz, we were the first party to issue the slogans of the general strike, disarming the bourgeoisie, arming the workers and immediately re-electing the political workers' councils. We also were the first, thanks to the strength of the Communist Party, to make these slogans a reality.[36]

However, a new danger appeared, precisely in the very region where the Communist initiatives seemed to be enabling a solid front of working-class resistance to the putschists to be created. An activist of the KPD(S) named Max Hoelz had during 1919 been the organiser of violent demonstrations of the unemployed in the Falkenstein region. Under threat of arrest, he went underground, where he met active elements in the Party opposition.

In this miserable Erzgebirge-Vogtland region, crushed beneath generalised unemployment, he had organised armed detachments, a kind of 'urban guerrilla', groups of unemployed or quite young people with weapons, who attacked the police or agents of the employers, and often seized the money in factories or banks to finance his troops.[37] In this crisis-ravaged region, after three arrests and escapes, Hoelz cut the figure of a modern-day Robin Hood.[38] On the news of the Kapp uprising, he attacked, forced open the prison gates at Plauen, recruited and summarily organised guerrilla units which he named 'red guards', and began to harass the Reichswehr. He organised raids against its isolated detachments, looted shops and banks, and spectacularly improved the food supply to the people of the workers' suburbs.[39] His 'activist' conception of action, the way in which he substituted commando raids for mass action, as well as the alarm which he provoked even in some of the working-class population, aroused the anxiety of Brandler and the Chemnitz Communists, who condemned him as an adventurist, and denounced some of his initiatives as provocative.[40]

---

[35] Brandler (op. cit., p. 1) wrote of control being exercised by the workers' council over a zone 100 kilometres across around the city, with the sole exception of the technical school, which the workers' militias surrounded.

[36] Ibid., p. 1.

[37] M. Hoelz, *Vom 'Weissen-Kreuz' zur Roten Fahne*, Berlin, 1929, pp. 51–65.

[38] Brandler, op. cit., p. 56.

[39] Hoelz, op. cit., pp. 85–112.

[40] Brandler, op. cit., pp. 54–60.

A similar phenomenon in the Ruhr attracted more numerous masses of workers, and gave rise to what was called a 'Red Army'. In Hagen, a committee of action was formed on the initiative of Independent activists, Stemmer, a miner, and Josef Ernst, a metalworker, and set up a 'military committee'. In a few hours, 2,000 armed workers marched on Wetter, where the workers were fighting the Free Corps.[41]

It seemed on 16 March that there was either fighting or preparation for it throughout Germany, except in the capital, where the military superiority of the army seemed overwhelming. The Red Army of the Ruhr workers was marching on Dortmund. The Free Corps and the Reichswehr held the centre of Leipzig against improvised detachments of workers. In Kottbus, Major Buchrucker ordered any civilian bearing arms to be shot on the spot. In Stettin, a committee of action on the Chemnitz model had been formed, and the struggle between the supporters and the opponents of the putsch took place in the garrison itself.[42]

Levi wrote to the Zentrale a very angry letter from the prison in Berlin where he had been held for several weeks. He criticised its passivity and lack of initiative, and its blindness to the possibilities which the struggle against the putsch offered to revolutionaries.[43] Moreover, over most of the country, apart from Berlin, the leading Communists reacted in a similar way to him. The activists in the Ruhr called for the arming of the proletariat, and for the immediate election of workers' councils from which the supporters of bourgeois democracy would be excluded.[44] The instructions drawn up by the Zentrale on the 13th received a cool reception everywhere, and its orders were destroyed.[45] Almost everywhere, without taking any notice of the instructions from the Zentrale, Communists called for a general strike, and played a part in organising it. Several opposition groups, however – notably that in Hamburg – took up a wait-and-see position which they justified by a refusal to join in common action with the 'social traitors'.[46] Neither in Berlin nor in Rühle's group in Dresden[47] did the ultra-leftists play any role. However,

---

[41] *Illustrierte Geschichte der deutschen Revolution*, op. cit., p. 496.
[42] Ibid., pp. 477–9, 489, 497.
[43] See Chapter 19.
[44] Essen district leaflet, 13 March, *Illustrierte Geschichte der deutschen Revolution*, op. cit., p. 494.
[45] Fischer, op. cit., p. 126.
[46] *Illustrierte Geschichte der deutschen Revolution*, op. cit., p. 481.
[47] Brandler, op. cit., pp. 4–5.

from various regions of Germany, opposition activists such as Appel from Hamburg and Karl Plattner from Dresden[48] came to join the workers fighting in the Ruhr.

In Berlin, Kapp, in desperation, negotiated with Vice-Chancellor Schiffer, who was representing the Bauer government. In the common interest, Kapp agreed that General Groener should attempt to mediate with President Ebert. But Ebert was in no hurry.[49] Kapp, confronted with the general strike, was in fact struggling 'against problems too great for human strength', as Benoist-Méchin put it.[50] In a sense, his government was in a vacuum. Bread and meat were in short supply in the capital. The head of the Reichsbank was refusing to pay out the ten million marks which Kapp was demanding of him.[51] On 16 March at one o'clock in the afternoon, Kapp gave the order that 'agitators and workers on picket lines were to be shot down from four o'clock onwards'.[52] This time, it was actually the big employers who reacted against a measure which could have unleashed civil war; Ernst von Borsig in person led a delegation to insist that Kapp should abandon any use of force. 'Unanimity is so great amongst the working class that it is impossible to distinguish the agitators from the millions of workers who have stopped work.'[53]

The workers in the Ruhr had recaptured Dortmund by six o'clock in the morning. During the night of 16–17 March, a regiment of pioneers mutinied in Berlin itself, and imprisoned its officers. Intervention by the spearhead of the putsch, the Ehrhardt naval brigade, was needed to free them.[54] Civil war was inevitable if the putschists persisted, and the victory of the working class was probable, both over them and over the government, not least because the latter's base and possibilities of action were narrowing hour by hour, as the army, whether putschist or 'neutral', had ceased to be reliable.

On 17 March, realising that he was defeated, Kapp fled. General von Lüttwitz came under pressure from officers more politically aware than himself to put an end to the adventure, and he too fled a few hours later, even leaving to Vice-Chancellor Schiffer the task of drafting his letter of explanation. His collaborators could no longer answer for their troops, and demanded that

---

[48] Bock, op. cit., biographies of these two militants, pp. 427, 438.
[49] Erger, op. cit., pp. 249–54.
[50] Benoist-Méchin, Volume 2, op. cit., p. 102.
[51] Erger, op. cit., p. 211.
[52] Ibid., p. 205.
[53] Benoist-Méchin, Volume 2, op. cit., p. 103, n. 2; Erger, op. cit., pp. 205–6.
[54] Benoist-Méchin, Volume 2, op. cit., p. 103.

command be handed over to a general who had not been compromised in the putsch. The man of the hour would be von Seeckt.[55] The putsch had lasted for no more than a hundred hours in all, and it was well and truly crushed by the response of the workers, and in the first place by their general strike.

But the consequences of the putsch were not exhausted. The first armed fights broke out in Berlin that day. Shots were exchanged in Neukölln, and barricades were raised by the workers at the entry to Kottbus. In Nuremberg, the Reichswehr fired on a demonstration of workers and killed twenty-two people; this sparked off a real insurrection. In Suhl, the workers' militia seized a Reichswehr training centre and took control of a substantial stock of arms and ammunition. In Dortmund, the police, controlled by the Social Democrats, took the side of the 'Red Army' against the Free Corps.[56] The general strike continued across the country, and at that point the question was whether Kapp's headlong flight would lead to the strike being called off, and at what cost, or whether the revolutionary wave which Kapp's putsch had so imprudently set in motion was leading to fresh civil war.[57] Amid the fears voiced on the Right, it is difficult to distinguish the genuine fears from the attempts to spread hysteria.

Indeed, whilst this time Germany was not covered by a network of elected workers' councils – Chemnitz and the Ruhr remained exceptional – it was nonetheless covered by a tight network of executive committees [Vollzugsräte], or action committees, formed by the workers' parties and trade unions. The struggle against the putschists and the organisation of defence led these committees to play the role of revolutionary centres, and this posed in a practical way, in the course of the general strike itself, the problem of power in general, and the more immediate question of the nature of the government.[58]

---

[55] Erger, op. cit., pp. 265–6, 277–8.
[56] *Illustrierte Geschichte der deutschen Revolution*, op. cit., pp. 475, 482, 484, 497.
[57] A communiqué from the Wolff telegraphic press agency on 17 March (cited in Erwin Könnemann, 'Zum Problem der Bildung einer Arbeiterregierung nach dem Kapp-Putsch', *Beiträge zur Geschichte der deutschen Arbeiterbewegung*, no. 6, 1963, pp. 904–21) mentions a governmental list that was in circulation and accepted as already semi-official: Däumig as Chancellor, Paul Levi at Foreign Affairs and Curt Geyer at the Interior. The despatch ended, 'There is no longer any doubt: there remains only one enemy – Bolshevism.'
[58] Mujbegović, op. cit., p. 210; K. Finker, 'Neue Wege und Erkenntnisse bei der Erforschung des Kampfes der deutschen Arbeiter gegen den Kapp-Putsch', *Beiträge zur Geschichte der deutschen Arbeiterbewegung*, no. 4, 1961, pp. 909–10.

The problem of the workers' government

The political consequences of the putsch ran very deep, even in the regions where neither workers' councils nor workers' militias were formed, even where the working people were content to follow the order to strike without taking up arms. For millions of Germans, the main lesson of the putsch was its demonstration of the bankruptcy of the Social-Democratic leadership. Noske, 'the generals' socialist', whom they discarded as soon as his job was done, was completely discredited, and his political career was at an end.

Moreover, it was the workers who had defeated the putschists, by a general strike which was started without the knowledge of the Majority Social-Democratic government, and in a certain sense in spite of it. During the struggle, activists of the different parties, who until that time had been opposing each other, drew closer together. For the first time since before the War they had fought side by side against the class enemy. The prestige of the trade-union leadership rose; Legien had issued the order for the general strike when Noske and Ebert ran away. From that point, the trade-union leaders were expected to take on political responsibilities.

There was deep confusion in the ranks of the SPD. The President, Otto Wels, posed the problem on 30 March in these terms: 'How are we going to get the Party out of the chaos into which it has been plunged by the common fight against reaction?'[59] In very many localities, the Social-Democratic activists and even their organisations had marched with the Communists and the Independents with slogans contrary to those of their national leadership. For example, in Elberfeld, a leader of the SPD had gone so far as to sign with the representatives of the Independents and the KPD(S) a call for struggle 'for the dictatorship of the proletariat'.[60] *Vorwärts* expressed the sentiment of nearly every German worker when it wrote on 18 March: 'The government must be rebuilt. Not to its right but to its left. We need a government which makes up its mind unreservedly to fight against the militarist, nationalist reaction, and which knows how to win the confidence of the workers as far as possible to its left.'[61]

It was clear before Kapp's flight that the bourgeoisie was trying to assemble a front of the Reichswehr and the governmental parties against the reawakening

[59] *Protokoll der Sitzung des SPD-Parteiausschusses vom 30, und 31–3 1920*, p. 4, quoted by Erger, op. cit., p. 291.
[60] Erger, op. cit., p. 291.
[61] *Vorwärts*, special edition, 18 March 1920.

of the working class. Vice-Chancellor Schiffer and General von Seeckt together issued in the name of the government an appeal for a return to calm, for national unity 'against Bolshevism'.[62] The SPD was torn between opposing tendencies. But this also happened in the USPD to some extent, particularly in places where its right-wing leaders had lined up with the Majority's capitulatory approach.[63] The USPD's activists expressed the united pressure of the working class, shoulder to shoulder in the strike, and the demand for guarantees at the level of government; the Party's press broadly reflected this response. The Party apparatus and the parliamentary group, however, were inclined to favour restoring the parliamentary coalition. The latter issued an appeal in which it declared that the continuation of 'the people's strike' after the leaders of the putsch had fled was a threat to the unity of the 'republican front'.[64] At the same time, a proclamation signed jointly by Schiffer and the Prussian Minister of the Interior, the Social Democrat Hirsch, assured everyone that the police and the Reichswehr had done their duty throughout, and had at no time been accomplices in the putsch.[65] This 'amnesty' was evidently necessary for order to be restored, and the government proclaimed a state of extreme emergency on 19 March.[66]

The government had been saved by the general strike. But would it use against the workers the generals who had refused to resist the putschists? Were Ebert and Noske to retain power? Had the workers fought for nothing else but to keep them there? The reply to these political questions depended largely on the leaders of the workers' parties and trade unions.

The workers had a very powerful weapon at their disposal: the general strike. Legien was aware of this. On 17 March, he called on the USPD Executive to send representatives to a meeting of the General Commission of the trade unions.[67] The Executive delegated Hilferding and Koenen, and Legien proposed

---

[62] Ibid.

[63] In Leipzig, for example, on 18 March, the Independent leader Richard Lipinski joined with the civil and military authorities in signing a 'cease-fire agreement', which was a real military and political capitulation. See the full text and Brandler's comments in Brandler, op. cit., pp. 48–9.

[64] Quoted in Erger, op. cit., p. 293, and in *Illustrierte Geschichte der deutschen Revolution*, op. cit., p. 471.

[65] *Vorwärts*, 20 March 1920, cited in *Illustrierte Geschichte der deutschen Revolution*, op. cit., p. 471.

[66] *Illustrierte Geschichte der deutschen Revolution*, op. cit., p. 471.

[67] W. Koenen, 'Zur Frage der Möglichkeit einer Arbeiterregierung nach dem Kapp-Putsch', *Beiträge zur Geschichte der deutschen Arbeiterbewegung*, no. 12, 1962, p. 347.

to them that a 'workers' government' be formed, made up of representatives of the workers' parties and the trade unions. He justified his proposal by explaining that from now on, no government could rule in Germany against the trade unions, and that in an exceptional situation the latter were ready to take on their responsibilities.

Clearly, neither the representatives of the Independents nor the railway worker Geschke, who had also been invited to the meeting, where he represented the KPD(S), could give a reply before they had consulted the responsible bodies in their parties, which they then did.[68] During the meeting of the Executive of the Independents, Koenen and Hilferding spoke in favour of accepting Legien's proposal, and of opening negotiations with a view to forming a workers' government. Crispien, who was Chairman of the Party and the leader of its right wing, protested that he could not possibly sit at the same table with people who 'had murdered workers', and that no discussion was possible with 'betrayers of the working class' such as the members of the General Commission. Däumig, the leader of the left wing, supported him, and said that he was ready to resign his function and even to leave the Party if the Executive engaged in such negotiations. Koenen and Hilferding did not find much support amongst their comrades. Stoecker and Rosenfeld, other leaders of the Left, expressed surprise at Koenen's views, and demanded simply that the Executive should not brusquely reject them, for fear of not being understood by the millions of striking workers. When the vote was taken, the categorical refusal which Crispien and Däumig proposed was carried by a large majority.[69]

But Legien did not withdraw from the game. On the next day, 18 March, despite the pressure on him from Social-Democratic elements close to the apparatus who urged him to call off the strike now that the putsch had been defeated, he prevailed upon the General Council to prolong it until the working class had received sufficient guarantees about the composition and the policies of the government. Laborious discussions began between the leaders of the trade unions and the representatives of the government. Legien warned his questioners that he would not hesitate, if he thought it necessary, to form a 'workers' government' himself, which would use force to prevent the return

---

[68] Ibid., p. 348.
[69] Ibid.

of the Bauer government in Berlin, even if this initiative were to lead to civil war, as he knew it might.[70]

Legien put forward a number of non-negotiable conditions. Noske must resign from the government of the Reich, as must two ministers, Heine and Oeser, from that of Prussia; trade-union delegates must have key posts in the government; the putschists and their accomplices must be severely punished, and the army and the police must be thoroughly purged. He repeated that there existed an immediate possibility of forming a workers' government with representatives of the trade unions and the two Social-Democratic Parties.

The trade-union leadership opened an unprecedented crisis in the SPD by its call for a general strike, and by its open opposition to the Party's leaders. This shook the Party to the very top of its apparatus, the Executive and the parliamentary group. But the attitude of the Independents was decisive. The problem was not simple for them. The Left was divided, with Däumig opposing Koenen. One section of the Right, including Crispien himself, went back on its first response on the evening of 17 March, when a new delegation from the Executive sought out Legien to tell him that they wanted to continue the discussions. Däumig, however, stood completely firm; he declared that he could not agree to the Party approving any 'workers'', government unless it called for the dictatorship of the proletariat and the régime of workers' councils.[71] Despite the opposition of his comrades of the same tendency who controlled the trade unions in Berlin, he carried the day. The majority of the Left agreed with him that the workers' government which Legien proposed would amount to nothing but a fresh version of 'the Noske régime', a new edition of the Ebert-Haase government of 1918.[72] As for the right wing, it finally reached its decision in the light of the risks involved in forming such a government under the fire of criticism from the Left and the threat of a split, in a situation in which it would become nothing more than a fragile left cover for the government.[73] Legien had to drop his proposal.

However, Legien still had to present to the government his conditions for resumption of work. On the morning of the 19th, after long negotiations, the

---

[70] This information comes from the record of the discussions between the trade-union leaders and the representatives of the Bauer government which was made by the Finance Minister, Südekum, cited in E. Könnemann, *Beiträge zur Geschichte der deutschen Arbeiterbewegung*, no. 2, 1966, p. 273.

[71] *Bericht über den 4 Parteitag der KPD*, op. cit., p. 38.

[72] *Freiheit*, 24 March 1920.

[73] Prager, op. cit., p. 218.

representatives of the government solemnly undertook to fulfil the conditions which Legien dictated, and which were called 'the nine points of the trade unions'. These were:

1. Recognition by the future government of the role of the trade-union organisations in the economic and social reconstruction of the country.

2. Disarming and immediate punishment of the rebels and their accomplices.

3. Immediate purge of all counter-revolutionaries from the state administration and state undertakings, and immediate reinstatement of all workers dismissed for trade-union or political activity.

4. Reform of the state on a democratic basis, in agreement and cooperation with the trade unions.

5. Full application of existing social legislation and adoption of new, more progressive laws.

6. Immediate resumption of measures to prepare for the socialisation of the economy, convocation of the socialisation commission, and immediate socialisation of the coal and potash mines.

7. Requisition of foodstuffs to control the food supply.

8. Dissolution of all counter-revolutionary armed formations. Formation of defence leagues on the basis of the trade-union organisations, with the units of the Reichswehr and the police which remained loyal at the time of the putsch to be unaffected.

9. Sacking of Noske and Heine.[74]

On this basis, the ADGB and the AFA decided to call for a return to work,[75] and most of the ministers and the parliamentarians made their way back to Berlin. But neither the Independents nor the Greater Berlin strike committee had given their agreement, and the decision remained on paper awaiting the meetings of the strikers, which were generally called for Sunday, 21 March.

Indeed, the agreement of the strikers was far from having been won. Many of the meetings decided to reject the decision of the trade-union confederations, believing that the government had given nothing but promises for which the workers had no guarantee, and that to endorse the decision would effectively be giving the government a blank cheque.[76] Furthermore, when 'government'

---

[74] Könnemann, 'Zum Problem', op. cit., p. 910, n. 19.
[75] Ibid., p. 910.
[76] *Illustrierte Geschichte der deutschen Revolution*, op. cit., p. 472.

troops had entered the suburbs of Berlin, there had been several violent confrontations with armed workers, exchanges of shots, and arrests.[77]

A messenger presented himself at the Greater Berlin strike committee bearing an appeal for help from the workers in the Ruhr who were under pressure from the Reichswehr. The representatives of the KPD(S), followed by many Independent workers, opposed ending the strike. Pieck and Walcher argued that they should protect the Ruhr workers and continue the movement until their security was ensured, that is, until the proletariat was armed. Then the question of the workers' government was raised publicly for the first time. Däumig denounced what he considered to be the manoeuvres of Legien and his 'government operation', the sole purpose of which was to pull the Independents into the parliamentary game and to provide a left-wing cover for the enfeebled coalition.[78] The Communists had no mandate on this question. They said that they were only learning about Legien's proposals in the meeting itself, and that they could speak only as individuals.[79]

Walcher emphasised that the sort of workers' government that the trade unions proposed would be a 'socialist government against Ebert and Haase', and that it did not need, contrary to what Däumig demanded, to announce formally that it recognised the dictatorship of the proletariat, in order to be, by its very existence, a step forward and a victory for the workers' movement. He turned to the trade-union delegates and said:

> If you take your undertakings seriously, if you really want to arm the workers and to disarm the counter-revolution, if you really want to purge the administration of all the counter-revolutionary elements, then that means civil war. In which case, it is not only obvious that we support the government, but still more that we shall be at the forefront of the struggle. If, on the contrary, you betray your programme and stab the workers in the back, then we – and we very much hope that we shall be supported by people coming from your ranks – we shall undertake the most resolute struggle, without reserve and with all the means at our disposal.[80]

---

[77] Notably in Henningsdorf (ibid., p. 476).

[78] *Bericht über den 4 Parteitag der KPD*, op. cit., p. 38.

[79] Könnemann ('Zum Problem', op. cit., p. 918, n. 41) suggests that Geschke, an ultra-left member of the Berlin leadership, who, according to Koenen, had been present at the meeting on the 17th, had not told the Zentrale what Legien proposed.

[80] J. Walcher, 'Die Zentrale der KPD(S) und der Kapp Putsch', *Die Kommunistische Internationale*, no. 1, 1926, p. 406.

At the end of a stormy session, it was finally decided, with the support of the KPD(S) delegates, to demand that the strike be continued until guarantees had been obtained, especially about the eighth point, the integration of workers in the forces of 'republican defence'.[81] At the end of the meeting, negotiations opened between the delegates of the two Social-Democratic Parties and the trade unions. The Majority Social-Democratic delegates had a vital interest in driving a wedge between the Communists and the Independents, and in ending the general strike. In the name of the Social-Democratic fraction, Bauer undertook to respect these four conditions: withdrawal of the Berlin troops to the line of the Spree; lifting of the state of siege; undertaking to take no offensive action against the armed workers, especially in the Ruhr; and enrolment in Prussia of working people in 'defence groups' under trade-union control.[82]

The real decision on stopping the general strike was in the hands of the Independents. The Communists could perhaps have reinforced the left wing of the USPD, but their Zentrale was in the throes of a full crisis. No sooner had circular 42 dated 22 March 1920 – which outlined the Party's new stance in respect of the formation of a workers' government – been issued to the Party's members,[83] than the Zentrale, after a stormy meeting lasting part of the night of the 21st and the morning of the 22nd, condemned its four representatives on the central strike committee for accepting the return to work on condition that workers were incorporated in the 'republican' formations, which it regarded as a trick, and for supporting the call for a 'workers' government'. By a small majority, it went on to carry a declaration addressed to the central strike committee:

> The Zentrale of the KPD declares that it disagrees with the demands formulated in the leaflet of the Greater Berlin central strike committee of 21 March, on several points. In particular, the demand for armed workers, civil servants and office workers to be enrolled in trustworthy republican or military formations. It declares, moreover, that it has not supported the proposal to form a coalition government between the trade unions and the USPD.[84]

---

[81] *Freiheit*, 24 March 1920.
[82] *Sozialdemokratische Korrespondenz*, no. 5, 1920, p. 45.
[83] *Die Internationale*, no. 1, 1920, p. 18; M.J. Braun (pseudonym of Bronski), *Die Lehren des Kapp Putsches*, Leipzig, 1920, pp. 30–2.
[84] *Bericht über den 4 Parteitag der KPD*, op. cit., p. 39.

This declaration was read to the strike committee at midday, and a few hours later the leadership of the USPD declared, against the opposition of Däumig, Stoecker, Koenen, Rosenfeld and Geyer, that it was satisfied with the new concessions made by the Social Democrats.[85] A statement, drafted during the evening of 22 March, was signed by Legien on behalf of the ADGB, Aufhäuser for the AFA, Juchacz for the SPD, and Crispien for the USPD, calling for work to be resumed in the light of the new concessions and promises by the government.[86] The trade-union leadership in Berlin supported Däumig, declared for 'interrupting' and against ending the strike, and refused to sign.[87]

The Zentrale of the KPD(S) met on the morning of the 23rd. It denounced what it called a capitulation, and called on the workers to continue the strike, for the Free Corps, the Reichswehr and the bourgeois paramilitaries to be disarmed, for the proletariat to be armed, for workers jailed for political offences to be freed, and for a conciliar republic.[88] However, people were beginning to return to work. Moreover, the Zentrale changed its position again, reversing yesterday's position on the workers' government, and accepting the position of Pieck and Walcher.[89] It emphasised that the Kapp Putsch signified that the coalition between the bourgeoisie and the Social Democrats had broken down, and that consequently the struggle against military dictatorship had as its aim 'the widening of the political power of the workers up to the point at which the bourgeoisie are crushed'. It restated that the dictatorship of the proletariat required a powerful Communist Party, supported by the masses, and specified:

> The present stage of the struggle, in which the proletariat has no adequate military force at its disposal, in which the Social-Democratic Party retains much influence amongst civil servants, office workers and other strata of the working people, in which the Independent Social-Democratic Party has the majority of the urban workers behind it, proves that the solid bases necessary for the dictatorship of the proletariat do not yet exist. For the deep strata of the proletarian masses to accept the Communist doctrine, a

---

[85] Naumann and Voigtländer, op. cit., p. 470.
[86] *Vorwärts*, 24 March 1920; *Illustrierte Geschichte der deutschen Revolution*, op. cit., p. 473.
[87] *Die Rote Fahne*, 26 March 1920.
[88] Ibid.
[89] According to Mujbegović (op. cit., p. 203), the new majority consisted of Pieck, Lange, Walcher, Thalheimer and Levi.

state of affairs has to be created in which political freedom is almost complete and the bourgeoisie is prevented from exerting its capitalist dictatorship.[90]

From this analysis, the Zentrale drew the conclusion that the formation of a workers' government would be desirable:

> The KPD believes that the formation of a socialist government free of the slightest bourgeois or capitalist element would create extremely favourable conditions for vigorous action by the proletarian masses. It would enable them to reach the maturity which they need in order to realise their political and social dictatorship. The Party declares that its work will retain the character of a loyal opposition as long as the government does not infringe the guarantees which ensure the freedom of political activity of the working class, resists the bourgeois counter-revolution by all possible means, and does not obstruct the strengthening of the social organisation of the working class. When we declare that the work of our party 'will retain the character of a loyal opposition', we mean that the Party will not prepare a revolutionary coup d'état, but will preserve complete freedom of action as far as political propaganda for its ideas is concerned.[91]

This was a declaration of great importance. It could change the balance of forces within the USPD and the Left as a whole. It was a belated change, not least because it was not generally known until 26 March, by which time the situation had altered considerably. On the morning of the 22nd, following the news of the first confrontations between the armed forces and workers immediately after the ending of the strike, negotiations had recommenced between the parties and trade unions. The leaders were again examining the possibility of forming 'a purely socialist government or a workers' government', as the *Sozialdemokratische Parteikorrespondenz* put it.[92] The Independents changed the position they had adopted on 17 March, and no longer demanded as a precondition a declaration by the government in favour of the dictatorship of the proletariat.[93]

On the same day, Malzahn presided over the meeting of the Greater Berlin factory councils. There Däumig defended the idea of 'interrupting' the strike,

[90] *Die Rote Fahne*, 26 March 1920.
[91] Ibid., *Bericht über den 4 Parteitag der KPD*, op. cit., p. 29.
[92] *Sozialdemokratische Parteikorrespondenz*, no. 5, 1920, p. 45.
[93] Krüger, *Die Diktatur oder Volksherrschaft*, p. 30, quoted by Könnemann, op. cit., p. 911; Franz Krüger was chairman of the Berlin district of the SPD.

whilst Pieck spoke in favour of continuing it. Däumig referred to his opposition to the idea of a workers' government. Pieck opposed him, and explained the position of his party:

> The situation is not yet ripe for a republic of councils, but it is ripe for a purely workers' government. As revolutionary workers, we ardently desire a purely workers' government. . . . The Independent Social-Democratic Party has rejected the workers' government, and consequently it has not managed to grasp what the interests of the proletariat are in a favourable combination of political events. . . . The workers' government will come; there is no other road to the republic of councils.[94]

There was a confused debate.[95] Däumig's motion was carried by a large majority. The strike was officially over. But there was not to be a workers' government. In the negotiations which followed, Crispien emphasised in vain that the KPD(S) Zentrale and the USPD Executive agreed on two points: they would on no account join a coalition government, and for the moment there was no question of a 'dictatorship of councils', whereas a purely workers' government was 'completely possible'.[96] The negotiations dragged on without result.

On 23 March, the USPD Executive had agreed on an eight-point programme which it advanced as a possible basis of agreement for a workers' government, and this was published on the 24th.[97] *Vorwärts* explained on the 25th that a workers' government, which it claimed was desired by the Majority, would only be possible if the bourgeois parties agreed to support it in the Reichstag, and that it would mean nothing more than the Independents joining the coalition. It concluded that the SPD would accept its responsibility to 'construct a government which would achieve the same results under a different name'.[98]

The Social-Democratic daily merely declared publicly a situation which already existed. The end of the strike had greatly strengthened the SPD's

---

[94] *Freiheit*, 24 March 1920.
[95] Both Rasch and Krause spoke, against each other, and both claimed to speak for the KPD(S) in Berlin. Pieck admitted that 'there were two Communist parties' (ibid.).
[96] Minutes of the discussions based on Südekum's notes, *Beiträge zur Geschichte der deutschen Arbeiterbewegung*, no. 2, 1966, p. 278. But we should note that Crispien suggested, in order to get the bourgeois parties to accept the formation of a government which excluded them, that they could get indirect representation if the Christian trade unions were brought in!
[97] *Freiheit*, 24 March 1920.
[98] *Vorwärts*, 25 March 1920.

position, and Ebert, who had now returned to Berlin, began discussions about widening the coalition. Legien vetoed the entry of Cuno, a businessman, into the Cabinet, and demanded that Schiffer, the Vice-Chancellor, be removed. This caused the scheme to break down, and Bauer's cabinet resigned.[99] The rules of the parliamentary game began to work again, and on 26 March, Ebert offered to Legien the position of Chancellor and the task of forming the new cabinet. The trade unions' General Commission rejected this offer. It considered that it could not, on its own, accept this governmental responsibility in the changed conditions, particularly under the fire of the attacks in the press, which had now reappeared and was every day violently denouncing the hidden influence of the 'counter-government' of the trade-union leaders.[100]

The way was now clear for a patching-up process. Ebert turned, that same day, to his fellow Social Democrat Hermann Müller.[101] The new government was formed on 27 March, with Müller as Chancellor, and Gessler, a Democrat, replacing Noske in command of the Reichswehr. A similar government was formed in Prussia. Däumig changed his position, and declared during a meeting of the factory councils in Berlin that 'only a purely socialist government based on the trust of the working people' could resolve the situation,[102] but he was too late. The opportunity had passed.

The declaration of 'loyal opposition' by the KPD(S) Zentrale had only one result: it provoked a commotion in the Party. This broke out when the Zentrale rejected it, by twelve votes to eight, and declared:

> The duty of the members of the KPD is to devote all their energies towards changing the real relations of forces by revolutionary means. Therefore, the question of some possible future governmental combination is of secondary interest in relation to the struggle of the proletariat to arm itself and to construct workers' councils.[103]

Meanwhile, the vacillations of the socialists and the Communists had made no small contribution to changing the real relation of forces, as events in the Ruhr were to emphasise further.

---

[99] Könnemann, 'Zum Problem', op. cit., p. 912.
[100] Varain, op. cit., p. 179.
[101] Könnemann, 'Zum Problem', op. cit., p. 915.
[102] *Freiheit*, 28 March 1920.
[103] *Bericht über den 4 Parteitag der KPD*, op. cit., p. 28.

The Reichswehr takes revenge

On the morrow of the putsch, the Ruhr stood in the van of the armed struggle and the organisation of workers' power. In a number of places, a network of workers' councils and action committees had taken power. The action committee in Hagen was a genuine revolutionary military leadership which could call on 100,000 armed workers. The workers' units went on the attack on 18 March, and the Reichswehr pulled back its scattered forces, one of which left behind for the workers of Düsseldorf 4,000 rifles, 1,000 machine-guns, cannon, mortars and ammunition.[104] Although the workers in the Ruhr appeared to be the masters during the following week, they were so far ahead of their comrades in the rest of the country that they were dangerously isolated. Social Democrats, Independents and even Communists everywhere else had willingly or unwillingly accepted the situation created by the return to work and the breakdown of the discussions about forming a workers' government. The delegates from the Ruhr, Wilhelm Düwell on 21 March, and Graul on the 23rd, described to the Berlin strike committee the situation in their region and the danger created by the shortage of food. On 23 March, the Zentrale sent Wilhelm Pieck to the scene.[105] Political divisions ran deep. The committee in Hagen was formed of Majority Social Democrats, Independents and two Communists, Triebel and Charpentier. However, their party had just disavowed them, because they agreed to open negotiations without being mandated to do so.[106] In Essen the executive committee, which was under Communist influence, reacted to Hagen's support for negotiations by considering how to outflank its committee.

On 18 March, the action committee in Hagen called on workers who were not armed to return to work. On 20 March, it made known its demands in respect of the Reichswehr to General von Watter, who had waited until 16 March to dissociate himself from von Lüttwitz: these were that the Reichswehr be disarmed and withdrawn from the whole industrial region, and that a militia be formed under the control of the workers' organisations. In the

---

[104] *Illustrierte Geschichte der deutschen Revolution*, op. cit., p. 500.

[105] Rather using than the article which appeared in *Die Kommunistische Internationale*, no. 15, under the same title, we have preferred to use here the manuscript contained in the Levi Archives under the same title, *Die Stellung der KPD zum Abbruch der bewaffneten Kämpfen im Rheinisch-Westfälischen Industriegebiet*, in which cuts were made for publication. This text, f. 1, specifies that Düwell's arrival on 21 March constituted the first contact between the Ruhr and Berlin since 13 March.

[106] *Die Stellung der KPD*, op. cit., f. 2.

meantime, 'public order would be ensured by armed formations of workers'.[107] Bauer replied by telegraph that these conditions were not acceptable, because von Watter and his forces had not taken the side of the putsch.[108] The Ministers Giesberts and Braun came to the support of Severing, the Reich's Commissioner, in negotiations aimed at an agreement based on the 'nine points of the trade unions'.[109]

The talks opened in Bielefeld on 23 March in the presence of a vast gathering of representatives of the councils in the principal cities, several mayors and the representatives of the workers' parties and trade unions, including Charpentier and Triebel, the two Communist members on the Hagen action committee. A small commission drew up a statement which all the participants finally approved on 24 March.[110] The representatives of the government confirmed in it that they agreed with the programme of the trade unions, and that they accepted a temporary collaboration between the military authorities and the workers' representatives whilst the terms of the agreement were fulfilled. Josef Ernst was attached to Severing and General von Watter.[111] It was expected that, in a first stage, the workers would retain under arms a limited number of men whom the authorities would control, and who would be recognised as auxiliary police. Most of the workers' arms would be handed in, and fighting was to stop immediately.[112]

These agreements were not respected in practice. Nonetheless, Wilhelm Pieck, who learned that they had been signed when he arrived in Essen, insisted that an armistice must be enforced which would enable the workers to retain their arms, and to organise solidly the militia which had provisionally been conceded to them.[113] But he failed to convince the members of the executive council in Essen, who did not regard themselves as bound by an agreement in which they had had no say. Moreover, the men from Duisburg and Mülheim, on the Left of this committee which the KPD(S) controlled and under the influence of the opposition Communists, together with the members

---

[107] *Illustrierte Geschichte der deutschen Revolution*, op. cit., p. 500; text in Benoist-Méchin, Volume 2, op. cit., p. 116.
[108] *Illustrierte Geschichte der deutschen Revolution*, op. cit., p. 500.
[109] C. Severing, *1919/1920 im Wetter- und Watterwinkel*, Bielefeld, 1927, p. 176. The ministers brought the information that the Dutch government had decided to cut off food supplies to the Ruhr because it was controlled by revolutionaries.
[110] Ibid., p. 177.
[111] *Illustrierte Geschichte der deutschen Revolution*, op. cit., p. 503.
[112] Text of the agreements, ibid., pp. 501–3; and Severing, op. cit., pp. 178–9.
[113] *L'Internationale comuniste*, no. 15, column 3364.

of the powerful local new 'unions', amongst whom anarchists had real influence, denounced the 'traitors' who had signed, and called for the struggle to be continued. There was a crowd of rival revolutionary authorities, six or seven 'military leaderships', and each was trying to outflank the others.[114]

On 24 March, the Essen executive council met in the presence of Josef Ernst and of a 'front-line' delegate from Wesel, where the workers were attacking the barracks. The representatives from Mülheim condemned any armistice in advance, but admitted that they were short of ammunition. The council refused to recognise the agreements, at which point the Hagen committee declared that it was dissolved, and repeated its order that fighting must end. This decision was ineffectual.[115] On the next day, 25 March, a meeting was held, again in Essen, of delegates of seventy workers' councils in the Ruhr, with the principal leaders of the 'Red Army'. Pieck spoke to emphasise that the agreements offered no guarantees, and he suggested that the workers should retain their arms in the meantime, although he warned against provoking fights. The assembly elected a central committee formed of ten Independents, one Majority Social Democrat and four Communists. Pieck said: 'We have not succeeded in convincing the front-line comrades that it would be better to stop fighting.'[116]

Two days later, however, the central council in Essen decided, against the opinion of its military leaders but in the light of the general situation, to demand that the government open armistice negotiations.[117] The next day, there was a conference in Hagen of delegates of the three workers' parties. Pieck spoke there to the effect that the situation was not ripe for a conciliar republic, but that they should fight to arm the proletariat, to disarm the bourgeoisie, and to reorganise and re-elect the workers' councils.[118] The decision was taken to negotiate, but also to prepare to resume the general strike in the event of an attack from the Reichswehr.[119] A second meeting of the councils, which was called for the 28th by the Essen central council and at which Levi

---

[114] *Illustrierte Geschichte der deutschen Revolution*, op. cit., p. 500.

[115] Ibid., p. 503; *Die Stellung der KPD*, op. cit., f. 7.

[116] *Die Stellung der KPD*, op. cit., f. 7. During this time, Levi in Berlin and Däumig succeeded in convincing the general assembly of workers' councils to call upon the trade unions to relaunch the call for a general strike (*Freiheit*, 28 March 1920). But this effort was in vain.

[117] *Illustrierte Geschichte der deutschen Revolution*, op. cit., p. 503.

[118] *Die Stellung der KPD*, op. cit., f. 7.

[119] Ibid., f. 8.

was present, confirmed this position.[120] But on the same day, Hermann Müller told the central council that he demanded as a precondition for any negotiations that the illegal authorities be wound up and the arms be handed in.[121]

Fighting continued during these days, and the central council did not succeed in imposing throughout the industrial region sufficient authority to make its policies effective. In Wesel, the barracks had been under siege for several days,[122] and the 'Red Army' chiefs in Wesel issued fiery summonses to battle which the central council criticised as 'adventurist'.[123] In Duisburg and Mülheim, 'unionist' elements threatened to sabotage the industrial installations and to 'destroy the plant' in the event of an advance by troops.[124]

A revolutionary executive committee, installed in Duisburg under the authority of the ultra-leftist Wild, decided to seize bank accounts and all foodstuffs, and called for the workers' councils to be elected exclusively by workers 'who stand for the dictatorship of the proletariat'.[125] Incidents began to break out between workers of opposed tendencies, supporters or adversaries of the armistice, and partisans or opponents of sabotage. A member of the opposition, Gottfried Karrusseit, issued inflammatory proclamations,[126] and signed them as 'Commander-in-Chief of the Red Army'. Pieck treated him as a 'crazed petty bourgeois'.

The central council in Essen was in no better position to guarantee a cease-fire than the Hagen action committee had been a few days earlier. General von Watter took advantage of this disunity and the internal differences in the workers' camp. He demanded from the Essen leaders that within 24 hours they hand in to him four heavy guns, 10 light guns, 200 machine-guns, 16 mortars, 20,000 rifles, 400 boxes of artillery shells, 600 mortar bombs and 100,000 cartridges. If the arms and ammunition were not handed over to him within the time limit, he would regard the workers' leaders as having refused

---

[120] Ibid., f. 11.
[121] Severing, op. cit., p. 186.
[122] Ibid., p. 184.
[123] *Die Stellung der KPD*, op. cit., f. 10.
[124] Levi was to say at the Fourth Congress of the KPD that these calls for sabotage set the mass of miners against those who advanced them, and broke the resistance (*Bericht über den 4 Parteitag der KPD*, op. cit., pp. 21–2).
[125] *Die Stellung der KPD*, op. cit., f. 9.
[126] Severing (op. cit., pp. 181–2) reproduced one of these proclamations and quoted another which announced two executions. Fischer (op. cit., p. 133) mentions the same proclamation without referring to Severing, and writes that Karrusseit was a 'member of the KAPD', which was not yet founded by that date. This means that Karrusseit was a member of the opposition in the KPD(S). Bock makes no reference to his role.

to disarm their forces, and having broken the agreement.[127] The Essen council replied to this provocative ultimatum by calling for a general strike.[128]

On 30 March, delegates from the Essen council were in Berlin, where they took part in a meeting which included the leaders of all the trade unions and workers' parties, including Pieck and Levi. They unanimously decided to demand from the Müller government that it take measures to ensure that the Bielefeld agreement was respected, and that the military authorities were rendered harmless. Five representatives, including Levi, were received by Chancellor Müller, and demanded from him that General von Watter be recalled.[129] Their effort was in vain. The Chancellor replied that the agreement had been one-sidedly broken, and he used the robberies, seizures of bank accounts and threats of sabotage to justify 'the maintenance of order'.[130]

When Pieck returned to Essen, he found a state of extreme confusion. A majority of the members of the central council had gone to Münster to negotiate with Severing, and nearly all of them had been arrested by the army on the way.[131] Nonetheless, another general assembly of the councils for the industrial region was held in Essen on 1 April, with 259 representatives from 94 councils.[132] Pieck, an Independent, Oettinghaus, and the representative from Mülheim, Nickel, reported on the events in Berlin, and the assembly adopted a position on the armistice conditions. It issued an appeal to defend and develop the network of workers' councils.[133]

On 3 April, von Watter's troops began their advance. They met only sporadic resistance because the confusion and disagreement between different leaders paralysed every slight attempt at coordinating the defence.[134] The behaviour of the soldiery when they were reoccupying the coalfield was such as to

---

[127] Text in Severing, op. cit., p. 187.

[128] Ibid., pp. 187–8.

[129] *Die Stellung der KPD*, op. cit., f. 13.

[130] Ibid., f. 14.

[131] Ibid., f. 14.

[132] Ibid., f. 16; 36 delegates were Social Democrats, 113 belonged to the Independents, and 109 to the KPD(S).

[133] Ibid., f. 20.

[134] It is true that Severing's account cannot be accepted without confirmation, but he gives examples of the disagreements. Josef Ernst, the Independent who led the Hagen committee, had gone to Mülheim for a discussion and only just escaped the execution with which the local leadership threatened him. In Dortmund, Brass escaped the same fate thanks to the intervention of Meinberg, a Communist (Severing, op. cit., pp. 184–6). The 'Red Army' had published a call for all the supporters of negotiation to be shot (p. 198).

provoke the anger even of Severing himself.[135] Soon, military courts were passing heavy prison sentences on militant workers accused of crimes or misdemeanours which were really requisitions or measures of struggle. A month after the putsch had been crushed by the general strike, the accomplices of the putschists took ample revenge in the Ruhr.[136]

The events of March 1920 were to have far-reaching effects. The Reichswehr had restored order, and the crisis in the workers' movement seemed to be reaching its peak. The Zentrale's vacillations, its evasions and its turns had prevented the KPD(S) from reaping the rewards it might have expected from the event. However, it was to try to deepen the crisis which surged up again in the Social-Democratic Parties.

On 26 March, Levi addressed the workers who supported or were influenced by Social Democracy, and the cadres and members of the trade unions, at the general assembly of the factory committees:

> When Kapp and von Lüttwitz staged their putsch and put the Ebert-Bauer régime in greater jeopardy than the Spartacists had ever done, they did not dare to call for armed struggle against them. Yet people wanted to fight them arms in hand. How could that happen? We should have made a fresh appeal to the forces which built the German Republic. We should have appealed to the working class, and put arms in their hands. That was perfectly possible. (Protests) Yes, it was perfectly possible. (Interruption: 'No!') It was possible, precisely as it was possible to call the workers to launch the general strike, to call them to arms. Just as it was possible in Rhineland-Westphalia to organise an army on the basis of the workers' own forces, so it became possible for the government to arm the proletariat elsewhere. But the government did not want to do that, because it knew that as soon as it repulsed the putsch of Kapp and von Lüttwitz thanks to the proletarian forces, it would at the same time be putting into the hands of the proletariat the means for it to reach its ultimate aim, and the workers would say: 'We are ready to defend the Republic, we are ready to take on its defence, but it is not enough for us to put Ebert and Bauer back on the throne!' I tell you that the Ebert-Bauer government would not take this

---

[135] Severing, op. cit., pp. 208ff.

[136] Ibid., pp. 208ff.; *Illustrierte Geschichte der deutschen Revolution*, op. cit., p. 508. Otto Brass made a very lively report to the Reichstag (*Freiheit*, 15 April 1920): some days later he was to be charged with 'high treason' for having given information to the foreign press about the military forces engaged in the Ruhr.

decision. It stayed with its old recipes, and tried to negotiate compromises with the forces before which it had fled to Dresden from Berlin. I think that, in this situation, it would have been completely wrong to speak of a 'new danger', because it was only the old danger that threatened from the first day, and which now has reached its critical stage, a stage in which the relationship of forces is so evenly balanced that very soon the question must be settled of knowing what force will take the state into its hands, and above all this state that we have here![137]

The split on the left wing of the KPD(S)

The Party was seriously affected by one of the first consequences of this period, which was not so much the putsch itself as the policy of the KPD(S) during and after it. This was the decision of the opposition to form a separate Communist Party. The abstentionism of the Zentrale in the first hours of the putsch, the unifying, defensive policy of Brandler in his fortress in Chemnitz,[138] the hesitation and fumbling of the Zentrale when faced with the perspective of a 'workers' government', its leaders' support for the Bielefeld agreement, and their condemnation of the adventurist activities in the Ruhr, all strengthened the activist current afresh, gave new life to the hopes of the ultra-leftists, and seemed to bear out their analyses of the 'opportunism' of the Zentrale's politics. Until then, the opposition had been in a process of disintegration, but it was now rejuvenating.

A conference of the German Communist opposition met in Berlin on 4–5 April, on the initiative of some Berlin activists and especially of Karl Schröder, who took advice from Hermann Gorter. In the difficult conditions of the time it brought together 11 delegates from Berlin and 24 from different districts in Brandenburg, the North, the North-West, Thuringia, West and East Saxony and Elberfeld-Barmen, and was jointly presided over by activists from the three principal groups, Hamburg, Berlin and Dresden. The delegates claimed

---

[137] Levi Archives, P60/6.

[138] Fischer (op. cit., p. 216) says that Brandler's reputation in the Party was bad because he was held responsible for the 'passivity' of the Communists in Chemnitz during the putsch. This was only the position of the ultra-leftists. Let us note a mistake by Fischer when she speaks of the legalistic attitude of Brandler at his trial 'after the putsch', which is evidently a confusion with the trial to which he was subjected on 6 June 1921, after the March Action. See Chapter 25.

to represent 38,000 members, perhaps over half of the Party's membership.[139] Against the opposition of Pfemfert and Otto Rühle,[140] the conference announced the foundation of the Communist Workers' Party of Germany (KAPD). It declared itself to be a member of the Communist International, whilst at the same time it condemned active work in bourgeois parliaments and the reformist trade unions as opportunist, and declared that 'the Levi Centre' had betrayed the party.[141]

In the theses which the new party adopted at its Founding Congress, it announced that it stood for the dictatorship of the proletariat. It defined the Communist Party as 'the brain and the weapon of the proletariat', and assigned to it the role of fighting opportunism and of developing the class consciousness of the proletariat, 'even at the cost of superficial and evident opposition on the part of the broad masses'. It presented itself as the model Communist Party in Western Europe, where the bourgeoisie was able to use democratic ideology as an essential weapon of defence. In order to organise struggles preparatory to the conquest of power, it advised that 'revolutionary factory councils' be formed and developed, as well as workplace 'unions'. Its appeal to the German working people emphasised:

> The KAPD is not a traditional party. It is not a party of leaders. Its essential work will consist of supporting the emancipation of the proletariat from every leadership. . . . The emancipation of the proletariat from every treacherous, counter-revolutionary policy of any sort of leader is the truest way to set it free.[142]

The Fourth Congress of the KPD(S) was held ten days after the emergence of the KAPD, and did not devote any time to the new party in its debates. The Communist leaders appear to have been convinced that the birth of an organisation based on the theories of Pannekoek, but containing in its ranks Wolffheim and Laufenberg as well as Rühle and Pfemfert, and that the best elements of the opposition, the Bremen Communists with Becker, refused to join was of secondary importance. They were looking in a different direction.

The general elections were held on 6 June. Their results conveyed indications of the political consequences of the upheaval in political and social relations

---

[139] Bock, op. cit., p. 228.
[140] Ibid., p. 283. Pfemfert and Rühle were hostile, not to the split, but to the very notion of a 'party'.
[141] *Programm der KAPD*, p. 3.
[142] 'Appeal to the German Proletariat', Bock, op. cit., p. 406.

which followed the putsch. The bourgeois parties together won 15 million votes, against 11 million for the workers' parties. The extremes were strengthened on both sides. The Centre lost more than 2.5 million votes and the Democrats 3.3 million, whilst the openly right-wing People's Party and the National Liberals gained over a million votes each. On the other side, the SPD had the worst losses. It received only six million votes and had 102 deputies as against the 11.9 million votes and 165 deputies it won in January 1919. The outstanding fact was the rise in votes for the USPD, whose vote rose from 2.3 million to over 5 million, and from 22 to 84 deputies, nearly equalling the old Majority Party, and outstripping it in all the industrial centres. The Communists obtained more modest results in their first participation in general elections: 589,000 votes and four deputies, including Zetkin and Levi.

The mass of the working-class electorate had moved for the first time. The ballot showed that the working people were moving sharply away from Social Democracy. But they were going mainly to the Independents, not the Communists. Here was a far more important lesson for the leaders of the KPD(S) than the emergence of the ultra-left KAPD.

Chapter Nineteen

The Communist Party at the Crossroads

The KPD(S) held its Fourth Congress on 14–15 April, soon after the Kapp Putsch and the general strike which had crushed it – in a state of illegality. This surprising situation can be explained by a sharp reversal in the general situation for which the KPD(S) bore its share of the responsibility. The policy of the KPD(S) during the Kapp episode was to become the subject of passionate debates, not only in Germany but in the whole Communist International.

A common criticism

One fact is clear; in the first hours of the putsch, the Zentrale had made a mistake of the first order when it announced on 13 March that the working class would not lift a finger to defend the bourgeois republic against the putschists. Even Béla Kun, whose unrepentant ultra-leftism did not lend itself to subtle distinctions, evoked in his analysis of the March events an opposition between what he called 'the democratic counter-revolution' and 'the anti-democratic counter-revolution'. He explained that the former, in order to defeat the latter, was able to resort to such 'revolutionary weapons' as the general strike and an appeal to the initiative of the proletariat.[1]

---

[1] B. Kun, 'Die Ereignisse in Deutschland', *Kommunismus*, no. 11, 1920, pp. 316–23; no. 12–13, pp. 345–51; no. 14, pp. 403–11; no. 15, pp. 438–44.

The first to accuse the Zentrale was Levi himself. On 13 March, he had begun serving a sentence in the Lehrerstrasse prison. He had learned in his cell about the putsch and the position which his comrades had taken. He had immediately sent a letter to the Zentrale,[2] in which he did not hesitate to declare that the proclamation of 13 March was 'a crime', 'a stab in the back for the greatest action of the German proletariat':[3]

> I cannot remain calm when I think that the opportunity for which we have been waiting for months has presented itself at last. The Right has committed a colossal blunder – and instead of profiting from the situation to ensure that our party has a leading role, as we did in 1918, we get this puerile absurdity! . . . I do not see how the Party can recover from such a blow.[4]

Levi said that the Communists should advance three essential slogans which the entire working class could take up and make its own: the arming of the proletariat; a struggle against the putschists until they unconditionally surrendered; and the immediate arrest of their leaders and accomplices:

> With these three slogans, the KPD would have given to the strike the perspective which it lacks today. With these slogans, people would soon see that what the Communist Party placed at the basis for its analysis was correct, namely that the Social Democrats would never take part, or at least would not be able to take part in the action through to the end. And then – but only then – the moment would come to show the masses who had betrayed their cause, who bore the responsibility for their setback. Then – but only then – when the masses had taken up our slogans and their 'leaders' had refused to lead them all the way, and had betrayed them, the course of events would have brought others into the leadership of the councils. Councils, congress of councils, republic of councils, abolition of the democratic republic. . . . And then, after six months of such a development, we would have had the republic of councils.[5]

No one thought of disputing this harsh judgement, not even the authors of the statement of 13 March. The leaders of the International believed it to have been an exceptionally serious mistake. They insisted, with Zinoviev at their

---

[2] *Die Kommunistische Internationale*, no. 12, 30 July 1920, columns 2145–8.
[3] Ibid., column 2143.
[4] Ibid., column 2144.
[5] Ibid., columns 2145–6.

head,[6] that Levi's letter be published in full in the journal of the International, where it opened a wide debate on the policy of the KPD(S) during and after the Kapp Putsch. The publication of this letter won increased authority for Levi, and destroyed a little more of that of his colleagues in the Zentrale.

Levi's position, however, was not completely adequate. It denounced the mistake – and its merit lay in having done so immediately – but it did not explain it. So there were some people who were to set about discovering what they called 'the roots' of the mistake. Kun, for example, attacked Radek's analysis of the speed of the revolution in the Western countries, on the ground that the putsch and the workers' reaction to it, with the accelerated radicalisation of the working class, had refuted it. He suggested that the KPD(S) was following a long-term perspective, and had let itself be surprised by the change of speed.[7] But Radek had no intention of becoming a scapegoat. In a long critical essay which followed Levi's article in the Comintern's journal,[8] he said that the Zentrale's appeal on 13 March was 'an unpardonable error'. Like Levi, he believed that 'the Communist Party must go along with and trust itself to the waves of the struggle, so as to deepen it and take it further forward'.[9]

Radek said that it was necessary to find out why the Party had refused to do this. The cause was to be found at the heart of the Zentrale itself, in the state of mind of the German leaders, their routinist political practice, and their incapacity to understand the turns in the objective situation. He went back to the problems which the dominating putschist and ultra-left tendencies posed in the Party in 1919, and the struggle which the Zentrale correctly waged against them. But this opposition to putschism had become systematic, and was now the basis of a new deviation, a tendency to passivity, a refusal to act: 'Anti-putschism with them has led to a kind of quietism; from not being able to win power in Germany – a fact which they established empirically in 1919 – they have drawn the conclusion in March 1920 that in general no action is possible, a conclusion which was already wrong a year before!'[10] Speaking from the viewpoint of the ECCI, he wrote:

---

[6] See the account, never repudiated, by Paul Levi, *Was ist das Verbrechen? Die Märzaktion oder die Kritik daran?*, Berlin, 1921, pp. 32–3.
[7] Kun, op. cit., p. 317.
[8] K. Radek, 'Die KPD während der Kapptage: Eine kritische Untersuchung', *Die Kommunistische Internationale*, no. 12, 30 July 1920, columns 2153–62.
[9] Ibid., column 2153.
[10] Ibid., column 2154.

It is not possible to give concrete directives from Moscow to the German Communist Party. We continue to believe that it has to work out its line for itself. But, just as the Moscow Executive Committee well understood in 1919 that the people who were resisting the putschists were right, so it has become clear to it today that doctrinaire propaganda against putschism is nothing more than a brake.[11]

The Fourth Congress of the KPD(S) was not to pay much attention to the blunder of 13 March. Walcher criticised it, and put the blame for it on the leaders of the Berlin district. In this connection, he mentioned the contributions of Budich and Friesland.[12] Thalheimer pleaded not guilty, and agreed in putting the blame for the false orientation on the Berliners. He mentioned the inadequacy of the links between the Zentrale and the rest of the Party, emphasised the weakness of the Party in Berlin, the only district where the leaders had been consulted, and admitted that their view had effectively prevailed in the declaration of 13 March, but stressed that the fear of again falling into 'putschist errors' played an important role in it. He declared: 'I resisted these objections, but it was impossible to clear them away all at once.'[13] As for Ernst Friesland, the leader in the Berlin district, he remained silent on this question,[14] and in this way tacitly recognised a responsibility which his biographers were to explain in terms of his ultra-leftism, 'the passivity of the isolated leftist'.[15]

It is of interest to note that the Congress showed hardly any interest in the problems raised, for example, by the practical policy of Brandler and the Chemnitz Communists against the putsch.[16] Whilst the introduction by Brandler to his pamphlet on the resistance to the putsch stressed that Communists had to seek above all to bring about a united workers' front, and in that way to deepen the crisis in the SPD and raise in it a left wing sympathetic to unity, the Congress – and Brandler himself – were silent on this point.[17]

---

[11] Ibid., columns 2155–6.
[12] *Bericht über den 4 Parteitag der KPD*, op. cit., p. 43.
[13] Ibid., pp. 32–3.
[14] Ibid., pp. 45–6.
[15] Brandt and Lowenthal, op. cit., p. 135.
[16] The book *Arbeitereinheit siegt über Militaristen*, Berlin, 1960, does not so much as mention Brandler's name.
[17] Brandler, op. cit., pp. 3–6.

A half-opened debate

The internal contradictions – the rebirth of putschism, and the 'opportunistic tendencies' of its opponents – were more clearly revealed by the other discussion, that about the slogan of a 'workers' government' posed by Legien's initiatives, and the declaration of 'loyal opposition' by the Zentrale in relation to a possible future 'purely socialist government'.

Neither Walcher nor Pieck had concealed their desire to see the Independents agree to join such a government. A few weeks later, the reconstruction of a coalition government between the SPD and its allies of the Centre and the Democratic Party revived their regrets. Already a strong minority in the Central Committee held the opinion that 'a workers' government which would definitely break from the bourgeois coalition, contribute to arming the workers and put in hand a serious struggle to disarm the bourgeoisie' would be desirable, to the extent that it could shorten and ease the long and painful road leading to the final objective, because it would rely on the working class being organised around its revolutionary workers' councils.[18] Similar conceptions underlay the positions of Pieck and Walcher, and of the comrades who drafted the declaration of 'loyal opposition'. For the first time in the history of the Communist movement, the problem was posed of a transitional form of government, which breaks from government of the parliamentary kind but is not yet the dictatorship of the proletariat, the conciliar republic.

There were many leading people in both the KPD(S) and the International who regarded all this as rank heresy. Kun wrote that belief in a 'purely workers' government' was the first of the three democratic illusions which showed themselves in March 1920 in the KPD(S). He said that support for what would at best be the result of a crisis of the bourgeois democracy meant simply going along with a 'reactionary utopia'.[19] One speaker after another repeated statements of this kind at the Party's Fourth Congress. Eulert expressed the opinion that such a government could only be 'reactionary and anti-working-class'.[20] Edwin Hoernle said that it would serve only to 'compromise the proletariat'.[21] Zetkin thought that it would have given the best of alibis

---

[18] This point of view was expressed in a resolution which Brandler moved at the Central Committee, *L'Internationale communiste*, no. 10, column 1643.
[19] Kun, op. cit., p. 410.
[20] *Bericht über den 4 Parteitag der KPD*, op. cit., p. 35.
[21] Ibid., p. 45.

to the Independents to avoid the fight for conciliar power.[22] In a confused way, they all more or less thought that the workers' government which Legien proposed would be essentially identical to the Ebert-Haase government of 1918.

But the discussion continued in the columns of the German and the international press, and showed that deeper differences existed. One of the most violent attacks came from Paul Frölich,[23] who argued that the hypothesis that 'the road from the governmental coalition to the council republic would pass through a socialist government' was 'completely anti-dialectical'.[24] He added that 'what claimed to be a Socialist Government' could be built only on the basis of a compromise between Social-Democratic and Independent leaders within the framework of parliament.[25] Ernst Meyer, who was much more moderate in form, declared in an open letter to the ECCI that the very hypothesis that there could exist 'an intermediary form between the dictatorship of the proletariat and that of the bourgeoisie' seemed 'hardly likely' to him,[26] and from this standpoint he also condemned the statement about 'loyal opposition', which did not conform to the mission and the task of a Communist Party.[27]

Radek's contribution was no less severe. He said that there was a link between the position which the Zentrale took on 13 March and its declaration of 'loyal opposition'. When the Party leaders adopted this declaration and the approval for a proposed workers' government, they had renounced their historic mission as revolutionary leaders, and behaved like 'abstract reasoners and not as fighters'.[28] Whereas the left Independents, who were developing towards communism, expressed by their refusal to join the government – the healthy reflex of proletarian revolutionaries who did not want to be allied to right-wing Social Democrats even in a government which pretended to be socialist – the Zentrale did what they could to induce them to accept this compromise by in effect assuring them that their historic mission was once more to dupe the proletariat.

---

[22] Ibid., p. 37.
[23] P. Frölich, 'Die Kappiade und die Haltung der Partei', *Die Internationale*, no. 24, 24 June 1920, pp. 19–31.
[24] Ibid., p. 28.
[25] Ibid.
[26] 'Offene Schreiben an der Exekutivkomitee', *Die Kommunistische Internationale*, no. 12, 30 July 1920, columns 2145–8.
[27] Ibid., column 2148.
[28] 'Die KPD während der Kapptage', op. cit., column 2158.

In Radek's opinion, the declaration of 'loyal opposition' deceived the masses by giving them illusions about the possibility of constructing a revolutionary government without first having disarmed the counter-revolutionaries. It had been interpreted as a declaration renouncing revolutionary violence at a moment precisely when it was necessary to summon the working class to fight and to receive 'sword in hand' a government which in reality was essentially directed against it.[29] The verdict was harsh: part of the Zentrale had substituted 'governmental cretinism' for the 'parliamentary cretinism' of the Social Democrats.[30]

The supporters of the declaration of 'loyal opposition' appeared timid in face of these charges. For example, Pieck defended himself energetically against having in any way compromised the Party, and declared that his sole aim had been to expose the Independents, whose refusal was based on their support for bourgeois democracy, and left the field clear for Ebert and Crispien. He repeated to the Congress that, in his understanding, the Independents had committed an act of cowardice when they placed their party interest above that of the revolutionary movement. At the same time, he declared that the Communists could not in any case take part in such a government, because they were the real supporters of the dictatorship of the proletariat.[31] Brandler contented himself with telling the Congress that the declaration had, at the moment when it was published, acted as a brake on the mass movement. He believed that a workers' government would be both desirable and possible on the basis of a mass movement leading to insurrection and the constructing of workers' councils.[32]

Thalheimer, for his part, did not avoid his critics, and even counter-attacked. He said that the declaration was a reply to a question posed by the masses. The Communists should not reply in a dogmatic fashion to the masses, but should help them to make their own experiences. In the eyes of the masses, the Independents were still a 'blank page'. Experience of a workers' government would have helped them to shed their illusions.[33] In reply to Frölich,[34] he accused him of suffering from a 'relapse into an infantile disorder', of neglecting

---

[29] Ibid., column 2159.
[30] Ibid., column 2160.
[31] *Bericht über den 4 Parteitag der KPD*, op. cit., pp. 37–40.
[32] Ibid., p. 55.
[33] Ibid., pp. 33–4.
[34] A. Thalheimer, 'Ein Rückfall von Kinderkrankheit', *Die Internationale*, no. 25, 24 July 1920, pp. 7–19.

the lessons of 1919, of the January events in Berlin and the Bavarian Revolution, and of losing sight of the fact that the main issue facing the Communists at the time was building their Party, the revolutionary party that was necessary for the final victory.[35] These were the same themes that Bronski (M.J. Braun) was to develop less skilfully when he wrote that the USPD, because it was 'not a Communist Party', had the duty to demonstrate the practical results of its principled position by accepting Legien's offers.[36] He traced a parallel between the Kornilov insurrection and the Kapp Putsch, and declared that the basis for the left-wing criticisms of the Zentrale lay in the wish 'to anticipate what would have to be faced on the road of struggle which the working class must travel, but to do so without their having had the necessary experience'.[37]

The position of Paul Levi

In appearance, Levi's position was more subtle. He did not actually state a view on the declaration of 'loyal opposition', taken by itself outside of any context. In his opinion, the initial mistake, the abstentionism of the Zentrale on 13 March and its passivity had the effect of depriving the KPD(S) of any real influence on events. The Independents had gained strength and an audience from these big mistakes; that being so, the Zentrale could hardly go beyond the declaration, which had reached the working people after they had resumed work, and which, for the Communists, was no more than a chance to explain the opportunities which they had bungled.[38] When Levi put the question in these terms, he was taking up the most comfortable position, because the declaration of 23 March could then appear to be the consequence of that of 13 March, for which he had no responsibility, and which he had been the first to denounce.

But Levi's prudence did not prevent him from being attacked. During the weeks which followed the Kapp Putsch, the general outlines of an offensive against him were being sketched. Frölich, in his article on the Kapp affair, directly challenged him by protesting against the interpretation which he gave to the phrase in the Spartacus programme to the effect that the Communists do not propose to seize power other than 'on the clearly expressed

---

[35] Ibid., pp. 12–13.
[36] Braun, op. cit., p. 20.
[37] Ibid., p. 23.
[38] *Bericht über den 4 Parteitag der KPD*, op. cit., pp. 48–9.

basis of the will of the great majority of the working class'.[39] In his conclusion, Frölich criticised Levi by name, together with what he called – in a style reminiscent of that of the KAPD – 'the high bureaucracy of the Party'.[40] Radek, from his side, was to open the attack on Levi in relation to the Bavarian and Hungarian Revolutions in 1919, and, without naming him, in relation to the criticism which he had made of the attitude of the Party during the Kapp Putsch. It was evident to every German reader that Levi most clearly represented the 'anti-putschist' tendency which Radek declared had descended into 'quietism'. In order that no doubt could remain – since Levi, after all, did not share the error of 13 March – Radek's criticisms ended with a violent attack on what he called 'Communist possibilism'.[41]

Radek by implication contradicted the perspectives which Levi had outlined in his letter to the Zentrale, and emphasised that one of the forms of this 'Communist possibilism' – which was merely the reverse side of the coin of putschism – consisted in tracing perspectives which expected 'stages' in the course of the revolution between bourgeois democracy and the proletarian dictatorship, which he thought would be most unlikely, and which he regarded as opportunism that dared not speak its name. The great danger was that the KPD(S) might embark 'on a centrist policy under the banner of Communism'. Everything showed that he thought Levi might one day be the standard-bearer for such a policy.[42]

Two simultaneous struggles were thus proceeding in the KPD(S) and the International. There was the theoretical debate, hardly formulated and in any case superficially treated, around the problem not so much of the workers' government as of the declaration of 'loyal opposition'. In this debate, various dogmatic accusers were confronting cautious defenders, concerned to bring out attenuating circumstances and to reject the charge of revisionism. At the same time, there was the increasingly open, straight fight between Radek and his supporters and Levi and his team in the Zentrale. Neither of these struggles was to be soon settled.

The theoretical debate was interrupted by the intervention of Lenin, in the form of an appendix, written in May, to his book 'Left-Wing' Communism. He vigorously condemned what he regarded as erroneous formulations about

---

[39] Frölich, 'Die Kappiade und die Haltung der Partei', op. cit., p. 27.
[40] Ibid., p. 31.
[41] 'Die KPD während der Kapptage', op. cit., column 2161.
[42] Ibid.

'bourgeois democracy which would not be the dictatorship of the bourgeoisie', or the use of the expression 'socialist government' in place of 'government of social-traitors'. But he quickly rose above the level of settling accounts and theological discussions, and asserted that the declaration of 'loyal opposition' was the product of an 'undoubtedly correct' tactic, 'quite correct both in its basic premises and in its practical conclusions'.[43] Some weeks later, after Lenin had read the criticism of the Zentrale written by Kun and published in *Kommunismus*, he wrote that Kun 'absolutely evades what is most important, that which constitutes the very gist, the living soul of Marxism – a concrete analysis of a concrete situation', and added:

> Since most of the urban workers have abandoned the Scheidemannites for the Kautskyites, and since, within the Kautskian party (a party 'independent' of correct revolutionary tactics), they are continuing to abandon its right wing in favour of the left, that is, in fact, of communism – since that is the case, is it permissible to take no account of the transitional and compromise measures to be adopted with regard to *such workers*? Is it permissible to disregard and to gloss over the experience of the Bolsheviks, who, in April and May 1917, pursued what was in fact a policy of compromise, when they declared that the Provisional Government (Lvov, Milyukov, Kerensky and the rest) could not be overthrown at once, since in the soviets they still had the backing of the workers and it was first of all necessary to bring about a *change in views* in the majority, or a considerable part, of those workers? I consider that impermissible.[44]

The verdict of Lenin was sufficient formally to close the half-opened debate. Whilst the declaration of 'loyal opposition' could be accepted as a correct but badly-formulated compromise position, the fact remained that the international Communist movement had by no means solved the problem of the workers' government with which circumstances had just confronted it.

Towards a mass Communist Party

All participants in the discussion, however much they might have disagreed about the timing, nonetheless agreed on the essential point, that it was

---

[43] V.I. Lenin, '"Left-Wing" Communism: An Infantile Disorder', *Collected Works*, Volume 31, Moscow, 1977, p. 109.
[44] V.I. Lenin, '*Kommunismus*', *Collected Works*, Volume 31, op. cit., p. 166.

necessary to construct in Germany a Communist Party capable of intervening directly in the class struggle, and capable of accepting its responsibilities by putting forward its own slogans; in other words, assuming a leading role. When Thalheimer refuted the arguments of Frölich, he mentioned the fact that henceforth two questions were concretely posed to the KPD(S): how to construct a strong and sufficiently united party (which raised the question of its relations with the USPD) and 'how to link the activity of this sufficiently strong and revolutionary party with that of the proletarian masses who are outside it, and that of the masses of the petty bourgeoisie'.[45] This twofold question would continue to arise over a long period.

There was one point on which all the Communists agreed immediately after the Kapp Putsch. Political life had revived, the Communists' period of retreat was in the past, and it was once again possible for them to fight successfully to win the core of the working class, and to take on the leading role to which they aspired. This was the issue, rather than the events of the preceding period, to which Levi devoted his interventions at the Fourth Party Congress. He did his best to provide an explanation of the movement which had developed deep within the German working class:

> The proletariat during these last 18 months has more or less separated in its heart from its old leadership, and more or less clearly turned towards Communism. But . . . such a movement within the working class cannot take place in the form of the awakening one fine morning of a proletariat which suddenly discovers that it is no longer with the Majority socialists but with the Independents or Communists. . . . It is necessary that some precise event take place that will arouse in the proletariat the awareness that its own feelings have changed.[46]

That was the point at which the intervention of the Party became necessary. Hence the need for the Party to be able simultaneously to make a correct analysis, and to maintain unfailing discipline. Levi regarded the existence within the Independent Party of a workers' vanguard, which pushed forward its left-wing leaders, as a crucial factor:

> It should be absolutely clear to us that it is the left wing of the Independents which provides the troops that will lead the revolutionary struggles. . . . We must be sure to address the masses of the Independent Party as if they were

---

[45] Thalheimer, 'Ein Rückfall von Kinderkrankheit', op. cit., p. 13.
[46] *Bericht über den 4 Parteitag der KPD*, op. cit., p. 23.

Communists. . . . The masses of the Independent Social-Democratic Party are ours in spirit and in blood. It would be absurd to come into collision with them, and, through them, with the proletarian masses.[47]

Ruth Fischer was an implacable adversary of Levi down the years, but she was later to confirm this diagnosis when she wrote:

The Kapp Putsch stimulated new impulses in the USPD. After a two-year experience with Lüttwitz, Seeckt, Watter, Ehrhardt, the workers were convinced that these men would not be disarmed by well-rounded formulas; they had lost their hope that the social-democratic government would act against the open and secret rearmament of the restoration. The mood prevailing in the spring of 1920 was: 'We need an organization able to cope with the excellently organised Free Corps and their allies in the army.'[48]

The Communist International, or rather, the Bolshevik Party, offered them the model for that. However, it was necessary for the Communists to repudiate many prejudices and habits which they had acquired during years of struggle against centrism, to overcome many inhibitions, and to reject many ready-made formulae. Levi seems to have been the only German leader at the Fourth Congress to express clearly the aim of winning the workers who formed the core of the USPD and the driving force of its left wing. Ernst Meyer did not deny that the USPD Left could progress towards Communism, but he declared that it would succeed in doing so only on condition that the Communists were able to 'hit it hard'.[49] Eulert, from Hamburg, where Ernst Thaelmann was one of the leaders of a very proletarian left wing, as well as Brandler himself, declared that, during the March events, they had not noticed any left wing in the USPD.[50] Friesland said that the supposed Left 'lacked revolutionary will'.[51] The majority of the speeches revealed in the old Spartacists a somewhat haughty attitude of disdain, alongside a sectarianism not free from naïveté, towards the 'masses' of the USPD. This attitude seems to have been reciprocated. The USPD's workers did not have much time for the German Communists, their quarrels, their hesitation-waltzes, their tiny organisation or the dogmatism which had led them to preach passivity in the face of the putschists in Berlin.

---

[47] Ibid., p. 51.
[48] Fischer, op. cit., p. 134.
[49] *Bericht über den 4 Parteitag der KPD*, op. cit., p. 42.
[50] Ibid., pp. 34, 54.
[51] Ibid., p. 46.

Chapter Twenty

Moscow and the German Revolutionaries

No sooner had the leaders of the KPD(S) considered that they had overcome the consequences of the mistakes which they had made ever since November 1918, especially at the time of the Founding Congress, when the early months of 1920 and especially the situation created by the Kapp-Lüttwitz Putsch revealed the most serious weakness of the young party, its inability to respond effectively to rapidly changing events. From another side, the debates at the Fourth Congress, which was held in clandestinity, brought to light that Paul Levi was relatively isolated in the Zentrale, and emphasised the obstacles raised on the road to the unification of the German revolutionaries – the USPD Left, KPD(S), KAPD – by the legacy of past differences and the sharpness of personal antagonisms. However, less than six months later, the USPD created the conditions for a fusion with the KPD(S), when it decided to join the Communist International.

The Bolsheviks, the International and Germany

The existence and the activity of the Communist International itself were a decisive factor in this development. In the final analysis, the mass of Independent workers and their left-wing leaders moved not towards the Spartacists, but, more simply, 'towards Moscow', as both supporters and critics were saying at the time.

For the Bolsheviks, the creation of a powerful International was a question of life and death. Nikolai Bukharin was to write in mid-1920, recalling the revolutionary struggles which had arisen in Europe since 1917 and their disappointing results:

> This shows that it is not possible for the Russian Revolution to be finally victorious without the victory of the international revolution. The victory of socialism is the only salvation for the world, its flesh mutilated and bled white. But without proletarian revolution in Europe, it is impossible for the socialist proletariat in Russia to have a lasting victory. . . . Revolutions are the locomotives of history. In backward Russia, the proletariat alone can climb aboard this locomotive, and become its irreplaceable driver. But it cannot remain forever within the limits set by the bourgeoisie: it seeks to seize power and build socialism. The problem which is posed in Russia will not be solved within the walls of the one nation. The working class is there encountering a rampart which can be broken only by the assault of the international workers' revolution.[1]

Bukharin concluded that the efforts of the Russians to construct the Communist International could only be understood in the light of this analysis: 'It is only to the extent that the proletariat is aware of the class organisation of international socialism, and gathers around it, that it is a revolutionary force, able to change the world, not only in intention, but in reality.'[2]

At first glance, the conditions were hardly favourable for an International to be constructed jointly by the Bolsheviks and the Spartacists. Lenin and Luxemburg were sharply opposed on fundamental questions, such as the role and the nature of the party, and then even on the necessity for revolutionaries to split the socialist movement. It was only the Russian Revolution which brought the two currents towards each other. In 1917 – if we exclude Radek, who was not really German – Lenin had not won a single German activist, whatever his influence on Levi or on certain people in Bremen may have been. It was the attractive force of the Russian Revolution, the prestige which the Bolsheviks won in their struggle, and the general hatred of the class enemy, in other words, the objective situation rather than the convergence of their outlooks, which had drawn the Bolshevik and Spartacist leaders towards one another.

---

[1] N.I. Bukharin, 'La Lutte des classes et la révolution russe', *Revue communiste*, no. 11, January 1921, pp. 385–6.
[2] Ibid., p. 386.

We must also concede that the relationship between the two parties was not helped by the fact that the Bolshevik German delegation to the Founding Congress of the KPD(S) was limited to two activists unfamiliar with the German movement, together with Radek, a man deeply suspect to many Spartacist leaders. Moreover, it was not by chance that the Bremen activists stressed the differences between Communism and Spartacism at this time, differences which Wolffheim and Laufenberg were to try to systematise, nor that a man such as Knief, doubtless the German activist who was nearest to the Bolsheviks, chose to stand aside from the foundation of the KPD(S). Moreover, the existence within the Spartacus League of a minority which opposed the use of the word 'Communist' in the name of the new party, and the mandate given by its leaders to its delegates to Moscow firmly to oppose the foundation of the Third International, not only revealed reservations, but also contributed to a certain ill-feeling, which foreboded difficult relations, marked at least with mutual distrust. The tragic deaths of Liebknecht and Luxemburg and their subsequent martyrs' halo made it difficult for the Bolsheviks to criticise their activity politically. But, finally and above all, the infrequent references to the German workers' movement in the press of the Russian Party and the International, or in Lenin's writings in 1918–19, reveal the lack of accurate information and regular political links, a context hardly favourable to the political clarification which would have been the necessary condition for agreement in analyses, perspectives and slogans.

There was not a single German activist on the ECCI when it was first set up. Those who did visit the Soviet Republic – Eduard Fuchs on the eve of the First Comintern Congress, Eberlein at the Congress itself, and Ernst Meyer during the following months – did not stay long. The KPD(S) was formally a member of the International, but in practice took an independent course, because the activists who had links with the Bolsheviks or were members of the Bolshevik Party with whom the KPD(S) had contact in Germany – such as Radek, Bronski and Zaks-Gladniev – were themselves cut off from all contact with the Soviet Republic. The first serious and regular link was not made until the autumn of 1919, when there arrived in Berlin a delegate from the ECCI whom history knows as 'Comrade Thomas', not having been able to penetrate the secret of his real identity.[3] The man who used this name had

---

[3] He was probably Jakob Reich, who was not a 'Bavarian communist', as E.H. Carr incorrectly writes (op. cit., p. 135). See the account he gave to Boris Nicolaevsky of

worked in 1917–18 in the Russian mission to Berne, from which he been expelled in November 1918. He returned to Russia, and was attached to the propaganda section under the executive of the soviets; he took part in preparing the Founding Congress of the Comintern, which appointed him to its Bureau. In Petrograd, he edited the *Communist International*, and under the pseudonym of James Gordon he published an article on Germany. In the early summer of 1919, he was sent to Berlin in order to set up a West European Secretariat of the Communist International. He was to explain this later in these laconic phrases: 'The activity of the Communist International had to be organised in the West, and particularly in Germany. This could not be done without assistance from veteran activists trained in clandestine work. They had to be sent from Moscow.'[4]

The emissary of the International was provided with a substantial amount of money and precious stones. He reached Berlin at the end of autumn, after an adventurous journey, and at once made contact with Radek[5] and with the KPD(S) Zentrale. He quickly succeeded in setting up publishing firms in Hamburg and Leipzig, one of which published *Die Kommunistische Internationale* in German. He helped arrange in Frankfurt-am-Main a conference of Western communist parties and groups, which approved theses prepared by Thalheimer that were very similar to those of the KPD(S)'s Heidelberg Congress. In collaboration with Radek, he formed a West European Bureau, made up of German members or contacts of the KPD(S), Radek himself, Thalheimer, Bronski, Münzenberg and Eduard Fuchs.[6]

It is difficult to regard this Bureau as an extension of the ECCI. In the same way that Bronski, who was sent by the Bolshevik Party, identified himself in Germany with the most anti-leftist elements in the Party, the West European Secretariat took up a sharp position against the ultra-left elements, and its theses produced at the end of 1919 showed it to be lagging a long way behind the ECCI and even the Founding Congress, because it called for 'founding'

---

the first years of the International and of his own activity in J. Freymond, *Contributions à l'histoire du Comintern*, Geneva, 1965, pp. 1–28. An English translation, Jakob Reich, 'The First Years of the Communist International', is in *Revolutionary History*, Volume 5, no. 2, Spring 1994, pp. 2–36. Lerner says that Thomas was really called Rubinstein (W. Lerner, *Karl Radek: The Last Internationalist*, Stanford, 1970, p. 196).

  [4] Reich, op. cit., p. 12.
  [5] Ibid. Thomas writes that Radek was then at liberty, whereas Radek (*November*, op. cit., p. 158) states that he was still in prison when they made contact.
  [6] Reich, op. cit., p. 15.

the International of the world revolution.[7] Thomas's arrival in Berlin helped to establish serious clandestine links between Berlin and Moscow, which were to enable the ECCI to be informed within a few weeks of events in Germany, and to organise clandestine visits.

Russian influence in Germany was limited to direct contacts with certain activists, such as Radek's contacts in Bremen, whom he succeeded in winning from the opposition and bringing back to the KPD(S).[8] In Berlin, Thomas was in contact with some activists in whom the Russians had confidence, especially Ernst Reuter-Friesland,[9] whose relations with the Berlin leaders of the opposition – Schröder in particular – were favourable to the plans of the ECCI for a reconciliation between the opposition and the Zentrale, even on the morrow of the Heidelberg Congress. The public debate which proceeded, at a distance, between Lenin and Thalheimer was only one aspect of the relations between the Spartacists and Bolsheviks in this period. However, contact between them proved difficult, and the relationship was thus sporadic. Immediately after the Kapp Putsch, a manifesto of the International, drafted in very general terms, hailed the victory of the general strike and the birth of the German Red Army.[10] Published in Moscow on 25 March 1920, it revealed the ignorance of the ECCI in respect of events in Germany.

The KPD(S)'s mistakes in respect of the Kapp Putsch were to force the ECCI to start actively intervening in its affairs. The first real intervention took place, as we have seen, in connection with the Zentrale's declaration of the Party being a 'loyal opposition' to a possible workers' government, which caused a major controversy in the Party. The affair brought to light important disagreements which arose within the ECCI itself and its 'small bureau'. The declaration of 'loyal opposition' was denounced by Radek, Bukharin, Kun and Zetkin, but in the end was supported by Lenin.

This first discussion was quickly curtailed after Lenin stated his position and suggested, to general agreement, that the debate be referred to the coming congress of the International. It raised issues which reappeared in all the great debates within the Communist International, with recourse, as points of reference, to quotations from Marx, even from Lenin, to examples drawn

---

[7] *Kommunisticheskii International*, no. 7–8, November-December 1919, column 1099–102.

[8] Karl Becker was present at the Fourth Congress of the KPD(S), held immediately after the foundation of the KAPD, from which he dissociated himself.

[9] Brandt and Lowenthal, op. cit., p. 131.

[10] *Pravda*, 25 March 1920.

from Bolshevik policy at this or that moment in Russian history, and the eternal comparison with the events of 1917 being the favoured weapons of the protagonists. Lenin himself set the example. He said that the Russian experience was a major asset in the discussion about ultra-leftism in 1920 and, for that reason, in the discussions about the method of constructing Communist Parties and the International.

The international struggle against the ultra-leftists

The fundamental discussion could only take place on an international level. The ultra-left current revealed itself most vigorously in Germany, and resulted in the first leftward split in a Communist Party, and the founding of the KAPD in April 1920. But the ultra-left tendency went far beyond Germany. Its influence penetrated the whole of the Western Communist movement. The principal theoreticians of the current were to be found in the Dutch Communist Party, the former leaders of the Tribunist group, Henriette Roland-Holst, Hermann Gorter and Anton Pannekoek, whose contribution to the international debate was to be fundamental.

A British ultra-leftist, Sylvia Pankhurst, provoked the first exchange on this basis. In July 1919, she wrote to Lenin, in the name of the British Workers' Socialist Federation, to seek his support for her organisation, which opposed any activity on the parliamentary plane. The misunderstanding is evident, and was commonplace in the conditions of the time. Lenin's reply was very diplomatic, and marked by concern to avoid useless quarrels. He suggested, provisionally, that two British Communist Parties be formed to organise the revolutionaries on the basis of their respective attitudes to elections and to the participation of Communists in bourgeois parliaments.[11] At the same time, a circular from the ECCI, dated 1 September 1919 and signed by Zinoviev, opened the discussion in the International.[12]

The ECCI was concerned to avoid both a dialogue of the deaf and a false debate about principles. It began by pointing out the framework within which the discussion should be carried on, namely; that the Russian Revolution had

---

[11] V.I. Lenin, 'Letter to Sylvia Pankhurst', *Collected Works*, Volume 29, op. cit., pp. 566–72.

[12] 'Der Parlamentarismus und der Kampf für die Sowjet', *Manifest, Richtlinien, Beschlüsse des ersten Kongresses. Aufrufe und Offene Schreiben des Exekutivkomitees bis zum Zweiten Kongress*, Hamburg, 1920, pp. 139–46.

traced a new line of cleavage in the workers' movement. The 'universal and unifying programme' of the Communists implied in effect 'recognition of the struggle for the dictatorship of the proletariat in the form of soviet power'. In these conditions, the discussion about Communists utilising bourgeois parliaments was obscure only because of a confusion between parliamentarism, as the expression of a political choice in favour of the parliamentary system, and the participation of revolutionaries in elected assemblies which they would use as platforms for their politics. Taking part in elections could not be regarded as an absolute rule, but there could be no question of rejecting it on principle. The circular declared: 'There is no basis for splitting on this secondary question.'[13]

Around this time, Rutgers, a Dutch Communist, arrived in Amsterdam from Moscow with the task of forming a West European Secretariat of the Communist International.[14] Rutgers' mission duplicated that of Thomas, which is not extraordinary if we consider the difficulty of communications and the need to ensure the most effective means of receiving material in Western Europe (the Amsterdam Bureau was also to deal with communications with America).[15] However, a serious conflict soon erupted between the Amsterdam bureau, animated by the Dutch Communists with their strong ultra-left tendencies, and the Berlin Secretariat, inspired by the KPD(S). An international conference organised by Rutgers met in Amsterdam on 3 February 1920, with the participation of mandated delegates from the Dutch Party and the different British groups, the American Louis Fraina, the Russian Mikhail Borodin, who had returned from Mexico, and unmandated delegates from Indonesia, China and Hungary, about twenty altogether.[16] There was no delegate from the KPD(S) or the Berlin Secretariat, and Zetkin said that they had only been informed of the conference on 31 January.[17] The conference met over four days, and then had to be interrupted, because the police had infiltrated an agent who recorded the debates, and the foreign delegates were arrested and expelled.[18]

The conference did not resume. Zetkin, who then arrived with Paul Frölich, Münzenberg and a Swiss delegate, was welcomed by the Dutch police, who

---

[13] Ibid., p. 146.
[14] Le Phare, no. 8, 1 April 1920, p. 387; Hulse, op. cit., p. 153.
[15] Bericht über den 4 Parteitag der KPD, op. cit., pp. 78–9.
[16] Hulse, op. cit., p. 154.
[17] Bericht über den 4 Parteitag der KPD, op. cit., p. 79.
[18] Hulse, op. cit., p. 155.

were well informed indeed. She protested indignantly to Rutgers and the others against the holding of a badly-prepared 'rump conference'.[19] The KPD(S) had other serious grounds for dissatisfaction. The conference adopted positions on the trade-union question which were very close to those of the German opposition, and moreover elected a bureau of three, all Dutch, Wijnkoop representing the Dutch Communist Party, Roland-Holst, a well-known ultra-leftist, and Rutgers himself, who had just aligned himself with the ultra-leftists in his own party.[20]

The Germans therefore drew the conclusion that this was an attempt to exclude them and to short-circuit the Berlin Secretariat. They emphasised that the delegates had not been given copies of the theses which the KPD(S) adopted at the Heidelberg Congress.[21] At any rate, the results of the conference were slight, and can be summed up in the decision to entrust to the Communist Party of USA the organisation of a sub-bureau for the American continent, and in an undertaking to organise a further conference in three months time.[22] It must be admitted that the activity of the Amsterdam Bureau contributed little to clarification. The Third Congress of the KPD(S) at Karlsruhe in February 1920 protested against its activities and initiatives.[23] The Amsterdam Bureau was soon to issue a public declaration against the policy of the KPD(S) during the period of the Kapp Putsch, and to line up with the KAPD.[24] During April, the ECCI closed down its mission:

> We are convinced that the differences with our Dutch comrades will soon be settled. Unlike the Second International, we do not conceal our differences, and we do not allow ourselves ambiguous formulations. On a number of questions (trade unions, parliament), the Dutch Bureau has adopted a position different from that of the Executive Bureau. It did not inform the Executive Committee of these differences before calling the international conference in Amsterdam. Consequently, the Executive Committee declares that the mandate of the Amsterdam Bureau has lost its validity, and thus revokes it. The functions of the Dutch Bureau are transferred to the West European Secretariat.[25]

---

[19] *Bericht über den 4 Parteitag der KPD*, op. cit., p. 81.
[20] Hulse, op. cit., p. 156.
[21] *Bericht über den 4 Parteitag der KPD*, op. cit., p. 79.
[22] Ibid., p. 82.
[23] Ibid., pp. 84–5.
[24] *Die Rote Fahne*, 22 April 1920.
[25] *Le Phare*, May–June 1920, pp. 484–5.

But, at much the same time, other signs of the international current evident in the Amsterdam Bureau appeared in the world Communist movement. One of its principal centres was to be formed around the review *Kommunismus*, which appeared in Vienna from the beginning of 1920 as an organ of the International directed towards South-East Europe. The Austrian Communist Party, like the Dutch Communist Party, represented a very isolated current in the working class of its country, with pronounced sectarian tendencies, as its conduct revealed in 1919, especially at the time of the Bettelheim incident.[26] Moreover, it was strongly influenced by the small group of Hungarian exiles who settled in Austria after the defeat of the Revolution in 1919, particularly by the former People's Commissar for Education, Georg Lukács. He was in violent factional opposition to Béla Kun,[27] but when the ultra-left current expressed itself in Western Europe, as much in the writings of Gorter and Pannekoek as in the positions of the KAPD and the British ultra-left groups, both men intervened to support it.

Lukács took up the question of parliamentarism[28] and disputed Lenin's viewpoint that it was a matter of tactics, rather than principles. Lukács saw it as a problem of knowing the precise relationship of forces. In a situation in which the working class was on the defensive, it should make use of parliamentary means to strengthen itself. However, when the working class was fully on the offensive, its duty was to create its own class organisms, the soviets. Under these conditions, participation in elections took on the appearance of renouncing a concrete revolutionary perspective, and opened the way to opportunism.[29] Lukács's article implicitly condemned participation in elections under the current conditions in Europe, and stood in opposition to the ECCI.[30]

Kun revealed strikingly similar tendencies.[31] He opposed what he called the 'syndicalist boycott', or 'passive boycott', in favour of the 'active boycott', which he defined as 'revolutionary agitation as broad as if the party were

---

[26] See Chapter 18.
[27] Borkenau, op. cit., pp. 175ff.
[28] G. Lukács, 'Die parlamentarische Frage', *Kommunismus*, no. 6, 1 March 1920, pp. 161–72; 'The Question of Parliamentarism', *Political Writings 1919–1929*, London, 1972, pp. 53–63.
[29] Ibid., pp. 164–9.
[30] Lukács was attacking the ideas which Lenin was to defend in *'Left-Wing' Communism* without yet knowing of them. Lenin was to say 'G.L.'s article is very left wing, and very poor. Its Marxism is purely verbal.' (Lenin, '*Kommunismus*', op. cit., p. 165)
[31] 'Die Durchführung', *Kommunismus*, no. 18, 8 May 1920, pp. 549–55.

taking part in elections, and as if its agitation and activity had the object of winning the largest number possible of proletarian votes'.[32] At the same time, the Italian Amadeo Bordiga also began to develop anti-trade-union and anti-parliamentarian themes which were to be the basis of the Italian Left, in his newspaper, *Il Soviet*.[33] The first Belgian communist organisation, grouped round Van Overstraeten in Brussels, in turn developed the same positions.[34]

Lenin against ultra-leftism

Lenin began to draft his pamphlet about ultra-leftism, *'Left-Wing' Communism: An Infantile Disorder*, as the conflict opened between the ECCI and the Amsterdam Bureau. With this pamphlet, the discussion ceased to be limited to Germany, and took on the form of a public international battle of ideas. Lenin's intention was to enable the emerging Communist Parties to benefit from the Bolsheviks' experience. He regarded Bolshevism as a condensation of worldwide revolutionary experience, as much in the art of attack as in that of defence. He did not wish, for all that, to make the Bolshevik experience the universal model, but he declared: 'Experience has proved that, on certain very important questions of the proletarian revolution, *all* countries will inevitably have to do what Russia has done.'[35] The international Communist movement, which was growing under the stimulus of the Russian Revolution, knew nothing of Bolshevism but the history of its struggle against opportunism. It still knew nothing of the struggle against what Lenin called 'petty bourgeois revolutionism'.[36]

In effect, the ultra-leftists denied the necessity for a revolutionary party, and permanently counterposed 'the masses' to their 'leaders'. Lenin said that this was a distinction which created a real danger for the revolutionary movement. For there existed, within the class, 'a semi-petty-bourgeois, opportunist "labour aristocracy"', whose 'leaders were constantly going over to the bourgeoisie'. These 'leaders' effectively had become 'separated from the "masses"', that is, 'the broadest strata of the working people, their majority, the lowest-paid workers'. It was the duty of the revolutionaries to work to

---

[32] Ibid., p. 552.
[33] See Bordiga's letters to the Communist International, 10 November 1919 and 11 January 1920, *Rivista Storica del Socialismo*, no. 27, 1966, pp. 183–8.
[34] *Le Phare*, 1 March 1920, pp. 334–5.
[35] Lenin, '"Left-Wing" Communism', op. cit., p. 31.
[36] Ibid., p. 32.

detach the masses from the 'social-traitor leaders'.[37] But they could not succeed in doing so unless they looked clearly at the situation: 'We can (and must) begin to build socialism, not with abstract human material, or with human material specially prepared by us, but with the human material bequeathed to us by capitalism.'[38]

The ultra-leftists relied on the obvious observation that the trade-union leaders were bound up with the bourgeoisie against the revolution, and called upon revolutionaries to leave the unions and fight to destroy them. However, it was essentially via the reformist trade unions that the reactionary leaders maintained their grip on the masses. The duty of revolutionaries, on the contrary, therefore, was to fight within the trade unions in order to challenge the reformist chiefs for the leadership of the masses: 'To refuse to work in the reactionary trade unions means leaving the insufficiently developed or backward masses of workers under the influence of the reactionary leaders, the agents of the bourgeoisie, the labour aristocrats, or "workers who have become completely bourgeois".'[39]

Lenin believed that it was unacceptable to refuse to join battle in the arena in which it should and could be won, when 'millions of workers' were for the first time passing from 'a complete lack of organisation to the elementary, lowest, simplest and . . . most easily comprehensible form of organisation, namely, the trade unions'. The task of the Communists was 'to *convince* the backward elements, to work *amongst* them, and not to *fence themselves off* from them'.[40] The ultra-leftists readily accused the workers of being counter-revolutionary: the fact was that they mistook '*their desire* . . . for objective reality', and that revolutionary tactics could not be built on 'a revolutionary mood alone'.[41]

As long as the Communists were not strong enough to dissolve the parliament, that is, as long as they had not convinced the majority of the working people that parliament was a fraud, they had the duty to be there, precisely in order to expose it, to utilise it in order to enlighten the workers who were being fooled by it. Lenin thought that if the KPD(S) had not developed immediately after the November Revolution, this was partly because

---

[37] Ibid., pp. 42–3.
[38] Ibid., p. 50.
[39] Ibid., p. 53.
[40] Ibid., p. 54.
[41] Ibid., pp. 58, 63.

in January 1919 it made the mistake of boycotting the elections to the National Assembly, and of permitting its members to abandon the reformist unions:

> Capitalism would not be capitalism if the proletariat *pur sang* were not surrounded by a large number of exceedingly motley types intermediate between the proletarian and the semi-proletarian. . . . From all this follows the necessity, the absolute necessity, for the communist party, the vanguard of the proletariat, its class-conscious section, to respond to changes of tack, to conciliation and compromises. . . . It is entirely a matter of *knowing how* to apply these tactics in order to *raise* – not lower – the *general* level of proletarian class-consciousness, revolutionary spirit, and ability to fight and win.[42]

In a word, Lenin believed that ultra-leftism was an 'infantile disorder' of Communism, and that its progress in Western Europe was not due to chance: 'In many countries of Western Europe, the revolutionary mood, we might say, is at present a "novelty" or a "rarity", which has all too long been vainly and impatiently awaited; perhaps that is why people so easily yield to that mood.'[43] The problem was all the more important in that the task of the revolutionaries in Western Europe was more difficult: '. . . it was easy for Russia, in the specific and historically unique situation of 1917, to *start* the socialist revolution, but it will be more difficult for Russia than for the European countries to *continue* the revolution and bring it to its consummation.'[44]

The West European Communists needed to understand that, as the writer Chernyshevsky said: 'Political activity is not like the pavement of Nevsky Prospekt.': 'We must strive at all costs to *prevent* the left communists and West European and American revolutionaries that are devoted to the working class from paying *as dearly* as the backward Russians did to learn this truth.'[45]

The frequency of the references to the theses of the German opposition and to the USPD, whose militant workers were moving towards Communism, showed that Lenin's preoccupation was to prevent the ultra-leftism of the German communist movement from being an obstacle to the gathering in a revolutionary party of all the militant workers, a minority of whom were in the two Communist Parties and the great majority in the USPD.

---

[42] Ibid., p. 74.
[43] Ibid., p. 63.
[44] Ibid., p. 64.
[45] Ibid., p. 71.

Hermann Gorter's reply

Gorter replied to Lenin on behalf of the ultra-leftists.[46] He deplored the publication of Lenin's pamphlet, which he believed would strengthen in the West the position of the opportunist socialist leaders who had already joined or were preparing to join the Third International. Gorter argued that Lenin was mistaken in mechanically transposing the Russian experience to the West, when Western and Eastern Europe formed two deeply different worlds. Unlike the Russian proletariat in 1917, the proletariat of the West could not count on the support of a mass of poor peasants, as this did not exist. It was completely isolated within society; and, for that reason, the efforts required from the masses for the success of the revolution were greater and the role of the leaders much less. The power of the Western proletariat in the revolutionary struggle could only be based on its quality. Therefore the role of Communists was first to 'raise the masses as a whole, and the individuals to a higher level, to educate them one by one to be revolutionary fighters, by making them realise . . . that all depends on them'.[47]

Gorter said that Lenin knew nothing about the real situation of the proletariat in Western Europe, and that he was nurturing illusions when he wrote that the vanguard had been won, or that the period of propaganda had passed. He said that, for decades, the Western workers had been deeply dependent ideologically on bourgeois culture, and particularly on bourgeois ideas about parliamentary democracy. Citing Pannekoek, Gorter said that the Western bourgeoisie had 'made a thorough impression on the thoughts and feelings of the masses'. The workers, organised in the disciplined ranks of the trade unions, under the illusion that the decisive battles could be won with ballots, had lost their capacity to act. To return it to them, it was necessary utterly to destroy their illusions, which obviously meant avoiding getting them stuck in these illusions by taking part in elections, and then to give them the means to act on their own initiative. Communists not only had to guard against strengthening the reformist trade unions by working in them, but were obliged

---

[46] H. Gorter, *Offener Brief an den Genossen Lenin. Eine Antwort auf Lenins Broschüre: Der Radikalismus, eine Kinderkrankheit des Kommunismus*, Berlin, 1920. We have used here the 1920 French translation, *Réponse à Lénine*, reprinted Paris, 1970, comparing it with the German text republished in A. Pannekoek and H. Gorter, *Organisation und Taktik der proletarischen Revolution*, Frankfurt, 1969. [We have used the English translation, *Open Letter to Comrade Lenin*, London, 1989 – Translator]

[47] Gorter, *Open Letter to Comrade Lenin*, op. cit., p. 10.

to destroy them because they formed an obstacle to action and to the development of the consciousness of the workers. In their place, Communists were to recommend an organisation based on the principles of the 'councils', which are revolutionary because 'here it is the worker himself who decides'; the 'workers' union', formed unlike the trade unions, not on the basis of the industry or the craft, but on that of the workplace. Lenin was seriously wrong when he called on the Communists of the Western countries to build 'mass parties'. Such parties would inevitably repeat the opportunist errors of Social Democracy. According to Gorter, it was necessary to concentrate every effort on creating and educating 'pure and firm kernels' of Communists.[48]

The months which followed the Kapp Putsch, during which the public polemic between Lenin and the ultra-leftists unfolded, also saw the development of secret negotiations in Moscow between representatives of the International and delegates from the KAPD, as well as a number of internal struggles within the apparatus of the Communist International. In Berlin, a struggle broke out between the West European Bureau and the Secretariat of the Youth International, which the Bureau accused of ultra-left and even semi-anarchist tendencies. Münzenberg accused the members of the West European Bureau of factional activities, and declared that it had refused to pass on to the ECCI documents and letters from the leadership of the Youth International.

However, in June, despite the efforts at conciliation made by the representative of the Russian Party on the Bureau, Abramovich-Zaleski (known as Albrecht), Münzenberg obtained the Bureau's unanimous support for a severe condemnation of the practices of Thomas and his staff.[49] In this way, a conflict developed which was to end a year later with Münzenberg being dismissed and the Youth International being placed under the supervision of the ECCI.[50] On the other hand, the apparatus of the International maintained contacts with the German leftists even in Berlin, over the head of the KPD(S) and perhaps even of the West European Bureau, through the intermediary of Felix Wolf, who was a member of the Bureau and of the Russian Party, and of Borodin, whom Babette Gross says was the Bureau's contact with the KAPD.[51]

Moreover, at the end of May 1920, discussions began in Moscow between the ECCI and representatives of the KAPD. Immediately after the KAPD was

---

[48] Ibid., pp. 14, 19, 38.
[49] Gross, op. cit., pp. 107–8.
[50] Ibid., pp. 177ff.
[51] Ibid., p. 116.

formed, two members of its leadership, Appel and Jung, travelled secretly to Soviet Russia, in order to establish contact with the International. When they arrived, after a tortuous journey of over a month, they were welcomed fraternally, but encountered a totally unambiguous opposition from all the Bolsheviks they met – including Lenin and Zinoviev – to the strategy and tactics which their party advocated in Germany. Lenin even showed them the still-unpublished manuscript of *'Left-Wing' Communism*.[52] After these meetings, the ECCI sent to Germany the *Open Letter of the Executive Committee of the Communist International to the Members of the KAPD*, dated 2 June 1920. In it the leaders of the International condemned the policy of the KAPD as 'the abandonment of communism', and declared: 'On all the important questions of principles and tactics arising today in Germany, it is not the KAPD but the KPD which is correct.'[53]

The ECCI considered that the issue should be properly settled at the Second Comintern Congress, and in the meantime it proposed that a provisional parity organisation bureau be formed in Germany, with equal representation from the two Communist Parties, and a delegate from the ECCI in the chair, in order – as the ECCI hoped – to form the preparatory stage for the reunification of the two Parties, which remained its objective.[54] However, the *Open Letter* did not reach Germany for several weeks. In the meantime, the KAPD, having received no news of Appel and Jung, sent to Moscow two other representatives to the Second Congress. This initiative, as well as the choice of delegates, was to pose the problem in new terms.

Debates about the Revolution of 1919

In the period between the Kapp Putsch and the Second Comintern Congress, a debate also developed about the revolutions in Bavaria and Hungary in 1919. This began just prior to the putsch, at the end of 1919, and brought Radek and his follower Frölich into opposition to Levi. Radek opened fire soon after he emerged from jail, when he made public the content of the discussions he had had with Levi on these questions during the autumn of 1919.[55] Like Lenin, he believed that the principal reason for the defeat of Kun

---

[52] Bock, op. cit., p. 253.
[53] J. Degras, *The Communist International 1919–1943*, Volume 1, London, 1956, p. 128.
[54] Bock, op. cit., p. 255.
[55] Radek, *Die Entwicklung*, op. cit.

and his Hungarian comrades was their inability, indeed their refusal, to create a genuine Communist Party, sharply separated from the persons, traditions and practices of Social Democracy, together with their spirit of conciliation not merely towards right-wing Social Democrats, but especially towards the centrists akin to the German Independents. Radek drew a comparison with Germany, and tried hard to demonstrate the centrist character of the politics of the leaders of the Independent leftists, of people such as Richard Müller and Däumig, characterised by oscillations between a tendency which he called 'putschist-Blanquist' immediately after January and March, and 'Proudhonist', opportunist conceptions in the interval. It was these oscillations, characteristic of centrism, which made these people the principal danger for a revolutionary leadership in a revolutionary period. Radek said that the defeats in Hungary and Bavaria could only be explained by the collaboration of the Communists with these centrists, the Bavarian Independents and the Hungarian left Social Democrats, who succeeded in depriving the leaders of the revolution of all determination and clear-headedness, and depriving the masses of a leadership.

This was also the viewpoint of Frölich. Under the pseudonym of Paul Werner, he devoted a pamphlet to the Bavarian Revolution, the ultimate defeat of which he explained by 'betrayal' by the Independents.[56] Radek soon returned to the Hungarian question in the preface which he drafted in January 1920 for the work by the Hungarian Communist, Béla Szanto.[57] Here he sharply criticised the view commonly accepted in the ranks of the Communists in Germany, to the effect that the Hungarian Council Republic had been an ideological construction, the result of an agreement at the top between Communists and Social Democrats, independent of the class action of the proletariat itself. Aiming directly at Levi and his comrades, he denounced the way in which they abused the passage in the Spartacists' programme which stated that the KPD(S) was not disposed to take power merely because Ebert-Scheidemann had run their course and had ended in a blind alley. He judged that this was appropriate and correct in Berlin in January 1919, but could not be raised to the level of a general principle of revolutionary action. He wrote: 'The conception of a simple collapse of the coalition of the bourgeois and the Social-Democratic parties in which the process of collapse of the

---

[56] P. Werner (Paul Frölich), *Die Bayrische Räterepublik. Tatsachen und Kritik*, Petrograd, 1920.

[57] B. Szanto, *Klassenkämpfe und Diktatur der Proletariats in Ungarn*, Vienna, 1920.

bourgeois state does not keep in step with that of marshalling the proletarian forces, is completely ahistorical.'[58] He believed that the German Communists in Bavaria, like those in Hungary, could not evade the duty of a revolutionary struggle for power, even when the international situation doomed the revolutions in Munich and Budapest to early defeat: 'We must be there, where the working class is fighting, where it is in struggle, whether we win or suffer defeat.'[59]

Radek waxed ironic at the expense of those whom he called 'political debaters', ready for battle only if 'history undertakes to ensure their victory'.[60] As he saw it, the Hungarian Communists could not ignore either the offers of unity from the Social Democrats, which corresponded to the deep aspirations of the proletariat, from the moment when the Social Democrats declared that they were for the dictatorship of the proletariat. But when the Communists agreed to unity, they should have fought at the same time against any illusions in a peaceful, non-violent victory. It was necessary to accept unity, but at the same time to erect gallows! That was the lesson he drew from the Russian Revolution and the Civil War; one must not be satisfied with theses, but act like revolutionaries. And in this case, the defeat would serve the proletarians of the rest of the world as an example and inspiration.

Levi, who was under direct attack, accepted the challenge. Like Luxemburg, he believed that the class consciousness of the proletariat was the necessary condition for the seizure of power. He declared:

> What is decisive is not the negative element on the side of the bourgeoisie, but the positive element on the side of the proletariat. . . . The positive signal for the seizure of power by the proletariat is located in the proletariat itself, and is expressed in the stage of revolutionary development which it has reached.[61]

Contrary to what Radek thought, there was no correlation between the degree of confusion and disorganisation reached by the bourgeoisie and the degree of clarity and organisation reached by the proletariat. The German example – the 'great illusion' of 'unity' in November 1918 – revealed this clearly: 'The

---

[58] K. Radek, 'Die Lehren der Ungarischen Revolution', *Die Internationale*, no. 21, 25 February 1920, p. 57.

[59] Ibid., p. 58.

[60] Ibid.

[61] P. Levi, 'Die Lehren der Ungarischen Revolution', *Die Internationale*, no. 24, 24 June 1920, p. 35.

proletariat did not respond with clarity and decisiveness to the momentary total impotence and confusion of the bourgeoisie, but, on the contrary, with equally great impotence and confusion.'[62] Levi tried to sharpen the thought of Luxemburg when he wrote:

> Normally a period of twilight lies between the bourgeois night and the proletarian day. . . . In such a situation, when the strength of the bourgeoisie may in certain cases have diminished to the point where it would already be possible for a very small minority to lay hands on power, we Communists are confronted with the first positive task which we have to accomplish: the organisation of the proletariat as a class in councils. I believe that the level reached by this process of organising the proletarian class – which, naturally, cannot precisely conform to a fixed scheme for the 'system of councils', but will consist of a succession of highs and lows, of demonstrations, interventions, struggles, etc – indicates the moment when the Communists must take power. I think that this is what Rosa Luxemburg wanted to express.[63]

Levi said that the error of the Hungarian Communists lay, therefore, in their desire to take power, and taking it, when the working class was not yet ready, when, as in Germany in 1918, its class consciousness was still obscured by tragic illusions about 'the unity of all the socialists'. Levi did not deny the necessity for class-based terror, but energetically opposed Radek's argument about the need to 'erect gallows':[64]

> To promote the erection of gallows as an essential method in the struggle to unite and weld together the proletariat at the moment of the formation of council power, to proceed to organise and consolidate the proletariat, not on the basis of 'the clear and unequivocal will of the great majority of the proletariat', of its 'conscious agreement with the ideas, the aims and the methods of struggle' of Communism, but on the basis of executing and hanging people, seems to me to be a most unfortunate method – I put it no more harshly than that. To my knowledge, the Russian Council Republic never placed the gallows in its emblem alongside the hammer and the sickle. I believe that this omission was not due to chance or mere bashfulness, but

---

[62] Ibid.
[63] Ibid., p. 36.
[64] Radek, 'Die Lehren der Ungarischen Revolution', op. cit., p. 59.

that it was the result of the fact that the Russian Council Republic was also constructed on bases other than those which comrade Radek proposes for Hungary. The way to ensure the cohesion of the proletariat as a class is no garland of roses, to be sure, but neither is it the hangman's rope.[65]

Levi added that the mistakes of the Communists in Bavaria were of another kind. The Bavarian Communists had been reorganised and purged by Leviné, and did not in fact let themselves be caught in the trap of socialist unity. Very correctly, they refused to support the 'monster' which the first council republic in Bavaria had been when it arose from an agreement amongst the anarchists, the Majority Social Democrats and the Independents. But they took power because the workers of Munich wanted it, and because, like Radek, they believed that their duty was to be with the masses of workers even when they were mistaken. Levi believed that the responsibility of the Communists lay not merely in maintaining solidarity with the masses at this or that moment, but in leading activities for the whole of the proletariat throughout the revolutionary period. What characterised the Communists was that they had a revolutionary aim, an overriding aim, and the responsibility of leading the workers to victory:

> To repeat the same slogans that the masses are already saying, without taking account of the vast context of the revolution is not a Communist, but an 'Independent' procedure. If we Communists have always unconditionally to adopt the same positions as the masses, if we have always to fight for whatever may be their aims at any given moment, we shall resign not only our political right to our own self-determination, we shall, moreover, repudiate our leading role in the revolution. We shall no longer be its head, but its tail.[66]

Levi turned against Radek the example of the Russian Revolution. He showed how the Bolsheviks had precisely this attitude in July 1917. They did not hesitate, in Petrograd, to take their stand against the stream and to defy temporary unpopularity in defence of a perspective which they believed to be correct. He quoted Lenin:

> It is not enough to be a revolutionary and an adherent of socialism or a communist in general. You must be able at each particular moment to find

---

[65] Levi, op. cit., p. 37.
[66] Ibid., p. 39.

the particular link in the chain which you must grasp with all your might in order to hold the whole chain and to prepare firmly for the transition to the next link. . . . From this point of view, it is by no means to retreat but, on the contrary, to lay an enduring hold on the revolution, when we issue tactical slogans which enable a certain or foreseeable defeat to be avoided.[67]

Levi's conclusion bore without any doubt the imprint of the disappointing years of 1918–19, for the experience of defeat had given him no liking for it:

Since the days of armed struggle in Berlin in January and March 1919, since the end of Munich and of Hungary, my faith in the miraculous virtues of defeat is broken. I do not believe that we are right to pass as lightly as Radek does over defeats as severe as the one suffered in Hungary. . . . I am afraid that, things being as they are, it will be a long time before the situation in Hungary permits the proletariat of that country to display this 'reinforced and deepened will' of which Radek speaks. I regard Hungary, like Munich, as a loss rather than a gain for the world revolution, and I cannot convince myself that it is acting as a Communist leadership to lead actions as if it did not matter whether their results provide us with gains or with losses. And I am still less disposed to say that we have to provoke a defeat if we cannot provoke a victory on the pretext that there can be something worthwhile in a defeat.[68]

The discussion about the Bavarian and the Hungarian Revolutions was by no means academic, especially in Germany. What Levi was opposing, through the arguments of Radek, was putschism, his chief *bête noire* in the Party, at least as much as the military form of Bolshevism in civil war which expressed itself through the arguments in favour of terror. This was what the Spartacists tended to regard as a sign of 'Blanquism', the temptation for the Party to substitute itself for the proletariat, the ultra-left illusion of the postwar years. People like Radek and Frölich scented in the hostility of Levi to putschism a tendency to wait upon events, an inclination to concentrate on propagandist activity alone, a subtle form of opportunism, which would in reality renounce revolutionary action, and always be delaying it for a more favourable combination of events, on the pretext of convincing and winning the majority

---

[67] Ibid. Levi is citing V.I. Lenin, 'The Immediate Tasks of the Soviet Government', *Collected Works*, Volume 27, op. cit., p. 274.
[68] Levi, op. cit., p. 40.

of the workers. For the moment, the differences were not fundamental, but there was a danger that they would become so.

Meanwhile, the main problem remained the construction of a Communist Party, how to win to Communism the hundreds of thousands of workers who had turned their backs on the party of Noske, Ebert and Scheidemann, and who formed the basis of the USPD, this centrist party which really, in the eyes of the leaders in Berlin and in Moscow alike, formed at that time the main obstacle to the winning to Communism of a substantial section of the working class.

The International and the Independents

This precise problem of winning the masses who followed the Independent leaders provided Lenin with the example which enabled him to demonstrate the necessity of compromise outlined in *'Left-Wing' Communism*. Against those who were for 'small hard solid nuclei', he wrote that recent events in Germany had confirmed the opinion which he had always defended, 'that German *revolutionary* social democracy . . . *came closest* to being the party the revolutionary proletariat needs in order to achieve victory'.[69] He saw the proof not only in the continuity between 'revolutionary social democracy' and the Spartacus League, which became the KPD(S), but in the internal evolution of the mass party, the USPD:

> Today, in 1920, after all the ignominious failures and crises of the war period and the early postwar years, it can be plainly seen that, of all the Western parties, the German revolutionary social democrats produced the finest leaders, and recovered and gained new strength more rapidly than the others did. This may be seen in the instances both of the Spartacists and the left proletarian wing of the Independent Social Democratic Party of Germany, which is waging an incessant struggle against the opportunism and spinelessness of the Kautskys, Hilferdings, Ledebours and Crispiens.[70]

However, in 1919, Lenin had been far from having so favourable an appreciation of the left wing of the USPD. In an article devoted to the Berne conference, he had vigorously attacked its spokesman, Däumig, whom he accused of

---

[69] Lenin, '"Left-Wing" Communism', op. cit., p. 34.
[70] Ibid.

'Byzantinism', of 'servility to the philistine prejudices of the petty bourgeoisie', whose 'leftism', he said, was 'not worth a brass farthing', and who he said, was amongst the 'cowardly philistines' and 'reactionary snivellers'.[71] This was the same mistrust that seemed to inspire the attitude of Radek prior to the Leipzig Congress.

The development of the USPD Left during 1919, the acceptance by the Party of the principle of the dictatorship of the proletariat, and the decision at Leipzig regarding the Third International had influenced the attitude of the ECCI, without having changed their fundamental attitude to the leaders of the Party's Centre and right wing. From that point onwards, the concern of the ECCI was to win the majority of the workers who followed the USPD to the idea of joining the Communist International, a factor which could not fail to have important consequences for the Party.

Just after the Leipzig Congress, Radek, on the eve of his return to Russia, had an official discussion with the USPD Executive about the prospects of joining the Communist International.[72] On 15 December 1919, Crispien wrote in the name of the Party to the ECCI in the same terms as he wrote to the socialist parties in Europe which were hostile to the Second International, proposing that an international conference be held either in Germany or Austria.[73] This showed that the Independent leaders wished to do everything to avoid facing the Russians alone.

The different organisms of the Comintern reacted in a way which revealed a certain lack of homogeneity. The West European Secretariat, based in Berlin, was the first to reply, in a rough way, as if the Leipzig Congress had not changed anything. It informed the Independents that they still had to prove their revolutionary credentials, and it refused any discussion with parties that still had 'social-patriots' in their ranks. It declared that it could only envisage public negotiations with the USPD, in which a pitiless political struggle would be waged.[74]

The ECCI's reply of 5 February 1920, signed by Zinoviev, was much more positive,[75] even if it consisted largely of a severe indictment of the USPD

---

[71] V.I. Lenin, 'The Heroes of the Berne International', *Collected Works*, Volume 29, Moscow, 1977, pp. 395–6.
[72] According to *Freiheit*, 25 June 1920.
[73] Text in *Freiheit*, 2 January 1920.
[74] *Spartakus*, no. 5–6, January 1920.
[75] *Die Rote Fahne*, 23, 26, 27, 28 April 1920.

leadership, accusing it of 'continually oscillating between open treachery of the Noske brand and the road of the revolutionary proletariat'. Zinoviev levelled many charges at the Independents, including the fostering of parliamentary illusions amongst the masses, frightening the German working people and turning them against the proletarian revolution by denouncing the terror in Soviet Russia, neglecting the anti-militarist struggle, and having accepted the dictatorship of the proletariat only in words. Like the West European Secretariat, the ECCI reproached the USPD leaders for their maintenance of relations with the Social-Democratic Parties, their refusal to support the struggles of the colonial peoples, the presence in their ranks of the likes of Kautsky, a declared adversary of Bolshevism, and, in particular, opening negotiations simultaneously with the Communist International and the centrist parties and 'sabotaging the decisions of the Leipzig Conference'.[76]

The appeal of the ECCI 'to the conscious German workers' to discuss this reply 'in public workers' meetings', and to demand 'clear and precise replies from the USPD's leaders' appeared to be a threat to engage in factional struggle and promote, from outside, a campaign to split the Party. Yet for all that, the ECCI did not burn its bridges, and declared that it was ready to receive in Moscow representatives of any party which declared itself ready firmly to break from the Second International. It even hinted at a range of possible concessions on its part when it stated:

> The ECCI is fully aware that it is necessary to take every peculiar feature into consideration, because the nature of revolutionary development is complex and specific. We are quite ready to enlarge the Third International, to take into consideration the experience of the proletarian movement in every country, and to improve and widen the experience of the proletarian movement in every country, to improve and widen the programme of the Third International on the basis of Marxist theory and of the worldwide experience of the revolutionary struggle.[77]

Nonetheless, matters remained stalled for some months as the result of a game of hide-and-seek, in which the USPD announced that it had not received from the ECCI a reply to its letter of 15 December 1919, and that it could not

---

[76] Already in *Freiheit* on 20 December 1919, Däumig had stressed the manifest hostility of his Party's press, and its dishonest, malicious and incomplete reports of the Leipzig Congress.

[77] *Die Rote Fahne*, 28 April 1920.

obtain the address where it could meet the West European Secretariat, which it regarded as its go-between in the negotiations with the ECCI, after having decided in principle to send a delegation to Moscow.[78] Many things had happened by the time that the negotiations recommenced – the Kapp Putsch and the workers' militant response, the revenge of the Reichswehr, the general elections, and, at the beginning of April, the foundation of the KAPD.[79] This was to complicate the task of the Communist negotiators even though it ultimately removed an obstacle to the improvement of relations between the KPD(S) and the USPD.[80]

Then, in early April 1920, Borodin presented himself at the central office of the USPD. He had been sent by the ECCI, and carried a letter of introduction from the West European Secretariat, as well as Zinoviev's letter of 5 February.[81] The Independent leaders expressed surprise at the delay in transmitting this document, but they did not publish it until 20 May, and then not in all their publications,[82] whereas the KPD(S) published it on 23 April. Crispien and Borodin met, but their conversation was confined to questions put by the former, who asserted the good faith of his comrades, and repeated his proposal to send a delegation, when the electoral campaign had ended, to open negotiations directly in Moscow.[83] The Communist press was now campaigning publicly for the Independents to join the Third International.[84] The left wing of the USPD took up a militant position, and Wilhelm Herzog entitled an editorial in *Forum*: 'From Leipzig to Moscow. Clarity at all costs!'[85] Moreover, Borodin agreed for Herzog to visit Moscow, which led to his being attacked in *Freiheit*.[86] Personal contacts continued in Berlin from 30 April, with the arrival of Alexander Shliapnikov, who was invited to attend a session of the

---

[78] *Freiheit*, 26 June 1920.

[79] See Chapter 18.

[80] The USPD right wing was to declare that there was 'a new element in the situation', but the Left saw here that its fiercest enemies on the Communist side had moved away.

[81] *Freiheit*, 26 June 1920.

[82] Ibid. The leadership of the USPD made the excuse of the electoral campaign and 'shortage of paper'.

[83] Stenographic report of these discussions, *Freiheit*, 26 June 1920.

[84] The documents brought by Borodin were published in the press of the KPD(S), and the Independents were accused of suppressing them.

[85] *Forum*, no. 7, April 1920, pp. 481–4, as an introduction to Zinoviev's letter of 5 February.

[86] He was to stay in the Soviet Union from May to August 1920. The attacks in *Freiheit*, together with the correspondence between Borodin, Radek and himself, are collected in 'Die Wut des Hilfergendinges', *Forum*, no 11, April 1920, pp. 866–70.

USPD Executive on 7 May. He categorically denied that the International demanded that the USPD expel any right-wing members prior to discussions being opened about its joining the International, or that fusion with the KPD(S) was a precondition for its joining it, as Crispien suggested.[87]

Things now speeded up. To the pressure behind the scenes and the desire for negotiations was added the public pressure of the International on the USPD activists through the Communist press and the Party's members. Radek wrote to the USPD in his capacity as the Secretary of the International expressing his surprise at the silence of its leaders, who had not replied to the letter of 5 February.[88] He protested against their failure to publish either it or their reply,[89] and he reiterated the proposal that they send a delegation to Moscow for direct negotiations, which for him would be the test of the sincerity of the USPD's leaders.[90] The USPD Executive replied by telegraph that it agreed to send delegates to Moscow. On 9 June, the West European Secretariat informed it of the agenda for the Comintern's Second World Congress, to which it was invited to send delegates, who were elected at its sessions held on 11 and 19 June.[91]

Relations between the Communist International and the USPD had been very close to a break, and in that same month of June, a letter from the ECCI, signed not only by Zinoviev and Radek but also by Lenin and other Russian leaders,[92] repeated the charge that the Independent leaders were sabotaging the Leipzig decisions. It was addressed to the USPD membership, and declared: 'Their attitude shows how correct we were when we stated that your admission to the Third International was possible only over the heads of your leaders.'[93] The appeal, which was directed to members and local and regional organisations of the USPD in order to encourage them to elect directly the delegates who would represent them in Moscow, indicated that the ECCI had decided that a split was a precondition for the USPD's joining the Communist International, the least certain and most costly means of recruiting the Party.

---

[87] *Freiheit*, 26 June 1920.
[88] *Die Rote Fahne*, 12 June 1920.
[89] It was to be published in *Freiheit* from 11 July 1920 onwards.
[90] See *Freiheit*, 31 May 1920.
[91] *Freiheit*, 27 June 1920.
[92] The undated text is in *Manifest, Richtlinien, Beschlüsse des ersten Kongresses*, op. cit., pp. 322–5 under the heading 'An alle Orts- und Landesorganisationen der USPD, an alle Arbeiter, die Mitglieder der USPD sind'.
[93] Ibid., p. 324.

Conversely, when the USPD nominated four official delegates, Crispien and Dittmann on one side and Stoecker and Däumig on the other, it left every possibility open. The KPD(S) had, however, taken up hard positions. The Central Committee voted on 17 June to demand that the USPD, in the event that it accepted the conditions for joining, give proof of its revolutionary credentials by expelling its right-wing leaders.[94] At the same time, the KPD(S) declared its determination to oppose the admission in any form whatever of the KAPD into the International: 'There is no place in Germany for two Communist Parties.'[95]

The question of the KAPD was also to give rise to differences within the Communist movement, with the West European Secretariat and the ECCI adopting conflicting positions. The former severely condemned the KAPD on 18 April, accusing it of having links with the supporters of the theory of 'national Bolshevism', and of having had contact with certain agents of the Kapp Putsch during the March events, in which they developed an adventurist approach, and advocated terrorism and sabotage.[96] The Secretariat contested the claim of the KAPD to be a member of the Third International so long as it assumed the right to make violent attacks on parties which were already members.[97] It was a categorical rejection of the KAPD. The ECCI's communiqué of 3 June, on the other hand, left the door open for the KAPD to return to the Communist movement, and to affiliate to the International.[98] The ECCI's open letter of 2 July to the members of the KAPD[99] reminded 'the revolutionary workers' in that party that the split in the KPD(S) was unnecessary, and that reunification remained possible if the KAPD really desired it. However, it

---

[94] *Die Rote Fahne*, 24 June 1920.

[95] Ibid.

[96] They were evidently aiming first at the Hamburgers, Wolffheim for his contacts with the officers of General von Lettow-Vorbeck – according to a statement by Brandler to O.E. Schüddekopf, he was even the General's secretary – but also Laufenberg, who, with Wolffheim, was said to have met Reventlow immediately before the putsch (O.E. Schüddekopf, *Linke Leute von Rechts*, Stuttgart, 1960, p. 435). Amongst the other leaders of the KAPD accused of such contacts was the Berlin worker, Fritz Rasch. *Freiheit* was to publish on 10 June 1920 a letter from one of the collaborators with Kapp in which he spoke of his talks with the 'Kappists' (letter from von Weimburg, 14 March 1920) declaring that General von Falkenhausen, 'was not opposed to conversation with Herr Rasch'. Rasch denied this (according to *Kommunistische Arbeiter-Zeitung*, reported in *Die Rote Fahne*, 16 June 1920).

[97] *Die Rote Fahne*, 22 April 1920.

[98] *Die Rote Fahne*, 15 June 1920.

[99] *Die Rote Fahne*, 13, 14, 16, 17, 20 and 21 July 1920.

demanded that the KAPD give guarantees about its intentions, including at the very least the expulsion of Wolffheim and Laufenberg and the supporters of 'national Bolshevism', who were compromised by their contacts with the military in March,[100] as well as of Otto Rühle, who was behaving as an open enemy of the Russian Revolution and the Bolshevik Party.[101] The ECCI repeated the positions of the International in favour of taking part in elections and of militant activity in the trade unions, and declared its agreement in principle with the KPD(S), which it again stressed was the only party of the Third International in Germany.

At the same time, the ECCI declared that it had been 'in complete disagreement' with the reasons which the leadership of the KPD(S) gave for its declaration of 'loyal opposition', and admitted that 'the Spartacist Zentrale had not always been either prudent or patient enough in its struggle against the opposition'.[102] Finally, it advanced concrete proposals with a view to reunification: the formation of a parity bureau including both parties, with a representative of the ECCI presiding, and the sending of a delegation from the KAPD to the Second Comintern Congress.[103]

The Second Comintern Congress was thus to take on the task of the reunification of the German Communists and the building of a mass Communist Party in Germany through the recruitment of all or at least part of the membership of the USPD to the Communist International. This was not an easy task. All the evidence shows that the ECCI wanted a total unification, in which the revolutionary combative spirit of the KAPD would be able to correct both the opportunist tendencies of the USPD, and the tendency of the leadership of the KPD(S) towards passivity.

---

[100] *Die Rote Fahne*, 17 July 1920.
[101] *Die Rote Fahne*, 20 July 1920. Otto Rühle had been in Russia since the end of May (Bock, op. cit., p. 255).
[102] *Die Rote Fahne*, 21 July 1920.
[103] Ibid. Merges had already set off for Moscow with the mandate to represent the KAPD, with Rühle, in the negotiations which began on 19 July (Bock, op. cit., p. 255).

Chapter Twenty-One

The Great Hopes of 1920

The First Comintern Congress had provided for only
limited participation by the non-Russian delegates,
who were mostly not mandated. The Second
Congress, however, saw an influx of foreign delegates.
For some months, the current in favour of joining
the Third International had been growing stronger
in all the socialist parties of the world. The Norwegian
and Italian parties had already given their support.
Mass parties as important as the French Socialist
Party and the Independent Social-Democratic Party
of Germany were knocking at the door of the
International, the attraction of which was likewise
being felt by syndicalist forces such as the Industrial
Workers of the World in America, and mass trade-
union organisations such as the CNT in Spain. This
political situation was matched, in these closing
months of the Civil War, with a favourable military
situation for the Soviet Republic.

At the end of April 1920, Marshal Pilsudski's
government in Poland attacked Soviet Russia,
reviving the Civil War which Baron Wrangel, backed
and financed by the French government, was leading
in the south-west of Russia. At first, the Soviet
government had feared a general attack by the
Entente in support of the Polish offensive, and Radek
had warned the Zentrale of the KPD(S) that the Polish
conflict opened up new, ominous perspectives. On
18 May, a manifesto of the ECCI launched an appeal

to the world proletariat for the defence by all means of Soviet Russia against 'White Poland'. But in July, the war took a turn which surprised many. The Red Army under the command of Mikhail Tukhachevsky routed the Polish army, counter-attacked, and marched on Warsaw.

An optimistic congress

At the opening session of the Second Comintern Congress on 19 July 1920, Zinoviev struck a solemn note: 'The Second Congress of the International entered history at the same moment as it opened. Remember this day. Know that it is the recompense for all our privations, for our hard, determined struggle. Tell your children, and explain what it meant. Hold the imprint of this hour in your hearts!'[1] Later he was to recall:

> In the congress hall hung a great map on which was marked every day the movement of our armies. And the delegates every morning stood with breathless interest before this map. It was a sort of symbol: the best representatives of the international proletariat with breathless interest, with palpitating heart, followed every advance of our armies, and all perfectly realised that, if the military aim set by our army was achieved, it would mean an immense acceleration of the international proletarian revolution.[2]

On this point, the foreign and the Russian delegates were in agreement. During the discussion of an appeal drafted by Paul Levi and addressed to the world proletariat on the subject of the Polish War, Ernst Däumig, one of the four delegates of the USPD, declared: 'Every kilometre which the Red Army wins . . . is a step towards the Revolution in Germany.'[3] The Russians modified the draft texts at the last minute to take into account what they regarded as a new conjuncture of events. For this reason, the resolution which Lenin drafted on tasks on 4 July which included the phrase: 'However, it does follow that the Communist Parties' current task consists not in accelerating the revolution, but in intensifying the preparation of the proletariat'[4] was charged in the draft finally submitted to the Congress to: 'The present task

---

[1] *Der Zweite Kongress der Kommunistischen Internationale*, op. cit., p. 14.
[2] Quoted in Carr, op. cit., p. 188.
[3] *Der Zweite Kongress der Kommunistischen Internationale*, op. cit., p. 370.
[4] V.I. Lenin, 'Theses on the Fundamental Tasks of the Second Congress of the Communist International', *Collected Works*, Volume 31, op. cit., p. 189.

of the Communist Parties is now to accelerate the revolution, without provoking it by artificial means before adequate preparation can have been made.'[5]

All this seemed to prove to the Communists that the postwar revolutionary wave, hitherto confined to the defeated countries, was in the process of extending to the victorious ones, France, Britain and Italy. From this viewpoint, the construction of real Communist Parties was becoming ever more urgent. For an approaching revolution, an organisation, an instrument, a leadership were needed very quickly. Lenin wrote:

> The Second International has definitely been smashed. Aware that the Second International is beyond hope, the intermediate parties and groups of the 'centre' are trying to lean on the Communist International, which is steadily gaining in strength. At the same time, however, they hope to retain a degree of 'autonomy' that will enable them to pursue their previous opportunist or 'centrist' policies. The Communist International is, to a certain extent, becoming the vogue. The desire of certain leading 'centre' groups to join the Third International provides oblique confirmation that it has won the sympathy of the vast majority of class-conscious workers throughout the world, and is becoming a more powerful force with each day.[6]

The requests of the centrist parties to join the International had to be examined with the greatest caution. If they were accepted unconditionally, it would be with the opportunist leaders at their head. The Bolsheviks thought that they had nothing to expect from such leaders but 'active sabotage of the revolution', as the experiences in Hungary and Germany had shown. There was not enough time to eliminate them by a political struggle from within. It was therefore necessary to take precautions in advance to prevent them bringing problems into the International, 'to put a lock . . . a solid guard on the door', as Zinoviev said.[7]

This concern, plus the need to concentrate the Bolshevik experience within a few points as an instrument of political clarification for parties joining the

---

[5] *Der Zweite Kongress der Kommunistischen Internationale*, op. cit., pp. 751–2. Meyer specified at a subsequent KPD congress that these changes had been made necessary by 'the situation of revolutionary crisis created by the offensive on Warsaw' (*Bericht über den 5 Parteitag der Kommunistischen Partei Deutschlands (Sektion der Kommunistischen Internationale), vom 1 bis 3 November in Berlin*, Berlin, 1921, p. 118).

[6] V.I. Lenin, 'The Terms of Admission into the Communist International', *Collected Works*, Volume 31, op. cit., p. 206.

[7] *Der Zweite Kongress der Kommunistischen Internationale*, op. cit., p. 696.

International, led the Russian Communists to propose to the Congress nineteen conditions with which applicants were to comply.[8] This applied both to existing members and to parties applying for admission, whether they were centrist, such as the USPD, which still included strong social-democratic currents, or ultra-leftist, such as the KAPD. These nineteen conditions were modified by the congress to become the celebrated 'Twenty-One Conditions', which expressed the Bolsheviks' conception of what a Communist Party should be.

The first duty of Communists was to give a 'genuinely Communist' character to their day-to-day agitation and propaganda. The objective of the dictatorship of the proletariat must be presented to the working masses in such a way that its indispensability would be clear from their day-to-day experience.[9] Reformist and centrist elements were to be systematically *dismissed* – the word is emphasised in the draft – from positions of responsibility in workers' organisations, and replaced by tested Communists, workers promoted from the rank and file if necessary. The activity of Communists could not be confined within the limits approved by bourgeois legality:

> In almost all the countries of Europe and America, the class struggle is entering the phase of civil war. In these conditions, Communists can place no trust in bourgeois legality. They must *everywhere* build up a parallel illegal organisation, which, at the decisive moment, will be in a position to help the party fulfil its duty to the revolution.[10]

In connection with this, Communists must carry out systematic agitational and propaganda work within the army, and create Communist cells in it. Refusal to carry on such activity, which would be partly illegal, was considered as incompatible with membership of the International. The Communist Parties must develop systematic agitational work directed at the working people of the countryside, relying upon workers who had preserved their rural connections.

One of the most important tasks facing Communists consisted of a determined break from both the social-patriotism of the reformists and the social-pacifism of the centrists. Communists must systematically demonstrate to the workers that, 'without the revolutionary overthrow of capitalism, no

---

[8] V.I. Lenin, 'The Terms of Admission into the Communist International', op. cit., pp. 207–11.

[9] Ibid., p. 207.

[10] Ibid., p. 208.

international arbitration courts, no talk about a reduction of armaments, no "democratic" reorganisation of the League of Nations will save mankind from new imperialist wars'.[11] The break from the reformists and the centrists must be carried through 'imperatively and uncompromisingly' in every party, particularly in respect of notorious reformist personalities like the Italian Turati. At the same time, the Communist Parties must resist the imperialist undertakings of their own bourgeoisie, and 'must support – in deed, not merely in word – every colonial liberation movement'.[12]

The ninth condition returned to the themes which were developed in the polemic against the ultra-leftists. It instructed the Communist Parties to work within the trade unions, by establishing cells within them that were 'completely subordinate to the party as a whole'. It was these cells – later to be called 'fractions' – which 'by their sustained and unflagging work, win the unions over to the communist cause' and 'unmask the treachery of the social-patriots and the vacillations of the centrists'. Within the unions, it was necessary to fight against 'the yellow Amsterdam International', and the International must do all that is possible to break the unions from Amsterdam, and strengthen 'the emerging international federation of red trade unions which are associated with the Communist International'.[13]

Communists must use bourgeois parliaments as platforms for revolutionary agitation, but must ensure the reliability of the parliamentary groups by purging them of unreliable elements, and subordinating them to the Party's Central Committee. The publishing and press departments of the Party must be under the control of the Central Committee.[14]

In matters of organisation, Communist Parties must be organised in conformity with the principle of democratic centralism. The thirteenth condition laid down:

> In this period of acute civil war, the communist parties can perform their duty only if they are organised in a most centralised manner, are marked by an iron discipline bordering on military discipline, and have strong and authoritative party centres invested with wide powers and enjoying the unanimous confidence of the membership.[15]

[11] Ibid.
[12] Ibid., p. 209.
[13] Ibid., pp. 209–10.
[14] Ibid., p. 210.
[15] Ibid.

Moreover, the leaders of Communist Parties needed to ensure the integrity of the rank and file by carrying out a periodic purge, which in the case of parties which carried on legal activities, meant systematically removing dubious members.

The fifteenth condition laid down that Communist Parties were obliged 'selflessly to help any Soviet republic in its struggle against counter-revolutionary forces'.[16]

The last four conditions spelt out the immediate requirements for parties that were either actual or prospective members of the International. They were to revise their former programmes to meet both national conditions and the decisions of the International, with the revisions being ratified by the ECCI. The decisions of the International's congresses and the ECCI were to be strictly followed. Every party which wished to join must call itself 'the *Communist* Party of the country in question (Section of the Third International)', in order to bring out clearly the difference between the Communist Parties and the old Socialist or Social-Democratic parties which had betrayed the working class. Lastly, they were all to convene their own congresses at the end of the World Congress in order to put on record that they accepted these conditions.[17]

These were draconian conditions, and they were further strengthened at the congress. They implied for every party of social-democratic or centrist origin, whether in the International or not, as well as for the ultra-left groups which wanted to join or to remain in the International, an early split on their part, as the Bolshevik leaders were well aware. Trotsky declared:

> There is no doubt that the proletariat would be in power in all countries, if there were not still between them [communist parties] and the masses, between the revolutionary mass and the advanced groups of the revolutionary mass, a large, powerful and complex machine, the parties of the Second International and the trade unions, which in the epoch of the disintegration, the dying of the bourgeoisie, placed their machine at the service of that bourgeoisie.... From now on, from this congress, the split in the world working class will proceed with tenfold greater rapidity. Programme against programme; tactic against tactic; method against method.[18]

---

[16] Ibid.

[17] Ibid., pp. 210–1.

[18] Speech on 7 August 1920 at a joint meeting of delegates to the World Congress, members of the Moscow Soviet, and representatives of trade unions and factory committees (Degras, op. cit., p. 110).

To be sure, no Communist underestimated the negative consequences of any split in the workers' movement. However, convinced as the Communists were that the world was in a period of 'sharp civil war', and that the time of the seizure of power was near, at least in the most advanced countries, they decided, without a real preliminary discussion, to apply these conditions.

The KAPD and the conditions for admission

The first consequence of this elaboration of the conditions for admission to the Communist International was to be a serious deterioration of the relations between the ECCI and the KAPD. At the end of May, with no news from Appel and Jung, or about the negotiations in Moscow, the KAPD sent Otto Rühle as its delegate to the Second Comintern Congress. His clandestine journey was followed by that of August Merges at the beginning of July.[19]

Rühle's political evolution was distancing him from Communism. He was hostile in principle from the beginning to the foundation of the KAPD as a 'party', and was very critical of what he observed in Russia under the dictatorship of war communism. He was appalled by what he saw as 'ultra-centralist' practices, and regarded as absurd and disastrous the desire of the Russians to apply such a system to Communist Parties and to the Communist International itself. Merges and Rühle sharply opposed the conditions for admission on the grounds that they were simultaneously opportunist and centralist. They regarded them as a barely improved repetition of the Zentrale's theses at the Heidelberg Congress of the KPD(S), which had split the Party. Rühle said: 'They were now a little amplified, a little more softened on the level of theory, and considerably strengthened on the level of centralism and dictatorship.'[20]

Confronted by their opposition, Radek said that there could be no question of admitting them to the Congress. Lenin and Zinoviev agreed, and Rühle and Merges leftists Moscow to return to Germany.[21] This setback did not suit the Bolsheviks and the members of the ECCI, for whom the presence of the ultra-leftists would have been valuable at the time of intense discussions with the centrists and rightists. A meeting of the ECCI immediately after the two German delegates had left decided to make a conciliatory proposal to them,

---

[19] Bock, op. cit., pp. 254–5.
[20] Ibid., p. 255.
[21] Ibid.

offering that they take part in the Congress not as full delegates, but in a consultative capacity. The two representatives of the KAPD received the proposal before they had left Soviet territory. They rejected it, and continued on their way.[22] This was ultimately a fortunate solution for the ECCI, because, as we shall see, when the delegation from the KPD(S) realised that the KAPD had been invited, they decided to leave the Congress if Merges and Rühle or any other KAPD leader took part in it, even in a consultative capacity![23]

The Independents and the conditions for admission

The USPD delegates took an active part in the conflict over the conditions for admission. The Russians, supported by the foreign Communist delegates, fought hard to convince – and, if necessary, to coerce – to ensure that the USPD would vote their way on this issue at its Party Congress. Dittmann and Crispien, who represented the USPD right wing and apparatus, felt that, although the Party press as a whole and most of the apparatus were hostile to joining the Comintern, the Left was growing rapidly, which meant that they were negotiating in a difficult position, at an international Communist congress held in the capital of the world revolution.

Dittmann said that he agreed with the theses proposed by the ECCI, although he advanced a number of objections. The first concerned the proclaimed aims of the parties which join the International:

> If our party adopted these theses in their present form, it would then lose its legal status. We believe that we must make use of legal means to rally the working masses . . . we know that the general strike is not enough to take power, and that armed insurrection is necessary. But if we say this openly in our theses, our party will immediately cease to be a legal party.[24]

He protested against a statement by Radek that the Independent leaders could any day be arrested and shot, and went on:

> We believe that we must use legal means as far as possible. We have over fifty daily papers. This press is a means of revolutionary propaganda and action which we must maintain, and which would be completely lost if we

---

[22] Ibid.
[23] *Bericht über den 5 Parteitag der KPD*, op. cit., pp. 27–9, 36.
[24] Report of the discussions on 25 July of the commission on the affiliation of the USPD to the Communist International, *Die Rote Fahne*, 2 September 1920.

fell into illegality. . . . The Communists know from experience how difficult it is for an illegal party to carry out propaganda work.[25]

He likewise raised other objections to the 'centralisation' of Communist Parties and the International:

> I was always in favour of strong centralisation in the old Social Democracy. But the experience of this bureaucratised Social Democracy alienated many revolutionary workers from centralisation. This is an understandable reaction against the centralised bureaucracy of the old Social Democracy. For that reason, we encounter a tendency hostile to the centralisation of the Party. For example, the Gotha Congress rejected control of the Party press by the Zentrale. This state of mind cannot be overcome overnight.[26]

Crispien declared that he agreed with the theses on four essential points: a centralised organisation of the International, the centralisation of the Party (which the USPD should be able to implement), and the drafting of a programme after a congress had enabled the Leipzig resolutions to be reconciled with the Moscow ones. As for its methods of struggle, he declared:

> We are living in the period of the struggle for power, and our movement must preserve its legal character. The masses would not understand an illegal party. We cannot declare ourselves openly for the arming of the proletariat. . . . We do not discount the possibility of working wholly in illegality. We wish to use every means to struggle, but we cannot declare it openly and officially.[27]

The Independent delegates came under fire from the ECCI's representatives. Zinoviev asked them whether they really believed that not declaring themselves in favour of illegal work would protect them against repression. Radek told them that no party aiming to be revolutionary could dispense with propaganda work in the army, and this necessitated an illegal apparatus. Ernst Meyer was sceptical about the declarations of Crispien and Dittmann that they agreed with the theses, and he demanded guarantees for the future. Zinoviev stressed that the promotion of revolutionary ideas was more important than running fifty daily papers, and he asked the Independent leaders to consider breaking from Hilferding.

[25] Ibid.
[26] Ibid.
[27] Ibid.

The Swiss delegate, Humbert-Droz, emphasised the international aspects of the question, the fact that elements in all the centrist parties retained contact with the Second International. He accused the right-wing centrists of aiming to corrupt the Third International from within, and drew the conclusion that the opportunist elements must be kept out. Crispien retreated without yielding, and gave a glimpse of a way out for the future: 'Our party has always evolved towards the left. It has already rid itself of its right wing. Bernstein has resigned. Kautsky has no influence, and no longer plays any role in the party. No one can say that Kautsky and Ströbel are building a right wing. They are alone and isolated.'[28] The resistance of Crispien and Dittmann to principles which the Communists regarded as fundamental led to a hardening in the Commission. In the seventh paragraph, it specifically added Kautsky and Hilferding to Turati and Modigliani as 'notorious reformists'. At the suggestion of Lenin himself, it inserted the obligation of the parties' press to publish the documents of the ECCI, and that a special congress be held within four months to approve the conditions for admission by the parties seeking admission.[29] The discussion on the conditions for admission continued on 29–30 July. Zinoviev was the rapporteur, and he emphasised that the International, which was a mere propaganda society, had to become an organisation of struggle, which implied a complete break from the outlook and the ideas of Kautsky.[30] Radek delivered a criticism of the policies of the USPD since November 1918.[31] Meyer dealt in particular with the USPD leadership's activities and positions since the Leipzig Congress, and declared his mistrust of all the Independent leaders' declarations; a revolutionary party proved itself in practice, and the USPD would not be able to pursue revolutionary practice if it did not rid itself of its opportunist elements.

The representative of the KPD(S) also made clear that he wanted a direct appeal from the ECCI to the Independent workers in order to organise the necessary split in the USPD.[32] Crispien and Dittmann spoke at the end of the first day. Crispien stressed the fact that his party essentially agreed with the theses of the International, but said that its policy of expulsions led to

---

[28] Ibid.
[29] Ibid.
[30] *Der Zweite Kongress der Kommunistischen Internationale*, op. cit., pp. 245–50.
[31] Ibid., pp. 256–61.
[32] Ibid., pp. 293–8.

splits, which were always damaging. His only criticism of the Russians was of their insistence that their experience was universally valid. He declared that terror was a circumstantial feature of the struggle for socialism of which Western countries would not need.[33] Dittmann vigorously answered Radek, and defended the USPD leadership, declaring that it had always been with the mass of the German workers.[34]

On the following day, Rakovsky took up Dittmann's justification of the policy of collaborating in the Ebert government. He declared: 'The German Independents, unfortunately, to the extent that they are represented here by comrades Dittmann and Crispien, seem to have forgotten nothing in the course of these last two or three years, but not to have learned anything either.'[35]

Lenin devoted himself to a short but incisive criticism of the method of thinking of Dittmann and Crispien, and did his best to show that it was entirely inspired by Kautsky's method.[36] Paul Levi referred to the terms which Crispien and Dittmann had used, in order to develop his ideas about the relations between the Party and the masses. He stressed that the Independents, who were seeking to be 'with the masses', committed a 'fundamental mistake' about the role of the Party, because they deprived it of its *raison d'être*, to be the revolutionary leadership of the masses.[37] Däumig expressed regret that the debates of the preceding day had led him to feel that the International was still made up only of sects. He protested against the caricature of his party that Radek in particular had made, recalled that it was always formed of two sharply opposed wings, and he emphasised past problems for which the Communists were to blame. He mentioned the foundation of the KPD(S) with 'undesirable' elements, but nonetheless declared that he unreservedly accepted the conditions for admission to the International, which he undertook to defend in the Party when he returned to Germany.[38]

Finally, Stoecker declared his surprise at Meyer's call for a split on the preceding day. He too emphasised the essential points of agreement between the USPD and the International, and reminded the Congress that the KPD(S) had for a long time voiced in Germany the ideas which were now those of

---

[33] Ibid., pp. 310–20.
[34] Ibid., pp. 320–9.
[35] Ibid., p. 334.
[36] Ibid., pp. 346–53.
[37] Ibid., pp. 353–62.
[38] Ibid., pp. 366–73.

the KAPD, which had now split from it. He supported acceptance of the conditions of admission, and ended with an appeal for unity in the ranks of the revolutionaries for the struggle that would be waged in a few months' time.[39]

The nineteen conditions became, successively, eighteen, with the amalgamation of two of them, and then twenty-one, with the acceptance of additional ones. These came from Humbert-Droz and Bordiga. They stated that a party joining the International must at the congress which endorsed its joining elect a central committee with at least two-thirds of its members having been in favour of joining the International prior to its Second Congress, and that, after the congress, anyone who opposed the twenty-one conditions would be expelled.[40]

Disagreements behind the scenes?

From then on, there was no longer any ambiguity about the question which faced the USPD. As the price for being accepted into the Communist International included the exclusion of Hilferding, Kautsky and other right-wingers, this effectively meant splitting the Party, because Crispien and Dittmann opposed it. Zinoviev, moreover, told them this clearly at one of the last meetings between the ECCI and the four Independent delegates.[41]

On this point, Levi expressed reservations during the debates in the Commission. He agreed with the conditions for admission, and voted for them along with the overwhelming majority of the Congress. But, behind closed doors, he stressed that he thought it important to avoid taking organisational measures which could assure an oppressive character. The struggle which was opening within the socialist parties throughout the world on the question of joining the Communist International would be a struggle without mercy. It was to the Communists' interest that it should appear clearly as a political struggle. To include clauses about organisation in the conditions for admission opened the danger of letting this struggle be diverted 'towards organisational matters, thus giving the trade-union bosses the chance that they desired to attack on this ground, while keeping silent about the political questions'. He therefore proposed that the questions about statutes and

---

[39] Ibid., pp. 374–82.
[40] Ibid., pp. 742–5. It is interesting here to note the role of Bordiga, who was one of the outstanding representatives of the ultra-left current of the International.
[41] Report of the discussion on 10 August, *Die Rote Fahne*, 10 October 1920.

other organisational points be relegated to a secondary level, and that every effort be concentrated on 'raising to the forefront the political conditions to be fulfilled'.[42]

Levi was clearly worried that Hilferding and others, with the help of Crispien and Dittmann, would use the Communist International's organisational strictures to prevent a large number of revolutionary workers from joining the KPD(S), as they would be able to hide the key political issues behind organisational factors. Levi did not seem to share entirely the optimism of the majority of the Congress about revolutionary perspectives in Europe. He insisted that the parties which joined the International had to be purged by means of a wide political discussion, but this was not an urgent matter because revolution was not on the immediate agenda. In the Commission, he defended Lenin's original text against the proposed new draft.[43] He annoyed Lenin and nearly all the delegates when he expressed pessimistic caution about the possibility of the German workers staging an uprising at the approach of the Red Army.[44]

There were other signs of growing tension between Levi and the Russian leaders, in particular Zinoviev. At the start of the Congress, this took the form of a sharp crisis over the decision of the ECCI to admit the KAPD to the debates. The Russian delegates, wishing to 'activate' the German Party, put forward this proposal, believing that the revolutionary fighters of the KAPD would soon be needed again in the ranks of the International. As soon as they arrived, the delegates of the KPD(S) met the Political Bureau of the Russian Party, whom they tried in vain to persuade to reverse their decision, and they then announced that they would leave the Congress if the KAPD delegates were admitted.[45] Radek supported them, and this position contrary to the discipline of the Russian Party resulted in his being removed from the post of ECCI secretary, which he had held since he returned from Germany.[46] The outburst soon calmed down when Rühle and Merges, the KAPD delegates, refused to take part in the Congress. But, in a general way, the attitude of the German delegation and the tone which their spokesman, Levi, used were severely condemned, both by Bukharin, who won over the rest of the

[42] 'Report of the Second World Congress', Levi Archives, P55/7, p. 8.
[43] *Die Rote Fahne*, 22 January 1922.
[44] M. Buber-Neumann, *Von Potsdam nach Moskau*, Stuttgart, 1958, p. 81.
[45] *Bericht über den 5 Parteitag der KPD*, op. cit., pp. 27–8, 125.
[46] A. Rosmer, *Lenin's Moscow*, London, 1987, p. 93.

ECCI against the Germans, and by Alfred Rosmer, who years later was to accuse them of having attempted a 'last-minute manoeuvre'.[47]

The Russians, especially Zinoviev and Bukharin, saw here proof of hostility towards them, that the Germans were clinging to the old quarrels and the old grievances of Luxemburg and Jogiches. They freely used against them, at any rate in the corridors, the criticism which already been heard both from within the German Party and from Radek about the 'lack of contact with the masses' and the 'exaggerated anti-putschism' of the Zentrale, which resulted in a passive outlook.[48] Levi was the first target, and he had to remind those who labelled him a 'right-winger' that he was the first in the leadership to criticise the passivity of the Zentrale at the time of the Kapp Putsch.[49] But he appears to have felt very bitter about these attacks, and confided to those near him that he was beginning to ask himself whether Luxemburg and Jogiches had not been right to oppose the formation of an International in which there was no effective counterweight to the influence of the Bolsheviks.[50] However, none of this came out in the sessions. Levi was elected to the ECCI as deputy to Meyer, who was elected by the Congress and was to stay in Moscow, where he would work in the 'small bureau'.

Another decision of the Second Comintern Congress was to have important consequences for the future of the German workers' movement. As Rosmer said, the trade-union question was discussed 'for a long time', but was 'the least fully and the least profitably treated question',[51] on the basis of a report by Radek who was notoriously incompetent to deal with the subject.[52] The resolution was adopted after a sharp debate, and against the opposition of the British and the Americans. It repeated the line which the ECCI had earlier adopted and had been summarised in the 'Twenty-One Conditions'. Whilst the Congress did not take a formal decision on the creation of a new trade-union international, it was whilst it was meeting that a provisional international committee was formed, with Lozovsky as its chairman, to call and prepare an 'international congress of red trade unions', intended to undertake the

---

[47] Ibid., p. 95.
[48] *Bericht über den 5 Parteitag der KPD*, op. cit., p. 28.
[49] Ibid., p. 35.
[50] W. Herzog, 'Journal de Russie', *Forum*, no. 5, April 1921, p. 278; statements by Brandler and Geyer in R. Lowenthal, 'The Bolshevisation of the Spartacus League', *St Anthony's Papers*, no. 9, p. 44.
[51] Rosmer, op. cit., p. 85.
[52] *Der Zweite Kongress der Kommunistischen Internationale*, op. cit., pp. 482ff.

struggle against the 'scab' Amsterdam trade-union international. The British historian E.H. Carr, comments that this was a 'fateful decision',[53] taken amid confusion, and one which was to serve the Social Democrats as a pretext to carry out a split in the trade unions, which was often their last resort, but which could be blamed on the Communists, who from this time were linked to the Red Trade-Union International.

The battle for the majority of the Independents

The debates at the Second Comintern Congress had been dominated by the concern of the leaders of the International about Germany, and by the 'Twenty-One Conditions' which had been devised to remove the right-wing Independents. In the political battle which followed this Congress, the ECCI engaged in the first of a series of struggles to win the workers who supported the socialist and centrist parties, a decisive stage on the road to constructing 'mass Communist Parties'. The ECCI threw its full weight and prestige into the fight to win the majority of the 800,000-strong USPD, with its broad range of organisations, its 54 daily papers, and, above all, its working-class cadres. The question was not limited to Germany, but was international scope, and was treated almost as a diplomatic negotiation between the USPD and the International, itself a product of the Russian Party and the Russian Revolution. The KPD(S), the heir of the Spartacus League, was relegated to the second division; the Russian activists of October 1917 addressed the German Independents's role. The whole issue revolved around Moscow directly.

The USPD delegation returned divided from the Congress. Däumig and Stoecker declared in favour of outright acceptance of the 'Twenty-One Conditions', which implied early fusion with the KPD(S). Dittmann and Crispien called on the Party's activists to reject these conditions, together with 'centralism' and 'Moscow dictatorship'. A preparatory conference for a Party congress showed that the USPD was divided between two virtually equal-sized tendencies.[54] Nearly the whole of the Party's apparatus and press, its elected representatives in the Reichstag and regional and local authorities, and an important section of its trade-union officials were against accepting the 'Twenty-One Conditions'. But the current in favour of Moscow grew

---

[53] Carr, op. cit., p. 207.
[54] Prager, in *Geschichte der USPD*, Berlin, 1921, p. 222, however, states that an overwhelming majority were going to declare for the conditions to be rejected.

stronger day by day. The direct support which it had in the KPD(S) enabled
it to react effectively, returning blow for blow, counterposing leadership to
leadership and apparatus to apparatus.[55] The Right understood that time was
on the side of the supporters of the International, and it did what it could
quickly to terminate a discussion in which it was being forced on to the
defensive. The Conference was to be prepared in five weeks, and it was finally
brought forward by a week, from 20 October to the 12th.[56]

On 29 September, the Presidium of the ECCI addressed an *Open Letter* to
all members of the USPD. This drew a balance sheet of the negotiations. It
explained that a process of differentiation was proceeding throughout the
world in the centrist parties, and that the Communist International was obliged
to accelerate and sharpen this process, in order free the militant workers in
these parties from the grip of the reformist leaders:

> We cannot accept into the Communist International all those who wish to
> join. In a certain sense, the Communist International has become fashionable.
> We do not want our Communist International to be like the bankrupt Second
> International. We open our doors wide to every proletarian revolutionary
> mass organisation. But we shall think ten times before we open the doors
> of the Communist International to newcomers from the camp of the petty-
> bourgeois bureaucrats and opportunists like Hilferding and Crispien.[57]

The ECCI insisted on the need for strong, centralised Communist Parties that
could lead the proletariat to victory in a civil war. Moreover:

> 'The principle of centralism is no less relevant on the international scale.
> The Communist International will be a centralised association of organisations,
> or it will not exist. . . . The imperialist war has created a situation in which
> every single important step forward by the working class in any country
> will have repercussions throughout the whole workers' movement and in
> the class struggle in every other country. All the fundamental questions

---

[55] The right exploited this argument to the full. It said that the 'neo-Communists'
were acting as traitors to the Party and agents for the KPD(S). At the National
Conference on 6 September, Dittmann told with indignation how in the Reichstag he
had 'surprised' a meeting between Levi, Geyer and Wilhelm Koenen (*USPD Protokoll
der Reichskonferenz*, 1920, p. 176).

[56] *Freiheit*, 17 September 1920. The Left voted against this, and issued a protest,
published by the KPD(S) in *Die Rote Fahne* on 21 September, which was to be denounced
as a proof of 'treachery'. The ECCI supported the protest (*Die Rote Fahne*, 30 September
1920).

[57] *Die Rote Fahne*, 12 October 1920.

of our life are now determined on the international scale. We need an
International to act as an international general staff of the workers in all
countries. We cannot transform the Communist International into a mere
letter-box. . . . There are historic circumstances when to force a split is the
sacred duty of every revolutionary.[58]

It concluded that the circumstances called precisely for a split, 'if we wish at
the decisive moment to be firm, united and resolute'.

The two tendencies of the USPD confronted each other in passionate debate
in every city in Germany. The main support for the left-wing Independents
came from the Communist press, because they had few papers of their own.
Their organ, *Kommunistische Rundschau*, began to appear only on 1 October.
On the Left, the fight was led by Levi, with Däumig, Stoecker, Curt Geyer
and Wilhelm Koenen. On the other side, the soul of the resistance was the
metalworkers' leader, Robert Dissmann,[59] himself a former supporter of the
Left, with Crispien and Dittmann. Dissmann organised the trade-union cadres
throughout the party against the Moscow 'splitters', who, he said, were
preparing with their red unions to split the unions as well as the parties.

People left and right made up their minds, as Zetkin put it, 'for or against
Moscow'.[60] All the unsolved questions of the workers' movement were
passionately debated in the most polemical forms. For the Right, the choice
was between the 'independence', the 'self-determination' of the socialist
parties, 'freedom of opinion', on the one side, and 'the dictates of the Moscow
Pope', 'colonisation' and even 'Asiatic barbarism', on the other. For the Left,
the choice was between 'opportunism', 'reformism' and 'class collaboration',
on the one side, and 'the centralised revolutionary organisation', 'discipline'
and 'class consciousness', on the other. The Right blamed the bankruptcy of
the Majority Social Democrats upon the bureaucratic centralisation and
omnipotence of their apparatus. The Left and the Communists retorted that
it was their opportunist, bourgeois and reformist outlook that permitted the

---

[58] *Die Rote Fahne*, 14 October 1920.
[59] In the trade unions, the line of cleavage with regard to Moscow passed through
the centre of the left wing. Otto Tost, Schliestedt, Urich and Ziska were with Dissmann
against Moscow, and were soon to receive reinforcement from a defector from the
KPD(S), Paul Lange. Osker, Rusch, Niederkirchner, Grylewicz, Richard Müller, Malzahn,
Neumann and Böttcher were in favour. The Left lost important trade-union positions
such as the local commission of the trade unions in Berlin and the editorship of
Metallarbeiter-Zeitung, which was taken from Richard Müller in July.
[60] C. Zetkin, 'Der Weg nach Moskau', *Die Rote Fahne*, 3 October 1920.

means to dominate the ends, placing the precious weapons of centralisation and discipline at the service of a policy that betrayed the working class. The Right drew attention to the role of the Communists in the putsches of 1919, and the Left replied by drawing attention to that of Ledebour at the time of the uprising of January 1919 in Berlin.[61]

The issues in the struggle were international. Each camp mobilised its allies in every possible country. In the end, the leading figures in this battle were not themselves German. The ECCI appointed to represent it in Germany Zinoviev, Lozovsky, who was already there, and Bukharin,[62] who in the end was not to come. The Right was supplemented by the old Menshevik, Julius Martov, the former comrade and later the adversary of Lenin, recently exiled from Russia, and by French Socialists, from the social-chauvinist Salomon Grumbach to the centrist Jean Longuet, the grandson of Marx.

The votes to appoint the delegates took place in a tense atmosphere, and led to extremely close results in all the important places. In Berlin, those endorsing the 'Twenty-One Conditions' won by 15,531 votes to 13,856, which gave 12 delegates to the Left against 11 for the Right. Amongst the former were the old revolutionary delegates, Heinrich Malzahn, who headed the list, Paul Eckert and Paul Scholze.[63] In several district or regional congresses the split took place even before the Congress. For example, in Württemberg, the supporters of the Left, led by Böttcher, withdrew as a sign of protest.[64] In the Lower Rhineland, the supporters of Crispien left the Congress, which having been placed in a minority, they declared to be 'illegal' and 'unconstitutional'.[65]

When Zinoviev disembarked at Stettin from the Estonian steamship *Wasa*, Curt Geyer could triumphantly announce him 'We have the majority.'[66] But it was a weak majority, which the Left itself estimated on the eve of the Congress to amount to barely 50,000 votes in all.[67]

---

[61] 'Georg Ledebour, die Revolution und die anderen', *Die Rote Fahne*, 5 September 1920, and Ledebour's reply (*Freiheit*, 25 September 1920, morning edition) provide interesting details on the events of January 1919.

[62] Letter from Zinoviev, dated 30 September, *Die Rote Fahne*, 2 October 1920.

[63] *Freiheit*, 5 October 1920, morning edition.

[64] *Freiheit*, 6 October 1920.

[65] *Freiheit*, 12 October 1920.

[66] G. Zinoviev, *Zwölf Tage in Deutschland*, Hamburg, 1921, p. 5.

[67] Ibid., p. 11.

The Halle Congress in October 1920

By the time the Special Congress of the USPD opened at Halle on 12 October, the Party had been pretty much rent asunder by the struggle for mandates during the preceding weeks. When Zinoviev entered the congress meeting-place, he noticed that there were really 'two parties in the hall'.[68] It was an astonishing spectacle, and this state of affairs was officially recognised by both tendencies, who drew the consequences in advance. The Presidium of the Congress itself was formed on a basis of parity, so that the Congress throughout had two Chairmen, Dittmann for the Right, and Otto Brass for the Left. The left Independents explained to Zinoviev that they had agreed to parity in all the organs of the Congress, including the Presidium and the Mandates Commission, because they feared that the Right would seize on the first pretext to split before a fundamental discussion, and could then blame the 'dictatorial methods' of the supporters of Moscow.[69] The discussion proceeded in a supercharged atmosphere, sometimes interrupted by violent disturbances. But, for most of the time, the delegates followed it passionately, understanding that, irrespective of their tendency, they were living through an event of historic importance for the workers' movement.

The Congress opened with the speeches of the Party's delegates to the Second Comintern Congress, in the order of Crispien, Däumig, Dittmann and Stoecker. But these were mere skirmishes. The battle really began when Zinoviev mounted the platform. He was to speak for more than four hours, in German, with much difficulty and a certain apprehension at the beginning, and then with an authority which enabled him to win his greatest oratorical triumph in an already distinguished career. He took up the five points on which the right Independents declared that they differed from the Bolsheviks: the Bolsheviks' agrarian policy, the national policy in the East, the trade-union question, the terror, and the role of the soviets.

He declared that, on the agrarian question, the Bolsheviks had followed the only line which could have led to the victory of the Revolution. When the opportunists opposed in the name of 'Marxism' the slogan of distributing the land, they showed the narrowness of their views, and, above all, their incapacity to grasp the worldwide character of the Revolution. For there would be no international proletarian revolution without the national and

---

[68] Ibid., p. 13.
[69] Ibid.

agrarian revolution in the East and Far East, no proletarian revolution in Europe without the armed uprising of the peasants in India and China. When the opportunists denied colonial problems, they, like the Social Democrats, were in fact supporting imperialism. This same fundamental attitude explained their diatribes against 'red terror' and the 'dictatorship' of the Party, because they had by no means devoted the same energy to defending the Russian proletariat against the 'white terror' which governments supported by their Social-Democratic brothers had set in motion. After the collapse of the Second International, the bourgeoisie retained one stronghold in the workers' movement: the trade-union federation based in Amsterdam, which had today become the prime enemy of the revolutionaries in the workers' movement.

Zinoviev said that the differences were not really about the 'Twenty-One Conditions' which the Communist International laid down: 'We are in the process of bringing about a split, not because you would like 18 conditions instead of 21, but because we disagree with you on the question of the world revolution, democracy and the dictatorship of the proletariat.'[70] He said that this congress reminded him of the congresses of the Russian Social Democrats at which Mensheviks and Bolsheviks confronted each other in the years after 1905. It was about world communism or reformism. At the side of Hilferding stood all the leaders of reformism, Kautsky and Dittmann, the former collaborators of Ebert, Grumbach, the French social-chauvinist, Julius Martov, of course, and 'the English Mensheviks, Henderson and MacDonald'. Zinoviev said that fear of revolution was the motivation behind their policies, even though they tried to hide this behind phrases about 'chaos' and 'famine' and everything that they thought went on in Russia. When Crispien was reporting on the Second Comintern Congress, he said that the socialist movement was then in the same situation as Marx and his comrades in 1849, 'as if', said Zinoviev, 'the world revolution could no longer come about in the near future'.[71]

Zinoviev said that the Right based its perspectives on the long-outdated prospect of peaceful development. The Right did not believe in the world revolution. It made ironic remarks about the 'fanaticism', the 'naïveté' and the 'illusions' of the revolutionaries: 'Can anyone doubt that, without what

---

[70] *Unabhängige Sozialdemokratische Partei: Protokoll über die Verhandlungen des ausserordentlichen Parteitags in Halle, vom 12 Bis 17 Oktober 1920*, Berlin, 1920, p. 156.
[71] Ibid., pp. 147–8.

they call this "fanaticism" of the masses, the liberation of the working class would be in the realm of impossibility?'[72]

The truth was otherwise. The President of the Third International declared: 'We are as we were in 1847!' Revolution was knocking on the door, both in the Balkans and in Great Britain, but especially in Germany. Throughout the whole of Western Europe, the situation was objectively revolutionary. The single bulwark which ensured the defence of the bourgeoisie was the labour aristocracy, with its trade-union and political leaders who paralysed the working class from within. It was this 'spearhead of the bourgeoisie' which had to be destroyed today if victory was to be won tomorrow. Acceptance by the Congress of the 'Twenty-One Conditions' would be the first step towards the victory of the proletarian revolution in Germany.

The difficult task of refuting arguments which undoubtedly influenced the Congress fell to Hilferding. He was a subtle theoretician, a follower of Kautsky, but not a popular leader, and the devastating attack by the Bolshevik leader forced him on to the defensive. He invoked the authority of Luxemburg to combat the conception of a centralised International and centralised parties, quoting at length her polemic against Lenin in 1904. To defend the policy of the Independents in 1918–20, he pleaded for 'realism', and even sought shelter behind Lenin who had said 'the republic is worth more the monarchy, and a bourgeois republic with a constituent assembly . . . is better than a republic without a constituent assembly'. In his opinion, the policy which the Bolsheviks advocated was a 'a gamble, a wager, on which it was impossible to build a party'.[73] It was false to say that the opponents of the 'Twenty-One Conditions' were opponents of the proletarian revolution, or even that they denied that the wave of revolution was rising at the time. He declared:

> Many tendencies towards a revolutionary development exist in Western Europe today, and it is our duty to direct and to lead them further. But, comrades, the course of this revolutionary development cannot be determined from outside. It depends on the relations of economic and social strength between the classes in the different countries, and it is utopian to suppose that one can speed it up by some slogan, through an impulsion from outside.[74]

---

[72] Ibid., p. 148.
[73] Ibid., p. 184.
[74] Ibid., p. 188.

He ended by denouncing the Communists' splitting policy as a catastrophe for the workers' movement, and the centralised International as a dangerous utopia.

The principals had spoken, and the stakes were down. The intervention of Martov was full of passion, as the old Menshevik warrior said that 'the Bolsheviks employ every means, however dubious and equivocal, to keep themselves in power',[75] and that they desired an International only in order to have at their disposal a docile instrument, but he was 'too Russian' to convince the delegates. The contribution of Lozovsky was entirely directed against the 'scab leaders' of the Amsterdam trade-union federation, and provoked indignant protests from Dissmann and his friends. This certainly caused anxiety to those who had essentially been won to the Communist theses, yet remained attached to the principle of trade-union unity. Finally, the Congress voted to accept the 'Twenty-One Conditions' for joining the Communist International by 237 votes to 156. Negotiations to fuse with the German Communist Party began.

The leaders of the right wing immediately decided to split. They challenged the right of the Congress to dissolve the Party, and decided to continue it.[76] However, at the same time, it was a momentary triumph for the Communist International, as well as a personal success for its President, Zinoviev. He was expelled from Germany, where in the end he spent only 12 days, and showed his delight in his account of the journey:

> We can, we must, say that the German proletariat is the first in Europe to get itself out of an unprecedented crisis, and to close its ranks. The old school has won. The work of the best German revolutionaries has not been in vain. A great Communist Party is born in Germany. This is going to lead to events of unprecedented historical importance.[77]

The President of the International emphasised that the workers made up a majority of the population in Germany, and that they were better organised than anywhere else. Until now, the masses had lacked a revolutionary organisation and a clear idea of their interests. The cause lay in the existence

---

[75] Ibid., p. 213.

[76] Prager (op. cit., pp. 226–9) gives a brief account of this debate with the full text of the *Manifesto of Independent Social Democracy to the German Proletariat*, proposed by Crispien and unanimously adopted.

[77] Zinoviev, *Zwölf Tage in Deutschland*, op. cit., p. 57.

of the 'labour aristocracy',[78] these hundred-thousand-odd trade-union officials who were 'the best white guard of German capital'.[79] It was necessary to drive them out in order to be able to wage the revolutionary struggle: 'The split was necessary and inevitable: it has happened. It remains for us to say: "Better late than never!"'[80] The split in the USPD opened the way to restoring revolutionary unity. A Communist Party of between 500,000 and 600,000 members would settle accounts with the reactionary leaders of the 'labour aristocracy'.[81] A page was turned in the history of the working class in Europe.

The birth of the United Communist Party

The Communist Party of Germany was ready to go forward. A few weeks after the Second Comintern Congress, it had changed its name, deleting the reference, now relegated to history, to the Spartacus League, and adopting the subtitle 'German Section of the Communist International'. In *Die Rote Fahne*, Levi hailed 'the end of the USPD' as a natural and necessary event. The Social-Democratic workers who in the course of the War, 'that first part of the Revolution', had cut their links with the old party, took along with them part of their pacifist, conservative leadership, who saw 'the alpha and omega' in returning to the Erfurt Programme as the basis for unifying all socialists: 'At Halle the Erfurt Programme, with its formal democracy, its "immediate demands", its revolution as a perspective for eternity, its "strategy of attrition", and its reformism was finally buried. It has done its job. Let it rest in peace!'[82]

The minority of the USPD, which remained around the leadership, with the largest part of the apparatus, the press, the elected representatives and, of course, the treasury, had its future with the Majority Social Democrats. As to the Left, it had gone over to Communism, and the time had come for the revolutionary fighters who had been divided since 1919 to come together. Levi wrote: '*Vorwärts* rejoices: "The End of the USPD!" Yes, the USPD is dead, along with the Erfurt Programme. But Communism is here.'[83]

---

78 Ibid., p. 82.
79 Ibid., p. 87.
80 Ibid., p. 84.
81 Ibid., p. 86.
82 *Die Rote Fahne*, 19 October 1920.
83 Ibid.

On 23 October, the Central Committee of the KPD(S) hailed the split in the USPD between the revolutionary majority and the right-wing minority, and declared in favour of the earliest possible fusion of the two German revolutionary organisations in one 'United Communist Party'.[84] On 24 October, the leadership of the left Independents elected at Halle issued an appeal to the Party and its members. It laid the blame on the Right for the 'crime' of having deliberately organised the split in order to break the front of the proletariat, and declared: 'We are the Party!' It continued: 'The road is open to unifying the conscious revolutionary proletariat, the road to constructing a powerful section of the Communist International. We shall follow this road!'[85] On 27 October, there appeared the first issue of the daily paper *Die Internationale*, 'Organ of the USPD (Left)'.

But the ECCI still hoped for a complete unification of the revolutionary forces in Germany, that is, of an Independent Party loyal to the Halle decisions and of the two Communist Parties, the KPD and the KAPD. It wrote to these three organisations:

> In practice, throughout Europe, the forces of the working class today are so powerful that the victory of the proletariat would present little difficulty if the working class were sufficiently prepared to fulfil its historic mission. What the working class today lacks is a clear theoretical orientation, consciousness of its own aims, and a clear understanding of the revolutionary road.[86]

The principal obstacle in Germany to acquiring this consciousness was, and remained, the 100,000 full-time trade-union officials who were in the service of the bourgeoisie. When the Halle Congress freed the workers' movement from the grip of this stratum, it 'opened the road to the victory of the proletarian revolution'.[87]

From this point of view, it is significant that the KAPD conveyed in its political statements the enormous impression made on its activists by the decisions, and especially the promises, of Halle. Its congress was held on 1–4 August 1920, and on the agenda was the call to resolve the principal difficulty in its relations with the ECCI by expelling from its ranks Wolffheim and

---

[84] *Die Rote Fahne*, 24 October 1920.
[85] Ibid.
[86] *Die Rote Fahne*, 25 October 1920.
[87] Ibid.

Laufenberg and the other supporters of 'national Bolshevism'.[88] Rühle, who had returned from Moscow full of anti-Bolshevik spite and anti-International hostility, virulently opposed to joining the International and fiercely denouncing the Russian-style 'party dictatorship' and 'the leaders' International', had brought about the formation of a current openly in favour of joining the International, in opposition to the tendency which he and Franz Pfemfert led. A large majority, essentially led by Karl Schröder and the Berlin group, had condemned as 'a serious mistake' the refusal of Merges and Rühle to take part in the Second Comintern Congress.

At the meeting of its Central Committee on 30–1 October, and following discussions at the beginning of the month with Zinoviev, the majority of the KAPD took another step forward. It expelled Rühle – as the ECCI had been asking since July, charging him with activity that aimed at destroying the Party. It decided to send to Moscow a solid delegation, representative of its new majority and new orientation, to negotiate directly with the ECCI. Schröder, Gorter and Rasch went to Moscow,[89] opening the perspective of overcoming the divisions within the left-wing forces.

Meanwhile, fusion between the left Independents and the KPD took place over a few weeks. To be sure, it did not happen in the form which the ECCI had hoped. In the legal battle which followed the Congress, the Independent apparatus, in other words, the right wing, succeeded in holding on to the essential material resources of the Party, its funds, premises and newspapers. It was estimated at the Fusion Congress in December that of the 800,000 members of the USPD immediately before the split,[90] about 400,000 joined the unified party.[91] The rest were dispersed amongst the individuals and groups who went back to Majority Social Democracy, or to the rump party which remained around Crispien, the apparatus of which was henceforth too

---

[88] Bock, op. cit., p. 280.

[89] Ibid., pp. 256–7.

[90] *Jahrbuch für Politik-Wirtschaft Arbeiterbewegung, 1922–23*, Hamburg, 1923, Pieck gives the figure of 893,000, including 135,000 women.

[91] In the course of the Third Comintern Congress, Radek was to specify that in the reports sent by the Zentrale to the ECCI at the time of the unification in December 1921, there had been a certain tendency to overestimate the membership figures, reckoned at around 500,000. According to him they did not exceed 350,000 (*Protokoll des III Kongresses der Kommunistischen Internationale (Moskau, 22 Juni bis 12 Juli 1921)*, Hamburg, 1921 p. 457). Pieck says that no more than 300,000 Independents actually joined the VKPD (*Jahrbuch, 1922–23*, op. cit., p. 647).

weighty for the members to support.[92] There were others, numbering several hundreds of thousands, who were broken or deeply scarred by the violence of the conflict, and decided to give up all political activity.

The process of fusion, which culminated in the Unification Congress of 4–7 December 1920, was progressively achieved through preparatory congresses held in November. In this way the revolutionary elements, whose division and dispersion had had such serious consequences in 1918–19, could be united in a single party. The Unification Congress provided a corrective to the Gotha Congress in 1917, and a reversal of the breakdown of January 1919 in the discussions between the Spartacists and the revolutionary delegates. It appeared to make it possible to overcome the consequences of the formation of the Communist Party in the unfavourable conditions of January 1919.

Within the new United Party, there were men of the prewar radical old guard, the nucleus of Luxemburg's faithful supporters, but also people who had always been left-wing Social Democrats, such as Däumig, Geyer, Hoffmann and Eichhorn, of whom Lenin said that they were 'the living ties' between the Party and the working masses whose confidence they enjoyed.[93] With them were the militant workers, the organising cadres of the class, the leaders of the big mass strikes in Berlin during the War, the builders of the workers' councils, and the nucleus of the Berlin revolutionary delegates during the War and the Revolution, such as Richard Müller, and people such as Wegmann, Eckert, Scholze, Malzahn and Paul Neumann, whom Lenin described as 'the steady, well-organised fighting rank and file of the revolutionary proletariat', and 'the basis and mainstay' of communism 'in the factories and trade unions'.[94]

The new party united these people with the Spartacist old guard, and with the activists from all over Germany who had led revolutionary struggles since 1917. Such people were Erich Wollenberg, who had survived from the Red Army of the workers' councils in Bavaria, Remmele the printer from Mannheim, the Koenen brothers, Bernhard and Wilhelm, from Halle, the Saxon printer Böttcher, Düwell from Zeitz, the Hamburg docker Ernst Thaelmann, the

---

[92] In 1922, the leaders of the USPD announced that they had 300,000 members, a figure which is probably overstated (*Jahrbuch, 1922–23*, op. cit., p. 643). In any case, reduced to a third or a quarter of its membership and subscription income, the USPD had great difficulty in maintaining the full-timers, newspapers and schools which had been supported by a party of nearly a million members.

[93] C. Zetkin, *Reminiscences of Lenin*, New York, 1934, p. 34.

[94] Ibid., p. 30.

metalworker Otto Brass from Remscheid, and Geyer, the former chairman of the Leipzig workers' council in 1919.

Ruth Fischer wrote that the Unification Congress was held 'in an atmosphere of ambiguity and obscurity'.[95] Her opinion was that the workers who had come with the left Independents tolerated the Spartacist theoreticians as inevitable appendages of the Third International, while, on the other hand, the Spartacist intellectuals were satisfied to accept, in the name of historical necessity, human material which they had long desired but which was too crude for their taste. This picture is too oversimplified to be true. The building worker Brandler was no less representative of the Spartacists than his friend the philosopher Thalheimer. The university teacher Karl Korsch, or Arthur Rosenberg, the historian of antiquity, were just as typical products of the USPD as the unpolished 'Teddy' Thaelmann, whose passionate speeches sometimes aroused laughter. The problem was to fuse quickly, in the course of common struggle, organisations which had hitherto fought separately. All party-building encounters such difficulties, neither more nor less serious than the problems that emerge between different generations or between different occupational environments.

For the new, combined Zentrale,[96] which was complemented by a Secretariat, the Unification Congress appointed two Chairmen. One was the former Independent, Däumig, and the other was Levi, on whom the Independents insisted.[97] The man who wanted to be the link between the currents led by Lenin and Luxemburg, the champion of struggle to win to Communism the revolutionary workers of the USPD, was a genuine symbol of this unification, and, no doubt, was its best hope. Despite the desire which he clearly expressed to retire from active political life, he understood this, and accepted it.[98]

---

[95] Fischer, op. cit., p. 146.

[96] The Independents were Däumig, Brass, Gäbel, Geyer, Hoffmann, Koenen, Remmele and Stoecker, and the Spartacists were Levi, Brandler, Heckert, Pieck and Zetkin.

[97] Radek said at the Third Comintern Congress that Levi's presence at the head of the Zentrale was for the Independents a demand in the form of an ultimatum ('ultimative Forderung') (*Protokoll des III Kongresses der Kommunistischen Internationale*, op. cit., p. 550).

[98] Here too, Radek's evidence is valuable despite his malevolence. Before the Halle Congress, he had already written to the German Zentrale to advocate 'fraternal' work with Levi. On his return from Halle, Zinoviev insisted that he should keep the leadership position, for he enjoyed the confidence of the left-wing Independents. Thalheimer and Radek had to persuade him against withdrawing at Frankfurt, as he wished, repeatedly saying to them: 'You can't carry a dog to the hunt in your arms.' (Radek, *Soll die Vereinigte KPD*, op. cit., pp. 104–5)

Chapter Twenty-Two

Paul Levi: A German Conception of Communism

Following the Halle Congress, and for the first time since the Communist International was founded, a mass Communist Party existed in one of the most advanced countries of Europe, Germany, the country which revolutionaries always regarded as the pivotal point of the world revolution. Had it been a victory for the Communist International, the prestige of which had played a central role in its establishment, or was it a personal triumph for Paul Levi, who, almost single-handed, had induced the reluctant KPD and the suspicious International to follow through to the end the political battle which he had been the first to foresee and to seek? The debate remains open. However, it is necessary at this stage to try to retrace the appearance of the first mass Communist Party, as it appears from the analyses of Levi, the man who conceived it.

The framework: the world revolution

The crucial link between the construction of a Communist Party and the Russian Revolution and the Bolshevik Party appeared in its clearest form in Germany. Levi declared at the Congress in December 1920 that united the KPD and the left Independents: 'This is not a German event. There no longer are any "German events" in the world revolution. What we are witnessing is the establishment of the first important member of the International formed according to the plan of the oppressed people alongside Soviet Russia.'[1]

Levi said that the working class of different countries did not advance in step with each other along the road from capitalism to socialism. The development of the world revolution would be as uneven as that of capitalism, and would differ from it. Thus, the USA, the most advanced country in the world within the framework of capitalism, was from the standpoint of workers' organisation at the most primitive stage, that of a single organisation – the One Big Union – the same idea as Chartism, which failed a century earlier in Britain at the dawn of the development of the working class. Likewise, the German working class saw the efforts of two generations of activists in the field of socialist education and political organisation reduced in a few years to nothing. The Russian proletariat, formed and organised under the iron heel of Tsarism, a numerically weak urban islet in an immense rural ocean, was the first to pose the question of the future of humanity in terms of the world revolution. The setbacks of the German Revolution could be explained in this setting: 'The greatest obstacle to the development of Communist forces in Western Europe has not been the bourgeoisie, but the workers' organisations themselves, and every revolutionary movement until today has broken itself against this rampart.'[2] It was thus important to understand thoroughly that, contrary to what the Bolsheviks appeared for a long time to believe, the German Revolution could not and must not follow the course of the Russian model of 1917:

> In no country in Western Europe will the revolution advance at the rapid pace at which, apparently, it rushed in Russia between February and November 1917. We say 'apparently', because we tend to forget that the Russian Revolution had already had its schooling ten years earlier, and that it could apply for the benefit of the proletariat the lessons learned in 1905, 1906 and 1907, in ten years of methodical work. Already, the single fact that we entered the revolution in Germany and in Western Europe without any Communist Parties, the fact that they had to be formed during the course of the revolution itself, and that precisely for this reason the errors, the defects, the imperfections and the half-measures of the proletariat were

---

[1] *Bericht über die Verhandlungen der USPD (Linke) und der KPD (December 1920)*, Berlin, 1921, p. 38.
[2] Levi Archives, P64/3, p. 14.

doubled and trebled during the revolution – all this precludes a course as clear and as straight as that which the Russian Revolution followed for seven months up to November 1917, and has followed since.[3]

Once this idea had been recognised, the need for a Communist Party in Germany was all the more clearly understood. Levi considered that the problem was not simply that of the German Revolution, but that of the world revolution in Germany. There were no parts of the world in which the class struggle would take on different aspects, or set itself different aims. The German bourgeoisie and German militarism were a real threat to the entire world revolution, and Germany was the arena in which the European proletariat would enter the decisive battle. For that reason, the role of the KPD would be decisive, and would have special importance for the world revolution. Every party in the International should learn from it, from its experience and its mistakes, and criticise it, not in relation to the Russian model, but in relation to its current concrete tasks. It was not a matter of starting the revolution in a backward country with the help of a firmly formed party, but of extending the revolution into a highly developed country in which the Communist Party had still to be constructed: 'Today we are in the course not only of a German revolution but the world revolution, and when we are faced with any possibility of action, we must never lose sight of any possibility of reaction, not merely here, but in respect of the world revolution.'[4]

Winning the proletariat

The Bolsheviks' advantage lay in the fact that between February and October 1917 they had won the majority of the proletariat in Russia to Communism. It was different in Germany in 1918–19. This was because the Revolution in November 1918 was less a victory of the proletariat than a collapse of the bourgeoisie. Levi was polemicising equally against Radek and against the ultra-leftists of the KAPD when he insisted that the development of the class-consciousness of the proletariat was the primary precondition in its fight for power. The Communists aimed to achieve this great task through the 'organising of the proletariat as a class in the councils'. The secret of the Bolsheviks' victory in Russia was the winning of the majority of the workers

---

[3] *Bericht über den 2 Parteitag der KPD*, op. cit., p. 61.
[4] 'Die Kehrseite', *Die Internationale*, no. 9–10, 4 April 1919, p. 13.

in the soviets. And, from this angle, their victory was a positive example. To quote from the theses which Levi had submitted to the Second Congress of the KPD(S):

> Before the conquest of power, it is of the most extreme importance both to strengthen the existing councils and to bring new ones into being. When we are doing this, we shall never lose sight of the fact that we cannot create or sustain councils or similar organisations by imposing rules or electoral regulations. They owe their existence solely to the revolutionary will and activity of the masses, and they form for the proletariat the ideological and organisational expression of its will to take power, exactly as parliament served for the bourgeoisie. This is precisely why the workers' councils are the historically designated channels for the revolutionary activities of the proletariat. Within the councils, the members of the German Communist Party must organise as a faction, in order to raise them, by means of appropriate slogans, to the height of their revolutionary tasks, and to win the leadership of them and of the mass of working class.[5]

The negative experience of the German Revolution – the Communists' refusal to sit alongside the Majority Social Democrats in the councils, their attempts to force decisions from outside, and the 'putschist' tendencies manifested in the early months of 1919 – served to confirm the positive experience of the victorious Russian Revolution. The revolutionary education of the proletariat could only take place through the work of a revolutionary party.

Levi and the German Communists believed in 1920 that history had finally settled the old polemic between Lenin and Luxemburg about the party. He wrote:

> We are dealing here with the old problem of the construction of socialist parties. I do not want to hide anything. We are dealing again with the old differences between Lenin and Rosa Luxemburg: 'How are Social-Democratic parties – to use the terminology of the time – to be built?' On that question, history has decided. Lenin was right. We too could form socialist or Communist parties by this ultra-rigorous selection. In a period of illegality, by very rigorous selection and simply by the mechanical process of adding one Communist to another, he formed a good party, and perhaps,

---

[5] *Bericht über den 2 Parteitag der KPD*, op. cit., p. 24.

comrades, if we had before us a period of ten years of illegality, perhaps we would decide to follow this path.[6]

The German Communists all believed, for the same reason, that history had likewise settled the quarrel about organisation and the necessary split between opportunists and revolutionaries:

> There is not a single Communist in Germany today who does not regret that the foundation of a Communist Party did not take place long ago, before the war, and that the Communists did not come together in 1903, even in the form of a small sect, and that they did not form a group, even a small one, which could at least have expressed clarity.[7]

But he refused to draw general conclusions from this observation. Splitting should not be raised to the level of a principle:

> In revolutionary epochs, when the masses are developing rapidly in a revolutionary direction, as against to periods in which the process of transformation is slower and is more painful, it can be advantageous for radical or Communist groups in opposition to stay within the large parties, so long as it remains possible for them to present themselves openly, and to carry on their agitation and propaganda work unhampered.[8]

Levi, who was influenced by the disaster of 1914, could never lose sight of the belief that the party is, at the end of the day, nothing more than an historical instrument for deciding a class conflict: 'The question for Communists is to have, not the largest party, but the most conscious working class. In this sense, the party is nothing, the revolution and the proletariat are everything.'[9]

Levi found himself in opposition on this point to most of the activists who formed his new party. For them, the Party was everything, because it was the instrument of their effectiveness, the irreplaceable tool which could give them victory.

The political atmosphere was greatly changed in the German working class after 1918, when the Russian example was conveyed in the magic effect of the words 'workers' council', and the recipe of armed insurrection to destroy

---

[6] 'The Beginning of the Crisis in the KPD and the International', 24 February 1921. Levi Archives, P64/3, p. 20.
[7] 'Der Parteitag des KP', *Die Internationale*, no. 26, 1 December 1920, p. 41.
[8] Levi Archives, P124/8, p. 3.
[9] 'Reinigung', *Die Internationale*, no. 15–16, 1 November 1919, p. 283.

the old state apparatus. The German workers wanted to have at their command some force more effective than the impotent workers' councils of 1918. They expected a radical change in their living conditions, which did not seem to them to be possible except by harking back to one of the strongest traditions of the workers' movement in their country, namely organisation, or, to use a different word, planning. It was to them whom Zinoviev addressed when he wrote:

> We have a way out, a hope. We are moving towards completely doing away with money. We pay wages in kind. We are bringing in free passenger transport in cities. We have free schools, free feeding-centres, even though for the present they are poor, we provide rent-free apartments and free lighting. We have introduced all this very slowly in the most difficult conditions. We have had to struggle all the time, but we have a way out, a vision and a plan.[10]

Here was a clear language for the Independent workers who joined the Spartacists in the ranks of the United Party. In fact, it was the only language to which they were ready to listen after years of disappointment, of the discovery that 'spontaneity' and the lack of organisation generated nothing but defeats, and of recognition of the vanity of hopes placed in elections. The persistence and continuity of the workers' Social-Democratic tradition of organisation contributed in these favourable circumstances to create an atmosphere in which they would see the building of the Party, with its strong apparatus, its cohesion, its discipline, its efficiency and its ability to organise and concentrate the workers' forces, as their essential aim.

The membership of the United Communist Party of Germany (VKPD), as the Party was now called, stood at several hundreds of thousands, and its leaders thought it had reached or passed the half-million. The Party had thirty-three daily papers, newspapers and specialised journals, it had a press correspondence service, and organised schools. It could call upon substantial material resources, 'men of good will', and the trust which its election results confirmed. In general, it could claim a quarter of the vote of the old SPD. It felt itself to be strong, and desired to become stronger.

---

[10] Zinoviev, *Zwölf Tage in Deutschland*, op. cit., p. 74. However, it should be noted that at this time he was expressing the aspirations of the Russian workers rather than those of the German working class.

The structure with which the party built immediately after the fusion combined the traditional, 'Social-Democratic characteristics of the old days' – the tradition of the 'old school' to which the Party appealed strongly – with the methods inspired by Bolshevism.[11] Its entire practice was centred upon the need to build the influence of Communism. One of the first specialised departments which was set up around the Zentrale was devoted to the work of Communist activists in the trade unions. The Gewerkschaftsableitung devoted itself to 'winning the unions' under the leadership of the Communist metalworkers, the nucleus of the old revolutionary delegates.[12] Another department was set up to undertake propaganda and organisation in rural areas, hitherto somewhat neglected. 'Specialists' sent by the ECCI helped to reorganise – and sometimes even to organise from scratch – clandestine apparatuses, in particular the so-called M-Apparat for military matters, and the N-Apparat for intelligence concerns.[13] Dozens of activists became full-timers, for the Party press and its businesses – printing and publishing establishments – or in its Secretariat, or even its secret apparatus. For them, as much for other members, the Party was everything, because it was the indispensable instrument of the coming revolution, and the apparatus was its nerve centre.

The Party and the International

The VKPD was born under the aegis of the Communist International, as Levi emphasised. For him, the International only really existed from 1920. Its proclamation in 1919 had been, in a certain sense, just an expression of the solidarity of the international proletariat with the Russian Revolution and Soviet Russia. It was only at its Second Congress in 1920 that it had equipped itself with a constitution, and had really been organised, as he said, as 'the party of the parties, that is, as a party which brings together and unites the Communist Parties of the world'.[14] Contrary to Luxemburg in 1918, the

---

[11] For details, see Chapter 28.

[12] Richard Müller took on the leadership of the Gewerkschaftsableitung. Alongside him were the most experienced of the working-class activists of the time, such as Brandler and Heckert, from the building industry, and the metalworkers Malzahn, Fritz Wolff, Walcher, Eckert (Mujbegović, op. cit., p. 341).

[13] Fischer (op. cit., p. 174) adds the groups Z (sabotage) and T (terror) on which our only information is from dubious sources.

[14] Levi Archives, P124/8, pp. 1–2.

leaders of the VKPD were not embarrassed by the fact that the formation of the International and the unification of the German Communists had both been engineered through the leaders of Soviet Russia. They saw history as a dialectical process; from that time on it would be through the agency of the Communist International that the world proletariat would succeed in assimilating the experiences of the different Communist Parties since the Russian Revolution, and that these Parties, in particular the German, would achieve the necessary homogeneity for the maintenance of the international organisation. Levi said:

> We believe that the Germans are not a chosen people, either for good or for evil. We believe that the experiences which we have had in Germany will be shared likewise by all the Western Parties. The same conflicts, exactly the same as in Germany, will be reproduced in France, in Britain and everywhere. They may perhaps take an easier course thanks to the price which we have paid for the apprenticeship.[15]

Likewise, with no apparent embarrassment, Levi openly criticised, just after the Second Comintern Congress, certain initiatives of his own Executive Committee which everyone knew to have been suggested and advocated by the leaders of the Russian Party. During the Congress, the German representatives strongly protested against the proposal by the Russians and adopted by the ECCI, to admit as visitors and as 'sympathising' organisations, bodies of an anarcho-syndicalist type. Levi said:

> Having learned from experience, we have opposed the idea of admitting to the Communist International elements which are not strictly Communist. . . . Guided by this idea, we have said that we shall not allow the clear and unitary line and the limpid ideas of Communism to be obscured by concessions to the Russians, whatever they may be.[16]

He admitted, moreover, the danger for the International which was arising from the pre-eminent role played by the ruling party in Russia. He declared:

> The Russian comrades are a state power and a mass organisation. As a state power, they have to undertake in relation to the bourgeoisie measures which they would never undertake as a party for the sake of the proletarian masses. . . . We can, of course, theoretically conceive that there is a risk here,

---

[15] Ibid., p. 3.
[16] Ibid.

the risk that if the link between the Communist International and the state power became very close, the Communist International would no longer act as a party or a super-party, as it were, inspired solely by the standpoint of Communism, but that it would become involved in the diplomatic game between the bourgeois forces of which the Bolsheviks must take account, not as a Party but as a state apparatus. . . . It is a theoretically conceivable risk, but I cannot imagine that it could become real. And I do not feel that it could become a reality, because of the identity which exists between the interests of the Communist International, on the one hand, and those of the Soviet Republic as a political state on the other hand, because the identity between the two, in a general way, is too great for a clash of interests to see the light.[17]

Moreover, the results of the Second Comintern Congress gave satisfaction to the German Communist leaders, and in particular to Levi, on the points which were at the centre of the internal and subsequently external discussions with the ultra-leftists of the German Communist movement. The Congress condemned the advocates – principally the Communist Party of Austria – of boycotting parliamentary elections. It declared that Communists must fight within reformist trade unions to challenge the opportunist leaders for the confidence of the workers. This seemed to them to confirm their own past positions which at the time had, on occasion, been sharply criticised in the leading circles of the International. We can understand why Levi's speech at the time of the Unification Congress of the German Communists sometimes took on a joyful note. On the level of programme, the Communist International was founded on the conception of Communism which he had advocated for the last two years. On the level of organisation the VKPD had become a mass party which could aim at winning the majority of the German workers to Communism.

However, the relationship between the German leadership, and in particular Levi, and the ECCI remained uncertain. Zinoviev, who as President of the International projected the experiences and the aims of the Russian Party, saw the problems of the class struggle in Germany in a way quite different from Levi. Zinoviev was marked by the experience of the preceding three years of Revolution and Civil War in Russia. He wrote in the first issue of *Kommunistische Rundschau*:

---

[17] Ibid., pp. 12–13.

Every conscious worker must understand that the dictatorship of the working class can be brought about only through the dictatorship of its vanguard, that is to say, of its Communist Party. . . . We do not simply need a Communist Party, we need a strongly centralised Communist Party, with iron discipline and military organisation.[18]

Conflict was inevitable between this conception and that of Levi, which was based more upon the working-class traditions of Germany.

---

[18] *Kommunistische Rundschau*, no. 1, 1 October 1920.

Chapter Twenty-Three

The First Steps of the Unified Communist Party

The year of 1920 saw both the end of the Civil War in Russia and the formation in Germany of a mass Communist Party. But 1921 was for world Communism the year of the Kronstadt uprising and of the first serious internal crisis of the Soviet Republic, the turn from War Communism to the New Economic Policy (NEP). After the conclusion of the Civil War in the autumn, the Russian Communists were plunged into discussions, including the debate about the trade unions, which expressed the confusion of people who saw decomposing before their eyes the country which for two years had been the battlefield of a ferocious conflict. Their eyes were fixed on their own problems, and they were not to understand immediately that the international situation had also changed. The time had passed of convulsive attacks by workers rendered desperate by suffering, and who felt power to be within their reach. Communists in every country had to admit that capitalism had stabilised itself, survived the postwar revolutionary crisis, and discovered new resources and a new capacity to endure.

The Communists' awareness of these new conditions and their willingness to accept them emerged in a piecemeal way, and involved a series of passionate arguments. The resistance to the reality which dissipated what Bukharin called 'the illusions of childhood'[1] took on tragically puerile forms.

---

[1] *Bolchevik*, no. 2, April 1924, p. 1.

Communists, rank-and-file and leaders alike, tried to compel the workers to fight. In their impatience, they rejected the methods that no longer seemed to function, and acted as if incantations and imprecations could produce miracles, as if it were enough to desire the revolution for it to happen . . .

The concrete perspectives of 1920

At the start of 1921, in a closed session of the VKPD's Central Committee, Radek summarised the political problems which had been raised during 1920, and described the great hopes of that summer:

> During the Polish War, the Executive believed that revolutionary movements were maturing in Western Europe, that in the drive toward the West the aim was not to impose Bolshevism at bayonet point, but only to break through the crust of the military might of the ruling classes, since there were already sufficient internal forces unleashed in Germany to keep things under control. The second cornerstone of the policy of the Executive was its assessment of the concrete situation in Germany. The Executive believed that in Germany things were already ripening for the seizure of political power. It was believed that once we held Warsaw there would no be further need to advance all the way to Germany.[2]

However, the 'German pattern' was not the only one on offer. Radek made this clear:

> There was another school of thought in the executive committee – the so-called South-Eastern tendency, which held that the break-through must be attempted, not in Germany, but somewhere else altogether, in countries with an explosive agricultural set-up, such as East Galicia, Romania, Hungary, and which was convinced that if we stood on the Drava and the Sava, the revolution in the Balkan states would be accelerated and the requisite agrarian hinterland would be created for the Italian Revolution. The creation of an agricultural hinterland is as crucial for the Italian Revolution as for the German Revolution.[3]

---

[2] Minutes of the Central Committee of the KPD, 28 January 1921, Levi Archives, P50/a5, reproduced in M. Drachkovich and B. Lazich, *The Comintern: Historical Highlights*, Stamford, 1966, p. 285. Radek is here setting out ideas which he personally had opposed.

[3] Ibid., p. 286.

However, the bulk of the members and, no doubt, of the Party cadres, had not concerned themselves with these finer points, and had placed their faith in the coming victory of the revolution in Western Europe.

The turn in the objective situation in 1920

In July 1921, recognising that the seizure of power was not on the immediate agenda, the Communist International adopted a new orientation. It was, however, a belated move, as the conditions influencing it had taken shape during the previous year. The summer offensive against Poland led by Tukhachevsky's Red Army had been only an illusion. For most Communists, his lightning counter-attack had sounded both the death-knell of capitalism in Europe and the call to insurrection. In a reverberating article calling for 'a policy of revolutionary offensive', Bukharin had argued that the Bolsheviks could and should export the revolution on the points of bayonets.[4] A 'provisional government' of veteran Polish Communists was waiting, ready to place itself at the head of the Polish workers, who were expected to rise up when their 'liberators' arrived.

The delegates to the Second Comintern Congress had shared these hopes. They had regarded Levi with suspicion because he continued to doubt whether the German workers would rise up when Budenny's cavalry arrived on Germany's eastern border. The recent past was clothed in new colours, rich in promise, in the light of the military operations; Jean Brécot wrote that the strike of French railway workers in May had marked 'the reawakening of proletarian consciousness in France' and 'the first step of the French proletariat towards international revolutionary action'.[5] Moreover, the revolutionary movement seemed to be spreading far beyond the frontiers of old Europe, the encirclement and the internal contradictions of which foreshadowed the inevitable socialist transformation. On 1 September, the first Congress of Peoples of the East was held in Baku. Indian, Chinese, Turkish, Iranian and Kurdish delegates applauded the fiery speeches by Zinoviev, Radek and Kun about the world revolution against imperialism. The Third International spread to the Middle and Far East.

---

[4] 'Über die Offensivtaktik', *Die Kommunistische Internationale*, no. 15, 1920, pp. 67–71.
[5] *Revue communiste*, no. 6, August 1920, pp. 504–5. Jean Brécot was the pseudonym of Gaston Monmousseau.

Whilst Zinoviev was cutting short his triumphant visit to Germany, events seemed to be speeding up. At the beginning of September, the workers in Northern Italy had started their great movement to occupy the factories, under the leadership of the factory councils and of the ideas of the small group of communists in Turin around *Ordine Nuovo* and Antonio Gramsci. Great class conflicts were approaching in Czechoslovakia, where the state undertook to defend the old leaders of Social Democracy against the Communists who wanted to wrest control of the Party from them. The recruitment of the German Independents to the International, and the probable adherence in the near future of the majority of the French Socialist Party, seemed to demonstrate that the upsurge which was carrying the masses of workers in all countries towards the Third International and its programme of proletarian revolution was irresistible.

Yet the negative balance sheet of 1920 was soon to be revealed. Those like Trotsky, Radek and some of the Polish Communists who had opposed the march on Warsaw, and had doubted the possibilities of the military export of the revolution, had been correct, and Lenin had erred. Not only had the Polish workers and poor peasants not risen, but they had fought beside their generals and their grandees, along with the advisers from the Entente, for their 'independence', against the Red Army. The victorious advance of the Red Army had given way to a headlong retreat, which led to an armistice. The Council of Action in Britain against intervention in Poland, which Lenin had hailed as the London Soviet, had not lasted beyond the end of the fighting. The railway workers' strike in France had been no more than the crest of the wave. In Italy, the right-wing social-democratic elements and trade-union leaders refused to get involved in the battle. The workers became sceptical and discouraged, and started to retreat, at which point the fascists, backed by a frightened bourgeoisie, began to make gains. In December, the strikers in Czechoslovakia were defeated arms in hand.

Lenin noted in December that 'the tempo of development of revolution in the capitalist countries' was 'far slower' than it had been in Russia.[6] But Zinoviev was telling the Italian Socialists that the proletarian revolution was imminent.[7] Perhaps he was convinced that a revolutionary victory on the part of the parties of the International would ensure that Russia could avoid

---

[6] V.I. Lenin, 'Speech Delivered at a Meeting of Activists of the Moscow Organisation of the RCP(B)', *Collected Works*, Volume 31, p. 441.

[7] R. Paris, *Histoire du fascisme en Italie*, Volume 1, Paris, 1962, p. 202.

having to initiate the NEP, which he accepted only reluctantly after having vigorously opposed it in the Russian Political Bureau.[8]

Zinoviev was, of course, applying the decisions of the Second Comintern congress. Around him, the apparatus of the International, the men on the ECCI, survivors of the Hungarian Revolution, red exiles in Moscow, plenipotentiaries of limited experience but wielding considerable authority, remained convinced that nothing essential had happened since the summer of 1920. In their quest to transform Communist Parties from what they perceived as left-wing social-democratic outfits into revolutionary organisations, they called on them to accelerate the imminent revolutionary upheavals.

Tension between Levi and the ECCI

Disagreements over the appreciation of the international situation were implied in Levi's reservations during the Second Comintern Congress in respect of both the conditions for admission and the immediate tasks of the Communist Parties. From this point of view, there can be no dispute that he was correct, and Lenin was wrong. But there was no need for this supplementary motive to feed the mistrust which the Russian members of the ECCI felt towards him. Meyer made this clear without equivocation to the KPD Congress: the Russian leaders, and especially Zinoviev, felt the 'reserve' of the Germans to be an expression of real distrust of them. They feared – no doubt following Radek – that the opposition of Levi and the Zentrale to putsches might be transformed into hostility and resistance to all action. This is why, more than ever, they wanted the fusion with the KAPD, which they thought would permit 'the sure and correct line' of the German Party to be invigorated with 'a little of the revolutionary fire' which was to be found 'in larger measure' in the ultra-left organisation.[9]

Levi's opponents hoped to catch him out on the question of the KAPD. In September 1920, Arkadi Maslow, a young intellectual of Russian origin who was trying to reconstruct a 'left' tendency in the VKPD in Berlin, wrote in *Kommunismus* to pose the question of unification of the proletarian forces in Germany from this point of view, and explicitly criticised Levi's position.[10]

---

[8] See the careful discussion on this point in Carr, op. cit., pp. 337–8.
[9] *Bericht über den 5 Parteitag der KPD*, op. cit., p. 27.
[10] A. Maslow, 'Die Proletarische Parteien Deutschlands und ihre Politik in der gegenwärtige Krise', *Kommunismus*, no. 36–37, pp. 1298–317.

A few weeks later, in the same journal, the Hungarian Lukács stressed the dangers for the German Revolution implied by a unification of Communists and Independents that excluded the KAPD. He declared that 'the revolutionary organisation of the masses' was 'possible only in the course of the revolution itself', and asked if the leaders of the new Unified Party really wanted to bring about the revolutionary mobilisation of the German proletariat.[11] These open attacks coincided with Radek's efforts directed towards left Independents such as Curt Geyer or Herzog to ensure their support for the ECCI in the event of a struggle against Levi, whom he presented as an 'opportunist' and a 'right-wing Communist'.[12] The German Party was sharply criticised at a meeting of the ECCI for not having tried to extend and generalise the electrical workers' strike in Berlin, which was led by one of its members, Wilhelm Sült.[13]

There was a sharp incident at the last Party Congress before the unification. Radek accused Levi of 'wanting to do nothing but educate Communists until the Party has white hairs on its super-intelligent head'.[14] Hugo Urbahns, a delegate from Hamburg, moved a resolution critical of the activity of the parliamentary group, which was evidently aimed at Levi.[15] It was rejected, but, at the Unification Congress, a draft manifesto, written by Levi and approved by the provisional Zentrale, was kept off the agenda in conditions

---

[11] G. Lukács, 'Der Parteitag der KPD', *Kommunismus*, no. 44, pp. 1562–4.

[12] W. Herzog, 'Russisches Tagebuch', *Forum*, no. 5, 7 April 1921, pp. 275, 278; C. Geyer, 'Zur Vorgeschichte des III Weltkongresses', *Sowjet*, no. 8–9, August 1921, p. 241. Geyer had been delegated immediately after the Unification Congress as a representative of the VKPD on the ECCI.

[13] Geyer, op. cit. The strike of the Berlin electricians was decided for 7 November by 1,800 votes to 60, and ended on 12 November by 704 to 600 on a manipulated vote. Its practical consequences had created an apocalyptic atmosphere in the capital, and it was the target of very violent attacks by the press and the government. The strike-breaking organisation Technische Nothilfe intervened, and this led to numerous incidents. Finally, the press campaign and threats of sackings and repression wore it down to defeat. The ultra-left elements criticised the Zentrale for not having issued the slogan of a general strike, which the latter regarded as adventurist (P. Levi, 'Die Lehren des Elektrizitätsstreiks', *Die Rote Fahne*, 12 November 1920. Fischer writes (op. cit., p. 119), that Sült, 'a quiet and discreet man, an intelligent and highly-skilled worker', wanted 'to resort to sabotage, even blowing up the power stations'. In the report which appeared in *Die Rote Fahne* on 12 November 1920 of a discussion by the delegates of the Berlin factory committees, Sült spoke to make clear his resolute opposition to sabotage, but also his determination to counterpose workers' violence to that of the 'scabs'. The higher authorities of Sült's union expelled him (*Die Rote Fahne*, 7 December 1920).

[14] *Bericht über den 5 Parteitag der KPD*, op. cit., p. 41.

[15] Ibid., p. 107.

which remain obscure,[16] to make room for a document by Radek which was introduced at the last moment. This declared in particular:

> Whereas a party which has an audience of only tens of thousands recruits its members mainly by propaganda, a party which organises hundreds of thousands and has an audience of millions must recruit mainly by what it does. The VKPD is strong enough to go alone into action when events permit and demand this.[17]

Levi stood by his point of view in his article on the Unification Congress:

> The introduction of Communism by the road of the proletarian dictatorship is the greatest task which has ever fallen to any class in history. It cannot be the task of a small part of that class or of a single, isolated party, but only that of the broad masses of the proletariat, of the class as such. The Communists, as the most advanced section of the proletariat, have not only to lead and to formulate as clearly as possible the struggles against the bourgeoisie, they must also be aware that they constitute only a fraction of the proletarian class. . . . The task of the Communists . . . is to win the hearts and minds of the proletarian class and all its organs, which today bind sections of the working class to the bourgeoisie.[18]

This indirect, discreet polemic was soon to turn into an open crisis.

The admission of the KAPD as a 'sympathising party'

Following the Halle Congress, when Zinoviev discussed with the Berlin leaders of the KAPD, relations between the ECCI and the German leftist party had resumed on a far more cordial level. Some in the KAPD, such as Gorter, believed that joining the International was possible, and that this would permit the KAPD to form a 'revolutionary-Marxist' tendency within it in opposition to the predominant 'revolutionary-opportunist' tendency.[19] The aim of the mission of the three delegates of the KAPD, Schröder, Rasch and Gorter, who went illegally to Russia in November, was to obtain for their

---

[16] E. Friesland, *Zur Krise unserer Partei*, Berlin, 1921, p. 21.
[17] *Bericht über die Verhandlungen des Vereinigungsparteitags der USPD (Linke) und der KPD (Spartakusbund)*, Berlin, 1921, p. 232.
[18] P. Levi, 'Der Vereinigungsparteitag', *Die Rote Fahne*, 4 December 1920.
[19] H. Gorter, 'Die KAPD und die 3 Internationale', *Kommunistische Arbeiter-Zeitung*, no. 162, 1920, cited in Bock, op. cit., p. 257.

party the status of a sympathising party, which would allow it to obtain material aid and international connections, without at the same time obliging it to revise its programme.[20]

The KAPD delegates had several discussions in Moscow with Lenin, Zinoviev, Trotsky and Bukharin, and took part in two sessions of the ECCI, which was enlarged for the occasion. On 24 November, Gorter presented the KAPD's report,[21] and Trotsky, on behalf of the ECCI, presented the International's counter-report, which was a real indictment. Trotsky said that the attitude of the ultra-leftists was not only 'puerile', but 'provincial', 'idealistic', and 'pessimistic', expressing their own powerlessness, especially that of the Dutch Communists, who had been reduced for years to the state of a sect. The ultra-leftists in general, and Gorter in particular, confused the minority of the proletariat – the labour aristocracy and bureaucracy, particularly in the trade unions – with the millions trapped in the apparatuses, who, they claimed, were 'bourgeoisified', but whom in reality they refused to emancipate. The Communists had to learn how to 'break the crust'. If the Western working class really was bourgeoisified, that would mean the end of the hopes of the revolutionaries. Gorter, like Pannekoek, was following the intellectual course of Bernstein; they scrutinised the situation within the advanced countries without taking the world situation into account. To have declared, as he did, that the British proletariat was 'isolated' was to neglect the fact that the world revolution had the dual character of proletarian revolution in the West and agrarian and national revolution in the East. The success of a revolution in a single country was no longer conceivable over a long period, and it was world revolution that was being discussed. Trotsky ended by declaring once again, in opposition to Gorter, that the Bolshevik experience of the mass party had to be completely assimilated in the world Communist movement on the basis of a global analysis.[22]

At the end of this discussion, the ECCI voted by an overwhelming majority in favour of the provisional admission of the KAPD as a 'sympathising party',

---

[20] Ibid.

[21] This report does not seem to have been published by the KAPD (Bock, op. cit., p. 258, n. 37). According to Trotsky's reply, it seems to have closely followed the analysis made by Pannekoek in 'World Revolution and Communist Tactics'. Rosmer (op. cit., pp. 113–14) gives an account of this session of the ECCI in which he took part.

[22] The complete text of Trotsky's counter-report is reproduced in *Piat'let Kominterna* (English edition, 'The Policy of the KAPD', *The First Five Years of the Communist International*, Volume 1, op. cit., pp. 174–89).

with a consultative vote, into the International. Zinoviev stressed in his closing speech: 'Logically there are only two solutions. In the long term, it is impossible to have two parties in one country. Either the KAPD will genuinely transform itself into a German Communist Party or it will cease to be one of ours even as a sympathiser.'[23]

The motion for admission opened the perspective of winning 'the best elements' of the KAPD. It restated the falsity of the KAPD's positions on parliaments and trade unions, and declared that the KAPD would have to fuse with the VKPD when it was formed.[24] The Third Congress of the KAPD in February 1921 was to approve its admission as a 'sympathising party' to the International. Nonetheless, at the December meeting of its Central Committee, it called for 'an irreconcilable struggle against opportunism in any form in the International', but it accepted, needless to say, the important financial support which the ECCI offered, and also agreed to form 'a collective for joint work' with the VKPD.[25]

The VKPD reacted violently to this, despite the ECCI's explanatory telegram which promised that the German working class would be publicly informed of the reasons for the KAPD's admission.[26] The Zentrale protested unanimously, and Levi penned an article in *Die Rote Fahne* entitled 'An Untenable Situation',[27] in which he discussed the attitude of the KAPD to the trade unions. He declared:

> The situation which the ECCI has created is not tolerable either for us, or for the KAPD, and for the Communist International it is a disaster of the greatest magnitude. . . . We are for rigorous international discipline, and for the Executive to have all the powers which the constitution of the Communist International confers upon it. But none of the provisions of the constitution of the Communist International compels us to recognise as a stroke of genius every decision of the ECCI, and we say openly: the decision of the Executive concerning the KAPD is not a stroke of genius, but very much the opposite.[28]

---

[23] *Protokoll des III Kongresses der Kommunistischen Internationale*, op. cit., p. 186.
[24] Resolution of 28 November 1920, *Komunisticheskii Internatsional*, no. 15, December 1920, column 3368; Degras, op. cit., p. 206.
[25] Bock, op. cit., pp. 258–9.
[26] On 2 February, Levi was to tell the Central Committee that this document had not yet arrived (Levi Archives, P64/3, f. 11).
[27] 'Eine unhaltbare Situation', *Die Rote Fahne*, 24 December 1920.
[28] Ibid.

Radek replied tartly, with a treacherous allusion to 'the old Social-Democratic aversion, deeply rooted, against working people who are not quite clearly revolutionary'.[29]

Levi then tried to move the debate to what he called 'tactical questions'. He concentrated on the fact that the passage from propaganda to action, which the unification with the left Independents had made possible, had to develop in Germany in a manner and in relation to conditions which the Russian Revolution never experienced. To be sure, the VKPD was a mass party, but this fact alone did not 'permit it to control totally, and without concern for other strata of the proletariat, the destiny of the German Revolution'. The Party, therefore, had to win the masses not only by propaganda, but by leading them through actions which would permit them to 'grasp their own interests through taking part in the struggle'. That was precisely what the Bolsheviks realised in the soviets of 1917. In the absence of councils, the German Communists should achieve it through work in the trade unions, where the great mass of the working people were organised: 'It is absolutely incorrect to treat the proletarian masses who are still on our right today with less consideration and patience than we have for the proletarian comrades in our class who believe themselves to be to our left.'[30]

Levi said the essential issue for the VKPD was to draw the masses into joint activities, without renouncing any Communist principles, but without frightening – particularly by alliances with elements tending towards anarchism – those proletarian masses to the right of the Party from whom it intended to recruit new members.

The *Open Letter*

The first important initiative in the direction of the policy which Levi outlined came from the rank-and-file of the VKPD.[31] In Stuttgart, the Party had won solid positions in the metalworkers' union, over which one of its members, Melcher, presided, and in the local trade-union federation. The local Communists were sensitive to the demands that were raised amongst the

---

[29] *Die Rote Fahne*, 29 December 1920.
[30] P. Levi, 'Taktische Fragen', *Die Rote Fahne*, 4 January 1921.
[31] This point was disputed by Robert Dissmann, who wrote in *Freiheit* of 26 January 1921 that the idea was suggested to Melcher, from Berlin, by the Communist Oskar Rusch.

non-Communist workers, in particular, their yearning for working-class unity. They secured the agreement of the trade-union bodies which they led for putting a demand to the national leadership of the metalworkers' union, the DMV, and the ADGB that they undertake immediately a joint struggle for concrete improvement in the workers' living conditions. A general meeting took place, in the course of which Melcher and his comrades received more support than Robert Dissmann, the right Independent, who appeared in person. The meeting demanded, in the name of the 26,000 members of the metalworkers' union in Stuttgart, that a joint struggle be organised around five basic demands:

- Lower prices for food.
- Opening the capitalists' books, and higher unemployment benefit.
- Lower taxes on wages and higher taxes on the rich.
- Workers' control of supply and distribution of raw materials and food.
- Disarming of reactionary gangs, and arming of the workers.

The Zentrale approved this initiative, and published the appeal of the Stuttgart metalworkers.[32] Moreover, it encouraged the organisation in every locality and workplace of workers' meetings to formulate common demands in this way, and to decide on means by which to fight for them.

A new tactic was taking form. Its outlines could be found since 1919 in the writings of Levi, Brandler, Radek and Thalheimer. Radek believed that this initiative from the metalworkers in Stuttgart should be taken up by the Party.[33] Levi was convinced at once, but the Zentrale showed a good deal of reluctance.[34] However, the district secretaries unanimously favoured the proposal when they were consulted,[35] and on 7 January 1921, the Zentrale agreed on the text of an *Open Letter* to be addressed to all the workers' organisations, parties and trade unions, in which it proposed to them the organisation of joint activity on the points on which agreement between them was possible. The *Open Letter*, published on 8 January, mentioned defence of the standard of living of the workers, the organisation of armed self-defence against

---

[32] *Die Rote Fahne*, 2, 10 December 1920.
[33] He declared to the Zentrale on 28 February: 'If I had been in Moscow, the idea would not even have crossed my mind.' (Levi Archives, P50/a5, cited in Drachkovich and Lazich, op. cit., p. 292) He was to state in *Soll die VKPD* (op. cit., p. 24), that the proposal was made at the Zentrale by 'the representative of the ECCI.'
[34] Radek (*Soll die VKPD*, op. cit., p. 24) stated that the opposition came from a 'section of the comrades who were former left Independents'.
[35] Ibid.

right-wing groups, a campaign to free workers in political detention, and the renewal of trade relations with Soviet Russia. It stated:

> When we propose this basis for action, we do not hide for a moment from ourselves nor from the masses that the demands which we have listed cannot end their poverty. Without giving up for a moment our propaganda amongst the masses for a struggle for the dictatorship, the only road to salvation, without ceasing to appeal to the masses and to lead them in the struggle at every favourable moment for the dictatorship, the United German Communist Party is ready for common action with the workers' parties to win the above-mentioned demands.
>
> 'We do not hide what separates us from the other parties and puts us in opposition to them. On the contrary, we declare that we do not seek from the organisations which we are addressing agreement in words alone to the activities which we propose, but action for the demands which we have listed. We put the question to them: 'Are you prepared to join without delay with us in the most ruthless struggle for these demands?' 'We expect an equally clear and unequivocal reply to this clear and unequivocal question. The situation calls for an urgent answer. That is why we shall wait until 13 January 1921 for your reply.
>
> 'If the parties and trade unions which we are addressing refuse to begin the struggle, the United German Communist Party will be obliged to carry it on alone, and it is convinced that the masses will follow it. Starting today, the United German Communist Party addresses all the proletarian organisations of the Reich and the masses grouped round them, calling on them to announce in public meetings that they are willing to defend themselves together against capitalism and reaction, and to defend jointly their common interests.'[36]

Whether this letter was drafted by Levi alone or in collaboration with Radek, or whether Radek drafted it, with or without the collaboration of Levi, it certainly expresses the political line which Levi had been defending for several months. For his part, Radek defended it with energy and conviction in an article which he wrote for *Die Internationale* under the pseudonym of Paul Bremer, called 'Building the Proletarian United Front of Struggle'.[37] He justified it by an analysis of the general political conjuncture:

[36] *Die Rote Fahne*, 8 January 1921.
[37] *Die Internationale*, nos. 1, 2, 1921, pp. 1–4, 10–16.

The Social-Democratic workers are full of democratic illusions. They still hope that they can improve their situation within the framework of bourgeois society, and regard the Communists as conscious disrupters of the workers' movement. They say: if the Communists had not organised the split in the working class, if the proletariat had remained united, it would have had a majority in the Reichstag, and all would have gone well. . . . It is clear that in this situation we cannot count on spontaneous unorganised movements in Germany, at any rate whilst the masses are not stirred up by outside events. Ten million workers belong to trade unions. Their eyes are fixed on the leaders, and they are awaiting slogans. . . . The Communist strategy must be to convince these broad masses of working people that the trade-union bureaucracy and the Social-Democratic Party not only refuse to fight for a workers' dictatorship, but do not even fight for the most fundamental day-to-day needs of the working class.[38]

Parties and trade unions refused to reply, or else rejected the appeal. But – despite what Western historians may say – it had a powerful echo alike from the workers and from the trade-union bureaucracy. The executive of the ADGB accused the Communists of trying to 'destroy the unions' by means of factional and anti-trade-union initiatives.[39] It threatened to expel local organisations which endorsed the *Open Letter*.[40] The leaders of the building trades union expelled Heckert and Brandler, as well as Bachmann, the chairman of the union branch in Chemnitz,[41] and organised a split-off local union in Halle.[42] The KPD Zentrale replied with the *Appeal to the Whole German Proletariat*,[43] in which it called on the workers to organise democratic assemblies in order to impose their demands on their leaders, and to declare their will to undertake a general struggle to win them. Such meetings took place, and the Communist proposals were approved by workers who were either not in parties or were members of one or other of the Social-Democratic Parties.

On 11 January 1921, the delegate meeting of the workers in the Vulkan naval shipyard in Stettin took place,[44] on 17 January, that of the production

---

[38] Radek, *Soll die VKPD*, op. cit., pp. 21–3.
[39] *Correspondenzblatt*, no. 8, 19 February 1921, p. 110.
[40] *Die Rote Fahne*, 16 February 1921.
[41] *Die Rote Fahne*, 19 January 1921.
[42] W. Raase, *Zur Geschichte der deutschen Gewerkschaftsbewegung, 1919–1923*, Berlin, 1967, p. 90.
[43] *Die Rote Fahne*, 21 January 1921.
[44] *Die Rote Fahne*, 15 January 1921.

workers and office staff at Siemens in Berlin, in the Busch Circus, on the 19th that of the railwaymen in Munich, and in the days which followed, meetings of the metalworkers in Danzig, Leipzig, Halle and Essen, of the railwaymen in Leipzig, Schwerin, Brandenburg and Berlin, the national congresses of the saddle-makers and the carpet weavers, the meeting of the miners in Dorstfeld, and a large workers' gathering in Jena, all fully endorsed the *Open Letter*, and called for a struggle to be organised around its demands.[45] The results of the elections in the unions and the factory councils that were held at the time bear witness to the response which the Communists received, and explain why the trade-union leaders were opposing it with bureaucratic methods.

In the elections in the woodworkers' union in Berlin, the Communists received 6,586 votes, against 5,783 for the Independents and 500 for the Majority Social Democrats. In the local branch of the metalworkers in Essen, 6,019 voted for the Communists, and 3,940 for the joint list of their opponents.[46] And there was a final success for the Communists and their *Open Letter* when on 26 February, the German trade unions presented to the government a programme of ten demands for the struggle against unemployment,[47] and warned that strikes and demonstrations might be organised and important sectors might to go into action.

However, the *Open Letter* came under many attacks from within the Communist movement. The KAPD said that it was 'opportunist and demagogic' and would merely produce illusions.[48] It was also the target of irony from the new Left in Berlin that was forming around the young intellectuals Fischer,[49] Maslow[50] and Friesland, and was attacked in *Kommunismus*.[51]

---

[45] *Die Rote Fahne*, passim; Raase, op. cit., pp. 89ff.; F. Knittel, 'Die mitteldeutsche Märzkämpfe im Jahre 1921, ihre Bedeutung und ihre Lehren', *Einheit*, no. 3, 1956, p. 17.

[46] *Graphischer Block*, no. 75, 15 February 1921.

[47] Raase, op. cit., p. 91.

[48] *Kommunistische Arbeiter Zeitung*, no. 61, according to *Freiheit*, 15 January 1921.

[49] Elfriede Friedländer had left Vienna with the reputation of being a right-wing element. Radek had been warned by Tomann that she was 'the Austrian Martov' (Radek, *November*, op. cit., p. 156). It was no doubt under the influence of Maslow that she became an ultra-leftist. Clara Zetkin, who shared a consistent and mutually very hostile relationship with her, said of her changing standpoints that 'her political positions varied with the vicissitudes of her sex life' (quoted in H. Weber, *Die Wandlung des deutschen Kommunismus*, Volume 2, op. cit., p. 118). It was during this period that she adopted the pseudonym of Ruth Fischer, from her mother's maiden name. She was to acquire German nationality only a year later through a marriage in Berlin with an activist named Golke (ibid.).

[50] Arkadi Maslow was the party name of Isaac Chereminsky. He had no connection with the workers' movement until the age of 26. In 1919, he made the acquaintance of Levi and Fischer, who won him to Communism.

[51] According to Mujbegović (op. cit., p. 260, n. 7), who was able to consult the

The *Open Letter* was sharply attacked by Zinoviev and Bukharin. Against opposition from Radek, they won the 'small bureau' of the ECCI to condemn it on 21 February 1921. Lenin intervened in the ECCI for this hasty decision to be revised. At his suggestion, the question was included with a number of other matters to be discussed in the run-up to the Third Comintern Congress.[52]

The differences within the German Zentrale and the ECCI on the German question turned thereafter on two different axes. On the one hand, the Russians, and especially Zinoviev, regarded Levi with increasing suspicion, whilst Radek seemed to concern himself with undermining Levi's authority within the Party. On the other hand, the Zentrale seemed to be in agreement with Radek on the central questions of the tactics of the moment, and opposed Zinoviev on this basis.

It appeared that a discussion was to open on the subject of the proletarian united front as a central aspect of Communist tactics, and when it did, Levi and Radek were to find themselves in the same camp, and come under attack together. But in the weeks which followed the publication of the *Open Letter*, a series of circumstances were to lead Levi and Radek to line up with two opposing camps.

---

minutes of the session of the Zentrale on 27 January 1921, left-wing criticisms were raised against the *Open Letter*, considering it to be 'opportunist'.

[52] Report of Curt Geyer, representative of the VKPD to the ECCI, to the Zentrale, quoted by Reisberg, 'Die Leninsche Politik der Aktionseinheit', *Beiträge zur Geschichte der deutschen Arbeiterbewegung*, no. 1, 1963, p. 62. Geyer mentioned in 1921 the position taken by the 'small bureau' and Lenin's intervention against it in *Sowjet*, no. 8–9, August 1921, p. 242, and the event was sufficiently well-known for references to be made to it at the Third as well as the Fourth and Fifth Comintern Congresses by the main individuals concerned.

Chapter Twenty-Four

The Split in the Italian Socialist Party

The crisis in the VKPD, the symptoms of which had been accumulating for months, finally exploded on a question that did not directly concern Germany – the split in the Italian Socialist Party (PSI) at its congress in Livorno. On the one hand, there were no 'national' problems alien to a Communist Party or an individual Communist. On the other, the battleground was all the more favourable to the adversaries of Levi, in that the representatives of the ECCI understood the Italian crisis better than the German leaders did.

The PSI had been the only social-democratic party in Europe to have stood aside in 1914 from the chauvinist current, although the renegade Benito Mussolini was prominent in it. The PSI had helped to organise the Zimmerwald Conference, and it played an important role there. It had been the first mass party to join the Communist International in 1919, even before the 'Twenty-One Conditions' were adopted. For that reason, it had retained in its ranks its reformists grouped around Turati. Its principal leader, Serrati, was in fact a left centrist, which had not prevented him from being one of the major figures at the Second Comintern Congress, in the course of which he had agreed with the 'Twenty-One Conditions', and had undertaken to apply them in Italy on condition that he would choose the time to proceed to expel Turati and his supporters.

However, his resolution seemed to weaken when he returned from Moscow. The defeat of the metalworkers' militant strike in the North in September 1920, when the workers occupied and ran the factories, for which the ECCI denounced the role of the reformists, could have provided the occasion to expel them. The ECCI demanded this with increasing insistence. But Serrati seemed to fear that a split in the Party, which could be clearly foreseen as the consequence of expelling Turati and his supporters, would be misunderstood by Socialists in Italy, and that it would only exacerbate the demoralisation following the end of the strikes.[1] He remained deaf to the injunctions of the ECCI, and argued that it was necessary to wait for a fresh example of the reformists' treachery, in order to get the best conditions for expelling them.[2] Of course, this resistance fed a growing suspicion on the part of the ECCI. It also led to indignant protests from the Left, led partly by Gramsci and his comrades of *Ordine Nuovo*, but also by Bordiga, who favoured boycotting the parliamentary elections, and by the deputy Bombacci, whose curious personality had given rise to many reservations on the part of delegates to the Second Comintern Congress.[3]

The affair was not confined to Italy. Serrati complained openly about the way in which the ECCI conceived the task of its representatives as informers on the Communist Parties, as well as the absence of control by the Parties over the information which reached the ECCI by this channel. Serrati went so far as to write: 'In this way there has been formed in the International a kind of red freemasonry. It operates in silence and mystery, and is all the more dangerous for being irresponsible.'[4]

On this point he found agreement with Levi, who had been deeply annoyed by discovering in Radek's office in Moscow reports on the VKPD addressed by Thomas to the ECCI.[5] It cannot be discounted that the ECCI imagined that a conspiracy, or at least some concerted action, between Levi and Serrati may have been envisaged. There names always appeared together when the ECCI discussed the 'rightist' danger in the International.[6]

---

[1] See a summary of his arguments in his letter to *L'Humanité*, 14 October 1920.
[2] Especially over a breach of discipline, which had not yet occurred.
[3] See Rosmer, op. cit., p. 73. Bombacci was to become a supporter of Mussolini.
[4] *Comunismo*, 15–31 December 1920, cited in *Revue communiste*, no. 12, February 1921, p. 510.
[5] Reich, op. cit., p. 19.
[6] C. Geyer, 'Zur Vorgeschichte des III Weltkongresses', *Sowjet*, no. 8–9, August 1921, p. 241.

All these problems were to be raised at the PSI's Congress which opened on 15 January 1921 in Livorno. The ECCI representatives, the Hungarian Mátyás Rákosi and the Bulgarian Kristo Kabakchiev,[7] were instructed to get the 'Twenty-One Conditions' applied without delay, especially the clause about excluding the reformists, with Serrati's support if possible, but without him if necessary.[8]

Three tendencies took shape in the course of the preparation for the Congress. The reformists demanded that anarchists and freemasons be excluded, opposed the dictatorship of the proletariat, and denounced 'the use of violence and illegal methods in the class struggle and in the fight for political power'.[9] The 'Communists', Bordiga, Gramsci and Bombacci, demanded that the 'Twenty-One Conditions' be put into operation immediately in their entirety, especially the expulsion of the reformists and the adoption of the name 'Communist Party'. Serrati, who led the 'Unity Communists' said that he accepted the 'Twenty-One Conditions', but wanted to interpret and apply them 'in conformity with the context and the history of the country'. Moreover, taking into account that the PSI had 'not smirched its banner during the War', he proposed that it should retain its Socialist title, 'in order to prevent the renegades of yesterday or of tomorrow from taking possession of the glorious name by which the proletarian masses know it'.[10]

After long discussions and without any regroupment appearing to be possible, the motions of each tendency were put to the vote. Serrati's motion received 98,028 votes, that of the 'Communists' received 58,173, and that of the reformists 14,695. Though the majority stated that the Party was a member of the Communist International, the 'Communist' minority left the hall, and proceeded to found the Italian Communist Party, the first congress of which opened in the same building on 21 January. Bordiga, Gramsci, Terracini and Bombacci were its most prominent leaders. Rákosi and Kabakchiev immediately recognised it as a section of the Communist International, the PSI being automatically expelled. The split was carried through, and the Communist International lost several hundred thousand revolutionary workers who stayed

---

[7] Originally Bukharin and Zinoviev were appointed, but they received no reply to their official request. See *Protokoll des III Kongresses der Kommunistischen Internationale*, op. cit., p. 167.

[8] Ibid., pp. 67–9; and K. Kabakchiev, 'Die Spaltung in der italienischen Sozialistischen Partei', *Die Internationale*, no. 2, 1921, pp. 16–22.

[9] Paris, op. cit., pp. 197, 200.

[10] Ibid., pp. 197–8, 200–1.

in the PSI with Serrati, or dropped out of political activity. Still more disturbing to the likes of Levi was that the banner of Communism in Italy passed into the hands of notorious ultra-leftists such as Bordiga. Robert Paris comments on the first consequences of the split at Livorno, coming on top of the defeat of the metalworkers in the North, that it 'was another military disaster like Caporetto in the face of the rise of fascism'.[11]

The Zentrale of the VKPD had discussed the situation in the PSI immediately before the Livorno Congress. Levi thought that a split was inevitable, but wanted everything to be done to push the line of cleavage as far to the right as possible, in order to retain in the International the majority of the workers influenced by Serrati, and to ensure that the Italian section did not fall under the exclusive control of the ultra-leftists. This is why, whilst he believed that Serrati had to be encouraged to agree to the exclusion of the supporters of Turati, he came out in favour of seeking an agreement with Serrati, even at the cost of certain concessions. The Zentrale agreed with him. He spoke to Radek immediately before he left for Italy; Radek was not yet aware of the ECCI's positions, and he took the view that the position of the Zentrale was correct. The two men agreed that a sharp conflict should be avoided in case the ECCI took a position different from theirs.[12] Levi had hardly set out for Italy when a telegram reached Berlin from Moscow calling for 'the most determined struggle to be waged' against Serrati.[13]

At Livorno, Levi was to find himself at once in conflict with the ECCI representatives. They rejected any change in Bordiga's motion which might enable the bloc behind Serrati to be split. Kabakchiev's speech at the Congress directed all its attacks at Serrati.[14] Levi had several private conversations with Serrati, in which, he claimed, he tried to convince him that the reformists had to be expelled,[15] but Rákosi later accused him of having encouraged Serrati to resist the ECCI, even by going so far as to show him a letter from Zetkin advocating this attitude.[16]

Levi restricted himself to a purely formal intervention of the 'fraternal greetings' kind, and departed without having either opened hostilities or

[11] Ibid., pp. 202–3.
[12] P. Levi, 'Wir und die Exekutive', *Die Rote Fahne*, 6 February 1921; *Der Beginn der Krise*, Levi Archives, P64/3, p. 16.
[13] Ibid.
[14] Levi Archives, P50 a3, cited in Drachkovich and Lazich, op. cit., pp. 278–9.
[15] Ibid., p. 276.
[16] *Protokoll des III Kongresses der Kommunistischen Internationale*, op. cit., p. 329.

supported the ECCI representatives, convinced that a grave mistake had been made. He believed that the ECCI was badly informed of the situation in the Italian Party. Serrati told him that Bombacci had gone so far as to embrace Turati openly in the parliament,[17] and Levi seems to have been convinced that, even if the ECCI's representatives had not exceeded their mandate, they had fulfilled their mission with excessive rigidity; but everything could be put right if the ECCI seriously studied the documents.[18] It was apparently in this spirit that he analysed the results of the Livorno Congress for *Die Rote Fahne*.

Levi's conclusions were critical. A split was inevitable, but not in the form which it took, because the best workers who supported the Third International now were outside its ranks, doubtless to the advantage of the centrists.[19] Radek replied to him at length, and coldly, three days later. The workers who were supporters of the International and yet had backed Serrati were supporters only in words, whilst the best revolutionary workers of Italy were those who were in the new Communist Party.[20]

The discussion was public, and the conflict broke into the open. It began with an outburst at a meeting of the Zentrale, for which Radek had asked urgently, and which was held on 25 January.[21] Levi was annoyed at the personal attacks on him in Radek's article, when the article which he – Radek – was attacking had put the position of the Zentrale. Radek was beside himself, and replied that Levi's article was 'a deliberate attack on the ECCI'. He threatened: 'Before you can attack us, we shall get in ahead of you and draw the sword against you.'[22] The tone of the attacks and the personal turn of Radek's criticisms were so sharp that Levi left the meeting. However, on the following day, Radek retreated and sent him a letter apologising for the form of his intervention.[23] Levi was not satisfied, and in a personal reply to Radek, he

---

[17] Report to the ECCI, Levi Archives, P50/a, p. 1.
[18] Ibid., p. 2.
[19] 'Der Parteitag der italienischen Partei', *Die Rote Fahne*, 23 January 1921 (unsigned article, dated 22 January 1921).
[20] 'Die Spaltung der Italienischen Sozialistischen Partei', *Die Rote Fahne*, 26 and 27 January 1921 (article signed 'PB', and also indicates Levi as the author of the article mentioned in note 19).
[21] According to Levi's report to the Central Committee on 4 February, Levi Archives, P64/3, pp. 16–17, where he does not explicitly indicate the date of the meeting, but provides details which enable it to be dated.
[22] Ibid., p. 16.
[23] Ibid. The text of this letter is not to be found in file P50 a, which contains Levi's reply.

reminded him of the circumstances in which had agreed – in the presence of Däumig – on the Italian question on the eve of his departure for Livorno, and how the new instructions from the ECCI had arrived when he was already on his journey. He protested against the interpretation which Radek placed on his article, and denied that he had wanted to attack the ECCI, whose mistakes would be corrected in Moscow itself, but he demanded precise replies from Radek. One related to the exact meaning of the threats levelled at him at the meeting of the 25th. The other was to know whether he, Levi, still had the confidence of the ECCI as leader of the German Party – yes or no?[24]

We do not have a reply from Radek, but the incident seems finally to have cleared the ground. The next meeting of the Zentrale was on 28 January. Radek was present, and the atmosphere was more relaxed. Radek (who appears in the report under the name of Max)[25] presented a long analysis of the political situation, and did not hide the disagreements which were starting to appear in the ECCI. In opposition to the ultra-leftists, whom he called 'the South-Easterners', he believed that Germany and Italy were the two decisive arenas in the European revolution. But everything depended on the ability of the Italian and German Communists to build mass movements, on their solidity and readiness to act. He admitted freely that the ECCI wanted by every means to 'activate' the VKPD, but he denied that this had anything to do with creating a diversion to shift attention from the internal difficulties of the Soviet Union. The important issue was whether the German and Italian Communists could take power before the threatening economic catastrophe descended in their countries. The ECCI wanted a closer relationship with the KAPD because it was concerned that the situation in the German Party was deteriorating. The ECCI judged that it was not ready for action, as was shown by the fact that the Zentrale had not discussed the *Open Letter* since 7 January.

Radek explained that he had reacted strongly against Levi because he had felt that the Party's solidarity with the ECCI was at stake:

---

[24] Levi Archives, P50 a4. This personal letter was to be published in *Freiheit* as early as 30 January! On 31 January, a statement by the Zentrale declared that the letter had been stolen, and that, it had become aware of it only through *Freiheit*. This is unlikely: in the discussions of 28 January (minutes in the Levi Archives, P50 a5), both Radek and Levi refer to their correspondence. The polemic was to continue, with the Communist press referring to the 'stolen letter', and the other newspapers to the letter which had been 'lost in the Reichstag', implying that Levi had lost it deliberately.

[25] Levi Archives, P50 a5, cited in Drachkovich and Lazich, op. cit., pp. 285–99.

What above all provoked the vigour of my polemic against Levi was not our disagreement on the Italian question, but above all the problem of relations with the Communist International as it appeared to me, not so much in what is printed, as what emerges in the real discussions. I do not need to say that I have not vowed blind allegiance to the Executive Committee. I have given and taken my share of blows, but there is criticism and criticism.[26]

He called on the German Zentrale to state clearly whether it agreed with the ECCI's general political line, which saw the principal danger as being on the right. It was then to discuss the question of the relations between the VKPD and the International, and advance concrete proposals. He argued:

The Communist International is not an isolated event, but a continuous process. In 1919, it was no more than a rallying-cry; today it has the support of a German party of half-a-million members. . . . In these conditions it is inadmissible to suppose that the Executive cannot be led to correct political mistakes by an open, clear, unequivocal policy, by saying: 'We don't agree.' It is still more serious to believe that we cannot even change the way that the International is organised.[27]

Far from unconditionally defending the ECCI, he stressed the difficulties which had been encountered, and the need for the leaders of the parties to make constructive criticisms:

There is much to be done to reduce the difficulties. In my opinion, the Executive's discomfort comes from the fact that it is located in a country which is going through a revolutionary struggle. We should not blame it for issuing orders, but because it does not intervene enough. It intervenes only when there is a sharp crisis. . . . We must express our criticisms and our opinions in a positive way. We must solve these questions on the level of the organisation. After the Russian Party, you are the largest party in the International, and you have the same share of responsibility as the Russian Party.[28]

Levi replied in a calm tone to this conciliatory intervention. But essentially he stood by what he had said in his personal letter of 27 January to Radek on the subject of the refusal to open up a political debate: 'The Executive will

---

[26] Ibid., p. 291.
[27] Ibid., p. 292.
[28] Ibid.

correct its mistakes. But this correction can only come from Russia.'[29] He said that he generally agreed with the opinions which Radek had expressed, and made it clear that he did not want the ECCI moved from Russia, but he did not share Radek's opinion about how to settle the present difficulties. He denied that he was sceptical, but stated his belief that there were two kinds of maladies, those which could be cured straight away with suitable treatment, and the others for which it was necessary to wait. The problems of the Party's relationship with the ECCI were of the second kind, and he explained why:

> My relations with Zinoviev have improved a little since his stay in Germany, but I must repeat here: we face a certain mistrust, and every effort we make to criticise mistakes will be interpreted solely as an act of opposition to the Communist International. . . . This discussion has opened my eyes: comrade Max got carried away during the discussion, and out came ideas which are alive and well in Moscow. Taking all these facts into account, I believe that we shall make the illness worse instead of encouraging a cure if all we do is express what are called 'positive criticisms'.[30]

Perhaps because he was counting on support from Lenin, and perhaps because he did not want to fight on issues that were beyond the concerns of his own party, Levi obstinately refused to enter into a confrontation, and Radek was to push this evasion to his own advantage. Two resolutions were on the table. Levi's resolution restated his principled agreement with the need to apply the necessary conditions for admission to the International and to expel the Italian reformists, but declared that the unity of the Italian Communists had to be maintained, which meant that the split from Serrati's faction was a mistake: 'The VKPD declares that, within the perspective of the unity of the Italian Communists, no price could be too high for accepting that the Italian reformists would still remain in the party.'[31]

Radek proposed a motion which approved the decisions of the ECCI, that is, the driving of Serrati's supporters into a position in which it was possible to write them off as 'centrists', and consequently to recognise the Italian Communist Party as the only party in Italy affiliated to the Communist International.[32]

---

[29] *Freiheit*, 30 January 1921; *Die Rote Fahne*, 2 February 1921.
[30] Levi Archives, P50 a5, cited in Drachkovich and Lazich, op. cit., pp. 293–4.
[31] Text in Radek, *Soll die Vereinigte KPD*, op. cit., pp. 47–8.
[32] Ibid., pp. 46–7.

Radek then addressed another letter to the Chairmen of the Party, Levi and Däumig. He regarded Levi's motion as unacceptable because it did not take a position on either the causes of the split at Livorno or the exclusion of Serrati and his group, which were accomplished facts. It spoke of Serrati and his group as though they were 'communists', but did not mention the 'Italian Communists' around Bordiga and Gramsci. He therefore regarded it as a declaration of hostility to both the Italian Communists and the ECCI, an attempt to introduce 'the practices of the USPD into the VKPD'. He counterposed his resolution to Levi's, and concluded: 'It would be better for the Chairman of the Party to be put for once in a minority in the Zentrale, than if the Zentrale were, out of a desire to support him, not merely to adopt a centrist position, but then to conceal it from the Party.'[33]

Driven into a corner, Levi took another step back, and withdrew his motion. Radek accepted an amendment moved by Zetkin. This inserted two paragraphs which called for the unification of the Italian Communist Party with 'the communist elements' in Serrati's group who had remained in the PSI.[34] This unanimity might appear contrived, but it had a real basis nonetheless. Zetkin, who supported the expulsion of the Turati tendency and reproached Serrati for having preferred the reformists to the revolutionaries, desired above all, as Levi did, to keep the door of the International open to Serrati and his supporters.[35] Nothing suggested that Radek disagreed. The incident which the Italian split had provoked therefore seemed closed. Levi, satisfied that Radek had not expressed the 'mistrust' which he feared and had regretted the form of his attacks, remained at the head of the Party.

In fact, Zetkin's resolution,[36] which was carried unanimously and without opposition from Radek, was about the need to improve the functioning of the ECCI and its relations with the Communist Parties. Moreover, it brought out the real problems, and gave hope that a positive way out of the crisis could be found. It did not dispute that the ECCI should be located in Moscow, 'the capital of the first proletarian state'. But it stressed the difficulties which this put in the way of its acting as a real leadership for the International, difficulties which resulted as much from the material problems of communication as from 'differences between the tasks of the Communist

---

[33] Ibid., pp. 48–50.
[34] Ibid. Text of the amended resolution in *Die Rote Fahne*, 2 February 1921.
[35] *Protokoll des III Kongresses der Kommunistischen Internationale*, op. cit., p. 283.
[36] *Die Rote Fahne*, 2 February 1921.

Party of a victorious proletariat and those of Communist Parties in countries where they must in the first place struggle for the dictatorship of the proletariat'. Zetkin therefore made practical proposals to overcome or at least alleviate these difficulties. The first consisted in increasing the numbers of representatives on the ECCI from parties with more than 100,000 members – a clear indication of the desire of the German leaders to prevent themselves from being submerged under the number of representatives of very small or émigré parties. The second was to send four representatives of the ECCI to Western Europe and America – at least two of whom should be from the Russian Party, mistrust of the others being obvious – whose task would be to inform the ECCI of the specific conditions in which the Communist Parties in the capitalist countries were operating. It would have been difficult to say more clearly that the ECCI was ill-informed. Finally, as a practical measure, and to overcome the disadvantages caused by the irregular publication of the journal *Communist International*, the resolution proposed the creation of a press correspondence service in several languages, which would enrich the press of the Parties, and facilitate communication and understanding between the ECCI and the parties of the International.[37]

However, forty-eight hours after the resolution was published, the ultra-leftist Friesland attacked it in *Die Rote Fahne*, on the grounds that it evaded the real problem, which was the transformation of the VKPD into a party of action.[38]

The Italian question was soon to re-erupt. Firstly, because Rákosi and Kabakchiev complained about the attitude of Levi at Livorno. They held him partly to blame for the resistance put up by Serrati,[39] which was to bring to a protest from the Italian Communists.[40] Secondly, because the affair was taking on an international dimension. When Jacques Mesnil reported on the Livorno Congress in *L'Humanité*, he stressed that the attitude of the ECCI was inspired by its belief in 'the imminence of the revolution', and posed the question: 'Is the situation *today* really as revolutionary as they think? Given the present situation, is it the best tactic to provoke a split which divides the youngest and most active communist elements from the mass of the Party?'[41]

---

[37] This was the origin of *International Press Correspondence* or *Inprekorr*, which was to appear in four languages.
[38] 'Zur Kritik der Partei', *Die Rote Fahne*, 4 February 1921.
[39] *Protokoll des III Kongresses der Kommunistischen Internationale*, op. cit., p. 329.
[40] Letter dated 28 January from Bordiga, *Die Rote Fahne*, 4 February 1921.
[41] *L'Humanité*, 25 January 1921.

A few days later, he went further, analysing and endorsing the accusations which Serrati made to the Communist Parties against the ECCI delegates.[42] He wrote that the attitude of these representatives could be explained only by what he saw as 'a fundamental theoretical mistake of the Bolsheviks: their blind belief in the virtue of centralisation'. He warned his own party: 'Serrati is right. Beware of *éminences grises!*'[43]

An international grouping was taking shape, or so it seemed to the members of the ECCI who were most alert to the 'rightists'. Immediately after the Livorno Congress, Serrati set out for Berlin, where he met Levi.[44] On Levi's advice, he wrote to the ECCI to demand a further enquiry into the Italian split. On his return, he stopped in Stuttgart to meet Zetkin, who approved of these initiatives.[45] And it certainly seemed that the resolution of the German Zentrale was such as to enable the attitude of the ECCI's representatives in Italy to be questioned.

Furthermore, the 'new leftists' in Berlin were trying to exploit the situation in order to press their advantage against Levi. Fischer, Friesland and Maslow repeatedly attacked, as much on the question of the KAPD – on which they agreed with the decision of the ECCI – and on the question of the Italian split, as on support for the slogan of 'alliance with Soviet Russia', which the Zentrale had advanced but which they regarded as a 'national-Bolshevik' slogan. During a meeting of Party leaders in Berlin, where he disputed with Fischer,[46] Levi commented on the resolution of the Zentrale in a sense which his opponents regarded as one-sided and exclusively favourable to Serrati.[47] The Left raised the problem of what it regarded as the 'ultra-centralism' of the Zentrale, and brought up the theme of 'bureaucratisation', which it linked to what it regarded as an 'opportunistic' policy.[48] Up against converging criticism from the ECCI and the Berlin organisation, the Zentrale was forced onto the defensive.[49]

---

[42] There had been an especially sharp conflict with Liubarsky, who was known as 'Carlo'.

[43] J. Mesnil, 'Le Congrès de Livourne', *Revue communiste*, no. 12, February 1921, pp. 509–11.

[44] *Protokoll des III Kongresses der Kommunistischen Internationale*, op. cit., pp. 286–7.

[45] Ibid., p. 287.

[46] See Fischer's speech in *Die Rote Fahne*, 10 February 1921; see also her article 'Die Rettung der deutschen Nation', in the next day's issue.

[47] *Die Rote Fahne*, 10 February 1921.

[48] See the resolution by Friesland and Fischer, and the article by Hort, 'Zentralismus und Bureaukratie', *Die Rote Fahne*, 15 February 1921.

[49] H. Brandler, 'Zur Organisationsfrage', *Die Rote Fahne*, 15 February 1921, evening edition.

To crown it all, when Rákosi was on his way back from Livorno, he stopped in Berlin to demand an explanation of the attitude taken up by Levi, whom he accused of being linked with Serrati, and of having made factional contacts with the Austrian and Yugoslav Parties in order to support Serrati's tendency against the ECCI. At a meeting of the Zentrale, Rákosi defended his policy at Livorno, and demanded that the Zentrale reverse its conciliatory resolution of 1 February.[50] He succeeded in convincing Thalheimer and Stoecker, who then moved a motion justifying both the split in the PSI and the need to struggle against Serrati, not merely for his refusal to exclude Turati's tendency, but for the PSI's positions on the national, agrarian and trade-union questions.[51] This motion was heavily defeated, and the Zentrale in this way endorsed its resolution of 1 February.[52]

But the ECCI did not give up. Rákosi also attended the meeting of the Central Committee on 22 February. He made a violent attack, denying Levi's statement that the greater part of the revolutionary workers had remained with Serrati, whilst the Communist Party only took semi-anarchist and syndicalist elements. He said that when Levi spread such slanders he was trying to deceive the German Party. In full cry, Rákosi then developed his own analysis. Whilst he did not repeat what he had said in private to Zetkin[53] – that the VKPD had too many members, and that a good number of its 400,000 should go – he declared that the split at Livorno should 'serve as an example', and that, if necessary, there would have to be 'splits, ten times over if need be, whether in Italy, France or Germany, in the interests of political clarity'.

Rákosi stressed that the International must have tempered cadres, and that the French Party, amongst others, needed to be seriously purged.[54] Levi saw Rákosi's statement as a declaration of war by the ECCI; he decided that the problem was no longer an accidental affair, as he had believed, but a political line which affected the construction of every Party. Zetkin expressed anger that Thalheimer and Stoecker, members of the Zentrale, should take upon themselves to raise before the Central Committee a motion which the Zentrale had expressly rejected. She saw in this operation a manoeuvre inspired by

---

[50] Levi Archives, P50 a7, under the heading 'Speech by Rakochin'.
[51] *Protokoll des III Kongresses der Kommunistischen Internationale*, op. cit., pp. 284–5.
[52] Ibid., p. 185.
[53] Ibid., p. 289.
[54] *Die Rote Fahne*, 26 February 1921.

Rákosi and, through him, by the ECCI, precisely one of those practices which gave credence to Serrati when he denounced the ultimatism and authoritarianism of the ECCI.[55] But the unexpected happened. By 28 votes to 23, the Central Committee adopted the Thalheimer-Stoecker motion, thus refusing to express confidence in Levi, and giving it instead to the emissary of the ECCI.[56] Levi was to say bitterly that the Central Committee had turned to the Delphic oracle to learn from the mouth of the priestess the real meaning of the events in Italy.[57]

This vote reopened the crisis on a higher level. At the session of the Central Committee the two Co-Chairmen of the Party, Levi and Däumig, with three members of the Zentrale, Clara Zetkin, Otto Brass and Adolf Hoffmann, resigned from the Zentrale. They submitted a written declaration that they were not in solidarity with Serrati and refused to be identified with him, but equally they refused to accept the positions of Rákosi and in that way to accept responsibility for policies aimed at 'creating more solid and pure parties by the method of mechanical splits'.[58] Brandler and Stoecker were elected as Chairmen of the Zentrale and Ernst Meyer, Frölich, Wegmann, Eberlein and Sievers joined the Zentrale to replace the members who had resigned. Frölich, Böttcher, Meyer and Sievers became Secretaries.[59] The new majority hastened to declare that it merely wanted the Party to cooperate loyally with the ECCI, and that it had no differences of principle with those who had resigned.[60] In reality, the factional struggle had only just begun, even though the new leaders of the VKPD were not yet aware of the fact. On 14 March Radek criticised them from Moscow for having treated Levi too kindly,[61] whilst at the Tenth Congress of the Russian Communist Party, Zinoviev in person rejoiced that Levi had been 'exposed', and declared that he had been 'fated' to have such a 'rightist' evolution.[62] War had indeed been declared.

---

[55] *Protokoll des III Kongresses der Kommunistischen Internationale*, op. cit., p. 285.
[56] Ibid., p. 286; Mujbegovic, op. cit., p. 267, n. 20.
[57] *Die Rote Fahne*, 1 March 1921.
[58] *Die Rote Fahne*, 28 February 1921.
[59] Mujbegovic, op. cit., p. 267, n. 22.
[60] *Die Rote Fahne*, 1 March 1921.
[61] Letter from Radek, Levi Archives, P55/3; *Sowjet*, no. 819, August 1921, pp. 248–9.
[62] *Die Kommunistische Internationale*, no. 16, 1921, pp. 555ff., but first published in Germany in *Freiheit*, 10 April 1921.

A political debate

From that time onwards, Levi fought the battle on the political level with great clarity. He demonstrated first that the differences began with very different appreciations of the world situation – something which he had not been able to see in the summer of 1920. The world situation was dominated by the importance of the bourgeois counter-offensive, which expressed itself in the ranks of the working class in the recovery of Social Democracy, especially in the trade unions. He stressed that in the Prussian elections half of the votes which had earlier been cast for the Independents had gone this time to the SPD. The principal concern of the VKPD should, therefore, be to avoid letting itself be isolated from the masses, and especially from the six million working people organised in the trade unions, a situation which was characteristic of Western Europe, but which the Russians had not experienced, and which they underestimated.

Another important difference appeared with the theory of the offensive. Although it had been discredited by the ill-fated march on Warsaw in the summer of 1920, it still had its supporters in Russia, particularly Bukharin. Levi declared: 'We cannot introduce the Soviet system mechanically, so to speak, at bayonet-point. The Soviet system has to rely on the revolutionary will of the proletariat in every country. Where that will is lacking, the proletarians receive the revolutionaries as oppressors.'[63]

All these problems were posed in Italy in the way that the split in the PSI developed. A split was necessary, but with Turati, not Serrati, and the representatives of the International had desired and prepared the split with Serrati. Indeed, the stakes were considerable; the problem was to hold in the party 100,000 workers who wanted to be communists, and it was a problem that would be faced in every country:

> There exist two ways, with these masses organisationally linked with the Third International, to reach a higher level of communist experience and communist will. One lies in educating them through fresh splits, and the other in politically educating these masses who have come towards us, going through this revolutionary period with them, and in this way reaching a higher level, with the masses and amongst the masses.[64]

---

[63] *Die Rote Fahne*, 10 February 1920.
[64] 'Wir und die Exekutive', *Die Rote Fahne*, 6 February 1921.

Levi said that the choice of the Russians – assuming that they were all in agreement – was to be explained by the tradition of Bolshevism, and the imprint left by its formation in illegality. In a mass party such as the workers' parties of the West, one could not proceed, as the successful split in the Independent Party had shown, 'to splits on the basis of resolutions, but only on the basis of political life', through activity and conviction produced by experience. After having made Serrati the figurehead of the International in Italy for two years, it was vain to hope to expose him in the eyes of the workers by a few 'open letters'. That was what the ECCI had done, and what it – fortunately – had not done in Germany. The Italian split was a dangerous precedent, the sign that the ECCI was in the process of going down the road of educating the Communist masses 'not by progressive education, but by mechanical splits'.[65]

Such practices were alien to the traditions of the revolutionary movement in the West. Levi had no doubt that they had been introduced from the Russian Party and the leadership which it exercised, through the ECCI, into the International. Levi denied that he was one of those who wanted to move the seat of the ECCI in order to remove it from the influence of the Russian leaders, but he stressed the isolation of the latter, the slow communications, the infrequency of personal meetings, and the difficulty which they had in forming an accurate appraisal of conditions in Western Europe. Moreover, the Bolshevik leaders stood at the head of a state, and inevitably were inclined to judge events from that position, at least initially.

This did not mean that the discussion with the Russians would be a dialogue of the deaf. Quite the contrary. Levi wanted a responsible discussion with them. But, for all these reasons, he refused to plunge into a factional struggle, which he was already being accused of doing. He sought the quickest possible clarification, which alone could spare the VKPD from the crisis and the factional struggles which would be so damaging to it:

> As you can see, the Italian question has now become a very serious issue for the German Party, with these consequences to which the representative of the Communist International has referred. We must understand very clearly how we can build and develop the German Communist Party, whether we want to remain together as a mass party, even if small groups break away from us to the right and to the left, whether we want to grow through

---

[65] 'Wir anderen', *Die Rote Fahne*, 1 March 1921.

united activity, or whether we want to reach a higher form of Communism by provoking a split, after a certain period of cohabitation, by the élite which has then taken shape. And I say this quite openly: there exist signs that in this Party some people are thinking about this second path.[66]

Events were soon to confirm this diagnosis.

---

[66] Levi Archives, P64/3, p. 23.

Chapter Twenty-Five

The March Action

Only a few weeks were to pass between Paul Levi's resignation from the chairmanship of the VKPD and his expulsion from the Party. These weeks were crucial in the history of German Communism and much about them remains obscure. Levi's opponents did not intend that the Italian affair should end with a mere change in the VKPD's leadership. When Radek returned to Moscow, he stopped being conciliatory, and sent to *Die Internationale* an article which indicated that the ECCI intended to carry the discussion to a conclusion, to what it called the 'activation' of the Party.[1] Radek declared that Levi only raised against the ECCI the bogey of a 'mechanical split' in respect of events in Italy because it had blamed him personally for the 'passivity' of the German leadership. Radek argued that the VKPD's old leadership 'had shown itself unable to move from the panic-stricken defensive in 1919 to the intensified offensive which the radicalisation of the Independent workers had made possible in 1920'.[2] It was clear: the VKPD was passing through a severe crisis, the proof of which was the fact that it did not act and merely confined itself to discussion, at a moment when nothing but action could highlight the problems of the day.[3] Radek gave the impression that the

---

[1] 'Die Krise in der VKPD', *Die Internationale*, no. 3, 1 March 1921, pp. 71–9.
[2] Ibid., p. 72.
[3] Radek dissociated himself from the personal opinions of Rákosi (ibid., p. 76).

ECCI wanted to 'activise' the VKPD, and break it from its routine of agitation and propaganda. The struggle against Levi was needed for that, and Radek blamed the 'conciliatory' attitude of Brandler, Stoecker and Thalheimer.

On 14 March, Radek spelt out his thoughts in a confidential letter addressed to Brandler, Frölich, Ernst Meyer and Böttcher, members of the Zentrale, as well as to Thalheimer and Felix Wolf:[4]

> Levi is trying to build a faction on the slogan of 'mass party or sect'. The swindle is that by implementing this line, he is engaged in dividing the Party in a catastrophic way, at a time when we can draw new masses around us by activising our policy. No one here is thinking of a mechanical split, nor of a split of any kind, in Germany. Our task is to bring to light the oppositions in the Party, and to make the left wing the leading force. Levi will soon go. But we must do all we can to prevent Däumig and Zetkin from going with him. . . .
>
> Everything depends on the world political situation. If the division between Germany and the Entente widens, and in the event of war with Poland, we shall speak. It is precisely because these possibilities exist that you must do all you can to mobilise the Party. One cannot start an action like firing a revolver. If today you do not do everything, by incessant pressure for action, to impart to the Communist masses the idea that they need to engage in action, you will again let slip a decisive moment. In this moment of political decisions of worldwide significance, think less about the 'radical' formula than about action, setting the masses in motion. In the event that war comes, think not about peace or about mere protests, but about taking up arms.[5]

Béla Kun's mission

We do not know the exact date when Kun arrived in Berlin, but only that it was around the end of February or the start of March. The new Chairman of the ECCI had been a Social-Democratic activist in Hungary before the War, and had been won to Bolshevism in 1917 when he was a prisoner of war. After secretly returning to Hungary, he had founded the Hungarian Communist Party. After being arrested, he emerged from jail to become Chairman of the

---

[4] Ibid., p. 79.
[5] Levi Archives, P55/3; *Sowjet (Unser Weg)*, no. 2/1, August 1921, pp. 248–9.

Council of Peoples' Commissars, and to lead the Party which had been formed by fusion with the Social Democrats. He succeeded in escaping after the council régime fell, and took refuge in Moscow, where he worked in the political section of the Red Army. He was strongly blamed for having had 'White' prisoners from Wrangel's army executed, in breach of the pledge given to them. Lenin spoke at first of having him shot, but finally was satisfied with sending him on a mission to Turkestan. Kun was a courageous but mediocre man. Lenin never concealed his low estimation of him, and that he was partly responsible, thanks to his opportunist errors, for the final collapse of the Hungarian conciliar republic. Perhaps it was for this reason that Kun thereafter proclaimed his leftism, and lost no opportunity to lambast the opportunists, particularly those in the VKPD, in the pages of *Kommunismus*. He was vigorously opposed amongst the Hungarian émigrés, criticised particularly for his use of factional methods, and for not shrinking either from threatening or corrupting people.[6] Nonetheless, he was an important figure, a member of the ECCI before the Second Comintern Congress, after which he became a member of the 'small bureau', and his work there caused him to be regarded as an unconditional supporter of Zinoviev. Two other collaborators of the ECCI arrived in Berlin at the same time, Josef Pogany, also a Hungarian, former president of the soldiers' council in Budapest, and the Polish Jew, Samuel Haifiz, who had come from the Zionist-socialist organisation, Poale Zion. He was known at this time as Guralski, and was to assume the name August Kleine in Germany.[7]

We must perhaps await the complete opening of the archives of the International and the Russian Party to learn the exact content of the mission in Germany which was entrusted to Kun, and to find out if he even had a specific mission. The documentation available gives no indication.[8] In April 1921, moreover, Curt Geyer, who represented the VKPD on the ECCI at the time declared that there had been no mention of this mission in the ECCI.

---

[6] Borkenau, op. cit., pp. 174–5.

[7] Borkenau (ibid.) mentions only Kun. Fischer (op. cit., p. 175) mentions only Kun and Guralski. The other authors (Carr, op. cit., p. 335; Brandt and Lowenthal, op. cit., p. 151; Flechtheim, p. 73) mention all three men. Gross (op. cit., p. 118) insists at length on the specific role of Pogany, who, she claims, was given the responsibility of putting an end to Willi Münzenberg's resistance to the ECCI in the Communist Youth.

[8] Mujbegović (op. cit., p. 269) refers on this point to the report of the meeting of the bureau of the ECCI on 22–23 February 1921, at which Kun and Guralski were present, and to the subsequent report by Curt Geyer.

Many years later, he stated that it had never been the subject of a meeting, or even mentioned in Moscow, at any rate in his presence.[9]

We can only suppose, in the light of Radek's letter, that the crisis in the VKPD was just one of the concerns of the leaders of the International. The sudden aggravation of tension in Europe – the ultimatum from the Entente demanding the disarming of the 'civic guards' in Germany, the extension of the Allied occupation zone, the advent of the plebiscite in Upper Silesia, and the military preparations in Poland – constituted a disquieting series of events. We have to reject the thesis that Kun's mission was connected with creating a diversion from the Kronstadt insurrection, which took place after he had left.[10] In the present state of information, the most likely explanation is that Kun acted on his own initiative, in the conviction that he would have the support and approval of the ECCI. In fact, people in Zinoviev's entourage were freely saying that, even if they were not victorious, great struggles by the international proletariat would permit Russia to avoid having to resort to the New Economic Policy.[11]

'Forcing the development of the Revolution'

As soon as Kun arrived, he set forth, in the course of individual discussions with the German Communist leaders, perspectives inspired by the theory of 'the revolutionary offensive', which was the vogue in Moscow, perspectives close to the model which Radek outlined in his letter. Kun also believed that the international crisis could not fail to worsen the conditions of life of the German proletariat, and that in this situation the VKPD must not maintain a passive or even expectant attitude. The German Communist leaders were to be taught that their Party could change the relation of forces by an active intervention, and that its duty was thus to tip the balance of the class struggle. It had to take the initiative, give an example through acts of resistance, and even, if necessary, 'force the development of the Revolution' by arousing a temporarily dormant working class. However, he encountered much resistance. Thomas describes his arrival and the beginning of his activity under the pseudonym of Spanior, and recounts a stormy interview in the presence of

---

[9] Interview given to Lowenthal, op. cit., p. 57, n. 117.
[10] A thesis put forward notably by Flechtheim, op. cit., p. 73.
[11] Lowenthal, op. cit., p. 63.

the Polish Communists, Warski and Lapinski.[12] Zetkin met him on 10 March, and was alarmed by what he said to her. She warned Levi, and thereafter refused to meet Kun except in the presence of a witness. Levi's turn to learn of the plans of the ECCI's delegate came on 14 March.[13]

The Central Committee met in Berlin on 16–17 March.[14] Kun does not appear to have spoken in support of his theses; everyone was convinced of the need to 'mobilise the masses', and only Malzahn did not share the general optimism about the inevitable approach of great proletarian struggles.[15] Brandler presented a statement inspired by the analysis made by the ECCI in Moscow, declaring:

> If the Revolution does not give a different turn to events, we shall soon have
> an Anglo-American war. . . . On 20 March, sanctions will be stiffened.
> Moreover, that very same day the referendum will be held in Silesia, and
> this seems likely to lead to conflicts between the Polish and the German
> bourgeoisie. . . . There's a 90 per cent chance of an armed conflict.[16]

He was vigorously supported by Frölich,[17] whose 'philosophy of action' in this dramatised international conjuncture led him to declare:

> We must by our activity do all we can to produce a breach [between the
> Entente and Germany], if necessary by a provocation. . . . What the Zentrale
> proposes now is a complete break from the past. Up to now, our tactic
> consisted in letting events take their course, and when a situation arose, we
> took our decisions within that setting. Today, we must ourselves forge the
> destiny of the Party and the Revolution.[18]

However, the Central Committee does not seem to have decided on this date to embark upon immediate action. Brandler was later to write:

---

[12] Freymond, op. cit., p. 25.
[13] These two discussions were referred to only by Levi in his speech at the May Central Committee meeting (Levi, *Was ist das Verbrechen?*, op. cit., p. 8).
[14] The report of this meeting in IML/ZPA 2/4, which Mujbegović consulted on, adds nothing essential, in her view, to the sources that are already known. The following quotations were made by Levi on the basis of this document, of which he had a copy.
[15] *Protokoll des III Kongresses der Kommunistischen Internationale*, op. cit., p. 553.
[16] Quoted in P. Levi, *Unser Weg: Wider den Putschismus*, Berlin, 1921, and in Levi Archives, P83/9, the text of which has in the margin of the quotation (p. 23) the handwritten note 'Brandler'.
[17] *Protokoll des III Kongresses der Kommunistischen Internationale*, op. cit., pp. 465, 553.
[18] Levi Archives, P83/9, p. 24, with the handwritten note 'Frölich'.

It was decided, in the event that the plebiscite in Upper Silesia led to an armed conflict, to appeal to the masses to struggle against this senseless adventure. Recognising that the sanctions provoked by the German government's passive resistance to the demands of the Entente or acceptance of these demands, could lead to more factories being closed and to production falling, the Central Committee decided, in the event that poverty forced the jobless and the laid-off workers to take to the streets, that it would do all it could to organise the struggle, to carry it on vigorously, and to set the masses in motion.[19]

The Central Committee voted to abandon its opposition on principle to partial strikes, and, further, decided to help widen the agricultural workers' struggles for higher wages. It considered that a partial victory in one sector, however exceptional, would restore confidence to the masses, and 'awaken their offensive spirit'. The politicisation of the strike movement would be effected under such slogans as 'Down with the Fehrenbach government! Alliance with Soviet Russia!', which would make unity possible. Finally, the Central Committee decided that the Party had to organise armed resistance if the government used the police or the Reichswehr to intervene against the mass strikes which they expected to occur.[20]

However, none of these activities was expected to be implemented immediately. The coming week was the run-up to the Easter holidays, and all the factories would be closed during 25–8 March. The Party was to use this interval to prepare itself for action during the week after Easter.[21] Then, before the meeting of the Central Committee ended, there arrived from Central Germany information which was to throw the original plan into confusion. The Oberpräsident of Prussian Saxony, the Social Democrat Hörsing, had just issued a statement announcing that he intended to have several industrial zones occupied by the police, including the mining district of Mansfeld-Eisleben, in order, as he put it, to 'clean up' the situation there.[22] The businessmen in these regions were complaining of frequent thefts, and the police were sometimes engaged in real battles with 'looters'. The official explanation Hörsing's measure was that it was to put a stop to the rise in

---

[19] H. Brandler, *War die Märzaktion ein Bakunisten-Putsch?*, Berlin-Leipzig, 1921, p. 20.
[20] Ibid., pp. 12–20.
[21] *Taktik und Organisation der revolutionären Offensive*, Leipzig-Berlin, 1921, p. 28; *Bericht über den 2 Parteitag der KPD*, op. cit., p. 61; Brandler, op. cit., pp. 16–17.
[22] *Die Rote Fahne*, 17 March 1921.

crimes ranging from theft to sabotage and attacks on the security staff in factories. However, there was no doubt that Hörsing's real aim was to disarm the workers – who had kept their weapons after the Kapp Putsch – and, at the same time, to break up a Communist stronghold. Although this news caught the Central Committee unprepared, it nonetheless in a certain way brought it relief. If we can believe Radek, Brandler was in the process of wondering whether they should not 'at some time provoke the enemy and take the initiative',[23] and Hörsing's action resolved this problem of conscience. The leftists seized the opportunity: Radek tells how Frölich 'came on the scene like a cavalry lieutenant, and declared: "Today we shall break from the tradition of the Party. Until now we have waited, and now we are taking the initiative and forcing the Revolution."'[24] The Party leaders in Halle, which incorporated the Mansfeld area, received the order to call a general strike as soon as the police occupied a factory, and to prepare at once for armed resistance.[25] The justification of the German leaders for their move to the general offensive was no longer the international situation, but Hörsing's attack on the working class.

The perspective which Kun had sketched out seemed to be in the process of realisation. After the Central Committee meeting closed, he persuaded Brandler to draft a statement to appear in *Die Rote Fahne* for the following day, 18 March, calling for the workers to be armed, which he justified by the refusal of the Bavarian government to disarm and dissolve the counter-revolutionary organisations of the Orgesch.[26] This appeal was reprinted several times up to 21 March in the central organ of the Party. Its connection with the Central Committee's appeal for resistance to Hörsing was not obvious.[27] Moreover, police detachments did not set off to invade the mining area until 19 March. On 20 March, *Die Rote Fahne* called on the German workers to support their brothers in Central Germany. An editorial, entitled 'Who Is Not With Me Is Against Me: A Word to Social-Democratic and Independent

---

[23] *Protokoll des III Kongresses der Kommunistischen Internationale*, op. cit., p. 463.
[24] Ibid.
[25] *Die Enthüllungen zu den Märzkämpfen*, Halle, 1922, p. 7.
[26] Lowenthal, op. cit., p. 61, following Brandler's account. The Orgesch (Organisation Escherich) was a right-wing terrorist organisation which had developed out of the Free Corps.
[27] See on this point B. Düwell, 'Disziplin und Grundsätze', *Sowjet*, no. 1, 1 May 1921, pp. 17–21.

Workers',[28] issued nothing less than an ultimatum to the non-Communist workers that they must choose their side in the rapidly-approaching struggles.

However, the response to these appeals seemed mediocre. On 18 March, the Zentrale had entrusted leadership of the action in the Halle-Merseburg district to two regional full-timers, Lemke and Bowitski.[29] On the 19th, the district committee met under the leadership of Fred Oelssner; the issue before it was to work out a way to push the situation 'in a revolutionary direction'.[30] On 20 March, Hörsing's troops continued their advance, and the Communist leaders continued to seek ways to arouse the spirit of struggle in the workers.[31] On the 21st, the strike began to spread in the districts occupied by the police, but the secretariat of the VKPD in Halle continued to hesitate before finally calling for a general strike throughout the district.[32] However, on the morning of 22 March, the strike was only partial. Reality did not correspond to the expectations of Kun and his supporters.

Armed clashes

Everything changed during the course of that day. First, Eberlein arrived in Halle, and explained to the local leaders that they must at all costs provoke an uprising in Central Germany, which would be the first stage of the Revolution. No means could be ruled out for shaking the workers out of their passivity, and he went so far as to suggest organising faked attacks on the VKPD or other workers' organisations, or kidnapping known leaders in order to blame the police and the reactionaries, and in this way provoke the anger of the masses. None of these projects was to be carried out after the failure of an attempt to blow up a munitions factory in Seesen.[33]

Things changed when Max Hoelz arrived in Halle on the evening of 21 March.[34] The hero of the armed struggles of March 1920 against Kapp's

---

[28] *Die Rote Fahne*, 20 March 1921.

[29] *Vorwärts*, 25 and 26 November 1921; *Die Enthüllungen zu den Märzkämpfen*, op. cit., p. 7.

[30] *Vorwärts*, 25 November 1921; *Die Enthüllunge zu den Märzkämpfen*, op. cit., p. 10.

[31] *Die Enthüllunge zu den Märzkämpfen*, op. cit., p. 19.

[32] *Die Rote Fahne*, 22 March 1921; *Taktik und Organisation der revolutionären Offensive*, op. cit., p. 137.

[33] *Vorwärts*, 25 and 26 November 1921; *Die Enthüllungen zu den Märzkämpfen*, op. cit., pp. 8, 16.

[34] See in particular S Ittershagen, 'Zur Rolle von Max Hoelz in den Kämpfen der mitteldeutschen Arbeiterschaft', *Die Märzkämpfe*, Berlin, 1956, pp. 105–11, as well as Hoelz's own version (op. cit.).

supporters had been expelled from the VKPD for adventurism after falling out with Brandler, and had lived in clandestinity, occasionally taking part in the expropriations carried out by such leaders of armed gangs as Karl Plättner, to finance the KAPD and its activities, legal and otherwise.[35] Shortly before the events of March 1921, Hoelz had been involved in the dubious business of an attempt to dynamite the Victoria column in Berlin on 13 March, which had provided the pretext for exceptional powers being given to Severing, the Prussian Minister of the Interior, and to Hörsing.[36] He appears to have joined the KAPD shortly before this, but he did not respect any Party discipline whatsoever, and had nothing but contempt for the people whom he called the 'politicians' of the VKPD and in particular for Brandler, his *bête noire*. When he arrived in the region, which he knew well, he addressed meetings of strikers, and began to recruit them to his armed bands.[37]

On the evening of the 22nd, Hoelz succeeded in forming his first nucleus in Eisleben, and armed it by disarming several policemen. The same night, he successfully attacked an arms depot, and then had enough weapons for any volunteers ready to join him. In forty-eight hours, his militia went over to armed action in the mining area, in the form of urban guerrilla warfare against soldiers and police, attacking banks, closing businesses, and extorting money from businessmen. The Chief Editor of the Communist newspaper in Mansfeld, Josef Schneider,[38] joined him, but generally the leaders and members of the VKPD were more restrained.[39] They similarly treated Karl Plättner, who appeared on the scene, and whose military role, though less known, was perhaps still greater.[40] The KAPD, on the contrary, claimed the credit for what he was doing, and its members hailed him as the hero of direct revolutionary action.[41]

The agreement which Kun arranged in Berlin for joint action between the two Communist Parties did not prevent rivalry breaking out between the VKPD and the KAPD on the ground. Whilst Eberlein was trying to mobilise

---

[35] Hoelz, op. cit., p. 142; on Plättner's 'expropriations', see Bock, op. cit., pp. 329–30.

[36] Hoelz, op. cit., pp. 138ff. The whole affair smells of police provocation.

[37] Ibid, p. 143. See also the very hostile article about Hoelz, 'Die Hölziade und ihre Ursachen!', *Freiheit*, 8 April 1921.

[38] Ibid.

[39] Apart from Lemke and Bowitski, who practically put themselves at his service.

[40] This is Bock's opinion, op. cit., p. 302. Plättner operated between Halle and Bitterfeld.

[41] Bock, op. cit., p. 297, cites 'Der Geist von Hölz ist wach!', *Kommunistische Arbeiter Zeitung*, no. 179, 1921.

his forces, two people sent by the KAPD from Berlin, Jung and Fritz Rasch, were doing the same in Halle.[42] The KAPD had a certain influence in this region, where an unsophisticated industrial proletariat still under rural influences was predominant. For nearly a year, one of its principal leaders, Peter Utzelman, had been active with the workers in the Leuna plant, amongst whom he had succeeded in founding a substantial union which produced its own newspaper.[43] On 21 March, the workers in this giant undertaking – which had a workforce of 12,000 – elected an action committee, of which Utzelman, elected under his pseudonym of Kempin, was chairman.[44] On 23 March, the plant was on strike, but the strike committee was divided by almost equally, between supporters of Kempin and those of the VKPD leader, Bernhard Koenen, who denounced his rival's 'provocations'.[45] Questions were raised. Were they to organise security services? Were the 2,000-odd armed workers in the factory to go over to the offensive in the region, or were they merely to hold this proletarian fortress? In the end, the armed workers in Leuna remained in their factory, their weapons unused, alarmed by the very adventurist extreme measures suggested by the leaders of the KAPD and their friends in the armed groups, cut off from the regional strike leaders, an isolated and eventually absurd stronghold.[46]

Throughout the rest of Germany, activists of both the VKPD and KAPD redoubled their efforts to arouse amongst the workers a massive wave of protest against the bourgeois offensive in Central Germany.[47] In Berlin, they organised a joint demonstration at which their speakers called for an immediate general strike, but the meeting was poorly attended. In Hamburg, on 23 March, a demonstration of unemployed led by Ernst Thaelmann occupied the docks, and elected an action committee.[48] On the morning of 24 March, the government proclaimed a state of emergency in Hamburg and Prussian Saxony, and gave Hörsing, who was appointed Reich Commissioner,

---

[42] F. Jung, *Der Weg nach unten*, Berlin, 1961, pp. 202ff.

[43] Bock, op. cit., p. 303.

[44] *Die Märzkämpfe 1921*, op. cit., p. 30.

[45] Ibid., p. 82. According to *Freiheit*, 5 April 1921 (evening edition), the Halle Communists who took Kempin for a provocateur had received every assurance to the contrary from their Zentrale.

[46] *Die Märzkämpfe 1921*, op. cit., pp. 80–2.

[47] Friesland was to complain on 7 April of the difficulties created by the KAPD which continually proposed 'provoking' action artificially by acts of terrorism or sabotage (Levi Archives, P83/9, p. 14).

[48] *Die Märzkämpfe 1921*, op. cit., p. 57.

exceptional powers to restore order. The Zentrale of the VKPD and the Central Committee of the KAPD replied on 24 March, the day before the factories closed for the Easter holidays, by issuing a call for a general strike.[49]

The decision was not reached unanimously. Members of both Parties' leaderships showed some scepticism about the workers' combativity. Friesland answered that Communists were obliged to fight, even alone if necessary.[50] Malzahn protested that the Party cut itself off completely from the masses when it called for a general strike under such circumstances. The fifty Communists, at most, who formed revolutionary nuclei in workplaces were going to see ranged against them the thousands of fellow-workers who in other circumstances would have readily followed them as they had earlier.[51] He was defeated and gave way, accepting the task of organising a general strike in the Ruhr.[52]

That Thursday, 24 March, the Communists used every means, including force, to attempt to set off a general strike. Groups of activists tried to occupy factories by surprise in order to prevent the entry of the great mass of non-Communist workers, whom they called 'scabs'. Elsewhere, groups of unemployed clashed with workers on their way to work or at the factories.[53] There were incidents in Berlin in several of the big factories, in the Ruhr and in Hamburg, where unemployed workers and dockers who had occupied the quays were driven out after a lively exchange of shots.[54] The general outcome was insignificant. Pessimistic estimates reckoned 200,000 strikers,[55] optimistic ones claimed half a million.[56] Some of the failures were bitterly disappointing, like that of Wilhelm Sült, who failed to win over his comrades in the power stations.[57] The joint demonstration of the VKPD and KAPD did not even attract 4,000 people in the Lustgarten,[58] whereas, a few weeks before, the

---

[49] Ibid., pp. 138–41; *Die Rote Fahne*, 24 March 1921.
[50] *Protokoll des III Kongresses der Kommunistischen Internationale*, op. cit., p. 553.
[51] Ibid., pp. 553–4.
[52] Ibid., p. 556.
[53] *Freiheit*, 22 March 1921, published the text of a leaflet issued by the Hamburg KPD which was an ultimatum for the disarming of the Orgesch: 'The unemployed will go and occupy the factories. The workers will obtain arms wherever they can, and will disarm the Orgesch wherever possible.'
[54] *Die Märzkämpfe*, op. cit., pp. 58–9.
[55] *Protokoll des III Kongresses der Kommunistischen Internationale*, op. cit., p. 251.
[56] According to Zinoviev, ibid., p. 184.
[57] *Die Rote Fahne*, 7 April 1921.
[58] 'A few hundred', according to *Freiheit*, 27 March 1921. The release of Friesland,

VKPD had received 200,000 votes in the elections. In Berlin, the strike was practically non-existent.[59]

Military and police reinforcements immediately flowed towards of the Mansfeld region. On 28 March, the Leuna works were bombarded, and the workers occupying them surrendered on the morning of 29 March.[60] In a final effort, Hoelz scattered his men in small groups. Against the orders of the Zentrale, the Communist leaders in the Ruhr gave the signal to return to work.[61] On 30 March, at the Central Committee, Franken, who represented the Ruhr, insisted that the order to return had to be issued at once. Brandler, Thalheimer, Stoecker and Heckert all inclined to that solution, but Eberlein insisted that they must try to 'hold out' still, and he carried the day.[62] It was only on 1 April that a call from the Zentrale gave the order to end the strike and an action that had long become hopeless.[63] On the preceding day, Sült, who was under arrest, had been shot whilst 'attempting to escape', in the police headquarters building.[64] His burial on 6 April was the occasion for the only demonstration by the mass of the Berlin proletariat during this period. The man whose initiatives had been decisive in the success in Berlin of the general strike against Kapp's supporters, gathered after his assassination the crowd of comrades who, for the first time, had not followed him when his party called on them to strike.[65]

On 30 March, *Pravda*, under the headline 'The German Revolution', hailed the German workers who were on the attack, it said, 'with the slogan of an alliance with Soviet Russia, under the leadership of the Communists, to aid the Soviet Republic.' It welcomed 'the combination of strikes and armed uprisings' which constituted 'the highest form of struggle known to the proletariat', and expressed delight that 'for the first time, the German proletariat has risen, with a Communist Party of half a million members at the head of

---

whose arrest had been one of the issues that led to the calling of the demonstration, doubtless contributed to this failure.

[59] Friesland admitted this on 7 April (Levi Archives, P83/9, p. 14).
[60] *Die Märzkämpfe*, op. cit., p. 102.
[61] Hoelz, op. cit., p. 162.
[62] *Protokoll des III Kongresses der Kommunistischen Internationale*, op. cit., p. 584. (Neumann) Neumann did not mention Eberlein, but Thalheimer, replying to him (ibid., p. 595), denied that the Zentrale was 'terrorised' by Eberlein.
[63] *Die Rote Fahne*, 4 April 1921.
[64] *Die Rote Fahne*, 1 April 1921.
[65] *Freiheit*, 7 April 1921; *Die Rote Fahne*, 7 April 1921.

the struggle'.[66] A few days later, Steklov, in *Izvestiia*, was already raising the question whether the German Communists did not bear the responsibility for a serious defeat by launching prematurely into a bid for power.[67] The action had ended, but the discussion was only beginning.

---

[66] *Pravda*, 30 March 1921.
[67] *Izvestiia*, 4 April 1921.

Chapter Twenty-Six

The Aftermath of a Defeat

The days which followed the defeat of the March
Action revealed the extent of the disaster which the
VKPD's leaders had inflicted upon their party. They
had not even been able to lead all their own members
into action. Some members publicly denounced the
strike. Many left the Party, sometimes noisily,
sometimes quietly slipping away. In a few weeks,
the party lost 200,000 members.[1] Moreover, it was
facing repression; its newspapers were being banned
or suspended, and its members being arrested,
sometimes held for a few hours or days, but often
charged and jailed for many months. The courts-
martial went to work with a vengeance; by the
beginning of June, it was calculated that of the strikers
or fighters in March there were already 400 sentenced
to some 1,500 years hard labour, and 500 to 800 years
in jail, eight to life imprisonment and four to death,
and there were still plenty awaiting trial.[2] Brandler,
the chairman of the Party, was sentenced to five years
imprisonment for high treason.[3]

---

[1] See Chapter 32. There were around 350,000 members at the beginning of March,
whereas in 1922 it was revealed that only 150,000 subscriptions had been paid in
August 1921.

[2] *Die Rote Fahne*, 9 June 1921. For six weeks, the KPD organ had been publishing
a regular 'balance-sheet'. F Knittel, in 'Die mitteldeutsche Märzkämpfe im Jahre 1921,
ihre Bedeutung und ihre Lehren', *Einheit*, no. 3, 1956, pp. 251–62, simply gives a total
of 2,500 years of imprisonment.

[3] *Die Rote Fahne*, 7 June 1921. See also *Der Hochverratprozess gegen Heinrich Brandler
vor dem ausserordentlichen Gericht am 6 Juni 1921 in Berlin*. Fischer (op. cit., p. 216)
locates this trial incorrectly as resulting from the Kapp Putsch, though she dates it

Tens of thousands of strikers lost their jobs, and were blacklisted by the employers. Moreover, in many factories and localities, the action of the authorities and the dismay of the workers led to the severing of the links between the Communists and the working class, links that had often only been recently forged.[4]

At this point it was not clear where the responsibility for the disaster lay. Many activists knew that on 17 March the Central Committee had decided only on a possible response to Hörsing's offensive in the Mansfeld region. Well into the 1960s, East German historians adhered almost entirely to the interpretation that viewed the March Action as a purely defensive reaction by the working people in Central Germany to a provocation on the part of the authorities.[5] This was indeed the first version to be put about, at least when defeat became evident. On 7 April, Friesland stated at a meeting of leading activists in Berlin that the Party had been obliged to respond to this offensive, but that conflicts had broken out in Central Germany against the intention and even the instructions of the Zentrale:

> In Berlin also we believed that armed insurrection could result only from a movement of the proletariat itself, that the general strike can only transform itself into armed struggle when it has really become a mass movement, but that at first we have to try to get the working class to clash with the employers.[6]

---

correctly. She asserts that Brandler defended himself more legalistically than politically. In fact, he told his judges that he accepted responsibility for all the decisions which the Zentrale had taken, which, to be sure, meant that he energetically denied that the party ever intended to stage a putsch. This was an essentially defensive stance. The people on the Left were to criticise him for having stated before the tribunal that the struggle for the dictatorship of the proletariat could be carried on within the framework of the Weimar Constitution. In a letter to the Zentrale on 17 June (*Sowjet*, no. 6, 1921, pp. 172–4), Brandler justified his attitude by the need to avoid playing into the hands of the governmental repression, and in this way to protect the activists. He insisted that his lawyer Weinberg assured him that he had been told by Pieck and Thalheimer that the Zentrale agreed with this method of defence. According to Mujbegović (op. cit., p. 280), who quotes the minutes of the meeting of the Zentrale on 15 July 1921, the Zentrale decided not to take a position as such on the conduct of Brandler, but to authorise those of its members who wished to do so to express their criticisms under their own names in the Party press. Here we have one of the first signs that the March coalition was breaking up.

[4] H. Malzahn, 'Die Märzaktion und unsere Gewerkschaftsarbeit', *Unser Weg (Sowjet)*, no. 2, 15 March 1921, pp. 35–8.

[5] See in particular *Die Märzkämpfe*, op. cit.

[6] 'Funktionärsitzung der VKP am 7 april in Kleiens Festsälen, Hasenkleide', Levi Archives P83/9, f11.

Immediately after the action was defeated, the 'errors' of the Mansfeld Communists, a few clumsy expressions and mistaken formulations in *Die Rote Fahne*, and the complications introduced into the conduct of the action by the KAPD, which was ready to use terrorism and provocation to start off a general strike and insurrection at all costs, explained, according to this spokesman of the Zentrale, how a correct policy had borne such disastrous fruits. He told the activists: 'I say that the blame lies in the failure of the working masses, who did not understand the situation, and did not give the reply that they should have given.'[7]

Levi's counter-attack

But Levi did not see things as Friesland presented them. During the vital days of March he was not in Germany. Immediately before the action, he had an angry discussion with Béla Kun, and then left for Italy, having, as he said, been assured that nothing important could happen before Easter. In Vienna, he learned of the March Action, and was thus able to appreciate the magnitude of the catastrophic turn which had been taken after he and his comrades had resigned from the Zentrale. Zetkin was to describe his initial reaction to Lenin and Trotsky:

> The unfortunate 'March Action' shook him to the depths. He firmly believed that the very existence of the Party was frivolously laid at stake, and everything for which Rosa, Karl, Leo and so many others gave their lives, squandered away. He cried, literally cried with pain at the thought that the Party was lost. He thought that it could only be saved by using the sharpest methods.[8]

He returned immediately to observe that Kun's theories had been put into practice, and that, on the pretext of 'forcing' the Party on to the offensive, the new leadership had led it to disaster. His first reflex was to write to Lenin, on 27 March. He reminded Lenin how much he himself had rejoiced at not holding a responsible position at the head of the Party, and assured him that his present attitude had nothing to do with the fact that others were now leading it: 'But the present leadership of the Party – I think I can say with certainty – is leading the Communist Party to complete collapse in six months

---

[7] Ibid., p. 17.
[8] Zetkin, *Reminiscences of Lenin*, op. cit., pp. 27–8.

at the most. This state of things, as well as the seriousness with which I
see the situation, has led me to write to you.'[9] He then described to Lenin
what had happened since Kun arrived, 'a comrade from the Communist
International',[10] and reported to him the discussions between Kun and Zetkin
and himself:

> The comrade explained: Russia found itself in an extraordinarily difficult
> situation. It was absolutely necessary that Russia be relieved by movements
> in the West, and, on that basis, that the German Party go immediately into
> action. Today, the VKPD had 500,000 members, and with that one could
> mobilise 1.5 million proletarians to bring down the government. He therefore
> favoured immediately joining battle with the slogan: 'Bring down the
> government!'[11]

He then recounted to Lenin how the March events had developed, insisting
that the actions that took place were not partial actions on the part of the
proletariat, but 'private undertakings by the Party', which resulted in the
Communists being mobilised against the rest of the working class, isolating
themselves, and strengthening the authority of the agents of the bourgeoisie
in the working class. He ended with an appeal to Lenin's authority:

> Since I regard the present situation of the Party not merely as difficult but,
> in the circumstances, as very dangerous, and in which the Party is in mortal
> danger, I turn personally to you, not knowing whether you are informed in
> detail of the policies of the Communist International, and beg that you will,
> on your part, reflect on this state of affairs and possibly act in consequence.
>
> Personally, I have no thought of opposing this policy of the International
> in Germany. I have already said to the representatives of the Executive, to
> whom I have explained my point of view, that I would do nothing which
> could thwart this action, because, after the recent events, I am only too well
> aware that my remarks would be listened to so that on the basis of them
> my listeners could label me an opportunist. Moreover, apart from my last
> meeting with the representative of the International, I have not lifted a finger
> against the policy of the Executive, and I simply await what follows. I shall
> now go no further except to write perhaps a pamphlet in which I shall state

---

[9] Levi Archives, P55/4, Levi, *Zwischen Spartakus und Sozialdemokratie*, op. cit., p. 37.
[10] Levi, *Zwischen Spartakus und Sozialdemokratie*, op. cit., p. 37, n. 1. Beradt unfortunately
indicates in a note that the person in question was . . . Rákosi!
[11] Levi, *Zwischen Spartakus und Sozialdemokratie*, op. cit., p. 38.

my point of view, but I shall make no criticism of the new leadership in Germany, nor of the Executive.

The comrades who bear the responsibility will not feel that I am obstructing them. But I ought to neglect nothing in these days and weeks which may be decisive for the German Party, and it is on this basis that I turn to you and beg that, if you approve even only partly of what I have said, you will undertake the necessary inquiry.[12]

However, the tempo of events speeded up, and on 2–3 April, Levi drafted his pamphlet. He submitted it to Zetkin, who judged it to be 'quite simply excellent',[13] and then tried twice to get a hearing from the Central Committee, which refused to listen to him.[14] On 7 April, at a meeting of cadres in Berlin, he did precisely what he had told Lenin he would not do, and delivered his first indictment of the policy of the Zentrale that had been inspired by the ECCI.[15]

Levi argued that any assessment of the March Action involved the fate not merely of Communism in Germany but that of the entire International: 'Such an action was completely impermissible from the standpoint of Communism.'[16] The contending positions of the debates on the split in the PSI reappeared, with all their concrete consequences and implications. There was Levi's position, rejected by the Zentrale, 'namely, that the actions could not be carried on by the Communist Party alone, and that they could only be carried out by the proletariat', and there was the other, which unfortunately had prevailed, which stated that 'the Communist Party could undertake activities on the basis of its own forces alone'.[17] This was the conception which had inspired the interventions on the Central Committee of people such as Frölich and Brandler, following Radek, and which had expressed itself in the appeal from the Zentrale, published on 18 March in *Die Rote Fahne*, which was nothing less than an appeal to arms: 'Every worker must defy the law, and obtain a weapon wherever he can find it.'[18]

Levi stressed that, at that point, there had not yet been any fighting in Central Germany. Only after these appeals had been repeated day after day

---

[12] Ibid., pp. 43–4.
[13] Beradt, op. cit., p. 49.
[14] Ibid., Levi Archives, P113/6.
[15] Report of the discussion, Levi Archives, P83/9.
[16] Ibid., f21.
[17] Ibid., f22.
[18] *Die Rote Fahne*, 18 March 1921.

was there any fighting: 'I tell you that what happened at Mansfeld was the necessary consequence of the gamble in Berlin.'[19] He counterposed the celebrated phrase in the *Communist Manifesto*, which points out that the communists have no interests separate from those of the working people, to the quotation from Bakunin which figured in the headline of the editorial of *Die Rote Fahne* for 20 March, and he accused the Party leadership of having adopted this typically anarchist conception, according to which one could 'make' the revolution simply because the Party was 'an organisation built on the devotion and the highest spirit of sacrifice of its members, and on the basis of a radical determination of its leaders'. He counterposed to this idea the Marxist conception according to which 'no Party, not even the most powerful, has the possibility of making the revolution over the heads of the rest of the proletariat'.[20] The German leaders had turned their backs on the Spartacist tradition as much as on that of Bolshevism, when, as Friesland had just admitted, they sent in the unemployed to attack the factories: 'There was yet another idea, that of making the revolution with the minority of the proletariat against its majority. . . . And there is now a fatal idea which underlies the other, that we also can organise strikes against the majority of the proletariat.'[21]

The result of this senseless policy was defeat, the importance of which lay not in the extent of the repression nor in the increased hatred of the bourgeoisie, but in the fact that 'a wall of distrust' stood from now on between the majority of the proletariat and the Communists.[22] This result was all the more damaging to the ability of the Communists to act and develop their influence because the relationship of class forces on the world scale had changed over the preceding year. The fascist offensive against the workers' organisations in Italy and the use of troops against striking miners in Britain were examples of the counter-offensive which the counter-revolution was mounting everywhere, a very serious matter.

Our Road

The Central Committee met secretly on 6–7 April. Zetkin demanded that it hear Levi, but it refused, and she proposed a motion criticising the Zentrale,

---

[19] Levi Archives, P83/9, f26.
[20] Ibid., f30.
[21] Ibid., f33.
[22] Ibid., f35.

and calling for a special congress. This was rejected by 43 votes to 6, with 3 abstentions.[23] The Committee then adopted another motion, by 26 votes to four, which justified the March Action on the grounds that an offensive tactic had been necessary, and laid the blame for the defeat on the 'treachery' of Social Democracy, and the 'passivity' of the working class. It ended with an appeal for discipline to be tightened: 'The Central Committee approves the political and tactical position which the Zentrale adopted, sharply condemns the passive and active resistance of some comrades as individuals during the action, and calls on the Zentrale to put the organisation on a war footing by all sufficient means.'[24] The first sanction was applied to Max Sievers, a member of both the Central Committee and the Zentrale, who was expelled for indiscipline from both bodies. It was clear that other heads were going to roll.

On 12 April, Levi's pamphlet *Unser Weg: Wider den Putschismus* [*Our Road: Against Putschism*] came off the presses.[25] It was a passionate indictment of the March Action and the ideas which had inspired it, and a presentation of Levi's general ideas about the revolution and the role of a Communist Party in an advanced country.

Levi said that the tempo of the Revolution was the crucial problem facing the German Communists. He took the objective conditions as given, with particular emphasis on the existence of the Communist International, and proposed to examine the subjective conditions. He noted briefly that the German bourgeoisie had now emerged from its postwar crisis, and had consolidated itself sufficiently to be able to stage a counter-attack. The position of the working class in the class struggle was of key importance. This had clearly improved, especially with the foundation of the VKPD, but the existence of a party of half a million members did not resolve the fundamental problem, the winning of the masses in order to take power.

From this point of view, Levi continued, the Party should not overestimate its successes. Not only had it been unable to reach the middle classes in order to group them behind the proletariat, but it still only enjoyed the allegiance

---

[23] Text of the motion presented by Zetkin in *Die Rote Fahne*, 30 April 1921; and *Unser Weg* (*Sowjet*), no. 1, 1 May 1921, pp. 4–10.

[24] *Die Rote Fahne*, 9 April 1921.

[25] According to Radek (*Soll die VKPD*, op. cit., p. 108), it was taken to the printer on 3 April, and, according to Levi at the Central Committee meeting of 4 May (*Was ist das Verbrechen?*, op. cit., p. 31), on 8 April, after the Central Committee had repeatedly refused to meet him.

of a minority of the proletariat. Without having electoral illusions, and whilst completely rejecting the old Social-Democratic argument about needing 51 per cent of the votes before starting the struggle for power, Levi believed that election results, as Lenin wrote, were an excellent 'thermometer' with which to assess the temperature of the masses. The figures were clear. Twenty per cent of the workers conscious enough to give their votes to a workers' party voted Communist. Study of trade-union membership revealed the same observation. The 500,000 members of the VKPD represented one-sixteenth of the working people organised in trade-unions. The Communists were therefore far from being a majority in the working class. By itself, this observation alone would suffice to condemn any premature attempt to take power. But it was necessary to go still further, by learning from the Bolsheviks' experience. Lenin wrote, in his pamphlet *Can the Bolsheviks Retain State Power?*:

> If the revolutionary party has no majority in the advanced contingents of the revolutionary classes and in the country, insurrection is out of the question. Moreover, insurrection, requires: 1) growth of the revolution on a country-wide scale; 2) the complete moral and political bankruptcy of the old government, for example the 'coalition' government; 3) extreme vacillation in the camp of all middle groups, that is, those who do *not* fully support the government, although they did fully support it yesterday.[26]

None of these supplementary conditions existed in Germany in 1921. Before the Bolsheviks seized power, they controlled at least half of the army, whilst the influence of the German Communists in the Reichswehr was nil. The Bolsheviks dominated the soviets in all the industrial centres, whilst the German Communists were in a majority in the proletariat solely in Central Germany, and even there their influence was falling.

Faced with such a relationship of forces, the duty of Communists was, of course, to work to create a revolutionary situation, which would enable them to speed up the conquest of the majority:

> We have always defended the idea that a political party can, and a Communist Party must, create situations of conflict *by the clarity and decisiveness with which it intervenes, by the vigour and the daring of its work of agitation and propaganda,* by the intellectual and organisational influence which it gains over the masses, in short, by *political* means.[27]

---

[26] V.I. Lenin, 'Can the Bolsheviks Retain State Power?', *Collected Works*, Volume 26, op. cit., pp. 133–4.

[27] P. Levi, *Unser Weg: Wider den Putschismus*, Berlin, 1921, p. 33.

Now, it was precisely this method, this tradition and these Marxist conceptions of the political struggle that for months had been under attack from those who proclaimed the need to 'break with the past', and to leave behind the days of passivity and purely propagandist activity. Levi said that the March Action had revealed what their new ideas meant: 'The innovation, which to be sure is a break with the past, of the Unified German Communist Party, is the idea that one can also create situations of conflict by non-political means, by police methods, by provocations.'[28]

Levi relied on quotations – anonymous ones – from members of the Zentrale in the session of 17–18 March, and on extracts from *Die Rote Fahne* to prove how this philosophy of the offensive led to the unemployed being set against other working people, and the Communists being forced, even when they were in a minority in their factories, to go out on strike and thereby lose their jobs, isolating them from their workmates, deliberately throwing away the influence they had already won, and in this way handing the factories over to the influence of the union bureaucrats. The crisis which was shaking the party could not be explained in any other way. A mass party could not be led in the way that Ludendorff led the Imperial army. One could not lead militant workers without taking account of what they felt, the feelings which they shared with the majority of their class, and the links which united them to the rest of the working people with whom they lived and struggled. The result was the March Action, 'the biggest Bakuninist putsch in history'.[29]

But the German Zentrale was not alone in being responsible for this disastrous policy. Levi attacked Kun, without actually naming him, regarding him as the initiator of the action:

> The initiative for this action did not come from the German Party. We do not know who bears the responsibility for it. It has already happened often enough that emissaries from the Executive Committee have exceeded their powers, that is, we have observed after the event that the emissaries had not been granted full powers to deal with this or that affair. . . . So there has been a certain pressure exerted on the Zentrale to launch itself into action, now, immediately and at all costs.[30]

The problem of the relations between the Party and the ECCI had to be approached: 'Not only because this catastrophic defeat of the Unified German

---

[28] Ibid., p. 33.
[29] Ibid., p. 39.
[30] Ibid., p. 51.

Communist Party also affects the Communist International, but, without going into details, because the Executive Committee of the Communist International bears at least part of the responsibility.'[31] Levi spelt out the material difficulties which obstructed links with Moscow; the ECCI was cut off from Western Europe. One of the causes of the present crisis lay in the solution which was adopted to overcome these difficulties, the despatch by the ECCI of 'trusties' to the national Parties with the task of supervising them. It was understandable that these men could not be chosen from amongst the best, from the Russian Party cadres, who were so indispensable in Russia itself. The men who were available and whom the ECCI sent – exiles from Central Europe – were at best mediocrities. To indicate Kun, Levi spoke of 'the man from Turkestan': the allusion is often misunderstood, but it stems from Lenin having Kun sent to Turkestan as a result of his conduct when Wrangel's army capitulated in Crimea. The Hungarian leader came out of disgrace only to be entrusted with the mission to Germany. Levi recalled what Rákosi had said in Berlin about the necessity of further splits in all the large Communist Parties, immediately after the Livorno Congress. Levi pointed out that Radek had disavowed them in a still-unpublished article, declaring that Rákosi had spoken 'only as an individual'. He commented:

> A very frivolous game is being played here. The method of sending abroad irresponsible people whose behaviour one can later, according to requirements, approve or disavow, is indeed a very convenient one, but even though it is hallowed by a long tradition in the Party, it is catastrophic for the Third International.[32]

The very attitude of the delegates from the ECCI towards the national Parties was an obstacle to the necessary political centralisation:

> They never work with the Party leadership in the country, but always behind its back, and often against it. They get a hearing in Moscow when others do not. It is a system which cannot possibly fail to undermine all confidence in joint work, either amongst comrades on the executive or in the member parties. These comrades are for the most part useless as political leaders, and moreover are quite insufficiently familiarised with these problems. A heart-breaking situation results. There is no political leadership coming from

---

[31] Ibid., p. 29.
[32] Ibid., p. 51.

the centre. All that the Executive does in that direction is to send appeals which reach us too late, and excommunications which come too soon. Such a political leadership on the part of the Communist International can lead to nothing but a catastrophe. . . . The Executive acts no differently than as a Cheka, projected beyond the frontiers of Russia – an impossible situation. To demand precisely a change, so as to prevent the incompetent hands of incompetent delegates from again grasping hold of the leaderships in the different countries, to call for a political leadership and to protest against a Party police does not mean demanding independence.[33]

Despite the vigour of his criticisms, Levi did not fundamentally question either the existence or the organisational principles of the Communist International. His conclusion proves this. He was expecting it to correct its errors, in the conviction that this meant defending in the current situation the ideas which Lenin and Trotsky had defended for years in the Bolshevik Party.

A severe reaction

But the ECCI was not ready for conciliation. On 4 April, it issued a statement regarding the resignation from the Central Committee of Levi, Zetkin, Däumig and others. It characterised this as 'desertion', and declared: 'The reason why comrade Levi and his group left the Zentrale of the German Communist Party was not the Italian question, but opportunist vacillations in respect of the policies for Germany and on the international level.'[34] The ECCI went on to express the hope that Levi's conduct would open the eyes 'of the comrades who had sided with him'. On 6 April, for the first time, the leading Committee adopted a position on the March Action, which it hailed as 'the first organised attack by the German proletariat' since March 1919, and ascribed its defeat to 'the inconceivable treachery of the Social-Democratic Party', and to the refusal of the Independents to plunge into the struggle at the side of the Communists. To the German Communists, the ECCI solemnly declared: 'The Communist International says to you: "You acted rightly. The working class can never win victory by a single blow. You have turned a new page in the history of the German working class. Prepare for new struggles."'[35]

---

[33] Ibid., p. 55.
[34] *Die Rote Fahne*, 14 April 1921.
[35] Degras, Volume 1, op. cit., pp. 217–18.

Thus encouraged, the Zentrale voted on 15 April to expel Levi from the Party, and demanded that he give up his seat as a deputy in the Reichstag. A declaration in bold type on the front page of *Die Rote Fahne* summed up its complaints against him.[36] He apparently had sent for printing on 3 April a pamphlet which contained falsehoods about and attacks upon the leadership of the Party and the representative of the International. He had refused to submit it before publication to the leading bodies of the Party, and had gone ahead on a day when the fighting was still continuing, and when repression was striking hard at the Party activists. He had publicly expressed opinions which were formally condemned by the Central Committee on 7–8 April. He had taken no part whatever in the actions which the leadership had called in March, and had written a pamphlet against the Communist fighters even when the fighting was going on. The Zentrale stressed that Levi was excluded for indiscipline, and declared that it did not question the right to criticise 'before and after the action': 'Criticism on the basis of the struggle and in full solidarity in the struggle is for the Party a vital necessity and a revolutionary duty. However, the position of Paul Levi is not a criticism based on the Party and on the struggle, but gives open support to its enemies.'[37]

There were some vacillations in the Zentrale. Ernst Meyer denounced in *Die Rote Fahne* 'Levi's road' towards the Independents,[38] and Maslow called him 'the German Serrati'.[39] Thalheimer, on the other hand, recalled the services which he had rendered and his eminent role in difficult moments:

> With Levi, the Communist movement in Germany also separates itself from a fragment of its own past. The Party is separating from a leader with immense, varied and brilliant qualities. But it is also leaving behind a leader who did not succeed in merging his whole being into the Party, so that his very personality was irrevocably engaged in the cause to which he devoted himself, that is, the Party in which it is incarnated. It is more than his life that he must give to the Party, it is his own personality, without reserve. Levi has not been able to do this.[40]

Levi immediately appealed to the Central Committee against the Zentrale's decision. On 16 April, eight well-known leaders and Party members holding

---

[36] *Die Rote Fahne*, 16 April 1921.
[37] Ibid.
[38] *Die Rote Fahne*, 15 April 1921.
[39] *Die Rote Fahne*, 15 April 1921 (evening edition).
[40] 'Das Oberste Gesetz', *Die Rote Fahne*, 16 April 1921.

responsibilities declared their solidarity with him, and offered themselves as guarantors that he was stating the truth – Däumig, Zetkin, Otto Brass and Adolf Hoffman, who had resigned with him from the Zentrale in February, Curt Geyer, the delegate of the Party in Moscow, and three leading figures in the trade-union commission, former leaders of the revolutionary delegates, Paul Neumann, Heinrich Malzahn and Paul Eckert.[41] There could be no disputing that a whole sector of the German leadership refused either to accept the expulsion of Levi or the reasons advanced for it. The Party crisis was now in public view.

On the same day, 16 April, Lenin finished the draft of a letter to Levi and Zetkin,[42] in reply to their letters at the end of March. On the burning question which was shaking the Party and was to shake the International, he wrote:

> As for the recent strike movement and the action in Germany, I have read absolutely nothing about it. I readily believe that the representative of the executive committee defended the silly tactics, which were too much to the left – to take immediate action 'to help the Russians': this representative is very often too left. I think that in such cases you should not give in, but should protest and immediately bring up this question officially at a plenary meeting of the executive bureau.[43]

Lenin did not yet know that Levi had published his pamphlet, but he was anxious about this project, and he criticised the two German leaders for having resigned from the Zentrale:

> But to withdraw from the central committee!!?? That, in any case, was the biggest mistake! If we tolerate the practice of responsible members of the central committee withdrawing from it when they are left in a minority, the communist parties will never develop normally or become strong. Instead of withdrawing, it would have been better to discuss the controversial question several times *jointly* with the executive committee. Now, comrade Levi wants to write a pamphlet, that is, to deepen the contradiction! What is the use of all this? I am convinced that it is a big mistake. Why not wait?

---

[41] *Die Rote Fahne*, 17 April 1921. The three latter activists had been accused of having sabotaged the strike, but had been cleared of this accusation in a statement by the Party Chairman Brandler and Stoecker to the Central Committee (Levi Archives, P83/9, f17).

[42] Levi Archives, P55/10, P63/3; V.I. Lenin, 'To Clara Zetkin and Paul Levi', *Collected Works*, Volume 45, Moscow, 1976, p. 124.

[43] Ibid., pp. 124–5.

The congress opens here on 1 June. Why not have a private conversation here, *before* the congress? Without public polemics, without withdrawals, without pamphlets on differences. We are so short of tried and tested forces that I am really indignant when I hear comrades announcing their withdrawal, etc. There is a need to do everything possible and a few things that are impossible to avoid withdrawals and aggravation of differences at all costs.[44]

These counsels came too late. The pamphlet was already published, and the Zentrale had expelled Levi.

What Is the Crime?

Levi was permitted to present his appeal in person before the Central Committee, and he renewed his attack. Once more he denounced the March Action and the responsibility borne by Kun – whom he never attacked by name – for the conception of the 'offensive' struggle as well as for the use of provocation. To the themes which he had already developed, both at the meeting on 7 April and in the pages of *Our Road*, this time he added some touches of stinging irony at the expense of the Zentrale, its evasions, and its retreat in the face of its responsibilities:

> The Zentrale says: 'I did not want that.' The Executive says: 'I did not want that.' The representatives of the Executive say: 'We did not want that.' Thus in the last analysis, it is evidently the workers who 'wanted that', and who advanced the thesis according to which it was necessary to force the revolution, and to go over from the 'defensive' to the 'offensive'.[45]

The rest of Levi's speech was a denunciation of the bad faith of his accusers, a criticism of the formal, mechanical conception of discipline in the name of which they attacked him, analyses which he supported with examples from the recent history of the international Communist movement. He said that his critics accused him of publishing extracts from the minutes of meetings of the leading bodies of the Party. He replied that Lenin had acted in the same way in 1917 in the public polemic against Zinoviev and Kamenev. His critics attacked him for his defeatism, a one-sided picture of the state of the Party, and catastrophic judgements. Levi replied by recalling the attitude of

---

[44] Ibid., p. 125.
[45] Levi, *Was ist das Verbrechen?*, op. cit., p. 17.

Zinoviev himself in 1917 – which had not led to his expulsion from the Bolshevik Party:

> Never I believe, have I put forward so catastrophically false an appreciation of the situation as comrade Zinoviev did in his appreciation of the situation in October 1917, when he declared that the seizure of power by the Bolsheviks would be a senseless putsch. I never resigned from my Party duties or refused my cooperation in any action as decisive as the action of October 1917 was for the existence of the Bolsheviks, as Zinoviev did then, so that he can present himself later on as the great accuser of the 'Mensheviks' and the 'undisciplined'.[46]

Levi reminded the members of the Party leadership how in the past he had wanted to confine to internal discussion his serious criticisms of the Zentrale at the moment of the Kapp Putsch, and how Zinoviev and the ECCI overrode his wishes as well as the personal reservations of the German leaders who were under attack at the time:

> The letter was published in *Communist International* at that time against my wishes. When I heard this publication being spoken of in Petersburg, I immediately opposed it, and said that this letter had not been written to be published. At that time, it was Zinoviev who said that when a Party committed such catastrophic stupidities as the German Party at the time of the Kapp Putsch, criticism of these stupidities was not a private affair.[47]

There were some who contrasted his attitude to that of Luxemburg, who did not reject responsibility for the street fighting in January 1919 in which Liebknecht and his supporters engaged against her advice. Levi replied that this attitude was to be explained

> . . . by a completely different perspective, namely that at that moment it was the broad masses who were mistaken, not a small circle of leaders who rushed to lose the masses who were not mistaken. There had been [in January 1919] a genuine mass movement, large, powerful and spontaneous, and there were more working people on one occasion in the Tiergarten in Berlin than intervened [in March 1921] in the whole of Germany.[48]

---

[46] Ibid., p. 35.
[47] Ibid., p. 32.
[48] Ibid., p. 33.

He turned to Liebknecht's former lieutenant, who had now become one of his accusers, and added: 'And I believe, comrade Pieck, that you must also know that comrade Rosa Luxemburg thought that she could not even go on working with Karl Liebknecht, so much did she condemn what he was doing. She had written nothing more . . . when death took away her pen.'[49] Levi therefore believed that he had not only not broken discipline when he published his pamphlet, but that he had acted in conformity with the highest imperative of revolutionary action. His opponents, moreover, had acted no differently, and had claimed before him the right which today they denied him: 'The Tenth Congress of the Russian Communist Party took place, if I am not mistaken, on 6 March of this year. About 15 March, we already had the reports on Europe, in which Zinoviev declared: "We have joined battle against Levi."'[50]

Levi attacked Pieck on the grounds that, it seemed deliberately, he confused the date of writing the pamphlet with that of its publication. He declared that it had been drafted on 3–4 April, but had been taken to the printers only on 8 April, after the Central Committee had once more announced that its policy had been correct, and had refused him the right to attend a session to present his criticism, whilst at the same time depriving him of every legitimate way to express his position in the Party on such a vital, burning question. He reminded them of the sanctions which had been summarily applied against his supporters since the action ended, adding that they proved that the Zentrale wanted to purge the Party, and declared that he had no intention of falling into the trap that had been laid for him: 'If you want a purge, I shall not let myself be expelled by you on the basis of a paragraph dealing with organisational questions.'[51]

From this point of view, it was absurd for the Party leaders to accuse Levi of having 'stabbed the Party in the back' by expressing himself openly after the end of the action. Silence on his part would have been criminal: 'When the Party is in danger, one's duty is to speak out. . . . This is not stabbing it in the back; it is the highest duty, when a party finds itself so deficient, to tell the truth. I do not want the Party to make such mistakes again, but, if that happens, I hope that there is someone present to act in the same way.'[52]

---

[49] Ibid.
[50] Ibid., p. 43.
[51] Ibid., p. 44.
[52] Ibid., p. 8.

Levi loudly demanded that the Party use the remedy which he had employed, a public, very loud, statement of position, because he believed it to be the only suitable way to combat the evil:

> Comrade Pieck said literally: 'But the worst is that Levi has sown distrust towards the Zentrale and the representatives of the Executive.' Yes I did that, I admit to the crime of high treason. I even add: in my pamphlet, I consciously went even further, I wanted to do more than sow distrust. . . . The Party had gone off the rails, and had placed itself in a fatal situation. Nothing but a surgical operation could at one stroke prevent new outbreaks of the illness, cut it short, as they say in medicine. This method was not to sow distrust of the Zentrale, but to expose and to chastise pitilessly this whole political crime, this whole betrayal of the principles which until now were those of the Party. It was to cut short the illness, and I freely acknowledge that I did it and intended to do it.[53]

Certain Communists honestly believed that such criticisms of the Party leadership or the International, even if they were justified, could be made only within the ranks of the Party, amongst Communists. They were wrong:

> It is completely wrong to think that communists can discuss their mistakes amongst themselves, far from indiscreet glances. The faults and mistakes of the Communists, along with their good qualities, form part of the political experience of the proletariat. They cannot and they must not deprive the masses of either the one or the other. If they made mistakes, they did not make them against the Party, even if these mistakes led to its ruin. If this is the only way in which the proletariat can learn the lesson of events, it must be so, because the Party is there for the proletariat and not vice versa.[54]

It was therefore in full awareness of the consequences of his actions that Levi had tried to give all the necessary publicity to his attack on the March 'crime', a blunder so gross that the lessons of it had to be drawn, and that these lessons made known outside the confines of the Party, rather than keeping it private for the sake of appearances. Here he seemed to be indirectly answering the proposals of Lenin in his letter of 16 April:

---

[53] Ibid., p. 31.
[54] Ibid., p. 44.

> I also understand perfectly why the [Comintern] Executive wants to leave over to the Third Congress the final decision about these problems of practical anarchism, which are by no means as new as the Executive claims. This, quite simply, is because it supposes that the German Party, which was alone in committing the stupidity, is also capable of penalising it at the end of the day. . . . But, in principle, this whole method, which consists of dragging the discussion from one committee to another, or from one small circle to another, on questions so serious for the Party, is, I repeat, completely consistent with the underlying conception which inspired the entire action – you can commit idiocies in a small circle, therefore you can correct them in a small circle. If there is anything to be learned from the March Action, it can only be learned on condition that the masses get to know and discuss the mistakes within the widest and the freest framework.[55]

Here was the fundamental difference, not only with the German leftists but, perhaps also, with the Russian Communists – though Levi did not risk a judgement on that point. In reality, it was about what a Communist Party in Western Europe ought to be, in a social context different from that in which the Bolshevik Party had operated in Russia:

> In Russia before the Revolution, the Communist Party had to form itself in a society in which the bourgeoisie was by no means fully developed. It had to form itself in a society in which the natural opposite pole to the proletariat, the bourgeoisie, existed as yet only sketchily, and in which its main adversary was agrarian feudalism. The situation is completely different in Western Europe. Here the proletariat faces a fully developed bourgeoisie and one of the consequences of this full development of the bourgeoisie, namely democracy. Under democracy, that is, under what has to be taken for democracy under the rule of the bourgeoisie, the organisation of the working people assumes different forms than under the feudal agrarian state, under absolutism.
>
> Thus, in Western Europe, the form of organisation cannot be other than that of an open mass party, of these *open mass parties* which therefore cannot be set in motion on the orders of a central committee, but only through that invisible fluid in which they exist, in psychological interaction with the whole of the rest of the proletarian mass. They do not move with response

---

[55] Ibid., pp. 28–9.

to commands; they move with the movement of those same proletarian classes of which they must later be the leaders and advisers. They depend on the masses as the masses do on them, and that is why, comrades, (and I shall speak about this later) it was a fatal mistake on the part of the Zentrale, after this action collapsed, to have made the attempt – which was not at all revolutionary – to dispose within a few committees of all the questions which were raised.[56]

To fail to understand this difference and to continue trying in Western Europe and especially in Germany to construct a Communist Party on the Russian model, was to run the risk of being unable to build a mass Communist Party, and especially of perpetuating the division in the workers' movement, which itself was based upon existing social cleavages within the working class:

> This fact alone carries in itself the grave danger that the working class may break up, that two strata, the organised and the unorganised, the Communist organisation and the non-Communist organisation, not only confront each other as politically separate bodies, but in a certain sense divide as distinct social realities, that one organisation includes different strata of the proletariat from the other, that the Communist Party is not what it should be, the organisation, to be sure, of a part of the proletariat, that of the most advanced proletarians, a part which permeates the whole proletariat, but, instead, that it becomes a party of the proletariat divided vertically according to factors of social differentiation.[57]

Differences in the coalition against Levi

Was this a clever foreboding of what, a few years later, would be the division of the German workers' movement in the face of the Nazis, the split between the unemployed Communists and the employed Social Democrats? This danger, for the moment, presented itself to Levi through Radek's articles and the conduct of the Zentrale. At this juncture, it seemed to him hardly likely that the orientation of the International would take that form; the numerous references to the authority and the writings of Lenin and Trotsky were not simple polemical devices, and Levi had some reason to think that the

---

[56] Ibid., pp. 20–1.
[57] Ibid., p. 21.

two Russian leaders were the most consistent 'Levites',[58] and also the most difficult to expel!

Nonetheless, the Central Committee endorsed his expulsion by 38 votes to seven, censured the eight leaders, including Däumig and Zetkin, who had said that his accusations were based on the truth,[59] removed Wegmann, after Sievers, from the Zentrale, accepted the resignation of Geyer, who had returned from Moscow and supported Levi, and replaced them with Walcher and Eberlein, two former Spartacists, and Emil Höllein, a former left Independent.[60]

Divisions were already appearing in the majority which had just expelled Levi. The 'new' Berlin Left, which had attracted attention by the force of its attacks since September 1920, revealed itself with renewed vigour. Maslow demanded that the apparatus of the International be reorganised, after which he thought its next step should be to wind up the West European Bureau.[61] Friesland, for his part, presented himself as an 'ultra', when he declared to the Central Committee:

> I regret that Levi was expelled only for breaking discipline. It is a whole world outlook which separates us from him. There exists no recipe to prevent us from cutting ourselves off from the masses. When we have a truly revolutionary task before us, it is our duty to fulfil it to the end.[62]

A few days later, the district congress in Berlin-Brandenburg showed the development of the Left in the VKPD. It was for the moment the leading wing of the Party, and it solidly held one of the most important districts in the country. Fischer presented to it a report in which she attacked 'opportunism in the International'. She detected the expression of this in statements about 'the stabilisation of capitalism', as well as in the resort to 'verbal actions' such as the VKPD had used increasingly 'during the period of the *Open Letter*'. The final resolution was adopted by an overwhelming majority. It stated: 'The March Action of the German Communists forms the first step since 1919 of Western European Communism towards a break with this policy.'[63]

---

[58] As Levi's supporters were called.
[59] *Die Rote Fahne*, 6 May 1921. The Central Committee had met on 3–5 May.
[60] *Bericht über die Verhandlungen des 2 (7) Parteitags der Kommunistischen Partei Deutschlands (Sektion der Kommunistischen Internationale), abgehalten in Jena vom 22 bis 26 August 1921*, Berlin, 1922, pp. 63–4.
[61] *Die Rote Fahne*, 10 May 1921.
[62] Ibid.
[63] *Die Rote Fahne*, 13 May 1921.

Rosenberg presented a report in which he drew the conclusion that the International should be more centralised, and that 'a fusion should be effected as quickly and as completely as possible' with the KAPD, stressing that this would be easier since the 'rightists' had left the VKPD. He suggested that this fusion be prepared by the immediate formation of a committee of action on a basis of parity by the leaders of the two Parties. The district congress gave to his motion the same number of votes as to Fischer and Geschke, who called for 'politicising the trade unions': over 200 against only a dozen.[64]

However, this was precisely the same moment as the leaders of the KAPD chose to attack the Zentrale of the VKPD. Indeed, in this very month of May 1921 there appeared, on its authority, a pamphlet, probably written by Gorter, entitled *Dr Levi's Road: The Road of the VKPD*. This put Levi and his opponents in the Zentrale on the same level. Gorter emphasised that the Party's attitude in March had in the end been nothing but the continuation of its opportunist past. If the March Action had not been a putsch, it was nonetheless correct to define the stance of the Zentrale – which went over in a few days from the most crass opportunism to armed insurrection – as putschist.[65] The KAPD press declared that there could no longer be any question of reunification with the VKPD; in mid-May a strong delegation, consisting of Appel, Schwab and Meyer, joined Reichenbach, who was already in Moscow.[66]

The definition of Communist policy now depended on the discussion at the Third Comintern Congress, which had begun several months early in the wake of the March Action. The German leadership had to prepare itself for this discussion, in order to be able to defend the basis for the March Action and the merits of the offensive tactic.

---

[64] *Die Rote Fahne*, 15 May 1921.
[65] Bock, op. cit., pp. 305–6.
[66] Ibid., p. 259.

Chapter Twenty-Seven
The Moscow Compromise

The leaders of the VKPD had no intention of going to Moscow as penitents. Confident of the support of the ECCI, the Berlin leftists forged forward, they spoke loudly and strongly, and tried hard to be both the theoreticians and the leading wing of the heterogeneous majority which had deposed Levi. Maslow declared as soon as the March Action ended:

> There is not much to be said about the principles which inspired the action. Roughly speaking, the situation was the following: our party was on the defensive, and was in that way losing its direction as a Communist Party. A party on the defensive is a Social-Democratic Party. If it wants to be a Communist Party, it must be on the offensive. Or else, it must say: 'We are opposed to all offensives!' But to say, 'We are against this or that action', is bluff.[1]

He wrote in *Die Internationale* a few days later: 'We have been asked what specifically new factors were represented by the March Action. We should reply: precisely what our enemies hold against us, namely that the Party plunged into battle without enquiring what the consequences would be.'[2] In the same vein, Fischer declared: 'A party of 500,000 members which

---

[1] Levi Archives, P83/9, second part, f17.
[2] A. Maslow, 'Probleme des III Weltkongresses', *Die Internationale*, no. 7, 1921, p. 142.

does not fight can only become a swamp, and that is precisely what it had already become.'[3] As for Arthur Rosenberg, he philosophised at an activists' meeting in Berlin: 'If you win, it is an insurrection, and if you lose it is a putsch.'[4]

Within a few days, the entire philosophy of the Left was apparently adopted by the Zentrale, which had been overwhelmed by events, and which, desperate for self-justification, was seeking an *a posteriori* explanation for its policies.

The theses of the VKPD

On 8 April, the Zentrale adopted theses drafted by Thalheimer, with the aim of drawing the lessons of the March Action.[5] The theses declared that the German bourgeoisie found itself in a deep crisis which led it to take action on two fronts: to strengthen the 'white' counter-revolution, and to tighten its links with the Social Democracy, in order to free its hands for a compromise with the Entente at the expense of the proletariat. In such a situation, the proletariat was obliged to take the offensive to avoid being paralysed in passivity. During the crises which had shaken the German bourgeoisie in the preceding years, the VKPD had not had sufficient forces to go beyond the stage of propaganda. Having become a mass party, it was obliged to do this and to call the proletariat to action, even at the risk of being followed by only a part of the working class. The action began after Hörsing attacked the workers of Central Germany. The choice was clear: Hörsing, the counter-revolution, on the one side, and the workers on the other. The VKPD had chosen to take its place in the camp of the workers, and the other workers' parties had chosen that of the counter-revolution. The VKPD had not, of course, succeeded in drawing all the German workers into the struggle, and certain strata of them stubbornly remained passive, refusing to act, and were now, no doubt, bound to accuse the Party of putschism and adventurism. However, the Zentrale declared:

> In periods of deep political tension, such actions, even if they result in a
> provisional defeat, are the preliminary conditions for future victories, and,
> for a revolutionary party, the only way to win the masses and to embark

---

[3] R. Fischer, 'War die Märzaktion eine Bettelheimerei?', *Die Internationale*, no. 6, 1921, p. 470.

[4] Levi Archives, P83/9, p. 27.

[5] *Die Rote Fahne*, 10 April 1921.

upon victorious revolutionary struggles is to make the objective political situation penetrate the consciousness of the masses.[6]

The March Action was a considerable step forward to the extent that it had in practice taken the offensive which alone could create the conditions for seizing power. The Zentrale regarded the consequences as positive. The class struggle was strengthened. The front of passivity and civil peace was broken. 'The USPD and the SPD and their trade-union bureaucracy had been exposed as counter-revolutionary forces.' The action had aroused the working people from their torpor. There had been international echoes which helped to 'expose the Mensheviks in every country'. The action had shown to the workers of all countries that there could not be 'a united front between the bourgeoisie and the proletariat', and that 'the German Revolution is a living reality'. After analysing the inadequacies of the Party on the plane of organisation, the theses declared:

> The VKPD must rid itself of the weaknesses of organisation and tactics shown in this first attempt. If it wants to fulfil its historic task, it must remain firmly on the line of the revolutionary offensive, which was at the basis of the March Action, and go forward on this road with determination and assurance.[7]

The pamphlet *Tactics and Organisation of the Revolutionary Offensive*, was published shortly afterwards. A collection of the principal articles on this theme, it was to be the manifesto of the new philosophy.[8] The delegates of the Zentrale prepared confidently for their stay in Moscow for the Third Comintern Congress, convinced that the Russians would receive them with all the respect due to courageous, far-sighted revolutionaries.

Radek, however, was far from satisfied with the conduct of the March Action. He wrote on 1 April to the German leaders:

> I am afraid that you may have acted several weeks too soon, I fear that it may have been a tactical mistake not to wait for the conflict between Germany and Poland to break out. . . . No doubt Levi is now going to spread the accusation of a putsch; he has found the formula, 'sect or mass party'.[9]

---

[6] 'Leitsätze über die Märzaktion', *Die Internationale*, no. 4, April 1921, p. 126.
[7] Ibid.
[8] *Taktik und Organisation der revolutionären Offensive*, op. cit.
[9] Letter from Radek to the Zentrale, 1 April 1921, Levi Archives, P56/2; *Sowjet (Unser Weg)*, no. 8–9, 3 August 1921, pp. 249–52.

On 7 April, Radek said in a fresh letter that 'the Old Man still hopes that the people are going to pull themselves together again', and that 'the Executive as such wants to hold back from declaring its own position against the Right until it exposes itself',[10] adding that, as far as he was concerned, he had decided to fight in the open. Thalheimer did his best to resist the ECCI's vacillations and doubts by presenting an optimistic picture: 'The March Action has acted on the Party like a confrontation with the sword. We have frightened or shocked all the rotten elements. The others are isolated individuals. Only a few, no doubt, will go across to the other side with Paul Levi. . . . The Party is recovering marvellously quickly.'[11]

At any rate, it is clear that Levi's gesture was regarded by many activists as an attack on the Party. Lenin told Zetkin: 'He tore the Party to pieces.'[12] The attack was utilised by all those who had accounts to settle and who preferred to attack him. The ECCI was clear on this point at least. On 26 April, it published a solemn declaration, signed by the most prestigious names, Zinoviev, of course, but also Lenin and Trotsky, as well as Bukharin, Radek, Rosmer . . . and Kun. This particularly stated:

> In regard to the celebrated pamphlet by Paul Levi there was complete unanimity. All members of the ECCI spoke of it with burning indignation. The general opinion was – Paul Levi is a traitor. In the name of the small bureau and the entire ECCI, comrade Zinoviev declared: 'It is an abominable lie that the ECCI or its representatives provoked the March rising. This fable was needed by the German counter-revolution, on whose side Levi stood.'[13]

At the same time, there was no longer any question in this proclamation of hailing the March Action as 'glorious'. The ECCI confined itself to declaring that, given the importance of the differences which had appeared on this question, it would be necessary to discuss it at the Third Comintern Congress.[14] The ECCI's resolution on the 'Levi case' struck a somewhat different tone from that of the proclamation itself:

---

[10] Letter of 7 April 1921, Levi Archives, P55/2; *Sowjet (Unser Weg)*, no. 8–9, 3 August 1921, pp. 252–5.

[11] Letter from Thalheimer to Radek, Levi Archives, P55/1; *Sowjet (Unser Weg)*, no. 8–9, 3 August 1921, pp. 255–7.

[12] Zetkin, *Reminiscences of Lenin*, op. cit., p. 27.

[13] Degras, Volume 1, op. cit., p. 219.

[14] Ibid., pp. 219–20.

> Having read Paul Levi's pamphlet *Unser Weg wider den Putschismus*, the
> ECCI ratifies the decision to expel Paul Levi from the United Communist
> Party of Germany and, consequently, from the Third International. Even if
> Paul Levi were nine-tenths right in his views of the March offensive, he
> would still be liable to expulsion from the Party because of his unprecedented
> violation of discipline and because, by his action, in the given circumstances,
> he dealt the Party a blow in the back.[15]

Levi might well be excluded for indiscipline, but the political problem was
still posed, and it would be tackled at the Third Comintern Congress.
Meanwhile, that problem was central to the concerns of all the Communist
leaders. Already an article written in Moscow by Radek on 10 May and
published in the international Communist press, showed that a turn was
being prepared and that the ECCI was not going to endorse with the theory
of the offensive. Radek started by condemning Levi's accusation that the
Zentrale had organised a putsch. The workers in Central Germany were under
attack and had spontaneously gone into battle against Hörsing's forces. The
Central Committee on 17 March had no other aim than 'to react against the
government's provocation': 'To talk of putschism is simply to cover up with
resounding phrases a pure and simple rejection of the offensive tactic of
Communism, and even of active defence.' Starting from that point, he
nonetheless developed a certain number of criticisms of the German leaders.
He accused them of having passed too quickly and directly from the
propagandism of the time of Levi and Däumig to that of active struggle. He
said that they had not 'held the workers in hand' and had 'allowed them to
act whilst the character of the movement was unclear', when no one knew
for sure whether the best response would have been a strike, and they had
talked about an 'offensive', when the action which the Zentrale was leading
was more of an 'offensive defence'.[16]

The positions adopted in the Russian Communist Party

Radek's change of position, as well as the evolution which his letters traced
out since the beginning of March, can be explained by the uncertainty in
Moscow. The March Action took place at the moment when Soviet Russia
was undergoing the worst crisis in its history. And, to that extent, the March

---

[15] *Die Rote Fahne*, 4 May 1921.
[16] *Bulletin communiste*, no. 24, 9 June 1921, pp. 398–400.

Action had passed almost unnoticed, even by leaders like Lenin, absorbed in the wide array of day-to-day economic and political difficulties. Lenin was probably alerted for the first time by Levi's letter of 27 March. The March Action then provided the occasion for one of his most important interventions in the life of the VKPD, and for the greatest political battle which he fought within the Communist International.

To be sure, during the Second Comintern Congress, Lenin had been one of the most optimistic about the immediate revolutionary prospects in Europe, and we recall his differences with Levi in the commission concerned with the formulation of the tasks of the Party in that period. Soon, however, the Russo-Polish War ended without the revolutionary uprising in Poland, which he, unlike Radek, Trotsky and some of the Polish leaders, had expected, and on which his prospects were based. The downturn was beginning in Italy, France and Britain. In December, Lenin allowed a more subtle appreciation to appear in his speeches. He admitted that the progress of the European revolution was more sluggish than that of the Russian Revolution, and, above all, that it would not be reasonable to count on its acceleration. He intervened little in the business of the International, but we know that he insisted to Zinoviev that a forthcoming enlarged ECCI must not follow the course of the 'small bureau' of the International, which on 21 February had condemned the VKPD's *Open Letter* as opportunist, and that the issue must be discussed.

At that time, Lenin's political activity was totally concerned with the internal problems of Soviet Russia. The Kronstadt insurrection took place in March 1921, as also did the Tenth Party Congress and the adoption of the New Economic Policy. We can feel sure that he paid more attention to these events than to the adventure in Germany, which followed them by a few days. The two questions, for all that, were no doubt linked, at any rate in the minds of such Russian leaders of the Party and the International as Bukharin and Zinoviev. We can regard it as plausible that those who supported the strategy of the 'offensive' in the International sincerely desired to break at all costs the isolation which doomed the Bolsheviks to the costly strategic retreat of the NEP, by forcing, if necessary, the development and artificially accelerating the speed of the revolution. Unfortunately, we know little of the political struggle which must have arisen in the leadership of the Russian Communist Party before March, apart from the fact that Bukharin defended the need to 'galvanise' the masses in order to provoke revolutionary explosions in Europe.[17]

---

[17] L.D. Trotsky, *The Third International After Lenin*, London, 1974, p. 67.

For the following months, we have available a testimony by Trotsky, taken from a declaration by him to the Russian Party's Political Bureau on 18 March 1926:

> There was a danger at that time that the policy of the Comintern would follow the line of the March 1921 events in Germany. That is, the attempt to create a revolutionary situation artificially – to 'galvanise' the proletariat, as one of the German comrades expressed it. . . . Before the congress, I wrote my impression of the March events to comrade Radek in a letter of which Vladimir Ilyich knew nothing. Considering the ticklish situation, and not knowing the opinion of Vladimir Ilyich and knowing that Zinoviev, Bukharin and Radek were in general for the German left, I naturally did not express myself publicly but wrote a letter (in the form of theses) to comrade Radek, asking him to give me his opinion. Radek and I did not agree. Vladimir Ilyich heard about this, sent for me, and characterised the situation in the Comintern as one involving the very greatest dangers. In appraising the situation and its problems, we were in full accord.
>
> After this conference, Vladimir Ilyich sent for comrade Kamenev, in order to assure a majority in the political bureau. There were then five members in the political bureau. With comrade Kamenev, we were three and consequently a majority, but in our delegation to the Comintern, there were, on one side, comrades Zinoviev, Bukharin and Radek; on the other, Vladimir Ilyich, comrade Kamenev and myself. And, by the way, we had formal sittings of these groups. Vladimir Ilyich said at that time: 'Well, we are forming a new faction.' During further negotiations as to the text of the resolutions to be introduced, I served as the representative of the Lenin faction whilst Radek represented the Zinoviev faction. . . . Moreover, comrade Zinoviev rather categorically accused Radek at that time of 'betraying' his faction in those negotiations; that is, of making presumably too great concessions. . . . Vladimir Ilyich conferred with me as to what we should do if the congress voted against us. Should we submit to the congress whose decisions might be ruinous, or should we not submit?[18]

The Russian leaders finally agreed on a compromise, which the delegation of the Russian Party would have to defend at the Congress, both against the leftists, Germans and others, and against the representatives of the pro-Levi

---

[18] L.D. Trotsky, *The Stalin School of Falsification*, London, 1974, pp. 26–7.

opposition in Germany, Zetkin, Neumann, Malzahn and Frankel, who were invited at the express demand of Lenin.[19] However, things did not go entirely as foreseen. Thalheimer was the first to arrive in Moscow, bearing theses which he had personally drafted and which the German Central Committee had adopted by 26 votes to 14. In particular, they declared: 'The Communist Party has for the first time and alone led the masses in struggle, not locally, but in the whole of Germany.'[20] The only mistake for which the German Party needed to take blame itself was of having waited too long. The enduring lesson of the March Action was that: 'If the Party wishes to fulfil its historic mission, it must remain faithful to the theory of the revolutionary offensive, which was the basis of the March Action, and it must advance resolutely along this road.'[21]

However, the group responsible for the March Action was already beginning to fragment in the light of the consequences of their policy. As Arnold Reisberg has stressed, Brandler, who accepted responsibility for the March Action as Chairman of the Zentrale, was very soon to start pondering the problems which it had caused, and to try to return to the policy of the *Open Letter*, which the arrival of Kun had rudely interrupted. In jail following the March Action, he reflected on the historical lessons of the recent events.[22] On 17 June, he wrote to the Zentrale demanding of his comrades that they reflect upon what Lenin had proposed in 1917, on the eve of seizing power, in his well-known pamphlet, *The Impending Catastrophe and How to Combat It*. He suggested that concrete slogans be adopted which could immediately mobilise the non-Communist working people, including 'compulsory reorganisation of industry under trade-union control, centralisation of the banks, control of industry, commerce and agriculture by the existing state and the factory committees', and concluded: 'We should finish with pure agitation. We must not be afraid of being less radical.'[23]

---

[19] Brandt and Lowenthal, op. cit., p. 167.

[20] *Die Rote Fahne*, 10 April 1921.

[21] Ibid.

[22] Brandler, *War die Märzaktion ein Bakunisten-Putsch?*, op. cit. Reisberg points out that Brandler wrote with reference to the slogan launched in 1921 of an alliance with Russia: 'We wanted the overthrow of the government and at the very least the formation of a workers' government.' (A. Reisberg, 'Zur Genesis der Losung Arbeiterregierungs in Deutschland, Das Jahr 1921', *Beiträge zur Geschichte der deutschen Arbeiterbewegung*, no. 6, 1965, p. 1027.)

[23] Brandler's letter was published in *Sowjet*, no. 6, 1921, pp. 172–4. Reisberg (op. cit., p. 1028) points out that Brandler was proposing 'the economic programme of a workers' government'.

When Thalheimer arrived in Moscow, he recognised that Brandler was apparently not alone in having retreated. No doubt he understood that his theses had not the slightest chance of being approved by the Russians.[24] He therefore gave up the tactics which had been prepared in Berlin, and, in agreement with Kun, decided to move amendments to the text of the Russian delegation, which Radek had been given to draft. At first, this new tactic succeeded. Radek introduced into his draft analyses remarks stamped with the seal of the theory of the offensive and even the outlook of its supporters, with its virulent denunciation of the 'Right' and the 'opportunists'.[25]

On 10 June, Lenin sharply criticised him in a letter to Zinoviev: 'The crux of the matter is that Levi in very many respects is *right politically*. . . . Thalheimer's and Béla Kun's theses are politically utterly fallacious.' Lenin considered that the amendments which Radek accepted were 'a classic example of Béla Kun's and Thalheimer's ineptitude' as much as of Radek's 'hasty complaisance'. The damage was great, and he let slip a disillusioned thought: 'What's to be done? I don't know. So much time and effort wasted.' However, he did not hesitate for a moment, and wrote to Zinoviev:

> . . . it is absurd and harmful to write and think that the propaganda period has ended and the period of action has started. The tactics of the Communist International should be based on a steady and systematic drive to win the *majority of the working class*, first and foremost *within the **old** trade unions*. . . . All those who have failed to grasp the necessity of the *Open Letter* tactic should be *expelled* from the Communist International within a month after its third congress. I clearly see my mistake in voting for the admission of the KAPD. It will have to be rectified as quickly and fully as possible.[26]

As for the March Action itself, Lenin reached some conclusions on the basis of the pamphlets of Levi and Brandler; all the shouting about it being an 'offensive action' was madness, and the very great mistake of the German leadership had been to call for a general strike when the government was obviously organising a provocation. But that purely defensive action could not be regarded as a putsch. Levi made an even greater mistake when he called it a putsch. Therefore it was necessary for sanctions to be applied to

---

[24] A. Reisberg, 'Ein neuer Brief VI Lenins über die Taktik der KI', *Beiträge zur Geschichte der deutschen Arbeiterbewegung*, no. 4, 1965, p. 687.

[25] Ibid.

[26] V.I. Lenin, 'Remarks on the Draft Theses on Tactics for the Third Congress of the Communist International', *Collected Works*, Volume 42, op. cit., p. 321.

him, perhaps suspension for six months, with the prospect of reintegration if he behaved loyally. But, at the same time, the madness of the theory of the offensive must be buried for good.

Cornering on two wheels

The turn in Comintern tactics was to be made very quickly. At the Tenth Conference of the Russian Communist Party in late May 1921, Radek presented the report on the tasks of the Third Comintern Congress of the International, and was a long way from the line which Lenin was defending. His analyses seemed to based on the perspectives outlined in the summer of 1920. In effect, he thought that the crisis which had broken out simultaneously in several Communist Parties was rooted in 'their feeling that the world revolution was in retreat', a feeling which underlay the analyses of Serrati and Levi. Radek believed that there was no retreat: 'If we reach the conclusion that the world revolution is in retreat, then we would have immediately to strike off the agenda the struggle for the immediate conquest of power.'[27]

In opposition to the thesis developed by Levi, Radek argued at the Russian Party Conference that 1920 had not marked a retreat of the revolutionary movement, but, on the contrary, an important acceleration: 'After our setback before Warsaw, many foreign capitalists believed that they could write off the revolution. But it was precisely at this moment that the long-awaited crisis broke out.' The years 1918–20 had been a time of preparation. The March Action had been purely defensive, but it had been positive because it was an action: 'Even a defeat in these circumstances means progress.' Its most positive result, in fact, was to demonstrate that the 'Right' – Levi and his comrades – were sabotaging the action of the Party: 'It is only today that our faith in the German Party is restored. . . . This proves that the Party is better than we believed it to be.'[28]

The conclusion is surprising, coming from a speaker who at the same moment denounced the 'white terror' at work in Germany, and condemned Levi's public initiative in such a context as a crime: 'The situation in Europe has changed in our favour . . . thanks to the growth and development of the Communist movement.'[29] That was in striking contrast to the theses on the

---

[27] *Bulletin communiste*, no. 28, 7 July 1921, p. 464.
[28] Ibid., pp. 465–6.
[29] Ibid., p. 468.

international situation which Trotsky and Varga were to present to the Third Comintern Congress, mandated by the ECCI on the position which Lenin had succeeded in getting accepted by the Bolsheviks' Central Committee. These theses started from observing that the economic crisis which broke out in 1920 reflected the deep crisis of the capitalist system, and expressed a reaction from the fictitious prosperity of the War years. But the central fact was that the workers' reactions had been dissipated, and this had prevented the crisis from leading to revolution. The theses recalled the stages of the great revolutionary wave which the World War had unleashed: the revolution in Russia in 1917, the revolution in Germany and in Austria-Hungary in 1918–19, the French railway workers' strikes in 1919 and 1920, the general strike in 1920 in Germany against the Kapp Putsch, the factory occupations in Northern Italy, and the general strike in Czechoslovakia. The theses concluded: 'This mighty wave, however, did not succeed in overthrowing world capitalism, not even European capitalism. During the year that elapsed between the second and third congresses of the Communist International, a series of working-class uprisings and battles have resulted in partial defeats.'[30] Therefore, the Communist International had to face the question of deciding whether a stabilisation of world capitalism had taken place, and whether new tactics had to be adopted to meet the new situation. The conclusion was clear: 'It is absolutely incontestable that on a world scale the open revolutionary struggle of the proletariat for power is at present passing through a slowing down in tempo.'[31]

Trotsky made the same point at the Congress: 'Today, for the first time, we can see and we can feel that we are not so close to our objective, the conquest of power, the world revolution. In 1919, we said: "It is a matter of months." Today we say: "It is a matter of years."'[32]

Coming after the interventions of Lenin in his preliminary discussions, Trotsky's speech had a precise implication. From the opening of the Congress, the two most prestigious leaders of the Bolshevik Party threw the weight of their authority into the discussion. Their intervention was undoubtedly necessary in order to defeat the bloc of ultra-leftists and neo-leftists.

---

[30] *Bulletin communiste*, no. 29, 14 July 1921, p. 480; L.D. Trotsky, 'Theses on the International Situation and the Tasks of the Comintern', *First Five Years of the Communist International*, Volume 1, op. cit., p. 291.

[31] Ibid., p. 312.

[32] *Protokoll des III Kongresses der Kommunistischen Internationale*, op. cit., p. 90.

How the Congress proceeded

Lenin and Trotsky had a simple aim. It was important to preserve the unity of both the German Party and the International, whilst at the same time ensuring that they undertook a radical political turn. Concretely, they were ready, on the one hand, to confirm the expulsion of Paul Levi, but only for 'indiscipline' and in order to avoid openly revealing the responsibility of the ECCI in the March Action, and, on the other hand, to pay homage to this action as 'a step forward', whilst they condemned the theory of the offensive, and attempted to prevent any repetition of it.

It was not an easy matter to put this plan into action, and it required much careful preparation and manoeuvring. Even as the Congress drew near, it was unclear whether Lenin and Trotsky would be able to win the majority of the delegates to their views. When Kun returned to Moscow, he worked hard to win the arriving foreign delegates to the theory of the offensive. Rosmer described in his memoirs how he made overtures, paid visits, had conversations and sought information, winning over the delegates from Belgium and Luxemburg, and reaching an agreement with the Italians who were already on his side.[33]

Lenin meanwhile resolutely awaited the thirty-three-strong German delegation.[34] Of the Party's leaders, only Meyer, Stoecker and Brandler were missing; the first two were running the leadership in Berlin, and Brandler was in jail. Zetkin, who was delegated to the Congress by the League of Communist Women, was the semi-official spokeswoman of the German opposition. Lenin had insisted that three other leaders of the opposition, Paul Neumann, Malzahn and Frankel, make the journey, and take part in the Congress with a consultative voice. Levi's friends had prepared carefully for the Moscow discussions, and had collected considerable documentation, including newspapers, leaflets, minutes of meetings and statements in evidence by activists. But they arrived empty-handed, because the files, which were packed in Zetkin's luggage, were seized at the German frontier by the Prussian police, acting on the orders of Severing.[35]

---

[33] Rosmer, op. cit., p. 146.

[34] Because the congress of the RILU was being held in Moscow, the Germans were in fact much more numerous. Mujbegovic (op. cit., p. 284, n. 54) estimates that there were some sixty German delegates in Moscow at this time.

[35] Fischer (op. cit., p. 178) says that the seizure was 'evidently' done 'with the tacit agreement' of Zetkin. This is a serious but groundless accusation. Nevertheless, Zetkin

Despite this incident, which at first made its task easier, the German delegation, which spoke for the VKPD majority, soon changed its tune. Heckert was received along with Rákosi by Lenin, and came out of the interview 'shattered'. Both men listened as Lenin accused them of political stupidity.[36] A first improvised discussion took place in Lenin's office. Vehemently and ironically, Lenin asked the supporters of the theory of the offensive how they thought the workers 'learnt' under the blows of repression and unemployment. Koenen replied sharply that 'their stomach sends the revolutionary energy to their heads'. From then on, Lenin interspersed all the criticisms of the Germans with the sarcastic remark: 'To be sure, with your ideas everything comes from the energy which the stomach communicates to the brain.'[37]

In a later meeting, Lenin shook the delegates of the German majority even harder:

> The provocation was as clear as day. And, instead of mobilising the masses of workers for defensive aims, in order to repel the attacks of the bourgeoisie and in that way to prove that you have right on your side, you invented your 'theory of the offensive', an absurd theory which offers to the police and every reactionary the chance to depict you as the ones who took the initiative in aggression, against which they could pose as the ones defending the people.[38]

Lenin attacked Kun severely, constantly taunting him with what he called his 'Kuneries', and ridiculed what he called the 'theoretical, historical and literary cosmetics' of the partisans of the offensive, on which he passed this summary verdict: 'Is it a theory anyway? Not at all, it is an illusion, it is romanticism, sheer romanticism.'[39] Heckert has borne witness to the disarray and resentment of the German majority, caught unawares by Lenin, who publicly baiting them in the presence of the other delegations, helpless objects

---

had made a mistake in taking the risk of carrying such documents, which would normally have been entrusted to the apparatus. She justified herself before the Zentrale on 30 November 1921, by explaining that she had been uncertain that the materials would really reach Moscow if she did not see to it herself, and added that several letters or telegrams which she had sent to the ECCI had either never arrived, or arrived only after a long delay. Mujbegović (op. cit., p. 315), who quotes these minutes, does not mention any reply to this argument, which was probably unanswerable.

[36] F. Heckert, 'Mes rencontres avec Lénine', *Lénine tel qu'il fut*, Volume 2, Moscow, 1959, p. 804.

[37] Ibid.

[38] Ibid.

[39] Zetkin, op. cit., p. 23.

of ridicule. According to Frölich, he complained about Lenin's terrifying 'meanness': no doubt he was not the only one.[40] Lenin gauged perfectly his need to defeat sharply the supporters of the offensive, whilst at the same time trying not to provoke excessive rancour amongst them. During his conversations with Zetkin, in the presence of Trotsky, he explained that if the Congress would 'utterly destroy' the theory of the offensive, he would at the same time give its supporters 'some crumbs of consolation'[41] – which meant that Zetkin and her friends would have to be satisfied with a compromise.

Such a compromise presupposed that the sanctions against Levi would be maintained. Lenin explained to Zetkin why they could not be avoided:

> He did not criticise, but was one-sided, exaggerated, even malicious; he gave nothing to which the party could usefully turn. He lacks the spirit of solidarity with the party. And it is that which has made the rank and file comrades so angry, and made them deaf and blind to the great deal of truth in Levi's criticism, particularly to his correct political principles.[42]

Levi had himself compromised what chances he had to convince his party:

> And so a feeling arose – it also extended to non-German comrades – in which the dispute concerning the pamphlet, and concerning Levi himself, became the sole subject of this contention, instead of the false theory and the bad practice of the 'offensive theory' and the 'leftists'. They have to thank Paul Levi that up to the present they have come out so well, much too well. Paul Levi is his own worst enemy.[43]

Though the essentials of the debate developed in this way behind closed doors, in Lenin's office, or during long sessions in the Commission, it inevitably had to be touched on during the full sessions, and there was a danger of incidents occurring as the sessions took place, even though the procedure which was adopted aimed as far as possible at avoiding them. For that reason,

---

[40] Heckert, op. cit., p. 805. Vassil Kolarov referred to quite a sharp clash at the time of the Executive meeting on 17 June between Lenin and Kun (V. Kolarov, 'V.I. Lenin na III Kongresse Kommunisticheskogo Internationala', *Voprosy Istorii*, no. 2, 1960, pp. 189–91).

[41] Zetkin, op. cit., p. 23. Zetkin's memoirs were published after the defeat of Trotsky and the Opposition in 1924, and do not mention the presence of Trotsky at these discussions. However Zetkin's letters to Levi at the time bear witness to this (Levi Archives, P113/18). For the rest, the memoirs are faithful to the accounts which she gave at the time.

[42] Zetkin, op. cit., p. 27.

[43] Ibid.

Zinoviev, who, as President of the International, had to present the report on its activities, did not have to deal with the March Action as such. Since he was judged to be too compromised by his links with Kun and his protection of the supporters of the offensive, he had to limit himself to explaining to the Congress how the ECCI had formulated a judgement on the action:

> We all agree with what Brandler wrote: it was not an offensive, but simply a defensive struggle. The enemy attack caught us by surprise. . . . Many mistakes were made, and many organisational weaknesses were revealed. Our comrades in the German Zentrale have not concealed these mistakes: they want to correct them. The question is whether we can *consider these struggles as a step forward, as an episode on the tormented road of the German working class, or whether indeed we must regard them as a putsch*. The Executive is of the opinion that *the March Action was not a putsch*. It is ridiculous to speak of a putsch when half a million workers were engaged in battle. . . . We must explain the mistakes clearly, and draw the lessons from them. We conceal nothing, but we are engaged neither in the politics of a coterie, nor in secret diplomacy. Our opinion is that the German Party has in general no need to be ashamed of this struggle, quite the contrary.[44]

Zinoviev had received a long appeal from Levi against his expulsion, but he neither read from it nor even acknowledged its existence at the Congress, and apart from this rather summary reply to Levi's arguments, the President of the International was to say nothing about the March Action.[45] Instead, at the end of the discussion on his report, a vote was taken on a general resolution to approve the sanctions which the ECCI had applied during the year. This way of settling the Levi case without having thoroughly discussed it aroused indignant protests from the German minority, and Zetkin attacked the procedure from the platform:

> In my opinion, the Levi case is not just a problem of discipline, it is chiefly and essentially a political problem. It can only be correctly judged or appreciated within the general political situation, and this is why I believe that it can only be really treated within the framework of our discussions on the tactics of the Communist Party, and in particular of our discussions on the March Action. . . . If Paul Levi is to be severely punished for his

---

[44] *Protokoll des III Kongresses der Kommunistischen Internationale*, op. cit., pp. 184–5.
[45] Levi Archives, P7/1.

criticism of the March Action and for the mistake which he unquestionably made on this occasion, then what punishment do they deserve who committed the mistakes themselves? The putschism about which we have made accusations did not lie in the actions of the masses in struggle. . . . It was in the brains of the Zentrale which led the masses in the struggle in this way.[46]

Radek was to deal with the question of the March Action during the debate on tactics.[47] In this way was expressed the ECCI's desire to avoid raking over the past, but also to preserve at all costs clarity for the future. He was hard on the German Zentrale, saying that it was taken by surprise by Hörsing's offensive, and that it had not understood that it should have organised effective solidarity action with the Mansfeld miners without hiding from the latter that they were not in a position to be victorious. It exacerbated the situation by issuing without due thought the call for a general strike, which did not correct any of its earlier mistakes, but merely exposed the weakness of the party. Finally, more seriously, instead of frankly recognising that it had been mistaken, the Zentrale had preferred to think up the theory of the offensive, in order to justify itself at all costs. Radek unleashed all his caustic wit against the German leaders, yet, like Zinoviev, drew the conclusion that despite everything, it would be wrong to call the March Action a putsch, and that it certainly represented 'a step forward'.[48]

Although the leaders of the International assuredly wanted to avoid it, it was impossible for the discussion to avoid touching on unpleasant and undesirable issues. The discussion amongst the Germans which followed Radek's report was a real display of dirty linen, during which Friesland, Heckert and Thaelmann showed themselves to be the most violent. Radek and Zetkin each accused the other of having contributed by their writings to the development of the theory of the offensive which they both condemned so sharply today.[49] None of the fundamental problems about the working of the ECCI and its relations with the Zentrale was touched upon. Kun was silent, and only intervened on the subject of the Congress agenda, recalling bitterly that he was part of the 'so-called Left'.[50] Once again, it was left to

---

[46] *Protokoll des III Kongresses der Kommunistischen Internationale*, op. cit., pp. 295–8.
[47] Ibid., pp. 455–84.
[48] Ibid., p. 472.
[49] Ibid., pp. 466, 599–600.
[50] Ibid., p. 651.

Zetkin to speak the unspeakable. She turned to Radek, and upbraided him: 'There are several people here whose conduct has been indecisive, hesitant and often unstable.'[51] Likewise, she posed the problem – about which she said 'it would be necessary to speak again' – of the ECCI representatives, and made a transparent allusion to Kun, without actually naming him:

> There remains one matter which we referred to in our analyses of the March Action. The representative of the Executive bears a large part of the responsibility for the way in which the March Action was handled, the representative of the Executive bears a large part of the responsibility for the incorrect slogans, for the incorrect positions taken up by the Party, or rather by its Zentrale. And no one knows that better than Radek himself.[52]

Having been pinned down like this, Radek at once protested from his seat that he had not been in Germany at the time. But that did not help him, because his challenger retorted: 'A few days ago, you declared, before witnesses, that as soon as you were informed, you told the representative of the Executive that his slogan was – I will not use the unparliamentary word which you did, but a weaker one – idiotic.'[53]

Zetkin also pleaded for Levi. Admitting that he had committed an act of indiscipline, she asked simply that he be treated in the same way as Zinoviev and Kamenev for their analogous mistake in 1917.[54] This was an allusion, displeasing to those concerned, but without doubt salutary for the Congress, to the attitude which had been adopted on the eve of the October insurrection by the man who, having now become President of the International, was portraying himself as the defender of discipline against Levi!

The political battle heated up only when the delegates of the German majority announced that, whilst they agreed with the theses as presented, they wished to include some amendments supported by the Austrian and Italian delegates. Quite clearly, this meant calling the initial compromise into question. They justified their attitude by saying that Trotsky's report gave the theses a 'rightist interpretation', which they wanted to correct.[55] The Polish delegate Michalak half-opened a window on the debates in the corridors

[51] Ibid., p. 279.
[52] Ibid., p. 297.
[53] Ibid.
[54] Ibid., pp. 292, 298.
[55] Ibid., p. 671.

when he admitted from the platform: 'Many comrades have said that Lenin has gone to the right, and Trotsky too.'[56]

Heckert attacked Lenin, and delivered a fiery defence of the March Action.[57] In the same vein, Thaelmann attacked Trotsky.[58] As for the Italian Terracini, he declared bluntly that it was not the small size of a party which prevented it from successfully leading a revolution, and he gave the example of the Bolshevik Party in 1917.[59]

At that point, Lenin launched his counter-attack, directed alike against the leftists in the International and the delegates of the KAPD. The latter had come in a large delegation with the evident aim of forming an international tendency. They intervened systematically during the debates on all the questions on the agenda, and submitted their own drafts on each of the points on which votes were taken. They made numerous contacts with the delegates, and distributed leaflets to them, in particular a brief history of their party.[60] They repeatedly asserted their anti-parliamentarism and opposition to militant work in the trade unions, and presented their criticism of the 'ultra-centralism' of the International and its parties. Immediately before Terracini, Appel spoke against Radek's report, and violently attacked the *Open Letter* of the VKPD, which he roundly condemned as invitably opportunist.[61] Lenin replied to Terracini, declaring that the amendments contained 'no Marxism, no political experience, and no reasoning'. Replying to the attacks from the KAPD, he said:

> To my deep regret and shame, I have already heard such views privately. But when, at the congress, after such prolonged debate, the *Open Letter* is declared opportunist – that is a shame and a disgrace. . . . The *Open Letter* is a model political step. This is stated in our theses, and we must certainly stand by it. It is a model because it is the first act of a practical method of winning over the majority of the working class. In Europe, where almost all the proletarians are organised, we must win the majority of the working class, and anyone who fails to understand this is lost to the communist

---

[56] Ibid., p. 522.
[57] Ibid., pp. 528–43.
[58] Ibid., pp. 633–8.
[59] Ibid., p. 505.
[60] Bock, op. cit., pp. 259–60.
[61] *Protokoll des III Kongresses der Kommunistischen Internationale*, op. cit., pp. 485–97, in particular p. 492. Appel is referred to by his pseudonym Hempel.

movement; he will never learn anything if he has failed to learn that much during the three years of the great revolution.[62]

He later answered Terracini, and, through him, all the ultra-leftists who appealed to the Bolshevik example to support their analyses:

> Comrade Terracini has understood very little of the Russian Revolution. In Russia, we were a small party, but we had with us in addition the majority of the Soviets of Workers' and Peasants' Deputies throughout the country. Do you have anything of the sort? We had with us almost half the army, which then numbered at least 10 million men. . . . If these views of comrade Terracini are shared by three other delegations, then something is wrong in the International! Then we must say: 'Stop! There must be a decisive fight! Otherwise the Communist International is lost!'[63]

Trotsky likewise categorically argued for the amendments to be rejected:

> From all this one gets the impression that the members of the German delegation still approach the issue as if it had to be defended at all costs, but not studied or analysed. . . . It is our duty to say clearly and precisely to the German workers that we consider this philosophy of the offensive to be the greatest danger. And in its practical application to be the greatest political crime. . . . You have broken with the opportunists and you are moving forward, but look around you: there exist in this world not only opportunists but also classes.[64]

In conformity with his agreement with Lenin before the Congress, Trotsky declared that he would make no further concessions 'to the Left', and that the theses themselves represented the extreme limit of compromise, beyond which he would not let himself be drawn: 'Right now, I want only to underscore that we view these theses as a maximum concession to a tendency represented here by many comrades, including comrade Thaelmann.'[65]

His threat to fight to the end if he and Lenin were put in a minority completed the rout of the attackers. All the motions referring to the March

---

[62] V.I. Lenin, 'Speech in Defence of the Tactics of the Communist International', *Collected Works*, Volume 32, op. cit., pp. 470, 472.

[63] Ibid., p. 471.

[64] L.D. Trotsky, 'Speech on Comrade Radek's Report on "Tactics of the Comintern" at the Third Congress', *First Five Years of the Communist International*, Volume 1, op. cit., pp. 326, 329, 332.

[65] *Protokoll des III Kongresses der Kommunistischen Internationale*, op. cit., p. 322.

Action were passed unanimously. Lenin and Trotsky could believe that they had both saved the International and repaired some of the damage which the ECCI had inflicted on the VKPD. Trotsky showed the importance of the issue in his account to the Congress of the Youth Communist International:

> As warriors of the revolution, we are convinced – and the objective facts corroborate us – that we as the working class, that we as the Communist International, will not only save our civilisation, the centuries-old product of hundreds of generations, but will raise it to much higher levels of development. However, from the standpoint of pure theory, the possibility is not excluded that the bourgeoisie, armed with its state apparatus and its entire accumulated experience, may continue fighting the revolution until it has drained modern civilisation of every atom of its vitality, until it has plunged modern mankind into a state of collapse and decay for a long time to come.[66]

The Third Comintern Congress appealed to all Communist Parties to turn towards the masses, to win the masses to Communism, in order to ensure, in the more or less near future, at the next crisis, the possibility of victory of the revolution and the construction of the dictatorship of the proletariat. This, in the eyes of Lenin and Trotsky, was the necessary condition for socialism to overcome barbarism.

Nonetheless, we may ask to what extent the foundation of the Red International of Labour Unions, the First Congress of which opened on 3 July, was really consistent with the new analysis of the situation. The RILU resulted from initiatives taken during the Second Comintern Congress, and its aim, if we are to believe Rosmer, one of its founders, was 'to unite in the same International both those union bodies which were already in a position to affiliate as a whole, and minorities which had been established within reformist trade unions, on the basis of the principle of affiliation'.[67]

The wish to destroy the reformist hegemony of the leaders of the Amsterdam trade-union federation was accompanied by the construction of another trade-union grouping under revolutionary leadership. However, the delicate tactics demanded by such an operation were perhaps too complicated to be easily understood and assimilated by all the partisans of the Communist International. According to Rosmer, the RILU congress was not well prepared, and dragged

---

[66] L.D. Trotsky, 'Report on the "Balance Sheet" of the Third Congress of the Third International', *First Five Years of the Communist International*, Volume 1, op. cit., pp. 351–2.
[67] Rosmer, op. cit., p. 155.

on in difficult debates concerned almost entirely with the relationship between the RILU and the Communist International. The final resolution that 'an organic linkage' between the Communist Party and the trade unions was 'highly desirable' proved to be a weapon in the hands of the reformist trade union leaders against the revolutionary minorities, whom they accused of working 'on the orders of the Party'. The fact that the RILU's resolution was consistent with two of the Comintern's 'Twenty-One Conditions', albeit formulated in different circumstances, enabled the reformists to present 'Leninism' as the resolute opponent of the idea of trade-union independence, a principle to which in many advanced countries the working people, including the revolutionaries amongst them, remained firmly attached.

A party torn asunder

The Third Comintern Congress devoted a special resolution to the VKPD. In the meetings outside formal sessions, the ECCI and the delegates of the two German tendencies signed a 'peace treaty' which expressed the hope that both sides would refrain from factionalism and thereby prevent the Party from disintegrating.

The dissension amongst the Germans during the Congress showed that the March Action had brought into focus the depth of the differences within the Party, not to mention the degree of animosity and even personal hatred, and the factional manoeuvring which constituted the day-to-day life of the Party. Paul Neumann read from the platform of the Congress a telegram which Thalheimer had sent to the members of the Zentrale who had remained in Berlin, demanding 'at all costs' that the supporters of the minority, Otto Brass and Anna Geyer, be prevented from coming to Moscow, in order to 'avoid the impression being given that they have forces behind them'.[68] Thalheimer's explanation revealed his embarrassment, and no one seems to have asked how Neumann had been able to obtain a telegram that was not addressed to him.[69] Neumann also accused Koenen, who strenuously denied it, of having known what was in of the telegram, and of having agreed at the same time to Zinoviev's request that he send another telegram calling for Brass and Geyer to come to Moscow.[70]

---

[68] *Protokoll des III Kongresses der Kommunistischen Internationale*, op. cit., p. 582.
[69] Ibid., pp. 594–5.
[70] Ibid., p. 582.

The atmosphere was thick with insults and accusations. Neumann declared: 'I am a real proletarian, and not one of those jugglers with theses like we have in Berlin and of whom one of the most eminent, comrade Maslow, is here.'[71] Malzahn's declaration that he and Neumann were members of the General Commission of the trade unions, where they represented the revolutionary minority of the metalworkers' union, was interrupted by the sarcastic remark: 'Now that really is significant!'[72] Radek interrupted to ask him where he was in January 1919. He replied that he was in an action committee and then in prison, from which he had escaped.[73] Radek accused Levi of having 'gone to ground' in moments of danger. Heckert accused Zetkin of having 'deserted' the Spartacus League at the start of 1919.[74] In the corridors, they said that Malzahn and Neumann had sabotaged the strike in Berlin in sympathy with the Mansfeld strikers,[75] and that Bernhard Düwell had actively opposed it, as had Richard Müller.[76] Malzahn's reply to these accusations was confirmed by Friesland, his political opponent, in respect of both Neumann and himself.[77] Zetkin answered Heckert with an account of her relations with the newly-formed Communist Party, from which she had stood apart only on the decision of the Zentrale led by Jogiches.[78] She reminded Radek, definitely a specialist in dirty tricks, that the Free Corps had put a price on Levi's head.[79] Richard Müller published in the newspaper of the Congress an indignant denial of the rumours about his role in the strike.[80] Malzahn attacked the intellectuals as 'scabs with pens';[81] branding Thalheimer,

---

[71] Ibid., p. 584.

[72] Ibid., p. 551.

[73] Ibid., p. 555.

[74] Ibid., p. 541.

[75] Twenty-five years later, Fischer (op. cit., p. 176) was to repeat: 'Some of Levi's friends – organisers of the Berlin metalworkers' union, Paul Malzahn and Paul Neumann – had toured the city's factories and called on the workers to abstain from striking in support of the Mansfeld strikers. In an outburst of indignation, the party demanded the immediate expulsion of Levi and these strike-breakers.' The fact is that, at the meeting on 7 April, Brandler, when Chairman of the Party, had already in a declaration to the Central Committee denied these rumours, which he regarded as slandering Malzahn, Neumann and Eckert, who had conducted themselves as disciplined revolutionaries (Levi Archives, P83/9, p. 19).

[76] In the same speech, Brandler left open the question of the attitude of Fritz Wolff, who was to be expelled, and that of Richard Müller.

[77] *Protokoll des III Kongresses der Kommunistischen Internationale*, op. cit., p. 556.

[78] Ibid., p. 668.

[79] Ibid., p. 296.

[80] *Moscou*, 30 June 1921.

[81] *Protokoll des III Kongresses der Kommunistischen Internationale*, op. cit., p. 555.

Frölich and Friesland as 'hair-splitters' with 'unhealthy obsessions'.[82] Radek witticised at the expense of Pannekoek, speaking of men who, thanks to observing the stars, no longer saw living workers.[83] Heckert and Rákosi talked of 'Herr Doktor Levi'. This extreme language on both sides expressed the hatred which from that time separated the two groups.

Lenin and the unity of the VKPD

Lenin still aimed to maintain the unity of the VKPD. All through the Congress, he did his best to calm people down, prepare the way for reconciliation, and soothe irritated susceptibilities. He said as much in his forthright way to Zetkin: 'You once wrote to me that we Russians should learn to understand Western psychology a little, and not thrust our hard, rugged methods upon people all at once. I took notice of that.'[84]

On the day after Heckert had made his violent attacks on Zetkin, Lenin succeeded in persuading him that, for that very reason, he was the one who should present to her the good wishes of the International on the occasion of her sixty-fourth birthday.[85] In the case of Levi, he showed himself very reserved in the Congress, and avoided declaring himself too categorically. But he had his plan. He declared to Zetkin:

> You know how highly I value Paul Levi and his capacity. . . . He proved true in the times of worst persecution, was brave, clever, unselfish. I believed that he was firmly bound to the proletariat, although I was aware of a certain coolness in his attitude to the workers. Something of a 'please keep your distance'. Since the appearance of his pamphlet, I have had doubts about him. I am afraid that there is a strong inclination towards solitariness and self-sufficiency in him, and something of literary vanity.[86]

Zetkin pleaded that his intentions were for the best. Lenin replied:

> I won't argue with you about that. . . . But you surely know that in politics we are not concerned with intentions, but with effects. . . . The congress will condemn Paul Levi, will be hard on him. That is unavoidable. But his

---

[82] Ibid., p. 556.
[83] Ibid., p. 444.
[84] Zetkin, op. cit., p. 37.
[85] *Protokoll des III Kongresses der Kommunistischen Internationale*, op. cit., pp. 741–6.
[86] Zetkin, op. cit., p. 27.

condemnation will be only on account of breach of discipline, not of his basic political principles. How could that be possible at the very moment when those principles will be recognised as correct? The way is open for Paul Levi to find his way back to us.... His political future lies in his own hands. He must obey the decision of the congress as a disciplined communist, and disappear for a time from political life.... He will come back to us with deeper knowledge, firm in his principles, and as a better, wiser party leader.

We must not lose Levi. For his own sake and for our cause. We are not overblessed with talent, and must keep as much of what we have as we can.... If Levi submits to discipline, bears himself well – he can, for example, write anonymously in the party press, or write some pamphlets – then in three or four months time I shall demand his readmission in an open letter.[87]

Lenin saw the main problem as 'knowing how to win the masses'. He repeated to Zetkin: 'We are not Xerxes, who had the sea scourged with chains.'[88] After the experiences of 1917–21, the Communists could no longer go on believing in a quick and easy victory:

That is why the congress had to make a clean sweep with the 'left' illusions that the world revolution will continue at its early stormy speed, that we shall be carried forward by a second revolutionary wave, and that it depends solely on the party and its actions to bring victory to our cause. Of course, it is easy to 'make' the revolution the 'glorious act of the party alone', without the masses, on paper and in the congress hall, in an atmosphere free from objective conditions. But that is not a revolutionary, but an entirely Philistine conception.[89]

Lenin advised Zetkin about the structure of the VKPD, which should take account of the necessity to bring together people of different ages and experience:

You must be strict with the young comrades who are still without any deep theoretical knowledge or practical experience, and at the same time you must be very patient with them.... It is particularly important for you to help capable comrades in our ranks who have already won their spurs in

---

[87] Zetkin, op. cit., pp. 28–9. See his letter to Zinoviev dated 10 June 1921, note 26 above.
[88] Ibid., p. 26.
[89] Ibid., p. 33.

the working-class movement. . . . You must have patience with them, too, and not imagine that the 'purity of communism' is endangered and lost if occasionally they lack the clear, sharp formulation of communist thought. . . . Think always of the masses, Clara, and you will come to the revolution as we came to it: with the masses, through the masses.[90]

He summed up on their parting:

Learn, learn, learn! Act, act, act! Be prepared, well and completely prepared, in order to be able to make full use, consciously and with all our forces, of the next revolutionary wave. That is our job. Untiring party agitation and party propaganda, culminating in party action, but party action free from the illusion that it can take the place of mass action. How did we Bolsheviks work amongst the masses, until we could say to ourselves: 'We have come so far! Forward! Therefore – to the masses! Win the masses as a preliminary to winning power.'[91]

When we read these lines, we cannot fail to perceive the wide gulf which separated Lenin, not only from the leaders of the VKPD, but even such close collaborators as Zinoviev and Radek. No doubt we have here a clue to his method of operation at the Third Comintern Congress, his awareness in those years of the need to take account of the human material around him, and also of the gap between the experience and political understanding of the Russian cadres whom he had educated, for better or worse, in an unceasing struggle over decades, and that of men who, in the advanced countries of Western Europe, were engaged in their first campaigns as apprentices to Bolshevisur at the head of young Communist Parties. Following Wilhelm Koenen's report, the Congress carried a detailed resolution on the structure and activities of Communist Parties. A year later, at the Fourth Comintern Congress, Lenin said:

The resolution is an excellent one, but it is almost entirely Russian, that is to say, everything in it is based on Russian conditions. This is its good point, but it is also its failing. It is its failing because I am sure that no foreigner can read it. I have read it again before saying this. In the first place, it is too long, containing 50 or more points. Foreigners are not usually able to read such things. Secondly, even if they read it, they will not understand it because

---

[90] Ibid., p. 34.
[91] Ibid., p. 26.

it is too Russian. Not because it is written in Russian – it has been excellently translated into all languages – but because it is thoroughly imbued with the Russian spirit. And thirdly, if by way of exception some foreigner does understand it, he cannot carry it out. . . . I have the impression that we made a big mistake with this resolution, namely, that we blocked our own road to further success. As I have said already, the resolution is excellently drafted. I am prepared to subscribe to every one of its 50 or more points. But we have not learnt how to present our Russian experience to foreigners. All that we said in the resolution has remained a dead letter. If we do not realise this, we shall be unable to move ahead.[92]

That was Lenin's last intervention in the Communist International, an organisation which had so far made little progress, and which was not to make any more in the future.

No historian or Sovietologist has been able to give any explanation of this setback other than that presented by Lenin himself in 1922. It foreshadowed the difficulties encountered by the German Communists after the death of the man who in 1921 had protected them from their own mistakes as well as from the mistakes of the emissaries of the ECCI.

---

[92] V.I. Lenin, 'Five Years of the Russian Revolution and the Prospects of the World Revolution', *Collected Works*, Volume 33, p. 430.

PART THREE

FROM THE CONQUEST OF THE MASSES TO A DEFEAT WITHOUT A FIGHT

Chapter Twenty-Eight

Unity Preserved With Difficulty

We cannot be surprised by the efforts of Lenin at the Third Comintern Congress to maintain the unity of the KPD.[1] Nothing was further from Lenin's thinking than that dogmatism which denies reality or tries to force it to correspond to its schemas. We would have to ignore Lenin's policy in the Russian Social-Democratic Labour Party between 1906 and 1912, his attitude towards the split in the KPD(S) at the Heidelberg Congress, his efforts to bring it nearer to the KAPD and the left-wing Independents in 1920, his concern after the March Action to reach a remedial compromise, in order to declare, as Levi was one of the first to do, that, for the Bolsheviks, splitting constituted one of the enduring and essential methods of constructing the revolutionary workers' movement.

The definitive break from the KAPD

One of the first results of the Third Comintern Congress was the termination of attempts to bring the KAPD back into the fold. Lenin had made himself the most constant defender of unity since the Heidelberg Congress, but then came to see this ultra-left current in a different light. Already on the eve

---

[1] The German Communist Party dropped the term 'United' from its name in mid-1921, and was thereafter known simply as the KPD. [Translator's note]

of the Congress he was thinking that it had been a serious mistake to call in 1920 for the KAPD to be admitted into the International as a sympathising section.[2] His opposition to Appel during the debates, and the way in which he linked the positions which the KAPD defended to those of the ultra-leftists in the International, probably indicate that he had become aware of the danger posed to the future of the International by the uniting of these two ultra-left wings, which seemed to be separated essentially by personal questions alone.

The speeches of the other members of the ECCI during the Congress clearly showed that a new position had been adopted. Zinoviev attacked an article by Gorter which said that the Bolshevik leaders were placing the interests of the Soviet state before the needs of the world revolution. He threatened: 'Such a policy is half-puerile and half-criminal, and you will take your place amongst the enemies of the proletarian republic.'[3] Radek broke in to shout: 'Gorter is already defending Kronstadt.'[4] In these conditions, it is hardly surprising that Radek and Zinoviev, in the name of the ECCI, demanded that the KAPD fuse with the KPD within three months, or be excluded from the International.[5]

The KAPD delegation had failed to win any of its objectives during the Congress, and it returned to Germany convinced that the idea of building a left-wing faction in the Third International was hopeless.[6] However, the decision to break from the International was referred to the national leadership of the KAPD by agreement between the two Parties. On 31 July 1921, its Central Committee took the first steps towards the construction of a Communist Workers' International, directed against the Communist International.[7] By this point, however, the KAPD had already largely decomposed. Many of the supporters of 'national Bolshevism' had moved a long way by then. Wendel returned to Social Democracy in the summer of 1920.[8] Wolffheim joined with officers and businessmen in the League for the Study of German Communism, which would take him in the direction of the Nazi grouplets.[9] Otto Rühle had become one of the most violent enemies of the International and of Communist perspectives, which he described in these words: 'Above: authority,

---

[2] See Chapter 27.
[3] *Protokoll des III Kongresses der Kommunistischen Internationale*, op. cit., p. 190.
[4] Ibid.
[5] Bock, op. cit., p. 262.
[6] Ibid.
[7] Ibid., p. 341.
[8] Ibid., p. 444.
[9] Ibid., p. 281.

bureaucratism, personality cult, dictatorship of leaders and power to command. Below: corpse-like discipline, subordination and standing to attention.'[10] He too, as defender of an 'anti-authoritarian' revolutionary orientation, moved far from the organised workers' movement. The remainder of the Party, behind Schröder and the Berlin group, survived until the next split.[11] Although the ultra-left current was not extinct, and was soon to revive in the very heart of the KPD, the KAPD was now in its death throes.

New theoretical problems

From 1921, the theoretical problems which faced the Communists were very different from those which the Bolsheviks had experienced before the War. In fact, on two occasions, first in 1905 and then in 1912, Lenin had attempted to build the RSDLP by splitting it, fighting against the 'liquidators' who wanted to dissolve the Party. After 1914, the question was posed on the global level. The Bolsheviks undertook to reconstruct the international workers' movement, a task which involved eliminating the leaders who had defected to the bourgeoisie, and gathering the working masses in new parties. Up to 1921, they believed that the revolution was imminent. Despite its crudity, a split was the only method by which to provide the masses, whose hands were reaching out for power, with a revolutionary leadership as rapidly as possible. But from the Third Comintern Congress, revolution was not considered as an imminent proposition anywhere. On the other hand, the split in the international workers' movement, which the Communists considered to be the quickest means to liquidate the opportunist past and to reunify the proletariat on a revolutionary basis, resulted in a lasting division between rival Internationals, parties and trade unions.

As the Bolsheviks still saw capitalism as facing its final crisis, their perspective continued to be the seizure of power, albeit in the longer term. However, that presupposed the victory of the revolutionary current over the reformist one within the workers' movement. But this victory, as no one doubted since the ultra-leftists had departed from the International, could not be won merely by the methods of theoretical discussion and propaganda. It depended

---

[10] Ibid., p. 286.

[11] This was to occur in March 1922, the date after which two rival groups, one in Berlin and the other in Essen, both claimed to be the KAPD (ibid., p. 244).

essentially on the ability of the revolutionaries to convince the masses through their own experience in action.

The situation in Germany is the best illustration of the difficulties which the Communists encountered during this period. The March Action showed that isolated action on the part of the Communists was definitely a negative factor in their development. It demoralised many activists by dooming them to defeat, whilst the rest of masses were repelled by the Communists' tactics, even when they were sympathetic to their aims, and were driven, if not directly towards the bourgeoisie, at least, where those organised in Social Democracy were concerned, into scepticism and passivity. The Communists recognised that, in order for the workers to recover confidence in their own strength, to have a concrete idea of what could be achieved, to establish contact with the reformist parties and unions, they must struggle against capitalism. But workers enter into struggle only when they feel that victory is possible. They then see the need to engage in general class struggle, even for limited objectives. The political and organisational division of the working class is an obstacle on that road. Workers who place confidence in one particular political or trade-union organisation are not generally prepared to take the supporters of the competing organisation at their word. Occasional exceptional circumstances apart, common action between organisations thus requires agreement at the leadership level. But, here too, there are immense obstacles, because the Communists have to propose agreements to those leaders whom they describe at the same time as 'traitors'. If they cease to denounce them, they facilitate future betrayals. If they continue to denounce them, they provide them with solid reasons for refusing collaboration altogether.

This is the contradiction which the policy of the united front set out to overcome. This policy was based on the conviction that the masses who followed the Social-Democratic leaders could be won to Communism if these leaders could be shown to betray the working class during the course of struggles which involved the organisations of the working class acting in common.

The strategy of the united front was implicit in the policy followed by the Bolshevik leaders in 1917 in the soviets, with their struggle to break the coalition between the working-class and bourgeois parties, and their call for soviet power. This represented a higher form of the united class front in struggle, although that particular terminology was not used at this point. Until the VKPD's *Open Letter* in 1921, Communists had above all conceived their struggle to unify the working class through eliminating the 'opportunist' leaders. Armed with the 'Twenty-One Conditions', the Communists were the initiators of splits, and the Social Democrats became the defenders of 'unity'. The strategy of the united front was implicit in the resolutions of the Third Comintern Congress, which appealed to the Parties to 'go to the masses'. The aim remained the same as during the revolutionary offensive of 1917–21 – to unify the working class under the banner of Communism, to overcome the split in the workers' movement through purging its opportunist leadership – but the methods had changed.

There is nothing that permits us to say that when the Bolsheviks formulated this new policy they were turning their back on the policy of the preceding period, and that they were accepting the idea of the unity of reformists and revolutionaries within one organisation. Nor does anything permit us to say that the proposals of Lenin to overcome the consequences of the division of the working class would be confined to the formulae which were used to define the united front in 1921–2. Illness was to rob him of the time needed to go further down that road, if he had wished, but in any case the necessities of the internal struggle in the Russian Communist Party posed a real risk that the discussion would be cut short at this stage. The resistance to the policy of the united front which was found in various Communist Parties, both from unrepentant leftists and from the so-called 'rightist' and 'opportunist' elements, showed that the International had already developed its own ideology, and that the man who had founded and inspired it had to take account of its routine, of the reflexes it had acquired, in a word, of its conservatism.

Levi's theses

Whilst the Third Comintern Congress was posing the strategy of the proletarian revolution in new terms, Paul Levi was completing a text entitled 'The Tasks of the Communists'.[12] Like Lenin and Trotsky, he recognised that the relation of forces between the classes on the world scale had been reversed, and he emphasised that, from this juncture, the Communists must adopt a long-term policy. This implied a certain number of revisions and corrections.

The first concerned trade-union policy. The RILU had been conceived on the basis of a policy which 'counted on a rapid advance of the revolution,

---

[12] 'Die Aufgaben der Kommunisten', *Sowjet*, no. 5, 1 July 1921, pp. 138–44.

and a rapid change in the attitude of the masses'. Now it was vital to call this into question. The same applied to the stance towards Social Democracy. Having become the party of reformism, that is, of class collaboration, it nonetheless retained – and, it appeared, would go on retaining for an indefinite period – a considerable level of trust amongst working people. Past hopes of excluding the opportunist leaders from the movement, and of quickly arriving at a revolutionary reunification after a series of splits, had to be postponed to a more-or-less distant future. There was now a new component on the international level – the simultaneous existence of two workers' parties, one reformist and the other revolutionary, the first far larger than the second. The division of the workers' ranks moreover contributed to the prostration of the masses, and to the frustration of their strong desire for unity.

Under such conditions, Communists had to take care not to sharpen the division in the class. On the contrary, they were obliged to work to unite in action the proletarians who were divided amongst different organisations. They had to 'enter into relations with the other proletarian parties and work jointly with them in practical struggles, whether parliamentary or extra-parliamentary', in other words, take up again the policy of the *Open Letter* of January 1921.

Levi believed that the increasingly vital issue of relations between the Communists and the other proletarian parties could not be settled on the basis of the experience of the Russian Revolution and the Bolsheviks, because the situation in Germany and generally in Western Europe was profoundly different:

> The fundamental difference between the corresponding relations in Germany, for example, and in Russia is as follows. In Russia, the development of the proletarian parties in the period of preparation for the revolution took place in illegality. The form which was adopted by the struggles between the proletarian parties was essentially that of written polemics and resolutions. That is in no way a criticism of the evolution of these parties, which was due to circumstances, but a simple observation. In Germany, it is different. In Germany, the discussions in the proletariat take place within the sectors of the vast proletarian movement. The first period of the Revolution, properly speaking, the period from the first open battles to the seizure of power by the Bolsheviks, was measured in months. In Germany, the struggles at the end of which the proletariat was, provisionally, unable to take power, lasted much longer.

The discussions developed in the forms of struggles between the Communists and a large section of the Independents on the one hand, and the Social Democrats on the other. In this context, it is useless to apportion blame; it is enough to observe that both sides were defeated, Social Democrats as well as Communists. . . . Politically then, the result was the same for all the parties of the proletariat – defeat. On the economic level, the same thing, exploitation continues. This means that the social body which constitutes the unity, the proletariat, continues to exist, it exists afresh, and that even if you introduce the most subtle point about 'the labour aristocracy', you cannot philosophise about a new form of Marxism. Anyone who disposes of the entirety of Social Democracy with the formula of the 'labour aristocracy' has a very poor acquaintance with the situation in Germany. However, there is something left to us, something valuable, from the past years. It is that today there is in the German working class a profound differentiation on the level of ideas. The idea of social reform is sharply separated from that of social revolution. Previously, there was no need of any proof for this. The draft programme of the Social-Democratic Party categorically provided it, whilst the resistance which it encountered in Social Democracy proves only that such differences are never as clear as some leaders of Social Democracy imagined, and that we cannot immediately put a name to everything in the world.[13]

This was the situation which forced the Communists to adopt a 'unitary' tactic:

Therefore, the ideas of social reform and of revolution have become separated, and oppose each other in the form of parties . . . and how should they stand in relation to each other? When Social Democracy placed itself at the service of the bourgeoisie in order to defend it in a time of open struggles . . . it necessarily aroused the struggle of the revolutionary masses against it. But now the front lies elsewhere. The Social-Democratic workers are again in the camp of the defeated, and economically in the camp of the exploited. Relations must be created which leave open at any time the possibility of joint struggle against the bourgeoisie, however rigorous may be the difference in the ideas or the separation between the parties. This means in the first place that we must introduce a certain rationing into the use of unnecessary epithets.[14]

---

[13] 'Der Parteitag der KPD', *Unser Weg (Sowjet)*, no. 8, 19 August 1921, pp. 236–7.
[14] Ibid., p. 237.

Levi stressed in this connection the disastrous effect which the use of a certain vocabulary produces on the German workers, ritual insults such as 'Menshevik' or 'traitor', uttering ready-made phrases which sounded fine in the offices of the ECCI, but which did not correspond to anything in the consciousness of the workers in Western Europe:

> This change of language may perhaps lead to the 'small bureau' of the ECCI criticising the German Communists for not using 'revolutionary language', but it can only raise their standing in the German proletariat. . . . It is true that this only concerns secondary aspects. We do not need to adopt the manners and the language of the court of Louis XIV. It is much more important to bring about, by most active participation in all the proletarian organisations – independently of the trade unions – a spirit of confidence in Communism and an atmosphere of proletarian solidarity. The most enthusiastic participation in everything that is proletarian, in the educational facilities, in the cooperatives, everywhere, that is the ground on which, despite all the divergent conceptions about objects and method, there develops the only spirit which can create a common front against the bourgeoisie.[15]

This proletarian united front was unprecedented in the history of the Communist movement, but Levi insisted that the situation which necessitated it was also new:

> The German Communists must be aware that the task of counterposing the idea of the social revolution under the form of a mass party to the idea of social reform under the form of a mass party, is a new one, without precedent in history. It has to be solved by the German Party itself, and will certainly not be solved by simply copying Russian recipes about Mensheviks and the like, which would be absurd.[16]

Was the KPD capable of carrying through the necessary turn, of showing the way to the other Communist Parties in Europe? Experience since the Livorno Conference had convinced Levi that it was not, that this party was not capable of any initiative:

> For the first time, a Communist Party could play the leading role in the political struggle, under the banner of the social revolution, and challenge a Social-Democratic party which is unequalled in cohesion, in clarity (in its

[15] Ibid., pp. 237–8.
[16] Ibid., p. 238.

own way) and unity. The German Revolution, even if it has produced no results, could provide the German proletariat with this party. The strategists of the March Action decided otherwise. Now, the United German Communist Party is a party that has lost many of its supporters, and, on the ideological plane, is nothing but a heap of ruins. Instead of trying to reconstruct it, its leaders have reached compromises, and put a seal on the collapse. The number of those who have preserved what they had is infinitely small. Perhaps it will happen – and, without a miracle, it will happen – that the Communist Party will share the fate of the river Tarim in Central Asia, which flows from the mountains rolling with abundant waters, becomes wider and deeper, but never reaches the sea. It is lost in the steppes of Siberia, as if it had never existed. In that case, destiny will have denied to the German proletariat the gift of a revolutionary party as homogeneous from the point of view of revolution as Social Democracy is from that of reformism.[17]

The first split to the right

A reconciliation between Levi and the International was not ruled out in principle. Lenin did all he could to keep the possibility open. Yet the opposite happened. Levi's expulsion was confirmed, it was followed by others, and the KPD once more went through a split.

At first, Levi remained deaf to the proposals from Lenin which Zetkin passed on to him. On 27 July, he wrote ironically to his friend, Mathilde Jacob: 'Some have returned from Mecca. Clara will come in a few days. Lenin has opened the prospect of pardon. I am to go to Mecca (Canossa). Trotsky spoke as sharply as I did . . . Lenin no less firm. Zinoviev all of a sudden has turned round, and Radek remains the same blackguard as ever.'[18]

When Zetkin returned, he wrote:

Clara has come with three proposals: firstly, many compliments (necessary, as old Jews say, for the Sabbath); secondly, that we stop producing our journal and organising; thirdly, six months' repentance and the prospect of forgiveness from Lenin for good conduct and hailing the omniscience of the Bolsheviks.[19]

---

[17] Ibid., p. 239.
[18] Levi Archives, P113/15, cited in Beradt, op. cit., p. 57.
[19] Levi Archives, P113/20, cited in ibid.

Was this a sign of deeply hurt feelings? Was it the 'vanity of a literary man' who refused to recognise his mistakes in matters which he regarded as secondary, whilst convinced that he was correct on essentials? Was it disgust at the baseness of some of the attacks on him, and the hatred that was suddenly exposed? Was it a feeling of isolation which made him in a few days an enemy of the party that had been his? Was it weariness and loss of heart and the end of an inner dialogue which led him to cut short the discussion by denouncing the organisational loyalty to which he had himself so often appealed?

These, no doubt, are some of the elements which explain his attitude. When he appealed to Lenin on 27 March, he hoped that Lenin would endorse him, would agree that his intervention in April was praiseworthy, and that he would disavow the manoeuvres of Zinoviev, the recantations of Radek, and the stupidities of Kun and Rákosi. Had Levi really tried to play a game of 'all or nothing' with Lenin? Had he thought that Lenin could possibly sacrifice not merely Zinoviev and Kun, but also the German activists who had trusted the ECCI representatives, for the sake of his hurt feelings? It appears rather that Levi had been evolving little by little, and that at the moment when the message of Lenin's outstretched hand reached him, he on his side had already passed a point of no return. Nonetheless, his disappointment was expressed in his comments on the Second Comintern Congress, where he felt that nothing but the authority of Lenin and Trotsky had prevented – in a very provisional way – the victory in the International of what he called the 'semi-anarchist' current:

> The International unfortunately does not consist of thousands of Lenins and Trotskys. Their opinion is very important, but is not decisive. And the much-decried 'Levites' have eternal truth on their side, as well as Lenin and Trotsky, but have against them the Party apparatus, the press, the organisation and the practical leadership on the Executive. That is why, in Germany, Lenin is grey theory, so to speak, and Béla Kun is practice.[20]

The results of the Congress of the International were actually expressed within the KPD in a less simplistic way. Fischer firmly opposed the Moscow compromise, because she could see quite clearly that it confirmed and sharpened the line of the Second KPD Congress, which she hoped to see

---

[20] Ibid., p. 240.

finally abandoned. Remaining in Germany during the debates in Moscow, she spent her energies in organising pressure from Berlin on the delegates to the Congress. On 2 July, 2,000 full-timers in the district supported the text of a telegram to Moscow which she suggested, denouncing the factional activities of the 'Levites', and calling for them to be expelled *en bloc*.[21] But she no doubt also felt the need to strengthen the morale of her supporters, at least one of whom, Friesland, had just been convinced by Lenin.

The Central Committee met in Berlin on 3–4 August. It confirmed by a large majority – with only four votes against – the support which the delegates to the Comintern Congress had given to the theses carried in Moscow, and endorsed the 'peace treaty'. But its concrete application proved to be difficult. The Zentrale wanted from the minority a clear, specific statement of a sharp break from Levi and the expellees as proof of their renewed support. In return, it proposed to coopt Zetkin and Malzahn onto the Zentrale, and three of their comrades onto the Central Committee.[22] Neumann, speaking for the minority, had quite different demands: he wanted the Zentrale to resign and be re-elected, new editorial committees to be appointed, a return to freedom of discussion and of criticism, and in particular the election of new delegates to the Party Congress to ensure that the debates and decisions in Moscow were sufficiently considered. The delegates had been elected before the Third Comintern Congress, in an atmosphere of a 'witch-hunt against the centrists', during the dominance of the now-abandoned 'theory of the offensive'.[23] Maslow led the battle against all compromises, and finally won over the Central Committee. The demands of the opposition and even the proposals of cooption advanced by the Zentrale were rejected.[24]

[21] *Die Rote Fahne*, 3 July 1920.

[22] *Bericht über die Verhandlungen des 2 (7) Parteitags der KPD*, op. cit., p. 64; P. Levi, 'Nach dem III Weltkongress', *Sowjet*, no. 7, p. 215; report of the session of the ECCI, 17 August 1921, *Die Tätigkeit der Exekutive und der Präsidiums der Exekutivkomitee der Kommunistischen Internationale vom 13 Juli 1921 bis 1 Februar 1922*, Petrograd, 1922, during which Karl Radek stated that the Moscow agreement provided merely that Zetkin should join the Zentrale, and Malzahn should join the Central Committee.

[23] Levi Archives, P113/15, cited in Beradt, op. cit.; *Sowjet*, no. 7, p. 215.

[24] Brandt and Lowenthal, op. cit., p. 175. About the behaviour of Maslow in this session of the Central Committee, Lenin wrote that he was 'playing at leftism' and wished 'to exercise himself in the sport of "hunting centrists"'. Lenin accused him of 'unreasonableness' and having 'more zeal than sense', adding that this phrase was putting it mildly (V.I. Lenin, 'A Letter to the German Communists', *Collected Works*, Volume 32, op. cit., p. 522).

This tenacious struggle evidently had backers in Moscow. Radek himself sent to *Die Rote Fahne* an article[25] in which he attacked Zetkin with what Lenin was to call his 'misplaced polemical zeal', accusing him of having 'gone to the length of saying something positively untrue'.[26] Even in Berlin, the current was so strong that Friesland, who loyally fought for what had been agreed in Moscow, was put in a minority by Maslow and Fischer in what had been his power-base: 90 votes against 33.[27] There can be no doubt that it was to Maslow and Fischer, thenceforward leaders of the Berlin-Brandenburg district, that Radek, the slayer of the opportunists, gave weighty support from Moscow.[28]

The confusion was such that the KPD's Jena Congress received no less than three official letters from Moscow, one from Radek,[29] one from Lenin[30] and one from the ECCI.[31] Radek warned the Party against the opportunists, and reminded it not to forget, in its struggle to win the masses, that the Social Democrats and the Independents were betrayers of the proletariat. Lenin explained at length why he had defended Paul Levi at the World Congress, and why the Party must at all costs stand by the 'peace treaty' which had been concluded in Moscow. The ECCI recalled the decisions of the World Congress, and rejected both the 'Mensheviks' of the Right and the 'brawlers' of the Left. On 17 August, a sharp discussion took place on the ECCI on the situation in the KPD, on the basis of a report by Radek which accused Neumann of violating the Moscow decisions and emphasised the danger from the Right. Kun declared that the information given revealed a new situation. He believed

---

[25] Karl Radek, 'Der 3 Weltkongress über die Märzaktion und die weitere Taktik', *Die Rote Fahne*, 14, 15 July 1921.

[26] Lenin, 'A Letter to the German Communists', *Collected Works*, Volume 32, op. cit., p. 516.

[27] Brandt and Lowenthal, op. cit., p. 176.

[28] Lenin specified that Radek's article had been sent to him by a Polish activist, which sheds some light on the alignments within the International (Lenin, 'A Letter to the German Communists', *Collected Works*, Volume 32, op. cit., p. 515).

[29] *Bericht über die Verhandlungen des 2 (7) Parteitags der KPD*, op. cit., pp. 174–81. Published separately under the title *Die innere Lage Deutschlands und die nächsten Aufgaben der KPD. Offener Brief an den 2 Parteitag der KPD*, Hamburg, 1921. This was a personal initiative by Radek, which he merely mentioned in his report to the Presidium on August 17 (*Die Tätigkeit*, op. cit., p. 102).

[30] *Bericht über die Verhandlungen des 2 (7) Parteitags der KPD*, op. cit.; Lenin, 'A Letter to the German Communists', op. cit., *Collected Works*, Volume 32, pp. 512–23.

[31] *Bericht über die Verhandlungen des 2 (7) Parteitags der KPD*, op. cit., pp. 155–74. The text drawn up by Zinoviev had been submitted to the 'small bureau', and approved in the course of the meeting on 13 August (*Die Tätigkeit*, op. cit., p. 86).

that the ECCI's letter was already overtaken by events, and proposed a motion which sharply declared that the struggle must be waged 'above all against the Right'. It was finally decided to send a telegram in this sense, which would be disclosed to the delegates only if absolutely necessary.[32]

The outcome of the Jena Congress was to reflect these contradictory pressures and tendencies. Not only did it essentially adopt Moscow's theses, but on many points it went further and clearly reverted to its January line of struggle for the workers' united front. In particular, it adopted a manifesto which contained demands that made possible a united front with the Social Democrats, including confiscation of the property of the former dynasties, control of industrial production by the factory committees, and transfer to the capitalists of the burden of reparations. The opposition came from Fischer, whose intervention formed the first 'manifesto' of the Left: without openly attacking the decisions of the Third Comintern Congress, she criticised the line which she once more regarded as opportunist. But at the same time, the congress revealed the desire of the majority to continue to settle accounts. It adopted an amendment by Thaelmann dissociating the Congress from Trotsky's criticism of the March Action, expelled Curt and Anna Geyer, and in that way precipitated the departure of three deputies who had been up to that point undecided, Däumig, Marie Mackwitz and Adolf Hoffmann, who were to join Levi in forming a Communist Working Collective (KAG) in the Reichstag, the very name of which signified a step towards a split. Nonetheless, the selection of the new leadership showed concern to follow a line close to that advised by Lenin: from Zetkin, who came from the 'Right', to Friesland, who came from the 'Left', every member of the Zentrale was a convinced supporter of the Moscow compromise. The new Party President was Ernst Meyer, with Friesland in the post of General Secretary.[33]

Levi saw nothing in the Jena Congress but a confirmation of his belief that a bureaucratic apparatus with semi-anarchistic ideas – two phenomena which he judged to be closely linked[34] – had now gained control of the KPD.

---

[32] Detailed report of this meeting of the ECCI in *Die Tätigkeit*, op. cit., pp. 100–4.
[33] Ibid., pp. 262–5, 408–15; W.T. Angress, *Stillborn Revolution*, Princeton, 1963, p. 209.
[34] 'Nach dem Parteitage. Das Ergebnis des Parteitages der KPD', *Sowjet*, no. 10, September 1921, pp. 265–8.

A second split to the right

The policy of the new Zentrale was to show that Levi's expectations were ill-founded. On 26 August, right-wing extremists murdered the Catholic deputy Mathias Erzberger. The KPD then plunged into what amounted to a policy of united struggle against the reactionaries, and it took part in demonstrations in several industrial cities organised by the other workers' parties.[35] In Thuringia, the September elections gave a majority in the Landtag to the workers' parties, and the KPD agreed to support a workers' coalition government formed by Majority Social Democrats and Independents, although it did not join it.[36] In October, the KPD advanced a four-point programme close to the demands of the trade-union confederation, and in this it particularly adopted the slogan of 'the confiscation of real values'.[37] On its behalf, Thalheimer declared the Party ready to support the Social-Democratic Parties in any policy aimed at winning 'positions of power' for the working class.[38] Levi at first saw nothing but duplicity in these contradictions, but soon had to correct his judgement.

Indeed, it was the new General Secretary, Friesland, who took the lead in the new policy, and consciously linked it to that of January 1921, and essentially to that of Levi and his group. Very quickly, the former ferocious lambaster of the 'Right' underwent some instructive experiences in his turn. Within a few weeks, he was treading the same path as Levi in the commanding positions of the Party. Like Levi, he came up against opposition from the ECCI and its initiatives, which he saw as obstacles to the Party's new policy. According to his biographers, he was behind the approach which Pieck and Heckert made on behalf of the Zentrale to the ECCI in September.[39] The German leaders asked that the ECCI give up the practice of public appeals and open letters, that there be more personal contacts between the KPD and the ECCI, and that the latter help them to consolidate their authority in the Party.

---

[35] *Die Rote Fahne*, 25, 27 August, 1 September 1921. The article 'Arbeiter Deutschlands! Werktätiges Volk', *Die Rote Fahne*, 29 August 1921, called for struggle for a 'proletarian united front'.

[36] *Die Rote Fahne*, 6 October 1921.

[37] *Die Rote Fahne*, 23, 25 October 1921. See also IML-ZPA, 3/1/25, 'An unsere Organisationen', 28 October 1921, pp. 51–4, cited in Mujbegović, op. cit., p. 309, n. 18.

[38] *Inprekorr*, no. 112, 29 November 1921, pp. 98–9.

[39] Brandt and Lowenthal, op. cit., p. 185.

The Zentrale asked that the RILU press stop its attacks on the trade unions and their reformist leaders, because they were used in Germany to present the Communists as splitters.[40] These themes echoed those which Levi had been developing for some months. Their rapprochement became even more flagrant after the conflict broke out between Friesland and the representatives of the International in Berlin, Felix Wolf, and especially Yelena Stasova, whose task, since the Jena Congress, was to take in hand 'organisational matters'. Once again, the problem of '*éminences grises*' was posed. Friesland went so far as to refer to the representatives as a 'counter-government' within the Party leadership itself.[41] Evidently, the question arose of how far the new German leadership – or at least part of it, including Friesland – was seeking a reconciliation with Levi and the KAG, and what the consequences would be for the KPD.

The developments in the KPD continued to divide the ECCI. The first report on the Jena Congress was given to the Presidium of the International by Heckert and Pieck on 18 September. Their main concern seems to have been the success of the Left in winning support amongst Berlin workers, to whom it was decided to address an open letter. On 24 September, Heckert, reporting to the ECCI, welcomed the expulsion by 273 votes out of 278, of Düwell and Geyer, but indicated that the letter which the ECCI had sent to the Congress had antagonised the Berlin organisation. On 1 November, the ECCI started to pay attention to the KAG, and appointed a commission of Radek, Heckert and Zinoviev to look at this issue.[42]

The KAG was now a major question for the Communist movement. On 3 November, the ECCI learned from Heckert that Däumig and Adolf Hoffmann had resigned from the KPD. Radek said that the German Communists had to 'hit the Right by every means'. Platten suggested sending Heckert and Pieck at once to the Zentrale.[43] They were anxious in Moscow about the absence of a reaction in Berlin to the appearance of 'a new centre of centrist regroupment'. Radek suggested sending a letter to the Zentrale expressing surprise at its passivity in the face of the KAG: 'Anyone who does not denounce what it really is . . . who is not fighting those people politically as enemies of

---

[40] Ibid., p. 186; Friesland, op. cit., p. 3.
[41] Brandt and Lowenthal, op. cit., p. 187.
[42] *Die Tätigkeit*, op. cit., pp. 202, 208–9, 243.
[43] Ibid., pp. 249–50.

Communism, is working for them and serving them as a spokesman within the Party.'[44]

The ultimatum thus addressed to the Zentrale demanded that those, like Malzahn and Neumann, who supported Friesland and still held responsible posts in the Party, must be challenged, not least because it was clear that they agreed in principle with Levi, and were suspected of having 'factional' links with him. At the Zentrale meeting a few days later, Heckert and Pieck arrived with a message from the ECCI which did not hide its distrust of Friesland. Eberlein proposed that Friesland be removed as General Secretary, and be replaced by Pieck.[45] The German leaders hesitated, the Zentrale rejected Eberlein's proposal, and wanted a more thoroughgoing political discussion to take place. A few days later, the Central Committee accepted Friesland's approach. It carried a resolution which condemned any attempt by the KAG to force a split, but advocated political discussions with its members.[46]

The First Conference of the KAG was held on 20 November, with Levi and Däumig to the fore. The Communist deputy Otto Brass was present, and had no hesitation in passing on information about the last session of the Central Committee.[47] The Conference adopted a manifesto which spelt out the conditions which would enable the KPD to 'win back the confidence of the masses': financial independence of the Party from the International; rejection of any future offers of subsidies; parity of control between the ECCI and the Zentrale on the publications of the International before their distribution in Germany; guarantees against any interference by the ECCI, open or otherwise, in the organisational affairs of the KPD; choice of a Communist orientation which would be 'clear and acceptable to revolutionary workers', an orientation which united the working class, and which excluded adventures like the March Action; and finally, a trade-union policy equally directed towards working-class unity.[48]

Friesland wrote an article for *Die Internationale* which constituted an overture to the KAG, and which also served as a warning to his opponents in the Party that the policy of the united front implied abandonment of the methods

---

[44] *Die Rote Fahne*, 16 November 1921.
[45] Brandt and Lowenthal, op. cit., p. 187; Friesland, op. cit., pp. 5–6.
[46] *Die Rote Fahne*, 22 November 1921; Ernst Friesland, 'Das Ergebnis des Zentralausschusses', *Die Internationale*, no. 17, 1 December 1921, pp. 592–3.
[47] Brandt and Lowenthal, op. cit., p. 189.
[48] 'Resolution der I Reichskonferenz der KAG', *Unser Weg (Sowjet)*, no. 15, 15 December 1921, p. 415.

of invective and excommunication.[49] The editors distanced themselves from this article in a prefatory note. Discreet references to the problems of relations between the International and the leadership of Communist Parties show that a working alliance had evolved between Levi and the man who had taken his place at the head of the KPD.

It was in the course of this realignment of forces within the Party and its leadership that a bomb exploded with the publication by *Vorwärts* from 25 November onwards of extracts from the documents which the Prussian police had found on 5 June in Zetkin's baggage.[50] Essentially, these consisted of minutes of meetings and statements by Communist activists and Party officials which had been collected for the ECCI's enquiry into the March Action. They furnished very convincing evidence of the provocative initiatives which some Communists had undertaken in March, suggestions for kidnapping people or faked attacks, and they particularly brought out the efforts of Eberlein to 'arouse' the workers in Central Germany.[51]

Even though these documents were published by the SPD, which itself received them from the Prussian Minister of the Interior, Severing, any Communist could easily see that they were authentic, and they were devastating for those responsible for the March Action. They also confirmed the most serious of the accusations which Levi had made during the preceding months. Their publication, and the shock which they inflicted on many militants who had honestly believed that Levi was a slanderer, moved Friesland towards making a decisive political clarification. The furore over Eberlein's role in the March Action encouraged Friesland to raise all the contentious political questions: the ECCI's interference in the affairs of the Party leadership,[52] the independence of the Party, the ultra-left conception of the struggle, and the

---

[49] 'Parteitaktische Bemerkungen', *Die Internationale*, no. 18–19, 15 December 1921, pp. 642–7.

[50] See Chapter 27, note 36.

[51] The KPD was to publish the complete documents the following year under the title *Die Enthüllungen zu den Märzkämpfen. Enthülltes und Verschwiegenes*, Halle, 1922.

[52] This question was at the centre of the struggle in the Zentrale. Mujbegović shows this clearly with quotations from the minutes of the leading committees. On 31 May, the Zentrale had expressed the desire to open discussions in Moscow on the matter of the choice of representatives of the International. The minutes on this point actually read: 'It must be stressed that it is necessary, if possible, to delegate comrades who know exactly the situation in the countries in question.' (IML-ZPA, 3/1, pp. 7–9) The minutes of the meeting of the Zentrale of 26 November read as follows: 'The comrades are of the opinion that it is easy to understand the need for fresh criticism of the Executive: up until now, and in many domains, the work has not been done as it

need for an honest recognition of errors which had been committed. His first indictment was directly aimed at Felix Wolf, whose relations with the ECCI were conducted over the heads of the Zentrale, and at Radek, whose semi-official letters to *Die Rote Fahne* on the eve of or immediately after meetings of the Central Committee effectively deprived the latter of its powers of decision.[53]

The problem of the Party's relationship with the ECCI arose again. Friesland declared: 'Through the pressure in personal matters on some members of the Zentrale and through private correspondence, etc., it is impossible to construct responsible leaderships of parties which can enjoy solid confidence amongst the masses of workers in their countries.'[54] The foundations for a fight seemed solid. On 28 November, Friesland met Malzahn and Neumann, and agreed to unite in calling for Eberlein to be expelled.[55] On 30 November, Malzahn, Neumann and Hauth of the trade-union department addressed to the Zentrale a statement which insisted that Eberlein be expelled, on the grounds that he was a mere tool within the KPD of a faction in the ECCI. The Hanau district adopted an analogous position.[56] Tensions were rising; it seemed that a real tempest would soon shake the Party.

However, a manifestation of Party solidarity was to cause a radically different result to that which the dissidents had expected. How could the Party attack one of its own leading members on the basis of documents published by the Social Democrats? This was the question around which differences revolved, which divided members throughout the Party, and which determined their attitude towards the issue.

The debate opened on 12 December at a meeting of the Party's Political Bureau.[57] Friesland, with the support of Ernst Meyer on this point, defended the thesis, popular with Levi's supporters, that the Zentrale should control

---

should have been.' However, the minutes go on to dissociate the meeting from Levi's criticisms of the ECCI, on the grounds that they 'were attacks on the work of the whole International, which the German Party – a member of the International – cannot support' (IML-ZPA, 3/1, p. 167).

[53] Friesland, op. cit., p. 10.

[54] Ibid.

[55] Ibid.

[56] Friesland, op. cit., p. 16. The Hanau leadership had already supported Levi at the time of his expulsion, and had expressed the view that he should be readmitted (*Die Rote Fahne*, 24 July 1921).

[57] Minutes of the session of the Political Bureau on 12 December, reproduced in Friesland, op. cit., pp. 16–23. Those present were Zetkin, Thalheimer, Pieck, Walcher, Remmele, Meyer, Friesland and Schmidt, plus 'Heinrich' (Süsskind), Editor-in-Chief of *Die Rote Fahne*, and 'Käte' (Katarina Rabinovich, alias Käte Pohl), Permanent Secretary of the Political Bureau (ibid., p. 16).

the International's German-language publications. His resolution was defeated by six votes to two, but five of his opponents, Zetkin, Thalheimer, Heckert, Pieck and Walcher, declared that whilst they fundamentally agreed with it, they refused to vote for it in order to avoid taking a position that would be an act of hostility to the ECCI.[58] Friesland then undertook to demonstrate that the principal danger to the Party came from the progress of the Left in Berlin. In his estimation, they had half of the active members of the Party behind them, and consequently the Zentrale should avoid taking a hard attitude to the KAG. Any policy that made things worse would propel the latter to the right, and open the way to the fragmentation of the Party.[59] He received no support. Felix Schmidt advocated fighting on two fronts: 'Friesland with the KAG and Fritzi with his KAPD.'[60] Pieck demanded that Friesland be removed and be replaced by a collective leadership. Walcher went further and demanded that Friesland be sent to Moscow.[61] When Friesland asked why they simply did not expel him from the Party, Pieck retorted: 'A strong Zentrale could and should expel Friesland. We are not a strong Zentrale, and we cannot do it point-blank.'[62] He supported Walcher's proposal. The important decisions were narrowly carried: five votes to three for removing Friesland from the post of General Secretary, and six to two for sending him to Moscow. Ernst Meyer voted against a motion which he believed to mean excluding Friesland from the Zentrale, but supported sending him to Moscow.[63]

However, as Friesland had announced at the Zentrale before the vote was taken, he refused to go into exile. On 20 December, with Brass and Malzahn, he drafted an appeal to Party members in which they denounced 'the pernicious influence of certain members of the ECCI' and the existing danger that 'the Communist International could be permanently compromised, and with it the very idea of an international centralised leadership of the revolutionary proletariat'.[64] Seventy-four active Party members, including many in trade-union positions, Niederkirchner, Franken and Fritz Winguth amongst them, called for those responsible for the provocations in March to resign, and for

[58] Ibid., p. 20.
[59] Ibid., pp. 17–19.
[60] Ibid., p. 1. 'Fritzi' refers to Ruth Fischer.
[61] Ibid., p. 23.
[62] Ibid. The proposal came from Heinrich Süsskind.
[63] Ibid., p. 23.
[64] Ibid., pp. 28–32.

all the documents in the affair to be published.[65] The appeal by Brass, Friesland and Malzahn reached the Zentrale on 22 December.[66] Friesland was helped by the metalworkers' union in Berlin to print 500 copies of a pamphlet entitled *On the Crisis in Our Party* for distribution to leading members. This reproduced the principal documents in the current discussion, with comments by Friesland, who for the first time in writing, in a document inevitably fated to leak out, attacked particularly Wolf and Radek himself, as representatives of the ECCI.[67] On 22 December, the Zentrale rejected the appeal of the three, and drafted a reply, which it then published.[68] At the same time, it published the documents of these oppositionists, whom it attacked as 'saboteurs' and 'splitters'.[69] Finally on 27 December, it expelled Friesland, and suspended from their functions those who had signed the various appeals.[70]

To be sure, many militants and Party functionaries shared the opinions of Levi or Friesland, or were receptive to their arguments. Since April, there had been as many protests against the policy of expulsions as against the March Action and the events in its aftermath. These protests came from the Spartacist old guard and the Independents as much as from the young, and the central body of the Communist Youth itself had protested. But it was not a matter of opinion that was at stake: the majority of these people refused to follow Friesland, just as they had not followed Levi, because they did not want to break their solidarity with the ECCI in the prevailing circumstances. They shared their views, but they baulked at following those whom they considered to be splitters. This was the position of old Emil Eichhorn and the veteran Independent from Halle, Kilian, of the trade-union activist Niederkirchner, of the activists from Hanau, such as the metalworker Rehbein, and those from Frankfurt, like Jakob Schloer, personally linked with Levi, of Jogiches's former follower Werner Hirsch, the young Communist Walter Gollmick, and the leaders of the Party in the Rhineland such as Franz Charpentier and Franz Dahlem.[71]

The ECCI devoted its meeting on 18 December mainly to the situation in the KPD. Remmele, who gave the report, said that Friesland had now come

---

[65] Ibid., pp. 23–7.
[66] Brandt and Lowenthal, op. cit., p. 198.
[67] Friesland, op. cit., p. 10.
[68] *Die Rote Fahne*, 24 December 1921.
[69] *Die Rote Fahne*, 25 December 1921.
[70] *Die Rote Fahne*, 28 December 1921.
[71] Weber, *Die Wandlung des deutschen Kommunismus*, Volume 2, op. cit., pp. 90–1, 104, 135, 140, 164, 181, 254, 277.

into the open. The KAG had aroused no echo in the Party outside the Zentrale and the trade-union department. But there was 'no clarity' on this matter in the Zentrale, because Friesland had not been expelled. The Russian representatives attacked with fury. Zinoviev said that the KAG was 'the most dangerous enemy', because it undermined the Party 'from within', and he insisted that anyone who discussed with Levi should be expelled without hesitation. Bukharin was even more violent. He said that the interests of political clarity demanded that the Levites be driven out of the Party, because their presence in its ranks made the application of the new united-front tactic extremely risky. Zinoviev expressed anxiety about a split to the left: 'If the Zentrale does not adopt a clear position towards these charlatans like Levi, and counter-revolutionary gangs like the KAG, we shall have ultra-left stupidities on the other side.'[72]

Zinoviev reminded the ECCI that the Zentrale had been elected by a 'left' congress, and that it was hesitant in dealing with the Right. Since Friesland and his supporters were making use of Lenin's position at the Third Comintern Congress, it was absolutely necessary for Moscow to take a stand and denounce the KAG as an agency of the bourgeoisie. Radek undertook to show that the differences were wider, that in particular there were vacillations in the Zentrale on the trade-union question, especially half-expressed reservations about the RILU. The German leadership, thus accused, had no defender. Only Brandler, who had just arrived in Moscow, opposed a public denunciation of the KAG. He thought it would be dangerous, if only because 'the Zentrale had not yet grasped the full extent of the political situation'. In fact, the stakes were down and the ECCI decided to throw its full weight in the balance when it entrusted to Radek, Bukharin and Remmele the task of drafting a letter to the Zentrale, which was approved on 10 January.[73]

The discussion in the KPD was harsh, but the forms of debate were respected. Friesland was given every chance to put his case to meetings of members, which one after another condemned him.[74] On the day of the Central Committee meeting which was to settle the question, *Die Rote Fahne* delivered the final blow by publishing the letter of the ECCI, signed by Lenin, Trotsky, Zinoviev, Bukharin and Radek amongst others, condemning as an 'enemy of the

---

[72] Ibid., pp. 329–34.
[73] Ibid., pp. 333–5, 375–86.
[74] Brandt and Lowenthal, op. cit., p. 201.

proletariat' anyone in the International who declared solidarity with Levi.[75] The Central Committee expelled Friesland and his supporters from the Party by forty votes to four.[76]

Thalheimer was to treat the affair with contempt when he addressed the ECCI, speaking of the departure of 'leaders without troops'.[77] It is true that many members who might have formed the basis of an opposition led by Friesland had left the Party immediately after the March Action. It is no less true that others, who agreed with him on many points, condemned and even voted to expel him. Nonetheless, Thalheimer was speaking there with surprising thoughtlessness. The people who were finally expelled in January 1922, like those who had been expelled or had left of their own accord immediately after the March Action, an important portion of whom were to return to Social Democracy by way of the rump USPD, were precisely those leading activists whose presence Lenin deemed necessary for the building of a revolutionary party in Germany.

Those who might dispute this judgement in view of the intellectual origins of Levi, Däumig, Adolf Hoffmann, Bernhard Düwell, Friesland or Kurt Geyer, could not deny that the departure or expulsion of Otto Brass, Richard Müller, Wegmann, Paul Neumann, Winguth, Malzahn or Paul Eckert was a loss. They were officers in that proletarian army the winning of whom had been seen at the time of the Halle Congress as a decisive stage in the battle to construct a mass Communist Party, and, for that reason, had been hailed as a triumph at the time.

The danger of a split to the left

The debate about the question of Levi, the KAG and finally Friesland had been dominated by fear of a twofold split. Expulsion of the 'Right' had been one of the demands of the 'Left', but the progress of the 'Left' strengthened the 'rightist' resistance, and the whole Party was in the end constantly

---

[75] *Die Rote Fahne*, 22 January 1922. This type of practice, an article by Radek or an open letter from the ECCI driving the Central Committee into a corner at the outset of its deliberations, was precisely an aspect of the 'means of pressure' expressly condemned by Friesland and his supporters.

[76] *Bericht über die Verhandlungen des III (8) Parteitages der Kommunistischen Partei Deutschlands (Sektion der Kommunistischen Internationale), abgehalten in Leipzig vom 28 Januar bis 1 Februar, 1923*, Berlin, 1923, p. 126.

[77] *Die Taktik der Kommunistischen Internationale gegen die Offensive des Kapitals*, Hamburg, 1922, p. 19.

threatened with an explosion.[78] From this viewpoint, the elimination or departure of the leaders of the 'Right' solved none of the current problems.

There was a deeply-rooted 'rightist' tendency amongst the leading activists of the KPD. No expulsions could eradicate it, and the events of 1921 had unquestionably strengthened it. There were many who did not want to condemn Levi and Friesland for their ideas, but could not accept acts of indiscipline and activities which divided the Communist movement and threatened solidarity with the Russian Party. The pressure of the ECCI had been able to win them to the Left in March 1921. The ensuing defeat, followed by the reprimands which they suffered in Moscow, had come as a real shock to many who had more or less resisted this pressure, such as Brandler, or who, like Frölich, had readily endorsed the theory of the offensive.

Activists such as Brandler, Thalheimer, Walcher and Meyer, who during the years of the KPD(S) had resisted 'leftism' with all their might, could now judge the seriousness of their relapse into this 'infantile sickness', and to see what it had cost. From then onwards, they would be resolute 'rightists', systematically persisting in an attitude of prudence, armed with precautions against the putschist temptation or even a simple leftist reflex. Convinced by the leadership of the International of the magnitude of their blunder, they lost confidence in their own ability to think, and often failed to defend their viewpoint, so that they systematically accepted that of the Bolsheviks, who had at least been able to win their revolutionary struggle.

The new German leadership, and in particular Meyer, who was to preside over the Zentrale for a year and came strongly under the influence of Radek, tried to find their bearings in the conditions pertaining in Germany within the terms of the analysis of the world situation outlined at the Third Comintern Congress. The revolutionary wave had receded, the seizure of power by the proletariat was not on the immediate agenda, and the bourgeois offensive was forcing the working class onto the defensive and into a desperate struggle to defend its very existence. The slogans of the united front had to correspond

---

[78] Mujbegović (op. cit., p. 314) quotes a report which sums up the problems which the appearance of the KAG and the advance of the Left posed to the German leaders: 'It is not impossible that the opposition could organise a new social revolutionary party with the KAG and the left wing of the Independents. Of course, today the leaders deny having such intentions, but if despite everything this were to happen, the remnants of the KPD would be thrown into the arms of the ultra-lefts round Ruth Fischer and Maslow, and eventually towards unification with the KAPD.'

to the concrete demands of the workers, whilst at the same time helping them to become aware of the necessity for the proletarian revolution.

In Germany in 1921–2, one of the elements in the formation of this awareness had to be the struggle to throw off the burden of reparations, which fell exclusively on the shoulders of the working class by means of taxes deducted from wages, whereas the industrialists and businessmen paid their taxes only months and years later, in depreciated marks. The idea that 'the capitalists ought to pay their share' was not peculiar to the Communists, but it could for that very reason unite the working class in struggle. Therefore the Zentrale advanced the demand of 'confiscation of real values' by the state, which would fall on bank accounts as well as shares, bonds and commercial and industrial property.[79]

The Zentrale made the point that 51 per cent confiscation of real values by the state would make possible effective control over production, whilst at the same time reparations could be paid without essentially coming out of wages. The aim of the KPD was to reveal clearly to the workers, through the struggle for 'the confiscation of real values', the nature of the capitalist state and government, and the need for a workers' government. At the same time, the Zentrale believed that this slogan, which every worker accepted and understood, could make it possible to unite large numbers of workers for the ensuing 'mass struggle' to challenge the grip of the great industrialists on the economy and political life.

Meyer and the Zentrale presented this policy as 'the German NEP'. They argued that the development of 'state capitalism' could in itself be a preparatory stage for the seizure of power and the dictatorship of the working class. In this way, Meyer and the Zentrale projected into Germany the policy of concessions to capitalist tendencies which had been operated in Russia by means of the NEP – at the very moment when the German state revealed its impotence before the barons of big business.

This policy was far from receiving enthusiastic acceptance in the ranks of the Party. In fact it could be easily understood only by the former Spartacists, who in 1919–20 had reflected upon means of proceeding towards taking power without immediately engaging in an armed struggle. Of the former

---

[79] The formal decision was taken by the Central Committee on 16–17 November 1921 (*Die Rote Fahne*, 22 November 1921) after the trade-union confederations had decided on 15 November on their 'Ten Demands', which in particular included the confiscation of 25 per cent of 'real values'. (*Korrespondenzblatt des ADGB*, 26 November 1921, p. 679).

left Independents, a good number of whom had deserted the Party, with Levi or individually, after the March Action, there remained only the most combative, often the most primitive, elements, those who fought in the March Action and who joined the Communist International because they wanted an immediate revolution. They did not like the new policy, as it was too much like the gradualism which they had rejected in the SPD and USPD. The prestige of the unsure, hesitant Party leaders, who went over from 'passivity' to 'ill-timed activity', was weakest amongst these members.

The new Left in Berlin was to take advantage of this new ultra-left current. Fischer, unlike Friesland, had not approved of the turn in the summer of 1921. She thought that the Third Comintern Congress had not taken any clear position on Levi's views, and had been unable to criticise the March Action without giving the impression that Levi had not been expelled merely for reasons of discipline.[80] Hostility to the policy defined at the Third Congress, which was seen as a retreat, an unjustified withdrawal, included also a severe criticism of the NEP as it was justified and applied in Russia. The theoreticians of the new Left considered that Lenin and his comrades had themselves fallen into opportunist error and taken the road of concessions to capitalism. Their policies elaborated in 1921 as a whole were a break from the revolutionary spirit of 1917, in so far as they implied extending the NEP to the rest of the world and renouncing the perspective of an early world revolution.[81] This new Left, which also saw world politics in Russian terms, made contact with the Workers' Opposition which Lenin and the Tenth Congress of the Russian Communist Party had condemned in March 1921.

During the summer of 1921, Maslow had several meetings in Arthur Rosenberg's flat in Berlin with Shliapnikov and Lutovimov, the former leaders of the Workers' Opposition, who were now employed in the Soviet foreign service. They also made contact with the KAPD.[82] Fischer and Maslow thought that the Russian leaders, in order to overcome gigantic difficulties, were not limiting themselves to internal concessions to capitalism on the economic level, but were also trying to find points of support abroad which would enable them to find a *modus vivendi* with imperialism. With such a perspective, the so-called policy of 'winning the masses' and the tactic of the workers' united front promoted by Meyer were no different from those of Levi. Their

---

[80] *Protokoll des vierten Kongresses der Kommunistischen Internationale, Petrograd-Moskau vom 5 November bis 5 Dezember 1922*, Hamburg, 1923, p. 80.
[81] Fischer, op. cit., p. 185.
[82] Ibid., pp. 181–2.

aim was to seek agreement with Social Democracy, and this process was helped considerably by their criticisms of genuine revolutionaries as 'ultra-leftists'.

The Left in the KPD emerged from the unification of two currents, the postwar generation of intellectuals, and the often politically uneducated workers who came from the left Independents. This left wing was completely outside control by the ECCI members who had sponsored and protected it whilst the struggle against Levi was being prepared, and it opposed the ECCI and the Bolshevik leaders themselves in the name of defending the Russian Revolution. Its supporters thought that the existence in Germany of a 'combat party' – or, at least, a left wing distinguished from the 'opportunist' Zentrale – could provide valuable help for those in Russia who were fighting opportunism and the tendencies towards accommodation with capitalism.[83] The Berlin Left was a real party within the Party, with its own features and characteristics.[84]

Lenin appears to have grasped perfectly the 'objective' causes for the development of the Left. He confided to Zetkin:

> I can well understand that in such a situation there should be a 'left opposition'. There are, of course, some CLP [KAPD] elements left, discontented, suffering workers who feel revolutionary, but are politically raw and confused. Things move forward so slowly. World history does

---

[83] Ibid., p. 182.

[84] The Berlin-Brandenburg district was led by intellectuals, Fischer, Maslow and Rosenberg – which was unusual in the KPD – and they were young, having played practically no role before 1919. Around them were still younger men and women, known as Fischer's 'Youth', who generally were very intelligent. For example there were Gerhard, Fischer's brother, Werner Scholem, who became district organiser in 1922, Lily Korpus who, aged 22, was in charge of women's work, and, of course, Heinz Neumann. In this team we first meet Moses Lurie, under the name Alexander Emel, who was later to be one of the trusted agents of the Communist International in Germany, and also a future defendant in the Moscow Trial in 1936. They were all of bourgeois or petty-bourgeois origin. All had completed brilliant university studies or interrupted them to become activists. But at the same time the Berlin Left was a working-class stronghold. Around Fischer were gathered survivors of the old nucleus of the revolutionary delegates who had not followed Levi and Friesland. There was Anton Grylewitz, Eichhorn's former deputy, Paul Schlecht, a tool-maker, Geschke, a railway worker, König, a metalworker and leaders of the opposition in the metalworkers' union, Kasper, a clerk, Grothe, a leader of the unemployed, Mahlow, a printer, and Max Hesse, a metalworker. These people had been leading organisers of the Berlin working class since at least 1916. The Berlin-Brandenburg district also brought out 'organisers', discreet but efficient apparatus figures, who firmly held the levers of command, such as Hans Pfeiffer or Torgler, men who looked like typical German civil servants. These people were from very diverse origins. Their characteristics differed, as did their later destinies, but they formed a very homogeneous team at this time.

not seem to hurry, but the discontented workers think that your party leaders don't want it to hurry. They make them responsible for the rate of the world revolution, cavil and curse. I understand all that.[85]

However, after a speech by Fischer at a meeting of the German delegates at the Fourth Comintern Congress, Lenin added:

> But what I don't understand is a leadership of the 'left opposition' such as I listened to. . . . No, such opposition, such leadership, does not impress me. But I tell you frankly that I am just as little impressed by your 'centre' which does not understand, which hasn't the energy to have done with such petty demagogues. Surely it is an easy thing to replace such people, to withdraw the revolutionary-minded workers from them and educate them politically. Just because they are revolutionary-minded workers, whilst radicals of the type in question are at bottom the worst sort of opportunists.[86]

However, whilst waiting for the Zentrale to be able to put into operation such a policy, it was necessary to avoid a split which would cost the KPD not only valuable cadres, but part of its shock troops and its youth. This was why Lenin devoted himself to reducing the danger of an explosion. In his letter of 14 August 1921 to the Jena Congress, he gave frank explanations to the German Communists of his own attitude at the Third Comintern Congress, particularly in respect of the Levi affair, which Levi himself had subsequently finally settled. He stressed that the new tactic did not mean an abandonment of the revolutionary struggle for power, but was intended to provide a better preparation for it:

> To win over the majority of the proletariat to our side – such is the 'principal task' . . . and that is possible, even if, formally, the majority of the proletariat follow bourgeois leaders, or leaders who pursue a bourgeois policy . . ., or if the majority of the proletariat are wavering. . . . Let us make more thorough and careful preparations for it; let us not allow a single serious opportunity to slip by when the bourgeoisie compels the proletariat to undertake a struggle; let us learn to determine correctly the moment when the *masses* of the proletariat *cannot but* rise together with us.[87]

---

[85] Zetkin, *Reminiscences of Lenin*, op. cit., p. 38.
[86] Ibid., pp. 38–9.
[87] Lenin, 'A Letter to the German Communists', *Collected Works*, Volume 32, op. cit., p. 522.

However, he insisted on the fact that, in order to be able to harness itself to this task, the KPD must set a limit to its internal conflicts, 'get rid of the quarrelsome elements on both sides', and 'get down to real work'. And on that point, he suggested that Maslow, who was 'playing at leftism' and devoting himself to the sport of 'hunting centrists', be sent with some of his friends to Russia, where they would find 'useful work' and: 'We would make men of them.'[88]

The only effect of this proposal was to provoke the indignation of the Left, who saw it as outside interference and even a threat, all the less tolerable because Maslow was of Russian origin. The Congress was to reject Lenin's suggestion.[89] Throughout the following year, however, the Left would maintain a faction in its strongholds in Berlin-Brandenburg and the Wasserkante, with its own policy, and often respecting discipline only in a very formal way. Fischer replaced Friesland in Brandenburg, and the lead in the Wasserkante was taken by Hugo Urbahns, at whose side the docker Thaelmann was becoming more and more important.[90] In the autumn of 1922, just before the Fourth Comintern Congress, the Berlin-Brandenburg district organised a conference in the Kliems-Festsäle, which formulated its own programme and appointed Fischer to defend it at the Moscow Congress.[91] This programme had the perspective of 'a return to the Second Congress' by way of cancelling the decisions of the Third.[92] The Zentrale easily denounced it as factional activity, and justified its call for sanctions by highlighting such activities as its contacts with the KAPD and the Russian Workers' Opposition.[93]

---

[88] Ibid., p. 519. Fischer (op. cit., pp. 182, 184) states that the German leaders were really at the origin of this proposal, and that they suggested it to Lenin. She wrote in particular (p. 184): '. . . the Spartacist leaders, as soon as they were unable to get their policy accepted by democratic party procedure, opened their drive for reformist communism by seeking Russian state intervention in the life of their party, contrary to the Comintern mores of the time. . . . When Ernst Meyer, Rosa's disciple, asked Lenin to eliminate Maslow from Germany *because of his Russian origin*, he introduced a new element into German communism' [my emphasis]. Even though the fundamental thesis which underlies this interpretation deserves a discussion which we shall develop only in the final part of the book, we must point out that no document confirms Fischer's statement. Moreover, a few months later, the leaders of the Zentrale proposed sending to Moscow Friesland, who, of course, was not of Russian origin.

[89] Fischer, op. cit., p. 182.

[90] See Chapter 32.

[91] Fischer, op. cit., p. 181.

[92] Zetkin, op. cit., p. 37.

[93] Fischer, op. cit., p. 181.

Despite Lenin's lack of sympathy for the leaders of the Left, he firmly opposed any action against them during the preparatory meetings for the Congress. He felt that the KPD could not survive another split.[94] At this point, his authority was sufficient to prevent a split occurring, and to compel the 'right-wing' Zentrale to accept the existence of the 'left' opposition.[95]

[94] Ibid., p. 186; Fischer's view is corroborated by Zetkin, op. cit., pp. 37ff. Amongst the Comintern leaders, Radek was the 'mentor' of the Right, but Zinoviev was to defend positions close to those of the Left on several occasions, at least in the course of 1922.

[95] Following the Jena Congress, the leading group around Meyer was for a short time called the 'conciliators', in so far as it tried to keep the door open for Levi. When the expulsion of the 'Levites' and then of the supporters of Friesland was carried through, these conciliators became in turn the 'Right'.

Chapter Twenty-Nine

A New Start

The KPD proved able to revive from a deep crisis, overcoming its internal differences, closing its ranks and winning back much of the ground it had lost. It was to accomplish this task in accord with the ECCI. Since the Third Comintern Congress, Lenin had managed to persuade the ECCI to accept the policy of 'winning the masses', which it then implemented, despite disagreements on interpretation between Lenin and Trotsky on the one side, and Bukharin and Zinoviev on the other. From December 1921, it was to engage in battle for the united front.

The united front: 'old target, new methods'

The Communists had opened the debate on the workers' united front in the International when the VKPD issued its *Open Letter* in January 1921 to the German labour movement. Lenin had secured the decision to develop it at the Third Comintern Congress, but the March Action had interrupted its implementation, and he needed all his strength to rout the supporters of the theory of the offensive, without, however, having the chance to counterpose to it a fully elaborated policy.

It is curious that the supporters of the theory of the offensive in the KPD had not openly rejected the tactic outlined in the *Open Letter*. In Germany, its only critic was the KAPD. The March Action and the ideas which inspired it stood in direct contradiction to this tactic, as Levi demonstrated so well. In any case, once the international tensions which made Radek believe that a new world war was imminent were relaxed, and once the debris of the March Action was cleared up, he could return to the line which he had inspired, and in the elaboration of which Brandler and Thalheimer had doubtless played no less a role than Levi.

Finally, the objective situation which in December 1920 had influenced the Stuttgart metalworkers to take the road of the *Open Letter*, from that time onwards produced the same results not only in Germany but more widely in Europe. The Communists were soon to see a striking sign of this in the international transport workers' conference held in Amsterdam on 15–16 November 1921. Its international leader, Edo Fimmen, had succeeded in getting the miners' and metalworkers' unions affiliated to the 'Amsterdam' trade-union federation to attend. The agenda of the conference was the struggle against war. At the end of the debates, the conference issued a call for disarmament and for an international struggle against militarism and against the capitalists' attack on workers' living standards, wages and political and organisational gains. A committee was appointed to organise action, anti-militarist propaganda and a concrete struggle against war. The conference adopted the idea, which had been raised before 1914, of an international strike as the answer to a declaration of war by governments, and the unions concerned believed that they could make this a complete defence against war. The Amsterdam conference also issued an appeal to 'mothers and women' to regard themselves as mobilised against war, in order to defend 'their husbands and children'.[1]

The Communist leaders considered that the very fact that such a conference was held was a demonstration of the depth of the workers' anxieties. In the weeks which followed, the ECCI drew the conclusions from the Third Comintern Congress and recent developments, and elaborated a line which was consistent on every point with the *Open Letter*. On 4 December 1921, it approved the report on the workers' united front presented by Zinoviev.[2] In February and March 1922, by a large majority, it confirmed and sharpened the new orientation.[3]

---

[1] *Bulletin communiste*, no. 5, 5 February 1922, pp. 90–1.
[2] Report and theses in *Bulletin communiste*, no. 2, 12 January 1922, pp. 26–33.
[3] Resolutions of the ECCI of 27 February and 4 March, *Bulletin communiste*, no. 18, 29 April 1922, p. 335.

The problem was to draw the necessary conclusions from the defeat of the postwar revolutionary wave. To be sure, that was due to the absence of a revolutionary party analogous to the one in Russia. But throughout those years, the Communist International had reckoned on Social Democracy being on the point of losing its influence, and on the working class having inexhaustible reserves of combativity. In reality, this was not so. Social Democracy had preserved its dominant position, and working people were demoralised. Consequently, the bourgeoisie had recovered the initiative. In order to reverse the relationship of forces, the Communists were obliged patiently to grasp all the means that enabled them to approach the masses, so as to be able to restore their will to struggle, and to raise their consciousness. These means existed, and, in the first place, were manifested in the fact that fresh strata of workers, recently awakened to political life, attributed their defeats solely to the division of the working class. In an article entitled 'Old Target, New Methods', Zinoviev emphasised this feeling: 'Workers feel physically, so to speak, that the strength of the proletariat lies in its mass, in its numbers.'[4] The crisis of the international workers' movement and the effect of what he called 'the burden of lost battles', led him to raise the problem of unity in the light of the fact that 'the tendency towards unity is the natural aspiration of the oppressed class'.[5]

In these conditions, the unity of the workers' organisations was a positive factor. In 1914 it was not so; on the contrary, when confronted by the treachery of the social-chauvinists, a split from them was obligatory. This split opened the way to 'organic differentiation'; the formation of Communist Parties was 'the only way to save the honour of socialism and defend the most elementary interests of the working class'.[6] But the Social Democrats took advantage of the fact that the Communists, as was their duty, had taken the initiative in the split, and portrayed them as 'splitters', and the problem of the split in the movement had to be reconsidered within this perspective.

Zinoviev drew a parallel between the stages in the construction of the Bolshevik Party and the problems which presented themselves to the International:

---

[4] G Zinoviev, 'Ancien but, voies nouvelles', *Bulletin communiste*, no. 6, 7 February 1922, p. 109.
[5] Ibid.
[6] Ibid.

During the fifteen years of our struggle against Menshevism, there were frequent circumstances in which a conflict arose between the Bolsheviks and Mensheviks about the 'unity' slogan, which in many ways recalls the present struggle in the European workers' movement. During the period of about fifteen years which passed between the foundation of Bolshevism and its victory (1903–17), Bolshevism never ceased to wage a systematic struggle against Menshevism. But at the same time, during the same period, we Bolsheviks often made agreements with the Mensheviks. The split between us and them had officially taken place in spring 1905, though it had been a reality since 1903. In January 1912, the official split between Mensheviks and Bolsheviks was confirmed again. But in 1906–7 and again in 1910, this total, official state of separation gave way to unity and semi-unity, not only in response to the vagaries of the struggle, but also under the pressure of great masses of workers . . . who were awakening to political activity, and insisted that we must renew our efforts to come together, in the belief that, if they could get the Bolsheviks and the Mensheviks united in one party, they would increase their ability to resist the great landed proprietors and the capitalists.[7]

The President of the International halted his parallel there. The possible organic reunion of the parties of the Second International and the Third International was excluded, because 'the War drew a line of demarcation between the old and the new periods of development of the workers' movement'. But the Communists must not only 'protect their organisations' and maintain the independence of the Communist Parties, but also 'genuinely march with the non-Communist masses', in order to win them to Communism. The new strata of the working class had to be convinced, from their own experience, of the reality behind the phrases of their reformist leaders. They would do so only if the Communists succeeded in organising a united struggle by all the workers.[8]

This was the political perspective contained in the appeal of the Communist International to the working people of the world that was issued on 1 January 1922.[9] It restated the principles of the International, that there was no way out for humanity other than through the proletarian revolution and the dictatorship of the proletariat, and it insisted on preserving of the organisational

---

[7] Ibid.
[8] Ibid., p. 112.
[9] *Bulletin communiste*, no. 3, 19 January 1922, pp. 46–8.

independence and the total freedom of criticism of the Communist Parties. But it declared: 'The Communist International and the Communist Parties wish patiently and fraternally to march on equal terms with all the other proletarians, even those who take their stand on the ground of capitalist democracy.'[10]

Radek had been one of the pioneers of the united front, and he was to become one of its most active propagandists, as much towards the German working class as towards the parties of the International. The line which the ECCI had just adopted in full clarity was for him the worthy result of assimilation by the workers' vanguard, the Communists, of the lessons of the revolutionary struggles of the preceding ten years. The bourgeoisie had experienced an unprecedented crisis, and its leading strata, unable immediately to adapt themselves to new and strange conditions, were disorganised and disoriented. However, their domination had been preserved, principally because of the help rendered by the Social-Democratic and trade-union leaderships, who were responsible for the fact that the working class lacked the clarity of view, consciousness and leadership which in Russia had made the Bolsheviks' victory a possibility. This was why the Communist International had the duty to organise a split in the Social-Democratic Parties and to bring the revolutionary minorities out of their ranks. The working-class movement drew its power from its very mass and from its role in the process of production. But an unorganised mass can only be transformed into an organised movement through the education of cadres – which was impossible in this period without the existence of genuine Communist Parties and a revolutionary International.

The fundamental question that was posed by the defeat of the first postwar revolutionary wave was the elaboration of a strategy that could enable the working class, especially in the advanced countries, to resist the international capitalist offensive against its living standards and its organisational and political gains, and from there to find a way out of the economic crisis. This is what lay behind the Comintern's change in tactics:

> The working class is divided today by profound differences on the questions
> of democracy or dictatorship, and on the means by which it can realise its
> final aims. But, it is united on the question of whether it must give up its
> piece of bread or a decent roof over its head.

---

[10] Ibid., p. 48.

On this question, a united front of the working class can be constructed little by little. The same proletarians who calmly and as spectators watched how capitalism rebuilt its régime, those who hoped that the strengthening of capitalism would lead to their situation being improved, are now seeing the rising wave of poverty, and they want to resist it. They still hope to be able to wage this defensive battle exclusively within the framework of capitalism. They still hope to be able to escape the necessity of waging this battle in a revolutionary way. But they want to defend their children's drop of milk. They want to defend the eight-hour day. They do not want their blood to be the miracle remedy which rejuvenates capitalism. It is through the economic struggles which come and go in the capitalist world that the united front of the proletariat will be slowly constructed. The Communist International, the party which represents the interests of the proletariat, cannot be indifferent to this.[11]

Radek did his utmost to show to the delegates to the Moscow Conference of the Russian Communist Party in March 1922 how the Communist Parties can and must work 'to win the masses' through the policy of the united front:

The Communist International is the vanguard of the masses. It fights for its programme and its ideal as a minority in the proletariat. But it can only realise its ideal if it wins the majority of the proletariat, and it cannot win this majority by mere propaganda for its ideas. Only if it knows how to become the leadership of the working class in its daily struggles can it win the working class to its ideas.[12]

He emphasised that there was no question here of a retreat or a lowering of the level of revolutionary struggle:

The participation of Communists in the struggle of the working class against poverty does not mean descending from the heights of revolutionary struggle towards the depths of opportunism; rather, it means that they want to guide the ascent of the proletariat towards the heights of the revolutionary struggle.[13]

In the countries of Western Europe, where the masses were organised in powerful reformist trade unions and an important section of them were

---

[11] K. Radek, *Genua, die Einheitsfront des Proletariats und die KI*, Hamburg, 1922, speech to the Moscow conference of the RCP(B) on 9 March 1922, pp. 69–70.
[12] Ibid., p. 70.
[13] Ibid.

members or supporters of Social-Democratic Parties, the first question to be posed was how Communists could win over the masses whilst opposing the leaders whom their target audience still followed. Radek gave a precise reply:

> In the long run, the revolutionary orientation will be victorious in the working class, even if the Social-Democratic organisations and the workers' bureaucracy oppose it. Yes, victory over Social-Democratic ideology is a necessary preliminary to the international victory of the proletariat. But that by no means indicates the road by which to win this victory.[14]

The real question facing Communists was this:

> How do we most easily reach the large numbers of non-Communist workers? Shall we succeed more easily by contenting ourselves with denouncing the Social-Democratic leaders in propaganda, whilst avoiding any contact with them? It is clear that this is the worst possible road. It means giving up the attempt to mobilise the masses for struggle. It means that we can act only with the support of those strata in the working class which are already Communist. It means that we call upon the masses to fight, but that, if at first they do not fight as consistently as we wish, we have to place ourselves on the outside whilst we criticise them. In that case, the working class will see us as those who divide its struggle, people who stand aside, tangled up in theories, unable to understand the need to gather together all the forces against the capitalist offensive. It will be quite different if we approach the workers as they are, with all their illusions, all their hesitations, and all their allegiances to the old leaders and old ideas, when we try to convince them while they are in the ranks of the old organisations.[15]

This was why the International was obliged to pursue the policy which had been previously undertaken in relation to the trade unions, and to reject any policy of splitting them, a policy as dangerous as that which sought to reconcile Social Democracy and Communism, and to overcome the effects of the split between the parties by means of unity agreements. The policy of the united front, through winning more and more important sections of the trade-union movement to this idea, would drive the Social-Democratic leaders into a corner and force them to use deceit in order to avoid openly opposing the

---

[14] Ibid., p. 71.
[15] Ibid., pp. 71–2.

aspirations of their members without engaging in a struggle in which they had everything to lose:

> Through experiencing the oscillations of the Social-Democratic Parties and their leaders, their working-class supporters will understand their policies more clearly, and will be increasingly forced to realise that Communism alone can be the torch of their struggle. To go to the leaders of the Social-Democratic parties with proposals for a joint struggle for the common interests of the working class does not in any way mean a retreat. Quite the contrary: it is to prepare the road to winning the majority of the working class to Communism, to make possible the advance of the Communist movement.[16]

Radek replied to the Social Democrats who accused the Communists of having adopted the united-front slogan as a simple tactical manoeuvre, declaring that, if they were sincere, all they had to do to defeat this tactic was to take the Communists at their word, by joining the struggle. The forthcoming conference in Berlin of the three Internationals was to give everyone the opportunity for a public presentation of their views.

The Conference of the Three Internationals

The Communists regarded high-level discussions amongst the leaders of the parties and trade unions as a vital part of the struggle for the united front. They accepted that what was necessary at the level of the parties was no less urgent at the level of the international general staffs. In the autumn of 1921, the question had been raised at the conference of the Labour Party in Britain and at the congress of the French Socialist Party, the SFIO, as well as by the organisations belonging to the Vienna Union of Socialist Parties, the so-called Two-and-a-Half International. On 12 December 1921, Radek, on behalf of the Communist International, wrote a letter in this sense to Friedrich Adler in Vienna.[17] In a resolution of 21 December 1921, the VKPD Zentrale in turn had informed the ECCI the that it would like its to hold a public session in Berlin, Vienna or some other great city in the West, where the agenda would include the question of common action with the other Internationals. It asked at the

---

[16] Ibid., p. 76.

[17] *Arbeiterzeitung* (Vienna), 1 February 1922, cited in A Reisberg, 'Lenin, die KPD und die Konferenz der drei Internationalen', *Beiträge zur Geschichte der deutschen Arbeiterbewegung*, no. 2, 1963, p. 251.

same time that the ECCI should immediately send proposals for joint action to the other Internationals.[18] In reply, the ECCI declared in favour of organising a world-wide workers' conference during the Genoa Conference, as the workers' reply to the attempts of the world's capitalists to reconstruct their system.[19]

The Second International did not reject the Communists' proposal, but pointed to the need, which it regarded as more urgent, for a conference of the socialist and Communist Parties of the West on the single question of reparations. The Vienna Bureau, for its part, came out for holding both conferences. In an appeal published on 15 January 1922,[20] in which it drew attention to the deterioration in workers' living standards, the rise in unemployment, the employers' counter-offensive, and the popular calls for working-class unity, it proposed to the leaders of the two main Internationals that a conference be held, with the agenda to cover the economic situation and the workers' struggles. The other two Internationals accepted this proposal, but the Amsterdam trade-union federation rejected it, refusing to sit at the same table as representatives of the RILU. The VKPD placed the international conference at the centre of its campaign for the united front.[21]

The work of the Conference of the Three Internationals began in Berlin on the morning of 2 April.[22] Some of the delegates, who had been once in the same parties and the same International, were meeting together for the first time since 1914. They sat around a T-shaped table, the transversal base of which was occupied by the delegation from the Vienna International, around the Austrian Friedrich Adler, flanked by Crispien, Bracke-Desrousseaux from France, and three representatives of the Russian Mensheviks, Yuli Martov, Fedor Dan and Rafail Abramovich. The representatives of the Second and Third Internationals faced each other, on either side of the central table.[23] On one side sat Vandervelde, the Belgian Socialist and former minister of the Belgian King, Tsereteli, former member of Kerensky's Provisional Government,

---

[18] *Die Rote Fahne*, 23 December 1921.
[19] Minutes of meeting of Zentrale of 16 January 1922, cited in Reisberg, op. cit., p. 251.
[20] *Freiheit*, 17 January 1922.
[21] Minutes of meeting of Political Bureau of 24 March 1922, cited in Reisberg, op. cit., p. 256.
[22] *Protokoll der Internationalen Konferenz des Drein Internationale Exekutiv-Komitees*, Vienna, 1922.
[23] Rosmer, op. cit., p. 179.

representing the Georgian Mensheviks, James Ramsay MacDonald, from the Labour Party, and Otto Wels, for the Majority Social Democrats in Germany. On the other side, flanking the white-haired Zetkin, sat Bukharin, Radek, the Yugoslav Vuyović, representing the Young Communist International, the Frenchman Rosmer representing the RILU in the delegation. Serrati represented his own party, the only non-member of an International to be invited, with a consultative vote.[24]

Had these people come to reach decisions together, and to commit themselves to joint undertakings? Their presence around the same table could be seen to offer a real promise to those who shared this great hope of working-class unity. After the opening speech by Adler, Zetkin opened fire in a preliminary declaration on behalf of the Communist International.[25] There should be no ambiguity in the Conference. No one was thinking of reconstructing an organic unity, which would be devoid of meaning. The Communists considered that those who had collaborated with the bourgeoisie were alone to blame for the split in the workers' movement. There would be no organic unity until the working class as a whole was engaged in the struggle to seize power. Nonetheless, the Communist International came to this conference because it hoped that the Conference would be able to help to coordinate workers' future struggles. That was why the circle of participation should be widened, to include not only the trade unions' international bodies, but also trade unions with no international affiliations, and, in general, those under anarchist leadership. At the moment when the capitalists were to meet at Genoa to settle the problems of humanity in their own way, the immediate aim of this conference should be to meet at the same time in order that the voice of the working people be heard, and in their name call the capitalists to account. Zetkin demanded that there should be added the agenda the subjects of preparations to struggle against war, organisation of relief for starving Soviet Russia, struggle against the Versailles Treaty, and reconstruction of regions devastated by the War.

Vandervelde – the Honourable Minister, as a disgusted Communist observer wrote[26] – undertook the role of prosecutor.[27] For his International, 'the question

---

[24] *Protokoll der Internationalen Konferenz des Drein Internationale Exekutiv-Komitees*, p. 7.
[25] Ibid., pp. 19–27.
[26] R. Albert, 'Impressions de séance', *Bulletin communiste*, no. 18, 29 April 1922, p. 342.
[27] *Protokoll der Internationalen Konferenz des Drein Internationale Exekutiv-Komitees*, pp. 28–42.

is to discover whether the proposed conference can be useful'.[28] The Socialists raised the question of confidence; they knew that the Communists were past-masters of the art of manoeuvre, and they refused to support any such operations. Before they could think of undertaking joint activity, they wanted to have guarantees that the Communists had come to the Conference willing to give up a certain number of practices which were not compatible with their new-found desire for unity. The Communist International must terminate its attacks on Social-Democratic leaders, its attempts to win over their supporters, and its factional practices, especially in the trade unions. It must likewise give a guarantee of the liberties that the ruling Communist Party in Russia should restore to the socialist parties which it had banned and persecuted, and publicly announce that it favoured the liberation of imprisoned Social Democrats and Socialist Revolutionaries in Russia, beginning with the Socialist Revolutionary leaders whose trial had just been announced. If these conditions were met, the leaders of the Second International would take note of the willingness of the Communists to restore confidence in themselves, and would agree unreservedly to discuss with them. But they refused to place on the agenda the revision of the Versailles Treaty, because they thought that this would be useful to the extreme right-wing elements in Germany who denounced it as an alien imposition.

Radek – whom the observer described as having 'a bony, hard profile, a harsh face, grey colour, vehement gestures and withering speech'[29] – replied by recalling what 'in his opinion' should have prevented Vandervelde from uttering the word 'confidence' – to begin with, his own speeches before and after August 1914, not forgetting the murder of Rosa Luxemburg and Karl Liebknecht under a socialist government, nor the execution of the twenty-six commissars of the Caucasian people in which the Labour Party was an accomplice. He added that the Communists did not come as accusers, but as activists who wanted to promote united action:

> We sit down at the same table with you, we want to fight at your side, and this struggle will decide whether it is a manoeuvre 'as you say' for the benefit of the Communist International, or a movement which will unify the working class. What you do will decide the significance of our action. If you fight in association with us, in association with the proletariat in

---

[28] Ibid., p. 34.
[29] Albert, op. cit., p. 343.

every country, if you fight, not for the 'dictatorship', because we do not believe that of you, but for a piece of bread and against the ever greater ruination of the world – then the proletariat will come together in this struggle, and we shall judge you, in the light not of a terrible past, but of the new facts. As long as these do not exist, we come to these negotiations with cold hearts, and we enter into joint activity profoundly mistrustful and sure that you will be found woefully lacking in this struggle.[30]

Radek saw the conditions which Vandervelde advanced as tantamount to starting a polemic and sabotaging joint activity: He added: 'No one will be able to predict the results should we draw nearer to each other in a common struggle. They will arise in the common struggle itself: that is why we call for the common struggle.'[31] Nonetheless, the Communist delegates were to make important concessions during the debates and discussions which followed. Thus, on the insistence of Radek and despite the reservations of Bukharin and Rosmer,[32] they proposed sending an international commission of enquiry to Georgia, and, above all, gave an the assurance that there would be no death sentences in the trial of the leading Socialist Revolutionaries, and that they could be defended by lawyers of their choice under the supervision of delegates from the other Internationals. In return, the Social-Democratic partners agreed to the formation of a permanent committee of nine members, the 'Committee of Nine',[33] to organise further conferences. They agreed on the principle of a general conference, which would not coincide with the Genoa Conference, and with organising during the general conference if possible, and in any case for May 1st 'powerful mass demonstrations with the greatest possible unity', for the eight-hour day, against unemployment, for unity of action, for the defence of the Russian Revolution and of 'starving Russia', 'for the formation of the united front of the proletariat in each country and in the International'.[34]

The Communist International and the Russian Communist Party were to keep the promises which their delegation had made on their behalf in Berlin.

---

[30] *Protokoll der Internationalen Konferenz des Drein Internationale Exekutiv-Komitees*, pp. 50–1.

[31] Ibid., p. 59.

[32] Rosmer, op. cit., p. 181.

[33] The nine appointed by the respective Executives after the Conference were Fritz Adler, Bracke, Crispien, Vandervelde, Wels, MacDonald, Zetkin, Radek and Frossard.

[34] *Protokoll der Internationalen Konferenz des Drein Internationale Exekutiv-Komitees*, pp. 143–6.

However, Lenin thought them excessive. In an article dictated on 3 April, entitled 'We Have Paid Too Much', he protested against the fact that Bukharin, Radek et al. had agreed to annul the death sentence for people found guilty of terrorism, without any equivalent concession, or one even approaching it, from the other side.[35] Nevertheless, Vandervelde and Theodore Liebknecht were to come to Moscow to defend the Socialist Revolutionaries, a defence which they abandoned almost at once.

The 'Committee of Nine' had only an ephemeral existence. The Social-Democratic Parties of the Second International refused to take a road which would have led them to break with the bourgeois parties. The ECCI, on its side, ratified the Berlin agreements, and mandated its delegates to suggest that a joint conference of the two trade-union Internationals be organised.[36] The VKPD launched a campaign of agitation to prepare, in line with the Berlin resolutions, for an international workers' congress and for joint meetings of members of the three parties to be held on 20 April. The SPD refused to participate in it. However, on 20 April, the joint demonstration organised by the Communists and the Independents brought together 150,000 people in Berlin.[37] In some cities, such as Düsseldorf, the local leaders of the SPD broke the ban, and demonstrated with the Communists and the Independents.[38]

The same day, in an 'appeal to the conscious working people of the whole world', the ECCI called for a struggle against the 'sabotage of the united front', and for committees to be set up to organise the international workers' congress.[39] At the same time, the ECCI publicly addressed the parties of the Second International, calling on them to denounce jointly the repressive measures taken by the German government against some of the Communist delegates to the Berlin Conference. Radek was expelled, and Felix Wolf, the secretary of the delegation, was arrested.[40] When the 'Committee of Nine' met in Düsseldorf on 29 May, the Social Democrats had already decided to refuse to endorse any new initiatives. The three Communists then presented to their partners what was a veritable ultimatum: either call an international

---

[35] V.I. Lenin, 'We Have Paid Too Much', *Collected Works*, Volume 33, op. cit., pp. 330–4.

[36] *Bericht über die Tätigkeit des Präsidiums und der Exekutive der KI für die Zeit vom 6 März bis 11 Juni 1922*, Hamburg, 1922, pp. 22–3.

[37] *Die Rote Fahne*, 21 April 1922.

[38] *Inprekorr*, no. 52, 22 April 1922, p. 418.

[39] *Bericht über die Tätigkeit*, op. cit., pp. 26ff.

[40] Letter from Clara Zetkin to Fritz Adler, 8 May 1922, *Correspondance internationale*, no. 36, 10 May 1922, p. 274.

conference or wind up the 'Committee of Nine'.[41] Faced with the social democrats' sustained refusal, they withdrew. The 'Committee of Nine' was at an end.

In spite of everything, the Conference of the three Internationals had helped the Vienna and Second Internationals to draw closer. They were to fuse in 1923 after the USPD had been reintegrated in the autumn of 1922 into the Unified Social-Democratic Party, as it became known for a time. In Germany, the conference contributed substantially and immediately to familiarising working people with the practice of the united front and the encouraging of joint activities at a rank-and-file level between Communists, Independents and Majority Social Democrats. The reunification of the Social Democrats was followed by the rebirth within the SPD of a left-wing tendency which generally favoured united action with the Communists.[42]

---

[41] Reisberg, op. cit., p. 263.

[42] Amongst the Independents who returned to Social Democracy in this period were a large number of former leading Communists, including Paul Lange, Paul Levi and his closest comrades-in-arms, Kurt Geyer, Düwell, Otto Brass, Malzahn, Neumann, etc. Levi had tried to counterpose to the perspective of Social-Democratic reunification that of a union of 'social revolutionaries', in which he hoped to include the non-leftist faction of the VKPD with all the Independents. But he was isolated on the Communist side, and he had neither the strength – nor, doubtless, the will – to maintain an 'independent nucleus' in these conditions. Georg Ledebour did that, with very questionable success. Nonetheless, Levi, who from now on obstinately opposed a 'split' and took care above all 'not to cut himself off from the masses', was to achieve the remarkable feat of being the intellectual inspiration of a 'new Left' in the SPD.

Chapter Thirty
The Rapallo Turn

A few days after the Conference of the Three Internationals, during the very course of the Genoa Conference, the prospect of which had figured so largely in its debates, a crucially important diplomatic event occurred. This was the signature of the Rapallo Treaty between Germany and Soviet Russia, the first realignment of forces since the World War, and, to a certain degree, a factor in producing new political relations in Germany itself.

The course which the dominant faction of the German bourgeoisie adopted at this juncture was to seek support, in the face of the Entente, and for limited purposes, through an alignment with Soviet Russia. The problem was not new. Since the end of the war, the supporters of the 'Western' and 'Eastern' orientations – that is, whether to orient Germany towards the Entente or Soviet Russia – had competed within the higher echelons of the civil service and the military. The policy of the Entente made the decision easier. The choice of diplomatic expediency coincided in a certain way with the policy of the KPD, with its campaign for links with Soviet Russia, which itself was an integral part of the defence of the Russian Revolution and of the struggle against Versailles. But the KPD was also categorically opposed to the 'Western' policy of Social Democracy, with its perspectives of collective security and maintaining peace through the League of Nations. The 'Rapallo policy' thus appeared as a supplementary factor of division – a highly impassioned one – between the workers' parties, and yet another obstacle to the KPD's policy of the united front.

The problem was complicated further by the role of Radek. He was at one and the same time a Soviet diplomat and the official spokesman of the Moscow government, and the 'mentor', on behalf of the ECCI, of the KPD. The same man who negotiated in Berlin, Genoa and Rapallo with Malzan, the head of the Eastern European department, and with Rathenau himself, intervened from Moscow to advise and guide the German Communists, and even to inspire its most important political decisions. Whether or not he confused the two roles intentionally or by accident is a completely secondary issue. More important is that his dual role influenced the interpretation of events, both by his contemporaries and by historians.

The German-Russian question

During the first years following the Russian Revolution, the problem of relations between Germany and Soviet Russia was not posed independently of the world revolution, which the Bolshevik leaders believed to be imminent. Lenin hardly conceived the mission of Joffe to be anything but a mission to provide revolutionary aid to the German revolutionaries, in the same way as Trotsky initially conceived his role as head of Soviet diplomacy as that of an agitator.

The 'ultras' of the Free Corps, those who fought in arms against the Soviet power in the Baltic states, reasoned essentially along the same lines. Revolutionary Russia was externally the number one enemy, just like Spartacism internally. This viewpoint was shared by the Entente – and was of direct advantage to the militarist elements in Germany. At this time, the *Times* wrote:

> The Allies at the time of the Armistice endeavoured to make use of this [German] army of occupation as a protection for Western Europe against the Bolshevists, and did not stipulate for an immediate evacuation, as there were then no local forces considered capable of making head against Bolshevik aggression.[1]

---

[1] 'German Baltic Schemes', *The Times*, 27 October 1919.

However, the defeat of the first wave of the German Revolution and the enforced conclusion of the Versailles Peace Treaty very quickly posed the problem in different terms.

An important pointer to this is provided by the quality and number of the visitors whom Radek received when he was in prison. His cell became a 'diplomatic salon'. There were military men such as General Reibnitz, Admiral Hintze and Colonel Max Bauer. There were industrialists such as Walter Rathenau and Felix Deutsch, and intellectuals such as Maximilian Harden and Otto Hoetzsch.[2] All of them, in one way or another, were fascinated by the man, but even more by the strength of the country he represented. This strength, to be sure, was political and military, but it also lay in its space, its markets and sources of raw materials, and in its potential as a field for investment, and even as an arsenal or training ground which would enable them to avoid the disarmament clauses in the Versailles Treaty. What attracted them was the fact that the interests of the two countries were complementary in the sense that they both opposed the 'dictated' Treaty.

No one who, like Radek, believed that the world revolution would be a long, complicated process, could neglect these perspectives. In these conditions, the isolation of Russia was a fact as important as its survival. Without jeopardising the world revolution, the Soviet state had the right and even the duty to utilise inter-imperialist contradictions to its advantage. Once the apocalypse of the immediate postwar period had ended and the revolution had been deferred, the diplomatic game recovered its appeal. Radek was quickly convinced of this, and wrote to the German Communists while still in prison:

> The problem of the foreign policy of Soviet Russia and, as long as the world revolution maintains its tardy pace, that of the other countries in which the working class may become victorious, lies in reaching a *modus vivendi* with the capitalist states. . . . The possibility of peace between capitalist states and proletarian states is not a utopia.[3]

A month later, during his period of release on probation, he wrote:

> Germany has suffered a defeat, but, despite that, its technical equipment and technical possibilities remain immense. . . . In Germany, because its

---

[2] Radek, *November*, op. cit., pp. 158–62.
[3] Radek, *Zur Taktik des Kommunismus: Ein Schreiben an den Oktoberparteitag der KPD*, op. cit., pp. 9–12.

foreign relations have been destroyed and its economy has collapsed, there are thousands of engineers who are unemployed and starving. They could be of the greatest service to Russia in rebuilding her national economy.[4]

This point of view coincided with the outlook of one of the men whose role in this matter was to be decisive – General von Seeckt. In January 1920, he wrote: 'To the extent that I regard the lasting aim of our policy to be future economic and political agreement with Great Russia, we must at least try not to arouse Russia against us.'[5]

The possibility of agreement between Germany and Soviet Russia was limited at this juncture. In the spring of 1920, Lenin wrote this clear condemnation of a policy which aimed at setting up preferential relations between Germany and Russia:

> The overthrow of the bourgeoisie in any of the large European countries, including Germany, would be such a gain for the international revolution that, for its sake, one can, and if necessary should, tolerate a *more prolonged existence of the Treaty of Versailles*. If Russia, standing alone, could endure the Treaty of Brest-Litovsk for several months, to the advantage of the revolution, there is nothing impossible in a Soviet Germany, allied to Soviet Russia, enduring the existence of the Treaty of Versailles for a longer period, to the advantage of the revolution.[6]

The turn of 1920–1

E.H. Carr has pointed out that it was in December 1920 that Lenin first discussed Germany in terms other than those of the world revolution. Indeed, at the Eighth Congress of Soviets, Lenin stressed that the survival of Soviet Russia was primarily dependent upon the disagreements amongst the imperialists:

> On the one hand, our existence depends on the presence of radical differences between the imperialist powers, and, on the other, on the Entente's victory and the Peace of Versailles having thrown the vast majority of the German nation into a situation it is impossible for them to live in. . . . [H]er only

---

[4] A Struthahn (K. Radek), *Die Auswärtige Politik Sowjet-Russlands*, Berlin, 1919, pp. 37–9, 44.

[5] F. von Rabenau, *Seeckt-Aus seinem Leben*, Leipzig, 1938–40, p. 252.

[6] Lenin, '"Left-Wing" Communism', *Collected Works*, Volume 31, op. cit., p. 77.

means of salvation lies in an alliance with Soviet Russia, a country towards which her eyes are therefore turning. . . . The German bourgeois government has an implacable hatred of the Bolsheviks, but such is its international position that, against its own desires, the government is driven towards peace with Soviet Russia.[7]

The German Minister for Foreign Affairs, Dr Simons, replied in January 1921: 'Communism as such is no reason why a German bourgeois, republican government cannot do business with the Soviet government.'[8]

In May 1921, a Soviet-German trade treaty was signed. Several mixed companies with German engineers and capital were to be set up, within the framework of the NEP and the policy of concessions. The German government was to send substantial help in the struggle against famine in the summer of 1921. Finally, secret negotiations started in respect of arms factories to be located on Russian territory, to evade the strictures of the Versailles Treaty.[9]

This development culminated in the 'flight' of the German and Russian delegates from the Genoa Conference on 16 April 1922. They met at Rapallo, and signed the treaty which put an end to the Entente hopes of a 'consortium' for jointly exploiting the concessions which the Russians offered. The Treaty wiped out the debts of both partners, the 'reparations' owed by the German government, and the 'compensation' owed by the Russian government for nationalised German property. It re-established consular and diplomatic relations, made Germany the 'most favoured nation' in Russian external trade (with the exception of the dependencies of the former Russian Empire). Finally, it looked forward to the two governments cooperating 'in a spirit of mutual goodwill in meeting the economic needs of both countries'.[10]

The Party and the International: reactions to Rapallo

The establishment of preferential links with Soviet Russia had been one of the favourite themes of Communist spokesmen, both in popular meetings and in the Reichstag, during the preceding years. Nonetheless, the conclusion of the Treaty came as a surprise to them. They do not appear to have expected

---

[7] V.I. Lenin, 'Report on Concessions Delivered to the RCP(B) Group at the Eighth Congress of Soviets', *Collected Works*, Volume 31, op. cit., pp. 475–6.

[8] *Stenographische Berichte des Reichstages Verhandlungen*, Volume 346, p. 1994.

[9] Lionel Kochan, *Russia and The Weimar Republic*, Cambridge, 1950, pp. 41–5.

[10] Ibid., pp. 52–3.

that the German bourgeois government would go so far as to sign such an agreement with the Russian government. The Social Democrats, for their part, hastened to stress the dangers of such an alliance. Crispien, speaking for the Independents, was to indict this agreement between the Bolsheviks and the 'government of heavy industry and finance capital', and to denounce the 'pro-capitalist' policy of the Russian government.[11]

The editors of *Die Rote Fahne* betrayed a certain embarrassment. Their first commentary devoted to the treaty stressed the fact that it represented a defeat for the Entente.[12] On the following day, Pieck declared at a demonstration in the Lustgarten that the German bourgeoisie had signed, 'not out of friendship, but under the pressure of cruel necessity, that is, under the blows of the Entente'.[13] For several weeks, nothing was said on the Treaty, until the debate in the Reichstag, during which Paul Frölich, the Communist spokesman, played down the content of the Treaty, and stressed that the Social Democrats and the Independents were really to blame for a situation which obliged the Russian revolutionaries to conclude treaties with a bourgeois state.[14]

The position of the Russian leaders was clearer. In an interview with an American journalist, Trotsky replied that there could be no question of regarding the Rapallo Treaty as an alliance against the other European states:

> Germany is separated from the Soviet Republic by the same fundamental contradictions in the systems of property as the countries of the Entente. This means that no one can speak of the Rapallo Treaty as any kind of offensive-defensive alliance to act as a counterweight to the pressure of other states. It is a matter of restoring the most elementary interstate and economic relations. Russia is ready today to sign a treaty based on the principles of Rapallo with any other country.[15]

On the following day, 19 May, the ECCI, which hailed the Treaty as having 'enormous historical importance', recalled that 'the bourgeois-Menshevik German government is a temporary thing', whilst 'the working class remains'. The fate of humanity was not to be decided by such treaties:

> In this sense the fate of humanity in the next few years will be determined by the successes of the German working class. The victory of the German

---

[11] *Stenographische Berichte des Reichstages Verhandlungen*, Volume 355, pp. 7716–17.
[12] *Die Rote Fahne*, 18 April 1922.
[13] *Die Rote Fahne*, 21 April 1922.
[14] *Stenographische Berichte des Reichstages Verhandlungen*, Volume 355, pp. 7738–40.
[15] *Izvestia*, 18 May 1922.

proletariat over 'its' bourgeoisie will involve unprecedented changes in the social structure of the whole of Europe. When the German proletariat destroys in its country the influence of the Second International and Two-and-a-Half International, a new chapter will open in the history of mankind.[16]

Rapallo: an obstacle to the Revolution?

Those, like the historian Lionel Kochan,[17] who think that Rapallo was a definite obstacle on the road of the German Revolution because of its implications for the Communist leaders, are arguing from a weak position. Angress stresses the fact that Radek, allegedly speaking at the Fourth Comintern Congress, 'not only foreshadowed his National-Bolshevist policy of a year later', but went on to suggest an interpretation of Rapallo as an alliance between Soviet Russia and Germany, both of whom wanted to 'revise' the Versailles Treaty and to oppose the Entente.[18] Even leaving aside the fact that Radek did not speak in this sense at that Congress,[19] the statements by him which are quoted, to the effect that Russia could only hold out as long as it had with 'the existence of Germany a counter-balance against the supremacy of the Allies',[20] are far from carrying conviction.

In reality, these historians rely upon Ruth Fischer's claim that the Rapallo policy implied a 'retreat' in Germany and thus a major turn in the policies of the Communist International, in which the theory advanced by the Hungarian economist Varga, that Germany was in the process of becoming 'an industrial colony' of the Entente through the system of reparations which Versailles imposed, is said to have played a central role. She neglects the reality of the economic and social facts, the double burden which weighed upon the German working class, to cope with both capitalist accumulation in Germany, and the payment of reparations:

> In the main, the theory of Germany's transformation into an industrial colony of the West was fabricated to implement the Treaty of Rapallo. In 1922–23, Varga, Bukharin and Radek were discovering a new role for the

---

[16] Degras, Volume 1, op. cit., p. 347.
[17] Who uses 'Rapallo versus Revolution?' as a chapter title in his *Russia and the Weimar Republic*.
[18] Angress, op. cit., pp. 238–9.
[19] Angress himself notes this, ibid., p. 239, n. 36.
[20] Quoted in Kochan, op. cit., pp. 55–6; Angress, op. cit., p. 239.

> German bourgeoisie, which they changed from the class enemy to a victim
> suffering almost as much as the German workers.[21]

The reality is that, since the Third Comintern Congress, the KPD had devoted
all its efforts, with the backing of the ECCI, to promoting the policy of the
united front, which precisely at this date was taking the form of a struggle
by the working people against poverty and reaction. Absolutely nothing –
apart from the dual role which Radek played – permits the declaration that
the united-front policy was dictated by the 'power' preoccupations of the
Russian government, or that the implications of Varga's analysis of Germany
constituted 'a fundamental revision of Lenin's analysis of the balance of class
forces in Germany'.[22]

---

[21] Fischer, op. cit., p. 199.
[22] Ibid., pp. 199–200.

Chapter Thirty-One

For the United Front Against Poverty and Reaction

During the discussions among the Internationals, the
SPD presented itself as the most obstinate in refusing
joint activity, and the KPD as the most determined
in seeking agreements. The Social-Democratic leaders
had decided to maintain with the bourgeois parties
of the Centre a coalition which they regarded
as a necessary bulwark against 'subversion' and
'adventure'. The Communist leaders took into account
that nothing but methodical campaigning for joint
actions, developing the policy of the *Open Letter* of
7 January 1921 could, in the first stage, break their
isolation and contribute to the rebirth of a left wing
in Social Democracy, which was essential for the
construction of the workers' united front.

The resolute orientation of Communist activists
towards work in the reformist trade unions began
to bear fruit with the revival of economic strikes.
Above all, 1922 was dominated by the rebirth
of a movement of factory councils, in which
the Communists exerted a real and sometimes
predominant influence.

The development of the organs of the united front

The factory councils first appeared in the
November Revolution and its aftermath. They
already played an important role in the first phase

of the revolutionary movement in 1918–19, especially in the Ruhr and Central Germany, where theirs had been the leading part in the great strikes in March 1919.

The reflux of the 'soviet' movement of workers' councils after the repression and the elections to the Constituent Assembly in early 1919, and the emergence of workers' economic demands, had made the workers' councils the arena for a struggle between the right and left wings in the labour movement. Article 65 of the Weimar Constitution, the law of 2 February 1920, had represented a wide-ranging attempt to integrate the working class into the structures of capitalism by transforming their organisations into appendages of the employers' authority through the *Mitbestimmingsrecht*, the right to participation and to consultation. The workers' organisations had rights in questions of administration and general policy of the firm's working conditions, hiring and firing,[1] and, in addition, they formed the electoral basis for the 'workers' section' of the membership of the Economic Council of the Reich. In practice, during the first years of their legal existence, they were little more than a duplication of the official trade-union structures, although they were confirmed by election.

Nonetheless, the fact that they were elected by all the working people in the firm, the 'industrial' character of their organisational form – in contrast to the trade-union organisation on the basis of 'trades' – meant that revolutionaries could make use of them. It was on this basis that Däumig developed his theory of the 'conciliar system', conceived as a kind of second economic power, erected in every enterprise, in opposition to the employers' authority, and rising to the summit of state power, by means of a pyramid of councils acting at every level.[2] On the purely political level, left Independents and Communists had attached a great deal of importance to the fact that people elected to factory councils had to be wage-earning workers in the enterprise concerned. This automatically ruled out the union full-timers, and rendered the members of the councils representatives who were very sensitive to pressure from the rank and file.

The German Communists, in line with the strategy of the International and with the resolution on factory councils carried during the Second Comintern

---

[1] Goetz-Girey, *Les Syndicats allemands après la guerre*, pp. 107–19.
[2] E. Däumig, *Das Rätesystem*, Berlin, 1919. This was a speech to the USPD Congress in March 1919.

Congress, placed the struggle for and around the factory committees at the centre of the strategic considerations in their factory work.[3] During the Party Congress in November 1920, just before the fusion with the Independents, the delegates had heard and discussed an important report by Brandler on this question. He said that the factory councils must be the workers' instrument to control production, stocktaking, accounting and records, which would help the workers to learn that the rule of the bourgeoisie had to be overthrown, and at the same time prepare them for their tasks under the dictatorship of the proletariat. For this reason, it was all the more necessary that the factory councils escape from the grip of the union bureaucrats, and become authentic organs of the workers' united front. Such a transformation was possible only through workers' struggle for real control and against the employers' plans to use the unemployed against those in work. By federating and centralising the councils, the workers could unite as a class in a framework of councils. This would enable them to confront the employers with their own proposals and demands, and in that way to contribute to the struggle for political power.[4]

The Communists were fighting on two fronts. They fought the trade-union bureaucrats, who tried to subordinate the councils to themselves by means of presenting trade-union lists in the elections. But they equally had to combat the 'unionist' or anarcho-syndicalist activists, who wanted to convert the factory councils into competitors to the trade unions. Since 1919, the Communists had been particularly concerned to organise factory councils on revolutionary perspectives, and through them to develop and politicise workers' economic struggles. They were at pains to organise local and regional congresses of factory councils in opposition to the 'official' organisation of factory councils as branches of the trade unions and basic elements of the system of elections to the Economic Council in Berlin, over which Emil Barth, the former Independent 'People's Commissar', presided.

The Communists presented this approach as the only way to break the power structure of the bosses in a single factory, and to encourage the members of councils and their electors to consider the problems of workers' control and class struggle on a national level. By the autumn of 1922, the Communists had won sufficient influence in several thousand factory councils to be able

---

[3] *The First Four Congresses of the Communist International*, pp. 56–7.
[4] *Die Rote Fahne*, 4 November 1920.

to hold and politically to dominate a national congress of the factory councils that November.[5]

The Communists' united-front policy, and their efforts to organise the working class around its own democratically-elected structures, inspired them to create, spread and develop the activity of the control committees [Kontrolausschuss] on the issues of prices and the struggle against speculation. These bodies were often formed on the initiative of the factory councils, and were usually elected by ad hoc workers' meetings. Their aim was to mobilise workers – especially women workers and housewives – as consumers. They organised petitions, demonstrations and sometimes punitive expeditions. They ensured links, exchanges of information and mutual support with the factory councils which represented the workers as producers. They tried to organise a practical struggle against the high cost of living. Through these control councils, the KPD had at its disposal instruments which may not have been as influential as the trade unions, but which enabled it by the end of 1922 to intervene in the daily struggles that were provoked by the constantly deteriorating economic and social conditions.

The KPD also worked within the committees of the unemployed. The trade-union organisations offered insurance and material support, but this was losing its value day by day as the crisis worsened and prices rose. Above all, the unions did not offer the unemployed any perspective of struggle. The Communists used their positions in the factory councils to demonstrate that in the last analysis capitalism was responsible for unemployment. The unemployed were often organised in parallel with the factory councils, or in local committees which remained closely linked to them. Perhaps more inclined towards general political thinking than employed workers, and more personally affected by the economic situation, which they saw as the result of capitalism, the unemployed were a favourable field of work, and the Party's influence amongst them was to grow. They gained cadres amongst them, and they won a great victory at the end of 1922 when they were joined by a well-known Social-Democratic activist, Edgar André, a leader of high quality, who had organised the unemployed workers' committee in Hamburg.[6]

---

[5] P. Maslowski, 'La Résurrection des conseils de fabrique', *Correspondance internationale*, no. 74, 30 September 1922, p. 508; H.J. Krusch, 'Zur Bewegung der revolutionären Betriebsräte in den Jahren 1922/1923', *Zeitschrifte für Gewissenschaft*, no. 2, 1963, pp. 260ff.

[6] *L'Internationale communiste*, no. 10–11, October–November 1936, p. 1342.

The united front in strikes

The Entente's ultimatum that insisted that the budget of the Reich had to be balanced to ensure its solvency and the payment of reparations, forced the government to implement severe fiscal measures and rigorous economies. Amongst the first people to be affected were the railway workers, 20,000 of whom were to be sacked, whilst the rest had to work longer hours.[7] There was a sharp response, and an independent federation of railway employees, a 'non-political organisation',[8] issued an order on 1 February 1922 for a strike in protest against the government's plans. The government responded energetically. The President of the Republic issued a decree that deprived the railway workers, as state employees, of their right to strike, and threatened serious punishments if the law were broken.[9] At that point, the defensive struggle, hitherto confined to the railway workers, took on a more general character. The question now was the right of state employees to strike, and, consequently, the right to strike in general. This is what the KPD immediately explained in an address to all workers' parties and trade unions with a proposal for joint action to defend the right to strike.[10]

However, on 4 February, the 'official' trade-union confederation, the ADGB, and the central clerical union, the AfA, as well as the railway workers' unions affiliated to them, denounced the initiative of the independent federation, and called upon the strikers to return to work.[11] Actually, the majority of the railway workers, manual and clerical, had already been on strike since 2 February, whilst the local leaders generally submitted to rank-and-file pressure and themselves led the movement. The call of the Social-Democratic trade unions met with only a weak response. The strike went ahead with the KPD alone supporting it;[12] the party called democratically-elected conferences and meetings in support, and mobilised its members to collect money for the strikers. At its suggestion, the federation which initiated the strike publicly

---

[7] Raase, op. cit., p. 106.
[8] It was the Reichsgewerkschaft Deutscher Eisenbahnbeamter und Angestellter (ibid.).
[9] Ibid.
[10] *Die Rote Fahne*, 2 February 1922; *Dokumente und Materialen*, Volume 2/7, Part 2, East Berlin, 1967, pp. 28–9.
[11] *Vorwärts*, 4 February 1922; *Dokumente und Materialen*, Volume 2/7, Part 2, op. cit., pp. 30–1.
[12] See the appeal to all workers, *Die Rote Fahne*, 5 February 1922; *Dokumente und Materialen*, Volume 2/7, Part 2, op. cit., pp. 31–3.

addressed the two Social-Democratic Parties and the two 'official' trade union Confederations, putting the problem before them in all its starkness. Since the government, supported by the majority of the deputies in the Reichstag, rejected the legitimate demands of the railway workers, the strikers had no prospect of winning within this framework. Were the trade unions and the workers' parties ready to form, if need be, a 'workers' government' which would set itself the task of satisfying the elementary demands of the working people? As the reply was negative, the federation resigned itself to ordering a return to work for 7 February, with, in return, only assurances from the employers about sackings.

The Communist press commented at length on all aspects of the railway workers' strike, showing that not only did the reformist parties and unions refuse to defend seriously the workers' elementary demands, but also that struggles which restricted themselves to the economic arena and did not succeed in spreading to the whole class were doomed to failure.[13]

The offensive of the government and the employers continued in other sectors, and soon provoked a militant response. The first struggle was in metalworking, where the employers tried to increase the working week by two hours to 48 hours. On 17 March, the metalworkers in Munich stopped work. Those of Nuremberg, Stuttgart and Frankfurt-am-Main soon followed. Around 150,000 metalworkers were on strike on 22 March.[14] This time, the DMV, the metalworkers' union affiliated to the ADGB, supported the striking workers, although without taking responsibility for the strikers' demands, or extending the strike nationally. The employers decided to reply in strength – they called in the strike-breakers from the Technische Nothilfe, and threatened to sack the strikers. The KPD emphasised that the metalworkers' defensive strike concerned the whole of the working class, and called for it to be extended to other sectors of the working class.[15] It organised demonstrations of solidarity

---

[13] *Correspondance internationale*, no. 10, 7 February 1922, pp. 73–6, special issue on the German railway workers' strike; circular from the Zentrale dated 11 February in *Dokumente und Materialen*, Volume 2/7, Part 2, op. cit., pp. 33–6. According to Mujbegović (op. cit., p. 321), the Zentrale meeting of 6 February 1922 made a self-criticism by taking note of the inadequacy of its efforts to promote within the working class the idea of the necessity of the general strike.

[14] *Die Rote Fahne*, 18, 20, 21, 22 March 1922; Raase, op. cit., p. 107.

[15] *Die Rote Fahne*, 1 April 1922; *Dokumente und Materialen*, Volume 2/7, Part 2, op. cit., pp. 43–5.

and above all collected money to enable the metalworkers to sustain a strike which the trade-union bureaucrats had evidently abandoned to its fate.[16]

The union leaders were careful to avoid anything which could appear as an attempt to break a strike which the rank and file pursued with such determination. The strikers were allowed to vote on every solution which emerged from arbitration, and for weeks turned them down with enormous majorities. The second of them, in the Stuttgart district, was rejected in a secret ballot by 40,654 votes to 1,892.[17] The bitterness of the struggle hardened attitudes in other sectors. In mid-April, the farm-workers in Thuringia and Halle-Merseburg struck for a week.[18] The demonstrations which followed the conference of the three Internationals were marked by this combativity. On 20 April, 150,000 people gathered in the Lustgarten in response to the call of the KPD and the USPD.[19] Many local organisations ignored the SPD's rejection of joint demonstrations. The strike of municipal workers in Berlin which broke out in the meantime aggravated the tension. The police opened fire on a demonstration on 20 May in front of the city hall. Four people were killed, and 25 were wounded. The KPD unsuccessfully appealed to the other workers' organisations for a 24-hour general strike in protest.[20]

The metalworkers' strike ended after nearly two months in a compromise favourable to the workers, the only possible outcome as long as their movement remained isolated. The working week was indeed to be lengthened to forty-eight hours, but the extra two hours were to be paid at overtime rates.[21] The intervention of the KPD in the succession of strikes since the beginning of the year had not been enough to organise successfully general resistance by the entire German working class to the offensive of the employers and the state. However, it helped to strengthen the Party's influence. The Party won the majority in important trade-union organisations, amongst the railway workers in Berlin with Geschke, in the building trades in Berlin with Kaiser, and in Düsseldorf, and amongst the metalworkers in Stuttgart.[22] By 29 votes to 18 they took the leadership of the trade-union council in Erfurt.[23] These

---

[16] Raase, op. cit., pp. 107–8.
[17] *Die Rote Fahne*, 21 April 1922.
[18] *Die Rote Fahne*, 7, 15 April 1922.
[19] *Die Rote Fahne*, 21 April 1922.
[20] *Die Rote Fahne*, 3 May 1922.
[21] *Correspondance internationale*, no. 44, 7 January 1922, p. 342.
[22] Raase, op. cit., p. 109.
[23] Ibid.

victories were not won without sharp battles. At the building workers' congress, held in Leipzig at the start of May, the union leaders invalidated the credentials of the delegates from Berlin and Leipzig, who had been won to the KPD. The Communists refused to submit to this violation of trade-union democracy. More than 2,000 building workers from the Leipzig district, led by Heckert, invaded the meeting-hall to register their protest, and tried to get the decision reversed. The leaders ended by getting the congress moved to Altenburg, where it could do its business 'in an orderly way', because the Communist minority could not organise street demonstrations there.[24] But when the Eleventh Congress of the ADGB met in Leipzig during 19–24 June, the Communists' proposals won widespread sympathy amongst the delegates who generally supported the Majority socialists. The policy of 'collaboration' was condemned by 345 votes to 327.[25] By an even larger majority the principle was carried that the ADGB was to be reorganised on an industrial basis, which would permit the craft unions, the bastions of the reformist bureaucracy, to be dismantled.[26]

The campaign after the assassination of Rathenau

On 24 June 1922, the Minister Walter Rathenau was struck down by an extreme right-wing squad from Organisation Consul, made up of ex-officers. He was a former head of the AEG trust, the spokesman in the Reichstag for the interests of processing industry – which in this period were often opposed to those of heavy industry – and one of those who signed the Rapallo Treaty with the Soviet Union. The Communists saw him as a redoubtable class enemy. The right-wing nationalists had picked him as a target because he was Jewish, and in order to terrorise those bourgeois elements who favoured external appeasement and accommodation to the Versailles Treaty. The murder followed hundreds of others, and came especially just after attacks on the Social Democrat Scheidemann on 4 June, and the Communist Thaelmann on 18 June.[27] The role played in this affair, as in many others, by accomplices in

---

[24] *Der Kommunistische Gewerkschafter*, no. 20, 20 May 1922, pp. 191–2.
[25] *Protokoll der Verhandlungen des II Kongresses der Gewerkschaften Deutschlands*, Berlin, 1922, pp. 517–19.
[26] Ibid., pp. 554–5. The resolution was moved by Dissmann. Although Mujbegović (op. cit., p. 345) says that the Communists obtained between 30 and 40 per cent of the votes, they had only 90 delegates at this congress.
[27] A. Reisberg, *Lenin und die Aktionseinheit in Deutschland*, East Berlin, 1964, p. 157.

the army and the police, the protection which the assassins enjoyed before and after the attack, and the nationalists' cries of triumph raised a wave of indignation, not only throughout the workers' movement, but in democratic opinion as a whole. Chancellor Josef Wirth declared in the Reichstag: 'The enemy is on the right.'[28] There was widespread fear that the assassination would be the prelude to another putsch. Resentment was directed at the Reichswehr, the police and the judicial system, all of which had been inherited from the Imperial régime. The demands that had been raised immediately after the Kapp Putsch reappeared, all the more vigorously as the passivity of successive governments appeared more striking. Ernst von Salomon, a man in the camp of the murderers, bears witness: 'An oppressive atmosphere weighed on the crowds, an atmosphere filled with foreboding, the precursor of panic, amid which a single gesture, a single word, would be enough to burst all the dykes of passion.'[29]

The KPD seized the opportunity offered by the situation to attempt to put into practice its united-front policy, this time with political slogans. Two hours after the news of the assassination broke, the Zentrale addressed in writing the two Social-Democratic Parties to propose a meeting to discuss concrete measures to be taken, and formulated eleven slogans:

- Banning of all nationalist meetings.
- Dissolution of nationalist and monarchist organisations.
- Dismissal of all monarchist officers in the Reichswehr and in the police, as well as higher civil servants and magistrates known for their nationalist views.
- Resignation of the minister Gessler and discharge of General von Seeckt.
- Arrest of Ludendorff, Escherich and the other leaders of the Orgesch.
- Amnesty for 'all revolutionary workers'.
- Banning of the monarchist publications which called for murders and for a struggle against the Republic.
- Creation of special courts made up of workers, office workers and unionised civil servants, with the duty to condemn and put an end to all the serious crimes inspired by the monarchists and the enemies of the workers.
- Energetic application of the Bielefeld agreements, especially point 8, which concerned workers' defence formations.

---

[28] *Verhandlungen des Reichstags, I Wahlperiode, 1920*, Volume 346, p. 8058.
[29] E. von Salomon, *Les Réprouvés*, p. 290, cited in Benoist-Méchin, op. cit., pp. 226–7.

- Repeal of the decree of 24 June concerning the state of emergency, and adoption of a decree in the sense of the preceding nine points, directed exclusively against the monarchists, the application of which would not be in the hands of the central authorities in the states.
- Formation of control committees, made up of workers, office workers and civil servants to supervise the application of these measures, to be elected by a congress of factory councils formed on the basis of meetings of factory committees to be convened immediately.

Furthermore, the KPD suggested to the other two parties that they agree on the slogan of a general strike throughout the country until the demands were completely satisfied.[30]

The situation was such that the leaders of the SPD at once agreed to the proposed meeting, which took place the same day at midnight, in view of the danger that they might be outflanked if the KPD and the Independents were allied.[31] The organisations represented there were the KPD, USPD, SPD, AFA, and the General Commission of the trade unions in Berlin.[32] They issued the call for a street demonstration on the following day, 25 June, as the prelude to a joint campaign which would be arranged at future meetings. On the same day, the vigorous demands of the Communist speakers, especially Walcher, led the Congress of the ADGB at Leipzig also to decide to join a united front 'to defend the Republic', and announced the slogan of a half-day general strike with demonstrations and meetings for Tuesday, 27 June.[33] On the 25th, the parties sat down for the first time with representatives of the ADGB, following the huge demonstration organised in the Lustgarten.[34] The Communists hailed this as a great victory and an important step on the road to constructing the workers' united front, even though the leaders of the other parties and the unions at once rejected some of their proposals, namely the call for an unlimited general strike, the formation of control committees, and the perspective of a workers' government.[35]

A significant factor was the militant stance adopted by the trade-union leaders under the pressure of the ADGB Congress. The reformist Leipart went

---

[30] A. Reisberg, 'Um die Einheitsfront nach dem Rathenaumoard', *Beiträge zur Geschichte der deutschen Arbeiterbewegung*, no. 5–6, 1963, p. 997.
[31] Ibid., f. 70.
[32] The entire leadership of the ADGB was attending its Eleventh Congress at Leipzig.
[33] *Vorwärts*, 25 June 1922.
[34] Reisberg, 'Um die Einheitsfront nach dem Rathenaumord', op. cit., p. 998.
[35] Ibid., p. 999.

so far as to say that his organisation was ready to use vigorous extra-parliamentary means, and to approve the Communists' conception of action.[36] At the same time, the reformists insisted that the various organisations must not try to outbid each other.[37] The Communists tried to get around this by declaring that they would regard the jointly agreed demands as minimum demands to be won by any and every means,[38] and this was accepted by the other organisations.

That evening, the representatives of the five organisations were received by Chancellor Wirth. He refused to change the decree which had already been read to the Reichstag, but undertook to expand it to meet the workers' demands.[39] They met again on 26 June to formulate the demands before the sitting of the Reichstag that day, and demanded that a special court be set up with only one law officer out of seven judges, that the monarchist and anti-Republican leagues be banned and dissolved, that the monarchist press, flag and colours be prohibited, that any attack, by action, writing or speech, on the flag or the colours of the Republic be heavily punished, that soldiers and police must not bear arms when off duty, that ex-officers must not wear uniform, and that the police and the magistrature in particular be rigorously purged.[40] They agreed to defer elaboration of measures in respect of the amnesty which the communists demanded.[41]

The first skirmishes between the representatives of the SPD and the KPD occurred during the course of this meeting. The former insisted that the Communists give a written declaration that they would not attack the democratic Republic 'by acts, or spoken word, or in writing'; also not to criticise their partners, and to withdraw a poster which abused the SPD. The KPD representatives refused, and the others went through the motions of leaving the meeting, but in the end resumed their place at the insistence of the trade-union representatives.[42] A few hours before the strike and the demonstrations planned for the 27th began, the five organisations signed the

---

[36] Ibid.
[37] Ibid.
[38] Ibid.
[39] Ibid., p. 1000.
[40] *Ist eine Einheitsfront mit den Kommunisten möglich?*, ADGB publication, Berlin, 1922, p. 4.
[41] According to Reisberg, 'Um die Einheitsfront nach dem Rathenaumord', op. cit., p. 1000, who gives no reference.
[42] Ibid., p. 1001.

'Berlin Agreement'. This repeated the essentials of the demands which had been presented to Chancellor Wirth. The ADGB and AFA had approved them, and only the KPD had any reservations.[43] They were:

- An amnesty.
- Prohibition of the monarchist leagues, meetings, processions, emblems and colours.
- Dissolution of anti-Republican armed groups.
- A purge of the state apparatus and the Reichswehr.[44]

The demonstrations on 27 June brought out millions of men and women in every large city at the unanimous call of the workers' organisations.[45] Von Salomon saw them like this: 'The crowds, massed under the floating banners, advanced like living walls of close-packed bodies. They filled the cities with the thunder of their tread, and made the air vibrate with the roar of their sullen anger.'[46]

There then began a race between the KPD, which wanted to force the other organisations into action, whilst taking advantage of the emotion and the impetus to build what it called organs of the united front, and the SPD, which tried to consolidate the coalition in the Reichstag by encouraging the People's Party deputies to vote for a 'law for the defence of the Republic', whilst at the same time blaming the Communists for breaking the united front. Despite the formal decisions of the National Committees of the SPD and the unions, control or action committees were formed on the initiative of the Communists in numerous localities, especially in Saxony and Thuringia, but also in Rhineland-Westphalia and Central Germany.[47]

In Zwickau, an action committee was formed of representatives of the unions and the workers' parties, and for several days exercised real power, based on a 'workers' security guard' of two hundred and fifty men.[48] In Thuringia, the leaders of the five organisations at the level of the region agreed

---

[43] Ibid., f. 25.

[44] *Die Rote Fahne*, 28 June 1922. *Dokumente und Materialen*, Volume 2/7, Part 2, op. cit., pp. 103–5.

[45] *Dokumente und Materialen*, Volume 2/7, Part 2, op. cit., pp. 103–5.

[46] Von Salomon, op. cit., p. 291, cited in Benoist-Méchin, op. cit., p. 227.

[47] Reisberg, 'Um die Einheitsfront nach dem Rathenaumord', op. cit., p. 1005, n. 37.

[48] G. Lange, 'Die Protestationen der Zwickauer Arbeiter gegen den deutschen Militarismus aus Anlass des Mordes an Walter Rathenau', *Beiträge zur Geschichte der deutschen Arbeiterbewegung*, no. 4, 1962, p. 961.

to form a central control committee.[49] However, the SPD managed to get included in the appeal for the huge demonstration planned for 4 July a warning against speeches by 'irresponsible' orators and 'provocateurs'. The representatives of the KPD refused to sign such a text, and the others published it without their signature.[50] The KPD protested strongly, and issued a special appeal supporting the joint demonstration, which the unions' paper refused to publish.[51] At the same time, it did its best to restart discussions, or at least to overcome differences by engaging in action. To that end, it advanced new proposals: for a general strike to obtain the fulfilment of the demands in the Berlin agreement; for the dissolution of the Reichstag, and new elections, in which the workers' parties would participate with the aim of winning a workers' majority in the Reichstag and forming a workers' government.[52] Resolutions to this effect were carried in many union branches and factory councils. The SPD was negotiating in the Reichstag with the People's Party for a 'law for the defence of the Republic': the latter refused to include an amnesty for the Communists who were sentenced after March 1921, and the SPD rejected the Communist proposals.[53]

The KPD then publicly accused the SPD of breaking the Berlin agreement, and began to publish the minutes of the discussions between the organisations.[54] On 4 July, the ADGB called upon the KPD to adhere to the demands which they had jointly drawn up.[55] The KPD Zentrale retorted by stressing that the difficulties arose from the fact that the Social Democrats were making concessions to their right-wing allies in the Reichstag, and that the united front could be ensured at a higher level if the five organisations called for the dissolution of the Reichstag and for new elections which would make possible a workers' majority and a workers' government.[56] The same day, the four organisations met without the KPD, and informed it that it had henceforth 'placed itself outside the united action'.[57]

The KPD replied with an appeal, entitled 'United Front in Spite of Everything!' and called for the formation of joint control committees and the

---

[49] Reisberg, 'Um die Einheitsfront nach dem Rathenaumord', op. cit., p. 1005, n. 37.
[50] *Ist eine Einheitsfront mit den Kommunisten möglich?*, op. cit., p. 12.
[51] Reisberg, 'Um die Einheitsfront nach dem Rathenaumord', op. cit., p. 1004.
[52] *Ist eine Einheitsfront mit den Kommunisten möglich?*, op. cit., p. 14.
[53] Reisberg, 'Um die Einheitsfront nach dem Rathenaumord', op. cit., p. 1003.
[54] *Die Rote Fahne*, 6 July 1922.
[55] *Ist eine Einheitsfront mit den Kommunisten möglich?*, op. cit., p. 13.
[56] *Die Rote Fahne*, 8 July 1922.
[57] *Ist eine Einheitsfront mit den Kommunisten möglich?*, op. cit., p. 20.

organisation of a struggle to apply the Berlin agreement.[58] New committees were effectively formed in Essen, Düsseldorf and Reinickendorf,[59] but in general the situation thereafter went in favour of the reformist leaders, who no longer feared being outflanked, and could thus devote themselves to a satisfactory settlement of the question on the parliamentary level.

Passing from concession to concession, from amendment to amendment in the course of the debate in the Reichstag, the law for the defence of the Republic ended by entrusting this task to the police and the courts. The KPD denounced its class character, and showed that the law would really be effective only against the working class and its organisations.[60] In the vote on 18 July, the Communist deputies voted against, with the extreme Right, and the SPD and USPD deputies voted for it, along with other bourgeois parties. An agreement between the Independents and the Majority led to a 'collective for parliamentary work', the prelude to an early fusion. The decision of the Independents to drop their formal refusal to participate in any coalition government, taken in the name of 'the defence of the Republic', was to facilitate the reunification. The KPD had been clearly isolated by its Social-Democratic opponents, who did their best to exploit and to divert against it the workers' aspiration for unity.

The disappointing results of this campaign provoked lively reactions within the KPD and the Third International. On the ECCI, Zinoviev uttered bitter criticisms of the way it had been handled by the Zentrale. In the end, he was mandated to inform the Germans of his personal remarks and suggestions, and to put questions for them to answer in order to inform the ECCI, which refused to send 'formal directives' about a problem with which it was badly acquainted. The letter was written on 18 July,[61] and said in particular:

> As far as we have been able to judge from *Die Rote Fahne*, your tactics during the early days were mediocre. You should not have shouted 'Republic! Republic!' under those conditions. You should rather, from the first minute, have explained to the masses that today Germany is a republic without republicans. In that moment of excitement, you should have shown to the

---

[58] *Die Rote Fahne*, 9 July 1922; *Dokumente und Materialen*, Volume 2/7, Part 2, op. cit., pp. 111–14.

[59] Reisberg, 'Um die Einheitsfront nach dem Rathenaumord', op. cit., p. 1007.

[60] *Die Rote Fahne* was banned for three weeks on 10 August, by virtue of this law (Reisberg, 'Um die Einheitsfront nach dem Rathenaumord', op. cit., p. 1007).

[61] Zinoviev quoted an extract from this letter in the course of the Fourth Comintern

broad masses of workers – who are less interested in the Republic than in their own economic interests – that the bourgeois republic not only offers no guarantee of the interests of the proletarian class, but that, especially in such circumstances, it actually offers the best form for oppressing the working masses. You should not blow the same trumpet as the Social Democrats or the Independents. The united front must never, never damp down the independence of our agitation. For us this is a condition *sine qua non*. We are ready to enter into negotiations with the people of the USPD and the SPD, not, however, as poor relations, but as an independent force which always preserves its own characteristics, and always explains the opinion of the Party to the masses, from A to Z.[62]

Zinoviev suggested that faced with the refusal of the other workers' organisations to act, the party should take the initiative, and launch a call for a strike of at least twenty-four hours.[63]

Zinoviev's position coincided broadly with that being voiced by Maslow, Fischer and the other leaders of the German Left. They accused the KPD's leaders of considering forging agreements amongst parties at the leadership level, and therefore being to blame for having isolated the Party from the masses, and making possible the Social-Democratic betrayal. The affair turned into a crisis when the Zentrale met on 22 July, following the arrival of Zinoviev's letter. Kleine, in his capacity as the representative of the ECCI, sat with the German leaders, and he violently attacked the Party's policy, declaring that the Zentrale's refusal to recognise its mistakes would open an exceptionally serious crisis in the Party. He said that on this point at least, he would support the left-wing critics, Maslow and Fischer. The Zentrale bowed to what Ernst Meyer said was really 'blackmail', and only Walcher and Heckert – who, significantly, were the Party's senior trade-union functionaries – remained at his side. Kleine repeated his attacks on the following day at the Central

---

congress (*Protokoll des vierten Kongresses der Kommunistischen Internationale*, op. cit., p. 198), presenting it as being dated 18 June – which was an impossibility. Angress (op. cit., p. 245, n. 52) suggests 28 June, which is proved impossible by documents published subsequently, in particular Ernst Meyer's letter to his wife, and the correspondence between Meyer and Zinoviev published by H. Weber, 'KPD und Komintern', *Vierteljahrshefte für Zeitgeschichte*, no. 2, 1968, pp. 185–8, where the references to Zinoviev's letter indicate the date of 18 July without any possible doubt.

[62] *Protokoll des vierten Kongresses der Kommunistischen Internationale*, op. cit., p. 198.

[63] Letter from Ernst Meyer to his wife Rosa Levine Meyer, dated 24 July 1922, from Rosa Leviné-Meyer's private archives, published in H. Weber, 'KPD und Komintern', *Vierteljahrshefte für Zeitgeschichte*, no. 2, 1968, p. 186.

committee, but Meyer fought back energetically and won. Maslow remained in a minority with four other left-wingers voting against Meyer's motion, although some ten members, like Kleine, voted for the part of the motion which listed the Party's forthcoming tasks, and abstained on the rest.[64]

This incident revealed both the influence which a representative of the ECCI could exert on the Zentrale, and the resistance which he could encounter. Above all, it showed how the long-term alliance of Zinoviev and the leftists on the ECCI with the German Left was a permanent and serious source of danger, all the more because the German leaders were always ready to confess to mistakes which they did not think they had made, in order to avoid a clash with the ECCI.[65] The poor results of the campaign following the assassination of Rathenau strengthened the attractiveness of the Left within the Party, and deepened the suspicions of many activists that the leadership was yet again being passive. The notorious 'theory of the offensive' resurfaced in the Party. As Remmele recounts, the Zentrale was bombarded with resolutions demanding a call for a general strike or an attack on the police headquarters.[66] We can see confirmation of this in the initiative of the leadership of the Berlin-Brandenburg district, which organised an attack on a public meeting of the extreme Right held in the Busch Circus on 15 October. The police intervened energetically, 50 of the Communist attackers were wounded, and one was killed. In the following days, the police arrested 50 people, including Brandler, Thalheimer and Pfeiffer, and raided *Die Rote Fahne* on 16 October.

The newspapers announced that the arrested activists would be prosecuted for 'breaches of civil peace', and could be sentenced to fifteen years hard labour.[67] But this time, the ECCI, despite its criticisms of the German Zentrale, did not side with the leftists.[68] At the Fourth Comintern Congress, Zinoviev

---

[64] A detailed account of these two meetings is to be found in Meyer's letter (see the preceding note). It is much more accurate than the report in *Die Rote Fahne* of 27 July 1922, which additionally claims that the votes were unanimous.

[65] According to Meyer, Pieck is said to have made a 'solemn declaration' in this sense to the Central Committee. Paul Böttcher was the only member of the Zentrale not to have changed his mind from one day to the next.

[66] Reisberg, 'Um die Einheitsfront nach dem Rathenaumord', op. cit., p. 1009.

[67] *Correspondance internationale*, no. 79, 18 October 1922, p. 608.

[68] According to Meyer, in a letter to his wife, Zinoviev had suggested a 24-hour strike at the least, but on his own initiative. There was no question of this at the Fourth Comintern Congress. The correspondence between Meyer and Zinoviev during this Congress leaves no doubt that this was a personal suggestion by Zinoviev. Radek was to say that 'if the Party had launched itself into action alone, this would have been a

said that the Berlin organisation had not shown itself at all in an intelligent light during this affair.[69]

The real defeat was elsewhere, in the factories and the streets, in the spreading disillusionment, which more clearly revealed the exasperation of a minority that was ready to act. Social Democracy had shown once more that under no circumstances would it break its coalition with the bourgeois parties, and that it was determined to use all its influence to prevent great class battles from taking place. Strengthened by this assurance and by the defeat of the workers' economic strikes in the spring and summer, the supporters of the 'strong hand' and the counter-attack could proceed. Hugo Stinnes expressed his requirements during a session of the Economic Council of the Reich, where he once again called for the working day to be lengthened, to meet the need to pay reparations, and to salvage the German economy: 'You cannot both lose the War and work two hours less. It's impossible. You must work, work and work again. . . . We should forbid for at least five years any strike in the firms which are vitally necessary to the national economy, and severely punish any infraction.'[70]

A new government was formed. Its head was Cuno, the former president of the Hamburg-Amerika shipping line. An ultimatum from Legien had excluded him from the Cabinet in March 1920. Now there were no Social-Democratic ministers. The government was clearly inclined to the right, and accepted Social-Democratic support whilst declaring that, if necessary, it could do without it. The victory of Mussolini in Italy encouraged the German capitalists to look again at the extreme right-wing groups, amongst which Adolf Hitler's National Socialist Workers' Party was beginning to emerge.[71]

---

more serious mistake than all those that have been made'. (*Protokoll des vierten Kongresses der Kommunistischen Internationale*, op. cit., p. 100). It was only in November, in the pre-Congress discussions, that Maslow and Urbahns were to learn from Zinoviev's own mouth of the existence of his letter of 18 July.

[69] *Protokoll des vierten Kongresses der Kommunistischen Internationale*, op. cit., p. 200.

[70] *Die Rote Fahne*, 11 November 1922. The Communist paper was to use the accounts which had appeared on the preceding day in *Vorwärts* and the *Berliner Tageblatt* of the speech which Stinnes had delivered behind closed doors. *Kreuzzeitung* was to protest on the same day against the interpretation which *Vorwärts* placed upon it, which gave the impression that Stinnes spoke against stabilising the mark. The full text of the speech was also published on 11 November in *Deutsche Allgemeine Zeitung*. In reality, the 'conditions' which Stinnes posed for the stabilisation of the mark, and especially the adoption of a 10-hour working day for the next 10 to 15 years, were well known (G. Hallgarten, *Hitler, Reichswehr und Industrie*, Frankfurt am Main, 1955, pp. 14–15 and n. 25, pp. 70–1).

[71] According to Konrad Heiden, *Adolf Hitler: Eine Biographie*, Zürich, 1937, p. 251,

The KPD did its utmost to overcome its isolation by organised campaigns, building and consolidating 'organs of the united front', control committees and especially factory councils, winning some considerable successes along the way. At the end of a campaign to reactivate these committees, it succeeded in mounting in November 1922 a National Congress of Factory Councils. Only a minority of the councils sent delegates, but some of them represented the most militant enterprises in Germany. On 22 November, this Congress adopted a programme which took up again the essentials of the 'transitional' demands of the KPD, and elected a standing committee presided over by the Berlin Communist, Hermann Grothe.[72]

Not all the consequences of this successful assembly were positive. Immediately after the Congress was held, Badische Anilin dismissed the three delegates who had represented the factory councils for its plants at Ludwigshaven. One of them was a Communist leader, popular in the Palatinate, Max Frenzel.[73] His dismissal provoked an exceptionally strong unofficial protest strike. The firm replied with a lock-out, and then re-employed people on the basis of new working conditions, reintroducing piece-work and compulsory overtime. The trade unions refused to make the strike official, and it only received the backing, throughout Germany, of the Communists and the factory committees which supported them. Nonetheless, it lasted for six weeks, but the strikers, exhausted, ultimately had to return to work well and truly beaten. The sacking of Max Frenzel and his two comrades was followed by the dismissal of some 2,000 strikers.[74]

The employers' offensive went hand in hand with the deepening of the economic crisis. Inflation accelerated, prices soared. Through November, the price of meat, eggs and margarine doubled, and that of butter and bread trebled. 'R. Albert', the pen-name of the irreplaceable chronicler of a whole

---

Ernst von Borsig was already contributing to the financing of the Nazi Party in this period. On 28 January 1923, the Zentrale of the KPD mentioned the Nazi danger in Bavaria.

[72] The programme is reproduced in *Dokumente und Materialen*, Volume 2/7, Part 2, op. cit., pp. 194–8. The Congress had brought together 856 delegates, of whom 657 were Communists (*Die Rote Fahne*, 27 November 1922).

[73] Weber, *Die Wandlung des deutschen Kommunismus*, Volume 2, op. cit., p. 125.

[74] Apart from *Die Rote Fahne*, which reported on the Palatinate strike every day throughout this period, see *Inprekorr*, and, in its French edition, *Correspondance internationale*, especially the articles of R. Albert, 'La Bataille industrielle du Palatinat', no. 97, 19 December 1922, p. 738; 'Les forces en présence dans le Palatinat', no. 98, 20 December 1922, pp. 746–7; 'Vaincus', no. 99, 23 December 1922, p. 755.

year's events in Germany,[75] wrote in *Inprekorr*, under the headline 'A Crumbling Society':

> Thirty-five million working people anxiously await winter, the killer of the poor. In less than two months, the average cost of living has more than trebled. The prices of necessities have risen five-fold. Since 1 October, rents have risen five-fold, postal charges have risen three- or four-fold, and rail and tramway fares have gone up. . . . Now they announce that the price of bread is going up four-fold.

He described the spectacle which Germany offered at the end of 1922. In working-class districts such as Neukölln and Moabit 'young, ashen faces, marked with the signs of tuberculosis and hunger . . . maimed people, beggars, prostitutes . . . and the feasting, the feasting of the rich.'[76]

Barbarism was installing itself in the country which until then had been the most advanced in Europe, with poverty all around the most advanced machinery and the most modern technology. As for the Communists, they thought that they had in their hands the means to change this crumbling world, the hope of all the most wretched was there, in the form of a mass Communist Party, a combat party.

---

[75] It seems very likely that this is the work of Victor Serge, one of whose pseudonyms was Albert. At that date, in Berlin, he was working as an editor of *Inprekorr*, and his personal style in the French edition stands out in contrast to the mediocre translations which accompany it.

[76] *Correspondance internationale*, no. 72, 23 September 1922, p. 561.

Chapter Thirty-Two
The 'Mass Communist Party'

The impact of the capitalist crisis and the altitude of Social Democracy and the trade unions would not necessarily result in a process of proletarian radicalisation, but could instead lead to passivity and ultimately resignation amongst a substantial part of the working class. The recent example of Italy showed the opportunities that the situation offered to big capital to consolidate its rule by resorting to the armed bands of fascism.

At the end of 1922, Brandler presented a political report to the KPD's Central Committee. He had just returned from Moscow, where he had been a member of the Presidium of the Communist International for nearly a year. He acknowledged that the KPD had made progress during the past year, but he insisted on the necessity to banish firmly that so-called 'intransigence' which revealed itself in 'an inability to draw direct inspiration from the workers', in a party which, he said, did not yet know 'how to adapt itself sufficiently to the thinking of the non-Communist working classes'.[1]

The composition of the KPD

The KPD had made considerable progress by the end of 1922, not only compared with its position in

[1] Extract from Brandler's report to the Central Committee, 13–14 December 1922, *Correspondance Internationale*, no. 99, 23 December 1922, p. 753.

1918–19, but also with its position in the months following the March Action in 1921. Its active membership had fallen dramatically by the summer of 1921, perhaps even lower than the figure, revealed only a year later, of 157,168 collected dues-payments,[2] which itself was derisory when one considers that immediately before the Halle Congress in late 1920, the membership of the USPD and KPD(S) stood at 893,000 and 78,715 respectively.[3] Even if we concede that the usually given figure of 450,000 members when the VKPD was founded was grossly optimistic,[4] we must nonetheless accept that the March Action led to a sharp fall in active members. This is clear from the tables drawn up by Hermann Weber. According to reliable statistics, the membership of the Halle-Merseburg district declined from 66,000 at the beginning of 1921 to 23,000 in mid-1922. Membership in the Lower Rhineland, around Düsseldorf, fell from 52,000 to 16,000, in Thuringia from 23,000 to 10,000, and in the North-West, around Bremen, from 17,000 to 4,000.[5]

The situation was improving at the end of 1922. Böttcher bases his figures on dues actually paid, and gives a membership figure for September 1922 of 218,195, of which 26,710 were women.[6] Pieck gives a figure of 255,863 for October.[7] Weber's statistical study gives the figure of 224,689 for the third quarter of 1922.[8] The numbers of contributions paid were less than the membership figures for October that were provided at the time by the local organisations, which totalled 328,017.[9] That method of calculation led the Party in 1921 to announce a membership of 359,613, a figure which was manifestly exaggerated.[10] We can draw the conclusion that after losing two-thirds of its effective membership immediately after March 1921, the KPD won – or won back – about 100,000 members during the rest of 1921 and 1922.

The Party's influence remained very unequal across the different regions of Germany. In Bavaria, for example, it had hardly more than 6,000 members, even though it claimed 8,000, and it had not recovered from the blows suffered in 1919.[11] On the other hand, it claimed about 50,000 members in Rhineland-

---

[2] *Correspondance Internationale*, no. 81, 25 October 1922, p. 624.
[3] *Jahrbuch für Politik-Wirtschaft Arbeiterbewegung 1922–23*, op. cit., pp. 642–7.
[4] *Correspondance Internationale*, no. 81, 25 October 1922, p. 624.
[5] Weber, *Die Wandlung des Deutschen Kommunismus*, Volume 1, op. cit., pp. 368–94.
[6] *Correspondance Internationale*, no. 11, 7 February 1923, p. 71.
[7] *Correspondance Internationale*, no. 81, 25 October 1922, p. 624.
[8] Weber, *Die Wandlung des Deutschen Kommunismus*, Volume 1, op. cit., p. 362.
[9] *Correspondance Internationale*, no. 81, 25 October 1922, p. 623.
[10] Ibid., p. 624.
[11] Weber, *Die Wandlung des Deutschen Kommunismus*, Volume 1, op. cit., pp. 383, 390 gives figures of 4,500 for the North, and 2,369 for the South. See also *Correspondance Internationale*, no. 41, 23 May 1923, p. 401.

Westphalia,[12] nearly 30,000 in the Berlin-Brandenburg district, nearly 20,000 in Erzgebirge-Vogtland, 23,000 in the Halle district and in the Wasserkante,[13] all of which were high as a percentage of the total population, but even higher as a percentage of the working class. It meant that there was one Communist for every 46 people in Halle, one for every 55 in Erzgebirge-Vogtland, one for 138 in the Wasserkante, one for 144 in Berlin-Brandenburg.[14] In relation to the working-class population, including women and children, there was one Communist for every 30 in Halle, one in 45 in the Erzgebirge, one in 50 in the Wasserkante, and one in 60 in Berlin-Brandenburg.[15] This unequal implantation resulted less from the recent political fluctuations than from the general history of the Party. Erzgebirge-Vogtland, which included Chemnitz, was a real stronghold because Brandler and Heckert enjoyed strong support within the working class, and had been able in 1919 to win over nearly all the Independent workers. Similarly, the big battalions of left Independents, won over in 1920, formed the mass Communist organisation in Central Germany and in the Wasserkante.

Only approximations are possible in respect of the social composition and composition by age and sex of the Party's members, as statistics for this period are lacking. But the elements of the available information are consistent. In this period, the KPD was above all a party of workers, and particularly of young workers. A wide range of writers agree that the Party's membership was at least 90 per cent working-class.[16] The Spartacus League and the old KPD(S) had never, local exceptions apart, had much presence in the industrial working class, but the left Independents had brought tens of thousands of factory workers into the Unified Party. Contemporary observers were struck by the working-class character of the meetings of delegates and cadres.[17]

---

[12] Including 16,389 for Lower Rhineland, 4,431 for Central Rhineland, and 18,523 for the Ruhr (Weber, *Die Wandlung des Deutschen Kommunismus*, Volume 1, op. cit., pp. 372, 374, 380).

[13] The precise figures are 29,273, 19,432, 23,263 and 23,263. It is somewhat surprising that these last two figures are identical (ibid., pp. 369–74).

[14] Ibid., pp. 369–71.

[15] Calculations based on Weber's figures.

[16] Zinoviev said: 'About 99 per cent workers.' (*Correspondance Internationale*, no. 61, 31 July 1923, p. 453).

[17] Robert Louzon wrote in *La Vie ouvrière* (28 April 1923): 'I had the chance to be present recently in Essen at a meeting of Communist shop-stewards. About a hundred were present, and all of them appeared to have left their factory a few hours earlier. Even in the most exclusively working-class areas in France, a meeting of branch secretaries and treasurers has never presented such a working-class character.'

Amongst them were many skilled workers, especially in metalworking, and the KPD cannot be compared in this respect to what it was to become ten years later, a party of unskilled workers and labourers.[18] There were considerably fewer women members, their number varying between one-sixth and one-twelfth of the total membership.[19]

The Communists were young. The overwhelming majority were men of the generation of the end and immediate aftermath of the War, in other words, that of the Russian Revolution and the November Revolution, led by men of the preceding generation.[20] Radek wrote on this subject:

---

[18] Weber studied the Party as it stood in 1924, and drew up the following table, which is all the more significant in that the proportion of non-proletarian elements is highest amongst the cadres (*Die Wandlung des Deutschen Kommunismus*, Volume 2, op. cit., p. 43).

Skilled workers	49%
Unskilled workers	11%
Office workers	10%
Peasants and day labourers	5.5%
Intellectuals	9.5%
Teachers	4%
Full-timers and Journalists	4%
Technicians	1.5%
Housewives	3.5%

Weber gives the following data in respect of the social origins of the parents of 120 of the cadres, from which the following table can be drawn:

Sons of workers	48%
Sons of office-workers	15%
Sons of peasants	12%
Sons of artisans	8.5%
Sons of intellectuals	4.5%
Sons of bourgeois	10%
Various	2%

[19] However, the past role of Luxemburg, the current role of Fischer and the prestige of Zetkin made the KPD a party in which women seemed to play a much more important role than in any other Communist Party. In fact, whilst several women – Rosi Wolfstein, Irmgaard Raasch, Martha Arendsee – worked in the Party's central departments, only one – Erna Halbe – occupied in 1923 a responsible post as Polleiter at a district level.

[20] Weber's study of 252 cadres shows that in 1924 the essential role was played by members who had come into political activity earlier than most of the members (*Die Wandlung des Deutschen Kommunismus*, Volume 2, op. cit., p. 43).

Date of entry into the workers' movement:

Before 1900	8%
1900–5	9%
1906–16	44%
Sub-total	61%
Between 1917 and 1920 from USPD	21%
From KPD(S)	15%
After 1920	2%
Sub-total	39%

The overwhelming majority of the proletarian masses who belong to the German Communist Party are workers who were aroused to political life by the Revolution after being shaken up by the War. The USPD did not become a party of a million members by recruiting from the SPD, but by an influx of new proletarian elements. The hundreds of thousands of Spartacists corresponded only to a very small part indeed of the former radical shock troops of the Party; the majority of them had been precipitated into political life by the thunder of the Revolution.[21]

These remarks need a little correction as regards cadres and the leadership. The most experienced activists, and, therefore the oldest, held responsible positions. The leading comrades in the large regions were between 30 and 40 years old.[22] Weber says that at the level of district leadership, a few people were over 40, such as Oelssner, the Polleiter in Silesia, who was 43, Eppstein, a leftist leader and Polleiter in Mid-Rhineland, who was 45, and Jakob Schloer, the Orgleiter of the Southern region, who was 44.[23] The great majority of the others were workers between 30 and 40, such as the building worker Siewert who led the Erzgebirge-Vogtland district, which he took in hand in 1920 at the age of 33, with the blacksmith Reissmann aged 36, and the cabinet-maker Grube, aged 30, at the head of the sub-district. These three men had begun life as activists in the trade unions or the SPD at the age of 17 or 18, and had six or seven years' militant activity behind them when the Great War broke out.[24]

In 1922, younger men appeared in the district leaderships. Hans Tittel, the Polleiter in Württemberg, was 28, and a prewar activist, Hans Weber, in the Palatinate, was 27. Willy Sachse, the secretary of the Halle-Merseburg district, the former comrade of Reichpietsch and Köbis (who had both been shot in 1917 for their participation in the sailors' revolutionary movement) was 26, as was Volk in Saxony, and Wollweber, also a former mutinous sailor,

---

In all, 62 per cent of these cadres had come to the Unified Party with the Independents, and 33 per cent with the KPD(S). Of the latter, 16 per cent were organised during the war by the Spartacists, and five per cent by the left radicals. Twelve per cent came directly to the KPD(S) at its foundation or afterwards.

[21] Radek, *Soll die VKPD*, op. cit., pp. 15–16.

[22] For example, Ernst Meyer, Stoecker, Dahlem, Felix Schmidt, Karl Schulz (see biographies in appendix).

[23] Weber, *Die Wandlung des Deutschen Kommunismus*, Volume 2, op. cit., pp. 239, 277.

[24] H.J. Krusch, *Um die Einheitsfront und eine Arbeiterregierung. Zur Geschichte der Arbeiterbewegung*, East Berlin, 1963, pp. 88–92.

who was 24. Very young men were less frequent, but there were some. Hausen became the secretary of the Lausitz district at 22, Fugger, Party leader in Düsseldorf at 25, and Herbert Müller, spokesman for the Communists in Ludwigshafen, at 22.[25]

The Central Committee elected in January 1923, and enlarged four months later, numbered 24 members. Fourteen of them were manual workers, metal-workers, building workers, printers, three were office-workers or draughtsmen, and only seven were journalists or Party officials of over five years standing – but even then this was a far higher proportion than for cadres of districts or localities. These non-workers, moreover, represented different generations. Clara Zetkin was the eldest at 66; she was the link with Social Democracy in its heroic period. Apart from her, only Pieck at 47, Remmele at 43, Brandler at 42 and Geschke at 41 had passed the 40 mark. The last three had been full-timers for only three years at the most. Four members of the Zentrale were under 30: Karl Becker and Walter Ulbricht at 29, and Ruth Fischer and Hans Pfeiffer at 28. All the others were between 30 and 40.

The KPD started to revive in 1922, and an inrush of very young cadres was felt, particularly in the Party's clandestine work and the press. Some important positions were entrusted to very young people. Otto Braun, who was born in 1900, was put in charge of training in the military apparatus of which Hans Kippenberger, at 25, was one of the leaders. In the same way, Heinz Neumann, who joined the Party at 18, joined the editorial staff of *Die Rote Fahne* in the following year. At 21, he was the secretary of the Mecklenburg district, and a regular contributor to *Inprekorr*, and he already played an important role in the clandestine apparatus, thanks no doubt to his knowledge of Russian, which he had learned during a stay in prison. Scholem was Editor of *Volksblatt* at 26, and in 1922, at 27, was Orgleiter in Berlin-Brandenburg. Erich Hausen, an electrical fitter and a member of the KPD at 18, joined the Central Committee at 21, and at 22 became the secretary in the Lausitz district.[26]

We notice particularly the youthfulness of the members with responsibilities in the press. None of the Chief Editors of Party papers in 1923 was over 40. Heinrich Süsskind had been Chief Editor of *Die Rote Fahne* for two years by the time he was 28. Adolf Ende was the Chief Editor of *Rote Echo* in Erfurt

---

[25] Weber, *Die Wandlung des Deutschen Kommunismus*, Volume 2, op. cit., pp. 128, 154, 227, 267, 324, 332, 337, 348.
[26] Ibid., pp. 154–5, 181–2, 233, 285–6.

at 24, and Martin Hoffmann, Chief Editor of *Echo des Ostens*, and Bernhard Meune, Chief Editor of the *Bergische Volksstimme*, were both only 22.[27]

The real leadership of the KPD, the Zentrale, was made up of men and women who were older, to be sure, but still youthful, and comparable in this respect only to the 'Montagne' in 1793, or the members of the Bolsheviks' Central Committee in 1917.[28] Nonetheless, they revealed a remarkable continuity in the history of the German workers' movement and its revolutionary wing. Most of its members could claim many years activity, if not in Social Democracy itself, at least in its youth wing. They nearly all entered militant activity between the ages of 16 and 20. Twenty-two of its 24 members had gone through this experience; the other two, Ruth Fischer and Guralski-Kleine, had also fought their first battles in the socialist movement when very young, one in Austria and the other in Poland.

Amongst these 'veterans' of prewar Social Democracy, fifteen were Spartacists who had joined during the war, and five were members from the same period of the revolutionary groups in Bremen and in Hamburg. Only one came from the youth movement exclusively, and nine came from the left wing of the Independents. Outside the Zentrale, we may note in the Central Committee or in the district committees and secretariats the exceptional case of the intellectuals, nearly all of the Left, who had come to Communism with the left Independents, and had entered into militant activity at a later age: Maslow was 26, Urbahns 28, Rosenberg 29, and Karl Korsch 33 when they joined the USPD at the end of the War.[29] They represented an important sector of the German revolutionary movement, the young intellectuals of bourgeois origin, disgusted by the War, who joined the camp of the organised workers. But they did not constitute the heart of the Party.

Structure and organisation

Like the Bolsheviks, the KPD demanded many sacrifices from its members, starting with significant membership dues, which stood in 1919 at a minimum of 15 pfennigs for women and young persons, and 30 pfennigs for everyone else. With inflation, it rose to a minimum of four marks in March 1922, and

---

[27] Ibid., pp. 108, 167, 218, 314.
[28] P. Broué, *Le Parti Bolchevique*, Paris, 1963, p. 90.
[29] Weber, *Die Wandlung des Deutschen Kommunismus*, Volume 2, op. cit., pp. 192, 213, 262, 329.

then to 15 marks that September. The Communist worker handed over to his party in this way the equivalent of one hour's work per week,[30] or about three times as much as the Social-Democratic or Independent activists. The dues-payment was progressive, and rose rapidly in step with the member's wages. We have to add extra contributions fixed by intermediary organisations, and special levies, voluntary in principle, announced in the course of political campaigns.

We may believe that the financial demands were a factor in consolidating the Party, keeping out dilettantes and birds of passage, but that they also may have discouraged the recruitment of workers in this period of crisis and decline of their living standards. Fischer records that the total of paid-up dues always fell below the actual number of members in these years, because payments were so often in arrears.

In the fields of organisation and internal functioning, the KPD prided itself as having been one of the first parties to combine both old and new practices. It stood in the tradition of the early socialist movement, but broke with the Social-Democratic practice established in 1905, whereby the basic units of the Party coincided with the boundaries of electoral districts. The Unification Congress took pains to establish a method of organisation which would be tighter than that of the KPD(S) or the USPD. The Party unit was based no longer on the electoral constituency, but in the economic sphere. The basic cell, accordingly, was the local group [Ortsgruppe], which coincided in principle with the workplace fractions [Betriebsfraktionen].[31] An important reorganisation occurred in May 1921, following a discussion of the weaknesses of the Party which the March Action had revealed. In every large locality the local group was divided up into districts, the districts into sub-districts, and the latter themselves divided into 'groups of ten', numbering between ten and twenty members. Special attention was paid to Party work in the factories, where a shop-steward or a factory council elected by the members led the work of the factory fraction. Thus each member belonged to two basic structures, the 'group of ten' and the fraction.[32]

The leading members at the higher levels of the Party were appointed by elections conducted on this dual base. The Party's shop-stewards in the

---

[30] Decision of the Central Committee, 15–16 May, *Die Rote Fahne*, 17 May 1922.

[31] H. Brandler, 'Die Organisation der Partei', *Die Rote Fahne*, 4 December 1920; *Die Internationale*, no. 26, 1 December 1920, pp. 33–7.

[32] Circular from the Zentrale on organisational questions, *Die Rote Fahne*, 1 June 1921.

workplaces elected the leaders of the districts, as well as half of the members of the executive committees of the local groups, the other half being elected directly at a general meeting of the local activists which included all the members of the various 'groups of ten'. The executive of the local group appointed in this way invited to all its deliberations, with consultative vote, the leaders of the various fractions, workplace fractions or fractions in mass organisations such as the Communist youth, Communist women, cooperatives, etc.[33] Despite this dual representation of members active in the fractions, the leadership took the view in 1922 that the attempts to organise factory work were still inadequate, and instituted a variety of measures intended to base the whole Party organisation on the workplace cells. At the start of 1923, the Zentrale created a special department with the task of systematically organising them, under the control of Walter Ulbricht.[34]

The local groups themselves were regrouped in districts, of which there were twenty-seven in 1922,[35] each with sub-districts. They tried to overcome this relative dispersion by regrouping several districts into what were actual regions.[36] At every level, the cadres, whether they were delegated for a particular situation, or responsible for a certain period, were elected and subject to recall at any time by the units which had elected them, whether committees or general meetings, conferences or congresses.

In accordance with the Bolshevik principle of democratic centralism, the supreme body of the Party was its Congress, which met at least once a year. The delegates to it were elected on the basis of pre-Congress discussions. In these discussions, different tendencies could confront each other and present their programmes and candidates at the same time. They had very wide freedom to express their differences, including at meetings of local groups in which they had no supporters.[37] In the intervals between Congresses, authority belonged to the Central Committee, which itself was made up of people

---

[33] Ibid.

[34] *Die Rote Fahne*, 17 May 1923; *Dokumente und Materialen*, Volume 7/2, Part 2, op. cit., pp. 329–30.

[35] They were Berlin-Brandenburg, Niederlausitz, Pomerania, East Prussia-Danzig, Silesia, Upper Silesia, Eastern Saxony, Erzgebirge-Vogtland, Western Saxony, Halle-Merseburg, Magdeburg-Anhalt, Thuringia, Lower Saxony, Mecklenburg, Wasserkante, North-West, Eastern Westphalia, Western Westphalia, Lower Rhineland, Central Rhineland, Hesse-Cassel, Hesse-Frankfurt, Palatinate, Baden, Württemberg, Northern Bavaria and Southern Bavaria.

[36] *Die Rote Fahne*, 2 June 1921.

[37] See, for example, Friesland's 'tour' in January 1922.

elected in two different ways. Some were directly elected by the Congress, but had to live where the leadership was resident, and they constituted the Zentrale. The others were also elected by the Congress, but from people nominated from the districts which they thus represented at the same time as they represented the Party as a whole. In this way, the Central Committee retained some features of the federal type of organisation which characterised the Spartacus League. Functionaries and delegates, whatever their functions, were closely dependent upon the base which elected them and had the right to recall them, and permanent Party workers were never in a majority in the executive organs outside the Central Committee.[38] The practice that meetings of full-timers or members actively debated great political problems was characteristic both of the Party and of the persistence of the Spartacist tradition.

In 1920, the Zentrale became aware of other important factors. It wanted to perfect its effectiveness by acquiring a more rational organisation, and, above all, a real professional apparatus. It divided itself into two working bodies, closely imitating the model recently adopted in Russia, a Political Bureau and an Organisation Bureau, each of which had in its ranks a member of the other to ensure permanent coordination of execution and decision.[39] In 1922, Ernst Meyer directed the former, and Wilhelm Pieck the latter.[40] They met three times a week.[41] The Zentrale created its own technical apparatus in the form of specialised departments, to which it recruited the best activists, such as the department for political work amongst women, led by Martha Arendsee; that for political work amongst children and adolescents, led by Edwin Hoernle;[42] that for local government affairs, led by Iwan Katz; that for the cooperatives, led by Karl Bittel; and that for work in the countryside, led by Heinrich Rau. Other services were not called departments but played an analogous role: education, led by the veteran Hermann Duncker; the Party press service, which was the ancestor of the well-known *agit-prop*, led by Alexander, who was known as Eduard Ludwig; and the legal bureau formed around Dr Felix Halle.[43]

---

[38] *Die Rote Fahne*, 4 December 1920.
[39] Ibid.
[40] Mujbegović, op. cit., p. 369.
[41] Ibid., p. 306, n. 8.
[42] Fischer, op. cit., pp. 172–3.
[43] Weber, *Die Wandlung des Deutschen Kommunismus*, Volume 2, op. cit., pp. 69, 76, 100, 150, 178, 253.

The trade-union department was by far the most important. It included a bureau for each of the trade-union sectors, led by the most experienced worker in each sector. The men who had proved themselves as mass leaders became professionals. It was led first by Richard Müller, Malzahn and Neumann, and then by Jakob Walcher and August Enderle. Melcher from Stuttgart headed the metalworkers' bureau, and Bachmann from Chemnitz headed the building workers' bureau.[44] Each bureau issued instructions to the Communist fractions in the corresponding unions on behalf of the department, and under the orders of the Zentrale.[45]

An apparatus of full-time professional workers was built up in this way. In 1921, the KPD had 223 full-timers, of whom 96 were 'political' and 127 'technical'; in 1922, there were 230, of whom 53 were 'political' and 177 'technical'.[46] The people who made up this staff did not all come from the same background. Some were old, experienced activists who carried political responsibilities, whilst others were not so well known, younger, brilliant or hard workers, who were essentially employed in technical duties which often also had a political purpose. By the side of the likes of Enderle, Hoernle, Melcher and Bachmann, veterans of at least a decade of political and industrial battles, we have from this time on to reckon with the role which was played in the corridors of the apparatus by little-known men or women, full-time technical personnel, such as Leo Flieg, the former leader of the Youth,[47] and Käthe Pohl,[48] who were secretaries to the Political Bureau, such as Fritz Heilmann, also a former member of the Youth, the Secretary to the Zentrale,[49] or again Heinz Neumann, who divided his activity between the press and the secret apparatus.[50] Such also, from 1921 onwards, was the role of the Russian Bolshevik Yelena Stasova, who came in May under the pseudonym of Lydia Lipnitskaya, acquired German nationality by a marriage of convenience, became Lydia Wilhelm, and was subsequently a member of the

---

[44] Ibid., pp. 64, 217.

[45] Fischer, op. cit., pp. 172–3.

[46] 'Kommunistische Bewegung in Deutschland 1921–1922', report by the KPD Zentrale to the ECCI, cited by Mujbegović, op. cit., p. 306, n. 8.

[47] Weber, Die Wandlung des Deutschen Kommunismus, Volume 2, op. cit., p. 121.

[48] She was the partner of August Kleine. Weber in 'KPD und Komintern', Viertel-jahrshefte für Zeitgeschichte, no. 2, April 1968, p. 185, n. 19, gives her the forename Katarina; in Die Wandlung des Deutschen Kommunismus, Volume 2, op. cit., p. 183, he calls her Lydia.

[49] Weber, Die Wandlung des Deutschen Kommunismus, Volume 2, op. cit., p. 157.

[50] Ibid., p. 233.

Organisation Bureau under the name of Herta.[51] This time saw the end of the tradition of the itinerant propagandists of the Spartacus period. Henceforth, they were incorporated into a new body of 'commissioners', whom the Zentrale sent into districts according to need, and who played there the role of travelling representatives.[52]

A tradition in the process of creation

The young Communist Party confronted the 'party-society' of old Social Democracy with its rituals, festivals, calendar and almost religious rhythm of life. It could not let itself appear as a party lacking a tradition, or without the apparatus necessary to build up around itself an ambiance, prestige, habits of thought, and ways of feeling. Already immediately after the unification and under pressure from Paul Levi, great efforts had been made in this direction.

The KPD had its ceremonies. Every year it organised big demonstrations to commemorate the assassination of Karl Liebknecht and Rosa Luxemburg, 'Karl and Rosa' as they were now called. The demonstrators carried huge portraits of their 'martyrs' – the celebrated drawing by Käthe Kollwitz of Liebknecht on his death-bed, with his head wrapped in a blood-stained bandage – chanted *Hoch* [up with] or *Nieder* [down with] three times in reply to the slogans pronounced by the group leaders, and sang the solemn *Martyrs' Song* in chorus. The First of May was the object of special preparation and presentation, but there were also the great 'International Days', the women's in March, and that of the youth in September. There were also 'Weeks'. The Communist tradition in many respects reproduced and continued that of Social Democracy, for example in the use of the term *Genosse* [comrade] between members, which was common to the two organisations.

The revolutionary song, whether a funeral hymn, a marching song or a song of battle, played a vital part in this tradition, as did the spoken chorus and the theatre. The tradition of the popular political song, the authentic revolutionary masses' song characteristic of the German workers' movement, was carried on in the twentieth century, and the KPD was one of those who benefited from it. Demonstrations and meetings began and ended with songs

---

[51] Brandt and Lowenthal, op. cit., p. 187; H. Stasova, 'Erinnerungen', *Beiträge zur Geschichte der deutschen Arbeiterbewegung*, no. 1, 1969, pp. 752ff.
[52] *Die Rote Fahne*, 2 June 1921.

in which the voices of the audience were guided and sustained by high quality choirs, made up of members and sympathisers, real detachments for agitation and propaganda.[53]

The Communist Youth had a particularly important place in this respect. At the end of 1922, it had 30,000 members between the ages of 14 and 25, organised in local groups, and from November whenever possible in workplace groups – electing their own leadership, the district and sub-district committees and the Central Committee.[54] As a Communist organisation, a member of the Communist Youth International, it sought to become a youth organisation and a mass organisation, and occupied itself with the leisure pursuits of young workers – sports, singing, theatre, long country walks, organised sung and spoken choruses. It also organised spectacular gatherings and marches, in an effort to group together available young workers and unemployed, and make them into fighters and cadres for the Party. A Communist Youth Congress was a genuine spectacle in itself, as is shown in the account by Manfred Uhlemann of the opening ceremony of the Seventh Congress of the Communist Youth on 31 March 1923, in Chemnitz:

---

[53] In the Communist repertory, alongside songs of an international character such as the *Internationale* itself, the *Song of the Survivors*, the *Song of the Partisans*, or *Warszawianka* – the German version of which, according to oral tradition, was written by Luxemburg – there were also traditional songs of the German workers' movement, some of which were to find a place in the repertory of the international Communist movement, for example the famous and already well-established *Brüder, zur Sonne, zur Freiheit!* – translated into French under the title *Marchons au pas, camarades!* – but also recent songs set to traditional tunes – often popular melodies or soldiers' songs – with words to fit the occasion inspired by contemporary episodes of the revolutionary struggle. *Im Januar um Mitternacht*, to the tune of a soldiers' song, evoked the struggles around *Vorwärts* in January 1919; the *Büxensteinlied*, to a tune of similar origin, referred to the battle around a publishing-house. *Auf, auf zum Kampf*, to a tune popular amongst soldiers, referred to the murder of Liebknecht and Luxemburg. The Red Army of the Ruhr in 1920 popularised *Schon seit langen, langen Jahren*, unpublished words and music by unknown authors, and *Die Rote Armee*, to a tune from the Russian Civil War which was also the basis for the Austrian Communist song *Wir sind die Arbeiter von Wien*. The Leuna struggles in March 1921 inspired *Bei Leuna sind wir gefallen*, adopting what was doubtless a popular tune in Bavaria in 1919. Inge Lammel ('Zur Rolle und Bedeuting des Arbeiterliedes', *Beiträge zur Geschichte der deutschen Arbeiterbewegung*, no. 3, 1962, pp. 726–42) has shown that two of the most famous songs of the KPD in 1923–33, *Es zog ein Rotgardist hinaus* and *Auf, junger Tambour, schlage ein*, originated in the struggles against the Kapp Putsch in the Ruhr in 1920, and in the Bavarian Revolution in 1919 respectively. In 1923 were to appear *Das ist die Rote Garde*, the song of the Milan strikers in 1919, adapted by Alfred Kurella, which became the anthem of the 'proletarian hundreds', as well as *Hunger in allen Gassen*, to a soldiers' tune, and *Die Rote Garde nennt man uns*, to the tune of a very old popular song, which entered the workers' repertory around 1900 (see in particular *Lieder des Rotenkämpferbundes*, no. 8 of the series *Das Lied im Kampf geboren*).

[54] M. Uhlemann, *Arbeiterjugend gegen Cuno und Poincaré*, East Berlin, 1960, p. 39.

> The inauguration ceremony . . . in the marble palace at Chemnitz was to
> show clearly the fire burned in the young men and women workers who
> came from every region of Germany. The delegations were welcomed by
> the workers of this industrial city, and came forward to the sound of their
> battle-songs, unfurling their red banners, into the huge, magnificently-
> decorated hall. After the triumphal march from *Aïda*, the *Robespierre Overture*,
> the recital of Gorky's *Song of the Stormy Petrel* and the oath of the Red Army
> soldier by the spoken chorus of the Communist Youth of Chemnitz, everyone
> stood to sing *The Internationale*. . . . The Congress delegates welcomed the
> representative of the Communist Youth International by singing *The March
> of the Red Guards*.[55]

The Communist Youth served the Party as both an elementary and high
school. It welcomed adolescents, and sometimes even children, and quite
young men received their apprenticeship in leadership in its ranks. Workers
or secondary-school students joined at 16 or even 15 years of age, as Albert
Norden did. Young people not yet 20 years old had responsibilities at
the local or regional level. The building-worker Fritz Grosse was district
secretary in Erzgebirge-Vogtland at 17. The metalworker Häbich was 18 when
he became an official in the Communist Youth in Frankfurt. The student Franz
Rotter (known as Krause) was 17 when he became the secretary of the Baden
district.[56]

This system enabled the Party to discover talented youth at an early age.
Able young workers could progress quickly up the hierarchy, and get their
apprenticeship in the responsibilities and tasks of leadership that the 'adult'
organisation could not provide directly. The young toolmaker Anton Saefkow
joined the Communist Youth at 17, entered its central leadership at 19, and
the Central Committee at 21. In 1922, an almost total renewal of the national
leadership took place. The generation educated during the War and immediately
after it by Willi Münzenberg – who were now between 20 and 30 years old
– progressed into the Party ranks, and there took on important responsibilities.
This was the case with Heilmann, Otto Unger and Leo Flieg. A new generation
took over the Youth leadership at the national level. Fritz Gäbler was President

---

[55] Ibid., pp. 67–8.
[56] Weber, *Die Wandlung des Deutschen Kommunismus*, Volume 2, op. cit., pp. 144, 147, 194, 236.

of the Communist Youth until May 1923, when he was 26; his successor was Heinz Pütz aged 25. Conrad Blenkle was Secretary at 23. Hermann Jakobs, a left-winger who was editor of *Die Junge Garde*, was 21 in 1922.[57] The Communist Youth were much fewer in numbers than the Party itself, but nonetheless played an important role, serving as a nursery for its cadres.

The influence of the Party

The extent of the Party's influence cannot easily be measured. The votes won in the elections enable us only to point to a ratio between the number of members and voters, which in some regions exceeded one in 20 or even one in 40. But we would need also to know how many votes were cast and the percentage of Communist votes in the factory council elections and the contests in the trade unions in order to establish an accurate idea of its influence.

The press was one of the Party's principal means of building its influence, and its print-runs provide valuable information. But it suffered from enormous difficulties in this period because of the economic crisis and inflation. In 1922, *Die Rote Fahne* considerably increased the number of its subscribers and doubled its print-run, but at the same time it suffered a deficit which it did not have when it began.[58] The Party had at its command a total of 38 daily papers – 17 of which were just regional editions – for which it received in all 338,626 subscriptions.[59] They were all fed by the Party's central press service, reproduced the same editorials, and made use of the same despatches. There were only 3,000 subscriptions for the party's theoretical journal, *Die Internationale*. The publication intended for the trade-union fractions, *Der Kommunistische Gerwerkschafter*, had a print-run of 38,000, and the figures for the women's weekly, *Die Kommunistin*, the peasants' newspaper *Der Pflug* (until it was suspended in 1922), and the bulletin on municipal affairs, *Kommune*,

---

[57] Ibid., pp. 78, 121, 130, 157, 171, 250, 267, 329.

[58] The monthly subscription – the only one possible in this situation – had risen from 10 marks to 300 marks in a year (*Correspondance Internationale*, no. 81, 25 October 1922, p. 624).

[59] Ibid. In *Jahrbuch für Politik-Wirtschaft Arbeiterbewegung 1922–1923*, op. cit., Pieck referred to 33 papers with 395,000 subscribers. The main party papers were *Hamburger Volkszeitung*, *Ruhr-Echo* (Essen), *Klassenkampf* (Halle), *Der Kämpfer* (Chemnitz), *Volkswille* (Suhl), *Sozialistische Republik* (Cologne), *Bergische Volksstimme* (Remscheid), and the numerous papers entitled *Arbeiterzeitung*.

were 29,000, 5,000 and 4,500 respectively. The magazines for children, *Das proletarische Kind*, and for adolescents, *Der Junge Genosse*, with a print-run of 30,000, did not have the same object as *Die Junge Garde*, the agitational organ of the Communist Youth.[60]

Another source of the influence of the KPD lay in its elected representatives. It had only 14 deputies in the Reichstag after 12 had left with Levi and, like him, had refused to resign their seats. But the majority had been elected on a USPD ticket before the birth of the VKPD, which in principle they represented.[61] The KPD had 66 deputies in the different Landtags, and 12,014 municipal councillors in 420 cities. It had a clear majority in 80 municipal councils, and was the largest single party in 170 others.[62] All these elected representatives were closely supervised and subject to a strict fraction discipline in the pure Social-Democratic tradition. They were both propagandists and agitators through their speeches in the elective assemblies, and tireless canvassers who attempted to win for the Party the support of the workers in whose interests they spoke.

The KPD's strength in the trade unions was constantly growing. It continued to play a role in the unions which were not members of the ADGB, such as the Union of Manual and Intellectual Workers which was formed in September 1921 through the fusion of the Free Workers Union (Gelsenkirchen), which had arisen out of the strikes in the Ruhr in 1919, with the small Union of Manual and Intellectual Workers. In 1922, it had some 80,000 members, essentially in the Ruhr and Upper Silesia, and above all sought joint action with the ADGB. Despite having been under strong syndicalist influence, the union had a Communist leadership, and in general followed the line of the party.[63] It joined the Red International of Labour Unions in 1922. The Union of Ship's Carpenters had written into its statutes its organic links with the KPD and the International.[64] The seamen's union which had been built in the ports and docks, also was a 'red' union which belonged to the RILU, and it was led by the Communist Walter.[65] We should add to these organisations the important sectors of workers who had been driven out of the 'free'

---

[60] *Correspondance Internationale*, no. 81, 25 October 1922, p. 624.
[61] Fischer, op. cit., p. 220.
[62] *Correspondance Internationale*, no. 81, 25 October 1922, p. 624.
[63] Raase, op. cit., p. 22, n. 34.
[64] Ibid., p. 98.
[65] Weber, *Die Wandlung des Deutschen Kommunismus*, Volume 2, op. cit., p. 336.

confederation with their leaders, like the 6,000 building workers who in Saxony remained behind Bachmann, Brandler and Heckert.[66]

Much more significant was the progress which the Communists made in the reformist trade unions. Despite the operation of a system of selecting delegates which favoured the Majority socialists, the Communists ensured that they were delegated to all the union congresses through the organisation and activity of substantial revolutionary minorities which they organised. At the National Congress of the ADGB, of a total of 694 delegates, there were 90 Communists, of whom 48 were metalworkers.[67] Despite the wave of expulsions which followed both the campaign in January 1921 for the *Open Letter* and the March Action, the Communists enjoyed a strong presence in all the big unions.[68] This explains why there were 46 militants amongst the 216 delegates at the railwaymen's congress, 35 out of 305 at that of the transport workers, and 41 out of 305 at that of the local government workers.[69] The Communists had clear majorities in 60 of the local trade-union councils, some in important centres of the working class such as Remscheid, Sollingen and Hanau, to name but a few.[70] Four hundred Communists held trade-union positions at least at workplace level, and their control extended to 997 trade-union organisations,[71] including the metalworkers' union branches at Stuttgart, Hanau and Friedrichshafen.[72]

The Communists were still clearly in a minority, but they were already candidates for political leadership in the unions, challenging the reformist leaders. Their militant activity was not confined to manual workers alone.

---

[66] Report to the RILU Congress, *Correspondance Internationale*, no. 23, 11 October 1922, p. 2.

[67] Ibid.

[68] Heckert wrote: 'In 1921, the Communist who was a member of a "cell" was simply expelled from the union. This year, the Congress of the German trade unions recognised, *de facto* if not *de jure*, the Communist fractions.' (*Correspondance Internationale*, no. 75, 4 October 1922.)

[69] Ibid.

[70] Some of the Communists' positions in the unions were due to the popularity of individual activists and, in a certain way, to local conditions. In Hanau, Karl Rehbein was already a Spartacist when he was elected as Secretary of the metalworkers' union. He retained this position until 1933, particularly during 1929–33, in which he left the KPD and returned to the SPD. He was deported to Dachau. He was proclaimed 'father of the city' by all the parties, including the KPD, and elected mayor until his death. The Communist Heinrich Galm had a similar standing at Offenbach. He was the son of an old Social-Democratic activist, and spokesman for the leather workers.

[71] Fischer, op. cit., p. 223.

[72] Weber, *Die Wandlung des Deutschen Kommunismus*, Volume 2, op. cit., pp. 254, 295.

They worked amongst teachers, either in the official union, or in the sections of an independent union, according to local conditions. They recruited teachers in primary and high schools, and even lecturers in universities[73] – the best-known were the philosopher Karl Korsch and the ancient historian Arthur Rosenberg[74] – and had a real influence over the lower ranks of university teachers, from amongst whom some full-timers were recruited, including the ex-serviceman Richard Sorge.[75] After great efforts, they finally succeeded in developing their political work in the student milieu, and constructed cells, the Communist student fractions, or *Kostufra*, and these too supplied cadres to the Communist Youth and to the KPD.[76]

The Party made a great effort to raise the political level of its members. Its units at every level met at least once a week, and general meetings were frequent. From 1921, systematic efforts were developed to educate the members theoretically and politically. In 1922, two central schools were held, one lasting three months, and the other one month. They were attended by 74 members, selected at the recommendation of the districts. Seven of these formed their own 'activist's school', and four travelling instructors serviced the analogous courses which were organised in the 16 districts which lacked the means to provide themselves with instructors for education.[77] In 1923, the Party was able, despite all kinds of difficulties, to organise in Jena a two-month school in which 32 students took part, chosen by the Central Committee, and all having experience of struggle, with 14 activists from other countries.[78]

---

[73] In 1924, Ausländer was to lead the teachers' fraction (ibid., p. 64).
[74] Ibid., pp. 192, 269.
[75] N. Chatel and A. Guérin, *Camarade Sorge*, Paris, 1965, p. 10.
[76] Weber, *Die Wandlung des Deutschen Kommunismus*, Volume 2, op. cit., pp. 171, 194, 233.
[77] *Correspondance Internationale*, no. 81, 25 October 1922, p. 624. The Leipzig Congress was to vote to organise evening classes throughout all Party bodies (*Bericht über die Verhandlungen des III (8) Parteitages der KPD*, op. cit., p. 429).
[78] G. Schumann, 'L'École communiste de Iéna', *Correspondance Internationale*, no. 74, 18 September 1923, p. 561. The programme of this two-month course was comprehensive. The economic section included the pre-capitalist economic forms, theories of value, surplus-value and the cost of production, capitalism and imperialism, the global economic situation (war, crises, social change and the reformist and Communist programmes). The historical section included study of the history of communism and of proletarian struggles up to the nineteenth century, the workers' movement from 1800 to 1914, the formation of the KPD, the Communist International, the revolutionary movement in Russia, and the development of Soviet Russia. The political section, which was regarded as the most important, had as its section headings Marxism, historical materialism, the conquest of power, the workers' government, and the

This summary picture calls for several remarks. In the first place, the Party press was hardly read at all outside its ranks. This phenomenon was especially clear in Rhineland-Westphalia, where the Party had 52,000 members and nine daily papers, with a total print-run of no more than 64,000 copies.[79] The leadership was aware of this deficiency. In order to remedy it, 'central' leaflets were regularly distributed, but it is hard to measure the response to them, because they were not sold but given away. In all, throughout 1922, 13 of these leaflets were produced in connexion with the Party's campaigns, in runs of between 1.4 and 4 million copies. In September 1922, the rising cost of paper forced the Party to produce smaller editions, which were printed in runs of between 500,000 and 1.4 million.[80] This was really a very low figure when we reflect that not every leaflet that is handed out actually is read. We have indeed to admit that the written propaganda of the Communists reached only a small proportion of the German workers. Leaflets and papers were more instruments for organising members and close sympathisers than tools for agitation and general propaganda.

Other remarks should be made about the education and training of members. The number who had passed through the courses at the central Party school in one year was extremely low – a total of 74 in a party of 250,000. Similarly, the theoretical organ of the Party was little read, despite being of interest to a Communist; only one per cent of the Party's members subscribed to it. No doubt, to be sure, we have there a proof of the predominantly working-class character of the Party. But it also confirms an occasional admission by the Party leaders: the polemics at a high theoretical level were followed and understood by only a few politically-educated cadres, amongst a large mass of members who were little interested in the theoretical discussions, and who were satisfied to follow in the internal debates their local 'chiefs' who were their organisers and leaders in the day-to-day struggle.[81]

---

dictatorship of the proletariat. Lastly, in the section entitled 'Communist Practice', were included 'specialisations', Party organisation, factory committees and control committees, cooperatives, the Reichstag, the Landtag, municipal councils, the press, the youth movement, etc. The students had 30 hours of classes a week, including four hours every morning, as well as 12 hours of practical work in smaller groups. The outbreak of the Cuno strike was to stop the completion of the course, when the students insisted on returning to their posts.

[79] Stoecker, op. cit., p. 347. The Central Committee meeting on 16 May 1923 was to discuss the need to increase the number of readers (*Die Rote Fahne*, 17 May 1923).

[80] Fischer, op. cit., p. 220.

[81] It is characteristic that each 'tendency' had its own clear territorial base; each district, without exception, aligned itself with its leaders.

Even though, in numbers, the KPD was the leading Communist Party in the world outside Russia, its members seem to have been relatively isolated in the working class. They were, to be sure, a coherent, active minority, but their influence appears to have spread widely amongst the politically organised workers only where they were able to organise or to lead trade-union struggles. Personalities counted for a very great deal; it was in everyday life, in the practice of the class struggle, that the influence of the Party could be marked, much more than through expounding their conception of the world, and through raising the level of workers' consciousness, which, as the Bolshevik example had shown, required numerous working-class cadres to be formed. From this viewpoint, the tactic of the united front was a progressive factor, and even represented a qualitative change, as it enabled the Communist activists to become organising cadres of the working class, whereas until then they had been no more than intelligent commentators upon events, or seemingly systematic critics of other political currents.

The reunification of Social Democracy through the return of the remaining Independents to 'the old firm' was in many ways negative for the KPD, but benefited the Communists insofar as the Independents were accustomed to joint activities with them, and were not systematically hostile to them. Within the newly unified SPD, they were a link with the mass of Social-Democratic workers. They also helped to facilitate the united front, the first steps of which were possible only through the work of organising cadres outside the KPD. In fact, only the existence of a serious left wing in the SPD enabled the Communists to endow their new central slogan of a workers' government with concrete reality.[82]

---

[82] This left wing developed essentially in Saxony. It rested on a solid working-class basis in the Zwickau region, around Max Seydewitz, and particularly around the old textile workers' leader, Georg Graupe (Krusch, op. cit., pp. 95–7). The historians in East Germany in the 1960s drew a distinction between two currents in the Social-Democratic Left, the 'Saxon' Left of Zeigner, Graupe, Seydewitz, etc, and that of Levi and Dissmann, which they regarded as a 'fake Left'.

Chapter Thirty-Three
The Workers' Government

The call for the united front of workers' organisations for the struggle against capitalism and for a workers' government was conceived with the idea of opening up perspectives for settling the question of power. Communists understood that, although the dictatorship of the proletariat was the ultimate aim, the slogan of a workers' government was at the core of the united-front strategy, which was intended to win the masses to the Communists' programme.

In Germany, the problem was posed in terms of parliamentary majorities, which represented a serious difficulty in relation to the theory of the state and to the traditional Communist hostility to parliamentarism. Together, the Communists, the Independents and the Social Democrats were not far from having an absolute majority in several Landtags, and a majority could not be ruled out after future elections to the Reichstag. If the KPD worked with the other socialist parties, it could not refuse to support or participate in socialist-led governments which excluded the representatives of the bourgeois parties and included in their programme the demands of the programme of the workers' united front. The question which Legien posed in March 1920 after the Kapp Putsch, and which had been set aside without proper discussion, now re-emerged following the turn in the Communist International in 1921.

The draft programme

The Zentrale considered that the Party required a new programme, which would draw on the experiences of the years of struggle, and would replace the Spartacus League's programme adopted at the Party's Founding Congress. A special commission comprising Brandler, Wilhelm Koenen, Ludwig, Zetkin and Thalheimer was charged with drafting it.[1] The draft was presented to the Central Committee on 15–16 October 1922, and adopted by 24 votes to 23, with the Left voting against what they regarded as an opportunist and revisionist document. The Party leaders then agreed to submit it for discussion to the Communist International.[2]

The draft declared that the Revolution and the seizure of power were imminent: 'Communism is no longer an affair of forecast and of the distant future. It is a reality and of immediate concern. Its reign has already begun.' From this point of view, the Russian experience was to serve as a guide. The October Revolution 'in all its stages' was 'a treasure-house of political strategy, a stimulating source of revolutionary energy, and a wealth of experiences of socialist construction'.[3]

The authors of the draft took the view that the period of the upward development of capitalism had finally ended when capital passed over from its pre-monopolistic to its current, imperialist phase. The historic significance of the Russian Revolution was that it showed that socialism was the sole road to salvation for humanity, threatened as it was by imperialist barbarism. In the struggle for socialism, the working class constituted the revolutionary class. Consequently, the working class was to lead the struggle of all the exploited against capitalist rule. The role of the Communists was to lead the working class with the aim of uniting its vanguard against the bourgeoisie because, as the *Communist Manifesto* had already pointed out, 'the communists have no interests separate from those of the proletariat as a whole'. They only formed its vanguard, the mission of which was to win the majority of the proletariat for Communism. The Communists were to struggle to win the masses without neglecting any of the means available to them:

> In order to win the majority of the working class, the Communist Party
> must make use of all the possibilities opened by bourgeois democracy,

---

[1] *Die Rote Fahne*, 20 October 1922.
[2] Krusch, *Um die Einheitsfront und eine Arbeiterregierung*, op. cit., p. 38.
[3] *Inprekorr*, 7 October 1922, pp. 1297, 1307.

namely parliament, municipal councils and administrations. It must seek
to win the proletarian mass organisations (trade unions and cooperatives)
in order to transform them from being supporters of mere reforms into a
solid phalanx that can attack the rule of the bourgeoisie.[4]

The aim of the Communists was to take the proletariat forward to establishing
its dictatorship and constructing a 'socialist unified republic of councils' in
Germany. During a period in which the immediate struggle for conciliar
power was not on the order of the day, a situation that had effectively existed
since the defeat in January 1919, the Communists' duty was to struggle to
transform the existing relation of social forces in order to recreate the
preconditions of this struggle. This was the object of what the draft programme,
taking up a favourite idea of Brandler's, called 'transitional slogans' which
the Communists were to elaborate and promote, in order to be in a position
'to base themselves on all the partial struggles and the partial aims' which
corresponded to the situation of the broad masses, 'so as to raise the level of
their consciousness'.[5] The programme emphasised:

> At a moment when the spontaneous movement of the mass of the proletariat
> has reached a certain level and scale, in which its opposition to the bourgeoisie
> and to the workers' leaders allied to them is growing stronger, but in which,
> however, the working class is not yet ready in its majority to leave the
> framework of bourgeois democracy, the slogan of a workers' government
> forms the appropriate means by which to achieve a new stage in separating
> the broad proletarian masses from the bourgeoisie, and a new point of
> departure on a higher level for its movement towards the proletarian
> dictatorship.[6]

Together with the political aspects of the call for a workers' government, there
were transitional demands which outlined measures that the masses were to
win by their own struggles, prior to the implementation of the dictatorship
of the proletariat, and which would be part of the programme of a workers'
government: the confiscation of real values, and majority participation by the
state in every firm; the unionisation or trustification of industry under workers'
control through the factory committees; the abolition of banking, technical
and commercial secrecy; the establishment of a state monopoly of the food

---

[4] Ibid., p. 1305.
[5] Ibid., pp. 1306–7.
[6] Ibid., p. 1307.

supply, and the introduction of rationing under workers' control; and a state monopoly of external trade and of banking under workers' control, exercised particularly by bank employees.[7]

These measures constituted a kind of state capitalism and did not go beyond the capitalist framework, but they would be a powerful element in radicalising and mobilising the masses, at the same time as they aroused resistance from the bourgeoisie, who themselves would take the initiative towards civil war. The draft programme spelt out: 'In the course of this struggle, the workers' government will be obliged, in order to survive, to overcome its own contradictory nature, to break up effectively the machine of the bourgeois state, and to place state power in the hands of the workers' councils.'[8]

Deepening or revision?

On 10 October 1921, immediately before the Central Committee met, the leadership of the KPD received from the ECCI a letter which sharply posed the question of the workers' government, and called for concrete answers. The ECCI suggested that the KPD should organise primarily around the ADGB's demand for the seizure of 'gold values', as this could create a campaign in which the workers' organisations could unite. The ECCI also called on the KPD to include this in its perspective for a workers' government, made up of representatives of the workers' parties and trade unions, which would place this demand in its programme. The ECCI believed that the KPD should be prepared to support such a government if it undertook to work to disarm the armed counter-revolutionary groups and to reorganise the Reichswehr under the control of the trade unions.[9]

The KPD leadership, and not only its left wing, continued to be reserved.[10] Soon, the ministerial crisis opened by the resignation of the Wirth cabinet was to pose the question concretely. The SPD fought for a grand coalition. The bourgeois centre parties tried to broaden the coalition towards the Right. The Zentrale drafted an appeal to the German workers which declared that no workers' party could assume the responsibility of helping even indirectly

---

[7] Ibid.

[8] Ibid.

[9] Cited in A. Reisberg, 'Zur Genesis der Lösung Arbeiterregierung', *Beiträge zur Geschichte der deutschen Arbeiterbewegung*, no. 6, 1965, p. 1031.

[10] Reisberg (ibid., p. 1034) mentions the fears of Meyer that they might find themselves again becoming a 'loyal opposition'.

to bring the spokesmen of heavy industry and the banks into the government. At the same time, it proposed a programme of struggle to include the seizure of real values;[11] the defence of the eight-hour day, the right to strike and to unionise; the disarmament and dissolution of the counter-revolutionary armed formations; the formation of workers' self-defence groups; and the purging of the state administration, the police, the army and the courts of all monarchist and counter-revolutionary elements.

The Zentrale explained that such a programme could never in fact be the work of a government which emerged from parliamentary combinations, but only that of 'a government which rested on the solid extra-parliamentary power of the proletariat'.[12] The Majority socialists and the Independents, who felt threatened and wanted to drive the Communists into a corner, then asked the KPD whether it would be ready to enter a 'purely socialist government'; they received a negative answer, and immediately broke off the discussions.[13]

However, the Communist leaders recognised the contradictory character of their position, which called on other workers' organisations to form a government in which they refused in advance to take part. An editorial in *Die Rote Fahne* explained that the Communists, who had already undertaken to confine themselves to 'loyal opposition' to 'a purely socialist government', would be ready to change their attitude if the latter seriously entered into a struggle against the bourgeoisie.[14]

The Zentrale then agreed to study every aspect of the question, and to submit to the Central Committee theses on the question of a workers' government, which would be published in the Party press before the meeting.[15] The proposed text set the tone for the Party's approach to the slogan of the workers' government; it started by observing that the proletariat could not undertake the struggle for power without previously having been liberated from its 'bourgeois-democratic illusions'.

---

[11] The call for the seizure of real values [*Erfassung der Sachwerte*] meant that part of the nation's real wealth – land, buildings, industrial plant, etc. – that was not affected by inflationary erosion, would be handed over to the state, thus giving the government the means to balance its budget and discharge its international liabilities. [Translator's note.]

[12] *Die Rote Fahne*, 25 October 1921.

[13] According to the report by Ernst Meyer to the Central Committee meeting of 16–17 November, quoted by Reisberg, *Lenin und die Aktionseinheit*, op. cit., p. 109.

[14] *Die Rote Fahne*, 26 October 1921.

[15] *Die Rote Fahne*, 12 November 1921.

The theses reflected all the past and present contradictions weighing on the Party, the sharp division between, on the one hand, its earlier condemnation of the declaration of 'loyal opposition' and recognition of the danger of compromise with the right-wing leaders of Social Democracy, and, on the other, the apparent logic which led from the strategy of the united front of the workers' organisations to the call for a government composed of these organisations which would fight for the realisation of their demands.

These contradictions revealed themselves in carefully balanced phrases, such as that which declared that a workers' government could 'form a bastion of the bourgeoisie against the proletarian masses', and another which said that a workers' government would be able to end the domination of the monopolies and in this way be a step forward for the workers in a situation in which the dictatorship of the proletariat and conciliar power were not on the agenda. The conclusion was cautious; the Communists would not oppose, and would indeed assist, the formation of a purely socialist government, to the extent that forming such a government partly depended upon them. They unreservedly supported socialist governments in the *Länder* as means to mobilise the masses:

> To the extent that the election of a purely bourgeois government, a coalition government or a 'purely socialist government' depends on the Communists, they will promote the election of a 'purely socialist government'. They will be obliged to support it in every measure which it takes in the interest of the working class.[16]

But the theses categorically excluded communist participation in such governments, believing that 'they could only play their revolutionary role if the Communists remained outside, and worked to push them forward by their criticism'.[17]

Here, too, the initiative was to come from the ECCI. On 7 November 1921, Radek sent to *Die Rote Fahne* an article devoted to this question, in which he broadly outlined a campaign for a workers' government in Germany. This call was 'the single practicable way to win the majority of the working class to the idea of the dictatorship of the proletariat'. The Communists were to elaborate a 'transitional programme', which could serve to move the masses from struggle to defend their immediate interests to understanding of the

---

[16] Ibid.
[17] Ibid.

need to struggle for power. In such a perspective, the formation of a workers' government would crown the work. For Radek, it was 'the concretisation of the tactic of the *Open Letter* in a new situation', and also 'the realisation of the slogan of the Third Comintern Congress: "To the Masses!"'[18]

On 10 November 1921, Radek addressed to the Zentrale a letter in which he attacked the conceptions inspiring its theses as 'schematic'. In so far as it was now clear that between the existing situation and the conciliar republic there would clearly be a period of transition, it was necessary to admit that the most efficacious form of transition was the workers' government, the intermediary stage between the dictatorship of the bourgeoisie and that of the proletariat. The Communists' promotion of the call for a workers' government did not in any way contradict their ultimate aim of a conciliar republic. On the contrary, it was the best means by which to approach and prepare for it. A Communist Party would actively use all its influence to help form a workers' government. Therefore, the Party must undertake in advance to support loyally a workers' government once it was established. Going further, Radek objected to the conception which was expressed in the Zentrale's theses stating that the KPD would not participate in a workers' government. He wrote:

> The Communist Party can join any government that is willing to struggle against capitalism. . . . The Party is not opposed in principle to participating in such a government. Of course, for its own part, it takes its stand on the basis of a conciliar government, but that does not indicate the road along which the working class is to advance towards a conciliar government. . . . The participation of the Communist Party in such a government would therefore depend on the specifics of the concrete situation.[19]

He suggested that the KPD should work out theses which were not 'Ninety Per Cent No!', and should give a positive response on this question, not 'tiresomely repeating old principles and old considerations', but taking a new step forward: 'This cannot be done unless the masses see that *we want to change things in the way that is possible today*, that is, not through propaganda about what divides us from them, but by realising and deepening what the masses believe to be a possible way out of this situation.'[20]

[18] *Die Rote Fahne*, 16 November 1921.
[19] Quoted in Reisberg, *Lenin und die Aktionseinheit*, op. cit., p. 115.
[20] Ibid., p. 116.

Radek made it clear that he was writing in his personal capacity, because he had not been able to consult Zinoviev, who was away, although he had discussed the matter with Lenin in the presence of Pieck, Heckert and Brandler. Lenin had agreed, with the reservation that he was not well informed and had not heard the counter-arguments.[21]

In the end, it was Radek's position which the Zentrale was to defend before the Central Committee,[22] where a lively debate developed, mainly stimulated by the opposition from Fischer. She vigorously criticised the notion of campaigning for economic demands, and counterposed to it the need of a political campaign for a 'socialist government', which she regarded as synonymous with the dictatorship of the proletariat: 'It is because today we cannot say "republic of councils", and even "political councils", that we have to clothe our Communist political slogans under the form of a "workers' government", which in fact means the same thing.'[23]

The Zentrale's new motion, which defined the slogan of a workers' government, was adopted by 31 votes to 15. It emphasised the need to support such a government, but did not mention any possible participation in it.[24] In fact, a turn was being made. On 8 December 1921, the Zentrale's circular no. 2 developed the slogan as it was subsequently presented in the Party's propaganda and agitational work:

> The drive towards the united front must find its political outlet in a socialist workers' government, which must replace the coalition government. . . . The KPD must say to the workers that it is ready to call for the formation of a socialist workers' government by all parliamentary and extra-parliamentary means, that it is likewise ready to join such a government, if it has the guarantee that this government represents the interests and the demands of the working class against the bourgeoisie, that it will really seize real values, will prosecute the Kappists, and free the revolutionary workers from jail, etc.[25]

On that very day, the striking railway workers adopted the slogan. It was taken up by the National Congress of Factory Councils, and defended everywhere by Communist activists as the key practical demand, the

---

[21] Ibid.
[22] Ibid., p. 117.
[23] Quoted in ibid., p. 118.
[24] *Die Rote Fahne*, 22 November 1921.
[25] Quoted in Reisberg, 'Zur Genesis der Lösung Arbeiterregierung', op. cit., p. 1038.

manifestation of the strategy of the united front on the governmental level, and the equivalent of the Bolsheviks' call in 1917 for the left-wing parties to break from their coalition with the bourgeoisie.

The problem of the socialist governments in the regions

However, the Communists took great care to stress that the workers' government must rest on an extra-parliamentary working-class base, and not on a simple parliamentary coalition. A practical problem was then raised in respect of the attitude to adopt when the workers' parties won a clear majority in a Landtag. Had they to deny the name of the workers' government to a 'purely socialist' government formed on the basis of the results of democratic elections, but without the appearance of the workers' councils for which a workers' government should clear the way? Should they support such governments? How could they justify to the workers, and particularly to the workers who wanted socialist governments, a refusal to vote for such a government if their action meant that the SPD joined a bourgeois coalition, or simply gave the power to the bourgeois parties? This question was posed very sharply in Saxony and Thuringia.

Already in November 1920, the electors in Saxony had sent a 'workers' majority to the Landtag: 49 'workers' deputies, of whom 27 were Majority Social Democrats, 13 were Independents and nine were Communists, against 47 deputies from bourgeois parties.[26] At that time, the left Social Democrats proposed a coalition government of the three workers' parties, but the KPD refused to join it on the basis of an experience which, it said, since 1918 had taught it that 'what was supposed to be a workers' government did nothing but look after the interests of the capitalist class'.[27] At the same time, it was concerned not to appear to be responsible for the return of the bourgeois parties to government in the region, and it instructed its deputies to vote for a socialist Prime Minister.[28] The situation was all the more awkward in that the Social-Democratic government in Saxony clearly declared that it would refuse to implement the measures which the Communists had demanded,[29]

---

[26] Krusch, op. cit., p. 65.
[27] Quoted in *Die Internationale*, no. 21, 1922, p. 472.
[28] *Die Rote Fahne*, 9, 10 December 1920.
[29] Reisberg, 'Zur Genesis der Lösung Arbeiterregierung', op. cit., p. 1031.

and thus the KPD had quite consciously given its votes to an opponent of the programme of the united front.

The question was posed much more sharply in June 1921. The KPD found itself faced with an unpleasant choice when the Social-Democratic government in Saxony proposed economic measures which it found unacceptable. The Communists could vote for the measures in order to keep the Social Democrats in office: if they voted against them, the government would fall, and could be replaced by a more reactionary one.[30] The Zentrale and the Central Committee were divided, with Ernst Meyer opposing Jakob Walcher, a supporter of 'conditional support', and could not reach a decision.[31] In the end, the Communist deputies in the Saxon Landtag settled the question by bailing out the Social-Democratic government.[32]

In September 1921, the elections to the Landtag in Thuringia gave a majority to the three workers' parties, and thus posed the same problem. The Independents proposed forming a workers' government. The KPD Political Bureau decided that its deputies would vote for a Social-Democratic or an Independent Prime Minister, and that they would support any workers' government which conducted 'a consistent working-class policy'.[33] The Zentrale and the Central Committee agreed. But they had to argue for their stance against strong opposition from the leading Communists in Thuringia, who refused either to endorse the policies of the Social Democrats or to help them become the government.[34] The KPD leftists fiercely opposed the leadership's policies, and regarded them as a first step towards a neo-revisionist slide into the opportunist conception of a parliamentary road to socialism. The perspectives of the Zentrale and the majority of the leadership actually went further, as W. Tür showed when he wrote: 'The workers' government is fully realisable in Germany. It is true that the workers' parties do not currently have a majority; nonetheless they could govern with the support of the masses, and the dissolution of parliament, followed by new elections, would certainly give them a majority.'[35]

The Landtag elections in Saxony in 1922 made a principled position absolutely necessary. Out of 96 elected deputies, there were 46 from bourgeois

---

[30] Ibid., p. 1032.
[31] Cited in ibid., p. 1032.
[32] Ibid., p. 1033.
[33] Cited in ibid.
[34] Cited in ibid.
[35] *Correspondance internationale*, no. 94, 6 December 1922, p. 716.

parties – 19 National Germans, 19 People's Party and 8 Democrats. The SPD won 40 deputies with a million votes, and the KPD won 10 deputies with 268,000 votes.[36] The Communists and Social Democrats together had a clear majority. Under the pressure of their left wing, led by Dr Erich Zeigner and the trade unionist Georg Graupe, the Social Democrats asked the Communists to form with them the government that they advocated in their programme.[37]

The question was sharply debated in the corridors and the commissions during the Fourth Comintern Congress. A news agency report announced that the Saxon government had been reconstructed, and that Brandler had joined it. The German delegation met, and Thalheimer declared that the decision was correct and inevitable. The Left protested. Forty-eight hours later, it was learned that the only subject which had been discussed was that of possible future entry by the Communists into the Saxon government. The discussion began again. This time it was known that the Social Democrats stubbornly rejected two points of the Communists' programme, the arming of the workers and the calling of a congress of factory councils in Saxony. Thalheimer and Meyer proposed that the Communists enter the government without insisting upon these two conditions. Ulbricht declared that, in Saxony, the slogan 'arm the workers' was meaningless, because every worker had a rifle. The delegation declared in favour of deleting these two points, and forming a socialist-Communist government, with four of the Left voting against.[38] At that point, the Russians intervened. For an entire evening they argued against Thalheimer and the German majority. Lenin, Trotsky, Radek and Zinoviev were unanimous. There was no question of yielding on this point. It had to be upheld. The Communists had to insist upon the Social Democrats accepting their demands in full, or else they would be politically disarming themselves. The Germans gave in to the pressure.[39]

The German leadership, twenty of the most important members of the KPD,[40] acted in accordance with the decision which the Russians had pushed

---

[36] R. Wagner, 'Der Kampf um die proletarische Einheitsfront und Arbeiterregierung in Sachsen unmittelbar nach dem VIII Parteitag der KDP', *Beiträge zur Geschichte der deutschen Arbeiterbewegung*, no. 4, 1963, p. 650.

[37] *Correspondance internationale*, no. 94, 6 December 1922, p. 716.

[38] *Die Lehren der deutschen Ereignisse. Das Präsidium des Exekutivkomitees der Kommunistischen Internationale zur deutschen Frage 1924*, Hamburg, 1924, p. 50.

[39] Ibid., pp. 64–5.

[40] Zinoviev (ibid., p. 64) refers to twenty leaders, 'die autoritative Vertretung' – the authoritative representation – present in Moscow at that date.

through in Moscow. They agreed in principle to join the government, but advanced the following programmatic conditions:

- Supply of foodstuffs at cheap rates to property-less people.
- Requisition of empty or under-occupied residences for the benefit of badly-housed families of workers.
- Reduction of the working day to eight hours.
- Obligation upon all between the ages of 18 and 58 to work.
- Amnesty for political prisoners, except counter-revolutionaries.
- Dissolution of the strike-breaking organisation.
- Organisation of workers' self-defence.
- Struggle against reaction, beginning with a purge of the administration.
- Obligation on the Landtag to endorse the decisions voted by the Saxon Congress of Factory Councils.
- Joint national campaign for a workers' government of the Reich.

The German Communists accepted the advice of the ECCI, and declared that they would join the government on condition that these demands be accepted. They emphasised that eight of these points already figured in the programme of the ADGB unions in Saxony.

The Social Democrats accepted all but the penultimate of these conditions.[41] To recognise that the factory councils had any competence in the field of legislation would be to give to the workers' government formed in this way a 'soviet flavour' which conflicted with the Weimar Constitution. The Communists stood firm, and a deadlock resulted. The Social Democrats alone formed a minority government around Buck, as Prime Minister, and Richard Lipinski. The leader of the Left, Dr Erich Zeigner, held the portfolio of justice. The moderation of the programme which the Cabinet proposed won the abstention of some Centre deputies, enough to ensure that it could take office. For the while, the prospect of a workers' government in Saxony became irrelevant.

Political science fiction?

At the end of 1922, there appeared in Moscow a book entitled *From NEP to Socialism* by Yevgeny Preobrazhensky, who during a decisive year had been Secretary of the Russian Communist Party. Written as a retrospective from

---

[41] *Correspondance internationale*, no. 94, 6 December 1922, p. 716.

1970, it was a scientific popularisation which undertook to explain the significance and the requirements of the New Economic Policy, whilst also representing an attempt to place it within the perspective of the world revolution, the last chapter being devoted to the German Revolution.

As the capitalist crisis dragged on, a first period was characterised by what Preobrazhensky called the 'spontaneous struggle by the working class for the system of state capitalism', in the course of which it advanced slogans in favour of the nationalisation of railways, mines and other key sectors of the economy. In parallel, the idea of a workers' government appeared. The worker-professor Minayev, who was responsible for the historical conference of 1970 which Preobrazhensky imagined (and which was already quoted at the beginning of this book) recounted the beginning of the German Revolution in these terms:

> In Austria and Germany, workers' governments were formed in face of bourgeois majorities in parliament, and in Germany the transition was completed through a struggle between the proletariat and reaction which had raised its head. Here appeared what was called the dual power, that is, the power of the workers' organisations on the one hand, and the purely formal power of the Reichstag on the other. In a period of extremely high cost of living, amid crisis and great agitation among the working class, expressed in demonstrations which clashed with the police and reactionaries, as also in general strikes, when it seemed that the whole structure of German capitalism was shaken to its very foundation, the Reichstag saw fit to declare by a majority of the bourgeois votes for the formation of a workers' government, and voted confidence in it when formed. This government, in which the leading role was played, of course, by the Scheidemannites, soon became *de facto* responsible not to the Reichstag, but to the Social Democratic Party and the trade union centres.[42]

The workers' government which was installed in this way would not represent the proletariat, but only its bureaucratic leaderships, and was really 'the last ditch of bourgeois society struggling against the real workers' power which had not yet arrived'.[43] The bourgeoisie was counting on it whilst it prepared its counter-attack, which would rely upon the use of determined fascist bands.

---

[42] E. Preobrazhensky, *From NEP to Socialism*, London, 1973, p. 107.
[43] Ibid., p. 108.

Moreover, it was expecting that the working class would quickly become disillusioned:

> The workers' party in power can do nothing to bring about a real improvement in the position of the working class, they will just compromise both themselves and the whole idea of a workers' government, and then the moment will come for the return to power of a purely bourgeois government . . .[44]

However, this calculation backfired, for although the masses became disillusioned with the reformists, a most undesired effect occurred:

> The reformists in power really did very soon compromise themselves in the eyes of the worker. . . . Very quickly, even the masses who had followed the Scheidemannites began to reproach their leaders for having done nothing, and not wishing to do anything, to squeeze the bourgeoisie and to go over to real socialist construction. These masses rapidly began to quit the camp of the reformists and pass over to that of the communists.[45]

The workers' government in power was being defied by the bourgeoisie, which it refused to fight. The economic crisis was getting worse, the class struggle was intensifying, and the masses, moving to the left, were increasingly demanding energetic action from their leaders. The principal result of the accession of the workers' government to power and of its impotence, then, was a crisis within the Social-Democratic masses. Our lecturer analysed it in these terms:

> Among the reformists, including their rank and file, three trends appeared. The first was for sabotaging the struggle against capitalism and dissuading the workers from decisive actions. The second was for carrying out all the urgently needed measures directed against the wealthy classes and against anarchy in production and distribution. But this group hoped to 'persuade' the wealthy to retreat without a fight. Finally, the third trend was definitely disappointed in reformism, and moved rapidly towards fusion with the Communists. To the first two groups belonged nearly all the trade union and party bureaucracy of the reformists, and also nearly all the reformist intelligentsia, while the majority of the rank and file of the reformist parties

---

[44] Ibid.
[45] Ibid.

and trade unions were drawn towards the third group. This swing to the left by the mass of the workers was especially marked at each successive election in the trade unions and in the councils of workers' deputies.[46]

In fact, workers' councils, firmly under control by the 'majority' reformists, had been formed everywhere after the workers' government took office. The focus of the struggle now was the removal of the reformists from the workers' movement. When the Communists won the majority in a soviet, they went over to action, dissolved the municipalities, fixed local rents and rates, and imposed labour-service. It was these measures as a whole, adopted by the local and soon by the regional soviets, which were to compel the bourgeoisie to resort to a test of strength, and to start a civil war. This was a desperate struggle which began with the armed uprising of the workers in the cities, followed by the conquest, mansion by mansion, estate by estate, of the German countryside. But the German civil war was also the signal for intervention by France and Poland, and for a European war. This was a civil war, because the workers across Europe rose to prevent their rulers from crushing the German workers.[47]

Preobrazhensky's essay reveals how most prominent Bolsheviks expected their perspectives to be fulfilled 'at the end of the 1920s',[48] within six or seven years, and outlines the developments which they expected, and for which they were already elaborating such slogans as that of a workers' government. The fact remains, however, that their estimations of the tempo of the European revolution were far from unanimous. Some of them appeared to be excessively pessimistic, and even infected with that 'opportunism' of which the Left freely accused the Russians at this time.

The question of tempo

The question of the tempo of the European revolution was the focus of the conflict between the leftists and their Bolshevik adversaries in the International. Trotsky, in a polemic in the columns of *Bolshevik* in late 1922 against the Austrian Friedländer, ventured a forecast on this point. He said that internal factors alone, the disarray of the German economy and the progress of the

---

[46] Ibid., p. 110.
[47] Ibid.
[48] Ibid., p. 107.

KPD, could make an optimistic observer expect decisive struggles to open quite soon, perhaps in less than a year. However, he expected delays: 'But it is absolutely self-evident that the threat of military occupation from the West will have a deterring effect upon the development of the German Revolution, until such time as the French Communist Party shows that it is capable and ready to checkmate this danger.'[49]

This did not mean that the German Revolution could not break out before the fall of the 'imperialist and aggressive' governments of France, Italy and Britain, but it did contradict Friedländer's forecasts that a revolution was imminent in Germany: 'And so there is hardly any ground for a categorical assertion that the proletarian revolution in Germany will triumph before the domestic and foreign difficulties plunge France into a governmental parliamentary crisis.'[50] In these conditions, the German Communists should beware of 'revolutionary radicalism' and 'leftism', which, according to Trotsky, only cover up 'pessimism and mistrust':

> For us the bourgeoisie is not a stone dropping into an abyss, but a living historical force which struggles, manoeuvres, advances now on its right flank, now on its left. And only provided we learn to grasp politically *all* the means and methods of bourgeois society, so as each time to react to them without hesitation or delay, shall we succeed in bringing closer that moment when we can, with a single confident stroke, actually hurl the bourgeoisie into the abyss.[51]

This discussion shows that the experience of recent years had caused Trotsky and the Russian leaders to be anxious, but it also conveys a certain optimism, as if the proletariat alone really had the means to avoid a premature engagement. In the same issue of *Bolshevik*, Radek tried to warn against the signs of impatience which were revealing themselves in the German proletariat and in the KPD under the blows of an increasingly difficult material situation. He wrote that these conditions should not lead the Communists to lose sight of the stages through which they must pass in their preparations for the seizure of power, stages over which they could not leap: 'The Communist

---

[49] 'Tomorrow', Trotsky-Friedländer correspondence, *Correspondance internationale*, no. 96, 13 December 1922, p. 735; L.D. Trotsky, 'Political Perspectives', *The First Five Years of the Communist International*, Volume 2, London, 1974, pp. 300–1.

[50] Ibid., p. 301.

[51] Ibid., p. 303.

Party must not forget that it does not yet represent the majority of the German working class, and that its immediate task is to win this majority, as well as new positions, with a view to the coming assault. . . . It must oppose "putschism" as much as passivity.'[52]

A few days later, the occupation of the Ruhr by French and Belgian troops was to upset the calculations of both parties.

---

[52] *Correspondance internationale*, no. 94, 6 December 1922, p. 715.

Chapter Thirty-Four

The Development of the Tactic

The Fourth Comintern Congress opened in November 1922. For the first time since its foundation, the International seemed to be in a position to reach agreement on the differences which had arisen during the three preceding years. Sixteen months had passed since the Third Congress; these had been rich in events and in lessons, marked by important progress, especially in Germany, but also by the sharpness of the struggles between tendencies within the International. Everything led, moreover, to Communists believing that they once more stood on the threshold of great class battles.

Radek drafted some preliminary remarks for the delegates.[1] He stressed the importance of the question of the programme, as it would thereafter be presented to the International. In his opinion, the previous years had shown Communists that they could not confine themselves, either in their propaganda or overall strategy, to general analyses of the period:

> The period of social revolution on the world level, which is likely to last for several decades, does not permit us, if only by its duration, to be content with general perspectives. It poses a

---

[1] These remarks were originally not intended for publication, but were nonetheless to appear in *Bulletin communiste*, no. 14, 5 April 1923, pp. 126–8, under the heading 'La Question du programme de l'IC'.

certain number of concrete questions to the Communist Parties, questions
which so far they have answered purely empirically. . . . Underlying them
all, there is the question of *the special character of the present phase of development
of the world revolution*, that of knowing whether we must advance transitional
demands which, whilst not proposing the dictatorship of the proletariat as,
for example, in the Spartacists' programme, will lead the working class into
struggles which will promote the dictatorship as their aim only after these
struggles have been sufficiently deepened and generalised.[2]

Radek suggested that there were three questions of principle which experience
posed to Communists. Firstly, could the Communists in the struggle against
bourgeois governments advance transitional demands which did not
correspond to what they themselves would do if they were in power? Secondly,
what should be their attitude to the questions of 'state capitalism' which arose
from the existence of tendencies towards monopoly or from workers' resistance
to reductions in wages? Finally, in what form, apart from general transitional
economic demands in respect of state capitalism and workers' control of
industry, was it correct to advance equivalent transitional *political* demands,
such as that for a workers' government?

Radek criticised the interpretation, which was current in the International –
and which Bukharin defended at the Congress – which relegated these
questions to the discussion on tactics:

> We do not accept this interpretation. To draw so sharp a distinction between
> questions of tactics and questions of programme has up to now been one
> of the characteristics of opportunism. Opportunism gladly watched over
> the 'purity' of the programme, in order to permit itself all kinds of disgraceful
> things in practical work, and in this way made the programme illusory and
> powerless.[3]

He therefore demanded from the Congress a clear description of the specific
character of the general situation facing the International in the given period,
between the second and the third waves of the world revolution. Using this
framework, he suggested that a transitional programme be drafted. This
would lay down slogans which would help to mobilise the working masses
with the prospect of the struggle for the dictatorship of the proletariat:

---

[2] Ibid., p. 126.
[3] Ibid., p. 127.

The world revolution could not triumph with a single blow. Whatever the pace of its development, we need a transitional programme. The task of a programme consists of tracing a line of demarcation between the efforts of a given party and those of the others. We distinguish ourselves from all the other workers' parties, not merely by the slogan of the dictatorship and Soviet rule, but also by our transitional demands. Whereas the demands of the Social-Democratic Parties are not only intended to be realised within capitalism, but also serve to reform it, ours aim to facilitate the struggle for the conquest of power by the working class, for the destruction of capitalism.[4]

The fact that the Russian delegation, following a long internal debate, had supported Radek against Bukharin,[5] and the fact that Radek had played the leading part in drafting resolutions on tactical questions, particularly in respect of Germany, gave the impression that the ECCI approached the discussion of these issues in the same way as Radek. Indeed, everyone accepted that the world revolution was on the agenda in Germany. Zinoviev stressed it again in his opening speech: 'If all the signs have not misled us, the road of the proletarian revolution which began in Russia goes by way of Germany.'[6]

The debates at the Fourth Congress

The ECCI considered that the course of the world revolution had not changed significantly since 1920. Radek's speech, entitled 'The Offensive of Capital', explained:

The main feature of the period in which we are living is that, even though the crisis of world capitalism has not yet been overcome, even though the question of power is at the centre of all the problems, the broadest strata of the proletariat have lost confidence in their ability to win power in the foreseeable future. They are forced back onto the defensive. . . . The conquest of power is not on the agenda as an immediate task for today. The retreat of the proletariat is not yet over.[7]

---

[4] Ibid., p. 128.
[5] On this point, see the statement signed by Lenin, Trotsky, Zinoviev, Radek and Bukharin, requesting deferment of the decision until the next Congress, *Protokoll des Vierten Kongresses der Kommunistischen Internationale*, op. cit., p. 542.
[6] Ibid., p. 37.
[7] Ibid., pp. 317–18.

As with previous Comintern Congresses, the debate on tactics was to become the main concern of the Fourth Congress. It was preceded by long preparatory discussions in the ECCI and the commissions. There were lively disagreements in which Zinoviev and Bukharin opposed Radek because they were apparently impressed by some of the arguments from the German Left, and particularly by the interpretation which it gave of the workers' government slogan. These disagreements were not to be clearly confirmed until later.[8]

There could be no doubt that the KPD leaders were the strongest supporters of the policy of the united front. Meyer spoke to insist on the necessity of top-level agreements in preparing and realising the united front. He stressed that none of the KPD's successes in that sphere would have been possible if the Berlin Conference and the discussions amongst the leaders of the parties had not opened the way to them. He opposed the opinion – which had been advanced by Zinoviev in the commission, as the debates at the Fifth Comintern Congress were to bear witness – that the workers' government was no more than a pseudonym for the dictatorship of the proletariat. He said: 'The workers' government is a slogan which we have formulated to win the workers to our cause, and to show that the working class needs to be united in its fight against the bourgeoisie.'[9]

Fischer, speaking for the Left, retorted that the tactic of the united front only reinforced the characteristic illusions of the German labour movement about 'workers' unity', and that its principal result during the preceding two years had been to drive the Independents into reunification with the Majority Social Democrats. She accused the KPD of having hidden its banner and abandoned its revolutionary line in its campaign after the assassination of Rathenau. She believed that there existed very concretely a danger that the KPD would again adopt a course towards opportunism and parliamentarism, in its desire to 'adopt a Western style'.[10]

Replying to Fischer, Radek firmly adhered to the explanation of the united front which he had developed against Vandervelde, and defended the correctness of his own thesis of the united struggle to defend 'the piece of bread': 'We engage in discussions with the Social Democrats in the knowledge that they will keep on deceiving us. And we warn the masses in advance so

---

[8] Especially in the debates at the Fifth Comintern Congress.
[9] *Protokoll des Vierten Kongresses der Kommunistischen Internationale*, op. cit., p. 76.
[10] Ibid., p. 82.

we don't appear to have been deceived. But we only break from the Social Democrats when we can do by ourselves what they refuse to do with us.'[11]

As regards the workers' government slogan, Radek likewise criticised Zinoviev's interpretation, which made it no more than a synonym for the dictatorship of the proletariat. Insisting that the workers' government could in no circumstances constitute a 'an innocent-looking soft pillow', he proclaimed: 'The workers' government is not the dictatorship of the proletariat. It is a possible transition towards the dictatorship of the proletariat.'[12] He criticised the purism of those who rejected the very idea of parliamentarism. He asserted that a workers' government could equally well arise from the struggle of the working masses outside parliament or from a parliamentary combination amongst workers' parties that emerged from a successful election. In any case, the essential factor was the influence of mass working-class action upon this government, and this was predicated upon the policy of the Communist Party. The slogan for a workers' government was based upon the experience of the struggles in the West. It took into account that the West differed from Russia, where the majority of the workers could be won directly to Communism, whilst in the West the workers showed strong allegiances to various parties. However, it was necessary to understand that the workers' government was not a necessity, but only an historical possibility, as Radek explained with his customary wit: 'It would be wrong to say that the evolution of man, from monkey to people's commissar, must necessarily pass through the stage of being a minister in the workers' government. But this variant is possible.'[13]

Therefore, speaking for the ECCI, Radek opposed both the intransigence of those who were for 'all or nothing', who accepted the idea of a workers' government only as a synonym for the dictatorship of the proletariat, and the opportunists who wished to retreat in the face of action and to use it as a 'parachute'. He ended by turning to the Left:

> The tactic of the united front is more difficult than the tactic we used in 1919 when we said: 'Bring Everything Down!' It is easier and more agreeable to bring everything down, but when you are not strong enough to do it,

---

[11] Ibid., p. 100.
[12] Ibid., p. 101.
[13] Ibid., p. 102.

when your only option is to go along this road, you have to do so convinced
that the dangers we face are from the Right, and that it is not us but the
Social Democrats whom this tactic harms.[14]

The final resolutions

The Congress endorsed the theses on the united front which the ECCI had
adopted at its meeting in December 1921. The tactic of the united front meant
that the Communist vanguard would march 'at the head of the day-to-day
struggles of the masses for their most immediate interests':

> The tactic of the united front is nothing other than the proposal made by
> the Communists to all workers, whether they are members of other parties
> or groups or of none, to fight alongside them, to defend the elementary and
> vital interests of the working class against the bourgeoisie. Every action
> for even the smallest demand is a source of revolutionary education,
> because the experience of combat will convince the working people of the
> necessity of the revolution, and will demonstrate the meaning of Communism
> to them.[15]

This meant concretely that the Communists should not hesitate to 'enter into
discussion with the traitors', but also that in no circumstances should the
united front be interpreted as a fusion of the workers' parties, nor should it
justify 'electoral deals'. The conditions for the success of this tactic, which
could have 'decisive significance for a whole period', was 'the existence of
independent Communist Parties and their complete freedom of action towards
the bourgeoisie and counter-revolutionary Social Democracy'.[16]

The resolution on tactics included a detailed section devoted to the workers'
government slogan. As a 'general propaganda slogan', it had particular
importance in the countries in which the relation of forces between the classes,
and especially the crisis of the bourgeoisie, placed it upon the agenda. The
slogan was 'an inevitable consequence of the entire united-front tactic', since
the Communists counterposed 'the united front of all workers and the political
and economic coalition of all workers' parties' against the rule of the bourgeoisie

---

[14] Ibid., pp. 102–3.
[15] Ibid., p. 1015.
[16] Ibid., p. 1014.

and for its overthrow, and 'any open or disguised coalition of the bourgeoisie with Social Democracy'.[17]

The workers' government, therefore, would arise from the struggle of the workers against the bourgeoisie. Its minimum programme was simple: 'Arm the proletariat, disarm the bourgeois counter-revolutionary organisations, install workers' control of production, place the bulk of the tax burden on the rich, and break the resistance of the counter-revolutionary bourgeoisie.'[18] The workers' government could never be a means of peaceful transition towards socialism, a recipe for avoiding civil war, even if it emerged from a favourable situation within the parliamentary framework:

> A government of this kind is possible only if it is born in the struggle of the masses themselves, if it draws support from workers' organisations which can fight, which are created by the broadest strata of the oppressed masses of workers. A workers' government which results from a deal in parliament can likewise provide the opportunity to revive the workers' revolutionary movement. But it naturally follows that the birth of a real workers' government and the continuance of a government which carries on a revolutionary policy must lead to the most desperate struggle and possibly to civil war against the bourgeoisie. The mere attempt by the proletariat to form a workers' government will from the beginning encounter the most violent resistance from the bourgeoisie. The slogan of a workers' government can concentrate and unleash revolutionary struggles.[19]

Participation by Communist Parties in workers' governments could be envisaged, so long as the other organisations provided guarantees that they really intended to fight against capitalism, and if the following conditions were observed: that participation was subject to the approval of the International, strict party control was maintained over the Communist members of the government, close contact was established between the latter and the 'revolutionary organisations of the masses', and the specific character and the absolute independence of the Communist Parties were maintained.[20]

---

[17] Ibid., pp. 1014–15.
[18] Ibid., p. 1016.
[19] Ibid.
[20] Ibid.

The resolution warned Communists against the dangers which, like any correct slogan or tactic, the workers' government slogan presented: 'Every bourgeois government is a capitalist government, but it is not true that every workers' government is an authentically proletarian government, that is, a revolutionary instrument of proletarian rule.'[21] In fact, several possibilities existed. There could happen, as in Australia and probably soon in Britain too, a 'liberal workers' government'. In 1918–19, Germany had experienced a 'Social-Democratic workers' government'. These were not revolutionary workers' governments, but 'disguised coalitions between the bourgeoisie and the counter-revolutionary workers' leaders':

> These 'workers' governments' are tolerated in critical periods by the enfeebled bourgeoisie, in order to deceive the proletariat about the true class character of the state, or even to divert the revolutionary offensive of the proletariat and to gain time with the help of corrupted workers' leaders. Communists must not take part in such governments. On the contrary, they must pitilessly demonstrate to the masses the real character of these false 'workers' governments'. In the period of capitalist decline, in which our main task is to win the majority of the proletariat for the revolution, these governments can objectively contribute to the process of decomposition of the bourgeois régime.[22]

The Congress noted three other kinds of workers' governments: a workers' and peasants' government, which could be foreseen as a possibility in Czechoslovakia or the Balkans; a workers' government with Communist participation; and finally, 'a real proletarian workers' government' which, 'in its purest form', could 'only be embodied in a Communist Party'. In the first two cases, Communists were ready to march with the working-class elements who had not yet recognised the dictatorship of the proletariat, and even, 'in certain conditions and under certain guarantees', to support a non-Communist workers' government: 'But Communists must explain to the working class that its liberation can be assured only by the dictatorship of the proletariat.'[23]

It was important clearly to understand that the different kinds of workers' governments in which Communists might participate were not the dictatorship of the proletariat: 'They do not yet constitute a necessary form of transition

---

[21] Ibid., p. 1017.
[22] Ibid.
[23] Ibid.

towards the dictatorship, but they can constitute a point of departure for winning that dictatorship. The complete dictatorship of the proletariat can be realised only by a workers' government formed by Communists.'[24]

The debates at Leipzig

The discussion was to continue at the KPD's Congress in Leipzig during 28 January–1 February 1923. The ECCI was represented by Kolarov and Radek, who had returned from Norway where he had tried to avert a split in he Communist Party which had been threatening for several months.[25] The Congress was obliged to express its attitude to the resolutions of the International, and the Left presented counter-statements, in opposition to the reports of Brandler and Meyer.

Meyer argued the case for the united-front tactic and the use to which the Zentrale had put it, whilst he recognised that opportunist errors had been committed during the campaign following Rathenau's assassination. He emphasised the importance of the gains which had been made by the discussions amongst the top Party leaders, and the ensuing responses amongst the rank-and-file Social-Democratic workers.[26] Brandler reported on the united front and the workers' government.[27] He began by emphasising the danger from fascism, the progress it was making, especially in Bavaria, and the deadly threat which it presented to the workers' movement. He said that the Party could lead a successful fight against fascism through the struggle for the united front:

> The tactic of the united front is not a simple propaganda formula. It is unquestionably a tactic for struggle. . . . We are convinced that we cannot wage the final struggle to overthrow the bourgeoisie and establish the dictatorship of the proletariat if we do not fight every day to relieve poverty, at every opportunity. . . . We know very well that the struggle for higher wages, lower rents and lower prices will not be enough to ensure the

---

[24] Ibid.
[25] He had intervened in the National Council of 5–6 January in order to define the 'autonomy' of the Norwegian Party within the framework of the statutes in such a way as to be acceptable to the minority which was hostile to the centralisation of the International (H.M. Lange and Meyer, *Det norske arbeiderpartis historie*, Volume 2, pp. 320ff.).
[26] *Bericht über die Verhandlungen des III (8) Parteitages der KPD*, op. cit., pp. 197–219.
[27] Ibid., pp. 314–33.

survival of the proletariat in this period of capitalist decadence, even for a short period, but nonetheless we shall wage this struggle against everyday difficulties, with modest results . . . in order to educate and to raise the offensive spirit and combative force of the working class, and to prepare it for the forthcoming battles.[28]

He added that the Communists would be ready when the Social-Democratic leaders, under the pressure of the masses, decided finally to stop being the left wing of the bourgeoisie, and became 'the right wing of the workers'.[29]

The final struggle could not succeed unless the working class united in a solid army. Brandler challenged the supporters of the Left, telling them that he was convinced that there was no disagreement on principles in the Party, but only on their application, and especially on estimating the risk of opportunism implicit in the tactic of the united front itself. For that reason, he stressed that 'concrete solutions' must be found to practical problems, and that the Party must conclude a discussion which would become futile.

Fischer once again attacked the Zentrale's approach, which she believed to be passive, opportunist and revisionist. She made great efforts to show that the interpretation which Brandler gave to the slogan of the workers' government was really an attempt to reconcile bourgeois democracy with the dictatorship of the proletariat.[30] Provocatively, she ended one of her speeches with the phrase: 'We shall carry on the fight; you can howl if you want to.'[31]

Maslow, opposing Brandler, was less polemical, but was ultimately more incisive, particularly in his criticism on the issue of the workers' government. He thought that the Zentrale had a purely parliamentary conception, and that its wish to reach top-level agreements revealed serious illusions about the leaders of Social Democracy. He accused the Zentrale of neglecting the important movement of the factory councils, and counterposed mobilisation at the base to agreements at the top:

> The creation of a workers' government is not predicated on rigid conditions, but depends in each given situation on the mass movement which poses the question of power, on the existence and possibility of developing the capacity of the workers for struggle, on the spirit of combativity of the

---

[28] Ibid., p. 318.
[29] Ibid., p. 328.
[30] Ibid., pp. 238–40.
[31] Ibid., p. 287.

proletarian organs of struggle (workers' councils and control committees), on the need for the working class to be armed . . . and on its need to end the defensive phase in order to go over to the attack.[32]

These were serious differences, and those who denied that they were about principles were being optimistic. The Left emphatically rejected the workers' government slogan, claiming that the Zentrale saw it as an alliance, at least a temporary one, with the leaders of Social Democracy, whom the Left considered to be by their very nature agents of the bourgeoisie, who would betray the proletariat if they joined a workers' government. The Left believed that the SPD was congenitally bound up with the counter-revolution, and that it could only make a monkey of Brandler's efforts to detach it from the bourgeoisie and turn it into the right wing of a bloc of workers' parties. Moreover, the Left clung to its original leftist conception of the offensive, and accepted defensive slogans only grudgingly. It rejected the very idea of transitional slogans, and only accepted demands such as the confiscation of real values and the formation of factory councils or control committees as measures heading up to a seizure of power in the short term. It could conceive of the workers' government itself only as being supported by the armed proletariat, and consequently being the first stage of the dictatorship of the proletariat, or – in very exceptional circumstances – the initial presentation of it. Such was the substance of the theses that the Left submitted to the vote of the Congress,[33] which rejected them in favour of those submitted by Brandler on behalf of the Zentrale, by 118 votes to 59.[34]

Brandler's theses

The theses on the tactic of the united front and the workers' government which the Congress approved were an attempt to apply to Germany the theses which had been endorsed at the Fourth Comintern Congress. They began by recalling that the struggle for power was a mass struggle, involving the working-class majority against the capitalist minority. The struggle for the united front, in the light of the class struggle, would begin by organising the revolutionary vanguard in a Communist Party, and continue by winning

---

[32] Ibid., p. 345.
[33] Ibid., pp. 142–50.
[34] Ibid., p. 375.

the workers organised in the trade unions and the reformist parties. But the Communist Party, which was 'a party of the masses, and their vanguard', had 'no object other than the class objective of the proletariat, the seizure of political power', for which it was obliged to win the confidence of the masses, by the actions which it organised, or in which it took part, as much as by the day-to-day work which it carried on in the workers' organisations.

The principal obstacle to the organising of the united front of the working class centred on the resolute hostility of the reformist Social-Democratic leaders. They continually attempted, by their policy of class collaboration, to prevent the proletariat from confront the bourgeois offensive. It was in the concrete struggle to organise the fight against the bourgeoisie that the Communists could win the trust of the working people, and expose the reformist leaders: 'The united-front tactic is not a manoeuvre for exposing the reformists. On the contrary, exposing the reformists is a method for uniting the proletariat into a close-knit fighting force.'[35]

The Communists were to be ready to fight at all times, and were to be prepared at any point to propose joint struggles to other workers' organisations, with the aim of forming a united front:

> The conception that a proletarian united front could be achieved by an appeal merely to the masses for struggle (only 'from below') or only by negotiations with the top-level committees ('from above') is anti-dialectical and static. The united front will develop much more through the living process of the class struggle, the awakening consciousness of the class, and the will to struggle on the part of ever-broader strata of the proletariat.[36]

Therefore, the struggle for the united front passed both through conquest of the existing mass organisations of the workers, such as trade unions and cooperatives, and through the construction of new organisations which would unite the class, such as factory councils, control committees and political workers' councils: 'The revolutionary united front organised in political workers' councils for the overthrow of the bourgeoisie is situated not at the beginning but at the conclusion of the struggle to win the masses to Communism.'[37]

The theses warned the KPD against the two deviations which had revealed themselves during the preceding months and weeks. The 'right' deviation

---

[35] Ibid., and *Dokumente und Materialen*, Volume 2/7, part 2, op. cit., p. 247.
[36] *Bericht über die Verhandlungen des III (8) Parteitages der KPD*, op. cit., pp. 247–8.
[37] Ibid., p. 248.

had expressed itself in excessive concessions to the reformists in the course of joint actions, a reluctance to declare the Communists' own positions, and particularly a tendency to refrain from leading the struggle within the reformist unions. The 'left' deviation continually expressed itself in the way the Party's line was applied in practice. It was characterised by stress on the united front 'from below'; declarations that the workers' government would be the dictatorship of the proletariat, and therefore could be a valid slogan only on the eve of the seizure of power; rejection of the necessity for transitional slogans to raise the consciousness of the masses; and a general allegation that the opportunist line of the KPD was a result of the application in Germany of the NEP in Soviet Russia. Hiding its inactivity behind phrases, it had created a leftist spirit in the Party, a latent hostility and mistrust towards the leadership, and towards centralism and discipline in general.

The theses then went on to show that the call for a workers' government was the only slogan which could unify Communist policy:

> The workers' government can appear only during the struggle of broad masses against the bourgeoisie, as a concession by the reformist leaders to the will to struggle of the working people. The workers' government can appear only in a period of mass proletarian struggles, in which the bourgeoisie is being heavily shaken by the struggle of the working class, owing to the inability of the former to overcome the economic crisis.
>
> The workers' government is neither the dictatorship of the proletariat, nor is it a peaceful, parliamentary advance towards it. It is an attempt by the working class, within the framework of bourgeois democracy (and in the first place with the means provided by it), to construct a working-class policy, supported by the proletarian organisations and mass movements, whereas the proletarian dictatorship consciously explodes the framework of democracy and destroys the apparatus of the democratic state, in order completely to replace it by proletarian organs.[38]

Turning, in accordance with the line of the Fourth Comintern Congress, to the hypothesis of a workers' government formed on the basis of a parliamentary victory of the workers' parties, the theses declared:

> The workers' government is neither a 'simplified revolution' nor a 'substitute dictatorship', which would weaken the resistance of the bourgeoisie, and

---

[38] Ibid., p. 25.

therefore benefit the reformists. It is a period of struggle, of violent struggle by the proletariat against the bourgeoisie, which will not willingly concede an inch to it. . . . The Communist Party declares that the workers' government is the only government which it can support in the current period of crucial proletarian struggle, the only one which can represent the interests of the proletariat without capitulating to the bourgeoisie, in opposition to coalition governments, or to Social-Democratic governments.[39]

The fate of workers' governments would ultimately depend upon the policy of the Communist Parties, and the way in which they were able to win the workers to Communism, and recognition of the need for the dictatorship of the proletariat:

To overcome the oscillations, the omissions and the mistakes of the workers' government by an ever more determined struggle of the united revolutionary front and its political organs, to free the workers from democratic and pacifist illusions, these are the tasks of the Communist Party in the period before and during the workers' government.[40]

The theses supported the idea that Communist representatives could, at a suitable juncture, join a workers' government:

Participation in the workers' government does not mean that the Communist Party will make any concessions that will detract from the revolutionary purpose of the proletariat, any deal or tactical manoeuvre, but will show that it is perfectly ready to struggle jointly with the reformist workers' parties when they show clearly that they wish to break from the bourgeoisie and to undertake jointly with the Communists a struggle for the demands of the hour.[41]

Amongst the necessary conditions for participation, the most important was recognition of the role which the organs of the proletarian united front were to play in legislative matters and the arming of the proletariat:

The determining factors for the Communist Party to participate in a workers' government are not the promises of the reformist leaders, but the analysis of the entire political situation, the relation of forces between the bourgeoisie

---

[39] Ibid., pp. 252–3.
[40] Ibid., p. 253.
[41] Ibid.

and the proletariat, the combativity of the proletarian masses, the existence of proper class organisms, the capacity of the reformist bureaucracy to resist, and, in the first place, the capacity of the Communist Party to lead the masses in struggle for their demands.[42]

The theses stressed that, like any participation of the proletariat in the system of the bourgeois-democratic state, the workers' government was only a means to an end, a stage for the proletariat 'in its struggle for its exclusive hegemony': 'The workers' government is by no means a necessary step, but it is a possible step in the struggle for political power.'[43]

The conclusion touched on the problem facing the workers in the various regions of Germany. The theses recalled the history of the issue, and the formation of Social-Democratic governments in the Landtags with the support of Communist votes, and declared:

> Workers' governments in regions can only appear in situations of acute political crisis, when the pressure of the masses is so strong that some of the Social-Democratic leaders decide to align themselves with those calling for a proletarian class policy. The workers' government in a region is a government of Social Democrats and Communists which rests on proletarian class organs. The political basis of this workers' government is not the bourgeois parliament, but the extra-parliamentary organs of the class. The KPD participates in these regional governments in order to construct bases for the struggle on the level of the Reich. The regional workers' governments must establish close relations with each other, and must form a red bloc against the capitalist government (be it purely bourgeois or a bourgeois-Social-Democratic coalition).[44]

Aftermath of the Congress

The opposition to Brandler's theses which had been displayed at the Congress, and the reservations which had been voiced in Moscow in the Commission and in the ECCI, account for the unease which could be felt after the Leipzig Congress. Events proceeded as if some of the leading elements in the International were susceptible to the arguments of Fischer, and were unhappy

---

[42] Ibid.
[43] Ibid.
[44] Ibid., pp. 254–5.

about the way in which the theses of the Fourth Comintern Congress were being developed in Germany. One example of this was the reproduction in the Communist press in various countries of a contribution to the discussion presented by Edwin Hoernle, a KPD delegate to the ECCI, which was in many respects a corrective to Brandler's position, seen as opportunist.[45]

Hoernle took up the issue in the same terms as Fischer had posed it: what was the role of the workers' government slogan in relation to the SPD members and the workers influenced by that party? He emphasised that the common aim of all Communists, whether of the Right or the Left, was to split Social Democracy and win its rank and file to the Communist Party. However, this could not be done at the beginning, but only at the outcome of revolutionary struggles. The workers' government could unleash such struggles. Hoernle stressed that, in order to achieve that end, the Communist Party must first of all 'treat the Social Democrats as they appear to the masses, that is, as honest people, in order that the masses themselves may be in a position to expose them'. This was the justification for the negotiations at leadership level.

Moreover, Hoernle tried to show that the principal task of a workers' government, far from confining itself to the framework of bourgeois democracy, worked to break it up, because it would have to bring about 'the formation, organisation and methodical centralisation of the workers' councils and the workers' defence corps, and the dissolution of the military and police formations and the bourgeois organs of justice and administration'.[46] He concluded with a more dialectical formula – one more acceptable also to the Left than Brandler's – to locate the workers' government in the interval between the bourgeois dictatorship and the proletarian dictatorship, and not 'in the framework of bourgeois democracy': 'The workers' government is no longer a bourgeois dictatorship without yet being a proletarian dictatorship. It forms a transitional step, amid a dialectical process of revolutionary development: whilst it exists, it proceeds to its own abolition.'[47] This was a brave attempt at a synthesis, but it was not enough to overcome the profound differences. Disagreements broke out when the KPD was confronted with the necessity to apply the tactic. In Saxony, the Buck government had been put in a minority

---

[45] Edwin Hoernle, 'Die Taktik der Einheitsfront aus dem Parteitag der KPD', *Die Internationale*, no. 6, 15 March 1923, pp. 179–85.
[46] Ibid., p. 183.
[47] Ibid., p. 285.

in the Landtag, and had just resigned. Paul Böttcher announced that the Saxon Communists had decided to help form a workers' government, and to do nothing that would give the Social Democrats any excuse for once more allying themselves with the bourgeoisie. Fischer at once retorted that his perspective, conceived without any reference to mass action, could not even claim in its favour the Congress resolutions, because it was situated on an exclusively opportunist and parliamentarian basis.[48]

The careful formulation of the Congress theses could not conceal the reality of the disagreement. It is true that Brandler and his supporters were obsessed by the necessity to win the majority of working people as they were, taking their illusions into account, and were seeking for a transitional slogan which these workers would accept, and that their idea of a workers' government was, at the beginning, no more than a parliamentary alliance with the SPD within the framework of the existing institutions – because it could not, for the moment, be otherwise. It is no less true that when Fischer and Maslow on their side used the terms 'united front' and 'workers' government', they meant that the former would be 'from below', and the latter would be another name for 'the dictatorship of the proletariat'. This aspect of their policy was part of the strategy that all the leftists had defended since 1918, and which the KPD had adopted on several occasions – at terrible cost – the revolutionary offensive that was to be launched regardless of the context, and the rejection of all transitional slogans. This road had led to isolation and defeat.

Thus the efforts of Lenin and the ECCI to encourage cooperation between the two tendencies, as the only means to make them overcome their differences, had been in vain.[49] Numerous incidents during the Leipzig Congress reflect this situation. Already, on the first day of the Congress, the tone of Fischer's attacks on the Zentrale, her denunciation of 'its passivity, its opportunism and its revisionism',[50] provoked lively reactions, especially from Stolzenburg, who presided over the Congress, and from Kleine, who represented the ECCI.[51] On the third day, she asked to make a personal statement, and took advantage

---

[48] *Bericht über die Verhandlungen des III (8) Parteitages der KPD*, op. cit., pp. 268ff.

[49] In a letter to Ernst Meyer dated 12 October 1922, Brandler spoke of the 'factional dirty tricks' of the Berlin people, and proposed suspending Fischer from her Party functions (cited in Weber, *Die Wandlung des deutschen Kommunismus*, Volume 1, op. cit., p. 45, n. 88). Ultimately, no action was taken against her.

[50] *Bericht über die Verhandlungen des III (8) Parteitages der KPD*, op. cit., p. 240.

[51] Ibid., p. 247.

682 • Chapter Thirty-Four

of it to deliver a fundamental speech on behalf of the Berlin-Brandenburg district. Stolzenburg claimed the right to stop her speaking. Maslow appealed to the Congress to unseat the Chairman.

The tumult calmed down only after a conciliatory speech by Pieck, who talked about a misunderstanding,[52] and the Congress returned to the agenda. The other incident happened during the closed sessions preparing the election of the Zentrale. The outgoing leadership proposed to increase the number of its members from 14 to 21, and submitted a list of 21 names. This list included none of the Left, but it also made an important concession by omitting Meyer, who had been the target of the attacks of the Left from the beginning. Meyer protested against the 'unprecedented' fact that the 'reservations' of certain districts against him had not been voiced during the Congress.[53] The Left demanded representation on the leadership consistent with its strength in the Party, where it had won one-third of the mandated votes. It announced that the delegates of the Berlin-Brandenburg, Wasserkante and Mid-Rhineland districts would not cast their votes. During a late-night session, Radek, with the support of Kolarov, threw the authority of the ECCI into the balance to persuade Brandler to include members of the Left in the Zentrale's list.[54]

---

[52] Ibid., p. 299.

[53] Weber, op. cit., p. 46.

[54] Fischer, a determined opponent of Radek, states without any corroboration that he intended to eliminate the leaders of the Left. She explains his final initiative and his search for a compromise by his awareness that he had 'gone too far'. In a letter which Radek addressed to Zetkin in December 1926 he was to explain that, in his opinion, 'Ruth Fischer, Maslow, Urbahns, Scholem represent a whole stratum of Communist workers', in whom was incarnated 'revolutionary impatience'. He expanded on this subject: 'We had to combat it in order to make clear to the Communist workers that a hopeless minority is in no position to capture power. But we did not want to separate ourselves from this mass, for it represented the hope of our class.' On the incident in the Congress, he stated: 'That is why, on my own initiative, I insisted at the Leipzig Convention of the Party that Ruth Fischer should be put on the Central Committee; the latter rejected the proposal. I wanted the left-wing representatives in the Central Committee so that they might constitute a counterbalance against the pure and simple daily politicians, against the comrades who did not understand the difference between a USPD and a Communist Party.' ('A Letter by Karl Radek to Clara Zetkin', *The New International*, Volume 1, no. 5, December 1934, p. 155.) This text, quoted by Fischer herself (op. cit., p. 509, n. 9), invalidates the idea about Radek's manoeuvring which she is trying to substantiate; Radek in fact was here taking a position against the policy of the ECCI, which was based on the attempt to exclude the Left – Ruth Fischer first and foremost – and to provoke a split. See also Angress, op. cit., pp. 275ff.; Peter Maslowski, *Thaelmann*, Leipzig, 1932, p. 42; E.H. Carr, *The Interregnum*, London, 1954, pp. 158–9. Finally, let us note that Fischer gave the lie to herself in advance when she stated to the ECCI in January 1924: 'The last-minute intervention by the representative of the Executive succeeded in avoiding a split.' (*Die Lehren der Deutschen Ereignisse*, op. cit., p. 51.)

However, despite resistance from, doubtless, Brandler, the new list of twenty-one names did in fact include three activists of the Left, Ewert, Lindau and Pfeiffer. But this concession was not enough to appease the opposition. They thought that Lindau was a moderate, and especially regarded Ewert as Radek's man.[55] Nine districts supported the Zentrale in presenting this list of candidates. The districts of Berlin, Wasserkante, Hesse-Frankfurt and Mid-Rhineland presented another list, which consisted merely of four leaders of the Left, Fischer herself, Geschke, Katz and König.[56] Finally, the East Prussian district presented Meyer alone.[57] In the end, the Zentrale's list was elected *en bloc* with a fairly comfortable majority.[58]

Although nothing was said about electing a Chairman, the newly-elected Zentrale nonetheless had a leader. The new head of the German Party was Heinrich Brandler. He was a building worker, aged 42, with a long record as a Social Democrat, and was also one of the rare members of the old Spartacist nucleus who was a trade-union leader and a 'mass' activist, a party-builder in Chemnitz, and an excellent organiser. He had already been called to the chairmanship of the VKPD immediately after Levi had resigned. In that capacity, he bore responsibility for the March Action, which led to his being arrested and sentenced. After his release, he spent several months in Moscow as a member of the Presidium of the International.

He was a short, thick-set man with a hump due to an accident at work, who spoke with a strong Saxon accent, a serious man with a broad, calm face, methodical and patient, a practical person rather than a theoretician, with a firm grip and cool temperament. In short, he was a workers' leader,

---

[55] Fischer (op. cit., pp. 225, 229–30) writes that the Zentrale's revised list included four candidates said to be from the Left, which is obviously a mistake. But the only name she gives is that of Ewert.

[56] Fischer (ibid.) speaks, without giving specific details, of Radek's 'manoeuvres' to prevent the candidacies of Maslow and Thaelmann, which in fact were not put forward. She says nothing of her own candidacy.

[57] Fischer (ibid.) asserts that Meyer had been eliminated at Radek's request, because he had rejected a proposal that he should help form a faction aligned with the ECCI within the KPD. In saying this, she forgets the attacks that she had made upon him.

[58] Fischer (ibid.) asserts that the left delegates abstained in the vote for the Zentrale, an assertion which cannot be supported, since at most 16 delegates abstained, whereas 59 had voted for the Left and against Brandler's theses. It is significant that Lindau, with 195 votes, and Pfeiffer, with 192, came top of the poll; the supporters of both the Zentrale and the Left had voted for them. Then came Zetkin, Eberlein, Frölich and Hoernle, then Brandler with 166 votes, which enables us to estimate that the number of leftists who took part in the vote was over 30. Ulbricht, with 117 votes, and Karl Becker, with 107, were those elected with the lowest number of votes (*Bericht über die Verhandlungen des III (8) Parteitages der KPD*, op. cit., p. 382).

in many respects very representative of the German movement, and of the most positive aspects of its Social-Democratic tradition. He enjoyed the confidence of the ECCI, even though they mistrusted his rancour against the 'Berliners', whom he had denounced since his return to Germany.[59] At his side were Party members like him, trade-union activists, leaders of masses, such as Heckert, Böttcher, Walcher, Koenen, Remmele and Stoecker, and of course, Zetkin. He also had with him a very different man, a theoretician, even an intellectual, whom history was to make his second self, August Thalheimer. He had a newly-arrived organiser, neither a speaker nor a writer, but efficient, the former cabinet-maker Walter Ulbricht. There was also Guralski, Zinoviev's agent (as some people plausibly said), who was elected to the Zentrale under his pseudonym of August Kleine. At their backs and in the wings was Radek, whose job was to follow events very closely, whether on the spot or in Moscow. He had promoted Brandler since at least November 1922, and worked with him to prepare the Leipzig Congress.

This new leadership, which seemed solid enough, and would have been in other times, took up its post on the eve of the breaking of a storm which would shake Germany to its very foundations.

---

[59] See note 49.

Chapter Thirty-Five

The Occupation of the Ruhr

For postwar Germany, 1923 was the *annus terribilis*. The consequences of the War let loose a crisis without precedent in an advanced capitalist country. Following the French decision in January 1923 to occupy the Ruhr, the economic difficulties of the previous two years were transformed into a tremendous social and political upheaval.

The problem of reparations and the Great Powers

Article 231 of the Versailles Treaty demanded that Germany pay reparations. This question quickly became the bone of contention between the victorious powers. From 1919, the British, Americans and French wrangled in the reparations commission. One interallied conference followed another, whilst German diplomacy did its best to turn these delays to its advantage.

In July 1920, the conference at Spa decided on the distribution amongst the allies of the sums to be collected, and on how to deal with defaults. In January 1921, the Paris conference decided that 42 annual payments were be made, some at a fixed rate, and others proportional to the receipts earned by German exports. The first London conference decided that Düsseldorf and Duisburg would be occupied as reprisals for non-payment of a debt of 20 million gold marks. The second London conference, in May 1921, fixed the total German debt at 132 billion gold marks (excluding the replacement of destroyed values) in fixed annual payments of two milliard gold marks, increased by a variable charge equal to 26 per cent of the total value of German exports. In July 1922, the German government pleaded for a moratorium, which the French government firmly refused. On 10 January 1923, despite the opposition of the other Allied states and the indignation of European public opinion, the Poincaré government ordered General Degoutte to occupy the Ruhr with troops, on the pretext of 'seizing a productive security'.

The disagreements between the Allied powers had nothing to do with different conceptions either of peace and political morality, or of the prospects for the future of Germany. The French industrialists sought to make good the ruin of their industries in the north of the country, and to feed the furnaces which they had acquired in Lorraine. German industry had lost three-quarters of the coal-field in Upper Silesia, but had to supply enormous quantities of coal to France in reparations.

The British coal-mining industry was threatened by these German deliveries, which halved its exports to France. French steel-makers particularly wanted furnace coke from the Ruhr. German heavy industry was short of ore, especially since the loss of the deposits in Lorraine. The possibility of an alliance between French and German heavy industry, of the formation of a Franco-German trust, could mean Britain being driven out of the European market, and losing important outlets for the products of its metalworking industries.

It was to realise this aim that the interests represented by the two big French banks, Union Parisienne and Banque de Paris et des Pays-Bas, and the Belgian Société Générale were working. Raymond Poincaré was the politician in this far-reaching operation, which could count on resolute supporters at all the control levers of the bourgeoisie. Since 1919, the French occupation authorities in Germany, Tirard, the chairman of the inter-Allied high commission in the Rhineland, and General de Metz, the commander of the forces in the Palatinate, had been busying themselves with encouraging a separatist tendency in the Rhineland. Since they could not really 'colonise' Germany, as the nationalists and the Communists said they were doing, they were thinking in Paris of breaking up the country. A Rhenish state which included the Ruhr could form a political prop for French domination in Europe, and the basis for Franco-German joint domination of the European market.

The USA resolutely opposed these plans in the name of the need to 'save Germany'. They tried to induce the French government to agree to reducing the level of reparations, and to drop the idea of breaking up Germany. The American capitalists declared that they were ready to provide Germany with the capital necessary for both its economic recovery and the payment of reparations. As Eugene Varga noted: 'The United States is the only country in the world which, even in a normal situation, is short of industrial manpower . . . the only country which can support the German industrial proletariat by giving it raw materials to work on in Germany itself.'[1] Britain firmly aligned itself with the USA, whose pressure alone could avert the disaster which it feared most. As Varga wrote: 'In opposition to the imperialist French continental system, every day the Anglo-American world-market system rises in greater solidarity.'[2]

At the end of 1922, the Poincaré government put forward a settlement plan. It proposed that the mark be stabilised – its continual devaluation was one means by which Germany tried to avoid the burden – and that measures be taken to balance the budget and to check the flight of capital and accumulation of foreign currency. The commission which had been set up in Berlin to supervise reparations payments would then in fact manage the finances of Germany with the power to 'veto expenditure which it considered to be undesirable, and to impose any kind of increase in revenue which it might believe to be realisable'. In this way, Germany would be subject to a more severe control than even Turkey before 1914. Moreover, the French government refused to allow any deferment of more than two years and, in general, any deferment of the cost of maintaining the occupation forces or of deliveries in kind. It demanded guarantees, such as the supervision of coal production and of the fulfilment of deliveries by an inter-Allied commission based in Essen, the deposit of guarantees in foreign currencies, and the power to requisition stocks.

'Passive resistance'

The day after French and Belgian troops occupied the Ruhr, the Cuno government announced that it would resist the foreign aggression. Ebert, the President, issued an appeal in this sense on 12 January 1923. On the 13th, the

---

[1] 'La situation en octobre-décembre 1922 – Les Plans de réparations français et anglais – Données principales', *Correspondance internationale*, no. 11, 7 February 1923, p. 67.
[2] Ibid.

Reichstag resolved by 284 votes to 12 to embark upon 'passive resistance'.[3] No German was to collaborate with the occupation authorities, and all reparation payments were forbidden. Incidents became more frequent as the occupation was extended. Shots were fired in Düsseldorf and Bochum, and there were sporadic strikes by railway workers and miners. The occupation authorities announced draconian measures to break this resistance. On 19 January, they arrested the mayor of Dortmund, and, on 27 January, the son of Fritz Thyssen. The German government appealed to the workers to take 'patriotic strike action', and threatened to regard as 'traitors' those who agreed to work for the occupiers. On 27 January, the French military authorities announced that they were taking over the operation of the railways in the Ruhr, which the strike had practically paralysed, and they managed to restart them by expelling 1400 German railwaymen from the region and issuing a large-scale appeal to French and Belgian railwaymen to replace them.[4] On 29 January, they proclaimed martial law, and extended the occupied zone to the Dutch frontier.[5]

The conflict became more violent from early February. Everything contributed to inflame the conflict: the decision of the Cuno government to call for passive resistance, the nationalist campaign in the popular press, and the reprisals which the occupiers were taking. All this helped to encourage the nationalist forces of the extreme Right. Cuno had the support of the big industrialists, and was obliged to give a free hand to the heads of the Reichswehr, whose complicity with the leaders of the nationalist gangs was scarcely hidden. On 26 January, Ludendorff issued a call to arms.[6] Volunteers from paramilitary groups and former members of the Free Corps flocked in from all over Germany to join, once more burning with nationalist fever. The Reichswehr generals coordinated all this with government approval. On 30 January, Chancellor Cuno and General von Seeckt met to discuss arming and mobilisation, and agreed on what their relations should be with the Orgesch.[7]

On the following day, the General met Jahnke, an notorious adventurer, who presented suggestions for sabotage of the railways. Another conversation, this time with Stinnes, dealt with financing these new activities. It was

---

[3] *Verhandlungen des Reichstags. I Wahlperiode 1920*, Volume 357, p. 9422.
[4] Badia, *Histoire de l'Allemagne contemporaine*, Volume 1, op. cit., p. 189.
[5] Angress, op. cit., p. 282.
[6] Fischer, op. cit., p. 196.
[7] Hallgarten, op. cit., p. 22.

at about this time that Lieutenant-Colonel von Stülpnagel was entrusted with the task of installing himself secretly in the occupied zone, in order to direct sabotage operations. He himself summed up his task as follows: 'It was a matter of changing the passive resistance into active resistance – a St Bartholemew's massacre – and organising it through the state as quickly as possible'.[8]

On 13 February, General von Seeckt had a discussion with representatives of the Ruhr industrialists and the heads of the Reichsbank. They declared that they were ready at once to provide 300 million marks to buy Austrian weaponry in Italy through the agency of Mussolini. On the 15th, von Seeckt met the leaders of the Orgesch. On the 17th, during a discussion with one of the directors of the Stinnes combine and the owner of the von Löwenstein mines, they decided to meet Ludendorff. On the 20th, at the home of the general manager of Stinnes, von Seeckt and Ludendorff met to discuss the conditions for collaboration between the Reichswehr and the activists of the extreme Right.[9]

This intense political activity led to a new revival of violence in the Ruhr. Rails were lifted, electricity and telephone cables were cut; there was more sabotage, which frequently paralysed industry and transport. The occupation forces hit back with numerous arrests after each incident, which was grist to the mill of the nationalists, whose aim was to arouse the whole population in a desperate struggle, which it would then control.

The SPD plunged headlong into this new *union sacrée* which the Franco-Belgian action provoked. In the name of the parliamentary group, Hermann Müller expressed his party's support for the policy of passive resistance,[10] despite the reservations which many of the deputies expressed even when it came to the vote.[11]

The KPD refused to be dragged into what it regarded as another capitulation before the German bourgeoisie, a repeat of the vote on 4 August 1914. In the Ruhr, it appealed to the workers to fight on two fronts, against the occupiers

---

[8] Ibid., pp. 22–4.
[9] Ibid., pp. 25–6.
[10] *Verhandlungen des Reichstags. I Wahlperiode 1920*, Volume 357, pp. 9424–8.
[11] According to Gunter Hortzschansky, the decision was won in the Party fraction by only 60 votes to 55 (*Der nationale Verrat der deutschen Monopolherren während des Ruhrkampfes 1923*, Berlin, 1960, p. 119). According to Stoecker, 67 deputies voted for passive resistance, 65 had left the hall before the vote was taken, and 14 had abstained from voting (*Correspondance internationale*, no. 5, 19 January 1923, p. 20).

and against their own bourgeoisie, who were misleading them. Communist propaganda denounced the swindle which led the German workers to be slaughtered for 'Stinnes's 50 per cent'.[12]

Radek commented ironically on 'the patriotism of the German chemical industry', and the agreement which Badisches Anilin had made with the French government about the sale of secrets of explosives manufacture and the establishment of an explosives factory in France within a few weeks of passive resistance being announced.[13] The Communists considered that their primary task was to ensure that the German working class, and in the first place the workers in the Ruhr, did not succumb to the lure of nationalism.

The desperate struggle between the legal German authorities and the occupation authorities centred around the workers in the Ruhr. The Communist activist Käthe Pohl[14] described the conflict:

> It was decisively important, both for the German bourgeoisie and for the French generals, to have the workers on their side. Both sides spared no expense in their efforts to attract the proletariat of the Ruhr into their camp. The French generals consciously exploited the hatred of the German working class for its masters. . . . On every occasion, the French generals would repeat that the French troops had come into the Ruhr against the bourgeoisie, and not against the workers. . . . Numerous French agents travelled throughout the Ruhr agitating in this sense. From the German side, the same efforts. When the French arrested the director of a factory, they would try to form a 'liberation committee' in the plant, made up of workers, and, if possible, to include a Communist worker. . . . Even more in fashion than 'liberation committees' was the protest strike. Whatever happened, a director arrested, a mayor sentenced or an official deported, they tried to start a strike by promising to pay the workers for the lost days' work.[15]

---

[12] There is an excellent summary of their arguments in Paul Frölich's article 'Sixty Per Cent Or 40 Per Cent', *Correspondance internationale*, no. 9, 30 January 1923, pp. 51–2. Stinnes had declared to the Economic Council: 'We could not form a trust along with Monsieur Loucheur, the French industrialist, in which our French partner held 60 per cent of the shares and we held 40 per cent.' (*Rheinisch Westfälische Zeitung*, 20 January 1933.)

[13] 'Le Patriotisme de l'industrie chimique allemande', *Correspondance internationale*, no. 18, 2 March 1923, p. 122.

[14] Käthe Pohl was the pseudonym of Katarina or Lydia Rabinovich, partner of Guralski Kleine. See Chapter 28, note 57.

[15] K. Pohl, 'L'Occupation de la Ruhr et la lutte du prolétariat allemand', *Bulletin communiste*, no. 10, 8 March 1923, pp. 158–9.

However, 'passive resistance' was soon to take on quite a different aspect from what the German government and army leaders had desired. The pressure of poverty, despite all kinds of threats, was the determining factor on the workers' side. They were aware that when they came out in solidarity with the employer, they were not fighting for their own interests. The factory councils in the Thyssen combine recalled their delegates who had agreed to vote alongside the employers for a motion demanding the release of Fritz Thyssen Junior.[16] The industrialists, although made wary by some vigorous actions on the part of the occupying authorities, did not lose sight of even their short-term material interests. Coal was not distributed to workers' families, as the Communists and, in many cases, the unions and the factory councils demanded. It remained stockpiled at the mines until the lorries came to collect it for the occupiers, and at best the employer went no further than an energetic protest. The industrialists' 'passive resistance' was looking increasingly like a charade.

Real tragedies developed in the workers' districts. High prices, rising unemployment and poverty provoked outbursts of anger and street demonstrations which the occupying forces put down. At Buer-Recklinghausen, they brought out tanks against a workers' procession. In Essen on 31 March, the 53,000-strong Krupp workforce stopped work at the news that an Allied commission was arriving, and then, learning that the French army was requisitioning the lorries which brought their food, they demonstrated directly against the occupation forces; several people were killed, and forty-two wounded.[17]

There was hardly any reaction from the workers when a few days later Gustav Krupp himself was arrested. They were indeed caught between two fires, and their spontaneous reactions, which were usually stirred up by acts of provocation, often led them to receive blows from both sides. On 13 April, at Mülheim, a crowd of workers took possession of the town hall by assault; under the leadership of Communists and anarcho-syndicalists, they appointed a workers' councils to supervise the distribution of foodstuffs, and to form a workers' militia.[18] The occupation authorities refrained from intervening, because the action was not directed against them, but they authorised the German police to enter their zone in order to restore order. The police

---

[16] *Correspondance internationale*, no. 9, 30 January 1923, p. 52.
[17] *Die Rote Fahne*, 1 April 1923. The central KPD organ stressed that one of those killed, a Communist named Josef Zander, had tried in vain to prevent the confrontation.
[18] Fischer, op. cit., p. 258.

recaptured Mülheim town hall on 21 April, after battles which left six dead and seventy wounded.[19]

Terrorists from the army and the Free Corps carried out more attacks and acts of sabotage with the aim of provoking reprisals which would rally the population around them in a nationalist reflex. A commando blew up a bridge near Essen. Soon a former member of a Free Corps was to be the first victim in the German nationalist cause. Leo Schlageter, who was charged with blowing up the railway near Düsseldorf, was arrested by the French authorities, and brought before a French court-martial. It sentenced him to death, and he was shot. This took place whilst the fighting was going on in Bochum. Pohl wrote:

> The German worker is obliged to begin his struggle against the occupation, and this makes his struggle against the German bourgeoisie very difficult. It enables those brigands, the German capitalists, to appear as national heroes, persecuted in the cause of the fatherland. The German proletariat can fight at the same time against German capitalism and French militarism only if it can count on the active, resolute help of the French working class.[20]

This, it appears, was the opinion of Zinoviev. He wrote to the leadership of the French section of the International that 'up to a certain point it held the destiny of the Communist International in its hands'.[21] The French Party had freed itself from its most right-wing tendency at the beginning of January when Ludovic-Oscar Frossard resigned, and it tried to campaign against the intervention, denounce the imperialist policy of Poincaré, affirm the solidarity of the French and German workers, and above all organise anti-militarist propaganda in favour of fraternisation between the German workers and the occupation troops. These efforts appear to have been fruitless. Marcel Cachin, Pierre Semard, Gaston Monmousseau and several others were arrested in January, following a conference in Essen.[22] Soon came the turn of Gabriel Péri, one of the leaders of the Communist Youth.[23] A new team of agitators left

[19] *Die Rote Fahne*, 22 April 1923.
[20] *Bulletin communiste*, no. 10, 8 March 1923, p. 159.
[21] Letter from Zinoviev, 2 February 1923, cited in J. Humbert-Droz, *L'Oeil de Moscou à Paris*, Paris, 1964, p. 187.
[22] *L'Humanité*, 21 January 1923.
[23] *L'Humanité*, 23 March 1923.

secretly for the Ruhr, led by another Communist Youth leader, Henri Lozeray,[24] but it was to fare no better. Despite the efforts of the Communist International to organise a European campaign against the occupation – of which the Frankfurt conference in March would have been the starting point – nothing came of it. The truth was that the workers in the Ruhr were totally cut off from the French proletariat, and to a large extent from the rest of the German proletariat. This state of affairs lay at the base of a new conflict which broke out in the KPD.

The difficulties of fighting on two fronts

The explosive situation developing in the Ruhr accentuated the differences that arose in the KPD. At the Leipzig Congress, Brandler had regarded the demand by the Left to discuss the political consequences of the Ruhr occupation as a sign of distrust in the Party leadership, and had kept it off the agenda. On 13 January, in the Reichstag, the Communist deputies refused to support the vote of confidence in the Cuno government. Their spokesman, Paul Frölich, attacked 'Cuno and Poincaré, the twin brothers', and condemned both the occupation of the Ruhr and the policy of 'passive resistance': 'We are at war and Karl Liebknecht taught us how the working class must carry out a war policy. He called for the class struggle against the war! This will be our slogan. No civil peace, but civil war!'[25]

On 23 February, an editorial drafted by the Zentrale in *Die Rote Fahne* endorsed this line. It was headlined: 'Fight Poincaré and Cuno on the Ruhr and on the Spree!' The battle of the Ruhr was presented as a conflict between bourgeoisies, 'on the backs of the German working class'.[26]

---

[24] G. Walter, *Histoire du Parti Communiste Français*, Paris, 1948, p. 137; H. Köller, *Kampfbündnis an der Seine, Ruhr und Spree*, Berlin, 1963, p. 180.

[25] *Stenographische Berichte des Reichstags Verhandlungen*, Volume 357, p. 9429.

[26] Fischer (op. cit., p. 263) writes that the day after the appearance of this headline in *Die Rote Fahne*, Radek sacked the two journalists responsible, one of whom was Gerhard Eisler, and had the headline repeated with the following modification: 'Against Cuno on the Spree and on the Ruhr Against Poincaré.' We have not found any such headline in any issue of *Die Rote Fahne*. Moreover, Fischer says the headline was in rhyme and printed in two lines: 'Against Cuno and Poincaré on the Ruhr and on the Spree', which is not the case. Erich Wollenberg, interviewed by Buchot about the events of 1923, gave virtually the same account, but replaced Radek's name by that of Thaelmann, describing him as a member of the Political Bureau, whereas he only joined the Zentrale three months later.

Nonetheless, there was great difficulty in applying the policy of struggle against Poincaré in the Ruhr without getting involved in either 'passive' or 'active' resistance, and in pursuing the struggle against Cuno without falling in with the game of certain syndicalist elements who were taking advantage of the opportunities that the French occupation offered to operate an ambiguous policy. On the day after the Essen massacre, *Die Rote Fahne* carried the headline: 'Workers Assassinated in Essen. Krupp Workers Victims of French Militarism and German Nationalist Provocations.'[27] A conference of factory councils met in Essen on 11 March, and Karl Becker, speaking for the Zentrale, insisted on the need to fight against the Ruhr occupation and the Versailles Treaty, especially by revolutionary propaganda in the ranks of the occupation forces. He repeated the slogans for the disarming of the counter-revolutionaries, the arming of the workers, a workers' government, and the formation of organs of the proletarian united front, control committees, factory councils and proletarian hundreds.[28] The same themes were repeated at the international conference in Frankfurt which was intended to coordinate international action against the occupation.[29] And it seemed as if the Communists all agreed with these slogans.

However, an article by Thalheimer, who was regarded as the Zentrale's theoretical brain, soon provoked a storm of protest in the Party and the International.[30] His central idea was that whatever their essential class identity, the roles of the French and German bourgeoisies were not the same. He said that the German bourgeoisie in its resistance was 'playing an objectively revolutionary role, against its own will', similar to that which Bismarck had played in his struggle for German unification between 1864 and 1870, and which Marx and Engels had recognised as such.

Thalheimer stressed that, whilst defeat of French imperialism in the World War had not been and could not have been a Communist aim, the situation was no longer identical, and 'the defeat of France in the Ruhr War' was 'a Communist objective'. Therefore, for the moment, the aim of the Communists coincided, to however limited a degree, with that of the German bourgeoisie, and their paths would only separate once the German bourgeoisie capitulated,

---

[27] *Die Rote Fahne*, 1 April 1923.
[28] *Die Rote Fahne*, 13 March 1923.
[29] *Die Rote Fahne*, 18, 20, 21 March 1923.
[30] A. Thalheimer, 'Einige taktische Fragen des Ruhrkrieges', *Die Internationale*, no. 4, 15 February 1923, pp. 907–1002; *Die Kommunistische Internationale*, no. 26, 1923.

as he expected it to do, to the French bourgeoisie. The German proletariat would then have to defeat its own bourgeoisie before concluding its victorious struggle against foreign imperialism.

The Czech Communists Neurath and Sommer vigorously opposed this analysis, which would lead the Communists to support their own bourgeoisie, if only temporarily, and they denounced the musty odour of the social-patriotism of 1914 which they sensed in it. The German Left appears to have taken a similar view.[31]

Did Thalheimer's article express the clear, considered, conscious orientation of the Zentrale? Was it directly inspired by Moscow, that is, by Radek, as Fischer declared?[32] The supporters of this idea have sought the reason for the defeats of the workers in this period in 'national Bolshevism', the alliance between Soviet Russia and German nationalism and militarism. They have cited in support of their interpretation a speech by Bukharin at the Fourth Comintern Congress:

> Can proletarian states form military blocs with bourgeois states on the basis of strategic suitability from the viewpoint of the proletariat as a whole? Here there is no difference between a loan and a military bloc, and I maintain that we are big enough to be able to conclude a military alliance with the bourgeoisie in one country in order to crush the bourgeoisie in another country. . . . In this kind of defence through a military alliance with bourgeois states, our comrades have the duty to contribute to the victory of such a bloc. If, in a later phase of development, the bourgeoisie of such an allied country is itself defeated, then other tasks appear [Laughter] which I do not need to explain to you: you will easily understand for yourselves.[33]

---

[31] A. Neurath, 'Eine verdächtige Argumentation'; Sommer 'Der Ruhrkrieg und die Aufgaben des deutschen Proletariats', *Die Internationale*, no. 2, 1 March 1923, pp. 110–13, 209ff. These articles were reproduced along with Thalheimer's in the same issue of *Kommunisticheski Internatsional*, no. 25, 7 June 1923, column 6857–6888, and, with a reply from Thalheimer, 'Noch einmal zu unserer Taktik im Ruhrkrieg', in *Bulletin*, no. 1 of the enlarged ECCI of 8 June, pp. 1–2 in French, English and German. Neurath was from the German minority in Czechoslovakia, one of the founders of the Communist Party of Czechoslovakia. Sommer was the pseudonym of another member of similar origin from the Czech Party, Dr Joseph Winternitz, known as 'Lenz', who had just settled in Germany and was to become one of the theoreticians of the Left (Weber, *Die Wandlung des deutschen Kommunismus*, Volume 2, p. 344).
[32] Fischer, op. cit., p. 281.
[33] *Protokoll des vierten Kongresses der Kommunistischen Internationale*, op. cit., p. 420. Fischer (op. cit., p. 279) does not quote the last sentence.

The thesis – which was to reappear with the approach of the Second World War under other conditions – was not as precise as Fischer and her disciples represented it, for there was nothing in it which constituted a deliberate abandonment by the International and its parties of the policy of the revolutionary destruction of the bourgeois state – quite the contrary. It is excessive, moreover, to make out of one phrase by Bukharin – which was delivered when he was presenting a report on the Comintern's programme, which, furthermore, was rejected – a credo of the fundamental political positions of the Russian Party and especially the International. The same applies to articles in *Izvestia* by Steklov, which are cited by Kochan:

> It is quite obvious that the toiling masses of Soviet Russia have no special sympathy for the bourgeois governments of Germany, still less for her reactionary imperialist elements. Nevertheless, Soviet Russia, *in her own vital interests*, cannot allow the final subjugation and destruction of Germany by an alliance of France and her vassals, of which Poland is the first. . . . A Polish attack on Germany at the present moment is a direct blow at Soviet Russia.[34]

This warning, directed towards White Poland, could not be interpreted as 'unqualified support' for the German bourgeoisie.[35] The author of this editorial, moreover, was careful to draw the distinction between the military and diplomatic needs of the Soviet state and the sympathies of the working masses. This proves that the Russian leaders, at this point, did not identify the allies of Soviet Russia with the allies of the world proletariat.[36]

It is not impossible that when Thalheimer wrote his article, he was preoccupied of finding a line of defence for Soviet Russia in the given

---

[34] Cited in Kochan, op. cit., p. 68.

[35] Ibid., p. 67.

[36] There is in Fischer's analyses and of the historians who follow her an anachronism that may or may not be deliberate. They project backwards into this period the contradictions between the policies of the USSR and the International and its parties which were to arise at the start of the Stalin era. It is significant in this connection that Fischer and Kochan are obliged, in order to support their theory, to resort to another quotation from Bukharin, when he was defending the idea of 'socialism in a single country', against the Left Opposition at the Fifteenth Conference of the Russian Party: 'When Germany was crushed, was enslaved, when she was in the position of a semi-colony . . . even the highest organs of the Soviet power . . . expressed their open sympathy for her. Then the German Communist Party posed the question in such a way that the possibility of defending the German fatherland against victorious Entente imperialism . . . was not excluded' (cited in Kochan, op. cit., p. 67, and in Fischer, op. cit., p. 280, with an inaccurate footnote).

conditions, a run-of-the-mill task for any Communist. But we think rather that, confronted by the nationalist passion that was raging in the Ruhr, he was searching for an acceptable theoretical explanation for the nationalist wave which was influencing the workers, including class-conscious workers, in order to orient the Party. No doubt he was also trying to emphasise the slow revolutionary development in Germany, and the disastrous character of the policy of the leftists who were always hunting for some short cut by which to bring about a revolutionary crisis.

Chapter Thirty-Six

Crisis in the KPD

The first result of the occupation of the Ruhr and the isolation of the working people in that region was to open up a new crisis within the KPD. In a few weeks, it led to the resurgence of old quarrels.

The success of the united front in Saxony

On 10 January, the Social-Democratic government in Saxony fell, and this provided the KPD with the opportunity for a vigorous campaign in favour of the united front and a workers' government. The Social-Democratic leaders in Saxony for the most part were in favour of a parliamentary alliance with the Democratic fraction in the Landtag, but some elements of the Left spoke out for an alliance with the Communists, which would give the Left an overall majority. The KPD systematically organised workers' assemblies in localities and workplaces. These served as an arena for an exchange of opinions in respect of the question of the government, and the Communists usually won the majority of those attending, including a section of the non-Communists, to their call for the immediate formation of a workers' coalition government in Saxony. At the same time, Communists attended Social-Democratic meetings, and asked if they could outline their party's proposals. On each occasion they received a substantial vote.[1]

---

[1] R. Wagner, 'Der Kampf um die proletarische Einheitsfront und Arbeiterregierung

Under the pressure of its Left, the Social-Democratic Executive in Saxony conceded that a special congress be called, which met on 4 March. Two days before, *Die Rote Fahne* published the text of a 'workers' programme' suggested by the KPD to the SPD in Saxony. In particular, it included confiscation without compensation of the property of the former royal family, arming of the workers, a purge of the judiciary, the police and the administration, severe measures against counter-revolutionary organisations, calling of a congress of factory councils, extension of the rights of the councils, confiscation of idle factories, a forced loan, and control of prices by elected committees.[2] Even though Dittmann supported the leaders of the Right, the Left won the day, and the congress agreed by 93 votes to 32 to reject any coalition with the Democrats, and to entrust the conduct of negotiations with the KPD to a 'commission of nine', led by Georg Graupe.[3]

The Communists then repeated the proposals which they had made to the old Social-Democratic leadership: arming of the workers, overall industrial control by factory councils, dissolution of the Landtag, and convocation of a congress of the factory councils. The left Social Democrats did not accept, any more than their predecessors, the step towards the 'sovietisation' of Saxony which convocation by the government of the congress of factory councils implied.[4] The Communists did not want to cut off any bridges; they withdrew the demand for the Landtag to be dissolved and the congress to be convened, and declared that they would support in the Landtag a single-party Social-Democratic government which excluded Buck, the leader of the right wing, and which undertook to authorise the formation of workers' defence groups, to organise consultative 'chambers of labour', in which the factory councils would be represented, and to declare an amnesty for political prisoners. An enlarged conference of the Saxon Social Democrats accepted these proposals on 19 March 1923, and on the same day, the Communists did likewise, despite the opposition of the Leipzig representatives.[5] A new government was formed on 21 March, with Erich Zeigner at its head, Liebmann at the Interior Ministry, and Graupe at the Ministry of Labour; the Landtag gave it a majority, with the Communists voting for.[6] On behalf of the Saxon

---

in Sachsen unmittelbar nach dem VIII Parteitag der KDP', *Beiträge zur Geschichte der deutschen Arbeiterbewegung*, no. 4, 1963, p. 651.

  [2] *Die Rote Fahne*, 2 March 1923.
  [3] Wagner, op. cit., pp. 653–4.
  [4] Ibid., p. 655.
  [5] Ibid.
  [6] Ibid., p. 357.

Communists, Böttcher welcomed this government as a step towards forming a workers' government and arming of the workers. The bourgeois deputies walked out of the Landtag in protest against what they called the 'Bolshevik programme' of the Zeigner government,[7] against which the big newspapers opened up a vast hostile campaign throughout Germany.

The Political Bureau of the KPD approved the decisions of the Saxon communists on 22 March, and decided to mount a nationwide campaign to make known what was happening in Saxony.[8] However, on 30 March, *Die Rote Fahne* published motions from Berlin and Berlin-Brandenburg which criticised as 'opportunist' the policy followed in Saxony, together with the reply of the Saxon leadership.[9]

On the edge of a split

The KPD Left regarded the overthrow of the majority in Saxon Social Democracy as a minor event, because they considered left-wing Social Democrats to be as treacherous as their right-wing colleagues. But for the leaders of the KPD, and for Radek, this was an event of profound significance, a confirmation that their line was correct. This is what Radek wrote for English readers:

> Even today the Social Democratic Party is the strongest party of the proletariat in Germany. This may cause disappointment and uneasiness, but it is nevertheless a fact, to which one attitude or another has to be taken. One might follow Levi . . . or one might take up arms against the traitors and be defeated, as happened to the German Communist Party in March 1921. One may also fight against this infamous fact day by day by educating the proletariat, mobilising the proletarian ranks.[10]

The conflict between the two tendencies was soon to be carried into the most explosive part of Germany, the Ruhr. Fischer went there after the Leipzig Congress, and devoted herself to organising the left-wing current, which then became stronger, and even expressed itself publicly, thus breaking Party discipline. The task as she saw it, was, faced with the imperialist invasion and the swindle of 'passive resistance', to push the workers forward to seize

---

[7] See Zeigner's statement of principles in *Verhandlungen des Sächsischen Landtages 1923*, pp. 717–20.

[8] Cited in Wagner, op. cit., p. 657.

[9] *Die Rote Fahne*, 30 March 1923.

[10] K. Radek, 'The Crucible of Revolution', *Communist Review*, Volume 3, no. 11, March 1923, p. 533, cited in Angress, op. cit., p. 305.

the factories and mines, and to take political power. Relying on the strong syndicalist traditions in the workers' movement and on the ultra-left currents both within and outside the Party, she tried to revive the idea of the Workers' Republic of the Ruhr, which had inspired the workers' struggles following the Kapp Putsch three years before.

According to Fischer, this Republic could have been 'the base from which a worker army would march into Central Germany, seize power in Berlin, and crush once and for all the nationalist counter-revolution'.[11] This was a seductive perspective for the leftists who had supported 'workers' unions', and it found an echo amongst the miners, if we are to believe Fischer, as well as in leading Party circles, where its principal advocate was Joseph Eppstein, one of the founders of the Party in the Ruhr, and the secretary of the mid-Rhine district.[12] But it was vigorously opposed by the supporters of the Zentrale, in the front rank of whom were Stolzenburg, the leader of the North Rhineland-Westphalia district, and Walter Stoecker, who was in charge of the Oberbezirk of the occupied zone and had the support of the metalworkers in Essen.

The conflict between these two tendencies was particularly violent throughout the whole region, because majorities were slight and the situation was difficult. The first public confrontation came at the Congress of the North Rhine-Westphalia District in Essen. Fischer and Ernst Thaelmann,[13] though strangers to the district, had managed despite Stolzenburg's opposition to get themselves delegated by local organisations which supported the Left. The Congress cancelled their credentials, but agreed that they could take part in its work and speak there on behalf of their own districts of Berlin-Brandenburg and Hamburg-Wasserkante. Fischer took advantage of this to deliver an attack of unprecedented violence on the 'opportunist' course of the Zentrale. She accused it of doing nothing but seeking an agreement with Social Democracy,

---

[11] Fischer, op. cit., p. 255.

[12] Eppstein was one of the radical leaders in the Ruhr before 1914. Imprisoned in 1919, he settled in Cologne, and, thanks to his gifts as an organiser, made the Central Rhineland from 1921 a bastion of the Left, after his election to the district secretariat to replace Dahlem, an associate of Levi. With him there was an efficient team: Peter Mieves, who was later revealed to be a police agent, the teacher Kerff, and Wilhelm Florin. In the other districts of the Rhineland, the Left held strong positions thanks to men such as Arthur König, the Dortmund leader, Kötter from Bielefeld, and Hans Kollwitz, who was to become the Ruhr secretary of the committee of factory councils.

[13] Thaelmann, a genuine proletarian, was more the symbol of the Hamburg Left than its boss. The true leader was Urbahns, one of whose chief lieutenants in 1923 was Philip Dengel, Editor of the *Hamburger Volkszeitung*.

the proof of this being shown in the struggle for a workers' government in Saxony. For the Ruhr, she proposed an immediate action programme, which included seizing the factories, installing workers' control of production, and the formation of workers' militias throughout the occupied zone. She argued that these demands were mere preparatory measures for the direct struggle for power, a struggle which at that moment was expressed in the call to bring down the Cuno government. She denounced the supporters of Brandler as 'friends of democracy' – a very serious accusation in the KPD at this period – and expressed herself in extreme language which seemed to show her readiness to force a split, going so far as to declare: 'A day will come when all the comrades will be behind us, and will drive out those who support democracy and keep their eyes fixed on the Weimar Constitution.'[14]

To oppose her, her old adversary Zetkin came to support Stoecker and Stolzenburg. She retorted that the Left's analysis did not in any way correspond to the reality of Germany at that time, and that if the line of the Left were applied, it would mean reverting to adventures of the putschist kind, which would lead through a premature offensive to the isolation and defeat of the proletariat of the Ruhr. Moreover, she warned, the initiatives for which the Left was calling would risk playing into the hands of the occupiers, whose agents were trying to make contact with local activists and leaders. In the end, the supporters of the Zentrale were narrowly successful, by 68 votes to 55.[15]

The threat of a split was reappearing. The strength and determination of the opposition in a crucially important region, the conduct of its activists in the Ruhr, and the aggressive attitude of Fischer herself, all showed that the crisis was serious and coming close to breaking-point. The Zentrale was disturbed;[16] after a heated discussion, it published a warning, couched in moderate terms, but nonetheless clear, entitled: 'This Must Stop!' It stated that the opposition was endangering the unity of the Party by its behaviour, not merely during the Essen Congress, but prior to it. The Zentrale did not wish to stifle the discussion, but declared that it was nevertheless resolved to defeat any attempts to provoke a split, whatever excuses or particular circumstances might be advanced to justify it.[17] On the following day, the

---

[14] *Die Rote Fahne*, 29 March 1923.
[15] Ibid.
[16] Report of the meeting of the Political Bureau on 27 March, discussion around Fischer's stance, cited by Mujbegović, op. cit., p. 397, n. 82.
[17] *Die Rote Fahne*, 30 March 1923.

Zentrale ran an article by Fischer in the Party's central newspaper, followed by a reply from Brandler.[18]

On the same day, Brandler was opening the Congress of the Communist Youth in Chemnitz, and issued a solemn warning:

> The Zentrale will try once more to reach an agreement with the opposition. We hope that the overwhelming majority of our comrades who support the opposition will join us in an honest attempt to find a solution which will save the party. However ... we cannot tolerate the repetition of incidents like those which have just occurred at the District Party Congress. We cannot permit another attempt to oppose the practical slogans of the Party during action, and to replace them by others which we have rejected. That would be to kill revolutionary battle discipline. Whoever infringes that is an enemy of the Party, and must be rendered harmless.[19]

At least some of the responsible members of the Left listened to what Brandler said. Eppstein was dismissed by the Zentrale and replaced by a more moderate leftist, Peter Maslowski.[20] On 10 April, four other important leftists, Arthur Ewert, a member of the Zentrale, Hans Pfeiffer, also a member of the Zentrale and secretary of the Berlin-Brandenburg organisation, Gerhard (really Gerhard Eisler), Fischer's brother, an alternate member of the Central Committee and a cadre of the district, and Heinz Neumann, renounced their solidarity with the leaders of the opposition, repudiated the essence of the theses of Fischer and Maslow, and advocated 'concentration' of the Party.[21] Neumann was a member of the editorial staff of *Die Rote Fahne* and *Inprekorr*, a member of the clandestine apparatus, a brilliant young man who had the ear of the Russians. In the Executive of the Berlin-Brandenburg district, the supporters of this 'Centre' won 10 votes in opposition to the 24 extremists of the Left.[22] On 22 April, Zinoviev invited, in the name of the ECCI, representatives of the Zentrale and the left opposition to a conference with the Bolshevik leaders in Moscow.[23]

---

[18] *Die Rote Fahne*, 31 March 1923.
[19] *Die Rote Fahne*, 1 April 1923.
[20] Weber, *Die Wandlung des deutschen Kommunismus*, Volume 2, op. cit., p. 111.
[21] 'Zur Lage und zu den Aufgaben der Partei', *Die Internationale*, no. 10, 15 May 1923, pp. 228–34. It was doubtlessly published here because *Die Rote Fahne* was banned during 8–21 April 1923.
[22] Weber, *Die Wandlung des deutschen Kommunismus*, Volume 1, op. cit., p. 48.
[23] Carr, *The Interregnum*, op. cit., p. 162, indicates that the text of this letter is to be found in the collection *Material zu den Differenzen mit der Opposition*, which we have not been able to consult.

A new compromise in Moscow

Lenin suffered his third stroke on 9 March. The ECCI attempted to resolve the crisis in the course of discussions which were held in Moscow early in May. Brandler and Böttcher represented the Zentrale, and Maslow, Fischer, Thaelmann and Gerhard Eisler represented the leftist minority.[24] Facing them, Trotsky, Bukharin, Zinoviev and Radek represented the Russian Communist Party.[25] We do not know the exact content of the discussions.[26] A long compromise resolution emerged. It declared in particular: 'The differences arise from the slow speed of revolutionary developments in Germany, and from the objective difficulties to which this leads, simultaneously feeding right and left deviations.'[27]

The ECCI characterised as 'right' errors certain formulations in the Leipzig resolution, such as the utilisation of the 'illusions, prejudices and needs' of the Social-Democratic workers, or the 'instruments of power available in a bourgeois state' that could possibly be used in the struggle for a workers' government. The ECCI said that these errors explained the dissatisfaction of 'healthy proletarian elements . . . inclining towards leftism'. It added, however, that the Zentrale was correct in resisting leftist tendencies, when, as in the Ruhr, they could have led to 'isolated struggles . . . where the Party would have suffered cruel defeats', or when, as in Saxony, they would have isolated the Party 'from large numbers of workers who are making their way towards us'. It ended: 'The struggle against leftist tendencies can be successfully fought only if the Zentrale eliminates, above all by a struggle against rightist elements, the causes of the revolutionary mistrust by the Left.'[28]

The ECCI condemned any moves towards factory occupations in the Ruhr in the absence of any revolutionary movement in the unoccupied zone, or of any sign of disintegration of the French occupation forces. Whilst it endorsed the Party's stance towards the Zeigner government, it regretted that it had

---

[24] Fischer (op. cit., p. 260) mentions only the first three. But *Die Rote Fahne*, 13 May 1923, mentions Gerhard, and a note in *Dokumente und Materialen*, Volume 7/2, Part 2, op. cit., p. 309, specifies that this was Gerhard Eisler; it is very unlikely that this omission was a matter of chance, since Fischer considered her brother had 'betrayed' the Left.

[25] Fischer, op. cit., p. 260.

[26] No minutes have ever been published, and the brief account given by Fischer seems to command little confidence.

[27] 'Resolution zu den Differenzen in der KPD', *Die Rote Fahne*, 13 May 1923; *Dokumente und Materialen*, Volume 7/2, Part 2, op. cit., p. 302.

[28] Ibid., pp. 303–4.

not yet succeeded in combining its struggle for a workers' government in Saxony with a struggle for a workers' government in Germany as a whole. Although it accepted that the German bourgeoisie was objectively contributing by its struggle against the Versailles Treaty to the disintegration of capitalist Europe, it recalled that this bourgeoisie was still waging a class struggle against the proletariat, and that it would not in any case defeat the Entente. The task of the KPD was to explain patiently to those influenced by nationalist ideology that 'only the working class, after its victory, will be in a position to defend German soil, the treasures of German civilisation, and the future of the German nation'.[29]

The resolution was carried unanimously, and, in order further to guarantee this political agreement, the ECCI recommended that a public discussion be opened in a bimonthly special supplement to *Die Rote Fahne*, that the leaders of the Left cease distributing their propaganda in districts where they had no influence,[30] and that the leaders of the Right propose to the next meeting of the Central Committee that the leaders of the Left who had been excluded from the Zentrale at Leipzig be coopted back onto it.

Unity recovered amid rising tension

During May, the aggravation of the international situation helped to consolidate the compromise which had been reached in the Party. On 2 May, Marshal Foch paid an official visit to Poland and inspected the army. On 8 May, Viscount Curzon, the British Foreign Secretary, addressed to the Soviet Union an ultimatum on the subject of the activity of its agents in Persia, Afghanistan and India. On 10 May, a White Russian assassinated the Russian diplomat Vorovsky in Switzerland. In the Soviet Union, there was considerable excitement. Zinoviev wrote that the die-hards in the imperialist camp were preparing a new offensive: 'The events in the Ruhr, the Curzon ultimatum,

---

[29] Ibid., pp. 304–7. Fischer (op. cit., p. 260) writes that the question of 'National Bolshevism was not brought up', whereas this passage in the resolution can be taken to be the foundation of what she calls a 'National Bolshevik' policy.

[30] *Dokumente und Materialen*, Volume 7/2, Part 2, op. cit., p. 308. It seems that in early 1923, the Left seriously encroached on some of the bastions of the Right. The anxiety of the Zentrale is revealed by the fact that its agents were sent to the districts in dispute: thus Hans Tittel left Württemberg for Thuringia, where he was elected Polleiter (Weber, *Die Wandlung des deutschen Kommunismus*, Volume 2, op. cit., p. 334).

the assassination of Vorovsky and the triumphant tour by Marshal Foch are links in the same chain.'[31]

On 13 May, the KPD attracted around 100,000 demonstrators in Berlin to protest against the assassination and the plans to attack Russia.[32] On 16 May, more than 150,000 people encircled the coffin of Vorovsky, which was en route to Moscow, in a gigantic torch-lit demonstration, about which Victor Serge was later to write that it 'marked the opening of the period of revolutionary mobilisation'.[33] Rykov and the Soviet ambassador Krestinsky stood at the side of Radek and the entire membership of the Zentrale. Radek delivered a fiery speech in which he appealed to the working people of Germany to come to the defence of the Russian Revolution.[34] The Central Committee met on both this and the following day. Brandler's speech, which stressed both the gravity of the international situation and the fascist danger in Germany itself, was followed merely by a short debate on matters of detail. In fulfilment of the Moscow agreement, Fischer, Geschke, Thaelmann and König were coopted to the Zentrale.[35] Agreement seems to have been reached on the basis of the formulation which Radek contributed on the day after the meeting: 'We are not in a position to institute the dictatorship of the proletariat because the necessary preconditions, the revolutionary will amongst the majority of the working class, do not yet exist'.[36]

But the Ruhr blew up once more on the following day. Franz Dahlem wrote: 'Hunger, which brings the wolf from the woods, brings the miners from the mine and the turner from the factory.'[37] The occasion was a sharp fall of the mark, following massive purchases of foreign currencies by the agents of Stinnes, and a sudden soaring of prices. An unofficial strike broke out, despite restraint by the unions, and the KPD had the greatest difficulty in controlling it. The movement began on 16 May, a central strike committee was eventually formed on 26 May, but it did not have sufficient authority to prevent sporadic street-fighting from occurring. Finally, on 29 May the Zentrale, which met in

---

[31] *Pravda*, 16 May 1923.
[32] It should be recalled that there were about 30,000 Communists in Berlin.
[33] V. Serge, *Memoirs of a Revolutionary*, London, 1967, p. 168.
[34] *Die Rote Fahne*, 17 May 1923.
[35] Ibid.
[36] *Die Rote Fahne*, 18 May 1923. Davidovich (op. cit., p. 79), drawing from the archives of the IML, Moscow, KPD collection, 1923–4, cites the speech of a left leader in the Ruhr, Unger, criticising the opportunism of the Zentrale.
[37] *Correspondance internationale*, no. 44, 1 June 1923, p. 824.

Essen at the same time as the central strike committee, agreed on a return to work on the basis of a 52.3 per cent wage increase. The Left agreed, and work quickly resumed.[38]

However, just as the Communists appeared to have agreed on the need for a prudent approach to the problems of the German Revolution, other people were under the impression that a revolutionary situation was in the offing. On 26 May, just after the first outbreaks at Gelsenkirchen, a senior German official, the deputy to the District President of Düsseldorf, Dr Lütterbeck, wrote to the French General Denvignes, to ask him to give authority to German police to enter the occupied zone in order to restore order:

> Events like those in Gelsenkirchen serve to encourage elements hostile to the state. New troubles will develop, and order, the necessary basis for culture and production, threatens to be overthrown for a quite long time. . . . The industrial region is too complex for us to risk a spark from one city becoming a flame . . . such as neither the Rhine nor the frontiers of Germany can stop. This danger hangs over the world. If the French High Command stands idly by, waiting inactively for the rioting to break out before responding, it will give the impression that France desires that German authority shall collapse . . . even at the cost of an uprising which would threaten European civilisation by placing the Ruhr in the hands of the populace. This game is dangerous to France herself. The army of occupation does not consist only of inanimate material, rifles, machine-guns and tanks. Men who have eyes and ears carry these weapons. They risk taking from the Ruhr dangerous seeds which will germinate in French territory.
>
> In the presence of these dangers, I take the liberty of emphasising the heavy responsibilities which the French High Command would incur if it showed itself to be indulgent towards anarchy. If it does not itself act, its duty is at least to leave the hands of the German authorities free to accomplish theirs. . . . I take the liberty of recalling in this connection that at the time of the Paris Commune, the German Command did all it could to meet the needs of the French authorities taking repressive action.[39]

---

[38] *Bericht über die Verhandlungen des IX Parteitags der Kommunistischen Partei Deutschlands (Sektion der Kommunistischen Internationale), abgehalten in Frankfurt a. M. vom 7 bis 10 April 1924,* Berlin, 1924, p. 11.

[39] *Die Rote Fahne,* 29 May 1923; *Correspondance internationale,* no. 44, 1 June 1923, pp. 825–6.

Chapter Thirty-Seven

An Unprecedented Pre-Revolutionary Situation

The crisis in Germany opened by the occupation of the Ruhr was the deepest which any advanced capitalist country had ever experienced. Poverty became general in a state based on the most modern industrial production. Nearly the whole of the working population suffered absolute pauperisation, and the petty bourgeoisie was ruined. The only privileges which survived were those of the owners of capital and the means of production. Speculation, corruption and prostitution triumphed. All measures of social security collapsed, and with them all democratic ideologies. All so-called moral values were ridiculed. Here was, in short, a fearful balance-sheet of failure and the obverse of a century of the amazing development and brilliant achievements of capitalism.

Runaway inflation

The most spectacular feature of the crisis of 1923 was the monetary inflation. The phenomenon was not new. It went back to the days immediately after the war, and had once been brought under control, in 1919. From 1921, the fall of the mark appears to have been central to the strategy of the German bourgeoisie. They returned to their former calculations in the belief that the monetary crisis was entirely due to the shortfall in exports, thinking that another fall in the mark would reduce their expenses, increase exports, encourage production and provide the conditions for economic recovery. The big industrialists proposed to re-establish a normal monetary situation by replacing state credit with their own, whilst at the same time demanding guarantees. But no government can safely give such guarantees when an organised working class exists. The Social-Democratic ministers obstructed every slightest hint by their partners in favour of accepting the proposals of Hugenberg and Stinnes.

It seems that from November 1921, the magnates of German industry decided that the general situation must deteriorate before it could improve; runaway inflation would wipe out the German debt, bring the state to its knees before them, exhaust the working people, and leave the great capitalists alone as masters of the situation. The mark fell steadily throughout 1922, and its fall became precipitous when the Ruhr was occupied. It would, however, be difficult to apportion precise responsibility for this collapse, one has to take into consideration the effects of increased government spending, together with panic, as well as any concerted policy.

In April 1922, the dollar was worth 1,000 marks; in October, 2,000; and in November, 6,000. On 4 January 1923, it was quoted at 8,000, on the 10th at 10,000 and on the 15th at 56,000 marks.[1] From that moment the curve rose madly, with more or less transitory halts, checks and spasmodic falls followed by sharp accelerations. On 17 May 1923, the dollar was quoted at 96,000 marks, and on 10 July, 200,000.[2] On 23 July, the dollar stood at 400,000, and on 28 July at one million.[3] On 7 August, it passed two million; on 9 August, 6.5 million;[4] on 5 September, a little under 20 million; on 6 September, 46 million; and on 7 September, 60 million.[5]

On 20 September, the dollar was worth 325 million marks.[6] In one year, the value of the mark had been divided by 162,500! At this level, figures lost their meaning. On 1 January 1923, there had been 1,654 million marks in circulation. By 15 August, the Reichsbank alone had issued bank notes for 116,402,548,057,000 marks.[7] The printing press worked unceasingly, and private

---

[1] *Correspondance internationale*, no. 13, 14 February 1923, p. 83.
[2] *Correspondance internationale*, no. 56, 13 July 1923, p. 415. The actual quotations were 266,000 in Danzig, 276,000 in New York, and only 187,000 in Berlin.
[3] *Correspondance internationale*, no. 61, 31 July 1923, p. 456.
[4] *Correspondance internationale*, no. 64, 15 August 1923, p. 478.
[5] *Correspondance internationale*, no. 71, 8 September 1923, p. 535.
[6] *Correspondance internationale*, no. 77, 28 September 1923, p. 582.
[7] *Correspondance internationale*, no. 70, 5 September 1923, p. 528.

presses were called upon to print one, two, five and 10 million mark notes,[8] and then 50 and 100 million mark notes.[9]

The rise in prices followed the same curve. On 3 February 1923, an egg cost 300 marks; on the 5th, 420;[10] on the 10th, 3,400; on the 11th, 4,400;[11] on the 27th, 7,000; on 5 August, 12,000;[12] and on the 8th, 30,000.[13] Shops had to mark up their prices from day to day, and then from hour to hour. The big stores employed people simply to add zeroes to marked prices, and they often lagged behind the actual figures. In fact, the only real transactions took place on the basis of gold or foreign exchange, preferably dollars. The paper mark was no longer of practical use, except for paying wages, when a fixed rate applied.

Economic and social consequences

The economic machine seized up irresistibly, bit by bit. The Reichsbank no longer gave credit except against material securities of stable value, but went on accepting payment in valueless paper, a good opportunity for speculators who had the necessary means. The rate of interest reached astronomical heights, 100 per cent for a 24-hour loan, 400 per cent for a month, and 5,000 per cent for a year. One might wonder whether anyone who lent for more than 24 hours was quite sane. In fact, no-one who possessed capital wanted to have anything in paper marks but his debts. The peasant refused to sell his crops. Shops were empty, and markets were deserted. The crisis took the form of a real internal blockade. Townspeople organised raids into the countryside, attacked farms and looted barns.

Real values, buildings, all kinds of goods and precious articles were at the base of immense fortunes and successes as brazen as they were fast. These things could be bought sometimes for sums which in figures were fabulous, but in reality were derisory. Anyone who did not possess them had no chance of getting them. Anyone who had a little, or assets which could not be divided up, risked losing everything. But anyone who already had enough could be sure of multiplying it ten-fold or even a hundred-fold. Large-scale traders,

[8] *Correspondance internationale*, no. 61, 31 July 1923, p. 456.
[9] *Correspondance internationale*, no. 64, 15 August 1923, p. 478.
[10] *Correspondance internationale*, no. 12, 9 February 1923, p. 75.
[11] *Correspondance internationale*, no. 56, 13 July 1923, p. 415.
[12] *Correspondance internationale*, no. 63, 7 August 1923, p. 470.
[13] *Correspondance internationale*, no. 64, 15 August 1923, p. 478.

industrialists and owners of large estates were seized with a buying frenzy and bought up all that they could. It is said that Stinnes acquired 1,300 firms in the most varied sectors of activity, and that he confessed that he could not give a full account of his own affairs. The export industries made fabulous profits. On the one hand, the low level of rents and wages, and the fall in the real value of their debts, enabled them to charge prices against which no one could compete, and, on the other, they were paid in foreign exchange. Large businesses could deposit capital abroad in foreign currencies. They set up firms in Switzerland, the Netherlands and South America to hide their gains, and created intermediary companies through nominees to enable them to evade the law against capital exports. In short, the big capitalists collected their profits in dollars or gold, and paid their debts in paper – to their very great benefit.

The petty bourgeoisie, on the contrary, were completely ripped off. People living on investments, pensioners and retired people or possessors of fixed incomes found themselves in poverty from one day to the next. In July 1923, an average pensioner received 10,800 marks, which allowed him to make two journeys on the tramway if he was shrewd enough to make them on the same day that he was paid.[14] The owners of blocks of flats saw their income from rents reduced to next to nothing. When they had no more resources, they sold. So gangs of dealers fell upon blocks of flats that they picked up very cheaply for a few kilos of paper marks. Office workers, paid by the month, experienced a fate similar to that of pensioners or recipients of fixed incomes. Even if their salaries paralleled the rise in prices, they did so at best with at least a month's delay, and this meant that their annual salaries were cut by between 50 and 90 per cent.

The workers were relatively better off because they were paid weekly. The gap between the 'rise' and the 'adjustment' was less important to them. Nonetheless, it was considerable at times. A metalworker who was earning 3,000 marks at the end of 1922 received 500,000 in March 1923, and then four million in July.[15] If we convert these marks into dollars, we find that his real wage had fallen from 30 dollars to 25 and then to 14 in a space of six months. According to the official indices, wages at that point were 3,300 times the 1914 level, whilst prices were 12,000 times higher. Thus the theoretical

---

[14] Ibid.
[15] *Correspondance internationale*, no. 61, 31 July 1923, p. 456.

purchasing power of the worker was one-quarter of what it had been before the War.[16] At the beginning of August 1923, wages were 87,000 times higher, and prices 286,000 times higher than in 1914.[17] And it should be remembered that the shops were often empty.

For the week of 27 July–2 August, the cost of living for a worker's family with two children was calculated at 5,158,912 marks for a week. This equalled the monthly pay of the father, provided that it was based on the previous week . . .[18] In October, a miner had to work one hour to buy an egg, and a fortnight to buy a pair of boots.[19] Unemployment was insignificant in the first months of 1923, but it spread: in September the proportion of the workforce which was totally unemployed stood at 7.06 per cent in the metalworking industries, 4.53 per cent in textiles, 12.9 per cent in printing, and 12.6 per cent in tailoring; the proportion of the workforce working part-time in these trades stood at 16.58, 36.19, 32.09 and 57.98 per cent.[20]

The number of homeless people continued to grow.[21] The night hostels were overflowing. 'Attacks on property' multiplied. Suicides reached record levels.[22] In most of the big cities, public transport closed down for lack of customers. For the same reason, all the public baths in Berlin were closed.[23] In this way, the overwhelming majority of the German population was declassed. It was not so much proletarianised as reduced to a sub-proletariat.

The political consequences

Inflation levelled down the living conditions of the working people, wiped out the labour aristocracy, and brought the best-paid specialists down to the level of labourers. There were no longer any differentiations of pay between different occupations or between different levels of skill within occupations, but only one uniformly wretched mass. The trade unions were collapsing, because the millions of marks which millions of members still paid in dues

---

[16] G. Castellan, *L'Allemagne de Weimar*, Paris, 1969, p. 156.
[17] *Correspondance internationale*, no. 64, 15 August 1923, p. 478.
[18] *Correspondance internationale*, no. 63, 7 August 1923, p. 471.
[19] *Correspondance internationale*, no. 83, 19 October 1923, p. 630.
[20] *Correspondance internationale*, no. 77, 28 September 1923, p. 582.
[21] *Correspondance internationale*, no. 12, 9 February 1923, p. 75. There were 40,000 more homeless people in Berlin in 1923 than in 1922.
[22] There were 2,700 attacks on property, and 150 suicides in Berlin in June (*Correspondance internationale*, no. 61, 31 July 1923, p. 456).
[23] *Correspondance internationale*, no. 70, 5 September 1923 p. 528.

could only pile up tons of worthless paper in their treasuries. The full-time officials were reduced to the level of tramps, and the welfare funds were empty of all real values. The newspapers sold for several dozens of millions of marks, but the paper on which to print them had to be paid for in gold. Lack of resources forced them to give up holding congresses. Bulletins, newspapers and journals disappeared. In this way departed *Die Neue Zeit*, in whose pages a whole period in the history of socialism was incarnated.[24]

The traditional trade-union practice of Social Democracy was empty of all content. Trade unionism was powerless, and collective agreements a joke. Working people left the unions, and often turned their anger against them, reproaching them for their passivity, and sometimes for their complicity in their plight. The collapse of the apparatuses of the trade unions and Social Democracy paralleled that of the state: what happened to notions of property, order and legality? How, in such an abyss, could anyone justify an attachment to parliamentary institutions, to the right to vote and universal suffrage? Neither the police nor the army escaped the infection. A whole world was dying. All the elements which only a year before had served as a basis for analysing German society had now been destroyed.

But despite the blows to the material basis of its apparatus, Social Democracy had not received a death blow, though its days were numbered. Already, against the right-wingers who saw the 'Bolshevik revolution' as even worse than the poverty which gripped the German workers, and who were again busy offering their services to oppose it, resistance was being organised, and a somewhat confused Left was arising. It was headed by people of several generations, with '1918 socialists' such as Erich Zeigner joining old-timers such as Paul Levi and Dissmann. This minority held factional meetings and emerged publicly as a political current. Levi, for example, declared: ' The question is posed to German Social Democracy: the dictatorship of the proletariat, or the dictatorship of the others. . . . The dictatorship of the proletariat is necessary. We must march with the Communists.'[25]

Differences appeared within Social Democracy around the problem of the united front. The movement was most vigorous in Saxony and in Thuringia, where it was led by some solidly-rooted trade-union cadres, but it showed itself everywhere. The Communists saw in it the long-awaited beginning of

---

[24] The last issue was dated 23 August 1923.
[25] Cited in *Correspondance internationale*, no. 74, 18 September 1923, p. 560.

the break of the bulk of workers from Social Democracy. During June, Zinoviev emphasised:

> What is new in the situation lies in the fact that the majority of organised workers in Western Europe are no longer *fundamentally* with Social Democracy, even though they may still be officially attached to it. The soul of the Social-Democratic workers is now much more with us: it is breaking free from the Social Democrats and coming nearer to us.[26]

Even someone who did not believe, as Zinoviev did, that 'the link of the great masses of workers with Social Democracy' was now holding 'by no more than a thread',[27] could not deny that the Communists were making progress. Arthur Rosenberg, who was little inclined retrospectively to share the lyrical illusions of his former comrades, was to write in his book on the formation and history of the Weimar Republic: 'At no moment were revolutionary aspirations so deep as in Germany during the summer of 1923.'[28]

It is a significant fact that neither the bourgeois parties nor the Social Democrats, who all made the ballot the basis for their political system, ever thought of facing the electors when they contemplated the scale of the economic and social catastrophe. There was one single election during the crisis period which enables us to judge the advance of Communist influence: the contest for the Landtag in the rural region of Mecklenburg-Strelitz in July 1923. The vote for the bourgeois parties dropped from 18,000 in 1920 to 11,000 in 1923. The Social-Democratic vote fell from 23,000 to 12,800, despite the reunification with the right Independents in the meantime. Finally, whilst the Independents, whom in 1920 one would have regarded as the 'extreme Left' had won in that year 2,257 votes, the Communists, standing for the first time in a region where they had no base, now received 10,853, or about a fifth of the total votes cast.[29]

The figures we have for membership of the Party and the organisations which it controlled are significant. The Communist Youth had 30,000 members in the autumn of 1922, but now had more than 70,000, in 500 local units.[30]

---

[26] G. Zinoviev, 'Un fait nouveau dans le mouvement ouvrier international', *Correspondance internationale*, no. 40, 8 June 1923, p. 337. Zinoviev gives as an example the fact the certain Communist demonstrations brought together two or three times as many people as the Party had in membership.

[27] Ibid., p. 338.

[28] A. Rosenberg, *Entstehung und Geschichte der Weimarer Republik*, Frankfurt am Main, 1955, p. 405.

[29] Ibid., p. 407; *Correspondance internationale*, no. 56, 13 July 1923, p. 415.

[30] *From Third to Fourth: a Report on the Activities of the YCI*, p. 39.

They brought together several hundreds of thousands of youth in their assemblies and marches.[31] The district of Erzgebirge-Vogtland, around Chemnitz, had, we are told, 15,394 members in September 1922, and 25,117 in September 1923, with 92 additional new local groups.[32] The Berlin district recruited 8,000, that of Halle 5,000, that of the Ruhr 3,000, and that of Thuringia 2,000.[33] The Party membership in Bremen doubled,[34] and that in mid-Rhineland gained 1,200 members in nine months.[35]

The numerical progress was accompanied by new organisational efforts. In the spring, the Party was resolutely turned towards the factories, and adopted new organisational forms which could help build its influence there. A new department attached to the Zentrale dealing with factory cells was created, in order systematically to replace the Communist workplace fractions with cells. The bulletin, *Der Partei-arbeiter*, gave information and directives on this task. In the Chemnitz district, the congress of 8–9 September decided to reorganise the Party on this basis.[36]

Considering the economic situation, the Communist press made remarkable progress. During July, *Die Rote Fahne* had a print-run of 60,000, well above that of *Vorwärts*,[37] and the *Hamburger Volkszeitung*'s print-run exceeded 35,000 from June.[38]

But the progress of the Party can be measured better by the links between the Party apparatus and the mass organisations. Between June and October, the number of Communist fractions inside the reformist trade unions rose from 4,000 to 6,000.[39] Methods of organisation had to be changed, because the trade-union department which Fritz Heckert led could no longer alone ensure efficient coordination. Starting in July, the Party created 'red cartels', which grouped at the local level the leaders of the Communist fractions in

---

[31] Uhlemann, op. cit., pp. 39, 130ff.

[32] R. Wagner, 'Zur Frage der Massenkämpfe in Sachsen im Frühjahr und Sommer 1923', *Zeitschrift für Geschichtswissenschaft*, no. 2, 1956, p. 256. The corresponding figures of 19,432 and 30,584 given by Weber are substantially different, but indicate progress of an identical nature (*Die Wandlung des deutschen Kommunismus*, Volume 2, op. cit., p. 373).

[33] Weber, op. cit., pp. 369–76.

[34] Weber, *Die Wandlung des deutschen Kommunismus*, Volume 1, op. cit., p. 50.

[35] *Die Rote Fahne*, 11 August 1923.

[36] *Der Kämpfer*, 11 September 1923, cited in Wagner, op. cit., p. 256.

[37] *Correspondance internationale*, no. 56, 13 July 1923, p. 414.

[38] Report no. 92 of the Reich Commissioner for public order, June 1923, cited in H. Habedank, *Zur Geschichte des Hamburger Aufstandes 1923*, Berlin, 1958, p. 75.

[39] Ibid., p. 69.

the reformist unions and the leading Communists in all the unions. In July, there were 1,100 of these cartels, and 2,100 in October, at which date the trade-union department had contact with fractions in 3,460 localities.[40] At the enlarged ECCI meeting in June, Jakob Walcher estimated that over 2.4 million workers were influenced by or were directly under the authority of Communists in the trade unions.[41] Heckert estimated that between 30 and 35 per cent of organised workers were influenced by the Party at that time, which corresponds to the figure of 2.5 million.[42]

The building trades union had 551,000 members and 749 centres for paying dues; the Communists in that union had 525 fractions, and a majority in 65 local groups which organised 67,200 workers. They were nearly on equal terms with the reformists in 230 local groups which organised 331,000 workers. In total, Walcher estimated that around 260,000 workers in the building trades followed the Communists.

The metalworkers' union, the DMV, was a real bastion of the Communist opposition in the trade unions. In June, according to Walcher, there were 500 Communist fractions in the 1.6 million-strong union, which had 750 centres for paying dues, and in total they estimated that 720,000 metalworkers supported the Communists.[43] They reckoned that their influence in 26 centres, grouping 500,000 workers, equalled that of the reformists. In a certain number of important places – Stuttgart, Halle, Merseburg, Jena, Suhl, Sollingen, Remscheid, etc. – the Communists had won a majority of the union's 260,000 members in these areas. The progress of the Communists was strikingly revealed in the elections of delegates to the congress of the DMV in July. The lists which the KPD backed were victorious in the principal industrial centres, winning one-third of the delegations and an absolute majority of votes. In Berlin, they won 54,000 votes, against 22,000 for the Social-Democratic lists,[44] in Halle, the figures were 2,000 against 500.[45] In June, Walcher, who did not underestimate the reformist grip on the unions, could nonetheless declare: 'We are well on the way to winning the trade unions on the field of organisation.'[46]

---

[40] Ibid.
[41] *Protokoll der Konferenz der Erweiterten Exekutive der Kommunistischen Internationale (Moskau, 12–23 Juni 1923)*, Hamburg, 1923, p. 196.
[42] *Bericht über die Verhandlungen des IX Parteitags der KPD*, op. cit., p. 358.
[43] *Protokoll der Konferenz der Erweiterten EKKI*, op. cit., p. 195.
[44] *Bericht über die Verhandlungen des IX Parteitags der KPD*, op. cit., p. 97.
[45] W. Ersil, *Aktionseinheit stürzt Cuno*, East Berlin, 1961, p. 149.
[46] *Protokoll der Konferenz der Erweiterten EKKI*, op. cit., p. 196.

The movement of factory councils developed extremely quickly during 1923, encouraged by the militant activity of the Communists as much as by the decomposition and passivity of the reformist trade unions. These were very flexible organisations, without full-time officials, led by rank-and-file workers who were nearer to the old Social-Democratic tradition of 'shop stewards' than the functionaries of the trade-union apparatus. They won the attention of important sections of the working class, and eventually undertook functions which had traditionally been devolved to the unions, along with other, more strictly political functions. From November 1922, the KPD's campaigns were partly pursued through the factory councils and their congresses at various different levels. The KPD prided itself on holding the majority in 2,000 factory councils, some of which, like that at the Leuna-Werke – where Bernhard Koenen won 60 per cent of the votes of the 12,000 workers – were very important.[47] The Congress of Factory Councils, which in August started the strike which brought down the Cuno government, claimed to represent, directly or indirectly, some 20,000 councils.[48]

The Chairman of the 'Committee of Fifteen', the action committee on the national level of the factory councils, was Hermann Grothe, a metalworker aged 35. He was a former member of the circle of revolutionary stewards, a Spartacist in 1917, for several years an organiser of committees of unemployed, a member of the KPD and of the Berlin Left. The movement of revolutionary factory councils – that is, of factory councils led by Communists – tended to adopt the same form of organisation: at the base in each factory the council was made up of two committees, one each representing production workers and office staff, the former having the preponderant voice. They organised by industry and by city, but during 1923 they built their organisation by districts and regions. Zinoviev wrote in October, on the basis of the information which reached him from Germany: 'The works committees are already taking part in Germany in settling such vital questions as food distribution, pay, fuel and the arming of the workers. They are becoming the principal lever of the revolution which is ripening before our eyes.'[49]

It was likewise under the influence and on the initiative of factory councils led by Communists that the control committees multiplied. These undertook to control the prices of essential foodstuffs and rents, and to combat speculation,

[47] Ersil, op. cit., p. 75.
[48] Ibid., p. 245.
[49] *Correspondance internationale*, no. 87, 2 November 1923, p. 662.

dealing and scarcity. They were made up of workers, including women workers and housewives,[50] and sometimes involved small traders and artisans in their activity.[51] Their network tried to mobilise the poorly-paid workers and especially women into uninterrupted activity by incessant propaganda and agitation.

The most remarkable of the Communists' initiatives in this period, however, was organising the proletarian hundreds. Since 1918, the need to arm the proletariat had always been present in the minds of the leaders of the Party. Launched afresh in the course of the campaign following the killing of Rathenau, the slogan of organising workers' self-defence began to be manifested in the campaign which followed the Ruhr occupation. This became an obvious necessity in the Ruhr itself, where the German police had been expelled and where Free Corps men continued to infiltrate, and then throughout the whole country. In Central Germany, *Klassenkampf* in Halle launched the first call to organise workers' self-defence groups.[52] They became a reality with the call of the regional congress of the factory councils on 11 March. But, by then, proletarian hundreds probably existed already in other places. In Chemnitz, 10 groups of them went into action on 9 March to prevent a nationalist meeting.[53] In Gera, four of these units marched on 4 March, and were followed in Zella-Mehls on 11 March by 4,000 men of the proletarian hundreds of Southern Thuringia.[54] In a few weeks, the movement spread throughout Germany, and in Berlin on 1 May, the traditional procession was led by the proletarian hundreds, 25,000 men with red armbands, a real workers' militia.[55]

The KPD paid very close attention to the proletarian hundreds. A special commission of three members, supervising their creation and practical organisation, was soon to become the military committee of the Party, under the direction of Ernst Schneller.[56] He had to take certain precautions; the Ministers of the Interior in some of the regions had followed the example of their colleague in Prussia, Severing, who had banned the hundreds on 13 May[57]

---

[50] See Chapter 27.
[51] Krusch, op. cit., p. 136.
[52] *Klassenkampf*, 28 February 1923.
[53] H. Gast, 'Die proletarischen Hundertschafter als Organe der Einheitsfront im Jahre 1923', *Zeitschrift für Geschichtswissenschaft*, no. 3, 1956, pp. 447–8; *Der Kämpfer*, 10 March 1923.
[54] Gast, op. cit., p. 448; *Der Kämpfer*, 15 March 1923.
[55] Ersil, op. cit., p. 95.
[56] Gast, op. cit., p. 457; Davidovich, op. cit., p. 133.
[57] Ersil, op. cit., p. 98.

along with an extreme-right paramilitary organisation.[58] Ultimately, they only developed on a large scale in Thuringia and Saxony, where they had the advantage of official protection and even of credits allocated by the left Social-Democratic governments. In mid-June, Paul Böttcher presented them in these terms:

> We are not playing a military game. Our hundreds have no military objective. . . . In case of provocation or a reactionary terrorist attack, they must be ready to react immediately. . . . The question of arming them has not yet arisen: the answer depends on the strength and the resolution which the movement shows. To act otherwise would be trying to arm the proletariat before it has effectively joined in the struggle for power. The hundreds can have no military purpose before the elementary conditions for that struggle have been realised in the factories.[59]

The Communists wanted to turn the proletarian hundreds into 'organs of the united front', and tried to bring Social-Democratic workers or non-party trade unionists into them. They naturally encountered the opposition of the Social-Democratic leaders, and even of some of their own people, who wanted them to be, in the Böttcher's words, 'troops armed for the conquest of power'. The Party's press and congresses repeated incessantly that the KPD opposed the creation of 'party hundreds'.[60]

A new explosion of nationalism

The Communists' progress was evident, though measurable only with difficulty. The advance of the nationalists of the extreme Right was much more spectacular. The original feature of it was its new colouration, popular or, to put it better, plebeian. The nucleus of their organisations remained the same as they had been when the War ended, the brawlers of the Free Corps, crazy adventurers, xenophobes, anti-Semites, beasts of prey who could not live without uniforms, arms and violence, mad and desperate people, the sad results of four years' war and a long period of indoctrination. However, from 1923, the nationalist movement changed its appearance. With Hitler and the National Socialists, Germany moved from the era of commandos to that of demagogues and mass action.

---

[58] Mujbegović, op. cit., p. 384.
[59] *Correspondance internationale*, no. 49, 19 June 1923, p. 362.
[60] Ibid.

Germany in 1923 was ideal territory for them. They could point out to the millions of declassed petty bourgeois and the suffering workers exactly who was to blame: the capitalists of the Entente, foreigners, Jews, Marxists, the 'November criminals' who had 'stabbed the glorious undefeated army in the back', the 'politicians', and the 'high priests' of the trade unions and the workers' parties, who deceived the working people, and used their formidable organisation to paralyse them and hand them over, bound hand and foot, to their enemies.

The Cuno government had offered a convenient target from the start of the crisis; here was parliamentary government, democracy, the Republic, its impotence and its divisions, in a word – betrayal. Germany betrayed had become a 'proletarian nation'; humiliated, scorned and trodden underfoot by the treachery of its leaders, whose thirst for power had made them provoke the defeat of 1918. To emerge from the abyss, a strong government and a united national will were needed, the dictatorship of a chief, a Führer, a German will, a German ideology, military discipline, strength, and redeeming and purifying violence.

Hitler had added the label 'National Socialist' to the name of the tiny organisation which he joined in 1920. This was to give to German nationalism the properly fascist character of a mass movement. The crisis of 1923 offered him an ideal opportunity. By now, nobody would admit, at least openly, being in favour of the parliamentary or the republican régime, nor of the capitalist system. He therefore had the opportunity to present his tactics in slogans, and to polish up the technique of his propaganda and activities. He recruited amongst the postwar generations, students, the unemployed and petty bourgeois who had become adults in a world without hope. The former warriors who, after being national heroes two years ago, had subsequently upset the bourgeois elements who were dreaming of a revival of their prosperity, were now their last hope, the only force able to resist the Communists, in the streets, in the schools, and even in the factories.

National Socialism confronted Bolshevism and the Communist International in a Germany that had been proletarianised in the extreme. This was the defensive weapon defence of the ruling classes since the beginning of the century. It was to present them with a dilemma which they were to avoid at the end of 1923, but which they were to face again, in an imperative form, between 1930 and 1933.

At the end of 1922 the National-Socialist Party had 15,000 members, and its shock troops, the SA, numbered 6,000. At the beginning of 1923, thanks to the efforts of a former member of the Free Corps, a Reichswehr officer named Röhm, who brought to it the support of the Reichswehr in Bavaria, it was able to conclude a pact with the other Bavarian nationalist organisations. Command of the SA was entrusted to a wartime hero of Germany's air force, Captain Hermann Goering. The organisation made sensational progress in the south, where it enjoyed the support of the authorities, plus abundant subsidies. On 1 May, 10,000 armed men marched near Munich. On 1 September, there were 70,000 in Nuremberg, reviewed by Hitler and Ludendorff. The fascist example inspired them, they talked of 'marching on Berlin'. On 12 September, Hitler declared: 'The November Parliament is nearing its end! The building is tottering! The structure is cracking! There is no longer any other alternative: the swastika or the Soviet star, the universal despotism of the International or the Holy Empire of the German nation.' Assemblies, meetings and processions followed one after another. Hitler became the head of the League of Struggle: his party, a member of this coalition of extreme right-wing groups, numbered 50,000 members, and the SA was armed to the teeth.

These were not the only paramilitary formations. With the approval of the Reichswehr and the subsidies of the magnates of heavy industry, an officer, Major Buchrucker, a former member of the Orgesch terrorist organisation, had formed in 1921, in the principal garrisons in Brandenburg, units of officers and NCOs provided with substantial armaments, with volunteer troops who underwent short periods of training. This Black Reichswehr was, in principle, illegal, but was in reality a semi-official formation with about 20,000 well-armed men, specialist units and modern equipment. Their state of mind was like that of the Free Corps from which they were directly descended; they burned impatiently as they awaited the signal to attack for the 'military dictatorship' which would liberate Germany from the yoke of the 'foreigner'.

The Communists confront the nationalists

Since the end of 1922, the Communists had become anxious about the development of the nationalist movement in general, and the progress of the Nazi Party in particular. In early December, Karl Becker had uttered a first cry of alarm. Fascism, recently victorious in Italy, was no less possible in Germany. In this highly industrialised country it had an insufficiently broad base, and big business would be making great efforts 'to neutralise a large part of the proletariat'. But fascism would be all the more serious a danger because the disillusion created by the Social Democrats would plunge layers of the working class into passivity. Only the success of a united front policy could nip it in the bud.[61]

Some weeks later, Hans Tittel devoted an article to the National-Socialist Workers' Party, noting the progress which it was making in southern Germany. It was financed by important capitalist groups, and was trying to win the sympathy of the apolitical popular masses. It was pan-German and anti-Semitic, and utilised demagogy against the parliamentary system and the 'high priests' of the parties and trade unions. It was recruiting widely in the middle class, and had a solid paramilitary organisation. Tittel stressed the need to organise armed proletarian resistance to this party, which was 'determined, well-financed, militarised and assured of the sympathy of the ruling classes'.[62]

The crisis accelerated its progress strikingly. Nazis, as they became known, had been elected to factory councils in Berlin and Upper Silesia. Böttcher declared: 'Fascism is pushing its roots into the working class.' The Communists had to understand that armed force was no longer enough to combat nationalism in its new form.[63]

The sharpened forms of the economic and social crisis were creating a new situation. Fascism in Germany was recruiting a basis amongst the petty bourgeoisie who were resisting being driven down into the proletariat. The Communists had to grasp this quickly. On 25 March, an article by Radek, entitled 'Powerless Germany', appeared in *Die Rote Fahne* in which he noted that, so far, the Communists had neglected 'fighting in the name of the whole people', and, in particular, in the name of the non-proletarian social strata which were being crushed by the capitalist crisis. This negligence explained why social strata who now had nothing to lose from the Revolution were joining the camp of the extreme Right.[64] Immediately after the Moscow compromise, the ECCI emphasised the importance of this question: 'The German Communist Party must make the nationalist masses of the petty bourgeoisie and the intellectuals clearly understand that the working class alone, once its victory has been won, will be able to defend German territory, the treasures of German culture and the future of the nation.'[65]

---

[61] Becker's article was originally published in *Bolshevik*, and reproduced in *Correspondance internationale*, no. 95, 9 December 1922, pp. 720–1.
[62] *Correspondance internationale*, no. 101, 30 December 1922, p. 763.
[63] *Correspondance internationale*, no. 49, 19 June 1923, p. 362.
[64] *Die Rote Fahne*, 25 March 1923.
[65] *Die Rote Fahne*, 13 May 1923; *Dokumente und Materialen*, Volume 7/2, Part 2, op. cit., p. 307.

On 17 May, a resolution of the Central Committee called on the Communists to attempt to attract the nationalistic petty-bourgeois masses away from fascism:

> We must go to the suffering masses of the proletarianised petty bourgeoisie who are bewildered and driven mad, and tell them the full truth: they can defend neither themselves nor the future of Germany unless they ally themselves with the working class to defeat the bourgeoisie. The road to victory over Poincaré and Loucheur goes first by way of victory over Stinnes and Krupp.[66]

At the end of May, the KPD commented on the appeal which Lütterbeck had addressed to the French occupation authorities. It addressed the 'petty-bourgeois masses whom nationalism inspires', civil servants and intellectuals:

> What do you intend to do about a government which, with the cynicism of a courtier, dares to ask French generals openly for their permission to massacre its German brothers? We are convinced that the nationalist masses of people are very largely made up of persons with honest and sincere convictions, but who are led astray, and do not realise that the Entente is not their only enemy.[67]

These appeals met with no echo from the Right, apart from favourable comment on the 'national sense' of the Communists in the journal of the nationalist intellectuals, *Gewissen*. Nonetheless, the appeals announced a policy which was destined to cause a sensation.

The fascist danger was at the centre of the discussions in June in the enlarged ECCI, rather than the question of the struggle for power in Germany. In his introductory speech on 12 June, Zinoviev confined himself to noting the progress of fascism, welcoming the common action which the Communist Parties of France and Germany had undertaken, and devoted only a minute or two to the situation in Germany, restricting himself to insisting that the call for a workers' government should be widened to a workers' and peasants' government.[68] Böttcher spoke merely to emphasise the successes which had been won in Germany thanks to the tactic of the united front, and in particular what he considered to be the 'ideological split in Social Democracy'. He

---

[66] *Die Rote Fahne*, 18 May 1923; *Dokumente und Materialen*, Volume 7/2, Part 2, op. cit., p. 322.

[67] *Die Rote Fahne*, 29 May 1923; *Dokumente und Materialen*, Volume 7/2, Part 2, op. cit., p. 335.

[68] *Protokoll der Konferenz der Erweiterten EKKI*, op. cit., p. 35.

stressed that 'the workers' government can arise from existing democratic institutions', declaring that the Communists had to 'face the possibility of a workers' government, a revolutionary coalition with Social Democracy and the trade unions . . . supported principally by the extra-parliamentary class organisations'.[69]

Radek left aside these old questions, to concentrate on underlining the importance of the 'national question' in Germany:

> It is significant that a Nazi journal violently attacks the common suspicions about the Communists; it says that the Communists are a combative party which is becoming more and more national-Bolshevik. In 1920, national Bolshevism meant an orientation towards certain generals. Today, it expresses the unanimous sentiment that salvation lies in the hands of the Communist Party. We alone can find a way out of the present situation in Germany. *To place the nation first means in Germany, as in the colonies, to perform a revolutionary act.*[70]

In his reply, Zinoviev echoed him, declaring that the article in *Gewissen* was 'the greatest possible compliment', and proved that the Party did not interpret 'its class character in a corporatist sense'.[71] On 15 June, Radek spoke on the development of the international situation during the preceding six months: 'The German working class and, with it, the German Revolution are under threat. . . . The poverty of the German workers is so deep that the watchword, "Don't let yourself be provoked", no longer has any effect, and it is clear that the German working class is going to have to fight.'[72] It was 'a difficult situation', because the German proletariat had to fight simultaneously against German fascism and French imperialism. This time, the discussion was frankly engaged. Neurath criticised the famous article by Thalheimer which stated that the German bourgeoisie could be playing a revolutionary role in international affairs, at least momentarily, despite itself.[73] He added: 'We have to overthrow the German bourgeoisie and establish a workers' and peasants' government. . . . It is in this way that we shall win to Communism the petty-bourgeois elements, who will not find that road if we compete with the nationalists.'[74]

---

[69] Ibid., p. 55.
[70] Ibid., pp. 66–7.
[71] Ibid., p. 101.
[72] Ibid., p. 127.
[73] See Chapter 33.
[74] *Protokoll der Konferenz der Erweiterten EKKI*, op. cit., p. 132.

Böttcher replied that the KPD had shown itself to be the revolutionary leadership of that class which alone could 'realise national independence'. To follow the line which Neurath advised would result in 'giving a powerful boost to fascism'.[75] Hoernle undertook to defend Radek: 'In order to bring down the Cuno government, the Party needs the masses and must take account of their ideology.' He advocated 'a living internationalism' in the place of 'an intransigent internationalism'.[76] In his reply, Radek emphasised the unique character of the German situation, 'the defeat of a great industrial nation reduced to the rank of a colony':

> The petty-bourgeois masses and the intellectuals and technicians who will play a big role in the revolution are in a position of national antagonism to capitalism, which is declassing them. . . . If we want to be a workers' party that is able to undertake the struggle for power, we have to find a way that can bring us near to these masses, and we shall find it not in shirking our responsibilities, but in stating that *the working class alone can save the nation*.[77]

After these skirmishes, it was only on 20 June, during the discussion on fascism, that the new line appeared in its full clarity. Zetkin, who was ill and had to be carried to the platform, gave the report. She emphasised that until then, the Communists had not known how to analyse fascism, which they had regarded more or less as a variant of white terror: 'Fascism is not the answer of the bourgeoisie to an attack by the proletariat; it is the punishment inflicted on the proletariat for not having continued the revolution begun in Russia.'[78] She saw in fascism the expression of the decadence of the capitalist economy, and a symptom of the decomposition of the bourgeois state. It recruited first amongst old soldiers and the proletarianised middle classes. Its bases rested on the disappointment caused by the delay in the coming of socialism, as well as amongst workers who despaired of the future of their own class. It was an instrument of the bourgeoisie, characterised by a programme which appeared to be revolutionary, adapted to the crude feelings of the masses, and by its systematic employment of force. The mistake of the Italian Communists was to see in fascism only a terrorist movement with military inspiration, and not to understand its social significance.

Zetkin added that the fight against fascism had to be waged on the military

---

[75] Ibid., p. 134.
[76] Ibid., p. 137.
[77] Ibid., pp. 147–8.
[78] Ibid., p. 205.

level, but it was not enough to oppose the storm-troopers with proletarian hundreds. If the Communists were to defeat fascism once and for all, they had to win over or neutralise some of its supporters, the elements whom the socialists had disillusioned, and to understand that they wanted to escape from poverty and open up for themselves new, exciting perspectives.

It was during the discussion on the report by Zetkin that Radek delivered his celebrated speech about Schlageter:

> Throughout the whole speech by our comrade Zetkin, I was obsessed by the name of Schlageter and his tragic fate. We need to remember him here when we are taking our position politically against fascism. The fate of this martyr of German nationalism must not be forgotten, or merely honoured in a passing word. He has much to teach us, us and the German people. We are not sentimental romantics who forget their hatred at the sight of a corpse, nor diplomats who say that before a tomb we must be silent or bestow praises on it. Schlageter was a valiant soldier of the counter-revolution. He deserves sincere homage on our part as soldiers of the revolution. . . . If those amongst the German fascists who want to serve their people loyally do not understand the meaning of the fate of Schlageter, then he has died in vain, and they can write on his tomb: 'The Wanderer into the Void!'[79]

He recalled the life and death of Schlageter, and addressed the fascists:

> Whoever will try to reduce the German people to slavery in the train of the speculators, the iron and coal kings, to precipitate it into adventures, will meet the resistance of the Communist workers. They will answer violence with violence. We shall fight by every means against those who through misunderstanding ally themselves to the mercenaries of capital. *However, we believe that the great majority of the masses who are stirred by nationalist feelings belong not in the camp of capital but in that of labour.* We seek to find the route to the masses, and we shall succeed in doing so. We shall do everything to ensure that men who, like Schlageter, were ready to give their life for a common cause, will become not *wanderers into the void, but wanderers into a better future for the whole of humanity*, so that they may generously shed their blood, not for the profit of the barons of iron and coal, but in the cause of the great working people of Germany, who are part of the family of the peoples fighting for their freedom.[80]

---

[79] Ibid., p. 240. See Chapter 35, note 24.
[80] *Protokoll der Konferenz der Erweiterten EKKI*, op. cit., p. 244.

The 'Schlageter line'

It was from this speech as its starting point that the KPD adopted what has come to be called the 'Schlageter line'. Radek developed it anew in several articles, in which it would take much myopia – or bad faith – to discern any wish to collude with Nazism.[81] For example, he wrote in *Die Rote Fahne* in July 1923:

> It is the duty of the German Communists to fight, arms in hand if necessary, against the fascist insurrection, which would be a calamity for the working class and for Germany. But at the same time, it is their duty to do all they can to convince the petty-bourgeois elements amongst the fascists, who are fighting against being pauperised, that Communism is not their enemy, but is the star which shows them the road to victory. . . . It is ridiculous to believe that we can defeat fascism simply arms in hand. . . . Socialism never was uniquely the struggle of the workers for their piece of bread. It has always sought to be a shining torch for all the wretched of the earth. . . . One of the greatest crimes of Social Democracy has been that it destroys all faith in socialism and in the strength of the popular masses.[82]

The Communists systematically sought discussion and public debate with the Nazis, especially amongst the students, who formed one of their bastions. The polemic or dialogue developed in the press. Count Reventlow replied to Radek in *Reichswart*, and Frölich replied to him. Möller van den Bruck then addressed Radek in *Gewissen*, and Radek in turn replied.[83] The KPD then published a brochure, *Schlageter: A Discussion*, based on this exchange and filled out with subsequent contributions from Reventlow and Radek, and did its best to distribute it systematically amongst Nazi members and sympathisers.[84] Communist speakers addressed nationalist audiences in the universities on the theme 'Why Did Schlageter Die?' in Göttingen, Jena and Berlin, where Fischer declared: 'The giant that will free Germany is there: it

---

[81] The source of that interpretation is to be found in the campaign in the French press at this time. Fischer's book contributed greatly to giving it credit.

[82] *Die Rote Fahne*, 27 July 1923.

[83] See in particular Reventlow, 'Mit Radek', *Reichswart*, 30 June 1923; Möller Van den Bruck, 'Der Wanderer ins Nichts', and 'Wirklichkeit', *Das Gewissen*, 30 July 1923; Radek, 'Dem Gewissen zur Antwort', *Die Rote Fahne*, 10 July 1923; 'Kommunismus und deutsche nationalistische Bewegung', *Die Rote Fahne*, 16–18 August 1923; 'Die Voraussetzung des Bündnisses mit Sowjetrussland', *Die Rote Fahne*, 2 September 1923.

[84] K. Radek, P. Frölich, Graf Ernst Reventlow, Möller Van den Bruck, *Schlageter: Eine Auseinandersetzung*, Berlin, 1923.

is the German proletariat, of which you are a part, and with which you should align yourselves.'[85] On 2 August, Remmele addressed a Nazi meeting in Stuttgart, and on the 10th a Nazi speaker addressed a Communist audience. Remmele said to the Nazis: 'They told you that Communism would take everything from you. But it is capitalism that has taken everything from you!'[86] These confrontations were often turning to the advantage of the Communists, and on 14 August, the Nazi leaders decided to put a stop to them.[87]

In parallel, the Communists stepped up their propaganda work towards non-proletarian layers affected by the crisis, in particular officers and policemen. In March, in order to reach the intellectuals, it had founded the League of Friends of Workers' International Relief, with personalities in the cultural world such as Maximilian Harden and Albert Einstein on the letterhead.[88] *Die Rote Fahne* carried an editorial entitled 'The Pauperisation of the Intellectual Proletariat',[89] and another, 'The Fate of the German Intelligentsia', describing the plight of doctors, lawyers, teachers and officials: 'Without the German working class, the German intelligentsia will perish. The destiny of the German working class is that of the German intelligentsia.'[90]

The results do not seem to have been very positive, and the influence of the KPD barely went beyond the limits of the working class. However, the dangers implicit in the new tactic were often exploited against it, especially by its Social-Democratic opponents. Communist orators sometimes let themselves get carried away in their desire to please their audiences, and made dangerous concessions to them, at any rate verbal ones, and the SPD tried to exploit the Schlageter line by denouncing collaboration between Communists and Nazis. *Vorwärts* accused Remmele of having told the Nazis on 10 August that the Communists preferred an alliance with them to one with the Social Democrats, and that they were ready, if necessary, to forge an alliance with the murderers of Liebknecht and Luxemburg.[91]

Vorwärts also accused Fischer of having used openly anti-Semitic language in Berlin,[92] and in this way initiated a legend which lives on actively today.

---

[85] *Die Rote Fahne*, 29 July 1923.
[86] Cited in *Bulletin communiste*, no. 41, 11 October 1923, p. 625.
[87] *Völkische Beobachter*, 14 August 1923, cited in ibid.
[88] Angress, op. cit., p. 346.
[89] *Die Rote Fahne*, 22 July 1923.
[90] *Die Rote Fahne*, 26 July 1923.
[91] Wenzel, op. cit., p. 116, n. 21; Angress, op. cit., p. 341, n. 66.
[92] *Vorwärts*, 22 August 1923, accused Fischer of having announced that 'all those who denounce Jewish capital' were 'already without knowing it class-fighters

In France, Salomon Grumbach, who was notorious in 1914–18 for his social-chauvinist opinions, undertook to spread it in *Le Populaire*, playing on the nationalism of the French workers to turn them against the German and French Communists. This campaign was not without success, which explains at least partly the isolation of the French Communist Party in the working class in its campaign of solidarity with the German workers. As the correspondence of the Swiss Communist Humbert-Droz bears witness,[93] it also led to much hesitation in the ranks of the French Party itself.[94]

However, the 'Schlageter line', which was accepted without apparent resistance throughout the KPD – Left and Right alike – corresponded to the needs of the time – and history has proved this to be correct – even if its application went awry at times. None of the German leaders in the period concealed this, and Böttcher explained it clearly:

> To the degree that the fascist movement develops in Germany, our party must revise its position towards it. As long as it was only at the stage of military formations, the defence of the working class consisted in counterposing proletarian violence to reactionary violence. The formation of organs of defence was at the basis of Communist propaganda. It became clear that this was not enough to resist fascism, a political movement with a social content. We have to fight it also on the level of ideology, first of all by counterposing to it our methods of preventing national ruin and economic enslavement, and then in stressing its role as an instrument of capital.[95]

[*Klassenkämpfer*]' and of having shouted: 'Yes, hang the Jewish capitalists from the lamp-posts . . . but . . . what about the big capitalists like Stinnes . . .?' Fischer did not send in a correction to *Die Rote Fahne*, according to Wenzel (op. cit., p. 118) and Angress (op. cit., p. 340, n. 62), but she did so a week later on a minor point in which *Vorwärts* had distorted her words. Over twenty years later, she wrote: 'I said that communism was for fighting Jewish capitalists only if all capitalists, Jewish and Gentile, were the object of the same attack' (Fischer, op. cit., p. 283, n. 16).

[93] Humbert-Droz's letters to Zinoviev, 14 June, 6, 20, 22 September (Humbert-Droz, op. cit., pp. 191–9).

[94] Humbert-Droz wrote to Zinoviev on 29 September 1923 that 'Monatte, for example, was convinced that the German party had taken the same road as the socialists in 1914' (ibid., p. 198). Rosmer, without challenging Radek's analysis, of which he seems rather to approve, nonetheless writes about the Schlageter speech: 'Radek's unbelievable declamation was not designed to ease the task of worker militants who had given their activity a carefully judged orientation. On the other hand, it was of great value to the social-democratic leaders who were remaining passive in the face of the advances of the national socialists, and were glad to have a pretext – which seemed excellent – to denounce the "collusion of the communist and fascist leaders"' (Rosmer, op. cit., pp. 224–5).

[95] *Correspondance internationale*, no. 49, 19 June 1923, p. 362.

In mid-1923, the 'Schlageter line' was but one of the methods of the Communists' policy of winning the masses, which they judged to be the precondition for the revolutionary struggle for power. In an article entitled 'The Road to the Abyss', Brandler summed up the policy and perspectives of his party at this point, and made clear precisely where their bastions in Saxony and Thuringia could be situated in them:

> The collapse of the German economy and state have brought about exceptional situations, as in Saxony and in Thuringia, where the bourgeoisie is not strong enough to prevent the formation of organs of struggle, control committees and proletarian hundreds, and in which the proletariat cannot completely crush the bourgeoisie because it is isolated in the middle of bourgeois Germany. . . . The plan of the bourgeoisie is to make the economic struggles of the working class degenerate into political struggles, so that they can crush the proletarian movement as they did in 1919. It is the duty of the Communist Party to foil this manoeuvre, and in the case of a general strike by miners and railwaymen, or of a fascist attack, to create a united movement with the precise demands which are formulated in the programme of the Congress of Factory Councils.[96]

Thus, at the end of June 1923, whilst the German Communists were totally convinced that the situation which the crisis had opened up in Germany was leading inevitably to revolution, they considered that they had sufficient time to strengthen their influence within and around the proletariat, an approach that enjoyed the full support of the ECCI. During the session of the enlarged ECCI in June, no one posed the conquest of power in Germany as an immediate task. Zinoviev declared: 'Germany is on the eve of revolution. This does not mean that revolution will come in a month or in a year. Perhaps much more time will be required.'[97]

---

[96] Ibid., p. 359.
[97] This quotation is translated from the Russian shorthand report, p. 103, and is quoted by Carr, *The Interregnum*, op. cit., p. 178. The German text is different: 'The KPD is a class party, but in the sense of the sort of revolutionary party that is necessary on the eve of revolution. There may be more episodes, but there is no doubt about the outcome of the struggle.' (*Protokoll der Konferenz der Erweiterten EKKI*, op. cit., p. 101.)

Chapter Thirty-Eight
The Overthrow of the Cuno Government

If, as Lenin believed, the essence of Marxism really lies in first knowing how to analyse a concrete situation correctly, then it was not easy to be a good Marxist in Germany in July 1923. There could be no disputing that the situation was pre-revolutionary. But, as such, it revealed many contradictory features. Moreover, the memory of past misadventures weighed heavily upon the judgement of the Communist leaders. The higher the stakes and the greater the real chances of victory, the greater the dangers of defeat appeared, and the more serious the reasons for temporising in order not to lose everything by engaging in battle too soon.

Rumours of civil war

After the relative respite in the Ruhr, the temperature did not cease to rise throughout the country from early June onward, as the economic crisis deepened, the mark collapsed, and prices soared. Strikes broke out, unofficial, disavowed by the trade unions, and opposed by the Social-Democratic leaders, who warned of the risks involved in rash actions and disorder that could only serve to increase the Communists' influence. The rising authority of the factory councils made itself felt in these strikes. Their All-Reich Action Committee, the 'Committee of Fifteen' over which Hermann Grothe presided, began to look like an alternative working-class leadership, a serious challenge to the leadership of the unions.

On 16 June, the Committee addressed a solemn appeal, in the name of the factory councils, to the working people, civil servants, clerical workers and intellectuals. It described the catastrophe that was threatening German society as a whole, and reaffirmed that the working class could tackle the root of the evil, the capitalist system: 'Only common struggle, only class struggle can bring you what you need simply to ensure that you survive. The working people are in motion. In the flood which the trade unions are today trying to stem and bring to a halt, important tasks fall to the factory councils.'[1] The Committee called on the factory councils to set up local and regional organisations, in order to provide 'objectives and leadership' to the working masses in the coming struggles. Committees to control prices and proletarian hundreds should be developed; with the factory councils, they would form the basis of the workers' government which alone could provide a positive way out of the crisis.

In fact, strikes and demonstrations broke out one after another. There were demonstrations by workers in Bautzen on 2 June,[2] and in Dresden and Leipzig on 7 June.[3] On the same day, over 100,000 miners and metalworkers were on strike in Upper Silesia, under the leadership of an elected strike committee[4] which included six Communists in its 26 members.[5] On 11 June, a strike of 100,000 agricultural workers broke out in Silesia – an unprecedented event[6] – followed by 10,000 day-labourers in Brandenburg.[7] Also on that day, a strike began in the mercantile marine in Emden, Bremen, Hamburg and Lübeck, called by the Seamen's Federation, which was part of the RILU, and was under Communist leadership.[8]

In Berlin, the metalworkers went into action.[9] There were 250,000 of them in the capital and the suburbs, of whom 153,000 were organised in the trade unions, and there were numerous small enterprises in which not even half

---

[1] *Die Rote Fahne*, 17 June 1923.
[2] *Die Rote Fahne*, 2 June 1923.
[3] *Die Rote Fahne*, 7 June 1923.
[4] *Die Rote Fahne*, 9 June 1923.
[5] Angress, op. cit., p. 352.
[6] *Die Rote Fahne*, 12 June 1923.
[7] *Die Rote Fahne*, 24 June 1923.
[8] *Die Rote Fahne*, 12 June 1923.
[9] *Die Rote Fahne*, 8 July 1923.

the workers were organised. The workers' pressure forced the union to call a strike ballot, and the response was massively favourable. The union then held a second ballot, this time to include non-members, and the majority for the strike was even greater than before. In the end, a strike call went out for the 60 largest firms, with a total workforce of 90,000. The employers immediately opened negotiations, but on 10 July there were 150,000 on strike, and the union leadership had been left behind in many factories. On the same day, the employers signed for a wage increase; from 9,800 marks for the last week in June to 12,000 for the first week in July. One clause provided for the formation of a parity commission to set up a price index, which would serve as the basis for compensation for the rising cost of living; the employers demanded this be kept secret to avoid any risk of the idea spreading. However, the results were there to be seen; the revised pay of the metalworkers from 10 July was 38 per cent higher than the amount for which the union had asked on 3 July, when the employers refused to pay up.[10]

The building trade workers soon had their turn, and then the woodworkers in the capital. The Communists in all areas played the leading role in starting the strike, and subsequently organised the return to work, not only in the trade-union meetings in which they often had a majority, but in the workers' assemblies open to all which they compelled the trade-union leaders to convene.

On 12 July, amid the upsurge of these economic strikes to defend wages, *Die Rote Fahne* published a resounding 'Call to the Party'.[11] It was drafted entirely by Brandler, and had been accepted on the 11th by the surprised Zentrale, despite many reservations. Brandler was alarmed by the progress of the nationalist extreme Right, and appalled by the report of a meeting during which the former leftist Wolffheim, who had defected to them, spoke of 'shooting the Communists'. He wanted to stir up the Party, and make it aware of the gravity of the situation.[12] The appeal declared that the situation was getting increasingly serious. The Cuno government was on the brink of collapse, and the hour of total crisis was approaching. The French and Belgians

---

[10] See Melcher's article on the metalworkers' strike in *Correspondance internationale*, no. 56, 13 July 1923, p. 416.

[11] *Die Rote Fahne*, 12 July 1923; *Dokumente und Materialen*, Volume 2/7, Part 2, op. cit., pp. 365–7.

[12] According to statements by Brandler to Wenzel and Carr, discussed in Angress, op. cit., p. 358, n. 109.

were promoting the separatist movement in the Rhineland, and Bavaria was on the point of seceding under an extreme right-wing government. The Reichswehr troops – in Bavaria at least – the Nazi storm troops and the Black Reichswehr were preparing for open civil war, after the harvest, against workers' Saxony and Thuringia, where left Social-Democratic governments were supporting the development of the movement of the factory councils, and tolerating that of the proletarian hundreds. The plans of the fascists were well known to the army chiefs, and met with their approval, to the leaders of the bourgeois parties, who encouraged them, and to the Social-Democratic leaders, who became their accomplices by remaining silent: 'We are heading for a serious fight; we must be completely ready to act! We must prepare ourselves and the masses without nervousness, calmly and with clear ideas.'[13] No one knew when the fascists would attack:

> We Communists can win this battle with the counter-revolution only if we succeed in leading the Social-Democratic and non-party workers into the struggle with us. . . . Our party must raise the combativity of its organisations to a height that can ensure that they are not taken unawares when civil war breaks out. . . . The fascists hope to win the civil war by overwhelming brutality and the most resolute violence. . . . Their attack can only be put down by red terror opposed to white terror. If the fascists, armed to the teeth, fire on our proletarian fighters, they will find us ready to wipe them out. If they put one striker in ten up against a wall, the revolutionary workers will shoot one fascist in five! . . . The Party is ready to fight shoulder to shoulder with anyone who sincerely agrees to fight under the leadership of the proletariat. Forward! Let us close the ranks of the proletarian vanguard! Into battle, in the spirit of Karl Liebknecht and Rosa Luxemburg![14]

The same issue of *Die Rote Fahne* announced the decision by the Zentrale to declare 29 July an 'Anti-Fascist Day' of the proletariat, and to organise demonstrations throughout Germany on that day. The moment appeared to have come to test the strength of the Party in large-scale street demonstrations, which in their turn could influence the course of political development, and in particular win the majority of the workers to Communism. This appeal to

---

[13] *Die Rote Fahne*, 12 July 1923; *Dokumente und Materialen*, Volume 2/7, Part 2, op. cit., p. 365.

[14] *Dokumente und Materialen*, Volume 2/7, Part 2, op. cit., pp. 365–7.

the Party was, however, criticised, especially amongst the cadres of the Right. Brandler was later to mention the rumours going around at this time: 'Brandler has gone mad. Once again he wants to stage a putsch.'[15]

The Anti-Fascist Day affair

The decision to organise a demonstration corresponded no doubt to the determination of the Zentrale to ensure its hold on the movement, but also to unify and centralise it. In any case, in the climate of the time, this demonstration could not fail to help heighten class confrontation. The press naturally denounced it immediately as a declaration of war, and the proof that the Communists were preparing for civil war.[16]

The Party press could issue denials, but its appeals for vigilance and its insistence on the need to mobilise the masses and the irresistible approach of the decisive moment helped maintain an oppressive atmosphere. Moreover, the Communists were not alone in preparing the Anti-Fascist Day. When we read the appeals to prepare and organise local demonstrations, we see that they had been able to win many trade unions and unaffiliated people to their project. Moreover, wherever the Communists had convinced the Social-Democratic organisations, there was a crowd of workers showing their readiness to follow them – and even to go ahead of them.

In Frankfurt-am-Main on 23 July there were violent scenes during a joint demonstration organised by the KPD and the Social Democrats. The demonstrators forced shops to close, stopped buses and accosted bourgeois-looking passers-by, making them carry placards and shout slogans.[17] The President of Hanover – Gustav Noske himself – used this as an excuse to ban the demonstration of 29 July in his state.[18] The Reich government called on the other states to follow his example. All agreed except Saxony and Thuringia. In Prussia, Severing, the Social-Democratic Minister of the Interior, banned the proposed demonstration in Potsdam.[19]

---

[15] *Die Lehren der deutschen Ereignisse*, op. cit., p. 31.
[16] Ersil (op. cit., p. 153) mentions articles from *Germania*, 19 July, *Deutsche Allgemeine Zeitung*, 12 July, and *Merseburger Tageblatt*, 14 July, denouncing 'a danger greater than the French troops on the Rhine and in the Ruhr'.
[17] *Die Rote Fahne*, 24 July 1923.
[18] Angress, op. cit., p. 364.
[19] Potsdam Archives I, Reichsministerium des Innern, no. 13, 212, p. 52, cited in Ersil, op. cit., p. 153.

All the old differences immediately reappeared within the Zentrale. Should they accept the ban? Should they proceed, but if so, how could they avoid running excessive risks, and even risking a premature battle? Brandler inclined towards an intermediate solution. To be sure, the KPD could now draw considerable forces behind it, but as it had not yet taken the leadership of any important mass movement, it must at all costs avoid the government's provocation, and, in short, evade the test of strength, but without capitulating. He proposed to maintain the slogan, and to demonstrate in Saxony, Thuringia and Baden, where they had not been banned, and also in Prussian Saxony, in the Ruhr and in Upper Silesia, where the authorities did not have the means to stop the demonstrations. In any case, the demonstrations would have to be protected by the proletarian hundreds bearing arms.[20] Fischer thought that the Party could not submit without losing face and the confidence of the workers, and insisted that the demonstration in Berlin must take place.[21]

The Berlin police under Severing were a formidable force, and the Communists' influence amongst the Berlin proletariat was far less than that of the Social Democrats. The danger existed – which was heightened in Brandler's judgement by the presence of leftists in the positions of command in the Berlin-Brandenburg districts – of falling into the trap of a provocation, and once again isolating the vanguard of the Berlin proletariat in a premature fight. Brandler pointed this out, and added – not, doubtless, without a certain irony – that the Zentrale could authorise the demonstration in Berlin only if the Party leaders in the capital could be sure that it would get sufficient armed protection. This counter-proposal so infuriated Fischer that she went so far as to call him a 'fascist' and an 'adventurer'! Brandler retreated, and proposed a strike against the prohibition of demonstrations, but this was rejected.[22] The Zentrale was plunged into deep confusion. The press continued to denounce the 'Bolshevik peril' and the intention of the Communists to stage a putsch on the occasion of the demonstration, and the majority of the Zentrale considered that they must at all costs avoid falling into the trap by agreeing to fight on the day and in the place chosen by the adversary. Nonetheless,

---

[20] *Die Lehren der deutschen Ereignisse*, op. cit., p. 32.
[21] Ibid., p. 55. It is curious that in *Stalin and German Communism*, Fischer devotes only five lines to the affair of the Anti-Fascist Day, and does not mention the positions which she held (op. cit., p. 287).
[22] *Die Lehren der deutschen Ereignisse*, op. cit., p. 32.

the decision to bow to the prohibition was so serious that Brandler did not want to take it alone, without the advice of the ECCI.[23]

The situation was confused in Moscow. The Twelfth Congress of the Communist Party had just ended. This was the first congress without Lenin, whose last article had appeared on 6 February, and who, following another stroke, had been completely paralysed since 9 March. For several months, conflicts had crystallised in the Political Bureau around economic questions. The 'scissors crisis' called for remedies; Trotsky proposed industrialisation and planning, which the majority rejected. Against him was the 'Troika', the alliance of Zinoviev, Kamenev and Stalin, who had been General Secretary since 1922. The differences between the Troika and Trotsky were not expressed during the Congress, but the former nonetheless faced severe criticism. Preobrazhensky and others denounced the stifling of democracy in the Party, the rise of the apparatus, and the spread of authoritarian methods of leadership. Bukharin and Rakovsky criticised Stalin for conducting a chauvinist policy of forced Russification. Moreover, Stalin's behaviour during the Georgian affair had encouraged Lenin to propose a bloc with Trotsky against him, and to embark on the struggle which on the eve of his final relapse was to lead him to break off personal relations with Stalin. But in Lenin's absence, Trotsky did not cross swords at the Congress with his opponents, whilst they were already organising a faction against him in the Political Bureau.

When Brandler's telegram arrived in Moscow, the majority of the Bolshevik leaders, including Zinoviev, Bukharin and Trotsky, were on holiday. Only Radek and the Finn Kuusinen, were at the ECCI.[24] The Bulgarian Communists had just repeated the KPD's blunders during the Kapp Putsch, and announced their neutrality in the conflict between Stambulisky's peasant-reformist government and Tsankov's military uprising.[25] Radek said that the Germans should beware of 'forcing the struggle' and of 'running to meet a defeat like that of July 1917 for fear of seeing repeated what happened in Bulgaria'.[26] Nonetheless, he consulted his colleagues who were on holiday. Trotsky refused

---

[23] Angress (op. cit., pp. 365–6, n. 131) discusses the question, which is unanswered, of whether the ECCI telegraphed its answer before or after the meeting of the Zentrale.

[24] *Cahiers du bolchevisme*, no. 11, 30 January 1925, p. 718. Kuusinen had been General Secretary of the Communist International since 5 December 1921 (*Die Tätigkeit*, op. cit., p. 320).

[25] See Carr, *The Interregnum*, op. cit., pp. 190–200.

[26] *Cahiers du bolchevisme*, no. 11, 30 January 1925, p. 718.

to express an opinion because he lacked information.[27] Zinoviev and Bukharin thought that it was necessary to defy the ban, and made this known to Radek:

> It is only by following the road which was traced in the appeal of 12 July that the Communist Party will be able to make itself recognised as the inspiration and the central rallying-point in the struggle of the proletariat against fascism. Otherwise, the regrettable experience in Italy and in Bulgaria will be repeated. There are already too many people hesitating in the German Communist Party.[28]

Stalin's opinion was completely the opposite. In a letter to Bukharin and Zinoviev, he declared that the Communists should carry out a temporary retreat:

> Should the Communists at the present stage try to seize power without the Social Democrats? Are they sufficiently ripe for that? That, in my opinion, is the question. When we seized power, we had in Russia such resources in reserve as a) the promise of bread; b) the slogan: the land to the peasants; c) the support of the great majority of the working class; and d) the sympathy of the peasantry. At the moment the German Communists have nothing of the kind. They have of course a Soviet country as neighbour, which we did not have; but what can we offer them? Should the government in Germany topple over now, in a manner of speaking, and the Communists were to seize hold of it, they would end up in a crash. That, in the 'best' case. Whilst at worst, they will be smashed to smithereens and thrown away back. The whole point is not that Brandler wants to 'educate the masse', but that the bourgeoisie plus the right-wing Social Democrats are bound to turn such lessons – the demonstration – into a general battle (at present all the odds are on their side) and exterminate them [the German Communists]. Of course, the fascists are not asleep; but it is to our advantage to let them attack first: that will rally the entire working class around the Communists (Germany is not Bulgaria). Besides, all our information indicates that in Germany fascism is weak. In my opinion, the Germans should be restrained and not spurred on.[29]

---

[27] Ibid. Trotsky never challenged Kuusinen's allegation.

[28] Ibid.

[29] Quoted in L.D. Trotsky, *Stalin*, New York, 1967, pp. 368–9. The whereabouts of the Russian original is unknown, but Stalin admitted the existence of this letter (*Sochineniya*, Volume 10, pp. 61–2, quoted in Carr, op. cit., p. 187, n. 1). According to

Faced with these contradictory opinions, Radek telegraphed to Brandler on the 26th: 'The Presidium of the Comintern advises the abandonment of street demonstrations on 29 July. . . . We fear a trap.'[30]

The Zentrale rallied to this position. In most places, the street demonstrations projected for the Anti-Fascist Day were replaced by indoor meetings, except in Saxony, Thuringia and the Württemberg region.[31] Nonetheless, very large numbers of people were involved. There were 200,000 in Berlin at 17 meetings,[32] between 50,000 and 60,000 in Chemnitz, 30,000 in Leipzig, 25,000 in Gotha, 20,000 in Dresden, and a total of 100,000 in the Württemberg region.[33] The Left denounced what it saw as a capitulation. The Zentrale congratulated itself on having frustrated the plans of the counter-revolution, which wanted on this occasion to develop a pogrom atmosphere. Meyer explained the decision:

> If the Communists had intended, as the government claims, to have begun the civil war on the 29th, no one could have stopped them. But they had no thought of joining battle at the moment chosen by the enemy. . . . The German Communist Party frustrated them by organising the demonstrations on the 29th in ways appropriate to local conditions, without incurring the reproach of having lightly risked the lives of its members and worker sympathisers. Revolutionary impatience will perhaps see a harmful retreat in this decision; our party knows very well that it cannot build its influence and confidence within the working class unless it says openly what it intends to do and why. The Communist Party is a party of the masses, and its tactics differ profoundly from the conspiracies and riots of the little counter-revolutionary organisations. It needs neither manoeuvres nor stratagems. . . . It will continue its work of agitation, propaganda and organisation.[34]

Fischer, this letter was published for the first time by Brandler and his friends in *Arbeiterpolitik*, 9 February 1929. Trotsky, both in *The Third International after Lenin* and *Stalin* – and contrary to what Carr writes (op. cit., p. 187, n. 1), apparently having consulted only the American edition of the latter work on this point – gives the date of 7 August. But the letter indisputably refers to the Anti-Fascist Day when it speaks of the 'demonstration' (the French edition of 1969 incorrectly renders this as *démonstration* rather than *manifestation*), and also inasmuch as it sweeps aside the arguments about Brandler's 'intentions'. It must therefore be recognised that this was not Stalin's reply to Radek's question, but rather a justification of his position on the Anti-Fascist Day addressed after the event to Bukharin and Zinoviev.

[30] Cited in Carr, op. cit., p. 187.
[31] Hortzschansky, op. cit., p. 164.
[32] *Die Rote Fahne*, 30 July 1923.
[33] Hortzschansky, op. cit., p. 164.
[34] Appeal by the Zentrale, *Die Rote Fahne*, 31 July 1923; *Dokumente und Materialen*,

The situation at the beginning of August

This call for calm and preparation seemed incongruous in the overheated atmosphere in Germany at the end of July and the beginning of August. On 26 July, *Kreuz-Zeitung* wrote: 'Without any doubt we are on the eve of another revolution – who could still be mistaken after seeing what is unfolding before our eyes.'[35] *Germania* stated the next day: 'Confidence in the government of the Reich is deeply shaken. . . . Discontent has reached a dangerous level. Fury is general. The atmosphere is electric. One spark and there will be an explosion. . . . This is the mood of 9 November.'[36] Communist publications apart, the entire press talked of 'the mood of November'.

On 29 July, a special conference of the Social-Democratic opposition was held in Weimar. Paul Levi and Kurt Rosenfeld attended, along with Dissmann, the leader of the metalworkers' union, and Max Urich, the leader of the metalworkers in Berlin. Levi was responsible for organising the conference. He spoke of the 'successes of the Communists', and the 'unpardonable blunders' of the SPD.[37] *Leipziger Volkszeitung* published the record of the meeting – this 'factional behaviour' was proof of the unsettling of the Party's apparatus – and reproduced the resolution which was carried, calling for a struggle to bring down the Cuno government opposing any possible participation by Social Democrats in a 'grand coalition' with the bourgeois parties.[38] This amounted both to rejecting in advance any parliamentary solution to the coming crisis, and to taking the road to the formation of a workers' government – a step which Levi had decided to take.

Radek developed the Communist line at length in his article 'Facing the Bankruptcy of the German Bourgeoisie: The Duties of the Communist Party',

---

Volume 2/7, part 2, op. cit., pp. 378–81. It was probably at this time – and not in May when Brandler had gone to Moscow and the 'patching-up' took place – in the atmosphere of renewed tension between the tendencies, that the episode mentioned by Radek in his letter to Zetkin of December 1926 took place. In fact he wrote, after having mentioned the incidents surrounding the election of the Zentrale at the Leipzig Congress: 'Later that summer, when Brandler, Thalheimer, Pieck, Guralsky and other members of the central committee wrote a letter to Zinoviev, Bukharin and me to demand the removal of Ruth Fischer and Maslow, and Brandler declared in a private letter to me that the patching-up will no longer work, I told him that I cannot go along with such insanity. He climbed down.' ('A Letter by Karl Radek to Clara Zetkin,' *The New International*, Volume 1, no. 5, December 1934, p. 155.)

[35] *Kreuz-Zeitung*, 26 July 1923.
[36] *Germania*, 27 July 1923.
[37] *Volksbote* (Zeitz), 31 July 1923.
[38] *Leipziger Volkszeitung*, 2 August 1923.

which appeared in *Die Rote Fahne* on 2 August. He argued that Germany was experiencing the second defeat of the bourgeoisie, which was obliged to capitulate in order to forestall mass uprisings and a revolution. Three essential facts characterised the situation. Firstly, the Communists were making fantastic progress. The Party was 'near to winning the majority of the active workers in the country', and was 'successfully winning the majority from the Social Democrats in numerous sectors, workplaces and localities'. Secondly, Social Democracy was in decline: 'It has ceased to be an active factor in public life. It is no longer the decisive factor in the counter-revolution. . . . It is an inert mass.' Thirdly, the fascist movement was decomposing, under the pressure of the Communists.

Was victory of the proletarian revolution on the immediate agenda? Everything seemed to point to that, but Radek insisted on the need to avoid fatalism, because this issue depended exclusively on the Party's activities. He stressed: '*The German bourgeoisie is organised like no other in the world. The Communist Party needs to be organised like no other.*' He came out firmly against the illusions of those who thought that the Russian model traced the road to follow:

> The Bolsheviks could take power with 70,000 members because the Russian bourgeoisie was not organised. Our German Party must have at least a million members – and soon. Our organisation must not be an electoral organisation, but a closed fist, united not only by the Communist ideal but also by the armour of our shock battalions, our proletarian hundreds. It is very possible that the German Communist Party may be called upon to act before having achieved these conditions. But it must work with all its might to ensure that it gives itself the best chances of success.

In the short run, the Party had to build the structures of the united front, to go forward with the left Social Democrats to build the factory councils, control committees and proletarian hundreds, and, through them, to promote the transitional demands which could mobilise the masses, namely, workers' control of production, the seizure of real values, and the formation of a workers' and peasants' government. It was no less essential to think seriously about how to win broad strata of the petty bourgeoisie: 'We need engineers, officers and bank clerks to get Germany out of her poverty.'

In concluding this article, dated 29 July and drafted in Moscow, Radek repeated that the moment to attack had not yet arrived:

> Do not let our enemies inflict partial defeats on us. Badly-prepared offensives can lead to defeats at the most propitious moment for action. If the adversary takes the offensive, he will be mistaken in all his calculations. Let us be ready, in that case, to oppose to him first a victorious resistance and then to defeat him. But do not let us seek a premature confrontation. Such is the situation in Germany. Such are the duties of the Communist Party. They demand the greatest efforts from it, confidence in its own strength, energy and enthusiasm, but also coolness, calm and good strategic calculation. Then the hour will come when the German comrades will be able to say: 'Audacity, more audacity and still more audacity!'[39]

These were the same themes, relying on the same analysis, that Brandler developed on 5–6 August before the Central Committee when he presented a motion on the political situation. The task of the Party, as he saw it, was to prepare for a 'defensive revolutionary struggle'. It must redouble its efforts to form a workers' united front with the trade unions and the SPD, which would lead to a workers' and peasants' government being established in Germany. Its concern was therefore to continue the campaign to win the workers still influenced by Social Democracy, and to obtain if not the sympathy, at least the benevolent neutrality of the lower strata of the petty bourgeoisie.

Fischer repeated her criticism of the 'opportunist' interpretation of the united front and the workers' government, accusing Brandler of repudiating the perspective of the dictatorship of the proletariat. Hugo Urbahns sharply criticised the slogan of the workers' and peasants' government which the enlarged ECCI had adopted in June, and, with their seven comrades of the Left, both Fischer and Urbahns abstained in the final vote.[40] Brandler said in a report that these seven abstentions were really no more than a personal protest against him as an individual. He quoted Fischer: 'Since the Leipzig Congress, the Party has developed in a direction which conforms to the wishes of the opposition. The opportunist danger still exists, but is very limited.'[41]

However, impatience was rising amongst the workers, and this was exacerbated by the disappointment which followed the retreat in July. Had the leaders of the KPD, as E.H. Carr believes, 'exhausted their repertory of

---

[39] *Die Rote Fahne*, 2 August 1923.
[40] *Die Rote Fahne*, 8 August 1923.
[41] *Correspondance internationale*, no. 64, 15 August 1923, p. 481.

words and ideas'? Was the KPD, as he thinks, 'not equipped, or not ready, for action'?[42] Had the Communists quite simply not succeeded – as Radek was to suggest later – in discovering that a new revolutionary wave was beginning to surge up before them, set as they were in the routine of propagandist work for the united front and the workers' government.[43] In fact, a few days later, the outbreak in Berlin of a wave of economic strikes was to create a new political situation that would take the Communists unawares, just as it took the political leaders of the German bourgeoisie and the Social-Democratic leadership.

The storm-warning

The Reichstag met on 8 August. Cuno's speech, which was several times interrupted by Communist deputies, appealed for a vote of confidence, and called for sacrifices, economies and work. Immediately after his speech, the Social Democrats demanded and were granted a suspension of the sitting and postponement of the discussion to the next day. Wilhelm Koenen, the spokesman for the KPD, shouted: 'Down with Cuno! This is the cry that we hear from every side!'[44]

The debate was resumed on 9 August. The hall was literally besieged by delegations of workers, whom the Assembly refused to receive. The Social-Democratic deputies announced that they would abstain from voting on the motion of confidence. It was learned that the workers in the Borsig plant in Berlin were on strike.[45] In Chemnitz, a demonstration of 150,000 called on the Cuno government to resign.[46] The debate proceeded, and on 10 August ended in a vote of confidence, with the Social Democrats abstaining, and the Communists voting against.[47] Koenen, from the speakers' platform, addressed to the working people of Germany a call for 'the mass movement of the working people to go forward, over the head of parliament, to form a workers' revolutionary government'.[48] The forecast was stormy.

---

[42] Carr, op. cit., p. 188.
[43] *Die Lehren der deutschen Ereignisse*, op. cit., pp. 14–15.
[44] *Verhandlungen des Reichstags. I Wahlperiode 1920*, Band 161, pp. 11748–9, 11761.
[45] *Die Rote Fahne*, 10 August 1923.
[46] Krusch, *Um die Einheitsfront und eine Arbeiterregierung*, op. cit., p. 251.
[47] *Verhandlungen des Reichstags. I Wahlperiode 1920*, Band 161, p. 11779.
[48] *Die Rote Fahne*, 11 August 1923.

At dawn, the strike had begun in the workshops of the Berlin metro.[49] A few minutes later, it was the turn of the printers, and above all, on the initiative of the Communist cell, that of the 8,000 workers in the national printing establishment.[50] The press for printing banknotes was stopped, and in a few hours the government would run out of means of payment. The big firms followed the movement, and Siemens stopped work, following Borsig.[51] The workers in eleven Berlin plants repeated in resolutions the Communists' demand for Cuno to be dismissed and a workers' government to be formed. Urban transport had completely stopped. Gas and electricity supplies were cut off. The strikes of the transport workers and the electricians provoked other stoppages of work, meetings and a growing agitation. In Hamburg, there was a total strike in the shipyards. There were workers' demonstrations in Crefeld and Aachen; the police intervened, and people were killed.[52]

The midday editions of the newspapers reported that the Reichsbank had run out of banknotes, and was closing its counters. *Vorwärts* appealed to the workers for calm. *Die Rote Fahne* published an appeal by the 'Committee of Fifteen':

> In every factory, passive resistance! Stop the pay trickery! Throw out the bankrupts! Throw out the usurers! For our labour, at least the peacetime pay! Ten million marks immediately to every worker, office worker or public employee, to make up for the high cost of living! Bread for those who work! Take over the food supply! Distribution by the trade unions and the workers' organisations! For a workers' and peasants' government! Workers, you must break out! The Cuno government is leading you to ruin! Form the united front of all the exploited in the struggle for your existence! Form workers' self-defence groups in all workplaces![53]

The Commission of the trade unions in Berlin held a special meeting on the evening of 10 August. Representatives of the Social-Democratic, Independent and Communist Parties were invited.[54] Otto Wels was present, along with Rudolf Breitscheid and Hertz. The Communists were represented by Fischer,

---

[49] Ersil, op. cit., pp. 242–3.
[50] *Verhandlungen des Reichstags. I Wahlperiode 1920*, Band 161, p. 11770.
[51] Ersil, op. cit., p. 214.
[52] Ibid.
[53] *Die Rote Fahne*, 10 August 1923.
[54] *Die Rote Fahne*, 11 August 1923; Fischer, op. cit., pp. 300–1; Wenzel, op. cit., p. 165; *Bericht über die Verhandlungen des IX Parteitags der KPD*, op. cit., pp. 12–13, 21.

Geschke and Heckert. The problem was whether the trade unions would support the spontaneously developing strike. It was a decision of historic importance. If the trade unions agreed and publicly endorsed it, the strike would be total and would sweep Cuno away. In that case the only solution would be to form a workers' government that included representatives of the trade unions. This was the same solution as Legien had suggested immediately after the Kapp Putsch, but coming this time in the midst of the offensive upsurge of the workers. The discussion was passionate. Eminent trade unionists, convinced reformists for decades – such as Gustav Sabath, whom Fischer mentions[55] – were inclined towards an initiative which they were aware would mean breaking with the bourgeoisie and the entire past of the trade-union movement.

The Social-Democratic leaders, with Wels at their head, argued in the contrary direction. The strike meant anarchy, an adventure, chaos. The government had just given serious undertakings to a delegation from their party. It was going to act; 50 million gold marks had been guaranteed by the large firms, to be spent on foodstuffs, and 200 million, on the same conditions, to strangle inflation. The Reichstag had just voted for increased taxes on incomes and companies. All this promised a rapid improvement of the economic situation, which the strike would definitely compromise. The Communists counterposed a motion calling for a three-day general strike with the objects of a minimum hourly wage of 0.6 of a gold mark, the dismissal of the Cuno government, and the formation of a workers' and peasants' government.[56] Did they really hope to convince the people to whom they were talking? When we read what Fischer had to say, we may doubt that:

> I wish the workers could see and hear your noble trade-union Commission.
> You have no idea what is going on out there, or you would not spout such
> rubbish. The movement is there: it is strong, and the question is simply to
> decide whether it will be led in a united way, with you, without you or
> against you.[57]

The union leaders were shaken by Wels's argument and the government's promises, and were hardly going to be won to action by such an attitude. In the end, they decided to reject the Communists' proposal.

---

[55] Fischer, op. cit., p. 300. Sabath had actually been a member of the USPD during 1919–22.
[56] Ibid.
[57] *Die Rote Fahne*, 11 August 1923.

On the evening of 10 August, the Political Bureau sent a circular to all the Party's districts to inform them that a 'powerful spontaneous mass movement of passive resistance and strikes' had broken out in Berlin. It announced that the assembly of delegates was to be held on the following day, and would decide on a three-day strike:

> The further development of the movement will depend on how it unfolds, and on the movement throughout the Reich. . . . The information which we have received shows that a situation like that in Berlin exists all over the country. Everywhere passive resistance and strikes. These movements must be methodically brought together, and we must take their leadership. . . . We must ensure that local committees of the ADGB take the head of the spontaneous movement. Where that is not happening, where the movement is spontaneous, time must not be wasted in lengthy negotiations, and the factory councils must lead and organise the movement.

The Party was to be prepared for any eventuality, particularly for being forced into illegality. However, for the moment, the perspective was as follows: 'It is possible that the Cuno government will be overthrown by the thrust of the strike, and replaced by a grand coalition. The SPD perhaps will try to apply a brake to the movement by joining the coalition.'[58]

The eleventh of August was Constitution Day, the fourth anniversary of the Weimar Constitution; there were shootings in Hanover, Lübeck and Neurode. At 10 o'clock in the morning in the two neighbouring halls of Neue Welte and Kliems Festsäle in Berlin, the delegates to the factory councils assembly arrived in cars or on motorbikes with red pennons. They had been convened during the night by the 'Committee of Fifteen', after the meeting of the trade-union leaders. The police did not intervene. In the name of the Committee, Grothe proposed a three-day general strike.[59] His proposal was adopted without great debate, along with a nine-point programme:

- Immediate dismissal of the Cuno government.
- Formation of a workers' and peasants' government.
- Requisition of foodstuffs and their fair distribution under the control of the workers' organisations.

---

[58] Political circular no. 18 from the Political Bureau, reproduced in Krusch, op. cit., pp. 328–9.

[59] Recollections of Erich Rochler, in *Unter der roten Fahne*, op. cit., p. 212; Ersil, op. cit., p. 245.

- Immediate official recognition of the workers' control committees.
- Lifting of the ban on the proletarian hundreds.
- Immediate fixing of the minimum hourly wage at 60 gold pfennigs.
- Immediate hiring of the unemployed for productive work.
- Ending of the state of emergency and the ban on demonstrations.
- Immediate liberation of workers jailed for political offences.[60]

In the afternoon, the KPD took up the appeal of the factory councils, which it published as a leaflet. The police confiscated the leaflet, relying on a decree passed the preceding day authorising the seizure of any printed matter calling for breaches of the public peace, or for the violent overthrow of the existing regime. The Social-Democratic parliamentary group was assembled urgently, drew some conclusions from the situation, and tried to correct the previous day's mistake. It declared that Cuno no longer enjoyed its confidence, but declared itself prepared, on the insistence of Wels and given the gravity of the situation, to join a grand coalition government,[61] which would be determined to 'make the rich pay', and to relieve the poverty of the working people. This was the death-blow to Cuno, who resigned.

There were violent disorders in every great industrial city to which the strike had spread. Grothe drafted directives on behalf of the Action Committee with a view to a general strike: the election of strike committees, the organisation of control committees and proletarian hundreds, appeals to workers' parties and trade unions for the formation of the workers' united front in order to prepare for a workers' and peasants' government, the disarming of the armed fascist groups by the proletarian hundreds, and propaganda for fraternisation directed at the soldiers and the police.[62]

On 12 August, there were clashes between demonstrators and the police in Hanover, Rotthausen and Gelsenkirchen, and 30 people were killed. On the 13th, there were more demonstrations, with more serious shootings, almost everywhere. Six people were killed in Wilhelmshaven, 20 in Hanover, 15 in Greisz, 10 in Aachen, 20 in Zeitz, 30 in Jena, one in Breslau, four in Crefeld, and four in Ratibor. In Halle and in Leipzig, the proletarian hundreds commandeered cattle in the surrounding countryside, slaughtered them, and organised the distribution of meat amongst the workers.[63]

---

[60] *Dokumente und Materialen*, Volume 2/7, Part 2, op. cit., pp. 404–5.
[61] *Vorwärts*, 12 August 1923.
[62] Ersil, op. cit., p. 283.
[63] *Correspondance internationale*, no. 64, 15 August 1923, p. 478.

The Central Committee went underground in the first hours of the strike, and left Berlin. Fritz Heckert alone remained in the capital, where he coordinated operations in liaison with the 'Committee of Fifteen'.[64] For 48 hours, after the wildcat strike had swept Cuno away, everything seemed possible.

However, during that time, serious negotiations had taken place between the parties, and Ebert, as President, had empowered Gustav Stresemann of the National People's Party to form the new government.[65] Four Social Democrats joined it, Robert Schmidt as Deputy Premier, Hilferding at Finance, Sollmann at the Interior, and Radbruch at Justice. The new government did not hide its intentions of negotiating with France and stabilising the mark, particularly by reforming the public finances and 'making the rich pay'.[66] In fact, within a few days, the workers' action had sufficiently scared the bourgeoisie and its representatives in the Reichstag to force them to make a decisive radical turn. The strategy, favoured by Cuno, of letting things deteriorate had led the ruling class to the edge of an abyss, and it decided to retreat. The Social Democrats agreed to collaborate once again in salvaging the bourgeois régime and society in exchange for the promise of fiscal measures directed at big business and a tighter watch on right-wing extremists. Stresemann calculated that their entry into the government could ensure him a few weeks' respite, which he would use to negotiate with the foreign powers over the Ruhr.

This is also what the Russian Communists thought in Moscow, or at any rate what Radek wrote. He thought that Stresemann, representing the middle bourgeoisie, was intending to try to negotiate his way out of the diplomatic blind alley, and to elaborate a reform of the Reich's finances at the cost of the bourgeoisie. The Social Democrats joined the grand coalition because they envisaged the possibility of their hoped-for 'middle way' opening up before them, the end of the fall of the mark and a fall in prices thanks to financial measures, negotiations with France, measures against the nationalists, and a reduction in the influence of the big industrialists. Radek judged the new Chancellor to be 'a much more experienced politician than Cuno', and

---

[64] Fischer, op. cit., p. 302.
[65] G. Stresemann, *Vermächtnis*, Volume 1, Berlin, 1932, p. 88.
[66] *Verhandlungen des Reichstags. I Wahlperiode 1920*, Band 361, pp. 11840ff.

concluded that the crisis was as serious as ever, but: 'It may well be that, despite it all, Herr Stresemann represents a stage which will bring the movement to a halt . . . a relative calming-down.'[67]

This was also the viewpoint of the German Zentrale. In their lengthy campaign of agitation they had presented the fall of Cuno as the preface to the formation of a workers' government. But now Cuno had gone, Social Democracy chose to play the card of the grand coalition, and had turned its back on any alliance with the Communists, making a workers' government impossible. Some time was necessary to deepen the crisis in Social Democracy. Albert wrote: 'A relative truce is now on the way. It will give the grand coalition the time to discredit itself more completely in the eyes of the petty bourgeoisie and the backward workers in whom the name of Hilferding still raises some vague hope.'[68]

The Congress of Factory Councils had called for the general strike to end on 13 August. Was it to be extended? This was the intention of the Action Committee, which called, in a proclamation signed by Grothe, for the general strike 'to be widened', and for 'a determined struggle to be undertaken against the grand coalition'.[69] No doubt he thought that the general strike, with its momentum, could also topple Stresemann, and bring in a workers' government. Brandler said that the Zentrale had tried to test that view by proposing to prolong the strike by a day. This was to prove impossible, and even the activists of the Left, he said, had to yield to the workers' refusal to pursue an action which seemed to them to have no purpose, now that Cuno had resigned, and in view of the promises made by his successors.[70]

A certain resistance to resuming work showed itself in the Political Bureau, and Böttcher, Pieck and Heckert opposed ending the strike.[71] *Die Rote Fahne* came out on the morning of 14 August with the headline 'Millions in the Streets, The Fight Goes On!'[72] But during the day it distributed a special edition, which called for a simultaneous, coordinated end to the strike. It

---

[67] *Die Rote Fahne*, 27 August 1923; *Correspondance internationale*, no. 68, 29 August 1923.

[68] *Correspondance internationale*, no. 64, 15 August 1923, p. 64.

[69] *Die Rote Fahne* (Lausitz), 14 August 1923; *Dokumente und Materialen*, Volume 2/7, Part 2, op. cit., pp. 406–7.

[70] *Die Lehren der deutschen Ereignisse*, op. cit., pp. 30–1.

[71] According to a report at the Political Bureau session of 13 August, summarised by Krusch, op. cit., pp. 297–8, n. 209.

[72] *Die Rote Fahne*, 14 August 1923 (morning edition).

explained that, faced with the opposition of the Social Democrats and the trade-union leaders, it was necessary to avoid continuing a forced action which risked ending in a fratricidal struggle.[73] The edition of 15 August was headlined: 'The Struggle Has Been Broken! Prepare the Next!' A sub-heading stressed 'Interruption, Not Conclusion'.[74] Brandler was later to emphasise, in self-defence, that the strike had not reached the same level in Berlin as it had in such bastions of the Party as Halle, Chemnitz and Dresden. The Saxon workers who had joined the strike after Cuno's fall had not engaged in the economic struggle as their comrades had in Berlin, but had embarked on a political strike, the beginning of the armed uprising for which the people in Berlin were not yet ready. The workers' army did not yet all march at the same pace.[75]

We can discuss the factors that led the Zentrale to its decision. Fischer says that Brandler never wanted a general strike that was not authorised by the ADGB[76] – which is nonsense, because this was from the start an unofficial strike. Ulbricht blamed the 'opportunists and traitors in the Zentrale' for not having fixed political objectives or called for the creation of a workers' government.[77] But the overthrow of Cuno, won by the strike, was one of its declared aims, and the conditions were obviously not ripe for the creation of a workers' government. Even though some resistance appeared in the factory councils, the Left does not seem to have strongly opposed the return to work. Fischer herself, whose sense of discipline was not particularly well-developed, spoke to the factory delegates to justify the ending of the strike,[78] which seems also to have met with Maslow's approval.[79] In reality, at the end of the three days, the strikers in Berlin thought that they had won their first objective: the resignation of Cuno. The strike slowly faded, flaring up day after day for another week from one plant or one region to another.

---

[73] *Die Rote Fahne*, 14 August 1923 (special edition).

[74] *Die Rote Fahne*, 15 August 1923; *Dokumente und Materialen*, Volume 2/7, Part 2, op. cit., pp. 407–9.

[75] *Die Lehren der deutschen Ereignisse*, op. cit., p. 31. *Klassenkampf*, 14 August 1923, called for the half-victory that had been achieved to be transformed into a total victory, and concluded: 'Down with Stresemann!'

[76] Fischer, op. cit., p. 302.

[77] Walter Ulbricht, *Zur Geschichte der deutschen Arbeiterbewegung*, Volume 1, Berlin, 1933, p. 126.

[78] *Die Rote Fahne*, 15 August 1923.

[79] Otto Wenzel, *Die Kommunistische Partei Deutschlands im Jahre 1923*, Berlin, 1955, p. 170.

A certain weariness appeared in the workers' ranks, and their opponents did not hesitate to take advantage of it. During the following week, some 200 strikers were arrested, and more than 100,000 were sacked. Severing in Prussia banned the 'Committee of Fifteen', against whom he brought an action, and they had to take refuge in Jena.[80] Everyone was aware that the strike, which had felled Cuno in 24 hours, was the main event in 'the inhuman year'. Some people concluded that it finally showed to the workers that they could not promote a policy which the Social Democrats opposed, and they saw the strike as the final flicker of the postwar militancy. Others drew the conclusion that it was a preparation for the last phase, the reaching of revolutionary consciousness by the masses, their turn to Communism, by having forced the bourgeoisie to stake everything on a renewed alliance with Social Democracy.

But what happened was the reverse of what both the leaders of the German bourgeoisie and those of the KPD and the Communist International had been led by their recent analyses to expect. The same parties that gave Cuno a vote of confidence on 10 August had to pitch him out 24 hours later, to cut their losses. The employers in the metalworking industries made haste to negotiate with the unions an agreement providing for a sliding scale of wages, which they had earlier stubbornly refused. The Communist leaders saw in the strike which brought down Cuno the sign that the situation was riper than they had believed. The bourgeoisie rushed to conclude a compromise which would free their hands on the international level for disposing of the threat of revolution. The Communists were to prepare hastily for a seizure of power which seemed to them to be demanded by the majority of the 'active proletariat'.

---

[80] Davidovich, op. cit., pp. 116–7; *Vorwärts*, 18 August 1923. Thalheimer later expressed the opinion that the Zentrale made a serious mistake in failing immediately to organise a counter-strike (*1923: Eine Verpasste Revolution?*, Berlin, 1931, p. 24).

Chapter Thirty-Nine

Preparing the Insurrection

The leaders of the Communist International were caught unawares by the strike against Cuno, which occurred whilst they were away on holiday. None of them had expected a movement of such dimensions, and the temporising tactics which had been adopted by the ECCI in June were now seen as plainly inadequate. It was clear that, from around 10 August, the masses were ready to engage in a struggle which their leaders did not believe to be as yet on the cards. But the tension could not continue indefinitely. The balance between the classes which was expressed in the formation of the grand coalition government could not last. Therefore, from mid-August, the leaders of the International, engaged in preparing an insurrection in Germany, were frantically attempting to make up for the time which they had lost since May.

The turn decided in Moscow

A full week passed before a meeting of the Russian Political Bureau was convened to discuss the German Revolution. Zinoviev received the first news about the strike and the resignation of the Cuno government whilst he was still on holiday in the Caucasus, and he applied himself to drafting theses, 'The Situation in Germany and our Tasks', which were completed on 15 August:

> The crisis is maturing. Decisive events are imminent. A new chapter in the history of the German Communist Party, and, consequently, of the entire International, is opening. The German Communist Party must direct itself quickly and resolutely towards the approaching revolutionary crisis. The crisis is ripening. The stakes are immense. The moment is nearing when audacity, more audacity and always audacity will be needed.[1]

The Cuno strike showed that the KPD had not yet been able to appreciate the real mood of the masses. It would be disastrous not to make the turn whilst there was still time. The Party was to cease holding back the masses for fear of premature battles, and henceforth must avoid acting as a brake on partial movements: 'It is impossible to keep our powder dry right up to the decisive battle. . . . It would be to show dogmatism and commit a serious political mistake if we delayed any attack until the moment of the decisive struggle.'[2]

Fischer, who we have every reason to believe was well-informed, writes that when Zinoviev drafted his theses he was coming out of a long period of hesitation and passionate discussion with Bukharin, Kuusinen and Piatnitsky.[3] Kuusinen and Radek himself understood when they read the theses that 'the revolution was knocking on the door in Germany'.[4]

Trotsky's attention had also been roused by the dimensions of the strike which had brought Cuno down. In order to obtain information which he had not received from the ECCI, he invited Walcher and Enderle, the German representatives at the head of the RILU, to visit him in the Crimea. After this meeting, Walcher returned to Germany, apparently to get further information for Trotsky.[5] At about the same time, the principal Russian leaders interrupted their holidays to discuss the German situation.

The Russian Political Bureau met on 23 August. For the first time since Lenin had fallen ill and been put out of action, the Bolshevik leaders had to

---

[1] Cited by O. Kuusinen, 'Un Exposé fallacieux des événements d'Allemagne', *Cahiers du bolchevisme*, no. 11, 30 January 1925, p. 178. The text of the theses has never been published. Even today official historians merely cite extracts.

[2] *Cahiers du bolchevisme*, no. 12, 6 February 1925, pp. 763–4.

[3] Fischer, op. cit., p. 305.

[4] *Cahiers du bolchevisme*, no. 11, 30 January 1925, p. 718.

[5] The information about this meeting comes from Wenzel (op. cit., p. 179), and is based on an account which Enderle gave him in 1952. Angress (op. cit., p. 392, n. 38) has laid stress on the improbabilities and exaggerations in this account, such as Trotsky's promise to send the Red Army into Germany. But there is other evidence of the presence of Walcher and Enderle on this date, and in my opinion there is no reason to doubt that the meeting actually took place.

reach a decision on a question of historical importance. They believed, as always, that it was the fate of the world revolution, of which their revolution was only the precursor, that was at stake. They would not by themselves take a decision which was the responsibility of the International and its leadership, although latter obviously would not be expected to demur from what the Moscow leaders had decided. The Political Bureau was augmented for the occasion by a number of experts, Piatakov and Tsiurupa, with Kuusinen and Radek as representatives of the ECCI, and Edwin Hoernle and Jakob Walcher, who were the resident German representatives in Moscow at this time.[6] No official record exists of this discussion, though many references have been made to it. The only precise evidence is that of Bazhanov; it includes no improbabilities, and has never been contradicted.[7]

Radek is said to have presented the principal report, which stated that the dimensions of the Cuno strike showed that the German Revolution had moved on to a new phase. There is no reason for us to think that he insisted on the necessity for prudence, which had been the central theme of his interventions during the preceding weeks, and he was almost certainly impressed with the agreement Zinoviev had reached on this issue with Trotsky. After Radek's report, Trotsky intervened vigorously. He had no doubt that the time was approaching for the decisive, direct struggle for power in Germany, for the German October. Only a few weeks remained for preparation, and everything was to be subordinated to this task. Zinoviev concurred, even if he preferred to count in months rather than in weeks, but nonetheless agreed with Bukharin and Trotsky that preparations must be made for the insurrection. Stalin was less outspoken, and showed a certain scepticism. He did not think that they could expect the victory of the German Revolution until the spring of 1924, but he did not insist on this view.

Despite these shadings of opinion, the Political Bureau thus believed that the crucial moment was well on the way in Germany, and it called upon the ECCI to take the necessary measures. The ECCI appointed a commission of four members to oversee the preparations, composed of Radek, Piatakov,

---

[6] The presence of Piatakov and Tsurupa, invited as experts on German matters, the former being also considered as a military expert, is indicated by B. Bajanov, *Avec Staline dans le Kremlin*, Paris, 1930, p. 190 together with that of Radek, which was to be expected. The presence of Kuusinen, Walcher and Hoernle is confirmed by evidence collected by Weber, *Die Wandlung des deutschen Kommunismus*, Volume 1, op. cit., p. 49.

[7] Bajanov, op. cit., pp. 190–8. The most recent official history of the Comintern is silent about this meeting.

Jozef Unshlikht, one of the heads of the secret services, and the trade unionist Vassili Shmidt,[8] and it immediately convened a special secret conference in Moscow, to which it invited, in addition to the permanent representatives of the KPD, Zetkin and Hoernle, Brandler, as Chairman of the Party, and representatives of the Left, including Fischer, Maslow and Thaelmann.[9]

When the delegates from Germany arrived, probably at the beginning of September, they were to find the atmosphere in the Soviet capital transformed by the revolutionary enthusiasm aroused by the approach of the German October.[10] The city was covered with posters appealing to young Russians to

---

[8] Ibid., pp. 195–6, as well as Wenzel (op. cit., pp. 193–4), who follows quite closely the information given by Erich Wollenberg. Angress (op. cit., p. 395) follows these two authors. For her part, Fischer (op. cit., p. 323) mentions Radek and Shmidt, but not Unschlikht and Piatakov, whom she replaces with Guralski-Kleine and Skoblevsky, who were in fact to fulfil responsibilities in Germany. Since this commission functioned in Russia even during the last days of October, at a time when Guralski and Skoblevsky had been working in Germany for some weeks, it is the first list which seems to be correct. Boris Souvarine mentions only Radek and Piatakov (B. Souvarine, *Staline*, Paris, 1935, p. 316). The presence of the latter is in no doubt, and in particular is confirmed, on the morrow of the defeat, by statements by Radek to the ECCI (*Die Lehren der deutschen Ereignisse*, op. cit., pp. 23ff.).

[9] The invitation to the leaders of the Left for a discussion in Moscow with Brandler and the Russian leaders was explained by the determination of the ECCI to force the two German tendencies to work together. Radek makes this clear in his letter of December 1926 to Zetkin: 'I sought to keep Brandler not out of friendship, although I value him highly and as a man he stands close to me, but because I was convinced that the left-wing comrades alone are not in a position to lead the party and to maintain its contact with broad masses. A communist party without the left-wing workers is threatened with the danger of becoming a USPD. A communist party without the collaboration of people like Brandler, Thalheimer, Walcher and the thousands of old Spartacus people courts the danger of becoming a KAPD.' ('A Letter by Karl Radek to Clara Zetkin', *The New International*, Volume 1, no. 5, December 1934, p. 156.) Fischer (op. cit., p. 313) thought that it was less of a question of enabling the leaders of the Left to join in the preparatory discussions than of enabling Radek to keep her and Maslow in Moscow. In fact, an important role was to be given to leading activists of her tendency who were involved in the preparations and then in the leadership of the insurrection. Thaelmann, plus two workers' leaders from the Berlin district, Grylewicz and Max Hesse, took part in all the discussions. Hesse was even sent to Saxony to supervise the preparations for the insurrection in October. But Radek was then trying, as he had been for months, to avoid a split, and to isolate Fischer and Maslow from the comrades of their tendency. It is undeniable that he succeeded, because Thaelmann at least was to return from Moscow, according to Fischer, filled with a 'new enthusiasm' for the agreed strategy, and because very few of the leading activists in Berlin expressed doubts about the validity of the plans adopted in Moscow (ibid., p. 328).

[10] According to Fischer (op. cit., p. 312), Brandler had the shock of his life on discovering posters about Germany on the streets of the Soviet capital. Everything seems to suggest that Brandler arrived first with his close collaborators, and that he was followed a few days later by the leaders of the Left. According to Mujbegović (op. cit., p. 398), the decision to send Fischer and Maslow to Moscow was taken by the Zentrale on 12 September.

learn German in order to serve the coming revolution.[11] Passionate meetings were being held every day in factories, schools and universities on the theme of the help which the German workers would require. Bukharin was applauded by the students when he called on them to throw their books aside and take up rifles.[12] Resolutions passed by mass meetings in factories declared that Russian workers were ready to give up increases in pay and even to accept reductions in order to help the German Revolution.[13] Units of the Red Army declared themselves ready to fly to the help of revolutionary Germany, to do their duty as 'the vanguard of the world revolution', and addressed resolutions in this sense to the German workers.[14] Two special funds were opened, a gold reserve, and a grain reserve. For the first, they were asked women to give up even their wedding rings.[15] For the second, the commissariat for trade planned the formation of a 'German reserve' of 60 million poods, to be stored near the western frontier.[16] The Political Bureau ordered the Party units to seek out members who knew German, in order to set up a military reserve that could serve as 'international brigades' in Germany.[17] The Communist Youth enthusiastically prepared for this revolutionary struggle; it would be the battle of their generation.[18] The press coined the slogans and hammered them home: the alliance of the 'German pile-driver' with 'Soviet bread' would conquer the world, and create a power of 200 million people, against whom no war would be possible.[19] The differences which for months had been poisoning the atmosphere in the Russian Party and the apathy which had been gaining ground seemed to disappear in the exhilarating breeze of the newly-revived prospects of world revolution. Radek himself let enthusiasm and lyricism carry him away. Several witnesses have left us accounts of episodes in this period. Alexander Barmin, a Red Army officer, heard Radek speak at the military academy:

---

[11] Fischer, op. cit., p. 312.

[12] Bessedovsky, *Revelations of a Soviet Diplomat*, p. 62, quoted by Angress, op. cit., p. 397.

[13] See on this point *Bericht über die Tätigkeit der Exekutive der KI vom IV bis V Weltkongress*, 1924, p. 8.

[14] See for example the resolution of the Kursk light infantry regiment addressed to the German Young Communists, published in *Die Junge Garde*, 7 October 1923.

[15] Wenzel, op. cit., p. 92.

[16] Bessedovsky, op. cit., p. 62, cited in Angress, op. cit., p. 397.

[17] Ibid.

[18] Wenzel, op. cit., p. 192.

[19] Cited in Angress, op. cit., p. 397.

Radek spoke to crowded halls, and people felt that he was completely absorbed in awaiting and thinking about these events. His dialectic introduced us to the economy, the history, the psychology and the way of life of the two conflicting Germanies, one of which, that of the working people, was to impose its law on the other, for the salvation of the nation and the progress of the universe. Radek was eloquent as always: as always he spoke in his indescribable accent, but his intelligence and his passion dominated everything.[20]

The turn in Germany

These sentiments were echoed in Germany. *Die Rote Fahne* published on 16 August a poem significantly entitled 'It Is Drawing Near'.[21] On 17 August, the central organ of the KPD attacked the Social-Democratic leaders, after Severing banned the Federal Committee of the Factory Councils in Berlin: 'We accept the challenge of the Social Democrats, and they will have to bear the consequences.'[22] On 19 August, it published a chapter from Gusev's pamphlet *The Lessons of the Civil War*, entitled 'Let the Proletariat Prepare!'.[23] On 21 August, under the title 'Preparations For a New Battle', it discussed the difficulties which workers were encountering in obtaining arms.[24] On the 24th, it published an appeal, 'To the Working People in the SPD and the USPD', calling on them to break with their parties and to join the KPD in 'the proletarian class struggle' and 'for the dictatorship of the proletariat'.[25]

The government and the police ended their policy of relative tolerance. After the Prussian government banned the Federal Committee of the Factory Councils in Berlin on 16 August,[26] the Württemberg government banned the regional congress of the KPD that was to be held on the 22nd.[27] The French occupation authorities banned the five Communist daily papers in the Ruhr and the occupied zone on the 24th. *Die Rote Fahne* was seized on the 26th, without even any reason being given. On the same day, the police searched the editorial offices, and arrested five of the staff. Severing banned the Central

---

[20] A. Barmine, *Vingt ans au service de l'URSS*, Paris, 1939, p. 217.
[21] *Die Rote Fahne*, 16 August 1923.
[22] *Die Rote Fahne*, 17 August 1923.
[23] *Die Rote Fahne*, 19 August 1923.
[24] *Die Rote Fahne*, 21 August 1923.
[25] *Die Rote Fahne*, 22 August 1923.
[26] *Vorwärts*, 17 August 1923.
[27] Angress, op. cit., pp. 408–9.

Council of the Factory Councils in Greater Berlin, which he accused of being no more than a cover for the KPD leadership in the city, whilst the daily *Hamburger Volkszeitung* was suspended for three days. The premises of *Die Rote Fahne* were searched again on the 29th, with two more arrests. Several warrants were issued, one for the arrest of Fischer, but the police could not find her.[28]

Meanwhile, the Political Bureau of the Russian Party had declared for the new course in Germany, and on 28 August it took the first measures in preparing for the insurrection by appointing a military council.[29] *Die Rote Fahne* clearly expressed the new line which Moscow had confirmed. On 1 September, the Zentrale issued an appeal to 'workers, office workers and public employees', proposing to them the Communist programme for workers' control of production, the confiscation of real values, and the formation of a government of workers and poor peasants.[30] Zinoviev welcomed the coming struggles in an article for International Youth Day: 'No power on earth can defeat twenty million proletarians.'[31]

On 2 September, an article in *Die Rote Fahne* by Radek appeared, entitled 'Hands Off Germany!', together with the text of a joint call by the ECCI and the Central Council of the RILU, adopted on the motion of Trotsky on 27 August. This stated that the situation created by the occupation of the Ruhr was getting worse, and that the condition of the proletariat in this economic chaos was becoming unbearable. The grand coalition which had been formed with the complicity of the Social Democrats had promised to tax the bourgeoisie and make the rich pay, but had begun its term by banning the central organs of the factory councils. These organisations were 'alone able to channel the spontaneous movement of the proletariat and thus prevent pointless clashes', at a time when the capitalists threatened to close the factories in order to bring the workers to their knees: 'They want to provoke the desperate working people into premature action, and to defeat them before they are ready to fight.' The appeal explained:

> The situation in Germany is becoming increasingly tense. If the numerous indices are reliable, revolution is on the way in Germany. The German

---

[28] Ibid., p. 409.
[29] *Die Kommunistische Internationale. Kurzer historischer Abriss*, East Berlin, 1970, p. 235.
[30] *Die Rote Fahne*, 1 September 1923.
[31] Ibid.

proletariat will have to face not only the armed force of its own bourgeoisie, but, at the moment when its own bourgeoisie attacks it, it runs the risk of being attacked in the rear by the bourgeoisie of the powers of the Entente and its vassal states.[32]

Therefore, the international proletariat would have to show effective solidarity to protect the German working class, by meetings, demonstrations, strikes and propaganda directed at the soldiers. A few days later, Lozovsky wrote in the German edition of the RILU publication: 'Revolution is knocking at Germany's door, and demanding entry. . . . We cannot fix the date of the German Revolution, but if we judge from the present situation, it is a question of months.' His conclusion looked forward to the moment, which was not far off, when the world revolution would form 'a territorial bloc from Vladivostok to the Rhine'.[33]

The preparatory discussions

Discussions on preparations for the German uprising were to continue for several weeks in Moscow.[34] The German Commission of the ECCI and the principal Russian leaders worked with the German representatives of the two tendencies who had been brought over to help with the preparations. Kuusinen and Radek, Zinoviev and Trotsky, Brandler, Eberlein, Fischer, Maslow, Thaelmann, Max Hesse and Grylewicz[35] devoted themselves to detailed analysis of the situation in Germany, outlining perspectives and refining slogans and technical preparations.

At the beginning there were no fundamental differences. To be sure, Fischer did not lay down her arms. On 12 September, just before she left for Moscow, she again criticised Brandler's 'opportunist' conception of the workers'

---

[32] *Die Rote Fahne*, 2 September 1923.

[33] *Die Rote Gewerkschaftsinternationale*, no. 9, September 1923, pp. 785–9.

[34] *Die Kommunistische Internationale* (op. cit., pp. 236–8) specifies that they began on 21 September and only ended on 4 October. Yet Thalheimer (*1923: Eine Verpasste Revolution?*, op. cit., p. 21) points out that Brandler had been in Moscow from the end of August. Why such a long delay? Thalheimer says: 'Because the majority of the Russian comrades were away.'

[35] The presence of Eberlein is confirmed in *Die Kommunistische Internationale* (op. cit., pp. 237–8), that of Hesse and Grylewicz by their own testimony, corroborated by third parties and reported by Weber, *Die Wandlung des deutschen Kommunismus*, Volume 2, op. cit., pp. 145, 160.

government slogan, accusing him of being 'oriented towards reformism' and of seeking reconciliation with the SPD.[36] But she thought that the only solution was to prepare to seize power, and that was the question being discussed in Moscow. Brandler, for his part, seemed convinced that a seizure of power was now on the agenda. Kuusinen was to write later that Brandler forecast that seizing power would be 'easy', and even that he had 'fallen into revolutionary fantasy'.[37] He presented it as 'a fully realisable task' at the Executive of the RILU, the time being right to take power,[38] although it should be noted that he was speaking here in an official capacity.

As for Brandler's real feelings, Fischer gives varying accounts. Sometimes she says that he gave fantastically optimistic information,[39] whereas at other times he was really opposed to any action,[40] and was looking for different plans. In fact, whilst Brandler did not question the perspective of revolution, he believed the estimations of most of his Russian comrades were 'too optimistic'.[41]

Several differences appeared during the preparatory meetings. The first was about whether it would be necessary to call at some specific moment for the formation of political workers' councils on the model of the soviets. Zinoviev said that the Russian Party should call, before the insurrection, for such councils to be elected, because they alone could form the basic elements for the new German workers' state.[42] Trotsky and Brandler, however, successfully argued that the factory councils would play the role of the soviets before the insurrection. Later on, Trotsky was to justify this decision: 'In view of the fact that the factory committees had already become in action the rallying centres of the revolutionary masses, soviets would only have been a parallel form of organisation, without any real content, during the preparatory stage.'[43] Moreover, the majority agreed with him that forming soviets ran the risk of distracting the attention of the activists from the material tasks of preparing the insurrection, and they would become targets for a government which

---

[36] Minutes of the Zentrale, 12 September 1923, cited by Mujbegoviĉ, op. cit., p. 398, n. 85 .

[37] *Cahiers du bolchevisme*, no. 11, 30 January 1925, p. 760.

[38] *Trud*, 22 September 1923, cited in Carr, *The Interregnum*, op. cit., p. 205.

[39] Fischer, op. cit., p. 313.

[40] Ibid., p. 317.

[41] Brandler to Trotsky, January 1924, L.D. Trotsky, *De la révolution*, Paris, 1963, p. 196.

[42] Wenzel, op. cit., pp. 182–3; L.D. Trotsky, 'Lessons of October', *The Challenge of the Left Opposition (1923–25)*, New York, 1975, p. 250.

[43] Ibid.

wanted to provoke the workers into a premature clash. The majority also agreed with him that 'the entire preparatory work for the insurrection' could be 'carried out successfully under the authority of the factory and shop committees', and that soviets would not have to be built until later, immediately after the insurrection, as part of its consolidation.[44]

However, whilst they agreed on the question of soviets, Trotsky and Brandler disagreed on the issue of fixing the date of the insurrection. The German Left, Zinoviev and Trotsky all insisted that a date be fixed, and the Political Bureau of the Russian Party first settled the question to this effect. But Brandler objected, and Radek supported him.[45]

Trotsky developed his ideas on this point in an article which appeared in *Pravda* on 23 September, entitled 'Can a Counter-Revolution or a Revolution be Made on Schedule?'. He began by referring to the recent counter-revolutions, Mussolini's coup d'état, Tsankov's coup in Bulgaria, and the Spanish *pronunciamiento*. They had occurred on a date fixed by their leaders, in the context of a favourable situation. He expressed the opinion that taking 'the waiting attitude in the face of the growing revolutionary movement' was 'to adopt essentially the point of view of Menshevism': '. . . the Communist Party has absolutely no use for the great liberal law according to which revolutions happen but are never made and therefore cannot be fixed for a specific date. From a spectator's standpoint this law is correct, but from the standpoint of the leader it is a platitude and a vulgarity'.[46] He painted a picture of a country which was undergoing 'a profound social crisis', in which the contradictions were aggravated to the extreme, in which the working class was in constant ferment, and in which the Party clearly had the support of an undeniable majority of working people and consequently of 'the most active, class-conscious and self-sacrificing elements of the proletariat' – the allusion is transparent. He declared that the sole duty of the Party was: '. . . to fix a definite time in the immediate future, a time in the course of which the favourable revolutionary situation cannot abruptly react against us, and then to concentrate every effort on the preparation of the blow, to subordinate the entire policy

---

[44] Ibid. Note on this point the agreement between Brandler, Radek, Trotsky and the German Left (*Protokoll fünfter Kongress der Kommunistischen Internationale, 17 Juni bis 8 Juli in Moskau*, Hamburg, 1925, p. 139).

[45] *Die Lehren der deutschen Ereignisse*, op. cit., p. 60.

[46] *Pravda*, 23 September 1923; *Vom Bürgerkrieg*, no. 3, n.d. [1923], pp. 1–7; L.D. Trotsky, 'Can a Counter-Revolution or a Revolution be Made on Schedule?', *The First Five Years of the Communist International*, Volume 2, op. cit., p. 349.

and organisation to the military object in view, so that this blow is dealt with maximum power.'[47] Therefore, he proposed to fix the symbolic date of 7 November, which seemed to him to take into account a reasonable interval for the necessary preparation and to present the indubitable advantage of enjoying the prestige of the October Revolution. But Brandler was immovable on this point. He believed that it was the German leadership, and it alone, which would be able to decide on the spot, with the fewest mistakes, the moment when they must strike. He was supported by Radek, and obtained approval that the choice of date for the insurrection be left to those who would lead it.[48]

Several personal disagreements gave rise to other equally sharp debates during the preparatory conferences. Brandler admired Trotsky, and was friendly with him despite their differences, and asked that the organiser of the Russian October be sent to Germany to lead the decisive battle in person. Zinoviev opposed this, and it is possible, as some have suggested, that he then proposed his own candidature, on the grounds that only the President of the International could be entrusted with such a mission.[49]

No one had forgotten that Trotsky had proved his ability in the insurrection in 1917 at the moment when Zinoviev had collapsed. But the Troika could not run the risk presented by either a success on the part of its rival or a failure on the part of its leader. It was thus almost unanimously decided quite simply to send to Germany at the last moment, in order to take supreme responsibility, the German Commission itself.[50]

Brandler raised another thorny problem. Despite the undertakings which Fischer and Maslow gave that they would be loyal to the Zentrale, he maintained his distrust of them. He considered that nothing must weaken the Zentrale at so crucial a moment, and demanded that the leaders of the Left should be removed from both the leadership and the Party itself during the decisive period, in order to prevent them from weakening it by their habitual factional initiatives. He suggested that the precedent be followed

---

[47] Ibid.

[48] *Die Lehren der deutschen Ereignisse*, op. cit., p. 60.

[49] This information comes from Brandler himself. It is reproduced in I. Deutscher, *The Prophet Unarmed*, London, 1959, pp. 111–12, 143; and in Wenzel, op. cit., p. 193. It is discussed by Angress, op. cit., p. 403, n. 65, who concludes that it is authentic.

[50] Angress, op. cit., p. 403. According to a letter from Brandler to Weber and K.H. Tjaden in October 1962, the supreme decision rested with a 'committee of three', Brandler, Thaelmann and Piatakov.

which Lenin created in 1921 when he had suggested that Maslow be retained in Moscow. He was supported by Trotsky on this point, but was strongly attacked by Bukharin and Radek.[51] After bitter discussions, Zinoviev narrowly succeeded in getting a compromise solution carried. Maslow alone would remain in Moscow, where a commission of the International was summoned to investigate certain accusations against him.[52]

Fischer was authorised to return to her place in Germany, but she was to be accompanied there by a 'supervisor' from the ECCI, the Russian Vassili Shmidt, a member of the German Commission, who was specially charged with seeing that discipline was respected by the Berlin-Brandenburg district organisation.[53]

When Brandler returned to Berlin and reported on the Moscow discussions to the Zentrale, he said that he was broadly satisfied. The report of the session of 12 October shows: 'Comrade Brandler gave a report on the general discussions as well as on the discussions with the opposition which took place in Moscow and with the Russian comrades. . . . There were no differences of opinion except where the fixing of dates was concerned.'[54]

The military preparations

Technical questions had an important place in the Moscow discussions, much to Fischer's annoyance.[55] But Trotsky was unyielding on this point, and spoke with the authority conferred by his prestige as the organiser of the victory in 1917. He wrote in *Pravda* recalling the technical preparations for the October insurrection:

---

[51] Speech of Zinoviev to the ECCI, 11 January 1924, *Die Internationale*, no. 2/3, 28 March 1924, p. 44. The corresponding paragraph does not appear in *Die Lehren der deutschen Ereignisse*. There is a reference to the attack on Fischer in *Cahiers du bolchevisme*, no. 11, 30 January 1925, p. 761.

[52] Fischer, op. cit., p. 323; Weber, *Die Wandlung des deutschen Kommunismus*, Volume 2, op. cit., p. 214. Some people in the KPD and in the International claimed that Maslow was in the service of the police. In February 1922, after he had been arrested in Berlin, he had declared that he was an agent of the Russian government, in the confidence of Trotsky and Radek. This seemed to him the best way to get released quickly, in view of the relations between the Russian and German governments. This did not save him from being sentenced to eight months in jail for using false papers (Weber, *Die Wandlung des deutschen Kommunismus*, Volume 2, op. cit., p. 214). The affair was brought up at the ECCI in September.

[53] Fischer, op. cit., p. 761.

[54] Minutes of the Zentrale, 12 October 1923, cited in Mujbegović, op. cit., p. 396, n. 80.

[55] Fischer, op. cit., p. 318.

The work of military preparation proceeds parallel with all the other work according to a rigid schedule. Therewith the party retains throughout absolute control of its military apparatus. To be sure, there is always a great deal that is entirely unforeseen, unexpected and spontaneous in the revolution; and we must of course make allowances for the occurrence of all such 'accidents' and adjust ourselves to them; but we can do this with greater success and certainty if our conspiratorial plan is thoroughly worked out beforehand. Revolution possesses a mighty power of improvisation, but it never improvises anything good for fatalists, bystanders and fools. Victory comes from the correct political evaluation, from correct organisation, and from the will to deal the decisive blow.[56]

The Military Apparatus of the KPD – the M-Apparat – could not meet the needs of the immense tasks that had to be carried out in such a short period. The Red Army placed at the disposal of the German Revolution one of its officers, of Latvian origin, a former worker named Rose, who was known as Piotr Alexandrovich Skoblevsky or Gorev.[57] He began to reorganise the Military Apparatus, which was renamed the Politico-Military Organisation (MP), for the insurrection. As Supreme Commander, or Reichsleiter, he was assisted by a Military Council, the Militärrat, with Ernst Schneller as Chairman, plus several members of the Zentrale. The territory of the Reich was divided into six regional politico-military commands, which corresponded to the military divisions. Each MP-Oberleiter, or regional commander, was supported by a technical adviser sent from the ECCI. Under their orders were the district and sub-district commanders, themselves at the head of Kampfleitungen, or combat detachments, with the task of organising, training and later leading into battle the proletarian hundreds.[58] The whole of the Politico-Military Organisation was placed under the authority of a political unit for preparing the insurrection, the Revko or Revkom, or Revolutionary Committee,[59] presided over by August Kleine, who had been sent to Germany by the ECCI in 1921, and had been elected to the Zentrale at the Leipzig Congress.

---

[56] Trotsky, 'Can a Counter-Revolution or a Revolution be Made on Schedule?', op. cit., pp. 352–3; Fischer, op. cit., pp. 452–3.

[57] Angress (op. cit., p. 417, n. 97) reviews the discussions about of the date of his arrival in Germany, which has been posited as September 1922, and January and September 1923.

[58] Wenzel, op. cit., pp. 194ff.; information from Wollenberg cited in H. Weber, *Von Rosa Luxemburg zu Walter Ulbricht*, Hanover, 1961, pp. 28–9.

[59] Russian authors, in particular Davidovich (op. cit., p. 134), give the title Revkom to local bodies, and reserve the term 'Kopf' [head] for the overall leadership.

The number of Russian officers and technicians sent to Germany to act as officers for the projected insurrection has often been exaggerated. Nearly all the technical cadres were Germans who had been trained as officers during the World War. They included Wilhelm Zaisser, who had gone over to the Ukrainian partisans in 1918 and had been one of the leaders of the fighting in the Ruhr in 1919 and 1920,[60] Albert Schreiner, known as Baumann,[61] Hans Kahle,[62] Erich Wollenberg, a former fighter in the Bavarian Red Army, Artur Illner, Albert Gromulat,[63] Hans Kippenberger, who was a very young man, a reserve lieutenant, and one of the most gifted and most intrepid leaders in the clandestine apparatus of the KPD. There were also the former officers or sergeants Karl Frank, Christian Heuck, Stefan Heymann, who was known as Dietrich, Lengnink, Merker, Strötzel,[64] and the former major in the old Imperial army Hans von Hentig.[65]

Some of them may have followed courses at military schools in Russia that concentrated upon the problems of civil war, but they had learned the essentials of their military knowledge during the Great War, and in the streets in 1919, 1920 and 1921. The former comrades in the M-Apparat could not attend to everything, and found themselves devolving key functions. Otto Bulian was put in charge of security, and Otto Braun took charge of training military cadres.[66] Specialists from the organisation were attached to them. Amongst these was Anton Grylewicz, the former deputy to Eichhorn in 1918, who took part in the technical preparations in Moscow. There was also Arthur Ewert, Ottomar Geschke, who worked in the Military Apparatus under the name of 'Polar Bear', and Melcher, who became 'Martin'.[67] Finally, they were reinforced by instructors, specialists and foreign Communists who had received appropriate training in Russia and had emerged as cadres in the Red Army, as well as Russian Communists. Their names are only rarely known.

Many of them already belonged or were on the point of being recruited to

---

[60] He was to be known in Spain as 'General Gomez'.
[61] To be known in Spain as 'Major Schindler'.
[62] To be known in Spain as 'Colonel Hans'.
[63] Weber, *Von Rosa Luxemburg zu Walter Ulbricht*, op. cit., p. 29.
[64] See Weber, *Die Wandlung des deutschen Kommunismus*, Volume 2, op. cit., for all these names.
[65] Wollenberg mentions 'Von H.' Fischer (op. cit., p. 315) records that 'as organiser of the party's military apparatus in Thuringia, he was charged with buying weapons'. There is much information about this curious person in O.E. Schüddekopf, *Linke Leute von Rechts*, op. cit., and especially on page 160 on his role in 1923.
[66] Weber, *Die Wandlung des deutschen Kommunismus*, Volume 2, op. cit., pp. 86, 89.
[67] Ibid., pp. 114, 134, 145, 217.

the intelligence services of the Red Army. However, we should mention Stein (whose real name was Manfred Stern),[68] 'Georg' (whose real name was Alexis Stetski),[69] the Yugoslav Communist Voya Vuyović, the leader of the Communist Youth International. There were the people in the Fourth Bureau, of whom history knows only the pseudonyms; Walter Krivitsky;[70] Alfred Krause and Ludwig, known also as Ignaz Reiss, who managed the security in Germany of the members of the delegation from the ECCI.[71] These foreign cadres – less than a hundred in all – had in principle no direct executive responsibility, and were simply technical advisers to the German 'politico-military' leaders at the highest levels.

During the first phase of the insurrection, the essential role was to fall to the workers' militias, the proletarian hundreds which had been patiently built up since the beginning of the year. Brandler estimated that they numbered between 50,000 and 60,000 men in Saxony alone.[72] Böttcher wrote in 1923 that their organisation was ten times more advanced in Saxony than elsewhere in Germany.[73] Fischer, on the other hand, considers that the proletarian hundreds only constituted a substantial force in the Ruhr.[74] It is not easy to evaluate their real strength, because in most of Germany they appeared in other guises. They were banned throughout Prussian territory from 15 May, and this undoubtedly obstructed their development, but they were maintained, or created in new forms, as 'stewards' or as clubs for youth and open air activities, which permitted them to practice drill, country marches and training in handling arms and in manoeuvres. The work of Helmut Gast has permitted their organisation to be better known.[75]

---

[68] Davidovich (op. cit., p. 233, n. 2) testifies that his first name was Manfred and not Lazar as had hitherto been believed. Wollenberg indicated the pseudonym Stein. Stern was to be known during the Spanish Civil War under the name of 'General Kléber'.

[69] Weber, *Die Wandlung des deutschen Kommunismus*, Volume 2, op. cit., p. 114.

[70] Whose book is to be consulted with caution. See W. Krivitsky, *In Stalin's Secret Service*, New York, 1939.

[71] For Krause and Ludwig, see E. Poretsky, *Les nôtres*, Paris, 1969. Ludwig, according to the author, who was his partner, was even in Dresden with Piatakov, whom he accompanied with a false passport, which had been prepared by the 'services', and which was identical to that of his companion.

[72] *Die Lehren der deutschen Ereignisse*, op. cit., p. 60.

[73] *Correspondance internationale*, no. 49, 19 June 1923, p. 363.

[74] Fischer, op. cit., p. 295.

[75] H. Gast, 'Die proletarischen Hundertschaften als Organe der Einheitsfront im Jahre 1923', *Zeitschrift für Geschichtswissenschaft*, no. 3, 1956, pp. 439–65.

In May 1923, there were about 300 proletarian hundreds in Germany. According to Gast this had increased to about 800 by October. This gives a total force of about 100,000 men, one-third in Saxony alone, and one-half of the total in Saxony and Thuringia together, where they were legally authorised.[76] When 25,000 men of the hundreds marched in Berlin on 1 May, they were still legal; and 1,000 marched in Dresden on the same day. On 9 September, 8,000 men marched in Dresden, and on 16 September, 5,000 in Leipzig. On 23 September, 800 men of the hundreds in the small villages of the Erzgebirge marched in Oelsnitz, and on 7 October, there was another march in the same city of 2,000.[77] Only one-fifth of the hundreds were made up exclusively of Communists. The others resulted from a united front between the KPD, the trade unions and, especially in Thuringia and Saxony, the SPD. In Leipzig, 40 per cent of the members came from the KPD, 20 per cent from the SPD, and 40 per cent from the unions.[78]

Their organisation closely followed the structure of working-class life. The basic unit was formed by the hundred of the factory or the city, which was itself divided into smaller detachments corresponding as far as possible to workplaces, workshops or small firms. Two sixes made up a group of a dozen. Three groups formed a column. Each hundred consisted of three columns, a detachment of scouts and a first aid group. Sixes, columns and hundreds elected their own leaders. Each hundred was led by a hundred-leader, an elected political head, assisted by a technical adviser elected from amongst men who had military training, mostly former officers or sergeants. Concern for unity often led the militia men to elect leaders from the two big workers' parties. In Saxony, as a general rule, the head of a hundred was a Communist, while his technical adviser was a Social Democrat. From this point of view, Gast emphasises the exception of the Zwickau-Plauen district: there the general staff was made up of seven leaders, four Social Democrats and three Communists, the Social Democrat Max Seydewitz being the district leader.[79] However, in general, the hundreds were under the control of the KPD's Military Apparatus, and Communist leaders, such as Theodor Neubauer in Thuringia and Ernst Schneller in Saxony, chaired the working meetings or the military gatherings.[80]

---

[76] Ibid., pp. 452–3; *Oktober*, no. 4, 1931, pp. 21–2.
[77] Gast, op. cit., p. 453.
[78] Ibid., p. 454.
[79] Ibid., p. 455.
[80] Ibid., pp. 448, 453.

Seen from the KPD's standpoint, the military forces which had been built up in a few months were a real achievement. In relation to German society as a whole, and to the forces of the Reichswehr, the police and the armed groups of the extreme Right, it still appeared very insufficient. But the Communists counted on a mass uprising of the working class, disintegration of the Reichswehr, and the overwhelming power of a general strike to ensure the victory of their hundreds, in which some already saw the elements of the future Red Army of Germany.

The question of weapons was one of the hardest to solve. The Organisation Bureau and Leo Flieg, the *éminence grise* of the Zentrale, maintained contact with one of the emissaries of the ECCI, Mirov-Abramov, a member of the OMS.[81] Mirov-Abramov had the advantage of being appointed to a post in the Russian embassy, which gave him a cover. Flieg also kept in touch with the Special Commission to buy arms and munitions, the Wumba.[82] A teacher and reserve officer, Nicholas Pfaff, working under the false name of 'Dr Winkler', arranged most of the purchases,[83] for which the conspirators apparently disposed of substantial sums in dollars.[84] It is difficult to evaluate the results: the estimates vary between 600 and 50,000 rifles, for example, which on the most favourable hypothesis means one rifle for every two fighters in the hundreds.[85] Revolvers appear to have been more numerous,[86] but machine-guns and heavier weapons were in very short supply. For the rest, they built up stocks of explosives, usually stolen from quarries at night. Some armouries or workshops of the Reichswehr were surprised and looted, but mostly were marked down for the big day, when arms would be obtained first by attacking police stations. In Saxony, the activists had set up a secret

---

[81] This was the Otdel Mezhdunarodnoi Svyazi or Department of International Relations attached to the ECCI.

[82] In full, the Waffen und Munitions-beschaffungsamt.

[83] Weber, *Die Wandlung des deutschen Kommunismus*, Volume 2, op. cit., p. 244. Other arms procurers he names are Christian Heuck and Paul Gmeiner (ibid., pp. 134, 161). Fischer (op. cit., p. 315) also mentions von Hentig in Thuringia.

[84] Ibid.

[85] Borkenau (op. cit., p. 250) speaks of 600 rifles, and Flechtheim (op. cit., p. 93, n. 1) mentions 11,000. The former Communist Walter Zeutschel, who went over to the Nazis, said that the Party had at its disposal 50,000 rifles in the whole of Germany (W. Zeutschel, *Im Dienst der Kommunistischen Terror-Organisation Tscheka in Deutschland*, Berlin, 1931, p. 92); whilst Brandler stated in Moscow that he had only 800 for Saxony (*Die Lehren der deutschen Ereignisse*, op. cit., p. 6). Brandler gave Wenzel (op. cit., p. 395) the figure of 395 rifles at the start of the insurrection in Hamburg.

[86] Zeutschel (op. cit., p. 23) writes that the insurgents in Hamburg had 80 rifles and twice as many revolvers.

factory to manufacture arms and ammunition.[87] Contacts had been made with officers, NCOs and soldiers in the Reichswehr who were expected to hand over arms depots to the insurgents at the last minute.

The mobilisation of the activists

The whole party was on a war footing. From the first days of September, with the help of several dozen specialists sent by the ECCI, tens of thousands of activists had gone underground. Members of the shock groups of the hundreds had left their factories, and known activists had changed their names and addresses. In all the big cities, men were sleeping, and sometimes spending entire days and nights, in apartments converted into dormitories or clandestine headquarters, where they studied maps of the cities and the region, and the location of the forces of order and of communications. Periodically, by action groups and hundreds, they carried out exercises in response to orders.

The activists who were detached in this way from their usual surroundings often came to think, act and behave in a purely conspiratorial manner. Fischer cites from memory a significant speech by Hans Pfeiffer in this connection:

> Comrades, under no circumstances should we proclaim a general strike. The bourgeoisie would find out what we are planning and would destroy us before we start. On the contrary, let us soften down our spontaneous movements. Let us hold back our groups in the factories and the unemployed organisations so that the government will think that the danger is over. And then – after they are lulled into an illusion of complete safety – let us strike in one night, quickly and decisively, arrest the government, storm the Reichswehr barracks, and ring the knell of the last battle.[88]

The naïveté of his plan is almost laughable. But it can be explained by the heat of the moment as much as by the intensity of the unprecedented efforts made by the activists. Albert, who lived through these weeks, wrote:

---

[87] Gast, op. cit., p. 457.
[88] Cited in Fischer, op. cit., p. 327.

There was no city in which they had not prepared conscientiously for the battle, with the detailed attention of men who were determined to give everything. Not a day without hard work, nor a night without a special task. Not a problem neglected. I know comrades who did not have a full night's sleep for long weeks. I have seen faces lined with exhaustion. Men's eyes still burned with the intense flame of their will. . . . The German Communist Party has given to the proletariat of the world the new, precious example of a formidable preparation for revolution.[89]

We owe to the same man this evocation of a Party meeting:

It is good to find gathered around the same table the faces of men who know what lies behind things, and who, in this long period of a people's suffering, every day replenish their will from their limitless hope. . . . A young, restrained voice exclaims: 'We already have entire divisions.' It is true that arms are lacking, but we shall find them in the barracks. Everyone has in his minds eye the map of Germany. 'Saxony, Thuringia, Hamburg and Berlin will hold . . . Russia!', 'Radek has written . . .' I noticed that the intellectuals – of whom I am one – are the most cautious. . . . For a long time they think, weigh the difficulties with persistent reasoning which sometimes has a highly destructive effect. A friend cuts our criticisms short; he says: 'I believe in the revolution because I want it, and I live with men who want it.' That man was a section organiser. He worked day and night.[90]

Voya Vuyović confided his optimism to Victor Serge: 'Voya believes that, on the day, we shall win: "Everything is going to be much better than in Russia . . ."'[91]

Fischer, many years later, recognised the resolute optimism of these tens of thousands of men who were scientifically preparing their revolution:

The official promise by the Russian Political Bureau to support the German uprising was enthusiastically accepted as decisive. The many Russian comrades in Germany, the unlimited funds (mostly in American dollars), the professional methods of preparation produced confidence. . . . These sober German workers were under a spell of revolutionary ecstasy.[92]

---

[89] R. Albert, 'Au seuil d'une révolution', *Clarté*, 15 February 1924, p. 97.
[90] R. Albert, 'Au seuil d'une révolution', *Clarté*, 1 February 1924, p. 63.
[91] Serge, op. cit., p. 170.
[92] Fischer, op. cit., p. 327.

The situation in September

Paradoxically, whilst the insurrection was being prepared, first in Moscow and then secretly in the German industrial centres, the crisis in Germany seems to have calmed down, or at any rate to have levelled off. At the end of August, Thalheimer was still writing that the time to act had not yet come:

> The hour for the workers' and peasants' government, for the first step towards the dictatorship of the proletariat, will come when the overwhelming majority of the working class wishes not only to break from the bourgeois coalition, but also to fight by every means for the formation of the workers' and peasants' government. It will also be necessary for important sections of the petty bourgeoisie to observe a benevolent neutrality towards the working class, and that the big bourgeoisie itself be divided. Moreover, it will be necessary that the class organisations of the proletariat – the factory councils, the control committees, the proletarian hundreds – shall have developed sufficiently to have become the preponderant authority amongst the masses. . . . Consequently, we shall have to travel a long road, both on the political and the organisational plane, before we meet the conditions which will ensure the victory of the working class. History will decide how long the necessary interval will be.[93]

On the basis of this analysis, the political developments did not seem to point to the approach of the great day. The German Zentrale appeared determined to correct the obvious excesses in the application of the Schlageter line. Voya Vuyović told Humbert-Droz that 'it had decided to modify this tactic and to moderate these bellicose declarations'.[94] However, as soon as the strike ended and Cuno had fallen, the Stresemann Cabinet did not hide its intention to demand sacrifices from everyone, including the wage-earners. The Chancellor and his Social-Democratic Finance Minister insisted that the overall volume of wages must fall, that work must be intensified and imports considerably increased. The bourgeois press campaigned for the eight-hour day to be abolished. The newspaper which was regarded as Stinnes's mouthpiece, *Deutsche Allgemeine Zeitung*, wrote on 8 September: 'The German people must work at least two more hours, with at least the same intensity as before the War.'[95]

---

[93] *Correspondance internationale*, no. 69, 31 August 1923, p. 619.
[94] Letter from Humbert-Droz to Zinoviev, 20 September 1923, referring to Vuyović's visit to Paris in early September, quoted in Humbert-Droz, op. cit., p. 195.
[95] *Deutsche Allgemeine Zeitung*, 8 September 1923.

It is true that the left opposition in the SPD continued to grow stronger. Its regional congress in Berlin declared that the policy of the grand coalition was bankrupt, demanded a return to class politics, and passed a vote of congratulation to Zeigner.[96] But at the same time, it showed that it could not stop the repression which the leaders of its own party were carrying out against the Communists. On the day after the publication of a joint appeal by the Communist International and the RILU, the Minister of the Interior of the Reich, the Social Democrat Sollmann, banned *Die Rote Fahne* and the Rostock *Volkswacht* for a week.[97]

However, the illegal or semi-legal press of the KPD did not surrender. When *Die Rote Fahne* re-appeared, it resumed its incendiary proclamations, with a headline on 15 September saying 'Down With the Régime of Blood and Famine!'.[98] On 21 September, it called for meetings and mass demonstrations to prepare a general strike for the overthrow of Stresemann, and the formation of a workers' and peasants' government.[99] On 23 September, the front page carried an article preparing for the insurrection headlined 'The Road of the Proletarian Revolution in Germany (Another Word to the Social-Democratic Workers)'.[100] Next day, the Berlin prefect of police banned *Die Rote Fahne* for a fortnight.[101]

In general, the streets in the German cities were calmer. The only notable incidents during these few weeks took place in Baden, with demonstrations and battles with the police in the small town of Lörrach.[102] The KPD leaders in Baden called for a general strike in Baden, but were disavowed by the Zentrale, which saw in this a risk of prematurely igniting the armed struggle in a peripheral region.[103] The Baden government agreed to withdraw its police forces from Lörrach and its environs, where calm was restored on 25 September.

By the end of September, the Stresemann government had completed two important stages towards fulfilling its aims of stabilisation and normalisation. On 26 September, the Chancellor announced that the government recognised the occupation of the Ruhr, and had decided to call off the campaign of passive

---

[96] *Vorwärts*, 25 September 1923.
[97] *Die Rote Fahne*, 4 September 1923.
[98] *Die Rote Fahne*, 15 September 1923.
[99] *Die Rote Fahne*, 21 September 1923.
[100] *Die Rote Fahne*, 23 September 1923.
[101] *Die Rote Fahne*, 24 September 1923.
[102] Angress, op. cit., p. 388; Habedank, op. cit., pp. 45–7; Wenzel, op. cit., pp. 203–5.
[103] Angress, op. cit., p. 426; Wenzel, op. cit., p. 216.

resistance. In this way it opened the road to the compromise desired by Washington and London.[104] Secondly, following a dizzy fall, during the week of 13–19 September, the mark was stabilised from the 22nd at about 100 million to the dollar.[105]

At this moment, the activities of the extreme Right seem to have been on the point of creating an entirely new situation. On 21 September, Hugo Stinnes informed the US ambassador that an anti-Communist movement was developing in Bavaria, supported by all the right-wing parties and an important number of moderates of the Centre. He made clear to his interlocutor that the industrialists supported this movement, the task of which would be to fight the Communists fiercely, and forcibly break any attempt at a general strike. He added that he hoped in this way to eliminate socialism as a politically possible mode of existence in Germany and what remained to do would be the immediate repeal of laws and decrees 'which hampered production and had no useful purpose'.[106] The events in Bavaria were soon to convince the ambassador that Stinnes was not mistaken.

On 26 September, in a coup d'état, von Kahr proclaimed himself Reichs-commissar General for Bavaria, and decreed martial law.[107] That night, Ebert responded to his initiative, and used Article 48 of the Constitution to proclaim martial law throughout Germany and hand executive power to the Reichswehr Minister Gessler, a Democrat, the civilian cover for General von Seeckt. The Social-Democratic ministers approved this decision, because of 'the reactionary danger from Bavaria'. Their Party press spoke of 'defending the Republic'. But on the 27th General von Lossow, the officer commanding the Reichswehr in Bavaria, placed himself under the orders of von Kahr. On the 28th, the latter abrogated in Bavaria the law 'to defend the Republic' which had been passed immediately after the assassination of Rathenau.[108]

The initiative seemed to have passed into the hands of the extreme Right. From Bavaria there resounded throughout Germany the crash of boots and the clanking of weapons from the well-organised and solidly equipped nationalist gangs, the grimly famous Free Corps of Ehrhardt and Rossbach, from Ludendorff who since January had felt his hour coming, and from Hitler

---

[104] Stresemann, op. cit., pp. 98, 100–128.
[105] *Correspondance internationale*, no. 77, 28 September 1923, p. 582.
[106] Hallgarten, op. cit., p. 64.
[107] Benoist-Méchin, Volume 2, op. cit., p. 295.
[108] Ibid., pp. 295–6.

and his troops. Rossbach had just succeeded in escaping from the fortress in which he had been confined. The Black Reichswehr was on the move, and on 1 October Major Buchrucker attempted a clumsy but revealing putsch in Küstrin.[109] People talked widely about 'a new crusade against Bolshevism', which would start from Munich and march on Berlin.

In certain respects, the situation recalled that which prevailed at the time of the Kapp Putsch: a three-cornered struggle, in which the nationalist bands and the armed workers seemed on the point of confronting the Reichswehr, without it being possible to decide which would be the first to open fire. The Reichswehr, which now legally ruled the state, announced its intention to 'defend the Republic' against its enemies on the Left and the Right, whilst the generals had firmly decided to avoid 'fratricidal strife', and to break the threat of revolution. The working class was exhausted by the sufferings of this terrible year, and, mesmerised by the threat from the nationalist gangs, allowed a régime of military dictatorship and martial law to be established, although it was to learn through experience that in the last analysis that régime would always be directed against it.

The KPD explained this in a manifesto to the German working class.[110] The ending of the resistance, which Stresemann had announced in the Reichstag, was the signal for a capitalist offensive against wages and the eight-hour day. Martial law, which had been proclaimed on the pretext of putting an end to the National Socialists' activities in Bavaria, and to separatism in the Rhineland, was in reality intended to liquidate the factory councils, and hit at the revolutionary movement whilst it was still assembling its forces.

But the fact that the initiative seemed to have passed from the working class to the fascists did not discourage the Communist leaders. They even counted on this threat to arouse the workers' combativity. They believed that the working people would rise up with them, as they had done in August, when the mask of the grand coalition would fall to reveal itself as the last refuge of the bourgeoisie. It was within the perspective of this armed uprising – the first to have been technically prepared by a Communist Party since October 1917 – that towards the end of September the details were being decided, in Moscow, of the plan which was intended to lead in a few weeks

---

[109] Ibid., pp. 270–8.
[110] 'Le KPD au peuple travailleur', *Correspondance internationale*, no. 56, supplement, 29 September 1923.

778 • Chapter Thirty-Nine

to the outbreak of the German October, to the second stage – after five years –
of the world revolution.

On 29 September, the Zentrale secretly sent to the district secretaries a
circular which left no doubt that the insurrection was drawing near:

> In workplaces and localities, *committees of action* must be formed immediately
> from representatives of the SPD, the USPD, the KPD, sports clubs, Factory
> Councils, trade unions and other workers' organisations. The task of the
> action committees is to undertake the struggle against martial law and
> against the dictatorship of Gessler and von Kahr, which the government
> supports. The immediate task is to prepare the general strike in every
> workplace and locality. . . . At the same time as they prepare for the general
> strike, the action committees must work out a plan to mobilise the working
> masses for the coming battles.[111]

---

[111] Cited in R. Wagner, 'Die revolutionäre Bewegung in den Bezirken Hessen-Frankfurt
und Baden im Herbst 1923', *Beiträge zur Geschichte der deutschen Arbeiterbewegung*, no.
7, 1965, p. 85.

Chapter Forty
Moscow's View of the German Revolution

On 12 October 1923, the first of a series of eight articles by Zinoviev under the heading of 'Problems of the German Revolution', appeared in *Pravda*. Six of these articles were to appear before the retreat was called. The articles, which had been translated and circulated by the KPD, were quickly withdrawn from circulation; they remain a valuable indication of the perspectives of the leaders of the Russian Communist Party and the Communist International towards the German October.

The characteristics of the German Revolution

The Bolsheviks had been waiting since 1917 for a revolution in Germany. They considered that they had not long to wait, and Zinoviev saw its victory as more or less guaranteed:

> The events in Germany are unfolding with a fateful inexorability. The road which cost the Russian Revolution twelve years from 1905 to 1917 will have been covered by the German Revolution in five years from 1918 to 1923. Events have been especially precipitate in recent days. First the 'coalition', then the 'grand coalition', then the 'Kornilov affair' (the events in Bavaria!) the ministry of the specialists, of 'personalities', and now something like a 'grand coalition' again –

in a word, incessant ministerial upheavals. This is 'on top'. But 'down below', amongst the masses, the movement is boiling over, and the battle which will quickly decide the fate of Germany is upon us. The proletarian revolution is knocking at the door in Germany: one must be blind not to see this.

The coming events will have a *world-historical* significance. We shall soon see that the autumn of 1923 marks a turning-point, not only for Germany, but for the whole of humanity. With trembling hands, the working class is turning the decisive page of the history of its world struggle. A new chapter in the history of the world proletarian revolution is opening.[1]

There could be no doubt about the social content of the imminent revolution. Statistics proved that in Germany the workers were twice as numerous as all the other social classes combined. Until now the majority of the workers had more or less followed counter-revolutionary Social Democracy, but were now in the process of turning away from it:

The coming German Revolution will be a proletarian class revolution; 22 million working people – the heart of the international working class and the initial capital of the world revolution. In 1917, Russia had at the most between 8 and 10 million workers, in a total population of 160 million. Germany has more than 20 million workers in a total population of 60 million. With us, the working class was only a very small minority. In Germany, on the contrary, it forms the principal element, the majority of the population. The German workers are almost without exception literate. They have been through a magnificent school of organisation. They are cultured. A high proportion of them served in the army during the imperialist war: the German army contained a large percentage of workers during 1914–18. This is why they will be the best soldiers of the revolution. With Social Democracy they have known a hard school, but they have also learned much there.[2]

The German Revolution would be taking place in a highly industrialised country, with a very high level of technology, in which the proletariat was highly trained. Historically speaking, the German proletariat, for this reason, no longer could take power prematurely, because the objective conditions for revolution had long been ripe. However, it should not be concluded that the

---

[1] G. Zinoviev, *Probleme der deutschen Revolution*, Hamburg, 1923, pp. 1–2.
[2] Ibid., pp. 6–7.

proletariat would be on the stage by itself. The petty bourgeoisie would also play a role. During the War and its aftermath, capitalism had dealt it terrible blows, and it suffered widespread pauperisation. It could only be favourable or at worst neutral towards the proletariat:

> The German Revolution will profit from the lessons of the Russian Revolution and will take care not to repeat its mistakes. From the first moment, it will take care not to lose sight of the enormous importance of the alliance between town and country, between the proletariat and the petty bourgeoisie. It will not resort to the total nationalisation of small-scale trade and small-scale industry. . . . From its first steps, the German revolutionary government will be obliged to do its utmost to win the sympathy of the little people, the intellectuals, the artisans and the poor and middle peasants. . . . It is precisely because the proletarian revolution in Germany possesses this solid foundation, and because the German proletariat will exert its total hegemony over events, that it will be able to permit itself the luxury of avoiding every action which would alienate the petty bourgeoisie.[3]

As for other questions, the Revolution would, as always, reveal unsuspected strengths: 'We cannot yet form any idea of the marvellous energy which twenty million tested, cultured, organised German proletarians will be able to apply in the final struggle for socialism.'[4]

The legend of collusion with the Nazis

Zinoviev showed how the Social-Democratic press of the whole world was doing its utmost to persuade the workers that there was collusion or even an alliance between Communists and nationalists in Germany. The explanation for this was very simple: the accusation was intended to justify in advance the armed intervention which French imperialism was considering against the German Revolution:

> The infamous role which was played in 1914 by the theory of 'national defence' in the imperialist war now backs up the legend of an alliance between Communism and nationalism. Its purpose is to discredit in advance the great German proletarian revolution. Even before it has occurred, they

---

[3] Ibid., p. 11.
[4] Ibid., p. 12.

are getting ready to slander it, to befoul it and to vilify it, as they have done for six years with the Russian Revolution.[5]

It was therefore of the utmost importance that the workers of the whole world understood that Germany was a defeated country, and was treated as such, trodden underfoot by the Entente, and this was why the nationalists' propaganda found a ready response. The German fascists were trying to exploit the agony, anxiety and despair of strata of the petty bourgeoisie to divert their anger from those who were really responsible, and to attract them towards nationalist passions in order to swell the ranks of the counter-revolution: 'The German Communists have more than the right, they have the imperious *duty* to win from bourgeois nationalism all the strata of the propertyless who have followed the fascists out of hatred – a legitimate and justified hatred – of the Entente which oppresses them.'[6]

The campaign which international Social Democracy launched against the German Communists demonstrated that imperialism was preparing to wage a counter-revolutionary war against Germany on the pretext that Germany was preparing a 'war of revenge'. A betrayal still more monstrous than that of August 1914 was thus being prepared. The Communists, like the German proletariat, wanted peace, but foreign intervention against the Revolution would clearly provoke the desperate resistance of all the vital forces of Germany, grouped around the proletariat.

The working class, Communists and Social Democrats

Zinoviev retraced the history of the German Revolution since 1918, and tried to show that, each time a proletarian victory had been possible, Social Democracy finally succeeded in guaranteeing, at least for a time, the survival of the bourgeoisie. He gave the reasons which made him think that it would not be the same this time.

The first reason was the fact that, especially since 1921, the German Communists had understood that they had to defer their projects of insurrection and seizing power, and were obliged above all to win the majority of the working class before they could carry through a victorious revolution. Zinoviev believed that they were very close to having succeeded in this in 1923. They

---

[5] Ibid., p. 17.
[6] Ibid., p. 19.

controlled the movement of the factory councils in more than 2,000 areas. They enjoyed a considerable influence in the trade unions – which they probably could not win completely until they had seized power. In August – and this was crucial – they enjoyed the clear majority in the strike committees in Berlin and Hamburg:

> Have we here yet a 'firm and lasting majority'? Perhaps we cannot say that. But there is no doubt: *we are moving that way*, and we shall soon be there. The state of mind of the masses can still change; it lacks stability. The feelings of millions of workers cannot be given once and for all. Part of them still hesitates, one foot already in the Communist camp and the other in that of Social Democracy. This is inevitable in a period of transition. It would be absurd to demand as a condition for success that every single worker shall have sworn loyalty to the Communist Party. It is during the course of the battle itself that the majority will complete taking its stand solidly behind the Communists.[7]

Zinoviev believed that, for the present, German Social Democracy had lost at least two-thirds of its supporters, and that its membership was now largely drawn from the more elderly workers. Hundreds of thousands of Social-Democratic workers were with the Communists in the factory councils and the proletarian hundreds, and were following the slogans of the KPD in breach of the discipline of their own party. Like the Socialist Revolutionaries during 1917, the SPD was cracking apart in the course of the Revolution.

From this point of view, the appearance of a left-wing tendency within its ranks was of great significance, not, of course, because its leaders could be trusted, but because it was a symptom, reflecting as in a distorting mirror the revolutionary state of mind of the proletarian masses. Most of the left-wing Social-Democratic leaders were 'old acquaintances' who at one moment or another in the past had betrayed the workers. It would be dangerous to let them play an independent role, and too much dependence upon them could be fatal to the proletarian revolution. But this did not mean, for all that, that their influence could be ignored; these Social-Democratic leftists personified the last illusions of an important section of the working class, and the revolution would be victorious only if the working class cured itself of these illusions: 'The time is near when the great majority of the working people, who today

---

[7] Ibid., p. 29.

still place such hope in this Social-Democratic Left, will convince themselves that the final struggle will have to be conducted not only without the Social-Democratic Right but also without the Left.'[8]

From this viewpoint, Zinoviev saw a dual purpose in the entry – which had just taken place – of representatives of the KPD into Zeigner's Saxon government:

> . . . to help the revolutionary vanguard in Saxony to strengthen its positions, to occupy a territory, to make Saxony a base of operations; to give the left Social Democrats the chance to expose themselves by their actions, and in this way to contribute to dissipating the illusions which they support. . . . The entry of Communists into the Saxon government is justified only if sufficient guarantees are given to us that the Saxon state is really going to serve the working class and begin to arm the tens of thousands of workers against Bavarian and pan-Germanist fascism, and that it really takes in hand the expulsion from the administration of the bourgeois elements often inherited from Wilhelm II, and that it will immediately take revolutionary economic measures against the bourgeoisie. If the present Saxon government succeeds in really making Saxony into a red territory, which could to a certain extent become a focus for concentrating the revolutionary proletarian forces in Germany, the German proletariat will know how to support its efforts. If, on the contrary, it does not do this, the German Communists must draw on the Dresden experience to denounce once more before the masses the lack of character of these leaders.[9]

As for the situation in Germany as a whole, the essential role rested with the Communist Party and its capacity for action:

> The German Communists have won, or are very close to having won, the majority of the numerous and powerful working class. This majority can neither strengthen nor temper itself by votes or discussions. It will complete its formation in the coming battles. The essential task of the Communist Party is to inculcate *by its activity* into the majority of German workers the conviction that the Communists, unlike in 1919 or 1921, are now leading into battle not just the vanguard, but the whole working class. And above all to inculcate into the working masses the conviction that the Communists' assumption of the leadership of the movement really ensures *victory*.[10]

---

[8] Ibid., p. 34.
[9] Ibid.
[10] Ibid., p. 36.

Trade unions, factory councils and soviets

Zinoviev was clear about the pernicious role of the trade unions. He said that between 1914 and 1919 they had been the determining element in the counter-revolution. Therefore, he had no doubt that, at the decisive moment, the leaders of the unions would line up on the other side of the barricades, in the camp of the ruling class. Moreover, the Communists would not win the apparatus of the trade unions any more easily than that of the state – and probably, as in Russia, would not succeed in doing so until after the victory of the Revolution. Nonetheless, the German Communists had been correct in continuing to fight in the trade unions, where they often could win the real majority, and, even certain sections of the apparatus, as in the metalworkers' union. It was through militancy in the trade unions that they had won their positions in the factory councils. Zinoviev recalled that, a few years earlier, these councils had been appendages of the reformist trade-union apparatus, and that it had become possible to transform them from the moment when the working people learnt that they could use them against the trade-union leaders:

> The spirit of the real class struggle is beginning to express itself in the factory councils. Throughout Germany, the factory councils are going through an unprecedented expansion. Little by little, they are taking over all the functions in the economic struggle which the scab unions have abandoned. They have taken over not only these functions, but also a large part of those connected with preparing the proletarian revolution. By doing so, the German factory councils today are very much akin to the workers' soviets in the period of the seizure of power.[11]

Throughout Germany they formed a closely-meshed network, led economic strikes, contributed to extending the committees controlling prices and rents, and organised the arming of the proletariat – the condition of victory – by way of organising the proletarian hundreds:

> We can say, in a general way, that the functions which were carried out in Russia, between February and October 1917, by the workers' soviets and factory councils, are being carried out in Germany today by the factory councils alone. In many respects they have become real workers' councils, and this is what confers upon them in Germany their real significance. It

---

[11] Ibid., p. 40.

is here where their general, international, character lies, valid for every workers' movement in any country at the beginning of the revolutionary period. The existence of such a movement of factory councils in Germany is the essential condition for the success of the proletarian revolution. To be victorious, the revolutionary fervour of the masses is not enough. For the proletarian revolution to be victorious and to establish itself, a organisational framework is necessary. And before the final uprising, it must build this organisational framework, which will form the basis on which the edifice of its soviet government will be built.[12]

He noted that the German factory councils were intervening in such matters as food supply, pay, fuel and arms, and were the principal driving force of the maturing revolution. Nonetheless, he stressed that it was unlikely that the dictatorship of the proletariat emerging from the German Revolution would take a different form to that in Russia:

Its form will no doubt be identical to ours, the soviet government. It won't be 'councils in the factories', that is to say, the independent management of the Siemens or the Halske factories, or of the Krupp enterprises, by the workers in these plants with a sovereign power of decision, but all power invested in the soviets, that is to say, *the whole management and whole power in the country, on the national scale, will be in the hands of the working class*.[13]

But he also declared that in the period of preparing the Revolution, the course of events in Germany would differ from that of Russia, because the German workers would not need to create new organisms. The authentic soviets, in the German form of workers' councils, would be present on the morrow of the Revolution.

Internal difficulties

Zinoviev recalled that the Communists had believed for a long time that the seizure of power in itself was not very difficult, but that the difficulties would begin immediately afterwards. Nonetheless, it was certain that the taking of power in Germany would not be easy. The fascist bourgeoisie could call on 600,000 men armed to the teeth; to be sure, they would not have the advantage

---

[12] Ibid., p. 45.
[13] Ibid., p. 46.

of enjoying popular sympathy, but they could inflict heavy blows in decisive places and at crucial junctures.

On the morrow of the insurrection, the German Revolution would encounter real difficulties. The big landed proprietors would withhold food from the cities, as would the better-off peasants. There would be a shortage of coal, not to mention difficulties with industry, unemployment and the agitation of counter-revolutionary elements. The government would above all have to wrestle with grave financial difficulties, inherited from the economy of capitalist Germany.

This perspective dictated a policy of prudence. The proletarian government would only proceed to nationalise large and medium industry to the extent that it could organise it effectively on socialist principles, 'not forgetting the good side of the Russian NEP'. Whilst it would deal carefully with the middle and poor peasants, it could at the same time count on grain consignments from Russia to feed the cities. To solve the problem of coal would be more difficult; no doubt it would have to consider agreements with French heavy industry, or large-scale purchases from Poland or Czechoslovakia. Unemployment would inevitably rise in the immediate future, but would partly be counteracted by forming a large Red Army. As for financial difficulties and counter-revolutionary agitation, Germany would deal with them generally as Soviet Russia did, taking account of changes dictated by circumstances:

> The internal difficulties of the German revolution on the morrow of the insurrection will be enormous, but not insuperable. It is indispensable today that the rising class and the Party to which the future belongs take them into consideration. But the total collective intelligence of the German revolutionary proletariat, the entire political experience of the Communist Party, the great revolutionary will, energy and enthusiasm, all the organisational strength of the proletarian vanguard, all the intellectual capacities of the heroic generation of the German proletarian revolution which today is coming to the fore – everything, absolutely everything that the working class possesses today, must be directed to the single objective: that of complete preparation for the final struggle.[14]

---

[14] Ibid., pp. 55–6.

The external difficulties

However considerable the internal difficulties awaiting the German Revolution, they were nonetheless minor compared with the external difficulties, which Zinoviev believed to be the real weakness in its armour.

The German Revolution would indeed have a significance and a reverberation like those of the Russian Revolution, but it would not have the advantage of the same favourable circumstances, namely, the size of the country and the fact that the imperialist powers were divided into two warring blocs. However, it would differ from the Russian Revolution in that it would not run the risk of being isolated, because it would not be the first victorious proletarian revolution. That said: 'The German proletariat must foresee the worst eventuality, and be ready for international imperialism to regard its Revolution not as a simple episode, but as an event which decides the fate of all bourgeois Europe, and immediately draws the practical conclusion.'[15]

Great Britain did not present an immediate threat, because it had no land army. France, on the contrary, had the men and matériel necessary for a counter-revolutionary fight. Nonetheless, if it declared war on the German Revolution, it would have to mobilise all its resources to overcome the desperate resistance of the German proletariat, and would expose itself at the same time to a domestic revolutionary counter-attack. Poland and Czechoslovakia could form the immediate force of the imperialists for intervention, but they were fragile – on both the social and national planes – and they would thus run enormous risks.

For this reason, whilst the German Revolution would mobilise the active international solidarity of the proletariat through the Communist Parties of France, Poland, Czechoslovakia and elsewhere, a proletarian Germany could not exclude in advance the possibility of being forced to sign a treaty along the lines of that signed at Brest-Litovsk. It would have to face the prospect of at least consenting to certain clauses of the Versailles Treaty, in order to obtain from France a pledge that its offensive be put off and the Ruhr evacuated. The German revolutionaries would resign themselves to signing such a treaty in full awareness of what they were doing, having learned from the Russian experience, more mature and experienced than the Russians were in 1918, and above all with clear consciousness of the threat to the Revolution from the international bourgeoisie. For the German working people wanted

---

[15] Ibid., p. 61.

peace, not war, but, if the international bourgeoisie chose war, the German proletariat would, despite everything, fight to victory.

The seventh of Zinoviev's articles on the problems of the German Revolution was written on 22 October. On the preceding day, the leaders of the Zentrale and the Revolutionary Committee had decided to call off the insurrection. As they stand, the six articles which the president of the International wrote in expectation of the German October clearly express the importance which the Bolshevik leaders attached to the events in Germany, and their certainty that they stood on the eve of the German Revolution.

Chapter Forty-One
The German October

Heinrich Brandler left Moscow at the end of September, returning to Germany to lead the battle. Ruth Fischer, who saw him depart, leaves us this description:

> As I left the Kremlin, I saw Trotsky bidding farewell to Brandler, whom he had accompanied from his residence inside the Kremlin to the Troitsky gate – an unusual gesture of extreme politeness. There they stood, in the sharp light of an autumn afternoon, the stocky Brandler, in his unpressed civilian suit, and the elegant Trotsky in his well-cut Red Army uniform. After the last words, Trotsky kissed Brandler tenderly on both cheeks in the usual Russian manner. Knowing both men well, I could see that Trotsky was really moved; he felt that he was wishing well the leader of the German revolution on the eve of great events.[1]

The time of waiting

Nobody could doubt that in that autumn, Germany stood on the brink of great events. The grand coalition government was in crisis, with the People's Party opposing any measures against Bavaria, and the

---

[1] Fischer, op. cit., p. 323.

Social Democrats opposing any official attack on the eight-hour day. Nonetheless, the Right unanimously demanded that Hilferding be dismissed, and after a ministerial reshuffle, he had given up his place to Luther, a businessman. But the Social Democrats had been promised that the eight-hour day would not be touched. And General von Seeckt had arrested the Black Reichswehr people who dreamed of playing at being Kappists, and threatened to detonate an explosion.

Why was the popular response so muted? Perhaps people were fearful of the ominous noises in Bavaria. At the beginning of September, there were 110,000 unemployed in Berlin; at the end of October there were 160,000, and 200,000 a few weeks later – and over two million in Germany as a whole.[2] During the week of 8–14 October, a Berlin metalworker earned 6.5 billion marks – worth between two and three dollars – hardly one-tenth of what he had earned a year before. On 16 October, an egg cost 110 million marks, or the hourly pay of a miner.[3] The system of indexing which had been won in August had helped in September to check the fall in the purchasing power of wages, but the time between working out the figures and their publication robbed the system of all meaning. On 11 October, *Vorwärts* actually condemned the trade unions for their passivity at a time when a 'wave of poverty and despair' was building up 'hour by hour'.[4] On the same day, a trade-union action committee was formed in Berlin.[5] However, the Communists had few illusions in the willingness of the trade-union leaders to act. Enderle wrote: 'It will depend on the combativity of the masses and the influence of the Communists whether or not the trade-union leaders follow the masses in their struggle.'[6]

A court near Potsdam acquitted von Kaehne, a country squire, who was charged with the murder of a worker who was collecting wood on his land. The accused declared that he 'was not afraid of firing on the rabble'.[7] Hunger stalked the cities. The Comintern's journal described the situation in October 1923:

---

[2] *Correspondance internationale*, no. 83, 19 October 1923, p. 630.
[3] Ibid., p. 631.
[4] *Vorwärts*, 11 October 1923.
[5] *Vorwärts*, 12 October 1923.
[6] *Correspondance internationale*, no. 86, 30 October 1923, p. 655.
[7] Quoted by Albert in *Bulletin communiste*, no. 42, 18 October 1923.

The street is grey in the morning. Sorry groups of poor women congregate in front of the dairies. They gather there, bringing folding seats or chairs and some sewing. . . . It is cold, and the damp penetrates the old clothes of the poor. They wait there for days at a time to buy a little margarine. Before them is the inevitable policeman in his green uniform, surly and sad with shame for his trade. A lorry full of potatoes passes. People immediately rush from both pavements. Some children clamber onto the back of the heavy vehicle and throw armfuls of the precious vegetables onto the road; these are gathered up at once. The driver accelerates. A policeman bawls, to no effect. I see a well-dressed gentleman, a minor office-worker perhaps, calmly gather up some potatoes and stuff them into his pockets. I see an old woman, grey-haired and bowed, rush to get her share. . . . The street is hungry. The faces of the street are filled with despair, anger and hatred. . . . Someone who saw one of these acts of looting told me about it. He was amazed at the spirit of order in these starving people. They looted methodically without smashing things or unnecessary jostling. They did not take articles of luxury, but bread, fats and footwear. People condemned to die of hunger were taking what they needed to live, being sharply returned to a primitive awareness of their right to live. It needed the intervention of the police for *expropriation* to degenerate into a riot.[8]

The Communists waited, silent and tightly-knit. Albert writes:

Loschlagen . . . Losschlagen means striking the blow that has been held back. Opening the attack. This word was on the lips of everyone on this side of the barricades. . . . In Thuringia, after the semi-secret meetings at which a Communist had spoken, workers – whom he did not know – gathered around him. A railway-worker asked him directly: 'When shall we go into action? When?'

October is cold. Drizzly rain and grey streets where in the workers' districts they stand for hours. Drivers, housewives, unemployed – who have neither shirts nor raincoats – discuss. In these angry groups, gathered at gloomy crossroads, far from the well-lit places where the police watch over the public welfare, I often hear stubborn talk about Russia. . . . I reflect that in the black sky of these poor people, one star at least has risen. . . . Fog, drizzle, rain and the first cold of October. Rooms without fire or bread. Shops guarded

---

8 *Correspondance internationale*, no. 84, 25 October 1923, p. 641.

by green-uniformed policemen, besieged from dawn until nightfall by
dejected crowds of women; sudden charges by the police with their short
carbines slung across their backs, down the main streets; motor lorries rush
by, bristling with rifles and gleaming military caps. At every door, surly
faces, and, in the restless evening, the newspapers report: 'Seven dead in
Beuthen . . . 12 dead in Sorau, 15 dead in Düsseldorf, six dead in Cologne . . .'.
The police are frightened; they are hungry too. But the police were not
created to distribute bread.[9]

The application of the plan

During these final days of September, the Communist leaders decided in
Moscow that representatives of the KPD should join the governments in
Saxony and Thuringia. The purpose was to occupy strategic positions in the
coming conflict. Radek summed up the plan which they adopted:

> The proletariat is taking the initiative in Saxony, starting from the defence
> of the workers' government which we are joining. In Saxony, it is going to
> use state power to arm itself, and, in this little proletarian province in mid-
> Germany, to build a wall between the Bavarian counter-revolution and the
> fascists in the north. At the same time, throughout the Reich, the Party is
> busily mobilising the masses.[10]

This plan had been discussed for several weeks. Brandler had strongly opposed
it. The left Social Democrats in Saxony were full of good will, to be sure, but
they could not be relied upon. During the summer, many incidents had
occurred between the proletarian hundreds and the police under the Social
Democrat Liebmann. In September, several dozen workers had lost their lives
in this way at the hands of the police in Leipzig. It was on the advice of the
ECCI itself that the KPD had several times refused to enter the Zeigner
government so long as the latter did not recognise the political role of the
factory councils. The entry of the Communists into the Saxon government
would be too sudden, and could not be explained to the Party's activists and
sympathisers without contradicting the reasons that had been given for the
earlier refusals to join it. Such a course of action would need to be patiently
explained, and would have to be achieved through a campaign that involved

[9] *Clarté*, no. 52, 1 February 1924.
[10] *Die Lehren der deutschen Ereignisse*, op. cit., p. 5.

the masses united in struggle, and not through a decision emerging from top-level negotiations.[11]

But Brandler appears to have been alone in his opinion. The other leading comrades resident in Moscow thought that the situation was developing so quickly that, if the Communists did not at once succeed in galvanising the resistance of the masses in Saxony and thereby provoking a general outbreak throughout Germany, they would hand the initiative to the head of the Reichswehr in Saxony, General Müller, who wielded all executive power, and the left Social Democrats would be unable to stand up to him on their own. Saxony had to become a solid proletarian base before he struck. The equipping of the proletarian forces of between 50,000 and 60,000 men, whom Brandler estimated could be armed within a week, had to be carried out.[12]

The decision was finally reached when Brandler was already on his way back to Germany. On 1 October, in the name of the ECCI, Zinoviev telegraphed to the Zentrale:

> As we believe that the situation is such that the decisive moment will come within four, five or six weeks, we judge it necessary to occupy immediately every position that can be useful to us. This situation obliges us to pose in a practical way the question of our joining the Saxon government. We should join it on condition that Zeigner's people are really ready to defend Saxony against Bavaria and the fascists. Carry through the arming of between 50,000 and 60,000 men at once. Ignore General Müller. The same in Thuringia.[13]

Negotiations immediately began between the Communists and the left Social-Democratic leaders in Saxony. The Communist press was banned or suspended almost everywhere. A leaflet issued by the factory councils entitled 'Mobilisation' was circulated on 7 October. It called on the workers to prepare a general strike as the means to respond to any counter-revolutionary attempt, to form action committees and self-defence groups, and to organise

---

[11] Ibid., p. 25.
[12] Ibid., pp. 60–1.
[13] Ibid. Fischer (op. cit., p. 335) reproduces this telegram without dating it. She introduces it in the course of an account which began with the entry of the Communists into Zeigner's government and went on with the decision by President Ebert to replace the government in Saxony with an executive appointed by the Reich. That decision was taken in mid-October. If readers were not warned, they might conclude that the telegram was sent immediately before the Reichswehr troops entered Saxony, in the third week of October, and that, as she states elsewhere (p. 335), Zinoviev was proposing in this telegram to present 'resolute armed resistance to the Reichswehr invasion'.

daily meetings in the factories and workplaces.[14] Brandler was back in Germany on 8 October, and on the same day Remmele delivered a speech in the Reichstag that evoked civil war:

> We know very well that the white dictatorship which rules over Germany today can only be destroyed by a red dictatorship. . . . The working classes have no choice other than to recognise that the reign of force can only be abolished by the means and methods which you yourselves use. . . . And when you make the workers aware that grenades and machine-guns are better weapons than all the speeches in parliament, that the weapons of the White dictatorship are more effective than ballots, then you are only yourselves creating the conditions for your own liquidation![15]

He announced to the deputies, like a challenge, that the Communists intended to join the governments in Saxony and Thuringia.[16] On 9 October, the representatives of the Zentrale, in which Brandler had resumed his place, presented a draft governmental programme for Saxony, in twenty points, which included the arming of the workers, the disarming of the bourgeois formations, workers' control over production, emergency measures to provide food, and a call to form a workers' government for the whole Reich.[17] The Saxon Social Democrats accepted it, and on 10 October, the Zeigner government was formed. It included three Communist ministers, Böttcher as Minister of Finance, Heckert as Minister for the Economy, and Brandler, who, having unsuccessfully asked for the portfolio of the Interior, became Ministerialdirektor, Head of the State Chancellery, which nonetheless gave him the right to oversee the police.[18] A declaration by the Zentrale explained this decision:

> The Zentrale of the German Communist Party has authorised three of its members, comrades Brandler, Böttcher and Heckert, to join the Saxon government. The working population stands face to face with the bloc of big capitalists, big landowners and monarchist generals. The dictatorship of the military and the big capitalists is preparing to strangle the working class. . . . *The formation in Saxony of a government of proletarian defence is a signal to the whole German working class.* . . . This first attempt to form, at this

---

[14] Cited in Habedank, op. cit., p. 72.
[15] *Stenographischer Bericht*, Volume 361, p. 12004.
[16] Ibid., p. 12005.
[17] *Protokoll des Fünften Kongress der Kommunistischen Internationale*, op. cit., p. 475.
[18] Apart from Zeigner, the Prime Minister, the Social-Democratic ministers were Ney, Fleissner, Graupe and Liebmann (*Sächsische Staatszeitung*, 11 October 1923).

gravest hour, with the left Social Democrats a joint government of proletarian defence, will be crowned with success if the Party mobilises the working class of the whole Reich with the same objective.[19]

On the same day, *Die Rote Fahne*, which reappeared for only 24 hours before being suspended permanently, published a letter by Stalin, the General Secretary of the Russian Party, to Thalheimer:

> The approaching revolution in Germany is the most important world event of our time. The victory of the German Revolution will have even more importance for the proletariat of Europe and America than the victory of the Russian Revolution six years ago. The victory of the German Revolution will shift the centre of the world revolution from Moscow to Berlin.[20]

Did the German leaders share the confidence expressed by Stalin? When we read the comments of Ernst Meyer, we may have our doubts:

> The working class is divided and paralysed by the coalition policy of the Social-Democratic Party and the class collaboration policy of the trade-union bureaucracy. The German proletariat is disarmed, and has been defeated several times since November 1918; it hesitates. The German workers have become distrustful of the leaders of all their organisations. . . . They are no longer confident. Nonetheless, today, either they surrender without a fight, as Social Democracy recommends, or they carry through a supreme, difficult and costly effort to shake off their heavy chains.[21]

But it was precisely because of this state of affairs that Meyer hailed the entry of the Communists into the Saxon government as an important victory: 'The smallest proletarian success consolidates the proletarian united front, and undermines the Social Democrats' policy of coalition with the bourgeoisie. It is in this sense that we understand the enormous importance of the formation of a workers' government in Central Germany.'[22]

On 13 October, three Communists, Neubauer, Tenner and Karl Korsch, joined the government of Thuringia, over which the Social Democrat Frölich presided.[23] Meyer commented:

---

[19] *Bericht über die Verhandlungen des X Parteitags der Kommunistischen Partei Deutschlands*, Berlin, 1925, p. 276.
[20] *Die Rote Fahne*, 10 October 1923, with facsimile of the original manuscript. [This letter does not appear in the appropriate volume of Stalin's *Works* – Translator.]
[21] *Correspondance internationale*, no. 82, 16 October 1923, p. 624.
[22] Ibid.
[23] *Allgemeine Thüringische Landeszeitung*, 17 October 1923.

> The Communist Party has taken on great responsibilities by making Central
> Germany the pivot of the approaching revolutionary struggles. The German
> proletariat can no longer bear disappointment. But we are convinced that Red
> Saxony and Thuringia will revive, strengthen and develop its revolutionary
> energies. Our party will show what a workers' government can do.[24]

However, the report which Brandler presented to the Zentrale on 12 October
already betrayed many anxieties:

> The Social Democrats in Saxony have decided, under the pressure of the
> masses, to form a coalition government with us. Our entry into the Saxon
> government permits us to regroup and prepare for civil war. . . . The military
> and organisational tasks set by our programme have been carried out . . . but
> the situation regarding arms is catastrophic. . . . Our duty is to temporise,
> and not to take part in isolated struggles.[25]

A time of observation

The entry of the Communists into the governments of Saxony and Thuringia
was a consequence partly of the aggressions of the Reichswehr. On 27
September, General Müller, the officer commanding Wehrkreis III, had
announced by a proclamation that he henceforth exercised full powers in
Saxony and that his troops had the task of ensuring public order. For the
immediate future, he announced that meetings and publications were subject
to prior authorisation by the military authorities, and he prohibited all street
demonstrations and strikes in the sectors which he judged to be 'necessary
for public life'.[26] However, Red Saxony did not submit, and the general went
on voicing threats without, however, calling his soldiers out of their barracks.
On 29 September, he proclaimed a reinforced state of siege, and on 5 October,
he banned all Communist publications.[27]

The workers' government, officially entitled a 'government of republican
and proletarian defence', was formed as though in response to these threats.
On 12 October Zeigner announced in the Landtag his intention to disarm the

---

[24] *Bulletin communiste*, no. 43, 25 October 1923, p. 779.
[25] Minutes of the meeting of the Zentrale, 12 October 1923, cited in Mujbegović,
op. cit., p. 401, n. 93.
[26] Cited in Davidovich, op. cit., p. 142.
[27] Ibid.

bourgeois formations and to strengthen the proletarian hundreds.[28] General Müller replied immediately by decreeing on 13 October that the hundreds and 'other similar organisations' were dissolved, and demanded that they surrender their weapons to the Reichswehr within three days.[29] His ban extended to the action committees which were being formed throughout Saxony with the participation of activists from the workers' parties and trade unions. The Zeigner government protested vigorously against the prohibition of the proletarian hundreds, and guaranteed that they were loyal to the constitution.[30] The Congress of the Hundreds in Saxony, planned for 14 October, was brought forward a day. It was attended by delegates from 155 units, and was held, despite the general's prohibition, in the suburbs of Chemnitz on 13–14 October.[31] Likewise, 150 delegates met on 14 October, on Saxon territory in Plauen, at the Congress of Bavarian Factory Councils.[32] The General's orders were openly defied.

In the days that followed, the left Social Democrats and the Communists held more and more mass meetings, and called on the workers to resist the threats and attempted intimidation by General Müller, ignore his orders and develop their hundreds. But the Zeigner government did nothing concrete to arm the hundreds. Whilst the government of the Reich hesitated between the contradictory pressures of Gessler – and of his adviser, Major von Schleicher – and the Social Democrats, General Müller continued to move his pawns forward. His men were still confined barracks, but on 16 October he informed Zeigner's government that he had ordered the police to place themselves directly under the orders of the Reichswehr commanders – and therefore to obey neither the Saxon Minister of the Interior, nor Zeigner himself![33] He began calling up reservists in Saxony. On the same day, at a large meeting in Leipzig, Böttcher, the Communist Minister for the Economy, appealed to the

---

[28] *Verhandlungen des Sächsischen Landtages*, 1923, Volume 2, pp. 1578, 1662. Already on 23 March, on the proposal of Zeigner, the Saxon Landtag had voted credits of 68 million marks for the arming of the proletarian hundreds (Mujbegović, op. cit., p. 383).

[29] *Schulthess Europäischer Geschichtskalender*, Munich, 1923, p. 192.

[30] Ibid., p. 193.

[31] Angress, op. cit., pp. 432–3; Gast, op. cit., pp. 461–2; Habedank, op. cit., p. 67; Davidovich, op. cit., p. 147; *Vossische Zeitung*, 18 October 1923. 'Aufruf des 1 Kongresses der sächsischen Abwehrorganisationen vom 13 Oktober 1923 in Ravenstein bei Chemnitz an die Werktätigen zum Eintritt in die Hundertschaften', *Dokumente und Materialen*, Volume 2/7, Part 2, op. cit., pp. 460–1.

[32] *Correspondance internationale*, no. 83, 19 October 1923, p. 630.

[33] *Verhandlungen des Sächsischen Landtages*, 1923, Volume 2, pp. 1606–7.

workers of Saxony to defy the military dictatorship, and to demand from their government that it immediately and fully arm the proletarian hundreds.[34] Red Saxony held firm.

The attitude of Social Democracy seemed at first inconsistent. Its leaders accepted without much difficulty the replacement of Hilferding by Luther in the government of the Reich. So the grand coalition continued: it was to a ministry including Social Democrats that Stinnes, Borsig and Thyssen made the demand on 8 October that the working day be lengthened, the social charges on the employers lightened, the subsidy on bread abolished, and the railways handed over to private companies.[35] On the 13th, Stresemann obtained full powers from the Reichstag – with the assent of the Social-Democratic deputies. But, on the 14th, the editorial in *Vorwärts* was devoted to an attack on martial law, which it declared to be 'intolerable', because, whilst it was officially justified by the necessities of the struggle against the reactionaries, it served only to open the struggle against the workers' movement, and, in the case of Saxony, against a constitutional government over which a Social Democrat presided.[36]

On the same day, the KPD's Political Bureau agreed on a programme of action to be submitted to the Congress of the Saxon Factory Councils, which the Saxon ministers Böttcher, Heckert and Graupe, had called for 21 October, and which was to be an important stage in preparing the All-German Congress of Factory Councils which the 'Committee of Fifteen' had just called for 9 November – a symbolic date.[37] The Zentrale issued a statement calling on the working people to struggle 'for a workers' government in Germany and elsewhere'.[38] *Die Rote Fahne* was once again suspended. *Rote Sturmfahne*, produced in secret but openly distributed, came out in its place. In Mannheim on 16 October, the trade unions called a 24-hour general strike. The Reichswehr intervened to prevent a street demonstration, and there were seven killed and 250 wounded. On 17 October, the military authorities secured the arrest of the members of the action committee of the unemployed at Altona.[39] In

---

[34] *Frankfurter Zeitung*, 18 October 1923; Habedank, op. cit., p. 79. Angress erroneously dates this speech to the 13th.

[35] Stresemann, op. cit., p. 116.

[36] *Vorwärts*, 14 October 1923.

[37] E. Zeissig, 'Der Entwurf eines Aktionsprogramms für die Chemnitzer Konferenz vom 21 Oktober 1923', *Beiträge zur Geschichte der deutschen Arbeiterbewegung*, no. 6, 1964, pp. 1060–5.

[38] Angress, op. cit., p. 433.

[39] *Correspondance internationale*, no. 84, 25 October 1923, p. 641.

the Saxon Landtag, the Communist deputy Arthur Lieberasch seemed to be sounding the charge:

> Against the ban on the hundreds . . . [and] the action committees, and the transfer of the police away from the Saxon government the Saxon working class should no longer rely on a few measures taken by its government. . . . Now it should say, not only in Saxony, but throughout Germany: Everyone join these defence formations! Arms into the hands of the working class! Build action committees all down the line! And then, throughout Germany, call for a general strike, and keep it going until the fascist organisations have been driven to the devil without respite or rest. The 15 to 20 million German working people are far more powerful than the 500,000 men in the Reichswehr and the fascists. Arms can also come to us through the back door if the poorly-paid soldiers of the Reichswehr realise that they too belong to the working class.[40]

However, on the same day, General Müller, having secured his grip on the police and in this way reduced the authority of the Zeigner government a little further, took a fresh step forward by directly attacking Zeigner. He wrote to him that hitherto he had acted in the conviction that they were working in accord, but that Böttcher's speech at Leipzig introduced a new element:

> I request you, Mr Prime Minister, to be so good as to comment on the declarations by Minister Böttcher, and to inform me clearly by 11 o'clock on 18 October whether the government as a whole is in agreement with the spirit and the letter of the declarations of Minister Böttcher, and whether it intends to conduct governmental affairs on these lines, or whether it wishes to act in conformity with my instructions. If this latter hypothesis is the case, I must require, in order to clarify the situation, that the Saxon government publish in the press a declaration on this point. Furthermore, I demand to be informed of the steps which the government proposes to take to prevent in the future fresh aberrations of the sort of which Minister Böttcher is undoubtedly guilty.[41]

The next day, *Vorwärts* again protested against the initiatives which General Müller was taking.[42] On this same evening, a gathering of delegates from the

---

[40] *Verhandlungen des Sächsischen Landtages*, 1923, Volume 2, pp. 1627–8.
[41] Ibid., p. 1622.
[42] *Vorwärts*, 18 October 1923; *Correspondance internationale*, no. 83, 19 October 1923, p. 631.

trade unions in Berlin resolved by 1,500 votes to 50 to declare a general strike in the event of the Reichswehr launching an attack in Saxony.[43] The leaders of the Prussian government itself, the Social Democrats Otto Braun and Severing, communicated to Ebert their uneasiness about the conduct of the Reichswehr in Saxony,[44] and demanded that the General be not given free rein.

Would the civil war which threatened to break out in Saxony spread immediately throughout Germany by means of a protest general strike? The Saxon industrialists declared that their security was threatened, and called for the Reichswehr to ensure their protection.[45] Böttcher, the Minister of the Economy in the Zeigner government, called on the Dresden banks to open a credit account for 150 billion gold marks to enable him to make the most urgent purchases of foodstuffs for the most deprived. They replied that the sum requested would be handed over . . . to General Müller.[46] *Vorwärts* again waxed indignant. Bavaria prohibited the sale of milk products to Saxony.[47]

Zeigner assured the Saxon Landtag that he was determined to resist. He categorically rejected the claims of General Müller, and said that he would not give him the honour of a reply. Then once more he attacked the Reichswehr and its Minister, Gessler.[48] He called on the Reich government to put a stop to the unconstitutional initiatives which General Müller, under the protection of his minister, was taking against the constitutional government of Saxony. He violently indicted the Reichswehr and particularly Gessler, recalling the attitude of the army during the Kapp Putsch, and the obstinate refusal of its leaders to agree to the democratisation which every government since 1920 had promised. He also attacked the military policy of the successive governments, and denounced the practice which had led to units such as the Black Reichswehr being formed, and to the shortening of the period of technical training in order to provide troops who would be of little use in a struggle against a European power but effective enough against workers. He laid

---

[43] *Die Rote Fahne*, 20 October 1923; *Dokumente und Materialen*, Volume 2/7, Part 2, op. cit., pp. 462–3.

[44] Braun, op. cit., p. 113.

[45] Verband Sächsischer Industrieller, *Denkschrift über den Terror der Arbeiter zur Erzwingung von Lebensmitteln oder Löhnerhöhungen*, Dresden, 1923, cited in Fischer, op. cit., p. 333.

[46] Stresemann, op. cit., p. 167.

[47] *Correspondance internationale*, no. 84, 25 October 1923, p. 640.

[48] Already in September he had accused the Cuno government of having tried to have him arrested, and had demanded the resignation of Gessler, who was compromised with the generals whom he was protecting with his authority.

emphasis on the political role and the ambitions of these semi-secret organisations which the government protected at the same time as it claimed the right to ban the proletarian hundreds in Saxony.[49]

Böttcher presented a very detailed account of the economic and social situation. He said that 700,000 people, or roughly one person in seven of the Saxon population, was in complete destitution or in urgent need of help. The controllers of the grain supply in the Reich had raised their prices by 41 per cent, and a blockade was effectively being erected around Red Saxony. He reported on the negotiations with the Workers' International Relief, which had promised to send 2,000 tonnes of grain immediately, and was looking into the possibility of sending 200,000 tonnes.[50] The Landtag rejected the general's ultimatum, and demanded the resignation of Gessler, who was covering the 'illegal' activities of the generals with his authority. A delegation of Social-Democratic members of the Landtag went to Berlin to meet the President of the Republic.

But on the same day at 11 o'clock, the notice which had been given to Zeigner expired, and General Müller addressed to him a still more threatening letter: 'Since you have not thought fit to reply to my communication of 17 October 1923, I respectfully inform you that I have so informed the Reich Minister of Defence, with a view to further action. With the assurance of my highest esteem. Müller, Lieutenant-General.'[51]

On 19 October, the following day, in the course of a meeting of the Cabinet, Stresemann briefly informed his ministers that units of the Reichswehr had received the order to invade Saxony and Thuringia, where they would be concentrated in order to 'intimidate the extremist elements and restore public order and security'.[52] On the same day, a message from the government assured Zeigner that the troops were being sent into Saxony in order to protect it from possible attacks on the part of the Bavarian extreme Right.[53]

---

[49] *Verhandlungen des Sächsischen Landtages*, 1923, Volume 2, pp. 1624ff.

[50] Ibid., pp. 1647–9. On this subject see the draft economic agreement between the free state of Saxony and the Soviet Union signed on 19 October by Böttcher and the Russian commercial attaché Stomoniakov (H. Hübsch, 'Der Entwurf eines Handelsvertrages zwischen der Sowjetunion und dem Freistaat Sachsen vom 19 Oktober 1923', *Beiträge zur Geschichte der deutschen Arbeiterbewegung*, special issue, 1965, pp. 135–9).

[51] *Verhandlungen des Sächsischen Landtages*, 1923, Volume 2, p. 1724.

[52] Stresemann, op. cit., p. 171, as well as the minutes of the cabinet quoted in Angress, op. cit., p. 439.

[53] *Verhandlungen des Sächsischen Landtages*, 1923, Volume 2, p. 1760.

On the same day, *Die Rote Fahne* was authorised to reappear in Berlin. In a communication to *Inprekorr*, the Communist deputy Bartz was reassuring. He said that the most diverse rumours were circulating about the government's intentions, but all talk about an early attack on Saxony was greatly exaggerated. Indeed, the government had probably not yet taken a decision. There were also what he called 'ups and downs' in the ranks of the working people.[54]

The fact was that the decision to attack Saxony had already been taken. General Müller ensured that Zeigner received a letter informing him – as always with the utmost politeness – that he had received instructions to 're-establish and maintain the conditions for constitutional order in the Saxon free state', and that he would communicate the reasons for this intervention directly to the population.[55] He did this immediately by means of posters. The hour had struck.

A few days later, Emil Höllein, another leading Communist, again announced it:

> The working class in Saxony, Thuringia and Central Germany is gravely, if not mortally, under threat. The immensity of the danger may at any moment provoke the spontaneous outbreak of a great revolutionary battle. It will depend on the widening and generalising of this battle whether the German Revolution will be defeated or victorious.

The left Social Democrats were at the point of decision: 'They will have to choose between struggle and betrayal.' The Communists, for their part, were confident:

> It is not only weapons that decide between victory and defeat; it is the state of mind of the combatants. Reaction is narrow-minded, despises the poor, desires to perpetuate the exploitation of man by man and military automatism, whilst the proletariat has the enthusiastic spirit of bearers of social revolution and the emancipation of mankind. . . . In every region of Germany, it feels itself stifled by the agonising heaviness of the atmosphere which precedes the storm. The purifying lightning, the lightning which sparks the conflagration, may strike at any moment. And then – woe to the conquered![56]

The man who wrote these lines was unaware that, at that very moment, his side was facing unequivocal defeat, without moreover having engaged in

---

[54] *Correspondance internationale*, no. 85, 26 October 1923, p. 642.
[55] *Die Rote Fahne*, 21 October 1923; Habedank, op. cit., p. 81.
[56] *Correspondance internationale*, no. 85, 26 October 1923, p. 648.

battle. Zinoviev was also unaware, and was continuing in *Pravda* his series of articles outlining the course of events that should follow the victory of the German October.

The Conference at Chemnitz

Rote Sturmfahne reported on 15 and 17 October on the negotiations which had been proceeding for over a week in Berlin regarding the formation of a joint action committee of the organisations of the SPD, KPD and the trade unions in the capital.[57] In Moscow, Zinoviev wrote that he hoped to receive at any moment the news that this agreement had been concluded, as it obviously would have a nationwide impact and significance.[58] In *Die Rote Fahne*, which had now reappeared, Brandler declared that the German working people would not let the Saxon proletariat be attacked. He ended: 'Now everything is ready!'[59] However, the Reichswehr had just set the date which he had refused to fix himself, the date for the decisive confrontation. As Carr remarks: 'It had fixed the date on which the communists must either act or confess their impotence.'[60]

On 20 October, the Revkom met in secrecy in Dresden. Despite the news which it had just received that some important arms stores in Berlin had been discovered by the authorities, it did not regard the situation as serious. Everything was in hand for the insurrection to develop as expected from the 23rd onwards. However, it was necessary that, before that date, the Saxon proletariat should appeal to the workers of Germany for help. The Revkom decided that the armed uprising should begin throughout the country with a general strike, for which the call would be issued, as the Communists proposed, from the Conference of Factory Councils called for 21 October, the very next day, in Chemnitz, to discuss the economic situation and social problems.[61]

Early in the morning on the 22nd, the KPD district secretaries from the entire country met Brandler, Böttcher and Heckert. The representatives of the Revkom revealed their plan. Very soon, at the suggestion of Brandler, the

---

[57] *Rote Sturmfahne*, 15, 17 October 1923.
[58] Zinoviev, *Probleme der deutschen Revolution*, op. cit., p. 72.
[59] *Die Rote Fahne*, 20 October 1923.
[60] Carr, *The Interregnum*, op. cit., p. 221.
[61] *Die Lehren der deutschen Ereignisse*, op. cit., p. 42. The Zentrale had prepared on 18 October a 'fighting programme' for the Conference (*Dokumente und Materialen*, Volume 2/7, part 2, op. cit., pp. 463–6), and a leaflet calling for workers' and peasants' governments, which would be dated 21 October (ibid., pp. 466–7).

Conference of the Factory Councils would issue a call for a general strike to defend proletarian Saxony and its workers' government against the Reichswehr. On Monday, there would be a comprehensive general strike throughout the Reich. On Tuesday, the special detachments, the shock troops and the proletarian hundreds would carry out the planned moves, attack barracks and police stations, occupy the centres of communications, railway stations, post offices and administrative buildings. Every leading Communist believed that they were within a few hours of the insurrection. The commission appointed by the ECCI, including Radek and Piatakov, was on its way to Dresden.[62]

Throughout that night, the proletarian hundreds mounted guard on the entrances to Chemnitz, against the possibility of a surprise attack by the Reichswehr.[63] But nothing happened. The young people in the shock units of the hundreds, in sports clothes with armbands and red five-pointed stars, guarded the doors of the meeting hall, and patrolled the streets of this great workers' city.[64] The delegates were there, 498 in all, of whom about 140 came from factory councils, 102 from various trade unions, 20 sent by the Saxon leadership of the ADGB, 79 delegated by control committees, 26 representing workers' cooperative societies, 15 from action committees, 16 from committees of unemployed, 66 from organisations of the KPD, seven from Social-Democratic organisations, and one Independent.[65]

The Conference opened with reports by three ministers, Graupe, the Social-Democratic Minister of Labour, and the Communists Böttcher and Heckert. All three laid emphasis on the very urgent problems of food supply, the gravity of the financial crisis, and unemployment, which was reaching catastrophic heights.[66] In the discussion, the great majority of speakers departed from the prescribed agenda. Numerous delegates spoke about the political situation in Saxony, and came out in favour of immediately organising struggle against the military dictatorship. Several called on the government to decide immediately to issue the call for a general strike against martial law and the Reichswehr's preparations.

---

[62] Habedank, op. cit., p. 85.

[63] Davidovich, op. cit., p. 160.

[64] Serge, op. cit., p. 171.

[65] *Vorwärts*, 23 October 1923, which is one of the rare reports of the debates at the conference.

[66] Davidovich, op. cit., p. 159, following the pamphlet *Gegen die Säbeldiktatur! Das Rote Sachsen ruft das deutsche Proletariat! Drei Reden von Fritz Heckert, Paul Böttcher und Georg Graupe gehalten auf der Chemnitzer Konferenz am 21 Oktober 1923.*

Then Brandler spoke. Perhaps he believed, in the light of the discussion so far, that his proposal would be enthusiastically adopted. He said briefly that working-class Saxony, under threat, must call the workers of Germany to its aid. Turning towards the left Social Democrats, he begged them to give up all hope, however vain, of a deal with the Reich government to protect Saxony. In order to break the sword which threatened the Saxon workers, a call should be sent out immediately for a general strike, which would be the fighting slogan for the whole working class. He stressed the need for unanimous agreement, and for the vote to be taken at once.[67]

At this point, the left Social Democrats hesitated. When Zeigner had protested against the arrival of troops and the call-up of reservists, the Reich government had given written assurances that these measures were directed against von Kahr and Hitler's Bavaria. General Müller had again made threatening noises towards Saxony, but so far had confined himself to threats. This could mean that the Social-Democratic ministers in the Reich government had ensured that he would move against the Bavarians rather than the Saxons. To agree to vote for Brandler's motion would make sense only if General Müller had received or were to receive a free hand, and this did not seem to be the case. In these conditions, they took the view that to launch suddenly, from such a gathering as this, the slogan of a general strike would be to plunge headlong into an adventure which would be likely to provoke an opponent whose exact intentions and potential were still unknown.

The left Social Democrats added that Brandler's plans would mean placing the Saxon government under the authority of the factory councils, and therefore meant repudiating the theme of 'loyalty to the constitution', so feeding the accusation that they were 'playing the Communists' game'. Moreover, the left Social Democrats were very well aware that the Communist leaders themselves – as their press bore witness – were not sure whether General Müller would go over to the attack, or whether the German workers were ready to hit back and to follow the order for the general strike. Moreover, the situation in Saxony was such that it was almost certain that the Communists would not decide to act alone. In short, the left Social Democrats recognised that everything rested on their attitude at this conference.

---

[67] The East German historian Habedank (op. cit., p. 86) asserts that Brandler made a unanimous vote a condition *sine qua non* for the general strike. There is no documentary evidence to confirm this interpretation.

Georg Graupe, the Minister of Labour, another veteran of the trade-union movement, replied to Brandler in the name of the left Social Democrats.[68] He said that the problem of defending workers' Saxony, like that of the repeated violations of the Constitution by the government and the heads of the Reichswehr, did indeed arise, but it would not be right for a conference alone, however representative of the Saxon workers' organisations, to decide on the response. Saxony had its government of 'republican and proletarian defence', which was what had to be defended. This government was responsible to an elected Landtag, in which the two great workers' parties were represented. Brandler himself was a member of it. Therefore, Graupe argued, it was for the government, and for it alone, for the moment, to consider what means of action to prescribe, on the basis of information which it alone possessed. To go over its head here would be to discredit it. Graupe was firm and categorical: if the Communists pressed the motion proposed by Brandler, he would quit the Conference with his Party comrades and leave the Communists to take on such a responsibility alone. However, as he was fully aware of the gravity of the situation, he added the proposal that a parity commission of members of the two Parties be elected to study the question of the general strike, and to report to the conference before it closed. Brandler then agreed to withdraw his motion and to support that of Graupe, which was unanimously adopted.[69]

The Commission at once set to work, and the entire Communist plan was blocked. The election of the Commission precluded an immediate appeal by the Conference for a general strike. It looked as though no decision for immediate action would emerge from Chemnitz. Above all, the Communists were profoundly disoriented. The reaction of the left Social-Democratic delegates seemed to show that the working class was not ready to fight.[70] No alternative plan existed, and the KPD's representatives could not but follow the current. The *ad hoc* Commission, with their agreement, presented proposals which, as Thalheimer was to write, constituted 'a first-class funeral'.[71] The Commission recognised the necessity of a general strike, and wished to launch it, and proposed that a parity action committee composed of five Communists

---

[68] *Vorwärts*, 23 October 1923.

[69] Ibid.

[70] This aspect of the matter was stressed by Thalheimer, in his retrospective self-exculpation, *1923: Eine Verpasste Revolution?*, op. cit., p. 26.

[71] Ibid.

and five Social Democrats be elected, to make immediate contact with the Party leaderships, the trade unions and the government, to examine and prepare with them the form to be taken by the call for a general strike. Only in the event that the government and the trade unions refused to take the initiative would the Action Committee be empowered to do so.[72]

The Chemnitz Conference thus ended without agreeing upon any action. The KPD's plan was blocked before it could be put into effect. Moreover, the means by which it was blocked put into question the entire analysis upon which the Communists had relied to justify it.

Retreat

The Zentrale met in Chemnitz on the same evening, in the presence of the military leaders and the 'advisers', but without Radek and his companions, who had travelled via Warsaw and Prague, and were in Dresden.[73] It concluded from its defeat at the Conference and from the collapse of the united front in Saxony that it would have to cancel its plan for an insurrection.[74]

The army's preparations took shape on the following day. General Müller's men left their barracks, and special trains brought in reinforcements. Brandler and his comrades met Radek, Piatakov and their comrades in a Saxon capital under siege. The German leader described the situation, and gave the reasons for the decision. He added, however, that it was not too late to reverse it, if the representatives of the ECCI did not agree with the decision and thought that the insurrection should go ahead as planned.[75]

But Radek also considered that the German Communists must retreat. After the defection of the left Social Democrats, there could be no question of applying a plan which presupposed their agreement. The armament of the proletarian hundreds in Saxony – 11,000 rifles – was already derisory, but what the party itself had – 800 rifles – was far more so.[76] It had to be recognised that Zeigner's government, despite the presence of three Communist ministers, had done nothing to arm the workers. Therefore the Communists could not possibly consider by themselves calling for an armed insurrection, when the

---

[72] *Vorwärts*, 23 October 1923.
[73] *Die Lehren der deutschen Ereignisse*, op. cit., p. 5.
[74] Ibid., pp. 5–6.
[75] Ibid., p. 6.
[76] Ibid.

proletariat was divided and unarmed. On this point, the representatives of the ECCI therefore supported Brandler, who drew their attention to the fact that they now shared the responsibility for the decision before the ECCI and the International as a whole.

However, Radek did not think that all was lost. If it were true that the Communists by themselves had not the strength to lead an armed uprising to victory, they had sufficient to lead a defensive struggle. He therefore suggested advancing the call for a general strike without aiming at transforming it into an armed uprising.[77] But this proposal met universal opposition. The Germans unanimously declared that if they dropped one call, they must drop the other, having regarded the insurrection as synonymous with the general strike.[78]

The discussion resumed on the following day, this time in Berlin at the Zentrale's meeting-place. Radek repeated his proposal for a general strike without the perspective of insurrection. Fischer proposed starting the general strike in Berlin, and aiming within two or three days at transforming it into an armed insurrection, particularly through initiatives in Kiel and in other cities. Brandler opposed both motions, and voted with Fischer against Radek's motion.[79] In practice, at the moment when General Müller's troops went into action against Zeigner's government, the KPD had no proposal for action to put to the German proletariat.

In this way, the plan built around 'Red Saxony' had collapsed in a few days, and with it the hopes for the victory of the proletarian revolution in Germany in October 1923. Nonetheless, the strategy was put into action in Hamburg.[80] The origin of the Communist rising in Hamburg is not yet clear.[81] Was it the premature departure from Chemnitz of Remmele, who did not know that the insurrection had been cancelled? Was it an attempt by the 'Left' to outflank the Zentrale, and to force the uprising, which had been planned first at Kiel and then 'forced back' to Hamburg? Were the initiatives an act of indiscipline or the result of misunderstandings or faulty communications? In any case, the Polleiter of the district, Hugo Urbahns, only returned from

---

[77] Ibid.

[78] Ibid., pp. 6–7.

[79] Ibid.

[80] See in particular the book by the Hamburg police chief in 1923, Lothar Danner, *Ordnungspolizei Hamburg: Betrachtungen zu ihrer Geschichte 1918 bis 1933*, Hamburg, 1958, as well as the works already mentioned by Habedank, Davidovich, etc.

[81] See Angress, op. cit., pp. 444–6, n. 57.

the Chemnitz Conference on the night of 22–3 October, at a moment when the local uprising was within a few hours of beginning. He would have been taken by surprise. Indeed, the operation of the armed uprising worked in accordance with the plan, within the framework of the general uprising as planned by the MP-Obleiter Nordwest, Albert Schreiner, and the local leader, Hans Kippenberger, in an extremely tense atmosphere.

Indeed, on 22 October, the Hamburg dockers, on the recommendation of the leaders of the ADGB, had demanded at a mass meeting that the workers' organisations, the parties and trade unions, issue a call for a general strike in the event of the Reichswehr attacking Saxony. During that night, from two o'clock onwards, detachments of armed Communists began to fell trees and cut telephone lines in order to interrupt communications. At five o'clock, the shock groups of the proletarian hundreds attacked police stations in the suburbs in order to obtain arms, and stormed ten or so of them without difficulty. To face several hundred poorly armed activists, there were at first only the local police and then detachments from the navy. But the mass of the workers did not stir, not even the dockers who were on strike. Work in the factories simply slowed down.

The news that the general uprising had been cancelled spread quickly. The local leadership recognised that they were isolated and organised a retreat, with the fighting gradually dying out until it ended in the suburb of Bambeck on the evening of the 24th. The principal military leader, Hans Kippenberger, faultlessly executed this military operation of disengagement, which enabled nearly all of the fugitives to avoid capture.[82] Nonetheless, 21 of the insurgents lost their lives, 165 were wounded, and 102 were taken prisoner, including Urbahns himself, who was to take the full and entire responsibility for the uprising at his trial, and to be celebrated throughout the entire International for his exemplary conduct before the court.[83]

---

[82] Kippenberger's report to the ECCI on the Hamburg insurrection is included in A. Neuburg, *Insurrection Armée*, Paris, 1978, pp. 83–99.

[83] *Correspondance internationale*, no. 12, 18 February 1925, p. 100, carried an account of this entitled 'The Words of an Insurgent', and subtitled, 'Better to burn in the fire of a revolution than to rot on the dung-heap of democracy', with extracts from his closing statement. The author of the preface, Erich Wollenberg, says (op. cit., p ix) that Urbahns received a personal letter expressing the Stalin's appreciation. His role in the insurrection was later to be wholly effaced from official history after he was expelled from the KPD in November 1926.

The Hamburg uprising was celebrated during the weeks that followed in an admirable piece of reporting thanks to Radek's young companion, the Russian Communist journalist Larissa Reissner.[84] It was later to form one of the foundations for the legend of Ernst Thaelmann, who apparently played no decisive role in it. At the time, it appeared as what it really was, a blunder or a misunderstanding, which could have been tragic, but which was settled at minimum cost, taking the whole situation into account. The Zentrale also saw it as proof that the decision reached at Chemnitz to retreat had been correct. Only one part of the KPD had fought, and had fought alone, whilst the great masses remained, if not indifferent, at least passive. The only armed combat in the Revolution of October 1923 consisted of a 'March Action' in one single city . . .

The Zentrale met on 23 October, and appointed a commission of seven members to draft a resolution on the situation and the tasks ahead. This was unanimously adopted on the 25th.[85] It declared:

> The social and political antagonisms grow increasingly sharp by the day. Each day may bring decisive battles between the revolution and the counter-revolution.
>
> The vanguard of the working class – the Communists and part of the Social-Democratic workers – wishes to engage in the struggle, but the working class as a whole is not ready to fight, despite its immense bitterness and appalling poverty.
>
> This is why it is necessary, by resolute agitation, to raise the reserves of the proletariat nearer to its vanguard. The party must develop a special approach that can help increase its influence amongst the strata of the proletariat which showed themselves disposed to fight, such as metalworkers, miners, railway workers, agricultural workers and clerks. The technical preparations must be continued with particular energy. In order to bring about the unity of the proletariat in the struggle, we must immediately begin discussions with Social Democracy at the central and local levels, in order either to force the Social Democrats to struggle, or to separate the Social-Democratic workers from their treacherous leaders.

---

[84] Having arrived in Germany in September 1923, Reissner was in Dresden on 21 October, with Radek; she went to Hamburg as soon as she heard of the outbreak of the insurrection. A few weeks later she returned to Soviet Russia with the manuscript of her work *Hamburg auf den Barrikaden* (Radek, preface to L. Reissner, *Oktober*, Berlin, 1926, pp. xviii, xix, xxiv).

[85] *Die Lehren der deutschen Ereignisse*, op. cit., p. 7.

In these circumstances, the Party must as far as possible restrain the comrades from armed struggle, in order to gain time for preparation. If, however, extensive proletarian struggles break out spontaneously, the Party will support them with every means at its disposal. It must also ward off the blows of the counter-revolution by means of mass struggles, such as demonstrations and political strikes. As far as possible, it must avoid armed struggle in these conflicts.

The Party throughout the Reich must call for protest strikes against the Stresemann ultimatum. Armed insurrection is ruled out during these activities. If the Social-Democratic Party in Saxony does not undertake to struggle against the Stresemann ultimatum, our comrades in the Saxon government must break with it, and engage in struggle against it.[86]

In a few days of discussion, Radek had thus succeeded in winning over the Zentrale to his views, and the KPD found itself, a few details apart, back on the line it had promoted when the Cuno strike broke out. Putting its preparations for insurrection on the back burner, it centred its policy on a defensive united front. But the general situation had changed. On the 26th, using martial law, General von Seeckt forbade any strike in Berlin.[87] At the Cabinet meeting of the Reich government on 27 October, the Reichswehr Minister, Gessler, together with Stresemann himself, forcefully argued in favour of armed intervention against Saxony, which they justified by the untenable situation of the troops and the need to demonstrate that a government which included Communists was not compatible with the spirit of the Constitution.[88] The Social-Democratic ministers gave way, and on the same day Stresemann addressed an ultimatum to Zeigner:

> The spirit of rebellion and violence which the Communist Party displays has been demonstrated by the declarations which your Ministerialdirektor (the head of the state chancellery) made in Chemnitz on 21 October. He publicly called for open opposition to the Reichswehr. . . . In the name of the federal government, I demand accordingly that you make arrangements for the government of the state of Saxony to resign, since, taking recent events into account, the participation of Communist members has become incompatible with the provisions of the Constitution.[89]

---

[86] Ibid., pp. 7–8.
[87] Stresemann, op. cit., pp. 171–84.
[88] Minutes of the Reich cabinet, quoted in Angress, op. cit., p. 454.
[89] Stresemann, op. cit., pp. 186–7.

The Chancellor told Zeigner that he had 24 hours in which to resign, and that, if a new government without Communists was not formed immediately, he would appoint a commissioner from the Reich for Saxony.[90] Radek wrote to Böttcher and Heckert, demanding that they do all they could to avoid yielding without resistance, and to call for a strike.[91] The Zentrale gave its approval. On 28 October, General Müller informed Zeigner that he had received the order to dismiss him, and forbade the Saxon Landtag to meet, in accordance with Article 48 of the Constitution.[92] On the same day, the SPD and KPD leaders in Chemnitz and the Erzgebirge-Vogtland jointly demanded of the Saxon government that it resist, issued an appeal to the working people of Saxony to hold themselves in readiness to start a general strike, and called on the workers of Germany to support the Saxon workers.[93]

On 29 October, Ebert, acting in accordance with Article 48, gave the Chancellor the authority 'to deprive of their functions the members of the government of the free state of Saxony, as well as those of the municipal or state administrations'.[94] The government appointed a People's Party deputy, Dr Heinze, as the Reich Commissioner.[95] A lively discussion began between them on whether the Reichswehr should enter the cities of Saxony with its bands playing.[96] When the Saxon ministers refused to give way, the Reichswehr expelled them by military force on 29 October at two o'clock in the afternoon. Böttcher put up a passive resistance, and was forcibly dragged down the steps of his ministry before being released in the street.[97] He declared that the government remained the sole legal authority, and appealed to the working people to support it.[98] The SPD, KPD, ADGB and a certain number of other workers' organisations issued an appeal for a three-day protest general strike.[99] In most workers' districts, there were clashes between the Reichswehr and

[90] Ibid.
[91] *Die Lehren der deutschen Ereignisse*, op. cit., p. 8.
[92] *Sächsische Staatszeitung*, 29 October 1923.
[93] *Schulthess Europäischer Geschichtskalender*, 1923, op. cit., p. 207.
[94] *Der Kämpfer*, 29 October 1923; *Dokumente und Materialen*, Volume 2/7, Part 2, op. cit., pp. 469–71.
[95] *Verhandlungen des Sächsischen Landtages*, 1923, Volume 2, p. 1862.
[96] This detail is given by H.J. Gordon, 'Die Reichswehr und Sachsen 1923', *Wehrwissenschaftliche Rundschau*, no. 12, December 1961, p. 686, n. 27.
[97] Böttcher told Davidovich the story of his expulsion (op. cit., pp. 276–7): he explained that he wanted to follow the example of 'the French revolutionary Mirabeau'.
[98] *Verhandlungen des Sächsischen Landtages*, 1923, Volume 2, p. 1845.
[99] Ibid., pp. 1845–6; this appeal was to be published in the press on 31 October.

the proletarian hundreds or demonstrating workers. The most serious seems to have been at Freiberg, where there were 27 killed.[100]

On 30 October, the SPD's Saxon leadership met along with the ministers and, probably, all the deputies. Zeigner resigned himself to stepping down, in order to permit an exclusively Social-Democratic government to be formed.[101] On the same day, General Müller authorised the Landtag to meet, the President read Zeigner's letter of resignation, and a new government was formed under Fellisch, a Social Democrat, who became the new Prime Minister.[102] The general strike lost its momentum within 24 hours, and had petered out by the end of the third day.

Elsewhere in Germany, there was a three-day strike in Frankfurt-am-Main called by all the workers' organisations.[103] In Berlin, during the meetings of the Zentrale, Radek tried in vain to reach an agreement to call demonstrations under the protection of the armed proletarian hundreds. He ran into resolute opposition from Fischer, who claimed that the masses were too disheartened by the events in Saxony and Hamburg to support any Communist initiative whatsoever.[104] There was not going to be a German revolution.

Who could describe better than Albert the experience of Communist activists during this climb-down, a defeat without a fight? Under the title 'Fifty Days Standing to Arms', we read:

> In Germany, in September, October and November, we lived through a profound revolutionary experience, still little known and often little understood. We were on the threshold of a revolution. The night watches were long. Zero hour was not signalled. . . . A silent and hardly probable drama. A million revolutionaries were ready, awaiting the word to attack. Behind them were millions of jobless, starving, bruised, desperate, a whole suffering people, murmuring: 'We too! We too!' The muscles of this crowd

---

[100] *Correspondance internationale*, no. 87, 2 November 1923, p. 663; E. Schneller 'Die Lehren des Oktober 1923', *Oktober*, no. 2, 1926, p. 31.

[101] Gordon, op. cit., p. 687. Dittmann and Wels had gone to Dresden to take the matter in hand.

[102] *Verhandlungen des Sächsischen Landtages*, 1923, Volume 2, p. 1841.

[103] R. Wagner, 'Die revolutionäre Bewegung in den Bezirken Hessen-Frankfurt und Baden im Herbst 1923', *Beiträge zur Geschichte der deutschen Arbeiterbewegung*, no. 7, 1965, p. 88.

[104] *Die Lehren der deutschen Ereignisse*, op. cit., p. 10. According to Angress (op. cit., pp. 251–2), Fischer finally let herself be persuaded. On 27 November, between 3,000 and 4,000 demonstrators gathered in the Lustgarten, only to disperse before the police arrived.

were tense, their hands gripped the rifles with which they were to oppose the armoured cars of the Reichswehr. . . . Nothing happened. There was nothing but the bloody clowning at Dresden, where a corporal with a few soldiers turned out of their ministries the workers' ministers who had made bourgeois Germany tremble. There were a few puddles of blood – sixty dead in all – on the streets of the industrial cities of Saxony. Now bankrupt Social Democracy can rejoice at having emerged from the massive and passive adventure, still ponderously loyal to its old abjurations.[105]

There were upheavals for a few more days in the SPD. A general meeting of Party officials in Berlin symbolically called for President Ebert to be expelled from the Party.[106] But the great hopes which Zinoviev had hailed were well and truly buried. Bourgeois Germany firmly grasped the reins again, and turned its back on the adventure of the 'inhuman year' by preparing a new policy of stabilisation. This required that the dissidents of the Right be liquidated, a task which the Reichswehr carried out. The Bavarian adventure, having played the part of a very useful bogey during the preceding stormy weeks, and having held the attention of the Social-Democratic activists, was cleared away in a few hours, with the arrest of Hitler and his accomplices. The future dictator was to draft *Mein Kampf* in jail. The German economy was soon reborn with an influx of American capital in a context favourable to the creation of profits, having been 'purged' by inflation. For all that, the fundamental questions remained unsolved. With the world crisis of 1929, and the massive withdrawal of the capital which had saved it, Germany was to experience a second economic and social catastrophe, which this time was to raise Hitler to power.

But by then the KPD would be very different. The fiasco of 1923, combined with the internal crisis of the Russian Party and the political struggle seen by historians as the battle for Lenin's succession, marked the end of a period in its history. From now on, the policies of the KPD were to be written almost entirely in Moscow, and in Russian.

[105] R. Albert, 'Cinquante jours de veillée d'armes', *Clarté*, no. 52, 1 February 1924, p. 66.

[106] *Die Volksstimme*, 2 November 1923, cited in Davidovich, op. cit., p. 233.

Chapter Forty-Two
Aftermath of Another Defeat

The defeat in October 1923, the 'German fiasco', constituted a decisive retreat of historic significance, but at first, it passed unnoticed. Zinoviev's series of articles on the German Revolution – in which the President of the Communist International continued imperturbably counting his chickens – continued until 30 October. It was only on that date that a few lines in the final article would suggest that anything like a defeat had happened.[1] Anyone who leafs through *Inprekorr* has to wait until the same date to find, from the pen of Albert, the sub-heading 'The Collapse of the Left Social Democrats' – an allusion to the retreat which had been decided nine days previously behind the scenes at the Chemnitz Conference.[2] The tone changed a few days later. People spoke of 'White Germany', a 'new betrayal' by the Social Democrats, and 'lost opportunities'. The KPD was declared illegal on 23 November, and its press was suspended across Germany. Activists were arrested one after another. The defeat was described in ever-stronger terms. It became one of the themes which divided the Russian leaders, who had already been engaged for some days in discussing the 'New Course'. This was the first violent open outburst of

---

[1] The article was entitled 'No Illusions' (Zinoviev, *Probleme der deutschen Revolution*, op. cit., pp. 97–104).
[2] *Correspondance internationale*, no. 89, 9 November 1923, p. 663.

the struggle between the Troika of Zinoviev, Kamenev and Stalin, and Trotsky and the so-called opposition of the 'Forty-Six', about democracy within the party, the relationship between the Old Bolsheviks and the younger generation, the power and role of the apparatus, and the growing tendency towards bureaucratisation.[3]

The October defeat was often mentioned after this time, but was never to be properly discussed. It became a weapon that was used in the settlement of accounts within the Russian Party, and in the struggle which the Russian Party leadership was waging through the ECCI to secure the support and subservience of the foreign Communist Parties.

The first reactions

The first reaction of Zinoviev was to provide an overall approval of the decision to retreat. He wrote:

> Events have shown that our calculations were exaggerated. . . . The KPD revealed many weaknesses and made a number of serious mistakes during those critical weeks, but we do not think it mistaken in not throwing the proletariat into a general battle in October. . . . The retreat should have been less passive. But the abstention from fighting a decisive battle was, in the circumstances, inevitable.[4]

The KPD's Central Committee met secretly in Berlin on 3–4 November. By 40 votes to 13, it adopted the theses which Brandler and Radek had drafted, and which the Zentrale had placed before it. These theses presented the recent events in Germany as meaning 'the end of the November Republic', and 'the victory of fascism over bourgeois democracy'. The workers had been taken by surprise. Whilst they had kept their eyes fixed on Bavaria and the threatening gestures of Ludendorff and Hitler, Ebert and the Imperial Cabinet had 'established fascism in the form of the dictatorship of General von Seeckt'. The general allowed 'the phantom of democratic parliamentarism to survive in order to hide a state of affairs which, if it were brought to light, would provoke defensive activities on the part of the working masses'. Social Democracy bore the entire responsibility for the passivity of the workers,

---

[3] Broué, *Le parti bolchevique*, op. cit., pp. 183–95.
[4] Cited in J. Degras, *The Communist International 1919–1943: Documents*, Volume 2, London, 1960, p. 64.

which was caused by its repeated betrayals, and by the illusions which it had succeeded in spreading at crucial junctures. However, no 'democratic' illusions could now exist in the face of the 'fascist' state. The 'fascist bourgeoisie' had intended and was intending to provoke the proletariat at a time when it was weakened and confused by the treachery of Social Democracy. The German bourgeoisie was out of breath. The unity of the proletarian front would be realised 'from below', and the elimination of the Social-Democratic leaders was, in the long run, inevitable in the continuing struggle.[5]

These theses were hastily drafted, and produced a first reaction from Zinoviev in *Pravda* on 23 November. The President of the Communist International took the view that the KPD was mistaken. Ebert and von Seeckt were two sides of the same coin. It was precisely 'because the proletariat was not in a position immediately to introduce its dictatorship' that 'the November Republic led to the dictatorship of von Seeckt', in whom Zinoviev, for his part, saw 'the Kolchak of Germany'. He concluded: 'It is now almost certain that Germany will have to go through a period of painful white terror, full of sacrifices for the proletariat. The road of the German Revolution is harder then we thought.'[6]

A first reply from Thalheimer reproached Zinoviev for again misusing an historical parallel which was necessarily an artificial one, but it did not take the debate beyond the framework of an almost academic discussion.[7] Nothing yet enabled the rising storm to be foreseen. If we can believe Radek, Zinoviev saw no reason by 7 November to proceed towards making changes in the leadership of the KPD.[8] On 1 December, he produced an article, 'The Second Wave of the International Revolution', which attempted to explain why the revolutionary character of the events in Germany had been overestimated, but he nowhere formulated any precise criticism of the KPD's leadership. Within a few days, however, everything was to change, under the pressure of the crisis in the Russian Communist Party.

---

[5] H.B. [Brandler], 'Die Tagung des Zentralausschusses', *Die Internationale*, no. 18, 30 November 1923, pp. 517–28.

[6] *Pravda*, 23 November 1923; *Bulletin communiste*, no. 49, 6 December 1923.

[7] *Correspondance internationale*, no. 1, 3 January 1924, pp. 3–4.

[8] Report of the Thirteenth Conference of the RCP(B), cited in Carr, *The Interregnum*, op. cit., p. 233.

The conflict in the Russian Communist Party

This crisis in the Russian Communist Party had been smouldering throughout the summer. The economic situation continued to deteriorate. Strikes had broken out. In September, the GPU arrested a number of Communists who had organised an unofficial campaign of public agitation. In parallel, the campaign of the Troika against Trotsky was proceeding. Skliansky, Trotsky's deputy, was removed from the War Commissariat and replaced by Voroshilov and Lashevich, supporters of the Troika. On 8 October, Trotsky addressed a letter to the Central Committee in which he denounced the rise of the bureaucracy in the Party and threatened to take the discussion to the rank and file. On 15 October, it was the turn of 46 leading Communists, including Piatakov and Radek, to address a letter in the same sense to the Central Committee. Indeed, the battle would no doubt have been joined sooner, had the hopes and the feverish preparations for the German October not absorbed energies and moderated impatience. The Central Committee was aware of this when, in its reply to Trotsky on 27 October, it attacked him for having taken such an initiative 'at a crucial moment for the development of the international revolution'.[9]

The public discussion opened in *Pravda* on 7 November. At first, conventional in tone, it became livelier when, on 28 November, Preobrazhensky intervened, and Zinoviev and Stalin replied. It reached a climax in the first few days of December, with the polemic between Stalin and Trotsky about the resolution which the Political Bureau had adopted on 5 December, on the subject of the need for a 'new course' in the Party. At that moment, the opposition's sails seemed to have caught the wind. The revolutionary mobilisation on the build-up to the German October had reawakened enthusiasm, and revived in the Red Army and amongst the Communist Youth a revolutionary state of mind favourable to the Opposition. The resolution which Preobrazhensky moved on 11 December at a meeting of activists in Moscow, which included a demand for freedom to organise groups within the Party, was only just defeated.[10]

It was probably during the same meeting[11] that Radek spoke in support of the theses of the opposition, and introduced the 'German question' indirectly, when he declared that the leaders of the most important parties in the

---

[9] Ibid., pp. 182–4.
[10] Broué, op. cit., pp. 185–9.
[11] Though Thalheimer gives the date as the 13th, with the precaution 'if I am not mistaken' (*1923: Eine Verpasste Revolution?*, op. cit., p. 11).

International, the French, German and Polish sections, agreed with Trotsky and the 'Forty-Six'.[12] This served to warn Zinoviev, who knew that friendly personal relations existed between Brandler and Trotsky and Radek; he understood the danger such an alliance at the heart of the International could pose to the Troika. This was the point when the 'German question' moved to the centre of the battle in the Russian Party.

The ECCI sent a very critical letter to the KPD around this time, at least after 2–3 December, when Zinoviev became aware of a letter from Fischer dated 22 November attacking Brandler, which had been intercepted by the German police.[13] Zinoviev started by calling into question the resolution of 4 November:

> The political error was a necessary consequence of your overestimation of the degree of political and technical preparation. We here in Moscow, as you must be well aware, regarded the entry of Communists into the Saxon government only as a military-strategic manoeuvre. You turned it into a political bloc with the 'left' Social Democrats, which tied your hands. We thought of your entry into the Saxon government as a way of winning a jumping-off ground from which to deploy the forces of our army. You turned participation in the Saxon Cabinet into a banal parliamentary coalition with the Social Democrats. The result was our political defeat. And what was still worse, there was an element of comedy in the business. We can stand a defeat in battle, but when a revolutionary party on the eve of revolt gets into a ridiculous position, that is worse than a defeat. In the Reich, the Party did not pursue a policy which could be and had to be the overture to decisive struggle. Not a single decisive revolutionary step. Not one even partially clear Communist speech. Not a single serious measure to expedite the arming of the Saxon workers, not a single practical measure to create soviets in Saxony. Instead of that, a 'gesture' by Böttcher; who declared that he would not leave the government building until he was ejected by force. No, comrades, that is not the way to prepare a revolution![14]

The preface to the German edition of Zinoviev's *Problems of the German Revolution*, dated 2 November, endorsed the tactic employed by the KPD in

---

[12] Ibid., p. 11. Zinoviev referred to Radek's speech on 6 January 1924 to the ECCI (*Inprekorr*, no. 20, 15 February 1924, p. 225).

[13] Angress, op. cit., p. 463.

[14] *Inprekorr*, no. 16, 4 February 1924; *Bulletin communiste*, no. 8, 22 February 1924, p. 209; Degras, op. cit., p. 65. The letter is not dated.

Saxony.[15] However, a note was appended to the pamphlet, in which Zinoviev condemned 'the banal parliamentary policy' which had been followed in the Zeigner government. For the first time, he publicly criticised the Communist members of the government for neither having armed the workers in their tens of thousands, nor having raised the question of nationalisation of industry, the arrest of speculators or the election of soviets.[16]

Trotsky developed the idea that the leadership of the International itself bore the responsibility for the set-back in Germany. In an article which had been circulating for over a week, which was published in *Pravda* on 28 and 29 December, and which was to appear a few weeks later in the pamphlet *The New Course*, he expressed his first thoughts, based on the declaration that during May–July 1923 Germany had experienced an unprecedented crisis:

> If the Communist Party had abruptly changed the pace of its work and had profited by the five or six months that history accorded it for direct political, organisational, technical preparation for the seizure of power, the outcome of the events could have been quite different from the one we witnessed in November. . . . It was only in October that it adopted a new orientation. But by then it had too little time to develop its dash. Its preparations were speeded up feverishly, the masses were unable to follow it, the lack of assurance of the party communicated itself to both sides, and at the decisive moment, the party retreated without giving battle. If the party surrendered its exceptional positions without resistance, the main reason is that it proved unable to free itself, at the beginning of the new phase (May–July 1923), from the automatism of its preceding policy, established as if it was meant for years to come, and to put forward squarely in its agitation, action, organisation and tactics the problem of taking power.[17]

A few days before, the Central Committee of the Polish Communist Party confirmed some of Radek's statements, and justified the apprehensions of Zinoviev by voicing its uneasiness at the Troika's attacks upon Trotsky:

> Only one thing is quite clear for us: the name of comrade Trotsky is for our party, for the whole International, for the whole revolutionary world proletariat, indissolubly bound up with the victorious October revolution,

---

[15] Zinoviev, op. cit., p. v.
[16] Ibid., pp. 105–9.
[17] Trotsky, *De la révolution*, op. cit., p. 58; Trotsky, 'The New Course', *The Challenge of the Left Opposition (1923–1925)*, op. cit., p. 95.

with the Red Army, with communism and world revolution. We cannot admit the possibility that comrade Trotsky could find himself outside the ranks of the leaders of the RKP [Russian Communist Party] and of the International. Nevertheless, we are perturbed by the thought that the disputes may go beyond the framework of the concrete problems under discussion, and some public utterances of responsible leaders of the party give reason for the gravest anxieties.[18]

In Moscow, Stalin began to take an interest in the discussions on Germany, after having stood back from them until now. He made contact with Maslow, who was still detained in Moscow by the Commission of Enquiry, and questioned him about the situation and the policies of the KPD. Soon he was to take Maslow under his wing. On every occasion, he praised Maslow's perspicacity and the firmness of his principles, and took in hand personally the leadership of the Commission of Enquiry, which ended by clearing Maslow of all suspicion.[19] This new alliance changed the balance of forces at least as much as the confusion amongst the Communists in Germany.

New alignments in the KPD

It was the debate within the Russian Party, rather than the German situation itself, which provided the setting for the discussion which Brandler opened in the KPD on 7 November. In December, three documents opposing each other were presented to the Zentrale. The first was by Fischer and her supporters, who declared that they supported Zinoviev's letter, the second was by Brandler and Thalheimer, who firmly rejected Zinoviev's criticisms, and the third was by the 'Centre' – Koenen, Kleine, Remmele and Eberlein – who took account of Zinoviev's criticisms without accepting Fischer's position. Fischer received six votes, Brandler and Thalheimer received two votes – their own, in the absence of Zetkin – and the Centre gathered those of the rest of the Zentrale, seventeen votes.[20]

The Centre represented those leading elements who supported Zinoviev and distanced themselves from Brandler, but refused to line up with the positions of the Left. In their opinion, 'the situation in Germany before and

---

[18] Quoted in Carr, *The Interregnum*, op. cit., pp. 234–5.
[19] Fischer, op. cit., p. 363.
[20] H. Brandler and A. Thalheimer, 'Erklärung', *Die Internationale*, no. 2/3, 28 March 1924, p. 135.

during the October events was objectively revolutionary to the highest degree'. The retreat which the Party made resulted from its own tactical and strategic mistakes, which themselves were consequences of 'an erroneous theoretical conception' and 'a false interpretation of the role of the Party'. They outlined these mistakes:

- Not having recognised sufficiently soon the significance of the great struggles of the workers previous to the strike against Cuno, and consequently not having modified the line of the Party accordingly.
- Not having begun the military preparations at latest when the Ruhr was occupied, which led subsequently to carrying out these preparations in a over-hasty manner.
- Having acted as a brake on the mass movements in September and October in order to conserve the workers' strength for the 'decisive blow'.
- Having had illusions about the left Social-Democratic leaders, and then having propagated these illusions.
- Having failed to use the positions that had been won in Saxony to mobilise the masses.
- Having made preparations with only the final battle in view, whilst rejecting and even discouraging the organisation of partial actions.
- Having made forecasts and calculations on a basis of abstract reasoning, which led the Party 'always to steal away in the face of a fight'.
- Having overestimated the importance of the number of rifles, and underestimated that of the will of the proletarian vanguard to fight.
- Having elaborated too rigid a plan on the basis of their incorrect calculations.

In the view of the centre grouping, the retreat without a fight, which was the direct result of all these mistakes, was a blunder in itself, to the extent that it had not been understood either by the Party or by the vanguard grouped around it, who 'were prepared in their minds for the final struggle', and because it had shaken the trust of the masses in the Communist Party. Nonetheless, the situation was still revolutionary, because 'the white dictatorship could not last long'. The Communists were to wait 'for a great upsurge in activity of the proletarian masses' within 'several months', the success of which was dependent upon the policies and activities of the Communist Party alone.[21]

---

[21] *Inprekorr*, no. 185, 28 December 1923, pp. 1564–6; 'Thesen zur Taktik des Oktoberrückzugs und zu den Nächsten Aufgaben der Partei', *Die Internationale*, no. 1, January 1924, pp. 14–19.

Brandler and Thalheimer were isolated, but they held firm in their belief that the retreat in October was 'inevitable and justified'. According to their theses, the causes of the defeat were 'of an *objective* nature, not to be attributed to tactical mistakes by the Party'.[22] They explained: 'The majority of the class *was no longer* disposed to fight for the November democracy . . . and *was not yet* ready to enter the struggle for the dictatorship of the workers' councils and for socialism'. The cardinal mistake was to have believed that the working class had been won to Communism. This mistake had been made by both the Zentrale and the ECCI. The criticisms which the Zentrale addressed to the ECCI had not been formulated in a sufficiently forceful manner,[23] and the ECCI had moreover ignored them.

The consequences of this blunder were that the date for the uprising was fixed too soon, that the importance of organising partial actions and above all of ensuring general political preparation was underestimated and neglected, and that there was insufficient coordination between political preparation and political and technical details. Moreover, the Party had not been able to take advantage of its positions in the Saxon government to sharpen the crisis in the SPD and to organise armed resistance. Brandler and Thalheimer believed that it was not possible for the moment to foresee how long the military dictatorship would continue, but that, in the immediate future, the Party should concentrate its efforts on combating the influence of Social Democracy, and on strengthening its organisation in the factories.[24]

The theses of the Left did not mince words. They declared at the outset:

> The objective situation in Germany in the period between the August strike and the October events was ripe for the conquest of power by the proletariat. . . . The chances of victory in October were very great. *But the party should have joined battle even at the risk of a defeat. This would have given the proletariat fine revolutionary traditions, identified with the Communist Party, thus preparing the way for our future victory.*

But the opposite had happened. The retreat without a fight demoralised the proletariat, and sowed confusion within the ranks of the Party. The causes

---

[22] This was Thalheimer's favourite theme, which he developed very persuasively in his pamphlet *1923, Eine verpasste Revolution?*, op. cit.

[23] This was Brandler's favourite theme, and is repeated over and over again in his letters.

[24] H. Brandler and A. Thalheimer, 'Theses zur Oktoberniederlage und zur gegenwärtigen Lage', *Die Internationale*, no. 1, January 1924, pp. 1–14; *Correspondance internationale*, no. 3, 16 January 1924, pp. 29–30.

of this failure were, firstly, the refusal by the Zentrale, up until October, and before actually being forced by the ECCI, to prepare members for the struggle for power; secondly, imperfect and insufficient technical-military preparation; thirdly, the use of the reformist united-front tactic, and the search for a 'misplaced' alliance with the left Social Democrats; fourthly, propaganda based on transitional slogans which led to failing to develop the 'Communist programme' amongst the masses; and fifthly, the breaking out of an internal struggle resulting from these mistakes. The Party must prepare itself, 'after an interval of a few months', for new struggles. For this reason, all the right-wing elements were to be eliminated from its leadership.[25]

The debate opened in confusion. The Left was faithful to itself, but the crucial factor was the disintegration of the Zentrale majority. The positions of the centre faction were unclear. Thalheimer did not miss the opportunity to remark that the Centre only criticised 'the retreat *without a fight*' and not 'the retreat itself': it was not Brandler's fault that the retreat was 'without a fight'. He denounced the revival, through the theses of the Centre, 'of the good old theory of the offensive, which, to succeed, needed two elements, the revolutionary will of the Party and the blue horizon of the vast spaces'. In his judgement – and this was pertinent – the theses of the Centre were the product of a compromise full of contradictions between 'leftist' premises and 'rightist' conclusions.[26] But the strength of the Centre's position lay elsewhere. On 27 December, the Political Bureau of the Russian Party condemned Radek, and adopted the same position:

> Comrade Radek directs his course entirely to support the *right* minority of the Central Committee of the KPD, and to disown the left wing of the Party – which objectively threatens a split in the German Party – whereas the Political Bureau of the Central Committee of the RKP bases its policy on support of the great majority of the Central Committee of the KPD and on collaboration with the Left, while criticising the errors of the Left and upholding what is correct in it, and at the same time criticising the gross errors of the Right.[27]

---

[25] 'Skizze zu Thesen über die Situation und über die Lage der Partei vorgelegt vom Polbüros der Bezirkleitung Berlin-Brandenburg', *Die Internationale*, no. 1, January 1924, pp. 54–7; *Correspondance internationale*, no. 4, 23 January 1924, pp. 33–4.

[26] A. Thalheimer, 'Réflexions sur les thèses du comité central du KPD', *Correspondance internationale*, no. 4, 23 January 1924, pp. 34–5.

[27] *VKP(B) v Rezoliutsiyakh*, Volume 1, 1941, p. 534, cited in Carr, *The Interregnum*, op. cit., p. 236.

The Political Bureau condemned Radek's attitude as 'factional', on the grounds that he had refused either to submit to the decisions or respect the discipline of his own party, on the pretext that his mandate as a member of the ECCI came not from the Russian Party, but from the World Congress of the International. Radek had prepared theses on the German question, which Trotsky and Piatakov had also signed, and which he had submitted directly to the ECCI, without going through the leadership of the Russian Party.[28]

The ECCI meeting in January 1924

The first battle took place on 11 January in the Presidium of the International. The Russian delegates were Zinoviev, Bukharin, Radek and Piatnitsky. Trotsky was ill, and could not participate. The Germans were there in force: Brandler, Walcher and Zetkin for the Right, Remmele, Pieck and Koenen for the Centre, and Thaelmann, Fischer and Arthur König for the Left.[29]

Radek reported as the representative of the ECCI in Germany. He began by recalling that the delegation of the ECCI had unanimously approved the October retreat, which the capitulation of the left Social Democrats and the impotence of the Saxon government had made necessary. He believed that an historic opportunity had been missed. He said that it should have been recognised before May at the latest that a revolutionary situation existed in Germany, and yet, despite all the evidence to this effect, the ECCI meeting in June had not discussed this matter. The leaders of the International – of whom he was one – therefore all shared the responsibility for not applying a plan that had become inapplicable to the situation in Germany. He stressed that every important decision had been taken by the ECCI or by its Presidium. Zinoviev knew this perfectly well, just as he knew that Brandler had been opposed to the Communists taking ministerial posts in Zeigner's government without the necessary political preparation, as had finally been decided. Radek declared that it was completely unacceptable that Zinoviev, who as President of the International bore the chief responsibility, should try to evade his responsibilities and be seeking to make Brandler and himself scapegoats, for reasons that had nothing to do with the matter in hand.[30]

---

[28] Ibid.; *Die Lehren der deutschen Ereignisse*, op. cit., p. 23. The text of these theses has never been published and remains unknown today.

[29] *Die Lehren der deutschen Ereignisse*, op. cit., passim.

[30] Ibid., pp. 5–23.

On the fundamental level, Radek developed some of the 'objective' reasons which dictated the decision to retreat in October:

> What is happening today within the German proletariat can only reflect the general situation in Germany, the collapse of all political activity, an extraordinary political passivity in every social class apart from the army. . . . A good workers' party, we are nowhere a good Communist Party. That is the outstanding feature of the situation.[31]

There was the beginning of an attempt at a serious analysis. But it stood no chance of being developed in the atmosphere prevailing in the Presidium after Zinoviev's speech for the prosecution on 12 January. The President of the International saw everything much more simply; it was Radek and Brandler who had been responsible for the KPD's mistakes, thanks to their opportunist positions. The first duty of the International was to change the KPD's leadership, because the old leadership was bankrupt, and because it was necessary to avoid the justified discontent of the workers who supported the Left from leading to a split. A commission was appointed to draft a report. Its chairman was Kuusinen, and it included five Germans, Maslow, Thaelmann, Remmele, Wilhelm Koenen and Pieck. Zetkin demanded that Brandler and Radek be included, but her proposal was defeated; a clear indication that the minds of the majority were already made up.[32]

The Thirteenth Conference of the Russian Communist Party opened immediately after the Presidium suspended its work. It revealed the severe defeat of the Opposition.[33] Zinoviev spoke on the German question. He stressed that there had been no fundamental disagreement within the Russian leadership in respect of the assessment that the situation in Germany was a genuinely revolutionary one. However, the disappointment was serious, and the primary error lay in a misestimation of the time-scale. As far as the past was concerned, he said that he had no wish to evade his own responsibilities, but he insisted on the fact that the Russian Political Bureau and the Central Committee had reached unanimous decisions on these questions. But then he emphasised the importance of the present differences; Radek and Brandler had transformed the entry of the Communists into the Zeigner government into a vulgar parliamentary deal. Already in July, Radek had reined in the German Party by advising it not to go onto the streets for the Anti-Fascist Day. Now, after

[31] Ibid., p. 13.
[32] Ibid., pp. 58–8081.
[33] Broué, op. cit., pp. 195–8.

the defeat, he was elaborating a whole philosophy to cover up for the opportunism of the Right. He, who in Russia liked to present himself as a 'leftist', today embodied the 'rightist' deviation in relation to Germany – which, according to Zinoviev, was no accident. With Piatakov, he had tried 'to introduce factional struggles into the International'.[34] Bukharin rounded off the indictment. In his opinion, Brandler was to blame for the defeat, because, instead of using the policy of the united front to break the influence of Social Democracy, he had used it merely to collaborate with Social Democracy.[35]

Radek defended himself vigorously. Yes, the situation had been revolutionary, but it was no less true that the Party had not been able to exploit it. The leadership of the International bore the same responsibilities as the German Zentrale. He recalled the past of such revolutionary-internationalist Communists as Brandler and Thalheimer, to show that they were themselves the victims of the weaknesses of both their own party and the International, for which they were not the only ones responsible. He accused Bukharin of cynically exploiting the ignorance of the delegates who did not know the German Party well, and challenged him by asking why, if Brandler was an opportunist and a rightist, did the ECCI not denounce him long ago? What was the ECCI saying and doing whilst Brandler was making his notorious mistakes? He asked the leaders: 'And do you want to accept responsibility only for victories and not for defeats?' He concluded that the only correction which the ECCI had made to the resolution of the Zentrale of 3 November had been to add to the slogans against fascism and Social Democracy that of 'Down with Brandler!'.[36]

In the end, the Conference unanimously – with one abstention, probably his own – instructed Radek to submit to the discipline of the Russian Party in the discussion on the German question in the International.[37]

The verdict of the International

On 19 January, Kuusinen's Commission presented its report to the Presidium. Its verdict was categorical; 'a mass of mistakes and omissions, to be imputed

---

[34] Extracts from Zinoviev's report to the Conference on the German question, *Bulletin communiste,* no. 8, 22 February 1924, pp. 205–10.
[35] Cited in Degras, op. cit., p. 70.
[36] Ibid., p. 71.
[37] Carr, *The Interregnum*, op. cit., p. 239.

in part to some opportunistic deviations' were committed in different fields. There was an error of appreciation: 'the Party recognised too late the maturity of the revolutionary situation', and 'the ECCI, on its side, did not give sufficient attention to the imminence of the dénouement'. There were tactical mistakes: holding back and deferring spontaneous movements, whilst not finding political aims to give them; failing to agitate for soviets; and neglecting to strengthen the factory councils and the action committees, in order to devote themselves to what was becoming merely in action by the Party when it should have involved the entire proletariat. There were omissions in political organisation: failing to recruit sufficiently to the Party, and insufficiently involving the masses in the technical preparations. There were mistakes in evaluating the various forces involved: an underestimation of the capacity of the Social Democrats to sabotage action, and illusions about the left Social Democrats and their capacities for action. There was an erroneous orientation towards Saxony alone, the error of staking everything on a single card, without having considered in advance either an alternative plan or a fallback position.

With breathtaking contempt for historical truth, the Commission imputed these mistakes as a whole to the KPD alone. The text did not hesitate to declare that the Party should have joined the Saxon government 'on the basis of a mass movement', and asserted that the Communist Ministers had displayed 'regrettable incapacity'.[38]

The Presidium carried the report by four votes against two, those of Zetkin and Radek, and then rejected an amendment from Pieck to the effect that, taking into account the circumstances as well as the mistakes that had already been made, the decision to retreat in October had been correct.[39]

With the ground thus cleared, the discussion was resumed on 21 January. Zinoviev was confident of victory, and, no doubt so as to avoid frightening the hesitant elements, he adopted a conciliatory air on this occasion, proclaiming himself ready to help the opposition, and taking up in his closing speech the substance of Pieck's amendment: 'It is not only because of the mistakes and weaknesses of the Party itself, but equally because of the weakness of the working class itself that the retreat was absolutely necessary in October. Of course, there are working people who will tell us that we let the opportunity

---

[38] Text of the resolution in *Die Lehren der deutschen Ereignisse*, op. cit., pp. 95–109.
[39] Ibid., p. 82. Radek and Zetkin alone voted for Pieck's amendment. Amongst the people who had been invited to attend the meeting of the Presidium, 10 voted for Pieck's amendment, and 11 against the resolution (ibid.).

slip.'[40] The concession was enough for the supporters of Brandler to seize the chance which was offered to them. They declared that they would vote for the resolution, Zetkin in order to preserve unity, and Radek (who was more disillusioned) out of traditional concern to maintain the solidarity of the ECCI in the eyes of the outside world. Nonetheless, they both regretted, as did Brandler, that the resolution did not admit explicitly, as Zinoviev had just admitted, that the retreat was necessary, and that it remained silent about the responsibilities of the Left.[41]

In the name of the Polish delegation, Prushniak, who also voted for the Presidium's resolution, commented that the ECCI was hiding its own responsibilities, and expressed regret at this attitude:

> Since Lenin, the most important leader of the revolutionary world proletariat, no longer takes part in the leadership of the International, and since the authority of Trotsky, a recognised leader of the revolutionary world proletariat, has been placed in question by the Russian Communist Party, the danger exists of the authority of the leadership of the Communist International being shaken. . . . We consider that the accusation of opportunism made against Radek, one of the most eminent leaders, is not only unjust, but is harmful in the highest degree to the authority of the leaders of the International. . . . The differences between the best-known leaders of the Communist International in their appreciation of the German Revolution are of the kind that are inevitable in a living revolutionary party.[42]

But the leading comrades, who claimed to stand by such principles, ended by supporting a resolution which formally contradicted them. Years later, Thalheimer wrote that the attitude of Zinoviev was explained by his wish to ward off the threats which Radek expressed about a Brandler-Trotsky-Radek alliance, and was to plead that in any case he was not guilty: 'Radek's declaration was pure invention on his part. No one had authorised him to say that we would defend Trotsky if he were attacked. . . . As soon as we learned of this, I wrote against Trotsky's viewpoint in *Die Internationale*.'[43]

The great issue for Zinoviev and his allies was power, the struggle against Trotsky and the Opposition, and the need to rebuild a prestige which had

---

[40] Ibid., p. 83.
[41] Ibid., pp. 84–7.
[42] Ibid., pp. 93–4.
[43] Thalheimer, op. cit., p. 11.

been seriously damaged in the affair. A few weeks later, Guralski-Kleine explained this clearly, and also showed that Brandler and Thalheimer's renunciation of Trotsky had not helped them:

> The alliance of Brandler and Thalheimer with Radek and Trotsky on the German question was not accidental. It raised fundamental questions; namely the de-Bolshevisation of the Russian Communist Party and the European parties, or the preservation of the Russian Communist Party and the Bolshevisation of the European Parties.[44]

The struggle against Brandlerism and Trotskyism

During the months which followed, the ECCI used the slogan of Bolshevisation in order to smother all the centres of resistance or criticism, and all possible support for Trotsky. In France, Souvarine, Monatte and Rosmer were eliminated in this way; in Poland, Warski, Walecki and Wera Kostrzewa. In Germany, there was profound disappointment amongst the KPD's rank and file, and this naturally turned against Brandler, to whom the majority of members were violently hostile. Zinoviev's attack made use of this sentiment without actually expressing it. As with those who had fought Lenin after the March Action and at the Third Comintern Congress in 1921, the main concern was that the ECCI and, behind it, the Russian Party must be above all criticism. The leaders of the national Parties would serve as scapegoats for the mistakes which they had made in common with the Russians.

The moral authority of the Russian Party was such that no one thought seriously of opposing the demands of its leaders. The result was that there quickly appeared Communist leaders who were characterised by a combination of a total lack of initiative – and, often, of political intelligence – and unconditional, blind submission to the directives, even if they contradicted each other, from Moscow. Thus, on 19 February, the German Central Committee approved the resolution of the Presidium, and appointed a new Zentrale, formed of two members of the Left and five of the Centre. Remmele replaced Brandler, with Thaelmann as a candidate member.[45] The new Zentrale at once took up a position against the 'Menshevik' and 'anti-Leninist' tendencies in

---

[44] *Die Internationale*, no. 4, 31 March 1924, p. 161.
[45] *Inprekorr*, 18 February 1924, pp. 244–8; *Geschichte der deutschen Arbeiterbewegung*, Volume 2, East Berlin, 1966, p. 20.

the Russian Opposition.[46] The furious attacks of the Left created a witch-hunting atmosphere in the Party, in which the centre tendency was quickly swamped.

The KPD's next Congress met secretly at Frankfurt-am-Main in April 1924. It was prepared in the worst possible conditions; 121,400 members – compared to 267,000 in September 1923 – elected 118 delegates, amongst whom only 11 were supporters of Brandler, and none of these actually voted for the document which he presented. The Left carried the day, along with a resolution calling for 'the traces of "Brandlerism" to be extirpated'. There were numerous clashes between Manuilsky, the delegate from the ECCI, and the leaders of the Left, who advocated systematic splits in the trade unions, and rejected the entire tactical approach of the Party since its Third Congress, which they saw as revolving solely around the winning of 'the most backward elements of the proletariat'.

Within this setting, a letter from Zetkin – which Manuilsky described as 'a provocation' – sounded like the last echo of the voices of those Communists who had devoted all their energy in trying to construct a revolutionary party in Germany: 'The revolutionary feeling of the masses had no political content, no political objective. It remained elemental and instinctive, and was not transformed into clear revolutionary understanding, into a resolute will to fight in a determined struggle.'

The duty of the Party was to give to it this consciousness and this will: that was where its failure lay. With its eyes fixed on 'the final struggle', it had not succeeded in mobilising the masses. On that level, both the left and right currents were to be rejected, the former because it expected that the offensive would play the role of Merlin the magician, and the latter because it counted on the left Social Democrats to do the work which the Party could not itself do. The German bourgeoisie had understood perfectly that the appearance of a workers' government in Saxony raised the problem of power throughout Germany, whilst the German proletariat had not understood this, because the Communist Party 'had done practically nothing to link the Saxon experience in the minds of the masses of the proletariat with the idea of the armed uprising'.

Zetkin added that the retreat had been necessary in October, and observed that the situation had continued to deteriorate thereafter because the leadership

---

[46] Cited in Degras, op. cit., p. 85.

had offered the Party no activities other than the witch-hunt against Brandler and his supporters. Her personal belief was that it would be impossible to build a genuine Communist Party in Germany without people like Brandler, Thalheimer, Walcher or Pieck playing a leading role in it.[47]

She was to repeat these arguments at the Fifth Comintern Congress, where she emphasised the responsibility of the ECCI, which was culpable at the very least, even from the viewpoint of those who agreed with it, for having given Brandler a free hand. Brandler admitted that perhaps the opportunity had been missed in August, but emphasised that amongst his accusers were the people who had led the Party in Berlin at the time. Radek struggled like a fiend; he interjected, interrupted and often struck home. Thalheimer reminded the Congress that he and Brandler had condemned the Russian Opposition, and declared that 'the leadership of the Russian Party in the International was an historical necessity'.[48] In closed session, Wera Kostrzewa, a Polish delegate, was to protest against 'the atmosphere of permanent struggle, tension and bitterness' which had been created in the International.[49] It was all in vain; Zinoviev continued to settle his scores. Social Democracy had become 'a wing of fascism', and the Saxon episode and the role of 'Radekism' and 'Brandlerism' showed the strength of Social-Democratic influence in the KPD and the International.[50]

A few months later, Stalin ventured for the first time to draft a report on the international situation, and to discuss the prospects of revolution in Western Europe, following the victory of those whom he called 'the revolutionary wing of the Communist Parties'. He said that the main difficulty lay in the fact that these parties were made up partly of men who had been 'formed out of former Social Democrats of the old school', and partly of young people who had not yet had 'sufficient revolutionary steeling'. They were confronted with a solid bourgeoisie, which had a 'tried and tested state apparatus' at its command, and which also enjoyed the help of 'hard-boiled' Social Democracy, which had an enormous influence on the working class. He added: 'To think that such communist parties can overthrow the European bourgeois system "overnight" is a great mistake. Hence the immediate task

---

[47] *Bericht über die Verhandlungen des IX Parteitags der KPD*, op. cit., pp. 85–96.
[48] *Protokoll fünfter Kongress der Kommunistischen Internationale*, op. cit., pp. 73–8, 84–7, 101–5.
[49] Cited in K.S. Karol, *Visa pour la Pologne*, Paris, 1958, p. 45.
[50] *Protokoll fünfter Kongress der Kommunistischen Internationale*, op. cit., pp. 131–5.

is to make the communist parties of the West really Bolshevik...' This task was possible now that 'the sad experience of the workers' government in Saxony' and the crushing of the Russian Opposition, 'a challenge to the mass of the party membership', had 'opened the eyes' of the Party members.[51]

Through the process of 'Bolshevisation', the KPD began to change into a party of a new type, which was soon to be known as Stalinist.[52]

---

[51] 'Sur la situation militaire', Part 2, *Bulletin communiste*, no. 45, 7 November 1924, p. 1053; J.V. Stalin, 'Concerning the International Situation', *Works*, Volume 6, London, 1975, pp. 304–5.

[52] See on this question, which falls outside our subject, the comprehensive work of Hermann Weber, frequently cited in these pages, *Die Wandlung des deutschen Kommunismus: Die Stalinisierung der KPD in der Weimarer Republik*, Volumes 1 and 2, op. cit.

PART FOUR

AN UNDERTAKING CONDEMNED BY HISTORY?

Chapter Forty-Three

History and Politics

The history of the German Communist movement
has, during the last half-century, been subjected more,
no doubt, than any other topic of contemporary
history to the day-to-day requirements of ideologies
and policies.

The Eleventh Congress of the KPD, which was
held in 1927, agreed that a history of the Party be
drafted and published.[1] On 29 February 1932,
Thaelmann, who by then was the Party's President
and all-powerful leader, announced that its drafting
was underway, up to the split of the Independents
at the Halle Congress and the winning of the left
Independents to the Third International.[2] This
undertaking was soon postponed indefinitely, as
much owing to the political problems involved in
writing such a history as to the victory of the Nazis
and their suppression of the KPD. It was necessary
to await the end of the Second World War to see the
first study, that by a non-Communist historian, Ossip
K. Flechtheim,[3] which was soon followed by that of
Ruth Fischer.[4] Whilst many historians in the West,
English or American, devoted themselves to retracing
the history of the early years of the KPD from one
angle or another, its history in the German Democratic

---

[1] *Bericht über die Verhandlungen des XI Parteitags der Kommunistischen Partei Deutschlands,*
Berlin, 1927, p. 416.
[2] E. Thaelmann, *Der revolutionäre Ausweg und die KPD,* p. 95.
[3] Flechtheim, op. cit.
[4] Fischer, op. cit.

Republic, the ruling party of which regarded itself as the successor to the KPD, was confined to a few paragraphs in the *History of the Communist Party of the Soviet Union (Bolsheviks) (Short Course)* dating from 1938, and to a selection of shortened and sometimes falsified documents and commentaries. It was necessary to wait until 1962–3 before the GDR and its leading party, the Socialist Unity Party (SED) – theoretically, the successor of the KPD – could offer to the younger generations an 'official' version of its history in the well known *Grundriss der Geschichte der deutschen Arbeiterbewegung*.[5]

Writing the history of the German Communist movement has met with the same difficulties as in the case of the other official Communist Parties; the periodical revisions of statements and analyses to meet the political requirements of the hour; the falsification or suppression of the role of members regarded as 'deviationists', 'traitors', or 'renegades'; the tendentious interpretation, falsification or elimination of documents; and the reconstruction of the past to meet ideological or tactical needs. One has to return to 1927 to find, from the pen of the former Spartacist Ernst Meyer, the last attempt at a scientific history of the early years of the KPD(S).[6] The author was almost immediately expelled as a 'conciliator', on the eve of his death early in 1930.

The majority of the pioneers of the KPD went over at one moment or another, particularly during the periods of so-called Bolshevisation and Stalinisation, into the ranks of the oppositions, which meant that they were retrospectively denied any 'positive' role. In this way, Paul Levi and Karl Radek disappeared from official history. They had been the most important leaders of the Party between 1918 and 1923, and were as completely eliminated from Bolshevik history as Trotsky had been, and whenever it was deemed necessary to mention their names, they were merely branded with the traditional epithets of 'enemies of the people', 'traitors' or 'renegades'. That is how Brandler and Thalheimer disappeared, as scapegoats for the defeat of 1923, and with them, the 'rightists', Walcher, Frölich and Böttcher, and the 'leftists' or 'ultra-leftists', Fischer and Maslow, Urbahns, Rosenberg and Korsch, and, lastly, 'conciliators' such as Meyer. In the great purge of 1936–9 in the Soviet Union or later in Europe during the Second World War, many other

---

[5] First published in draft form, with introduction by Ulbricht, in two special numbers of *Einheit* in August and September 1962.

[6] His work, entitled 'Kommunismus', was published in *Volk und Reich der deutschen*, Volume 2, Berlin, 1929.

leaders who had long been devoted to the Stalin faction of the KPD disappeared – executed or dead in prison, including Hugo Eberlein, Heinz Neumann, Remmele, Kippenberger, Flieg, Leow, Schulte, Schubert and Münzenberg.[7]

Throughout these years, the history of the KPD was entirely in the hands of such leaders as Wilhelm Pieck and Walter Ulbricht, whose role had been central in its history after 1923 as agents of the Stalinist faction, and who had led the struggle against the old guard. Their business was to justify themselves, to establish that they had promoted the correct position at every stage of the past, and above all to present a picture of that past which conformed to the exigencies of both their hold over the Party apparatus and of the influence of the Russian Party in the International. The history of the KPD became a series of conscious efforts managed from above – that is, from the Stalinist leadership in the Russian Party – to eliminate 'petty-bourgeois tendencies' and 'deviations', the burden of the Social-Democratic tradition, that is, according to the Stalinist model, 'the activities of the class enemy'. It had to minimise, suppress or misrepresent the role of all those who at any moment had found themselves in any grouping other than that of the Stalinist faction, to magnify and to exalt the role of that faction's agents in the KPD, going so far, in the case of Thaelmann up to 1933 and of Ulbricht later, as to indulge in manifestations of the 'cult of the personality'.

This task was incompatible with publishing the full texts of authentic documents. This explains why so little was produced by the historical institutes in the GDR in the early years, when even that could be dangerous, after Stalin had denounced the 'bureaucrats' who needed 'pieces of paper' to write history, and who attached importance to 'written documents'.[8]

The mere mention of oppositionists who had been crushed in the past

---

[7] Weber, *Die Wandlung des deutschen Kommunismus*, Volume 1, op. cit., p. 357; Volume 2, op. cit., various biographies.

[8] In a letter to *Proletarskaiia Revoliutsiia* in 1934, Stalin had attacked the historian Slutsky, who was accused of having written that Lenin had not oriented himself before 1914 towards a break with the opportunists of the Second International, and that he regarded Kautsky as an 'orthodox' Marxist, and then for having observed that Lenin did not support the German Left against the Centre. Slutsky's argument that no one had discovered the documents to support Stalin's thesis aroused the wrath of the latter: 'Who, except hopeless bureaucrats, can rely on written documents alone? Who, except archive rats, does not understand that a party and its leaders must be tested primarily by their *deeds* and not merely by their declarations?' (J.V. Stalin, 'Some Questions Concerning the History of Bolshevism', *Works*, London, 1975, Volume 13, p. 99.)

risked resuscitating before the eyes of younger generations a conception of Bolshevism and the Party, of its aims and its methods, of its very nature, which were very different from those which everyday life and official speeches presented. It would have been imprudent to recall that the Communist International in Lenin's time had the world revolution as its aim, not the construction of socialism in a single country, or that the Bolsheviks had not believed in the messianic predestination of the Russian people in general and their party in particular, but, on the contrary had regarded the Russian Revolution as the first – and the easiest – stage in a revolutionary process which could be successful only on a world scale. It was dangerous, especially after 1956 and the explosive rebirth of the workers' councils in Poland and Hungary, to allow the younger generations to know that the German Revolution of the workers' and soldiers' councils had taken on the characteristics of a strictly soviet revolution, and that at that point there simply did not exist in Germany a party anything like the image which the Stalinist history-writers presented of the Bolshevik Party, the invincible phalanx, 'centralised and moulded in a single block', with its cadres 'tempered by Marxism-Leninism' and its infallible apparatus, a retrospective projection of the all-powerful SED, the single party of the GDR. It was, finally, impossible to retrace the efforts of the German Communists, with the support of the leaders of the Russian Revolution, to construct in Germany a party of a Bolshevik type adapted to German conditions, when this organisation was in reality, in the early years of its history, based on traditions of proletarian democracy, the recognition of tendencies and even of organised factions, the practice of general meetings of members and leaders, that of minority reports, broad discussions, the opening of the press to oppositional currents, and the representation of minorities in the leading bodies.

The history of Bolshevism is very rich in examples which reveal it, on a certain number of essential points, as being the very opposite of Stalinism, which claimed to be its rightful heir and successor. That of German Communism is perhaps even richer from this point of view. Already at the beginning of the 1930s, Stalin was attacking the personality and role of Luxemburg, in order to whip the Russian historians into line,[9] and to crush

---

[9] In his letter against Slutsky, Stalin allowed himself to 'criticise' the left Social Democrats, Parvus and Luxemburg, and what he called their 'semi-Menshevik hotchpotch' (ibid., p. 94). He attacked Slutsky for defending them because he himself was a 'Trotskyist', and Trotskyism was 'the advanced detachment of the counter-

Radek's theory of the formation of the world Communist movement through the historic blending of 'currents'.[10] This attack had to be made, in order to impose the dogma of omniscient 'Bolshevism' and 'Leninism', constructed in a conscious struggle against Social Democracy.

One of the constant features of the Stalinist period had been the bitter tone of the attacks on those who 'overestimated' Luxemburg. She and her Spartacist comrades were all the more suspect because they had criticised the Bolshevik leadership, and often declared their profound attachment to workers' democracy and to mass initiative. From this viewpoint, even the 'rehabilitation' of Social Democracy was easier, as we see from how carefully old Social-Democratic personalities such as Friedrich Ebert Junior were treated when the SED was being set up.

The process of de-Stalinisation was to change this situation somewhat. Researchers were encouraged by the (albeit limited) opening of the archives in the Soviet Union, and by the attacks of the new leadership on the 'cult of the personality', and on Stalin himself. They were under the pressure of the outburst of curiosity which the younger generations had displayed since 1953, and especially since 1956. They thus attempted to create a more scientific

revolutionary bourgeoisie'. Stalin concluded that this 'certain liberalism in the attitude towards the Trotskyists and Trotskyist-minded people' was 'deeply mistaken and harmful' (ibid., p. 101). In a lecture on a 'Bolshevik study' of the history of the Party, on 1 December 1931, Kaganovich stated that 'on a number of fundamental questions . . . Rosa Luxemburg did not agree with the Bolsheviks, and was near to the Centre', and that 'she was nearer to Trotsky and to the Trotskyists' (*Correspondance internationale*, no. 114, 23 December 1931, p. 1257).

[10] In the course of the lecture mentioned in the previous note, Kaganovich declared: 'Radek also spoke to the Marxist historians' fraction. It emerged from his lecture that the Communist International took into its ranks all that was best in the workers' movement, and that we should not forget in the Communist International the currents and the streams which emptied themselves into the Bolshevik Party. Radek should understand what this theory of streams represents. . . . He must understand that the theory of rivulets lays the basis for the freedom of groups and factions. If we tolerate a rivulet, we have also to give it the possibility of having its course. No, comrades, our party is not a reservoir of muddy streams, it is a river so powerful that it cannot preserve any rivulet, for it is fully capable of making all the obstacles in our path disappear.' (Ibid., p. 1260.) Let us recall what Radek wrote, on behalf of the International, in 1919: 'The Communist International is not, as people like Lloyd George, Clemenceau, Scheidemann and Hilferding suppose, an ingenious product of the Soviet government. . . . It is the regroupment of all the revolutionary tendencies of the old International, those that declared and strengthened themselves during the war. It is not only the Bolsheviks who sowed the seeds of it . . . but likewise . . . Debs, De Leon, the heroic fighters of the IWW . . ., Jules Guesde, Loriot and Monatte . . ., Rosa Luxemburg, Warski, Tyszka . . ., the Dutch Tribunists who were laughed at at the time . . . the work which we, German left radicals, have accomplished during ten years.' (Radek, *Die Entwicklung*, op. cit., p. 62.)

history, one which could confront the writings of Western historians, whilst it still continued to be inspired with 'Party spirit', that is, to conform to the political requirements which the regime dictated.

These were the conditions in which the production and then the discussion were to develop of the first official version of any substance of the history of the KPD, the so-called *Grundriss*, by way of which, for the first time, the theses of the leaders were to be questioned, even though partially and indirectly.

In 1957, the historian and old Communist Robert Leibbrand used the columns of *Einheit* to attack the Stalinist theses contained in the notorious *History of the CPSU(b) (Short Course)*. He criticised the Stalinist account, according to which the November Revolution of 1918 had been 'not a socialist but a bourgeois revolution', which presented the workers' and soldiers' councils, not as organs of dual power like soviets, but as 'an obedient tool of the bourgeois parliament', because they were 'dominated' by the Social Democrats, the Independents and other German Mensheviks.[11] Leibbrand saw the German Revolution as a defeated 'socialist revolution', 'in its historical tasks, its fundamental forces and the aims of the proletariat'. He argued that to characterise it as a 'bourgeois revolution' was equivalent to 'an underestimation, a diminution of this great movement of the German proletariat'.[12]

The attempt by Leibbrand was soon supported by another historian, a veteran and a still more prestigious one, because this was the old Spartacist, Albert Schreiner, who wrote in an historical journal that, after studying the question deeply, he was giving up 'his' former interpretation of the November Revolution as a 'bourgeois revolution'.[13] Then Roland Bauer, a young historian, made use of contemporary documents of the November Revolution in both the German and Russian languages, and particularly of writings by Lenin and Liebknecht – which were, of course, unassailable. He vigorously attacked the Stalinist thesis of the 'bourgeois revolution', which everyone knew to be endorsed by Walter Ulbricht. Bauer summed up the fundamental opposition

---

[11] *Geschichte der Kommunistischen Partei der Sowjetunion (Bolschewiki. Kurzer Lehrgang)*, Moscow, 1939; *History of the Communist Party of the Soviet Union (Bolsheviks) (Short Course)*, Moscow, 1939, pp. 231, 279.

[12] R. Leibbrand, 'Zur Diskussion über den Charakter der Novemberrevolution', *Einheit*, no. 1, January 1957, pp. 107–8. Leibbrand had in 1923 been the young secretary of the Communist Youth in Halle and a member of the committee which ran the strike against Cuno in August 1923 (Ersil, op. cit., pp. 80, 322).

[13] A. Schreiner, 'Auswirkungen der Grossen Sozialistischen Oktoberrevolution auf Deutschland vor und während der Novemberrevolution', *Zeitschrift für Geschichts-wissenschaft*, no. 1, 1958, p. 32.

between these theses, that of the 'democratic-bourgeois revolution' and the 'non-victorious proletarian revolution', and emphasised that the latter was also 'the former interpretation by Marxist historians'.[14] An ever-widening circle of historians supported the latter view, and his conclusion is quite precise: 'The November Revolution had the character of an unfinished, defeated proletarian revolution. Such an appreciation is consistent both with the opinion of Marx, Engels and Lenin about the proletarian revolution, as well as the appreciations of the November Revolution by the Spartacus League and the German Communist Party.'[15]

This discussion, which was basic but full of profound implications and consequences, was quickly closed down by the heavy hand of authority. Ulbricht put a stop to the debate which was to have taken place in the Political Bureau when he declared, in the columns of the Party organ, *Neues Deutschland*, that the only interpretation 'consistent with the viewpoint of Marxism-Leninism' of the November Revolution was that of a 'democratic-bourgeois revolution fought with the means and methods of the proletariat'. He formally denounced 'the erroneous opinion defended by some historians about the socialist character of the November Revolution'.[16] The former thesis thus reaffirmed remained thereafter at the foundation of the official history, and the next version of the history of the KPD presented no substantial modifications of the Stalinist history contained in the *Short Course*. Brandler and his comrades were still 'enemies of the Party' and 'right-wing opportunists', and Fischer's tendency were 'sectarian ultra-lefts, enemies of the Party'. However, Ulbricht who belonged to Brandler's group in 1923, and Thaelmann, who was a follower of Fischer and Maslow, were presented as the 'healthy', 'revolutionary' forces, who fought to defend the revolutionary Marxist viewpoint within the KPD. Whilst the minutes of the Leipzig Congress record in full a speech by Ulbricht entirely devoted to a polemic against Fischer and her 'leftist' interpretations of the relation of forces in Germany,[17] the editors of the *Grundriss* wrote: 'Already in 1923, at the height of the postwar revolutionary crisis, Walter Ulbricht appeared as one of the leaders of the Party who at the Leipzig Congress stood out against the right-opportunist revision of the

---

[14] R. Bauer, 'Über den Charakter der Novemberrevolution', *Zeitschrift für Geschichtswissenschaft*, no. 1, 1958, p. 142.

[15] Ibid., p. 168.

[16] *Neues Deutschland*, 18 June 1958.

[17] *Bericht über die Verhandlungen des III (8) Parteitages der KPD*, op. cit., pp. 356–7.

Marxist-Leninist theory of the state by the Brandler-Thalheimer group.'[18]

Ulbricht was concerned with the cult of his own personality, but he did not lose sight of his political objectives, which were to defend the status quo on which the justification for his position stood. In a speech to the Central Committee at the time of the debate on the *Grundriss*, he declared:

> I have the advantage of having actively and consciously taken part in the leadership in two periods of the history of the German workers' movement. During this speech, when I deal with a certain number of questions of strategy and tactics, do not rely only on my theoretical knowledge nor on a systematic exploitation of my various experiences, but also on my personal participation in these great battles of the German working class.[19]

That is how he wanted to truncate the debate – which, in fact, remained wide open – about the links of Bolshevism with the left radicals in Bremen and the Spartacists. This important question had been approached by Wilhelm Eildermann and Karl Dreschsler[20] during the de-Stalinisation period. They declared:

> It is . . . false to say that the Bremen leftists had the greatest political clarity on the question of the party in the German revolutionary workers' movement. . . . It was the Spartacus League which was the closest to the Bolsheviks. Its activity influenced directly or indirectly all the German revolutionary groups, and found strong support in the movement, particularly from Lenin and the Bolsheviks. To put the Spartacus League on the same level as the Bremen radical Left, or simply to overestimate the Bremen group, does not therefore correspond to the facts of history.[21]

Hermann Weber produced a criticism of the *Grundriss* in 1964, entitled *Ulbricht Falsifies History*.[22] He observed that the problem here was not simply for Ulbricht to declare that the undisputed leader of the SED could have belonged only to the most consistent and therefore the historically most important group, a necessity which in his eyes tipped the balance of history in favour

---

[18] *Einheit*, no. 6, June 1963, p. 5.
[19] *Einheit*, August 1962 (special issue), p. 5.
[20] *Die Oktoberrevolution in Deutschland*, proceedings of a meeting of historians, held on 25–30 November 1957 in Leipzig, p. 223.
[21] *Einheit*, August 1962 (special issue), pp. 28–30.
[22] H. Weber, *Ulbricht fälscht Geschichte: Ein Kommentar mit Dokumenten zum Grundriss der Geschichte der deutschen Arbeiterbewegung*, Cologne, 1964.

of the Spartacus League. Above all, his problem was, throughout the 'revised' history, to defend a fundamental principle which could never be challenged: 'There can never be more than *one* group which acts correctly, *one* which has "the leading role" and *one* correct political line, which supports its right to political leadership.'[23]

In fact, in a speech a large part of which was devoted to denouncing conceptions which he treated as 'revisionist', Ulbricht admitted, on his own account and on that of his party, to one single revision, but a substantial one, when he proclaimed:

> The defeat of the German working class in the course of the November Revolution and the defeats of the revolutionary uprisings of the proletariat in the other imperialist states after the First World War have shown that the working class could not erect the dictatorship of the proletariat at a single stroke in the countries which have well-developed systems of state monopoly capitalism.[24]

As Weber notes, we can hear the leader of the SED declaring that the road of Germany towards socialism could not and cannot be anything other than what it is, in the GDR under the leadership of Walter Ulbricht. Moreover, this entirely justifies – despite the essence of the thought of Marx, Lenin and Luxemburg – all the past policy of constructing 'socialism in a single country', the suicidal policy which the Stalinist International dictated to the KPD between 1931 and 1933, not to speak of the recent policy of the Communist Parties in the framework of 'peaceful coexistence', of 'the struggle for advanced democracy', and of the 'parliamentary roads to socialism'.

Like Heinz Habedank, who was one of the first to attempt to rehabilitate the use of 'written documents' in his history of the Hamburg uprising,[25] researchers still risk today running into a veto from the political leaders.[26] As in the Soviet Union, historical research cannot be separated from the political consequences which they imply. The work of Arnold Reisberg on the role of Lenin in elaborating the policy of the workers' united front,[27] which established the role and personality of Radek for readers in the GDR, and did justice to

---

[23] Ibid., p. 110.
[24] *Einheit*, August 1962 (special issue), p. 33.
[25] Habedank, op. cit.
[26] We must remember that this book was first published in 1971. [Translator's note]
[27] In particular his *Lenin und die Aktionseinheit in Deutschland*, as well as the series of articles on the subject in *Beiträge zur Geschichte der deutschen Arbeiterbewegung*.

Brandler, cannot fail to provoke reflections and questions, despite the cautious language with which they are surrounded.

Moreover, we should take note that, on the central point of the perspectives of the proletarian revolution in the advanced countries, the revision in the field of theory which Ulbricht formulated has been supported, with various shadings of difference, in the principal works of historiography in the West. Thus, Werner Angress writes at the end of his study of the KPD in those years:

> They thought of this revolution as inspired and spearheaded by themselves, but carried out by the mass of German workers. This vision was shattered during the weeks after the collapse of the Empire and after January 1919 ceased to be a feasible undertaking. It was a tragedy for the KPD and, indeed, for the Weimar Republic that the German communists were unable to accept the finality of their defeat. Their several bids for power, which ended only with the close of 1923, were doomed to certain failure, and the party could have found little comfort in the thought that theirs was not the only abortive attempt at revolution in the history of modern Germany.[28]

Richard Lowenthal's study, 'The Bolshevisation of the Spartacus League', is unquestionably a pioneering work. It moves in the same direction. On the history of the KPD itself, he paints in black and white what the writers in the East paint in white and black, and draws the conclusion that it was the ECCI which introduced into the German Communist movement the 'organisational techniques' which he enumerates as

> the deliberate mixing of different elements to create a less homogeneous and more pliable leadership; the encouragement of the formation of 'wings' which Comintern could then play against each other; the incorporation in party documents of general key phrases which could later be applied as yardsticks for measuring the performance of the leaders; the gradual building up of inner-party legends about recalcitrant leaders in order to discredit them, first by whispering, then publicly through the mouths of opponents, finally by open use of Comintern's authority.[29]

Above all, like Ulbricht himself, he explains the setback to the revolutionary party in Germany by the impossibility of a revolution in an industrially developed country:

---

[28] Angress, op. cit., p. 475.
[29] Lowenthal, op. cit., p. 68.

The transfer of authority to Comintern was based on the failure of all non-Bolshevik revolutionary movements in Europe. The leftward drift of the communist rank and file sprang from the impossibility of maintaining in the long run a separate revolutionary party with a 'Luxemburgist' concept of its role. But both circumstances really expresseed the fact – more obvious today than at the time – that the basic expectation of Rosa Luxemburg, and the non-Bolshevik revolutionary Marxists generally, had been disproved by history; the expectation that the working class of industrially advanced Europe would be increasingly revolutionised by its own experience. . . . In the last analysis, the heirs of Rosa Luxemburg were defeated by the 'Bolshevisers', because their own vision of the proletarian revolution had no future.[30]

Unlike many of the other Western historians, Lowenthal draws the necessary distinction between the International in the time of Lenin and the International which was placed in the following years under the rod of Stalin: 'If Lenin could have foreseen the final outcome of the process which we have designated as the Bolshevisation of the communist parties, he might well have sincerely objected to that term. But, judging not by conscious intentions but by historical consequences, he would have been wrong.'[31]

Our personal opinion is that Walter Ulbricht, Richard Lowenthal and Werner Angress were mistaken in thinking that Lenin and Luxemburg made a fundamental mistake in believing that a proletarian revolution could occur and be victorious in an advanced country. We believe that the German Communist Party could have been victorious, even though it was defeated. There does not exist any Book of Destiny, in which the victory of the Russian October and the defeat of the German October, and the victory of Stalin and then Hitler, could have been written in advance. It is human beings who make history.

---

[30] Ibid., pp. 69–70.
[31] Ibid., p. 71.

Chapter Forty-Four

Grafting Bolshevism onto German Stock

In the years covered by this study, the German
Communist Party developed from the Spartacus
League, through the Communist Party of Germany
(Spartacists) and the United Communist Party of
Germany, to become finally the Communist Party of
Germany. This history is not an epic in black and
white of a struggle between the 'good' and the 'bad',
whether the latter were right-wing opportunists or
left-wing sectarians. Nor is it the slow death agony
of a socialist, revolutionary sector of the German
workers' movement in the embrace of a foreign
organisation which consciously aimed at emptying
it of its class content. The KPD represents one
experience in the long struggle of the German
working class movement for its consciousness and
its existence. The KPD cannot be understood apart
from the crisis of Social Democracy, a crisis which
for a long time haunted the latter in all its deeds,
and which was revealed publicly during 1914 and
the years which followed.

German Social Democracy had been, and to a large
measure still was in 1914, the expression of the
German workers' movement, with its characteristically
serious attitude to organisation, the strict discipline
which it demanded from its members, who were
organised in fractions, and the coexistence of a
minimum programme which called for reformist
practices with the programme of the proletarian

revolution, which was put on the back burner for a whole historical period. The First World War put an end to this compromise, which had been painfully assembled during the years of Germany's expansion, and had been preserved with difficulty during the prewar years. The War compelled a choice to be made between the two perspectives which had been presented as complementary, but which the situation had rendered contradictory. The pursuit of the struggle for the minimum programme – or at least to defend gains already made – could seem to lead along the road of the *union sacrée* in times of war, but it was clear that the revolutionary perspective, on the contrary, lay through struggle – in illegality if necessary – against the War and through preparing for civil war.

The crisis of German Social Democracy set free elements which had been fused within it for several decades. Old currents reappeared; the 'corporatism' of craft unions seeking an agreement with the employers in order to obtain privileges; Bernsteinian 'revisionism' and its links with the democratic and nationalist movement; 'syndicalism', which threw overboard parliamentary 'illusions', preached the organisation of 'the rank and file', and hailed the virtues of 'spontaneity' as opposed to the vices of 'organisation'. So-called 'centrist' currents oscillated between the inevitable choices; they all expressed both the continuity of the Social-Democratic traditions, and resistance to adaptation in the face of changes in the objective situation; they all expressed conservatism as a defensive reflex in the face of crisis, like a wish to return to what they believed to have been the golden age of the old status quo. Leftism was at one and the same time an old current and a new response. It was a wholesale rejection of the past, and a childish desire to force the course of events, to reject all compromises and even any transition; it was over-simplified, maximalist, impatient, peremptory utopianism, to which, nonetheless, the aberrant character of the policies of the 'government socialists' lent a certain attractiveness.

The Russian Revolution intervened in this crisis, indirectly at first, but then directly and decisively. Bolshevism was, in a certain sense, an experience and a doctrine external, not to say alien, to the German workers' movement. The Bolshevik Party was constructed on the basis of specifically Russian conditions. But Bolshevism never felt itself to be specifically Russian. Lenin described Bolshevism as having been born on the basis of the world-wide experience of Social Democracy, within the context of the concrete conditions of the struggle in the Tsarist Empire. Moreover, the victory of the Russian Revolution proved the validity of the maximum programme of Social Democracy, the Marxist perspective of the proletarian revolution as the first concrete stage in the realisation of socialism. In any case, for German revolutionaries, irrespective of the group or grouplet to which they belonged, Bolshevism was first and foremost the theory and practice which led the Russian workers to victory.

There were no German 'Bolsheviks' before the revolution of October 1917 in Russia. Radek, to be sure, was very close to Lenin. His differences with Lenin were neither more nor less than those of others such as Bukharin or Piatakov. But it is difficult to regard Radek in that period as a German activist, even though it was his personal connections which ensured the links between the Zimmerwald Left and the German internationalists.[1] The left-wing radicals in Bremen, with whom Radek worked, were to a certain extent fascinated and dazzled by the Bolshevik experience, which they claimed to support. But, with their theory of 'industrial unions', their instinctive leftism in trade-union and electoral questions, they were no doubt nearer to the leftists in the Russian movement, whom Lenin had fought for years even within his own faction, than to what can be called Bolshevism. On the other hand, the Spartacists could hold views close to those of the Bolsheviks on a certain number of important tactical points, such as utilising parliamentary platforms and carrying out oppositional work in opportunist trade unions. But, for all that, they found it no easier over the course of many years to assimilate the Bolshevik conception of the party. They were hostile to centralisation, which they believed to be inevitably bureaucratic, or at least a source of bureaucracy. They were attached to spontaneity, they identified the working class with its political movement, and they opposed the conception of the labour aristocracy, which Lenin, Radek and others used to justify what they saw as the historical necessity for revolutionaries deliberately to split the Social-Democratic movement.

Yet Spartacists, leftists of every shade and Bolsheviks were all convinced that the revolutionary struggle needed to be organised on an international scale. The prestige of the Russian Revolution, combined with the proclamation of the Communist International, brought them together, heterogeneous as their theories and practices were, into the camp over which flew the banner

---

[1] And even if in his pamphlet *Die Entwicklung* (op. cit.) he presents himself as a German activist. For her part, Luxemburg is described there as a Polish activist!

of Moscow. From that moment, it became inevitable – and in the eyes of many desirable – that Bolshevism should graft itself onto the crisis-ridden body of the German workers' movement, as the theory and practice of the victorious Revolution, and that it should take hold of its revolutionary currents, without Russifying them, but, on the contrary, 'Germanising' itself, by passing on to them, not ready-made solutions, but its experience and its general line.

The old guard of the Spartacists, particularly Luxemburg and Jogiches, regarded Lenin first and foremost as the leader of the indefatigable Bolshevik faction with its intrigues and its ultimata, as the leader of a small group with which they had been locked for years in struggle, but this old guard had now largely gone. The younger people who succeeded them saw in Lenin above all the revolutionary guide and theoretician, the man who had been able to foresee the degeneration of the old firm and to save his party from it, the only man who could begin to realise the maximum programme, the world revolution. So this graft of Bolshevism onto the left wing of the German movement seemed to them all to be historically necessary as the correct, dialectical restoration of international experience, enriched by victory in one of its sections. The Russian revolutionaries were giving back to the German revolutionaries the gains which they had inherited from German Social Democracy, the inheritance which they had invested profitably. The 'Bolshevisation' of the German Communist Party in the years which interest us here was not the mechanical transposition of prescriptions for organisation, slogans and instructions which it was to become in later years. It was an effort to translate Bolshevism into the German language, into the thinking of the German workers, into German socialist practice. It was the attempt to create in Germany as elsewhere a Communist organisation, and that was the term that was used – not 'Bolshevik', which specifically referred to the Russian branch of the movement.

The Founding Congress of the KPD (Spartacists) on 1 January 1919 presented the spectacle of an organisation which bore little resemblance to a party, and had nothing in common with what a Communist Party in Germany could and should have been. In other words, the KPD(S) when it was formed was effectively both Spartacist and leftist, a living contradiction. However, the Second Congress, in Heidelberg in October 1919, showed a profound transformation, at least in the attitudes of the leading team. The resolutions were the first systematic attempt to secure adoption of the principles and tactics of the Bolsheviks in Russia. This was a considerable step forward in comparison with the First Congress, when we bear in mind that the Bolshevik party had not always been the mass party which it then was, and that it had also over the years experienced splits and had been as small as the KPD(S) was immediately after the Heidelberg Congress. This is all the more remarkable because the Bolsheviks did not precisely recognise themselves in the Heidelberg decisions, and, when they discussed with Lenin, Levi and Thalheimer appeared to be more Bolshevik than the Bolsheviks themselves.

The graft took perfectly in the period which the Heidelberg Congress opened. Not only did the Russian experience, concentrated in the 'Twenty-One Conditions', begin to influence the contours and the functioning of the German Party, but the inverse is equally true. The experience of the class struggle in Germany, as it had been more or less assimilated in the leadership of the KPD, was to introduce a number of themes and positions of the highest importance into the Communist International. Lenin, in *'Left-Wing' Communism: An Infantile Disorder*, did no more than to systematise the themes which Radek and Levi had developed against the German opposition and the KAPD, although, no doubt, with wider vision and less rancour. It was the experience through which the leadership of the KPD had lived and the manner in which it found its way towards the question of the workers' government after the Kapp Putsch, particularly in respect of Legien's proposals, that were to introduce this thenceforth essential slogan into the body of the doctrine of the International.

It was the initiative of the metalworkers of Stuttgart in their struggle against the left Social Democrat Dissmann which inspired the *Open Letter* of January 1921. Here we find for the first time the policy of the workers' united front clearly formulated. It had been applied in Russia in 1917, but was not yet an integral part of Bolshevik doctrine, and it was the struggle to organise the united front of the workers, Communist and non-Communist alike, in Germany, which was to lead to the appearance, first in the debates in the International and then in its programme, of the idea of transitional slogans and demands, the purpose of which was to fill, in the arsenal of Communist theory, the place which had been left empty by the collapse of the old separation between maximum and minimum programmes, which went back to the SPD's Erfurt Programme of 1891.

Nonetheless, the graft did not fail to produce some antibodies. These were the German leftists, who paid many compliments to Bolshevism, but who refused to recognise it, and fought against it as hard as they could, in the belief that it was 'opportunist', 'right-wing' and 'capitulatory', when Levi presented it to them translated into German. It was the leftists in the International and, behind Zinoviev and Bukharin, the *apparatchiki* of the ECCI, who vigorously opposed all these German innovations, and denounced systematically in them the pressure of the environment, the weight of opportunism and the influence of Social Democracy. Against both of them, and against the conservatism which tends to adopt the theory and practice of yesterday, as if the world never changed and Communists had nothing to learn from life,[2] Lenin always limited the damage, discouraged hasty condemnations, succeeded in deferring poorly-formulated discussions, in order to propose, not a compromise, but a synthesis between the old principles and the new conditions.

The state of German society, the brutal cynicism of its political morals, the reaction against the bureaucratic strait-jacket imposed by the SPD and the trade unions, the hatred of the military caste, the junkers and the labour bureaucrats, continued all the time to produce leftist currents. After Laufenberg, the 'national Bolshevik', was expelled from the KPD(S), Münzenberg supported the boycott of parliament, and, on the morrow of the Heidelberg Congress, Béla Kun discovered the virtues of an active boycott. After the 'putschists' of 1919 had been expelled, the very people who expelled them had become, by 1921, enthusiasts for a revival in a new guise of their old theory of the offensive. For every one such as Friesland, whom Lenin convinced at the Third Comintern Congress, how many followers of Fischer and Maslow, intellectuals revolted by the War, unpolished and combative workers, whose strategy was simple and whose tactics expressed impatience, and who were always wanting to take up arms in an insurrection, were constantly ready to denounce the 'opportunism' of the Russians or the KPD's leadership, and to write off altogether the 'opportunism' of the New Economic Policy and the united front, the concessions to the capitalists in the USSR and transitional demands? There, too, Lenin played the role of a mediator. He had been unable in 1919 to prevent the split and the expulsion of the ultra-leftists, but he did not cease to hold out a hand to the activists of the KAPD, without sparing them in the fundamental discussions, and, from 1921 onwards, he extended his protection

---

[2] Radek (op. cit., pp. 21–2) had already written in 1919 that a Communist Party must always be aware that 'it was not the revolution which had to learn from the party, but the party from the revolution'.

to the leftists behind Fischer, whom he tried at all costs to keep in the ranks of the International.

The German Communist Party was constructed in opposition to Social Democracy, but also in a certain sense within it, and, in any case, in relation to it. Indeed, Social Democracy was not unchangeable. In 1918–19, it had presented to the Communist and Independent activists the repugnant features of the 'Party of Noske'. After 1920, it freed itself, at least in appearance, from its most compromising associations. People such as Lensch and Winnig had openly gone over to the class enemy, and had been expelled, whilst Noske had been pushed to one side. The SPD had learned something from the Kapp Putsch; it openly proclaimed itself to be reformist, that is, to be opposed to revolution but, at its Congress at Görlitz, it made an effort to present itself once more as a workers' party. It existed in order to win workers to a reformist policy, which would be reasonable and realistic; it would oppose the adventurism and irresponsibility of the 'Moscowteer' revolutionaries. Its reunification in 1922 with the right-wing minority of the Independents also helped to give it a new image. From that time onwards, with its left wing which consented to discuss and to act jointly with the Communists, the SPD was once again able to influence its hostile brother, to exert pressure on it directly or indirectly, to attract it or to attract elements from it, especially in the unions where the activists of both Parties worked side by side. This pressure from Social Democracy, taken together with the very lively desire of the masses for working-class unity – which was sometimes almost made a fetish – explain in a certain way the echo in Germany of the policy of the united front, or at any rate of the way in which it was understood in certain sectors of the KPD. At least as much as the fact that some leading Communists held responsible positions in the trade unions, these pressures were to strengthen the 'rightist' tendencies in the Party in 1923.

In this way, the KPD seemed to have been building itself up between two tendencies, perpetually renewed. These tendencies, one 'right' and the other 'left', grew out of the reality of society. They struggled against each other, but they also complemented each other. The successive leaderships of the Party unceasingly tried to effect a synthesis between them. The logic of both of them alike would lead the Party to disaster, either as a sect isolated by the policy of putschism, the theory of the offensive – or in dissolution within a general unity, the price of conceding too much in order to forge a united front at any price. The Party was a permanent battleground, yet, for all that, no one might draw the conclusion that it was weak, or that it did not sufficiently influence events and the workers' struggles. The Bolshevik Party, indeed, had undergone the same difficulties. It had experienced the same permanent crisis, which became still sharper in the period of the Revolution, if we recall that on the eve of the insurrection the desperate rightist resistance of Zinoviev and Kamenev followed the manifestation of leftism of July 1917, and preceded that of March 1918.

As a whole, the KPD was a living organism. What had been Luxemburg's 'baby' had proved itself worthy of surviving. It not only screamed, it grew. We find the proof of this, not only on the level of the elaboration of theory, the putting forward of new slogans, and progress in defining methods and clarifying intermediary objectives, but also in the daily life of the organisation, in particular in the coexistence of the right and left tendencies in the Party, with all the shadings of the Centre. This coexistence was not an objective but a fact, it was not a model, but a datum. It was institutionalised in the constitution and practice of the Party in the form that the right of tendencies was recognised – and even factions, which in 1923 replaced tendencies, were tolerated – groups which had their own discipline and which concluded 'compromises' with each other that were backed by the ECCI. This coexistence took the concrete form that everyone participated in the debates which preceded great decisions, through the custom which allowed minorities the right to put forward counter-statements, within every organ and at every level, to have representation at every committee, including executives, and to speak freely not only within the Party, but publicly in its press, when they had serious differences from the policy of the leadership.

The permanence of these tendencies with contours approximately fixed, could, it is true, be interpreted as proof that the organism had an artificial character; a federation of currents does not constitute a party. In fact, whilst the contours of the tendencies remained largely identical in relation to the great problems of strategy and tactics, the people who incarnated them were not always the same. In Switzerland, Levi had been hostile to participating in elections, and was apparently a supporter in 1918–19 of 'industrial unions' and opposed to work in the existing unions. At the Heidelberg Congress in October 1919, he was a new convert to the theses that were endorsed. At the Foundation Congress, at the end of 1918, Frölich was a perfect example of a leftist on all the essential questions of the moment. He was partially convinced in 1919 in the course of his work with Levi on the Zentrale, but relapsed into leftism in 1921. After that, Radek spoke seriously to him and guided his thinking, and he then became a resolute rightist.

Friesland, whose position was hardly worked out when he began his activity in the Party in December 1918, accepted the principal responsibility in 1920, at the time of the Kapp Putsch, for the passivity of the central leadership, and for its call for the workers to refuse to defend the government. The following autumn he was the spearhead of the attacks on Levi's opportunism, and a fervent supporter of the initiatives of the International towards the KAPD. In March 1921, he supported the theory of the offensive, and was taken in hand by Lenin at the Third Comintern Congress in June 1921, returning to Germany a supporter of the application of the Moscow compromise. No doubt, this evolution cannot be explained in terms of his having a docile attitude towards the ECCI; when it pushed him into becoming General Secretary, he quickly became an opponent of its interference in the affairs of the German Party, and some months later became the organiser of an opposition based almost point by point on the theses of Levi, of whom he had been one of the most violent critics. Brandler was deeply rooted in trade-union work, and inspired the construction of a mass party in his stronghold in Chemnitz; he was the spiritual father of the united front from 1919 onwards, but he was also the chairman of the Zentrale which launched the March Action in 1921, before becoming the leader of the Right in 1922. He and Thalheimer were with Levi against Frölich, and then with Frölich against Levi.

Social pressures constantly bore down on these people. It was the refraction of these pressures in the consciousness of the activists which inspired the political discussions, contributed to the tendencies, and fed the contradictions from which a policy was elaborated in order to overcome them. But there was not always any direct connection between the environment, tradition, education, origin or activity of the activists and the positions which they adopted in the political conflicts in the Party. It is, of course, true that, in general, the places where the Left was traditionally strongest, such as Berlin, the Wasserkante and Central Rhineland, were strongholds of the left Independents, whilst the bastions of the Right, such as Württemberg, the North-West, the Erzegbirge and West Saxony, were where the Spartacists had been influential. But the relationship was not always direct. For example, the former left Independent leaders in the Central Rhineland nearly all supported Levi in the crisis in 1921. It was their departure with him which handed the district over to the influence of the new leftists. It is true that the former left

Independents in 1919–20 who were well entrenched in trade-union work, the old Berlin revolutionary shop-stewards such as Eckert, Wegmann, Brass, Neumann, Malzahn and Winguth left the VKPD in 1921. But, at that point, their leaders were Levi, the old Spartacist, and Friesland, whom the Bolsheviks themselves won directly to Communism. The people who then took over the leadership of the Zentrale were not only the nucleus of the old Spartacists (Pieck, Brandler, Thalheimer, Walcher and Eberlein), but also other leaders of the former left Independents, such as Stoecker, Remmele, Koenen and Böttcher. There is perhaps just one consistent factor; this is that the intellectuals who came to Communism belatedly, and essentially through their experience of the War, were until 1923 all on the Left – but they were not the only ones.

The life of the KPD – its external activity as well as its internal life, its political life and its interventions – was the product of the dialectic of theory and practice, or, if you like, analysis and action. We observe that the organisation, as it were, constantly manifested conservatism, a tendency to refuse to see that reality had changed, an attachment to old slogans and a great dislike of taking new positions. Levi was correct in 1919 when he denounced the putschist tendencies as a mortal danger to his party, but he went on denouncing them long after they had already been toned down. Despite the profound change in the international situation immediately after the Second Comintern Congress in July–August 1920, the International and the KPD blithely persisted with the old orientation, as if the perspective of imminent revolution was still valid, even after the armistice between Poland and Soviet Russia, and even after the strikes in France, Britain, Italy and Czechoslovakia had been defeated and European capitalism was beginning to become stabilised. Levi was the first to notice the change, and Lenin and Trotsky then successfully encouraged the International to recognise it.

What was the role of the International and its weight in the life and struggles of the KPD? The answer is not simple. It is true that, in March 1921, Kun was acting with the full authority of a representative of the ECCI and the Russian Communist Party. But, in 1919, the putschists had not needed emissaries from Moscow before they went into action. The VKPD adhered blindly to its theory of the offensive after the March Action. Would it have understood its mistakes if Lenin had not held back its delegates in Moscow in June 1921? And were they not heading towards the early destruction of the Communist Parties in Europe, in leftist adventures in the style of Kun, if the International, thanks to the authority of Lenin and Trotsky, had not called a halt? Yet even that authority was not enough to hold in the ranks of the KPD such a man as Paul Levi, who could still have played a useful role in it.

In 1919, Thalheimer used the language of an equal when he was answering Lenin on the problems of the Independents and the split at Heidelberg. Yet, a few months later, he was to bear the responsibility for a huge blunder, the declaration of 13 March 1920, at the start of the Kapp Putsch, that the workers should not act against it. He never subsequently tried to justify this action. The following year, he set off for Moscow, confident of his orientation, but came back severely admonished, and convinced this time too that he had been sadly mistaken. In fact, the German Communists never raised the question of transitional slogans – in particular that of the workers' government – during this period. It was the old revisionist Social Democrat, Legien, the trade-union bureaucrat, who devised the latter, under the pressure of the mobilised workers, the day after the Kapp Putsch began. The Communist leaders were sunk deep in their routine activities; they were divided and went off the rails somewhat; their declaration of 'loyal opposition', despite being repudiated almost as soon as it was launched, was no more than a prudent taking of a position. A few remarks from Lenin were enough to bring them back to a hasty condemnation of it. But two years later, it was Radek (with Lenin's support) who from Moscow encouraged and nagged at them to abandon this road and to follow consistently a policy which they agreed to be correct, but which they had properly grasped only little by little, a policy which they had let their opponents suggest, and which for a long time they hesitated to adopt.

The fact is that, throughout this whole period, confronted with the succession of defeats in Germany, the Russian victory exerted a great influence upon the German Communists. In Russia, too, the situation was complicated. Lenin said repeatedly that the Bolshevik experience served as a model, but in 1922 he criticised the Third Comintern Congress in 1921 for having adopted resolutions that were written and thought out in Russian, which were not properly translated, and which were inappropriate and incomprehensible to those who had not lived through the Russian experience. Lenin's methods of dealing with German questions can be taken as exemplary from this point of view, although Radek's were not always so, and Zinoviev's never were. Lenin intervened only on particularly important issues. When he plunged into the depths of the struggle at the Third Comintern Congress, he had nothing to guide him but two slim pamphlets, one by Levi and the other by Brandler. Immediately after the March Action, he admitted his ignorance, and wrote to Levi that he knew only what he, Levi, had personally confided in him. He admitted to Levi that he could well believe, even without proof in Kun's 'Kuneries'. But Kun had been sent to Berlin by Zinoviev, and Radek, who had just left Berlin, was writing letters of advice to Levi's opponents . . .

The question then arises of the apparatus of the International and that of the Party. Many Communists regarded the crystallisation of a solid 'bureaucratic' apparatus as the origin of the degeneration of Social Democracy. The apparatus of full-time officials, built by Ebert, had removed the rights of the SPD's members, smuggled revisionist conceptions into its electoral practice, and, under the rubric of 'adaptation', tried to integrate itself into the bourgeois state. Already in 1916, Liebknecht was sharply critical of this centralising, authoritarian apparatus, which made organisation an end in itself.[3] This theme remained at the heart of the propaganda of the Spartacists and the leftists, and was the central preoccupation of every delegate at the Foundation Congress of the Communist Party in December 1918. The apparatus was held to blame for everything, from the passivity of the proletariat to its lack of reaction against the World War. From this negative experience, this instinctive, almost manichean certitude, leftism drew its strength after 1919; someone such as Otto Rühle, for example, could draw from it arguments against organisation as such, in support of an anti-authoritarian philosophy that worshipped spontaneity. This tradition, this mistrust of the apparatus and centralisation, remained alive throughout the early years of the KPD, as we can see from the vitality of the practice of members' meetings and the jealous concern of the local organisations to retain their right to control their elected full-time officials and their press. The KAPD systematically attacked the KPD as 'an organisation of leaders', but *Die Rote Fahne* did not ever hide the existence, at this time, of a certain apprehension in the ranks of the KPD(S) about a 'Party bureaucracy'.[4] At the Fifth Congress of the KPD in November 1922, Hermann Duncker declared that the principal lesson of the Russian Revolution was the necessity for a 'rigorously organised' revolutionary party,[5] whereat Hans Tittel, a delegate from Württemberg, shouted: 'We want no bureaucratic

---

[3] K. Liebknecht, *Politische Aufzeichnungen aus seinem Nachlass*, Berlin, 1921, p. 17. This passage was suppressed in the East-German edition of Liebknecht's writings until 1968.

[4] *Die Rote Fahne*, 4 February 1920.

[5] *Bericht über den 5 Parteitag der KPD*, op. cit., p. 38.

centralism, we want a democratic centralism!',[6] and the district which he represented submitted a resolution to this effect.[7]

Nonetheless, it was in the enthusiasm which immediately followed the unification with the left Independents that the Communists proceeded to build an apparatus, both legal and clandestine. Everyone saw it as the obvious price to be paid for efficiency. From this point of view, the Russian example, that passion for efficient centralisation which developed during the Civil War to the point that the Party was really militarised, did not seem to contradict the German experience. Against the general staff of the bourgeoisie, they needed a workers' general staff, specialists against bourgeois specialists, and an army against the bourgeois army. Levi, like Thalheimer, Stoecker or Däumig, attacked the right Independents, who talked about 'autonomy' and 'decentralisation', and denounced the 'dictatorship of the Communist *apparatchiki* over the Party'. The Unified Party was constructed on the basis of democratic centralism on the Bolshevik model, adapted to German conditions and traditions. Discipline in action was required, but discussion always remained possible. The Party was centralised, but its centralisation was democratic. In January 1922, Friesland was completely free to go and defend his position in every meeting against the positions of the leadership, before rank-and-file members or their delegates. Like Levi before him, Friesland was expelled because he broke discipline, but only after he had had every opportunity to say what he wished to the rank-and-file base of the Party as well as to the Central Committee which took the final decision. In any case, like Levi, he had made up his mind to split. No one can blame the KPD when it locked the door which both Levi and Friesland had chosen of their own free will to slam behind them.

During this whole period, the apparatus of full-timers posed no problems other than those posed in Russia by the corps of professional revolutionaries in the time of the struggle against Tsarism, who could not be imagined as the ancestors of professional bureaucrats, except at the price of greatly distorting reality. The KPD employed few full-timers, hardly more than two hundred.[8] They received the pay of an average skilled worker, and had no privileges,

---

[6] Ibid., p. 40.
[7] Ibid., p. 107.
[8] See above, Chapter 32, and Brandler's letter cited in Weber, *Die Wandlung des deutschen Kommunismus*, Volume 1, op. cit., p. 308.

apart from being the first to be arrested, prosecuted and sentenced, and, when shooting started, to be the first to fall.

The KPD, despite its strength its participation in elections and many successes in them, was never assimilated into the society of Weimar Germany. As a revolutionary party, it was a foreign body in the world of Weimar, to which it was bound only by its implacable aim of destroying it. People joined the apparatus young, and competed to excel. Whilst the pre-1914 Social-Democratic apparatus had been a means of individual advancement in society, and often an intermediate stage between the factory and a seat in the Reichstag, the KPD's apparatus was open only to the best fighters, the most self-sacrificing, who committed their whole lives to the struggle.

Levi was criticised precisely because he did not want to devote himself body and soul to the cause, but always tried to guard his private life. The people in the KPD's apparatus, legal or illegal, were convinced revolutionaries; that was why they became professional workers for the Revolution. Apart from the specialists in the illegal apparatus, whose political role was far from being decisive, the Communist functionaries were strictly accountable. They could be recalled. They were not all-powerful bureaucrats. When Friesland accepted the compromise with Moscow, he was eliminated by the activists from the leadership of the Berlin-Brandenburg district on returning from the Third Comintern Congress in 1921. Ernst Meyer, who the day before had still been the Chairman of the Party and then a delegate to the ECCI, was eliminated in the secret ballot for the Zentrale at the Leipzig Congress in 1923.

In fact, the most severe critics of the KPD, whether contemporaries such as Levi or Friesland, or former activists trying to do the job of historians, such as Fischer and Lowenthal, do not put into question for this period the apparatus of the KPD, but only the international apparatus, the emissaries of the ECCI on the one hand, and the close financial dependence of the KPD on the International and the ECCI on the other. There were frequent disagreements with the emissaries; it was the same in the other Parties, for example in Italy and France. There was the incident after the Second Comintern Congress between Thomas and Levi, which Radek appears to have prepared by letting Levi read Thomas's reports. There were the rows in the Zentrale and the Central Committee between Levi and Mátyás Rákosi, just after the Livorno Congress of the Italian Communist Party in January 1921. After Levi departed, there were clashes between Kun and other German leaders.

Nonetheless, the ECCI did not unconditionally support its own people. In the end, both Rákosi and Kun were repudiated, the former by Radek, almost on the spot, and the latter by Lenin in person before the delegates to a Comintern Congress. Moreover, it is not clear that all the emissaries, (even if there were few people of value among the 'red émigrés'), shared the same conception of the relations between the KPD and the ECCI. Felix Wolf was close to Levi, and shared his criticisms of the ECCI. At the beginning of the Second Comintern Congress in 1920, did not Radek himself, the Secretary of the International, support the KPD in the KAPD affair, taking a position on that occasion opposed to the position of his own party in Russia? New conflicts broke out in 1921 between Friesland and Stasova, and in 1922 between Meyer and Kleine. But Stasova's job was as a specialist in organisation, rather than a political chief, whilst Kleine may have reported to Zinoviev, but was not his agent, and hardly played any determining role in elaborating Comintern policies, since, whilst he bullied the Zentrale into criticising itself, he found himself in a minority on the Central Committee. In 1923, Brandler was infuriated by the references of his left critics to Zinoviev's remark that a workers' government would be a synonym for the dictatorship of the proletariat; he replied from the platform: 'We do not have any lords and masters, and we are not bound by the personal opinions of comrade Zinoviev.'[9]

The advisers whom the ECCI sent during the preparation for the insurrection in 1923, Russian or not, restricted themselves to their role as technicians. The German Zentrale took the decisions on the spot, and the responsible German politico-military people were given the job of effectively leading the insurrection. It is true that the most important decisions to be reached, from early September, were reached in Moscow, but they do not appear to have been imposed on the German leadership, who accepted them, shared responsibility for them, and tried to apply them.

It was only from 1924 onwards, as a result of the factional struggle in the Russian Party and on the occasion of the defeat of the German Revolution, that these practices were to change, and that the Russian leaders, through the ECCI, were to decide that Brandler, Thalheimer and those whom they called the 'rightists' had to carry the responsibility for the fiasco. The practice of scapegoating was entering a new era.

In the period of 1919–23 with which we are concerned, the KPD was several times sharply criticised by Moscow for its political mistakes. It usually accepted

---

[9] *Bericht über die Verhandlungen des III (8) Parteitages der KPD*, op. cit., p. 373.

these criticisms, though not without having discussed them. But this discussion and political battle was not accompanied by a reshuffle of leaders. The nucleus remained, regardless of the mistakes it might have made; it drew new elements into itself at all times, such as those working-class cadres who came from the left Independents and to whose formation so much care had been devoted. The ECCI may have been severe in its criticisms, but, under the pressure of Lenin, it was very concerned at the same time to preserve the continuity of the leadership and the conception of the development of its responsible elements, of the formation of leaders, a process which must necessarily entail the making of mistakes and their subsequent correction. That was how it was done in Lenin's party. It was not to be the same under the regime of Bolshevisation, which was applied from 1924 under the iron rod of Ruth Fischer.

From Paul Levi in 1921 to Hermann Weber today, people have liked to underline the degree of material dependence of the KPD on the International, and through it, on the Russian Communist Party. Friesland, a year after the polemics at Halle in 1920, wrote on the banner of his opposition the slogan of 'material independence'. We do not have the documents necessary to put into figures the contribution of the ECCI to the budget of the German Party, and to evaluate the consequences and implications of this aid, and the relationship to which it gave rise. However, we cannot in any event deny that this aid continued for a long time. In 1919, Eberlein made a clear reference to it in his report at the Heidelberg Congress.[10] He said that it was limited, but it constituted a proof of international solidarity. The KPD had the right to receive help from the Russian Party. The duty of revolutionary organisations – including the SPD at one time – to help materially foreign activists and parties had always been recognised. There was no further questioning of this at following congresses, when to all appearances the ECCI's contributions were increasing.

In the pauperised conditions in Germany at this time, the dues, high as they were, levied on the activists, who lived on starvation wages or unemployment benefit, did not permit the development of self-financing Party activities. In 1923, even the SPD's coffers were empty. *Die Neue Zeit* disappeared, and the powerful metalworkers' union had to cancel its annual conference for lack of resources. In these conditions, the KPD could not on the basis of

---

[10] *Bericht über den 2 Parteitag der KPD*, op. cit., pp. 28–9.

its own resources have intervened as an organised force with the necessary means of propaganda and activity. Brandler was to point out later that, in 1923, the material help of the ECCI permitted the Party to maintain 27 daily papers, and to pay 200 full-time workers. With its own resources, the KPD could have maintained only four papers and barely a dozen employees.[11]

But, if legal activity is expensive, illegal activity is even more so. No German Communist contested the necessity for the illegal clandestine Party apparatus, the existence of which was required by the 'Twenty-One Conditions'. The Party was reduced to illegality for several months in 1919, in the weeks which followed the Reichswehr's revenge in the aftermath of the Kapp Putsch, immediately after the March Action in 1921, and again after November 1923. For all that, it did not cease to live and to act, and for that purpose premises were necessary, a reliable system of clandestine couriers, and clandestine print-works. A party which is preparing to take power needs an even more secret military apparatus, better concealed and therefore more expensive. The KPD needed information about the extremist organisations of the far Right and the Black Reichswehr, it needed to organise the purchase of arms, it needed to train specialists, it needed elementary military training for the members of armed groups, it needed to establish secret ways of crossing frontiers, to create secret networks, to organise the fabrication of false papers, and so on. These could be undertaken in the conditions of Germany at the time only with resources which a workers' party, even of several hundreds of thousands of members, was without doubt unable to collect for itself, even with a businessman of genius like Münzenberg, who was really to build up his 'trust' in quite a different economic period.

The real question here is not the amount of help the KPD received from the ECCI, nor whether it was absolutely necessary; the real question is whether this aid prevented the KPD from elaborating the necessary political strategy in Germany. From this point of view, no Communist demanded absolute 'independence' – not even Levi or Friesland, before they had finally decided to break from the KPD.

The lessons of the bankrupt nature of Social Democracy were clear to everyone; the victory of the revolution could be ensured only by a world party of socialist revolution. The Communist International was formed with precisely this type of party in mind. Levi was supported when he posed in

---

[11] Letter cited in Weber, op. cit., p. 308.

very restrained terms the question of the role and influence of the Russian Party in the International. It was not against the Russian comrades that the leaders raised their objections, but against the 'Turkestanis', less experienced, incompetent émigrés. Those who protested against the initiatives of Kun or Rákosi did not query the existence of the International, but only how it functioned.

The Second Comintern Congress tried to trace the general outlines of this functioning. The International was to be a world party, of which the parties in each country constituted only the national sections. Its functioning was to be governed by the rules of democratic centralism. This meant that its sovereign body was the Congress of Delegates elected by the different sections, meeting frequently, properly prepared, the decisions of which would take precedence over those of the Congresses or the Central Committees of national sections. In the interval between the meetings of Congresses, the powers of the Congress were entrusted to the ECCI – the equivalent of the Central Committees of the sections and of the German Zentrale – composed of members elected by the Congress in accordance with their abilities, and who ceased to be representatives of their parties and became those of the whole International.

The world party needed a world leadership, but this could only be developed and refined through its own participation in activities on a global scale. This ambitious programme, however, was never realised. It is true that Comintern Congresses met frequently, every year between 1919 and 1922. The Founding Congress lasted only four days – it was hardly more than a symbolic meeting – but the Second lasted 25 days, the Third 20 days, and the Fourth 31 days. They actually lasted much longer, because the official debates were preceded by introductions, preliminary discussions and meetings of commissions. The Congresses were the scene of many intense political disputes, and the most important decisions were made after such sharp debates, rather than being decided in advance.

Things were different, however, with the ECCI. Even if we overlook the Executive which was improvised at the end of the First Congress, it is clear that the Comintern never managed to put into operation a leadership which even remotely resembled the international leadership it required. The delegates to the Second Congress elected an Executive, and the choice of the Frenchman Rosmer, who was not even a member of the French Socialist Party, which was at its Tours Congress to join the International with a majority of its membership, indicates that they wanted to create an international leadership which would not be federal, and would in no way be a collection of figures representing each his own national party. This Executive included a German member, Ernst Meyer, a significant choice. Meyer was one of the old Spartacist nucleus, and was without doubt representative of the KPD(S). But he was not one of its most important leaders, there was nothing to suggest that he had the necessary qualities for a full leadership role in the International. The only German who could take on such responsibilities was Levi. No one – including Levi himself – thought for a moment of making him a permanent member of the ECCI. Everyone regarded his presence in Germany as vital for the construction of the KPD, and his election as substitute-member for Meyer was merely symbolic.

The greatest reservations about establishing a real Executive at the Second Comintern Congress were to be heard from the German Party and, more precisely, from Levi. He did not want foreign members to live in Moscow and work permanently on the ECCI. He suggested that it should meet once a quarter. This proposal was opposed by Zinoviev in a commission, and was finally defeated.[12] Immediately after Livorno, Levi and Zetkin raised questions about the functioning of the ECCI and its relations with the parties, and Radek also pleaded with the Zentrale to assume its responsibilities:

> Let us insist that the Executive has representatives, comrades experienced in European affairs, and we shall then have an Executive ten times more effective. . . . There is no choice. Either we say that we hush our consciences and only take them out from time to time to show them in public at Congresses, or we give up every kind of scepticism and send responsible comrades – it being understood that they should not stay too long and must be rapidly rotated, so that they are not cut off from their parties for too long. You must find people to send to Moscow.[13]

Levi's reply shows how far he saw the relations between the KPD and the ECCI from a purely diplomatic viewpoint. He proposed to instruct the German representatives on the ECCI 'not to engage in hard discussions'.[14] In February 1921, the ECCI responded to the wish of the German Zentrale, which had not supported Levi in his suspicious reserve. The ECCI voted to enlarge its

---

[12] *Bericht über die Verhandlungen des 2 (7) Parteitags der KPD*, op. cit., pp. 594–6.
[13] Levi Archives, P50/a5, reproduced in Drachkovich and Lazich, op. cit., p. 292.
[14] Ibid., pp. 293–4.

'small bureau', which soon became its Presidium. One representative after another from the KPD served on the ECCI and the Presidium for periods of about three months: Kurt Geyer, Wilhelm Koenen, Fritz Heckert, Frölich, Pieck in 1921, Walcher, Eberlein, Zetkin, Hoernle and Böttcher were to participate in this way, fully but for a short time, in the work of the leadership of the International. Brandler was also to sit on the ECCI and the Presidium from November 1921 to August 1922.

However, these stays in Moscow were to pose new problems. Did not Lenin demand that Maslow be sent, so that, as he said openly, he could 're-educate' him politically? And did this not raise cries of outrage amongst the German Left? The same intentions inspired the Zentrale's proposal in December 1921 to send Friesland to Moscow as a delegate. This was new; seen in this light, the ECCI ceased to be regarded as the leadership of the International and the framework in which its leaders were educated, and became a school for the re-education of Communist leaders whose political deviations made them, for the time being, undesirable.

Immediately after *Vorwärts* published its revelations about the March Action, Eberlein took refuge in Moscow to escape from the series of attacks he faced for his mistakes – and was coopted on to the ECCI! In the same period, the designation of Zetkin was now no more than of symbolic value, as she was already elderly and seriously ill. She was obliged to give up day-to-day activity, and really represented the past rather than the future of German and international Communism on the ECCI. Brandler, in the Presidium, was only nominally there in 1923. He went to Russia following his release from jail, but soon returned to Germany to carry out the functions of the Party's Chairman, which required his full-time attention. It was the same after the Fourth Comintern Congress. Stoecker, who was appointed to work in the Secretariat of the ECCI, did no more than pass through Moscow before returning to undertake the highest responsibilities in the occupied Ruhr.

In these conditions, there was no real international leadership. The ECCI elected at each Congress, each with its 'small bureau' or Presidium and its Secretariat, was perpetually being recast. The foreign leaders of legal parties were only passing visitors, unaccustomed to the day-to-day work. The institution of 'Enlarged Executive' Meetings aimed at correcting to some extent this disadvantage; they effectively assembled the principal leaders of the national sections two or three times a year around the nucleus of the ECCI. But even here the delegates were really no more than the representatives of their national sections, not the elected representatives of the International as a whole. The day-to-day work of the ECCI passed largely out of the control of its elected or coopted members in the foreign Communist Parties, and was taken over by a small group of specialists.

The Russian nucleus on the ECCI was very small. It is true that it included the big names of the Bolshevik Party, but the conditions in Soviet Russia at the time afforded them little time for the affairs of the International and the problems of the world revolution, crucial though they were. Zinoviev was President of the International, but he was also a member of the Political Bureau of the Russian Party and Chairman of the Petrograd Soviet. Trotsky devoted most of his time to the Red Army and to general problems, rather than to the International's sections, other than the French Party, which he supervised. Only Radek (who did not lack responsibilities in the Russian Party in the fields of education and publicity) devoted an important part of his activity to the International and the KPD.

Radek nonetheless combined this responsibility with that of being the semi-official representative of the Russian government to the German government at decisive moments, and a diplomatic function was hardly compatible with that of a revolutionary leader. Even before Lenin fell ill he experienced much difficulty in keeping himself informed about events in Germany, and did not conceal the gaps in his information. After 1922, he no longer played any role in the International. At the decisive moment, on the eve of the anti-fascist demonstration in July 1923 which the Prussian government banned, the reactions of the principal Russian leaders are significant. Trotsky had no opinion, because, as he said, his information was scanty; if Stalin had an opinion, he reluctantly showed that he was as badly informed about the particular situation as he was about Germany in general. The Bolshevik leaders returned from their holidays to the historic discussion on 23 August, but Brandler and his comrades had to wait for three weeks into September before they could begin the concrete preparations for the insurrection.

The day-to-day work of the ECCI actually rested on the shoulders of a small number of full-time functionaries who belonged to the Bolshevik Party – and the best elements of them were taken up until 1921, with the Civil War – and on the shoulders of exiles, the Hungarians Kun, Pogany and Rudniansky (the last of whom, it is said, vanished with military funds), the Bulgarians Dimitrov, Kabakchiev, Minev and then Kolarov, the Poles, and Kuusinen from Finland. Their experience was limited, not to say rudimentary, and many showed

distinct leftist tendencies. They knew little about the workers' movement of
Western Europe, and, on the other hand, were convinced of the superiority
of the Russian experience, with which they felt closely identified.

Between the Congresses, which were treated with great seriousness by the
leaders of the International, and which constituted a distillation of their
experience and knowledge, it was, therefore, a small nucleus of inexperienced
people, whom nothing had prepared for playing a role as international leaders,
who assumed the current tasks of the ECCI around Radek, a one-man band,
a journalist of great talent, and a sincere but erratic Communist. The evidence
of Geyer, when he was a member of the 'small bureau' in the period preceding
the March Action, enables us to conclude that Kun's mission to Berlin was
not even discussed, important as it was, within this highest committee. This
leads us to believe that, between Congresses, the International never functioned
as an proper international organisation with its own genuine existence, but
was always an appendage of the leadership of the Bolshevik Party.

Already in 1920, Levi had raised, on his return from Moscow, the problem
of the hegemony of the Russian Party within the International. This issue
was made all the more delicate by the fact that the leaders of the Russian
Party and the International were also the leaders of the Soviet state, and that
Communists considered that Russia was the revolutionary fortress which was
to be defended as the most sacred duty. But this hegemony was regarded by
all as both normal and transitory. Lenin himself said: 'Leadership in the
revolutionary proletarian International has passed for a time – for a short
time, it goes without saying – to the Russians, just as at various periods of
the nineteenth century it was in the hands of the British, then of the French,
then of the Germans.'[15]

Every Communist hailed the Russians for having been able to carry through
a revolution, seizing and wielding power. Their authority grew stronger as
years passed, and as the other Parties failed in their struggle for power in
their own countries. After Liebknecht and Luxemburg were killed, and after
Paul Levi left the movement, there was no person in the international
Communist movement, and in particular in Germany, comparable to the
Bolshevik leaders.

However, this does not imply that the German leaders merely tailed after

---

[15] V.I. Lenin, 'The Third International and Its Place in History', *Collected Works*,
Volume 29, op. cit., p. 311.

the Russians. The neo-leftists of 1921 defended their theses boldly. Meyer and Brandler did not hesitate to reject arguments based on the authority of such figures as Zinoviev. In April 1923, four German activists, Gerhard Eisler, Heinz Neumann, Hans Pfeiffer and Arthur Ewert, called for a more complete alignment of the KPD on the Russian Party; most probably because they saw in Bolshevism the way to achieve the greater effectiveness that they desired in their own party. But it was through this kind of reaction that, in the longer term, a real domination by the Russian apparatus was being prepared.

The fact remains that relations between the KPD and the Russian Party between 1919 and 1922 followed almost constantly the same pattern: a sharp conflict at the level of proposals made or initiatives taken by the Germans; a vigorous critique by the leaders of the ECCI; and then an intervention by Lenin, who while making some formal criticisms, judged the German initiative acceptable, and called for a discussion to be opened. Amongst the leaders of the International and the Russian Party, Lenin seems to have been the only one – always followed by or in agreement with Trotsky – to concern himself with understanding the German initiatives and problems, with seeking, not a compromise, but a synthesis, and with desperately fighting against splits in the KPD.

When Lenin was confronted by Levi in 1919 with the expulsion of the ultra-leftists from the KPD, he did his utmost, albeit unsuccessfully, to reconcile the KAPD with the International. In 1920, he supported the declaration of 'loyal opposition' and the position of the Zentrale in respect of the call for a workers' government, and unreservedly supported the polemic against the leftists, and the effort to win the left-wing Independents. He successfully undertook the defence of the *Open Letter* of 7 January 1921 against Bukharin and Zinoviev. He fought to keep Levi in the Party. By sheer force of moral authority, he imposed the Moscow compromise; he checked the leftists in their attack upon the 'centrists', and stopped Meyer from expelling them for their factional activity. Lenin was no longer on the scene from early 1923, and the KPD's factional struggles were then integrated with the internal quarrels in the Russian Party, of which they were simultaneously the reflection, the pretext and the excuse. No one in Germany, nor in the International, was able to play the role which Lenin had intermittently played, that of working ceaselessly to adapt the policy of the Party to economic, social and political realities, to homogenise its ranks, to educate its leading cadres, and to build it without stifling differences, in short, to help the graft to take.

In the history of the KPD between 1918 and 1923, only two men seem at certain moments to have been able to play the necessary role of theoretician and guide, of team-builder, of master and arbiter, which Lenin played in the International. The first was Levi, the Spartacist irregular, and the other was Radek, the Bolshevik irregular. The transfer of the moral authority of Levi to Radek was already significant of the difficulties encountered in the construction of the KPD's leadership, and of the close political dependence of the latter on Moscow, where Radek lived for most of the time, whilst Levi had only one short stay there in three years.

Chapter Forty-Five
Paul Levi: The Lost Opportunity?

Was Paul Levi a Communist? This question needed to be asked from the moment when he refused to take the hand which Lenin extended to him by way of his correspondence with Clara Zetkin.

Radek regarded Levi not as a Communist but as a bourgeois dilettante playing at revolution.[1] Trotsky compared him to Frossard and Serrati, as no more than one of the many left-wing Social Democrats who were caught up by the Russian Revolution and carried by the mass movement beyond their own limitations, but whom the ebb tide was to return to the fold.[2] Finally, the historian Richard Lowenthal regards Levi's adherence to Communism as a misunderstanding due to his ignorance of the reality of Russia; as a disciple of Luxemburg, he could believe himself to be a comrade-in-arms of the Bolsheviks only because he had never really understood what Bolshevism was.[3] This is also the essential opinion of the historians of the GDR, who, when we clear away the traditional epithets and insults of 'traitor' and 'renegade', regard him as no more than a 'class enemy' and a potential traitor, even when he was a leader of the KPD.[4]

---

[1] Radek, *Soll die Vereinigte KPD*, op. cit.
[2] L.D. Trotsky, 'Bilan d'une période', *Le Mouvement communiste en France (1919–1939)*, Paris, 1967, pp. 27–32; 'Trotzkis Brief', *Unser Weg (Sowjet)*, 15 February 1922, pp. 82–4; 'Preface to *The Communist Movement in France*', *The First Five Years of the Communist International*, Volume 2, op. cit., pp. 334–40.
[3] Lowenthal, op. cit.
[4] The commonest descriptions are 'right-wing opportunist' and 'renegade'. The

There are two witnesses against this opinion. There is Zetkin, who agreed with Levi, shared his reservations and his criticisms, and defended him tirelessly until he arrogantly rejected the compromise for which she had worked with her usual energy.[5] She remained a member of the KPD and the International until her death in Moscow in 1933, and at the moment when the first signs of triumphant Stalinism were appearing, continued to think and write that the opinions which Levi and she had defended during 1919–21 were within the framework of customary differences within the Communist movement.

The other opinion is that of Lenin himself. He wrote in August 1921, five months after Levi was expelled, about his attitude in 1916: 'At that time Levi was *already* a Bolshevik.'[6] As the years passed, we can even detect from the pen of Trotsky the beginning of a revision of his judgement of 1923, when he quoted the opinion of Lenin: 'The man has lost his head entirely. . . . He, at least, had something to lose: one can't even say that about *the others*.'[7]

Underlying Lowenthal's thesis is the notion, common to the majority of the Western historians who have tackled the subject, firstly, that Bolshevism was a specifically Russian, if not 'Asiatic', ideology and practice in the socialist movement, and that consequently a man of the education and Marxist culture of Levi could only have been able to regard himself as a Communist through a misunderstanding. However, the real target here is Luxemburg and, with her, the entire revolutionary wing of the German Social Democracy, which these historians attempt in this way to detach from the Bolshevik family.

Certain other historians, however, regard the development of socialism in its dialectical movement. They believe that the progress which Social Democracy made during the pre-1914 economic and social sphere explains both the development of bureaucratisation, with the tightening of the grip of the apparatus over the Party, and the emphasis which Luxemburg placed on the role of the spontaneity of the masses. They also believe that the uneven

---

volume devoted to 1919 in *Dokumente und Materialen zur Geschichte der Deutschen Arbeiterbewegung* does not once mention the name of the leader of the KPD at the time! Arnold Reisberg, whose *Lenin und die Aktionseinheit in Deutschland* does not deny the role of Radek in the history of the KPD, refers to 'the opportunist and treacherous policy' of Levi, who was soon 'to reveal himself as a renegade' (op. cit., p. 87).

[5] Zetkin, *Reminiscences of Lenin*, op. cit., bears the date 'end of January 1925' (p. 64).

[6] V.I. Lenin, 'A Letter to the German Communists', *Collected Works*, Volume 32, op. cit., p. 517.

[7] L.D. Trotsky, 'What Next?', *The Struggle Against Fascism in Germany*, Harmondsworth, 1975, p. 179.

development of Russian society, and the specific position of the workers' movement within the autocratic framework, explain why the Bolsheviks could find the formula which would enable the proletariat to wage a successful revolutionary struggle – and which would be all the more possible in the advanced countries – by placing the accent on the role of a tightly-knit, disciplined vanguard leading the movement of the masses. In that case, the differences between Lenin and Luxemburg appeared not as the expression of currents of irreconcilable ideas, but as two branches of the same revolutionary-socialist current. On this hypothesis, Levi's failure does not show that the Bolsheviks were congenitally unable, like their non-Russian comrades, to build a 'world party of the socialist revolution', but that the Russian Revolution was an ill-fated venture which nonetheless contains important lessons for the socialist movement.

We shall not omit to mention that there is a third position which often underlies this discussion. This is the doctrine that there is no salvation for the workers' movement without a mechanical submission to the instructions of the leaders of the Communist Parties, which themselves come down, in the last analysis, to those of the Russian Communist Party.

In order to answer the question which Levi's case raises, it is useful to recall the political conflicts which brought him into opposition to one or another committee or group of leaders of the International or the Bolshevik Party.

Levi first took his stand on a determined hostility to the ultra-left current which called on revolutionaries to abstain from voting in elections and to leave the trade unions. These positions appeared first at the Founding Congress of the KPD(S), then in the ranks of the ultra-left opposition, and from 1920 onwards in the KAPD. The way in which Levi carried on the struggle against the ultra-left was strongly criticised, particularly by Radek and Lenin. They both regretted that Levi provoked the split in the Party by expelling the opposition. After this, his analysis of the tempo of the German Revolution at the Heidelberg Congress brought him into sharp opposition with the viewpoint of such Russian leaders as Bukharin. Levi clashed with the same people immediately after the Kapp Putsch in 1920, when he supported the declaration of 'loyal opposition' which the KPD(S) made in response to the trade-union leaders' plans for a workers' government. That same year, he was the most outspoken of the German Communists in their unsuccessful protest against the admission into the International of the KAPD as a 'sympathising party'.

A whole series of disagreements revolved around the question of discipline. On the international scene, Levi denounced the role which the ECCI emissaries, the 'éminences grises', played in relation to the leaderships of the national sections. At the Italian Socialist Party Congress in Livorno, he was convinced that the role played by Rákosi and Kabakchiev was disastrous, but he respected discipline and remained silent. Yet he subsequently brought the discussion into the open before the Berlin activists, and then in the columns of *Die Rote Fahne*. He opposed Rákosi's pressure and his open intervention in the KPD's affairs, which he denounced as interference that was not justified by any decision of a regular body in the International. When put in a minority in the Zentrale in early 1921, he resigned his responsibilities. A few days later, he believed his duty as a Communist was to criticise publicly the March Action in his pamphlet *Unser Weg: wider den Putschismus*, for which he was expelled from the Party, a decision that was endorsed by the ECCI.

Further differences concerned the relationship between the Party and the working class as a whole. He challenged any mechanistic interpretation of this relationship, insisting that the Party should not issue orders to the working class like a general staff to its troops. The Party should guide, explain, point out the road, and suggest slogans. It should not attempt to command, and it had neither the right nor the ability to call on the workers to stage an armed uprising when the majority of the class did not think the situation demanded it.

Levi's final difference was perhaps the most decisive in the succession of events which led to his break with the International, and was the one that was most closely connected with what was happening at the time. Already in the summer of 1920, when the Bolsheviks were convinced that a pre-revolutionary situation was arising, Levi believed that the revolutionary wave in Europe had already passed, that capitalism had begun to revive, and, consequently, that the proletarian revolution was not on the immediate agenda. He told Lenin frankly that the arrival of the Red Army on the borders of Germany after a victorious campaign in Poland would be very unlikely to encourage the German workers to take up arms for 'the final conflict.' Moreover, he did not believe that the Polish workers would rise up against their own government. It was on the basis of this analysis that he proposed the strategy of the united front, which was based on the requirements of a defensive struggle and on the elementary aspirations of the workers, who were deeply distressed by the split in the socialist movement, and he supported the *Open*

Letter of January 1921, which was to be sharply criticised by the ECCI and within various Communist Parties.

These were differences which were perfectly normal and admissible in this period within Communist Parties and the International. It is true that on almost all these points, Levi clashed with the ECCI, or at least with its permanent nucleus, the small group of Russian leaders around Zinoviev and Bukharin, as well as with the leftists in Germany and in the Hungarian Communist Party. But it is interesting, and more significant, to compare Levi's positions with those of other leaders such as Lenin and Trotsky, for example, or even with those of Zinoviev and Bukharin in other circumstances. In that case, his opposition ceases to give the impression of having been systematic, and one can no longer see in it a principled opposition to Bolshevism.

None of the Bolsheviks, and Lenin least of all, shared the fundamental political orientation of the German ultra-leftists. Lenin's *'Left-Wing' Communism: An Infantile Disorder* illustrates and develops in a polemical style the arguments which Levi himself had advanced during and after the Second Congress of the KPD(S). In reality, the difference was about one precise point: whether at the time a split in the Party was the right way to settle this political problem. In the given conditions, Lenin opposed the idea of a split, whereas Levi carried it through. But no one in the International was to return directly to this question. Moreover, Lenin did not know the concrete conditions in Germany as well as Levi, and, from the viewpoint of Bolshevism, the success shown by the winning at Halle of the majority of the USPD to the Communist International, for which the credit was largely due to Levi, justified retrospectively his 'disruptive' action in 1919. When Zinoviev and Bukharin, as well as Kun, Maslow and others, violently criticised the declaration of 'loyal opposition' to a workers' government, Lenin, whilst regretting the incorrect formulation, made clear that it was 'quite correct both in its basic premise and its practical conclusions',[8] which corresponded exactly with Levi's position.

As far as discipline was concerned, Levi's behaviour in March 1921 was quite consistent with the spirit and letter of the statutes of the International and its parties, as well as with the practice of the Bolsheviks and of Communists throughout the world. Had not Zinoviev in 1917 and Bukharin in 1918

---

[8] V.I. Lenin, ' "Left-Wing" Communism: An Infantile Disorder', *Collected Works*, Volume 31, op. cit., p. 109.

polemicised, not only within the Bolshevik Party but publicly in its press and even outside it, against decisions which the Central Committee had reached in their presence, but with which they disagreed? Had not the Left Communists in 1918 announced that they no longer intended to recognise the authority of the Central Committee until a special congress on the question of the Brest-Litovsk Treaty had met? And did they encounter any disciplinary punishment? Levi had been criticised for opposing the emissaries of the Communist International, but was one not to see the French Communist Party demanding and getting the recall of delegates from the ECCI whom it declared to be unwelcome?

Even the publication of *Unser Weg* could not be regarded as an unusual and criminal action in the Communist movement of that period. Though the pamphlet did not attack the particular role of any individual leader, it certainly criticised the policy of the Party, but it did so *after* the March Action had taken place. In 1917, Zinoviev and Kamenev had denounced the October uprising *in advance*, in the Menshevik journal, *Novaia Zhizn*. This 'mistake' did not put them outside the Party, and they were removed only for a short time from positions of responsibility. On this point, Levi had a weighty argument. In 1920, the leaders of the Communist International themselves, and particularly Zinoviev, desired, against Levi's opposition, the publication in full of the letter he had written from prison condemning the actions of the leadership of the KPD(S) during the Kapp Putsch. In fact, on the question of discipline, Lenin expressed only one serious criticism of Levi; that when, in February, he resigned from the Chairmanship of the Party and the Zentrale, he abandoned his responsibilities at the head of the Party, and ceased to fight for his ideas at the post which the Congress had entrusted to him, in the name of a parliamentary conception of relations within the leadership.

The debates at the Third Comintern Congress helped to clarify the relationship between a Communist Party and the working class. It is clear that Levi had a conception which differed from the ideas expressed by the leftists, by Zinoviev and Bukharin, amongst others, who were silent at the Congress after being defeated politically in the Russian Party, as well by those who spoke, such as Terracini or Thalheimer. Lenin whipped them with language that allowed no confusion, as sharply as in his conversations with Zetkin. No, the Communists were not like Xerxes 'who had the sea scourged with chains'.[9] No! The Bolsheviks could never have been able to take power

---

[9] Zetkin, op. cit., p. 26.

if they had believed, like Terracini, who spoke, or like Rákosi, who remained silent, that a party-sect could lead to power masses whom they had not previously won over by their words and actions. These differences on Levi's part – not with the whole International, not with Bolshevik doctrine, not even with its current leadership, but with a conception which had inspired the ECCI for a few months, and which furthermore was merely that of a tendency around Zinoviev and Kun – he shared with Lenin and Trotsky themselves.

There is no doubt that the most important difference concerned the possibilities of revolution in 1920. In the summer of that year, Levi was perhaps the only Communist leader in the world to have formed the opinion that the postwar revolutionary wave had ended. But the leaders of the International soon came, one after another, to the same conclusion. The first was Radek, who refused to share the illusions of Lenin about revolutionary prospects in Poland.[10] Lenin had come to understand the realities of the situation by November that year, and Trotsky and Kamenev soon followed. The last people to understand that the situation had changed were the leaders of the International, Zinoviev and his immediate collaborators – a group whom Radek called the 'South-Eastern Tendency', who gave up their optimistic view only after the debates in the Russian Political Bureau between March and August 1921.

We should stand up for him. Levi was not expelled because he was a 'deviationist', as Annie Kriegel writes.[11] He was expelled for breaching discipline when he published *Unser Weg*. This measure of expulsion was not a disguised condemnation of some deviation – a 'Luxemburgist' conception of the party, or of the relations between party and masses – because Levi defended the same conception that Lenin was successfully to promote at the Third Comintern Congress. Lenin spoke the truth when he told Zetkin that the 'Levites' left Moscow with a great political victory. Levi had been essentially right, not least against Lenin, who freely admitted it. Lenin criticised him only on the grounds that he had not fought sufficiently strongly for his ideas, that he had deserted his post when he resigned as Party Chairman, and above all, that he had infringed discipline through breaking the solidarity of the Party when he published his pamphlet. That was the reason for his exclusion – 'Disziplinbruch' – breach of discipline.

---

[10] Ibid., p. 18.
[11] She adds: 'He was then expelled for an opportunist deviation.' (Humbert-Droz, op. cit., footnote, p. 103.)

Sometimes another explanation is advanced, namely, that the political differences which Levi expressed could certainly not justify his expulsion, but it was necessary precisely because he was correct against the Russian leaders of the International. The breach of discipline immediately after the March Action is then seen as simply providing the pretext for getting rid of a man whose intelligence and independence of mind made him dangerous.

Every witness agrees that Levi's personality was never completely acceptable to the Communists in Germany and Russia, or to the foreign Communists who came into contact with him. Levi was from the upper bourgeoisie, and remained there in his lifestyle. His taste for collecting *objets d'art* upset the professional revolutionaries as much as his successes with women in the smart set. This explains Radek's charge of his being a dilettante, as he never ceased to practice as a lawyer, and always maintained an extra-Party personal life.

Levi was an intellectual, a highly-cultured man with a lively intelligence, and he knew it. Radek reproached him for his arrogance, his supercilious behaviour, and the distance at which he held worker comrades. Alfred Rosmer, who would be least likely to be suspected of wanting to justify at all costs the decisions of Moscow, bears witness in the same sense. To the arrogance of a German intellectual, Levi added that of a Social Democrat, aware of having been educated in the best of schools; he spoke with a certain disdain about the backwoodsmen whom he had to meet at the Second Comintern Congress, those Spanish anarchists or anarcho-syndicalists half-a-century behind. It was not by accident that people such as Heckert and Thaelmann demonstrated a sour hostility at the Third Comintern Congress when the man who earlier had been 'Comrade Levi' was classically referred to as 'Herr Doktor'. Lenin and Trotsky felt the same, the former when he condemned Levi's 'certain coolness in his attitude to the workers',[12] and Trotsky when he spoke of his 'egocentricity'.[13]

Finally, let us note a remark by Radek in his indictment of Levi. It was despite himself that Levi became a Communist leader. He had to be begged to accept the leadership of the KPD(S) after Luxemburg and Liebknecht were murdered. Later on, he would take any opportunity to try to get away. In

---

[12] Zetkin, op. cit., p. 27.

[13] *Die Rote Fahne*, 13 January 1922, cited by Levi, 'Trotskis Brief', *Unser Weg (Sowjet)*, 15 February 1922, pp. 82–4, Levi Archives H 3/4.

April 1920, following the Kapp Putsch, he only agreed to retain his functions because he could not deny that his presence was important when the Party had so badly blundered, but he himself fixed a time-limit, that of winning the left wing of the USPD, which he willingly admitted was a venture he could manage better than anyone else. Afterwards, at the Fusion Congress, he again announced that he intended to withdraw, and agreed not to do so only because those who had joined from the USPD demanded that he remain, as they saw in him a guarantee of the sincerity of the fusion. Was this just the affectation of a man who liked being persuaded? Radek did not think so. He saw in Levi a man who could not totally devote himself to the working class and the socialist revolution, and who knew that in the end he would not be able to be loyal to them.

This aspect of Levi's personality was one which he confirmed in circumstances which Radek could not mention, particularly during the struggles within the International itself. During the Second Congress, in the summer of 1920 when the delegates believed that they were meeting in Moscow for the last time, as the centre of the revolution would soon be in the West, Levi remained silent, and only spoke when Lenin put a question to him. He did not carry through his criticisms of the amendment which Lenin moved to Russian Party's the theses on the structure of the International. He claimed that any problems were merely a matter of drafting, and he accepted the 'Twenty-One Conditions' without hesitation. Yet, he was one of the very few who could foresee the dangers inherent in them, and he understood that they were destined to 'Bolshevise', by summary and forceful means, parties which were still heavily under the influence of Social Democracy, with the perspective of imminent revolution, a prospect which he considered to be most unlikely. He confined himself to formulating a few reservations in the commission and then in the plenary session. But he did not fight for his ideas, he merely took note, just as later he did not prevent Rákosi from executing the Italian Socialist Party by applying to it the 'Twenty-One Conditions'.

How can we fail to be tempted to follow Lenin when he accused Levi of 'abandoning his post' in February 1921, leaving the field clear for leaders whose conceptions he believed to be dangerous alike for the KPD and the International? How are we to understand that he could leave the commanding positions in the KPD to people who had just revealed their political weakness by bowing without discussion to the demands of the likes of Rákosi? Would the March adventure have been possible if Levi had still been at the head of the KPD, or if it had been he and Däumig, instead of Brandler and Stoecker, who received Kun and his lieutenants a few days later?

Levi knew that Kun was in Berlin, and he knew his dangerous impulses and political ineptness. Why, in these conditions, did he travel to Italy, breaking his journey when he received the news from Berlin, but placing himself far from the centres of decision at an essential time? We are tempted to think that Levi, in early 1921, before the March Action, had already decided to draw back from being a leader of the International, and wished to become an intelligent, ironic commentator, a role which history ultimately denied him. To be sure, Lenin had several times declared that he was ready to resign his leading responsibilities, but this was to fight amongst the Party's rank and file, not to go on his travels.

This, no doubt, was the real reason for Lenin's attitude to Levi. Lenin was preoccupied above all else at this time with constructing the International and parties worthy of the name of Communist. The indiscipline of Zinoviev in 1917, and of Bukharin in 1918, had certainly placed the unity of the Party in jeopardy for a while, but the danger vanished when the orientation which they had opposed proved to be successful. Despite their seriousness and the fact that they had occurred quite recently, these differences lay in the past and no longer presented problems to the Russian comrades. But Lenin judged differently the situation in the KPD in 1921. In Lenin's opinion, Levi was guilty of 'lacking the spirit of solidarity with the party': he 'tore the party to pieces'.[14]

The March Action itself, as much as its defeat, had been a hard experience for the German Communists. From one day to the next, the Party had asked them, in the name of Communist discipline, to hurl themselves into an action which they suspected of being unprepared, putting themselves in danger of repression, with most of them losing their jobs, and some of them spending years in a prison or fortress. Many of them – perhaps two out of every three – had wavered. Those who had stood firm were aware both of the extent of the disaster and of the need to believe that, despite everything, they had conducted themselves well, and done their duty as Communists. Hence the new outburst of leftism amongst the majority of the leaders and activists in the weeks which followed the March Action, and hence the

---

[14] Zetkin, op. cit., p. 27.

common insistence on discipline, which was the only possible justification for their having obeyed initiatives that had proved to be disastrous.

Levi was denouncing 'putschism', 'adventurism' and 'leftism' at the very moment when the Social Democrats and other anti-Communists were taking up the same refrain, and when repression was severe. In the eyes of the unfortunate March fighters, he personified the 'scab', breaker of action and of discipline. Coming from a leader who of his own accord had abandoned his responsibilities a few weeks earlier, this attitude must have seemed still more unpardonable. Since he had not fought with all his strength to prevent the March Action, his subsequent denunciation of it seemed to be that of a renegade who was satisfied to see events confirm his worst forecast.

But Lenin's severity had no doubt still deeper causes. In that year, 1921, not only was the unity and the very existence of the recently-formed VKPD at stake, but those of the entire Communist movement. The turn of 1921 was the first radical turn in the International since it was established. It had been formed in the wake of the postwar revolutionary wave. It had recruited its fighters from activists who were convinced that the revolution would be the work of their time and their generation. This was even more true for the members of the International's apparatus. Limited as Kun might have been, he had the excuse that he had not been prepared for the stabilisation of capitalism, which anyway was barely perceptible in 1920. He had been a prisoner of war in 1917, and Chairman of the Council of People's Commissars in Hungary two years later; he had experienced defeat after victory, exile, and then the Civil War as a political commissar, and its aftermath in starving Turkestan. How could he have conceived, when he arrived in Berlin as the envoy of the ECCI, that this heroic period had ended? In fact, the Communists had been swimming for a year against the stream, struggling with the reality of the new conditions, with the resolutions of the Second Comintern Congress in their hands. Both Lenin and Trotsky judged that it was impossible to get the delegates to the Third Congress to admit that they, their parties and the International as a whole had been mistaken in their perspective of an early conquest of power. Nor did they think it possible to persuade the delegates to the Third Congress to admit that Levi – who had broken solidarity with their struggle and sufferings – had been right, completely alone, against the Party and the International. Lenin explained this clearly to Zetkin, saying that Levi's attitude had to be condemned, in order to prevent those who had opposed him, and had remained loyal to their party in the worst moments, from sinking into despair.

The terms in which the problem confronted the Russian Communist Party were hardly different. Even though it was accepted, the New Economic Policy aroused much opposition and anxiety. Did not people talk about 'a return to capitalism'? The concessions to the peasants, coming after the condemnation of the Workers' Opposition, did not reassure the activists, who themselves were steeped in the conviction that the Russian Revolution would be either worldwide or doomed to failure. Without doubt, it is incorrect to say, as Heckert implied, that the March insurrection could be explained as an attempt to compensate for Kronstadt.[15]

However, the hypothesis which holds that the March Action may have resulted from Zinoviev's desperate attempts to spark the world revolution, and thus enable Russia to avoid the necessity of the NEP, is far from improbable. Trotsky says that the compromise on the international situation had only been won in the Russian Party after much manoeuvring and arguing in corridors. Kamenev was coopted to the Political Bureau when he had been secretly won to Lenin's point of view. The bloc of Lenin, Trotsky and Kamenev made it possible for Zinoviev's group to be defeated, and a series of concessions to be won from Radek, whom Zinoviev was to accuse of having 'betrayed' him. However, although the Russians decided that a compromise was necessary, it could not be reached at the expense of principles, nor at that of condemning the theory of the offensive. But that was what would have happened if they had exonerated Levi. No one in the Russian Party could have thought of doing so – Bukharin and Zinoviev, who had been defeated, no more than Lenin and Trotsky, who presented themselves as arbitrators.

Levi had initially sought Lenin's support, and seems to have been unable to understood the basis for his altitude. Certainly, it would be unjust to accept unreservedly the picture of Levi which Radek and other contemporaries presented. First of all, after Levi was expelled, he never ceased to be a socialist or to attract the hatred of the bourgeoisie. This proves that, whilst he did not sacrifice his personal tastes for the sake of militant activity, he did not sacrifice militant activity – less rewarding as it may have been after he broke with the Communists – to his personal tastes. Besides, it cannot be disputed that he

---

[15] According to Carr (*The Bolshevik Revolution*, Volume 3, op. cit., p. 335, n. 2), Heckert voiced this interpretation of the March Action at the All-Russian Congress of Trade Unions in May 1921. Flechtheim (op. cit., p. 73) was later to develop the thesis that there was a link between the Kronstadt insurrection and the March Action, but this does not stand up to a careful study of the dates.

knew how to attract and retain the confidence of worker activists of great value, such as Malzahn, Neumann and Franken, whom Lenin admired, and who he said were 'the steady, well-organised fighting rank and file of the revolutionary proletariat'.[16] An amateur does not get results like that!

But, for the rest, when Levi rejected Lenin's proposals which Zetkin passed on to him, when he refused to silence his personal pride as the price for recognition of a political victory, which should be infinitely more important to a Communist, he seemed to have demonstrated convincingly that he himself no longer believed in the ideas which he had defended against Zinoviev and the others since 1920, or in rectifying the International. Had he suddenly come to feel himself to be a foreign body in the Communist movement, under the pressure of the clamour and the denunciations? However that may be, if Levi had really been a Communist, a Bolshevik, as Lenin said, he had ceased to be one or – what may come to the same thing – to regard himself as one, during 1921.

After he had 'lost his head' in this sense, this remarkably lucid man was thereafter to accumulate mistakes of judgement and make incorrect forecasts. He said that the 'leftists' would eliminate Lenin and Trotsky and that the 'Bakuninists' would take over the leadership of the KPD, which would then be incapable of ever applying the tactic of the united front.

The fact remains that, during 1918–21, Levi was the only Communist leader outside Russia whose intransigent character and political penetration made him an interlocutor who could discuss with the Russian leaders on an equal basis, and that no one was able to fill the gap once he was expelled. He was the only person who posed in political terms the problem of Communism immediately after the victory of the revolution in Russia, how to graft onto the old solidly and deeply rooted tree of the Western workers' movement the living graft of the revolutionary advance of 1917 and of conciliar power. There was to be no one after him to face the Russians but plagiarists and parrots, as he put it, apart from those who hesitated and remained silent, resigned in advance to being condemned as wrong.

The personal adventure of Levi in 1921 symbolised in this way the first setback suffered by the Communist International, and was an integral part of it. The Comintern was unable to achieve its ambition of becoming the 'world party of the socialist revolution'. The Bolsheviks were unable to bring

---

[16] Zetkin, op. cit., p. 30.

about in the West, in this short space of time, the creation of Communist Parties which could pursue in a conscious and systematically organised way the aim of the seizure of state power by the proletariat, of revolutionary organisations which would not be pale transpositions of the Russian model, but parties that were as deeply rooted in the social reality and traditions of struggle and thought in their respective countries as the Bolshevik Party was in Russia.

Communism in 1918–21 was a living organism in which were many shades of difference. Levi was the living expression of a German colouration. People who try to counterpose Levi to Communism in this period forget that history has seen the cohabitation of the Social Democracy of Bebel and that of Ebert, the thought of Lenin and 'Leninism', Leninism and Stalinism, Luxemburg and 'Luxemburgism'. Such a perspective would mean depriving Levi of his real historic dimension, that of a missed opportunity.

Chapter Forty-Six
Karl Radek: The Confusion of Styles?

Karl Radek was a unique character in the history of the Communist movement, and is a key figure for anyone wishing to study the first years of the Communist International. Despite being a prolific writer, today he is almost forgotten, but during the years following the Russian Revolution he was one of the most important leaders in the International, and was effectively its Secretary for some months between his release from prison in Germany and the Second Comintern Congress. Moreover, he was the mentor of the KPD until 1923, and was appointed by the ECCI to deal with 'German questions' in the same way that Trotsky was assigned 'French questions'. Recent studies by H. Schurer and Warren Lerner have perhaps opened the way for works devoted to him, and we must now hope that the numerous 'Radek' files in East Germany and the Soviet Union, access to which was refused to us, will be opened.

The best portrait of him is without doubt that from the brush of the German journalist Wilhelm Herzog in 1920:

> Karl Radek . . . has been elected secretary of the Third Communist International. His lively and ever-active mind is feverishly at work. His brain, filled with German romanticism (and a touch of Polish Judaism), is rich in irony and energy. Every day he writes two editorials, one for *Pravda* and one for *Izvestia*, and often another text as well,

which is transmitted by radio from Christiania. Every day, he is visited by a dozen delegates from other parts of the world. He advises and instructs. He presides at the meetings of the Third International, and takes part in the conferences of the Executive Committee, of the Central Committee of the Party and of numerous other bodies. He lectures at the Workers' University and to the officers of the Red Army. He speaks at meetings and at congresses of the central and local Soviets. All this without ever being superficial or unreflective, but after solid preparation, as a very competent man, very serious but never lacking wit. He masters his problem, lays hold of it, explains it and analyses it. It is a feast to listen to him. He overflows with ideas and with a rare knowledge of men and things. He knows every date, every leader and even every individual of any importance in the workers' movement throughout the world. Hence an immense historical culture and a very clear knowledge of world political relations.

He has a sparkling style. Although, to be sure, he does not command Russian as if it were his native language, we admire his articles for their clarity and their striking imagery. His quicksilver mind reacts to all the concerns of human life, political and intellectual. In short, he is an exceptionally talented man, a born propagandist and an agitator whom nothing can restrain or stop. He knows no compromise when the problem is to influence the hostile or the still-indifferent world, to infect it and to impregnate it with the idea of the world revolution. With Bukharin, Osinsky and others, he belongs to the younger generation of the Bolsheviks (that is, of the revolutionary Marxists). This extraordinary strategist of the class war, this dreaded terrorist, loves German literature; he knows Goethe, Heine, Kleist, Friedrich von Gentz and the romantics, Büchner and Grabbe, he loves Conrad Ferdinand Meyer, and quotes verses from Stefan Georg and Hugo von Hofmannsthal.[1]

This is a flattering portrait, but no doubt a truthful one, though perhaps it should be slightly filled out with a reference to his physical ugliness and his neglect of his dress. Count Kessler describes him as 'something between Puck and Wolf, a bit of a street Arab . . . Mephisto'. 'A cross between a professor and a bandit', wrote the British spy-cum-diplomat, Bruce Lockhart. The man was attractive for his wit, the liveliness of his repartee, the sharp sense of

---

[1] W. Herzog, 'Russisches Notizbuch', *Das Forum*, no. 11, August 1920, pp. 805–7.

humour which he never forgot to use at his own expense, the breadth of his culture and intellectual curiosity, and in short, despite the aggressiveness of his manner of speaking, his graciousness, sensitivity and an undeniable vulnerability.

First and foremost, Radek was a freelancer. He had his own distinct personality when he appeared in the German Social-Democratic movement. In fact, he had had some revolutionary experience, in a period when the leaders of the German Party had nothing in this field but what they had read about the Paris Commune or the revolutions of 1848. But Radek had hardly emigrated before he returned to Poland at the beginning of the upheavals in 1905, and had replaced Leo Jogiches before he was twenty years old as chief editor of the newspaper of the Polish Social Democrats. He then had experience of prison. He later settled in Germany, and won a reputation as a polemicist and theoretician by his attacks on Kautsky at the Copenhagen Congress of the Second International and in *Die Neue Zeit*. He specialised in studies of imperialism, and devoted himself to demonstrating that inter-imperialist rivalries would lead to a world war. He based upon this perspective his theory of world revolution – a theme dear to the Bolsheviks, but not familiar to the members of the SPD. His talent won him fame as a journalist, but he remained isolated in Germany, and increased his isolation still more by supporting the opposition in the Warsaw committee of the SDKPiL against Luxemburg and Jogiches.

He paid for both his celebrity and his isolation in what became known as the 'Radek affair'. He had committed the imprudence of attacking both the SPD's apparatus and its Southern revisionists. In 1912, Bebel launched a ferocious attack on him at the Chemnitz Congress, and the support of the Poles made possible his expulsion from both the SPD and the Polish Party in the following year on charges concerning his personal behaviour. He resisted courageously, did not hesitate to move to Berlin in order the better to defend himself, and published his defence with the help of a handful of friends. The international commission of enquiry, the so-called 'Paris commission', cleared him, and in the course of the affair he won the support of Lenin and Liebknecht as well as that of Trotsky. But the First World War prevented his trial from being properly reviewed, and, as Schurer notes, he remained 'a marked man for the majority of the German socialists'.[2]

---

[2] H. Schurer, 'Radek and the German Revolution', Part 1, *Survey*, no. 53, October 1964, p. 62.

There was no place for him in 1914 in Germany, where the internationalist nucleus was made up of his worst adversaries. He emigrated to Switzerland, deeply discouraged, and disappointed Trotsky, who had great hopes for him:

> I hoped to find in him one who shared my views. . . . But I was surprised
> to learn from our conversations that he never conceded the possibility of a
> proletarian revolution in connection with the war, and, generally speaking,
> in the near future. 'No', he replied, 'for this the productive forces of mankind,
> taken as a whole, are not sufficiently developed.'[3]

Radek soon, however, recovered his bearings in the milieu of the émigré internationalists, and attracted the attention of Lenin, who hoped to make contact with the German internationalists through him. He urged him to work on the international journal which he hoped would act as the focus for an international regroupment. At Zimmerwald, Radek sided with the minority; but the Germans refused to put their signature alongside his. At Berne, Zetkin became violently angry when she realised that he was there.[4] Without question, he was still in quarantine.

Although he was close to the Bolsheviks, Radek nonetheless distanced himself from Lenin, who attacked him in strong terms for his 'spirit of intrigue', and even for his 'vileness'. He polemicised with Lenin on the question of the right of nations to self-determination, and condemned the Easter Rising of 1916 in Ireland. At the same time, on German issues, he defended the necessity for a split in Social Democracy, and for the revolutionaries to be independently organised. Through Radek's articles in *Arbeiterpolitik*, Lenin's themes on the treachery of the labour aristocracy, the necessity for a split in Social Democracy, and the transformation of the imperialist conflict into a civil war, made their way into the German far Left. A Spartacist delegate quoted from him at the Foundation Congress of the USPD, and provoked a lively response from the gathering. Radek was still in a certain sense an outlaw in the German movement, but his isolation was gradually breaking down.

The Russian Revolution of 1917 sharply changed his standing. He left on the same train as Lenin, but was refused admission into Russia. He settled in Stockholm, organising the Bolsheviks' international links, and directing propaganda into Germany. He arrived at Petrograd on the day following the

---

[3] Trotsky, *My Life*, op. cit., p. 246.
[4] Schurer, op. cit., p. 63.

uprising, and was at once recognised as an authentic Bolshevik. As Vice-Commissar for Foreign Affairs, he was at Brest-Litovsk confronting the German diplomats and generals, and organised both the distribution of Bolshevik propaganda amongst the prisoners of war and fraternisation at the front. His attention was always turned towards Germany, and when he was refused recognition as the official representative of the Soviet régime, he crossed the frontier illegally and arrived in Berlin in early December 1918 as the representative of the Bolshevik Party.

We have seen how Radek's reactions were strongly influenced by the Russian experience, and noted the positions which he adopted in the first phase of the German Revolution. A powerless spectator in the course of it, he was convinced that the Bolshevik school was superior. He was arrested and could have feared for his life for a few weeks, but he stood his ground throughout his interrogation. Then his situation changed; he became a prisoner of distinction, his cell became a political salon, and he received political figures, generals and business chiefs, everyone who saw him as a semi-official representative of the Russian government, and who wanted to seek information or to influence him. The bohemian outlaw showed himself to be an able diplomat, able to charm or impress the people with whom he talked, and who was beginning to think in terms of high foreign policy, to see the possibilities of alliances, and to impose himself as an *éminence grise*.

For all that, Radek did not for a moment lose sight of the problems of the KPD, which he had seen being born and then losing its leadership role within a few days. It was especially Levi whom he attempted to convince of the need to win the masses, to turn away from infantile leftism, to work in the trade unions, and to use the opportunities provided by electoral and parliamentary platforms. His writings from 1919 brought together the arguments of a polemic against the 'infantile disorder' of leftism, and Lenin was to add nothing essential to it. Radek agreed with Levi on general perspectives and on the line of the Heidelberg theses, which perhaps he helped to draft, but nonetheless distrusted him, and criticised him sharply for having organised a split in the new Party, and also for attacking the Communists in Hungary and Bavaria from a standpoint which he believed to be opportunist.

When he returned to Russia, he became the Secretary of the International, and took principal responsibility for German issues. He demonstrated his independence at the Second Comintern Congress when he supported the KPD(S) against the ECCI and the Russian Party on the matter of the invitation to the KAPD to attend. This show of independence – he regarded himself as responsible to the International, and not to his own party – caused the Russians to remove him from his post as Secretary. At the same time, the summer of 1920, he was one of the rare Communist leaders who did not share Lenin's optimism about the revolutionary perspectives in Poland and Germany. Lenin later said: 'Radek predicted how it would turn out. He warned us. I was very angry with him, and accused him of "defeatism". But he was right in his main contention.'[5]

As far as Germany was concerned, Radek was very reserved in his opinion of the KPD's leaders. He was one of the sharpest critics of the attitude of the Zentrale after the Kapp Putsch, violently condemned the declaration of 'loyal opposition', and polemicised directly or via Frölich against Levi throughout the year. He was at first hostile to establishing closer relations with the left Independents, but came around clearly to the idea, and supported Levi on this issue. At the same time, he seems to have intrigued in order to find amongst the leaders of the left Independents, if not in the Zentrale itself, supporters or counterweights to what he regarded as Levi's harmful influence. He opposed Levi at the Unification Conference, but joined with him in drafting the *Open Letter*, which caused him to be attacked by Zinoviev, Bukharin and Kun, and he developed his critique of leftism by elaborating the theory of the proletarian united front.

It becomes difficult to understand Radek's political aims after February 1921. He was sharply opposed to the leftist and divisive initiatives of the delegates of the ECCI to Livorno, but was appalled by the behaviour of Levi, when he allowed himself to be removed from the Party leadership, opening the way for his worst leftist opponents. On the eve of the March Action, he engaged himself from Moscow in 'activating' the Party, but cautiously criticised the form which 'activation' took – the March Action inspired by Kun – as soon as he heard about it.

In the confusion which prevailed for some months in the leadership of the Russian Communist Party and the International, Radek seemed rather to take the side of the Russian leftists – for which Lenin was to reproach him – but a little to the right of Zinoviev, who was to reproach him for having sold out in the compromise which was concluded on the eve of the Third Comintern

---

[5] Zetkin, op. cit., p. 18.

Congress with Lenin and Trotsky – whereas Lenin then reproached him for having leaned 'too far to the left'. His hesitations can be observed between the Conference of the Russian Party and the Third Comintern Congress itself, at which, finally, it was his behaviour that facilitated the leftist counter-offensive in the amendments presented by Thalheimer and Terracini.

After the Third Comintern Congress, Radek seemed to be one of those in Moscow who wanted to restart the war against the centrists, and Lenin reproached him for a public attack on Zetkin. He furiously attacked Levi and then Friesland in terms akin to those used by the Berlin Left. In fact, from February 1921, his attitude was to be in contradiction with his recognised political temperament, his appreciation of the international situation, and his pessimism about the tempo of the world revolution. He was a resolute opponent of the leftists, but seems suddenly to have joined them, though only to support them half-way. Can we explain this turn by the anxieties which the explosive international situation caused, the threatening danger of war which he perceived, as his letters to the Zentrale suggest? Did he only want to avoid a conflict with Zinoviev, who clearly was strengthened by the unlimited support of Lenin? Did he merely think it possible and convenient to take advantage of the circumstance to get rid of Levi, whom he regarded as unreliable, without rejecting his line? For the present, we must accept that we cannot clear up the mystery of this period, which indeed shows him open to the charge of being erratic, if not opportunist. In any case, it is hard to agree with Schurer when he sees a 'new Radek' emerge at the end of 1921. It was only the resurgence of the old Radek, after six months' confusion, faithful to his earlier analyses about the slow revolutionary tempo in the West, the need to construct a party patiently by winning the masses, and to struggle unceasingly to build the workers' united front by fighting around economic demands and 'transitional' slogans.

The year of 1922 saw him playing a particularly important role on the diplomatic scene on behalf of the Soviet government, in discussions with General von Seeckt and the diplomat von Malzan, which led to the Rapallo Treaty being concluded. Radek was the real if unofficial representative of the Kremlin in Germany, and in certain respects he identified himself with a foreign policy with which the International did not concur. Within the International, he was one of those who devoted themselves, within the framework of the strategy of the workers' united front, to discovering revolutionary 'new roads', transitional slogans such as the workers' government, of which he was, if not the father, at least the godfather. Unlike Zinoviev, he attached great importance to the victory of fascism in Italy, and drew from it conclusions, which were to emerge openly in 1923, about how the proletariat should act when it was confronted concretely for a whole historical period with the alternative of socialism or fascism, the modern translation of Marx's alternative of socialism or barbarism. Contrary to what Schurer thinks, the perspectives which Radek developed in 1923 were in no way an abandonment of his analyses of the role of the labour aristocracy as an agency of the bourgeoisie in the workers' movement. In Radek's opinion, it was precisely in that year and in Germany that the economic crisis destroyed the very foundation of the labour aristocracy and equalised the workers' living conditions by driving them down, making it possible for the class to be reunified under the banner of Communism.

We have also pointed out the erroneous nature of the traditional interpretation of Radek's 'Schlageter line'. This has been interpreted as an attempt to revive 'national Bolshevism', or even, as Schurer writes, as proof of 'the new interest in nationalism as a potential revolutionary factor'.[6] The concern of Radek, who believed that the majority of the working class had been virtually won over to Communism, was to deprive counter-revolutionary nationalism, Nazism, of its mass base in the petty-bourgeoisie, who had been driven mad by the economic and social crisis and national humiliation. Schlageter, who was fighting on the side of the counter-revolution, deserved the admiration of the revolutionaries for his courage and spirit of sacrifice, but he was only, as Radek said, 'the wanderer into the void', whilst the Communists held the keys to the future.

However, a new contradiction in Radek's political behaviour appeared in the course of 1923. Right up to the unofficial strike which swept away the Cuno government, he firmly opposed all the impatience and the leftist impulses within the KPD, and assumed almost alone the responsibility for refusing to defy the ban on street demonstrations on 29 July. He then appears to have moved without discussion to supporting Trotsky's opinion that the uprising had to be prepared, and himself put forward the proposal at the Political Bureau on 23 August. On this point, however, in the present state of the documentation, we must decline to give a precise answer. Was Trotsky's personal influence sufficient to convince him of the need to make a turn

---

[6] H. Schurer, 'Radek and the German Revolution', Part 2, *Survey*, no. 55, April 1965, p. 135.

because the situation had changed? Did he agree, in the light of his earlier experiences, to change an opinion which had not been formed on the spot? Did he, as perhaps in 1921, keep silent about his real convictions and suppress his own impulses, for lack of assurance or confidence in his own judgement, or, on the contrary, through opportunism, in order to follow the dominant current at the top? Did he really, as Schurer suggests, act and speak against his own convictions which he knew to be sound?

This problem cannot be tackled if we do not take into account the fact that the German leaders – especially Brandler – shared the same attitude, remaining silent about their reservations, and sometimes even obligingly feeding the illusions of their comrades. This is what Radek suggested when he said at the ECCI that the fundamental problem was that the KPD was 'an excellent workers' party', but was not yet a Communist Party, that the turn in August had been made too late, and that the German Communists had not grasped the depth of passivity into which the collapse of Social Democracy had dragged the mass of the working class.

Radek was not at Chemnitz when they decided to cancel the uprising. But he subsequently approved the decision, accepting his full responsibilities, as Brandler demanded from him. This time, he did not try to evade the clash with his comrades on the ECCI and with the leaders of the Russian Party, but, on the contrary, deliberately provoked it. He defended himself step by step, with great firmness, before the enlarged ECCI at which he featured as the accused. It was only at the last moment and, as he said, out of respect for tradition, that he gave way and supported the resolution which made Brandler and himself the scapegoats for the defeats in 1923.

Radek's intellectual gifts cannot be denied, nor can his courage in the face of the ruling class, in prison or in illegality, be questioned. But his political courage within his own party is more debatable. He was brilliant, effective and resolute when the political line was clear, when he knew that his position was secure, whether through general agreement or the soundness of the views of those for whom he was speaking, but he revealed very sharp vacillations, in the form of striking twists and turns, as soon as the ground no longer felt solid under his feet, when conflicts were raging at the head of the International or the Russian Party, or as soon as something new had to be created in a hard political battle. He was a brilliant interpreter – populariser if you like – and scintillating commentator on someone else's political thought, but he showed uncertainty when the responsibility for directing – and especially for reorienting – depended on his own initiative. He could ensure that a political line determined by the International would be intelligently applied, and was successful in leading the German Party 'by proxy', in times when there were no sharp political problems, but not in a period of crisis, when a fully rounded political leader must accept all his responsibilities, including that of fighting within his own party for what he believes to be the correct line.

Fifteen years later, immediately after the great public trial in Moscow, where the accused Radek put on an amazing performance, as accuser and accomplice, before the prosecutor Vyshinsky, Trotsky was to deliver a severe judgement on him. It does, however, provide the necessary corrective to Herzog's panegyric:

> Radek . . . is merely a journalist. He possesses the brilliant traits of this category, and all its faults as well. Radek's education may perhaps best be characterised as extremely erudite. His definitive knowledge of the Polish movement, his long participation in the German social democracy, his attentive study of the world press, especially English and American, broadened his mental horizon, invested his mind with greater mobility and armed it with an innumerable variety of examples, comparisons, and, in the last analysis, anecdotes. Radek, however, lacks that quality which Ferdinand Lassalle called 'the physical force of the mind'. Radek was always more of a guest than a fundamental participant among different sorts of political groupings. His mind is too impulsive and mobile for systematised work. From his articles one may gather a great deal of information; his paradoxes are likely to illuminate a question from an unexpected angle; but Radek was never an independent politician.[7]

In short, the man whom the Communist International could offer during 1919–23 as a political mentor to the KPD, the man upon whom rested the historic mission of forging in Germany a revolutionary leadership composed of people capable of finding the right direction amid problems of revolutionary strategy and tactics, lacked the necessary qualities. He could not give to the cadres of the KPD what he did not possess himself, namely, deep political self-confidence, based on an analysis constantly tested against a changing situation, continuity in activity, firmness in defence of his ideas, attachment to principles, and rejection of dogmatism. Under the aegis of this man, and in spite of his conscious efforts, the German Communist leaders could not attain maturity.

---

[7] L.D. Trotsky, 'A New Moscow Amalgam', *Writings of Leon Trotsky 1936–37*, New York, 1978, p. 118.

Chapter Forty-Seven

Balance Sheet of a Defeat

The fiasco of Germany's 'failed October' in 1923 was to mark a decisive turn in postwar history. At this pivotal point for Europe, the initiative passed back into the hands of the bourgeoisie, who were not to lose it again. Within the Communist International, beginning with the Russian Communist Party itself, the defeat of 1923 represented, if not the starting-point, at least the decisive acceleration in a process of degeneration the most negative aspects of which can often be directly linked to the greatest hopes of this inhuman year.

No doubt it is by no means an accident that even today the international Communist movement has not devoted to this unprecedented disaster the minimum attention which it affords to victories or even to defeats of less importance. A revolution that had been lost, the attempt at an uprising in 1923, was not subjected to a genuine discussion after the event. It is hardly remembered today that this discussion started, but never ran its full course. Of all the contemporary Marxists, only Trotsky, in the Russian Communist opposition, and Paul Levi, who was then in the left wing of Social Democracy, tried to produce a summary explanation.

Trotsky returns to the German affair

In 1924, Trotsky referred again to the German situation in 1923, in the well-known work *The Lessons of*

October, which served as a preface to the collection of his writings and speeches entitled *1917*. As he had declared in *The New Course* at the end of 1923, he believed that Germany had presented, in this terrible year, an exceptionally favourable opportunity for the victory of the proletarian revolution, and he sought the causes of this defeat in the Party itself. He wrote:

> The Bulgarian revolution ought to have been a prelude to the German revolution. Unfortunately, the bad Bulgarian prelude led to an even worse sequel in Germany itself. In the latter part of last year, we witnessed in Germany *a classic demonstration of how it is possible to miss a perfectly exceptional revolutionary situation of world-historic importance.*[1]

Trotsky said that the first mistake of the German Communist leaders had been an inaccurate estimate of the armed forces of the class enemy: an underestimation during the pre-revolutionary period, and an overestimation during the revolutionary period before the insurrection:

> So long as the slogan of insurrection was approached by the leaders of the German Communist Party mainly, if not solely, from an agitational standpoint, they simply ignored the question of the armed forces at the disposal of the enemy (Reichswehr, fascist detachments, police, etc.). It seemed to them that the constantly rising revolutionary flood tide would automatically solve the military question. But when the task stared them in the face, the very same comrades who had previously treated the armed forces of the enemy as if they were non-existent, went immediately to the other extreme. They placed implicit faith in all the statistics of the armed strength of the bourgeoisie, meticulously added to the latter the forces of the Reichswehr and the police, then they reduced the whole to a round number – half a million and more – and so obtained a compact mass force, armed to the teeth, and absolutely sufficient to paralyse their own efforts.
>
> '*No doubt the forces of the German counter-revolution were much stronger numerically* and, at any rate, better organised and prepared than our own Kornilovites and semi-Kornilovites. But so were the effective forces of the German revolution. The proletariat composes the overwhelming majority of the population in Germany. . . . In Germany, the insurrection would have immediately blazed in scores of mighty proletarian centres.[2]

---

[1] L.D. Trotsky, 'Leçons d'octobre', *Cahiers du bolchevisme*, no. 5, 19 December 1924, pp. 313–4; L.D. Trotsky, 'Lessons of October', *The Challenge of the Left Opposition (1923–1925)*, op. cit., p. 201.

[2] Ibid., pp. 230–1.

Comparing the course of the German Revolution of 1923 with that of the Russian Revolution in 1917, he laid stress on the growth within the two revolutionary parties of apprehension and hesitation as the decisive moment neared. He recalled the opposition by Zinoviev and Kamenev to the insurrection, and concluded that what had happened in Germany was the development of similar hesitations in the Party leadership, which in the end had communicated themselves to the masses. He rejected the schema of the German Left, which counterposed masses of workers impatiently pawing the ground to timorous leaders, and wrote:

> The strength of a revolutionary party increases only up to a certain moment, after which the process can turn into the very opposite. The hopes of the masses change into disillusionment as a result of the party's passivity, while the enemy recovers from his panic and takes advantage of this disillusionment. We witnessed such a decisive turning point in Germany in October 1923.[3]

Trotsky returned to the question in greater detail a few years later in 'The Draft Programme of the Communist International: A Criticism of Fundamentals', which emphasised the responsibility of the KPD leadership:

> We have already stated above that in our epoch of abrupt turns the greatest difficulty for a revolutionary leadership lies in being able to feel the pulse of the political situation at the proper moment, so as to catch the abrupt contingency, and to turn the helm in due time. Such qualities of a revolutionary leadership are not acquired simply by swearing fealty to the latest circular letter of the Comintern. They can be acquired, if the necessary theoretical prerequisites exist, by personally acquired experience and genuine self-criticism.[4]

Trotsky considered that such a turn, which had 'violent revolutionary consequences', occurred in Germany in 1923, from the time when the French and Belgians occupied the Ruhr. But:

> The leadership of the Comintern did not take this into consideration at the right time. The German Communist Party still continued to follow its one-sided interpretation of the slogan of the third [Comintern] congress which had firmly drawn it away from the threatening road to putschism. . . . It was not easy to achieve the sharp turn from the tactics of the March days of

---

[3] Ibid., p. 233.
[4] L.D. Trotsky, *The Third International After Lenin*, op. cit., p. 69.

1921 to a systematic revolutionary activity in the press, meetings, trade unions and parliament. After the crisis of this turn had been weathered, there arose the danger of the development of a new one-sided deviation of a directly opposite character. The daily struggle for the masses absorbs all attention, creates its own tactical routine, and diverts attention away from the strategic tasks flowing from changes in the objective situation.[5]

The key to the German situation in 1923 lay in the hands of the Communists:

It became quite clear that the German bourgeoisie could extricate itself from this 'hopeless' situation only if the Communist Party failed to understand in due time that the position of the bourgeoisie was 'hopeless', and if the party failed to draw all the necessary revolutionary conclusions. Yet it was precisely the Communist Party, holding the keys in its hands, that opened the door for the bourgeoisie with this key.[6]

It is true that, in October 1923, the German workers did not march into battle. This was neither an accident nor an unconnected phenomenon which contradicted the analysis which held that Germany was in the midst of a revolutionary situation:

After all the German proletariat had gone through in recent years, it could be led to a decisive struggle only if it were convinced that this time the question would be decisively resolved and that the Communist Party was ready for the struggle and capable of achieving the victory. Not only the rights but also the lefts, despite the fact that they had fought each other very bitterly, viewed rather fatalistically the process of revolutionary development up to September–October 1923.[7]

In the end, there were two weaknesses in the German leadership which explained the fiasco: its fatalism – the belief that the Revolution would in some way develop by itself, independently of the leadership's own policy – and its hesitation at the decisive moment: 'In Germany, the leadership as a whole vacillated and this irresolution was transmitted to the party and through it to the class.'[8]

---

[5] Ibid., pp. 69–70.
[6] Ibid., p. 70.
[7] Ibid.
[8] Ibid., p. 75.

Trotsky drew from the experience of Germany in 1923 some lessons which he believed were as essential for the world revolutionary movement as those of October 1917, and which, like them, bore on the problem of revolutionary leadership: 'There are epochs during which even Marx and Engels could not drive historical development forward a single inch; there are other epochs during which men of much smaller calibre, standing at the helm, can check the development of the international revolution for a number of years.'[9] Trotsky considered that this specific application of a general law occurred in Germany:

> It is here that the danger arises that the policy of the party leadership and of the party as a whole does not correspond to the conduct of the class and the exigencies of the situation. During a relatively languid course of political life, such incongruities are remedied, even if with losses, but without a catastrophe. But in periods of acute revolutionary crisis, it is precisely *time* that is lacking to eliminate the incongruity and to redress the front, as it were, under fire. The periods of the maximum sharpening of a revolutionary crisis are by their very nature transitory. The incongruity between a revolutionary leadership (hesitation, vacillation, temporising in the face of the furious assault of the bourgeoisie) and the objective tasks, can lead in the course in a few weeks and even days to a catastrophe and to a loss of what took years of work to prepare. . . . By the time the leadership succeeds in accommodating itself to the situation, the latter has already changed; the masses are in retreat and the relationship of forces worsens suddenly.[10]

What Trotsky called 'the crisis of the revolutionary leadership on the eve of the transition to the armed insurrection' was in his opinion 'a general danger'. It resulted from the pressure of 'the material and ideological terror of the bourgeoisie at the decisive moment' on 'certain elements of the party tops and the middle stratum of the party'.[11] In 1917, Lenin succeeded, thanks to his 'stern energy' in overcoming the hesitation of the upper strata of the Party due to this pressure. In 1923, and despite the existence of the International, nothing like this happened. Hesitation led to defeat.

---

[9] Ibid., p. 73.
[10] Ibid., p. 74.
[11] Ibid.

Paul Levi's opinion

At this juncture, Levi had been back for over a year in Social Democracy, where he was leading a left-wing current, and he drafted the preface to the first German edition of *The Lessons of October*. Like Trotsky, he judged that the events in Germany in 1923 constituted the greatest economic and social catastrophe ever provoked by the capitalist system:

> Such a total undermining of every social condition in the short space of a few months as occurred at that time in Germany, has perhaps not yet been seen anywhere else. Out of the ocean of tears represented by the war in the Ruhr emerged a small stratum of capitalists with increased economic power and increased lust for political power, and who had begun to undertake a terrible sorting out within their own capitalist ranks. The earlier inflationary bloodletting faded away, and the 'honest ones', who had not grasped the possibility of the Ruhr robberies in good time, were brought to their knees. The middle class, both those in industry and the intellectuals, lost their economic foundations. The workers saw their wages in gold pfennigs drastically reduced, and this effect on their economic basis also meant that all their organisational structures, trade unions, cooperatives and so forth, were brought to their knees.[12]

Like Trotsky, Levi believed that the necessity of a revolution and the seizure of power by the proletariat had never been so evident as in 1923. They faced one of those historic situations in which, logically, power should have changed hands and passed in Germany from the bourgeoisie to the proletariat, as in October 1917 in Russia. However, Levi thought that Trotsky was wrong when he believed even for a moment that the KPD could have played in Germany the role of revolutionary leadership which the Bolsheviks had been able to assume in Russia. With savage bitterness, he declared Trotsky's hypothesis to be improbable:

> So when all three preconditions coincide, when the German situation is wholly comparable to the Russian one, when the Communist International has become the most flawless organisation ever created, and when Gregory Zinoviev has become a politician of great stature and not just an idiot of European fame, there we have it: nevertheless, even if all that occurred, the

---

[12] P. Levi, 'Introduction to Trotsky's *The Lessons of October*, *Revolutionary History*, Volume 5, no. 2, Spring 1994, p. 63.

KPD has still not yet earned the legal title to put itself forward as the force which could shape the state after that catastrophe.[13]

In Russia, the Bolsheviks had won their audience and authority amongst the masses on the basis of the policies which they had understood and approved since February 1917, and which gave them their legitimacy in October. Revolutionaries could and should have carried out such a policy in Germany, and thereby put themselves in a similar position:

> In the tragic circumstances in Germany such a policy was not so difficult to put forward. As pointed out, there was of course the previous experience of the World War; it took really no more than that to demonstrate how this war in the Ruhr was a shameless bout of plunder by German capitalists against German non-capitalists, and the end of this policy must ensure that the social classes who suffered by it turn on the originator of the policy.[14]

Instead of this simple, clear policy, the masterminds of the KPD had preferred to plunge headlong into what they claimed to be their 'new' theories about 'national oppression'. Radek had delivered his notorious speech about Schlageter, the 'wanderer into the void', and Zinoviev had warned the Communists against national nihilism. Every zealous Party full-timer repeated and caricatured these themes, which really spread confusion in the minds of German working people, and encouraged the demagogic undertakings of the extreme Right. The proletariat did not comprehend any of this, and that explained its passivity:

> And the result of all this was that, instead of a strong proletarian force at the end of the war in the Ruhr, there was a nationalist-communist stench which poisoned the whole of Germany. The national socialists lay claim to the same right which the communists assert, to be the heirs of the foundering Germany: the one presents itself as national-communist, and the other as communist-nationalist, so at bottom both were the same.[15]

However, during 1923, Levi had supported the call for a workers' government in Germany, and gave his backing to the workers' government in Saxony, because he saw this as the only possible means both to oppose the grand coalition and to help the working class to overcome in common struggle the

---

[13] Ibid., p. 64.
[14] Ibid.
[15] Ibid., p. 65.

inhibitions and the fears caused by the divisions in its ranks. During August 1923, when he was rallying the Social-Democratic Left, he believed that one practical task for Social Democracy was to find a new form of the dictatorship of the proletariat:

> Do not let us believe that the form which it has taken in Russia is the finished product. We do not believe that its Russian form is a model which is valid for all countries. . . . This is the starting-point for the tasks of Social Democracy. It must successfully promote the idea of the dictatorship of the proletariat in conditions very different from those in Russia, in conditions that are much more characteristic of the proletarian revolution in the capitalist countries. It will be necessary to link the dictatorship of the proletariat much more to given state structures. It could take form first in a government of a parliamentary minority, which could convert a 'minus' on the level of its strength in parliament into a 'plus' on that of its social power.[16]

This tends to prove that despite all his warnings and his criticism of the, national, policy of the KPD, Levi could still regard the German situation as revolutionary, and in the end could endorse the efforts of the KPD to find transitional slogans at the governmental level.[17]

The congenital weaknesses of the KPD

In fact, despite his desire to demonstrate that the KPD had become completely bankrupt before undergoing the test of battle, Levi did not deny the underlying basis of Trotsky's analysis. To write that the 'national-communist' policy during the summer of 1923 spread confusion in the ranks of working people, to declare, as he later did, that the German Communist leaders had not been capable of acting in any other way than as 'stupid plagiarists' of the Bolsheviks,[18] merely emphasises the manifestations of the weakness of a party which had not been able to raise itself, in the exceptional circumstances of the time, to the height of its historic tasks. From this point of view, there is significance in what Radek said at the Central Committee on 1 February 1921: 'The affair of the *Open Letter* is typical. If I had been in Moscow, the idea would never have occurred to me.'

---

[16] 'Über die gegenwärtige Aufgaben der Partei', *Sozialistische Politik und Wirtschaft*, 7 September 1923.

[17] He was to return to this question a number of times, in particular in 'Bei den Kommunisten', *Sozialistische Politik und Wirtschaft*, 17 April 1924.

[18] 'Der neue Kommunistendreh', *Sozialistische Politik und Wirtschaft*, 18 June 1925.

The men who controlled the policy of the KPD were not in Berlin, but in Moscow. It was the Germans themselves, those who were in Germany, who asked them, as in the case of the Anti-Fascist Day, to take for them decisions which they did not feel able to take themselves, and which, furthermore, they were not to follow through as they should have done. Radek pointed out on 1 February 1921 to the German leaders that their Central Committee had not yet found time for a serious discussion of the *Open Letter*, its political significance and the political perspectives which it opened up. The single important initiative during 1923 in Germany came from Brandler, when he drafted the 12 June appeal to the Party. Not only did this initiative provoke lively reactions amongst the cadres, who treated Brandler as 'mad', but he himself, moreover, was unable after this gesture to outline perspectives based on the situation in the country.

It is no less significant that it was the Political Bureau of the Russian Party which initiated the turn in the policy of the KPD in August, and that this analysis could be made by Trotsky on the basis of information from Walcher and Enderle, who themselves waited for his verdict to draw the political conclusions from the material which they themselves had supplied. In Moscow in September 1923, Brandler admitted without too much hesitation that they could see in Moscow what he himself had not seen in the country in which he led a revolutionary party of many hundreds of thousands of members.

One weakness of the KPD lay in the 'demagogues' of its Left, specimens of an intellectual bohemia, expert in handling revolutionary phrases, but unable to weigh up a situation, or to grasp the link which would enable the whole chain to be taken in hand. They attracted good militant workers but also – as Zetkin emphasised in her letter to the Frankfurt Congress – petty-bourgeois elements, adventurers and even vulgar anti-Semites, not to mention quite a few dilettantes, alien to the workers' movement.[19]

A further weakness lay in the leaders of the KPD's right wing, tossed between their own instinctive appreciation of a situation and their reflexes towards prudence on the one hand, and, on the other, the voluntarist principle of a pseudo-Bolshevism, reduced to a caricature of itself in the armed insurrection. It lay in Brandler's permitting himself be led in March 1921 by the likes of Kun, and holding his tongue in Moscow in September 1923 as Radek had done in August, instead of fighting to the end for his views.

---

[19] See Chapter 42.

Yet another weakness, in a general way, lay in the cadres who were devoted, self-sacrificing and courageous in the face of the ruling class, but were almost incapable of thinking for themselves, perpetually marching with an ear cocked in the direction of Moscow, from where advice was received as if it were the law and the prophets.

But we must not forget that the KPD's leaders had only had a few years' experience, amidst difficult conditions. Levi, who was a lawyer in 1914, and a typical left-wing intellectual, was not really integrated into the workers' movement. He took the crushing responsibility in early 1919 of leading the new Communist Party at a crucial moment of the world revolution. The Bolshevik leaders knew his limitations, feared his dilettantism and individualism, but nonetheless used all their influence to keep him at the head of the party. No one else in Germany could do better than he. And it was not by accident either, that the German internal security services in 1923 instructed their embassy in Moscow to refuse to issue a visa to Radek permitting him to return to Germany whilst that country was in a state of effervescence. This man excelled the leaders of the KPD by a mile.

The KPD had workers' leaders, tested organisers such as Brandler and Walcher, theoreticians such as Thalheimer, people able to coordinate strikes, organise demonstrations, and lead forces of stewards who could both fight and die at their posts. It could call upon good speakers for its mass meetings and its parliamentary debates, underground workers who were skilful conspirators, talented journalists, people who could write books and could aim machine-guns. But there was no one who, with his ear to the ground, heard the grass grow, as Lenin liked to say, no one who could find the way forward in a practical situation. There was no Lenin, and, taking into consideration the abilities of the second-rank personalities in the prewar left opposition in the SPD, there was nothing in the history of the Party or in that of the German proletariat that made likely the emergence within a few years of people able to lead a successful revolution against the most conscious and determined bourgeoisie in Europe, if not the world. Levi said in 1920 that the principal mistake of the German revolutionaries was their refusal before 1914 to organise independently on the political level, even if the organisation so created would have had to exist as a sect.[20] In 1926, in his letter to Zetkin, Radek expressed the same judgement:

[20] Levi Archives, P124/8.

On the anniversary of the death of Karl and Rosa, I spoke at a meeting of the Moscow Youth League, at which you too were scheduled to speak. I prepared for my speech, thumbed through old articles by Rosa, and it is my deep conviction that we left radicals in Germany awakened not too early but too late, fought against the dangers not too sharply but too weakly.[21]

The weaknesses of the KPD were, in short, the reflection of those of Social Democracy as it had developed before the First World War. A society within society, it was perfectly integrated by a principled opposition and a practical adaptation which offered experience, responsibilities and tasks, not to those who were capable of making history with the workers, but only to those who wanted to take part in politics by making use of the workers.

The conservative character of the trade-union bureaucracy and the SPD's apparatus had turned the most combative elements amongst the workers against the concepts of centralisation and organisation. The Communist leaders who emerged from prewar Social Democracy carried all its imprint in their tendency to passivity, and in their propensity for tailing behind events. We must largely reject the accusations which most historians direct against the leadership of the Communist International in this respect. For it was in large part the mediocrity of the people in the KPD which sustained in Germany the success, the prestige, and then the authority, and, finally, the despotism of Moscow in relation to that party. As long as the perspective of the world revolution remained the central preoccupation of the Bolshevik leaders, this hiatus could be regarded as temporary, and the hope of overcoming it was realistic. But the degeneration of the Russian Revolution was to become a decisive factor in such a propitious climate. Stalin's faction, which gradually assumed power in the Russian Party, domesticated the KPD, and received from this powerful party only a feeble opposition, even when Moscow's directives resulted in it implementing criminally aberrant policies in the face of the mortal danger posed by the rise of Nazism.

In the brief period of the history of the KPD which we have studied here, one of the most striking facts is certainly the dead-end posed by leftism and by all the theories based on what has been claimed to be Luxemburgism, about the spontaneity of the masses. Revolutionary impatience, the tragic illusion that small groups of determined fighters, active minorities, can

---

[21] 'A Letter by Karl Radek to Clara Zetkin', *The New International*, Volume 1, no. 5, December 1934, p. 156.

substitute themselves for the activity of the great masses, the belief in the virtue of 'exemplary actions', emerge at every moment during the history of the KPD. They too are the price paid for the years of the exclusive domination of Social-Democratic practice in the workers' movement, and of the weakness even of the KPD, insufficiently able to respond rapidly to the revolutionary aspirations of the active minority of the proletariat. And these initiatives by minorities, inside and often outwith the KPD enabled the active and organised factions in the German bourgeoisie to cope on a number of occasions with difficult situations, and to make effective use of one of their essential assets, a division within the ranks of the working class.

The defeat of the KPD in 1923 ultimately did not represent the defeat of Bolshevism, Spartacism or, still less, Communism. It was the defeat of the whole German socialist movement, of which the KPD tried – too late in relation to the development of the world crisis – to be the driving force for its reunification under the banner of the proletarian revolution.

What remains of the history of the KPD belongs to another chapter, all the principal lines of which this time start in Moscow. Henceforth there was to be no consistent attempt to construct a mass revolutionary Communist Party, to utilise the strength of the German workers' movement, its concentration, cultural level and organisation, in the struggle for power and the implementation of the dictatorship of the proletariat.

After a few years of stabilisation, thanks to the injection of American credits, the German economy recovered its vigour, and brilliantly developed its productive apparatus. Then it was struck by the world crisis of 1929, in a different economic and social form from that of 1923, but just as deep and just as potentially revolutionary. This time, it was the armed gangs of the SA and the SS who were victorious. They were to send side by side to the scaffolds and the concentration camps, Communists and Social Democrats, Independents and reformists, Stalinists and leftists, Brandlerites and Trotskyists. In that period, the Party which had inherited the name of the KPD was no longer the party of Levi, Brandler, Radek or Maslow, and did not in the least resemble the revolutionary instrument of the proletariat which they had all wanted to build.

By now, the KPD was a 'party of the new type', subject to the authority of its charismatic chief, Ernst Thaelmann, an apparent proletarian replica of the Führer, infallible and all-powerful, but in reality merely an imitation of the Soviet Union's 'leader of genius', specially made for use in Germany. The KPD was nothing but an apparatus intended to accomplish the tasks assigned to it to meet the needs of the foreign policy of the Soviet bureaucracy, which no longer concerned itself with organising the German Revolution, but, on the contrary, feared an event which would threaten to overturn the precarious status quo upon which its survival was predicated.

In the tradition of the *apparatchiki* of Social Democracy, and in conformity with the Russian model of 1927–8, the all-powerful hierarchy of the Secretaries – the Polleiters of the districts through whom passed control, correspondence and leadership – depended entirely on a Secretariat of a few members who directly headed the different central departments, and concentrated in their hands control over the entire Party on every level. An apparatus of 8,000 full-timers was enough to hold a party of which the membership was constantly changing and being replaced, in which the veterans of the years of revolutionary struggle were no longer more than a handful, and through which passed the youth and the unemployed – sometimes before joining the Nazi Party, which, for its part, enabled them to live and promised that it would fight. The KPD was sufficiently powerful for it to paralyse in its own ranks and in the whole working class the aspiration for a united front against Nazism, but it was a broken reed when in 1933 Hitler's gangs succeeded in taking hold of the essential machinery of the state apparatus, and was to be smashed within a few days along with the rest of the workers' organisations and the gains of half a century of the Social-Democratic and trade-union movement.

Whilst men like Stoecker, Schneller, Neubauer, Becker and Thaelmann were dying on the gallows, under the executioner's axe, or in Hitler's prisons and concentration camps, others of their comrades-in-arms, such as Werner Hirsch, Leo Flieg, Remmele, Eberlein, Süsskind, Kippenberger, Leow and Heinz Neumann were dying in the prisons or cellars of Stalin's GPU.

This final defeat was the conclusion of two battles, separate but nonetheless closely linked by their origins and their consequences. The former had unfolded in the factories and streets of Germany's industrial cities between 1918 and 1923. The other battle had taken place within the Russian Communist Party between 1923 and 1927, and had ended with the victory of Stalin and his bureaucratic apparatus. These two lost battles, defeats of the world proletariat in arenas of vital strategic importance, expressed the tragic weakness of the proletariat on the territory of organisation and theory, and pointed to the only way to overcome this weakness, the construction of a real International.

At the end of this work, may we be permitted to apply to the world revolution the remark which Trotsky formulated at the end of his *History of the Russian Revolution*:

Capitalism required 100 years to elevate science and technique to the heights, and plunge humanity into the hell of war and crisis. To socialism, its enemies allow only 15 years to create and furnish a terrestrial paradise. We took no such obligation upon ourselves. We never set these dates. The process of vast transformations must be measured by an adequate scale.[22]

In this perspective, the history of the Communist Party of Germany during the early years of the Communist International ceases to be a history of lost illusions, and becomes the prehistory of a struggle which continues to this day.

---

[22] Trotsky, *History of the Russian Revolution*, op. cit., p. 1192.

CHRONOLOGY

Date	World Events	Germany	Revolutionary Movement in Germany	International Revolutionary Movement	Russian Revolutionary Movement
1914					
August	4: Outbreak of First World War. German offensive, battle on the frontiers. 27: Two Socialists in French government.	Social-Democratic parliamentary fraction votes for war credits.	4: Meeting of internationalists around Luxemburg.	1: Serbian Socialists vote against war credits.	8: Bolshevik deputies vote against war credits. Manifesto of the Bolshevik CC against the War.
September	Battle of the Marne.		21: Liebknecht states he was wrong to vote for military credits.		6–7: Bolshevik Conference at Berne adopts Lenin's theses on the War.
October	Beginning of trench warfare.				
December			2: Liebknecht alone against military credits in the Reichstag.		
1915					
January					Bolshevik deputies and leaders sentenced.
February	Fighting in Champagne, on the Yser, in Argonne (February–March).		7: Liebknecht called up. 18: Luxemburg arrested.		Bolshevik Conference at Berne confirms the defeatist line (27 February–4 March)

Table (*cont.*)

Date	World Events	Germany	Revolutionary Movement in Germany	International Revolutionary Movement	Russian Revolutionary Movement
March		18: Liebknecht and Rühle vote against war credits	4: First conference of the opposition in Berlin.	26–28: International Socialist Women's Conference at Berne.	
April			14: First issue of *Die Internationale*.	5–7: Young Socialists' International Conference at Berne.	
May	23: Italy enters the war.		27: Liebknecht's leaflet: 'The enemy is at home'.		
September	Bulgaria enters the war. Allied offensive in Champagne and Artois.			5–8: International Socialist Conference at Zimmerwald.	
December			21: 18 'centrist' deputies against military credits.		
1916					
January			1: Conference of *Die Internationale* in Berlin adopts Luxemburg's theses.		
February	Battle of Verdun (February–June).		Publication of the *Junius Pamphlet*.	5–8: Preparation of the Second Zimmerwald Conference.	

April		14–30: International Socialist Conference at Kienthal.
May	1: Workers' demonstrations for peace	1: Liebknecht in uniform distributes leaflets.
June	27–30: Strikes and demonstrations in support of Liebknecht.	28: Liebknecht sentenced.
July	Allied offensive on the Somme (July–October).	
September	21–23: SPD national conference.	1: First Spartacus letter.
October	17–19: *Vorwärts* seized by army, handed back to SPD Executive.	
November	Resumption of the battle of Verdun (November–December).	
1917		
January		7: SPD opposition conference in Berlin. 18: All oppositionists expelled from SPD.
February	1: Beginning of submarine war.	10–12: February Revolution. Tsarism falls.

Table (*cont.*)

Date	World Events	Germany	Revolutionary Movement in Germany	International Revolutionary Movement	Russian Revolutionary Movement
March			5: The Spartacist Conference declares in favour of forming a party with the centrists; the 'left radicals' are opposed.		
April	6: USA enters War. Offensive on the Chemin des Dames; Mutinies in the French Army (April–July).	16–23: Big strikes in Berlin and Leipzig.	6–8: Gotha Congress; formation of USPD.		16: Lenin arrives in Petrograd; April Theses.
May				13: Split in Sweden; Left Socialist Party formed.	
July					20–22: Provisional Government suppresses peace demonstrations by Petrograd workers.
August		2: Sailors' demonstrations. 25: Sailors' leaders sentenced.			
September		5: Köbis and Reichpietsch shot.			

October	24: Italian catastrophe at Caporetto.		
November			7: Insurrection in Petrograd. 8: Lenin in power.
December	4: German-Russian armistice. 22: Brest-Litovsk peace talks begin.	5–12: Stockholm Conference.	
1918			
January	Strikes in Austro-Hungary.	28–31: Strikes in Berlin and other working-class centres.	
February			Debate on peace in Russian Party.
March	3: Signature of Brest-Litovsk Treaty.		6–8: Seventh Congress of RSDLP which becomes Russian Communist Party (Bolshevik).
April	German offensive in the West (March–June).	28: Joffe, Soviet ambassador in Berlin.	
May			
July	Second battle of the Marne.		
August	Allied victory at Montdidier.		
September	30: Armistice with Bulgaria.		15: Start of the Civil War.

Table (*cont.*)

Date	World Events	Germany	Revolutionary Movement in Germany	International Revolutionary Movement	Russian Revolutionary Movement
October	30: Revolution in Vienna; fall of Austro-Hungarian Empire. 31: Armistice with Turkey.	1: German army leaders call for peace. 2: Max von Baden's government set up with two SPD ministers. 30: Agitation in the navy; demonstration at Stuttgart.	1: Joint conference of Spartacists and left radicals calls for socialist revolution and power to the councils. 21: Liebknecht released.		
November	2: Austro-Italian armistice. 11: Rethondes armistice. 12: Proclamation of the Austrian Republic. 16: Proclamation of the Hungarian Republic.	3: Kiel sailors mutiny. 5–9: Revolutionary wave; workers' and soldiers' councils set up. 9: Revolution in Berlin; Ebert becomes Chancellor. 10: Ebert and the SPD-USPD cabinet given authority by councils. 16: Agreement between unions and employers.	11: Organisation of Spartacus League with a Zentrale.	3: Foundation of Austrian CP. 5: Foundation of Greek Socialist Workers Party. Foundation of Hungarian CP.	
December	4: Beginning of formation of Free Corps. 6: Council of People's Commissioners decides to convene National Assembly.		7: Armed Spartakus demonstration in Berlin. 29: USPD ministers resign. Appeal to Noske as War Minister.	16: Foundation of Polish CP.	Russian CP sends Radek to Germany.

			30: Congress of German communists, Spartacists and left radicals, attended by Radek.
	Failed counter-revolutionary putsch in Berlin. 10: Ebert hails the 'undefeated' front-line troops. 16–21: Congress of Councils declares for the National Assembly. 23–24: Armed clashes between sailors and soldiers in Berlin. 25: Workers' demonstrations; *Vorwärts* building occupied. 29: USPD ministers resign. Appeal to Noske as war minister.		
1919			
January	18: Opening of Peace Conference.	4: Removal of Eichhorn 5: Demonstration in Berlin; buildings occupied. 6–12: Free Corps restore order in Berlin. 15: Murder of Liebknecht and Luxemburg. 26: National Assembly elections.	1: End of KPD(S) Founding Congress.
February		Free Corps begin to cover the country.	12: Radek arrested.

Table (cont.)

Date	World Events	Germany	Revolutionary Movement in Germany	International Revolutionary Movement	Russian Revolutionary Movement
		11: Ebert elected President; Scheidemann coalition government in office. Strike in the Ruhr.			
March	21: Proclamation of the Council Republic in Hungary.	1: Free Corps in Halle. 3–8: General strike and repression; 'bloody week' in Berlin. 31: Ruhr general strike begins.	2–6: Special USPD Congress in Berlin. 3: Ban on *Die Rote Fahne*. 10: Arrest and murder of Jogiches; Paul Levi takes leadership of KPD(S).	2–6: International Socialist Conference which proclaims itself First Congress of Communist International. Bulgarian Social-Democratic Party (Narrows) affiliates to CI.	White offensive under Kolchak (April–June).
April	Mutinies in the French Black Sea fleet. 28: Founding pact of League of Nations.	7: First Council Republic in Bavaria. 8–14: Second Congress of Councils in Berlin. 13: Second Council Republic in Bavaria, led by Communists.	8: Zentrale takes refuge in Leipzig.	10: Foundation of Dutch CP.	
May	1: General strike in France. 7: Versailles Peace Conference dictates terms to the German delegation.	1: Free Corps take Munich; repression. 11: Free Corps take Leipzig. 28: End of Ruhr general strike.	11: Zentrale leaves Leipzig for Berlin.	Bulgarian Social-Democratic Party becomes CP.	

Month				International
June	28: Versailles Treaty signed.	20: Scheidemann resigns; railway strike begins. 22: National Assembly ratifies acceptance of Versailles Treaty. Bauer coalition government in office. 30: Tenth Congress of ADGB.		
July	3: End of railway strike.			
August	1: Liquidation of the Hungarian Council Republic.	16–17: KPD(S) Congress at Frankfurt-am-Main; start of conflict between Levi and ultra-Left.	31: Foundation of Communist Workers' Party of USA.	
September			9–10: USPD Jena Congress.	White offensive against Petrograd (September–October).
October		Left opposition with Dissmann at head of metalworkers' union.	20–24: KPD(S) Second, 'Heidelberg' Congress. Levi obtains expulsion of ultra-leftists.	
November			USPD Congress at Leipzig (30 November–6 December); shift to left.	Establishment of Amsterdam Bureau of CI for Western Europe.
December			5: Radek freed. 12: *Die Rote Fahne* reappears.	

Table (*cont.*)

Date	World Events	Germany	Revolutionary Movement in Germany	International Revolutionary Movement	Russian Revolutionary Movement
1920					
January	10: Birth of League of Nations.	Demonstration outside the Reichstag, shooting leaves 42 dead.	17: Radek leaves.	Conference organised by the leftist Amsterdam Bureau. Radek becomes Secretary of the CI.	
February			25–26: KPD(S) Third Congress at Karlsruhe.	Amsterdam Bureau dissolved.	
March		13: Kapp Putsch. 14: General strike begins. 17: Kapp flees; Legien calls for government of workers' parties and unions. 22: End of general strike. 24: Bielefeld agreements. 26: Legien refuses position of Chancellor. 27: Hermann Müller becomes Chancellor.	13: KPD(S) Zentrale refuses to defend government. 23: Declaration of 'loyal opposition'.		
April	24: Russo-Polish War begins.	3: Reichswehr offensive in the Ruhr.	4–5: Opposition conference in Berlin; KAPD founded. 14–15: KPD(S) Fourth Congress in Berlin.	15: Foundation of Spanish CP.	Lenin publishes *Left-Wing Communism*.

May	1–29: French railway strike.			23: Foundation of Indonesian CP.	
June		6: Reichstag elections; progress made by Right and USPD. 25: Fehrenbach (Centre) government takes office.			
July			KPD(S) delegates to CI Congress protest at presence of KAPD representatives.	15: Preparatory conference for founding of RILU (19 July–7 August). Second CI Congress. Adoption of '21 Conditions'.	
August	Red Army at gates of Warsaw.			1: Foundation of British CP.	Radek removed from CI Secretariat for supporting KPD against Russian Party.
September	Metalworkers' strikes and factory occupations in Northern Italy.			10: Foundation of Turkish CP.	
October	12: Russo-Polish peace treaty.		12–17: USPD Congress in Halle accepts '21 Conditions'.	13: Foundation of Iranian CP. Radek in Germany (clandestinely).	
November	14: Destruction of Wrangel's army. End of Civil War.		1–3: KPD(S) Fifth Congress, now KPD (Section of CI).	28: KAPD admitted to CI as 'sympathising' party.	

Table (cont.)

Date	World Events	Germany	Revolutionary Movement in Germany	International Revolutionary Movement	Russian Revolutionary Movement
December			4–7: Fusion Congress between KPD and left wing of USPD; birth of VKPD; Levi and Däumig Co-Chairman. 24: Levi protests at admission of KAPD to CI as a 'sympathising party'.	25–30: French Socialist Party Congress at Tours; majority supports affiliation to CI and '21 Conditions'.	Start of debate on trade-union question.
1921					
January			7: KPD *Open Letter* to other workers' organisations. 21: First incident between Radek and Levi.	15: Livorno Congress of Italian SP opens. 21: Italian SP splits; PCI founded.	
February		26: Unions formulate ten demands.	22: Levi and Däumig resign; Brandler chairman of VKPD. Béla Kun in Berlin.	21: Small bureau of CI condemns *Open Letter*.	Radek in Russia.
March	20: Plebiscite in Upper Silesia.	16–17: Hörsing's offensive in Central Germany. 19: Police enter Mansfeld region. Fighting in Central	16–17: VKPD CC decides on 'activation' of Party, and prepares defensive action against Hörsing. 18: VKPD's call to arms.		2–17: Kronstadt rising. 8–16: Tenth Congress of Bolshevik Party; ban on factions, measures for workers' democracy, adoption of NEP.

Month						
April	British miners' strike (April–June).	Germany; incidents elsewhere. 29: Murder of Sült. 30: End of March Action.	21: Hoelz launches urban guerrilla struggle. VKPD calls general strike. 27: Levi's letter to Lenin.	8: Theses on March Action and appearance of the theory of the offensive. 12: Levi publishes *Unser Weg*. 5: Levi expelled from VKPD.		16: Anglo-Russian trade agreement.
May		Fehrenbach resigns; Wirth takes over.			8: Foundation of Romanian CP. 14–16: Foundation of Czechoslovak CP.	Conflict in the Russian party; Lenin-Trotsky bloc against the ultra-leftists (May–June).
June	Foundation of CGTU, establishing trade-union split in France.		6: Brandler sentenced.		17: Lenin against Kun on the ECCI. Third CI Congress; turn 'to the masses' (23 June–12 July).	
July					1: Foundation of Chinese CP. 3: First RILU congress.	
August		26: Murder of Erzberger.		3–4: VKPD CC has difficulty in adopting Moscow compromise. 22–26: Second (Seventh) KPD Congress at Jena; Meyer and Friesland lead Party.		

Table (*cont.*)

Date	World Events	Germany	Revolutionary Movement in Germany	International Revolutionary Movement	Russian Revolutionary Movement
September			Development of Berlin Left; Friesland moves towards Levi (September–October)		
October		22: Social Democrats enter Wirth's government.		ECCI poses problem of workers' government.	
November		25: Beginning of *Vorwärts'* revelations on March Action.	16-17: KPD CC adopts slogan of 'confiscation of real values'. 20: First conference of Levi's KAG.		
December			20: Friesland, removed from his post, appeals to Party members.	4: ECCI declares in favour of the workers' united front. 8: ECCI supports struggle to the end against KAG.	
1922					
January			22: Friesland expelled.		Radek's secret mission to Germany on Russo-German military cooperation.

February	6: Treaty of Washington.	1–7: Railway strike.	22: KAG joins USPD.	First Enlarged ECCI Meeting; adoption of theses on the workers' united front (24 February–3 March).	
March		22: Metalworkers' strike begins.			Eleventh Congress of Bolshevik Party (27 March–2 April)
April	2–5: Conference of the Three Internationals in Berlin. 10–19: Genoa Conference. 16: Russo-German Rapallo Treaty.			Radek in Germany as representative of Russian CP and CI (April–May).	3: Stalin becomes Party General Secretary.
May				7–11: Second Enlarged ECCI Meeting.	26: Lenin's first stroke.
June		4: End of metalworkers' strike. 19–24: ADGB Congress at Leipzig. 24: Murder of Rathenau. 27: Berlin agreements between workers' organisations.			
July		18: Law for defence of the Republic.	8: KPD excluded from united front.		
August	Failure of general strike in Italy.				Georgian affair (August–September).
September		24: SPD-USPD reunification.			

Table (*cont.*)

Date	World Events	Germany	Revolutionary Movement in Germany	International Revolutionary Movement	Russian Revolutionary Movement
October	20: Mussolini takes power in Italy.				
November		21: Cuno government takes office without Social Democrats (24 November–6 December). Strikes in the Palatinate.		Fourth CI Congress, approves slogan of the workers' government, confirms strategy of united front (5 November–5 December).	
December					16: Lenin's second stroke. 25: Lenin dictates 'Testament'. 30: Soviet Constitution adopted.
1923					
January	11: Occupation of Ruhr by French and Belgian troops; start of passive resistance. Demonstrations, strikes & sabotage.		Eighth KPD Congress at Leipzig; sharp conflict between the Left and the new leadership, especially Brandler. (28 January–1 February).	Radek visits Germany secretly (January–February).	4: Lenin dictates postscript, recommending removal of Stalin.
March		21: Zeigner socialist government in office in Saxony with Communist support.	26: Violent confrontations between tendencies at Essen regional congress.		6: Lenin breaks with Stalin. 9: Lenin's third stroke.

Month					
April	17-25: Twelfth Party Congress; sharp attacks on Stalin.	ECCI obtains agreement between KPD Left and Right in Moscow.			
May	Radek visits Berlin legally.		26: Execution of Schlageter.		8: Curzon ultimatum to Soviet Union.
June	12-23: Third Enlarged ECCI meeting; Radek's Schlageter speech.				9: Stambulisky's peasant government overthrown in Bulgaria, Communist Party remains neutral.
July	Scissors Crisis; social unrest, strikes (July–August).	26: Radek advises Zentrale to cancel demonstration.	12: Zentrale's appeal to Party. Decision to call anti-fascist demonstration on 29 July. Demonstration banned in several states.		
August	15: Zinoviev draws up theses on German Revolution. 23: Politbureau calls on ECCI to prepare insurrection in Germany.	6: Decision to prepare an insurrection in Bulgaria.	28: Zentrale appoints Military Committee for insurrection.	9: General strike against Cuno begins. 11: Cuno resigns. 12: Stresemann government takes office with Social Democrats.	19-28: Bulgarian insurrection crushed. 26: End of passive resistance in Ruhr.
September			21: Start of preparatory conference for German insurrection.	26: Martial law; secession in Bavaria. 27: General Müller's threats in Saxony.	
October	8: Trotsky's letter on Party democracy. 15: Letter of the 46.	1: Zinoviev's telegram advocating Communists enter Zeigner's government in Saxony. 4: End of preparatory	8: Brandler returns. 20: Final preparations for insurrection by Revkom. 21: Zentrale decides	1: Failed putsch by the Black Reichswehr. 1-6: Stresemann reshuffles cabinet to the right.	

Table (*cont.*)

Date	World Events	Germany	Revolutionary Movement in Germany	International Revolutionary Movement	Russian Revolutionary Movement
		10: Brandler, Böttcher, Heckert join Zeigner's government. 13: Stresemann obtains full powers; workers' government in Thuringia; Congress of Proletarian Hundreds in Saxony. 16 Böttcher calls for arming of proletariat. 17: General Müller's ultimatum. 19: Government decides to act against Saxony. 21: Chemnitz conference: left Social Democrats refuse to call for general strike. 23–24: Hamburg insurrection. 29: Dismissal of Zeigner; Reichswehr drives out Saxon ministers.	to abandon insurrection.	conference. 10–16: Founding Congress of Red Peasant International. 22: Radek in Germany clandestinely. 22: Pyatakov and Radek approve decision to retreat.	
November		8–9: Failed putsch in Munich.	3–4: KPD CC adopts Brandler's theses.	4: Letter from ECCI to KPD Zentrale.	7: Opening of public debate in Party.

December			8: Trotsky's letter on the 'New Course'.
	30: Marx government takes office, without Social Democrats.		
1924			16–18: Thirteenth Party Conference condemns Opposition, ensures authority of Zinoviev-Kamenev-Stalin Troika. 21: Lenin dies.
January		Constitution of 'centre' tendency. Brandler isolated.	11: First meeting of CI Presidium on German question. 19–21: Resolution of CI Presidium on Germany, condemning errors of Radek and Brandler.
February		19: Brandler replaced by Remmele.	Massive and unselective recruitment into Party: 'Lenin enrolment'.
April	16: German government accepts Dawes Plan.	7–10: Ninth KPD Congress in Frankfurt am Main; the Left takes the leadership.	
May			23–31: Thirteenth Party Congress confirms authority of Troika.
June			Fifth CI Congress on theme of struggle against the 'Right' and for Bolshevisation (17 June–18 July).

Table (*cont.*)

Date	World Events	Germany	Revolutionary Movement in Germany	International Revolutionary Movement	Russian Revolutionary Movement
July					Trotsky revives subject of German defeat of 1923 in *Lessons of October*.
October					Start of campaign against Trotsky.
December					Stalin introduces idea of 'socialism in one country'.

Bibliography

A. Bibliographies

Bibliographie zur Geschichte der Kommunistischen und Arbeiterparteien, vol. II, *Deutschland*, t. I, *K.PD. (Gründung bis 1946) und S.E.D.* East Berlin, I.M.L., 531 pp., roneoed.

Bibliographie zur Geschichte der Novemberrevolution, East Berlin (I.M.L.), 1959, 292 + 70 pp., roneoed.

Colloti, Enzo, *Die Kommunistische Partei Deutschlands 1918–1933. Ein bibliographischer Beitrag*, Milan, 1961, 217 pp.

Eberlein, Alfred, *Die Presse der Arbeiterklasse und der soziale Bewegung*, Berlin, 4 vol, 1968–1969, 2122 pp.

Farbman, N.V., "Izuchenie v SSSR noveishei istorii germanskogo rabochego dvizheniia (Obzor literatury)", in *Germanskoe rabochee dvizhenie v noveishsee vremia*, Moscow, 1962, pp. 282–303.

Herting, Günter, *Bibliographie zur Geschichte der Kommunistischen Internationale 1919–1934*, East Berlin (I.M.L.), 1960, 200 pp.

Procacci, G., "L'Internazionale Comunista dal I al VII Congreso 1919–1935", *Annali*, Milan, 1958, pp. 283–315.

Sworakowski, Witold, *The Communist International and its Front Organisations. A Research Guide and Checklist of Holdings in American and European Libraries*, Stanford, 1965, 493 pp.

B. Specialist Journals

Annali, published by the Feltrinelli Institute, Milan.

Archiv für die Geschichte des Sozialismus und der Arbeiterbewegung (ed. Karl Grünberg), Leipzig, 1911–1930.

Archiv für Sozialgeschichte, published by the Friedrich Ebert Foundation, Hanover.

Beiträge zur Geschichte der deutschen Arbeiterbewegung, published by the Institute of Marxism-Leninism, East Berlin. (Abbr. *BzG*.)

International Review of Social History, published by the International Institute of Social History, Amsterdam.

Internationale Wissenschaftliche Korrespondenz zur Geschichte, roneoed monthly bulletin of the history commission of the Friedrich Meinecke Institute of the Free University of West Berlin.

Le Mouvement social, published by the French Institute of Social History, Paris.

Rivista Storica del Socialismo, Milan.

Survey. A Journal for Soviet and East European Studies, London.

Vierteljahrshefte für Zeitgeschichte, published by the Institute of Contemporary History, Munich.

Wissenschaftliche Zeitschrift der Karl Marx Universität, Leipzig.

Wissenschaftliche Zeitschrift der Martin Luther Universität Halle-Wittenberg, Halle.

Zeitschrift für Geschichtswissenschaft, East Berlin (abbrev. Z/G).

Voprosy Istorii K.PPS., published by the Moscow Institute of Marxism-Leninism.

C. Archives

a) *Private Archives*

Paul Levi archives, Buttinger Library, New York. Main files:

P 7   Documents on the 3rd Congress of the CI.
P 19–1   KPD (S) circular, June 11, 1919.
P 19–2   Letter to all, from Levi, November 28, 1919.
P 40   Documents concerning the expulsion of Levi from the VKPD.
P 50–4   Manuscript: *Wer wollte den Januarputsch?* by Levi.

P 50–16   KPD(S) circulars No. 2, and June 13, 1919 (3?).
P 50   Documents on the split in the PSI.
P 54   Documents and reports on the Kapp Putsch.
P 55   Correspondence between Levi, Radek and Lenin, 1919–1921.
P 55–9   Minutes of the KPD(S) Conference in August 1919.
P 63   Correspondence between Levi, Lenin and Zetkin, 1921.
P 64   Materials on the crisis of the VKPD in 1921.
P 70   Documents on the Congress of the VKPD at Iena (1921).
P 83–6   Notes on the 3rd Congress of the CI.
P 83–9   Report on the meeting of cadres from the Berlin district, April 7, 1921.
P 88   Documents on the crisis in the Italian party.
P 89–6   Levi's correspondence with Brass, Franken & Wegmann (1921).
P 113   Documents and material on the March Action and the 3rd. Congress of the
          CI; correspondence with Warski and Zetkin about Rosa Luxemburg's
          manuscript.
P 124   Documents about the 2nd Congress of the CI.
P 124–8   Levi's report to the 2nd Congress about the KPD(S).
P 125   Documents on the founding of the KPD(S)
P 126   Documents on the origins of the CI.
P 126–6   Levi's report on the 2nd Congress of the CI.
P 129–3   KPD(S) circulars No. 5 (n.d.), No. 6 (December 2, 1919), No. 11 (January
          1920).
P 129–4   Manuscript: *Geschichte der Partei* by Levi.
P 129–8   KPD(S) circulars No. 19 (August 1, 1920), No. 20 (October 5, 1920).

b) *Government Archives*

St. Antony's College collection of German foreign ministry reports: "Akten betreffend
   den russischen Bolschewik Karl Radek (Sobelsohn)", film No. 38.
Bundesarchiv, Koblenz: *Akten Reichskanzlei,* "Akten betreffend Kommunistische Partei",
   vols 1–6.
Staatsarchiv, Düsseldorf: files Nos. 16, 681 to 15, 692.
Stattsarchiv, Bremen: files 2E – 3K 13 – 4 13 – 4 49.

c) *Party Archives*

We were not able to get access to the KPD archives deposited at the Institute of
Marxism-Leninism of the Central Committee of the SED in East Berlin (IML-ZPA),
and we have been able to use only extracts or occasional photocopies. The following
files are to be found there:

Minutes of the meetings of the CC (Zentralausschuss)

2/1   CC of 27.1.1921
2/2   CC of 22–24.2.1921
2/3   CC of 16–17.3.1921
2/4, 2/5   CC of 7–8.4.1921
2/6   CC of 3/5.5.1921
2/7   CC of 2–3.8.1921
2/8, 2/8/1 & 2/8/2   CC of 16–17.11.1921, and a letter from Radek of 10.11.1921
2/13, 2/14   CC of 1923

Minutes of the Zentrale and of the Polburo

3   Zentrale of 18.8.1921, with Heckert's report on the 3rd Con-
                        gress of the CI.
3/1   Zentrale from 24.5.1921 to 21.12.1921
3/2   Zentrale from 7.12.1921 to 15.2.1922
3/1/5   Polburo from September to December 1921
3/1/6   Zentrale 1922
3/1/7, 3/1/22. 3/1/27   Zentrale 1923
3/1/14   Stenographic record of the Brandler trial.
3/1/15   Polburo of 12/16.9.1921

3/1/16   Report of the Zentrale to the Executive on organisational questions.
3/1/17   Political report of the Zentrale to the Executive for the period 1921–1922.
3/1/25   Circular from the Zentrale (1921).
3/1/27   Circular from the Zentrale (1923).
3/2   Zentrale in 1922
3/2/39   Organisational circulars 1922.
3/2/40   Organisational circulars 1923.
3/3   Zentrale in 1923 (12–16.9.1923, 12.10.1923).
3/8   Central Committee of November 1921.
3/10   Reports from the 22 districts on the general strike and the struggle against Kapp.
539   Meeting of the Executive of the CI of 22/23.2.1921.
538   Circular No. 1, 1921, from the Zentrale.
10/14   Report by Curt Geyer on the Executive to the Zentrale.
12/198   Circular No. 2, 1921, from the Zentrale.
15/1/144 Letter to the Zentrale from the leaders of the districts of Dresden and Chemnitz, 7.5.1923.
17/1/151 Reports from the leaders of the Zwickau district (1923).

In the "KPD Collection" of the Moscow IML, the missing information on the year 1923 is to be found at shelf-mark F 495/19/70.

D. Congress Reports

a) *USPD*

Protokoll über die Verhandlungen des Gründungsparteitags der USPD 1917 in Gotha. Appendix: *Bericht über die gemeinsame Konferenz der Arbeitsgemeinschaft und der Spartakusgruppe von 7.1.1917 in Berlin*, Berlin, 1921, 129 pp. (Abbrev. *Protokoll USP 1917*).

Unabhängige Sozialdemokratische Partei: Protokoll über die Verhandlungen des ausserordentlichen Parteitags in Leipzig, 30 November to 6 December 1919, Berlin, n.d., 560 pp.

Unabhängige Sozialdemokratische Partei: Protokoll über die Verhandlungen des ausserordentlichen Parteitags in Halle, October 12 to 17, 1920, Berlin 1920, 310 pp. (Abbrev. *Protokoll USP Halle*).

b) *KPD(S), VKPD, KPD*

Bericht über den Gründungsparteitag der Kommunistischen Partei Deutschlands (Spartakusbund) 30 December 1918 to 1 January 1919, Berlin, n.d. (1919), 56 pp. (Abbrev. *Bericht 1 . . .*)

Der Gründungsparteitag der KPD. Protokoll und Materialen (collected and introduced by Hermann Weber, on the basis of the documents in the Paul Levi archive), Frankfurt am Main, 1969, 346 pp. (Abbrev. *Der Gründungsparteitag.*)

Bericht über den 2. Parteitag der Kommunistischen Partei Deutschlands (Spartakus bund) October 20 to 24, 1919, n.p. (Berlin), n.d. (1919), 68 pp. (Abbrev. *Bericht 2 . . .*).

Bericht über den 3. Parteitag der Kommunistischen Partei Deutschlands February 25 & 26, 1920, n.p. (Berlin), n.d. (1920), 90 pp. (Abbrev. *Bericht 3 . . .*).

Bericht über den 4. Parteitag der Kommunistischen Partei Deutschlands April 14 & 15, 1920, n.p. (Berlin), n.d. (1920), 110 pp.

Bericht über den 5. Parteitag der Kommunistischen Partei Deutschlands (Sektion der Kommunistischen Internationale) November 1–3, 1920 in Berlin, Berlin, 1921, 196 pp. (Abbrev. *Bericht 5 . . .*).

Bericht über die Verhandlungen des Vereinigungsparteitags der USPD (Linke) und der KPD (Spartakusbund) held in Berlin, 4 to 7 December, 1921, Berlin, 1921, 334 pp.

Bericht über die Verhandlungen des 2 Parteitags der Kommunistischen Partei Deutschlands (Sektion der Kommunistischen Internationale), held in Jena, 22–26 August 1921, Berlin, 1922, 454 pp. (Abbrev. *Bericht II (7) . . .*).

Bericht über die Verhandlungen des III (8) Parteitages der Kommunistischen Partei Deutschlands (Sektion der Kommunistischen Internationale), held in Leipzig from January 28 to February 1, 1923, Berlin, 1923, 454 pp. (Abbrev. *Bericht III (8) . . .*).

c) *International*

Der I Kongress der Kommunistischen Internationale. Protokoll der Verhandlungen in Moskau vom 2 bis 19 März 1919, Hamburg, 1921, 202 pp. *Der I Kongress der Kommunistischen Internationale*, op. cit.
Der zweite Kongress der Kommunistischen Internationale. Protokoll der Verhandlungen vom 19 Juli in Petrograd und vom 23 Juli bis 7 August 1920 in Moskau, Hamburg, 1921, 798 pp. (Abbrev. *Protokoll des II . . .*).
Protokoll des III Kongresses der Kommunistischen Internationale (Moscow, 22 June to 12 July 1921), Hamburg, 1921, 1086 pp.
Protokoll des vierten Kongresses der Kommunistischen Internationale. Petrograd-Moscow from 5. November 5. to December 1922, Hamburg, 1923, 1088 pp. (Abbrev. *Protokoll des IV . . .*).
Protokoll fünfter Kongress der Kommunistischen Internationale, 17 June to 8 July in Moscow, Hamburg, 1925.
Protokoll der Internationalen Konferenz des Drein Internationale Exekutiv-Komitees, Vienna, 1922, 52 pp.

d) *Unions*

Protokoll der Verhandlungen des 10. Kongresses der Gewerkschaften Deutschlands, Nuremberg, June-July 1918: Berlin, 1919, 699 pp.
Protokoll der Verhandlungen des 11. Kongresses der Gewerkschaften (1. Bundestag der ADGB), Leipzig, June, 1922: Berlin, 1922, 640 pp.
Die vierzehnte ordentliche Generalversammlung des Deutschen Metallarbeiterverbandes in Stuttgart 1919: Stuttgart, 1919, 447 pp.
Die fünfzehnte ordentliche Generalversammlung des Deutschen Metallarbeiterverbandes in Jena 1921: Stuttgart, 1921, 478 pp.
Verband der Deutschen Buchdrucker. Protokoll der 10. Generalversammlung, June 1920 in Nuremberg: Berlin, 1920, 335 pp.
Verband der Deutschen Buchdrucker. Protokoll der 11. Generalversammlung, July 1922 in Leipzig: Berlin, 1922, 239 pp.

e) *Councils*

Allgemeine Kongress der Arbeiter- und Soldaten- Räte Deutschlands, from 16. to 21. December in the House of Representatives in Berlin, Stenographic Report: Berlin, n.d. (1919), 216 pp.

f) *Parliamentary Debates*

Verhandlungen des Reichstages. XIII Legislative period. II. Session. Stenographic report, Berlin, 1914–1918. (Abbrev. *Stenographische Berichte . . .*).
Verhandlungen des Reichstags. I Wahlperiode 1920, Volumes 306–310, 340–351. (Abbrev. *Verhandlungen des Reichstages*)
Verhandlungen des Sächsischen Landtags. 2. Election periods, vol. I & II.

E. Contemporary Newspapers, Bulletins & Journals

Die Aktion, ed. Franz Pfemfert, Berlin Wilmersdorf 1918 (7th year), 1923.
Arbeiterpolitik, Wochenschrift für wissenschaftlichen Sozialismus, Bremen, 1916–19.
Der Arbeiterrat. Organ der Arbeiterräte Deutschlands. Berlin, 1919–1920.
Bote der Russischen Revolution. Organ der ausländischen Vertretung des ZK der SDAPR(B), Nos. 1 to 11 (September 15–November 28, 1917).
Bulletin communiste. Organ of the comité de la IIIe Internationale (1920), then of the Parti Communiste, SFIC, 1921–23.
Bulletin des IV. Kongress der Kommunistichen Internationale, Moscow, 1922, Nos 1–31 (November 11–December 12).
Bulletin der Erweiterten Exekutive der Kommunistischen Internationale, Moscow, 1922, Nos. 1–16, June 8–26, 1923.

La Correspondance Internationale, French edition of the CI Information Bulletin, 1920–3, see *Internationale Presse-Korrespondenz*. (Abbrev. *Corr. int.*)

Correspondenzblatt der Generalkommission der Gewerkschaften Deutschlands, Berlin, 1918–19; then becomes *Korrespondenzblatt des Allgemeinen Deutschen Gewerkschaftsbundes*, Berlin, 1920–3.

Deutsche Allgemeine Zeitung, news daily (Stinnes combine), Berlin, 1918 (47th year) to 1923.

Das Forum, monthly journal published by W. Herzog, Berlin, 1919 (2nd year) to 1920.

Freiheit, Berlin organ of the USPD, then central daily organ from November 15, 1918 to September 30, 1922.

Graphischer Block, organ of the union for the printing industry, No. 6, September 1, 1919–1920.

Hamburger Volkszeitung, Hamburg daily of the USPD, then of the KPD, 1919–23.

Die Internationale, Zeitschrift für Praxis und Theorie des Marxismus, No. 1, April 15, 1915; reappeared on May 30, 1919 as theoretical organ of the KPD, Berlin, 1919–23.

Die Internationale, Zentralorgan der USPD (Linke), daily paper of the USPD Left, Berlin, October 27 to December 31, organ of the VKPD December 8–31.

Internationale Presse-Korrespondenz (Inprekorr), German edition of the daily bulletin of the CI, Berlin, 1921–3.

Die Junge Garde, weekly of the Communist Youth, with various subtitles: central organ of the SJD (from November 27, 1918 to August 1919), of the FSJD (September 1919 to October 1920), of the KJD (October 1920 to January 1921), then of the KJD, section of the Communist Youth International from January 1921: Berlin, 1918–23.

Der Junge Genosse. Internationale Zeitung für Arbeiterkinder. Published by the Executive of the ICJ, Berlin, 1921–3.

Jugend-Internationale. Kampf-Organ der Kommunistischen Jugend-Internationale. Monthly from June 1919 to 1923.

Der Kämpfer. Organ der KPD Bezirk Sachsen, Chemnitz, 1919–1922.

Kommunismus. Zeitschrift der Kommunistischen Internationale für die Länder Südosteuropas; subsequently *Zeitschrift der KI* (June 19, 1920 to October 16, 1921), Vienna, 1920–1.

Der Kommunist. Flugzeitung der Internationalen Kommunisten Deutschlands, Bremen, 1918–20.

Die Kommunistin. Frauenorgane der Kommunistischen Partei Deutschlands, Stuttgart, from May 1919 to 1923.

Kommunistische Arbeiterzeitung. Organ der KAPD, Berlin, 1921–2.

Der Kommunistische Gewerkschafter. Wochenzeitung für die Tätigkeit der Kommunisten in den Gerwerkschaften und Betriebsräten, from September 1921, *für die Kommunisten in den* etc., Berlin, 1921–3.

Die Kommunistische Internationale, organ of the Executive Committee of the Communist International, Petrograd, then Moscow, 1919–23 (French edition, *L'Internationale communiste*; Russian edition, *Kommunisticheskii Internatsional*).

Kommunistische Partei-Korrespondenz, Leipzig, Berlin, No. 1–13, April 15 to July 10, 1919; bimonthly from October 1, 1921 to August 1923.

Kommunistische Räte-Korrespondenz, weekly, May 1919 to December 1920.

Kommunistische Rundschau, published by Däumig, Stoecker, Geyer, USPD (Linke), Berlin, Nos 1–6, October–December, 1920.

Leipziger Volkszeitung, Leipzig daily of USPD, then of VSPD, 1917–1923.

Moscou, French language organ of the 4th CI Congress, Moscow, 1922, Nos 1–44, November 11–December 12.

Der Parteiarbeiter. Monatschrift für die Praxis revolutionärer Organisationsarbeit (cadre magazine of the KPD), August 1923.

Ruhr-Echo, Essen daily of USPD, then of KPD, 1919–23.

Die Rote Fahne, central organ of the Spartakus League, then of the KPD(S), of the VKPD and finally the KPD, Berlin, 1918–23.

Sozialdemokratische Partei-Korrespondenz, 1918–23.

Sozialistische Politik und Wirtschaft, organ of the Social-Democratic Left, published by Paul Levi, Berlin, 1923–8 (Abbrev. *SPW*).

Sozialistiche Republik, Cologne daily of the USPD, then of the KPD, 1923.

Spartakusbriefe, republished by the IML of the Central Committee of the SED, Berlin, 1958, 475 pp.
Unser Weg (Sowjet). Zeitschrift für Kommunistische Politik. (From May to June 1921: *Sowjet. Kommunistische Zeitschrift.* Bimonthly, Berlin, 1922 (3rd year) to 1922.
Vom Bürgerkrieg, liberal organ published by E. Schneller, Berlin, 1923, Nos 1–4.
Vorwärts. Berliner Volksblatt. Zentralorgan der Sozialdemokratischen Partei Deutschlands, daily of the SPD, 1917–23.
Vossische Zeitung, daily newspaper, 1918–23.

F. Published Documents

Beinert, Heinz, *Zum 50. Jahrestag der Ermordung von Rosa Luxemburg und Karl Liebknecht.* Eine Dokumentation der Liebknecht-Luxemburg Gesellschaft, East Berlin, 1968, 81 pp.
Bericht der Exekutive der Kommunistischen 'Internationale (15. Dezember 1922–15. Mai 1923), Moscow, 1923, 82 p.
Bericht über die Tätigkeit des Präsidiums und der Exekutive der Kommunistischen Internationale für die Zeit vom 6. März bis 11. Juni 1922, Hamburg, 1922, 142 p.
Beschlüsse des zweiten Parteitages der K.P.D. abgeordneten vom 22. bis 26. August im Jena, Berlin, 1921, 39 p.
Über die Bildung der kommunistischen Zellen und Arbeitsgruppen, Hamburg, 1921, 16 p.
Die Bildung der linkssozialdemokratischen Regierung in Sachsen. Eine Materialzusammenstellung, Berlin, 1923, 58 p.
Degras, Jane, *The Communist International 1919–1943.* Documents. Vol. I, *1919–1923*, London, 1956, 463 p.; vol. II, *1923–1928*, London, 1960, 584 p.
Dokumente und Materialen zur Geschichte der deutschen Arbeiterbewegung, Reihe II (1914–1945): vol. I, *Juli 1914–Oktober 1917*, East Berlin, 1958, 760 p.; vol. II, *November 1917–Dezember 1918*, 1957, 770 p.; vol. III, *Januar 1919–Mai 1919*, 1958, 500 p.; vol. VII, half-vol. 1, *Februar 1919–Dezember 1921*, 1966, 651 p.; half-vol. 2, *Januar 1922–Dezember 1923*, 1966, 523 p. (Abbrev: *Dok. u. Mat.*)
Der Dolchstossprozes in München, Oktober-November 1925. Eine Ehrenrettung des deutschen Volkes. Zeugen und Sachverständigenaussagen. Eine Sammlung von Dokumenten, Munich, 1925.
Drahn, Ernst and Leonhard, Susanne, *Unterirdische Literatur im revolutionären Deutschlands während des Weltkrieges*, Berlin, 1920, 200 p.
Die Enthüllungen zu den Märzkämpfen: Enthülltes und Verschwiegenes, Halle, 1922, 40 p.
Gankin and Fisher, *The Bolsheviks and The World War; The Origins of the Third International*, Stanford, 2ᵉ ed., 1960, 856 p.
Grünberg, Carl, *Die Internationale und der Weltkrieg I, Vor dem Kriege und während der ersten Kriegswochen*, Leipzig, 1916, 318 p.
Hannover-Drück, Elisabeth, and Hannover Heinrich, *Der Mord an Rosa Luxemburg und Karl Liebknecht. Dokumentation eines politischen Verbrechens*, Frankfurt/M., 1965, 185 p.
Haussmann, Arno, *Morgenrot über der Spree. Feuilletons und Reportagen aus der Berliner Arbeiterpresse 1918–1933*, East Berlin, 1933, 185 p.
Jahrbuch für Politik = Wirtschaft Arbeiterbewegung, Hamburg, 1922–3, 1923–4.
Kolb, Eberhard (with R. Rürup), *Der Zentralrat der deutschen sozialistischen Republik, 19. Dezember 1918–8. April 1919, vom ersten zum zweiten Rätekongress*, Leiden, 1968, 830 p. (Abbrev: *Der Zentralrat.*)
Könnemann, Erwin, 'Protokolle Albert Südekums aus den Tagen nach dem Kapp-Putsch', *BzG*, 1966 nᵒ 2, pp. 262–78.
Lay, K., *Appelle einer Revolution. Das Ende der Monarchie. Das revolutionäre Interregnum. Die Rätezeit. Dokumente aus Bayern zum Jahr 1918/1919*, Munich, 1968, 125 p.
Der Ledebour-Prozess. Gesamtdarstellung des Prozesses gegen Ledebour wegen Aufruhr . . . vor dem Geschworenengericht Berlin Mitte Mai–Juni 1919. Auf Grund des amtlichen Stenogramm, Berlin, 1919, 831 p.
Die Lehren des deutschen Ereignisse. Das Präsidium des Exekutivkomitees der Kommunistischen Internationale zur deutschen Frage 1924, Hamburg, 1924, 120 p. (Abbrev: *Die Lehren . . .*)

Manifest, Richtlinien, Beschlüsse der ersten Kongresses. Aufrufe und offene Schreiben des Exekutivkomitees bis zum zweiten Kongress, Hamburg, 1920, 379 p.

Matthias, Erich, and Morsey, Rudolf, *Die Regierung des Prinzen Max von Baden*, Düsseldorf, 1962, 784 p.

Matthias, Erich and Pikart, Eberhard, *Die Reichstagsfraktion der deutschen Sozialdemokratie 1898 bis 1918*, Düsseldorf, 1966, 2 vol., vol. II, 600 p.

Matthias, Erich (with Rudolf Morsey), *Der Interfraktionnelle Ausschuss 1917/1918*, Düsseldorf, 1967, 1 624 p.

—— (intro. with Susanne Miller and H. Potthoff), *Die Regierung der Volksbeauftragten 1918–1919*, Düsseldorf, 1969, t. I, 408 p., t. II, 400 p.

Der Meuchelmord en Karl Liebknecht und Rosa Luxemburg (Tatsachen-material), K.P.D.(S), s. 1., n.d., 16 p.

Michaelis, H. and Schraepler, E., *Ursachen und Folgen vom deutschen Zusammenbruch 1918 und 1945 bis zur Staatlichen Neuordnung Deutschlands in der Gegenwart*, Berlin, grand in-8°: vol. I, *Die Wende des ersten Weltkrieges und der Beginn der innerpolitischen Wandlung (1916–1958)*, 1958, 454 p.; II, *Der militärische Zusammenbruch und das Ende des Kaiserreichs*, 1958, 454 p.; II, *Der militärische Zusammenbruch und das Ende des Kaiserreichs*, 1958, 594 p.; III, *Der Weg in die Weimarer Republik*, 1958, 628 p.; IV, *Die Weimarer Republik. Vertragserfüllung und innere Bedrohung 1919–1922*, 1960, 439 p.; V, *Die Weimarer Republik. Das kritische Jahr 1923*, 1960, 571 p.

Der Mord an Karl Liebknecht und Rosa Luxemburg. Zusammenfassende Darstellung des gesamten Untersuchungsmaterials mit ausführlichen Prozessberichten, Berlin, 1920, 115 p.

Neuberg, A., *Der bewaffnete Aufstand. Versuch einer theoretischen Darstellung*, Zurich, 1928: French trans., Paris, 1970, *L'Insurrection armée*, 284 p.

Die proletarische Einheitsfront. Aufruf der Exekutive der Kommunistischen Internationale und der Exekutive der Rote-Gewerkschats Internationale (Moskau 1. Januar 1922). Leitsätze über die Einheitsfront (einstimmig genommen von der Exekutive der Kommunistischen Internationale am 28. Dezember 1921), s. 1., 1922, 25 p.

Protokoll der Konferenz der Erweiterten Exekutive der Kommunistischen Internationale (Moskau 12.–23. Juni 1923), Hamburg, 1923, 336 p.

Ritter, Gerhard, A. and Miller, Susanne *Die deutsche Revolution 1918–1919*, Frankfurt/M., 1968, 380 p.

Schmolze, Gerhard (ed), *Revolution und Räterepublik in München 1918/1919 in Augenzeugenberichten*, Düsseldorf, 1969, 426 p.

Schneider, Dieter and Kuda, Rudolf, *Arbeiterräte in der Novemberrevolution. Ideen, Wirkungen, Dokumente*, Frankfurt/M., 1968, 173 p.

Schulthess Europäischer Geschichtskalender, Munich, *1919*, 616 p., *1920*, 416 p., *1921*, 680 p., *1922*, 881 p., *1923*, 718 p.

Stern Leo, *Die Auswirkungen der grossen sozialistischen Oktoberrevolution auf Deutschland*, East Berlin, 1959, 4 vol., 2031 p.

Stresemann, Gustav, *Vermächtnis. Der Nachlas in drei Bänden*, edited by H. Bernhard, vol. I, *Vom Ruhrkrieg bis London*, Berlin, 1932, 643 p.

Die Tätigkeit der Exekutive und des Präsidiums der Exekutivkomitee der Kommunistischen Internationale vom 13. Juli 1921 bis 1. Februar 1922, Petrograd, 1922, 410 p.

Tivel, A., *Pjat' let Kominterna v resheniiakh i tsifrakh*, Moscow, 1924, 123 p.

Weber, Hermann, *Der deutsche Kommunismus. Dokumente*, Cologne, 1963, 629 p.

——, *Die Kommunistische Internationale. Eine Dokumentation*, Hanover, 1966, 416 p.

Der Weg der Revolution, Berlin, 1920, 20 p. (*Letter from Lenin, Circular from Executive, Postface by Thalheimer.*)

Zeman, Z.A.B., *Germany and the Revolution in Russia 1915–1918, Documents from the Archives of the German Foreign Ministry*, London, 1958, 157 p.

G. Biographies

Becher, Johannes, R., *Walter Ulbricht. Ein deutscher Arbeitersohn*, East Berlin, 1958, 228 p.

Beradt, Charlotte, *Paul Levi. Ein demokratischer Sozialist in der Weimarer Republik*, Frankfurt/M., 1969, 156 p.

Besson, Waldemar, *Friedrich Ebert. Verdienst und Grenze*, Göttingen, 1963, 94 p.

Brandt, Willy, and Lowenthal, Richard, *Ernst Reuter. Ein Leben für die Freiheit. Eine Politische Biographie*, Munich, 1957, 760 p.

Bredel, Willi, *Ernst Thälmann. Ein Beitrag zu einem politischen Lebensbild*, East Berlin, 1950, 168 p.

Dahlem, Franz, 'Warum er "Genosse Zelle" hiess' (on Ulbricht), *BzG*, 1963, n° 2, pp. 264–70.

Deutscher, Isaac, *Trotsky*, vol. III, *The Prophet Unarmed*, London, 1959, 490 p.

Dornemann, Luise, *Clara Zetkin; ein Lebensbild*, East Berlin, 1959, 457 p.

Erpenbeck, Fritz, *Wilhelm Pieck. Ein Lebensbild*, East Berlin, 1951, 172 p.

Frölich, Paul, *Rosa Luxemburg. Gedanke und Tat*, Paris, 1939, 269 p.; French trans. *Rosa Luxemburg*. Paris, 1965, 390 p.

Gross, Babette, *Willi Münzenberg. Eine politische Biographie*, Stuttgart, 1967, 352 p.

Gruber, Helmut, 'Levi and the Comintern', *International Communism in the Era of Lenin*, pp. 391–407.

Hammer, Franz, *Theodor Neubauer. Ein Kämpfer gegen den Faschismus*, East Berlin, Second ed., 1967, 204 p.

Hohendorf, Gerd, *Revolutionäre Schulpolitik und marxistische Pädagogik im Lebenswerk Clara Zetkins*, East Berlin, 1962, 196 p.

Ilberg, Hanna, *Clara Zetkin. Aus dem Lehren und Wirken einer grossen Sozialistin*, East Berlin, 1956, 220 p.

Kerff, Willy, *Karl Liebknecht 1914 bis 1916. Fragment einer Biographie*, East Berlin, 1967, 337 p.

Kiessling, Wolfgang, *Ernst Schneller. Lebensbild eines Revolutionärs*, East Berlin, 1960, 243 p.

Kotowski, Georg, *Friedrich Ebert. Eine politische Biographie*. Vol. I: *Der Aufstieg eines deutschen Arbeiterführers 1871–1917*, Wiesbaden, 1963, 280 p.

Ledebour, Minna, *Georg Ledebour. Mensch und Kämpfer*, Zurich, 1954, 169 p.

Leipart, Theodor, *Carl Legien. Ein Gedenkbuch*, Berlin, 1929, 187 p.

Lerner, Warren, *Karl Radek. The Last Internationalist*, Stanford, 1970, 240 p.

Maslowski, Peter, *Thälmann*, Leipzig, 1932, 94 p.

Mehnert, Wolfgang, *Der Beitrag Edwin Hoernles zum Schulpolitischen und Pädagogischen Kampf der K.P.D. in der Zeit der Weimarer Republik (1919–1929)*, East Berlin, 1958, 176 p.

Meyer, Karl W., *Karl Liebknecht: Man without a Country*, Washington, 1957, 180 p.

Müller, Sonja, *Theodor Neubauer*, East Berlin, 1964, 127 p.

Nettl, J.P., *Rosa Luxemburg*, 2 vols., London, 1966, 984 p.

Œlssner, Fred, *Rosa Luxemburg, eine kritische biographische Skizze*, East Berlin, 1951, 218 p.

Ossietzky, Carl von, 'Paul Levi', *Die Weltbühne*, n° 8, 18 February 1930, pp. 280–2.

Osterroth, Franz, *Biographisches Lexikon des Sozialismus*, vol. I, *Verstorbene Persönlichkeiten*, Hanover, 1960, 368 p. + 35.

Schleifstein, Joseph, *Franz Mehring. Sein marxistische Schaffen 1891–1919*, East Berlin, 1959, 356 p.

Schumacher, Horst, *Sie nannten ihn Karski*, East Berlin, 1964, 194 p.

Schumacher, Horst, and Tych, Feliks, *Julian Marchlewski. Eine Biographie*, East Berlin, 1966, 345 p.

Schurer, H., 'Radek and the German Revolution', *Survey*, n° 53, October 1964, pp. 59–69, and n° 55, April 1965, pp. 126–140.

Stern, Carola, *Ulbricht. Eine politische Biographie*, Cologne, 1964, 357 p.

Werner, Paul (pseud. of P. Frölich), *Eugen Léviné*, Berlin, 1922, 58 p.

Zeman, Z.A.B., and Scharlau, W.B., *The Merchant of Revolution. The Life of Alexander I. Helphand (Parvus) 1867–1924*, London, 1965, 306 p.

N.B. – When finishing the manuscript, we were unfortunately not able to consult the first part of the biography of Walter Stoecker which was announced as forthcoming.

Stoecker, Helmuth, *Walter Stoecker. Die Frühzeit eines deutschen Arbeitersführers 1891–1920*, East Berlin.

H. Autobiographies, Memoirs, Remembrances

Beckers, Hans, *Wie ich zum Tode verurteilt wurde. Die Marinetragödie im Sommer 1917*, Leipzig, 1928, 116 p.

Braun, Otto, *Von Weimar bis Hitler*, Hamburg, 1949, 311 p.

Buber-Neumann, Margarete (pseud. of Faust, Margarete), *Von Potsdam nach Moskau: Stationen eines Irrweges*, Stuttgart, 1958, 477 p.

Globig, Fritz, *. . . aber verbunden sind wir mächtig. Aus der Geschichte der Arbeiterjugendbewegung*, East Berlin, 1958, 336 p.

Groener, General Wilhelm, *Lebenserinnerungen. Jugend-Generalstab-Weltkrieg* (Intro. by Frh. Hiller von Gärtringen), Göttingen, 1957, 584 p.

Guilbeaux, Henri, *Du Kremlin au Cherche-Midi*, Paris, 1933, 270 p.

Haupt, Georges, and Marie, Jean-Jacques (intro), *Les Bolcheviks par eux-mêmes*, Paris, 1969, 398 p.

Hoelz, Max, *Vom 'Weissen Kreuz' zur Roten Fahne: Jugend-Kampf und Zuchthauserlebnisse*, Berlin, 1929, 392 p.

Jannack, Carl, *Wir mit der roten Nelke. Ein Arbeiterveteran erzählt*, Bautzen, 1959, 288 p.

Heckert, Fritz, 'Mes rencontres avec Lénine', *Lénine tel qu'il fut. Souvenirs de contemporains*, vol. II, Moscow, 1959, pp. 802–809.

Jung, Franz, *Der Weg nach Unten*, Berlin, 1961, 482 p.

Keil, Wilhelm, *Erlebnisse eines Sozialdemokraten*, Stuttgart, 1947, 477 p., and 1948, 726 p.

Krivitsky, Walter G., *In Stalin's Secret Service. An Exposé of Russia's Secret Policies by the former Chief of the Soviet Intelligence in Western Europe*, New York, 1939, 273 p.; French trans. *Agent de Staline*, Paris, 1940, 320 p.

Léviné, Rosa, *Aus der Münchener Rätezeit*, Berlin, 1925, 76 p.

Löbe, Paul, *Erinnerungen eines Reichstagspräsidenten*, Berlin, 1949, 173 p.

Lüttwitz, Walter, Freiherr von, *Im Kampf gegen die Novemberrevolution*, Berlin, 1934, 139 p.

Maercker, Ludwig R.G., *Vom Kaiserheer zur Reichswehr. Geschichte der freiwilliger Landjäger Korps*, Leipzig, 1922, 398 p.

Max, Prinz von Baden, *Erinnerungen und Dokumente*, Stuttgart-Berlin, 1928, 699 p.

Mühsam, Eric, *Von Eisner bis Léviné. Die Enstehung der bayerische Räterepublik. Persönlichen Rechenschaftsbericht über die revolutionäre Ereignisse in München vom 7.XI.1918 bis zum 13.IV.1919*, Berlin, 1929, 70 p.

Müller, Hermann, *Die Novemberrevolution*, Berlin, 1931, 286 p.

Müller, Richard, *Vom Kaiserreich zur Republik*, 2 vol.: I, *Ein Beitrag zur Geschichte der revolutionären Arbeiterbewegung während des Weltkrieges*, Berlin, 1924, 219 p.; II, *Die Novemberrevolution*, Berlin, 1925, 296 p.

——, *Der Bürgerkrieg in Deutschland. Geburtswehen der Republik*, Berlin, 1925, 244 p.

Münzenberg, Willi, *Die dritte Front*, Berlin, 1930, 398 p.

1918. Erinnerungen von Veteranen der deutschen Gewerkschaftsbewegung an die November-revolution 1914–1920, Berlin, 1949, 446 p.

Noske, Gustav, *Von Kiel bis Kapp. Zur Geschichte der deutschen Revolution*, Berlin, 1920, 210 p.

Œhme, Walter, *Damals in der Reichskanzlei. Erinnerungen aus den Jahren 1918–1919*, East Berlin, 1958, 366 p.

——, *Die Weimarer Nationalversammlung. Erinnerungen*, East Berlin, 1962, 404 p.

Paetel, Karl O., 'Der deutsche Nationalbolschewismus 1918–1932; Ein Bericht', *Aussenpolitik*, April 1952, n° 4, pp. 229–42.

Payer, Friedrich, *Von Bethmann-Hollweg bis Ebert. Erinnerungen und Bilder*, Frankfurt/M., 1923, 304 p.

Poretski, Elisabeth, *Les nôtres. Vie et mort d'un agent soviétique (Ignace Reiss)*, Paris, 1969, 304 p.

Radek, Karl, 'Nojabr', Iz vospominaii', *Krasnaja Nov'*, 1926, n° 10, pp. 140–176; German trans.: 'November. Eine kleine Seite aus meinen Erinnerungen', in 'Karl Radek in Berlin' by O.E. Schüddekopf, *Archiv für Sozialgeschichte*, vol. II, 1962, pp. 119–66.

——, «Avtobiografija», *Entsiklopeditcheskii slovar'*, Seventh ed., vol. XLI, Second Part, Moscow, Institut Granat, 1929, pp. 138–69. French trans. (with some cuts) in Haupt and Marie, *op. cit., supra*, pp. 321–39.

Reichenbach, Bernhard, 'Moscow 1921. Meetings in the Kremlin', *Survey*, n° 53, October 1964, pp. 16–22.

Scheidemann, Philip, *Der Zusammenbruch*, Berlin, 1921, 251 p.

——, *Memoiren eines Sozialdemokraten*, 2 vol., Dresden, 1928, 443 p.

Serge, Victor (pseud. of Kibaltchich), *Mémoires d'un révolutionnaire*, Paris, 1951, 416 p.

Severing, Carl, *1919/1920 im Wetter- und Watterwinkel. Aufzeichnungen und Erinnerungen*, Bielefeld, 1927, 253 p.

Severing, Carl, *Mein Lebensweg*, 2 vol., Cologne, 1950, 465 and 525 p.

Toller, Ernst, *Eine Jugend in Deutschland*, Amsterdam, 1933, 287 p.

Trotsky, Léon, *Ma Vie*, 3 vol., Paris, 1930, 220, 272, 344 p.

Unter der roten Fahne. Erinnerungen alter Genossen, East Berlin, 1958, 332 p.

Valtin, Jan (pseud. of Krebs), *Out of the Night*, New York, 1941, 749 p.; French trans. *Sans Patrie ni Frontières*, Paris, 1947, 788 p.

Vorwärts und nicht vergessen. Erlebnisseberichte aktiver Teilnehmer der November-revolution 1918–1919, East Berlin, 1958, 584 p. (Abbrev: *Vorwärts und . . .*)

Witzmann, Georg, *Thüringen von 1918–1933. Erinnerungen eines Politikers*, Meisenheim / Glain, 1958, 184 p.

Wollenberg, Erich, *Als Rot-Armist vor München. Reportage aus der Münchener Räterepublik*, Berlin, 1929, 160 p.

Wrobel, Kurt, *Der Sieg der Arbeiter und Matrosen im Dezember 18 in Berlin. Berliner Arbeiterveteranen berichten über ihren Kampf in der Novemberrevolution*, Berlin, 1958, 64 p.

Zeigner, Erich, 'Politischer Rückblick auf das Jahr 1923', *Sozialistische Einheit*, 24 March 1956.

Zetkin, Clara, *Erinnerungen an Lenin*, Vienna-Berlin, 1925, 85 p.; French trans. *Souvenirs sur Lénine*, Paris, 1926, 67 p.

Zeutschel, Walter, *Im Dienst der Kommunistischen Terrororganisation. Tscheka in Deutschland*, Berlin, 1931, 159 p.

Zikelsky, Fritz, *Das Gewehr in meiner Hand. Erinnerungen eines Arbeiter-veteranen*, East Berlin, 1958, 197 p.

I. Contemporary Works

Adler, Max, *Demokratie und Rätesystem*, Vienna 1919. French trans. *Démocratie and conseils ouvriers*, Preface by Y. Bourdet, Paris, 1966, 164 p.

Adler, Victor, *Briefwechsel mit August Bebel und Karl Kautsky*, Vienna, 680 p.

Barth, Emil, *Aus der Werkstatt der deutschen Revolution*, Berlin, 1919, 158 p.

Bernstein, Eduard, *Die deutsche Revolution, I – Geschichte der Entstehung und ersten Arbeitsperiode der deutschen Republik*, Berlin, 1921, 198 p.

Brandler, Heinrich, *Durch die Räte zur Einheit der Arbeiterklasse und zum Kommunismus*, Chemnitz, 1919, 14 p.

——, *Die Aktion gegen den Kapp-Putsch in Westsachsen*, Berlin, 1920, 93 p.

——, *War die Märzaktion ein Bakunisten-Putsch?*, Berlin-Leipzig, 1921, 88 p.

——, *Der Hochverrats-Prozess gegen Heinrich Brandler vor dem ausserordentlichen Gericht am 6. Juni 1921 in Berlin*, Leipzig-Berlin, 1921, 46 p.

Braun, M.J. (pseud of Bronski), *Die Lehren des Kapp-Putsches*, Leipzig, 1920, 32 p.

Bremer, Karl, *Der nahende Zusammenbruch der deutschen Bourgeoisie und der K.P.D.*, Hamburg, 1921, 36 p.

Crispien, Artur, *Programm und Taktik der U.S.P.D. in ihrer Geschichtliche Entwicklung* (speech), Berlin, 1920, 86 p.

Däumig, Ernst, *Das Rätesystem* (Speech at Congress of U.S.P.D. in March 1919), Berlin, 1919, 38 p.

Dittmann, Wilhelm, *Revolutionäre Taktik*, Berlin, 1920, 32 p.

Eichhorn, Emil, *Meine Tätigkeit im Berliner Polizeipräsidium und mein Anteil an den Januar-Ereignissen*, Berlin, 1919, 104 p.

Eisner, Kurt, *Die halbe Macht den Räten. Ausgewählte aufsätzen und Reden*, Cologne, 1969, 292 p.

Fischer, *Die Revolutions-Kommandantur Berlin*, Berlin, 1922, 84 p.

Frank, Karl, *Der Fall Levi in der Dritten Internationale*, Vienna, 1921, 15 p.

Friesland, Ernst, *Zur Krise unserer Partei*, Berlin 1921, 32 p.

Frölich, Paul, *Zehn Jahre Krieg und Bürgerkrieg, I. Der Krieg*, Berlin, 1924, 243 p.

Frölich, Paul, and Schreiner, Albert, *Die deutsche Sozialdemokratie. Vierzehn Jahre im Bunde mit dem Kapital*, Berlin, 1928, 173 p.

Geyer, Curt, *Sozialismus und Rätesystem*, Leipzig, 1919, 32 p.

——, *Für die dritte Internationale! Die U.S.P.D. am Scheideweg*. Berlin, 1920, 77 p.

——, *Der Radikalismus in der deutschen Arbeiterbewegung. Ein soziologischer Versuch*, Jena, 1923, 111 p.

——, *Drei Verderber Deutschlands. Zur Geschichte Deutschlands und der Reparationsfrage 1920–1924*, Berlin, 1924, 230 p.

Gorter, Hermann, *Die Klassenkampforganisation des Proletariats*, Berlin, 1919, 88 p.

——, *Der Imperialismus, der Weltkrieg und der Sozialdemokratie*, Munich, 1919, 135 p.

——, *Offenen Brief an der Genossen Lenin. Eine Antwort auf Lenins Broschüre 'Der Radikalismus, ein Kinderkrankheit des Kommunismus*, Berlin, 1920, 88 p. French trans. *Réponse à Lénine*, Paris, 1920, reprint, 1970, 112 p.

Goussev (Gussew S.J.), *Die Lehren des Bürgerkrieges*, Hamburg, 1921, 96 p.

Gruber, Helmut (ed), *International Communism in the Era of Lenin. A documentary History* (Extract from documents of the CI, Lenin, Radek, Levi, Frölich, Szanto, Bettelheim; Gorter, Serrati, R. Fischer, Brandler, etc.), New York, 1966, 512 p.

Heckert, Fritz (Gekkert), 'Germanija v oktjabre 1923 k istorii K.P.G.', *Kommunistitcheskii International*, 1934, n° 5, pp. 55–64.

Hoel, Max, *Anklagerede gegen die bürgerliche Gesellschaft. Gehalten vor dem Moabiter Sondergericht am 22. Juni 1921 in Berlin*, Berlin, 1921, 20 p.

Ist eine Einheitsfront mit dem Kommunisten möglich? Denkschrift über die Verhandlungen der Gewerskchaften mit den Arbeiterparteien über den Schutz der Republik (A.D.G.B. Publication), Berlin, 1922, 280 p.

Karski, Julian (pseud. of Marchlewski), *Die Sozialisierung des Bergbaus*, Essen, 1919, 31 p.

Kools, Frits (ed.), *Die Linke gegen die Parteiherrschaft*, Olten and Fribourg/Brisgau, 1970, 640 p. (Texts by Pannekoek, Gorter, Laufenberg, Wolffheim, Rühle, Schröder, Hoelz, etc.)

Korsch, Karl, *Arbeitsrecht für Betriebsräre (1922)*, new ed., Frankfurt/M., 1967, 152 p.

Landauer, Gustav, *Aufrut zum Sozialismus*, Third ed., Berlin, 1920, 155 p.

Laufenberg, Heinrich, *Zwischen der ersten und zweiten Revolution*, Hamburg, 1919, 48 p.

——, *Die Hamburger Revolution*, Hamburg, 1919, 32 p.

——, *Massen und Führer*, Hamburg, 1919, 27 p.

——, *Arbeiterklasse und Staatsgewalt*, Hamburg, 1919, 15 p.

——, *Was heisst Sozialisierung?*, Hamburg, 1919, 16 p.

Laufenberg, Heinrich and Wolffheim, Fritz, *Revolutionärer Volkskrieg oder konterrevolutionärer Bürgerkrieg? Erste kommunistische Adresse an das deutsche Proletariat*, Hamburg, 1919, 16 p.

—— and ——, *Moskau und die deutsche Revolution. Eine kritische Erledigung der bolschewistischen Methoden*, Hamburg, n.d., 48 p.

—— and ——, *Nation und Arbeiterklasse*, Hamburg, 1920, 20 p.

Lenin, V.I. *Œuvres*, translation Editions de Moscow.

Levi, Paul (with pseud. of Caius), *Generalstreik und Noske-Blut-Bad in Berlin*, Berlin, 1919, 19 p.

——, *Unser Weg. Wider den Putschismus*. En annexe: Karl Radek, *Die Lehren eines Putschversuches*, Berlin, 1921, 64 p.

——, *Was ist das Verbrechen? Die Märzaktion oder die Kritik daran?*, Berlin, 1921, 44 p.

——, *Zwischen Spartakus und Sozialdemokratie*. Aufsätze und Reden (Text/edited by Charlotte Beradt), Frankfurt/M., 1969, 338 p.

Liebknecht, Karl, *Klassenkampf gegen den Krieg*, Berlin, n.d. (1919), 109 p. (Abbrev: *Klassenkampf*.)

——, *Politische Aufzeichnungen aus seinem Nachlass* (Writings of 1917–18, introduced and edited by Franz Pfemfert), Berlin, 1921, 160 p.

——, *Gesammelte Reden und Schriften*, East Berlin, vol. VIII, *August 1914 bis April 1916*, 1966, 655 p., vol. IX, *Mai 1916 bis 15. Januar 1919*, 1968, 734 p.

——, *Militarisme, guerre and révolution* (selected texts), Paris, 1970, 270 p.

Lozovski, A. (Losovskii), *Aufgaben und Entwicklung der Betriebsräte in Russland* (Selected texts Speech to Berlin Congress of Factory Councils), Berlin, 1920, 31 p.

——, *Eroberung oder Zerstörung der Gewerkschaften?* (Speech given in Berlin), Leipzig, 1920, 14 p.

—— and Brandler, Heinrich, *Der Kampf der Kommunisten in den Gewerkschaften*, (Report to the Executive of the CI in February–March 1922), Berlin, 1922, 35 p.

Ludwig, E. (pseud. of Alexander), *Die Rolle der Arbeiterräte in der deutschen Revolution*, Berlin, 1919, 19 p.

Luxemburg, Rosa, *Massenstreik, Partei und Gewerkschaften*, Leipzig, 1919, 68 p.

——, *Die Krise der Sozialdemokratie* (*Junius-Broschüre*), Berlin, 1916, 96 p.; French trans. *La Crise de la social-démocratie*, Bruxelles, 1970, 250 p.

——, *Briefe aus dem Gefängnis*, Berlin, 1920, 48 p.

——, *Die russische Revolution. Eine kritische Würdigung* (*Intr. Paul Levi*), Berlin, 1922, 120 p.

——, *Briefe an Freunde*, Zurich, 1950, 226 p.

——, *Im Kampf gegen den deutschen Militarismus*, I.M.L., East Berlin, 1960, 264 p.

——, *Ich war, ich bin, ich werde sein* (Writings and Speeches on November Revolution), East Berlin, 1958, 144 p.

——, *Ausgewählte Reden und Schriften*, 2 vol., East Berlin, 1951, 751 and 741 p.

——, *Politische Schriften* (Introduced by O.K. Flechtheim), Frankfurt/M., 1966, 232 p., II., 1966, 208 p., III., 1967, 246 p.

Marchlewski, Julian, *Das Rätesystem*, Essen, 1910, 16 p.

——, *Was ist Bolschewismus?*, Basel, 1920, 20 p.

Marchlewski, (voir Karski).

Münzenberg, Willi, *Von der Revolte zur Revolution. Eine Antwort auf Kautsky's «Weitertreiben der Revolution»*, Berlin, 1919, 32 p.

Neubauer, Theodor, *Aus Reden und Aufsätzen* (Introduced by Müller and Sieber), s. 1., n.d., 156 p.

Neumann, Paul, *Hamburg unter der Regierung des Arbeiter- und Soldatenräte. Tätigkeitsbericht, erstattet im Auftrage der Exekutive der Arbeiterrats Gross-Hamburgs*, Hamburg, 1919, 143 p.

Pannekoek, Anton, *Die taktische Differenzen in der Arbeiterbewegung*, Hamburg, 1909, 132 p.

Pannekoek (see Kools, *op. cit., supra*, and Bricianer, *infra*).

Pannekoek, Anton, and Gorter, Hermann, *Organisation und Taktik der proletarischen Revolution* (Texts selected and introduced by M. Bock), Frankfurt/M., 1969, 254 p.

Paquet, Alfons, *Der Geist der russischen Revolution*, Leipzig, 1919, 110 p.

Pawlowski, Eugen (pseud. of E. Varga), *Der Bankrott Deutschlands*, Hamburg, 1921, 189 p.

Pieck, Wilhelm, *Gesammelte Reden und Schriften*, East Berlin, vol. I, *August 1904 bis Januar 1919*, 1959, 24–527 p.; vol. II, *Januar 1919 bis April 1925*, 1959, 18–539 p.

Préobrajensky, *Ot Nepa k Sotsialismu*, Moscow, 1922; French trans. *De la N.É.P. au socialisme* (*Vues sur l'avenir de la Russie and de l'Europe*), (Preface by P. Naville), Paris, 1966, 123 p.

Radek, Karl, *In den Reihen der deutschen Revolution 1909–1919*, Munich, 1921, 464 p.

—— (v. Struthahn).

——, *Die Entwicklung der Weltrevolution und die Taktik der Kommunistischen Parteien im Kampfe für die Diktatur des Proletariats*, Berlin, 1919, 66 p.

——, *Zur Taktik des Kommunismus*: *Ein Schreiben an den Oktober-Parteitag der K.P.D.*, Berlin, 1919, 12 p.

——, *Die Masken sind gefallen. Eine Antwort an Crispien, Ditmann und Hilferding*, s. 1., 1920, 38 p.

——, *Der Weg der Kommunistischen Internationale*, Hamburg, 1921, 86 p.

——, *Rosa Luxemburg, Karl Liebknecht, Leo Jogiches*, Hamburg, 1921, 48 p.

——, *Soll die Vereinigte Kommunistische Partei Deutschlands eine Massenpartei der revolutionärer Aktion oder zentristische Partei des Wartens sein?*, Hamburg, 1921, Second ed., 120 p. (Abbrev: *Soll de V.K.P.D.?*)

——, *Genua, die Einheitsfront des Proletariats und die Kommunistische Internationale*, Hamburg, 1922, 78 p.

——, *Vorwort*, pp. VII–XXVII to Reissner, Larissa, *Oktober*, Berlin, 1932, 522 p.

Radek, Karl and Thalheimer, August, *Gegen den Nationalbolschewismus*, s. l., 1920, 48 p.

Radek, Karl, Frölich, Paul, Reventlow, Graf Ernst, and Möller Van den Bruck, *Schlageter. Eine Auseinandersetzung*, Berlin, 1923, 60 p.

Reissner, Larissa, *Hamburg auf den Barrikaden 1923*, Berlin, n.d., 85 p.; new ed. East Berlin, 1960, 174 p.

Schneider, Josef, *Die blutige Osterwoche im Mansfelder Land. Tatsachen-material aus den Märzaktion*, Vienna, 1922, 96 p.

Sender, Tony, *Diktatur über das Proletariat, oder Diktatur des Proletariats. Dar Ergebnis von Moskau*, Frankfurt/M., 1920, 16 p.

Struthahn, Arnold (pseud. of Radek), *Die Diktatur der Arbeiterklasse und der Kommunistische Partei*, s. l., 1919, 15 p.

——, *Die Entwicklung der deutschen Revolution und die Aufgaben der Kommunistischen Partei*, Stuttgart, 1919, 64 p.

——, *Die Auswärtige Politik des deutschen Kommunismus und der Hamburger National-Bolschewismus*, Berlin, 1919.

Szanto, Béla, *Klassenkämpfe und die Diktatur des Proletariats in Ungarn* (Introduction by Karl Radek), Vienna, 1920, 100 p.

Taktik und Organisation des revolutionären Offensive. Die Lehren der März-Aktion, Leipzig-Berlin, 1921, 146 p.

Thalheimer, August, 'Der proletarische Klassenkampf in Deutschland in Jahre 1922', *Jahrbuch für Politik, Wirtschaft und Arbeiterbewegung 1922/1923*, Hamburg, pp. 607–11.

——, 'Die Arbeiterparteien in Deutschland 1922 bis 1924', *Jahrbuch für Politik, Wirtschaft, und Arbeiterbewegung 1923/1924*, Hamburg, pp. 591–605.

——, *1923, Eine verpasste Revolution? Die deutsche Oktoberlegende und die wirkliche Geschichte von 1923*, Berlin, 1931, 32 p.

Troeltsch, Ernst, *Spektator-Briefe. Aufsätze über die deutsche Revolution und die Weltpolitik 1918/1922*, Tübingen, 1924, 321 p.

Trotsky, Léon, *Pjat' let Kominterna*, 2 vol., Moscow, 1924–1925, 612 p. English trans.: *The First Five Years of the Communist International*, vol. I, New York, 1945, 374 p., vol. II, London, 1953, 384 p.

——, 'Leçons d'Octobre', in *Cahiers du bolchevisme*, n° 5 (19 December 1924) and 6 (25 December 1924), Paris, pp. 313–336 and 396–411; and in *Staline contre Trotsky*, Paris, 1965, pp. 30–82.

——, *L'Internationale communiste après Lénine*, new ed. 2 vol., Paris, 1969, 592 p.

Ulbricht, Walter, *Zur Geschichte der deutschen Arbeiterbewegung*, vol. I, *1918–1933*, Eighth ed., East Berlin, 1933, 688 p.

Umbreit, Paul, *Die deutsche Gewerkschaften im Weltkrieg*, Berlin, 1917, 122 p.

Varga, Eugen, *Die Krise der kapitalistischen Weltwirtschaft*, Hamburg, 1921, 64 p.

Warski, Adolf (pseud. of Warszawski), *Rosa Luxemburgs Stellung zu den taktischen Problemen der Revolution*, Hamburg, 1922, 38 p.

Der Weg des Dr Levi, der Weg der V.K.P.D. (KAPD attributed to pamphlet Gorter), Berlin, 1921, 32 p.

Der Weisse Terror. Skizze aus dem Blutherrschaft Ebert-Scheidemann-Noske, Stuttgart, 1919, 16 p.

Werner, Paul (pseud. of P. Frölich), *Die bayrische Räterepublik. Tatsachen und Kritik*, Petrograd, 1920, 195 p.

Wolffheim, Fritz, *Betriebsorganisation oder Gewerkschaft?*, Hamburg, 1919, 14 p.

Zetkin, Clara, *Der Weg nach Moskau*, Hamburg, 1920, 31 p.

——, *Der Kampf der kommunistischen Parteien gegen Kriegsgefahr und Krieg*, Hamburg, 1922, 54 p.

——, *Um Rosa Luxemburgs Stellung zur russischen Revolution*, Hamburg, 1923, 224 p.

——, *Gegen Poincaré und Cuno. Eine kommunistische Antwort im Reichstag auf der Regierungserklärung der Reichskanzlers Cuno*, Berlin, 1923, 20 p.

——, *Ausgewählte Reden und Schriften*, East Berlin, vol. I, *Auswahl aus den Jahren 1889 bis 1917*, 1957, 799 p.; vol. II, *Auswahl aus den Jahren 1918 bis 1923*, 1960, 748 p.; vol. III, *Auswahl aus den Jahren 1924 bis 1933*, 1960, 640 p.

Zinoviev (German spelling used for the name of this author: Sinowjew), *Der Krieg und die Krise des Sozialismus*, Vienna, 1924, 667 p.

Zinoviev, G., *Brennende Tagesfragen der internationalen Arbeiterbewegung*, Petrograd, 1920, 107 p.

——, *Die Weltrevolution und die Kommunistische Internationale* (Speech to Halle Congress, s. l., 1920, 68 p.

——, *Zwölf Tage in Deutschland* (Account of his trip in Germany at the time of the Halle Congress), Hamburg, 1921, 91 p.

——, *Probleme der deutschen Revolution*, Hamburg, 1923, 109 p.

——, *Fünf Jahre Kommunistische Internationale*, Hamburg, 1924, 75 p.

J. Historical Works and Essays

Abendroth, Wolfgang, *Aufstieg und Krise der deutschen Arbeiterbewegung*, Frankfurt/M., 1964, 144 p.

——, *Sozialgeschichte der europäischen Arbeiterbewegung*, Frankfurt/M., 1966, Second ed., 191 p.

Anderle, A., *Die deutsche Rapallo-Politik. Deutsch-sowjetische Beziehungen 1922–1929*, Halle, 1962, 248 p.

Anderson, Evelyn, *Hammer oder Amboss. Zur Geschichte der deutschen Arbeiterbewegung* (Translated from English), Nuremberg, 1948, 244 p.

Angel, Pierre, *Edouard Bernstein and l'évolution du socialisme allemand*, Paris, 1961, 462 p.

Angermüller, Hans Heinrich, 'Die Bedeutung der I. und II. Kongresses der Kommunistische Internationale für die Entwicklung der K.P.D. zur revolutionären Massenpartei', *Wissenschaftliche Zeitschrift der Martin-Luther Universität Halle-Wittenberg* (*Gesellschaft und sprachwissenschaftliche Reihe, 1958–1959*, pp. 47–60).

Angress, Werner T., *Stillborn Revolution: The Communist Bid for Power in Germany, 1921–1923*, Princeton, 1963, 514 p.

——, 'Weimar Coalition and Ruhr Insurrection, March–April 1920: a Study of Government Policy', *The Journal of Modern History*, XXIX, n° 1, March 1957, pp. 1–20.

Arndt, Helmuth, Seifert, Gerhard, 'Zur Gründung der K.P.D.', *Wissenschaftliche Zeitschrift der Karl-Marx Universität*, 1957–8, n° 4, pp. 313–24.

Ay, Karl Ludwig, *Die Enstehung einer Revolution. Die Volksstimmung in Bayern während des Ersten Weltkrieges*, Berlin, 1968, 230 p.

Badia, Gilbert, *Histoire de l'Allemagne contemporaine*, vol. I, *1917–1933*, Paris, 1962, 342 p.

——, 'L'attitude de la gauche social-démocrate dans les premiers mois de la guerre (août 1914–avril 1915)', *Le Mouvement social*, n° 49, October–December 1964, pp. 81–105.

——, *Les Spartakistes. 1918: l'Allemagne en révolution*, Paris, 1966, 298 p.

——, *Le Spartakisme. Les dernières années de Rosa Luxemburg and de Karl Liebknecht 1914–1919*, Paris, 1967, 438 p.

——, 'Allemagne, novembre 1918: Kurt Eisner devant le comité exécutif des conseils berlinois', *Revue d'histoire moderne and contemporaine*, XV (1968), pp. 340–361.

Bartel, Walter, *Die Linken in der deutschen Sozialdemokratie im Kampf gegen Militarismus und Krieg*, East Berlin, 1958, 640 p.

——, 'Die Spartakusgruppe im Kampf der deutscher Arbeiterklasse für die schnelle Beendigung des Krieges nach dem Januarstreik 1918', *ZfG*, 1964, n° 5, pp. 799–816.

Bauer, Roland, 'Die besten Deutschen verteidigten die Oktoberrevolution und lernten von ihr', *BzG*, 1962, n° 4, pp. 901–15.

——, 'Ueber den Charakter der Novemberrevolution', *ZfG*, 1958, n° 1, pp. 142–68.

Beckert, Siegfried, 'Die Linken in Chemnitz im Kampf gegen den Opportunismus für die Herausbildung einer revolutionären Partei', *BzG*, 1967, n° 1, pp. 109–18.

Beckmann, E., *Der Dolchstossprozess, in München vom 19. Oktober bis 20. November 1925. Verhandlungsberichte und Stimmungsbilder nach Berichten in die Münchener Zeitung*, Munich, 1925, 232 p.

Benoist-Méchin, *Histoire de l'armée allemande*, 2 vol., Paris, 1936, 470 and 684 p.

Bergsträsser, Ludwig, *Die Geschichte der politischen Parteien in Deutschland*, Munich, Tenth recast ed. 1960, 363 p.

Berlau, Joseph A., *The German Social-Democratic Party 1914–1921*, Oxford, 1950, 374 p.

Berthold, Lothar and Neef, Helmut, *Militarismus und Opportunismus gegen die Novemberrevolution. Das Bündnis der rechten Führung mit der O.H.L. (November–Dezember 1918). Eine Dokumentation*, East Berlin, 1958, 218 p.

Berthold, Lothar, 'Die Erforschung der Geschichte der Arbeiterbewegung in der Weimarer Republik', *ZfG*, 1960, special issue, pp. 358–380.

Berthold, Walter, 'Die Kämpfe der Chemnitzer Arbeiter gegen die militarische Konterrevolution im August 1919', *BzG*, 1962, n° 1, pp. 127–38.

Beutel, Horst, 'Die November-Revolution von 1918 in Leipzig und die Politik der Leipziger U.S.P.D.-Führung bis zum Eimarsch der Konterrevolutionären Truppen des Generals Maercker am 12 Mai 1919', *Wissenschaftliche Zeitschrift der Universtät Leipzig*, G.u.S.R. VII, 1958, pp. 385–411.

Beutel, Hans and Zeitz, Alfred, *Die Novemberrevolution 1918 und die Gründung der Kommunistischen Partei in Brandeburg*, Brandeburg-Havel, 1958, 63 p.

Beyer, Hans, *Von der Novemberrevolution zur Räterepublik in München*, East Berlin, 1957, 184 p.

Bock, Hans Manfred, *Syndikalismus und Linkskommunismus von 1918 bis 1923. Zur Geschichte und Soziologie der Kommunistischen Arbeiterpartei Deutschlands (K.A.P.D.), der Allgemeinen Arbeiterunion (A.A.U.D.) und der Freien Arbeiterunion (F.A.U.D.)*, Meisenheim/Glain, 1969, 480 p.

Borkenau, Franz, *Der europäische Kommunismus. Seine Geschichte von 1917 bis zur Gegenwart*, Bern, 1952, 540 p.

——, *World Communism. A History of the Communist International*, new ed. Michigan, 1962, 442 p.

Bosl (introduced by), *Bayern im Umbruch. Die Revolution von 1918, ihre Voraussetzungen, ihr Verlauf und ihre Folgen*, Munich, 1969, 603 p.

Bracher, Karl Dietrich, *Die Auflösung der Weimarer Republik*, Stuttgart, 1955, 754 p.

Brauer, Erwin, *Der Ruhraufstand von 1920*, Berlin, 1930, 112 p.

Braunthal, Julius, *Geschichte der Internationale*, Hanover, vol. I, 1961, 404 p., vol. II, 1963, 618 p.

Bricianer, Serge, *Pannekoek et les conseils ouvriers*, Paris, 1969, 306 p.

Brjunin, V.G., *Die erste Widerhall in der deutschen Arbeiterbewegung auf die Grosse Oktoberrevolution und den Friedenvorschlag der Sowjetregierung*, East Berlin (trans. from Russian), 1957, 44 p.

Buber-Neumann, Margarete (pseud. of Faust, Margarete), *Kriegsschauplätze der Weltrevolution. Ein Bericht aus der Praxis der Komintern, 1919–1943*, Stuttgart, 1967, 522 p.

Bücher, Hermann, *Finanz und Wirtschaftsentwicklung Deutschlands in den Jahren 1921 bis 1925*, Berlin, 1925, 203 p.

Buchheim, Karl, *Die Weimarer Republik. Grundlagen und politische Entwicklung*, Munich, 1960, 140 p.

Buchot, J.C., *Erich Wollenberg raconte: la 'révolution' allemande de 1923* (D.E.S. Grenoble, 1968, 110 p. dact.).

Burgelin, Henri, *La Société allemande 1871–1968*, Paris, 1969, 440 p.

Buse, D.K., 'Ebert and the Coming of World War I: A Month from his Diary', *International Review of Social History*, 1968, n° 3, pp. 430–48.

Carr, E.H., *The Bolshevik Revolution 1917–1923*, Fifth part, *Soviet Russia and the World*, vol. III, London, 1952, 614 p.

——, *The Interregnum 1923–1924*, London, 1954, 932 p.

Castellan, Georges, *L'Allemagne de Weimar*, Paris, 1969, 444 p.

Chelike, V.F., 'Natchalo Martovskhikh boev 1919 v Berline', *Nojabr'skaja Revoljuaja* Moscow, 1960, pp. 169–98.

Colloti, Enzo, 'Sinistra radicale e spartachisti nelle socialdemocrazia tedesca attraverso le Spartakus-Briefe', *Annali*, 1961, pp. 11–89.

Colm, Gerhard, *Beitrag zur Geschichte und Soziologie der Ruhraufstandes vom März–April 1920*, Essen, 1921, 142 p.

Comfort, Richard A., *Revolutionary Hamburg. Labor Politics in the Early Weimar Republic*, Stanford, 1966, 226 p.

Coper, Rudolf, *Failure of a Revolution*, Cambridge, 1954, 294 p.

Danner, Lothar, *Ordnungspolizei Hamburg: Betrachtungen zu ihrer Geschichte 1918 bis 1933*, Hamburg, 1958, 252 p.

Davidovitch, D.S., *Revoljutsionnii Krisis 1923 g. v. Germanii i Gamburskoe vostanie*, Moscow, 1963, 336 p.

Degras, Jane, 'United Front Tactics in the Cominter 1921–1928', *International Communism*, *St-Anthony's Papers*, n° 9, pp. 9–22.

Dix, Rudolf, 'Deutsche Internationalisten bei der Errichtung und Verteidigung der Sowjetmacht 1917–1921', *BzG*, 1966, n° 3, pp. 491–506.

Dorst, Tankred and Neubauer, Helmut (eds.), *Die Münchener Räterepublik. Zeugnisse und Kommentar*, Frankfurt/M., 1966, 192 p.

Drabkin, J.S., *Die Novemberrevolution 1918 in Deutschland*, Berlin 1968, 593 p.

Drachkovitch, Milorad and Lazitch, Branko, *The Comintern: Historical Highlights, Essays, Recollections, Documents*, Stanford-London, 1966, 430 p.

Drechsler, Hanno, *Die Sozialistische Arbeiterpartie Deutschlands (S.A.P.D.). Ein Beitrag zur Geschichte der deutschen Arbeiterbewegung um Ende der Weltkrieges*, Meisenheim/Glain, 1965, 406 p.

Dünow, Wilhelm, *Der Rotekämpferbund*, Berlin 1958, 101 p.

Ehrt, Adolf and Schweicert, Julius, *Entfesselung der Unterwelt. Ein Querschnitt durch der Bolschewisierung Deutschlands*, Berlin, 1933, 326 p.

Eildermann, Willi, 'Die Märzaktion 1921 im Mitteldeutschland und ihre Lehren', *Einheit*, 1951, n° 10, pp. 648–59.

Einhorn, Marion, 'Zur Rolle der Räte im November und Dezember 1918', *ZfG*, 1956, n° 3, pp. 545–59.

Einige Probleme der Novemberrevolution 1918 in Deutschland unter besonderer Berücksichtigung der Ereignisse im Kreis Weissenfelde, Zum 40. Jahrestag der Novemberrevolution und der Gründung der K.P.D., Weissenfeld, 1958, 24 p.

Eisner, Erich, *Gegen die Bürger in Marxpelz. Die anti-Autoritären 'Linken' in der Arbeiterbewegung*, Cologne, 1968, 94 p.

Erdmann, Lothar, *Die Gewerkschaften im Ruhrkampf* (A.D.G.B.), Berlin, 1924, 224 p.

Erger, Johannes, *Der Kapp-Lüttwitz Putsch. Ein Beitrag zur deutschen Innenpolitik 1919–1920*, Düsseldorf, 1967, 365 p.

Ersil, Wilhelm, *Aktionseinheit stürzt Cuno. Zur Geschichte des Massenkampfes gegen die Cuno-Regierung 1923*, East Berlin, 1961, 400 p.

Eyck, Erich, *Geschichte der Weimarer Republik*, Stuttgart, vol. I, *Vom Zusammenbruch des Kaisertums bis zur Wahl Hindenburgs 1918–1925*, 1954, 468 p.

Fabian, Walter, *Klassenkampf um Sachsen. Ein Stück Geschichte 1918–1930*, Löbau, 1930, 200 p.

Finker, Kurt, 'Aus dem Kampf der Internationalen Arbeitershilfe in Deutschland', *BzG*, 1964, n° 5, pp. 928–36.

Fischer, Ruth, *Stalin and German Communism. A Study in the Origins of the State Party*, Cambridge, MA., 1948, 688 p.

Flechtheim, Ossip K., *Die K.P.D. in der Weimarer Republik*, Offenbach, 1948, 296 p.

——, *Die K.P.D. in der Weimarer Republik* (Introduction by Hermann Weber), Frankfurt/M., 1969, 360 p.

Freymond, Jacques (ed.), *Contributions à l'histoire du Comintern*, Geneva, 1965, 265 p.

Friedländer, Henry Egon, 'Conflict of Revolutionary Authority: Provisional Government Versus Berlin soviet', *International Review of Social History*, 1962, n° 2, pp. 163–76.

Gast, Helmut, 'Die proletarischen Hunderstschaften als Organe der Einheitsfront im Jahre 1923', *ZfG*, 1956, n° 3, pp. 439–65.

Gätsch, Helmut, *Die Freien Gewerkschaften in Bremen 1919–1933*, Bremen, 1969, 169 p.

Gatzke Hans W., 'Russo-German Military Collaboration during the Weimar Republic', *The American Historical Review*, LXIII, n° 3, April 1958, pp. 565–97.

Gebler, Joachim, 'Die Novemberrevolution 1918 und die Bewegung der Lehrerräte, dargestellt am Beispiel der Lehrerbewegung in Leipzig', *Wissenschaftliche Zeitschrift der Karl-Marx Universität Leipzig*, 1965, n° 2, pp. 197–203.

Germanskoe rabotchee dvijenie v novejsee vremia, Moscow, 1962, 313 p.

Geschichte der deutschen Arbeiterbewegung-Chronik, East Berlin, vol. I, *Von den Anfängen bis 17*, 1965, 366 p., vol. II, *Von 1917 bis 1945*, 1966, 552 p.

Gessler, Otto, *Reichswehrpolitik in der Weimarer Zeit*, Stuttgart, 1958, 582 p.

Golovacev, F.F., *Rabotchee dvijenie i sotsial-demokratija Germanii v gody pervoj mirovj vojny (avgust 1914–oktjabr' 1918 g)*, Moscow, 1960, 565 p.

Gordon, Harold J., 'Die Reichswehr und Sachsen 1923', *Wehrwissenschaftliche Rundschau*, 1961, n° 12, pp. 677–92.

——, *The Reichswehr and the German Republic 1919–1926*, Princeton, 1957, 480 p.

Görlitz, *November 1918. Bericht über die deutsche Revolution*, Hamburg, 1968, 224 p.

Gorski, Günter, 'Zur These vom "ersten deutschen Arbeiterrat" in Leipzig und über das Ausmass des Mitteldeutschen Antikriegsstreiks 1917', *BzG*, 1964, n° 4, pp. 634–40.

Gotsche, Otto, *Die Märzaktion 1921 in Mitteldeutschland und ihre historische Bedeutung*, East Berlin, 1956, 84 p.

Gottschalch, Wilfried, *Strukturveränderung der Gesellschaft und politisches Handeln in der Lehre von Rudolf Hilferding*, Berlin, 1962, 287 p.

Grau, Roland, 'Zur Rolle und Bedeutung des Roten Soldatenbundes', *Zeitschrift für Militärgeschichte*, 1968, n° 6, pp. 718–32.

Grebing, Helga, *Geschichte der deutschen Parteien*, Wiesbaden, 1962, 184 p.

Grotewohl, Otto, *Dreissig Jahre später. Die Novemberrevolution und die Lehren der Geschichte der deutschen Arbeiterbewegung*, Berlin, 1952, 168 p.

Grundriss der Geschichte der deutschen Arbeiterbewegung, Fourth ed., 1964, Berlin, 304 p.

'*Grundriss der Geschichte der deutschen Arbeiterbewegung*'. *Kritik einer Legende.* (Contributions by F. Schaeppler, H. Skrzypczak, S. Bahne, Kotowski), Berlin, 1964, 83 p.

Die Gründung der Kommunistischen Partei Deutschlands. Protokoll der wissenschaftliche Tagung des Instituts für Gesellschaftswissenschaft der Parteihochschule 'Karl Marx' und des Instituts für Marxismus-Leninismus beim Z.K. der S.E.D. am 22–23. Januar 1959 in Berlin anlässlich des 40 Jahrestages der Gründung des K.P.D., Berlin, 1959, 244 p.

Guillen, Pierre, *L'Allemagne de 1848 à nos jours*, Paris, 1970, 255 p.

Gumbel, E.J., *Vier Jahre politischer Mord*, Berlin, 1922, 152 p.

Habedank, Heinz, 'Der Kampf für die zehn Forderungen des A.D.G.B. im Jahre 1921', *Die Arbeit* (East Berlin), 1963, n° 9, pp. 46–9.

——, *Zur Geschichte des Hamburger Aufstandes 1923*, Berlin, 1958, 250 p.

Haffner, Sébastien, *Die verratene Revolution*, Munich, 1970, 364 p.

Hagelweide, Gert, *Die publistische Erscheinungsbild des Menschen im Kommunistischen Lied. Eine Untersuchung der Liedpublizistik der K.P.D. (1919–1933) und der S.E.D.*, Berlin, 1968, 371 p.

Haimson, L.H., *Russian Marxists and the Origins of Bolshevism*, Cambridge, 1955, 256 p.

Hallgarten, Georg, *Hitler, Reichswehr und Industrie. Zur Geschichte der Jahre 1918–1933*, Frankfurt/M., Second ed., 1955, 139 p.

Hammer, Franz, *Freistaat Gotha im Kapp-Putsch. Nach Dokumenten und Erinnerungen alter Mitkämpfer erzählt*, East Berlin, 1955, 123 p.

Hanisch, Wilfred, *Die Hundertschaften der Arbeitewehr. Die proletarischen Hundertschaften 1923 in Sachsen*, Berlin, 1958, 105 p.

Hartenstein, *Der Kampfeinsatz der Schutzpolizei bei inneren Unruhen. Schilderung der Hamburger Oktoberunruhen 1923*, Berlin, 1926, 193 p.

Heidegger, Dr Hermann, *Die deutsche Sozialdemokratie und der national Staat (1870–1920). Unter besonderer Berücksichtigung der Kriegs- und Revolutionsjahre*, Göttingen, 1956, 401 p.

Heidorn, Gunter and Kretzchmar, Rudolf, *Rostocker Arbeiter schlugen den Kapp-Putsch nieder*, Rostock, 1955, 127 p.

Heininger, König and Tuchsheerer, *Œkonomisch-historische Aufsätze zur Novemberrevolution und zur Gründung der K.P.D.*, Berlin, 1958. 136 p.

Hennicke, Otto, *Die Rote Ruhrarmee*, Berlin, 1957, 120 p.

Hermann, Rudolf and Schmücking Arnult, 'Die Ausnahmegericht zur Unterdrückung der mitteldeutschen Märzkämpfe im Jahre 1921', *Wissenschaftliche Zeitschrift der Martin-Luther Universität Halle Wittenberg*, special issue 1958–9, I, pp. 127–40.

Hoegner, Wilhelm, *Die verratene Republik. Geschichte der deutschen Gegenrevolution*, Munich, 1958, 397 p.

Hortzschansky, Gunter, *Der nationale Verrat der deutschen Monopolherren, während des Ruhrkampfes 1923*, Berlin, 1960, 327 p.

Hübsch, Hans 'Der Entwurf eines Handelsvertrages zwischen der Sowjetunion und dem Freistaat Sachsen vom 19. Oktober 1923', *BzG*, 1965, special issue, pp. 135–139.

Hulse, James W., *The Forming of the Communist International*, Stanford, 1964, 276 p.

Humbert-Droz, Jules, *Der Krieg und die Internationale. Die Konferenzen von Zimmerwald und Kienthal*, Zurich, 1964, 262 p.

Hunt, Richard N., *German Social-Democracy 1918–1933*, London, 1964, 292 p.

Illustrierte Geschichte der deutschen Revolution, Berlin, n.d., (1929), 21 × 27 cm, 528 p. (Written by P. Frölich, Lindau and Thomas.) (Abbrev: *Ill. Gesch.*).

Illustrierte Geschichte der Novemberrevolution in Deutschland (Publication of the I.M.L.), Berlin, 1968, 391 p. (Abbrev: *Ill. Gesch.* II.)

Imig, Werner, 'Zur Hilfe Lenins für die deutschen Linken bei der Durchsetzung der marxistisch-leninistischen Staatsaufflassung 1915 bis Oktober 1918', *BzG*, 1963, n° 5–6, pp. 803–19.

Ittershagen, Siegfried, 'Die Leitsätze des 2. Parteitages der K.P.D.', *BzG*, 1963, n° 5–6, pp. 829–39.

Ittershagen, Siegfried and Wimmer, H.K.W., 'Zur Entwicklung der Strategie und Taktik der K.P.D. der Novemberrevolution bis zur Brüsseler Konferenz', *BzG*, 1963, n° 1, pp. 32–52 and n° 2, pp. 228–46.

James, Cyril L.R., *World Revolution 1917–1936. The Rise and Fall of the Communist International*, London, n. d. (1937), 429 p.

Kabaktschieff, Christo, *Die Enstehung und Entwicklung der Komintern. Kurzer Abriss der Geschichte der Komintern*, Hamburg, 1929, 174 p.

Kleen, Walter, 'Über die Rolle der Räte in der Novemberrevolution', *ZfG*, 1956, n° 2, pp. 344–66.

Klein, Fritz, *Die diplomatische Beziehungen Deutschlands zur Sowjetunion 1917–1932*, East Berlin, 1953, 190 p.

Knittel, Fritz, 'Die mitteldeutsche Märzkämpfe im Jahre 1921, ihre Bedeutung und ihre Lehren', *Einheit*, 1956, n° 3, pp. 251–62.

Kochan, Lionel, *Russia and the Weimar Republic*, Cambridge, 1950, 190 p.

Koenen, Wilhelm, 'Zur Frage der Möglichkeit einer Arbeiterregierung nach dem Kapp-Putsch', *BzG*, 1962, n° 2, pp. 342–52.

Kolarov, Vassil, 'V.I. Lenin na III. Kongresse Kommunistitcheskogo Internatsionala', *Voprosy Istorii K.P.P.S.*, 1960, n° 2, pp. 189–91.

Kolb, Eberhard, *Die Arbeiterräte in der deutschen Innenpolitik (1918–1919)*, Düsseldorf, 1962, 432 p.

Kolbe, Helmut, 'Die Herausbildung der Kommunistischen Partei Deutschlands unter der Einfluss der grossen sozialistischen Revolution', *ZfG*, 1958, special issue, pp. 84–109.

——, 'Aussenpolitisches Programm des Gründungsparteitages der K.P.D.', *Deutsche Aussenpolitik*, 1958, n° 11, pp. 1033–41.

——, 'V.I. Lenin Werk "Der 'linke Radikalismus', die Kinderkrankenheit im Kommunismus", eine bedeutende Hilfe für die junge Kommunistische Partei Deutschlands', *BzG*, 1960, n° 2, pp. 255–75.

Köller, Heinz, *Kampfbündnis an der Seine, Ruhr und Spree. De gemeinsame Kampf der K.P.F. und K.P.D. gegen die Ruhrbesetzung 1923*, Berlin, 1963, 348 p.

Könnemann, Erwin, 'Zur Problem der Bildung einer Arbeiterregierung nach dem Kapp. Putsch' *BzG*, n° 5/6, 1963, pp. 904–21.

Die Kommunistische Internationale. Kurzer historischer Abriss (I.M.L. and Moscow), East Berlin, 1970, 718 p.

Koszyk, Kurt, *Zwischen Kaiserreich und Diktatur. Die sozialdemokratische Presse von 1914 bis 1933*, Heidelberg, 1958, 276 p.

Krivoguz, I.M., 'V.I. Lenin in germanskoe levye sotsial-democraty v gody pervoj mirovoj vojny', in *Velika sila leninskhikh idej*, Moscow, 1960, pp. 342–68.

——, '*Spartak' i obrazovanie kommunistitcheskoj partii Germanii*, Moscow, 1962, 239 p.

Kruppa, Reinhold, *Die Niederlausitz greift zur Waffe. Die Abwehr des Kapp-Putsches in der Niederlausitz*, Berlin, 1957, 80 p.

Krusch, Hans Joachim, *Um die Einheitsfront und eine Arbeiterregierung Zur Geschichte der Abeiterbewegung im Bezirk Erzgebirge-Vogtland unter besonderer Berücksichtigung des Klassenkampfes im Zwickau-Œlsnitzer Steinkohlrevier von Januar bis August 1923*, East Berlin 1963, 400 p.

——, 'Zur Bewegung der revolutionären Betriebsräte in den Jahren 1922–1923', *ZfG*, n° 2, pp. 374–6.

——, 'Zur Losung der Arbeiterregierung Anfang 1923', *BzG*, 1964, n° 2, pp. 276–8.

——, 'Zu den Ergebnisse der Einheitsfrontpolitik der K.P.D. im Industriegebiet von Zwickau unter besonderer Berücksichtigung der Lage in der S.P.D. (Ende 1922 bis Mais 1923)', *BzG*, 1965, special issue, pp. 37–55.

Kuckuk, Peter (ed.), *Revolution und Räterepublik in Bremen*, Frankfurt/M., 1969, 182 p.

Kuczynski, Jürgen, *Die Geschichte der Lage der Arbeiter in Deutschland von 1978 bis in die Gegenwart*, vol. I, 2nd Part (Seventh Expanded ed.), Berlin, 1954, 353 p.

——, *Der Ausbruch der ersten Weltkrieges und die deutsche Sozialdemokratie. Chronik und Analyse*, East Berlin, 1957, 252 p.

——, *Die Geschichte der Lage der Arbeiter unter dem Kapitalismus*. Vol. 5, vol. I, *Die Geschichte der Lage der Arbeiter in Deutschland vom 1789 bis zum Gegenwart. Darstellung von 1917/1918 bis 1932–1933*, Berlin 1966, 279 p.

Kulinytsch, I.M., and Koschyk, M.M., *Die deutsche Spartakusgruppe in der Ukraine 1918/1919*, East Berlin, 1961, 128 p.

Küster, Heinz, 'Die Rolle der "Roten Fahne" bei der Vorbereitung der Gründung der K.P.D.', *ZfG*, 1963, n° 8, pp. 1466–84.

Küster, Heintz, Nimtz, Walter, and Wimmer, Walter, 'Der Kampf des Spartakusbundes in der Novemberrevolution 1918 für die Losung der nationalen sozialen Lebensfragen des deutschen Volkes', *BzG*, n° 5/6, 1964, pp. 789–802.

Lammel, Inge, 'Zur Rolle und Bedeutung des Arbeiterlieder', *BzG*, 1962, n° 3, pp. 726–42.

Lange, Günter, 'Die protestaktionen der Zwickauer Arbeiter gegen den deutschen Militarismus aus Anlass des Mordes an Walter Rathenau im Sommer 1922', *BzG*, n° 4, 1962, pp. 950–64.

Laschitza, Horst, 'Zum internationalen Widerhall von Karl Liebknechts Kampfaktionen 1914/1915 gegen den imperialistischen Krieg', *BzG*, 1962, n° 1, pp. 102–6.

Lazitch, Branko, *Lénine and la IIIᵉ Internationale*, Neuchâtel, 1950, 226 p.

Lenzner, S.I., 'Berlinkskij Savet v period martovskikh revoljutsionnykh boev 1919 g. v Berline', in *Germanskoe rabotchee dvijenie v novejsee*, pp. 7–42.

Leuna, Kämpfendes: Geschichte des Kampfes der Leuna-Arbeiter, vol. I, *1916–1933*, East Berlin, 1961, 608 p.

Lindau, Rudolf, *Revolutionäre Kämpfe 1918–1919. Aufsätze und Chronik*, East Berlin, 1960, 268 p.

Lipinski, Richard, *Der Kampf un die politische Macht in Sachsen*, Leipzig, 1926, 95 p.

Lösche, Peter, *Der Bolschewismus im Urteil der deutschen Sozialdemokratie 1903–1920*, West Berlin, 1967, 306 p.

Lowenthal, Richard, 'The Bolshevisation of the Spartacus League', in *International Communism, St-Antony's Papers*, n° 9, pp. 23–71.

Lucas, Erhard, *Frankfurt unter der Herrschaft des Arbeiter- und Soldatenräte*, Frankfurt/M., 1969, 150 p.

——, *Märzrevolution im Ruhrgebiet. Bewaffneter Arbeiteraufstand März/April 1920*, Frankfurt/M., 1970, 300 p.

Luther, Karl Heinz, 'Die nachrevolutionäre Machtkämpfe in Berlin November 1918 bis März 1919', *Jahrbuch für die Geschichte Mittel und Ostdeutschlands*, 1959, n° 8, pp. 187–221.

Lutz, Ralph Haswell, *The German Revolution 1918–1919*, Stanford, 1968, 186 p.

Malanowski, Wolfgang, *Novemberrevolution 1918. Die Rolle der S.P.D.*, Frankfurt/M., 1969, 190 p.

Mammach, Klaus, *Der Einfluss der russischen Februarrevolution und der Grosse Sozialistischen Oktoberrevolution auf die deutsche Arbeiterklasse Februar 1917–Oktober 1918*, East Berlin, 1955, 152 p.

Die Märzkämpte 1921, East Berlin, 1956, 188 p.

Meisel, Gerhard, 'Zur Entwicklung der Rätebewegung von 1919 bis. 1921, unter besonderer Berücksichtigung der wirtschaftlichen Organisation', *BzG*, 1966, n° 2, pp. 209–26.

Mitchell, Allan, *Révolution in Bavaria 1918–1919. The Eisner Regime and the Soviet Republic*, Princeton, 1965, 374 p.

Morenz, Ludwig and Münz, Erwin, *Revolution und Räteherrschaft in München*, Munich, 1969, 135 p.

Mujbegović, Véra, *Komunisticka Partija Nemake v Periodu Posleratne Krize 1918–1923*, Belgrade, 1968, 493 p.

Müller, Hermann, 'Die Bedeutung der Gründung der I.A.H. im Jahre 1921 für die Entwicklung der Solidarität der deutschen Arbeiterklasse mit Sowjetrussland', *BzG*, 1962, n° 3, pp. 642–56.

Naumann, Horst, 'Ob edinenie revoljutsionnogo kryla nevazisimoj sotsial-demokratija partii c K.P.G.' in *Germanskoe rabotchee dvijenie v novejsee vremia*, pp. 74–97.

——, 'Die Bedeutung des II. Weltkongresses der Kommunistischen Internationale für die Vereinigung des revolutionären Flügels der U.S.P.D. mit der K.P.D.', *BzG*, 1960, n° 3, pp. 466–87.

Naumann, Horst and Voigtländer, Fred, 'Zum Problem einer Arbeiterregierung nach dem Kapp-Putsch', *BzG*, 1963, n° 3, pp. 461–74.

Neubauer, Helmut, *München und Moskau 1918–1919. Zur Geschichte der Rätebewegung in Bayern*, Munich, 1958, 100 p.

—— (ed.), *Deutschland und die Russische Revolution*, Stuttgart, Berlin, Cologne, 1968, 112 p.

Nimtz, Walter, *Die Novemberrevolution 1918 in Deutschland*, Berlin, 1962, 248 p.

Nipperdey, Thomas, *Die Organisation der deutschen Parteien vor 1918*, Düsseldorf, 1961, 454 p.

Nojabrs'kaja Revoljustsija v Germanii, Moscow, 1960, 514 p.

Nollau, Günther, *Die Internationale. Wurzeln und Erscheinungsformen des proletarischen Internationalismus*, Cologne, 1969, 344 p.

Norden, Albert, *Zwischen Berlin und Moskau. Zur Geschichte der deutsch-sowjetischen Beziehungen*, East Berlin, 1954, 387 p.

Noske, Gustav, *Erlebtes aus Aufstieg und Niedergang einer Demokratie*, Offenbach/M., 1947, 323 p.

Obermann, Karl, *Die Beziehungen des amerikanischen Imperialismus zum deutschen Imperialismus in der Zeit der Weimarer Republik*, Berlin, 1952, 168 p.

Œckel, Heinz, *Die revolutionäre Volswehr 1918–1919. Die deutsche Arbeiterklasse im Kampf um die revolutionäre Volkswehr (November 1918 bis Mai 1919)*, East Berlin, 1968, 328 p.

——, 'Über die Militärpolitik der K.P.D. in der Periode der revolutionären Nachkriegskrise 1919–1923', *Militärwesen*, 1964, n° 1, pp. 75–84.

Œrtzen, Peter von, 'Die grossen Streiks der Ruhrbergarbeiterschaft im Frühjahr 1919', *Vierteljahrshefte für Zeitgeschichte*, 1958, n° 2, pp. 231–62.

Œrtzen, Peter von, *Betriebsräte in der Novemberrevolution. Eine politik-wissenschaftliche Untersuchung über Ideengewalt und Struktur der betrieblichen und wirtschaftlichen Arbeiterräte in der deutschen Revolution 1918/1919*, Düsseldorf, 1964, 377 p.

Opel, Fritz, *Der deutsche Metallarbeiterverband während des ersten Weltkrieges und der Revolution*, Hanover, Frankfurt/M., 1958, 144 p.

Osterroth, Franz and Schuster, Dietrich, *Chronik der deutschen Sozial-demokratie*, Hanover, 1963, 672 p.

Ostwald, Hans, *Sittengeschichte der Inflation. Ein Kulturdokument aus den Jahren des Marksturzes*, Berlin, 1931, 280 p.

Petzold, Joachim, *Die Dolchstosslegende. Eine Geschichtesfälschung im Dienst des deutschen Imperialismus und Militarismus*, Berlin, 1963, 148 p.

Plener, Ulla, 'Die Märzkonferenz der Spartakusgruppe – ein Markstein auf dem Wege zur Gründung der K.P.D.', *BzG*, 1961, n° 4, pp. 821–41.

Polzin, Martin, *Kapp-Putsch in Mecklemburg. Junkertum und Landproletariat in der revolutionären Krise nach den 1. Weltkrieges*, Rostock, 1966, 333 p.

Prager, Eugen, *Geschichte der U.S.P.D. Enstehung und Entwicklung der Unabhängigen Sozialdemokratischen Partei Deutschlands*, Berlin, 1921, 240 p.

Puchta, Gerhard, 'Der Arbeiter- und Soldatenrat Leipzigs von November 1918 bis vor den II Rätekongress Anfang April 1919', *Wissenschaftliche Zeitschrift der Universität Leipzig*, 1957–8, pp. 363–84.

Raase, Werner, *Zur Geschichte der deutschen Gewerkschaftsbewegung 1919–1923*, Berlin, 1967, 166 p.

Radczun, Günter, 'Einige Probleme der Haltung Rosa Luxemburgs zur proletarische Revolution (Zu Flechtheims Rosa Luxemburgs Edition "Die Russische Revolution")', *BzG*, 1966, n° 1, pp. 9–22.

Reichenbach, Bernhard, 'Zur Geschichte der K.A.P.D.', *Archiv für die Geschichte der Sozialismus und der Arbeiterbewegung*, Leipzig, 1928, XIII, pp. 117–40.

Reisberg, Arnold, 'Die Leninsche Politik der Aktionseinheit und ihre Anfänge in Deutschland', *BzG*, 1963, n° 1, pp. 53–71.

——, 'Lenin, die K.P.D. und die Konferenz der drei Internationalen in Berlin 1922', *BzG*, 1963, n° 2, pp. 247–63.

——, 'Um die Einheitsfront nach dem Rathenaumord', *BzG*, 1963, n° 5/6, pp. 995–1009.

——, *Lenin und die Aktionseinheit in Deutschland*, East Berlin, 1964, 200 p.

——, 'Zur Genesis der Losung Arbeiterregierung in Deutschland (Das Jahr 1921)', *BzG*, 1965, n° 6, pp. 1025–38.

——, 'Lenin und die Zimmerwalder Bewegung', *ZfG*, 1964, n° 5, pp. 777–98.

Renouvin, Pierre, *L'Empire allemand 1890–1918* (4 vol.).

Retzlaw, Karl, *Spartakus, Gezeiten der Revolution*, Munich, 1969, 500 p.

Ritter, Gerhard, *Die Arbeiterbewegung im Wilhelminischen Reich. Die S.P.D. und die Freien Gewerkschaften 1890–1900*, Berlin, 1959, 225 p.

Rosenberg, Arthur, *Entstehung und Geschichte der Weimarer Republik*, Frankfurt/M., 1955, 502 p.

Rosenfeld, Günter, *Sowjetrussland und Deutschland 1917–1922*, East Berlin, 1960, 423 p.

Rosmer, Alfred, *Moscou sous Lénine. Les origines du communisme*, Paris, 1953, 316 p.

Roth, Günter, *The Social-Democrats in Imperial Germany. A Study in Working-class Isolation and National Integration*, Totowa, 1963, 352 p.

Rückert, Otto, 'Die Linken im Reichstagswahlkreis Potsdam-Spandau-Osthavelland (unter besonderer Berücksichtigung des Wirkens Karl Liebknecht im Wahlkreis)', *BzG*, 1965, special issue, pp. 84–101.

Ruge, Wolfgang, *Die Stellungsnahme der Sowjetunion gegen die Besetzung des Ruhrgebietes*, East Berlin, 1962, 198 p.

Runkel, Ferdinand, *Die deutsche Revolution. Beitrag zur Zeitgeschichte*, Leipzig, 1919, 232 p.

Rürup, Reinhard, *Probleme der Revolution in Deutschland 1918/1919*, Wiesbaden, 1968, 59 p.

Ryder, A.J., *The German Revolution of 1918. A Study of German Socialism in War and Revolution*, Cambridge, 1967, 304 p.

Sayous, André, 'L'Epuisement économique de l'Allemagne entre 1914 and 1918', *Revue historique*, January–March 1940, pp. 66–75.

Schabrod, Karl, *Generalstreik rettet die Weimarer Republik. Wie der Arbeiterschaft vor 40 Jahren der Kapp-Putsch zerschlug*, Düsseldorf, 1960, 44 p.

Schade, Franz, *Kurt Eisner und die bayrische Sozialdemokratie*, Hanover, 1961, 200 p.

Schneider, Kurt, 'Die Herausbildung der Leipziger Liebknechtgruppe und ihre Entwicklung zu einem Glied des Spartakusgruppe (1914–1916)', *BzG*, 10, n° 5, pp. 763–76.

——, 'Der Streik der Leipziger Arbeiter gegen den imperialistischen Krieg im April 1917 und die Haltung der Leipziger U.S.P.D. Führung', *BzG*, 1963, n° 2, pp. 274–81.

Schorske, Carl E., *The German Social-Democracy 1905–1917. The Development of the Great Schism*, Cambridge, 1955, 358 p.

Schreiner, Albert and others, *Revolutionäre Ereignisse und Probleme in Deutschland während der Periode der Grossen Sozialistischen Oktoberrevolution 1917/1918*, East Berlin, 1957, 354 p.

Schröder, Wolfgang, 'Die erste "Arbeiterregierung" auf deutschem Boden. Das Sächsische Kabinett Zeigner', *Wissenschaftliche Zeitschrift der Hochschule für Verkehrwwesen*, 1958–9, n° 1–2.

——, *Klassenkampf und Gewerkschaftseinheit. Die Herausbildung und Konstituierung des gesamtnationalen deutschen Gewerkschaftsbewegung und der General-kommission der Gewerkschaften Deutschlands*, Leipzig, 1965, 400 p.

Schüddekopf, O.E., *Linke Leute von Rechts. Nationalbolschevismus in Deutschland von 1918 bis 1953*, Stuttgart, 1960, 548 p.

——, *Das Heer und die Republik. Quellen zur Politik der Reichswehrführung 1918–1933*, Hanover, Frankfurt/M., 1955, 326 p.

——, 'Karl Radek in Berlin', presentation of 'November', *Archiv für Sozialgeschichte*. V. Radek (Biographies).

Schüller, Richard, Kurella Alfred and Chitarov, *Geschichte der Kommunistischen Jugendinternationale*, Berlin, 1929–1930, 3 vol., 224, 256 and 240 p.

Schulz, Eberhard, *Dokumente und Materialen zur Geschichte der Arbeiterbewegung im Bezirk Halle*, vol. I (*1917–1933*), Halle, 1965, 181 p.

——, 'Die Entwicklung der K.P.D. zu einer revolutionäre Massenpartei und die Rolle des linken Flügels in der U.S.P.D. im Bezirk Halle-Merseburg (1920)', Halle, 1958, 85 p.

Schunke, Joachim, *Schlacht um Halle. Die Abwehr des Kapp-Putsches in Halle und Umbegung*, East Berlin, 1956, 110 p.

Schwaab, Dagmar, 'Die Sächsischen Organisationen des Verbands der ausgeschlossenen Bauarbeiter Deutschlands und die Forderung nach einer Arbeiterregierung', *Wissenschaftliche Zeitschrift der Hochschule für Architektur und Bauwesen*, Weimar, 1966, n° 1, pp. 1–4.

Schwarz, Albert, *Die Weimarer Republik*, Constance, 1958, 232 p.

Schwenk, Paul, 'Lenin, Mehring und das Niederbarnimer Referentenmaterial', *BzG*, 1960, n° 1, pp. 158–63.

Seidel, Richard, *Die Gewerkschaftsbewegung und das Rätesystem*, Berlin, 1919, 64 p.

Seleznev, K.L., 'Bolcheviktskaja agitacija i revoljutsionnoe dvijenie v Germanskoj Armii vostoshnoe fronte v 1918 g', *Nojabr'skraja Revoljucija*, pp. 271–328.

Slonimski, M., *Eugen Léviné. Erzählung.* East Berlin, 1949, 103 p.

Spectator, *Die Geschichte der Berliner Fünftagregierung*, Leipzig, 1920, 96 p.

Spethmann, Hans, *Der Ruhrkampf 1923 bis 1925*, Berlin, 1933, 274 p.

Stampfer, Friedrich, *Die ersten 14 Jahren der deutschen Republik*, Karlsbad, 1936, 636 p.

Stern, Leo, *Der Einfluss der grossen sozialistischen Oktober revolution auf Deutschland und die deutsche Arbeiterbewegung*, East Berlin, 1958, 384 p.

——, *Die Auswirkungen der grossen sozialistischen Oktoberrevolution auf Deutschland*, East Berlin, 1959, vol, I.

——, 'Zur Vorgeschichte der Gründung der K.P.D.', *Wissenschaftliche Zeitschrift der Martin-Luther Universität Halle-Wittenberg*, 1954, n° 1, pp. 11–28.

——, 'Razgrom Kappovskogo puttcha. Resultat edinstva dejstvij rabotchego klassa', *Germanschoe rabotchee divjenie . . .*, pp. 44–72.

Tjaden, K.H., *Struktur und Funktion der 'K.P.D.-Opposition' (K.P.O.). Eine organisationssoziologische Untersuchung zur 'Rechts'-Opposition im deutschen Kommunismus zur Zeit der Weimarer Republik*, Maisenheim/Glain, 1964, 235 p.

Tormin, Walter, *Zwischen Rätediktatur und sozialer Demokratie. Die Geschichte der Rätebewegung 1918–1919*, Düsseldorf, 1954, 150 p.

Uhlemann, Manfred, *Arbeiterjugend gegen Cuno und Poincaré. Das Jahr 1923*, East Berlin, 1960, 336 p.

Varain, J. *Freie Gewerkschaften, Sozialdemokratie und Staat. Die Politik der General-kommission unter der Führung Carl Legiens (1890–1920)*, Düsseldorf, 1956, 298 p.

Vermeil, Edmond, *L'Allemagne contemporaine, sociale, politique, culturelle (1890–1950)*, Paris, 1952. Vol. I, *Le Règne de Guillaume II (1890–1918)*, 384 p. Vol. II, *La République de Weimar and le Troisième Reich (1918–1950)*, 444 p.

Vietzke and Wohlgemuth, *Deutschland und die deutsche Arbeiterbewegung in der Zeit der Weimarer Republik (1919–1933)*, East Berlin 1966, 523 p.

Vidil, Charles, *Les Multineries de la marine allemande (1917–1918)*, Paris, 1931, 207 p.

Volkmann, E.O., *La Révolution allemande (1918–1920)*, Paris, 1933, 310 p.

Wagner, Raimund, 'Zur Frage der Massenkämpfe in Sachsen im Frühjahr und Sommer 1923', *ZfG*, 1956, n° 2, pp. 246–64.

——, 'Über die Chemnitzer Konferenz und die Widerstandaktionen der sächsischen Arbeitermassen gegen den Reichswehreinmarsch im Oktober 1923', *BzG*, 1961, special issue, pp. 188–208.

——, 'Der Kampf um die proletarische Einheitsfront und Arbeiterregierung in Sachsen unmittelbar nach dem VIII. Parteitag der K.P.D.', *BzG*, 1963, n° 4, pp. 647–57, and n° 5/6, pp. 922–32.

——, 'Die revolutionäre Bewegung in den Bezirken Hessen-Frankfurt und Baden im Herbst 1923', *BzG*, 1965, n° 1, pp. 84–95.

Waldman, Eric, *The Spartacist Uprising of 1919 and the Crisis of the German Socialist Movement. A Study of the Relation of Political Theory and Practice*, Milwaukee, 1958, 248 p.

Weber, Helmut, 'Neue Dokumente zur Politik der deutschen Linken 1915 und 1916', *BzG*, 1965, n° 4, pp. 661–69.

Weber, Hermann, *Von Rosa Luxemburg bis Walter Ulbricht. Wandlungen des deutschen Kommunismus*, Hanover, 1961, 112 p.

——, *Ulbricht fälscht Geschichte. Ein Kommentar mit Dokumenten zum 'Grundriss der Geschichte der deutschen Arbeiterbewegung'*, Cologne, 1964, 180 p.

——, 'Zu den Beziehungen zwischen der K.P.D. und der Kommunistischen Internationale. Dokumentation' (Documents from the private archives of Rosa Meyer-Léviné), *Vierteljahrshefte für Zeitgeschichte*, Munich, 1968, n° 2, pp. 178–208.

——, *Die Wandlung des deutschen Kommunismus. Die Stalinisierung der K.P.D. in der Weimarer Republik*, Frankfurt/M., 1969, vol. I, 466 p., vol. II, 428 p. (Abbrev: Weber, *Die Wandlung*.)

Wenzel, Otto, *Die Kommunistische Partei Deutschlands im Jahre 1923* (Thesis, Free University of Berlin, 1955).

Wheeler-Bennett, J.W., *The Nemesis of Power. The German Army in Politics (1918–1945)*, London, 1954, 829 p.

Wimmer, Walter, *Das Betriebsrätegesetz von 1920 und das Blutbad vor dem Reichstag*, Berlin, 1960, 68 p.

Winkler, Erwin, *Die Bewegung der Berliner revolutionären Obleute im ersten Weltkrieg. Enstehung und Entwiklung bis 1917*, East Berlin, 1964, 53 p.

——, 'Die Berliner Obleutebewegung im Jahre 1916', *ZfG*, 1968, n° 11, pp. 1422–42.

Wohlgemuth, Heinz, *Burgkrieg, nicht Burgfriede! Der Kampf Karl Liebknechts, Rosa Luxemburg und Ihrer Anhänger um die Rettung der deutschen Nation in den Jahren 1914–1916*, East Berlin, 1963, 320 p.

——, *Die Enstehung der Kommunistischen Partei Deutschlands*, East Berlin, 1968, 364 p.

Wollenberg, Erich, *Der Apparat: Stalins Fünfte Kolonne*, Bonn, Third ed., 1952, 148 p.

Wrobel, Kurt, *Die Volksmarinedivision*, Berlin, 1957, 144 p.

Zeisler, Kurt, *Aufstand in der deutschen Flotte. Die revolutionäre Matrosen bewegung im Herbst 1918*, East Berlin, 1956, 91 p.

Zeissig, Eberhard, 'Der Entwurf eines Aktionsprogramms für die Chemnitzer Konferenz vom 21. Oktober 1923', *BzG*, 1964, n° 6, pp. 1060–5.

Biographical Details*

Alexander, Eduard (known as E. Ludwig, 1881–1945). Lawyer, member of Spartacus League and of KPD at its foundation; head of Zentrale's press service in 1922, editor of economics page of *Die Rote Fahne*. Removed from his responsibilities in 1929 as 'conciliator', arrested in August 1944, and died during transport.

André, Edgar (1894–1936). Born in the Rhineland, brought up in Belgium, building worker, member of Socialist Young Guard. Conscripted, prisoner of war in France in 1918; docker in Hamburg, joined SPD; then unemployed, organised unemployed committee in Hamburg, joined KPD at end of 1922. Very prominent activist in Hamburg in 1923. Organised League of Red Fighters, which he led in Hamburg. Nicknamed 'Red General', strongly hated by the Nazis, arrested in March 1933, tortured, sentenced to death, and beheaded on 4 November 1936.

Arendsee, Marta (1885–1953). Worked in bookshops, member of SPD in 1906, organiser of women's movement from 1907; in opposition in 1914, member of Niederbarnim group, delegate to Berne in 1915. Member of USPD in 1917 and VKPD in 1920. On editorial staff of *Die Kommunistin* from 1922, elected to trade-union commission at Leipzig. Close to KPD Right, worked in Workers' International Relief. Arrested in 1933, released in 1934, emigrated to USSR with her husband Paul Schwenk, who was arrested there; worked for Soviet radio in Moscow. Returned to Germany in 1945, member of leadership of SED until 1947.

Artelt, Karl (1890–). Metalworker member of SPD in 1908. Led mutiny in Kiel and Baltic sailors' council in November 1918. Member of USPD, leader of councils in Brunswick in 1919. Member of USPD Left, in VKPD in 1920. Occupied various secondary responsibilities in KPD; veteran of SED, lived in DDR.

Bachmann, Otto (1887–). Building worker trade-union secretary in Breslau in 1908, chairman in Chemnitz during 1919–21, founding member of KPD. Expelled from trade-union and became secretary of 'red trade union', put in charge of builders' section of Zentrale's trade-union department. Chairman of union of stonemasons expelled from ADGB from September 1923. After 1926, was a leader of red unions; in 1927, was first Communist mayor in Germany, at Ölsnitz. Expelled in 1929 as rightist. Continued to support Brandler, active in KPO. Emigrated in 1933, and probably died in exile.

Barth, Emil (1879–1941). Metalworker and Social Democrat. Discharged from army in 1917. Member of USPD. Replaced Richard Müller at head of group of revolutionary delegates after strike in January 1918. Member of Executive of Councils, People's Commissar in November–December 1918, disowned by his comrades. Chairman of Factory Councils in 1921. Remained in USPD in 1920, returned to SPD in 1922. Then returned to anonymity.

Bartz, Wilhelm (1881–1929). Printer, joined union and SPD in 1900; attended Party School in 1910–11; full-time Party worker and journalist. Joined USPD

---

* These biographical details were compiled in 1971 and have not been updated for this edition.

in 1919. Joined VKPD in 1920. Protested against March Action, but did not follow Levi or Friesland. Worked on *Inprekorr* in 1921, joint chairman of KPD parliamentary fraction in Reichstag in 1922. Member of Left in 1923. Joined centre tendency in 1925.

Becker, Karl (1894–1942). Printer, son of activist, member of Socialist Youth in 1909 and SPD in 1912. During war was a leader of radical Left in Dresden and then in Bremen. Arrested in 1917, freed by November Revolution, was leader of a workers' council. Delegate from IKD to founding conference of KPD. Supported ultra-left majority. Co-leader of opposition in 1919 and co-founder of Allgemeine Arbeiter Union. Expelled at Heidelberg, did not join KAPD, returned to KPD(S) under Radek and Frölich's influence in March 1920. Made several visits to Moscow. From 1921 was editor of *Hamburger Volkszeitung*, in 1923 in charge of the Wasserkante and North-West region, member of right tendency. Appears to have gone underground at end of 1923 and taken refuge in Moscow. Returned in 1925, member of 'conciliator' group, elected to Prussian Landtag in 1928. Made 'self-criticism'. Went underground in 1933, then emigrated to France. Betrayed by Vichy, condemned to death, executed in Plötzensee.

Blenkle, Konrad (1901–43). Bakery worker, from working-class family; joined Youth in 1919 and KPD(S) in 1920; worked for Soviet embassy in Berlin; became secretary of Communist Youth in 1923, supported KPD Left. Chairman of Communist Youth and member of Central Committee in 1924; deputy in 1928; in disgrace thereafter. Worked illegally in 1933–4. Emigrated and led some illegal work in Germany, from Copenhagen. Arrested, sentenced to death, executed in Plötzensee.

Böttcher, Paul (1891–). Printer, member of Socialist Youth in 1907, chairman of Leipzig group in 1908, member of SPD, youth full-timer at trade-union level. Opposed War. Joined USPD in 1917, Chief Editor of *Sozialdemokrat* in Stuttgart in 1920. In USPD Left, head of trade-union left opposition. Joined VKPD in 1920. Kidnapped by supporters of Kapp during putsch. In February 1921, Chief Editor of *Die Rote Fahne*, member of the Zentrale in August 1921. In 1923 chairman of parliamentary fraction in Saxony, secretary of West Saxony district, favoured support for and joining workers' government. Minister for the Economy in Zeigner's government in October 1923, driven from his ministry by Reichswehr. Member of right opposition, expelled from KPD in 1929, founder, with Brandler, of KPO; in exile in Switzerland during 1933–46. Arrested on return to Germany, taken to USSR after sentence *in absentia* to two years in jail, held in various camps and prisons until 1955. Released that year, returned to DDR and admitted to SED in 1956; Chief Editor of *Leipziger Volkszeitung* until he retired in 1968. According to Hermann Weber, Böttcher worked for Soviet intelligence services from 1927, and arrested in Switzerland for this reason.

Brandler, Heinrich (1881–1967). Building worker, born in the Sudetenland, of Austrian nationality, lame since early youth owing worker to accident at work, trade-union activist 1897, sentenced for violence in 1900. Joined SPD in 1901, worked until 1904 in Hamburg, where he led building workers' union, then in Bremen during 1904–8, where he was active in trade union and Socialist Youth. In Switzerland during 1908–14. In Chemnitz in June 1914, secretary of the building workers' union. Expelled from SPD with Heckert in 1915, driving force in Spartacus group, joined USPD in 1917 despite reservations. Deported from Germany as foreigner in October 1918, he acquired

German nationality thanks to Eisner's government in Bavaria. Returned to Chemnitz, founded there both *Der Kämpfer* and most powerful local organisation of KPD(S). Supported Levi against ultra-Left, organised election of workers' councils in Chemnitz immediately after Kapp Putsch, and was chairman of Chemnitz workers' council, where he developed ideas foreshadowing those of the workers' united front. Elected to Zentrale in April 1920 and reported to Unification Congress on questions of organisation. Took Levi's place as KPD Chairman in February 1921 and assumed Party leadership during March Action. In June, sentenced to five years imprisonment in a fortress. Released in November, spent some time in Moscow as member of Comintern Presidium. Returned to Germany in autumn 1922, carried out functions of General Secretary. In 1923 stood at head of KPD, and attacked by Left, whose expulsion he urged many times in vain. Head of State Chancellery of Zeigner's government, after having taken part in Moscow in preparations for insurrection. Communist spokesman at Chemnitz Conference, called off insurrection after left Social Democrats retreated. Held responsible for defeat in Germany in 1923, and tried in vain to assert that he did not support Left Opposition in Russia. In Moscow until October 1928, returned to Germany against KPD's decision, expelled in January 1929. Founded KPO, but did not join SAP. Emigrated to France, interned during 1939–40, took refuge in Cuba during 1941–7, then in Britain, returned to Germany in 1949, and settled in Hamburg where he led Arbeiterpolitik group.

Brass, Otto (1875–1960). File-cutter, in SPD in 1897. Cashier in insurance firm, then administrator of newspaper. Leader of radical wing in the Ruhr, co-founder of USPD. Chairman in 1919 of council of workers and soldiers in Remscheid, delegate to Berlin in December. USPD deputy at Weimar. Organised strike in the Ruhr in 1919 and struggle against Kapp in 1920, which led to his being charged with high treason. In USPD Left, Joint Chairman of the Halle Congress. Elected to VKPD Zentrale, resigned at same time as Levi and Däumig in February 1921. As minority delegate in Moscow immediately after March Action, publicly supported Levi for months following his expulsion, and, with Friesland and Malzahn, organised new right opposition. Expelled in January 1922, returned that year with Levi to USPD and then to SPD. From then until 1933 played minor role, but placed under surveillance by the Nazis. Arrested in 1945 for underground activity, liberated by Red Army. In leadership of SPD in Russian zone, signed appeals for reconstitution of free trade unions and for fusion of Social-Democratic and Communist Parties. On this basis, he was co-founder of SED.

Braun, M.J. (Miechislaw Bronski, 1882–1937). Polish, Social Democrat in 1902, took part in 1905 Revolution, served a year in prison. Emigrated to Switzerland in 1907, active in Swiss Social-Democratic Party and, in opposition to Luxemburg and Jogiches, supported Warsaw Committee, which Radek also supported. Close to Lenin, took part in Zimmerwald and Kienthal Conferences, a leader of Zimmerwald Left. Accompanied Lenin in 'sealed train' in April 1917, took part in Russian Revolution. Appointed consular representative in Berlin in 1918, made contact with German revolutionaries. Deported in November. Returned to Germany in 1919, was member of Western European Secretariat and leadership of KPD(S) under a pseudonym. Sharply criticised for Zentrale's position at beginning of Kapp Putsch and recalled to Moscow shortly afterwards. Lectured at University of Moscow, active in Polish Communist Party, joining its Political Bureau. Arrested and executed during purges.

Budich, Willi (1890–1941). Son of peasant, studied to become engineering technician, member of SPD in 1910, joined Spartacus League during War, and, under name 'Brandt', was one of Jogiches' principal collaborators in underground organisation. Joined USPD in 1917, arrested in March 1918, and set free by November Revolution. Organised League of Red Soldiers in November 1918, seriously wounded and lost an arm as a result of the shooting on 6 December. Took part in Munich Soviet Republic in March 1919, member of its Executive Committee under the name of 'Dietrich'. Shared with Friesland and other Berlin leaders responsibility for appeal of 13 March 1920. Was also in USSR in that year, and received military training. Arrested in 1921, escaped and returned to USSR. His role in 1923 is not known. In Moscow, was in leadership of International Workers' Relief, and then, under the name of Gerbilski, Soviet trade representative in Vienna. Returned to Germany in 1929, arrested in 1933, released, and once more emigrated. Arrested in 1937 during purges, and died in prison in 1941 or 1942.

Charpentier, Fritz (1869–1928). After business studies, became businessman and representative. Joined SPD before war. Joined USPD in 1917, and KPD in 1920. Disowned by KPD for having agreed without its authority to Bielefeld agreements following Kapp Putsch. He joined Levi in KAG, but broke with him and continued to be Party secretary in Elberfeld. Played important role in 1923 in preparing for insurrection in the Ruhr. Hunted by police, took refuge in USSR. In Leningrad, supported Left Opposition. The Social-Democratic press announced that he had been executed, which KPD denied.

Cohn, Oskar (1869–1937?). Son of Jewish traders, lawyer, member of SPD, deputy in 1912. Supported the majority in 1914 and served at front as non-commissioned officer. Discharged in 1917, joined USPD, defended sailors and strikers before tribunals. In 1918 was legal adviser to Russian ambassador Joffe. In January 1919, acted as conciliator in January days. Later in right wing of USPD and went back to SPD in 1922. In 1933 took refuge in USSR, arrested in purges, and disappeared.

Creutzburg, August (1892–1940?). Painter and lacquer worker, member of SPD in 1908. In army during 1912–18. Joined USPD in 1917 and VKPD in 1920, secretary in Jena. KPD leader in Magdeburg district in 1923. A real 'commissar' of the KPD leadership, played important role in expelling each successive opposition. Leading figure in apparatus from 1929. Emigrated in 1933 and reached USSR in 1935, arrested in 1937, and said to be one of the prisoners whom Stalin handed over to Hitler.

Crispien, Artur (1875–1946). Painter and decorator, Social Democrat, became journalist. Joined *Die Internationale* group on its foundation; arrested in 1915 and put in army. Joined centrist opposition during its formation and became USPD leader when it was founded. People's Commissar in November–December 1918. Leader of USPD Right, stayed with it despite vote at Halle, returned to SPD with it in 1922. Emigrated to Switzerland in 1933, died there without returning to Germany.

Dahlem, Fritz (1892–). Son of railway worker, worked as stable lad. In SPD in 1913. Chairman of Socialist Youth in Cologne in 1914. Conscripted into army during 1914–18, joined USPD in 1917, member of soldiers' council in 1918. Worked as journalist in Cologne, member of USPD Left, joined VKPD in 1920, represented Central Rhineland on Central Committee. Supported Levi, openly backed his positions in Party press without being punished, but then broke with him. In France during July–October 1922. At beginning of

1923 was secretary [*Obersekretär*] for entire Rhineland. Deported by French occupying authorities, then worked in Party press and organisation department. Member of Politbureau in 1929, deputy during 1928–33. Compromised with oppositions to Ulbricht and Pieck at head of Party. Emigrated in 1933, fought in International Brigades in Spain during 1936–9, interned in France in 1939, handed over to German government in September 1941, held for eight months in Gestapo headquarters cell, then in Mauthausen until 1945. Reached Moscow and then Germany with Pieck. Leader of SED and East-German state. Dismissed from all functions in May 1953, rehabilitated in 1956.

Däumig, Ernst (1868–1922). Of bourgeois origin, joined French Foreign Legion. Joined SPD well before war, journalist on *Vorwärts* in 1911. Joined opposition in 1914. Co-founder of USPD and Chief Editor of *Freiheit* in 1917–18. Coopted in 1918 into nucleus of revolutionary delegates to undertake military preparations for November insurrection. Member of Executive of Councils in November, opposed formation of KPD(S) and adhesion of revolutionary shop-stewards, unsuccessfully opposed putschist elements in January 1919. Leader of USPD Left and theoretician of 'conciliar system'. Secured rejection of Legien's proposals for workers' government following Kapp Putsch. Delegate to Third Comintern Congress, supported 'Twenty-One Conditions'. Elected joint chairman of VKPD with Levi in December 1920, resigned position with Levi in February 1921. Joined KAG, refused to surrender his mandate as KPD deputy. Died soon after Levi and KAG joined USPD.

Dissmann, Robert (1878–1926). Turner, leader at age of 22 of metalworkers' union in Barmen-Elberfeld. In 1905 secretary of metalworkers' union in Frankfurt-am-Main and of SPD in Hanau in 1908. Candidate of left opposition for SPD Executive in 1911. Joined opposition in 1914, member of USPD from its foundation. Chairman of metalworkers' union in October 1919, leader of trade-union left opposition, broke with left Independents on issue of trade-union independence, and opposed before and during Halle Congress affiliation to Comintern. Stayed with rump USPD and in 1922, in alliance with Levi, unsuccessfully opposed return to SPD. In 1923 organised left opposition with Levi in SPD. One of leaders of Social-Democratic Left and trade-union leader, died of heart attack.

Dittmann, Wilhelm (1874–1954). Cabinet maker, member of SPD in 1898, journalist in 1899, deputy in 1912. In opposition during War, particularly attacked censorship. Co-founder of USPD, had contact with the sailor Reichpietsch. Sentenced to five years imprisonment in a fortress after January 1918 strike. Amnestied in October, became People's Commissar in November and December. Leader of USPD Right, returned to SPD in 1922. In 1933 emigrated to Switzerland, where he remained until 1951.

Dorrenbach, Heinrich (1888–1919). Office worker, Social Democrat, secretary of association of office workers in the Rhineland in 1910. Volunteered for army in 1914, became second lieutenant. Reduced to ranks and discharged in 1917, active in strikes of January 1918. In November, tried to organise Red Guard, and then took command of People's Naval Division. Associated with Liebknecht, advocated insurrection in January 1919, and was disavowed by the sailors. Took refuge in Brunswick where he barely escaped capture by the Free Corps; arrested in Eisenach, killed 'whilst trying to escape'.

Duncker, Herman (1874–1960). Son of business people, had higher education, became doctor of philosophy. Member of SPD in 1893, journalist in 1903, travelling speaker, then in 1911 taught with Luxemburg at Central Party

School. Member of internationalist nucleus in August 1914 and of Internationale group and then of Spartacus League. Member of KPD(S) Zentrale at its foundation, re-elected to it in January 1919, but not in 1920. Became Secretary of Independent government in Gotha region. Asthmatic, he then devoted himself to intellectual tasks and education of activists. Arrested in 1933, spent a year in concentration camp, managed to flee to Denmark in 1936. Reached USA in 1941. Opposed to German-Soviet Pact in 1939. Returned to East Germany in 1947, was member of SED, professor and dean.

Duncker, Käte (née Doell, 1871–1953). Teacher, Social Democrat in 1900, associated with Clara Zetkin, organiser of Socialist Women. Married Hermann Duncker, whom she won to socialism. Worked with him in internationalist nucleus, on Zentrale in 1918, where she was in charge of work amongst women. Elected to Zentrale in 1919, not re-elected in 1920. Held no more responsible positions after that. Emigrated to USA in 1938, and returned with her husband in 1947 to resettle in East Germany.

Düwell, Bernhard (1891–). Higher studies in commerce. Conscripted into army during 1914–18. Joined USPD in 1917, journalist in Zeitz in 1918. Commissar of councils in Merseberg. Helped organise strike in Central Germany in 1919, deputy to National Assembly. In USPD Left, in Party's central press service, joined VKPD in 1920. Supported Levi, expelled in August 1921. Joined KAG and then USPD and SPD in 1922. Later fate unknown.

Eberlein, Hugo (1887–1944). Industrial draughtsman, trade-unionist in 1905, in SPD in 1906. Member of opposition nucleus in August 1914, organiser of group responsible for an important SPD Berlin group. Joined USPD in 1917. Member of Zentrale in November 1918 in charge of finances, active in workers' council in Neukölln. Elected to KPD(S) Zentrale at its foundation, delegate under the name Max Albrecht to Comintern Foundation Congress, unsuccessfully defended KPD(S) thesis opposing its 'premature' foundation, and abstained in the vote. Enjoyed confidence of ECCI, which entrusted money to him, and was a leader of M-Apparat. Played important role in organising 'provocations' during March Action. Compromised by revelations in *Vorwärts*, took refuge in Moscow, from where he returned at unknown date, still working in underground apparatus. Supported Brandler. Supported centre tendency at end of 1923, associated with 'conciliators' in 1928, eliminated from Politbureau and then from Central Committee, retained his seat in Prussian Landtag (1921–33) and appears to have worked in international apparatus. Emigrated to France in 1933, was arrested there and deported, went to USSR. Arrested in 1937, deported and included in 1940 in list of prisoners to be handed over to Germany, died shortly afterwards of pulmonary asthma without being transported. According to other sources died in 1944.

Eckert, Paul (1883–). Metalworker, member of SPD before 1914. Leader and organiser during War of group of revolutionary shop-stewards, member of USPD in 1917. Member of action committee of strikers in January 1918, of Executive of Councils in November, delegate to Congress of Councils in December. Participated as an 'invited visitor' at KPD(S) Founding Congress, but stayed in USPD, a leader of left wing. Joined VKPD in 1920, was member of its trade-union department. Supported Levi, joined KAG after expulsion, then USPD and SPD in 1922. Played secondary role from 1922. In East Germany after 1945, SED member and 'veteran'.

Egelhofer, Rudolf (1897–1919). Son of worker, conscripted into navy. Organiser of clandestine action with Reichpietsch in 1917, condemned to hard labour. Freed by November Revolution, organised detachment of revolutionary sailors. Head of Red Army in Bavaria, shot without trial by Free Corps.

Eichhorn, Emil (1863–1925). Son of artisan, glassworker, member of SPD in 1881, Party full-timer in 1893, head of its press office during 1908–17. Joined USPD in 1917, organised its press office, and led 'information' section of Soviet Rosta agency. On 9 November 1918, occupied the police headquarters and surrounded himself with worker activists. His dismissal on 5 January 1919 sparked January uprising and repression. Took refuge by air in Brunswick. USPD deputy in Constituent Assembly. On USPD Left, joined VKPD in 1920. Supported Levi in 1921, joined KAG, but returned to KPD. Remained KPD deputy in Reichstag until his death.

Eildermann, Willi (1897–). Son of SPD full-timer. Youth organiser, internationalist in 1914. Conscripted during 1916–18. Joined KPD(S) in 1919. Communist journalist, particularly in 1923 on *Klassenkampf* in Halle. Worked underground in Germany in 1933. In International Brigades in Spain during 1937–8. Interned until 1942, served in British army during 1942–4. Returned to USSR. Professor of history in DDR, member of SED, supported theses about origins of KPD which Ulbricht condemned.

Eisler, Gerhart (1897–1968). Son of professor in Vienna, brother of Ruth Fischer. Officer in Hungarian army in 1918, joined Communist Party in 1919, collaborated on *Kommunismus*. Active in Germany from 1921 under name of Gerhardt, collaborated on *Die Rote Fahne* and in Berlin district organisation. Broke from Left in April 1923 with Ewert, Pfeiffer and Heinz Neumann, supporter of centre tendency after October. Member of apparatus, linked to conciliators, then entered Comintern apparatus, which he served in China and USA. Jailed in 1948, returned to DDR in 1949. Appears to have been intended for trial during Cold War years, but was saved by death of Stalin. Fulfilled important functions up to his death.

Eisner, Kurt (1878?–1919). Of Jewish family from Galicia, born in Berlin, broke off his studies to work in Social-Democratic press. Editor on *Vorwärts* in 1898, literary critic. Revisionist, dismissed in 1903, lived by his pen. In 1914 opposed war on pacifist grounds, joined USPD in 1917, organised network of delegates in Munich factories. Sentenced to eight months in jail after January 1918, leader of Bavarian Revolution in November, Prime Minister of Bavaria, assassinated 21 February 1919.

Enderle, August (1887–1959). Mechanic, trade-unionist and SPD member in 1905. Full-timer in 1910. Oppositionist during War, member of USPD in 1917, joined KPD(S) as individual. Organised Communist fraction in metal-workers' union, delegate to Second RILU Congress. In Moscow during 1922–3, gave information to Trotsky about situation in Germany. Collaborated in KPD trade-union commission, excluded as rightist in 1928, founded KPO with Brandler, joined SAP in 1932. In exile in Sweden in 1933, returned to Germany in 1945, joined SPD and until his death worked in trade-union press.

Eppstein, Eugen (1878–1943). Son of Jewish traders. Had business training, worked in commerce. In SPD in 1897, in opposition in 1914, organiser of Spartacus League in the Ruhr. Secretary from 1920 of Central Rhineland district. Stalwart of Fischer-Maslow left wing, replaced by Dahlem, re-elected in February 1923, dismissed by Zentrale. Reinstated after October 1923, deputy and secretary of North-West district in 1924. Then joined left opposition, left KPD in 1928, co-founder of Leninbund. Emigrated to France in 1933, arrested by Gestapo, deported from Drancy to Lublin-Majdanek, where he was murdered.

Ewert, Arthur (1890–1959). Son of small peasant, saddle-maker. Trade unionist and SPD member in 1908. Went to Canada before war, served a year in jail there for a political offence. Returned to Germany in 1920, joined KPD in Berlin, then became secretary of Hesse district, in Frankfurt. Tended to be associated with Left, but regarded as 'lukewarm'. Elected to Zentrale in January 1923 in Leipzig. In April, attacked Left with Pfeiffer and Heinz Neumann. Military head of Oberbezirk West in 1923. In 1925 was member of centre tendency, on Central Committee, Zentrale and Politbureau. In illegality during 1926–8, candidate member of Comintern Presidium, resident in Moscow during 1928–9. Purged along with conciliators, worked in Comintern apparatus. Represented ECCI in China during 1929–34, then sent to Brazil. Arrested in 1935, was tortured, lost his reason, nevertheless sentenced to 13 years imprisonment. Repatriated to Germany in 1947, and diagnosed incurable. Still denounced as an 'agent' in 1956, but finally honoured at his death in psychiatric hospital.

Fischer, Ruth (Elfriede Eisler, successively married Friedländer, Golke, Pleuchot, 1895–1961). Daughter of Viennese professor Eisler, student of philosophy and political economy, joined Social Democracy in 1914, brought together revolutionary elements in student milieu. In 1918 made contact with Russian representatives in Vienna, received funds enabling her to found weekly journal *Der Weckruf*. First member of Austrian Communist Party founded on 3 November 1918, imprisoned for several weeks after November days. Removed in May 1919 from revolutionary leadership, strongly criticised as rightist after defeat of Bettelheim. Left Austria for Berlin in August. Associated with leaders of KPD(S), especially Levi, and then influenced by Maslow – who was to be her life-long companion – took leadership of left opposition. Under pseudonym of Ruth Fischer was a leader of Berlin-Brandenburg district from 1921. Acquired German nationality in early 1923 by marriage to Golke. A beautiful woman and an exceptional orator, became in 1921 champion of 'theory of the offensive' and opponent of Moscow Compromise. Delegated by KPD Left to Fourth Comintern Congress. Provoked crisis in KPD at beginning of 1923 by her passionate speeches, but in May accepted compromise dictated by ECCI, and joined Zentrale. From July, resumed her opposition, took part in Moscow in preparation for insurrection, declared in favour of maintaining slogan of armed uprising, but opposed general strike following Chemnitz Conference. Supported by Zinoviev and anti-Brandler current in KPD, reached leadership of Party in 1924 and became leader of chorus for 'Bolshevising' Communist Parties. However, in 1925 came out in favour of withdrawing Communist candidate in second round of presidential elections, and was disavowed by ECCI. Obliged to stay in Moscow in 1925–6, replaced in Berlin by Thaelmann, and expelled in August 1926. Founder of the Leninbund and other oppositional groupings. Exiled in France in 1933, acquired French nationality by another marriage, arranged by Doriot. In Spain in June 1940, then in Cuba, then finally in USA in 1941, taking part in various anti-Communist activities. Naturalised as American, returned to France in 1956, and died in Paris.

Flieg, Leo (1893–1939). From Jewish family, office worker in commerce. Active in Socialist Youth from 1908, became bank employee. Conscripted in 1914, employed as secretary in General Staff, whilst also member of Spartacus League and youth organisation. Secretary to Jogiches, arrested in March 1918, freed by November Revolution. Organiser of Young Communist International and member of Executive up to 1922. Then secretary to KPD Politbureau, and in 1923 responsible for contacts in Berlin with OMS. Influential behind scenes in KPD up to 1933, then emigrated to Moscow, later to Paris. Recalled to Moscow in 1937, considered refusal but returned, arrested on arrival and probably murdered in 1939.

Frank, Karl (1893–). Son of small industrialist in Vienna, officer cadet during 1909–13. Then at university, became doctor of philosophy, joined Socialist Students. Called up into army as lieutenant, discharged in 1916. Joint founder of Austrian Communist Party, settled in Berlin in 1920, collaborated on *Die Internationale*. In 1923 responsible for preparing uprising in Bavaria, arrested and escaped. Imprisoned during 1924–5, was journalist in 1929. Expelled in 1929, joined KPO, then SAP, then SPD in 1933. Worked in illegality during 1933–8, then settled in USA, teaching psychology.

Franke, Otto (1877–1953). Erector-mechanic in Berlin. In SPD in 1898. Revolutionary delegate and organiser of Spartacus League during War. Agent of Liebknecht in October 1918. Member of Berlin workers' and soldiers' council. Played subordinate role in KPD apparatus. Collaborated with Pieck. Arrested in 1933, released, emigrated to Britain, returned to East Germany in 1946, joined SED.

Friesland, Ernst (known as Reuter, 1889–1953). Son of merchant marine officer, Social Democrat, dismissed as teacher for political activity. Organised pacifist league in 1914. Conscripted in 1915, prisoner of war in Russia in 1916, formed prisoners' committee in 1917, became Communist in German section of Bolshevik Party and met Lenin. Commissar of Volga Germans in 1918, returned secretly to Germany with Radek and Felix Wolf in December, took pseudonym of Reuter. Secretary in Upper Silesia, then in Berlin-Brandenburg after Heidelberg split. Co-led KPD(S) Left during 1920–1. Won by Lenin to support Moscow Compromise, he defended it at Jena, and became General Secretary. Moved in a few weeks towards positions of his former opponent Levi, organised right opposition, expelled in January 1922. Rejoined SPD directly in 1922. Emigrated to Turkey, then to Scandinavia. Returned to Germany after 1945, member of SPD from 1948 to his death, Mayor of West Berlin during Cold War.

Frölich, Paul (alias Paul Werner, 1884–1953). Second of 11 children in workers' family. Technical commercial studies, worked as office worker in commerce. Self-educated and studied at SPD schools, joined SPD in 1902. Journalist from 1908 in Altona, from 1910 in Hamburg, associated with Bremen militants, Knief, Radek and Pannekoek. In 1914 journalist on Bremen *Bürgerzeitung*. Conscripted as non-commissioned officer and discharged in 1916, joint founder of *Arbeiterpolitik*, delegate at Kienthal, member of Zimmerwald Left, close to Lenin, recalled into army at end of 1916. In summer 1918 was arrested for anti-militarist activity and interned in psychiatric hospital, liberated by November Revolution. Leader of IKD, spokesman for leftists at KPD(S) Foundation Congress, and elected to Zentrale. Took part in Bavarian Revolution and spent some time in clandestinity. Re-elected to Zentrale, criticised Levi's passivity in 1920, in 1921 became a defender of 'theory of the offensive'. Secretary of Zentrale in 1921–2. Deputy from 1921. Supported Brandler in 1923. Teacher in KPD school until 1928, then expelled as right-winger. Joint founder of KPO. Left it for SAP. Arrested in 1933, released after nine months in concentration camp, succeeded in emigrating to Czechoslovakia, then Belgium and France. Interned in 1939, got visa for USA, lived there until 1950, returned to West Germany and joined SPD.

Gäbel, Otto (1885–1953). Bookbinder, in SPD in 1905. In 1914 published opposition's first documents with his comrades in Niederbarnim group. Member of Spartacus League, did not join KPD(S) on its foundation, but remained in USPD, in leadership of Left. Joined VKPD in 1920, elected to Zentrale. In December 1921 supported Brass against Zentrale, but did not join KAG. Then in charge of *Kommunistische Partei-Korrespondenz* and Secretary of Reichstag fraction. Municipal councillor in Berlin. Compromised in financial scandal, expelled from KPD in 1929, and later sentenced to prison. No subsequent political role, died in West Berlin.

Geschke, Ottomar (alias Eisbär, 1882–1957). Metalworker working on railways, in SPD in 1910. After 1914 in opposition; led youth group. Member of Spartacus League, in USPD on foundation, member of group of revolutionary stewards. On KPD Central Committee in 1921. Chairman of Berlin railwaymen, three times re-elected after union leadership annulled election, finally expelled from union. Second secretary of organisation of Berlin-Brandenburg district in 1921, supported Left. Coopted to Zentrale in May 1923, played important role in M.-Apparat. Second and then first secretary for organisation in KPD, led 'Bolshevisation' process. Then broke with Left and backed Thaelmann. Arrested in 1933, held in various camps, chaired in 1945 international committee of Buchenwald. Secondary role after 1945 in KPD and SED.

Geyer, Curt (1891–1967). Son of pioneer Saxon Social Democrat. Higher studies in economics and history. On editorial staff of *Vorwärts* in 1914 and then of Party paper in Würzburg. Member of USPD in 1917, of Leipzig council in 1918, chaired it in 1919. Deputy in National Assembly. Leader of USPD Left, supported joining Comintern. On VKPD Zentrale in 1920, represented Party on ECCI and 'small bureau'. Supported Levi, expelled in August 1921, followed him into KAG, USPD and SPD. Unlike other 'Levites' and Levi himself, did not join left opposition in SPD. In 1933 emigrated and settled in Britain, where he was on SPD Executive in exile. For a long time correspondent of German newspapers, retired in West Germany.

Glöbig, Fritz (1882–). One of 11 children of a worker. Injured at age of four by tram. Engraver, trade-unionist and member of Socialist Youth in 1908, joined Spartacus League during War whilst continuing activity in Socialist Youth. Member of KPD(S) on foundation, one of first leaders of German Communist Youth. Employed in Soviet embassy in 1922. Journalist in Bremen in 1923. Worked as journalist in Germany up to 1930, then settled in Moscow. Arrested in 1937, spent many years in concentration camp. Returned to Germany in 1955, admitted to SED.

Gorter, Hermann (1864–1927). Dutch, son of pastor. Studied classical literature, high-school teacher, wrote thesis on Aeschylus. Member of Dutch Social Democracy in 1896, opponent of revisionism, defender of 'mass strike', collaborator on *Tribune* in 1907. Expelled in 1909, co-founder of leftist SPD. Opposed War in 1914, joined Zimmerwald Left, co-founder of Dutch Communist Party in 1918. In Germany at end of 1918, became theoretical leader of ultra-left wing of KPD(S) in 1919–20. Member of Amsterdam Bureau of Communist International, came into conflict with Secretariat and then ECCI. Co-founder in April 1920 of KAPD, wrote reply to Lenin's *Left-Wing Communism*. In November negotiated in Moscow status of KAPD as 'sympathising' party. In April 1921 criticised VKPD's March Action. In 1922 after split in KAPD, led 'Essen Group'. Died whilst travelling in Belgium. Essential literary and poetical works have been published since his death.

Grothe, Hermann (1888–). Metalworker. In SPD in 1907. Conscripted in 1914, hospitalised during 1916–17, discharged. Member of revolutionary shop-stewards in Marienfelde, entrusted amongst others with task of preparing November insurrection. Active amongst unemployed in 1919. From 1922, president of national council of workers' councils. KPD full-timer during 1924–33; jailed under Hitler for two-and-a-half years, lived in East Berlin.

Grylewicz, Anton (1885–1971). Son of worker, mechanic. In SPD in 1912. Two years on Eastern Front, wounded and discharged. Toolmaker in Berlin factory, joined USPD and revolutionary delegates. Assistant to Eichhorn at police headquarters, played important role in January 1919. Deputy-Chairman and then Chairman of USPD in Greater Berlin in 1920, leader of USPD Left. Secretary of Berlin-Brandenburg organisation in 1921. Took part in 1923 in Moscow in preparing plans for insurrection. Leader of KPD Left, member of Zentrale in 1924, several times sentenced. Expelled from Party in 1927. Became leader of Trotskyists in Germany. Published Trotsky's writings in Germany. In 1933 arrested in Prague in connection with frame-up aimed at implicating him in espionage. Cleared, reached France in 1937 and Cuba in 1941, where he worked as cabinet-maker until 1955. Retired to West Berlin.

Haase, Hugo (1863–1919). Of Jewish origin from East Prussia, 'the poor people's lawyer' in Koenigsberg, Social Democrat. Deputy in 1897, SPD Chairman in 1911, in Reichstag fraction in 1912. Opposed vote for war credits in 1914, but submitted in interests of discipline. Spokesman for centrist minority from 1916. Leader of USPD from its foundation, People's Commissar in November-December 1918. Leader of USPD Right, assassinated on Reichstag steps by nationalist.

Hausen, Reich (1900–). Son of worker, electrician-fitter. Conscripted in 1918, in USPD in 1919, in VKPD in 1920. Secretary of Lausitz district in 1922, member of Central Committee in 1923. Played important role in preparing insurrection in 1923. Served 20 months imprisonment, then was secretary in Silesia. Accuser of Thaelmann in Wittorf affair, expelled in December 1928. Organiser and leader of KPO, arrested and sentenced in 1934, emigrated to France when released. Interned, went to USA in 1941 and settled there.

Heckert, Fritz (1884–1936). Son of worker, building-worker. In SPD in 1902, itinerant worker, settled in Berlin and Bremen, then in Switzerland during 1908–11, where, through his wife, contacted Bolsheviks. In 1912 in Chemnitz, led builders' union and brought in Brandler. Created strong Spartacus group, joined USPD which he led locally. Arrested in October 1918, chaired workers' and soldiers' council in Chemnitz in November. Member of KPD(S) at its foundation, brought into it USPD organisation in Chemnitz. Candidate member of Zentrale in 1919, full member in 1921, assistant in trade-union department of Zentrale. Important role in clandestine preparations in 1923. Minister for the Economy in Zeigner's government in Saxony in October 1923. Member of KPD right wing, joined centre tendency, elected to Politbureau in 1928. Member of Comintern Presidium from 1928, representative on RILU, and later in the Communist International. Was seriously wounded in 1931 by SA. Died in Moscow, his funeral urn placed in Kremlin wall.

Hesse, Max (1895–1964). Son of metalworker, co-founder of metalworkers' union, mechanic, member of Socialist Youth in 1910, worked in Scandinavia, then in Siemens. Conscripted in 1914, three times wounded, discharged in 1916, member of group of revolutionary shop-stewards. Recalled to army, deserted, sentenced to six years imprisonment, freed by November Revolution. Member of workers' council in Spandau. In KPD(S) at its foundation. In jail during March-September 1919. Leader of VKPD in Charlottenburg, and chairman of Lorenz workers' council during 1920–3. Member of KPD Left, took part in Moscow in discussions in September 1923, then sent to Saxony. Member of ECCI during 1924–6, in left opposition, reproved in 1927 and then expelled. Co-founder of Leninbund. Returned to SPD in 1929, chairman of it in Charlottenburg and of a works' council. Arrested in 1933, escaped from Oranienburg, emigrated to Netherlands, arrested, was not identified, escaped in 1944, returned to Germany in 1947.

Hirsch, Werner (1899–1937?). Son of Jewish banker. In USPD in 1917, then in Spartacus League, where he supported Jogiches. Arrested at beginning of 1918, freed and conscripted into navy. Took part in Kiel mutinies, helped organise People's Naval Division. Delegate to KPD(S) Foundation Congress. Distanced himself from Party after Levi was expelled, became press correspondent in Vienna. Returned to KPD in Germany in 1924, as journalist in 1926. Chief Editor of *Die Rote Fahne* in 1930, secretary to Thaelmann in 1932. Arrested in 1933, freed in 1934, wrote a pamphlet on Nazi camps. Went to USSR in 1937, arrested as 'spy' and shot.

Hoelz, Max (1889–1933). Son of worker, sawyer of timber. Emigrated to Britain in 1905, became mechanic. In army in 1914, seriously wounded, joined USPD, worked on railways. In 1919 organised unemployed in the Vogtland, and practised 'direct action'. In KPD in 1919, began 'urban guerrilla' operations, which he developed on large scale at time of Kapp Putsch. Hunted by police, came close to KAPD when in clandestinity. Organised armed struggle in Mansfeld region in March 1921. Arrested, escaped, recaptured and sentenced to life imprisonment. Set free in 1928, made lecture tour, went to Moscow in 1929. Accidentally drowned; hypothesis that he was assassinated has often been advanced.

Hoernle, Edwin (1883–1952). Son of pastor, studied theology. Pastor for three months during 1909, joined SPD in 1910, associated with Mehring and Luxemburg, then journalist in Stuttgart with Westmeyer. Member of Spartacus League nucleus during War, several times arrested, sent to front and wounded. Member of USPD in 1917, of KPD(S) at its foundation. Imprisoned during January-June 1919. Specialised in work amongst children and adolescents. Member of Zentrale in 1923, member of ECCI and candidate member of Comintern Presidium. Supported centre tendency in 1924, but protested against exclusion of leftists, worked during 1928–33 in campaigns department of Zentrale. Emigrated to USSR in 1933, member of Freies Deutschland committee during War, returned to Germany in 1945, and filled important posts until his death.

Hoffmann, Adolf (1858–1930). Son of worker, gilder, then metalworker. In SPD when Exceptional Laws in operation. Journalist, then publisher for SPD in 1893. In 1900 deputy to Prussian Landtag; very popular. In Reichstag in 1904. Pacifist in 1914, opposed both majority and revolutionaries. In USPD in 1917, played important role in strikes in January 1918. Minister of Education in November 1918. On USPD Left, in VKPD and member of Zentrale in 1920. Supported Levi, followed him into KAG and USPD, but not into SPD. Remained up to his death in USPD fragment which maintained its independence.

Höllein, Emil (1880–1929). Son of worker, emigrated to Belgium, toolmaker. In SPD in 1905. At front during 1915–18. In USPD in 1917, Chief Editor of its daily paper in Jena. On USPD Left, in VKPD in 1920, elected to Zentrale after Levi resigned. Responsible in 1923 for links between KPD and French Communist Party. Arrested, released shortly afterwards, very ill, thereafter played only secondary role.

Jannack, Karl (1891–). Illegitimate child, worked as farm labourer and then as cobbler. In SPD in 1909. Soldier during 1913–16. Gassed and discharged, at this time associated in Bremen with Arbeiterpolitik group. Arrested, volunteered to join army and served as soldier up to November Revolution. Co-founder of IKD, member of KPD(S) at its foundation. Leader of Conciliar Republic in Bremen, then secretary of KPD(S) North-West district. Expelled after Heidelberg with ultra-leftists. Did not join KAPD, rejoined KPD(S) and resumed his responsibilities. Member of Central Committee after 1920. In 1922 secretary of ADGB trade unions in Remscheid. In 1923 secretary for trade-union work in KPD Rhineland-South Westphalia district, firm supporter of Brandler against Left. Expelled in 1924 for factional activity, re-admitted in 1925, worked for Workers' International Relief. Illegal after 1933, then accused of having joined Nazis. Arrested in 1940, offered to 'redeem' himself. In Buchenwald until end of war. After 1945 in DDR, member of SED.

Jogiches, Leo (also known as Tyszka, Grosovsky, Johannes Kraft, Otto Engelmann, Krumbagel, etc., 1867–1919). Son of rich Jewish family in Lithuania, joined clandestine revolutionary movement when very young, first arrested in 1888. In Switzerland in 1890, in Zürich met Rosa Luxemburg, who was to be his partner until 1906 and his comrade-in-arms until her death. Founded with her Polish Social-Democratic Party, which he led in emigration from Germany from 1897. Returned to Poland in 1905, played important role in Revolution, arrested and sentenced to six years hard labour, escaped, returned to Germany. Broke politically from Lenin on some Russian Party questions immediately before War; sharp conflict with Radek about Polish Party. Member of internationalist nucleus in 1914, co-editor of *Spartacus Letters*, organiser of Spartacus League, supported entry into USPD. Arrested in March 1918, set free by the Revolution, became a leader of Zentrale. Opposed foundation of KPD(S) and immediate break from USPD. Elected to Zentrale at Founding Congress. Opposed Liebknecht's policy in January 1919, and called upon him, unsuccessfully, to repudiate it publicly. Arrested and murdered in March 1919 'whilst trying to escape'.

Jung, Franz (1888–1963). Higher studies, literary activities in expressionist movement. Deserted in 1914, joined Aktion group. Joined KPD(S) at Foundation Congress, in its left wing. In KAPD in 1920, delegate to Second Comintern Congress. Organiser of KAPD's fighting groups, played important role during March Action, hunted by police, took refuge in USSR. Returned to Germany after 1923, correspondent of various journals, emigrated to USA, returned in 1945, thereafter merely literary activity.

Katz, Ivan (1889–1956). Son of businessman, higher technical studies. In Socialist Youth in 1906, worked as metal-worker for one year, then as assistant in how and economics college. Member of SPD before War, remained there until end of 1919, when he joined USPD. In VKPD in 1920, leader of 'communes' department attached to Zentrale in 1922, supporter of Left. Member of Politbureau in 1924, then delegate to Moscow. Organised ultra-left opposition in 1925, expelled in January 1926. Arrested in 1934, set free, again arrested in 1940, escaped and lived illegally until 1940, arrested and deported to Auschwitz. After war spent short time in KPD and SED, in 1950 founded 'Titoite' party.

Kilian, Otto (1879–1945). Printer, in SPD in 1902, full-timer in 1906, then journalist. Conscript during 1915–18, joined USPD in 1917. Chairman of workers' council in Halle, in 1918, sentenced in March 1919 to three years imprisonment, amnestied. On USPD Left, in VKPD in 1920. Opposed March Action, remained in Party, then activist of the Left, expelled in 1927, made 'self-criticism', readmitted, resigned and organised Leninbund. Arrested in 1933, in a concentration camp, died of typhus in Bergen-Belsen shortly before end of War.

Kippenberger, Hans (also known as Leo and Alfred Langer, 1898–1937). Secondary education, bank employee. Lieutenant during war. Resumed studies after war, worked as press correspondent. In USPD in 1918, in VKPD in 1920. Joined clandestine apparatus in 1922, played important role in 1923 in military preparations, and had leading role in Hamburg uprising. Took refuge in Moscow, studied in military school. In illegality in Germany during 1924–8, organised KPD's Military Apparatus. Deputy in Reichstag during 1928–33. Important role in illegality in Germany during 1933–5, recalled to Moscow, shot after secret trial on 3 October 1937. Officially rehabilitated in USSR in May 1957, but not in DDR.

Kleine, August (Samuel Haifiz, also known as Guralski, 1885–1960). Son of poor Jewish family, born in Lodz. Higher studies during which he joined Jewish Poale Zion movement. Emigrated to Vienna, went to Russia, active in Menshevik ranks in February 1917. Joined Bolsheviks at end of 1918, joined Comintern apparatus. In Germany in 1921 with Béla Kun just before March Action. Representative of ECCI in 1922 with KPD, elected to Zentrale in 1923. Responsible for politico-military preparations for insurrection in Germany in 1923, leader of Kopf. Organiser of centre tendency after October retreat. Recalled to Moscow in 1924 after his group was defeated by KPD Left. Member of United Opposition behind Zinoviev, sent on mission to South America. Arrested during purges, freed after death of Stalin, died in 1960, according to DDR sources.

Knief, Johann (1880–1919). Petty-bourgeois family, teacher. In SPD, journalist in Bremen in 1905. Pupil of Pannekoek. Organiser of opposition in 1914, founded *Arbeiterpolitik* in 1916, then in ISD which became IKD in 1918, supported splitting from right-wing Social Democrats, and announced himself to be a Bolshevik, remaining in contact with Radek. Emigrated to Holland in 1917 or 1918, collaborated with Gorter and Pannekoek, polemicised against Spartacists, whom he condemned for joining USPD. Hostile to fusion with Spartacus League, refused to be delegate to Foundation Congress of KPD(S). Seriously ill, died in April 1919 following operation.

Kobis, Alwin (1892–1917). Son of worker, stoker in navy. Organiser of revolutionary sailors in 1917 with Reichpietsch. Sentenced to death, shot in September 1917.

Koenen, Bernhard (1889–1964). Son of socialist carpenter. Trade unionist in 1906, in SPD in 1907. Itinerant worker in Europe and North Africa. Conscript during 1914–16. Worked at Leuna-Werke, vice-chairman of workers' council in 1918. On USPD Left. In VKPD in 1920, delegate to the Second Comintern Congress. Played important role in March Action, in which he opposed KAPD's initiatives. Represented ECCI in France and Belgium during 1921–2. In 1923 candidate member of KPD Central Committee. Member of centre tendency, then 'conciliator', capitulated in 1929, given subordinate functions. Attacked by SA in 1933, left for dead, blinded in one eye, succeeded in emigrating, took refuge in USSR. Arrested in 1937, freed in 1939, rearrested for having disclosed tortures to which he had been subjected. Reintegrated into KPD in 1940, coopted to Central Committee in 1942, returned to Germany in 1945, occupied important posts in SED and DDR, ambassador to Prague.

Koenen, Wilhelm (1886–1963). Brother of Bernhard. Business studies, worked in SPD bookshop, joined Party in 1904. Full-timer from 1907. Student at Party school in 1911. In USPD in 1917, commissar of workers' and soldiers' council in Halle-Merseburg in 1918, leader of strike in Central Germany in 1919. On USPD Left, in VKPD 1920, twice delegated, in 1921 and 1922, to Moscow, where he presented draft Comintern constitution to its Fourth Congress. Defended March Action, then Moscow Compromise. Joined centre tendency, capitulated in 1929. In 1933 emigrated to Czechoslovakia, France, Britain. Returned to Germany in 1945, held important posts. Criticised in 1953, demoted to subordinate functions until his death.

Köhler, Max (1897–). Son of worker, painter. Member in 1911 of Socialist Youth, in SPD in 1915, joined Spartacus League, led its youth organisation in Berlin 1916. Sentenced to six years imprisonment in 1917. Co-founder of Communist Youth, member of KPD on its foundation, held national and international responsibilities. Appointed head of trade-union department of Zentrale in 1923. Expelled in 1928 as rightist, member of KPO and then SAP. Arrested, released, led underground SAP. Arrested in 1933, sentenced to three years imprisonment. Emigrated 1937. Lived illegally in Denmark during War, returned to Germany postwar, joined SPD.

Kolarov, Vassili (1877–1950). Member of Bulgarian Social-Democratic Party in 1897, a leader of 'Narrow' faction, pro-Bolshevik. Deputy in 1913. Co-founder of Bulgarian Communist Party in 1919. Represented ECCI at Jena Congress in 1921. Member of ECCI from December 1922, then of Comintern Presidium and Orgbureau. Finally took refuge in Moscow after insurrection in Bulgaria in September 1923. Lived in USSR during 1923–45, worked in apparatus of Comintern and Russian Communist Party. Deputy Prime Minister, then Prime Minister in Bulgaria after War.

König, Artur (1884–). Worker, self-educated, became bookseller. In SPD in 1904, settled in the Ruhr. Conscript during 1916–18, joined Spartacus League. In KPD(S), which he led in Essen from its foundation, played important role at head of Ruhr Red Army in 1920. Member of Central Committee, Orgleiter of Oberbezirk West in 1923, coopted to Zentrale in May as leader of Left. Treasurer of Zentrale in 1924, expelled after 1925 with left, later fate unknown.

Korsch, Karl (1886–1961). Son of bank manager. Higher studies in Germany and Britain. Member of Fabian Society in London during 1912–14. Officer during 1914–18, joined USPD in 1917. In VKPD in 1920. Professor of Law in Jena. In October 1923, Minister of Justice in Thuringia. Published *Marxism and Philosophy* in 1923. Deputy in Reichstag during 1924–28, delegate to Fifth Comintern Congress, led ultra-left opposition, expelled in 1926. Emigrated, settled in USA.

Béla Kun (1886–1939). Hungarian, office worker, Social Democrat in 1902, journalist, then full-timer. Prisoner of war in Russia, joined Bolshevik Party in 1917, at end of 1918 founded Hungarian Communist Party a few months before heading short-lived Soviet Republic in Hungary in 1919. Took refuge in Moscow, political commissar in Red Army. Organiser of left current and *Kommunismus* during 1920–1. Joined Comintern small bureau in 1921, arrived in Germany just before March Action, for which he is generally seen as being responsible. Functionary in Comintern apparatus, arrested in 1937, executed without trial. Rehabilitated in 1956.

Kuusinen, Otto (1881–1964). Finnish, Social-Democratic student, teacher of philosophy in 1905, took part in Revolution. Deputy and leader of Centre in Social-Democratic Party of Finland. Member of Provisional Government in 1918, joined Communist movement after defeat of Revolution, founded Communist Party of Finland. From 1921, Secretary of ECCI. Functionary in Comintern to 1939, then in Russian Party. Took part in de-Stalinisation process.

Lange, Paul (1880–1951). Office worker. In SPD in 1900, leader of office-workers' union. Member of Spartacus League during War, on Zentrale in 1918. Left KPD after disagreeing with its trade-union policy in 1920, just before unification with USPD Left. Joined USPD and then, in 1922, SPD. Member of SPD left opposition with Levi, playing an unobtrusive role; in SED in 1946.

Laufenberg, Heinrich (1872–1932). Son of Catholic family in the Rhineland. Doctor of philosophy, went from Catholic Centre Party to SPD. Journalist in Düsseldorf during 1904–8, given task of writing history of workers' movement in Hamburg, and settled there. Organised left opposition there in 1914. Chairman of workers' and soldiers' council in Hamburg during 1918–19, organiser of 'united communists', at First Congress of Councils in December 1918. Supporter of revolutionary 'unions', excluded from KPD(S) at Heidelberg. Member of KAPD, excluded in 1919 after having developed national Bolshevism theses with Wolffheim. Accused of having contacts with the Kappist generals in 1920. Later fate unknown.

Ledebour, Georg (1850–1947). Teacher, actor, then journalist. Deputy for Pankow, well-known for his interruptions, prewar radical, centrist during war, hostile to Bolsheviks and Spartacists. Member of USPD in 1917 and of its Berlin organisation in 1918, leader of circle of revolutionary stewards. Joint Chairman of Revolutionary Committee in January 1919, charged with high treason, accused of putschism by Communists. Broke with USPD Left in 1920 on question of joining Comintern. Stayed in USPD in 1920, returned to SPD in 1922. Emigrated to Switzerland in 1933, died there after War.

Leow, Willi (1887–1937). Son of worker, carpenter. In SPD in 1904, joined Spartacus League during War, already youth organiser. Arrested in March 1918, freed by November Revolution. Occupied various functions in clandestine apparatus before 1923. Vice-President and real organiser of League of Red Front Fighters in 1924, deputy in 1928, member of Central Committee in 1929. Emigrated in 1933, in USSR in 1934, arrested in 1937, probably executed without trial that year.

Levi, Paul (also known as Paul Hartstein, Paul Hartlaub, 1883–1930). Son of Jewish banker. Studied law in Berlin, Grenoble, Heidelberg. Lawyer in Frankfurt, member of SPD in 1906. Defended Luxemburg in 1913, member of nucleus around her in 1914. Conscripted, discharged in 1916, settled in Switzerland, associated with Radek, then with Lenin, member of bureau of Zimmerwald Left. Declared in favour of split from social-chauvinists and centrists in 1917. Supported Lenin's journey across Germany in 1917. Recalled to army, again discharged, leader of Spartacus League in 1918. Member of Zentrale, close collaborator of Luxemburg. Opposed initiatives of Liebknecht in January 1919, and made head of Zentrale in March. Opened struggle against ultra-Left, organised split at Heidelberg. President of VKPD in 1920, resigned in February 1921, publicly condemned March Action. Expelled in April, founded KAG, and in 1922 joined USPD, then SPD. In August 1923 organised a conference of Social-Democratic left opposition. Deputy until his death, organiser of 'new Left' and *Sozialistische Politik und Wirtschaft*, then *Der Klassenkampf*. Committed suicide by throwing himself out of window during fever.

Levien, Max (1885–1937). Son of Jewish trader born in Moscow. Studied in German school in Russia, then at university in Germany. In Russia in 1905, Socialist Revolutionary, emigrated, continued studies in Switzerland, where he was associated with Bolsheviks but gave up political work. Finished studies in Germany, acquired German nationality. Conscript during 1914–18. Spartacist leader in Munich during 1918–19, chairman of soldiers' council in Munich. Leading role in Bavarian Soviet Republic. Took refuge in Vienna and then in USSR, where he worked in Comintern apparatus. From 1924 'protected' German Left in Moscow, associated with Maslow. Executed during purges.

Leviné, Eugen (1883–1919). Son of Jewish businessman, born in St Petersburg. Secondary and higher studies in Germany after 1897. Took part as Socialist Revolutionary in 1905 Revolution. Arrested in 1906 and 1908, harshly treated. Continued studies in Germany, joined SPD. Conscripted during 1914–16, joined USPD, worked in Russian Rosta agency. Member of Spartacus League, organiser in Rhineland, delegate to councils congress. Sent to First Comintern Congress, but unable to get to Russia. Entrusted with reorganising KPD(S) in Bavaria, purging pro-anarchist leftists. Leader of second Soviet Republic in Munich, condemned to death and shot.

Lieberasch, Arthur (1881–1966). Son of worker, metal-worker. Trade unionist in 1899, in SPD in 1906, in USPD in 1918, led strike in Leipzig in 1918, led workers' council in November Revolution. On USPD Left, in VKPD in 1920. Supported Brandler in 1923. Stalwart of KPD Right, expelled in 1929, co-founder of KPO, emigrated to Switzerland in 1933. Returned to Leipzig, admitted to SED in 1947, expelled in 1951, readmitted and rehabilitated after death of Stalin.

Liebknecht, Karl (1871–1919). Son of Wilhelm Liebknecht, SPD founder. Lawyer in Berlin in 1906, SPD member since 1900, leader of Socialist Youth, sentenced for anti-militarist activity. Deputy in Reichstag in 1912, voted for war credits in August 1914 to avoid breaking discipline, then standard-bearer of revolutionary opposition to war. Conscripted, organised anti-War demonstration on 1 May 1916, sentenced to four years imprisonment in a fortress. Amnestied in October 1918, took part in preparations for insurrection. Leader of Spartacus League, then of KPD(S) at its foundation. One of those who inspired uprising of January 1919. Arrested and murdered by his captors.

Lindau, Rudolf (1888–). Son of saddler, transport worker. In SPD in 1907. Leader of left radicals in Hamburg during War, remained in KPD(S) when KAPD split off. Secretary of the Wasserkante district in 1921. Member of Left, moderated position, elected to Zentrale in 1923, worked in organisation department. Joined centre group in 1924, journalist and historian, in Moscow during 1933–45, director of Party school in Berlin, dismissed in 1950, author of historical works.

Luxemburg, Rosa (1871–1919). Born in Poland of impoverished Jewish family. Emigrated to Zürich in 1888, met Jogiches and with him founded

Polish Social-Democratic Party. Settled in Germany, naturalised thanks to marriage of convenience. Polemicised against revisionists. Returned to Poland during 1905 Revolution, arrested and freed on bail. Lecturer in central SPD school in Berlin from 1907. Broke with Kautsky and centre tendency of SPD in 1912. In August 1914 organised resistance to social-chauvinism, founded Internationale group. Twice imprisoned, freed by November Revolution, strove to maintain Spartacus League, of which she was theoretical leader, within USPD. Edited *Die Rote Fahne*. Member of Zentrale, opposed January uprising, arrested and murdered along with Liebknecht.

Malzahn, Heinrich (1884–1957). Son of worker, mechanic. In SPD in 1906, in left opposition in metalworkers' union. Member of group of revolutionary shop-stewards. In USPD in 1917, member of strikers' action committee in January 1918, and of Executive of Councils in November 1918. Chairman of Berlin Committee of Factory Councils. USPD deputy in 1920, co-led USPD Left. In VKPD and in trade-union commission in 1920. Opposed March Action, but organised strike in the Ruhr. Defended Levi at Third Comintern Congress. Organised right opposition with Brass and Friesland, expelled in January 1922, returned to USPD, then to SPD. Later political role of no great importance. Imprisoned by Nazis during 1940–5.

Marchlewski, Julian (known as Karski and as Johannes Kämpfer, 1866–1925). Born in Poland, secondary education, then dye-worker. Underground activist in 1888, emigrated, resumed studies, took part in formation of Polish Social-Democratic Party with Luxemburg, continued to be associated with her in Germany, where he settled in 1893. Member of Spartacist nucleus, imprisoned during 1916–18, freed as Russian citizen abroad at request of Soviet government, returned in February 1919 and advised Commission of the Nine in the Ruhr. Escaped, returned to Russia, then to Poland, where he was in leadership of Communist Party. Declined offer in 1921 of leading position in KPD. Settled in Moscow, leader of Workers' Relief International.

Maslow, Arkadi (Isaac Chereminsky, 1893–1941). Born in Elisabetgrad of rich Jewish family, which took up residence in Germany in 1899. Brilliant, very eclectic studies: natural sciences, music, physics under Einstein. No connection with workers' movement before 1914. Interned as resident foreigner, volunteered for work with Russian prisoners, then served as Russian interpreter in German army. Resumed studies in Berlin in 1919, made acquaintance of Levi and Fischer, who won him to Communism, active in KPD under pseudonym Maslow; elected to Central Committee in November 1920 as representative of 'Russian section', already leader of Left. Prominent in attacks on Levi, supported March Action and theory of the offensive, opponent of Moscow compromise, for which Lenin suggested, unsuccessfully, that he be sent to Russia. Arrested in 1922, proclaimed himself to be Russian agent, which got him into difficulties with KPD but did not save him from being sentenced to eight months in jail. Spokesman of Left at Leipzig Congress, elected to Central Committee. Summoned to Moscow in September 1923 for preparations insurrection, held there by Commission of Enquiry. Cleared by Commission presided over by Stalin, returned to Germany in January 1924. Member of Politbureau in April, and leader of KPD with Fischer. Arrested in May 1925, not released until July 1926. Meanwhile, had taken a position opposing formation of red trade unions and in favour of withdrawing KPD candidate in second round of presidential elections. Attacked by ECCI in

September 1925, expelled in August 1926. Co-founder and leader of Leninbund. Emigrated to Paris with Fischer in 1933, stayed until 1940, not authorised to enter USA, settled in Cuba, where he died, killed in road accident. Fischer was to attribute his death to Stalin's assassins.

Maslowski, Peter (1893–). Tailoring worker, in USPD in 1917, member of League of Red Soldiers in 1918, of VKPD in 1920. In 1923 secretary of Central Rhineland district in Cologne, leader of moderate Left. Joined centre tendency in 1924, active journalist, twice elected deputy, several times sentenced. Emigré in 1933, broke with KPD after his friend Münzenburg was expelled. Lived illegally in Grenoble, France during War, in contact with Trotskyists. Returned to Germany in 1945, and joined SPD.

Mehring, Franz (1846–1919). Son of bourgeois family. Writer and liberal journalist, joined SPD in period of anti-socialist persecution. Author of works of history and literary criticism. Longtime Chief Editor of *Leipziger Volkszeitung* and editorial writer in *Die Neue Zeit*. Associated with Luxemburg, joined her when she broke from Kautsky. Member of internationalist nucleus in 1914, Spartacist, showed sympathy for Bolsheviks in 1917. In bad health, did not take part in foundation of KPD(S), of which he became member. Deeply affected by murder of Liebknecht and Luxemburg, died a few weeks later.

Melcher, Erich (1892–1944). Son of worker, toolmaker. In SPD in 1910, conscript during 1912–17, then worked in Daimler factories in Stuttgart, joined Spartacus League and USPD. Co-founder of KPD(S) in Württemberg, first president of metalworkers' union in Stuttgart in 1919, responsible for *Open Letter* in January 1921, expelled from union in May. Stayed briefly in Moscow, then head of metalworkers' section in trade-union department of Zentrale. Secretary for trade-union questions in Berlin-Brandenburg district in spring 1923. Led 'security' department during preparations for insurrection in 1923. Removed as rightist, imprisoned during July 1924–August 1926, Polleiter in Dresden, expelled as rightist in 1928. In KPO then SAP. Illegal work under Hitler, jailed 1934 to end of 1936, arrested in August 1937, deported to Buchenwald, where clandestine KPD leadership treated him as 'enemy of party'. Died during transport.

Merges, August (1870–1933). Son of worker, tailor. In SPD towards 1890, held various responsibilities. Associate of Thalheimer, member of Spartacus group in Brunswick, where in November 1918 he was chairman of workers' council and President of Socialist Republic of Brunswick. After revolutionary movement was crushed, joined KAPD, which he represented in Moscow at Second Comintern Congress. In minority in KAPD until 1921, then joined KPD. Murdered by SS in 1933.

Meyer, Ernst (1887–1930). Son of locomotive driver. Higher studies, narrow religious training. Polemicised against socialists, ended by joining SPD in 1908. Presented thesis in 1910, worked as statistician. Journalist on *Vorwärts* at beginning of 1913, where he edited art and literature sections. Friend of Luxemburg, oppositionist in August 1914. Tubercular, not conscripted, stalwart of Spartacus League during War, despite several arrests. On Zentrale in 1918, elected to KPD(S) Zentrale at its foundation. Principal Party leader with Levi, Chief Editor of *Die Rote Fahne*, then Secretary of Politbureau in 1921, and Chairman of Party. Very hostile to Left, but criticised on ECCI for opportunist positions, gave place to Brandler when latter returned in August 1922. Not re-elected to the Zentrale in 1923. Secretary of Oberbezirk South during preparation of insurrection in 1923. Leader of centre tendency in 1924, then of 'conciliators'. Openly opposed Comintern's ultra-left line in 1929, died early in 1930.

Möller, Werner (known as Nauffacher, 1888–1919). Son of worker, tin-smith, joined SPD when very young, became writer. In 1914 in Borchardt's Berlin group, helped lead ISD. Nine months in prison in 1915, leader of ISD in Berlin, collaborator in *Arbeiterpolitik*. IKD leader, and leader of Berlin ultra-leftists. Led occupation of *Vorwärts* building, and helped to defend it in January 1919. Murdered by Free Corps soldiers.

Müller, Richard (1890–). Son of worker, turner. Responsible for turners' branch of metalworkers' union in Berlin. In 1914 led opposition to War, organised network of revolutionary stewards, led strikes in June 1916, April 1917 and January 1918. Conscripted. President of Executive of Councils in November 1918, resisted convocation of National Assembly. Opposed entry of revolutionary stewards into KPD(S), protested against initiatives which led to January uprising. Led strike of March 1919 in Berlin. Leader of left opposition in trade unions and USPD. In VKPD in 1920, supported Levi in 1921, resigned and gave up all political activity. Later fate unknown.

Münzenberg, Willi (1887–1940). Son of inn-keeper, itinerant worker at age of 12. In Socialist Youth in 1906. In Switzerland from 1910, where he led Socialist Youth. Was then associated with Bolsheviks, and reorganised leadership of Young Socialist International. Several times imprisoned, expelled from Switzerland in 1918. From November 1918, member of USPD and Spartacus League in Stuttgart, organised National Conference of Socialist Youth (Left) in Berlin in December. Delegate to First Congress of Councils. Member of KPD(S) on its foundation, under arrest for five months in 1919, organised 'buffer group' between Levi and leftists at Heidelberg Congress. Secretary of Young Communist International until 1921, in conflict several times with ECCI. In 1921 put in charge of organising Workers' International Relief. Founded network of businesses, the 'Münzenberg Trust', to help Comintern. Deputy during 1924–33, emigrated to France, refused to go to Russia when summoned, expelled from KPD in 1938. Interned in 1940, freed when French army collapsed, assassinated near Saint-Marcellin.

Neubauer, Theodor (known as Lorenz, 1890–1945). Son of nationalist civil servant. Higher education, worked as teacher. Doctorate in 1913, active in National Liberal Party. Volunteered for army in 1914. Lieutenant in 1915, gassed in 1917. Member of 'party of the German Fatherland', joined Democratic Party in 1918. Developed rapidly leftwards, in USPD at end of summer 1919, and in KPD in 1920. Still a teacher Communist minister in Fröhlich government in October 1923. Went into illegality, active on Left, up to 1927. Journalist, deputy from 1928, specialist in foreign affairs, many stays in Moscow. Arrested in 1933, freed in 1939, organised secret group. Arrested in 1944, sentenced to death, executed in 1945.

Neumann, Heinz (1902–1937?). Son of bourgeois family, revolted against it, sent to special school at age of 15. Secondary education, then higher studies in philosophy. Joined Socialist Youth in 1918, KPD in 1920; recruited by Friesland, trained by Thalheimer. Worked in KPD press office, on *Inprekorr* and *Die Rote Fahne* from 1922. Sentenced to six months in prison, learned Russian, which enabled him that year to be first German leader to have personal relations with Stalin. Member of left opposition in 1923, broke with it in April, played important role in M- and Z-Apparat during preparations for insurrection. Secretary of Mecklenburg district, arrested, escaped.

Represented KPD in Moscow in 1925, contributed to elimination from KPD leadership of Zinoviev's protégés. Sent on mission to China in 1927, organised Canton Commune with Lominadze. One of few leaders to support Thaelmann in Wittorf affair in 1928, became Chief Editor of *Die Rote Fahne* and Party leader. Until 1932 was Stalin's spokesman in KPD, then deported opposed his policies, lost all positions, and sent to Spain. Recognised his factional activities in 'self-criticism' in 1934, arrested in Switzerland, deported to USSR, arrested in April 1937, and executed without trial.

Neumann, Paul (1888–). Son of worker, metalworker. SPD member when very young, in circle of revolutionary delegates in 1916, in USPD in 1917, member of Revolutionary Committee in January 1918. Organised left opposition in metalworkers' union. On USPD Left, joined VKPD in 1920. Opposed decisions which Central Committee took in March 1921, supported Levi. Delegate of 'Right' at Third Comintern Congress. Organiser with Brass of right opposition; worked with Brass in Zentrale's trade-union department. Supported Friesland, excluded in January 1922. Returned to USPD in 1922, and then to SPD. Later activity and fate unknown.

Niederkirchner, Michaël (1882–1949). Son of stonemason, born in Hungary. Plumber, in Hungarian Social-Democratic Party in 1903, in SPD in Berlin in 1905. In USPD in 1917, in VKPD in 1920. Secretary of plumbers' trade-union from 1921. Supported Levi, protested in 1921 against condemnation of KAG. Pillar of KPD Right in 1923. Remained very popular union leader, member of Central Committee in 1927 and 1929. Arrested in 1933, deported as foreigner; in USSR, from where he returned in 1945, to fill several important positions.

Osterloh, Hermann (1886–1961). Son of worker, metalworker, in SPD in 1908. Conscripted in 1914, prisoner in Russia, joined Bolshevik Party in 1917. Arrested and turned back at German frontier in December 1918, returned only in 1919, active in Bremen as secretary concerned with peasant questions. KPD full-timer in various posts, expelled as rightist in 1928, joined SPD in 1930, worked in factory. Sentenced to eight years in camp in 1934. Leader of SPD in Bremen after War.

Pannekoek, Anton (known as Harper and Horner, 1873–1960). Of Dutch origin, higher studies in astronomy, in Dutch Social Democracy in 1902, formed its left wing from 1905, and led Tribune group; excluded in 1909, founded leftist SDP. Settled in Germany after 1905, lived in Bremen for many years, educated many activists there. Prewar polemic against Kautsky. Returned to Netherlands in 1914, member of Zimmerwald Left, co-founder of Dutch Communist Party in 1918, supported IKD in Germany, then became theoretician of German ultra-Left. Inspired KAPD's programme in 1920, and was its theoretician. Following crises in KAPD, resumed scientific activities, published authoritative works; continued to inspire activity of council communists in Holland and elsewhere.

Peters, Bruno (1884–). Son of worker, toolmaker. In SPD before war, secretary of Charlottenburg circle in 1916, and member of Spartacus group, member of circle of revolutionary stewards. In USPD in 1917, led April 1917 strike in DMW plant in Berlin. Arrested in January 1918, liberated by November revolution, chairman of workers' council in Frankfurt-an-der-Oder. Member of KPD(S) on its foundation, on control commission afterwards. In SED in 1946; had secondary role for long time.

Pfeiffer, Hans (1895–1968). Son of worker, toolmaker. In SPD in 1913, won to anarchism in Switzerland. Returned to Social Democracy before 1914. Discharged during War, active in Berlin in connection with youth groups around Münzenberg, joined Spartacists. In USPD in 1917, in KPD on its foundation. Specialist in organisation, secretary of Berlin-Brandenburg district from 1919, in charge of organisation. Elected to Zentrale in January 1923, broke from Left in April. Imprisoned for a year in 1924–5, opposed Left, held organisational responsibilities in Berlin, then Moscow and Prague. Arrested in 1933, sentenced to three years in jail in 1934. Returned to work in factory. Obscure member of KPD and SED after War.

Pfemfert, Franz (1879–1954). Writer, editor of *Die Aktion*, left critic of SPD before war, leading figure in expressionist literature during War, founded in 1915 'anti-national socialist party'. Joined KPD(S) at its foundation, placed *Die Aktion* in service of ultra-left current, joined KAPD in April 1920, defended 'unions'. Expelled from KAPD at beginning of 1921, maintained left criticism of workers' parties. After 1923 applied himself to creating 'Spartacus League Mark 2', personally associated with Trotsky, came close to theses defended by International Left Opposition. Emigrated in 1933 to Prague, then Paris, in 1940 to New York. Settled in 1941 in Mexico, where he was photographer, and died there.

Pieck, Wilhelm (1876–1960). Son of labourer, carpenter. Trade unionist in 1894, in SPD in 1895, worked until 1906 as carpenter in Bremen and during 1906–10 in apparatus of local Party. In Berlin in 1910 responsible for Party education. Worked with Ebert, but stood on Left of SPD. Member of Internationale group in 1914, arrested in May 1915, conscripted in October, sentenced for refusal to obey orders in August 1917 to 18 months in prison. Deserted and escaped into Holland in January 1918. Returned in November, was coopted by Liebknecht to circle of revolutionary shop-stewards. Elected to Zentrale of Spartacus League, then to that of KPD(S), Liebknecht's right-hand man in January 1919, arrested with him, released soon afterwards, under arrest again during July-November 1919. His first arrest was to give rise to accusations against him which are rather improbable. One of authors in 1921 of declaration of loyal opposition, did his best to get compromise in the Ruhr, as mandated by Zentrale. On KPD Right, supported Brandler, agent of ECCI, to which he was delegated particularly in 1921. Supported centre tendency in 1924, led Workers' International Relief, and then, in 1926, the Berlin district. Made self-criticism and submitted to Stalin in 1929, was member of ECCI from 1928, of Comintern Secretariat and Presidium from 1931, for a long time Comintern Secretary for the Balkans. In Paris during 1933–8. In Moscow in 1938, worked with Committee for a Free Germany during War. Returned in 1945 as KPD chairman. SED chairman in 1946, DDR President from its foundation in 1949 to his death.

Plattner, Karl (1893–1933). Son of worker, printer. In Socialist Youth before War, in SPD in 1914, organiser of youth during War, sentenced to 18 months in prison for leaflet supporting Liebknecht's actions. Founder of IKD in Dresden in 1918, member of workers' and soldiers' council of Dresden, then resigned from it. Member of KPD(S) on its foundation and activist of ultra-left wing. Played important role in Republic of Councils in Bremen in 1919, and in struggle against Kappists in the Ruhr in 1920. Foundation member of KAPD, head of its fighting organisation, organised 'expropriations' to finance Party; important role in fighting in March 1921, organised urban guerrillas, arrested in 1921 and sentenced in 1923 to 10 years in fortress. Amnestied in 1928, rejoined KPD. According to Hermann Weber, died in

Buchenwald; according to Hans Bock, was shot down when trying to cross Czechoslovak frontier.

Pogany, Josef (known as Pepper, 1886–1937). Social-Democratic journalist, joined Hungarian Communist Party, President of Soldiers' Council in Budapest in 1919. After defeat, took refuge in Moscow, collaborator of ECCI, accompanied Kun to Berlin in 1921, carried on struggle against rightist current in youth organisation. Played no further role in Germany. Organised Communist Party of the USA, under name of Pepper. Arrested and liquidated during Stalinist purges.

Pohl, Kathe (Katarina or Lydia Rabinovich, 1892–). Born in St Petersburg. Partner of Guralski-Kleine, active in Germany under pseudonym. Secretary to KPD Politbureau in 1921, collaborated on *Inprekorr*, played role in the Ruhr in 1923. Supported centre tendency in 1924, appears to have ceased all political activity; all trace of her is lost.

Radek, Karl (Karl Bernardovich Sobelson, known as Parabellum, Arnold Struthahn, Paul Bremer, Max, 1885–1940?). Son of Jewish family in Austrian Galicia. Studied in Poland, then in Vienna and Switzerland. Active at age of 18 in underground movement, met Jogiches in 1904, played important role in 1905 Revolution. Arrested in 1906, escaped, reached Germany in 1908, wrote in SPD press in Leipzig, then in Bremen, and became known through his controversy with Kautsky. Expelled from Polish Party in 1912 at instigation of Jogiches and Luxemburg, and from SPD in 1913 following much-publicised 'scandal'. Emigrated to Switzerland 1914, took part in Zimmerwald and Kienthal Conferences, collaborated in *Arbeiterpolitik*, and played important role in forming Zimmerwald Left. Close to Lenin, in conflict with him on national question. Left Switzerland with him, organised in Stockholm Bureau of Bolsheviks' Central Committee with task of revolutionary propaganda in Germany. In Petrograd in October 1918, Vice-Commissar for Foreign Affairs, took part in Brest-Litovsk discussions, and organised Bolshevik propaganda directed at German prisoners of war and troops. Secret mission to Berlin in December 1919, took part in Founding Conference of KPD(S), giving support to decision to found it. Unsuccessfully opposed initiatives of Liebknecht in January 1919. Arrested in February, enjoyed favourable treatment after some months. Set free at end of year, he became ECCI Secretary, from which job he was removed for having supported Levi and KPD against his own party in KAPD affair. Co-author of *Open Letter* of January 1921 with Levi, opened struggle against him, and, up to Third Comintern Congress, supported KPD Left, which he had earlier opposed. From then, was KPD's guide and principal political leader, at same time as being USSR's semi-official diplomatic representative in contact with ruling circles in Germany. Supported decision to withdraw Brandler in October 1923. Selected as scapegoat for 1923 defeat, after he had moved to support Left Opposition in USSR. Rector of University of the Peoples of the East in Moscow, important member of United Opposition during 1926–7, expelled and exiled internally, capitulated in 1929. Journalist, accuser and accused in second Moscow Trial in 1937, sentenced only to imprisonment, died in concentration camp.

Rákosi, Mátyás (1892–1971). Son of comfortably-placed Jewish family. Studied in Budapest, then in Germany and England. Member of Socialist Youth in 1911. Conscript in 1914, prisoner of war in Russia, member of group which, with Kun, adhered to Communism. Returned to Hungary at beginning of 1918; People's Commissar of Soviet Republic in 1919. Took refuge in Moscow, worked in Comintern apparatus, which he represented notably at Livorno Congress. His intervention in KPD Zentrale provoked crisis and resignation of Levi. From 1922 member of Comintern Secretariat. Sent on secret mission to Hungary in 1925, arrested and sentenced, exchanged in 1940 for Hungarian flags taken in 1848. Russian citizen, lived in USSR during 1940–44, returned with Russian army as General Secretary of Hungarian Party. Compelled to resign in July 1956 after protracted resistance. Left Hungary for USSR after Revolution of October 1956. Expelled from Hungarian party, in which he had been incarnation of Stalinism, in August 1962. Died in USSR.

Rau, Heinrich (1899–1961). Son of peasant. Metalworker. In Socialist Youth in 1913. Spartacist in 1916. Member of USPD in 1917, in KPD(S) at its foundation. Leader in Stuttgart in 1919–20. In Berlin in 1920 as head of agricultural department of Zentrale. Editor of *Der Pflug*. Retained Party functions until 1932. Arrested in 1933, two years in jail, emigrated to Czechoslovakia, then to USSR. Commissar and then Commander of Eleventh International Brigade in Spain. Interned in France in 1939. Handed over to Gestapo in 1942, deported to Mauthausen. Minister and member of SED Politbureau after war, specialist in economic questions.

Reichenbach, Bernhard (born 1888). Son of comfortably-off family. Higher studies, leader of socialist students. Conscript during 1915–17, joined USPD in 1917, worked in its press office until 1919; in 1920, associated with Schröder, went over to KAPD, delegate to Third Comintern Congress. Member of Essen group after split in KAPD in 1922. In SPD in 1924, in SAP in 1931, emigrated to Britain in 1935, living there from then.

Reichpietsch, Max (1894–1917). Mechanic, conscripted into navy in 1914. In 1917 organised revolutionary sailors and made contact with USPD leaders in Berlin. Shot in September 1917.

Remmele, Hermann (1880–1939). Son of small-scale miller. In SPD in 1897, organiser of youth and illegal anti-militarist activity in Ludwigshafen. Student at SPD school in 1907–8, then full-timer in Mannheim, member of Left. Conscript during 1914–18, organised opposition whilst on leave in Mannheim, delegate to USPD Foundation Congress. Council chairman in Mannheim in 1919, leader of Conciliar Republic in 1919. Then in Stuttgart, leader of USPD Left. In VKPD in 1920, elected to Zentrale. Important role in preparing insurrection in 1923; courier of Zentrale indirectly, at least, responsible for outbreak of Hamburg insurrection. Supported centre tendency, then Thaelmann's faction, member of Comintern Presidium, a principal leader of KPD until 1932, came out against Thaelmann. Emigrated to Moscow in 1933, con-fessed in 1934 to 'factional' activity, arrested in 1937. According to some, he was murdered immediately; according to others, he lost his reason.

Rogg, Ulrich (1888–1938?). Bakery worker. In SPD before War, then in Spartacus group. One of its organisers in the Ruhr. Important role in events in Duisburg in 1919. In 1923 a KPD cadre in Halle region. In Russia in 1925, arrested and sentenced when he returned to Germany, gave up all political activity.

Rosenberg, Arthur (1889–1945). Son of Jewish business people in Berlin. Brilliant higher studies in ancient history. Assistant in University of Berlin in 1914. Joined USPD when demobilised in 1918. In VKPD in 1920, worked on *Inprekorr*. Member of Berlin Left and leadership of Berlin-Brandenburg district, theoretician of theory of the offensive from 1921. Member of Zentrale and

Politbureau in 1924–5, then leader of ultra-left opposition, joined Thaelmann in 1926. Resigned from KPD in 1927, returned to chair in University of Berlin, led League of the Rights of Man. Dismissed in 1933, emigrated to Britain, taught in University of Liverpool. Settled in 1937 in Brooklyn, USA, continued to teach and produce historical works.

Ruck, Fritz (1895–1959). Son of carpenter, printer. Active in Socialist Youth, on Left of SPD in 1913. Conscript during 1915–16, discharged, joined USPD as Spartacist, collaborated on *Sozialdemokrat* in Stuttgart. A leader of November Revolution there. Member of editorial staff of *Die Rote Fahne* in 1921, supported Brandler in 1923. Expelled in 1929 as right-winger. In SAP in 1932. Emigrated in 1933 to Switzerland and in 1937 to Sweden. Joined Social Democrats. Author of children's books. President of printers' union in West Germany after War.

Rühle, Otto (1874–1943). Teacher, psychologist, educator. In SPD in 1900, journalist in 1902. Deputy in Reichstag in 1912. Joined Liebknecht in open opposition in 1915, spoke in favour of splitting SPD. Spartacist, then leader of IKD in 1917. Resigned in November 1919 from Dresden council of workers and soldiers. Spokesman at KPD(S) Foundation Congress for ultra-left majority. Defended 'unionism', joined KAPD when it was founded. Delegate to Second Comintern Congress, spoke against 'Twenty-One Conditions', refused to take part, repudiated and expelled by KAPD in November. Promoter of 'unionist', anti-authoritarian tendency. Returned in 1923 to SPD. Devoted himself to valuable scientific works, emigrated in 1933, in Mexico in 1936, helped organise Dewey Commission of Enquiry into Moscow Trials, had discussions with Trotsky, devoted his last years to painting.

Rusch, Oskar (1884–). Metalworker, delegate and 'agent' of SPD in Berlin factory in 1914. Social-Democratic member of Executive of Councils in November 1918, joined USPD after Congress of the Councils in December. Later, leader of metalworkers' union and trade unions in Berlin, particularly during Kapp Putsch. On USPD Left, removed from his responsibilities. In VKPD in 1920. Left in 1921, returned to SPD in 1922. Later dates and facts unknown.

Sachse, Willy (1896–1944). From petty-bourgeois family, technical studies. Conscripted into navy in 1914. Organiser of revolutionary sailors in 1917, sentenced to death, but sentence commuted to hard labour. Freed by November Revolution, joined USPD and then VKPD in 1920. In 1923 secretary of Halle-Merseburg district. Important functions in KPD apparatus up to 1928, when he resigned. From 1933, organised resistance group to Hitler régime. Arrested in January 1942, executed in August 1944.

Schliestedt, Heinrich (1883–1938). Metalworker, active in trade union, in left tendency before War. In USPD in 1917, organiser of struggles in the Ruhr in 1919–20. On USPD Left, opposed joining Comintern. Returned to SPD in 1922. Underground organiser under Hitler, killed accidentally when returning from conference abroad.

Schloer, Jakob (1888–1956). Café waiter, in SPD from 1911. Associated with Levi, Spartacist in Frankfurt during War, co-founder of KPD(S) in Mannheim. Supported KAG in 1921, remained in Party. In apparatus in South Germany in 1923. Secretary-general of Red Aid in 1926, expelled as rightist in 1929, émigré in 1933, admitted to KPD and then SED after War, expelled in 1951, readmitted in 1955.

Schmidt, Felix (1885–1932). Printer, in SPD in 1904, led left opposition in Bremen during War, and IKD in 1918, leader of left wing. Remained in KPD(S) when ultra-Left split off. Treasurer of Zentrale from 1921. In 1923 took leadership of Oberbezirk South-West. In Red Aid in Moscow during 1924–6, excluded in 1929, went to KPO and then to SAP. Died following an operation.

Schneller, Ernst (1890–1940). Son of railway worker, orphaned at age of five. Became schoolteacher. In SPD in 1920, joined KPD after Kapp Putsch. In 1921 belonged to Levi's tendency. A leader of preparations for insurrection in 1923, commanded proletarian hundreds in Saxony. Joined centre tendency and then left wing. On Zentrale in 1924, in charge of military questions, then of theoretical matters, became champion of 'the struggle against Trotskyism and Luxemburgism'. Joined Thaelmann's leadership, but removed after Wittorf affair. Arrested in 1933, sentenced to six years, executed in Sachsenhausen.

Scholem, Werner (1895–1940). Son of printing worker, higher studies in history and law. In Socialist Youth in 1912, in SPD in 1913. Conscripted in 1914, sentenced in 1917 for anti-militarist activity. In USPD in 1917, journalist in Halle. In VKPD in 1920, worked on *Die Rote Fahne*. Arrested after March 1921, played important role as organiser in Berlin district, supported Left in 1923. Member of Zentrale and Politbureau, responsible posts in Organisation Bureau in 1923, *de facto* KPD leader with Fischer until 1925, when he co-led ultra-Left. Expelled in 1926, joint organiser of Leninbund, worked with organ of German Trotskyist opposition. Arrested in 1933, executed in 1940.

Schreiner, Albert (1892–). Son of worker who became SPD full-timer. Mechanic. In SPD in 1910, member of Spartacus group during War. Minister of War in government of Württemberg for a few days. A leader of Military Apparatus in 1923, M. Leiter in Wasserkante. In military school in Moscow in 1924, then leader of League of Red Front Fighters. Expelled in 1929 as rightist. Member of KPO. Returned to KPD in October 1932, left it immediately. Emigrated to France in 1933, fought in Spain as Chief of Staff of Twelfth International Brigade. In France during 1939–41, then in Morocco, Mexico and USA. Returned in 1946 to East Germany, frequently in conflict with leadership on questions of history.

Schröder, Karl (1885–1950). Son of teacher, higher studies in philosophy. In SPD in 1913. In Spartacus League during War. Helped run *Die Rote Fahne* in 1918. Ultra-leftist, theoretician of revolutionary workplace organisations. Leader of Berlin district, expelled from KPD(S), prominent initiator in founding KAPD. Close collaborator with Gorter in 1920. Travelled with him to Moscow, when he obtained admission of KAPD into Comintern as sympathising party. At end of 1921, organised information bureaux and International of Left Communists. Led KAPD in Essen after split of 1922. Returned to SPD in 1924. Literary critic on *Vorwärts*. Organised former KAPD members in SPD, and in 1936 formed illegal organisation, Red Fighters. Sentenced to hard labour, organised education in West Berlin after 1945, went over to East, joined SED.

Schubert, Hermann (1886–1938). Son of worker, miner, then itinerant worker. In SPD in 1907. Trade-union responsibilities. In USPD in 1917, in VKPD in 1920. Followed courses at Lenin School in Moscow in 1923. A leader of projected insurrection in Thuringia. Arrested, escaped, lived illegally in the Ruhr. Member of left wing, then supported Thaelmann against Fischer; from 1933 lived illegally, defended former sectarian line against Pieck and Ulbricht. Removed in 1935, arrested in Moscow in 1937, and executed.

Schulte, Fritz (1890–1943). Son of worker, worked in chemical industry. In USPD in 1918. In VKPD in 1920, led red trade-union. Member of right wing, called Thaelmann an 'idiot'. Joined Left in 1924, then organised red trade unions. Took part in Politbureau. In Moscow in 1935, removed from Central Committee, arrested and executed.

Schulz, Karl (1884–1933). Son of worker, blacksmith. In SPD in 1905, leader of Socialist Youth. At SPD school during 1912–13, then journalist. Joined Spartacus League during War, founder and leader of Red Soldiers' League. Delegate to Foundation Congress of KPD(S), founder of Party in Pomerania and Mecklenburg. In 1923 secretary of Oberbezirk North. Hunted by police, took refuge in Moscow during 1924–8. Conciliator, accepted penalties against group. Arrested at time of Reichstag fire, died in Spandau as a result of ill-treatment.

Schumann, Georg (1886–1945). Son of stonemason, toolmaker. In SPD in 1905, leader of Socialist Youth. At SPD school in 1912–13, then journalist. During War joined Internationale group, arrested in 1915 and conscripted. Sentenced by military court to 12 years hard labour. Freed by November Revolution, led Spartacus League and then KPD(S) in Leipzig. The most popular leader in Central Germany, member of right wing. Moved to centre tendency in 1924. Worked in RILU in Moscow during 1925–6, then in jail in Germany during 1926–7. Conciliator, made 'self-criticism' in 1929. Arrested in 1933, deported to Sachsenhausen until 1939. Resumed factory work, soon became leader of important communist resistance group, which declared, in opposition to Free German Committee in USSR, its support for socialism. Arrested in 1944, tortured at length, executed in January 1945.

Schwab, Alexander (1887–1943). Son of master carpenter. Printer. In SPD in 1907, Spartacist during War. Associated with Schröder in Berlin, co-founder of KAPD. Sympathised with national Bolshevism, left KAPD in September 1920, returned to SPD.

Serrati, Giacinto Menotti (1874–1926). Became Socialist activist at very young age, pioneer of Italian Socialism. Leader of maximalist wing during War, Chief Editor of *Avanti* in 1915, delegate to Zimmerwald and Kienthal. Arrested in 1917, supporter of break with Second International and of joining Third International from 1919. Elected at Second Comintern Congress to ECCI, resisted application of 'Twenty-One Conditions' by his party. Remained with Italian Socialist Party after Livorno Congress. Was readmitted with some of his supporters to Comintern and Italian Communist Party in 1924, member of latter's Central Committee until he died.

Siewert, Robert (1887–). Son of carpenter, building worker. In SPD in 1906. Worked in Switzerland where he knew Lenin, Brandler and Heckert. Conscripted during 1914–18, worked illegally for Spartacus League. Organised and led soldiers' council. Joined KPD(S) on return, organised activities in Erzegebirge. Supporter of Brandler, member of Central Committee, political secretary for Erzgebirge-Vogtland in 1923. Right oppositionist, expelled in 1929, joined KPO, worked on *Arbeiterpolitik*. Arrested in 1933, rejoined KPD in Buchenwald. Held posts in DDR after War, dismissed in 1950 because of his past, forced to make 'self-criticism' in 1951.

Sommer, Josef (Joseph Winterritz, alias Lenz, 1896–1952). Son of professor, studied in Britain, then in Prague. Conscripted in 1917, socialist in 1918, in Communist Party of Czechoslovakia in 1920. Doctor of philosophy, active in KPD from 1923, attacking right wing, and appearing to be theoretician of Left. Responsible for propaganda in 1924, candidate member of Central Committee, low-level posts in apparatus during 1925–8, returned to heading propaganda in 1931. Made 'self-criticism' after having attacked Thaelmann and Stalin. Emigrated to Czechoslovakia in 1934, to Britain in 1939, worked for Communist Party of Great Britain. Returned in 1948, headed the Marx-Engels Institute. Severely criticised in 1951, returned to Britain, where he died.

Sorge, Richard (alias Sonter, alias Ika, 1895–1944). Son of engineer, born in Russia. Higher studies; volunteered in 1914, three times wounded. In USPD in 1918, in VKPD in 1920. Teacher in Aachen, dismissed in 1922. Lecturer in Frankfurt in 1923, member of KPD's secret Military Apparatus. In charge of security at Congress in 1924, seconded to Moscow, worked for Comintern, then in Fourth Bureau of the Red Army. Mission to China during 1931–2. Returned to Germany in 1933, joined Nazi Party, got himself accredited as war correspondent to Japan, organised information network which in particular was to warn Stalin in advance of German aggression of June 1941. Arrested in October 1944, executed in November. His mission has been recognised and role celebrated since an article in *Pravda* on 4 September 1964.

Stern, Manfred (alias Stein, alias Kleber, 1896–1954). Born in Bukovina, activist before War, conscripted in Austro-Hungarian army in 1916, prisoner of war, won to Communism, fought in ranks of Red Army, especially in Siberia. In Germany as military technician in 1921 and 1923, under name of Stein. From 1927 to 1936, was military adviser in China. Appointed in Spain to command International Brigades and in defence of Madrid under name of General Kléber. Arrested on recall in 1937 and long believed to have been executed. According to Russian sources, which do not seem to deny his long imprisonment, he died in 1954.

Stoecker, Walter (1891–1939). Son of engineer, began higher studies. In SPD in 1908, active in youth movement and from 1912 led socialist students in Cologne. In contact with Münzenberg in 1914. Conscripted during 1915–18. In USPD in 1917. Leader of councils in Cologne in 1918–19. Deputy Secretary of USPD in June 1919, a leader of left wing, delegate to Third Comintern Congress. Elected to VKPD Zentrale in 1920, Chairman of Party after Levi resigned. In retirement during 1921–3. Elected to Zentrale in 1923, Secretary of Oberbezirk West in 1923. Joined centre tendency, Chairman of parliamentary fraction in Reichstag during 1924–32. Arrested at time of Reichstag fire, sent to various camps, died of typhus in Buchenwald.

Sturm, Fritz (Samuel Markovich Zaks-Gladniev, 1890–1937?). Born in Russia, Bolshevik. Came to Hamburg in 1919. Member of IKD, then of KPD(S), belonged to left wing. Did not join KAPD. Arrested in 1920 and expelled. Settled in Leningrad. Supported Bukharin in 1928, arrested and seems to have been executed as terrorist in 1937.

Süsskind, Heinrich (alias Heinrich, alias Kurt, 1890–1937). Son of rabbi, born in Poland. Studied in Vienna, in Germany in 1917, studies in history. In 1919 worked in youth movement, joined KPD(S). Subject to expulsion from Germany, went underground, worked on *Die Rote Fahne*, becoming its Chief Editor at age 26 in December 1921. Member of Zentrale. Arrested and forced to leave Germany, in Russia in 1922 and 1923. Resumed his position at beginning of 1923, replaced in June by Thalheimer, sent to Leipzig. Member of Left, then of Thaelmann's group, conciliator in 1928, made 'self-criticism', emigrated to Prague in 1933, then in USSR, where he was arrested and executed.

Tenner, Albin (1885–1967). Son of painter on porcelain, started work at age of 14, became teacher. Conscript during 1914–18. In USPD in 1918, member of Land government in Gotha. In VKPD in 1920. A Communist leader in

Thuringia, member of Central Committee in 1923, Minister for the Economy in Frölich's government in October 1923. Expelled in 1925, then readmitted, again expelled in 1929; in KPO, then in SAP. Emigrated to Holland, where he died.

Teuber, Heinrich (1872–1928). Miner, union president in 1910, leader of trade-union left opposition. In USPD in 1917, in VKPD in 1920, expelled with Malzahn and Brass, returned to USPD and then SPD in 1922.

Thaelmann, Ernst (1886–1944). Son of greengrocer, left paternal home when very young, became stoker in cargo ship. Worked in New York, then returned to Germany and did various jobs, including as docker. In SPD in 1903, member of left wing, opponent of trade-union bureaucrats. Conscripted during 1915–18, in USPD in 1918. Leader of USPD Left in Hamburg, in VKPD in 1920, mobilised unemployed to impose strike in March 1921. Defended theory of the offensive against Lenin and Trotsky at Third Comintern Congress. Member of Central Committee, a standard-bearer of Left. Coopted to Zentrale in May 1923. Important role in Hamburg insurrection in October 1923. Member of Zentrale and Politbureau in 1924, President of Party after Fischer and Maslow were eliminated, endangered by Wittorf affair, supported by Stalin. Arrested in March 1933, executed in Buchenwald in August 1944.

Thalheimer, August (1884–1948). Son of Jewish trader. Higher studies in philosophy, especially in Oxford and Strassburg. In SPD in 1904, Chief Editor in Göppingen in 1909, linked with Radek, Luxemburg, Mehring and Westmeyer. Member of Internationale group, active in Spartacus group during War, conscripted during 1916–18, played important role in November Revolution in Stuttgart, and was for short time member of Land government. Fought ultra-Left in 1919–20, but in 1921 defended theory of the offensive. Member of Zentrale since 1918. Theoretician of KPD in 1923, sceptical about chances of Revolution. Held responsible, with Brandler, for the defeat, held in Moscow 1924–8, where he taught at Sun-Yat-Sen University. Expelled in 1929, co-founder of KPO, emigrated to France in 1933, interned in 1939, found refuge in Cuba in 1941, died in exile, for lack of authorisation to live either in Germany or in France.

Thomas, Wendelin (1884–). Son of peasant, ship's boy and then sailor. In SPD in 1910. Conscripted during 1914–18, member of Committee of Revolutionary Sailors in 1918, joined USPD. In VKPD in 1920. Sentenced in 1921. Important role in preparations for insurrection in 1923. Worked in Comintern apparatus during 1925–8, imprisoned in Germany during 1928–30, left KPD in 1933. Emigrated to USA, where he joined Dewey Commission of Enquiry into Moscow Trials. Not to be confused with 'Comrade Thomas', Comintern envoy to Berlin, about whom nearly nothing is known.

Tittel, Hans (1894–). Son of worker, lithographer. In Socialist Youth in 1909, in SPD in 1912, a leader of radicals in Württemberg in 1914. With Spartacus League, jailed for eight months and conscripted. Leader of KPD(S) in Stuttgart and leading member of right wing. Political secretary in Thuringia in 1923. Imprisoned during 1923–4, headed Zentrale press bureau from 1926, excluded at end of 1928 as rightist. Joined KPO. Emigrated in 1933, expelled from KPO in 1939, went to USA, returned to West Germany in 1962.

Toller, Ernst (1883–1939). Son of Jewish trader, born in Russia, higher studies especially at Grenoble. In army in 1914, wounded and discharged. Pacifist, associated with Eisner. President of USPD in Munich in 1917. Commander of Red Army in Bavaria in 1919, sentenced to five years imprisonment. When released, joined KPD, but devoted himself to literature and theatre. Committed suicide in New York.

Tost, Otto (?–?). Metalworker in Berlin, conscripted into navy, then discharged. In USPD in 1917, member of circle of revolutionary stewards and action committee of strikers in April 1917 and January 1918. Again conscripted, organised People's Naval Division in Cuxhaven, which he led for short while. President of metalworkers' trade-union and secretary of unions in Berlin in October 1919, on USPD Left, supported Dissmann and opposed joining Comintern. Remained in USPD at Halle, and returned to SPD in 1922.

Ulbricht, Walter (1893–). Son of Social-Democratic tailor, carpenter. In SPD in 1912. In 1914 in Leipzig, member of Liebknecht's group, led by Schumann. Conscripted in 1915–18, two months in jail for desertion. Joined KPD(S) after its foundation, journalist, had task of getting arms to workers in March 1921. Political secretary of Thuringia district in June 1921, supported Brandler, elected to Zentrale in 1923, Revkom organiser. Supported centre tendency, put in charge of putting Party on factory cells basis and Bolshevisation. In Moscow in 1924. Various missions for ECCI in Vienna and Prague. At top level after Wittorf affair. Represented Party in Moscow in 1928–9, member of Central Committee and Politbureau from 1929. Succeeded Thaelmann after his arrest in 1933, formed bloc with Pieck against his supporters for Popular Front policy. In USSR in 1937, during War founded Free German Committee. Returned to Germany in 1945, leader of KPD and SED, 'strong man' of Pankow régime. Retired in May 1971.

Unger, Otto (1893–1937?). Worked in bookshops, in SPD in 1912, active in Socialist Youth, leader of Communist Youth in 1921, supported Left, criticised Brandler at beginning of 1924. Leader in Hamburg during 1926–8, conciliator, disciplined in 1928, sent to USSR, arrested and executed in 1937.

Urbahns, Hugo (1890–1947). Son of peasant, teacher, socialist sympathiser before war. In army in 1914. Joined Spartacus League in 1918, then KPD leader in Wasserkante, conspicuous leftist from 1921. Secretary of Wasserkante district in 1923. Arrested in January 1924, sentenced in January 1925, released in October. Supported Left, expelled in November 1926. Leader of Leninbund, in favour of workers' united front against Nazism. Emigrated in 1933, expelled from Sweden at time of Moscow Trials, unable to get a visa to anywhere, died in Sweden.

Utzelmann, Peter (alias Kempin, 1894–). Son of worker, carpenter. In Socialist Youth in 1908, in SPD in 1912. Conscripted into navy in 1915, member of People's Naval Division in 1918, joined KPD(S) on its foundation, sided with ultra-Left. Helped found KAPD, leader in Leuna works in March Action. Sentenced to hard labour for life in 1921, amnestied in 1923, left KAPD. In SPD in 1928, organised Red Front Fighters, expelled in 1932, under arrest during 1936–8, held important posts in DDR until 1950, when he went to West Germany.

Walcher, Jacob (1887–). Son of worker, turner. In SPD in 1906. Student at SPD school during 1910–11. Then journalist in Stuttgart. Organiser of Left, then of Spartacus group in Stuttgart in 1914, arrested in 1915, sent into army. Chairman of Founding Congress of KPD(S), won over half of USPD in Stuttgart. Member of Zentrale in 1920, supporter of general strike against Kapp, member of strike leadership, supporter of workers' government line. Secretary of Zentrale in 1921, responsible for trade-union work, represented Germany at

RILU in 1923, gave Trotsky information about situation in Germany. Demoted as rightist, in Moscow during 1924–6, expelled in 1928, in KPO and then SAP. Emigrated in 1933, close to Trotsky briefly, then moved away to join London Bureau. Interned in France in 1939, reached USA in 1941, took part in Council for a Democratic Germany. Returned to East Germany in 1946, admitted into SED, demoted from all positions in 1949, then expelled from SED. Rehabilitated and readmitted in 1956.

Wegmann, Paul (1889–1945). Metalworker in Berlin, in SPD before War. With Richard Müller, organised circle of revolutionary shop-stewards. In USPD in 1917. Member of Action Committee in November 1918, then of Executive Committee, spokesman for Left at Congress of Councils in December. Leader of left wing in trade unions and USPD. In VKPD in 1920, joined Zentrale after Levi resigned. In opposition with Friesland and Malzahn, expelled in January 1922, returned to USPD in same year, then to SPD. Became specialist on problems of youth for municipality of Berlin, and gave up all political activity. Arrested in 1933, died of typhus in Bergen-Belsen.

Wendel, Friedrich (1886–1960). Son of master carpenter, printer. In SPD in 1907, joined Spartacus League during War in Berlin, led left wing in KPD(S) in 1919. Co-founder of KAPD, sympathetic to national Bolshevism, returned to SPD in 1920. Became Social-Democratic journalist. Went to ground during Nazi period, employed by city of Kiel and member of SPD until he died.

Westmeyer, Friedrich (1873–1916). Worker, Party secretary in Stuttgart, leader of Württemberg radicals, personal friend of Luxemburg and Clara Zetkin. Organised resistance in 1914, arrested, conscripted, died in military hospital.

Weyer, Paul (1887–1943). Son of worker, metalworker. In SPD in 1910, in USPD in 1917, whilst a leader of revolutionary shop-stewards. Close to Spartacists, remained in USPD in 1919, joined VKPD in 1920. Leftist, a leader of Berlin-Brandenburg district. In 1924 led movement to leave trade unions. Expelled in September 1924. Subsequently rejoined SPD.

Winguth, Fritz (1892–1948). Son of worker, mechanic. In Socialist Youth in 1908, in SPD in 1912. Organiser of youth and Spartacus League during War. Vice-president of USPD in Neukölln in 1917, member of revolutionary stewards. Full-time official of metalworkers' union in 1919. On KPD(S) Central Committee in 1920. Supported Levi and expelled like him in 1921, followed him into USPD and then SPD. Secretary of metalworkers' union in 1933. Organised resistance group with Brass in 1933, worked in East Germany in 1945, but not admitted to SED.

Wolf, Felix (Nicolas Krebs, alias Rakov, alias Inkov, 1890–1937?). Son of German worker settled in Russia. Railway worker, Bolshevik in 1917, Communist organiser of prisoners of war. In Germany with Radek in December 1919. Comintern functionary, returned to Germany with Kun in February 1921. Deported from Germany in 1922. Diplomatic representative in Vienna under pseudonym of Inkov. Associated with Opposition, expelled in 1933, arrested and executed in 1937.

Wolffheim, Fritz (?–1936?). Journalist, collaborator with IWW organ in San Francisco in 1912–13. In Germany in 1913, worked with Laufenberg and with him led ultra-leftists in Hamburg during War. Theoretician of industrial 'unions', joined KPD(S), there defended ultra-left theories which called into question role of Communist Parties. Spokesman for opposition which was expelled at Heidelberg Congress. Shortly afterwards became publicist for national Bolshevism with Laufenberg. Accused of being in contact with some Kappist officers who were considering alliance with USSR against West. Joined KAPD at its foundation, expelled in August 1920. Co-founder of Communist League, then of Union for the Study of German Communism, with nationalistic elements. Linked to Nazis in 1923. Led various small groups, apparently in contact with left wing of Nazi Party, led by Strasser. Arrested under Nazism, died in concentration camp.

Wolfstein, Rosi (1888–). Daughter of businessman, commercial studies. In Socialist Youth in 1907, in SPD in 1908. Pupil of Luxemburg at SPD school in 1912–13. Active in Youth and in Spartacus League during War. In USPD in 1917, member of Düsseldorf council in 1918, Secretary of Foundation Congress of KPD(S). Candidate member of Zentrale from 1921. From 1924, devoted herself, with husband Paul Frölich, to publishing Luxemburg's works. Expelled in 1929. In KPO and then SAP. Emigrated in 1933, in USA during 1941–50. In SPD when she returned to Frankfurt.

Wollenberg, Erich (1892–). Son of doctor, medical student. In army in 1914, lieutenant, five times wounded. In USPD in 1918. Commanded detachment of revolutionary sailors in Koenigsberg. A commander of Red Army in Bavaria in 1919. Several times arrested and escaped. Transferred from Koenigsberg to the Ruhr in 1923, politico-military head of the South-West during summer. Military studies in Moscow, various posts of command in Red Army up to 1927. Again in USSR, teaching from 1928. Clandestine leader of Red Front Fighters in Germany in 1931, again arrested. Criticised KPD leadership, expelled in 1933 with Felix Wolf. Emigrated to France in 1934, collaborated with various anti-Nazi groups, arrested in 1940, took part in Resistance in Morocco, arrested, freed by Allied landing. Press officer for USA in Bavaria in 1946. Freelance journalist.

Wollweber, Ernst (1898–1967). Son of miner, docker, in Socialist Youth in 1915. Conscripted in 1916, stoker, in leadership of Kiel mutiny in 1918. In KPD in 1919. District secretary in Hesse-Kassel from 1921, member of Central Committee. Organised merchant seamen's trade-union. From 1932 head of underground apparatus, controlled all links between emigration and Germany from Copenhagen, then from Sweden, where he was arrested in 1943 and expelled to USSR. In East Germany in 1945, member of KPD, head of state security, member of SED Central Committee until 1958.

Zaisser, Wilhelm (1893–1958). Schoolteacher in the Ruhr. Conscripted, lieutenant, joined Ukrainian partisans in 1918 with his men. Played role in Military Apparatus, particularly in the Ruhr, in 1920, 1921 and 1923. Student at Military Academy in Moscow in 1924. Military adviser to Chiang Kai-Shek in China up to 1930. Commanded an International Brigade in Spain under name of General Gomez. In USSR in 1940, led political re-education of German officers in 'anti-fascist school'. Member of KPD, then of SED, Minister for State Security in DDR during 1950–3. Compelled to retire after June 1953 rising.

Zeigner, Erich (1886–1961). Son of bourgeois family. Studied law. Deputy judge in 1908, conscript during 1917–19. Presiding judge, joined SPD in 1919. Led Left in Saxony, where he was Minister of Justice in 1921, favoured alliance with KPD. Prime Minister in Saxony in April 1923, obtained entry of KPD in October its government of republican and proletarian defence. Denounced Reichswehr's activities. Deposed by it and imprisoned. After trial, resumed functions as magistrate. Dismissed in 1933, became accountant. Mayor of Leipzig in 1946, honoured as forerunner by SED of which he became member.

Zetkin, Clara (née Eisner, by marriage Gundel, 1857–1933). Daughter of schoolteacher, won to Marxism by Russian, Ossip Zetkin, whom she married and who died in 1889. Emigrated during 1880–90, collaborated on *Sozial-demokrat*, presented report on work amongst women at Foundation Congress of Second International in 1889. Secretary of Women's Secretariat of International, founder and Chief Editor of *Gleichheit*. One of the best-known figures of international socialist movement and German Left. Member of internationalist nucleus from August 1914, arrested immediately after Berne Conference, removed from *Gleichheit* in 1916. In USPD as Spartacist in 1917, declared solidarity with Bolsheviks. Not present at KPD(S) Founding Congress, joined Party some months later. Deputy, member of Zentrale, supported Levi in 1921 and Brandler in 1924. Was kept in KPD for prestige purposes, despite evident disagreements. Spent last years in Moscow; sympathised with Bukharinist right wing. Delivered opening speech in Reichstag in August 1932 with violent attack on Nazism. Died in Moscow.

HISTORICAL MATERIALISM BOOK SERIES

ISSN 1570–1522

1. ARTHUR, C.J. The New Dialectic and Marx's *Capital*.
   ISBN 90 04 12798 4 (2002, hardcover), 90 04 13643 6 (2004, paperback)
2. LÖWY, M. The Theory of Revolution in the Young Marx. 2003.
   ISBN 90 04 12901 4
3. CALLINICOS, A. Making History. Agency, Structure, and Change in Social Theory. 2004. ISBN 90 04 13627 4
4. DAY, R.B. Pavel V. Maksakovsky: The Capitalist Cycle. An Essay on the Marxist Theory of the Cycle. Translated with Introduction and Commentary. 2004. ISBN 90 04 13824 2
5. BROUÉ, P. The German Revolution, 1917-1923. 2005.
   ISBN 90 04 13940 0
6. MIÉVILLE, C. Between Equal Rights. A Marxist Theory of International Law. 2005. ISBN 90 04 13134 5
7. BEAUMONT, M. Utopia Ltd. Ideologies of Social Dreaming in England 1870-1900. 2005. ISBN 90 04 14296 7